PROFESSIONAL
JAVASCRIPT® FOR WEB DEVEL[

T0094248

Continues

PROFESSIONAL

JavaScript® for Web Developers

PROFESSIONAL

JavaScript® for Web Developers

Fifth Edition

Matt Frisbie

WILEY

*To my wonderful and patient wife, Jordan, whom
I assured three books ago that I wasn't going to
write any more books.*

ABOUT THE AUTHOR

MATT FRISBIE has worked in web development for over a decade. During that time, he has worked as an independent software consultant, a startup co-founder, an engineer at a Big Four tech company, and the first engineer at a Y Combinator startup that would eventually become a billion-dollar company. He also maintains a popular open-source project. At Google, Matt worked on both the AdSense and AMP platforms; his code still runs on most of the planet's web browsing devices. Prior to this, Matt was the first engineer at DoorDash, where he helped lay the foundation for a company that has become the leader in online food delivery. Matt has written four other books: *Building Browser Extensions (Apress, 2022); Professional JavaScript for Web Developers, fourth edition (Wiley, 2019); Angular 2 Cookbook (Packt, 2017);* and *AngularJS Web Application Development Cookbook (Packt, 2014).* He also recorded several video series. He is a frequent guest on podcasts, speaks at frontend meetups, and is a level-1 sommelier. Matt majored in Computer Engineering at the University of Illinois Urbana-Champaign. You can reach him on Twitter as `@mattfriz` or on the Web at `mattfriz.com`.

ABOUT THE TECHNICAL EDITOR

BEN LUO is a software engineer with experience in full-stack web development, natural language processing, and DevOps. Ben, whose professional interests lie in the healthcare domain, is a proponent for user-conscious and accessible UI design in clinical and patient-facing applications. He holds a Master of Science in computer science from the University of Illinois Chicago.

Ben plays competitive fighting games and is involved in community organization efforts for online tournaments. In addition, he enjoys building and using mechanical keyboards and stenotypes. As an avid tinkerer, he is involved in the development of open-source firmware for both custom arcade video game controllers and mechanical keyboards.

ACKNOWLEDGMENTS

THANKS TO WILEY FOR allowing me to continue as the steward of this book. Writing consecutive editions of *Professional JavaScript for Web Developers* has been a complete privilege. Thanks to the Wiley staff, specifically Jim Minatel, who offered me the opportunity.

Special thanks to Patrick Walsh for helping bring this book to fruition. Having a great primary editor makes the process so much more enjoyable, and he was terrific to work with. I'd also like to thank everyone who provided feedback on the book's drafts: Ben Luo, Archana Pragash, Judy Flynn, Pete Gaughan, Ashirvad Moses, and everyone else behind the scenes. This book would be nothing without your efforts.

Finally, I'd like to thank John Hubberts for writing the Foreword. I have been close friends with John for nearly 20 years, and it did not take me long to learn he has a ferociously hungry mind and an infectious passion for technology and engineering. I am honored that he agreed to contribute to this book.

CONTENTS

CHAPTER 13: THE DOCUMENT OBJECT MODEL

CHAPTER 19: ERROR HANDLING AND DEBUGGING

FOREWORD

During nearly a decade at Amazon, I worked on a wide variety of projects including a petabyte-scale customer analytics cluster, an airport for drones, computer vision labeling tools, an open-source smart home specification, and even fitness watch firmware. None of these projects were inherently rooted in client-side web dynamism, but each of them had some facet that eventually involved JavaScript, either by necessity or by virtue of it being the best tool for the job.

Fifteen or even 10 years ago, a generalist software engineer with a career analogous to mine might have never had reason to learn JavaScript at more than a surface level, but today JavaScript has established itself as the lingua franca of the programming world. In 2022, JavaScript remained GitHub's most used language for the ninth year in a row, not even including Typescript contributions, which independently came in fourth.

React Native is exposing many career mobile developers to JavaScript, and Electron is doing the same for desktop applications. My work at Roboto exposes me to a number of robotics companies, and I can say with high confidence that there are even people out there building robots in Node. And of course, in the web development world, JavaScript is king.

JavaScript is not going anywhere, and as such it's a great investment for any software professional to become an expert practitioner and develop a deep understanding and intuition around the language. I've known Matt for close to two decades, and in that time, I haven't met another engineer who could better fill a 1,000-page technical document with poignant wisdom without wasting a word.

When I first met Matt, he didn't have his current wealth of early career accolades, such as being the first engineer at DoorDash, publishing multiple successful technical books, founding his own ventures, or working on extremely high-scale, public-facing projects at Google—back then he was just a nerdy teenager who could hit the high register on trumpet and was great at math.

Obviously a lot has changed in the time since, but two things that haven't are Matt's inherent curiosity and his ability to explain anything he truly understands to anyone who will listen. He's the kind of engineer who will lose sleep at night over not understanding the minutia about how something incredibly specific works, which is exactly the kind of person you want writing a technical reference. At the same time, his wealth of hands-on experience as an engineer, engineering leader, and entrepreneur gives him an excellent sense of what points need to be played up and what minutia can live in the margins.

This book is packed with pragmatic examples and tidbits of knowledge that will make you a better JavaScript developer whether you read for 20 minutes or 20 hours. I've gleaned some useful tips from every edition that I've read, and I'm excited for what you'll learn approaching this with fresh eyes!

—JOHN HUBBERTS
Founding Principal Engineer at Roboto

INTRODUCTION

A tech lead at Google once shared with me a compelling perspective on JavaScript: It's not really a programming language. The ECMA-262 specification *defines* JavaScript, but there is no single true *implementation* of it. Web browsers and their JavaScript engines all implement this specification as they see fit. Chrome has Blink/V8, Firefox has Gecko/SpiderMonkey, and Safari has WebKit/JavaScriptCore. What's more, the language swims in an ocean of supplementary specifications that govern APIs for everything that JavaScript touches: the DOM, network requests, system hardware, storage, events, files, cryptography, and *hundreds* of others. Therefore, JavaScript is more accurately characterized as a constellation of ECMAScript implementations buttressed by an API buffet.

The first edition of this book was published in 2005. Microsoft was still pushing its rogue JScript, Internet Explorer had over a 90 percent browser market share, mobile browsers were in the Stone Age, and jQuery wouldn't be released for another year. At the time this fifth edition was written in 2023, major browsers have coalesced around the ECMA-262 specification, over 70 percent of Internet traffic uses a Chromium-based browser, mobile browser traffic exceeds desktop traffic, and modern web development largely comprises manipulating frameworks like React and Angular.

Most web developers would identify the release of ECMAScript 6 as JavaScript's Cambrian explosion. Pre-ES6, the language advanced in infrequent and irregular lurches. A dire lack of critical language constructs led to ugly patterns, hacks, and fragmented workarounds. Post-ES6, the language enjoys more sophisticated and useful syntactical tools. Annual ECMAScript editions ensure the language addresses developer needs and stays abreast of industry trends. Modern JavaScript is beginner-friendly, is applicable in almost any domain, has an enormous development community, and enjoys a rich library of developer tools. As a result, developers flock to the language in droves: the *Stack Overflow 2022 Developer Survey* listed JavaScript as the most popular programming language for the 10th consecutive year.

In this book, JavaScript is covered from its very beginning in the earliest Netscape browsers to the present-day incarnations flush with support for a dizzying spectrum of browser technologies. The book covers many advanced topics in meticulous detail, yet it ensures the reader understands how to use these topics and where they are appropriate. In short, you learn how to apply JavaScript solutions to problems faced by web developers everywhere.

WHO THIS BOOK IS FOR

This book is aimed at three groups of readers:

➤ Experienced developers familiar with object-oriented programming who are looking to learn JavaScript as it relates to traditional OO languages such as Java and C++

➤ Web application developers attempting to enhance the usability of their websites and web applications

➤ Novice JavaScript developers aiming to better understand the language

In addition, familiarity with the following related technologies is a strong indicator that this book is for you:

➤ Compiled languages such as Java, C++, and Rust

➤ Interpreted languages such as Python, PHP, and Ruby

➤ HTML and CSS

This book is not aimed at beginners lacking a basic computer science background or those looking to add some simple user interactions to websites. These readers should instead refer to *A Smarter Way to Learn JavaScript* by Mark Myers (ASmarterWayToLearn.com, 2014).

WHAT THIS BOOK COVERS

Professional JavaScript for Web Developers, fifth edition, provides a developer-level introduction, along with the more advanced and useful features of JavaScript.

The book begins with an exploration of how JavaScript originated and evolved into what it is today. A detailed discussion of the components that make up a JavaScript implementation follows, with specific focus on standards such as ECMAScript and the Document Object Model (DOM).

Building on that base, the book moves on to cover basic concepts of JavaScript, including classes, promises, iterators, and proxies. This is followed by an in-depth examination of events, animations, forms, errors, and JSON.

The last part of the book is focused on the newest and most important additions to the language. This includes fetch, modules, web workers, service workers, and a collection of emerging APIs.

HOW THIS BOOK IS STRUCTURED

This book comprises the following chapters:

1. **What Is JavaScript?**—Explains the origins of JavaScript: where it came from, how it evolved, and what it is today. Concepts introduced include the relationship between JavaScript and ECMAScript, the Document Object Model (DOM), and the Browser Object Model (BOM). A discussion of the relevant standards from the European Computer Manufacturer's Association (ECMA) and the World Wide Web Consortium (W3C) is also included.

2. **JavaScript in HTML**—Examines how JavaScript is used in conjunction with HTML to create dynamic web pages. Introduces the various ways of embedding JavaScript into a page and includes a discussion surrounding the JavaScript content-type and its relationship to the `<script>` element.

3. **Language Basics**—Introduces basic language concepts, including syntax and flow control statements. Explains the syntactic similarities of JavaScript and other C-based languages and points out the differences. Type coercion is introduced as it relates to built-in operators. Covers all language primitives, including the `Symbol` type.

4. **Variables, Scope, and Memory**—Explores how variables are handled in JavaScript given their loosely typed nature. A discussion of the differences between primitive and reference values is included, as is information about execution context as it relates to variables. Also, a discussion about garbage collection in JavaScript covers how memory is reclaimed when variables go out of scope.

5. **Basic Reference Types**—Covers all of the details regarding JavaScript's built-in reference types, such as `Date`, `Regexp`, primitives, and primitive wrappers. Each reference type is discussed both in theory and in how they relate to browser implementations.

6. **Advanced Reference Types**—Continues the book's coverage of built-in reference types with `Object`, `Array`, `Map`, `WeakRef`, `WeakMap`, `Set`, and `WeakSet`.

7. **Iterators and Generators**—Introduces iterators and generators and discusses both in terms of their most fundamental behavior as well as how they are used in relation to existing language constructs.

8. **Objects, Classes, and Object-Oriented Programming**—Explains how to use classes and object-oriented programming in JavaScript. Begins with an in-depth discussion of the JavaScript Object type and continues into coverage of prototypal inheritance. Following this is a complete discussion of classes and how they are a close sibling of prototypal inheritance.

9. **Proxies and Reflect**—Introduces two closely related concepts: Proxy and the Reflect API. These can be used to intercept and shim additional behavior into fundamental operations within the language.

10. **Functions**—Explores one of the most powerful aspects of JavaScript: function expressions. Topics include closures, the `this` object, the module pattern, the creation of private object members, arrow functions, default parameters, and spread operators.

11. **Promises and Async/Await**—Introduces two new closely related asynchronous programming constructs: the `Promise` type and `async/await`. The chapter begins with a discussion of the asynchronous JavaScript paradigm and continues into coverage of how promises are used and their relationship to async functions.

12. **The Browser Object Model**—Introduces the Browser Object Model (BOM), which is responsible for objects allowing interaction with the browser itself. Each of the BOM objects is covered, including window, document, location, navigator, and screen.

13. **The Document Object Model**—Introduces the Document Object Model (DOM) objects available in JavaScript as defined in DOM Level 1. Features an in-depth exploration of the entire DOM and how it allows developers to manipulate a page.

14. **DOM Extensions**—Explains how other APIs, as well as the browsers themselves, extend the DOM with more functionality such as the Selectors API, the Element Traversal API, and HTML5 extensions. Discusses how DOM Levels 2 and 3 augmented the DOM with additional properties, methods, and objects. Includes coverage of DOM4 additions such as resize, intersection, and mutation observers.

15. **Events**—Explains the nature of events in JavaScript, where they originated, and how the DOM redefined how events should work.

16. **Animation and Graphics with Canvas**—Discusses the `<canvas>` tag and how to use it to create on-the-fly graphics. Both the 2D context and the WebGL (3D) context are covered, providing you with a good starting point for creating animations and games. Includes coverage of both WebGL1 and WebGL2.

17. **Scripting Forms**—Explores using JavaScript to enhance form interactions and work around browser limitations. Discussion focuses on individual form elements such as text boxes and select boxes and on data validation and manipulation.

18. **JavaScript APIs**—Covers an assortment of JavaScript APIs, including Atomics, Encoding, File, Blob, Notifications, Streams, Timing, Web Components, and Web Cryptography.

19. **Error Handling and Debugging**—Discusses how browsers handle errors in JavaScript code and presents several ways to handle errors. Debugging tools and techniques are also discussed for each browser, including recommendations for simplifying the debugging process.

20. **JSON**—Introduces the JSON data format. Discusses browser-native JSON parsing and serialization as well as security considerations when using JSON.

21. **Network Requests and Remote Resources**—Explores all of the most ways that data and assets are requested by the browser via the Fetch API.

22. **Client-Side Storage**—Discusses how to detect when an application is offline and provides various techniques for storing data on the client machine. Begins with a discussion of the most commonly supported feature, cookies, and then discusses newer functionality such as Web Storage and IndexedDB.

23. **Modules**—Discusses the module pattern and its implications on codebases. Following this, the chapter covers module loaders such as CommonJS, AMD, and UMD. Ends with detailed coverage on the ECMAScript module pattern and how to use it properly.

24. **Workers**—Covers dedicated workers, shared workers, and service workers in-depth. Includes a discussion of how workers behave both at the operating system and browser level, as well as strategies for how best to use the various types of workers.

25. **Best Practices**—Explores approaches to working with JavaScript in an enterprise environment. Techniques for better maintainability are discussed, including coding techniques, formatting, and general programming practices. The chapter also covers execution performance and introduces several techniques for speed optimization. Last, the chapter covers deployment issues, including how to create a build process.

WHAT YOU NEED TO USE THIS BOOK

To run the samples in the book, you need the following:

➤ Any modern operating system, such as Windows, Linux, or Mac OS

➤ Any modern browser, such as Chrome, Firefox, Edge, Safari, or Opera

The complete source code is available for download from www.wiley.com/go/projavascript5e

1

What Is JavaScript?

WHAT'S IN THIS CHAPTER?

➤ Review of JavaScript history

➤ What JavaScript is

➤ How JavaScript and ECMAScript are related

➤ The different versions of JavaScript

DOWNLOADS FOR THIS CHAPTER

Please note that all the code examples for this chapter are available as a part of this chapter's code download on the book's website at www.wiley.com/go/projavascript5e.

When JavaScript first appeared in 1995, its main purpose was to handle some of the input validation that had previously been left to server-side languages such as Perl. Prior to that time, a round-trip to the server was needed to determine if a required field had been left blank or an entered value was invalid. Netscape Navigator sought to change that with the introduction of JavaScript. The capability to handle some basic validation on the client was an exciting new feature at a time when use of telephone modems was widespread. The associated slow speeds turned every trip to the server into an exercise in patience.

Since that time, JavaScript has grown into an important feature of every major web browser on the market. No longer bound to simple data validation, JavaScript now interacts with nearly all aspects of the browser window and its contents. JavaScript is recognized as a full programming language, capable of complex calculations and interactions, including closures, anonymous (lambda) functions, and even metaprogramming. JavaScript has become such an important part of the web that even alternative browsers, including those on mobile phones and those designed for users with disabilities, support it. Even Microsoft, with its own client-side scripting language called VBScript, ended up including its own JavaScript implementation in Internet Explorer from its earliest version.

The rise of JavaScript from a simple input validator to a powerful programming language could not have been predicted. JavaScript is at once a very simple and very complicated language that takes minutes to learn but years to master. To begin down the path to using JavaScript's full potential, it is important to understand its nature, history, and limitations.

A SHORT HISTORY

As the web gained popularity, a gradual demand for client-side scripting languages developed. At the time, most Internet users were connecting over a 28.8 kbps modem even though web pages were growing in size and complexity. Adding to users' pain was the large number of round-trips to the server required for simple form validation. Imagine filling out a form, clicking the Submit button, waiting 30 seconds for processing, and then being met with a message indicating that you forgot to complete a required field. Netscape, at that time on the cutting edge of technological innovation, began seriously considering the development of a client-side scripting language to handle simple processing.

In 1995, a Netscape developer named Brendan Eich began developing a scripting language called Mocha (later renamed as LiveScript) for the release of Netscape Navigator 2. The intention was to use it both in the browser and on the server, where it was to be called LiveWire.

Netscape entered into a development alliance with Sun Microsystems to complete the implementation of LiveScript in time for release. Just before Netscape Navigator 2 was officially released, Netscape changed LiveScript's name to JavaScript to capitalize on the buzz that Java was receiving from the press.

Because JavaScript 1.0 was such a hit, Netscape released version 1.1 in Netscape Navigator 3. The popularity of the fledgling web was reaching new heights, and Netscape had positioned itself to be the leading company in the market. At this time, Microsoft decided to put more resources into a competing browser named Internet Explorer. Shortly after Netscape Navigator 3 was released, Microsoft introduced Internet Explorer 3 with a JavaScript implementation called JScript (so called to avoid any possible licensing issues with Netscape). This major step for Microsoft into the realm of web browsers in August 1996 is now a date that lives in infamy for Netscape, but it also represented a major step forward in the development of JavaScript as a language.

Microsoft's implementation of JavaScript meant that there were two different JavaScript versions floating around: JavaScript in Netscape Navigator and JScript in Internet Explorer. Unlike C and many other programming languages, JavaScript had no standards governing its syntax or features, and the two different versions only highlighted this problem. With industry fears mounting, it was decided that the language must be standardized.

In 1997, JavaScript 1.1 was submitted to the European Computer Manufacturers Association (Ecma) as a proposal. Technical Committee #39 (TC39) was assigned to "standardize the syntax and semantics of a general purpose, cross-platform, vendor-neutral scripting language" (www .ecma-international.org/memento/TC39.htm). Made up of programmers from Netscape,

Sun, Microsoft, Borland, NOMBAS, and other companies with interest in the future of scripting, TC39 met for months to hammer out ECMA-262, a standard defining a new scripting language named ECMAScript (often pronounced as "ek-ma-script").

The following year, the International Organization for Standardization and International Electrotechnical Commission (ISO/IEC) also adopted ECMAScript as a standard (ISO/IEC-16262). Since that time, browsers have tried, with varying degrees of success, to use ECMAScript as a basis for their JavaScript implementations.

JAVASCRIPT IMPLEMENTATIONS

Though JavaScript and ECMAScript are often used synonymously, JavaScript is much more than just what is defined in ECMA-262. Indeed, a complete JavaScript implementation is made up of the following three distinct parts (see Figure 1.1):

➤ The Core (ECMAScript)

➤ The Document Object Model (DOM)

➤ The Browser Object Model (BOM)

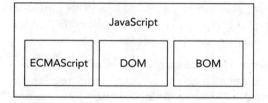

FIGURE 1.1: Components of JavaScript

ECMAScript

ECMAScript, the language defined in ECMA-262, isn't tied to web browsers. In fact, the language has no methods for input or output whatsoever. ECMA-262 defines this language as a base upon which more-robust scripting languages may be built. Web browsers are just one *host environment* in which an ECMAScript implementation may exist. A host environment provides the base implementation of ECMAScript and implementation extensions designed to interface with the environment itself. Extensions, such as the Document Object Model (DOM), use ECMAScript's core types and syntax to provide additional functionality that's more specific to the environment. Other host environments include NodeJS, a server-side JavaScript platform, and the increasingly obsolete Adobe Flash.

What exactly does ECMA-262 specify if it doesn't reference web browsers? On a very basic level, it describes the following parts of the language:

➤ Syntax

➤ Types

- ➤ Statements
- ➤ Keywords
- ➤ Reserved words
- ➤ Operators
- ➤ Global objects

ECMAScript is simply a description of a language implementing all of the facets described in the specification, and JavaScript implements ECMAScript.

ECMAScript Editions

The different versions of ECMAScript are defined as *editions* (referring to the edition of ECMA-262 in which that particular implementation is described). The first edition of ECMA-262 was essentially the same as Netscape's JavaScript 1.1 but with all references to browser-specific code removed and a few minor changes: ECMA-262 required support for the Unicode standard (to support multiple languages) and that objects be platform-independent (Netscape JavaScript 1.1 actually had different implementations of objects, such as the Date object, depending on the platform). This was a major reason why JavaScript 1.1 and 1.2 did not conform to the first edition of ECMA-262.

The second edition of ECMA-262 was largely editorial. The standard was updated to get into strict agreement with ISO/IEC-16262 and didn't feature any additions, changes, or omissions. ECMAScript implementations typically don't use the second edition as a measure of conformance.

The third edition of ECMA-262 was the first real update to the standard. It provided updates to string handling, the definition of errors, and numeric outputs. It also added support for regular expressions, new control statements, try-catch exception handling, and small changes to better prepare the standard for internationalization. To many, this marked the arrival of ECMAScript as a true programming language.

The fourth edition of ECMA-262 was a complete overhaul of the language. In response to the popularity of JavaScript on the web, developers began revising ECMAScript to meet the growing demands of web development around the world. In response, Ecma TC39 reconvened to decide the future of the language. The resulting specification defined an almost completely new language based on the third edition. The fourth edition includes strongly typed variables, new statements and data structures, true classes and classical inheritance, and new ways to interact with data.

As an alternate proposal, a specification called "ECMAScript 3.1," was developed as a smaller evolution of the language by a subcommittee of TC39, who believed that the fourth edition was too big of a jump for the language. The result was a smaller proposal with incremental changes to ECMAScript that could be implemented on top of existing JavaScript engines. Ultimately, the ES3.1 subcommittee won over support from TC39, and the fourth edition of ECMA-262 was abandoned before officially being published.

ECMAScript 3.1 became ECMA-262, fifth edition, and was officially published on December 3, 2009. The fifth edition sought to clarify perceived ambiguities of the third edition and introduce additional functionality. The new functionality includes a native JSON object for parsing and serializing JSON data, methods for inheritance and advanced property definition, and the inclusion of a new strict mode that slightly augments how ECMAScript engines interpret and execute code. The fifth edition saw a maintenance revision in June 2011; this was merely for corrections in the specification and introduced no new language or library features.

The sixth edition of ECMA-262—colloquially referred to as ES6, ES2015, or ES Harmony—was published in June 2015, and contained arguably the most important collection of enhancements to the specification since its inception. ES6 added formal support for classes, modules, iterators, generators, arrow functions, promises, reflection, proxies, and a host of new data types.

ES6 also marked the beginning of annual releases of ECMAScript editions. As a result, ECMAScript editions gradually ceased to be referred to by an incrementing integer (ES5, ES6) and began to be referred to by the year of their release (ES2020, ES2021). Recent editions have included features such as additional string and array methods, async/await, dynamic module imports, and new numerical types.

What Does ECMAScript Conformance Mean?

ECMA-262 lays out the definition of ECMAScript conformance. To be considered an implementation of ECMAScript, an implementation must do the following:

➤ Support all "types, values, objects, properties, functions, and program syntax and semantics" as they are described in ECMA-262.

➤ Support the Unicode character standard.

Additionally, a conforming implementation may do the following:

➤ Add "additional types, values, objects, properties, and functions" that are not specified in ECMA-262. ECMA-262 describes these additions as primarily new objects or new properties of objects not given in the specification.

➤ Support "program and regular expression syntax" that is not defined in ECMA-262 (meaning that the built-in regular-expression support is allowed to be altered and extended).

These criteria give implementation developers a great amount of power and flexibility for developing new languages based on ECMAScript, which partly accounts for its popularity.

The Document Object Model

The *Document Object Model* (DOM) is an application programming interface (API) for XML that was extended for use in HTML. The DOM maps out an entire page as a hierarchy of nodes. Each part of an HTML or XML page is a type of node containing different kinds of data. Consider the following HTML page:

```html
<html>
    <head>
        <title>Sample Page</title>
    </head>
    <body>
        <p> Hello World!</p>
    </body>
</html>
```

This code can be diagrammed into a hierarchy of nodes using the DOM (see Figure 1.2).

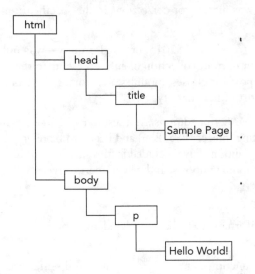

FIGURE 1.2: Example DOM node hierarchy

By creating a tree to represent a document, the DOM allows developers an unprecedented level of control over its content and structure. Nodes can be removed, added, replaced, and modified easily by using the DOM API.

Why the DOM Is Necessary

With Internet Explorer 4 and Netscape Navigator 4 each supporting different forms of Dynamic HTML (DHTML), developers for the first time could alter the appearance and content of a web page without reloading it. This represented a tremendous step forward in web technology but also a huge problem. Netscape and Microsoft went separate ways in developing DHTML, thus ending the period when developers could write a single HTML page that could be accessed by any web browser.

It was decided that something had to be done to preserve the cross-platform nature of the web. The fear was that if someone didn't rein in Netscape and Microsoft, the web would develop into two distinct factions that were exclusive to targeted browsers. It was then that the World Wide Web Consortium (W3C), the body charged with creating standards for web communication, began working on the DOM.

DOM Levels

DOM Level 1 became a W3C recommendation in October 1998. It consisted of two modules: the DOM Core, which provided a way to map the structure of an XML-based document to allow for easy access to and manipulation of any part of a document, and the DOM HTML, which extended the DOM Core by adding HTML-specific objects and methods.

> **NOTE** *that the DOM is not JavaScript-specific and indeed has been implemented in numerous other languages. For web browsers, however, the DOM has been implemented using ECMAScript and now makes up a large part of the JavaScript language.*

Whereas the goal of DOM Level 1 was to map out the structure of a document, the aims of DOM Level 2 were much broader. This extension of the original DOM added support for mouse and user-interface events (long supported by DHTML), ranges, and traversals (methods to iterate over a DOM document), and support for Cascading Style Sheets (CSS) through object interfaces. The original DOM Core introduced in Level 1 was also extended to include support for XML namespaces.

DOM Level 2 introduced the following new modules of the DOM to deal with new types of interfaces:

➤ **DOM views**—Describes interfaces to keep track of the various views of a document (the document before and after CSS styling, for example)

➤ **DOM events**—Describes interfaces for events and event handling

➤ **DOM style**—Describes interfaces to deal with CSS-based styling of elements

➤ **DOM traversal and range**—Describes interfaces to traverse and manipulate a document tree

DOM Level 3 further extends the DOM with the introduction of methods to load and save documents in a uniform way (contained in a new module called DOM Load and Save) and methods to validate a document (DOM Validation). In Level 3, the DOM Core is extended to support all of XML 1.0, including XML Infoset, XPath, and XML Base.

Presently, the W3C no longer maintains the DOM as a set of levels, but rather as the DOM Living Standard, snapshots of which are termed DOM4. Among its introductions is the addition of Mutation Observers to replace Mutation Events.

> **NOTE** *When reading about the DOM, you may come across references to DOM Level 0. Note that there is no standard called DOM Level 0; it is simply a reference point in the history of the DOM. DOM Level 0 is considered to be the original DHTML supported in Internet Explorer 4.0 and Netscape Navigator 4.0.*

Other DOMs

Aside from the DOM Core and DOM HTML interfaces, several other languages have had their own DOM standards published. The languages in the following list are XML-based, and each DOM adds methods and interfaces unique to a particular language:

➤ Scalable Vector Graphics (SVG) 1.0

➤ Mathematical Markup Language (MathML) 1.0

➤ Synchronized Multimedia Integration Language (SMIL)

Additionally, other languages have developed their own DOM implementations, such as Mozilla's XML User Interface Language (XUL). However, only the languages in the preceding list are standard recommendations from W3C.

The Browser Object Model

The Internet Explorer 3 and Netscape Navigator 3 browsers featured a *Browser Object Model* (BOM) that allowed access and manipulation of the browser window. Using the BOM, developers can interact with the browser outside of the context of its displayed page. What made the BOM truly unique, and often problematic, was that it was the only part of a JavaScript implementation that had no related standard. This changed with the introduction of HTML5, which sought to codify much of the BOM as part of a formal specification. Thanks to HTML5, a lot of the confusion surrounding the BOM has dissipated.

Primarily, the BOM deals with the browser window and frames, but generally any browser-specific extension to JavaScript is considered to be a part of the BOM. The following are some such extensions:

- ➤ The capability to pop up new browser windows
- ➤ The capability to move, resize, and close browser windows
- ➤ The navigator object, which provides detailed information about the browser
- ➤ The location object, which gives detailed information about the page loaded in the browser
- ➤ The screen object, which gives detailed information about the user's screen resolution
- ➤ The performance object, which gives detailed information about the browser's memory consumption, navigational behavior, and timing statistics
- ➤ Support for cookies
- ➤ Custom objects such as `XMLHttpRequest`

Because no standards existed for the BOM for a long time, each browser has its own implementation. There are some *de facto* standards, such as having a window object and a navigator object, but each browser defines its own properties and methods for these and other objects. With HTML5 now available, the implementation details of the BOM are expected to grow in a much more compatible way. A detailed discussion of the BOM is included in the Chapter 12, "The Browser Object Model."

SUMMARY

JavaScript is a scripting language designed to interact with web pages and is made up of the following three distinct parts:

- ➤ ECMAScript, which is defined in ECMA-262 and provides the core functionality
- ➤ The Document Object Model (DOM), which provides methods and interfaces for working with the content of a web page
- ➤ The Browser Object Model (BOM), which provides methods and interfaces for interacting with the browser

There are varying levels of support for the three parts of JavaScript across the five major web browsers (Edge, Firefox, Chrome, Safari, and Opera). Support for recent ECMAScript features is generally good across all browsers. Support for the DOM varies, but Level 3 compliance is increasingly normative. The BOM, codified in HTML5, can vary from browser to browser, though there are some commonalities that are assumed to be available.

2

JavaScript in HTML

WHAT'S IN THIS CHAPTER?

➤ Using the `<script>` element

➤ Comparing inline and external scripts

➤ Examining how document modes affect JavaScript

➤ Preparing for JavaScript-disabled experiences

DOWNLOADS FOR THIS CHAPTER

Please note that all the code examples for this chapter are available as a part of this chapter's code download on the book's website at www.wiley.com/go/projavascript5e.

The introduction of JavaScript into web pages immediately ran into the web's predominant language, HTML. As part of its original work on JavaScript, Netscape tried to figure out how to make JavaScript coexist in HTML pages without breaking those pages' rendering in other browsers. Through trial, error, and controversy, several decisions were finally made and agreed upon to bring universal scripting support to the web. Much of the work done in these early days of the web has survived and become formalized in the HTML specification.

THE *<SCRIPT>* ELEMENT

The primary method of inserting JavaScript into an HTML page is via the `<script>` element. This element was created by Netscape and first implemented in Netscape Navigator 2. It was later added to the formal HTML specification. There are eight attributes for the `<script>` element:

➤ `async`—Optional. Indicates that the script should begin downloading immediately but should not prevent other actions on the page such as downloading resources or waiting for other scripts to load. Valid only for external script files.

➤ `charset`—Optional. The character set of the code specified using the `src` attribute. This attribute is rarely used because most browsers don't honor its value.

➤ `crossorigin`—Optional. Configures the CORS settings for the associated request; by default, CORS is not used at all. `crossorigin="anonymous"` will configure the request for the file to not have the credentials flag set. `crossorigin="use-credentials"` will set the credentials flag, meaning the outgoing request will include credentials.

➤ `defer`—Optional. Indicates that the execution of the script can safely be deferred until after the document's content has been completely parsed and displayed. Valid only for external scripts.

➤ `integrity`—Optional. Allows for verification of Subresource Integrity (SRI) by checking the retrieved resource against a provided cryptographic signature. If the signature of the retrieved resource does not match that specified by this attribute, the page will error and the script will not execute. This is useful for ensuring that a Content Delivery Network (CDN) is not serving malicious payloads.

➤ `language`—Deprecated. Originally indicated the scripting language being used by the code block (such as "JavaScript," "JavaScript1.2," or "VBScript"). Most browsers ignore this attribute; it should not be used.

➤ `src`—Optional. Indicates an external file that contains code to be executed.

➤ `type`—Optional. Replaces language; indicates the content type (also called MIME type) of the scripting language being used by the code block. Traditionally, this value has always been "`text/javascript`," though both "text/javascript" and "text/ecmascript" are deprecated. JavaScript files are typically served with the "application/x-javascript" MIME type even though setting this in the type attribute may cause the script to be ignored. Other valid values are "application/javascript" and "application/ecmascript." If the value is "module," the code is treated as an ES6 module and only then is eligible to use the import and export keywords.

There are two ways to use the `<script>` element: embed JavaScript code directly into the page or include JavaScript from an external file.

To include inline JavaScript code, place JavaScript code inside the `<script>` element directly, as follows:

```
<script>
  function sayHi() {
    console.log("Hi!");
  }
</script>
```

The JavaScript code contained inside a `<script>` element is interpreted from top to bottom. In the case of this example, a function definition is interpreted and stored inside the interpreter environment. The rest of the page content is not loaded and/or displayed until after all of the code inside the `<script>` element has been evaluated.

When using inline JavaScript code, keep in mind that you cannot have the string "*</script>*" anywhere in your code. For example, the following code causes an error when loaded into a browser:

```
<script>
  function sayScript() {
    console.log("</script>");
  }
</script>
```

Because of the way that inline scripts are parsed, the browser sees the string "</script>" as if it were the closing </script> tag. This problem can be avoided easily by escaping the "/" character, as in this example:

```
<script>
  function sayScript() {
    console.log("<\/script>");
  }
</script>
```

The changes to this code make it acceptable to browsers and won't cause any errors.

To include JavaScript from an external file, the src attribute is required. The value of src is a URL linked to a file containing JavaScript code, like this:

```
<script src="example.js"></script>
```

In this example, an external file named example.js is loaded into the page. The file itself need only contain the JavaScript code that would occur between the opening <script> and closing </script> tags. As with inline JavaScript code, processing of the page is halted while the external file is interpreted. (There is also some time taken to download the file.) In XHTML documents, you can omit the closing tag, as in this example:

```
<script src="example.js"/>
```

This syntax should not be used in HTML documents because it is invalid HTML and won't be handled properly by some browsers, most notably Internet Explorer.

> **NOTE** *By convention, external JavaScript files have a .js extension. This is not a requirement because browsers do not check the file extension of included JavaScript files. This leaves open the possibility of dynamically generating JavaScript code using a server-side scripting language, or for in-browser transpilation into JavaScript from a JavaScript extension language such as TypeScript or React's JSX. Keep in mind, though, that servers often use the file extension to determine the correct MIME type to apply to the response. If you don't use a .js extension, double-check that your server is returning the correct MIME type.*

It's important to note that a <script> element using the src attribute should not include additional JavaScript code between the <script> and </script> tags. If both are provided, the script file is downloaded and executed while the inline code is ignored.

One of the most powerful and most controversial parts of the `<script>` element is its ability to include JavaScript files from outside domains. Much like an `<img>` element, the `<script>` element's `src` attribute may be set to a full URL that exists outside the domain on which the HTML page exists, as in this example:

```
<script src="http://www.somewhere.com/afile.js"></script>
```

When the browser goes to resolve this resource, it will send a GET request to the path specified in the `src` attribute to retrieve the resource—presumably a JavaScript file. This initial request is not subject to the browser's cross-origin restrictions, but any JavaScript returned and executed will be. Of course, this request is still subject to the HTTP/HTTPS protocol of the parent page.

Code from an external domain will be loaded and interpreted as if it were part of the page that is loading it. This capability allows you to serve up JavaScript from various domains, if necessary. Be careful, however, if you are referencing JavaScript files located on a server that you don't control. A malicious programmer could, at any time, replace the file. When including JavaScript files from a different domain, make sure you are the domain owner, or the domain is owned by a trusted source. The `<script>` tag's `integrity` attribute gives you a tool to defend against this.

Regardless of how the code is included, the `<script>` elements are interpreted in the order in which they appear in the page so long as the `defer` and `async` attributes are not present. The first `<script>` element's code must be completely interpreted before the second `<script>` element begins interpretation, the second must be completed before the third, and so on.

Tag Placement

Traditionally, all `<script>` elements were placed within the `<head>` element on a page, as in this example:

```
<!DOCTYPE html>
<html>
  <head>
  <title>Example HTML Page</title>
  <script src="example1.js"></script>
  <script src="example2.js"></script>
  </head>
  <body>
    <!-- content here -->
  </body>
</html>
```

The main purpose of this format was to keep external file references, both CSS files and JavaScript files, in the same area. However, including all JavaScript files in the `<head>` of a document means that all of the JavaScript code must be downloaded, parsed, and interpreted before the page begins rendering (rendering begins when the browser receives the opening `<body>` tag). For pages that require a lot of JavaScript code, this can cause a noticeable delay in page rendering, during which time the browser will be completely blank. For this reason, modern web applications typically include all JavaScript references in the `<body>` element, after the page content, as shown in this example:

```
<!DOCTYPE html>
<html>
  <head>
    <title>Example HTML Page</title>
```

```
    </head>
    <body>
      <!-- content here -->
      <script src="example1.js"></script>
      <script src="example2.js"></script>
    </body>
  </html>
```

Using this approach, the page is completely rendered in the browser before the JavaScript code is processed. The resulting user experience is perceived as faster because the amount of time spent on a blank browser window is reduced.

Deferred Scripts

HTML 4.01 defines an attribute named `defer` for the `<script>` element. The purpose of defer is to indicate that a script won't be changing the structure of the page as it executes. As such, the script can be run safely after the entire page has been parsed. Setting the `defer` attribute on a `<script>` element signals to the browser that download should begin immediately but execution should be deferred:

```
  <!DOCTYPE html>
  <html>
    <head>
      <title>Example HTML Page</title>
      <script defer src="example1.js"></script>
      <script defer src="example2.js"></script>
    </head>
    <body>
      <!-- content here -->
    </body>
  </html>
```

Even though the `<script>` elements in this example are included in the document `<head>`, they will not be executed until after the browser has received the closing `</html>` tag. The HTML5 specification indicates that scripts will be executed in the order in which they appear, so the first deferred script executes before the second deferred script, and both will execute before the `DOMContentLoaded` event (see the Chapter 15, "Events," for more information). In reality, though, deferred scripts don't always execute in order or before the `DOMContentLoaded` event, so it's best to include just one when possible.

As mentioned previously, the `defer` attribute is supported only for external script files. This was a clarification made in HTML5, so browsers that support the HTML5 implementation will ignore `defer` when set on an inline script.

Asynchronous Scripts

HTML5 introduces the `async` attribute for `<script>` elements. The async attribute is similar to `defer` in that it changes the way the script is processed. Also similar to `defer`, async applies only to external scripts and signals the browser to begin downloading the file immediately. Unlike `defer`, scripts marked as `async` are not guaranteed to execute in the order in which they are specified. For example:

```
  <!DOCTYPE html>
  <html>
    <head>
      <title>Example HTML Page</title>
      <script async src="example1.js"></script>
```

```
      <script async src="example2.js"></script>
    </head>
    <body>
      <!-- content here -->
    </body>
</html>
```

In this code, the second script file might execute before the first, so it's important that there are no dependencies between the two. The purpose of specifying an asynchronous script is to indicate that the page need not wait for the script to be downloaded and executed before continuing to load, and it also need not wait for another script to load and execute before it can do the same. Because of this, it's recommended that asynchronous scripts not modify the DOM as they are loading.

Asynchronous scripts are guaranteed to execute before the page's load event and may execute before or after DOMContentLoaded (see the Chapter 15 for details). Using asynchronous scripts also confers to your page the implicit assumption that you do not intend to use document.write—but good web development practices dictate that you shouldn't be using it anyway.

Dynamic Script Loading

You are not limited to using static <script> tags to retrieve resources. Because JavaScript is able to use the DOM API, you are more than welcome to add script elements, which will, in turn, load the resources they specify. This can be done by creating script elements and attaching them to the DOM:

```
let script = document.createElement('script');
script.src = 'myscript.js';
document.head.appendChild(script);
```

Of course, this request will not be generated until the HTMLElement is attached to the DOM, and therefore not until this script itself runs. By default, scripts that are created in this fashion are asynchronous.

Resources fetched in this fashion will be hidden from browser preloaders. This will severely injure their priority in the resource fetching queue. Depending on how your application works and how it is used, this can severely damage performance. To inform preloaders of the existence of these dynamically requested files, you can explicitly declare them in the document head:

```
<link rel="subresource" href="myscript.js">
```

INLINE CODE VERSUS EXTERNAL FILES

Although it's possible to embed JavaScript in HTML files directly, it's generally considered a best practice to include as much JavaScript as possible using external files. Keeping in mind that there are no hard and fast rules regarding this practice, the arguments for using external files are as follows:

➤ **Maintainability**—JavaScript code that is sprinkled throughout various HTML pages turns code maintenance into a problem. It is much easier to have a directory for all JavaScript files so that developers can edit JavaScript code independent of the markup in which it's used.

➤ **Caching**—Browsers cache all externally linked JavaScript files according to specific settings, meaning that if two pages are using the same file, the file is downloaded only once. This ultimately means faster page-load times.

One notable consideration when configuring how external files are requested is their implication on request bandwidth. With SPDY/HTTP2, the per-request overhead is substantially reduced insofar as it may be advantageous to deliver scripts to the client as lightweight independent JavaScript components.

For example, your first page might have the following:

```
<script src="mainA.js"></script>
<script src="component1.js"></script>
<script src="component2.js"></script>
<script src="component3.js"></script>
...
```

A subsequent page loaded might have the following:

```
<script src="mainB.js"></script>
<script src="component3.js"></script>
<script src="component4.js"></script>
<script src="component5.js"></script>
...
```

On the initial request, if the browser supports SPDY/HTTP2, it will be able to efficiently retrieve a number of files from the same endpoint, and it will enter them into the browser cache on a per-file basis. From the perspective of the browser, retrieval of these individual resources over SPDY/HTTP2 should have approximately the same latency as delivering a monolithic JavaScript payload.

On the second page request, because you segmented your application into lightweight cacheable files, some of the components that the second page also depends upon are already in the browser cache.

Of course, this assumes the browser supports SPDY/HTTP2, which is only a valid assumption for modern browsers. Monolithic payloads may be more appropriate if your aim is to include support for older browsers.

DOCUMENT MODES

Internet Explorer 5.5 introduced the concept of document modes through the use of doctype switching. The first two document modes were *quirks mode*, which made Internet Explorer behave as if it were version 5 (with several nonstandard features) and *standards mode*, which made Internet Explorer behave in a more standards-compliant way. Though the primary difference between these two modes is related to the rendering of content with regard to CSS, there are also several side effects related to JavaScript.

Since Internet Explorer first introduced the concept of document modes, other browsers have followed suit. As this adoption happened, a third mode called *almost standards mode* arose. That mode has a lot of the features of standards mode but isn't as strict. The main difference is in the treatment of spacing around images (most noticeable when images are used in tables).

Quirks mode is achieved in all browsers by omitting the doctype at the beginning of the document. This is considered poor practice because quirks mode is very different across all browsers, and no level of true browser consistency can be achieved without hacks.

Standards mode is turned on when one of the following doctypes is used:

```
<!-- HTML 4.01 Strict -->
<!DOCTYPE HTML PUBLIC "-//W3C//DTD HTML 4.01//EN"
```

```
"http://www.w3.org/TR/html4/strict.dtd">

<!-- XHTML 1.0 Strict -->
<!DOCTYPE html PUBLIC
"-//W3C//DTD XHTML 1.0 Strict//EN"
"http://www.w3.org/TR/xhtml1/DTD/xhtml1-strict.dtd">
<!-- HTML5 -->
<!DOCTYPE html>
```

Almost standards mode is triggered by transitional and frameset doctypes, as follows:

```
<!-- HTML 4.01 Transitional -->
<!DOCTYPE HTML PUBLIC
"-//W3C//DTD HTML 4.01 Transitional//EN"
"http://www.w3.org/TR/html4/loose.dtd">

<!-- HTML 4.01 Frameset -->
<!DOCTYPE HTML PUBLIC
"-//W3C//DTD HTML 4.01 Frameset//EN"
"http://www.w3.org/TR/html4/frameset.dtd">

<!-- XHTML 1.0 Transitional -->
<!DOCTYPE html PUBLIC
"-//W3C//DTD XHTML 1.0 Transitional//EN"
"http://www.w3.org/TR/xhtml1/DTD/xhtml1-transitional.dtd">

<!-- XHTML 1.0 Frameset -->
<!DOCTYPE html PUBLIC
"-//W3C//DTD XHTML 1.0 Frameset//EN"
"http://www.w3.org/TR/xhtml1/DTD/xhtml1-frameset.dtd">
```

Because almost standards mode is so close to standards mode, the distinction is rarely made. People talking about "standards mode" may be talking about either, and detection for the document mode (discussed later in this book) also doesn't make the distinction. Throughout this book, the term *standards mode* should be taken to mean any mode other than quirks.

Earlier versions of HTML were verbose because it was Standard Generalized Markup Language (SGML) based and required a reference to a document type definition (DTD). DTDs became obsolete, so HTML5 massively simplified this syntax. The following is now the preferred document mode syntax:

```
<!DOCTYPE html>
```

THE *<NOSCRIPT>* ELEMENT

Of particular concern to early browsers was the graceful degradation of pages when the browser didn't support JavaScript. To that end, the <noscript> element was created to provide alternate content for browsers without JavaScript. Although all modern browsers support JavaScript, this element is still useful for browsers that explicitly disable JavaScript.

The <noscript> element can contain any HTML elements, aside from <script>, that can be included in the document <body>. Any content contained in a <noscript> element will be displayed under only the following two circumstances:

➤   The browser doesn't support scripting.

➤   The browser's scripting support is turned off.

If either of these conditions is met, then the content inside the `<noscript>` element is rendered. In all other cases, the browser does not render the content of `<noscript>`.

Here is a simple example:

```
<!DOCTYPE html>
<html>
  <head>
    <title>Example HTML Page</title>
    <script ""defer="defer" src="example1.js"></script>
    <script ""defer="defer" src="example2.js"></script>
  </head>
  <body>
    <noscript>
      <p>This page requires a JavaScript-enabled browser.</p>
    </noscript>
  </body>
</html>
```

In this example, a message is displayed to the user when the scripting is not available. For scripting-enabled browsers, this message will never be seen even though it is still a part of the page.

SUMMARY

JavaScript is inserted into HTML pages by using the `<script>` element. This element can be used to embed JavaScript into an HTML page, leaving it inline with the rest of the markup, or to include JavaScript that exists in an external file. The following are key points:

➤ To include external JavaScript files, the `src` attribute must be set to the URL of the file to include, which may be a file on the same server as the containing page or one that exists on a completely different domain.

➤ All `<script>` elements are interpreted in the order in which they occur on the page. The code contained within a `<script>` element must be completely interpreted before code in the next `<script>` element can begin so long as `defer` and `async` attributes are not used.

➤ For nondeferred scripts, the browser must complete interpretation of the code inside a `<script>` element before it can continue rendering the rest of the page. For this reason, `<script>` elements are usually included toward the end of the page, after the main content and just before the closing `</body>` tag.

➤ You can defer a script's execution until after the document has rendered by using the `defer` attribute. Deferred scripts always execute in the order in which they are specified.

➤ You can indicate that a script need not wait for other scripts and also not block the document rendering by using the `async` attribute. Asynchronous scripts are not guaranteed to execute in the order in which they occur in the page.

By using the `<noscript>` element, you can specify that content is to be shown only if scripting support isn't available on the browser. Any content contained in the `<noscript>` element will not be rendered if scripting is enabled on the browser.

3

Language Basics

WHAT'S IN THIS CHAPTER?

➤ Reviewing syntax

➤ Working with data types

➤ Working with flow-control statements

➤ Understanding functions

DOWNLOADS FOR THIS CHAPTER

Please note that all the code examples for this chapter are available as a part of this chapter's code download on the book's website at `www.wiley.com/go/ projavascript5e`.

At the core of any language is a description of how it should work at the most basic level. This description typically defines syntax, operators, data types, and built-in functionality upon which complex solutions can be built. As previously mentioned, ECMA-262 defines all of this information for JavaScript in the form of a pseudolanguage called ECMAScript.

ECMAScript as defined in ECMA-262 is implemented with increasing uniformity across all major browsers. A decade ago, major browsers had widely divergent support for some ECMAScript features. Today, features included in the annual ECMAScript editions are usually supported by all major browsers in less than a year.

> **NOTE** *Support for various ECMAScript features can be checked on* `https://caniuse.com`.

SYNTAX

ECMAScript's syntax borrows heavily from C and other C-like languages such as Java and Perl. Developers familiar with such languages should have an easy time picking up the somewhat looser syntax of ECMAScript.

Case-Sensitivity

The first concept to understand is that everything is case-sensitive; variables, function names, and operators are all case-sensitive, meaning that a variable named `test` is different from a variable named `Test`. Similarly, `typeof` can't be the name of a function because it's a keyword (described in the next section); however, `"Typeof"` is a perfectly valid function name.

Identifiers

An *identifier* is the name of a variable, function, or function argument. Identifiers may be one or more characters in the following format:

- ➤ The first character must be a letter, an underscore (_), or a dollar sign ($).
- ➤ All other characters may be letters, underscores, dollar signs, or numbers.

Letters in an identifier may include extended ASCII or Unicode letter characters such as À and Æ, though this is not recommended.

By convention, ECMAScript identifiers use camel case, meaning that the first letter is lowercase and each additional word is offset by a capital letter, like this:

```
firstSecond
myCar
doSomethingImportant
```

Although this is not strictly enforced, it is considered a best practice to adhere to the built-in ECMAScript functions and objects that follow this format.

> **NOTE** *Keywords, reserved words, "true," "false," and "null" cannot be used as identifiers. See the section "Keywords and Reserved Words" coming up shortly for more detail.*

Comments

ECMAScript uses C-style comments for both single–line and block comments. A single–line comment begins with two forward-slash characters, such as this:

```
// single line comment
```

A block comment begins with a forward slash and asterisk (/*) and ends with the opposite (*/), as in this example:

```
/* This is a multi-line
comment */
```

Strict Mode

ECMAScript 5 introduced the concept of *strict mode*. Strict mode is a different parsing and execution model for JavaScript, where some of the erratic behavior of ECMAScript 3 is addressed and errors are thrown for unsafe activities. To enable strict mode for an entire script, include the following at the top:

```
"use strict";
```

Although this may look like a string that isn't assigned to a variable, this is a pragma that tells supporting JavaScript engines to change into strict mode. The syntax was chosen specifically so as not to break ECMAScript 3 syntax.

You may also specify just a function to execute in strict mode by including the pragma at the top of the function body:

```
function doSomething() {
  "use strict";
  // function body
}
```

Strict mode is effectively the assumed modality in modern JavaScript. ES6 modules and classes automatically apply strict mode without the "use strict" directive. Furthermore, modern code compilers and bundlers such as Webpack will automatically insert the directive.

Statements

Statements in ECMAScript are terminated by a semicolon, though omitting the semicolon makes the parser determine where the end of a statement occurs, as in the following examples:

```
let sum = a + b     // valid even without a semicolon - not recommended
let diff = a - b;   // valid - preferred
```

Even though a semicolon is not required at the end of statements, you should always include one. Including semicolons helps prevent errors of omission, such as not finishing what you were typing, and allows developers to compress ECMAScript code by removing extra white space (such compression causes syntax errors when lines do not end in a semicolon). Including semicolons also improves performance in certain situations because parsers try to correct syntax errors by inserting semicolons where they appear to belong.

Multiple statements can be combined into a code block by using C-style syntax, beginning with a left curly brace ({) and ending with a right curly brace (}):

```
if (test) {
  test = false;
  console.log(test);
}
```

Control statements, such as `if`, require code blocks only when executing multiple statements. However, it is considered a best practice to always use code blocks with control statements, even if there's only one statement to be executed, as in the following examples:

```
// valid, but error-prone and should be avoided
if (test)
  console.log(test);

// preferred
if (test) {  console.log(test);
}
```

Using code blocks for control statements makes the intent clearer, and there's less chance for errors when changes need to be made.

KEYWORDS AND RESERVED WORDS

ECMA-262 describes a set of reserved *keywords* that have specific uses, such as indicating the beginning or end of control statements or performing specific operations. By rule, keywords are reserved and cannot be used as identifiers or property names. The complete list of keywords for ECMA-262, sixth edition is as follows:

```
await break case catch class const continue
debugger default delete do else export
extends false finally for function if import
in instanceof let new null return super switch
this throw true try typeof var void while
with yield
```

The specification also describes a set of *future reserved words* that cannot be used as identifiers or property names. Though reserved words don't have any specific usage in the language, they are reserved for future use as keywords.

The following is the complete list of future reserved words defined in ECMA-262:

```
Always reserved:

enum


Reserved in strict mode:

arguments eval implements interface package private protected public static
```

VARIABLES

ECMAScript variables are loosely typed, meaning that a variable can hold any type of data. Every variable is simply a named placeholder for a value. There are three keywords that can be used to declare a variable: `var`, `const`, and `let`.

The var Keyword

To define a variable, use the var operator (note that var is a keyword) followed by the variable name (an identifier, as described earlier), like this:

```
var message;
```

This code defines a variable named message that can be used to hold any value. (Without initialization, it holds the special value undefined, which is discussed in the next section.) ECMAScript implements variable initialization, so it's possible to define the variable and set its value at the same time, as in this example:

```
var message = "hi";
```

Here, message is defined to hold a string value of "hi". Doing this initialization doesn't mark the variable as being a string type; it is simply the assignment of a value to the variable. It is still possible to not only change the value stored in the variable but also change the type of value, such as this:

```
var message = "hi";
message = 100;  // legal, but not recommended
```

In this example, the variable message is first defined as having the string value "hi" and then overwritten with the numeric value 100. Although it's not recommended to switch the data type that a variable contains, it is completely valid in ECMAScript.

var Declaration Scope

It's important to note that using the var operator to define a variable makes it local to the function scope in which it was defined. For example, defining a variable inside of a function using var means that the variable is destroyed as soon as the function exits, as shown here:

```
function test() {
  var message = "hi";  // local variable
}
test();
console.log(message); // error!
```

Here, the message variable is defined within a function using var. The function is called test(), which creates the variable and assigns its value. Immediately after that, the variable is destroyed so the last line in this example causes an error. It is, however, possible to define a variable globally by simply omitting the var operator as follows:

```
function test() {
  message = "hi";  // global variable
}
test();
console.log(message); // "hi"
```

By removing the var operator from the example, the message variable becomes global. As soon as the function test() is called, the variable is defined and becomes accessible outside of the function once it has been executed.

> **NOTE** *Although it's possible to define global variables by omitting the* var *operator, this approach is not recommended. Global variables defined locally are hard to maintain and cause confusion because it's not immediately apparent if the omission of* var *was intentional. Strict mode throws a* ReferenceError *when an undeclared variable is assigned a value.*

If you need to define more than one variable, you can do it using a single statement, separating each variable (and optional initialization) with a comma like this:

```
var message = "hi",
    found = false,
    age = 29;
```

Here, three variables are defined and initialized. Because ECMAScript is loosely typed, variable initializations using different data types may be combined into a single statement. Though inserting line breaks and indenting the variables isn't necessary, it helps to improve readability.

When you are running in strict mode, you cannot define variables named eval or arguments. Doing so results in a syntax error.

var Declaration Hoisting

When using var, the following is possible because variables declared using that keyword are hoisted to the top of the function scope:

```
function foo() {
  console.log(age);
  var age = 26;
}
foo();  // undefined
```

This does not throw an error because the ECMAScript runtime technically treats it like this:

```
function foo() {
  var age;
  console.log(age);
  . age = 26;
}
foo();  // undefined
```

This is "hoisting," where the interpreter pulls all variable declarations to the top of its scope. It also allows you to use redundant var declarations without penalty:

```
function foo() {
  var age = 16;
  var age = 26;
  var age = 36;
  console.log(age);
}
foo();  // 36
```

let Declarations

`let` operates in nearly the same way as `var`, but with some important differences. Most notable is that `let` is block scoped, but `var` is function scoped.

```
if (true) {
  var name = 'Bob';
  console.log(name);   // Bob
}
console.log(name);     // Bob

if (true) {
  let age = 26;
  console.log(age);    // 26
}
console.log(age);      // ReferenceError: age is not defined
```

Here, the `age` variable cannot be referenced outside the `if` block because its scope does not extend outside the block. Block scope is strictly a subset of function scope, so any scope limitations that apply to `var` declarations will also apply to `let` declarations.

A `let` declaration also does not allow for any redundant declarations within a block scope. Doing so will result in an error:

```
var name;
var name;
let age;
let age;  // SyntaxError; identifier 'age' has already been declared
```

The JavaScript engine will keep track of identifiers used for variable declarations and the block scope they were declared inside, so nesting using identical identifiers will not throw errors because no redeclaration is occurring:

```
var name = 'Alice';
console.log(name);  // 'Alice'
if (true) {
  var name = 'Bob';
  console.log(name);  // 'Bob'
}

let age = 30;
console.log(age);  // 30
if (true) {
  let age = 26;
  console.log(age);  // 26
}
```

The declaration redundancy errors are not affected if `let` is mixed with `var`. The different keywords do not declare different types of variables—they just specify how the variables exist inside the relevant scope.

```
var name;
let name;  // SyntaxError

let age;
var age;   // SyntaxError
```

Temporal Dead Zone

Another important behavior of `let` distinguishing it from `var` is that `let` declarations cannot be used in a way that assumes hoisting:

```
// name is hoisted
console.log(name);  // undefined
var name = 'Bob';

// age is not hoisted
console.log(age);  // ReferenceError: age is not defined
let age = 26;
```

When parsing the code, JavaScript engines will still be aware of the `let` declarations that appear later in a block, but these variables will be unable to be referenced in any way before the actual declaration occurs. The segment of execution that occurs before the declaration is referred to as the "temporal dead zone," and any attempted references to these variables will throw a `ReferenceError`.

Global Declarations

Unlike the `var` keyword, when declaring variables using `let` in the global context, variables will not attach to the `window` object as they do with `var`.

```
var name = 'Bob';
console.log(window.name);  // 'Bob'

let age = 26;
console.log(window.age);  // undefined
```

However, `let` declarations will still occur inside the global block scope, which will persist for the lifetime of the page. Therefore, you must ensure your page does not attempt duplicate declarations in order to avoid throwing a `SyntaxError`.

Conditional Declaration

When using `var` to declare variables, because the declaration is hoisted, the JavaScript engine will happily combine redundant declarations into a single declaration at the top of the scope. Because `let` declarations are scoped to blocks, it's not possible to check if a `let` variable has previously been declared and conditionally declare it only if it has not.

```
<script>
  var name = 'Alice';
  let age = 26;
</script>

<script>
  // Suppose this script is unsure about what has already been declared in the page.
  // It will assume variables have not been declared.

  var name = 'Bob';
  // No problems here, since this will be handled as a single hoisted declaration.
  // There is no need to check if it was previously declared.

  let age = 36;
  // This will throw an error when 'age' has already been declared.
</script>
```

Using a `try`/`catch` statement or the `typeof` operator are not solutions, as the `let` declaration inside the conditional block will be scoped to that block.

```
<script>
  let name = 'Alice';
  let age = 36;
</script>

<script>
  // Suppose this script is unsure about what has already been
declared in the page.
  // It will assume variables have not been declared.

  if (typeof name === 'undefined') {
    let name;
  }
  // 'name' is restricted to the if {} block scope,
  // so this assignment will act as a global assignment
  name = 'Bob';


  try (age) {
    // If age is not declared, this will throw an error
  }
  catch(error) {
    let age;
  }
  // 'age' is restricted to the catch {} block scope,
  // so this assignment will act as a global assignment
  age = 26;
</script>
```

Because of this, you cannot rely on a conditional declaration pattern.

> **NOTE** *Not being able to use* `let` *for conditional declaration is a good thing, as conditional declaration is a bad pattern to have in your codebase. It makes it harder to understand program flow. If you find yourself reaching for this pattern, chances are very good that there is a better way to go about writing it.*

let Declaration in *for* Loops

Prior to the advent of `let`, `for` loop definition involved using an iterator variable whose definition would bleed outside the loop body:

```
for (var i = 0; i < 5; ++i) {
  // do loop things
}
console.log(i);  // 5
```

This is no longer a problem when switching to `let` declarations, as the iterator variable will be scoped only to the `for` loop block:

```
for (let i = 0; i < 5; ++i) {
  // do loop things
}
console.log(i);  // ReferenceError: i is not defined
```

When using `var`, a frequent problem encountered was the singular declaration and modification of the iterator variable:

```
for (var i = 0; i < 5; ++i) {
  setTimeout(() => console.log(i), 0)
}
// You might expect this to console.log 0, 1, 2, 3, 4
// It will actually console.log 5, 5, 5, 5, 5
```

This happens because the loop exits with its iterator variable still set to the value that caused the loop to exit: 5. When the timeouts later execute, they reference this same variable, and consequently `console.log` its final value.

When using `let` to declare the loop iterator, behind the scenes the JavaScript engine will actually declare a new iterator variable each loop iteration. Each `setTimeout` references that separate instance, and therefore it will `console.log` the expected value: the value of the iterator variable when that loop iteration was executed.

```
for (let i = 0; i < 5; ++i) {
  setTimeout(() => console.log(i), 0)
}
// console.logs 0, 1, 2, 3, 4
```

This per-iteration declarative behavior is applicable for all styles of for loops, including for-in and for-of loops.

const Declarations

`const` behaves identically to that of `let` but with one important difference—it must be initialized with a value, and that value cannot be redefined after declaration. Attempting to modify a `const` variable will result in a runtime error.

```
const age = 26;
age = 36;  // TypeError: assignment to a constant

// const still disallows redundant declaration
const name = 'Bob';
const name = 'Alice';  // SyntaxError

// const is still scoped to blocks
const name = 'Bob';
if (true) {
  const name = 'Alice';
}
console.log(name);  // Bob
```

The const declaration is only enforced with respect to the reference to the variable that it points to. If a const variable references an object, it does not violate the const constraints to modify properties inside that object.

```
const person = {};
person.name = 'Bob';  // ok
```

Even though the JavaScript engine is creating new instances of let iterator variables in for loops, and even though const variables behave similarly to let variables, you cannot use const to declare for loop iterators:

```
for (const i = 0; i < 10; ++i) {}  // TypeError: assignment to constant variable
```

However, if you were to declare a for loop variable that is not modified, const is allowed—precisely because a new variable is declared for each iteration. This is especially relevant in the case of for-of and for-in loops:

```
let i = 0;
for (const j = 7; i < 5; ++i) {
  console.log(j);
}
// 7, 7, 7, 7, 7

for (const key in {a: 1, b: 2}) {
  console.log(key);
}
// a, b

for (const value of [1,2,3,4,5]) {
  console.log(value);
}
// 1, 2, 3, 4, 5
```

Declaration Styles and Best Practices

The introduction of let and const in ECMAScript 6 bring objectively better tooling to the language in the form of increased precision of declaration scope and semantics. It is no secret that the bizarre behavior of var declarations caused the JavaScript community to pull its collective hair out for years as a result of all the problems it caused. In the wake of the introduction of these new keywords, there are some increasingly common patterns emerging that can improve code quality.

Don't Use *var*

With let and const, most developers will find that they no longer need to use var in their codebase anywhere. The patterns that emerge from restricting variable declaration to only let and const will serve to enforce higher codebase quality thanks to careful management of variable scope, declaration locality, and const correctness.

Prefer *const* Over *let*

Using const declarations allows the browser runtime to enforce constant variables, as well as for static code analysis tools to foresee illegal reassignment operations. Therefore, many developers feel it is to their advantage to, by default, declare variables as const unless they know they will need to reassign its value at some point. This allows for developers to more concretely reason about values that they know will never change, and also for quick detection of unexpected behavior in cases where the code execution attempts to perform an unanticipated value reassignment.

DATA TYPES

There are seven simple data types (also called *primitive types*) in ECMAScript: Undefined, Null, Boolean, Number, BigInt, String, and Symbol. There is also one complex data type called Object, which is an unordered list of name–value pairs. Because there is no way to define your own data types in ECMAScript, all values can be represented as one of these eight. Having only eight data types may seem like too few to fully represent data; however, ECMAScript's data types have dynamic aspects that make each single data type behave like several.

The *typeof* Operator

Because ECMAScript is loosely typed, there needs to be a way to determine the data type of a given variable. The typeof operator provides that information. Using the typeof operator on a value returns one of the following strings:

- ➤ "undefined" if the value is undefined

- ➤ "boolean" if the value is a Boolean

- ➤ "string" if the value is a string

- ➤ "number" if the value is a number

- ➤ "object" if the value is an object (other than a function) or null

- ➤ "function" if the value is a function

- ➤ "symbol" if the value is a Symbol

- ➤ "bigint" if the value is a BigInt

The typeof operator is called like this:

```
let message = "some string";
console.log(typeof message);    // "string"
console.log(typeof(message));   // "string"
console.log(typeof 95);         // "number"
```

In this example, both a variable (message) and a numeric literal are passed into the typeof operator. Note that because typeof is an operator and not a function, no parentheses are required (although they can be used).

Be aware there are a few cases where typeof seemingly returns a confusing but technically correct value. Calling typeof null returns "object," as the special value null is considered to be an empty object reference.

> **NOTE** *Technically, functions are considered objects in ECMAScript and don't represent another data type. However, they do have some special properties, which necessitates differentiating between functions and other objects via the* typeof *operator.*

The Undefined Type

The Undefined type has only one value, which is the special value undefined. When a variable is declared using var or let but not initialized, it is assigned the value of undefined as follows:

```
let message;
console.log(message == undefined);   // true
```

In this example, the variable message is declared without initializing it. When compared with the literal value of undefined, the two are equal. This example is identical to the following:

```
let message = undefined;
console.log(message == undefined);   // true
```

Here the variable message is explicitly initialized to be undefined. This is unnecessary because, by default, any uninitialized variable gets the value of undefined.

> **NOTE** *Generally speaking, you should never explicitly set a variable to be undefined. The literal undefined value is provided mainly for comparison and wasn't added until ECMA-262, third edition, to help formalize the difference between an empty object pointer (null) and an uninitialized variable.*

Note that a variable containing the value of undefined is different from a variable that hasn't been defined at all. Consider the following:

```
let message;    // this variable is declared but has a value of undefined

// make sure this variable isn't declared
// let age

console.log(message);   // "undefined"
console.log(age);       // causes an error
```

In this example, the first console.log displays the variable message, which is "undefined". In the second console.log, an undeclared variable called age is passed into the console.log() function, which causes an error because the variable hasn't been declared. Only one useful operation can be performed on an undeclared variable: you can call typeof on it (calling delete on an undeclared variable won't cause an error, but this isn't very useful and in fact throws an error in strict mode).

The `typeof` operator returns "undefined" when called on an uninitialized variable, but it also returns "undefined" when called on an undeclared variable, which can be a bit confusing. Consider this example:

```
let message;    // this variable is declared but has a value of undefined

// make sure this variable isn't declared
// let age

console.log(typeof message);  // "undefined"
console.log(typeof age);      // "undefined"
```

In both cases, calling `typeof` on the variable returns the string `"undefined"`. Logically, this makes sense because no real operations can be performed with either variable even though they are technically very different.

> **NOTE** *Even though uninitialized variables are automatically assigned a value of undefined, it is advisable to always initialize variables. That way, when* `typeof` *returns* `"undefined,"` *you'll know that it's because a given variable hasn't been declared rather than was simply not initialized.*

The value undefined is falsy; therefore, you are able to more succinctly check for it wherever you might need to. Bear in mind, however, that many other possible values are also falsy, so be careful in scenarios where you need to test for an exact value of undefined rather than just a falsy value:

```
let message;    // this variable is declared but has a value of undefined
// 'age' is not declared

if (message) {
  // This block will not execute
}

if (!message) {
  // This block will execute
}

if (age) {
  // This will throw an error
}
```

The Null Type

The Null type is the second data type that has only one value: the special value `null`. Logically, a null value is an empty object pointer, which is why `typeof` returns "object" when it's passed a null value in the following example:

```
let car = null;
console.log(typeof car);   // "object"
```

When defining a variable that is meant to later hold an object, it is advisable to initialize the variable to null as opposed to anything else. That way, you can explicitly check for the value null to determine if the variable has been filled with an object reference at a later time, such as in this example:

```
if (car != null) {
    // do something with car
}
```

The value undefined is a derivative of null, so ECMA-262 defines them to be superficially equal as follows:

```
console.log(null == undefined);    // true
```

Using the equality operator (==) between null and undefined always returns true, though keep in mind that this operator converts its operands for comparison purposes (covered in detail later in this chapter).

Even though null and undefined are related, they have very different uses. As mentioned previously, you should never explicitly set the value of a variable to undefined, but the same does not hold true for null. Any time an object is expected but is not available, null should be used in its place. This helps to keep the paradigm of null as an empty object pointer and further differentiates it from undefined.

The null type is falsy; therefore, you are able to more succinctly check for it wherever you might need to. Bear in mind, however, that many other possible values are also falsy, so be careful in scenarios where you need to test for an exact value of null rather than just a falsy value:

```
let message = null;
let age;

if (message) {
  // This block will not execute
}

if (!message) {
  // This block will execute
}

if (age) {
  // This block will not execute
}

if (!age) {
  // This block will execute
}
```

The Boolean Type

The Boolean type is one of the most frequently used types in ECMAScript and has only two literal values: true and false. These values are distinct from numeric values, so true is not equal to 1, and false is not equal to 0. Assignment of Boolean values to variables is as follows:

```
let found = true;
let lost = false;
```

Note that the Boolean literals `true` and `false` are case–sensitive, so True and False (and other mix-ings of uppercase and lowercase) are valid as identifiers but not as Boolean values.

Though there are just two literal Boolean values, all types of values have Boolean equivalents in ECMAScript. To convert a value into its Boolean equivalent, the special `Boolean()` casting function is called, like this:

```
let message = "Hello world!";
let messageAsBoolean = Boolean(message);
```

In this example, the string message is converted into a Boolean value and stored in `messageAsBoolean`. The `Boolean()` casting function can be called on any type of data and will always return a Boolean value. The rules for when a value is converted to true or false depend on the data type as much as the actual value. The following table outlines the various data types and their specific conversions.

DATA TYPE	VALUES CONVERTED TO TRUE	VALUES CONVERTED TO FALSE
Boolean	`true`	`false`
String	Any nonempty string	`""` (empty string)
Number	Any nonzero number (including infinity)	`0`, NaN (See the "NaN" section later in this chapter.)
Object	Any object	`null`
Undefined	n/a	`undefined`

These conversions are important to understand because flow-control statements, such as the `if` state-ment, automatically perform this Boolean conversion, as shown here:

```
let message = "Hello world!";
if (message) {
   console.log("Value is true");
}
```

In this example, the `console.log` will be displayed because the string message is automatically con-verted into its Boolean equivalent (`true`). It's important to understand what variable you're using in a flow-control statement because of this automatic conversion. Mistakenly using an object instead of a Boolean can drastically alter the flow of your application.

The Number Type

The ECMAScript Number data type uses the IEEE–754 format to represent both integers and floating-point values (also called double–precision values in some languages). To support the various types of numbers, there are several different number literal formats.

The most basic number literal format is that of a decimal integer, which can be entered directly as shown here:

```
let intNum = 55;  // integer
```

Integers can also be represented as binary (base 2), octal (base 8), or hexadecimal (base 16) literals. For a binary literal, the 0b prefix must be followed by a sequence of 1s and 0s:

```
let binaryNum1 = 0b110;   // binary for 6
let binaryNum2 = 0b333;   // invalid binary - SyntaxError
```

An octal literal can be defined both implicitly and explicitly. For the implicit declaration, the first digit must be a zero (0) followed by a sequence of octal digits (numbers 0 through 7). If a number out of this range is detected in the literal, then the leading zero is ignored and the number is treated as a decimal, as in the following examples:

```
let octalNum1 = 070;    // octal for 56
let octalNum2 = 079;    // invalid octal - interpreted as 79
```

An octal literal can also be defined explicitly, with a 0o prefix:

```
let octalNum3 = 0o70;    // octal for 56
let octalNum4 = 0o79;    // invalid octal - SyntaxError
```

Octal literals are invalid when running in strict mode and will cause the JavaScript engine to throw a syntax error. To create a hexadecimal literal, you must make the first two characters 0x (case insensitive), followed by any number of hexadecimal digits (0 through 9, and A through F). Letters may be in uppercase or lowercase. Here's an example:

```
let hexNum1 = 0xA;    // hexadecimal for 10
let hexNum2 = 0x1f;   // hexadecimal for 31
```

Numbers created using binary, octal, or hexadecimal format are treated as decimal numbers in all arithmetic operations.

> **NOTE** *Because of the way that numbers are stored in JavaScript, it is actually possible to have a value of positive zero (+0) and negative zero (–0). Positive zero and negative zero are considered equivalent in all cases but are noted in this text for clarity.*

Floating-Point Values

To define a floating-point value, you must include a decimal point and at least one number after the decimal point. Although an integer is not necessary before a decimal point, it is recommended. Here are some examples:

```
let floatNum1 = 1.1;
let floatNum2 = 0.1;
let floatNum3 = .1;    // valid, but not recommended
```

For very large or very small numbers, floating-point values can be represented using *e-notation*. E-notation is used to indicate a number that should be multiplied by 10 raised to a given power. The format of e-notation in ECMAScript is to have a number (integer or floating-point) followed by an uppercase or lowercase letter E, followed by the power of 10 to multiply by. Consider the following:

```
let floatNum = 3.125e7;   // equal to 31250000
```

In this example, `floatNum` is equal to 31,250,000 even though it is represented in a more compact form using e-notation. The notation essentially says, "Take 3.125 and multiply it by 10⁷."

E-notation can also be used to represent very small numbers, such as 0.00000000000000003, which can be written more succinctly as 3e–17. By default, ECMAScript converts any floating-point value with at least six zeros after the decimal point into e-notation (for example, 0.0000003 becomes 3e–7).

Floating-point values are accurate up to 17 decimal places but are far less accurate in arithmetic computations than whole numbers. For instance, adding 0.1 and 0.2 yields 0.30000000000000004 instead of 0.3. These small rounding errors make it difficult to test for specific floating-point values. Consider this example:

```
if (a + b == 0.3) {       // avoid!
   console.log("You got 0.3.");
}
```

Here, the sum of two numbers is tested to see if it's equal to 0.3. This will work for 0.05 and 0.25 and for 0.15 and 0.15. But if applied to 0.1 and 0.2, as discussed previously, this test would fail. Therefore you should never test for specific floating-point values.

> **NOTE** *It's important to understand that rounding errors are a side effect of the way floating-point arithmetic is done in IEEE-754–based numbers and is not unique to ECMAScript. Other languages that use the same format have the same issues.*

Numeric Separators

All numbers can use a single underscore as a numeric separator for increased readability. The underscore can appear as many times as needed in a number literal—the interpreter will silently ignore them:

```
let oneMillion = 1_000_000;
let binary = 0b0100_0000;
let float = 1_000.000_001;
```

The underscore cannot start or end a number literal, cannot reside next to a decimal, and cannot follow a leading 0:

```
let invalid1 = _101;   // ReferenceError, _101 interpreted as variable name
let invalid2 = 101_;   // SyntaxError
let invalid3 = 0_01;   // SyntaxError
let invalid4 = 1._4;   // SyntaxError
```

Range of Values

Not all numbers in the world can be represented in the ECMAScript Number data type because of memory constraints. The smallest number that can be represented in ECMAScript is stored in `Number.MIN_VALUE` and is 5e–324 on most browsers; the largest number is stored in `Number.MAX_VALUE` and is 1.7976931348623157e+308 on most browsers. If a calculation results in a number that cannot be represented by JavaScript's numeric range, the number automatically gets the special value of Infinity. Any negative number that can't be represented is –Infinity (negative infinity), and any positive number that can't be represented is simply Infinity (positive infinity).

If a calculation returns either positive or negative Infinity, that value cannot be used in any further calculations, because Infinity has no numeric representation with which to calculate. To determine if a value is finite (that is, it occurs between the minimum and the maximum), there is the `isFinite()` function. This function returns `true` only if the argument is between the minimum and the maximum values, as in this example:

```
let result = Number.MAX_VALUE + Number.MAX_VALUE;
console.log(isFinite(result));  // false
```

Though it is rare to do calculations that take values outside of the range of finite numbers, it is possible and should be monitored when doing very large or very small calculations.

> **NOTE** *You can also get the values of positive and negative Infinity by accessing* `Number.NEGATIVE_INFINITY` *and* `Number.POSITIVE_INFINITY`. *As you may expect, these properties contain the values –Infinity and Infinity, respectively.*

NaN

There is a special numeric value called NaN, short for *Not a Number*, which is used to indicate when an operation intended to return a number has failed (as opposed to throwing an error). For example, taking the square root of a negative number typically causes an error in other programming languages, halting code execution. In ECMAScript, taking the square root of a negative number returns NaN, which allows other processing to continue.

The value NaN has a couple of unique properties. First, any operation involving NaN always returns NaN (for instance, NaN /10), which can be problematic in the case of multistep computations. Second, NaN is not equal to any value, including NaN. For example, the following returns false:

```
console.log(NaN == NaN);  // false
```

For this reason, ECMAScript provides the `isNaN()` function. This function accepts a single argument, which can be of any data type, to determine if the value is "not a number." When a value is passed into `isNaN()`, an attempt is made to convert it into a number. Some nonnumerical values convert into numbers directly, such as the string "10" or a Boolean value. Any value that cannot be converted into a number causes the function to return true. Consider the following:

```
console.log(isNaN(NaN));     // true
console.log(isNaN(10));      // false - 10 is a number
console.log(isNaN("10"));    // false - can be converted to number 10
console.log(isNaN("blue"));  // true - cannot be converted to a number
console.log(isNaN(true));    // false - can be converted to number 1
```

This example tests five different values. The first test is on the value NaN itself, which, obviously, returns `true`. The next two tests use numeric 10 and the string "10," which both return `false` because the numeric value for each is 10. The string "blue," however, cannot be converted into a number, so the function returns `true`. The Boolean value of `true` can be converted into the number 1, so the function returns `false`.

> **NOTE** *Although typically not done,* `isNaN()` *can be applied to objects. In that case, the object's* `valueOf()` *method is first called to determine if the returned value can be converted into a number. If not, the* `toString()` *method is called and its returned value is tested as well. This is the general way that built-in functions and operators work in ECMAScript and is discussed more in the "Operators" section later in this chapter.*

Number Conversions

There are three functions to convert nonnumeric values into numbers: the `Number()` casting function, the `parseInt()` function, and the `parseFloat()` function. The first function, `Number()`, can be used on any data type; the other two functions are used specifically for converting strings to numbers. Each of these functions reacts differently to the same input.

The `Number()` function performs conversions based on these rules:

➤ When applied to Boolean values, `true` and `false` get converted into 1 and 0, respectively.

➤ When applied to numbers, the value is simply passed through and returned.

➤ When applied to null, `Number()` returns 0.

➤ When applied to undefined, `Number()` returns NaN.

➤ When applied to strings, the following rules are applied:

> ➤ If the string contains only numeric characters, optionally preceded by a plus or minus sign, it is always converted to a decimal number, so Number("1") becomes 1, Number("123") becomes 123, and Number("011") becomes 11 (note: leading zeros are ignored).

> ➤ If the string contains a valid floating-point format, such as "1.1," it is converted into the appropriate floating-point numeric value (once again, leading zeros are ignored).

> ➤ If the string contains a valid hexadecimal format, such as "0xf," it is converted into an integer that matches the hexadecimal value.

> ➤ If the string is empty (contains no characters), it is converted to 0.

> ➤ If the string contains anything other than these previous formats, it is converted into NaN.

➤ When applied to objects, the `valueOf()` method is called and the returned value is converted based on the previously described rules. If that conversion results in NaN, the `toString()` method is called and the rules for converting strings are applied.

Converting to numbers from various data types can get complicated, as indicated by the number of rules there are for Number(). Here are some concrete examples:

```
let num1 = Number("Hello world!");   // NaN
let num2 = Number("");               // 0
let num3 = Number("000011");         // 11
let num4 = Number(true);             // 1
```

In these examples, the string "Hello world" is converted into NaN because it has no corresponding numeric value, and the empty string is converted into 0. The string "000011" is converted to the number 11 because the initial zeros are ignored. Last, the value true is converted to 1.

> **NOTE** *The unary plus operator, discussed in the "Operators" section later in this chapter, works the same as the* Number() *function.*

Because of the complexities and oddities of the Number() function when converting strings, the parseInt() function is usually a better option when you are dealing with integers. The parseInt() function examines the string much more closely to see if it matches a number pattern. Leading white space in the string is ignored until the first non–white space character is found. If this first character isn't a number, the minus sign, or the plus sign, parseInt() always returns NaN, which means the empty string returns NaN (unlike with Number(), which returns 0). If the first character is a number, plus, or minus, then the conversion goes on to the second character and continues on until either the end of the string is reached or a nonnumeric character is found. For instance, "1234blue" is converted to 1234 because "blue" is completely ignored. Similarly, "22.5" will be converted to 22 because the decimal is not a valid integer character.

Assuming that the first character in the string is a number, the parseInt() function also recognizes the various integer formats (decimal, octal, and hexadecimal, as discussed previously). This means when the string begins with "0x," it is interpreted as a hexadecimal integer; if it begins with "0" followed by a number, it is interpreted as an octal value.

Here are some conversion examples to better illustrate what happens:

```
let num1 = parseInt("1234blue");   // 1234
let num2 = parseInt("");           // NaN
let num3 = parseInt("0xA");        // 10 - hexadecimal
let num4 = parseInt(22.5);         // 22
let num5 = parseInt("70");         // 70 - decimal
let num6 = parseInt("0xf");        // 15 - hexadecimal
```

All of the different numeric formats can be confusing to keep track of, so parseInt() provides a second argument: the radix (number of digits). If you know that the value you're parsing is in hexadecimal format, you can pass in the radix 16 as a second argument and ensure that the correct parsing will occur, as shown here:

```
let num = parseInt("0xAF", 16);      // 175
```

In fact, by providing the hexadecimal radix, you can leave off the leading "0x" and the conversion will work as follows:

```
let num1 = parseInt("AF", 16);   // 175
let num2 = parseInt("AF");       // NaN
```

In this example, the first conversion occurs correctly, but the second conversion fails. The difference is that the radix is passed in on the first line, telling `parseInt()` that it will be passed a hexadecimal string; the second line sees that the first character is not a number and stops automatically.

Passing in a radix can greatly change the outcome of the conversion. Consider the following:

```
let num1 = parseInt("10", 2);    // 2 - parsed as binary
let num2 = parseInt("10", 8);    // 8 - parsed as octal
let num3 = parseInt("10", 10);   // 10 - parsed as decimal
let num4 = parseInt("10", 16);   // 16 - parsed as hexadecimal
```

Because leaving off the radix allows `parseInt()` to choose how to interpret the input, it's advisable to always include a radix to avoid errors.

> **NOTE** *Most of the time you'll be parsing decimal numbers, so it's good to always include 10 as the second argument.*

The `parseFloat()` function works in a similar way to `parseInt()`, looking at each character starting in position 0. It also continues to parse the string until it reaches either the end of the string or a character that is invalid in a floating-point number. This means that a decimal point is valid the first time it appears, but a second decimal point is invalid and the rest of the string is ignored, resulting in "22.34.5" being converted to 22.34.

Another difference in `parseFloat()` is that initial zeros are always ignored. This function will recognize any of the floating-point formats discussed earlier, as well as the decimal format (leading zeros are always ignored). Hexadecimal numbers always become 0. Because `parseFloat()` parses only decimal values, there is no radix mode. A final note: if the string represents a whole number (no decimal point or only a zero after the decimal point), `parseFloat()` returns an integer. Here are some examples:

```
let num1 = parseFloat("1234blue");   // 1234 - integer
let num2 = parseFloat("0xA");        // 0
let num3 = parseFloat("22.5");       // 22.5
let num4 = parseFloat("22.34.5");    // 22.34
let num5 = parseFloat("0908.5");     // 908.5
let num6 = parseFloat("3.125e7");    // 31250000
```

The BigInt Type

The `BigInt` data type is a primitive for dealing with large integers that exceed `Number` `.MAX_SAFE_INTEGER`. Under the hood, the BigInt primitive allocates an object in memory to represent arbitrarily large integers that cannot fit inside a CPU register. Instead of the typical IEEE–754 64-bit format, the JavaScript engine represents one large number with a collection of smaller values that *can* fit into a CPU register. Each BigInt is a signed integer.

> **NOTE** *Use a BigInt value only when dealing with values greater than 2^53.*

A BigInt can be created either by appending "*n*" to the end of an integer literal or with the `BigInt()` function:

```
let bigintA = 12345n;
let bigintB = BigInt(12345);
let bigintC = BigInt(0x12345);
let bigintD = BigInt("12345");
let bigintE = BigInt("0o12345");
```

As shown above, the `BitInt()` function can be passed a number literal (or string equivalent) in binary, octal, decimal, or hexadecimal format.

A BigInt is similar to a Number, but the two types cannot be mixed when using arithmetic or bitwise operators. Furthermore, a BigInt cannot be used with any built-in `Math` methods:

```
123n + 123n;        // ok

123 + 123n;         // TypeError
Math.round(123n);   // TypeError
```

Conversion

Integer values can be converted to and from the BigInt format, but because the underlying representation in memory is fundamentally different, a loss of precision may occur. The BigInt type is incompatible with non-integers:

```
123n === BigInt(123);   // true
123 === Number(123n);   // true

// Note loss of precision
Number(BigInt(10000000000054321));   // 10000000000054320
Number(54321n + BigInt(1E16));       // 10000000000054320

BigInt(0.5);   // RangeError
```

Operators

BigInt supports *nearly* all the arithmetic, unary, and bitwise operators used by the Number type. Note with `bigintB` that the remainder from a division operation is automatically rounded down:

```
let bigintA = 10n ** 2n;   // 100n
let bigintB = 100n / 3n;   // 33n
let bigintC = 16n | 8n;    // 24n
let bigintD = -8n + -8n;   // -16n
```

There are two operators that are not supported:

➤ The zero-fill right shift `>>>` operator is not supported.

➤ The unary `+` operator is not supported.

Although mixing Number and BigInt is not allowed with arithmetic and bitwise operators, you can still use comparison operators and sorting between the types:

```
4n > 3;  // true

[5n, 1, 3n].sort();  // [1, 3n, 5n]
```

Static Methods

BigInt features two static methods, `asIntN` and `asUintN`, for clamping integers. Clamping an integer means truncating it to a given number of least significant bits:

➤ `BigInt.asIntN(bits, bigint)` clamps to a signed integer.

➤ `BigInt.asUintN(bits, biting)` clamps to an unsigned integer.

A BigInt is represented as a two's complement number in memory, so clamping methods must be used carefully. As shown in the following examples, the output may be dramatically different than the input number even though the total number of bits is reduced:

```
// Clamps 00011000 to 1000
BigInt.asIntN(4, 24n);    // -8n
BigInt.asUintN(4, 24n);   // 8n

// Clamps 11111111 to 1111
BigInt.asIntN(4, -1n);    // -1n
BigInt.asUintN(4, -1n);   // 15n

// Clamps 00010000 to 10000
BigInt.asIntN(5, 16n);    // -16n

// Clamps 00010000 to 010000
BigInt.asIntN(6, 16n);    // 16n
```

JSON

BigInt does not support JSON serialization, but the built-in JSON global can be provided with `replacer` and `reviver` methods to convert in and out:

```
let data = {
  bigNumber: 1234n
};

JSON.stringify(data);  // TypeError

const replacer = (k, v) => typeof v === 'bigint' ? v.toString() : v;

JSON.stringify(data, replacer);
// {"bigNumber": "1234" }

const reviver = (k, v) => k === "bigNumber" ? BigInt(v) : v;

JSON.parse(`{"bigNumber": "1234"}`, reviver);
// { bigNumber: 1234n }
```

The String Type

The String data type represents a sequence of zero or more 16-bit Unicode characters. Strings can be delineated by either double quotes ("), single quotes ('), or backticks (`), so all of the following are legal:

```
let firstName = "John";
let middleName = 'Jacob';
let lastName = `Jingleheimerschmidt`
```

Unlike some languages in which using different quotes changes how the string is interpreted, there is no difference in the syntaxes in ECMAScript. Note, however, that a string beginning with a certain character must end with the same character. For example, the following will cause a syntax error:

```
let firstName = 'Alice";  // syntax error - quotes must match
```

Character Literals

The String data type includes several character literals to represent nonprintable or otherwise useful characters, as listed in the following table:

LITERAL	MEANING
\n	New line
\t	Tab
\b	Backspace
\r	Carriage return
\f	Form feed
\\	Backslash (\)
\'	Single quote (')—used when the string is delineated by single quotes. Example: 'He said, \'hey.\''.
\"	Double quote (")—used when the string is delineated by double quotes. Example: "He said, \"hey.\"".
\`	Backtick (`)—used when the string is delineated by backticks. Example: `He said, \`hey.\``.
\xnn	A character represented by hexadecimal code *nn* (where *n* is a hexadecimal digit 0-F). Example: \x41 is equivalent to "A".
\unnnn	A Unicode character represented by the hexadecimal code *nnnn* (where *n* is a hexadecimal digit 0-F). Example: \u03a3 is equivalent to the Greek character Σ.

These character literals can be included anywhere with a string and will be interpreted as if they were a single character, as shown here:

```
let text = "This is the letter sigma: \u03a3.";
```

In this example, the variable text is 28 characters long even though the escape sequence is 6 characters long. The entire escape sequence represents a single character, so it is counted as such.

The length of any string can be returned by using the length property, as follows:

```
console.log(text.length);   // 28
```

This property returns the number of 16-bit characters in the string.

> **NOTE** *If a string contains double–byte characters, the* `length` *property may not accurately return the number of characters in the string. Mitigation strategies for this are detailed in the Chapter 5, "Basic Reference Types."*

The Nature of Strings

Strings are immutable in ECMAScript, meaning that once they are created, their values cannot change. To change the string held by a variable, the original string must be destroyed and the variable filled with another string containing a new value, like this:

```
let lang = "Java";
lang = lang + "Script";
```

Here, the variable lang is defined to contain the string "Java." On the next line, lang is redefined to combine "Java" with "Script," making its value "JavaScript." This happens by creating a new string with enough space for 10 characters and then filling that string with "Java" and "Script." The last step in the process is to destroy the original string "Java" and the string "Script," because neither is necessary anymore.

Converting to a String

There are two ways to convert a value into a string. The first is to use the toString() method that almost every value has. This method's only job is to return the string equivalent of the value. Consider this example:

```
let age = 11;
let ageAsString = age.toString();       // the string "11"
let found = true;
let foundAsString = found.toString();   // the string "true"
```

The toString() method is available on values that are numbers, Booleans, objects, and strings. (Yes, each string has a toString() method that simply returns a copy of itself.) If a value is null or undefined, this method is not available.

In most cases, toString() doesn't have any arguments. However, when used on a number value, toString() actually accepts a single argument: the radix in which to output the number. By default, toString() always returns a string that represents the number as a decimal, but by passing in a radix, toString() can output the value in binary, octal, hexadecimal, or any other valid base, as in this example:

```
let num = 10;
console.log(num.toString());     // "10"
console.log(num.toString(2));    // "1010"
console.log(num.toString(8));    // "12"
console.log(num.toString(10));   // "10"
console.log(num.toString(16));   // "a"
```

This example shows how the output of `toString()` can change for numbers when providing a radix. The value 10 can be output into any number of numeric formats. Note that the default (with no argument) is the same as providing a radix of 10.

If you're not sure that a value isn't null or undefined, you can use the `String()` casting function, which always returns a string regardless of the value type. The `String()` function follows these rules:

➤ If the value has a `toString()` method, it is called (with no arguments) and the result is returned.

➤ If the value is `null`, "null" is returned.

➤ If the value is `undefined`, "undefined" is returned.

Consider the following:

```
let value1 = 10;
let value2 = true;
let value3 = null;
let value4;

console.log(String(value1));    // "10"
console.log(String(value2));    // "true"
console.log(String(value3));    // "null"
console.log(String(value4));    // "undefined"
```

Here, four values are converted into strings: a number, a Boolean, null, and undefined. The result for the number and the Boolean are the same as if `toString()` were called. Because `toString()` isn't available on null and undefined, the `String()` method simply returns literal text for those values.

> **NOTE** *You can also convert a value to a string by adding an empty string (" ") to that value using the plus operator (discussed in the "Operators" section later in this chapter).*

Template Literals

It is also possible to define strings using template literals. This is accomplished using the backtick (`` ` ``) delimiter. Unlike their single and double quoted counterparts, template literals respect new line characters, and can be defined spanning multiple lines:

```
let myMultiLineString = 'first line\nsecond line';
let myMultiLineTemplateLiteral = `first line
second line`;

console.log(myMultiLineString);
// first line
// second line"

console.log(myMultiLineTemplateLiteral);
// first line
// second line

console.log(myMultiLineString === myMultiLinetemplateLiteral);    // true
```

As the name suggests, template literals are especially useful when defining templates, such as HTML:

```
let pageHTML = `
<div>
<a href="#">
    <span>Jake</span>
  </a>
</div>`;
```

Because template literals will exactly match the whitespace inside the backticks, special care will need to be applied when defining them. A correctly formatted template string may appear to have improper indentation:

```
// This template literal has 25 spaces following the line return character
let myTemplateLiteral = `first line
                         second line`;
console.log(myTemplateLiteral.length);   // 47

// This template literal begins with a line return character
let secondTemplateLiteral = `
first line
second line`;
console.log(secondTemplateLiteral[0] === '\n'); // true

// This template literal has no unexpected whitespace characters
let thirdTemplateLiteral = `first line
second line`;
console.log(thirdTemplateLiteral[0]);
// first line
// second line
```

Interpolation

One of the most useful features of template literals is their support for interpolation, which allows you to insert values at one or more places inside a single unbroken definition. Technically, template literals aren't strings, they are special JavaScript syntactical expressions that evaluate into strings. Template literals are evaluated immediately when they are defined and converted into a string instance, and any interpolated variables will be drawn from its immediate scope.

This can be accomplished using a JavaScript expression inside ${}:

```
let value = 5;
let exponent = 'second';

// Formerly, interpolation was accomplished as follows:
let interpolatedString =
  value + ' to the ' + exponent + ' power is ' + (value * value);

// The same thing accomplished with template literals:
let interpolatedTemplateLiteral =
  `${ value } to the ${ exponent } power is ${ value * value }`;

console.log(interpolatedString);            // 5 to the second power is 25
console.log(interpolatedTemplateLiteral);   // 5 to the second power is 25
```

The value being interpolated will eventually be coerced into a string, but any JavaScript expression can safely be interpolated. Nesting template strings is safe with no escaping required:

```
console.log(`Hello, ${ `World` }!`);  // Hello, World!
```

`String()` is invoked to coerce the expression result into a string:

```
let foo = { toString: () => 'World' };
console.log(`Hello, ${ foo }!`);        // Hello, World!
```

Invoking functions and methods inside interpolated expressions is allowed:

```
function capitalize(word) {
   return `${ word[0].toUpperCase() }${ word.slice(1) }`;
}
console.log(`${ capitalize('hello') }, ${ capitalize('world') }!`);  //
Hello, World!
```

Additionally, templates can safely interpolate their previous value:

```
let value = '';
function append() {
  value = `${value}abc`
  console.log(value);
}
append();  // abc
append();  // abcabc
append();  // abcabcabc
```

Template Literal Tag Functions

Template literals also support the ability to define *tag functions*, which are able to define custom interpolation behavior. The tag function is passed the individual pieces after the template has been split by the interpolation token and after the expressions have been evaluated.

A tag function is defined as a regular function and is applied to a template literal by being prepended to it, as shown in the code that follows. The tag function will be passed the template literal split into its pieces: the first argument is an array of the raw strings, and the remaining arguments are the results of the evaluated expressions. The return value of this function will be the string evaluated from the template literal.

This is best demonstrated by example:

```
let a = 6;
let b = 9;

function simpleTag(strings, aValExpression, bValExpression, sumExpression) {
  console.log(strings);
  console.log(aValExpression);
  console.log(bValExpression);
  console.log(sumExpression);

  return 'foobar';
```

```
    }
    let untaggedResult = `${ a } + ${ b } = ${ a + b }`;
    let taggedResult = simpleTag`${ a } + ${ b } = ${ a + b }`;
    // ["", " + ", " = ", ""]
    // 6
    // 9
    // 15

    console.log(untaggedResult);  // "6 + 9 = 15"
    console.log(taggedResult);    // "foobar"
```

Because there are a variable number of expression arguments, using the spread operator to combine them into a single collection is usually prudent:

```
    let a = 6;
    let b = 9;

    function simpleTag(strings, ...expressions) {
      console.log(strings);
      for(const expression of expressions) {
        console.log(expression);
      }

      return 'foobar';
    }
    let taggedResult = simpleTag`${ a } + ${ b } = ${ a + b }`;
    // ["", " + ", " = ", ""]
    // 6
    // 9
    // 15

    console.log(taggedResult);  // "foobar"
```

For a template literal with n interpolated values, the number of expression arguments to the tag function will always be n, and the number of string pieces in the first argument will always be exactly $n + 1$. Therefore, if you wished to "zip" the strings and the evaluated expressions together into the default returned string, you could do so as follows:

```
    let a = 6;
    let b = 9;

    function zipTag(strings, ...expressions) {
      return strings[0] +
             expressions.map((e, i) => `${e}${strings[i + 1]}`)
                        .join('');
    }

    let untaggedResult =    `${ a } + ${ b } = ${ a + b }`;
    let taggedResult = zipTag`${ a } + ${ b } = ${ a + b }`;

    console.log(untaggedResult);  // "6 + 9 = 15"
    console.log(taggedResult);    // "6 + 9 = 15"
```

Raw Strings

It is also possible to use template literals to give you access to the raw template literal contents without being converted into actual character representations, such as a new line or Unicode character. This can be done by using the `String.raw` tag function, which is available by default.

```
// Unicode demo
// \u00A9 is the copyright symbol
console.log(`\u00A9`);              // ©
console.log(String.raw`\u00A9`);   // \u00A9

// Newline demo
console.log(`first line\nsecond line`);
// first line
// second line

console.log(String.raw`first line\nsecond line`);  // "first line\nsecond line"

// This does not work for actual newline characters: they do not
// undergo conversion from their plaintext escaped equivalents
console.log(`first line
second line`);
// first line
// second line

console.log(String.raw`first line
second line`);
// first line
// second line
```

The raw values are also available as a property on each element in the string piece collection inside the tag function:

```
function printRaw(strings) {
  console.log('Actual characters:');
  for (const string of strings) {
    console.log(string);
  }

  console.log('Escaped characters;');
  for (const rawString of strings.raw) {
    console.log(rawString);
  }
}

printRaw`\u00A9${ 'and' }\n`;
// Actual characters:
// ©
// (newline)
// Escaped characters:
// \u00A9
// \n
```

The Symbol Type

Symbols are primitive values, and symbol instances are unique and immutable. The purpose of a symbol is to be a guaranteed unique identifier for object properties that does not risk property collision.

Although they may seem to share some similarities with private properties, symbols are not intended to offer private property behavior (especially because the Object API offers methods to easily discover symbol properties). Instead, symbols are intended to be used as unique tokens that can be used to key special properties with something other than a string.

Basic Symbol Use

Symbols are instantiated using the `Symbol()` function. Because it is its own primitive type, the `typeof` operator will identify a symbol as symbol.

```
let sym = Symbol();
console.log(typeof sym);  // symbol
```

When invoking the function, you can provide an optional string that can be used for identifying the symbol instance when debugging. The string you provide is totally separate from the symbol's definition or identity:

```
let genericSymbol = Symbol();
let otherGenericSymbol = Symbol();

let fooSymbol = Symbol('foo');
let otherFooSymbol = Symbol('foo');

console.log(genericSymbol == otherGenericSymbol);  // false
console.log(fooSymbol == otherFooSymbol);          // false
```

Symbols do not have a literal string syntax, and this is central to their purpose. The specification governing how symbols operate allows you to create a new Symbol instance and use it to key a new property on an object with the guarantee that you will not be overwriting an existing object property—irrespective of whether it is using a string or symbol as a key.

```
let genericSymbol = Symbol();
console.log(genericSymbol);  // Symbol()

let fooSymbol = Symbol('foo');
console.log(fooSymbol);        // Symbol(foo);
```

Importantly, the `Symbol()` function cannot be used with the `new` keyword. The purpose of this is to avoid symbol object wrappers, as is possible with `Boolean`, `String`, and `Number`, which support constructor behavior and instantiate a primitive wrapper object:

```
let myBoolean = new Boolean();
console.log(typeof myBoolean);  // "object"

let myString = new String();
console.log(typeof myString);   // "object"

let myNumber = new Number();
console.log(typeof myNumber);   // "object"

let mySymbol = new Symbol();  // TypeError: Symbol is not a constructor
```

Should you want to utilize an object wrapper, you can make use of the `Object()` function:

```
let mySymbol = Symbol();
let myWrappedSymbol = Object(mySymbol);
console.log(typeof myWrappedSymbol);   // "object"
```

Using the Global Symbol Registry

In scenarios where different parts of the runtime would like to share and reuse a symbol instance, it is possible to create and reuse symbols in a string-keyed global symbol registry.

This behavior can be achieved using `Symbol.for()`:

```
let fooGlobalSymbol = Symbol.for('foo');
console.log(typeof fooGlobalSymbol);   // symbol
```

`Symbol.for()` is an idempotent operation for each string key. The first time it is called with a given string, it will check the global runtime registry, find that no symbol exists, generate a new symbol instance, and add it to the registry. Additional invocations with the same string key will check the global runtime registry, find that a symbol does exist for that string, and return that symbol instance instead.

```
let fooGlobalSymbol = Symbol.for('foo');          // creates new symbol
let otherFooGlobalSymbol = Symbol.for('foo');     // reuses existing symbol

console.log(fooGlobalSymbol === otherFooGlobalSymbol);   // true
```

Symbols defined in the global registry are totally distinct from symbols created using `Symbol()`, even if they share a description:

```
let localSymbol = Symbol('foo');
let globalSymbol = Symbol.for('foo');

console.log(localSymbol === globalSymbol);   // false
```

The global registry requires string keys, so anything you provide as an argument to `Symbol.for()` will be converted to a string. Additionally, the key used for the registry will also be used as the symbol description.

```
let emptyGlobalSymbol = Symbol.for();
console.log(emptyGlobalSymbol);   // Symbol(undefined)
```

It is possible to check against the global registry using `Symbol.keyFor()`, which accepts a symbol and will return the global string key for that global symbol, or undefined if the symbol is not a global symbol.

```
// Create global symbol
let s = Symbol.for('foo');
console.log(Symbol.keyFor(s));   // foo

// Create regular symbol
let s2 = Symbol('bar');
console.log(Symbol.keyFor(s2));   // undefined
```

Using `Symbol.keyFor()` with a non-symbol will throw a `TypeError`:

```
Symbol.keyFor(123);   // TypeError: 123 is not a symbol
```

Using Symbols as Properties

Anywhere you can normally use a string or number property, you can also use a symbol. This includes object literal properties and `Object.defineProperty()`/`Object.defineProperties()`. An object literal can only use a symbol as a property inside the computed property syntax.

```
let s1 = Symbol('foo'),
    s2 = Symbol('bar'),
    s3 = Symbol('baz'),
    s4 = Symbol('qux');

let o = {
  [s1]: 'foo val'
};
// Also valid:   o[s1] = 'foo val';

console.log(o);
// {Symbol(foo): foo val}

Object.defineProperty(o, s2, {value: 'bar val'});

console.log(o);
// {Symbol(foo): foo val, Symbol(bar): bar val}

Object.defineProperties(o, {
  [s3]: {value: 'baz val'},
  [s4]: {value: 'qux val'}
});

console.log(o);
// {Symbol(foo): foo val, Symbol(bar): bar val,
//  Symbol(baz): baz val, Symbol(qux): qux val}
```

Just as `Object.getOwnPropertyNames()` returns an array of regular properties on an object instance, `Object.getOwnPropertySymbols()` returns an array of symbol properties on an object instance. The return values of these two methods are mutually exclusive. `Object.getOwnPropertyDescriptors()` will return an object containing both regular and symbol property descriptors. `Reflect.ownKeys()` will return both types of keys:

```
let s1 = Symbol('foo'),
    s2 = Symbol('bar');

let o = {
  [s1]: 'foo val',
  [s2]: 'bar val',
  baz: 'baz val',
  qux: 'qux val'
};

console.log(Object.getOwnPropertySymbols(o));
// [Symbol(foo), Symbol(bar)]

console.log(Object.getOwnPropertyNames(o));
```

```
// ["baz", "qux"]

console.log(Object.getOwnPropertyDescriptors(o));
// {baz: {...}, qux: {...}, Symbol(foo): {...}, Symbol(bar): {...}}

console.log(Reflect.ownKeys(o));
// ["baz", "qux", Symbol(foo), Symbol(bar)]
```

Because a property counts as a reference to that symbol in memory, Symbols are not lost if directly created and used as properties. However, declining to keep an explicit reference to a property means that traversing all the object's symbol properties will be required to recover the property key:

```
let o = {
  [Symbol('foo')]: 'foo val',
  [Symbol('bar')]: 'bar val'
};

console.log(o);
// {Symbol(foo): "foo val", Symbol(bar): "bar val"}

let barSymbol = Object.getOwnPropertySymbols(o)
            .find((symbol) => symbol.toString().match(/bar/));

console.log(barSymbol);
// Symbol(bar)
```

Well-Known Symbols

ECMAScript includes a collection of *well-known symbols* that are used throughout the language to expose internal language behaviors for direct access, overriding, or emulating. These well-known symbols exist as string properties on the `Symbol` factory function.

One of the primary utilities of these well-known symbols is redefining them as to alter the behavior of the native language constructs. For example, because it is known how the for-of loop will use the `Symbol.iterator` property on whatever object is provided to it, it is possible to provide a custom definition of `Symbol.iterator`'s value in a custom object in order to control how for-of behaves when provided with that object.

There is nothing special about these well-known symbols, they are regular string properties on the `Symbol` global that key an instance of a symbol. Each well-defined symbol property is non-writeable, non-enumerable, and non-configurable.

> **NOTE** *In discussions about the ECMAScript specification, you will frequently see these symbols referred to by their specification names, which are prefixed with @@. For example, @@iterator refers to* `Symbol.iterator`.

Symbol.asyncIterator

Per the ECMAScript specification, this symbol is used as a property for "A method that returns the default `AsyncIterator` for an object. Called by the semantics of the for-await-of statement." It is used to identify the function that implements the asynchronous iterator API.

Language constructs such as the for-await-of loop make use of this function to perform asynchronous iteration. They will invoke the function keyed by `Symbol.asyncIterator` and expect it to return an object which implements the iterator API. In many cases, this will take the form of an `AsyncGenerator`, an object which implements this API:

```
class Foo {
  async *[Symbol.asyncIterator]() {}
}

let f = new Foo();

console.log(f[Symbol.asyncIterator]());
// AsyncGenerator {<suspended>}
```

Specifically, the object produced by the `Symbol.asyncIterator` function should sequentially produce a `Promise` via its `next()` method. This can be through explicit `next()` method definition or implicitly through an async generator function:

```
class Emitter {
  constructor(max) {
    this.max = max;
    this.asyncIdx = 0;
  }

  async *[Symbol.asyncIterator]() {
    while(this.asyncIdx < this.max) {
      yield new Promise((resolve) => resolve(this.asyncIdx++));
    }
  }
}

async function asyncCount() {
  let emitter = new Emitter(5);

  for await(const x of emitter) {
    console.log(x);
  }
}

asyncCount();
// 0
// 1
// 2
// 3
// 4
```

Symbol.hasInstance

This symbol is used as a property for a method that determines if a constructor object recognizes an object as one of the constructor's instances and is called by the semantics of the instanceof operator.

The instanceof operator provides a way of determining if an object instance has a prototype in its prototype chain. Typical use of the instanceof is as follows:

```
function Foo() {}
let f = new Foo();
console.log(f instanceof Foo);   // true

class Bar {}
let b = new Bar();
console.log(b instanceof Bar);   // true
```

In ES6, the instanceof operator is using a Symbol.hasInstance function to evaluate this relationship. The Symbol.hasInstance keys a function which performs the same behavior but with the operands reversed:

```
function Foo() {}
let f = new Foo();
console.log(Foo[Symbol.hasInstance](f));   // true

class Bar {}
let b = new Bar();
console.log(Bar[Symbol.hasInstance](b));   // true
```

This property is defined on the Function prototype, and therefore it is automatically available by default to all function and class definitions. Because the instanceof operator will seek the property definition on the prototype chain like any other property, it is possible to redefine the function on an inherited class as a static method:

```
class Bar {}
class Baz extends Bar {
  static [Symbol.hasInstance]() {
    return false;
  }
}

let b = new Baz();
console.log(Bar[Symbol.hasInstance](b));   // true
console.log(b instanceof Bar);             // true
console.log(Baz[Symbol.hasInstance](b));   // false
console.log(b instanceof Baz);             // false
```

Symbol.isConcatSpreadable

Per the ECMAScript specification, this symbol is used as a property for "A Boolean valued property that if true indicates that an object should be flattened to its array elements by Array.prototype. concat()." The Array.prototype.concat method in ES6 will select how to join an array-like object to the array instance based on the type of object it is passed. The value of Symbol.isConcatSpreadable allows you to override this behavior.

Array objects by default will be flattened into the existing array; a value of false or falsy value will append the entire object to the array. Array-like objects by default will be appended to the array; a value of true or truthy value will flatten the array-like object into the array instance. Other objects which are not array-like will be ignored when Symbol.isConcatSpreadable is set to true.

```
let initial = ['foo'];

let array = ['bar'];
console.log(array[Symbol.isConcatSpreadable]);        // undefined
console.log(initial.concat(array));                   // ['foo', 'bar']
array[Symbol.isConcatSpreadable] = false;
console.log(initial.concat(array));                   // ['foo', Array(1)]

let arrayLikeObject = { length: 1, 0: 'baz' };
console.log(arrayLikeObject[Symbol.isConcatSpreadable]);    // undefined
console.log(initial.concat(arrayLikeObject));              // ['foo', {...}]
arrayLikeObject[Symbol.isConcatSpreadable] = true;
console.log(initial.concat(arrayLikeObject));              // ['foo', 'baz']

let otherObject = new Set().add('qux');
console.log(otherObject[Symbol.isConcatSpreadable]);      // undefined
console.log(initial.concat(otherObject));                 // ['foo', Set(1)]
otherObject[Symbol.isConcatSpreadable] = true;
console.log(initial.concat(otherObject));                 // ['foo']
```

Symbol.iterator

This symbol is used as a property for a method that returns the default iterator for an object and is called by the semantics of the for-of statement. It is used to identify the function that implements the iterator API.

Language constructs such as the for-of loop make use of this function to perform iteration. They will invoke the function keyed by `Symbol.iterator` and expect it to return an object which implements the iterator API. In many cases, this will take the form of a Generator, an object which implements this API:

```
class Foo {
  *[Symbol.iterator]() {}
}

let f = new Foo();

console.log(f[Symbol.iterator]());
// Generator {<suspended>}
```

Specifically, the object produced by the `Symbol.iterator` function should sequentially produce values via its `next()` method. This can be through explicit `next()` method definition or implicitly through a generator function:

```
class Emitter {
  constructor(max) {
    this.max = max;
    this.idx = 0;
  }

  *[Symbol.iterator]() {
    while(this.idx < this.max) {
      yield this.idx++;
    }
  }
}
```

```
  }

  function count() {
    let emitter = new Emitter(5);

    for (const x of emitter) {
      console.log(x);
    }
  }

  count();
  // 0
  // 1
  // 2
  // 3
  // 4
```

> **NOTE** *Iterator definition is covered in depth in the Chapter 7, "Iterators and Generators."*

Symbol.match

This symbol is used as a property for a regular expression method that matches the regular expression against a string and is called by the `String.prototype.match()` method. The `String.prototype.match()` method will use the function keyed by `Symbol.match` to evaluate the expression. The regular expression prototype has this function defined by default, and therefore all regular expression instances are valid parameters to the `String` method by default:

```
console.log(RegExp.prototype[Symbol.match]);
// Æ' [Symbol.match]() { [native code] }

console.log('foobar'.match(/bar/));
//   ["bar", index: 3, input: "foobar", groups: undefined]
```

Providing something other than a regular expression to this method will cause it to be converted to a `RegExp` object. If you wish to circumvent this behavior and have the method use the parameter directly, it is possible to pass something other than a regular expression instance to the `match()` method by defining a `Symbol.match` function to supplant the behavior that would otherwise be exhibited by the regular expression. This function has a single parameter which is the string instance upon which `match()` is invoked. The return value is unrestricted:

```
class FooMatcher {
  static [Symbol.match](target) {
    return target.includes('foo');
  }
}

console.log('foobar'.match(FooMatcher));   // true
console.log('barbaz'.match(FooMatcher));   // false

class StringMatcher {
  constructor(str) {
    this.str = str;
```

```
  }

  [Symbol.match](target) {
    return target.includes(this.str);
  }
}

console.log('foobar'.match(new StringMatcher('foo')));  // true
console.log('barbaz'.match(new StringMatcher('qux')));  // false
```

Symbol.replace

This symbol is used as a property for a regular expression method that replaces matched substrings of a string and is called by the `String.prototype.replace()` method. The `String.prototype.replace()` method will use the function keyed by `Symbol.replace` to evaluate the expression. The regular expression prototype has this function defined by default, and therefore all regular expression instances are valid parameters to the `String` method by default:

```
console.log(RegExp.prototype[Symbol.replace]);
// Æ' [Symbol.replace]() { [native code] }

console.log('foobarbaz'.replace(/bar/, 'qux'));
// 'fooquxbaz'
```

Providing something other than a regular expression to this method will cause it to be converted to a `RegExp` object. If you wish to circumvent this behavior and have the method use the parameter directly, it is possible to pass something other than a regular expression instance to the `replace()` method by defining a `Symbol.replace` function to supplant the behavior that would otherwise be exhibited by the regular expression. This function has two parameters, the string instance upon which `replace()` is invoked and the replacement string. The return value is unrestricted:

```
class FooReplacer {
  static [Symbol.replace](target, replacement) {
    return target.split('foo').join(replacement);
  }
}

console.log('barfoobaz'.replace(FooReplacer, 'qux'));
// "barquxbaz"

class StringReplacer {
  constructor(str) {
    this.str = str;
  }

  [Symbol.replace](target, replacement) {
    return target.split(this.str).join(replacement);
  }
}

console.log('barfoobaz'.replace(new StringReplacer('foo'), 'qux'));
// "barquxbaz"
```

Symbol.search

This symbol is used as a property for a regular expression method that returns the index within a string that matches the regular expression and is called by the `String.prototype.search()` method. The `String.prototype.search()` method will use the function keyed by `Symbol.search` to evaluate the expression. The regular expression prototype has this function defined by default, and therefore all regular expression instances are valid parameters to the `String` method by default:

```
console.log(RegExp.prototype[Symbol.search]);
// Æ' [Symbol.search]() { [native code] }

console.log('foobar'.search(/bar/));
// 3
```

Providing something other than a regular expression to this method will cause it to be converted to a `RegExp` object. If you wish to circumvent this behavior and have the method use the parameter directly, it is possible to pass something other than a regular expression instance to the `search()` method by defining a `Symbol.search` function to supplant the behavior that would otherwise be exhibited by the regular expression. This function has a single parameter which is the string instance upon which `search()` is invoked. The return value is unrestricted:

```
class FooSearcher {
  static [Symbol.search](target) {
    return target.indexOf('foo');
  }
}

console.log('foobar'.search(FooSearcher));   // 0
console.log('barfoo'.search(FooSearcher));   // 3
console.log('barbaz'.search(FooSearcher));   // -1

class StringSearcher {
  constructor(str) {
    this.str = str;
  }

  [Symbol.search](target) {
    return target.indexOf(this.str);
  }
}

console.log('foobar'.search(new StringSearcher('foo')));   // 0
console.log('barfoo'.search(new StringSearcher('foo')));   // 3
console.log('barbaz'.search(new StringSearcher('qux')));   // -1
```

Symbol.species

This symbol is used as a property for a function valued property that is the constructor function that is used to create derived objects. This is most commonly used for build-in types which expose methods that instantiate derived objects for the return value of an instance method. Defining a static getter method with `Symbol.species` allows you to override the prototype definition for the newly created instance:

```
class Bar extends Array {}
class Baz extends Array {
```

```
    static get [Symbol.species]() {
      return Array;
    }
  }

  let bar = new Bar();
  console.log(bar instanceof Array);   // true
  console.log(bar instanceof Bar);     // true
  bar = bar.concat('bar');
  console.log(bar instanceof Array);   // true
  console.log(bar instanceof Bar);     // true

  let baz = new Baz();
  console.log(baz instanceof Array);   // true
  console.log(baz instanceof Baz);     // true
  baz = baz.concat('baz');
  console.log(baz instanceof Array);   // true
  console.log(baz instanceof Baz);     // false
```

Symbol.split

This symbol is used as a property for a regular expression method that splits a string at the indices that match the regular expression and is called by the `String.prototype.split()` method. The `String.prototype.split()` method will use the function keyed by `Symbol.split` to evaluate the expression. The regular expression prototype has this function defined by default, and therefore all regular expression instances are valid parameters to the `String` method by default:

```
console.log(RegExp.prototype[Symbol.split]);
// ƒ' [Symbol.split]() { [native code] }

console.log('foobarbaz'.split(/bar/));
// ['foo', 'baz']
```

Providing something other than a regular expression to this method will cause it to be converted to a `RegExp` object. If you wish to circumvent this behavior and have the method use the parameter directly, it is possible to pass something other than a regular expression instance to the `split()` method by defining a `Symbol.split` function to supplant the behavior that would otherwise be exhibited by the regular expression. This function has a single parameter which is the string instance upon which `split()` is invoked. The return value is unrestricted:

```
class FooSplitter {
  static [Symbol.split](target) {
    return target.split('foo');
  }
}

console.log('barfoobaz'.split(FooSplitter));
// ["bar", "baz"]

class StringSplitter {
  constructor(str) {
    this.str = str;
```

```
  }
  [Symbol.split](target) {
    return target.split(this.str);
  }
}

console.log('barfoobaz'.split(new StringSplitter('foo')));
// ["bar", "baz"]
```

Symbol.toPrimitive

This symbol is used as a property for a method that converts an object to a corresponding primitive value and is called by the `ToPrimitive` abstract operation. There are a number of built-in operations which will attempt to coerce an object into a primitive value: a string, a number, or an unspecified primitive type. For a custom object instance, it is possible to divert this behavior by defining a function on the instance's `Symbol.toPrimitive` property.

Based on a string parameter provided to the function (either string, number, or default), you are able to control the returned primitive:

```
class Foo {}
let foo = new Foo();

console.log(3 + foo);        // "3[object Object]"
console.log(3 - foo);        // NaN
console.log(String(foo));    // "[object Object]"

class Bar {
  constructor() {
    this[Symbol.toPrimitive] = function(hint) {
      switch (hint) {
        case 'number':
          return 3;
        case 'string':
          return 'string bar';
        case 'default':
        default:
          return 'default bar';
      }
    }
  }
}
let bar = new Bar();

console.log(3 + bar);        // "3default bar"
console.log(3 - bar);        // 0
console.log(String(bar));    // "string bar"
```

Symbol.toStringTag

This symbol is used as a property for "A String valued property that is used in the creation of the default string description of an object. Accessed by the built-in method `Object.prototype` `.toString()`."

Object identification via the `toString()` method will retrieve the instance identifier specified by `Symbol.toStringTag`, defaulting to `Object`. Built-in types have this value already specified, but custom class instances require explicit definition:

```
let s = new Set();

console.log(s);                         // Set(0) {}
console.log(s.toString());             // [object Set]
console.log(s[Symbol.toStringTag]);   // Set

class Foo {}
let foo = new Foo();

console.log(foo);                       // Foo {}
console.log(foo.toString());           // [object Object]
console.log(foo[Symbol.toStringTag]); // undefined

class Bar {
  constructor() {
    this[Symbol.toStringTag] = 'Bar';
  }
}
let bar = new Bar();

console.log(bar);                       // Bar {}
console.log(bar.toString());           // [object Bar]
console.log(bar[Symbol.toStringTag]); // Bar
```

Symbol.unscopables

Per the ECMAScript specification, this symbol is used as a property for "An object valued property whose own and inherited property names are property names that are excluded from the `with` environment bindings of the associated object." Setting this symbol so it keys an object mapping a corresponding property to true will prevent a `with` environment binding, as shown here:

```
let o = { foo: 'bar' };

with (o) {
  console.log(foo);  // bar
}

o[Symbol.unscopables] = {
  foo: true
};

with (o) {
  console.log(foo);  // ReferenceError
}
```

> **NOTE** *It's not recommended to use* `with`, *so using* `Symbol.unscopables` *is also not recommended.*

The Object Type

Objects in ECMAScript start out as nonspecific groups of data and functionality. Objects are created by using the new operator followed by the name of the object type to create. Developers create their own objects by creating instances of the `Object` type and adding properties and/or methods to it, as shown here:

```
let o = new Object();
```

This syntax is similar to Java, although ECMAScript requires parentheses to be used only when providing arguments to the constructor. If there are no arguments, as in the following example, then the parentheses can be omitted safely (though that's not recommended):

```
let o = new Object;  // legal, but not recommended
```

Instances of `Object` aren't very useful on their own, but the concepts are important to understand because, similar to `java.lang.Object` in Java, the `Object` type in ECMAScript is the base from which all other objects are derived. All of the properties and methods of the `Object` type are also present on other, more specific objects.

Each `Object` instance has the following properties and methods:

➤ `constructor`—The function that was used to create the object. In the previous example, the constructor is the `Object()` function.

➤ `hasOwnProperty(propertyName)`—Indicates if the given property exists on the object instance (not on the prototype). The property name must be specified as a string (for example, `o.hasOwnProperty("name")`).

➤ `isPrototypeof(object)`—Determines if the object is a prototype of another object.

➤ `propertyIsEnumerable(propertyName)`—Indicates if the given property can be enumerated using the `for-in` statement (discussed later in this chapter). As with `hasOwnProperty()`, the property name must be a string.

➤ `toLocaleString()`—Returns a string representation of the object that is appropriate for the locale of execution environment.

➤ `toString()`—Returns a string representation of the object.

➤ `valueOf()`—Returns a string, number, or Boolean equivalent of the object. It often returns the same value as `toString()`.

Because Object is the base for all objects in ECMAScript, every object has these base properties and methods.

> **NOTE** *Technically speaking, the behavior of objects in ECMA-262 need not necessarily apply to other objects in JavaScript. Objects that exist in the browser environment, such as those in the Browser Object Model (BOM) and Document Object Model (DOM), are considered host objects because they are provided and defined by the host implementation. Host objects aren't governed by ECMA-262 and, as such, may or may not directly inherit from* Object.

OPERATORS

ECMA-262 describes a set of *operators* that can be used to manipulate data values. The operators range from mathematical operations (such as addition and subtraction) and bitwise operators to relational operators and equality operators. Operators are unique in ECMAScript in that they can be used on a wide range of values, including strings, numbers, Booleans, and even objects. When used on objects, operators typically call the `valueOf()` and/or `toString()` method to retrieve a value they can work with.

Unary Operators

Operators that work on only one value are called *unary operators*. They are the simplest operators in ECMAScript.

Increment/Decrement

The increment and decrement operators are taken directly from C and come in two versions: prefix and postfix. The prefix versions of the operators are placed before the variable they work on; the postfix ones are placed after the variable. To use a prefix increment, which adds 1 to a numeric value, you place two plus signs (++) in front of a variable like this:

```
let age = 29;
++age;
```

In this example, the prefix increment changes the value of age to 30 (adding 1 to its previous value of 29). This is effectively equal to the following:

```
let age = 29;
age = age + 1;
```

The prefix decrement acts in a similar manner, subtracting 1 from a numeric value. To use a prefix decrement, place two minus signs (--) before a variable, as shown here:

```
let age = 29;
--age;
```

Here the age variable is decremented to 28 (subtracting 1 from 29).

When using either a prefix increment or a prefix decrement, the variable's value is changed before the statement is evaluated. (In computer science, this is usually referred to as having a *side effect*.) Consider the following:

```
let age = 29;
let anotherAge = --age + 2;

console.log(age);         // 28
console.log(anotherAge);  // 30
```

In this example, the variable `anotherAge` is initialized with the decremented value of age plus 2. Because the decrement happens first, age is set to 28, and then 2 is added, resulting in 30.

The prefix increment and decrement are equal in terms of order of precedence in a statement and are therefore evaluated left to right. Consider this example:

```
let num1 = 2;
let num2 = 20;
let num3 = --num1 + num2;
let num4 = num1 + num2;
console.log(num3);   // 21
console.log(num4);   // 21
```

Here, num3 is equal to 21 because num1 is decremented to 1 before the addition occurs. The variable num4 also contains 21, because the addition is also done using the changed values.

The postfix versions of increment and decrement use the same syntax (++ and --, respectively) but are placed after the variable instead of before it. Postfix increment and decrement differ from the prefix versions in one important way: the increment or decrement doesn't occur until after the containing statement has been evaluated. In certain circumstances, this difference doesn't matter, as in this example:

```
let age = 29;
age++;
```

Moving the increment operator after the variable doesn't change what these statements do, because the increment is the only operation occurring. However, when mixed together with other operations, the difference becomes apparent, as in the following example:

```
let num1 = 2;
let num2 = 20;
let num3 = num1-- + num2;
let num4 = num1 + num2;
console.log(num3);   // 22
console.log(num4);   // 21
```

With just one simple change in this example, using postfix decrement instead of prefix, you can see the difference. In the prefix example, num3 and num4 both ended up equal to 21, whereas this example ends with num3 equal to 22 and num4 equal to 21. The difference is that the calculation for num3 uses the original value of num1 (2) to complete the addition, whereas num4 is using the decremented value (1).

All four of these operators work on any values, meaning not just integers but strings, Booleans, floating-point values, and objects. The increment and decrement operators follow these rules regarding values:

➤ When used on a string that is a valid representation of a number, convert to a number and apply the change. The variable is changed from a string to a number.

➤ When used on a string that is not a valid number, the variable's value is set to NaN. The variable is changed from a string to a number.

➤ When used on a Boolean value that is false, convert to 0 and apply the change. The variable is changed from a Boolean to a number.

➤ When used on a Boolean value that is true, convert to 1 and apply the change. The variable is changed from a Boolean to a number.

➤ When used on a floating-point value, apply the change by adding or subtracting 1.

➤ When used on an object, call its valueOf() method to get a value to work with. Apply the other rules. If the result is NaN, then call toString() and apply the other rules again. The variable is changed from an object to a number.

The following example demonstrates some of these rules:

```
let s1 = "2";
let s2 = "z";
let b = false;
let f = 1.1;
let o = {
  valueOf() {
    return -1;
  }
};

s1++;  // value becomes numeric 3
s2++;  // value becomes NaN
b++;   // value becomes numeric 1
f--;   // value becomes 0.10000000000000009 (due to floating-point inaccuracies)
o--;   // value becomes numeric -2
```

Unary Plus and Minus

The *unary plus and minus operators* are familiar symbols to most developers and operate the same way in ECMAScript as they do in high-school math. The unary plus is represented by a single plus sign (+) placed before a variable and does nothing to a numeric value, as shown in this example:

```
let num = 25;
num = +num;
console.log(num);  // 25
```

When the unary plus is applied to a nonnumeric value, it performs the same conversion as the `Number()` casting function: the Boolean values of `false` and `true` are converted to 0 and 1, string values are parsed according to a set of specific rules, and objects have their `valueOf()` and/or `toString()` method called to get a value to convert.

The following example demonstrates the behavior of the unary plus when acting on different data types:

```
let s1 = "01";
let s2 = "1.1";
let s3 = "z";
let b = false;
let f = 1.1;
let o = {
  valueOf() {
    return -1;
  }
};

s1 = +s1;  // value becomes numeric 1
s2 = +s2;  // value becomes numeric 1.1
s3 = +s3;  // value becomes NaN
b = +b;    // value becomes numeric 0
f = +f;    // no change, still 1.1
o = +o;    // value becomes numeric -1
```

The unary minus operator's primary use is to negate a numeric value, such as converting 1 into –1. The simple case is illustrated here:

```
let num = 25;
num = -num;
console.log(num);   // -25
```

When used on a numeric value, the unary minus simply negates the value (as in this example). When used on nonnumeric values, unary minus applies all of the same rules as unary plus and then negates the result, as shown here:

```
let s1 = "01";
let s2 = "1.1";
let s3 = "z";
let b = false;
let f = 1.1;
let o = {
  valueOf() {
    return -1;
  }
};

s1 = -s1;  // value becomes numeric -1
s2 = -s2;  // value becomes numeric -1.1
s3 = -s3;  // value becomes NaN
b = -b;    // value becomes numeric 0
f = -f;    // change to -1.1
o = -o;    // value becomes numeric 1
```

The unary plus and minus operators are used primarily for basic arithmetic but can also be useful for conversion purposes, as illustrated in the previous example.

Bitwise Operators

The next set of operators works with numbers at their very base level, with the bits that represent them in memory. All numbers in ECMAScript are stored in IEEE–754 64-bit format, but the bitwise operations do not work directly on the 64-bit representation. Instead, the value is converted into a 32-bit integer, the operation takes place, and the result is converted back into 64 bits. To the developer, it appears that only the 32-bit integer exists because the 64-bit storage format is transparent. With that in mind, consider how 32-bit integers work.

Signed integers use the first 31 of the 32 bits to represent the numeric value of the integer. The 32nd bit represents the sign of the number: 0 for positive or 1 for negative. Depending on the value of that bit, called the *sign bit*, the format of the rest of the number is determined. Positive numbers are stored in true binary format, with each of the 31 bits representing a power of 2, starting with the first bit (called bit 0), representing 2^0, the second bit represents 2^1, and so on. If any bits are unused, they are filled with 0 and essentially ignored. For example, the number 18 is represented as 00000000000000 000000000000010010, or more succinctly as 10010. These are the five most significant bits and can be used, by themselves, to determine the actual value (see Figure 3.1).

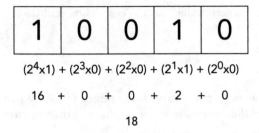

$(2^4 \times 1) + (2^3 \times 0) + (2^2 \times 0) + (2^1 \times 1) + (2^0 \times 0)$

$16 \ + \ 0 \ + \ 0 \ + \ 2 \ + \ 0$

18

FIGURE 3.1: Breakdown of binary integer representation

Negative numbers are also stored in binary code but in a format called *two's complement*. The two's complement of a number is calculated in three steps:

1. Determine the binary representation of the absolute value (for example, to find –18, first determine the binary representation of 18).

2. Find the one's complement of the number, which essentially means that every 0 must be replaced with a 1, and vice versa.

3. Add 1 to the result.

Using this process to determine the binary representation –18, start with the binary representation of 18, which is the following:

```
0000 0000 0000 0000 0000 0000 0001 0010
```

Next, take the one's complement, which is the inverse of this number:

```
1111 1111 1111 1111 1111 1111 1110 1101
```

Finally, add 1 to the one's complement as follows:

```
1111 1111 1111 1111 1111 1111 1110 1101
                  1
-----------------------------------------
1111 1111 1111 1111 1111 1111 1110 1110
```

So the binary equivalent of –18 is 11111111111111111111111111101110. Keep in mind that you have no access to bit 31 when dealing with signed integers.

ECMAScript does its best to keep all of this information from you. When outputting a negative number as a binary string, you get the binary code of the absolute value preceded by a minus sign, as in this example:

```
let num = -18;
console.log(num.toString(2));  // "-10010"
```

When you convert the number –18 to a binary string, the result is –10010. The conversion process interprets the two's complement and represents it in an arguably more logical form.

> **NOTE** *By default, all integers are represented as signed in ECMAScript. There is, however, such a thing as an unsigned integer. In an unsigned integer, the 32nd bit doesn't represent the sign because there are only positive numbers. Unsigned integers also can be larger, because the extra bit becomes part of the number instead of an indicator of the sign.*

When you apply bitwise operators to numbers in ECMAScript, a conversion takes place behind the scenes: the 64-bit number is converted into a 32-bit number, the operation is performed, and then the 32-bit result is stored back into a 64-bit number. This gives the illusion that you're dealing with true 32-bit numbers, which makes the binary operations work in a way similar to the operations of other languages. A curious side effect of this conversion is that the special values NaN and Infinity both are treated as equivalent to 0 when used in bitwise operations.

If a bitwise operator is applied to a nonnumeric value, the value is first converted into a number using the Number() function (this is done automatically), and then the bitwise operation is applied. The resulting value is a number.

Bitwise NOT

The bitwise NOT is represented by a tilde (~) and simply returns the one's complement of the number. Bitwise NOT is one of just a few ECMAScript operators related to binary mathematics. Consider this example:

```
let num1 = 25;        // binary 00000000000000000000000000011001
let num2 = ~num1;     // binary 11111111111111111111111111100110
console.log(num2);    // -26
```

Here, the bitwise NOT operator is used on 25, producing –26 as the result. This is the end effect of the bitwise NOT: it negates the number and subtracts 1. The same outcome is produced with the following code:

```
let num1 = 25;
let num2 = -num1 - 1;
console.log(num2);       // -26
```

Realistically, though this returns the same result, the bitwise operation is much faster because it works at the very lowest level of numeric representation.

Bitwise AND

The bitwise AND operator is indicated by the ampersand character (&) and works on two values. Essentially, bitwise AND lines up the bits in each number and then, using the rules in the following truth table, performs an AND operation between the two bits in the same position.

BIT FROM FIRST NUMBER	BIT FROM SECOND NUMBER	RESULT
1	1	1
1	0	0
0	1	0
0	0	0

A bitwise AND operation returns 1 if both bits are 1. It returns 0 if any bits are 0.

As an example, to AND the numbers 25 and 3 together, use the following code:

```
let result = 25 & 3;
console.log(result);  // 1
```

The result of a bitwise AND between 25 and 3 is 1. Why is that? Take a look:

```
25 = 0000 0000 0000 0000 0000 0000 0001 1001
 3 = 0000 0000 0000 0000 0000 0000 0000 0011
---------------------------------------------
AND = 0000 0000 0000 0000 0000 0000 0000 0001
```

As you can see, only one bit (bit 0) contains a 1 in both 25 and 3. Because of this, every other bit of the resulting number is set to 0, making the result equal to 1.

Bitwise OR

The bitwise OR operator is represented by a single pipe character (|) and also works on two numbers. Bitwise OR follows the rules in this truth table:

BIT FROM FIRST NUMBER	BIT FROM SECOND NUMBER	RESULT
1	1	1
1	0	1
0	1	1
0	0	0

A bitwise OR operation returns 1 if at least one bit is 1. It returns 0 only if both bits are 0.

Using the same example as for bitwise AND, if you want to OR the numbers 25 and 3 together, the code looks like this:

```
let result = 25 | 3;
console.log(result);    // 27
```

The result of a bitwise OR between 25 and 3 is 27:

```
25 = 0000 0000 0000 0000 0000 0000 0001 1001
 3 = 0000 0000 0000 0000 0000 0000 0000 0011
----------------------------------------------
OR = 0000 0000 0000 0000 0000 0000 0001 1011
```

In each number, four bits are set to 1, so these are passed through to the result. The binary code 11011 is equal to 27.

Bitwise XOR

The bitwise XOR operator is represented by a caret (^) and also works on two values. Here is the truth table for bitwise XOR:

BIT FROM FIRST NUMBER	BIT FROM SECOND NUMBER	RESULT
1	1	0
1	0	1
0	1	1
0	0	0

Bitwise XOR is different from bitwise OR in that it returns 1 only when exactly one bit has a value of 1 (if both bits contain 1, it returns 0).

To XOR the numbers 25 and 3 together, use the following code:

```
let result = 25 ^ 3;
console.log(result);  // 26
```

The result of a bitwise XOR between 25 and 3 is 26, as shown here:

```
25 = 0000 0000 0000 0000 0000 0000 0001 1001
 3 = 0000 0000 0000 0000 0000 0000 0000 0011
----------------------------------------------
XOR = 0000 0000 0000 0000 0000 0000 0001 1010
```

Four bits in each number are set to 1; however, the first bit in both numbers is 1, so that becomes 0 in the result. All of the other 1s have no corresponding 1 in the other number, so they are passed directly through to the result. The binary code 11010 is equal to 26. (Note that this is one less than when performing bitwise OR on these numbers.)

Left Shift

The left shift is represented by two less-than signs (<<) and shifts all bits in a number to the left by the number of positions given. For example, if the number 2 (which is equal to 10 in binary) is shifted 5 bits to the left, the result is 64 (which is equal to 1000000 in binary), as shown here:

```
let oldValue = 2;            // equal to binary 10
let newValue = oldValue << 5; // equal to binary 1000000 which is decimal 64
```

Note that when the bits are shifted, five empty bits remain to the right of the number. The left shift fills these bits with 0s to make the result a complete 32-bit number (see Figure 3.2).

"Secret" sign bit   The number 2

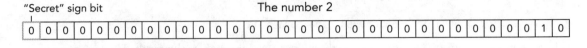

The number 2 shifted to the left five bits (the number 64)

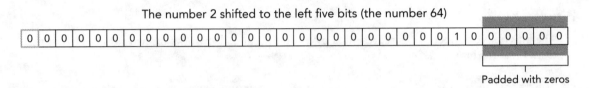

Padded with zeros

FIGURE 3.2: Before and after left shift operation

Note that left shift preserves the sign of the number it's operating on. For instance, if −2 is shifted to the left by five spaces, it becomes −64, not positive 64.

Signed Right Shift

The signed right shift is represented by two greater-than signs (>>) and shifts all bits in a 32-bit number to the right while preserving the sign (positive or negative). A signed right shift is the exact opposite of a left shift. For example, if 64 is shifted to the right five bits, it becomes 2:

```
let oldValue = 64;              // equal to binary 1000000
let newValue = oldValue>> 5;  // equal to binary 10 which is decimal 2
```

Once again, when bits are shifted, the shift creates empty bits. This time, the empty bits occur at the left of the number but after the sign bit (see Figure 3.3). Once again, ECMAScript fills these empty bits with the value in the sign bit to create a complete number.

"Secret" sign bit   The number 64

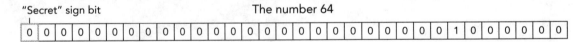

The number 64 shifted to the right five bits (the number 2)

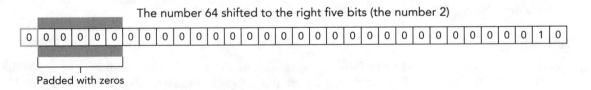

Padded with zeros

FIGURE 3.3: Before and after right shift operation

Unsigned Right Shift

The unsigned right shift is represented by three greater-than signs (>>>) and shifts all bits in a 32-bit number to the right. For numbers that are positive, the effect is the same as a signed right shift. Using the same example as for the signed-right-shift example, if 64 is shifted to the right five bits, it becomes 2:

```
let oldValue = 64;              // equal to binary 1000000
let newValue = oldValue>>> 5;   // equal to binary 10 which is decimal 2
```

For numbers that are negative, however, something quite different happens. Unlike signed right shift, the empty bits get filled with zeros regardless of the sign of the number. For positive numbers, it has the same effect as a signed right shift; for negative numbers, the result is quite different. The unsigned-right-shift operator considers the binary representation of the negative number to be representative of a positive number instead. Because the negative number is the two's complement of its absolute value, the number becomes very large, as you can see in the following example:

```
let oldValue = -64;             // equal to binary 11111111111111111111111111000000
let newValue = oldValue>>> 5;   // equal to decimal 134217726
```

When an unsigned right shift is used to shift –64 to the right by five bits, the result is 134217726. This happens because the binary representation of –64 is 111111111111111111111111111000000, but because the unsigned right shift treats this as a positive number, it considers the value to be 4294967232. When this value is shifted to the right by five bits, it becomes 00000111111111111111111111111111110, which is 134217726.

Boolean Operators

Almost as important as equality operators, Boolean operators are what make a programming language function. Without the capability to test relationships between two values, statements such as if. . .else and loops wouldn't be useful. There are three Boolean operators: NOT, AND, and OR.

Logical NOT

The logical NOT operator is represented by an exclamation point (!) and may be applied to any value in ECMAScript. This operator always returns a Boolean value, regardless of the data type it's used on. The logical NOT operator first converts the operand to a Boolean value and then negates it, meaning that the logical NOT behaves in the following ways:

➤ If the operand is an object, `false` is returned.

➤ If the operand is an empty string, `true` is returned.

➤ If the operand is a nonempty string, `false` is returned.

➤ If the operand is the number 0, `true` is returned.

➤ If the operand is any number other than 0 (including `Infinity`), `false` is returned.

➤ If the operand is `null`, `true` is returned.

➤ If the operand is `NaN`, `true` is returned.

➤ If the operand is `undefined`, `true` is returned.

The following example illustrates this behavior:

```
console.log(!false);    // true
console.log(!"blue");   // false
console.log(!0);        // true
console.log(!NaN);      // true
console.log(!"");       // true
console.log(!12345);    // false
```

The logical NOT operator can also be used to convert a value into its Boolean equivalent. By using two NOT operators in a row, you can effectively simulate the behavior of the `Boolean()` casting function. The first NOT returns a Boolean value no matter what operand it is given. The second NOT negates that Boolean value and so gives the true Boolean value of a variable. The end result is the same as using the `Boolean()` function on a value, as shown here:

```
console.log(!!"blue");   // true
console.log(!!0);        // false
console.log(!!NaN);      // false
console.log(!!"");       // false
console.log(!!12345);    // true
```

Logical AND

The logical AND operator is represented by the double ampersand (&&) and is applied to two values, as in this example:

```
let result = true && false;
```

Logical AND behaves as described in the following truth table:

OPERAND 1	OPERAND 2	RESULT
true	true	true
true	false	false
false	true	false
false	false	false

Logical AND can be used with any type of operand, not just Boolean values. When either operand is not a primitive Boolean, logical AND does not always return a Boolean value; instead, it does one of the following:

➤ If the first operand is an object, then the second operand is always returned.

➤ If the second operand is an object, then the object is returned only if the first operand evaluates to `true`.

➤ If both operands are objects, then the second operand is returned.

➤ If either operand is `null`, then `null` is returned.

➤ If either operand is `NaN`, then `NaN` is returned.

➤ If either operand is `undefined`, then `undefined` is returned.

The logical AND operator is a short-circuited operation, meaning that if the first operand determines the result, the second operand is never evaluated. In the case of logical AND, if the first operand is `false`, no matter what the value of the second operand, the result can't be equal to true. Consider the following example:

```
let found = true;
let result = (found && someUndeclaredVariable);  // error occurs here
console.log(result);  // this line never executes
```

This code causes an error when the logical AND is evaluated, because the variable `someUndeclaredVariable` isn't declared. The value of the variable `found` is `true`, so the logical AND operator continued to evaluate the variable `someUndeclaredVariable`. When it did, an error occurred because `someUndeclaredVariable` is not declared and therefore cannot be used in a logical AND operation. If `found` is instead set to `false`, as in the following example, the error won't occur:

```
let found = false;
let result = (found && someUndeclaredVariable);  // no error
console.log(result);  // works
```

In this code, the `console.log` is displayed successfully. Even though the variable `someUndeclaredVariable` is undefined, it is never evaluated because the first operand is `false`. This means that the result of the operation must be `false`, so there is no reason to evaluate what's to the right of the `&&`. Always keep in mind short-circuiting when using logical AND.

Logical OR

The logical OR operator is represented by the double pipe (||) in ECMAScript, like this:

```
let result = true || false;
```

Logical OR behaves as described in the following truth table:

OPERAND 1	OPERAND 2	RESULT
true	true	true
true	false	true
false	true	true
false	false	false

Just like logical AND, if either operand is not a Boolean, logical OR will not always return a Boolean value; instead, it does one of the following:

➤ If the first operand is an object, then the first operand is returned.

➤ If the first operand evaluates to `false`, then the second operand is returned.

➤ If both operands are objects, then the first operand is returned.

➤ If both operands are `null`, then `null` is returned.

➤ If both operands are `NaN`, then `NaN` is returned.

➤ If both operands are `undefined`, then `undefined` is returned.

Also like the logical AND operator, the logical OR operator is short-circuited. In this case, if the first operand evaluates to true, the second operand is not evaluated. Consider this example:

```
let found = true;
let result = (found || someUndeclaredVariable);   // no error
console.log(result);   // works
```

As with the previous example, the variable someUndefinedVariable is undefined. However, because the variable found is set to true, the variable someUndefinedVariable is never evaluated and thus the output is "true." If the value of found is changed to false, an error occurs, as in the following example:

```
let found = false;
let result = (found || someUndeclaredVariable);   // error occurs here
console.log(result);   // this line never executes
```

You can also use this behavior to avoid assigning a null or undefined value to a variable. Consider the following:

```
let myObject = preferredObject || backupObject;
```

In this example, the variable myObject will be assigned one of two values. The preferredObject variable contains the value that is preferred if it's available, whereas the backupObject variable contains the backup value if the preferred one isn't available. If preferredObject isn't null, then it's assigned to myObject; if it is null, then backupObject is assigned to myObject. This pattern is used very frequently in ECMAScript for variable assignment and is used throughout this book.

Multiplicative Operators

There are three multiplicative operators in ECMAScript: multiply, divide, and modulus. These operators work in a manner similar to their counterparts in languages such as Java, C, and Perl, but they also include some automatic type conversions when dealing with nonnumeric values. If either of the operands for a multiplication operation isn't a number, it is converted to a number behind the scenes using the Number() casting function. This means that an empty string is treated as 0, and the Boolean value of true is treated as 1.

Multiply

The multiply operator is represented by an asterisk (*) and is used, as one might suspect, to multiply two numbers. The syntax is the same as in C, as shown here:

```
let result = 34 * 56;
```

However, the multiply operator also has the following unique behaviors when dealing with special values:

➤   If the operands are numbers, regular arithmetic multiplication is performed, meaning that two positives or two negatives equal a positive, whereas operands with different signs yield a negative. If the result cannot be represented by ECMAScript, either Infinity or –Infinity is returned.

➤   If either operand is NaN, the result is NaN.

➤ If Infinity is multiplied by 0, the result is NaN.

➤ If Infinity is multiplied by any finite number other than 0, the result is either Infinity or -Infinity, depending on the sign of the second operand.

➤ If Infinity is multiplied by Infinity, the result is Infinity.

➤ If either operand isn't a number, it is converted to a number behind the scenes using Number() and then the other rules are applied.

Divide

The divide operator is represented by a slash (/) and divides the first operand by the second operand, as shown here:

```
let result = 66 / 11;
```

The divide operator, like the multiply operator, has special behaviors for special values. They are as follows:

➤ If the operands are numbers, regular arithmetic division is performed, meaning that two positives or two negatives equal a positive, whereas operands with different signs yield a negative. If the result can't be represented in ECMAScript, it returns either Infinity or -Infinity.

➤ If either operand is NaN, the result is NaN.

➤ If Infinity is divided by Infinity, the result is NaN.

➤ If zero is divided by zero, the result is NaN.

➤ If a nonzero finite number is divided by zero, the result is either Infinity or -Infinity, depending on the sign of the first operand.

➤ If Infinity is divided by any number, the result is either Infinity or -Infinity, depending on the sign of the second operand.

➤ If either operand isn't a number, it is converted to a number behind the scenes using Number() and then the other rules are applied.

Modulus

The modulus (remainder) operator is represented by a percent sign (%) and is used in the following way:

```
let result = 26 % 5;   // equal to 1
```

Just like the other multiplicative operators, the modulus operator behaves differently for special values, as follows:

➤ If the operands are numbers, regular arithmetic division is performed, and the remainder of that division is returned.

➤ If the dividend is an infinite number and the divisor is a finite number, the result is NaN.

➤ If the dividend is a finite number and the divisor is 0, the result is NaN.

➤ If `Infinity` is divided by `Infinity`, the result is `NaN`.

➤ If the dividend is a finite number and the divisor is an infinite number, then the result is the dividend.

➤ If the dividend is zero and the divisor is nonzero, the result is zero.

➤ If either operand isn't a number, it is converted to a number behind the scenes using `Number()` and then the other rules are applied.

Exponentiation Operator

The exponentiation operator (`**`) is equivalent to `Math.pow()`.

```
console.log(Math.pow(3, 2);        // 9
console.log(3 ** 2);               // 9

console.log(Math.pow(16, 0.5);     // 4
console.log(16** 0.5);             // 4
```

The operator also gets its own exponentiate assignment operator, `**=`, which performs the exponentiation and subsequent assignment of the result:

```
let squared = 3;
squared **= 2;
console.log(squared);  // 9

let sqrt = 16;
sqrt **= 0.5;
console.log(sqrt);     // 4
```

Additive Operators

The additive operators, add and subtract, are typically the simplest mathematical operators in programming languages. In ECMAScript, however, a number of special behaviors are associated with each operator. As with the multiplicative operators, conversions occur behind the scenes for different data types. For these operators, however, the rules aren't as straightforward.

Add

The add operator (`+`) is used just as one would expect, as shown in the following example:

```
let result = 1 + 2;
```

If the two operands are numbers, they perform an arithmetic add and return the result according to the following rules:

➤ If either operand is `NaN`, the result is `NaN`.

➤ If `Infinity` is added to `Infinity`, the result is `Infinity`.

➤ If −`Infinity` is added to −`Infinity`, the result is −`Infinity`.

➤ If `Infinity` is added to −`Infinity`, the result is `NaN`.

➤ If +0 is added to +0, the result is +0.

➤ If −0 is added to +0, the result is +0.

➤ If −0 is added to −0, the result is −0.

If, however, one of the operands is a string, then the following rules apply:

➤ If both operands are strings, the second string is concatenated to the first.

➤ If only one operand is a string, the other operand is converted to a string and the result is the concatenation of the two strings.

If either operand is an object, number, or Boolean, its `toString()` method is called to get a string value and then the previous rules regarding strings are applied. For `undefined` and `null`, the `String()` function is called to retrieve the values "undefined" and "null," respectively.

Consider the following:

```
let result1 = 5 + 5;    // two numbers
console.log(result1);         // 10
let result2 = 5 + "5";  // a number and a string
console.log(result2);         // "55"
```

This code illustrates the difference between the two modes for the add operator. Normally, 5 + 5 equals 10 (a number value), as illustrated by the first two lines of code. However, if one of the operands is changed to a string, "5," the result becomes "55" (which is a primitive string value) because the first operand gets converted to "5" as well.

One of the most common mistakes in ECMAScript is being unaware of the data types involved with an addition operation. Consider the following:

```
let num1 = 5;
let num2 = 10;
let message = "The sum of 5 and 10 is " + num1 + num2;
console.log(message);  // "The sum of 5 and 10 is 510"
```

In this example, the message variable is filled with a string that is the result of two addition operations. One might expect the final string to be "The sum of 5 and 10 is 15"; however, it actually ends up as "The sum of 5 and 10 is 510." This happens because each addition is done separately. The first combines a string with a number (5), which results in a string. The second takes that result (a string) and adds a number (10), which also results in a string. To perform the arithmetic calculation and then append that to the string, just add some parentheses like this:

```
let num1 = 5;
let num2 = 10;
let message = "The sum of 5 and 10 is " + (num1 + num2);
console.log(message);  // "The sum of 5 and 10 is 15"
```

Here, the two number variables are surrounded by parentheses, which instruct the interpreter to calculate its result before adding it to the string. The resulting string is "The sum of 5 and 10 is 15."

Subtract

The subtract operator (-) is another that is used quite frequently. Here's an example:

```
let result = 2 - 1;
```

Just like the add operator, the subtract operator has special rules to deal with the variety of type conversions present in ECMAScript. They are as follows:

➤ If the two operands are numbers, perform arithmetic subtract and return the result.

➤ If either operand is NaN, the result is NaN.

➤ If Infinity is subtracted from Infinity, the result is NaN.

➤ If –Infinity is subtracted from –Infinity, the result is NaN.

➤ If –Infinity is subtracted from Infinity, the result is Infinity.

➤ If Infinity is subtracted from –Infinity, the result is –Infinity.

➤ If +0 is subtracted from +0, the result is +0.

➤ If –0 is subtracted from +0, the result is –0.

➤ If –0 is subtracted from –0, the result is +0.

➤ If either operand is a string, a Boolean, null, or undefined, it is converted to a number (using Number() behind the scenes) and the arithmetic is calculated using the previous rules. If that conversion results in NaN, then the result of the subtraction is NaN.

➤ If either operand is an object, its valueOf() method is called to retrieve a numeric value to represent it. If that value is NaN, then the result of the subtraction is NaN. If the object doesn't have valueOf() defined, then toString() is called and the resulting string is converted into a number.

The following are some examples of these behaviors:

```
let result1 = 5 - true;   // 4 because true is converted to 1
let result2 = NaN - 1;    // NaN
let result3 = 5 - 3;      // 2
let result4 = 5 - "";     // 5 because "" is converted to 0
let result5 = 5 - "2";    // 3 because "2" is converted to 2
let result6 = 5 - null;   // 5 because null is converted to 0
```

Relational Operators

The less-than (<), greater-than (>), less-than-or-equal-to (<=), and greater-than-or-equal-to (>=) relational operators perform comparisons between values in the same way that you learned in math class. Each of these operators returns a Boolean value, as in this example:

```
let result1 = 5> 3;   // true
let result2 = 5 < 3;  // false
```

As with other operators in ECMAScript, there are some conversions and other oddities that happen when using different data types. They are as follows:

➤ If the operands are numbers, perform a numeric comparison.

➤ If the operands are strings, compare the character codes of each corresponding character in the string.

> ➤ If one operand is a number, convert the other operand to a number and perform a numeric comparison.

> ➤ If an operand is an object, call `valueOf()` and use its result to perform the comparison according to the previous rules. If `valueOf()` is not available, call `toString()` and use that value according to the previous rules.

> ➤ If an operand is a Boolean, convert it to a number and perform the comparison.

When a relational operator is used on two strings, an interesting behavior occurs. Many expect that less-than means "alphabetically before" and greater-than means "alphabetically after," but this is not the case. For strings, each of the first string's character codes is numerically compared against the character codes in a corresponding location in the second string. After this comparison is complete, a Boolean value is returned. The problem here is that the character codes of uppercase letters are all lower than the character codes of lowercase letters, meaning that you can run into situations like this:

```
let result = "Brick" < "alphabet";  // true
```

In this example, the string "Brick" is considered to be less than the string "alphabet" because the letter *B* has a character code of 66 and the letter *a* has a character code of 97. To force a true alphabetic result, you must convert both operands into a common case (upper or lower) and then compare like this:

```
let result = "Brick".toLowerCase() < "alphabet".toLowerCase();  // false
```

Converting both operands to lowercase ensures that "alphabet" is correctly identified as alphabetically before "Brick."

Another sticky situation occurs when comparing numbers that are strings, such as in this example:

```
let result = "23" < "3";  // true
```

This code returns true when comparing the string "23" to "3." Because both operands are strings, they are compared by their character codes (the character code for "2" is 50; the character code for "3" is 51). If, however, one of the operands is changed to a number as in the following example, the result makes more sense:

```
let result = "23" < 3;  // false
```

Here, the string "23" is converted into the number 23 and then compared to 3, giving the expected result. Whenever a number is compared to a string, the string is converted into a number and then numerically compared to the other number. This works well for cases like the previous example, but what if the string can't be converted into a number? Consider this example:

```
let result = "a" < 3;  // false because "a" becomes NaN
```

The letter "a" can't be meaningfully converted into a number, so it becomes NaN. As a rule, the result of any relational operation with NaN is false, which is interesting when considering the following:

```
let result1 = NaN < 3;   // false
let result2 = NaN>= 3;   // false
```

In most comparisons, if a value is not less than another, it is always greater than or equal to it. When using NaN, however, both comparisons return false.

Equality Operators

Determining whether two variables are equivalent is one of the most important operations in programming. This is fairly straightforward when dealing with strings, numbers, and Boolean values, but the task gets a little complicated when you take objects into account. Originally ECMAScript's equal and not-equal operators performed conversions into like types before doing a comparison. The question of whether these conversions should, in fact, take place was then raised. The end result was for ECMAScript to provide two sets of operators: *equal* and *not equal* to perform conversion before comparison, and *identically equal* and *not identically equal* to perform comparison without conversion.

Equal and Not Equal

The equal operator in ECMAScript is the double equal sign (==), and it returns true if the operands are equal. The not-equal operator is the exclamation point followed by an equal sign (!=), and it returns true if two operands are not equal. Both operators do conversions to determine if two operands are equal (often called *type coercion*).

When performing conversions, the equal and not-equal operators follow these basic rules:

➤ If an operand is a Boolean value, convert it into a numeric value before checking for equality. A value of false converts to 0, whereas a value of true converts to 1.

➤ If one operand is a string and the other is a number, attempt to convert the string into a number before checking for equality.

➤ If one of the operands is an object and the other is not, the valueOf() method is called on the object to retrieve a primitive value to compare according to the previous rules.

The operators also follow these rules when making comparisons:

➤ Values of null and undefined are equal.

➤ Values of null and undefined cannot be converted into any other values for equality checking.

➤ If either operand is NaN, the equal operator returns false and the not-equal operator returns true. Important note: even if both operands are NaN, the equal operator returns false because, by rule, NaN is not equal to NaN.

➤ If both operands are objects, then they are compared to see if they are the same object. If both operands point to the same object, then the equal operator returns true. Otherwise, the two are not equal.

The following table lists some special cases and their results:

EXPRESSION	VALUE
null == undefined	true
"NaN" == NaN	false
5 == NaN	false
NaN == NaN	false
NaN != NaN	true
false == 0	true
true == 1	true
true == 2	false
undefined == 0	false
null == 0	false
"5" == 5	true

Identically Equal and Not Identically Equal

The identically equal and not identically equal operators do the same thing as equal and not equal, except that they do not convert operands before testing for equality. The identically equal operator is represented by three equal signs (===) and returns true only if the operands are equal without conversion, as in this example:

```
let result1 = ("55" == 55);   // true - equal because of conversion
let result2 = ("55" === 55);  // false - not equal because different data types
```

In this code, the first comparison uses the equal operator to compare the string "55" and the number 55, which returns true. As mentioned previously, this happens because the string "55" is converted to the number 55 and then compared with the other number 55. The second comparison uses the identically equal operator to compare the string and the number without conversion, and of course, a string isn't equal to a number, so this outputs false.

The not identically equal operator is represented by an exclamation point followed by two equal signs (!==) and returns true only if the operands are not equal without conversion. For example:

```
let result1 = ("55" != 55);   // false - equal because of conversion
let result2 = ("55" !== 55);  // true - not equal because different data types
```

Here, the first comparison uses the not-equal operator, which converts the string "55" to the number 55, making it equal to the second operand, also the number 55. Therefore, this evaluates to false because the two are considered equal. The second comparison uses the not identically equal operator. It helps to think of this operation as saying, "Is the string 55 different from the number 55?" The answer to this is yes (true).

Keep in mind that while `null == undefined` is `true` because they are similar values, `null === undefined` is `false` because they are not the same type.

> **NOTE** *Because of the type conversion issues with the equal and not-equal operators, it is recommended to use identically equal and not identically equal instead. This helps to maintain data type integrity throughout your code.*

Conditional Operator

The conditional operator is one of the most versatile in ECMAScript, and it takes on the same form as in Java, which is as follows:

```
variable = boolean_expression ? true_value : false_value;
```

This basically allows a conditional assignment to a variable depending on the evaluation of the `boolean_expression`. If it's `true`, then `true_value` is assigned to the variable; if it's `false`, then `false_value` is assigned to the variable, as in this instance:

```
let max = (num1> num2) ? num1 : num2;
```

In this example, `max` is to be assigned the number with the highest value. The expression states that if `num1` is greater than `num2`, then `num1` is assigned to `max`. If, however, the expression is `false` (meaning that `num1` is less than or equal to `num2`), then `num2` is assigned to `max`.

Nullish Coalescing Operator

The nullish coalescing operator `??` provides a concise way to handle *nullish* (`null` or `undefined`) values in expressions. It is a binary operator that returns the right-hand operand if the left-hand operand is either `null` or `undefined`. Otherwise, it returns the left-hand operand. It can be used as follows:

```
variable = expression ?? nullish_fallback_value;
```

Without the use of `??`, the above expression could be expressed using a conditional operator as follows:

```
variable = expression !== null && expression !== undefined ? expression :
nullish_fallback_value;
```

The `??` operator is particularly useful in situations where you need to be careful when assigning defaults for falsy values. Prior to the introduction of the `??`, the `||` operator was typically used to assign a default value, but its behavior was sometimes undesirable when dealing with falsy values. The following example compares the behavior of these operators:

```
const values = [null, undefined, 0, ""];

console.log(values.map(x => x || "default"));
```

```
// ["default", "default", "default", "default"]

console.log(values.map(x => x ?? "default"));
// ["default", "default", 0, ""]
```

Assignment Operators

Simple assignment is done with the equal sign (=) and simply assigns the value on the right to the variable on the left, as shown in the following example:

```
let num = 10;
```

Compound assignment is done with one of the multiplicative, additive, or bitwise–shift operators followed by an equal sign (=). These assignments are designed as shorthand for such common situations as this:

```
let num = 10;
num = num + 10;
```

The second line of code can be replaced with a compound assignment:

```
let num = 10;
num += 10;
```

Compound-assignment operators exist for each of the major mathematical operations and a few others as well. They are as follows:

➤ Multiply/assign (*=)

➤ Exponentiation/assign (**=)

➤ Divide/assign (/=)

➤ Modulus/assign (%=)

➤ Add/assign (+=)

➤ Subtract/assign (-=)

➤ Left shift/assign (<<=)

➤ Signed right shift/assign (>>=)

➤ Unsigned right shift/assign (>>>=)

➤ Bitwise OR/assign (|=)

➤ Bitwise AND/assign (&=)

➤ Bitsize XOR/assign (^=)

➤ Logical OR/assign (||=)

➤ Logical AND/assign (&&=)

➤ Nullish coalescing/assign (??=)

These operators are designed specifically as shorthand ways of achieving operations. They do not represent any performance improvement.

Comma Operator

The comma operator allows execution of more than one operation in a single statement, as illustrated here:

```
let num1 = 1, num2 = 2, num3 = 3;
```

Most often, the comma operator is used in the declaration of variables; however, it can also be used to assign values. When used in this way, the comma operator always returns the last item in the expression, as in the following example:

```
let num = (5, 1, 4, 8, 0);   // num becomes 0
```

In this example, num is assigned the value of 0 because it is the last item in the expression. There aren't many times when commas are used in this way; however, it is helpful to understand that this behavior exists.

STATEMENTS

ECMA-262 describes several statements (also called *flow-control statements*). Essentially, statements define most of the syntax of ECMAScript and typically use one or more keywords to accomplish a given task. Statements can be simple, such as telling a function to exit, or complicated, such as specifying a number of commands to be executed repeatedly.

The *if* Statement

One of the most frequently used statements in most programming languages is the if statement. The if statement has the following syntax:

```
if (condition) statement1 else statement2
```

The condition can be any expression; it doesn't even have to evaluate to an actual Boolean value. ECMAScript automatically converts the result of the expression into a Boolean by calling the Boolean() casting function on it. If the condition evaluates to true, statement1 is executed; if the condition evaluates to false, statement2 is executed. Each of the statements can be either a single line or a code block (a group of code lines enclosed within braces). Consider this example:

```
if (i> 25)
    console.log("Greater than 25.");  // one-line statement
else {
    console.log("Less than or equal to 25.");  // block statement
}
```

It's considered best coding practice to always use block statements, even if only one line of code is to be executed. Doing so can avoid confusion about what should be executed for each condition.

You can also chain if statements together like so:

```
if (condition1) statement1 else if (condition2) statement2 else statement3
```

Here's an example:

```
if (i> 25) {
    console.log("Greater than 25.");
} else if (i < 0) {
```

```
    console.log("Less than 0.");
} else {
    console.log("Between 0 and 25, inclusive.");
}
```

The *do-while* Statement

The `do-while` statement is a post-test loop, meaning that the escape condition is evaluated only after the code inside the loop has been executed. The body of the loop is always executed at least once before the expression is evaluated. Here's the syntax:

```
do {
    statement
} while (expression);
```

And here's an example of its usage:

```
let i = 0;
do {
    i += 2;
} while (i < 10);
```

In this example, the loop continues as long as `i` is less than 10. The variable starts at 0 and is incremented by two each time through the loop.

> **NOTE** *Post-test loops such as this are most often used when the body of the loop should be executed at least once before exiting.*

The *while* Statement

The `while` statement is a pretest loop. This means the escape condition is evaluated before the code inside the loop has been executed. Because of this, it is possible that the body of the loop is never executed. Here's the syntax:

```
while(expression) statement
```

And here's an example of its usage:

```
let i = 0;
while (i < 10) {
    i += 2;
}
```

In this example, the variable `i` starts out equal to 0 and is incremented by two each time through the loop. As long as the variable is less than 10, the loop will continue.

The *for* Statement

The `for` statement is also a pretest loop with the added capabilities of variable initialization before entering the loop and defining postloop code to be executed. Here's the syntax:

```
for (initialization; expression; post-loop-expression) statement
```

And here's an example of its usage:

```
let count = 10;
for (let i = 0; i < count; i++) {
  console.log(i);
}
```

This code defines a variable `i` that begins with the value 0. The for loop is entered only if the conditional expression (`i < count`) evaluates to true, making it possible that the body of the code might not be executed. If the body is executed, the postloop expression is also executed, iterating the variable `i`. This for loop is the same as the following:

```
let count = 10;
let i = 0;
while (i < count) {
  console.log(i);
  i++;
}
```

Nothing can be done with a `for` loop that can't be done using a `while` loop. The for loop simply encapsulates the loop-related code into a single location.

It's important to note that there's no need to use the variable declaration keyword inside the for loop initialization. However, the overwhelming majority of the time you will find that the iterator variable is not useful after the loop completes. In these cases, the cleanest implementation is to use a `let` declaration inside the loop initialization to declare the iterator variable because its scope will be limited to only the loop itself.

The initialization, control expression, and postloop expression are all optional. You can create an infinite loop by omitting all three, like this:

```
for (;;) {  // infinite loop
  doSomething();
}
```

Including only the control expression effectively turns a `for` loop into a `while` loop, as shown here:

```
let count = 10;
let i = 0;
for (; i < count; ) {
  console.log(i);
  i++;
}
```

This versatility makes the `for` statement one of the most used in the language.

The *for-in* Statement

The `for-in` statement is a strict iterative statement. It is used to enumerate the non-symbol keyed properties of an object. Here's the syntax:

```
for (property in expression) statement
```

And here's an example of its usage:

```
for (const propName in window) {
    document.write(propName);
}
```

Here, the `for-in` statement is used to display all the properties of the BOM window object. Each time through the loop, the `propName` variable is filled with the name of a property that exists on the `window` object. This continues until all of the available properties have been enumerated. As with the `for` statement, the `const` operator in the control statement is not necessary but is recommended for ensuring the use of a local variable that will not be altered.

Object properties in ECMAScript are unordered, so the order in which property names are returned in a `for-in` statement cannot necessarily be predicted. All enumerable properties will be returned once, but the order may differ across browsers.

Note that the `for-in` statement simply doesn't execute the body of the loop if the variable representing the object to iterate over is `null` or `undefined`.

The *for-of* Statement

The `for-of` statement is a strict iterative statement. It is used to loop through elements in an iterable object. Here's the syntax:

```
for (property of expression) statement
```

And here's an example of its usage:

```
for (const el of [2,4,6,8]) {
    document.write(el);
}
```

Here, the `for-of` statement is used to display all the elements inside the four-element array. This continues until each element in the array has been looped over. As with the `for` statement, the `const` operator in the control statement is not necessary but is recommended for ensuring the use of a local variable that will not be altered.

The `for-of` loop will iterate in the order that the iterable produces values via its `next()` method. This is covered in-depth in the *Chapter 7*.

Note that the `for-of` statement will throw an error if the entity that it is attempting to iterate over does not support iteration.

> **NOTE** *The for-of statement is extended as a `for-await-of` loop to support async iterables which produce promises. This is covered in depth in the Chapter 7.*

Labeled Statements

It is possible to label statements for later use with the following syntax:

```
label: statement
```

Here's an example:

```
start: for (let i = 0; i < count; i++) {
    console.log(i);
}
```

In this example, the label start can be referenced later by using the break or continue statement. Labeled statements are typically used with nested loops.

The *break* and *continue* Statements

The break and continue statements provide stricter control over the execution of code in a loop. The break statement exits the loop immediately, forcing execution to continue with the next statement after the loop. The continue statement, on the other hand, exits the loop immediately, but execution continues from the top of the loop. Here's an example:

```
let num = 0;

for (let i = 1; i < 10; i++) {
    if (i % 5 == 0) {
        break;
    }
    num++;
}

console.log(num);   // 4
```

In this code, the for loop increments the variable i from 1 to 10. In the body of a loop, an if statement checks to see if the value of i is evenly divisible by 5 (using the modulus operator). If so, the break statement is executed and the loop is exited. The num variable starts out at 0 and indicates the number of times the loop has been executed. After the break statement has been hit, the next line of code to be executed is the console.log, which displays 4. The number of times the loop has been executed is four because when i equals 5, the break statement causes the loop to be exited before num can be incremented. A different effect can be seen if break is replaced with continue like this:

```
let num = 0;

for (let i = 1; i < 10; i++) {
    if (i % 5 == 0) {
        continue;
    }
    num++;
}

console.log(num);   // 8
```

Here, the console.log displays 8, the number of times the loop has been executed. When i reaches a value of 5, the loop is exited before num is incremented, but execution continues with the next iteration, when the value is 6. The loop then continues until its natural completion, when i is 10. The final value of num is 8 instead of 9 because one increment didn't occur due to the continue statement.

Both the `break` and `continue` statements can be used in conjunction with labeled statements to return to a particular location in the code. This is typically used when there are loops inside of loops, as in the following example:

```
let num = 0;

outermost:
for (let i = 0; i < 10; i++) {
    for (let j = 0; j < 10; j++) {
    if (i == 5 && j == 5) {
      break outermost;
    }
    num++;
  }
}

console.log(num);   // 55
```

In this example, the `outermost` label indicates the first `for` statement. Each loop normally executes 10 times, meaning that the `num++` statement is normally executed 100 times and, consequently, `num` should be equal to 100 when the execution is complete. The `break` statement here is given one argument: the label to break to. Adding the label allows the `break` statement to break not just out of the inner `for` statement (using the variable `j`) but also out of the outer `for` statement (using the variable `i`). Because of this, `num` ends up with a value of 55, because execution is halted when both `i` and `j` are equal to 5. The `continue` statement can be used in the same way, as shown in the following example:

```
let num = 0;

outermost:
for (let i = 0; i < 10; i++) {
    for (let j = 0; j < 10; j++) {
    if (i == 5 && j == 5) {
      continue outermost;
    }
    num++;
  }
}

console.log(num);   // 95
```

In this case, the `continue` statement forces execution to continue—not in the inner loop but in the outer loop. When `j` is equal to 5, `continue` is executed, which means that the inner loop misses five iterations, leaving `num` equal to 95.

Using labeled statements in conjunction with `break` and `continue` can be very powerful but can cause debugging problems if overused. Always use descriptive labels and try not to nest more than a few loops.

The *with* Statement

The `with` statement sets the scope of the code within a particular object. The syntax is as follows:

```
with (expression) statement;
```

The `with` statement was created as a convenience for times when a single object was being coded to over and over again, as in this example:

```
let qs = location.search.substring(1);
let hostName = location.hostname;
let url = location.href;
```

Here, the location object is used on every line. This code can be rewritten using the `with` statement as follows:

```
with(location) {
    let qs = search.substring(1);
    let hostName = hostname;
    let url = href;
}
```

In this rewritten version of the code, the `with` statement is used in conjunction with the location object. This means that each variable inside the statement is first considered to be a local variable. If it's not found to be a local variable, the location object is searched to see if it has a property of the same name. If so, then the variable is evaluated as a property of location.

In strict mode, the `with` statement is not allowed and is considered a syntax error.

> **WARNING** *It is widely considered a poor practice to use the* `with` *statement in production code because of its negative performance impact and the difficulty in debugging code contained in the* `with` *statement.*

The *switch* Statement

Closely related to the `if` statement is the `switch` statement, another flow-control statement adopted from other languages. The syntax for the `switch` statement in ECMAScript closely resembles the syntax in other C-based languages, as you can see here:

```
switch (expression) {
    case value1:
        statement
        break;
    case value2:
        statement
        break;
    case value3:
        statement
        break;
    case value4:
        statement
        break;
    default:
        statement
}
```

Each case in a `switch` statement says, "If the expression is equal to the value, execute the statement." The `break` keyword causes code execution to jump out of the switch statement. Without the `break` keyword, code execution falls through the original case into the following one. The `default` keyword indicates what is to be done if the expression does not evaluate to one of the cases. (In effect, it is an `else` statement.)

Essentially, the switch statement prevents a developer from having to write something like this:

```
if (i == 25) {
  console.log("25");
} else if (i == 35) {
  console.log("35");
} else if (i == 45) {
  console.log("45");
} else {
  console.log("Other");
}
```

The equivalent switch statement is as follows:

```
switch (i) {
  case 25:
    console.log("25");
    break;
  case 35:
    console.log("35");
    break;
  case 45:
    console.log("45");
    break;
  default:
    console.log("Other");
}
```

It's best to always put a `break` statement after each case to avoid having cases fall through into the next one.

Although the switch statement was borrowed from other languages, it has some unique characteristics in ECMAScript. First, the `switch` statement works with all data types (in many languages it works only with numbers), so it can be used with strings and even with objects. Second, the case values need not be constants; they can be variables and even expressions.

> **NOTE** *The* switch *statement compares values using the identically equal operator, so no type coercion occurs (for example, the string "10" is not equal to the number 10).*

FUNCTIONS

Functions are the core of any language because they allow the encapsulation of statements that can be run anywhere and at any time. Functions in ECMAScript are declared using the `function` keyword or arrow syntax, followed by a set of arguments and then the body of the function.

> **NOTE** *In-depth function coverage can be found in the Chapter 10, "Functions."*

The basic function syntax is as follows:

```
function functionName(arg0, arg1,...,argN) {
   statements
}
```

Here's an example:

```
function sayHi(name, message) {
   console.log("Hello " + name + ", " + message);
}
```

This function can then be called by using the function name, followed by the function arguments enclosed in parentheses (and separated by commas, if there are multiple arguments). The code to call the `sayHi()` function looks like this:

```
sayHi("Alice", "how are you today?");
```

The output of this function call is, "Hello Alice, how are you today?" The named arguments name and message are used as part of a string concatenation that is ultimately displayed in a `console.log`.

Functions in ECMAScript need not specify whether they return a value. Any function can return a value at any time by using the return statement followed by the value to return. Consider this example:

```
function sum(num1, num2) {
   return num1 + num2;
}
```

The `sum()` function adds two values together and returns the result. Note that aside from the return statement, there is no special declaration indicating that the function returns a value. This function can be called using the following:

```
const result = sum(5, 10);
```

Keep in mind that a function stops executing and exits immediately when it encounters the return statement. Therefore, any code that comes after a return statement will never be executed. For example:

```
function sum(num1, num2) {
   return num1 + num2;
   console.log("Hello world");  // never executed
}
```

In this example, the `console.log` will never be displayed because it appears after the `return` statement.

It's also possible to have more than one return statement in a function, like this:

```
function diff(num1, num2) {
   if (num1 < num2) {
     return num2 - num1;
   } else {
     return num1 - num2;
   }
}
```

Here, the `diff()` function determines the difference between two numbers. If the first number is less than the second, it subtracts the first from the second; otherwise it subtracts the second from the first. Each branch of the code has its own `return` statement that does the correct calculation.

The `return` statement can also be used without specifying a return value. When used in this way, the function stops executing immediately and returns `undefined` as its value. This is typically used in functions that don't return a value to stop function execution early, as in the following example, where the `console.log` won't be displayed:

```
function sayHi(name, message) {
  return;
  console.log("Hello " + name + ", " + message);  // never called
}
```

> **NOTE** *Best practices dictate that a function either always returns a value or never returns a value. Writing a function that sometimes returns a value causes confusion, especially during debugging.*

Strict mode places several restrictions on functions:

➤ No function can be named `eval` or `arguments`.

➤ No named parameter can be named `eval` or `arguments`.

➤ No two named parameters can have the same name.

If any of these occur, it's considered a syntax error and the code will not execute.

SUMMARY

The core language features of JavaScript are defined in ECMA-262 as a pseudolanguage named ECMAScript. ECMAScript contains all of the basic syntax, operators, data types, and objects necessary to complete basic computing tasks, though it provides no way to get input or to produce output.

Understanding ECMAScript and its intricacies is vital to a complete understanding of JavaScript as implemented in web browsers. The following are some of the basic elements of ECMAScript:

➤ The basic data types in ECMAScript are Undefined, Null, Boolean, Number, BigInt, String, and Symbol.

➤ There is also a complex data type, Object, that is the base type for all objects in the language.

➤ A strict mode places restrictions on certain error-prone parts of the language.

➤ ECMAScript provides a lot of the basic operators available in C and other C-like languages, including arithmetic operators, Boolean operators, relational operators, equality operators, and assignment operators.

➤ The language features flow-control statements borrowed heavily from other languages, such as the if statement, the for statement, and the switch statement.

Functions in ECMAScript behave differently than functions in other languages:

➤ There is no need to specify the return value of the function because any function can return any value at any time.

➤ Functions that don't specify a return value actually return the special value undefined.

Variables, Scope, and Memory

WHAT'S IN THIS CHAPTER?

➤ Working with primitive and reference values in variables

➤ Understanding execution context

➤ Understanding garbage collection

The nature of variables in JavaScript, as defined in ECMA-262, is quite unique compared to that of other languages. Being loosely typed, a variable is literally just a name for a particular value at a particular time. Because there are no rules defining the type of data that a variable must hold, a variable's value and data type can change during the lifetime of a script. Though this is an interesting, powerful, and problematic feature, there are many more complexities related to variables.

PRIMITIVE AND REFERENCE VALUES

ECMAScript variables may contain two different types of data: primitive values and reference values. *Primitive values* are simple atomic pieces of data, while *reference values* are objects that may be made up of multiple values.

When a value is assigned to a variable, the JavaScript engine must determine if it's a primitive or a reference value. The seven primitive types were discussed in the previous chapter: Undefined, Null, Boolean, Number, BigInt, String, and Symbol. These variables are said to be accessed *by value*, because you are manipulating the actual value stored in the variable.

Reference values are objects stored in memory. Unlike other languages, JavaScript does not permit direct access of memory locations, so direct manipulation of the object's memory space is not allowed. When you manipulate an object, you're really working on a *reference* to that object rather than the actual object itself. For this reason, such values are said to be accessed *by reference*.

> **NOTE** *In many languages, strings are represented by objects and are therefore considered to be reference types. ECMAScript breaks away from this tradition.*

Dynamic Properties

Primitive and reference values are defined similarly: a variable is created and assigned a value. What you can do with those values once they're stored in a variable, however, is quite different. When you work with reference values, you can add, change, or delete properties and methods at any time. Consider this example:

```
let person = new Object();
person.name = "Alice";
console.log(person.name);  // "Alice"
```

Here, an object is created and stored in the variable person. Next, a property called name is added and assigned the string value of "Alice." The new property is then accessible from that point on, until the object is destroyed or the property is explicitly removed.

Primitive values can't have properties added to them even though attempting to do so won't cause an error. Here's an example:

```
let name = "Alice";
name.age = 27;
console.log(name.age);  // undefined
```

Here, a property called age is defined on the string name and assigned a value of 27. On the very next line, however, the property is gone. Only reference values can have properties defined dynamically for later use.

Note that the instantiation of a primitive type can be accomplished using only the primitive literal form. If you were to use the new keyword, JavaScript will create an Object type, but one that behaves like a primitive. Here's an example to distinguish between the two:

```
let name1 = "Alice";
let name2 = new String("Bob");
name1.age = 27;
name2.age = 26;
console.log(name1.age);  // undefined
console.log(name2.age);  // 26
console.log(typeof name1); // string
console.log(typeof name2); // object
```

Copying Values

Aside from differences in how they are stored, primitive and reference values act differently when copied from one variable to another. When a primitive value is assigned from one variable to another, the value stored on the variable object is created and copied into the location for the new variable. Consider the following example:

```
let num1 = 5;
let num2 = num1;
```

Here, num1 contains the value of 5. When num2 is initialized to num1, it also gets the value of 5. This value is completely separate from the one that is stored in num1 because it's a copy of that value.

Each of these variables can now be used separately with no side effects. This process is diagrammed in Figure 4.1.

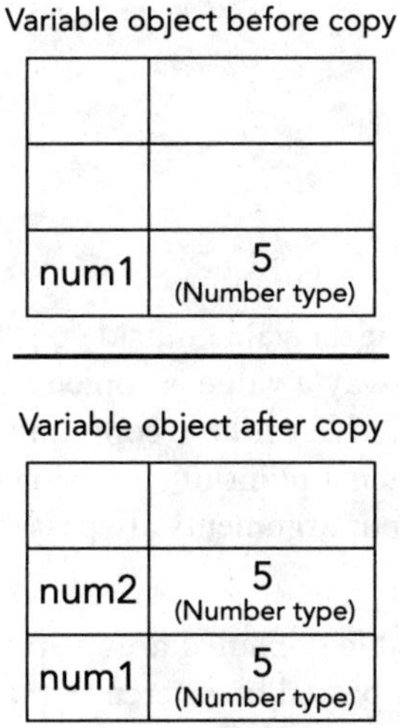

Variable object before copy

num1	5 (Number type)

Variable object after copy

num2	5 (Number type)
num1	5 (Number type)

FIGURE 4.1: Variable object before and after copy

When a reference value is assigned from one variable to another, the value stored on the variable object is also copied into the location for the new variable. The difference is that this value is actually a pointer to an object stored on the heap. Once the operation is complete, two variables point to exactly the same object, so changes to one are reflected on the other, as in the following example:

```
let obj1 = new Object();
let obj2 = obj1;
obj1.name = "Alice";
console.log(obj2.name);   // "Alice"
```

In this example, the variable obj1 is filled with a new instance of an object. This value is then copied into obj2, meaning that both variables are now pointing to the same object. When the property name is set on obj1, it can later be accessed from obj2 because they both point to the same object. Figure 4.2 shows the relationship between the variables on the variable object and the object on the heap.

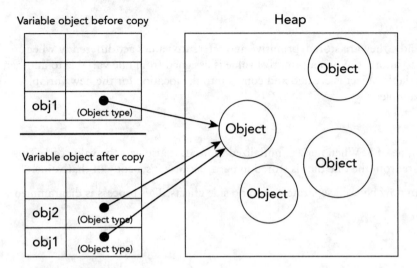

FIGURE 4.2: Relationship between variable objects and the heap

Argument Passing

All function arguments in ECMAScript are passed by value. This means that the value outside of the function is copied into an argument on the inside of the function the same way a value is copied from one variable to another. If the value is primitive, then it acts just like a primitive variable copy, and if the value is a reference, it acts just like a reference variable copy. This is often a point of confusion for developers because variables are accessed both by value and by reference, but arguments are passed only by value.

When an argument is passed by value, the value is copied into a local variable (a named argument and, in ECMAScript, a slot in the arguments object). When an argument is passed by reference, the location of the value in memory is stored into a local variable, which means that changes to the local variable are reflected outside of the function. (This is not possible in ECMAScript.) Consider the following example:

```
function addTen(num) {
    num += 10;
    return num;
}

let count = 20;
let result = addTen(count);
console.log(count);    // 20 - no change
console.log(result);   // 30
```

Here, the function `addTen()` has an argument, `num`, which is essentially a local variable. When called, the variable `count` is passed in as an argument. This variable has a value of 20, which is copied into the argument `num` for use inside of `addTen()`. Within the function, the argument `num` has its value changed by adding 10, but this doesn't change the original variable count that exists outside of the function. The argument `num` and the variable count do not recognize each other; they only happen to have the same value. If num had been passed by reference, then the value of count would have changed to 30 to reflect the change made inside the function. This fact is obvious when using primitive values such as numbers, but things aren't as clear when using objects. Take this, for example:

```
function setName(obj) {
   obj.name = "Alice";
}

let person = new Object();
setName(person);
console.log(person.name);   // "Alice"
```

In this code, an object is created and stored in the variable person. This object is then passed into the setName() method, where it is copied into obj. Inside the function, obj and person both point to the same object. The result is that obj is accessing an object by reference, even though it was passed into the function by value. When the name property is set on obj inside the function, this change is reflected outside the function, because the object that it points to exists globally on the heap. Many developers incorrectly assume that when a local change to an object is reflected globally, that means an argument was passed by reference. To prove that objects are passed by value, consider the following modified code:

```
function setName(obj) {
   obj.name = "Alice";
   obj = new Object();
   obj.name = "Greg";
}

let person = new Object();
setName(person);
console.log(person.name);   // "Alice"
```

The only change between this example and the previous one is that two lines have been added to setName() that redefine obj as a new object with a different name. When person is passed into setName(), its name property is set to "Alice." Then the variable obj is set to be a new object and its name property is set to "Greg." If person were passed by reference, then person would automatically be changed to point to the object whose name is "Greg." However, when person.name is accessed again, its value is "Alice," indicating that the original reference remained intact even though the argument's value changed inside the function. When obj is overwritten inside the function, it becomes a pointer to a local object. That local object is destroyed as soon as the function finishes executing.

> **NOTE** *Think of function arguments in ECMAScript as nothing more than local variables.*

Determining Type

The typeof operator, introduced in the previous chapter, is the best way to determine if a variable is a primitive type. More specifically, it's the best way to determine if a variable is a string, number,

Boolean, or `undefined`. If the value is an object or `null`, then `typeof` returns "object," as in this example:

```
let s = "Alice";
let b = true;
let i = 22;
let u;
let n = null;
let o = new Object();

console.log(typeof s);    // string
console.log(typeof i);    // number
console.log(typeof b);    // boolean
console.log(typeof u);    // undefined
console.log(typeof n);    // object
console.log(typeof o);    // object
```

Although `typeof` works well for primitive values, it's of little use for reference values. Typically, you don't care that a value is an object—what you really want to know is what type of object it is. To aid in this identification, ECMAScript provides the `instanceof` operator, which is used with the following syntax:

```
result = variable instanceof constructor
```

The `instanceof` operator returns true if the variable is an instance of the given reference type (identified by its prototype chain, as discussed in the Chapter 8, "Objects, Classes, and Object-Oriented Programming"). Consider this example:

```
console.log(person instanceof Object);    // is the variable person an Object?
console.log(colors instanceof Array);     // is the variable colors an Array?
console.log(pattern instanceof RegExp);   // is the variable pattern a RegExp?
```

All reference values, by definition, are instances of Object, so the `instanceof` operator always returns `true` when used with a reference value and the `Object` constructor. Similarly, if `instanceof` is used with a primitive value, it will always return `false`, because primitives aren't objects.

EXECUTION CONTEXT AND SCOPE

The concept of execution context, referred to as *context* for simplicity, is of the utmost importance in JavaScript. The execution context of a variable or function defines what other data it has access to, as well as how it should behave. Each execution context has an associated *variable object* upon which all of its defined variables and functions exist. This object is not accessible by code but is used behind the scenes to handle data.

The global execution context is the outermost one. Depending on the host environment for an ECMAScript implementation, the object representing this context may differ. In web browsers, the global context is said to be that of the window object (discussed in the Chapter 12, "The Browser Object Model"), so all global variables and functions defined with var are created as properties and methods on the window object. Declarations using let and const at the top level are not defined in the global context, but they are resolved identically on the scope chain. When an execution context has executed all of its code, it is destroyed, taking with it all of the variables and functions defined within it (the global context isn't destroyed until the application exits, such as when a web page is closed or a web browser is shut down).

Each function call has its own execution context. Whenever code execution flows into a function, the function's context is pushed onto a context stack. After the function has finished executing, the stack is popped, returning control to the previously executing context. This facility controls execution flow throughout an ECMAScript program.

When code is executed in a context, a *scope chain* of variable objects is created. The purpose of the scope chain is to provide ordered access to all variables and functions that an execution context has access to. The front of the scope chain is always the variable object of the context whose code is executing. If the context is a function, then the *activation object* is used as the variable object. An activation object starts with a single defined variable called arguments. (This doesn't exist for the global context.) The next variable object in the chain is from the containing context, and the next after that is from the next containing context. This pattern continues until the global context is reached; the global context's variable object is always the last of the scope chain.

Identifiers are resolved by navigating the scope chain in search of the identifier name. The search always begins at the front of the chain and proceeds to the back until the identifier is found. (If the identifier isn't found, typically an error occurs.)

Consider the following code:

```
var color = "blue";

function changeColor() {
  if (color === "blue") {
    color = "red";
  } else {
    color = "blue";
  }
}

changeColor();
```

In this simple example, the function changeColor() has a scope chain with two objects in it: its own variable object (upon which the arguments object is defined) and the global context's variable object. The variable color is therefore accessible inside the function, because it can be found in the scope chain.

Additionally, locally defined variables can be used interchangeably with global variables in a local context. Here's an example:

```
var color = "blue";

function changeColor() {
  let anotherColor = "red";

  function swapColors() {
    let tempColor = anotherColor;
    anotherColor = color;
```

```
        color = tempColor;

        // color, anotherColor, and tempColor are all accessible here
    }

    // color and anotherColor are accessible here, but not tempColor
    swapColors();
}

// only color is accessible here
changeColor();
```

There are three execution contexts in this code: global context, the local context of `changeColor()`, and the local context of `swapColors()`. The global context has one variable, `color`, and one function, `changeColor()`. The local context of `changeColor()` has one variable named `anotherColor` and one function named `swapColors()`, but it can also access the variable `color` from the global context. The local context of `swapColors()` has one variable, named `tempColor`, that is accessible only within that context. Neither the global context nor the local context of `changeColors()` has access to `tempColor`. Within `swapColors()`, though, the variables of the other two contexts are fully accessible because they are parent execution contexts. Figure 4.3 represents the scope chain for the previous example.

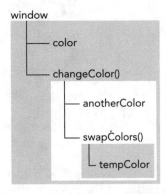

window

FIGURE 4.3: Example scope chain for nested functions

In this figure, the rectangles represent specific execution contexts. An inner context can access everything from all outer contexts through the scope chain, but the outer contexts cannot access anything within an inner context. The connection between the contexts is linear and ordered. Each context can search up the scope chain for variables and functions, but no context can search down the scope chain into another execution context. There are three objects in the scope chain for the local context of `swapColors()`: the `swapColors()` variable object, the variable object from `changeColor()`, and the global variable object. The local context of `swapColors()` begins its search for variable and function names in its own variable object before moving along the chain. The scope chain for the `changeColor()` context has only two objects: its own variable object and the global variable object. This means that it cannot access the context of `swapColors()`.

> **NOTE** *Function arguments are considered to be variables and follow the same access rules as any other variable in the execution context.*

Scope Chain Augmentation

Even though there are only two primary types of execution contexts, global and function (the third exists inside of a call to eval()), there are other ways to augment the scope chain. Certain statements cause a temporary addition to the front of the scope chain that is later removed after code execution. There are two times when this occurs, specifically when execution enters either of the following:

➤ The catch block in a try-catch statement

➤ A with statement

Both of these statements add a variable object to the front of the scope chain. For the with statement, the specified object is added to the scope chain; for the catch statement, a new variable object is created and contains a declaration for the thrown error object. Consider the following:

```
function buildUrl() {
  let qs = "?debug=true";

  with(location){
    let url = href + qs;
  }

  return url;
}
```

In this example, the with statement is acting on the location object, so location itself is added to the front of the scope chain. There is one variable, qs, defined in the buildUrl() function. When the variable href is referenced, it's actually referring to location.href, which is in its own variable object. When the variable qs is referenced, it's referring to the variable defined in buildUrl(), which is in the function context's variable object. Inside the with statement is a variable declaration for url, which becomes part of the function's context and can, therefore, be returned as the function value.

Variable Declaration

ECMAScript variables can either be function scoped or block scoped. Furthermore, a block scoped variable can be declared as a const.

Function Scope Declaration Using var

When a variable is declared using var, it is automatically added to the most immediate context available. In a function, the most immediate one is the function's local context; in a with statement, the most immediate is the function context. If a variable is initialized without first being declared, it gets added to the global context automatically, as in this example:

```
function add(num1, num2) {
  var sum = num1 + num2;
  return sum;
}
let result = add(10, 20);   // 30
console.log(sum);           // causes an error: sum is not a valid variable
```

Here, the function `add()` defines a local variable named `sum` that contains the result of an addition operation. This value is returned as the function value, but the variable `sum` isn't accessible outside the function. If the `var` keyword is omitted from this example, `sum` becomes accessible after `add()` has been called, as shown here:

```
function add(num1, num2) {
  sum = num1 + num2;
  return sum;
}

let result = add(10, 20);   // 30
console.log(sum);           // 30
```

Here, the variable `sum` is initialized to a value without ever having been declared using `var`. When `add()` is called, `sum` is created in the global context and continues to exist even after the function has completed, allowing you to access it later.

> **NOTE** *Initializing variables without declaring them is a very common mistake in JavaScript programming and can lead to errors. It's advisable to always declare variables before initializing them to avoid such issues. In strict mode, initializing variables without declaration causes an error.*

A `var` declaration will be brought to the top of the function or global scope and before any existing code inside it. This is referred to as "hoisting." This allows you to safely use a hoisted variable anywhere in the same scope without consideration for whether or not it was declared yet. However, in practice, this can lead to legal yet bizarre code in which a variable is used before it is declared. Here is an example of two equivalent code snippets in the global scope:

```
var name = "Jake";

// This is equivalent to:

name = 'Jake';
var name;
```

Here is an example of two equivalent functions:

```
function fn1() {
  var name = 'Jake';
}

// This is equivalent to:
function fn2() {
  var name;
  name = 'Jake';
}
```

You can prove to yourself that a variable is hoisted by inspecting it before its declaration. The hoisting of the declaration means you will see undefined instead of ReferenceError:

```
console.log(name);  // undefined
var name = 'Jake';

function() {
  console.log(name);  // undefined
  var name = 'Jake';
}
```

Block Scope Declaration Using *let*

Declaring variables with let operates much in the same way as var, but it is scoped at the block level. Block scope is defined as the nearest set of enclosing curly braces {}. This means if blocks, while blocks, function blocks, and even standalone blocks will be the extent of the scope of any variable declared with let.

```
if (true) {
  let a;
}
console.log(a);  // ReferenceError: a is not defined

while (true) {
  let b;
}
console.log(b);  // ReferenceError: b is not defined

function foo() {
  let c;
}
console.log(c);  // ReferenceError: c is not defined
                 // This should be unsurprising, as
                 // a var declaration would also throw an Error

// This is not an object literal, this is a standalone block.
// The JavaScript interpreter will identify it as such based on its contents.
{
  let d;
}
console.log(d);  // ReferenceError: d is not defined
```

In a similar departure from the behavior of var, let cannot be declared twice inside the same block scope. Duplicate var declarations are simply ignored; duplicate let declarations throw a SyntaxError.

```
var a;
var a;
// No errors thrown

{
  let b;
  let b;
}
// SyntaxError: Identifier 'b' has already been declared
```

The behavior of `let` is especially useful when using iterators inside loops. Iterator declarations using `var` will bleed outside the loop after it completes, which is frequently a very undesirable behavior. Consider these two examples:

```
for (var i = 0; i < 10; ++i) {}
console.log(i);   // 10

for (let j = 0; j < 10; ++j) {}
console.log(j);   // ReferenceError: j is not defined
```

`let` is technically hoisted in the JavaScript runtime, but because of the "temporal dead zone," you are prevented from using the variable above its actual declaration. Therefore, for the purposes of writing JavaScript, let is not hoisted in the same way as var.

Constant Declaration Using *const*

A variable declared using `const` must be initialized to some value. Once declared, it cannot be reassigned to a new value at any point in its lifetime.

```
const a;   // SyntaxError: Missing initializer in const declaration

const b = 3;
console.log(b);   // 3
b = 4;   // TypeError: Assignment to a constant variable
```

Apart from its `const` rule enforcement, `const` variables behave identically to `let` variables:

```
if (true) {
  const a = 0;
}
console.log(a);   // ReferenceError: a is not defined

while (true) {
  const b = 1;
}
console.log(b);   // ReferenceError: b is not defined

function foo() {
  const c = 2;
}
console.log(c);   // ReferenceError: c is not defined

{
  const d = 3;
}
console.log(d);   // ReferenceError: d is not defined
```

The `const` declaration only applies to the top-level primitive or object. In other words, a `const` variable assigned to an object cannot be reassigned to another reference value, but the keys inside that object are not protected.

```
const o1 = {};
o1 = {};   // TypeError: Assignment to a constant variable;

const o2 = {};
o2.name = 'Jake';
console.log(o2.name);   // 'Jake'
```

If you wish to make the entire object immutable, you can use `Object.freeze()`, although attempted property assignment will not raise errors; it will just silently fail:

```
const o3 = Object.freeze({});
o3.name = 'Jake';
console.log(o3.name);  // undefined
```

Because `const` declarations imply that the value is of a single type and immutable, the JavaScript runtime compiler can replace all instances of it with its actual value instead of performing a variable lookup through a lookup table. The Google Chrome V8 engine performs such an optimization.

> **NOTE** *If your development process isn't too materially affected by it, best practices dictate that you use* `const` *as often as possible unless you really need a variable that can undergo reassignment. This will allow you to catch an entire vein of reassignment bugs much earlier than you normally would.*

Identifier Lookup

When an identifier is referenced for either reading or writing within a particular context, a search must take place to determine what identifier it represents. The search starts at the front of the scope chain, looking for an identifier with the given name. If it finds that identifier name in the local context, then the search stops and the variable is set; if the search doesn't find the variable name, it continues along the scope chain. (Note that objects in the scope chain also have a prototype chain, so searching may include each object's prototype chain.) This process continues until the search reaches the global context's variable object. If the identifier isn't found there, it hasn't been declared.

To better illustrate how identifier lookup occurs, consider the following example:

```
var color = 'blue';

function getColor() {
  return color;
}

console.log(getColor());  // 'blue'
```

When the function `getColor()` is called in this example, the variable `color` is referenced. At that point, a two-step search begins. First `getColor()`'s variable object is searched for an identifier named `color`. When it isn't found, the search goes to the next variable object (from the global context) and then searches for an identifier named `color`. Because `color` is defined in that variable object, the search ends.

Given this search process, referencing local variables automatically stops the search from going into another variable object. This means that identifiers in a parent context cannot be referenced if an identifier in the local context has the same name, as in this example:

```
var color = 'blue';

function getColor() {
  let color = 'red';
```

```
    return color;
  }

  console.log(getColor());  // 'red'
```

Using block scoped declarations does not change the search process, but it can add extra levels to the lexical hierarchy:

```
  var color = 'blue';

  function getColor() {
    let color = 'red';
    {
      let color = 'green';
      return color;
    }
  }

  console.log(getColor());  // 'green'
```

In this modified code, a local variable named `color` is declared inside the `getColor()` function. When the function is called, the variable is declared. When the second line of the function is executed, it knows that a variable named `color` must be used. The search begins in the local context, where it finds a variable named `color` with a value of `'green'`. Because the variable was found, the search stops and the local variable is used, meaning that the function returns `'green'`. Any lines of code appearing after the declaration of `color` as a local variable cannot access the global color variable without qualifying it as `window.color`. If one of the operands is an object and the other is not, the `valueOf()` method is called on the object to retrieve a primitive value to compare according to the previous rules.

> **NOTE** *Variable lookup doesn't come without a price. It's faster to access local variables than global variables because there's no search up the scope chain. JavaScript engines are getting better at optimizing identifier lookup, however, so this difference may end up negligible in the future.*

GARBAGE COLLECTION

JavaScript is a garbage-collected language, meaning that the execution environment is responsible for managing the memory required during code execution. In languages such as C and C++, keeping track of memory usage is a principle concern and the source of many issues for developers. JavaScript frees developers from worrying about memory management by automatically allocating what is needed and reclaiming memory that is no longer being used. The basic idea is simple: figure out which variables aren't going to be used and free the memory associated with them. This process is periodic, with the garbage collector running at specified intervals (or at predefined collection moments in code execution). The process of garbage collection is an approximate and imperfect solution because the general problem of knowing whether some piece of memory is needed is "undecidable," meaning it cannot be solved by an algorithm.

Consider the normal life cycle of a local variable in a function. The variable comes into existence during the execution of the function. At that time, memory is allocated on the stack (and possibly on the heap) to provide storage space for the value. The variable is used inside the function and then the function ends. At that point, this variable is no longer needed, so its memory can be reclaimed for later use. In this situation, it's obvious that the variable isn't needed, but not all situations are as obvious. The garbage collector must keep track of which variables can and can't be used so it can identify likely candidates for memory reclamation. The strategy for identifying the unused variables may differ on an implementation basis.

Performance

The garbage collector runs periodically and can potentially be an expensive process if there are a large number of variable allocations in memory, so the timing of the garbage-collection process is important. In particular, on mobile devices with limited system memory, garbage collection can noticeably degrade the speed and framerate of rendering. You cannot know when garbage collection is coming, so the best strategy is to organize your code in such a way that it allows garbage collection to do its job to the best of its ability whenever it is scheduled to run.

Modern garbage collectors decide when to run based on a collection of heuristics that are measured from the JavaScript runtime environment. These heuristics will vary by engine, but they will all be approximately based upon the size and number of objects that have been allocated. For example, from a V8 blog post in 2016: "At the end of a full garbage collection, V8's heap growing strategy determines when the next garbage collection will happen based on the amount of live objects with some additional slack."

Managing Memory

In a garbage-collected programming environment, developers typically don't have to worry about memory management. However, JavaScript runs in an environment where memory management and garbage collection operate uniquely. The amount of memory available for use in web browsers is typically much less than is available for desktop applications, and even more so for mobile browsers. This is more of a security feature than anything else, ensuring that a web page running JavaScript can't crash the operating system by using up all the system memory. The memory limits affect not only variable allocation but also the call stack and the number of statements that can be executed in a single thread.

Keeping the amount of used memory to a minimum leads to better page performance. The best way to optimize memory usage is to ensure that you're keeping around only data that is necessary for the execution of your code. When data is no longer necessary, it's best to set the value to null, freeing up the reference—this is called *dereferencing* the value. This advice applies mostly to global values and properties of global objects. Local variables are dereferenced automatically when they go out of context, as in this example:

```
function createPerson(name){
  let localPerson = new Object();
  localPerson.name = name;
  return localPerson;
```

```
    }

    let globalPerson = createPerson("Alice");

    // do something with globalPerson

    globalPerson = null;
```

In this code, the variable `globalPerson` is filled with a value returned from the `createPerson()` function. Inside `createPerson()`, `localPerson` creates an object and adds a `name` property to it. The variable `localPerson` is returned as the function value and assigned to `globalPerson`. Because `localPerson` goes out of context after `createPerson()` has finished executing, it doesn't need to be dereferenced explicitly. Because `globalPerson` is a global variable, it should be dereferenced when it's no longer needed, which is what happens in the last line.

Keep in mind that dereferencing a value doesn't automatically reclaim the memory associated with it. The point of dereferencing is to make sure the value is out of context and will be reclaimed the next time garbage collection occurs.

Performance Boosts with const and let Declarations

Because `const` and `let` are scoped to a block instead of a function, depending on how your code is organized this may signal to the garbage collector that an allocated variable is eligible for cleanup far sooner than it would have been when using `var`. This would occur in situations when the block scope terminates far sooner than the function scope.

Hidden Classes and the delete Operation

The most popular browser engine is the V8 JavaScript engine. This engine utilizes "hidden classes" when compiling the interpreted JavaScript code into actual machine code, and if you are writing performance-sensitive code, this might matter to you.

During runtime, V8 will associate hidden classes for every object created to keep track of the shape of its properties. Objects that are able to share the same hidden class will have better performance, and V8 will optimize for this but may not always be able to. Consider the following code snippet:

```
function Article() {
    this.title = 'Inauguration Ceremony Features Kazoo Band';
}

let a1 = new Article();
let a2 = new Article();
```

Behind the scenes, V8 will configure the two class instances to share the same hidden class. This makes sense because they share a constructor and prototype. Suppose you then appended the following line to the end of this code:

```
a2.author = 'Jake';
```

Now, the two `Article` instances will have two divergent hidden class implementations. Depending on the frequency of this operation and the size of the hidden classes, this can have meaningful impacts on performance.

The solution, of course, is to avoid JavaScript's ready-fire-aim dynamic property assignment and instead declare all properties inside the constructor, as shown here:

```
function Article(opt_author) {
  this.title = 'Inauguration Ceremony Features Kazoo Band';
  this.author = opt_author;
}

let a1 = new Article();
let a2 = new Article('Jake');
```

Now, the two instances will behave in essentially the same way (not counting the return values of hasOwnProperty), and they will also share a hidden class, potentially yielding improved performance. Bear in mind though that using the `delete` keyword can generate the same hidden class fragmentation. This is demonstrated here:

```
function Article() {
  this.title = 'Inauguration Ceremony Features Kazoo Band';
  this.author = 'Jake';
}

let a1 = new Article();
let a2 = new Article();

delete a1.author;
```

At the end of this snippet, the two instances will no longer share a hidden class even though they use a unified constructor. Dynamic deletion of a property will yield the same effect as dynamic addition. Best practices dictate that unwanted properties should be set to `null`. It will allow the hidden classes to remain intact and shared, and it has the same effect on removing references for the benefit of the garbage collector.

```
function Article() {
  this.title = 'Inauguration Ceremony Features Kazoo Band';
  this.author = 'Jake';
}

let a1 = new Article();
let a2 = new Article();

a1.author = null;
```

Memory Leaks

Poorly written JavaScript can yield some sneaky and insidious memory leaks. On devices with limited memory, or in the context of functions that are called many times, this can cause big problems. Overwhelmingly, memory leaks in JavaScript are caused by unwanted references.

One of the most common and easily fixed memory leaks is accidentally declaring global variables. In the following code, the name variable is not prefixed with a declaration keyword:

```
function setName() {
  name = 'Jake';
}
```

In this example, the interpreter will handle this as `window.name = 'Jake'`, and, of course, properties set on the `window` object will never be cleaned up if the `window` object itself is not cleaned up. This is easily fixed by prefixing the declaration with `var`, `let`, or `const`, which will all go out of scope at the end of the function's execution.

Interval timers can also quietly cause memory leaks. In the following code, the code sets an interval, which references a variable provided through a closure:

```
let name = 'Jake';
setInterval(() => {
  console.log(name);
}, 100);
```

As long as this interval timer is running, the handler function containing a reference to name remains allocated. The garbage collector recognizes this and therefore is unable to clean up the outer variable.

JavaScript closures are an exceedingly common way to leak memory without realizing it. Consider the following example:

```
let outer = function() {
  let name = 'Jake';
  return function() {
    return name;
  };
};
```

This leaks the memory allocated for name. This code creates an internal closure, so as long as the outer function exists, the name variable cannot be cleaned up because there will be a persistent reference to it through that closure. If the contents of the name variable were extremely large instead of just a short string, major problems could result.

Static Allocation and Object Pools

At the very end of the JavaScript performance spectrum, you may find yourself wanting to squeeze the very last bit of performance juice out of the browser. To accomplish this, a good place to focus is on minimizing the number of garbage collection operations the browser performs. Because you do not directly control when garbage collection occurs, you can instead optimize around the heuristics that browsers use when scheduling garbage collection. In theory, if you can responsibly use allocated memory and at the same time obviate superfluous garbage collection, then you will be able to make performance gains that would otherwise be lost freeing memory.

One important metric measured by the browser to decide when to schedule garbage collection is the rate of object churn. If lots of objects are being instantiated and then going out of scope, the browser will schedule garbage collections more aggressively, which of course will slow down the application. Consider the following example, a two dimensional vector addition function:

```
function addVector(a, b) {
  let resultant = new Vector();
  resultant.x = a.x + b.x;
  resultant.y = a.y + b.y;
  return resultant;
}
```

When invoked, this function creates a new object on the heap, modifies it, and returns it to the caller. If the lifetime of this vector object is short, it will soon lose all its references and be eligible for garbage collection. If this vector addition function is called frequently, the garbage collection scheduler will see this high rate of object churn, and garbage collection will be scheduled more frequently.

Instead of this dynamic vector creation, suppose you changed the method to use an existing vector object:

```
function addVector(a, b, resultant) {
   resultant.x = a.x + b.x;
   resultant.y = a.y + b.y;
   return resultant;
}
```

Of course, this requires the resultant vector argument to be fresh and instantiated somewhere else, but the behavior of this function is the same. Where then to create a vector while avoiding the gaze of the garbage collector heuristics?

One strategy is to use an object pool. At some point in initialization, you will create an object pool that manages a collection of recyclable objects. Your application can request an object from this pool, set its properties, use it, and return it to the pool when it's done. Because no object instantiation is occurring, garbage collection heuristics won't measure an uptick in object churn, and garbage collection will occur less frequently. An object pool pseudo-implementation might look something like this:

```
// vectorPool is the existing object pool
let v1 = vectorPool.allocate();
let v2 = vectorPool.allocate();
let v3 = vectorPool.allocate();

v1.x = 10;
v1.y = 5;
v2.x = -3;
v2.y = -6;

addVector(v1, v2, v3);

console.log([v3.x, v3.y]);  // [7, -1]

vectorPool.free(v1);
vectorPool.free(v2);
vectorPool.free(v3);

// If the objects had properties referencing other objects,
// those would need to be set to null here as well
v1 = null;
v2 = null;
v3 = null;
```

If the object pool only allocates vectors as necessary (which creates new ones when they don't exist and reuses ones that already exist), this implementation is essentially a greedy algorithm that will have monotonically increasing yet static memory. This pool must maintain the collection using some structure, and a good choice is an `Array`. However, the implementation using an array must be designed carefully as to not incur additional garbage collection. Consider the following example:

```
let vectorList = new Array(100);
let vector = new Vector();
vectorList.push(vector);
```

Because JavaScript uses dynamically sized arrays, the engine will delete the array of size 100 and create a new array of size 200. The garbage collector will see this deletion and may be encouraged to run sooner because of it. This dynamic allocation can be avoided by creating an appropriately sized array upon initialization, which will enable you to avoid the aforementioned resizing operation. It will require, however, that you gain a sense of how large this array should be.

> **NOTE** *Static allocation is an extreme form of optimization. It will yield performance gains when your application's performance is hindered by garbage collection overhead, but this will be the case very infrequently. In most cases, this is a form of premature optimization and is not appropriate.*

SUMMARY

Two types of values can be stored in JavaScript variables: primitive values and reference values. Primitive values have one of the seven primitive data types: Undefined, Null, Boolean, Number, BigInt, String, and Symbol. Primitive and reference values have the following characteristics:

➤ Primitive values are of a fixed size and so are stored in memory on the stack.

➤ Copying primitive values from one variable to another creates a second copy of the value.

➤ Reference values are objects and are stored in memory on the heap.

➤ A variable containing a reference value actually contains just a pointer to the object, not the object itself.

➤ Copying a reference value to another variable copies just the pointer, so both variables end up referencing the same object.

➤ The `typeof` operator determines a value's primitive type, whereas the `instanceof` operator is used to determine the reference type of a value.

All variables, primitive and reference, exist within an execution context (also called a scope) that determines the lifetime of the variable and which parts of the code can access it. Execution context can be summarized as follows:

➤ Execution contexts exist globally (called the global context), within functions, and within blocks.

➤ Each time a new execution context is entered, it creates a scope chain to search for variables and functions.

➤   Contexts that are local to a function or block have access not only to variables in that scope but also to variables in any containing contexts and the global context.

➤   The global context has access only to variables and functions in the global context and cannot directly access any data inside local contexts.

➤   The execution context of variables helps to determine when memory will be freed.

JavaScript is a garbage-collected programming environment where the developer need not be concerned with memory allocation or reclamation. JavaScript's garbage-collection routine can be summarized as follows:

➤   Values that go out of scope will automatically be marked for reclamation and will be deleted during the garbage-collection process.

➤   Dereferencing variables helps not only with circular references but also with garbage collection in general. To aid in memory reclamation, global objects, properties on global objects, and circular references should all be dereferenced when no longer needed.

5

Basic Reference Types

WHAT'S IN THIS CHAPTER?

➤ Working with objects

➤ Understanding basic JavaScript data types

➤ Working with primitives and primitive wrappers

DOWNLOADS FOR THIS CHAPTER

Please note that all the code examples for this chapter are available as a part of this chapter's code download on the book's website at www.wiley.com/go/projavascript5e.

A reference value (object) is an instance of a specific *reference type*. In ECMAScript, reference types are structures used to group data and functionality together and are often incorrectly called *classes*. Although technically an object-oriented language, ECMAScript lacks some basic constructs that have traditionally been associated with object-oriented programming, including classes and interfaces. Reference types are also sometimes called *object definitions* because they describe the properties and methods that objects should have.

> **NOTE** *Even though reference types are similar to classes, the two concepts are not equivalent. To avoid any confusion, the term "class" is not used in the rest of this chapter.*

Again, objects are considered to be *instances* of a particular reference type. New objects are created by using the new operator followed by a *constructor*. A constructor is simply a function whose purpose is to create a new object. Consider the following line of code:

```
let now = new Date();
```

This code creates a new instance of the Date reference type and stores it in the variable now. The constructor being used is Date(), which creates a simple object with only the default properties and methods. ECMAScript provides a number of native reference types, such as Date, to help developers with common computing tasks.

> **NOTE** *Functions are a reference type, but they are too broad of a topic for this chapter and therefore have an entire chapter devoted to them. Refer to the Chapter 10, "Functions."*

THE DATE TYPE

The ECMAScript Date type is based on an early version of java.util.Date from Java. As such, the Date type stores dates as the number of milliseconds that have passed since midnight on January 1, 1970 UTC (Universal Time Code). Using this data storage format, the Date type can accurately represent dates 285,616 years before or after January 1, 1970.

To create a date object, use the new operator along with the Date constructor, like this:

```
let now = new Date();
```

When the Date constructor is used without any arguments, the created object is assigned the current date and time. To create a date based on another date or time, you must pass in the millisecond representation of the date (the number of milliseconds after midnight, January 1, 1970 UTC, the Unix epoch). To aid in this process, ECMAScript provides two methods: Date.parse() and Date.UTC().

The Date.parse() method accepts a string argument representing a date. It attempts to convert the string into a millisecond representation of a date. ECMA-262 defines which date formats Date .parse() should support, filling in a void left by the third edition. All implementations must now support the following date formats:

➤   month/date/year (such as 5/23/2019)

➤   month_name date, year (such as May 23, 2019)

➤   day_of_week month_name date year hours:minutes:seconds time_zone (such as Tue May 23 2019 00:00:00 GMT-0700)

➤   ISO 8601 extended format YYYY-MM-DDTHH:mm:ss.sssZ (such as 2019-05-23T00:00:00) For instance, to create a date object for May 23, 2019, you can use the following code:

```
let someDate = new Date(Date.parse("May 23, 2019"));
```

If the string passed into `Date.parse()` doesn't represent a date, then it returns NaN. The `Date` constructor will call `Date.parse()` behind the scenes if a string is passed in directly, meaning that the following code is identical to the previous example:

```
let someDate = new Date("May 23, 2019");
```

This code produces the same result as the previous example.

The `Date.UTC()` method also returns the millisecond representation of a date but constructs that value using different information than `Date.parse()`. The arguments for `Date.UTC()` are the year, the zero-based month (January is 0, February is 1, and so on), the day of the month (1 through 31), and the hours (0 through 23), minutes, seconds, and milliseconds of the time. Of these arguments, only the first two (year and month) are required. If the day of the month isn't supplied, it's assumed to be 1, while all other omitted arguments are assumed to be 0. Here are two examples of `Date.UTC()` in action:

```
// January 1, 2000 at midnight GMT
let y2k = new Date(Date.UTC(2000, 0));

// May 5, 2005 at 5:55:55 PM GMT
let allFives = new Date(Date.UTC(2005, 4, 5, 17, 55, 55));
```

Two dates are created in this example. The first date is for midnight (GMT) on January 1, 2000, which is represented by the year 2000 and the month 0 (which is January). Because the other arguments are filled in (the day of the month as 1 and everything else as 0), the result is the first day of the month at midnight. The second date represents May 5, 2005, at 5:55:55 PM GMT. Even though the date and time contain only fives, creating this date requires some different numbers: the month must be set to 4 because months are zero-based, and the hour must be set to 17 because hours are represented as 0 through 23. The rest of the arguments are as expected.

As with `Date.parse()`, `Date.UTC()` is mimicked by the `Date` constructor but with one major difference: the date and time created are in the local time zone, not in GMT. However, the `Date` constructor takes the same arguments as `Date.UTC()`, so if the first argument is a number, the constructor assumes that it is the year of a date, the second argument is the month, and so on. The preceding example can then be rewritten as this:

```
// January 1, 2000 at midnight in local time
let y2k = new Date(2000, 0);

// May 5, 2005 at 5:55:55 PM local time
let allFives = new Date(2005, 4, 5, 17, 55, 55);
```

This code creates the same two dates as the previous example, but this time both dates are in the local time zone as determined by the system settings.

ECMAScript also offers `Date.now()`, which returns the millisecond representation of the date and time at which the method is executed. This method makes it trivial to use `Date` objects for code profiling, such as:

```
// get start time
```

```
    let start = Date.now();

    // call a function
    doSomething();

    // get stop time
    let stop = Date.now(),
      result = stop - start;
```

Inherited Methods

As with the other reference types, the `Date` type overrides `toLocaleString()`, `toString()`, and `valueOf()`, though unlike the previous types, each method returns something different. The `Date` type's `toLocaleString()` method returns the date and time in a format appropriate for the locale in which the browser is being run. This often means that the format includes AM or PM for the time and doesn't include any time-zone information (the exact format varies from browser to browser). The `toString()` method typically returns the date and time with time-zone information, and the time is typically indicated in 24-hour notation (hours ranging from 0 to 23). The following displays the format for `toLocaleString()` and `toString()` when representing the date/time of February 1, 2019, at midnight PST (Pacific Standard Time) in the "en-US" locale:

> `toLocaleString()` — 2/1/2019 12:00:00 AM

> `toString()` — Thu Feb 1 2019 00:00:00 GMT-0800 (Pacific Standard Time)

Modern browsers have converged to output the same strings for these two methods. When using legacy browsers, there are differences between the formats that browsers return for each method. These differences mean `toLocaleString()` and `toString()` are useful only for debugging purposes, not for display purposes.

The `valueOf()` method for the `Date` type doesn't return a string at all because it is overridden to return the milliseconds representation of the date so that operators (such as less-than and greater-than) will work appropriately for date values. Consider this example:

```
    let date1 = new Date(2019, 0, 1);    // "January 1, 2019"
    let date2 = new Date(2019, 1, 1);    // "February 1, 2019"

    console.log(date1 < date2);   // true
    console.log(date1> date2);   // false
```

The date January 1, 2019, comes before February 1, 2019, so it would make sense to say that the former is less than the latter. Because the milliseconds representation of January 1, 2019, is less than that of February 1, 2019, the less-than operator returns true when the dates are compared, providing an easy way to determine the order of dates.

Date-Formatting Methods

There are several `Date` type methods used specifically to format the date as a string. They are as follows:

➤ `toDateString()`—Displays the date's day of the week, month, day of the month, and year in an implementation-specific format.

➤ `toTimeString()`—Displays the date's hours, minutes, seconds, and time zone in an implementation-specific format.

➤ `toLocaleDateString()`—Displays the date's day of the week, month, day of the month, and year in an implementation- and locale-specific format.

➤ `toLocaleTimeString()`—Displays the date's hours, minutes, and seconds in an implementation-specific format.

➤ `toUTCString()`—Displays the complete UTC date in an implementation-specific format.

The output of these methods, as with `toLocaleString()` and `toString()`, varies widely from browser to browser and therefore can't be employed in a user interface for consistent display of a date.

> **NOTE** *There is also a method called* `toGMTString()`, *which is equivalent to* `toUTCString()` *and is provided for backwards compatibility. However, the specification recommends that new code use* `toUTCString()` *exclusively.*

Date/Time Component Methods

The remaining methods of the `Date` type (listed in the following table) deal directly with getting and setting specific parts of the date value. Note that references to a UTC date mean the date value when interpreted without a time-zone offset (the date when converted to GMT).

METHOD	DESCRIPTION
`getTime()`	Returns the milliseconds representation of the date; same as `valueOf()`.
`setTime(milliseconds)`	Sets the milliseconds representation of the date, thus changing the entire date.
`getFullYear()`	Returns the four-digit year (2019 instead of just 19).
`getUTCFullYear()`	Returns the four-digit year of the UTC date value.
`setFullYear(year)`	Sets the year of the date. The year must be given with four digits (2019 instead of just 19).
`setUTCFullYear(year)`	Sets the year of the UTC date. The year must be given with four digits (2019 instead of just 19).
`getMonth()`	Returns the month of the date, where 0 represents January and 11 represents December.
`getUTCMonth()`	Returns the month of the UTC date, where 0 represents January and 11 represents December.
`setMonth(month)`	Sets the month of the date, which is any number 0 or greater. Numbers greater than 11 add years.

continues

(continued)

METHOD	DESCRIPTION
setUTCMonth(month)	Sets the month of the UTC date, which is any number 0 or greater. Numbers greater than 11 add years.
getDate()	Returns the day of the month (1 through 31) for the date.
getUTCDate()	Returns the day of the month (1 through 31) for the UTC date.
setDate(date)	Sets the day of the month for the date. If the date is greater than the number of days in the month, the month value also gets increased.
setUTCDate(date)	Sets the day of the month for the UTC date. If the date is greater than the number of days in the month, the month value also gets increased.
getDay()	Returns the date's day of the week as a number (where 0 represents Sunday and 6 represents Saturday).
getUTCDay()	Returns the UTC date's day of the week as a number (where 0 represents Sunday and 6 represents Saturday).
getHours()	Returns the date's hours as a number between 0 and 23.
getUTCHours()	Returns the UTC date's hours as a number between 0 and 23.
setHours(hours)	Sets the date's hours. Setting the hours to a number greater than 23 also increments the day of the month.
setUTCHours(hours)	Sets the UTC date's hours. Setting the hours to a number greater than 23 also increments the day of the month.
getMinutes()	Returns the date's minutes as a number between 0 and 59.
getUTCMinutes()	Returns the UTC date's minutes as a number between 0 and 59.
setMinutes(minutes)	Sets the date's minutes. Setting the minutes to a number greater than 59 also increments the hour.
setUTCMinutes(minutes)	Sets the UTC date's minutes. Setting the minutes to a number greater than 59 also increments the hour.
getSeconds()	Returns the date's seconds as a number between 0 and 59.
getUTCSeconds()	Returns the UTC date's seconds as a number between 0 and 59.

(continued)

METHOD	DESCRIPTION
`setSeconds(seconds)`	Sets the date's seconds. Setting the seconds to a number greater than 59 also increments the minutes.
`setUTCSeconds(seconds)`	Sets the UTC date's seconds. Setting the seconds to a number greater than 59 also increments the minutes.
`getMilliseconds()`	Returns the date's milliseconds.
`getUTCMilliseconds()`	Returns the UTC date's milliseconds.
`setMilliseconds(milliseconds)`	Sets the date's milliseconds.
`setUTCMilliseconds (milliseconds)`	Sets the UTC date's milliseconds.
`getTimezoneOffset()`	Returns the number of minutes that the local time zone is offset from UTC. For example, Eastern Standard Time returns 300. This value changes when an area goes into Daylight Saving Time.

THE REGEXP TYPE

ECMAScript supports regular expressions through the `RegExp` type. Regular expressions are easy to create using syntax similar to Perl, as shown here:

```
let expression = /pattern/flags;
```

The pattern part of the expression can be any simple or complicated regular expression, including character classes, quantifiers, grouping, lookaheads, and backreferences. Each expression can have zero or more flags indicating how the expression should behave. Three supported flags represent matching modes, as follows:

➤　`g`—Indicates global mode, meaning the pattern will be applied to all of the string instead of stopping after the first match is found.

➤　`i`—Indicates case-insensitive mode, meaning the case of the pattern and the string are ignored when determining matches.

➤　`m`—Indicates multiline mode, meaning the pattern will continue looking for matches after reaching the end of one line of text.

➤　`y`—Indicates sticky mode, meaning the pattern will only look at the string contents beginning at `lastIndex`.

➤　`u`—Indicates Unicode mode is enabled.

➤　`s`—Indicates singleline mode, meaning the wildcard character `"."` will match line break characters.

➤　`d`—Indicates the result of a match should contain the start and end indices for each capture group.

A regular expression is created using a combination of a pattern and these flags to produce different results, as in this example:

```
// Match all instances of "at" in a string.
let pattern1 = /at/g;

// Match the first instance of "bat" or "cat", regardless of case.
let pattern2 = /[bc]at/i;

// Match all three-character combinations ending with "at", regardless of case.
let pattern3 = /.at/gi;
```

As with regular expressions in other languages, all *metacharacters* must be escaped when used as part of the pattern. The metacharacters are as follows:

```
( [ { \ ^ $ | ) ] } ? * + .
```

Each metacharacter has one or more uses in regular-expression syntax and so must be escaped by a backslash when you want to match the character in a string. Here are some examples:

```
// Match the first instance of "bat" or "cat", regardless of case.
let pattern1 = /[bc]at/i;

// Match the first instance of "[bc]at", regardless of case.
let pattern2 = /\[bc\]at/i;

// Match all three-character combinations ending with "at", regardless of case.
let pattern3 = /.at/gi;

// Match all instances of ".at", regardless of case.
let pattern4 = /\.at/gi;
```

In this code, pattern1 matches all instances of "bat" or "cat", regardless of case. To match "[bc]at" directly, both square brackets need to be escaped with a backslash, as in pattern2. In pattern3, the dot indicates that any character can precede "at" to be a match. If you want to match ".at", then the dot needs to be escaped, as in pattern4.

The preceding examples all define regular expressions using the literal form. Regular expressions can also be created by using the RegExp constructor, which accepts two arguments: a string pattern to match and an optional string of flags to apply. Any regular expression that can be defined using literal syntax can also be defined using the constructor, as in this example:

```
// Match the first instance of "bat" or "cat", regardless of case.
let pattern1 = /[bc]at/i;

// Same as pattern1, just using the constructor.
let pattern2 = new RegExp("[bc]at", "i");
```

Here, pattern1 and pattern2 define equivalent regular expressions. Note that both arguments of the RegExp constructor are strings (regular-expression literals should not be passed into the RegExp constructor). Because the pattern argument of the RegExp constructor is a string, there are some instances in which you need to double-escape characters. All metacharacters must be double-escaped, as must characters that are already escaped, such as \n (the \ character, which is normally escaped in strings as \\ becomes \\\\ when used in a regular-expression string). The following table shows some patterns in their literal form and the equivalent string that would be necessary to use the RegExp constructor.

LITERAL PATTERN	STRING EQUIVALENT
/\[bc\]at/	"\\[bc\\]at"
/\.at/	"\\.at"
/name\/age/	"name\\/age"
/\d.\d{1,2}/	"\\d.\\d{1,2}"
/\w\\hello\\123/	"\\w\\\\hello\\\\123"

It is also possible to copy existing regular expression instances and optionally modify their flags using the constructor:

```
const re1 = /cat/g;
console.log(re1);  // "/cat/g"

const re2 = new RegExp(re1);
console.log(re2);  // "/cat/g"

const re3 = new RegExp(re1, "i");
console.log(re3);  // "/cat/i"
```

Capture groups can be accessed by index, which is a terrific exercise in frustration because indices offer no context as to what they actually contain:

```
const text = '2018-03-14';

const re = /(\d+)-(\d+)-(\d+)/;

console.log(re.exec(text));
// ["2018-03-14", "2018", "03", "14"]
```

Named capture groups allow for associating a valid JavaScript identifier with a capture group that can then be retrieved from the groups property of the result:

```
const text = '2018-03-14';

const re = /(?<year>\d+)-(?<month>\d+)-(?<day>\d+)/;

console.log(re.exec(text).groups);
// { year: "2018", month: "03", day: "14" }
```

RegExp Instance Properties

Each instance of RegExp has the following properties that allow you to get information about the pattern:

1. global—A Boolean value indicating whether the g flag has been set.

2. ignoreCase—A Boolean value indicating whether the i flag has been set.

3. unicode—A Boolean value indicating whether the u flag has been set.

4. sticky—A Boolean value indicating whether the y flag has been set.

5. lastIndex—An integer indicating the character position where the next match will be attempted in the source string. This value always begins as 0.

6. multiline—A Boolean value indicating whether the m flag has been set.

7. source—The string source of the regular expression. This is always returned as if specified in literal form (without opening and closing slashes) rather than a string pattern as passed into the constructor.

8. flags—The string flags of the regular expression. This is always returned as if specified in literal form (without opening and closing slashes) rather than a string pattern as passed into the constructor.

9. dotAll—A Boolean value indicating whether the s flag has been set.

10. hasIndices—A Boolean value indicating whether the d flag has been set.

These properties are helpful in identifying aspects of a regular expression; however, they typically don't have much use, because the information is available in the pattern declaration. Here's an example:

```
let pattern1 = /\[bc\]at/i;

console.log(pattern1.global);     // false
console.log(pattern1.ignoreCase); // true
console.log(pattern1.multiline);  // false
console.log(pattern1.lastIndex);  // 0
console.log(pattern1.source);     // "\[bc\]at"
console.log(pattern1.flags);      // "i"

let pattern2 = new RegExp("\\[bc\\]at", "i");

console.log(pattern2.global);     // false
console.log(pattern2.ignoreCase); // true
console.log(pattern2.multiline);  // false
console.log(pattern2.lastIndex);  // 0
console.log(pattern2.source);     // "\[bc\]at"
console.log(pattern2.flags);      // "i"
```

Note that the source and flags properties of each pattern are equivalent even though the first pattern is in literal form and the second uses the RegExp constructor. The source and flags properties normalize the string into the form you'd use in a literal.

RegExp Instance Methods

The primary method of a `RegExp` object is `exec()`, which is intended for use with capturing groups. This method accepts a single argument, which is the string on which to apply the pattern, and returns an array of information about the first match or `null` if no match was found. The returned array, though an instance of `Array`, contains two additional properties: `index`, which is the location in the string where the pattern was matched, and `input`, which is the string that the expression was run against. In the array, the first item is the string that matches the entire pattern. Any additional items represent captured groups inside the expression (if there are no capturing groups in the pattern, then the array has only one item). Consider the following:

```
let text = "mom and dad and baby";
let pattern = /mom( and dad( and baby)?)?/gi;

let matches = pattern.exec(text);
console.log(matches.index);    // 0
console.log(matches.input);    // "mom and dad and baby"
console.log(matches[0]);       // "mom and dad and baby"
console.log(matches[1]);       // " and dad and baby"
console.log(matches[2]);       // " and baby"
```

In this example, the pattern has two capturing groups. The innermost one matches `" and baby"`, and its enclosing group matches `" and dad"` or `" and dad and baby"`. When `exec()` is called on the string, a match is found. Because the entire string matches the pattern, the index property on the matches array is set to 0. The first item in the array is the entire matched string, the second contains the contents of the first capturing group, and the third contains the contents of the third capturing group.

The `exec()` method returns information about one match at a time even if the pattern is global. When the global flag is not specified, calling `exec()` on the same string multiple times will always return information about the first match.

```
let text = "cat, bat, sat, fat";
let pattern = /.at/;

let matches = pattern.exec(text);
console.log(matches.index);        // 0
console.log(matches[0]);           // cat
console.log(pattern.lastIndex);    // 0

matches = pattern.exec(text);
console.log(matches.index);        // 0
console.log(matches[0]);           // cat
console.log(pattern.lastIndex);    // 0
```

The pattern in this example is not global, so each call to `exec()` returns the first match only (`"cat"`). `lastIndex` remains unchanged in nonglobal mode.

With the global g flag set on the pattern, each call to `exec()` moves further into the string looking for matches, as in this example:

```
let text = "cat, bat, sat, fat";
```

```
let pattern = /.at/g;

let matches = pattern.exec(text);
console.log(matches.index);        // 0
console.log(matches[0]);           // cat
console.log(pattern.lastIndex);    // 3

matches = pattern.exec(text);
console.log(matches.index);        // 5
console.log(matches[0]);           // bat
console.log(pattern.lastIndex);    // 8

matches = pattern.exec(text);
console.log(matches.index);        // 10
console.log(matches[0]);           // sat
console.log(pattern.lastIndex);    // 13
```

This pattern is global, so each call to exec() returns the next match in the string until the end of the string is reached. Note also how the pattern's lastIndex property is affected. In global matching mode, lastIndex is incremented after each call to exec(). lastIndex tracks the index of the character that appears immediately to the right of the last match.

With the sticky y flag set on the pattern, each call to exec() will search for a match in the string only at lastIndex—nowhere else. The sticky flag overrides the global flag.

```
let text = "cat, bat, sat, fat";
let pattern = /.at/y;

let matches = pattern.exec(text);
console.log(matches.index);        // 0
console.log(matches[0]);           // cat
console.log(pattern.lastIndex);    // 3

// There is no match starting at character index 3, so exec() will return null
// exec() finding no matches resets lastIndex to 0
matches = pattern.exec(text);
console.log(matches);              // null
console.log(pattern.lastIndex);    // 0

// Advancing lastIndex will allow a sticky regex exec() to find the next match:
pattern.lastIndex = 5;
matches = pattern.exec(text);
console.log(matches.index);        // 5
console.log(matches[0]);           // bat
console.log(pattern.lastIndex);    // 8
```

Another method of regular expressions is test(), which accepts a string argument and returns true if the pattern matches the argument and false if it does not. This method is useful when you want to know if a pattern is matched, but you have no need for the actual matched text. The test() method is often used in if statements, such as the following:

```
let text = "000-00-0000";
let pattern = /\d{3}-\d{2}-\d{4}/;

if (pattern.test(text)) {
  console.log("The pattern was matched.");
}
```

In this example, the regular expression tests for a specific numeric sequence. If the input text matches the pattern, then a message is displayed. This functionality is often used for validating user input, when you care only if the input is valid, not necessarily why it's invalid.

The inherited methods of `toLocaleString()` and `toString()` each return the literal representation of the regular expression, regardless of how it was created. Consider this example:

```
let pattern = new RegExp("\\[bc\\]at", "gi");
console.log(pattern.toString());        // /\[bc\]at/gi
console.log(pattern.toLocaleString());  // /\[bc\]at/gi
```

Even though the pattern in this example is created using the `RegExp` constructor, the `toLocaleString()` and `toString()` methods return the pattern as if it were specified in literal format.

> **NOTE** *The* `valueOf()` *method for a regular expression returns the regular expression itself.*

PRIMITIVE WRAPPER TYPES

Three special reference types are designed to ease interaction with primitive values: the `Boolean` type, the `Number` type, and the `String` type. These types can act like the other reference types described in this chapter, but they also have a special behavior related to their primitive-type equivalents. Every time a primitive value is read, an object of the corresponding primitive wrapper type is created behind the scenes, allowing access to any number of methods for manipulating the data. Consider the following example:

```
let s1 = "some text";
let s2 = s1.substring(2);
```

In this code, `s1` is a variable containing a string, which is a primitive value. On the next line, the `substring()` method is called on `s1` and stored in `s2`. Primitive values aren't objects, so logically they shouldn't have methods, though this still works as you would expect. In truth, there is a lot going on behind the scenes to allow this seamless operation. When `s1` is accessed in the second line, it is being accessed in read mode, which is to say that its value is being read from memory. Any time a string value is accessed in read mode, the following three steps occur:

1. Create an instance of the `String` type.

2. Call the specified method on the instance.

3. Destroy the instance.

You can think of these three steps as they're used in the following three lines of ECMAScript code:

```
let s1 = new String("some text");
let s2 = s1.substring(2);
s1 = null;
```

This behavior allows the primitive string value to act like an object. These same three steps are repeated for Boolean and numeric values using the `Boolean` and `Number` types, respectively.

The major difference between reference types and primitive wrapper types is the lifetime of the object. When you instantiate a reference type using the `new` operator, it stays in memory until it goes out of scope, whereas automatically created primitive wrapper objects exist for only one line of code before they are destroyed. This means that properties and methods cannot be added at runtime. Take this for example:

```
let s1 = "some text";
s1.color = "red";
console.log(s1.color);   // undefined
```

Here, the second line attempts to add a color property to the string `s1`. However, when `s1` is accessed on the third line, the `color` property is gone. This happens because the `String` object that was created in the second line is destroyed by the time the third line is executed. The third line creates its own `String` object, which doesn't have the color property.

It is possible to create the primitive wrapper objects explicitly using the `Boolean`, `Number`, and `String` constructors. This should be done only when absolutely necessary because it is often confusing for developers as to whether they are dealing with a primitive or reference value. Calling `typeof` on an instance of a primitive wrapper type returns `"object"`, and all primitive wrapper objects convert to the Boolean value `true`.

The `Object` constructor also acts as a factory method and is capable of returning an instance of a primitive wrapper based on the type of value passed into the constructor. For example:

```
let obj = new Object("some text");
console.log(obj instanceof String);   // true
```

When a string is passed into the `Object` constructor, an instance of `String` is created; a number argument results in an instance of `Number`, while a Boolean argument returns an instance of `Boolean`.

Keep in mind that calling a primitive wrapper constructor using `new` is not the same as calling the casting function of the same name. For example:

```
let value = "25";
let number = Number(value);   // casting function
console.log(typeof number);       // "number"
let obj = new Number(value);  // constructor
console.log(typeof obj);          // "object"
```

In this example, the variable `number` is filled with a primitive number value of 25 while the variable `obj` is filled with an instance of `Number`.

Even though it's not recommended to create primitive wrapper objects explicitly, their functionality is important in being able to manipulate primitive values. Each primitive wrapper type has methods that make data manipulation easier.

The Boolean Type

The `Boolean` type is the reference type corresponding to the Boolean values. To create a Boolean object, use the `Boolean` constructor and pass in either `true` or `false`, as in the following example:

```
let booleanObject = new Boolean(true);
```

Instances of `Boolean` override the `valueOf()` method to return a primitive value of either `true` or `false`. The `toString()` method is also overridden to return a string of `"true"` or `"false"` when called. Unfortunately, not only are Boolean objects of little use in ECMAScript, but they can actually be rather confusing. The problem typically occurs when trying to use `Boolean` objects in `Boolean` expressions, as in this example:

```
let falseObject = new Boolean(false);
let result = falseObject && true;
console.log(result);  // true

let falseValue = false;
result = falseValue && true;
console.log(result);  // false
```

In this code, a `Boolean` object is created with a value of `false`. That same object is then ANDed with the primitive value `true`. In Boolean math, `false && true` equals `false`. However, in this line of code, it is the object named `falseObject` being evaluated, not its value (`false`). As discussed earlier, all objects are automatically converted to true in Boolean expressions, so `falseObject` actually is given a value of `true` in the expression. Then, `true && true` is equal to `true`.

There are a couple of other differences between the primitive and the reference `Boolean` types. The `typeof` operator returns `"boolean"` for the primitive but "object" for the reference. Also, a `Boolean` object is an instance of the `Boolean` type and will return true when used with the `instanceof` operator, whereas a primitive value returns `false`, as shown here:

```
console.log(typeof falseObject);        // object
console.log(typeof falseValue);         // boolean
console.log(falseObject instanceof Boolean);  // true
console.log(falseValue instanceof Boolean);   // false
```

It's very important to understand the difference between a primitive Boolean value and a `Boolean` object—prefer to never use the latter.

The Number Type

The `Number` type is the reference type for numeric values. To create a `Number` object, use the `Number` constructor and pass in any number. Here's an example:

```
let numberObject = new Number(10);
```

As with the `Boolean` type, the `Number` type overrides `valueOf()`, `toLocaleString()`, and `toString()`. The `valueOf()` method returns the primitive numeric value represented by the object, whereas the other two methods return the number as a string. The `toString()` method optionally accepts a single argument indicating the radix in which to represent the number, as shown in the following examples:

```
let num = 10;
console.log(num.toString());      // "10"
console.log(num.toString(2));     // "1010"
console.log(num.toString(8));     // "12"
console.log(num.toString(10));    // "10"
console.log(num.toString(16));    // "a"
```

Aside from the inherited methods, the Number type has several additional methods used to format numbers as strings.

The toFixed() method returns a string representation of a number with a specified number of decimal points, as in this example:

```
let num = 10;
console.log(num.toFixed(2));   // "10.00"
```

Here, the toFixed() method is given an argument of 2, which indicates how many decimal places should be displayed. As a result, the method returns the string "10.00", filling out the empty decimal places with zeros. If the number has more than the given number of decimal places, the result is rounded to the nearest decimal place, as shown here:

```
let num = 10.005;
console.log(num.toFixed(2));   // "10.01"
```

The rounding nature of toFixed() may be useful for applications dealing with currency, though it's worth noting that arithmetic operations between multiple floating point values may not produce exact results—for example, 0.1 + 0.2 = 0.30000000000000004.

> **NOTE** *The* toFixed() *method can represent numbers with 0 through 20 decimal places. Some browsers may support larger ranges, but this is the typically implemented range.*

Another method related to formatting numbers is the toExponential() method, which returns a string with the number formatted in exponential notation (aka e-notation). Just as with toFixed(), toExponential() accepts one argument, which is the number of decimal places to output. Consider this example:

```
let num = 10;
console.log(num.toExponential(1));   // "1.0e+1"
```

This code outputs "1.0e+1" as the result. Typically, this small number wouldn't be represented using e-notation. If you want to have the most appropriate form of the number, the toPrecision() method should be used instead.

The `toPrecision()` method returns either the fixed or the exponential representation of a number, depending on which makes the most sense. This method takes one argument, which is the total number of digits to use to represent the number (not including exponents). Here's an example:

```
let num = 99;
console.log(num.toPrecision(1));  // "1e+2"
console.log(num.toPrecision(2));  // "99"
console.log(num.toPrecision(3));  // "99.0"
```

In this example, the first task is to represent the number 99 with a single digit, which results in `"1e+2"`, otherwise known as 100. Because 99 cannot accurately be represented by just one digit, the method rounded up to 100, which can be represented using just one digit. Representing 99 with two digits yields "99" and with three digits returns "99.0". The `toPrecision()` method essentially determines whether to call `toFixed()` or `toExponential()` based on the numeric value you're working with; all three methods round up or down to accurately represent a number with the correct number of decimal places.

> **NOTE** *The* `toPrecision()` *method can represent numbers with 1 through 21 decimal places. Some browsers may support larger ranges, but this is the typically implemented range.*

Similar to the `Boolean` object, the `Number` object gives important functionality to numeric values but really should not be instantiated directly because of the same potential problems. The `typeof` and `instanceof` operators work differently when dealing with primitive numbers versus reference numbers, as shown in the following examples:

```
let numberObject = new Number(10);
let numberValue = 10;
console.log(typeof numberObject);           // "object"
console.log(typeof numberValue);            // "number"
console.log(numberObject instanceof Number); // true
console.log(numberValue instanceof Number);  // false
```

Primitive numbers always return `"number"` when `typeof` is called on them, whereas `Number` objects return `"object"`. Similarly, a `Number` object is an instance of `Number`, but a primitive number is not.

The *isInteger()* Method and Safe Integers

The `isInteger()` method is capable of discerning whether or not a number value is stored as an integer or not. This is useful when a trailing decimal 0 may mask whether or not the number is actually stored in floating point format:

```
console.log(Number.isInteger(1));     // true
console.log(Number.isInteger(1.00));  // true
console.log(Number.isInteger(1.01));  // false
```

The IEEE 754 number format has a distinct numerical range inside which a binary value can represent exactly one integer value. This numerical range extends from `Number.MIN_SAFE_INTEGER`, or $-2^53 + 1$, to `Number.MAX_SAFE_INTEGER`, or $2^53 - 1$. Outside this range, you may attempt to store an integer, but the IEEE 754 encoding format means that this binary value may also alias to a completely different number. To ascertain if an integer is inside this range, the `isSafeInteger()` method allows you to easily check this:

```
console.log(Number.isSafeInteger(-1 * (2 ** 53)));        // false
console.log(Number.isSafeInteger(-1 * (2 ** 53) + 1));    // true

console.log(Number.isSafeInteger(2 ** 53));               // false
console.log(Number.isSafeInteger((2 ** 53) - 1));         // true
```

The String Type

The `String` type is the object representation for strings and is created using the `String` constructor as follows:

```
let stringObject = new String("hello world");
```

The methods of a `String` object are available on all string primitives. All three of the inherited methods—`valueOf()`, `toLocaleString()`, and `toString()`—return the object's primitive string value.

Each instance of `String` contains a single property, length, which indicates the number of characters in the string. Consider the following example:

```
let stringValue = "hello world";
console.log(stringValue.length);    // "11"
```

This example outputs "11", the number of characters in "hello world". Note that even if the string contains a double-byte character (as opposed to an ASCII character, which uses just one byte), each character is still counted as one.

The `String` type has a large number of methods to aid in the dissection and manipulation of strings in ECMAScript.

The JavaScript Character

JavaScript strings consist of 16 bit code units. For most characters, each 16 bit code unit will correspond to a single character. The length property indicates how many 16 bit code units occur inside the string:

```
let message = "abcde";

console.log(message.length);  // 5
```

Furthermore, the `charAt()` returns the character at a given index, specified by an integer argument to the method. Specifically, this method finds the 16 bit code unit at the specified index and returns the character that corresponds to that code unit:

```
let message = "abcde";

console.log(message.charAt(2));  // "c"
```

JavaScript strings use a hybridized strategy of two Unicode encodings: UCS-2 and UTF-16. For characters which can be encoded with 16 bits (U+0000 to U+FFFF), these two encodings are effectively identical.

> **NOTE** *For in-depth coverage of character encoding, check out Joel Spolsky's excellent blog post:* www.joelonsoftware.com/2003/10/08/the-absolute-minimum-every-software-developer-absolutely-positively-must-know-about-unicode-and-character-sets-no-excuses.
>
> *Another good resource is Mathias Bynens' blog post:* https://mathiasbynens.be/notes/javascript-encoding.

You can inspect the character encoding of a given code unit with the `charCodeAt()` method. This method returns the code unit value at a given index, specified by an integer argument to the method. This method is demonstrated here:

```
let message = "abcde";

// Unicode "Latin small letter C" is U+0063
console.log(message.charCodeAt(2));  // 99

// Decimal 99 === Hexadecimal 63
console.log(99 === 0x63);            // true
```

The `fromCharCode()` method is used for creating characters in a string from their UTF-16 code unit representation. This method accepts any number of numbers and returns their character equivalents concatenated into a string:

```
// Unicode "Latin small letter A" is U+0061
// Unicode "Latin small letter B" is U+0062
// Unicode "Latin small letter C" is U+0063
// Unicode "Latin small letter D" is U+0064
// Unicode "Latin small letter E" is U+0065

console.log(String.fromCharCode(0x61, 0x62, 0x63, 0x64, 0x65));  // "abcde"

// 0x0061 === 97
// 0x0062 === 98
// 0x0063 === 99
// 0x0064 === 100
// 0x0065 === 101

console.log(String.fromCharCode(97, 98, 99, 100, 101));          // "abcde"
```

For characters in the range of U+0000 to U+FFFF, `length`, `charAt()`, `charCodeAt()`, and `fromCharCode()` all behave exactly as you would expect them to. This is because every character is represented by exactly 16 bits, and each of these methods are all operating on 16 bit code units. As long as there is parity between character encoding size and code unit size, these methods will behave as expected.

This parity breaks down when expanding into the realm of Unicode supplementary character planes. The idea for this concept is relatively straightforward: 16 bits can only uniquely represent 65,536 characters. This is enough to cover most language character sets and is referred to as the *Basic Multilingual Plane* (BMP). In order to introduce even more characters, Unicode defined a strategy which used an additional 16 bits per character to select a *supplementary* or *astral plane*. Using two 16 bit code units per character is referred to as a *surrogate pair*.

With the introduction of this convention, the previously discussed string methods begin to break down. Consider the following example, which uses a smiley face emoji – a character which is encoded using a surrogate pair:

```
// The "smiling face with smiling eyes" emoji is U+1F60A
// 0x1F60A === 128522
let message = "ab☺de";

console.log(message.length);          // 6

console.log(message.charAt(1));       // b
console.log(message.charAt(2));       // <?>
console.log(message.charAt(3));       // <?>
console.log(message.charAt(4));       // d

console.log(message.charCodeAt(1));   // 98
console.log(message.charCodeAt(2));   // 55357
console.log(message.charCodeAt(3));   // 56842
console.log(message.charCodeAt(4));   // 100

console.log(String.fromCharCode(0xD83D, 0xDE0A));  // ☺

console.log(String.fromCharCode(97, 98, 55357, 56842, 100, 101));  // ab☺de
```

These methods are still treating each 16 bit code unit like a separate character, when in fact the code units at index 2 and 3 need to be considered together as a single surrogate pair to form a single character. The `fromCharCode()` method is still working correctly using the two code units separated because this method is literally assembling the string from a provided binary representation. The browser is able to correctly parse the surrogate pair (which was assembled as two separate code units) and correctly interpret it as a single smiley face Unicode character.

To correctly parse a string containing both single-code unit and surrogate pair characters, the `codePointAt()` method can be used instead of the error-prone `charAt()`. As is the case with `charAt()`, this method accepts a 16 bit code unit index and returns the code point at that index. A *code point* refers to the full Unicode identifier for a single character. The code point for `"c"` is 0x0063. The code point for "☺" is 0x1F60A. Code points may either require 16 or 32 bits to fully represent them, and the `codePointAt()` method will identify the full code point beginning at the specified code unit.

```
let message = "ab☺de";

console.log(message.codePointAt(1));  // 98
console.log(message.codePointAt(2));  // 128522
console.log(message.codePointAt(3));  // 56842
console.log(message.codePointAt(4));  // 100
```

Notice in this example how a code point can be incorrectly identified if targeted at a code unit index that is not the start of a surrogate pair. This is only problematic for one-off character inspection, and can be averted by traversing the string from left to right and advancing the proper number of code units per iterator. The iterator for a string is intelligent enough to identify surrogate pair code points:

```
console.log([..."ab☺de"]);  // ["a", "b", "☺", "d", "e"]
```

Just as charAt() has an analogue in codePointAt(), fromCharCode() has an analogue in fromCodePoint(). This method accepts any number of code point numbers and returns their character equivalents concatenated into a string:

```
console.log(String.fromCharCode(97, 98, 55357, 56842, 100, 101));  // ab☺de
console.log(String.fromCodePoint(97, 98, 128522, 100, 101));        // ab☺de
```

The *normalize()* Method

Some Unicode characters can be encoded in more than one way. Sometimes, a character can be represented by either a single BMP character or a surrogate pair. For example, consider the following:

```
// U+00C5: Latin capital letter A with ring above
console.log(String.fromCharCode(0x00C5));        // Å

// U+212B: Angstrom sign
console.log(String.fromCharCode(0x212B));        // Å

// U+0041: Latin captal letter A
// U+030A: Combining ring above
console.log(String.fromCharCode(0x0041, 0x030A));  // Å
```

Comparison operators do not care about the visual appearance of characters, and so these three will be considered distinct:

```
let a1 = String.fromCharCode(0x00C5),
    a2 = String.fromCharCode(0x212B),
    a3 = String.fromCharCode(0x0041, 0x030A);

console.log(a1, a2, a3);  // Å, Å, Å

console.log(a1 === a2);  // false
console.log(a1 === a3);  // false
console.log(a2 === a3);  // false
```

Unicode accounts for this by offering four normalization forms by which characters such as this one can be normalized into a consistent format irrespective of their character code derivation. These four normalization forms, Normalization Form D (NFD), Normalization Form C (NFC), Normalization Form KD (NFKD), and Normalization Form KC (NFKC), can be applied to a string using the normalize() method. This method should be provided with a string identifier to specify which normalization form to apply: NFD, NFC, NFKD, or NFKC.

> **NOTE** *The specifics of each of these normal forms is out of the scope of this text. Refer to* http://unicode.org/reports/tr15 *for additional details.*

It is possible to determine if a string is already normalized by checking it against the return value of `normalize()`:

```
let a1 = String.fromCharCode(0x00C5),
    a2 = String.fromCharCode(0x212B),
    a3 = String.fromCharCode(0x0041, 0x030A);

// U+00C5 is the NFC/NFKC normalized form of 0+212B
console.log(a1 === a1.normalize("NFD"));    // false
console.log(a1 === a1.normalize("NFC"));    // true
console.log(a1 === a1.normalize("NFKD"));   // false
console.log(a1 === a1.normalize("NFKC"));   // true

// U+212B is non-normalized
console.log(a2 === a2.normalize("NFD"));    // false
console.log(a2 === a2.normalize("NFC"));    // false
console.log(a2 === a2.normalize("NFKD"));   // false
console.log(a2 === a2.normalize("NFKC"));   // false

// U+0041/U+030A is the NFD/NFKD normalized form of 0+212B
console.log(a3 === a3.normalize("NFD"));    // true
console.log(a3 === a3.normalize("NFC"));    // false
console.log(a3 === a3.normalize("NFKD"));   // true
console.log(a3 === a3.normalize("NFKC"));   // false
```

Selecting a normal form will allow for the comparison operator to behave as expected between identical characters:

```
let a1 = String.fromCharCode(0x00C5),
    a2 = String.fromCharCode(0x212B),
    a3 = String.fromCharCode(0x0041, 0x030A);

console.log(a1.normalize("NFD") === a2.normalize("NFD"));    // true
console.log(a2.normalize("NFKC") === a3.normalize("NFKC"));  // true
console.log(a1.normalize("NFC") === a3.normalize("NFC"));    // true
```

String-Manipulation Methods

Several methods manipulate the values of strings. The first of these methods is `concat()`, which is used to concatenate one or more strings to another, returning the concatenated string as the result. Consider the following example:

```
let stringValue = "hello ";
let result = stringValue.concat("world");

console.log(result);       // "hello world"
console.log(stringValue);  // "hello"
```

The result of calling the `concat()` method on `stringValue` in this example is "hello world"—the value of `stringValue` remains unchanged. The `concat()` method accepts any number of arguments, so it can create a string from any number of other strings, as shown here:

```
let stringValue = "hello ";
```

```
let result = stringValue.concat("world", "!");

console.log(result);        // "hello world!"
console.log(stringValue);   // "hello"
```

This modified example concatenates `"world"` and `"!"` to the end of `"hello"`. Although the `concat()` method is provided for string concatenation, the addition operator (+) is used more often and, in most cases, actually performs better than the `concat()` method even when concatenating multiple strings.

ECMAScript provides three methods for creating string values from a substring: `slice()`, `substr()`, and `substring()`. All three methods return a substring of the string they act on, and all accept either one or two arguments. The first argument is the position where capture of the substring begins; the second argument, if used, indicates where the operation should stop. For `slice()` and `substring()`, this second argument is the position before which capture is stopped (all characters up to this point are included except the character at that point). For `substr()`, the second argument is the number of characters to return. If the second argument is omitted in any case, it is assumed that the ending position is the length of the string. Just as with the `concat()` method, `slice()`, `substr()`, and `substring()` do not alter the value of the string itself—they simply return a primitive string value as the result, leaving the original unchanged. Consider this example:

```
let stringValue = "hello world";
console.log(stringValue.slice(3));        // "lo world"
console.log(stringValue.substring(3));    // "lo world"
console.log(stringValue.substr(3));       // "lo world"
console.log(stringValue.slice(3, 7));     // "lo w"
console.log(stringValue.substring(3,7));  // "lo w"
console.log(stringValue.substr(3, 7));    // "lo worl"
```

In this example, `slice()`, `substr()`, and `substring()` are used in the same manner and, in most cases, return the same value. When given just one argument, 3, all three methods return "lo world" because the second `"l"` in `"hello"` is in position 3. When given two arguments, 3 and 7, `slice()` and `substring()` return "lo w" (the `"o"` in `"world"` is in position 7, so it is not included), while `substr()` returns "lo worl" because the second argument specifies the number of characters to return.

There are different behaviors for these methods when an argument is a negative number. For the `slice()` method, a negative argument is treated as the length of the string plus the negative argument.

For the `substr()` method, a negative first argument is treated as the length of the string plus the number, whereas a negative second number is converted to 0. For the `substring()` method, all negative numbers are converted to 0. Consider this example:

```
let stringValue = "hello world";
console.log(stringValue.slice(-3));        // "rld"
console.log(stringValue.substring(-3));    // "hello world"
console.log(stringValue.substr(-3));       // "rld"
console.log(stringValue.slice(3, -4));     // "lo w"
console.log(stringValue.substring(3, -4)); // "hel"
console.log(stringValue.substr(3, -4));    // "" (empty string)
```

This example clearly indicates the differences between three methods. When `slice()` and `substr()` are called with a single negative argument, they act the same. This occurs because –3 is translated into

7 (the length plus the argument), effectively making the calls slice(7) and substr(7). The substring() method, on the other hand, returns the entire string because –3 is translated to 0.

When the second argument is negative, the three methods act differently from one another. The slice() method translates the second argument to 7, making the call equivalent to slice(3, 7) and so returning "lo w". For the substring() method, the second argument gets translated to 0, making the call equivalent to substring(3, 0), which is actually equivalent to substring(0,3) because this method expects that the smaller number is the starting position and the larger one is the ending position. For the substr() method, the second argument is also converted to 0, which means there should be zero characters in the returned string, leading to the return value of an empty string.

String Location Methods

There are two methods for locating substrings within another string: indexOf() and lastIndexOf(). Both methods search a string for a given substring and return the position (or –1 if the substring isn't found). The difference between the two is that the indexOf() method begins looking for the substring at the beginning of the string, whereas the lastIndexOf() method begins looking from the end of the string. Consider this example:

```
let stringValue = "hello world";
console.log(stringValue.indexOf("o"));       // 4
console.log(stringValue.lastIndexOf("o"));   // 7
```

Here, the first occurrence of the string "o" is at position 4, which is the "o" in "hello". The last occurrence of the string "o" is in the word "world", at position 7. If there is only one occurrence of "o" in the string, then indexOf() and lastIndexOf() return the same position.

Each method accepts an optional second argument that indicates the position to start searching from within the string. This means that the indexOf() method will start searching from that position and go toward the end of the string, ignoring everything before the start position, whereas lastIndexOf() starts searching from the given position and continues searching toward the beginning of the string, ignoring everything between the given position and the end of the string. Here's an example:

```
let stringValue = "hello world";
console.log(stringValue.indexOf("o", 6));       // 7
console.log(stringValue.lastIndexOf("o", 6));   // 4
```

When the second argument of 6 is passed into each method, the results are the opposite from the previous example. This time, indexOf() returns 7 because it starts searching the string from position 6 (the letter "w") and continues to position 7, where "o" is found. The lastIndexOf() method returns 4 because the search starts from position 6 and continues back toward the beginning of the string, where it encounters the "o" in "hello". Using this second argument allows you to locate all instances of a substring by looping callings to indexOf() or lastIndexOf(), as in the following example:

```
let stringValue = "Lorem ipsum dolor sit amet, consectetur adipisicing elit";
let positions = new Array();
let pos = stringValue.indexOf("e");

while(pos> -1) {
  positions.push(pos);
```

```
    pos = stringValue.indexOf("e", pos + 1);
}

console.log(positions);  // "3,24,32,35,52"
```

This example works through a string by constantly increasing the position at which `indexOf()` should begin. It begins by getting the initial position of "e" in the string and then enters a loop that continually passes in the last position plus one to `indexOf()`, ensuring that the search continues after the last substring instance. Each position is stored in the positions array so the data can be used later.

String Inclusion Methods

ECMAScript includes three additional methods for determining if a string is included inside another string: `startsWith()`, `endsWith()`, and `includes()`. All methods search a string for a given substring and return a Boolean indicating whether it is not included. The difference between them is that `startsWith()` checks for a match beginning at index 0, `endsWith()` checks for a match beginning at index (`string.length - substring.length`), and `includes()` checks the entire string.

```
let message = "foobarbaz";

console.log(message.startsWith("foo"));  // true
console.log(message.startsWith("bar"));  // false

console.log(message.endsWith("baz"));    // true
console.log(message.endsWith("bar"));    // false

console.log(message.includes("bar"));    // true
console.log(message.includes("qux"));    // false
```

The `startsWith()` and `includes()` methods accept an optional second argument that indicates the position to start searching from within the string. This means that the methods will start searching from that position and go toward the end of the string, ignoring everything before the start position. Here's an example:

```
let message = "foobarbaz";

console.log(message.startsWith("foo"));      // true
console.log(message.startsWith("foo", 1));   // false

console.log(message.includes("bar"));        // true
console.log(message.includes("bar", 4));     // false
```

The `endsWith()` method accepts an optional second argument that indicates the position that should be treated as the end of the string. If this value is not provided, the length of the string is used by default. When a second argument is provided, the method will treat the string as if it only has that many characters:

```
let message = "foobarbaz";

console.log(message.endsWith("bar"));     // false
console.log(message.endsWith("bar", 6));  // true
```

The *trim()* Method

ECMAScript features a `trim()` method on all strings. The `trim()` method creates a copy of the string, removes all leading and trailing white space, and then returns the result. For example:

```
let stringValue = "  hello world   ";
let trimmedStringValue = stringValue.trim();
console.log(stringValue);          // "  hello world   "
console.log(trimmedStringValue);   // "hello world"
```

Note that since `trim()` returns a copy of a string, the original string remains intact with leading and trailing white space in place.

Also available are the `trimLeft()` and `trimRight()` methods that remove white space only from the beginning or end of the string, respectively.

`trimStart()` and `trimEnd()` allow for targeted white space removal. These methods are intended to replace `trimLeft()` and `trimRight()`, which have ambiguous meaning in the context of right-to-left languages such as Arabic and Hebrew.

These two methods are effectively the opposite of `padStart()` and `padEnd()` with a single space character. The following example adds white space to a string and then removes it on either side:

```
let s = '   foo   ';

console.log(s.trimStart()); // "foo   "
console.log(s.trimEnd());   // "   foo"
```

The *repeat()* Method

ECMAScript features a `repeat()` method on all strings. The `repeat()` method accepts a single integer argument count, copies the string count times, and concatenates all the copies.

```
let stringValue = "na ";
console.log(stringValue.repeat(16) + "batman");
// na na na na na na na na na na na na na na na na batman
```

The *padStart()* and *padEnd()* Methods

The `padStart()` and `padEnd()` methods will copy a string and, if the length of the string is less than the specified length, add padding to either side of a string to extend it to a certain length. The first argument is the desired length, and the second is the optional string to add as a pad. If not provided, the U+0020 'space' character will be used.

```
let stringValue = "foo";

console.log(stringValue.padStart(6));        // "   foo"
console.log(stringValue.padStart(9, "."));   // "......foo"

console.log(stringValue.padEnd(6));          // "foo   "
console.log(stringValue.padEnd(9, "."));     // "foo......"
```

The optional argument is not limited to a single character. If provided a multiple-character string, the method will use the concatenated padding and truncate it to the exact length. Additionally, if the length is less than or equal to the string length, the operation is effectively a no-op.

```
let stringValue = "foo";

console.log(stringValue.padStart(8, "bar"));   // "barbafoo"
console.log(stringValue.padStart(2));          // "foo"

console.log(stringValue.padEnd(8, "bar"));     // "foobarba"
console.log(stringValue.padEnd(2));            // "foo"
```

String Iterators and Destructuring

The string prototype exposes an `@@iterator` method on each string, which allows for iteration through individual characters. Manual use of the iterator works as follows:

```
let message = "abc";
let stringIterator = message[Symbol.iterator]();

console.log(stringIterator.next());   // {value: "a", done: false}
console.log(stringIterator.next());   // {value: "b", done: false}
console.log(stringIterator.next());   // {value: "c", done: false}
console.log(stringIterator.next());   // {value: undefined, done: true}
```

When used in a `for-of` loop, the loop will use this iterator to visit each character in order:

```
for (const c of "abcde") {
  console.log(c);
}

// a
// b
// c
// d
// e
```

The string iterator becomes especially useful since it allows for interoperability with the destructuring operator. This allows you to easily split a string by its characters:

```
let message = "abcde";

console.log([...message]);  // ["a", "b", "c", "d", "e"]
```

String Case Methods

The next set of methods involves case conversion. Four methods perform case conversion: `toLowerCase()`, `toLocaleLowerCase()`, `toUpperCase()`, and `toLocaleUpperCase()`. The `toLowerCase()` and `toUpperCase()` methods are the original methods, modeled after the same methods in `java.lang.String`. The `toLocaleLowerCase()` and `toLocaleUpperCase()` methods are intended to be implemented based on a particular locale. In many locales, the locale-specific methods are identical to the generic ones; however, a few languages (such as Turkish) apply special rules to Unicode case conversion, and this necessitates using the locale-specific methods for proper conversion. Here are some examples:

```
let stringValue = "hello world";
console.log(stringValue.toLocaleUpperCase());  // "HELLO WORLD"
console.log(stringValue.toUpperCase());        // "HELLO WORLD"
console.log(stringValue.toLocaleLowerCase());  // "hello world"
console.log(stringValue.toLowerCase());        // "hello world"
```

This code outputs `"HELLO WORLD"` for both `toLocaleUpperCase()` and `toUpperCase()`, just as `"hello world"` is output for both `toLocaleLowerCase()` and `toLowerCase()`. Generally speaking, if you do not know the language in which the code will be running, it is safer to use the locale-specific methods.

String Pattern-Matching Methods

The `String` type has several methods designed to pattern-match within the string. The first of these methods is `match()` and is essentially the same as calling a `RegExp` object's `exec()` method. The `match()` method accepts a single argument, which is either a regular-expression string or a `RegExp` object. Consider this example:

```
let text = "cat, bat, sat, fat";
let pattern = /.at/;

// same as pattern.exec(text)
let matches = text.match(pattern);
console.log(matches.index);       // 0
console.log(matches[0]);          // "cat"
console.log(pattern.lastIndex);   // 0
```

The array returned from `match()` is the same array that is returned when the `RegExp` object's `exec()` method is called with the string as an argument: the first item is the string that matches the entire pattern, and each other item (if applicable) represents capturing groups in the expression.

When using the global flag, `match()` will only return an array of matches—all capture groups are lost. To preserve capture groups when matching multiple values, use `matchAll()` instead. It accepts only global regular expressions and returns a `RegExpStringIterator` iterable of each `match()` therein. This distinction is demonstrated here:

```
const text = "abcdeazcde";

console.log(text.match(/a(.)c/));
// ['abc', 'b', index: 0, input: 'abcdeazcde', groups: undefined]

console.log(text.match(/a(.)c/g));
// ['abc', 'azc']

console.log([...text.matchAll(/a(.)c/g)]);
// [
//.   ['abc', 'b', index: 0, input: 'abcdeazcde', groups: undefined],
//.   ['azc', 'z', index: 5, input: 'abcdeazcde', groups: undefined]
// ]
```

Another method for finding patterns is `search()`. The only argument for this method is the same as the argument for `match()`: a regular expression specified by either a string or a `RegExp` object. The `search()` method returns the index of the first pattern occurrence in the string or –1 if it's not found. `search()` always begins looking for the pattern at the beginning of the string. Consider this example:

```
let text = "cat, bat, sat, fat";
let pos = text.search(/at/);
console.log(pos);  // 1
```

Here, `search(/at/)` returns 1, which is the first position of "at" in the string.

To simplify replacing substrings, ECMAScript provides the `replace()` method. This method accepts two arguments. The first argument can be a `RegExp` object or a string (the string is not converted to a regular expression), and the second argument can be a string or a function. If the first argument to `replace()` is a string, then only the first occurrence of the substring will be replaced. There are two ways to replace all instances of a substring: provide a regular expression with the global flag specified, or use `replaceAll()`:

```
const text = "cat, bat, sat, fat";
let result = text.replace("at", "ond");
console.log(result);  // "cond, bat, sat, fat"

result = text.replace(/at/g, "ond");
console.log(result);  // "cond, bond, sond, fond"

result = text.replaceAll("at", "ond");
console.log(result);  // "cond, bond, sond, fond"
```

In this example, the string `"at"` is first passed into `replace()` with a replacement text of `"ond"`. The result of the operation is that `"cat"` is changed to `"cond"`, but the rest of the string remains intact. By changing the first argument to a regular expression with the global flag set, each instance of `"at"` is replaced with `"ond"`. `replaceAll()` mirrors the global flag behavior.

When the second argument is a string, there are several special character sequences that can be used to insert values from the regular-expression operations. ECMA-262 specifies the following table of values.

SEQUENCE	REPLACEMENT TEXT
$$	$
$&	The substring matching the entire pattern. Same as `RegExp.lastMatch`.
$'	The part of the string occurring before the matched substring. Same as `RegExp.rightContext`.
$`	The part of the string occurring after the matched substring. Same as `RegExp.leftContext`.
$n	The nth capture, where n is a value 0–9. For instance, $1 is the first capture, $2 is the second, and so on. If there is no capture then the empty string is used.
$nn	The nnth capture, where nn is a value 01–99. For instance, $01 is the first capture, $02 is the second, and so on. If there is no capture then the empty string is used.

Using these special sequences allows replacement using information about the last match, such as in this example:

```
let text = "cat, bat, sat, fat";
result = text.replace(/(.at)/g, "word ($1)");
console.log(result);  // word (cat), word (bat), word (sat), word (fat)
```

Here, each word ending with `"at"` is replaced with `"word"` followed in parentheses by what it replaces by using the $1 sequence.

The second argument of `replace()` or `replaceAll()` may also be a function. When there is a single match, the function gets passed three arguments: the string match, the position of the match within the string, and the whole string. When there are multiple capturing groups, each matched string is passed in as an argument, with the last two arguments being the position of the pattern match in the string and the original string. The function should return a string indicating what the match should be replaced with. Using a function as the second argument allows more granular control over replacement text, as in this example:

```
function htmlEscape(text) {
  return text.replace(/[<>"&]/g, function(match, pos, originalText) {
    switch(match) {
      case "<":
        return "&lt;";
      case ">":
        return "&gt;";
      case "&":
        return "&amp;";
      case "\"":
        return "&quot;";
    }
  });
}

console.log(htmlEscape("<p class=\"greeting\">Hello world!</p>"));
// "&lt;p class=&quot;greeting&quot;&gt;Hello world!&lt;/p&gt;"
```

Here, the function `htmlEscape()` is defined to escape four characters for insertion into HTML: the less-than, greater-than, ampersand, and double-quote characters all must be escaped. The easiest way to accomplish this is to have a regular expression to look for those characters and then define a function that returns the specific HTML entities for each matched character.

The last string method for dealing with patterns is `split()`, which separates the string into an array of substrings based on a separator. The separator may be a string or a `RegExp` object. (The string is not considered a regular expression for this method.) An optional second argument, the array limit, ensures that the returned array will be no larger than a certain size. Consider this example:

```
let colorText = "red,blue,green,yellow";
let colors1 = colorText.split(",");        // ["red", "blue", "green", "yellow"]
let colors2 = colorText.split(",", 2);     // ["red", "blue"]
let colors3 = colorText.split(/[^\,]+/);   // ["", ",", ",", ",", ""]
```

In this example, the string `colorText` is a comma-separated string of colors. The call to `split(",")` retrieves an array of those colors, splitting the string on the comma character. To truncate the results to only two items, a second argument of 2 is specified. Last, using a regular expression, it's possible to get an array of the comma characters. Note that in this last call to `split()`, the returned array has an empty string before and after the commas. This happens because the separator specified by the regular expression appears at the beginning of the string (the substring `"red"`) and at the end (the substring `"yellow"`).

The *localeCompare()* Method

The last method is `localeCompare()`, which compares one string to another and returns one of three values as follows:

1. If the string should come alphabetically before the string argument, a negative number is returned. (Most often this is –1, but it is up to each implementation as to the actual value.)

2. If the string is equal to the string argument, 0 is returned.

3. If the string should come alphabetically after the string argument, a positive number is returned. (Most often this is 1, but once again, this is implementation-specific.)

Here's an example:

```
let stringValue = "yellow";
console.log(stringValue.localeCompare("brick"));  // 1
console.log(stringValue.localeCompare("yellow")); // 0
console.log(stringValue.localeCompare("zoo"));   // -1
```

In this code, the string "yellow" is compared to three different values: `"brick"`, `"yellow"`, and `"zoo"`. Because `"brick"` comes alphabetically before `"yellow"`, `localeCompare()` returns 1; "yellow" is equal to "yellow", so `localeCompare()` returns 0 for that line; and "zoo" comes after "yellow", so `localeCompare()` returns –1 for that line. Once again, because the values are implementation-specific, it is best to use `localeCompare()` as shown in this example:

```
function determineOrder(value) {
  let result = stringValue.localeCompare(value);
  if (result < 0) {
    console.log(`The string 'yellow' comes before the string '${value}'.`);
  } else if (result> 0) {
    console.log(`The string 'yellow' comes after the string '${value}'.`);
  } else {
    console.log(`The string 'yellow' is equal to the string '${value}'.`);
  }
}

determineOrder("brick");
determineOrder("yellow");
determineOrder("zoo");
```

By using this sort of construct, you can be sure that the code works correctly in all implementations.

The unique part of `localeCompare()` is that an implementation's locale (country and language) indicates exactly how this method operates. In the United States, where English is the standard language for ECMAScript implementations, `localeCompare()` is case-sensitive, determining that uppercase letters come alphabetically after lowercase letters. However, this may not be the case in other locales.

SINGLETON BUILT-IN OBJECTS

ECMA-262 defines a built-in object as "any object supplied by an ECMAScript implementation, independent of the host environment, which is present at the start of the execution of an ECMA-Script program." This means the developer does not need to explicitly instantiate a built-in object; it is already instantiated. You have already learned about most of the built-in objects, such as Object, Array, and String. There are two singleton built-in objects defined by ECMA-262: Global and Math.

The Global Object

The `Global` object is the most unique in ECMAScript because it isn't explicitly accessible. ECMA-262 specifies the `Global` object as a sort of catchall for properties and methods that don't otherwise have an owning object. In truth, there is no such thing as a global variable or global function; all variables and functions defined globally become properties of the `Global` object. Functions covered earlier in this book, such as `isNaN()`, `isFinite()`, `parseInt()`, and `parseFloat()`, are actually methods of the `Global` object. In addition to these, there are several other methods available on the `Global` object.

URI-Encoding Methods

The `encodeURI()` and `encodeURIComponent()` methods are used to encode URIs (Uniform Resource Identifiers) to be passed to the browser. To be valid, a URI cannot contain certain characters, such as spaces. The URI-encoding methods encode the URIs so that a browser can still accept and understand them, replacing all invalid characters with a special UTF-8 encoding.

The `encodeURI()` method is designed to work on an entire URI (for instance, `www.wrox.com/ illegal value.js`), whereas `encodeURIComponent()` is designed to work solely on a segment of a URI (such as `illegal value.js` from the previous URI). The main difference between the two methods is that `encodeURI()` does not encode special characters that are part of a URI, such as the colon, forward slash, question mark, and pound sign, whereas `encodeURIComponent()` encodes every nonstandard character it finds. Consider this example:

```
let uri = "http:// www.wrox.com/illegal value.js#start";

// "http:// www.wrox.com/illegal%20value.js#start"
console.log(encodeURI(uri));

// "http%3A%2F%2Fwww.wrox.com%2Fillegal%20value.js%23start"
console.log(encodeURIComponent(uri));
```

Here, using `encodeURI()` left the value completely intact except for the space, which was replaced with `%20`. The `encodeURIComponent()` method replaced all nonalphanumeric characters with their encoded equivalents. This is why `encodeURI()` can be used on full URIs, whereas `encodeURIComponent()` can be used only on strings that are appended to the end of an existing URI.

> **NOTE** *Generally speaking, you'll use* `encodeURIComponent()` *much more frequently than* `encodeURI()` *because it's more common to encode query string arguments separately from the base URI.*

The two counterparts to `encodeURI()` and `encodeURIComponent()` are `decodeURI()` and `decodeURIComponent()`. The `decodeURI()` method decodes only characters that would have been replaced by using `encodeURI()`. For instance, `%20` is replaced with a space, but `%23` is not replaced because it represents a pound sign (#), which `encodeURI()` does not replace. Likewise, `decodeURIComponent()` decodes all characters encoded by `encodeURIComponent()`, essentially meaning it decodes all special values. Consider this example:

```
let uri = "http%3A%2F%2Fwww.wrox.com%2Fillegal%20value.js%23start";

// http%3A%2F%2Fwww.wrox.com%2Fillegal value.js%23start
console.log(decodeURI(uri));

// http:// www.wrox.com/illegal value.js#start
console.log(decodeURIComponent(uri));
```

Here, the `uri` variable contains a string that is encoded using `encodeURIComponent()`. The first value output is the result of `decodeURI()`, which replaced only the %20 with a space. The second value is the output of `decodeURIComponent()`, which replaces all the special characters and outputs a string that has no escaping in it. (This string is not a valid URI.)

> **NOTE** *The URI methods* `encodeURI()`, `encodeURIComponent()`, `decodeURI()`, *and* `decodeURIComponent()` *replace the escape() and* `unescape()` *methods, which are deprecated in the ECMA-262 third edition. The URI methods are always preferable, because they encode all Unicode characters, whereas the original methods encode only ASCII characters correctly. Avoid using* `escape()` *and* `unescape()` *in production code.*

The *eval()* Method

The final method is perhaps the most powerful in the entire ECMAScript language: the `eval()` method. This method works like an entire ECMAScript interpreter and accepts one argument, a string of ECMAScript (or JavaScript) to execute. Here's an example:

```
eval("console.log('hi')");
```

This line is functionally equivalent to the following:

```
console.log("hi");
```

When the interpreter finds an `eval()` call, it interprets the argument into actual ECMAScript statements and then inserts it into place. Code executed by `eval()` is considered to be part of the execution context in which the call is made, and the executed code has the same scope chain as that context. This means variables that are defined in the containing context can be referenced inside an `eval()` call, such as in this example:

```
let msg = "hello world";
eval("console.log(msg)");  // "hello world"
```

Here, the variable msg is defined outside the context of the eval() call, yet the call to console
.log() still displays the text "hello world" because the second line is replaced with a real line of
code. Likewise, you can define a function or variables inside an eval() call that can be referenced by
the code outside, as follows:

```
eval("function sayHi() { console.log('hi'); }");
sayHi();
```

Here, the sayHi() function is defined inside an eval() call. Because that call is replaced with the
actual function, it is possible to call sayHi() on the following line. This works the same for variables:

```
eval("let msg = 'hello world';");
console.log(msg);  // "hello world"
```

Any variables or functions created inside of eval() will not be hoisted, as they are contained within
a string when the code is being parsed. They are created only at the time of eval() execution.

In strict mode, variables and functions created inside of eval() are not accessible outside, so these
last two examples would cause errors. Also, in strict mode, assigning a value to eval causes an error:

```
"use strict";
eval = "hi";  // causes error
```

> **NOTE** *The capability to interpret strings of code is very powerful but also very
> dangerous. Use extreme caution with eval(), especially when passing user-entered
> data into it, as this method exposes a large attack surface for XSS exploits. A mis-
> chievous user could insert values that might compromise your site or application
> security.*

Global Object Properties

The Global object has a number of properties, some of which have already been mentioned in this
book. The special values of undefined, NaN, and Infinity are all properties of the Global object.
Additionally, all native reference type constructors, such as Object and Function, are properties of
the Global object. The following table lists all of the properties.

PROPERTY	DESCRIPTION
undefined	The special value undefined
NaN	The special value NaN
Infinity	The special value Infinity
Object	Constructor for Object
Array	Constructor for Array
Function	Constructor for Function

PROPERTY	DESCRIPTION
Boolean	Constructor for Boolean
String	Constructor for String
Number	Constructor for Number
Date	Constructor for Date
RegExp	Constructor for RegExp
Symbol	Pseudo-constructor for Symbol
Error	Constructor for Error
EvalError	Constructor for EvalError
RangeError	Constructor for RangeError
ReferenceError	Constructor for ReferenceError
SyntaxError	Constructor for SyntaxError
TypeError	Constructor for TypeError
URIError	Constructor for URIError

The Window Object

Though ECMA-262 doesn't indicate a way to access the Global object directly, web browsers implement it such that the window is the Global object's delegate. Therefore, all variables and functions declared in the global scope become properties on window. Consider this example:

```
var color = "red";

function sayColor() {
  console.log(window.color);
}

window.sayColor();  // "red"
```

Here, a global variable named color and a global function named sayColor() are defined. Inside sayColor(), the color variable is accessed via window.color to show that the global variable became a property of window. The function is then called directly off of the window object as window.sayColor(), which pops up the console.log.

> **NOTE** *The window object does much more in JavaScript than just implement the ECMAScript Global object. Details of the window object can be found in Chapter 12, "The Browser Object Model."*

Another way to retrieve the Global object is to use the following code:

```
let global = function() {
  return this;
}();
```

This code creates an immediately-invoked function expression that returns the value of this. As mentioned previously, the this value is equivalent to the Global object when a function is executed with no explicit this value specified (either by being an object method or via call()/apply()). Thus, calling a function that simply returns this is a consistent way to retrieve the Global object in any execution environment.

The Math Object

ECMAScript provides the Math object as a common location for mathematical formulas, information, and computation. The Math object offers a number of properties and methods to help these computations.

> **NOTE** *The computations available on the Math object execute faster than if you were to write the computations in JavaScript directly because computations available on the Math object use more efficient implementations in the JavaScript engine and processor instructions. A side-effect of this is that precision of these operations may vary between browsers, operating systems, instruction sets, and hardware.*

Math Object Properties

The Math object has several properties, consisting mostly of special values in the world of mathematics. The following table describes these properties.

PROPERTY	DESCRIPTION
Math.E	The value of e, the base of the natural logarithms
Math.LN10	The natural logarithm of 10
Math.LN2	The natural logarithm of 2
Math.LOG2E	The base 2 logarithm of e
Math.LOG10E	The base 10 logarithm of e
Math.PI	The value of π
Math.SQRT1_2	The square root of ½
Math.SQRT2	The square root of 2

Although the meanings and uses of these values are outside the scope of this book, they are defined in the ECMAScript specification and available when you need them.

The *min()* and *max()* Methods

The Math object also contains many methods aimed at performing both simple and complex mathematical calculations.

The `min()` and `max()` methods determine which number is the smallest or largest in a group of numbers. These methods accept any number of parameters, as shown in the following example:

```
let max = Math.max(3, 54, 32, 16);
console.log(max);  // 54

let min = Math.min(3, 54, 32, 16);
console.log(min);  // 3
```

Out of the numbers 3, 54, 32, and 16, `Math.max()` returns the number 54, whereas `Math.min()` returns the number 3. These methods are useful for avoiding extra loops and `if` statements to determine the maximum value out of a group of numbers.

To find the maximum or the minimum value in an array, you can use the spread operator as follows:

```
let values = [1, 2, 3, 4, 5, 6, 7, 8];
let max = Math.max(...values);
```

Rounding Methods

The next group of methods has to do with rounding decimal values into integers. Four methods—`Math.ceil()`, `Math.floor()`, `Math.round()`, and `Math.fround()`—handle rounding in different ways as described here:

➤ The `Math.ceil()` method represents the ceiling function, which always rounds numbers up to the nearest integer value.

➤ The `Math.floor()` method represents the floor function, which always rounds numbers down to the nearest integer value.

➤ The `Math.round()` method represents a standard round function, which rounds up if the number is at least halfway to the next integer value (0.5 or higher) and rounds down if not. This is the way you were taught to round in elementary school.

➤ The `Math.fround()` method returns the nearest single precision (32 bits) floating point representation of the number.

The following example illustrates how these methods work:

```
console.log(Math.ceil(25.9));   // 26
console.log(Math.ceil(25.5));   // 26
console.log(Math.ceil(25.1));   // 26

console.log(Math.round(25.9));  // 26
console.log(Math.round(25.5));  // 26
console.log(Math.round(25.1));  // 25

console.log(Math.fround(0.4));  // 0.4000000059604645
console.log(Math.fround(0.5));  // 0.5
```

```
console.log(Math.fround(25.9));   // 25.899999618530273

console.log(Math.floor(25.9));    // 25
console.log(Math.floor(25.5));    // 25
console.log(Math.floor(25.1));    // 25
```

For all values between 25 and 26 (exclusive), `Math.ceil()` always returns 26 because it will always round up. The `Math.round()` method returns 26 only if the number is 25.5 or greater; otherwise it returns 25. Last, `Math.floor()` returns 25 for all numbers between 25 and 26 (exclusive).

The *random()* Method

The `Math.random()` method returns a random number between the 0 and the 1, including 0 but not including 1. This is a favorite tool of websites that are trying to display random quotes or random facts upon entry of a website. You can use `Math.random()` to select numbers within a certain integer range by using the following formula:

```
number = Math.floor(Math.random() * total_number_of_choices + first_possible_value)
```

The `Math.floor()` method is used here because `Math.random()` always returns a decimal value, meaning that multiplying it by a number and adding another still yields a decimal value. So, if you wanted to select a number between 1 and 10, the code would look like this:

```
let num = Math.floor(Math.random() * 10 + 1);
```

You see 10 possible values (1 through 10), with the first possible value being 1. If you want to select a number between 2 and 10, then the code would look like this:

```
let num = Math.floor(Math.random() * 9 + 2);
```

There are only nine numbers when counting from 2 to 10, so the total number of choices is nine, with the first possible value being 2. Many times, it's just easier to use a function that handles the calculation of the total number of choices and the first possible value, as in this example:

```
function selectFrom(lowerValue, upperValue) {
    let choices = upperValue - lowerValue + 1;
    return Math.floor(Math.random() * choices + lowerValue);
}

let num = selectFrom(2,10);
console.log(num);   // number between 2 and 10, inclusive
```

Here, the function `selectFrom()` accepts two arguments: the lowest value that should be returned and the highest value that should be returned. The number of choices is calculated by subtracting the two values and adding one and then applying the previous formula to those numbers. So it's possible to select a number between 2 and 10 (inclusive) by calling `selectFrom(2,10)`. Using the function, it's easy to select a random item from an array, as shown here:

```
let colors = ["red", "green", "blue", "yellow", "black", "purple", "brown"];
let color = colors[selectFrom(0, colors.length-1)];
```

In this example, the second argument to `selectFrom()` is the length of the array minus 1, which is the last position in an array.

> **NOTE** *The* `Math.random()` *method is fine for the purposes demonstrated here. If you need to use random number generation for cryptographic purposes (which requires higher entropy in the inputs to the generator) prefer instead to use* `window.crypto.getRandomValues()`.

Other Methods

The Math object has a lot of methods related to various simple and higher-level mathematical operations. It's beyond the scope of this book to discuss the ins and outs of each or in what situations they may be used, but the following table enumerates the remaining methods of the Math object.

METHOD	DESCRIPTION
`Math.abs(x)`	Returns the absolute value of x
`Math.exp(x)`	Returns `Math.E` raised to the power of x
`Math.expm1(x)`	Equivalent to `Math.exp(x) - 1`
`Math.log(x)`	Returns the natural logarithm of x
`Math.log1p(x)`	Equivalent to `1 + Math.log(x)`
`Math.pow(x, power)`	Returns x raised to the power of `power`
`Math.pow(...nums)`	Returns the square root of the sum of the squares of each number in `nums`
`Math.clz32(x)`	Returns the number of leading zeroes of a 32-bit integer x
`Math.sign(x)`	Returns 1, 0, -0, or -1 indicating the sign of x
`Math.trunc(x)`	Returns the integer component of x, removing any decimals
`Math.sqrt(x)`	Returns the square root of x
`Math.cbrt(x)`	Returns the cubic root of x
`Math.acos(x)`	Returns the arc cosine of x
`Math.acosh(x)`	Returns the hyperbolic arc cosine of x
`Math.asin(x)`	Returns the arc sine of x
`Math.asin(x)`	Returns the hyperbolic arc sine of x
`Math.atan(x)`	Returns the arc tangent of x
`Math.atanh(x)`	Returns the hyperbolic arc tangent of x
`Math.atan2(y, x)`	Returns the arc tangent of y/x

continues

(continued)

METHOD	DESCRIPTION
`Math.cos(x)`	Returns the cosine of x
`Math.sin(x)`	Returns the sine of x
`Math.tan(x)`	Returns the tangent of x

Even though these methods are defined by ECMA-262, the results are implementation-dependent for those dealing with sines, cosines, and tangents, because you can calculate each value in many different ways. Consequently, the precision of the results may vary from one implementation to another.

SUMMARY

Objects in JavaScript are called reference values, and several built-in reference types can be used to create specific types of objects, as follows:

➤ Reference types are similar to classes in traditional object-oriented programming but are implemented differently.

➤ The `Date` type provides information about dates and times, including the current date and time and calculations.

➤ The `RegExp` type is an interface for regular-expression support in ECMAScript, providing most basic and some advanced regular-expression functionality.

One of the unique aspects of JavaScript is that functions are actually instances of the `Function` type, meaning functions are objects. Because functions are objects, functions have methods that can be used to augment how they behave.

Because of the existence of primitive wrapper types, primitive values in JavaScript can be accessed as if they were objects. There are three primitive wrapper types: `Boolean`, `Number`, and `String`. They all have the following characteristics:

➤ Each of the wrapper types maps to the primitive type of the same name.

➤ When a primitive value is accessed in read mode, a primitive wrapper object is instantiated so that it can be used to manipulate the data.

➤ As soon as a statement involving a primitive value is executed, the wrapper object is destroyed.

There are also two built-in objects that exist at the beginning of code execution: `Global` and `Math`. The `Global` object isn't accessible in most ECMAScript implementations; however, web browsers implement it as the `window` object. The `Global` object contains all global variables and functions as properties. The `Math` object contains properties and methods to aid in complex mathematical calculations.

Advanced Reference Types

WHAT'S IN THIS CHAPTER?

➤ Working with objects

➤ Working with arrays and typed arrays

➤ Working with Map, WeakMap, Set, and WeakSet types

> **DOWNLOADS FOR THIS CHAPTER**
>
> Please note that all the code examples for this chapter are available as a part of this chapter's code download on the book's website at www.wiley.com/go/projavascript5e.

THE OBJECT TYPE

Up to this point, most of the reference-value examples have used the Object type, which is one of the most commonly used types in ECMAScript. Although instances of Object don't have much functionality, they are ideally suited to storing and transmitting data around an application.

There are two ways to explicitly create an instance of Object. The first is to use the new operator with the Object constructor like this:

```
let person = new Object();
person.name = "Matt";
person.age = 29;
```

The other way is to use *object literal* notation. `Object` literal notation is a shorthand form of object definition designed to simplify creating an object with numerous properties. For example, the following defines the same person object from the previous example using object literal notation:

```
let person = {
  name: "Matt",
  age: 29
};
```

In this example, the left curly brace (`{`) signifies the beginning of an object literal because it occurs in an *expression context*. An expression context in ECMAScript is a context in which a value (expression) is expected. Assignment operators indicate that a value is expected next, so the left curly brace indicates the beginning of an expression. The same curly brace, when appearing in a *statement context*, such as follows an `if` statement condition, indicates the beginning of a block statement.

Next, the `name` property is specified, followed by a colon, followed by the property's value. A comma is used to separate properties in an object literal, so there's a comma after the string `"Matt"` but not after the value 29 because `age` is the last property in the object. Including a comma after the last property is allowed in all modern browsers.

Property names can also be specified as strings or numbers when using object literal notation, such as in this example:

```
let person = {
  "name": "Matt",
  "age": 29,
  5: true
};
```

This example produces an object with a name property, an age property, and a property 5. Note that numeric property names are automatically converted to strings.

It's also possible to create an object with only the default properties and methods using object literal notation by leaving the space between the curly braces empty, such as this:

```
let person = {};  // same as new Object()
person.name = "Matt";
person.age = 29;
```

This example is equivalent to the first one in this section, though it looks a little strange. Prefer to use object literal notation only when you're going to specify properties for readability.

> **NOTE** *When defining an object via object literal notation, the* `Object` *constructor is never actually called.*

Though it's acceptable to use either method of creating Object instances, developers tend to favor object literal notation because it requires less code and visually encapsulates all related data. In fact, object literals have become a preferred way of passing a large number of optional arguments to a function, such as in this example:

```
function displayInfo(args) {
  let output = "";

  if (typeof args.name == "string"){
    output += "Name: " + args.name + "\n";
  }

  if (typeof args.age == "number") {
    output += "Age: " + args.age + "\n";
  }

  alert(output);
}

displayInfo({
  name: "Matt",
  age: 29
});

displayInfo({
  name: "Greg"
});
```

Here, the function `displayInfo()` accepts a single argument named `args`. The argument may come in with a property called `name` or `age` or both or neither of those. The function is set up to test for the existence of each property using the `typeof` operator and then to construct a message to display based on availability. This function is then called twice, each time with different data specified in an object literal. The function works correctly in both cases.

> **NOTE** *This pattern for argument passing is best used when there are a large number of optional arguments that can be passed into the function. Generally speaking, named arguments are easier to work with but can get unwieldy when there are numerous optional arguments. The best approach is to use named arguments for those that are required and an object literal to encompass multiple optional arguments.*

Although object properties are typically accessed using *dot notation*, which is common to many object-oriented languages, it's also possible to access properties via *bracket notation*. When you use bracket notation, a string containing the property name is placed between the brackets, as in this example:

```
alert(person["name"]);  // "Matt"
alert(person.name);     // "Matt"
```

Functionally, there is no difference between the two approaches. The main advantage of bracket notation is that it allows you to use variables for property access, as in this example:

```
let propertyName = "name";
alert(person[propertyName]);  // "Matt"
```

You can also use bracket notation when the property name contains characters that would be either a syntax error or a keyword/reserved word. For example:

```
person["first name"] = "Matt";
```

Because the name `"first name"` contains a space, you can't use dot notation to access it. However, property names can contain nonalphanumeric characters—you just need to use bracket notation to access them.

Generally speaking, dot notation is preferred unless variables are necessary to access properties by name.

> **NOTE** *Chapter 8, "Objects, Classes, and Object-Oriented Programming," has extensive coverage on the* `Object` *type.*

THE ARRAY TYPE

After the Object type, the Array type is probably the most used in ECMAScript. An ECMAScript array is very different from arrays in most other programming languages. As in other languages, ECMAScript arrays are ordered lists of data, but unlike in other languages, they can hold any type of data in each slot. This means that it's possible to create an array that has a string in the first position, a number in the second, an object in the third, and so on. ECMAScript arrays are also dynamically sized, automatically growing to accommodate any data that is added to them.

Creating Arrays

Arrays can be created in several basic ways. One is to use the `Array` constructor, as in this line:

```
let colors = new Array();
```

If you know the number of items that will be in the array, you can pass the count into the constructor, and the length property will automatically be created with that value. For example, the following creates an array with an initial length value of 20:

```
let colors = new Array(20);
```

The `Array` constructor can also be passed items that should be included in the array. The following creates an array with three string values:

```
let colors = new Array("red", "blue", "green");
```

An array can be created with a single value by passing it into the constructor. This gets a little bit tricky because providing a single argument that is a number always creates an array with the given number of items, whereas an argument of any other type creates a one-item array that contains the specified value. Here's an example:

```
let colors = new Array(3);       // create an array with three items
let names = new Array("Greg");   // create an array with one item, the string "Greg"
```

It's possible to omit the new operator when using the Array constructor. It has the same result, as you can see here:

```
let colors = Array(3);       // create an array with three items
let names = Array("Greg");   // create an array with one item, the string "Greg"
```

A second way to create an array is by using *array literal* notation. An array literal is specified by using square brackets and placing a comma-separated list of items between them, as in this example:

```
let colors = ["red", "blue", "green"];   // Creates an array with three strings
let names = [];                          // Creates an empty array
let values = [1,2,];                     // Creates an array with 2 items
```

In this code, the first line creates an array with three string values. The second line creates an empty array by using empty square brackets. The third line shows the effects of leaving a comma after the last value in an array literal: values is a two-item array containing the values 1 and 2.

> **NOTE** *As with objects, the* Array *constructor isn't called when an array is created using array literal notation.*

The Array constructor also has two additional static methods to create arrays: from() and of(). from() is used for converting array-like constructs into an array instance, whereas of() is used to convert a collection of arguments into an array instance.

The first argument to Array.from() is an *arrayLike* object, which is anything that is iterable or has a property length and indexed elements. This type can be used in an abundance of different ways:

```
// Strings will be broken up into an array of single characters
alert(Array.from("Matt"));   // ["M", "a", "t", "t"]

// Sets and Maps can be converted into a new array instance using from()
const m = new Map().set(1, 2)
                   .set(3, 4);
const s = new Set().add(1)
                   .add(2)
                   .add(3)
                   .add(4);

alert(Array.from(m));   // [[1, 2], [3, 4]]
alert(Array.from(s));   // [1, 2, 3, 4]

// Array.from() performs a shallow copy of an existing array
const a1 = [1, 2, 3, 4];
```

```
const a2 = Array.from(a1);
alert(a1);           // [1, 2, 3, 4]
alert(a1 === a2);    // false


// Any iterable object can be used
const iter = {
  *[Symbol.iterator]() {
    yield 1;
    yield 2;
    yield 3;
    yield 4;

  }
};
alert(Array.from(iter));  // [1, 2, 3, 4]

// The arguments object can now easily be casted into an array:
function getArgsArray() {
  return Array.from(arguments);
}
alert(getArgsArray(1, 2, 3, 4));  // [1, 2, 3, 4]

// from() will happily use a custom object with required properties
const arrayLikeObject = {
  0: 1,
  1: 2,
  2: 3,
  3: 4,
  length: 4
};
alert(Array.from(arrayLikeObject));  // [1, 2, 3, 4]
```

`Array.from()` also accepts a second optional map function argument. This allows you to augment the new array's values without creating an intermediate array first, which is the case if the same were performed with `Array.from().map()`. A third optional argument specifies the value of `this` inside the map function. The overridden `this` value is not applied inside an arrow function:

```
const a1 = [1, 2, 3, 4];
const a2 = Array.from(a1, x => x**2);
const a3 = Array.from(a1, function(x) {return x**this.exponent}, {exponent: 2});
alert(a2);   // [1, 4, 9, 16]
alert(a3);   // [1, 4, 9, 16]
```

`Array.of()` will convert the list of arguments into an array. This serves to replace the common pre-ES6 method of converting the arguments object into an array using the unwieldy `Array.prototype` `.slice.call(arguments)`:

```
alert(Array.of(1, 2, 3, 4));  // [1, 2, 3, 4]
alert(Array.of(undefined));    // [undefined]
```

Array Holes

Initializing an array with an array literal allows you to create "holes" using sequential commas. ECMAScript will treat the value at the index between the commas as a hole. An array of holes might be created as follows:

```
const options = [,,,,,];  // Creates an array with 5 items
alert(options.length);    // 5
alert(options);           // [,,,,,]
```

Methods and iterators introduced in ES6 behave differently than methods present in earlier ECMAScript editions. ES6 additions will universally treat the holes as an existing entry with a value of undefined:

```
const options = [1,,,,5];

for (const option of options) {
  alert(option === undefined);
}
// false
// true
// true
// true
// false

const a = Array.from([,,,]);  // Array of 3 holes created with ES6's Array.from()
for (const val of a) {
  alert(val === undefined);
}
// true
// true
// true

alert(Array.of([,,,]));  // [undefined, undefined, undefined]

for (const [index, value] of options.entries()) {
  alert(value);
}
// 1
// undefined
// undefined
// undefined
// 5
```

Conversely, methods available before ES6 will tend to ignore the holes, although exact behavior can vary slightly between methods:

```
const options = [1,,,,5];

// map() will skip the holes entirely
```

```
alert(options.map(() => 6));  // [6, undefined, undefined, undefined, 6]

// join() treats holes as empty strings
alert(options.join('-'));      // "1----5"
```

> **NOTE** *Due to their bizarre behavior and performance issues, avoid using array holes in your code. Prefer to use an explicit* undefined *in place of a hole.*

Indexing into Arrays

To get and set array values, you use square brackets and provide the zero-based numeric index of the value, as shown here:

```
let colors = ["red", "blue", "green"];  // define an array of strings
alert(colors[0]);                       // display the first item
colors[2] = "black";                    // change the third item
colors[3] = "brown";                    // add a fourth item
```

The index provided within the square brackets indicates the value being accessed. If the index is less than the number of items in the array, then it will return the value stored in the corresponding item, as colors[0] displays "red" in this example. Setting a value works in the same way, replacing the value in the designated position. If a value is set to an index that is past the end of the array, as with colors[3] in this example, the array length is automatically expanded to be that index plus 1 (so the length becomes 4 in this example because the index being used is 3).

The number of items in an array is stored in the length property, which always returns 0 or more, as shown in the following example:

```
let colors = ["red", "blue", "green"];  // creates an array with three strings
let names = [];                         // creates an empty array

alert(colors.length);  // 3
alert(names.length);   // 0
```

A unique characteristic of length is that it's not read-only. By setting the length property, you can easily remove items from or add items to the end of the array. Consider this example:

```
let colors = ["red", "blue", "green"];  // creates an array with three strings
colors.length = 2;
alert(colors[2]);  // undefined
```

Here, the array colors starts out with three values. Setting the length to 2 removes the last item (in position 2), making it no longer accessible using colors[2]. If the length were set to a number greater than the number of items in the array, the new items would each get filled with the value of undefined, as in this example:

```
let colors = ["red", "blue", "green"];  // creates an array with three strings
colors.length = 4;
alert(colors[3]);  // undefined
```

This code sets the length of the colors array to 4 even though it contains only three items. Position 3 does not exist in the array, so trying to access its value results in the special value `undefined` being returned.

The `length` property can also be helpful in adding items to the end of an array, as in this example:

```
let colors = ["red", "blue", "green"];  // creates an array with three strings
colors[colors.length] = "black";        // add a color (position 3)
colors[colors.length] = "brown";        // add another color (position 4)
```

The last item in an array is always at position `length-1`, so the next available open slot is at position `length`. Each time an item is added after the last one in the array, the length property is automatically updated to reflect the change. That means `colors[colors.length]` assigns a value to position 3 in the second line of this example and to position 4 in the last line. The new `length` is automatically calculated when an item is placed into a position that's outside of the current array size, which is done by adding 1 to the position, as in this example:

```
let colors = ["red", "blue", "green"];  // creates an array with three strings
colors[99] = "black";                   // add a color (position 99)
alert(colors.length);                   // 100
```

In this code, the colors array has a value inserted into position 99, resulting in a new length of 100 (99 + 1). Each of the other items, positions 3 through 98, doesn't actually exist and so returns `undefined` when accessed.

> **NOTE** *Arrays can contain a maximum of 4,294,967,295 items, which should be plenty for almost all programming needs. If you try to add more than that number, an exception occurs. Trying to create an array with an initial size approaching this maximum may cause a long-running script error.*

The `at()` method was introduced to make it easier to access elements within an array, especially when working with negative indices. The method takes an integer argument and returns the element at that position within the array. Positive indices work as expected, while negative indices count from the end of the array, with -1 representing the last element, -2 representing the second to last element, and so on.

```
let colors = ["red", "blue", "green"];

console.log(colors.at(0));       // "red"
console.log(colors.at(-1));      // "green"
console.log(colors.at(-2));      // "blue"
console.log(colors.at(100));     // undefined
console.log(colors.at(-100));    // undefined
```

Detecting Arrays

A classic ECMAScript problem is determining whether a given object is an array. When dealing with a single web page, and therefore a single global scope, the `instanceof` operator works well:

```
if (value instanceof Array){
    // do something on the array
}
```

The one problem with `instanceof` is that it assumes a single global execution context. If you are dealing with multiple frames in a web page, you're really dealing with two distinct global execution contexts and therefore two versions of the `Array` constructor. If you were to pass an array from one frame into a second frame, that array has a different constructor function than an array created natively in the second frame.

To work around this problem, ECMAScript offers the `Array.isArray()` method. The purpose of this method is to definitively determine if a given value is an array regardless of the global execution context in which it was created. Consider the following example:

```
if (Array.isArray(value)){
    // do something on the array
}
```

Iterator Methods

Three methods are exposed on the `Array` prototype that allow you to inspect the contents of an array: `keys()`, `values()`, and `entries()`. `keys()` will return an iterator of the array's indices, `values()` will return an iterator of the array's elements, and `entries()` will return an iterator of index/value pairs:

```
const a = ["foo", "bar", "baz", "qux"];

// Because these methods return iterators, you can funnel their contents
// into array instances using Array.from()
const aKeys = Array.from(a.keys());
const aValues = Array.from(a.values());
const aEntries = Array.from(a.entries());

alert(aKeys);      // [0, 1, 2, 3]
alert(aValues);    // ["foo", "bar", "baz", "qux"]
alert(aEntries);   // [[0, "foo"], [1, "bar"], [2, "baz"], [3, "qux"]]
```

It is very easy to split out the key-value pairs inside a loop using destructuring:

```
const a = ["foo", "bar", "baz", "qux"];

for (const [idx, element] of a.entries()) [
    alert(idx);
    alert(element);
}
// 0
// foo
// 1
// bar
```

```
// 2
// baz
// 3
// qux
```

Copy and Fill Methods

Two methods, `fill()` and `copyWithin()`, respectively allow for batch fill and copy inside an array. Both methods have a similar function signature in that they allow you to specify a range within an existing array instance using an inclusive start and exclusive end index. Arrays that use this method will never be resized.

The `fill()` method allows you to insert the same value into all or part of an existing array. Specifying the optional start index instructs the fill to begin at that index, and the fill will continue to the end of the array unless an end index is provided. Negative indices are interpreted from the end of the array; another way to think of this is that negative indices have the array length added to them to calculate a positive index:

```
const zeroes = [0, 0, 0, 0, 0];

// Fill the entire array with 5
zeroes.fill(5);
alert(zeroes);    // [5, 5, 5, 5, 5]
zeroes.fill(0);   // reset

// Fill all indices>=3 with 6
zeroes.fill(6, 3);
alert(zeroes);    // [0, 0, 0, 6, 6]
zeroes.fill(0);   // reset

// Fill all indices>= 1 and < 3 with 7
zeroes.fill(7, 1, 3);
alert(zeroes);    // [0, 7, 7, 0, 0];
zeroes.fill(0);   // reset

// Fill all indices >=1 and < 4 with 8
// (-4 + zeroes.length = 1)
// (-1 + zeroes.length = 4)
zeroes.fill(8, -4, -1);
alert(zeroes);    // [0, 8, 8, 8, 0];
```

`fill()` silently ignores ranges that exceed the boundaries of the array, are zero length, or go backwards:

```
const zeroes = [0, 0, 0, 0, 0];

// Fill with too low indices is noop
zeroes.fill(1, -10, -6);
alert(zeroes);    // [0, 0, 0, 0, 0]

// Fill with too high indices is noop
zeroes.fill(1, 10, 15);
```

```
alert(zeroes);    // [0, 0, 0, 0, 0]

// Fill with reversed indices is noop
zeroes.fill(2, 4, 2);
alert(zeroes);    // [0, 0, 0, 0, 0]

// Fill with partial index overlap is best effort
zeroes.fill(4, 3, 10)
alert(zeroes);    // [0, 0, 0, 4, 4]
```

Unlike `fill()`, `copyWithin()` instead performs an iterative shallow copy of some of the array and overwrites existing values beginning at the provided index. However, it uses the same conventions with respect to start and end indices:

```
let ints,
    reset = () => ints = [0, 1, 2, 3, 4, 5, 6, 7, 8, 9];
reset();

// Copy the contents of ints beginning at index 0
// to the values beginning at index 5.
// Stops when it reaches the end of the array either in the source
// indices or the destination indices.
ints.copyWithin(5);
alert(ints);  // [0, 1, 2, 3, 4, 0, 1, 2, 3, 4]
reset();

// Copy the contents of ints beginning at index 5
// to the values beginning at index 0.
ints.copyWithin(0, 5);
alert(ints);  // [5, 6, 7, 8, 9, 5, 6, 7, 8, 9]
reset();

// Copy the contents of ints beginning at index 0 and ending at index 3
// to values beginning at index 4.
ints.copyWithin(4, 0, 3);
alert(ints);  // [0, 1, 2, 3, 0, 1, 2, 7, 8, 9]
reset();

// The JS engine will perform a full copy of the range of values before inserting,
// so there is no danger of overwrite during the copy.
ints.copyWithin(2, 0, 6);
alert(ints);  // [0, 1, 0, 1, 2, 3, 4, 5, 8, 9]
reset();

// Support for negative indexing behaves identically to fill() in that negative
// indices are calculated relative to the end of the array
ints.copyWithin(-4, -7, -3);
alert(ints);  // [0, 1, 2, 3, 4, 5, 3, 4, 5, 6]
```

`copyWithin()` silently ignores ranges that exceed the boundaries of the array, are zero length, or go backwards:

```
let ints,
    reset = () => ints = [0, 1, 2, 3, 4, 5, 6, 7, 8, 9];
```

```
reset();

// Copy with too low indices is noop
ints.copyWithin(1, -15, -12);
alert(ints);    // [0, 1, 2, 3, 4, 5, 6, 7, 8, 9];
reset()

// Copy with too high indices is noop
ints.copyWithin(1, 12, 15);
alert(ints);    // [0, 1, 2, 3, 4, 5, 6, 7, 8, 9];
reset();

// Copy with reversed indices is noop
ints.copyWithin(2, 4, 2);
alert(ints);    // [0, 1, 2, 3, 4, 5, 6, 7, 8, 9];
reset();

// Copy with partial index overlap is best effort
ints.copyWithin(4, 7, 10)
alert(ints);    // [0, 1, 2, 3, 7, 8, 9, 7, 8, 9];
```

Spread Operator

The spread operator allows you to expand the elements of an array into individual elements, making it easier to merge, copy, or insert elements from one array into another. Using the spread operator, you can merge two or more arrays into a single array:

```
let array1 = [1, 2, 3];
let array2 = [4, 5, 6];

let mergedArray = [...array1, ...array2];
console.log(mergedArray); // [1, 2, 3, 4, 5, 6]
```

The spread operator can also be used to create a shallow copy of an array:

```
let originalArray = [1, 2, 3];
let copiedArray = [...originalArray];

console.log(copiedArray); // [1, 2, 3]
```

The flexible syntax of the spread operator allows for sophisticated array operations. For example, you can mix slicing and spreading to interleave arrays:

```
let array1 = [1, 2, 4];
let array2 = [3];

let combinedArray = [...array1.slice(0, 2), ...array2, ...array1.slice(2)];
console.log(combinedArray); // [1, 2, 3, 4]
```

Rest Operator

The rest operator is used to collect the remaining elements of an array into a new array. It is typically used in function parameters or destructuring assignments.

The rest operator can be used to collect an unknown number of function arguments into an array:

```
function sum(...numbers) {
  return numbers.reduce((total, num) => total + num, 0);
}

console.log(sum(1, 2, 3, 4, 5)); // 15
```

The rest operator can also be used in destructuring assignments to collect remaining elements of an array:

```
let [first, second, ...rest] = [1, 2, 3, 4, 5];

console.log(first);  // 1
console.log(second); // 2
console.log(rest); // [3, 4, 5]
```

Conversion Methods

As mentioned previously, all ECMAScript objects have toLocaleString(), toString(), and valueOf() methods. The toString() and valueOf() methods return the same value when called on an array. The result is a comma-separated string that contains the string equivalents of each value in the array, which is to say that each item has its toString() method called to create the final string. Take a look at this example:

```
let colors = ["red", "blue", "green"];  // creates an array with three strings
alert(colors.toString());  // red,blue,green
alert(colors.valueOf());  // red,blue,green
alert(colors);  // red,blue,green
```

In this code, the toString() and valueOf() methods are first called explicitly to return the string representation of the array, which combines the strings, separating them by commas. The last line passes the array directly into alert(). Because alert() expects a string, it calls toString() behind the scenes to get the same result as when toString() is called directly.

The toLocaleString() method may end up returning the same value as toString() and valueOf(), but not always. When toLocaleString() is called on an array, it creates a comma-delimited string of the array values. The only difference between this and the two other methods is that toLocaleString() calls each item's toLocaleString() instead of toString() to get its string value. Consider the following example:

```
let person1 = {
  toLocaleString() {
    return "Matthew";
  },

  toString() {
    return "Matt";
  }
```

```
  };

  let person2 = {
    toLocaleString() {
      return "Grigorios";
    },

    toString() {
      return "Greg";
    }
  };

  let people = [person1, person2];
  alert(people);                    // Matt,Greg
  alert(people.toString());         // Matt,Greg
  alert(people.toLocaleString());   // Nikolaos,Grigorios
```

Here, two objects are defined, person1 and person2. Each object defines both a toString() method and a toLocaleString() method that return different values. An array, people, is created to contain both objects. When passed into alert(), the output is "Matt,Greg" because the toString() method is called on each item in the array (the same as when toString() is called explicitly on the next line). When toLocaleString() is called on the array, the result is "Matthew,Grigorios" because this calls toLocaleString() on each array item.

The inherited methods toLocaleString(), toString(), and valueOf() each return the array items as a comma-separated string. It's possible to construct a string with a different separator using the join() method. The join() method accepts one argument, which is the string separator to use, and returns a string containing all items. Consider this example:

```
  let colors = ["red", "green", "blue"];
  alert(colors.join(","));     // red,green,blue
  alert(colors.join("||"));    // red||green||blue
```

Here, the join() method is used on the colors array to duplicate the output of toString(). By passing in a comma, the result is a comma-separated list of values. On the last line, double pipes are passed in, resulting in the string "red||green||blue". If no value or undefined is passed into the join() method, then a comma is used as the separator.

> **NOTE** *If an item in the array is* null *or* undefined, *it is represented by an empty string in the result of* join(), toLocaleString(), toString(), *and* valueOf().

Stack Methods

One of the interesting things about ECMAScript arrays is that they provide a method to make an array behave like other data structures. An array object can act just like a stack, which is one of a group of data structures that restrict the insertion and removal of items. A stack is referred to as a *last-in-first-out* (LIFO) structure, meaning that the most recently added item is the first one removed. The insertion (called a *push*) and removal (called a *pop*) of items in a stack occur at only one point: the top of the stack. ECMAScript arrays provide push() and pop() specifically to allow stack-like behavior.

The push() method accepts any number of arguments and adds them to the end of the array, return-ing the array's new length. The pop() method, on the other hand, removes the last item in the array, decrements the array's length, and returns that item. Consider this example:

```
let colors = new Array();              // create an array
let count = colors.push("red", "green"); // push two items
alert(count);                          // 2

count = colors.push("black");   // push another item on
alert(count);                   // 3

let item = colors.pop();   // get the last item
alert(item);               // "black"
alert(colors.length);      // 2
```

In this code, an array is created for use as a stack [note that there's no special code required to make this work; push() and pop() are default methods on arrays]. First, two strings are pushed onto the end of the array using push(), and the result is stored in the variable count (which gets the value of 2). Then, another value is pushed on, and the result is once again stored in count. Because there are now three items in the array, push() returns 3. When pop() is called, it returns the last item in the array, which is the string "black". The array then has only two items left.

The stack methods may be used in combination with all of the other array methods as well, as in this example:

```
let colors = ["red", "blue"];
colors.push("brown");          // add another item
colors[3] = "black";           // add an item
alert(colors.length);          // 4

let item = colors.pop();       // get the last item
alert(item);                   // "black"
```

Here, an array is initialized with two values. A third value is added via push(), and a fourth is added by direct assignment into position 3. When pop() is called, it returns the string "black", which was the last value added to the array.

Queue Methods

Just as stacks restrict access in a LIFO data structure, queues restrict access in a *first-in-first-out* (FIFO) data structure. A queue adds items to the end of a list and retrieves items from the front of the list. Because the push() method adds items to the end of an array, all that is needed to emulate a queue is a method to retrieve the first item in the array. The array method for this is called shift(), which removes the first item in the array and returns it, decrementing the length of the array by one. Using shift() in combination with push() allows arrays to be used as queues:

```
let colors = new Array();              // create an array
let count = colors.push("red", "green"); // push two items
alert(count);                          // 2

count = colors.push("black");   // push another item on
```

```
alert(count);                           // 3

let item = colors.shift();  // get the first item
alert(item);                // "red"
alert(colors.length);       // 2
```

This example creates an array of three colors using the `push()` method. The highlighted line shows the `shift()` method being used to retrieve the first item in the array, which is `"red"`. With that item removed, `"green"` is moved into the first position, and `"black"` is moved into the second, leaving the array with two items.

ECMAScript also provides an `unshift()` method for arrays. As the name indicates, `unshift()` does the opposite of `shift()`: it adds any number of items to the front of an array and returns the new array length. By using `unshift()` in combination with `pop()`, it's possible to emulate a queue in the opposite direction, where new values are added to the front of the array and values are retrieved off the back, as in this example:

```
let colors = new Array();                    // create an array
let count = colors.unshift("red", "green");  // push two items
alert(count);                                // 2

count = colors.unshift("black");  // push another item on
alert(count);                     // 3

let item = colors.pop();  // get the first item
alert(item);              // "green"
alert(colors.length);     // 2
```

In this code, an array is created and then populated by using `unshift()`. First "red" and "green" are added to the array, and then `"black"` is added, resulting in an order of `"black"`, `"red"`, `"green"`. When `pop()` is called, it removes the last item, `"green"`, and returns it.

Reordering and Sorting Methods

Two methods deal directly with the ordering of items already in the array: `reverse()` and `sort()`. As one might expect, the `reverse()` method simply reverses the order of items in an array. Consider the following example:

```
let values = [1, 2, 3, 4, 5];
values.reverse();
alert(values);  // 5,4,3,2,1
```

Here, the array's values are initially set to 1, 2, 3, 4, and 5, in that order. Calling `reverse()` on the array reverses the order to 5, 4, 3, 2, 1. This method is fairly straightforward but doesn't provide much flexibility, which is where the `sort()` method comes in.

By default, the `sort()` method puts the items in ascending order—with the smallest value first and the largest value last. To do this, the `sort()` method calls the `String()` casting function on every item and then compares the strings to determine the correct order. This occurs even if all items in an array are numbers, as in this example:

```
let values = [0, 1, 5, 10, 15];
values.sort();
alert(values);  // 0,1,10,15,5
```

Even though the values in this example begin in correct numeric order, the sort() method changes that order based on their string equivalents. So even though 5 is less than 10, the string "10" comes before "5" when doing a string comparison, so the array is updated accordingly. Clearly, this is not an optimal solution in many cases, so the sort() method allows you to pass in a *comparison function* that indicates which value should come before which.

A comparison function accepts two arguments and returns a negative number if the first argument should come before the second, a zero if the arguments are equal, or a positive number if the first argument should come after the second. Here's an example of a simple comparison function:

```
function compare(value1, value2) {
    if (value1 < value2) {
        return -1;
    } else if (value1> value2) {
        return 1;
    } else {
        return 0;
    }
}
```

This comparison function works for most data types and can be used by passing it as an argument to the sort() method, as in the following example:

```
let values = [0, 1, 5, 10, 15];
values.sort(compare);
alert(values);  // 0,1,5,10,15
```

When the comparison function is passed to the sort() method, the numbers remain in the correct order. Of course, the comparison function could produce results in descending order if you simply switch the return values like this:

```
function compare(value1, value2) {
    if (value1 < value2) {
        return 1;
    } else if (value1> value2) {
        return -1;
    } else {
        return 0;
    }
}

let values = [0, 1, 5, 10, 15];
values.sort(compare);
alert(values);  // 15,10,5,1,0
```

Alternately, the compare function can be shortened and defined as an inline arrow function:

```
let values = [0, 1, 5, 10, 15];
values.sort((a, b) => a < b ? 1 : a > b ? -1 : 0);
alert(values);  // 15,10,5,1,0
```

In this modified example, the comparison function returns 1 if the first value should come after the second and −1 if the first value should come before the second. Swapping these means the larger value will come first and the array will be sorted in descending order. Of course, if you just want to reverse the order of the items in the array, reverse() is a much faster alternative than sorting.

> **NOTE** *Both* `reverse()` *and* `sort()` *return a reference to the array on which they were applied.*

A much simpler version of the comparison function can be used with numeric types and objects whose `valueOf()` method returns numeric values (such as the `Date` object). In either case, you can simply subtract the second value from the first as shown here:

```
function compare(value1, value2){
    return value2 - value1;
}
```

Because comparison functions work by returning a number less than zero, zero, or a number greater than zero, the subtraction operation handles all of the cases appropriately.

> **NOTE** *ECMAScript's* `sort()` *is stable, meaning that equal items in the unsorted list will remain in the same relative order in the sorted list.*

Developers usually find that ECMAScript's `sort()` method is unintuitive, so the following table is a quick reference for common sort patterns:

SORT ORDER	SORT SNIPPET	RESULT
Ascending numbers	`arr.sort((a,b) => a - b)`	`[1,2,3]`
Descending numbers	`arr.sort((a,b) => b - a)`	`[3,2,1]`
Ascending strings	`arr.sort((a, b) => a` `.localeCompare(b))`	`["a","b","c"]`
Descending strings	`arr.sort((a, b) => b` `.localeCompare(a))`	`["c","b","a"]`
Ascending number property	`arr.sort((a,b) => a.foo` `- b.foo)`	`[{foo: 1}, {foo: 2},` `{foo: 3}]`
Ascending string property	`arr.sort((a, b) => a.foo` `.localeCompare(b.foo);};`	`[{foo:"a"},{foo:"b"},` `{foo:"c"}]`
Ascending string property, with empty values appearing last	`arr.sort((a, b) => {` `  if (a.foo === "") return 1;` `  if (b.foo === "") return -1;` `  return a.foo` `.localeCompare(b.foo);` `});`	`[{foo:"a"},{foo:"b"},` `{foo:""}]`

Manipulation Methods

There are various ways to work with the items already contained in an array. The concat() method, for instance, allows you to create a new array based on all of the items in the current array. This method begins by creating a copy of the array and then appending the method arguments to the end and returning the newly constructed array. When no arguments are passed in, concat() simply clones the array and returns it. If one or more arrays are passed in, concat() appends each item in these arrays to the end of the result. If the values are not arrays, they are simply appended to the end of the resulting array. Consider this example:

```
let colors = ["red", "green", "blue"];
let colors2 = colors.concat("yellow", ["black", "brown"]);

alert(colors);    // ["red", "green","blue"]
alert(colors2);   // ["red", "green", "blue", "yellow", "black", "brown"]
```

This code begins with the colors array containing three values. The concat() method is called on colors, passing in the string "yellow" and an array containing "black" and "brown". The result, stored in colors2, contains "red", "green", "blue", "yellow", "black", and "brown". The original array, colors, remains unchanged.

You can override this force-flattening default behavior by specifying a special symbol on the argument array instance, Symbol.isConcatSpreadable. This will prevent the concat() method from flattening the result. Conversely, setting the value to true will force array-like objects to be flattened:

```
let colors = ["red", "green", "blue"];
let newColors = ["black", "brown"];
let moreNewColors = {
  [Symbol.isConcatSpreadable]: true,
  length: 2,
  0: "pink",
  1: "cyan"
};

newColors[Symbol.isConcatSpreadable] = false;

// Force the array to not be flattened
let colors2 = colors.concat("yellow", newColors);

// Force the array-like object to be flattened
let colors3 = colors.concat(moreNewColors);

alert(colors);    // ["red", "green","blue"]
alert(colors2);   // ["red", "green", "blue", "yellow", ["black", "brown"]]
alert(colors3);   // ["red", "green", "blue", "pink, "cyan"]
```

The next method, slice(), creates an array that contains one or more items already contained in an array. The slice() method may accept one or two arguments: the starting and stopping positions of the items to return. If only one argument is present, the method returns all items between that position and the end of the array. If there are two arguments, the method returns all items between the start position and the end position, not including the item in the end position. Keep in mind that this operation does not affect the original array in any way. Consider the following:

```
let colors = ["red", "green", "blue", "yellow", "purple"];
let colors2 = colors.slice(1);
let colors3 = colors.slice(1, 4);

alert(colors2);  // green,blue,yellow,purple
alert(colors3);  // green,blue,yellow
```

In this example, the colors array starts out with five items. Calling `slice()` and passing in 1 yields an array with four items, omitting `"red"` because the operation began copying from position 1, which contains `"green"`. The resulting `colors2` array contains `"green"`, `"blue"`, `"yellow"`, and `"purple"`. The `colors3` array is constructed by calling `slice()` and passing in 1 and 4, meaning that the method will begin copying from the item in position 1 and stop copying at the item in position 3. As a result, `colors3` contains `"green"`, `"blue"`, and `"yellow"`.

> **NOTE** *If either the start or end position of* `slice()` *is a negative number, then the number is subtracted from the length of the array to determine the appropriate locations. For example, calling* `slice(-2, -1)` *on an array with five items is the same as calling* `slice(3, 4)`. *If the end position is smaller than the start, then an empty array is returned.*

Perhaps the most powerful array method is `splice()`, which can be used in a variety of ways. The main purpose of `splice()` is to insert items into the middle of an array, but there are three distinct ways of using this method. They are as follows:

➤ **Deletion**—Any number of items can be deleted from the array by specifying just two arguments: the position of the first item to delete and the number of items to delete. For example, `splice(0, 2)` deletes the first two items.

➤ **Insertion**—Items can be inserted into a specific position by providing three or more arguments: the starting position, 0 (the number of items to delete), and the item to insert. Optionally, you can specify a fourth parameter, fifth parameter, or any number of other parameters to insert. For example, `splice(2, 0, "red", "green")` inserts the strings `"red"` and `"green"` into the array at position 2.

➤ **Replacement**—Items can be inserted into a specific position while simultaneously deleting items, if you specify three arguments: the starting position, the number of items to delete, and any number of items to insert. The number of items to insert doesn't have to match the number of items to delete. For example, `splice(2, 1, "red", "green")` deletes one item at position 2 and then inserts the strings `"red"` and `"green"` into the array at position 2.

The `splice()` method always returns an array that contains any items that were removed from the array (or an empty array if no items were removed). These three uses are illustrated in the following code:

```
let colors = ["red", "green", "blue"];
let removed = colors.splice(0,1);    // remove the first item
alert(colors);                       // green,blue
alert(removed);                      // red - one item array

// insert two items at position 1
removed = colors.splice(1, 0, "yellow", "orange");
alert(colors);    // green,yellow,orange,blue
alert(removed);   // empty array

// insert two values, remove one
removed = colors.splice(1, 1, "red", "purple");
alert(colors);    // green,red,purple,orange,blue
alert(removed);   // yellow - one item array
```

This example begins with the `colors` array containing three items. When `splice()` is called the first time, it simply removes the first item, leaving `colors` with the items `"green"` and `"blue"`. The second time `splice()` is called, it inserts two items at position 1, resulting in colors containing `"green"`, `"yellow"`, `"orange"`, and `"blue"`. No items are removed at this point, so an empty array is returned. The last time `splice()` is called, it removes one item, beginning in position 1, and inserts `"red"` and `"purple"`. After all of this code has been executed, the colors array contains `"green"`, `"red"`, `"purple"`, `"orange"`, and `"blue"`.

Search and Location Methods

ECMAScript offers two strategies for searching inside an array instance: searching by strict equivalence, and searching with a predicate function.

ECMAScript's strict equivalence lookup methods are `indexOf()`, `lastIndexOf()`, and `includes()`. Each of these methods accepts two arguments: the item to look for and an optional index from which to start looking. The `indexOf()` and `includes()` methods start searching from the front of the array (item 0) and continue to the back, whereas `lastIndexOf()` starts from the last item in the array and continues to the front.

`indexOf()` and `lastIndexOf()` each return the position of the item in the array or –1 if the item isn't in the array. `includes()` returns a Boolean indicating if at least one element in the searched array matched the provided element. An identity comparison is used when comparing the first argument to each item in the array, meaning that the items must be strictly equal as if compared using `===`. Here are some examples of this usage:

```
let numbers = [1, 2, 3, 4, 5, 4, 3, 2, 1];

alert(numbers.indexOf(4));          // 3
alert(numbers.lastIndexOf(4));      // 5
alert(numbers.includes(4));         // true

alert(numbers.indexOf(4, 4));       // 5
alert(numbers.lastIndexOf(4, 4));   // 3
alert(numbers.includes(4, 7));      // false

let person = { name: "Matt" };
```

```
let people = [{ name: "Matt" }];
let morePeople = [person];

alert(people.indexOf(person));        // -1
alert(morePeople.indexOf(person));    // 0
alert(people.includes(person));       // false
alert(morePeople.includes(person));   // true
```

ECMAScript also allows you to define a predicate function that will be invoked at each index. The return value of the function determines if the element at that index is considered a match.

A predicate function takes the form predicate(element, index, array), where element is the current element in the array being examined, index is the index of element inside the array, and array is the array instance. A truthy return value indicates a match.

The two methods that make use of this are find() and findIndex(). Both begin searching at the lowest index in the array; find() returns the first matching element, and findIndex() returns the index of the first matching element. Both methods also accept a second optional argument that allows you to specify the value of this inside the predicate.

```
const people = [
  {
    name: "Matt",
    age: 27
  },
  {
    name: "Matt",
    age: 29
  }
];

alert(people.find((element, index, array) => element.age < 28));
// {name: "Matt", age: 27}

alert(people.findIndex((element, index, array) => element.age < 28));
// 0
```

Neither method will continue searching once a match has been found.

```
const evens = [2, 4, 6];

// Last element of array will never be inspected after match is found
evens.find((element, index, array) => {
  alert(element);
  alert(index);
  alert(array);
  return element === 4;
});
// 2
// 0
// [2, 4, 6]
// 4
// 1
// [2, 4, 6]
```

Iterative Methods

ECMAScript defines five iterative methods for arrays. Each of the methods accepts two arguments: a function to run on each item and an optional scope object in which to run the function (affecting the value of this). The function passed into one of these methods will receive three arguments: the array item value, the position of the item in the array, and the array object itself. Depending on the method, the results of this function's execution may or may not affect the method's return value. The iterative methods are as follows:

- ➤ every()—Runs the given function on every item in the array and returns `true` if the function returns `true` for every item.

- ➤ filter()—Runs the given function on every item in the array and returns an array of all items for which the function returns `true`.

- ➤ forEach()—Runs the given function on every item in the array. This method has no return value.

- ➤ map()—Runs the given function on every item in the array and returns the result of each function call in an array.

- ➤ some()—Runs the given function on every item in the array and returns `true` if the function returns `true` for any one item.

These methods do not change the values contained in the array.

Of these methods, the two most similar are `every()` and `some()`, which both query the array for items matching some criteria. For `every()`, the passed-in function must return `true` for every item in order for the method to return `true`; otherwise, it returns `false`. The `some()` method, on the other hand, returns `true` if at least one of the items causes the passed-in function to return `true`. Here is an example:

```
let numbers = [1, 2, 3, 4, 5, 4, 3, 2, 1];

let everyResult = numbers.every((item, index, array) => item> 2);
alert(everyResult);  // false

let someResult = numbers.some((item, index, array) => item> 2);
alert(someResult);   // true
```

The next method is `filter()`, which uses the given function to determine if an item should be included in the array that it returns. This method is very helpful when querying an array for all items matching some criteria. For example, to return an array of all numbers greater than 2, the following code can be used:

```
let numbers = [1, 2, 3, 4, 5, 4, 3, 2, 1];

let filterResult = numbers.filter((item, index, array) => item> 2);
alert(filterResult);   // [3,4,5,4,3]
```

The `map()` method also returns an array. Each item in the array is the result of running the passed-in function on the original array item in the same location. This method is helpful when creating arrays whose items correspond to one another or when performing work using each element of an array. For example, you can multiply every number in an array by two and are returned an array of those numbers, as shown here:

```
let numbers = [1, 2, 3, 4, 5, 4, 3, 2, 1];

let mapResult = numbers.map((item, index, array) => item * 2);

alert(mapResult);    // [2,4,6,8,10,8,6,4,2]
```

The last method is `forEach()`, which simply runs the given function on every item in an array. There is no return value and it is essentially the same as iterating over an array using a `for` loop. Here's an example:

```
let numbers = [1, 2, 3, 4, 5, 4, 3, 2, 1];

numbers.forEach((item, index, array) => {
  // do something here
});
```

All of these array methods ease the processing of arrays by performing a number of different operations.

Reduction Methods

ECMAScript offers two reduction methods for arrays: `reduce()` and `reduceRight()`. Both methods iterate over all items in the array and build up a value that is ultimately returned. The `reduce()` method does this starting at the first item and traveling toward the last, whereas `reduceRight()` starts at the last and travels toward the first.

Both methods accept two arguments: a function to call on each item and an optional initial value upon which the reduction is based. The function passed into `reduce()` or `reduceRight()` accepts four arguments: the previous value, the current value, the item's index, and the array object. Any value returned from the function is automatically passed in as the first argument for the next item. The first iteration occurs on the second item in the array, so the first argument is the first item in the array and the second argument is the second item in the array.

You can use the `reduce()` method to perform operations such as adding all numbers in an array. Here's an example:

```
let values = [1, 2, 3, 4, 5];
let sum = values.reduce((prev, cur, index, array) => prev + cur, 0);

alert(sum);  // 15
```

The first time the callback function is executed, `prev` is 1 and `cur` is 2. The second time, `prev` is 3 (the result of adding 1 and 2), and `cur` is 3 (the third item in the array). This sequence continues until all items have been visited and the result is returned. 0 is passed as the second argument to define the initial value; otherwise, `reduce()` will error when called on an empty array. Note that, when the array is empty with 0 passed as the second argument, or when the array has only one element without 0 passed as the second argument, the callback in the first argument is not called.

The `reduceRight()` method works in the same way, just in the opposite direction. Consider the following example:

```
let values = [1, 2, 3, 4, 5];
let sum = values.reduceRight(function(prev, cur, index, array){
  return prev + cur;
});
alert(sum); // 15
```

In this version of the code, `prev` is 5 and `cur` is 4 the first time the callback function is executed. The result is the same, of course, because the operation is simple addition.

The decision to use `reduce()` or `reduceRight()` depends solely on the direction in which the items in the array should be visited. They are exactly equal in every other way.

Flattening Methods

The Array prototype has `flat()` and `flatMap()` methods to make array flattening operations much easier. Without these methods, flattening arrays is a nasty business that involves either an iterative or recursive solution.

> **NOTE** `flat()` and `flatMap()` are strictly limited to flattening nested arrays. Nested iterable objects such as Map and Set will not be flattened.

The following is an example of how a simple recursive implementation might look without using these new methods:

```
function flatten(sourceArray, flattenedArray = []) {
  for (const element of sourceArray) {
    if (Array.isArray(element)) {
      flatten(element, flattenedArray);
    } else {
      flattenedArray.push(element);
    }
  }

  return flattenedArray;
}

const arr = [[0], 1, 2, [3, [4, 5]], 6];

console.log(flatten(arr))
// [0, 1, 2, 3, 4, 5, 6]
```

In many ways, this example resembles a tree data structure; each element in an array behaves like a child node, and non-array elements are leaves. Therefore, in this example the input array is a tree of height 2 with 7 leaves. Flattening this array is in essence an in-order traversal of the leaves.

It is sometimes useful to be able to specify how many levels of array nesting should be flattened. Consider the following example, which modifies the initial implementation and allows for the flattening depth to be specified:

```
function flatten(sourceArray, depth, flattenedArray = []) {
  for (const element of sourceArray) {
    if (Array.isArray(element) && depth > 0) {
      flatten(element, depth - 1, flattenedArray);
    } else {
      flattenedArray.push(element);
    }
  }

  return flattenedArray;
}


const arr = [[0], 1, 2, [3, [4, 5]], 6];

console.log(flatten(arr, 1));
// [0, 1, 2, 3, [4, 5], 6]
```

The `Array.prototype.flat()` method accepts a depth argument (defaulting to a depth of 1) and returns a shallow copy of the `Array` instance flattened to the specified depth. This is demonstrated here:

```
const arr = [[0], 1, 2, [3, [4, 5]], 6];

console.log(arr.flat(2));
// [0, 1, 2, 3, 4, 5, 6]

console.log(arr.flat());
// [0, 1, 2, 3, [4, 5], 6]
```

Because a shallow copy is performed, arrays with cycles will copy values from the source array when flattening:

```
const arr = [[0], 1, 2, [3, [4, 5]], 6];

arr.push(arr);

console.log(arr.flat());
// [0, 1, 2, 3, 4, 5, 6, [0], 1, 2, [3, [4, 5]], 6]
```

The `Array.prototype.flatMap()` method allows you to perform a map operation before flattening the array. `arr.flatMap(fn)` is functionally equivalent to `arr.map(fn).flat()`, but `arr.flatMap()` is more efficient since the browser only must perform a single traversal.

The function signature of `flatMap()` is identical to `map()`. A simple example is as follows:

```
const arr = [[1], [3], [5]];

console.log(arr.map(([x]) => [x, x + 1]));
// [[1, 2], [3, 4], [5, 6]]

console.log(arr.flatMap(([x]) => [x, x + 1]));
// [1, 2, 3, 4, 5, 6]
```

`flatMap()` is especially useful in situations where a non-array object's method returns an array, such as `split()`. Consider the following example, where a collection of input strings is split into words and joined into a single word array:

```
const arr = ['Lorem ipsum dolor sit amet,', 'consectetur adipiscing elit.'];

console.log(arr.flatMap((x) => x.split(/[\W+]/)));
// ["Lorem", "ipsum", "dolor", "sit", "amet", "", "consectetur", "adipiscing",
// "elit", ""]
```

A handy trick (albeit one that may incur a performance hit) is to use an empty array to filter out results after a map. The following example extends the preceding example to strip out the empty strings:

```
const arr = ['Lorem ipsum dolor sit amet,', 'consectetur adipiscing elit.'];

console.log(arr.flatMap((x) => x.split(/[\W+]/)).flatMap((x) => x || []));
// ["Lorem", "ipsum", "dolor", "sit", "amet", consectetur", "adipiscing", "elit"]
```

Here, each empty string in the results is first mapped to an empty array. When flattening, these empty arrays are effectively skipped in the array that is eventually returned.

TYPED ARRAYS

The typed array is a construct designed for efficiently passing binary data to native libraries. There is no actual "TypedArray" type in JavaScript—rather, the term refers to a collection of specialized arrays that contain numeric types. To understand how to use the typed array, it is helpful to first understand its intended purpose.

History

As web browsers gained adoption, it was not difficult to foresee that the ability to run complex 3D applications inside of them would be in demand. As early as 2006, browser vendors including Mozilla and Opera began to experiment with a programming platform for rendering graphics-intensive applications inside the browser without requiring any plugins. The goal was to develop a JavaScript API that could make use of a 3D graphics API and GPU acceleration to enable rendering of complex graphics on a `<canvas>` element.

WebGL

The eventual JavaScript API was based on the OpenGL for Embedded Systems (OpenGL ES) 2.0 specification, a subset of OpenGL that specializes in 2D and 3D computer graphics. The new API, named the Web Graphics Library (WebGL), saw its 1.0 release in March 2011. With it, developers were able to write graphics-intensive application code that could natively be interpreted by any WebGL-compliant web browser.

In initial versions of WebGL, a fundamental mismatch between JavaScript arrays and native arrays caused performance issues. The graphics driver APIs often did not want numbers passed to them in JavaScript's default double floating point format. Furthermore, the graphics driver APIs expected arrays of numbers to be passed to them in a binary format, which of course is nothing like the JavaScript array's format in memory. Therefore, each time an array was passed between WebGL and the

JavaScript runtime, the WebGL binding would perform the expensive operation of allocating a new array in the destination environment, iterating over the array in its current format, and casting the number into an appropriate format in the new array.

Emergence of Typed Arrays

This, of course, was untenable, and Mozilla solved this problem by implementing `CanvasFloatArray`, a C-style array of floating point numbers that offered a JavaScript interface. Using this type allowed the JavaScript runtime to allocate, read, and write an array that could be passed directly to and from the graphics driver API. The `CanvasFloatArray` would eventually be reshaped into the `Float32Array`, which was the first "type" available for typed arrays as they currently exist.

Using ArrayBuffers

`Float32Array` is actually one type of "view" that allows the JavaScript runtime to access a block of allocated memory called an `ArrayBuffer`. The `ArrayBuffer` is the fundamental unit referred to by all typed arrays and views.

> **NOTE** *The* `TypedArrayBuffer` *is a variant of the* `ArrayBuffer` *that can be passed between execution contexts without performing a copy. Refer to Chapter 24, "Workers," for coverage of this type.*

`ArrayBuffer` is a normal JavaScript constructor that can be used to allocate a specific number of bytes in memory.

```
const buf = new ArrayBuffer(16);   // Allocates 16 bytes of memory
alert(buf.byteLength);             // 16
```

An `ArrayBuffer` can never be resized once it is created. However, you are able to copy all or part of an existing `ArrayBuffer` into a new instance using `slice()`:

```
const buf1 = new ArrayBuffer(16);
const buf2 = buf1.slice(4, 12);
alert(buf2.byteLength);   // 8
```

`ArrayBuffer` is in some ways similar to the C++ `malloc()`, with several notable exceptions:

➤ When `malloc()` fails to allocate, it returns a `null` pointer. If `ArrayBuffer` allocation fails, it throws an error.

➤ A `malloc()` call can take advantage of virtual memory, so the maximum size of the allocation is only bounded by the addressable system memory. `ArrayBuffer` allocation cannot exceed `Number.MAX_SAFE_INTEGER` ($2 \wedge 53$) bytes.

➤ A successful `malloc()` invocation performs no initialization of the actual addresses. Declaring an `ArrayBuffer` initializes all the bits to 0s.

➤ Heap memory allocated by `malloc()` cannot be used by the system until `free()` is invoked or the program exits. Heap memory allocated by declaring an `ArrayBuffer` is still garbage collected—no manual memory management is required.

The contents of an `ArrayBuffer` cannot be read or written with only a reference to the buffer instance. To read or write data inside, you must do so with a view. There are different types of views, but they all refer to binary data stored in an `ArrayBuffer`.

DataViews

The first type of view that allows you to read and write an `ArrayBuffer` is the `DataView`. This view is designed for file I/O and network I/O; the API allows for a high degree of control when manipulating buffer data, but it offers reduced performance compared to different view types as a result. A `DataView` does not assume anything about the buffer contents and is not iterable.

A `DataView` must be created to read from and write to an `ArrayBuffer` that already exists. It can use the whole buffer or only part of it, and it maintains a reference to the buffer instance and where in the buffer the view begins.

```
const buf = new ArrayBuffer(16);

// DataView default to use the entire ArrayBuffer
const fullDataView = new DataView(buf);
alert(fullDataView.byteOffset);        // 0
alert(fullDataView.byteLength);        // 16
alert(fullDataView.buffer === buf);  // true

// Constructor takes an optional byte offset and byte length
//    byteOffset=0 begins the view at the start of the buffer
//    byteLength=8 restricts the view to the first 8 bytes
const firstHalfDataView = new DataView(buf, 0, 8);
alert(firstHalfDataView.byteOffset);        // 0
alert(firstHalfDataView.byteLength);        // 8
alert(firstHalfDataView.buffer === buf);  // true

// DataView will use the remainder of the buffer unless specified
//    byteOffset=8 begins the view at the 9th byte of the buffer
//    byteLength default is the remainder of the buffer
const secondHalfDataView = new DataView(buf, 8);
alert(secondHalfDataView.byteOffset);        // 8
alert(secondHalfDataView.byteLength);        // 8
alert(secondHalfDataView.buffer === buf);  // true
```

To read from and write to the buffer through a `DataView`, you will require the use of several components:

➤   The byte offset at which you wish to read or write. This can be thought of as a sort of "address" within the `DataView`.

➤   Which `ElementType` the `DataView` should use for conversion between the `Number` type in the JavaScript runtime and the binary format in the buffer.

➤   The endianness of the value in memory. Defaults to big-endian.

ElementType

The `DataView` makes no assumptions about what data type is stored inside the buffer. The API it exposes forces you to specify an `ElementType` when reading or writing, and the `DataView` will dutifully perform the conversion to execute that read or write.

ECMAScript supports 10 different `ElementType` values:

ELEMENTTYPE	BYTES	DESCRIPTION	C EQUIVALENTS	RANGE OF VALUES
Int8	1	8-bit signed integer	➤ signed char ➤ int8_t	-2^7 to 2^7-1
Uint8	1	8-bit unsigned integer	➤ unsigned char ➤ uint8_t	0 to 2^8-1
Int16	2	16-bit signed integer	➤ short ➤ int16_t	-2^{15} to $2^{15}-1$
Uint16	2	16-bit unsigned integer	➤ unsigned short ➤ uint16_t	0 to $2^{16}-1$
Int32	4	32-bit signed integer	➤ int ➤ int32_t	-2^{31} to $2^{31}-1$
Uint32	4	32-bit unsigned integer	➤ unsigned int ➤ uint32_t	0 to $2^{32}-1$
Float32	4	32-bit IEEE-754 floating point	➤ float	$-3.4E+38$ to $+3.4E+38$
Float64	8	64-bit IEEE-754 floating point	➤ double	$-1.7E+308$ to $+1.7E+308$
BigInt64	8	64-bit signed integer	➤ signed long long ➤ int64_t	-2^{63} to $2^{63}-1$
BigUint64	8	64-bit unsigned integer	➤ unsigned long long ➤ uint64_t	0 to $2^{64}-1$

The `DataView` exposes get and set methods for each of these types, which use a `byteOffset` to address into the buffer for reading and writing values. Types can be used interchangeably, as demonstrated here:

```
// Allocate two bytes of memory and declare a DataView
const buf = new ArrayBuffer(2);
```

```
const view = new DataView(buf);

// Demonstrate that the entire buffer is indeed all zeroes
// Check the first and second byte
alert(view.getInt8(0));    // 0
alert(view.getInt8(1));    // 0
// Check the entire buffer
alert(view.getInt16(0));   // 0

// Set the entire buffer to ones
// 255 in binary is 11111111 (2^8 - 1)
view.setUint8(0, 255);
// DataView will automatically cast values to the designated ElementType
// 255 in hex is 0xFF
view.setUint8(1, 0xFF);

// The buffer is now all ones, which when read as a
// two's complement signed integer should be -1
alert(view.getInt16(0));   // -1
```

Big-Endian and Little-Endian

The buffer's bytes in the previous example were intentionally symmetrical to avoid the issue of endianness. "Endianness" refers to the convention of byte ordering maintained by a computing system. For the purposes of DataViews, there are only two conventions supported: *big-endian* and *little-endian*. Big-endian, also referred to as "network byte order," means that the most significant byte is held in the first byte, and the least significant byte is held in the last byte. Little-endian means the least significant byte is held in the first byte, and the most significant byte is held in the last byte.

The native endianness of the system executing the JavaScript runtime will determine how it reads and writes bytes, but a DataView does not obey this convention. A DataView is an unbiased interface to a segment of memory and will follow whatever endianness you specify. All DataView API methods default to the big-endian convention but accept an optional final Boolean argument that allows you to enable the little-endian convention by setting it to true.

```
// Allocate two bytes of memory and declare a DataView
const buf = new ArrayBuffer(2);
const view = new DataView(buf);

// Fill the buffer so that the first bit and last bit are 1
view.setUint8(0, 0x80);   // Sets leftmost bit to 1
view.setUint8(1, 0x01);   // Sets rightmost bit to 1

// Buffer contents (spaced for readability):
// 0x8   0x0   0x0   0x1
// 1000  0000  0000  0001

// Read a big-endian Uint16
// 0x80 is the high byte, 0x01 is the low byte
// 0x8001 = 2^15 + 2^0 = 32768 + 1 = 32769
alert(view.getUint16(0));   // 32769

// Read a little-endian Uint16
// 0x01 is the high byte, 0x80 is the low byte
// 0x0180 = 2^8 + 2^7 = 256 + 128 = 384
```

```
alert(view.getUint16(0, true));  // 384

// Write a big-endian Uint16
view.setUint16(0, 0x0004);

// Buffer contents (spaced for readability):
// 0x0  0x0  0x0  0x4
// 0000 0000 0000 0100

alert(view.getUint8(0));  // 0
alert(view.getUint8(1));  // 4

// Write a little-endian Uint16
view.setUint16(0, 0x0002, true);

// Buffer contents (spaced for readability):
// 0x0  0x2  0x0  0x0
// 0000 0010 0000 0000

alert(view.getUint8(0));  // 2
alert(view.getUint8(1));  // 0
```

Corner Cases

A `DataView` will only complete a read or write if there is sufficient buffer space to do so; otherwise it throws a `RangeError`:

```
const buf = new ArrayBuffer(6);
const view = new DataView(buf);

// Attempt to get a value that partially extends past end of buffer
view.getInt32(4);
// RangeError

// Attempt to get a value past the end of the buffer
view.getInt32(8);
// RangeError

// Attempt to get a value past the end of the buffer
view.getInt32(-1);
// RangeError

// Attempt to set a value that extends past end of buffer
view.setInt32(4, 123);
// RangeError
```

A `DataView` will make a best effort to cast a value into the appropriate type when writing to a buffer, falling back to 0. If it cannot, it will throw an error:

```
const buf = new ArrayBuffer(1);
const view = new DataView(buf);

view.setInt8(0, 1.5);
```

```
alert(view.getInt8(0));  // 1

view.setInt8(0, [4]);
alert(view.getInt8(0));  // 4

view.setInt8(0, 'f');
alert(view.getInt8(0));  // 0

view.setInt8(0, Symbol());
// TypeError
```

Typed Arrays

Typed arrays are another form of an `ArrayBuffer` view. Though it is similar in concept to a `DataView`, a typed array is distinguished in that it enforces a single `ElementType` and obeys the system's native endianness. In exchange, it offers a much broader API and better performance. Typed arrays are designed for efficiently exchanging binary data with native libraries like WebGL. Because the binary representation of typed arrays is in an easily digestible format for the native operating system, JavaScript engines are able to heavily optimize arithmetic, bitwise, and other common operations on typed arrays, and as a result they are extremely fast to use.

Typed arrays can be created to read from an existing buffer, initialized with their own buffer, filled with an iterable, or filled from an existing typed array of any type. They can also be created using `<ElementType>.from()` and `<ElementType>.of()`:

```
// Creates a buffer of 12 bytes
const buf = new ArrayBuffer(12);
// Creates an Int32Array that references this buffer
const ints = new Int32Array(buf);
// The typed array recognizes it needs 4 bytes per element,
// and therefore will have a length of 3
alert(ints.length);  // 3

// Creates an Int32Array of length 6
const ints2 = new Int32Array(6);
// Each number uses 4 bytes, so the ArrayBuffer is 24 bytes
alert(ints2.length);             // 6
// Like DataView, typed arrays have a reference to their associated buffer
alert(ints2.buffer.byteLength);  // 24

// Creates an Int32Array containing [2, 4, 6, 8]
const ints3 = new Int32Array([2, 4, 6, 8]);
alert(ints3.length);             // 4
alert(ints3.buffer.byteLength);  // 16
alert(ints3[2]);                 // 6

// Creates an Int16Array with values copies from ints3
const ints4 = new Int16Array(ints3);
// The new typed array allocates its own buffer, and each value
// is converted to its new representation at the same index
alert(ints4.length);             // 4
alert(ints4.buffer.byteLength);  // 8
```

```
alert(ints4[2]);                    // 6

// Creates an Int16Array from a normal array
const ints5 = Int16Array.from([3, 5, 7, 9]);
alert(ints5.length);                // 4
alert(ints5.buffer.byteLength);     // 8
alert(ints5[2]);                    // 7

// Creates a Float32Array from arguments
const floats = Float32Array.of(3.14, 2.718, 1.618);
alert(floats.length);               // 3
alert(floats.buffer.byteLength);    // 12
alert(floats[2]);                   // 1.6180000305175781
```

Both the constructor and instances expose a BYTES_PER_ELEMENT property that returns the size of each element in that type of array:

```
alert(Int16Array.BYTES_PER_ELEMENT);   // 2
alert(Int32Array.BYTES_PER_ELEMENT);   // 4

const ints = new Int32Array(1),
      floats = new Float64Array(1);

alert(ints.BYTES_PER_ELEMENT);         // 4
alert(floats.BYTES_PER_ELEMENT);       // 8
```

Unless a typed array is initialized with values, its associated buffer is filled with zeroes:

```
const ints = new Int32Array(4);
alert(ints[0]);  // 0
alert(ints[1]);  // 0
alert(ints[2]);  // 0
alert(ints[3]);  // 0
```

Typed Array Behavior

In most ways, typed arrays behave like their regular array counterparts would. Typed arrays support nearly all of the Array operators, methods, and properties. Methods that return a new array will return a new typed array with the same element type:

```
const ints = new Int16Array([1, 2, 3]);
const doubleints = ints.map(x => 2*x);
alert(doubleints instanceof Int16Array);   // true
```

Typed arrays have a Symbol.iterator defined, meaning that for-of loops and spread operators can also be used:

```
const ints = new Int16Array([1, 2, 3]);
for (const int of ints) {
  alert(int);
}
// 1
// 2
// 3

alert(Math.max(...ints));  // 3
```

Merging, Copying, and Changing Typed Arrays

Typed arrays still use array buffers as their storage, and array buffers cannot be resized. Therefore, the following methods are not supported by typed arrays:

➤ concat()

➤ pop()

➤ push()

➤ shift()

➤ splice()

➤ unshift()

However, typed arrays do offer two new methods that allow you to copy values in and out of arrays quickly: set() and subarray().

set() copies the values from a provided array or typed array into the current typed array at the specified index:

```
// Create an int16 array of length 8
const container = new Int16Array(8);

// Copy in typed array into first four values
// Offset default to an index of 0
container.set(Int8Array.of(1, 2, 3, 4));
alert(container);  // [1,2,3,4,0,0,0,0]
// Copy in normal array into last four values
// Offset of 4 means begin inserting at the index 4
container.set([5,6,7,8], 4);
alert(container);  // [1,2,3,4,5,6,7,8]

// An overflow will throw an error
container.set([5,6,7,8], 7);
// RangeError
```

subarray() performs the opposite operation of set(), returning a new typed array with values copied out of the original. Providing the start and end indices is optional:

```
const source = Int16Array.of(2, 4, 6, 8);

// Copies the entire array into a new array of the same type
const fullCopy = source.subarray();
alert(fullCopy);  // [2, 4, 6, 8]

// Copy the array from index 2 on
const halfCopy = source.subarray(2);
alert(halfCopy);  // [6, 8]

// Copy the array from index 1 up until 3
const partialCopy = source.subarray(1, 3);
alert(partialCopy);  // [4, 6]
```

Typed arrays don't have a native ability to concatenate, but ample tools are available in the typed array API that one can be constructed manually:

```
// First argument is the type of array that should be returned
// Remaining arguments are all the typed arrays that should be concatenated
function typedArrayConcat(typedArrayConstructor, ...typedArrays) {
  // Count the total elements in all arrays
  const numElements = typedArrays.reduce((x,y) => (x.length || x) + y.length);

  // Create an array of the provided type with space for all elements
  const resultArray = new typedArrayConstructor(numElements);

  // Perform the successive array transfer
  let currentOffset = 0;
  typedArrays.map(x => {
    resultArray.set(x, currentOffset);
    currentOffset += x.length;
  });

  return resultArray;
}

const concatArray =  typedArrayConcat(Int32Array,
                                      Int8Array.of(1, 2, 3),
                                      Int16Array.of(4, 5, 6),
                                      Float32Array.of(7, 8, 9));
alert(concatArray);  // [1, 2, 3, 4, 5, 6, 7, 8, 9]
alert(concatArray instanceof Int32Array);  // true
```

Underflow and Overflow

Overflow and underflow of values in typed arrays will not spill over into other indices, but you still must take into account what element type the array considers its entries. Typed arrays will accept only the relevant bits that each index in the array can hold, irrespective of the effect it will have on the actual numerical value. The following demonstrates how underflow and overflow are handled:

```
// Signed ints array of length 2
// Each index holds a 2's complement signed integer which can
// range from -128 (-1 * 2^7) to 127 (2^7 - 1)
const ints = new Int8Array(2);

// Unsigned ints array of length 2
// Each index holds an unsigned integer which can range from
// 0 to 255 (2^7 - 1)
const unsignedInts = new Uint8Array(2);

// Overflow bits will not spill into adjacent indices.
// The index only takes the least significant 8 bits
unsignedInts[1] = 256;     // 0x100
alert(unsignedInts);       // [0, 0]
unsignedInts[1] = 511;     // 0x1FF
```

```
alert(unsignedInts);      // [0, 255]

// Underflow bits will be converted to their unsigned equivalent.
// 0xFF is -1 as a 2's complement int (truncated to 8 bits),
// but is 255 as an unsigned int
unsignedInts[1] = -1  // 0xFF (truncated to 8 bits)
alert(unsignedInts);   // [0, 255]

// Overflow in 2's complement occurs transparently.
// 0x80 is 128 in unsigned int but -128 in 2's complement int
ints[1] = 128;    // 0x80
alert(ints);      // [0, -128]

// Underflow in 2's complement occurs transparently.
// 0xFF is 255 in unsigned int but -1 in 2's complement int
ints[1] = 255;    // 0xFF
alert(ints);      // [0, -1]
```

In addition to the element types, there is also an additional "clamped" array type, Uint8ClampedArray, which prevents overflow in either direction. Values above its maximum value of 255 will be rounded down to 255, and values below 0 will be rounded up to 0.

```
const clampedInts = new Uint8ClampedArray([-1, 0, 255, 256]);
alert(clampedInts);  // [0, 0, 255, 255]
```

According to Brendan Eich, "Uint8ClampedArray is totally a historical artifact of the HTML5 canvas element. Avoid unless you really are doing canvas-y things."

THE MAP TYPE

The ECMAScript Map is a collection reference type that introduces true key-value behavior into the language. Much of what it offers is an overlap with what is provided by the Object type, but there are subtle differences between the Object and Map types that should be taken into account when selecting one for use.

Basic API

An empty Map is instantiated with the new keyword:

```
const m = new Map();
```

If you wish to populate the Map when it is initialized, the constructor optionally accepts an iterable object, expecting it to contain key-value pair arrays. Each pair in the iterable argument will be inserted into the newly created Map in the order in which they are iterated:

```
// Initialize map with nested arrays
const m1 = new Map([
  ["key1", "val1"],
  ["key2", "val2"],
  ["key3", "val3"]
]);
```

```
alert(m1.size);  // 3

// Initialize map with custom-defined iterator
const m2 = new Map({
  [Symbol.iterator]: function*() {
    yield ["key1", "val1"];
    yield ["key2", "val2"];
    yield ["key3", "val3"];
  }
});
alert(m2.size);  // 3

// Map expects values to be key-value whether they are provided or not
const m3 = new Map([[]]);
alert(m3.has(undefined));  // true
alert(m3.get(undefined));  // undefined
```

Key-value pairs can be added after initialization with `set()`, queried with `get()` and `has()`, counted with the `size` property, and removed with `delete()` and `clear()`:

```
const m = new Map();

alert(m.has("firstName"));   // false
alert(m.get("firstName "));  // undefined
alert(m.size);               // 0

m.set("firstName", "Matt")
 .set("lastName", "Frisbie");

alert(m.has("firstName"));  // true
alert(m.get("firstName"));  // Matt
alert(m.size);              // 2

m.delete("firstName");  // deletes only this key-value pair

alert(m.has("firstName"));  // false
alert(m.has("lastName"));   // true
alert(m.size);              // 1

m.clear();  // destroys all key-value pairs in this Map instance

alert(m.has("firstName"));  // false
alert(m.has("lastName"));   // false
alert(m.size);              // 0
```

The `set()` method returns the Map instance, so it is possible to chain multiple set operations together, including on the initial declaration:

```
const m = new Map().set("key1", "val1");

m.set("key2", "val2")
 .set("key3", "val3");

alert(m.size);  // 3
```

Unlike an `Object`, which can only use numbers, strings, or symbols as keys, a `Map` can use any JavaScript data type as a key. It uses the *SameValueZero* comparison operation (defined inside the ECMAScript specification and not available in the actual language) and is mostly comparable to using strict object equivalence to check for a key match. As with `Object`, there is no restriction on what is contained in the value.

```
Const m = new Map();

const functionKey = function() {};
const symbolKey = Symbol();
const objectKey = new Object();

m.set(functionKey, "functionValue");
m.set(symbolKey, "symbolValue");
m.set(objectKey, "objectValue");

alert(m.get(functionKey));  // functionValue
alert(m.get(symbolKey));    // symbolValue
alert(m.get(objectKey));    // objectValue

// SameValueZero checks mean separate instances will not collide
alert(m.get(function() {}));  // undefined
```

As with strict equivalence, objects and other "collection" types used for keys and values remain unchanged inside a `Map` when their contents or properties are altered:

```
const m = new Map();

const objKey = {},
      objVal = {},
      arrKey = [],
      arrVal = [];

m.set(objKey, objVal);
m.set(arrKey, arrVal);

objKey.foo = "foo";
objVal.bar = "bar";
arrKey.push("foo");
arrVal.push("bar");

alert(m.get(objKey));  // {bar: "bar"}
alert(m.get(arrKey));  // ["bar"]
```

The use of the *SameValueZero* operation may introduce unexpected collisions:

```
const m = new Map();

const a = 0/"",  // NaN
      b = 0/"",  // NaN
      pz = +0,
      nz = -0;

alert(a === b);    // false
```

```
alert(pz === nz);   // true

m.set(a, "foo");
m.set(pz, "bar");

alert(m.get(b));    // foo
alert(m.get(nz));   // bar
```

> **NOTE** *There is an excellent writeup on* SameValueZero *and other ECMAScript equality conventions on the Mozilla documentation site:* `https://developer` `.mozilla.org/en-US/docs/Web/JavaScript/Equality_comparisons_and_` `sameness.`

Order and Iteration

One major departure from the `Object` type's conventions is that `Map` instances maintain the order of key-value insertion and allow you to perform iterative operations following insertion order.

A `Map` instance can provide an Iterator that contains array pairs in the form of `[key, value]` in insertion order. This iterator can be retrieved using `entries()`, or the `Symbol.iterator` property, which references `entries()`:

```
const m = new Map([
  ["key1", "val1"],
  ["key2", "val2"],
  ["key3", "val3"]
]);

alert(m.entries === m[Symbol.iterator]);   // true

for (let pair of m.entries()) {
  alert(pair);
}
// [key1,val1]
// [key2,val2]
// [key3,val3]

for (let pair of m[Symbol.iterator]()) {
  alert(pair);
}
// [key1,val1]
// [key2,val2]
// [key3,val3]
```

Because `entries()` is the default iterator, the spread operator can be used to concisely convert a `Map` into an array:

```
const m = new Map([
  ["key1", "val1"],
  ["key2", "val2"],
  ["key3", "val3"]
]);

alert([...m]); // [[key1,val1],[key2,val2],[key3,val3]]
```

To use a callback convention instead of an iterator, `forEach(callback, opt_thisArg)` invokes the callback for each key-value pair. It optionally accepts a second argument, which will override the value of this inside each callback invocation.

```
Const m = new Map([
    ["key1", "val1"],
    ["key2", "val2"],
    ["key3", "val3"]
]);

m.forEach((val, key) => alert(`${key} -> ${val}`));
// key1 -> val1
// key2 -> val2
// key3 -> val3
```

`keys()` and `values()` return an iterator that contains all keys or all values in the Map in insertion order:

```
const m = new Map([
    ["key1", "val1"],
    ["key2", "val2"],
    ["key3", "val3"]
]);

for (let key of m.keys()) {
    alert(key);
}
// key1
// key2
// key3

for (let key of m.values()) {
    alert(key);
}
// value1
// value2
// value3
```

Keys and values exposed inside an iterator are mutable, but the references inside the Map cannot be altered. However, this does not restrict changing properties inside a key or value object. Doing so will not alter their identity with respect to the Map instance:

```
const m1 = new Map([
    ["key1", "val1"]
]);

// String primitive as key is unaltered
for (let key of m.keys()) {
    key = "newKey";
    alert(key);              // newKey
    alert(m.get("key1"));    // val1
```

```
  }

  const keyObj = {id: 1};

  const m = new Map([
    [keyObj, "val1"]
  ]);

  // Key object property is altered, but the object still refers
  // to the same value inside the map
  for (let key of m.keys()) {
    key.id = "newKey";
    alert(key);             // {id: "newKey"}
    alert(m.get(keyObj));   // val1
  }
  alert(keyObj);            // {id: "newKey"}
```

Choosing Between Objects and Maps

There are some important differences between objects and maps that may influence when one is chosen over the other.

Keys

The Object type can only use integers, strings, or symbols as keys. A Map may use any type as the key.

Memory Profile

The engine-level implementation of Object and Map will obviously differ between browsers, but the amount of memory required to store a single key-value pair scales linearly with the number of keys. Bulk addition or removal of key-value pairs is also governed by how the engine implements memory allocation for that type. Results may vary by browser, but given a fixed amount of memory, a Map will be able to store roughly 50 percent more key-value pairs than an Object.

Insertion Performance

Inserting a new key-value pair into an Object versus a Map is a roughly comparable operation, but insertion into a Map will generally be slightly faster across all browser engines. For both types, the speed of an insertion does not scale linearly with the number of key-value pairs in the Object or Map. If your code is heavy on insert operations, Map instances offer superior performance.

Lookup Performance

Unlike insertion, looking up a key-value pair in an Object versus a Map is a roughly comparable operation at scale, but a smaller number of key-value pairs favor Object instances in some situations. In situations where an Object instance is being used like an array (for example, consecutive integer properties), the browser engine can perform optimizations such as more efficient layout in memory—this is never possible with a Map. For both types, lookup speed does not scale linearly with the number of key-value pairs in an Object or Map. If your code is heavy on lookup operations, in some scenarios it may be more advantageous to use an Object.

Delete Performance

The performance of the delete operation on Object properties is notorious for being horrendous, and this is still very much the case in many browser engines. Workarounds for pseudo-deleting object properties include assigning undefined or null as the property value, but in many cases this is an obnoxious or unsuitable compromise. Across most browser engines, the Map delete() operation is faster than insert and lookup. If your code is heavy on delete operations, the Map type is the overwhelming favorite.

THE SET TYPE

Set is a collection reference type that introduces set behavior into the language. A Set in many ways behaves more like an augmented Map, as much of the API and behavior is shared.

Basic API

An empty Set is instantiated with the new keyword:

```
const m = new Set();
```

If you wish to populate the map when it is initialized, the constructor optionally accepts an iterable object containing elements to be added into the newly created Set instance.

```
// Initialize set with array
const s1 = new Set(["val1", "val2", "val3"]);
alert(s1.size);  // 3

// Initialize set with custom-defined iterator
const s2 = new Set({
  [Symbol.iterator]: function*() {
    yield "val1";
    yield "val2";
    yield "val3";
  }
});
alert(s2.size);  // 3
```

Values can be added after initialization with add(), queried with has(), counted with the size property, and removed with delete() and clear():

```
const s = new Set();

alert(s.has("Matt"));     // false
alert(s.size);            // 0

s.add("Matt")
 .add("Frisbie");

alert(s.has("Matt"));     // true
```

```
alert(s.size);                // 2

s.delete("Matt");

alert(s.has("Matt"));     // false
alert(s.has("Frisbie"));  // true
alert(s.size);            // 1

s.clear();  // destroys all values in this Set instance

alert(s.has("Matt"));     // false
alert(s.has("Frisbie"));  // false
alert(s.size);            // 0
```

The add() method returns the Set instance, so it is possible to chain multiple operations together, including on the initial declaration:

```
const s = new Set().add("val1");

s.set("val2")
 .set("val3");

alert(s.size);  // 3
```

Like Map, a Set can contain any JavaScript data type as a value. It uses the *SameValueZero* comparison operation (defined inside the ECMAScript specification and not available in the actual language) and is mostly comparable to using strict object equivalence to check for a key match. There is no restriction on what is contained in the value.

```
Const s = new Set();

const functionVal = function() {};
const symbolVal = Symbol();
const objectVal = new Object();

s.add(functionVal);
s.add(symbolVal);
s.add(objectVal);

alert(s.has(functionVal));    // true
alert(s.has(symbolVal));      // true
alert(s.has(objectVal));      // true

// SameValueZero checks mean separate instances will not collide
alert(s.has(function() {}));  // false
```

As with strict equivalence, objects and other "collection" types used for values remain unchanged inside a set when their contents or properties are altered:

```
const s = new Set();

const objVal = {},
      arrVal = [];

s.add(objVal)
```

```
    .add(arrVal);

objVal.bar = "bar";
arrVal.push("bar");

alert(s.has(objVal));   // true
alert(s.has(arrVal));   // true
```

The add() and delete() operations are idempotent. Delete() returns a Boolean indicating if that value was present in the set.

```
Const s = new Set();

s.add('foo');
alert(s.size);   // 1
s.add('foo');
alert(s.size);   // 1

// Value was present in the set
alert(s.delete('foo'));   // true

// Value was not present in the set
alert(s.delete('foo'));   // false
```

Order and Iteration

Sets maintain the order of value insertion and allow you to perform iterative operations following insertion order.

A Set instance can provide an iterator that contains the set contents in insertion order. This iterator can be retrieved using values(), its alias keys(), or the Symbol.iterator property, which references values():

```
const s = new Set(["val1", "val2", "val3"]);

alert(s.values === s[Symbol.iterator]);   // true
alert(s.keys === s[Symbol.iterator]);     // true

for (let value of s.values()) {
  alert(value);
}
// val1
// val2
// val3

for (let value of s[Symbol.iterator]()) {
  alert(value);
}
// val1
// val2
// val3
```

Because values() is the default iterator, the spread operator can be used to concisely convert a set into an array:

```
const s = new Set(["val1", "val2", "val3"]);

alert([...s]); // [val1,val2,val3]
```

`entries()` returns an iterator that contains a two-element array containing a duplicate of all values in the `Set` in insertion order:

```
const s = new Set(["val1", "val2", "val3"]);

for (let pair of s.entries()) {
  alert(pair);
}
// [val1,val1]
// [val2,val2]
// [val3,val3]
```

To use a callback convention instead of an iterator, `forEach(callback, opt_thisArg)` invokes the callback for each value. It optionally accepts a second argument, which will override the value of `this` inside each callback invocation.

```
Const s = new Set(["val1", "val2", "val3"]);

s.forEach((val, dupVal) => alert(`${val} -> ${dupVal}`));
// val1 -> val1
// val2 -> val2
// val3 -> val3
```

Changing properties of values in a `Set` does not alter the value's identity with respect to the `Set` instance:

```
const s1 = new Set(["val1"]);

// String primitive as value is unaltered
for (let value of s1.values()) {
  value = "newVal";
  alert(value);           // newVal
  alert(s1.has("val1"));  // true
}

const valObj = {id: 1};

const s2 = new Set([valObj]);

// Value object property is altered, but the object still exists
// inside the set
for (let value of s2.values()) {
  value.id = "newVal";
  alert(value);           // {id: "newVal"}
  alert(s2.has(valObj));  // true
}
alert(valObj);            // {id: "newVal"}
```

WEAK REFERENCES

JavaScript is a garbage-collected language, which means that it automatically manages the allocation and deallocation of memory for objects. When an object is no longer being used, the garbage collector frees up the memory it was using so it can be used for other purposes. However, in some cases, we might want to keep a reference to an object without preventing it from being garbage collected. This kind of reference is called a *weak reference*. A weak reference is a type of reference that does not prevent an object from being garbage collected. This means that if the only reference to an object is a weak reference, the garbage collector will free up the memory used by the object.

WeakRef

In JavaScript, objects can be weakly referenced with the `WeakRef` class. Its constructor takes a single argument, the target object that should be weakly referenced:

```
let obj = { name: "Matt" };
let weakRef = new WeakRef(obj);
```

This target cannot be changed after instantiation. To access the target that is being weakly referenced, use its `deref()` method. This method returns the target or returns `undefined` if the target has been garbage collected. The following example demonstrates what you would see before and after garbage collection takes place:

```
let obj = { name: "Matt" };
let weakRef = new WeakRef(obj);

console.log(weakRef.deref());  // { name: "Matt" }
obj = null;

// Eventually, the browser will garbage collect the target object

// After GC occurs:
console.log(weakRef.deref());  undefined
```

> **NOTE** *If you run the preceding code, it is unlikely that you will see your browser garbage collect the target object. Browsers wait as long as possible to perform garbage collection (GC), and the developer console can actively prevent GC from happening.*

FinalizationRegistry

Sometimes, you might want to perform some cleanup or finalization when an object is about to be garbage collected. This is where the `FinalizationRegistry` object comes in. The `FinalizationRegistry` allows us to define a callback function that will be called just before an object is garbage collected. Objects can be added and removed to the registry with `register()` and `unregister()`.

To register an object, the `register()` method is passed the target object and a *held value* that will be passed to the handler when GC is about to occur. Here's an example:

```
let obj = { name: "Matt" };
let finalizationRegistry = new FinalizationRegistry((heldValue) => {
  console.log(`Cleaning up object: ${heldValue}`);
```

```
  });

  finalizationRegistry.register(obj, "My held value");

  obj = null;

  // After GC:
  // "Cleaning up object: My held value"
```

To unregister an object, call `unregister()` and pass it the registered object:

```
  let obj = { name: "Matt" };
  let finalizationRegistry = new FinalizationRegistry((heldValue) => {
    console.log(`Cleaning up object: ${heldValue}`);
  });

  finalizationRegistry.register(obj, "My held value");

  obj = null;

  finalizationRegistry.unregister(obj);

  // After GC:
  //   <no output>
```

`FinalizationRegistry` is a feature that requires careful consideration and should be avoided if possible. Some things to consider:

➤ The behavior of garbage collection in JavaScript is not guaranteed and may vary depending on the engine and version used.

➤ The use of cleanup callbacks is not recommended for essential program logic because the timing and occurrence of their execution are dependent on the JavaScript engine's implementation.

➤ It is likely that major implementations will execute cleanup callbacks at some point during program execution, but they may occur substantially after the related object was reclaimed.

➤ Certain situations, such as shutting down a program entirely, may prevent the execution of cleanup callbacks altogether.

THE WEAKMAP TYPE

The `WeakMap` is a collection reference type that introduces augmented key-value behavior into the language. The `WeakMap` type is a cousin to the `Map` type, and its API is a strict subset of `Map`. The "weak" designation describes how JavaScript's garbage collector treats keys in a `WeakMap`.

Basic API

An empty `WeakMap` is instantiated with the `new` keyword:

```
  const wm = new WeakMap();
```

Keys in a `WeakMap` can only be of type `Object` or inherit from `Object`—all other attempts to set a key with a non-object will throw a `TypeError`. There are no restrictions on the type of the value.

If you wish to populate the WeakMap when it is initialized, the constructor optionally accepts an iterable object, expecting it to contain valid key-value pair arrays. Each pair in the iterable argument will be inserted into the newly created WeakMap in the order in which they are iterated:

```
const key1 = {id: 1},
      key2 = {id: 2},
      key3 = {id: 3};
// Initialize WeakMap with nested arrays
const wm1 = new WeakMap([
  [key1, "val1"],
  [key2, "val2"],
  [key3, "val3"]
]);
alert(wm.get(key1));  // val2
alert(wm.get(key2));  // val2
alert(wm.get(key3));  // val3

// Initialization is all-or-nothing, a single bad key will
// throw an error and abort the initialization
const wm2 = new WeakMap([
  [key1, "val1"],
  ["BADKEY", "val2"],
  [key3, "val3"]
]);
// TypeError: Invalid value used as WeakMap key
typeof wm2;
// ReferenceError: wm2 is not defined

// Primitives can still be used with an object wrapper
const stringKey = new String("key1");
const wm3 = new WeakMap([
  stringKey, "val1"
]);
alert(wm3.get(stringKey));  // "val1"
```

Key-value pairs can be added after initialization with set(), queried with get() and has(), and removed with delete():

```
const wm = new WeakMap();

const key1 = {id: 1},
      key2 = {id: 2};

alert(wm.has(key1));  // false
alert(wm.get(key1));  // undefined

wm.set(key1, "Matt")
  .set(key2, "Frisbie");

alert(wm.has(key1));  // true
alert(wm.get(key1));  // Matt

wm.delete(key1);  // deletes only this key-value pair

alert(wm.has(key1));  // false
alert(wm.has(key2));  // true
```

The set() method returns the WeakMap instance, so it is possible to chain multiple set operations together, including on the initial declaration:

```
const key1 = {id: 1},
      key2 = {id: 2},
      key3 = {id: 3};

const wm = new WeakMap().set(key1, "val1");

wm.set(key2, "val2")
  .set(key3, "val3");

alert(wm.get(key1));   // val1
alert(wm.get(key2));   // val2
alert(wm.get(key3));   // val3
```

Weak Keys

The "weak" designation stems from the fact that keys in a WeakMap are "weakly held," meaning they are not counted as formal references that would otherwise prevent garbage collection. An important distinction for the WeakMap is that the value reference is *not* weakly held. As long as the key exists, the key-value pair will remain in the map and count as a reference to the value—thereby preventing it from being garbage collected.

Consider the following example:

```
const wm = new WeakMap();

wm.set({}, "val");
```

Inside set(), a fresh object is initialized and used as a key to a dummy string. Because there are no other references to this object, as soon as this line is finished executing, the object key will be free for garbage collection. When this occurs, the key-value pair will disappear from the WeakMap, and it will be empty. In this example, because there are no other references to the value, this key-value destruction will also mean that the value is eligible for garbage collection.

Consider a slightly different example:

```
const wm = new WeakMap();

const container = {
  key: {}
};

wm.set(container.key, "val");

function removeReference(){
  container.key = null;
}
```

Here, the container object maintains a reference to the key in the WeakMap, so the object is ineligible for garbage collection. However, as soon as removeReference() is invoked, the last strong reference to the key object will be destroyed, and garbage collection will eventually wipe out the key-value pair.

Non-Iterable Keys

Because key-value pairs in a WeakMap can be destroyed at any time, it does not make sense to offer the ability to iterate through the key-value pairs. This also excludes the ability to destroy all key-value pairs at once using clear(), which is not part of the WeakMap API. Because iteration is not possible, it is also not possible to retrieve a value from a WeakMap instance unless you have a reference to the key object. Even if code has access to the WeakMap instance, there is no way to inspect its contents.

The reason that WeakMap instances restrict keys to only objects is to preserve the convention that values can only be retrieved from a WeakMap with a reference to the key object. If primitives were allowed, the WeakMap instance would have no way of differentiating between the string primitive that was initially used to set the key-value pair and an identical string primitive that was initialized later—an undesirable behavior.

Utility

Because WeakMap instances do not interfere with garbage collection, they are a terrific tool for cleanup-free metadata association. Consider the following example, which uses a regular Map:

```
const m = new Map();

const loginButton = document.querySelector('#login');

// Associates some metadata with the node
m.set(loginButton, {disabled: true});
```

Suppose after this code executes, the page is changed by JavaScript and the login button is removed from the DOM tree. Because a reference exists inside the Map, the DOM node will linger in memory in perpetuity until explicitly removed from the Map, or until the Map is destroyed.

If, instead, a WeakMap was used, as shown in the following code, the node's removal from the DOM would allow the garbage collector to free the allocated memory immediately (assuming no other lingering references to the object).

```
const wm = new WeakMap();

const loginButton = document.querySelector('#login');

// Associates some metadata with the node
wm.set(loginButton, {disabled: true});
```

THE WEAKSET TYPE

WeakSet is a collection reference type that introduces set behavior into the language. The WeakSet type is a cousin to the Set type, and its API is a strict subset of Set. The "weak" designation describes how JavaScript's garbage collector treats values in a weak map.

Basic API

An empty `WeakSet` instance is instantiated with the `new` keyword:

```
const ws = new WeakSet();
```

Values in a `WeakSet` can only be of type or inherit from `Object`—all other attempts to set a value with a non-object will throw a `TypeError`.

If you wish to populate the `WeakSet` when it is initialized, the constructor optionally accepts an iterable object, expecting it to contain valid values. Each value in the iterable argument will be inserted into the newly created `WeakSet` in the order in which they are iterated:

```
const val1 = {id: 1},
      val2 = {id: 2},
      val3 = {id: 3};
// Initialize WeakSet with nested arrays
const ws1 = new WeakSet([val1, val2, val3]);

alert(ws1.has(val1));   // true
alert(ws1.has(val2));   // true
alert(ws1.has(val3));   // true

// Initialization is all-or-nothing, a single bad value will
// throw an error and abort the initialization
const ws2 = new WeakSet([val1, "BADVAL", val3]);
// TypeError: Invalid value used in WeakSet
typeof ws2;
// ReferenceError: ws2 is not defined

// Primitives can still be used with an object wrapper
const stringVal = new String("val1");
const ws3 = new WeakSet([stringVal]);
alert(ws3.has(stringVal));   // true
```

Values can be added after initialization with `add()`, queried with `has()`, and removed with `delete()`:

```
const ws = new WeakSet();

const val1 = {id: 1},
      val2 = {id: 2};

alert(ws.has(val1));   // false

ws.add(val1)
  .add(val2);

alert(ws.has(val1));   // true
alert(ws.has(val2));   // true

ws.delete(val1);   // deletes only this value

alert(ws.has(val1));   // false
alert(ws.has(val2));   // true
```

The `add()` method returns the `WeakSet` instance, so it is possible to chain multiple add operations together, including on the initial declaration:

```
const val1 = {id: 1},
      val2 = {id: 2},
      val3 = {id: 3};

const ws = new WeakSet().add(val1);

ws.add(val2)
  .add(val3);

alert(ws.has(val1));  // true
alert(ws.has(val2));  // true
alert(ws.has(val3));  // true
```

Weak Keys

The "weak" designation stems from the fact that values in a `WeakSet` are "weakly held," meaning they are not counted as formal references, which would otherwise prevent garbage collection.

Consider the following example:

```
const ws = new WeakSet();

ws.add({});
```

Inside `add()`, a fresh object is initialized and used as a value. Because there are no other references to this object, as soon as this line is finished executing, the object value will be free for garbage collection. When this occurs, the value will disappear from the `WeakSet`, and it will be empty.

Consider a slightly different example:

```
const ws = new WeakSet();

const container = {
  val: {}
};

ws.add(container.val);

function removeReference(){
  container.val = null;
}
```

Here, the container object maintains a reference to the value in the `WeakSet` instance, so the object is ineligible for garbage collection. However, as soon as `removeReference()` is invoked, the last strong reference to the value object will be destroyed, and garbage collection will eventually wipe out the value.

Non-Iterable Values

Because values in a `WeakSet` can be destroyed at any time, it does not make sense to offer the ability to iterate through the values. This also excludes the ability to destroy all values at once using `clear()`, which is not part of the `WeakSet` API. Because iteration is not possible, it is also not possible to retrieve a value from a `WeakSet` instance unless you have a reference to the value object. Even if code has access to the `WeakSet` instance, there is no way to inspect its contents.

`WeakSet` instances restrict keys to only objects in order to preserve the convention that values can only be retrieved from a `WeakSet` with a reference to the value object. If primitives were allowed, the `WeakSet` would have no way of differentiating between the string primitive that was initially used to set the value and an identical string primitive that was initialized later—an undesirable behavior.

Utility

Like `WeakMap`, `WeakSet` is useful when you wish to track an object without preventing its garbage collection. Consider the following example, which uses a regular `Set`:

```
const disabledElements = new Set();

const loginButton = document.querySelector('#login');

// Tags the node as "disabled" by adding it to the corresponding set
disabledElements.add(loginButton);
```

Here, it is possible to check if an element is disabled by seeing if it exists inside `disabledElements`, which can be done in constant time. However, if the element is removed from the DOM, its presence inside this Set will prevent garbage collection from reallocating its memory.

To allow the garbage collection to reallocate the element's memory a `WeakSet` can instead be used:

```
const disabledElements = new WeakSet();

const loginButton = document.querySelector('#login');

// Tags the node as "disabled" by adding it to the corresponding set
disabledElements.add(loginButton);
```

Now, when any element in the `WeakSet` is removed from the DOM, the garbage collector will ignore its presence inside the `WeakSet` when considering it for garbage collection.

ITERATION AND SPREAD OPERATORS

Iterators and the spread operator are especially useful in the context of collection reference types. These new tools allow for easy interoperability, cloning, and modification of collection reference types.

> **NOTE** *Chapter 7, "Iterators and Generators," offers more coverage on exactly how iterators work.*

As shown earlier in the chapter, `Array`, `Map`, `Set`, and all typed arrays define a default iterator. This means that all support ordered iteration and can be passed to a `for-of` loop:

```
let iterableThings = [
  Array.of(1, 2),
  typedArr = Int16Array.of(3, 4),
  new Map([[5, 6], [7, 8]]),
  new Set([9, 10])
];


for (const iterableThing of iterableThings) {
  for (const x of iterableThing) {
    console.log(x);
  }
}

// 1
// 2
// 3
// 4
// [5, 6]
// [7, 8]
// 9
// 10
```

This also means that all these types are compatible with the spread operator. The spread operator is especially useful as it performs a shallow copy on the iterable object. This allows you to easily clone entire objects with a succinct syntax:

```
let arr1 = [1, 2, 3];
let arr2 = [...arr1];

console.log(arr1);         // [1, 2, 3]
console.log(arr2);         // [1, 2, 3]
console.log(arr1 === arr2); // false
```

Constructors which expect an iterable object can just be passed the iterable instance to be cloned:

```
let map1 = new Map([[1, 2], [3, 4]]);
let map2 = new Map(map1);

console.log(map1);  // Map {1 => 2, 3 => 4}
console.log(map2);  // Map {1 => 2, 3 => 4}
```

It also allows for partial array construction:

```
let arr1 = [1, 2, 3];
let arr2 = [0, ...arr1, 4, 5];

console.log(arr2);  // [0, 1, 2, 3, 4, 5]
```

The shallow copy mechanism means that only object references are copied:

```
let arr1 = [{}];
```

```
let arr2 = [...arr1];

arr1[0].foo = â€˜barâ€™;
console.log(arr2[0]);  // { foo: â€˜barâ€™ }
```

Each of these collection reference types support multiple methods of construction, such as the `Array` `.of()` and `Array.from()` static methods. When combined with the spread operator, this makes for extremely easy interoperability:

```
let arr1 = [1, 2, 3];

// Copy array into typed array
let typedArr1 = Int16Array.of(...arr1);
let typedArr2 = Int16Array.from(arr1);
console.log(typedArr1);  // Int16Array [1, 2, 3]
console.log(typedArr2);  // Int16Array [1, 2, 3]

// Copy array into map
let map = new Map(arr1.map((x) => [x, â€˜valâ€™ + x]));
console.log(map);  // Map {1 => â€˜val 1â€™, 2 => â€˜val 2â€™, 3 => â€˜val 3â€™}

// Copy array in to set
let set = new Set(typedArr2);
console.log(set);  // Set {1, 2, 3}

// Copy set back into array
let arr2 = [...set];
console.log(arr2);  // [1, 2, 3]
```

SUMMARY

JavaScript supports a range of advanced reference types that allow for handling collections of data and managing object references. Objects are unordered collections of key-value pairs, where the keys are strings or symbols and the values can be any data type. Objects have many built-in methods that allow developers to manipulate and iterate over an object's properties.

Arrays are ordered collections of values, which can be of any data type. Arrays have many built-in methods that allow developers to add, remove, and manipulate array elements.

Typed arrays are collections of values of a specific type, such as `Int32Array` or `Float64Array`. These are useful for working with binary data and performant numeric operations.

JavaScript allows for weak references to objects. Weak references do not prevent the garbage collector from reclaiming the referenced object, making them useful for tracking objects that are no longer needed by the program. These features are important for memory management and can help prevent memory leaks in large and complex applications.

`WeakRef` provides a way to create a weak reference to an object, while `FinalizationRegistry` allows for cleanup code to be executed when the object is no longer needed. `WeakSet` and `WeakMap` are collections that only allow weak references to their elements, which can be useful for managing object relationships that should not prevent garbage collection.

7

Iterators and Generators

The term "iteration" is derived from the Latin *itero*, meaning "repeat" or "do again." In the context of software, "iteration" means repetitively performing a procedure multiple times, in sequence, and usually with an expectation of termination. The ECMAScript specification introduces two high-level features—iterators and generators—to allow for cleaner, faster, and easier iteration.

INTRODUCTION TO ITERATION

In JavaScript, one of the simplest examples of iteration is a counting loop:

```
for (let i = 1; i <= 10; ++i) {
  console.log(i);
}
```

Loops are a fundamental iterative tool because they allow you to specify how many iterations should occur and what should occur during each iteration. Each loop iteration will finish execution before another begins, and the order in which each iteration occurs is well-defined.

Iteration can occur over ordered collections of items. (Consider "ordered" in this context to imply there is an accepted sequence in which all the items should be traversed, with a definitive beginning and end item.) In JavaScript, the most common example of this ordered collection is an array.

```
let collection = ['foo', 'bar', 'baz'];

for (let index = 0; index < collection.length; ++index) {
  console.log(collection[index]);
}
```

Because an array has a known length, and because each item in that array can be retrieved via its index, the entire array can be traversed in order by incrementing the range of possible indices.

The fundamental procedure occurring in such a loop is not ideal for several reasons:

➤ **Iterating through the data structure requires a specific knowledge of how to use the data structure.** Each item in the array can only be retrieved by first referencing the array object and then retrieving an item at a specific index using the `[]` operator. This does not generalize to other data structures.

➤ **The order of traversal is not inherent to the data structure.** Incrementing an integer to access sequential indices is specific to the array type and does not generalize to other data structures that have an implicit ordering.

ES5 introduced the `Array.prototype.forEach` method, which is closer to what is needed (but still not an ideal solution):

```
let collection = ['foo', 'bar', 'baz'];

collection.forEach((item) => console.log(item));
// foo
// bar
// baz
```

This solves the problem of separately tracking an index and retrieving items via the array object. However, there is no way to terminate this iteration, the method is limited to arrays, and the callback structure is unwieldy.

With earlier versions of ECMAScript, performing iteration required the use of loops or other auxiliary constructs, which is an increasingly messy affair as code complexity scales. Many languages have addressed this problem with a native language construct that allows iteration to be performed without specific knowledge of how the iteration was actually occurring, and the solution is the *iterator pattern*. Python, Java, C++, and many other languages offer first-class support for this pattern.

THE ITERATOR PATTERN

The *iterator pattern* (specifically in the context of ECMAScript) describes a solution in which something can be described as "iterable" and can implement a formal Iterable interface and is consumed by an iterator.

The concept of an "iterable" is intentionally abstract. Frequently, the iterable will take the form of a collection object like an array or set, both of which have a finite number of countable elements and feature an unambiguous order of traversal:

```
// Arrays have finite countable elements
// In-order traversal visits each index in increasing index order
let arr = [3, 1, 4];

// Sets have finite countable elements
// In-order traversal visits each value in insertion order
let set = new Set().add(3).add(1).add(4);
```

However, an iterable does not have to be linked to a collection object. It can also be linked to something that only behaves like an array—such as the counting loop from earlier in the chapter. The values generated in this loop are transient, and yet such a loop is performing iteration. Both this counting loop and an array can behave as an iterable.

> **NOTE** *Transient iterables can be implemented as* generators, *which are covered later in the chapter.*

Anything that implements the Iterable interface can be "consumed" by an object that implements the Iterator interface. An iterator is a separate object created on demand and intended for a single use. Each iterator is associated with an iterable, and the iterator exposes an API to iterate through the associated iterable a single time. The iterator doesn't need to understand the structure of the iterable it is associated with; it only must know how to retrieve sequential values. This separation of concerns is what makes the Iterable/Iterator convention so useful.

The Iterable Protocol

Implementing the Iterable interface requires both the capability to self-identify as supporting iteration and the capability to create an object that implements the Iterator interface. In ECMAScript, this means it must expose a property, the "default iterator," keyed with the special `Symbol.iterator` key. This default iterator property must refer to an iterator factory function, which will produce a new iterator when invoked.

Many built-in types implement the Iterable interface:

➤ Strings

➤ Arrays

➤ Maps

➤ Sets

➤ The arguments object

➤ Some DOM collection types like NodeList

Checking for the existence of this default iterator property will expose the factory function:

```
let num = 1;
let obj = {};

// These types do not have iterator factories
console.log(num[Symbol.iterator]);  // undefined
console.log(obj[Symbol.iterator]);  // undefined

let str = 'abc';
let arr = ['a', 'b', 'c'];
let map = new Map().set('a', 1).set('b', 2).set('c', 3);
let set = new Set().add('a').add('b').add('c');
let els = document.querySelectorAll('div');

// These types all have iterator factories
console.log(str[Symbol.iterator]);  // f values() { [native code] }
console.log(arr[Symbol.iterator]);  // f values() { [native code] }
console.log(map[Symbol.iterator]);  // f values() { [native code] }
console.log(set[Symbol.iterator]);  // f values() { [native code] }
console.log(els[Symbol.iterator]);  // f values() { [native code] }

// Invoking the factory function produces an Iterator
console.log(str[Symbol.iterator]());  // StringIterator {}
console.log(arr[Symbol.iterator]());  // ArrayIterator {}
console.log(map[Symbol.iterator]());  // MapIterator {}
console.log(set[Symbol.iterator]());  // SetIterator {}
console.log(els[Symbol.iterator]());  // ArrayIterator {}
```

You do not necessarily need to explicitly invoke this factory function to produce an iterator. Anything that implements this protocol is automatically compatible with any language features that accept an iterable. These native language constructs include:

➤ for...of loop

➤ Array destructuring

➤ The spread operator

➤ Array.from()

➤ Set construction

➤ Map construction

➤ Promise.all(), which expects an iterable of promises

➤ Promise.race(), which expects an iterable of promises

➤ The yield* operator, used in generators

Behind the scenes, these native language constructs are invoking the factory function of the provided iterable to create an iterator:

```
let arr = ['foo', 'bar', 'baz'];

// for...of loops
for (let el of arr) {
  console.log(el);
}
// foo
// bar
// baz

// Array destructuring
let [a, b, c] = arr;
console.log(a, b, c);  // foo, bar, baz

// Spread operator
let arr2 = [...arr];
console.log(arr2);  // ['foo', 'bar', 'baz']

// Array.from()
let arr3 = Array.from(arr);
console.log(arr3);  // ['foo', 'bar', 'baz']

// Set constructor
let set = new Set(arr);
console.log(set);  // Set(3) {'foo', 'bar', 'baz'}

// Map constructor
let pairs = arr.map((x, i) => [x, i]);
console.log(pairs);  // [['foo', 0], ['bar', 1], ['baz', 2]]
let map = new Map(pairs);
console.log(map);  // Map(3) { 'foo'=>0, 'bar'=>1, 'baz'=>2 }
```

An object still implements the Iterable interface if a parent class up the prototype chain implements the interface:

```
class FooArray extends Array {}
let fooArr = new FooArray('foo', 'bar', 'baz');

for (let el of fooArr) {
  console.log(el);
}
// foo
// bar
// baz
```

The Iterator Protocol

An iterator is a single-use object that will iterate through whatever iterable it is associated with. The Iterator API uses a `next()` method to advance through the iterable. Each successive time `next()` is invoked, it will return an IteratorResult object containing the next value in the iterator. The current position the iterator is at cannot be known without invoking the `next()` method.

The next() method returns an object with two properties: done, which is a Boolean indicating if next() can be invoked again to retrieve more values, and value, which will contain the next value in the iterable or undefined if done is true. The done:true state is termed "exhaustion." This can be demonstrated with a simple array:

```
// Iterable object
let arr = ['foo', 'bar'];

// Iterator factory
console.log(arr[Symbol.iterator]);  // f values() { [native code] }

// Iterator
let iter = arr[Symbol.iterator]();
console.log(iter);  // ArrayIterator {}

// Performing iteration
console.log(iter.next());  // { done: false, value: 'foo' }
console.log(iter.next());  // { done: false, value: 'bar' }
console.log(iter.next());  // { done: true, value: undefined }
```

Arrays are iterated in order by creating an iterator and invoking next() until it ceases to produce new values. Note how the iterator does not know how to retrieve the next values inside the iterable, nor does it know how large the iterable is. Once the iterator reaches the done:true state, invoking next() is idempotent:

```
let arr = ['foo'];
let iter = arr[Symbol.iterator]();
console.log(iter.next());  // { done: false, value: 'foo' }
console.log(iter.next());  // { done: true, value: undefined }
console.log(iter.next());  // { done: true, value: undefined }
console.log(iter.next());  // { done: true, value: undefined }
```

Each iterator represents a one-time ordered traversal of the iterable. Different instances are not aware of each other and will independently traverse the iterable:

```
let arr = ['foo', 'bar'];
let iter1 = arr[Symbol.iterator]();
let iter2 = arr[Symbol.iterator]();

console.log(iter1.next());  // { done: false, value: 'foo' }
console.log(iter2.next());  // { done: false, value: 'foo' }
console.log(iter2.next());  // { done: false, value: 'bar' }
console.log(iter1.next());  // { done: false, value: 'bar' }
```

An iterator is not bound to a snapshot of the iterable; it merely uses a cursor to track its progress through the iterable. If the iterable is mutated during iteration, the iterator will incorporate the changes:

```
let arr = ['foo', 'baz'];
let iter = arr[Symbol.iterator]();

console.log(iter.next());  // { done: false, value: 'foo' }

// Insert value in the middle of array
```

```
arr.splice(1, 0, 'bar');

console.log(iter.next());  // { done: false, value: 'bar' }
console.log(iter.next());  // { done: false, value: 'baz' }
console.log(iter.next());  // { done: true, value: undefined }
```

> **NOTE** *An iterator maintains a reference to the iterable object, so be aware that the iterator's existence will prevent garbage collection of the iterable object.*

The term "iterator" can be somewhat nebulous because it refers to a generalized iteration concept, an interface, and formal iterator-type classes. The following example compares an explicit iterator implementation and a native iterator implementation:

```
// This class implements the Iterable interface.
// Invoking the default iterator factory will return
// an iterator object that implements the Iterator interface.
class Foo {
  [Symbol.iterator]() {
    return {
      next() {
        return { done: false, value: 'foo' };
      }
    }
  }
}
let f = new Foo();

// Logs an object which implements the Iterator interface
console.log(f[Symbol.iterator]());  // { next: f() {} }


// The Array type implements the Iterable interface.
// Invoking the default iterator of an Array type
// will create an instance of ArrayIterator.
let a = new Array();

// Logs an instance of ArrayIterator
console.log(a[Symbol.iterator]());  // Array Iterator {}
```

Custom Iterator Definition

Like the Iterable interface, any object that implements the Iterator interface can be used as an iterator. Consider the following example where a Counter class is defined to iterate a specific number of times:

```
class Counter {
  // Counter instance should iterate <limit> times
  constructor(limit) {
    this.count = 1;
    this.limit = limit;
```

```
    }

    next() {
      if (this.count <= this.limit) {
        return { done: false, value: this.count++ };
      } else {
        return { done: true, value: undefined };
      }
    }

    [Symbol.iterator]() {
      return this;
    }
  }

  let counter = new Counter(3);

  for (let i of counter) {
    console.log(i);
  }
  // 1
  // 2
  // 3
```

This satisfies the Iterator interface, but this implementation isn't optimal because each class instance can be iterated only once:

```
  for (let i of counter) { console.log(i); }
  // 1
  // 2
  // 3

  for (let i of counter) { console.log(i); }
  // (nothing logged)
```

In order to allow for creating multiple iterators from a single iterable, the counter must be created on a per-iterator basis. To address this, you can return an iterator object with the counter variables available through a closure:

```
  class Counter {
    constructor(limit) {
      this.limit = limit;
    }

    [Symbol.iterator]() {
      let count = 1,
          limit = this.limit;
      return {
        next() {
          if (count <= limit) {
            return { done: false, value: count++ };
          } else {
            return { done: true, value: undefined };
          }
        }
      };
    }
```

```
    }

    let counter = new Counter(3);

    for (let i of counter) { console.log(i); }
    // 1
    // 2
    // 3
    for (let i of counter) { console.log(i); }
    // 1
    // 2
    // 3
```

Every iterator created in this way also implements the Iterable interface. The `Symbol.iterator` property refers to a factory that will return the same iterator:

```
    let arr = ['foo', 'bar', 'baz'];
    let iter1 = arr[Symbol.iterator]();

    console.log(iter1[Symbol.iterator]);  // f values() { [native code] }

    let iter2 = iter1[Symbol.iterator]();

    console.log(iter1 === iter2);         // true
```

Because every iterator also implements the Iterable interface, they can be used everywhere an iterable is expected, such as a `for...of` loop:

```
    let arr = [3, 1, 4];
    let iter = arr[Symbol.iterator]();

    for (let item of arr) { console.log(item); }
    // 3
    // 1
    // 4

    for (let item of iter) { console.log(item); }
    // 3
    // 1
    // 4
```

Early Termination of Iterators

The optional `return()` method allows for specifying behavior that will execute only if the iterator is closed prematurely. "Closing" an iterator occurs when the construct performing the iteration wishes to indicate to the iterator that it does not intend to finish traversing until exhaustion. Scenarios where this might happen include the following:

➤   A `for...of` loop exits early via `break`, `continue`, `return`, or `throw`.

➤   A destructuring operation does not consume all values.

The `return()` method must return a valid IteratorResult object. A simple iterator implementation should just return `{ done: true }`, as the return value is only used in the context of generators, which is discussed later in the chapter.

As shown in the code that follows, a built-in language construct will automatically invoke the return() method once it identifies that there are further values that need to be iterated over that will not be consumed.

```
class Counter {
  constructor(limit) {
    this.limit = limit;
  }

  [Symbol.iterator]() {
    let count = 1,
        limit = this.limit;
    return {
      next() {
        if (count <= limit) {
          return { done: false, value: count++ };
        } else {
          return { done: true };
        }
      },
      return() {
        console.log('Exiting early');
        return { done: true };
      }
    };
  }
}

let counter1 = new Counter(5);

for (let i of counter1) {
  if (i > 2) {
    break;
  }
  console.log(i);
}
// 1
// 2
// Exiting early


let counter2 = new Counter(5);

try {
  for (let i of counter2 {
    if (i > 2) {
      throw 'err';
    }
    console.log(i);
  }
} catch(e) {}
// 1
// 2
```

```
// Exiting early


let counter3 = new Counter(5);

let [a, b] = counter3;
// Exiting early
```

If an iterator is not closed, then you are able to pick up iteration where you left off. For example, Array Iterators are not closable:

```
let a = [1, 2, 3, 4, 5];
let iter = a[Symbol.iterator]();

for (let i of iter) {
  console.log(i);
  if (i > 2) {
    break
  }
}
// 1
// 2
// 3

for (let i of iter) {
  console.log(i);
}
// 4
// 5
```

Because the `return()` method is optional, not all iterators are closable. Whether or not an iterator is closable can be ascertained by testing if the return property on the iterator instance is a function object. However, merely adding the method to a non-closable iterator will *not* make it become closable, as invoking `return()` does not force the iterator into a closed state. The `return()` method will, however, still be invoked.

GENERATORS

Generators are a delightfully flexible construct that offers the ability to pause and resume code execution inside a single function block. The implications of this ability are profound; it allows for, among many other things, the ability to define custom iterators and implement coroutines.

Generator Basics

Generators take the form of a function, and the generator designation is performed with an asterisk. Anywhere a function definition is valid, a generator function definition is also valid:

```
// Generator function declaration
function* generatorFn() {}

// Generator function expression
```

```
let generatorFn = function* () {}

// Object literal method generator function
let foo = {
  * generatorFn() {}
}

// Class instance method generator function
class Foo {
  * generatorFn() {}
}

// Class static method generator function
class Bar {
  static * generatorFn() {}
}
```

> **NOTE** *Arrow functions cannot be used as generator functions.*

The function will be considered a generator irrespective of the whitespace surrounding the asterisk:

```
// Equivalent generator functions:
function* generatorFnA() {}
function *generatorFnB() {}
function * generatorFnC() {}

// Equivalent generator methods:
class Foo {
  *generatorFnD() {}
  * generatorFnE() {}
}
```

When invoked, generator functions produce a generator object. Generator objects begin in a state of suspended execution. Like iterators, these generator objects implement the Iterator interface and therefore feature a next() method, which, when invoked, instructs the generator to begin or resume execution.

```
function* generatorFn() {}

const g = generatorFn();

console.log(g);        // generatorFn {<suspended>}
console.log(g.next);   // f next() { [native code] }
```

The return value of this next() method matches that of an iterator, with a done and value property. A generator function with an empty function body will act as a passthrough; invoking next() a single time will result in the generator reaching the done:true state.

```
function* generatorFn() {}

let generatorObject = generatorFn();

console.log(generatorObject);          // generatorFn {<suspended>}
console.log(generatorObject.next());   // { done: true, value: undefined }
```

The `value` property is the return value of the generator function, which defaults to `undefined` and can be specified via the generator function's return value.

```
function* generatorFn() {
  return 'foo';
}

let generatorObject = generatorFn();

console.log(generatorObject);         // generatorFn {<suspended>}
console.log(generatorObject.next());  // { done: true, value: 'foo' }
```

Generator function execution will only begin upon the initial `next()` invocation, as shown here:

```
function* generatorFn() {
  console.log('foobar');
}

// Nothing is logged yet when the generator function is initially invoked
let generatorObject = generatorFn();

generatorObject.next();  // foobar
```

Generator objects implement the Iterable interface, and their default iterator is self-referential:

```
function* generatorFn() {}

console.log(generatorFn);
// f* generatorFn() {}
console.log(generatorFn()[Symbol.iterator]);
// f [Symbol.iterator]() {native code}

console.log(generatorFn());
// generatorFn {<suspended>}
console.log(generatorFn()[Symbol.iterator]());
// generatorFn {<suspended}

const g = generatorFn();

console.log(g === g[Symbol.iterator]());
// true
```

Interrupting Execution with *yield*

The `yield` keyword allows generators to stop and start execution, and it is what makes generators truly useful. Generator functions will proceed with normal execution until they encounter a `yield` keyword. Upon encountering the keyword, execution will be halted and the scope state of the function will be preserved. Execution will only resume when the `next()` method is invoked on the generator object:

```
function* generatorFn() {
  yield;
}

let generatorObject = generatorFn();

console.log(generatorObject.next());  // { done: false, value: undefined }
console.log(generatorObject.next());  // { done: true, value: undefined }
```

The `yield` keyword behaves as an intermediate function return, and the yielded value is available inside the object returned by the `next()` method. A generator function exiting via the `yield` keyword will have a `done` value of `false`; a generator function exiting via the `return` keyword will have a `done` value of `true`:

```
function* generatorFn() {
  yield 'foo';
  yield 'bar';
  return 'baz';
}

let generatorObject = generatorFn();

console.log(generatorObject.next());  // { done: false, value: 'foo' }
console.log(generatorObject.next());  // { done: false, value: 'bar' }
console.log(generatorObject.next());  // { done: true, value: 'baz' }
```

Execution progress within a generator function is scoped to each generator object instance. Invoking `next()` on one generator object does not affect any other:

```
function* generatorFn() {
  yield 'foo';
  yield 'bar';
  return 'baz';
}

let generatorObject1 = generatorFn();
let generatorObject2 = generatorFn();


console.log(generatorObject1.next());  // { done: false, value: 'foo' }
console.log(generatorObject2.next());  // { done: false, value: 'foo' }
console.log(generatorObject2.next());  // { done: false, value: 'bar' }
console.log(generatorObject1.next());  // { done: false, value: 'bar' }
```

The `yield` keyword can only be used inside a generator function; anywhere else will throw an error. Like the function `return` keyword, the `yield` keyword must appear immediately inside a generator function definition. Nesting further inside a non-generator function will throw a syntax error:

```
// valid
function* validGeneratorFn() {
  yield;
}

// invalid
function* invalidGeneratorFnA() {
  function a() {
    yield;
  }
}

// invalid
function* invalidGeneratorFnB() {
  const b = () => {
    yield;
  }
```

```
  }

  // invalid
  function* invalidGeneratorFnC() {
    (() => {
      yield;
    })();
  }
```

Using a Generator Object as an Iterable

You will infrequently find the need to explicitly invoke `next()` on a generator object. Instead, generators are much more useful when consumed as an iterable, as shown here:

```
function* generatorFn() {
  yield 1;
  yield 2;
  yield 3;
}

for (const x of generatorFn()) {
  console.log(x);
}
// 1
// 2
// 3
```

This can be especially useful when the need to define custom iterables arises. For example, it is often useful to define an iterable, which will produce an iterator that executes a specific number of times. With a generator, this can be accomplished simply with a loop:

```
function* nTimes(n) {
  while(n--) {
    yield;
  }
}

for (let _ of nTimes(3)) {
  console.log('foo');
}
// foo
// foo
// foo
```

The single generator function parameter controls the number of loop iterations. When n reaches 0, the `while` condition will become falsy, the loop will exit, and the generator function will return.

Using *yield* for Input and Output

The `yield` keyword also behaves as an intermediate function parameter. The `yield` keyword where the generator last paused execution will assume the first value passed to `next()`. Somewhat confusingly, the value provided to the first `next()` invocation is not used, as this `next()` is used to begin the generator function execution:

```
function* generatorFn(initial) {
  console.log(initial);
  console.log(yield);
  console.log(yield);
```

```
  }
  let generatorObject = generatorFn('foo');

  generatorObject.next('bar');   // foo
  generatorObject.next('baz');   // baz
  generatorObject.next('qux');   // qux
```

The `yield` keyword can be simultaneously used as both an input and an output, as is shown in the following example:

```
  function* generatorFn() {
    return yield 'foo';
  }

  let generatorObject = generatorFn();

  console.log(generatorObject.next());        // { done: false, value: 'foo' }
  console.log(generatorObject.next('bar'));   // { done: true, value: 'bar' }
```

Because the function must evaluate the entire expression to determine the value to return, it will pause execution when encountering the `yield` keyword and evaluate the value to yield, `foo`. The subsequent `next()` invocation provides the `bar` value as the value for that same `yield`, and this in turn is evaluated as the generator function return value.

The `yield` keyword is not limited to a one-time use. An infinite counting generator function can be defined as follows:

```
  function* generatorFn() {
    for (let i = 0;;++i) {
      yield i;
    }
  }

  let generatorObject = generatorFn();

  console.log(generatorObject.next().value);   // 0
  console.log(generatorObject.next().value);   // 1
  console.log(generatorObject.next().value);   // 2
  console.log(generatorObject.next().value);   // 3
  console.log(generatorObject.next().value);   // 4
  console.log(generatorObject.next().value);   // 5
  ...
```

Suppose you wanted to define a generator function that would iterate a configurable number of times and produce the index of iteration. This can be accomplished by instantiating a new array, but the same behavior can be accomplished without the array:

```
  function* nTimes(n) {
    for (let i = 0; i < n; ++i) {
      yield i;
    }
  }

  for (let x of nTimes(3)) {
    console.log(x);
  }
  // 0
  // 1
  // 2
```

Alternately, the following has a slightly less verbose `while` loop implementation:

```
function* nTimes(n) {
  let i = 0;
  while(n--) {
    yield i++;
  }
}

for (let x of nTimes(3)) {
  console.log(x);
}
// 0
// 1
// 2
```

Using generators in this way provides a useful way of implementing ranges or populating arrays:

```
function* range(start, end) {
  while(end> start) {
    yield start++;
  }
}

for (const x of range(4, 7)) {
  console.log(x);
}
// 4
// 5
// 6

function* zeroes(n) {
  while(n--) {
    yield 0;
  }
}

console.log(Array.from(zeroes(8)));  // [0, 0, 0, 0, 0, 0, 0, 0]
```

Yielding an Iterable

It is possible to augment the behavior of `yield` to cause it to iterate through an iterable and yield its contents one at a time. This can be done using an asterisk, as shown here:

```
// generatorFn is equivalent to:
// function* generatorFn() {
//    for (const x of [1, 2, 3]) {
//      yield x;
//    }
// }
function* generatorFn() {
  yield* [1, 2, 3];
}

let generatorObject = generatorFn();

for (const x of generatorFn()) {
```

```
    console.log(x);
}
// 1
// 2
// 3
```

Like the generator function asterisk, whitespace around the yield asterisk will not alter its behavior:

```
function* generatorFn() {
  yield* [1, 2];
  yield *[3, 4];
  yield * [5, 6];
}

for (const x of generatorFn()) {
  console.log(x);
}
// 1
// 2
// 3
// 4
// 5
// 6
```

Because yield* is effectively just serializing an iterable into sequential yielded values, using it isn't any different than placing yield inside a loop. These two generator functions are equivalent in behavior:

```
function* generatorFnA() {
  for (const x of [1, 2, 3]) {
    yield x;
  }
}

for (const x of generatorFnA()) {
  console.log(x);
}
// 1
// 2
// 3

function* generatorFnB() {
  yield* [1, 2, 3];
}

for (const x of generatorFnB()) {
  console.log(x);
}
// 1
// 2
// 3
```

The value of yield* is the value property accompanying done:true of the associated iterator. For vanilla iterators, this value will be undefined:

```
function* generatorFn() {
  console.log('iter value:', yield* [1, 2, 3]);
}

for (const x of generatorFn()) {
  console.log('value:', x);
}
// value: 1
// value: 2
// value: 3
// iter value: undefined
```

For iterators produced from a generator function, this value will take the form of whatever value is returned from the generator function:

```
function* innerGeneratorFn() {
  yield 'foo';
  return 'bar';
}
function* outerGeneratorFn(genObj) {
  console.log('iter value:', yield* innerGeneratorFn());
}

for (const x of outerGeneratorFn()) {
  console.log('value:', x);
}
// value: foo
// iter value: bar
```

Recursive Algorithms Using yield*

yield* is especially useful when used in a recursive operation, where the generator can yield itself. Consider the following example:

```
function* nTimes(n) {
  if (n> 0) {
    yield* nTimes(n - 1);
    yield n - 1;
  }
}

for (const x of nTimes(3)) {
  console.log(x);
}
// 0
// 1
// 2
```

In this example, each generator is first yielding each value from a newly created generator object, and then yielding a single integer. The result of this is that the generator function will recursively decrement the counter value and instantiate another generator object, which at the top level will have the effect of creating a single iterable that returns incremental integers.

Using recursive generator structure and `yield*` allows for elegantly expressing recursive algorithms. Consider the following graph implementation, which generates a random bidirectional graph:

```
class Node {
  constructor(id) {
    this.id = id;
    this.neighbors = new Set();
  }

  connect(node) {
    if (node !== this) {
      this.neighbors.add(node);
      node.neighbors.add(this);
    }
  }
}

class RandomGraph {
  constructor(size) {
    this.nodes = new Set();

    // Create nodes
    for (let i = 0; i < size; ++i) {
      this.nodes.add(new Node(i));
    }

    // Randomly connect nodes
    const threshold = 1 / size;
    for (const x of this.nodes) {
      for (const y of this.nodes) {
        if (Math.random() < threshold) {
          x.connect(y);
        }
      }
    }
  }

  // This is just for debug purposes
  print() {
    for (const node of this.nodes) {
      const ids = [...node.neighbors]
                    .map((n) => n.id)
                    .join(',');

      console.log('${node.id}: ${ids}');
    }
  }
}

const g = new RandomGraph(6);

g.print();
// Example output:
// 0: 2,3,5
// 1: 2,3,4,5
```

```
// 2: 1,3
// 3: 0,1,2,4
// 4: 2,3
// 5: 0,4
```

The graph data structure is well-suited for recursive traversal, and using a recursive generator allows you to do exactly that. To do so, the generator function must accept an iterable, yield each value in that iterable, and recurse on each value. A simple utilization of this would be to test if a graph is connected, meaning that there are no nodes that cannot be reached. This test can be accomplished by beginning at one node and exhaustively attempting to visit every node. The result is a very succinct implementation of a depth first traversal:

```
class Node {
  constructor(id) {
    ...
  }

  connect(node) {
    ...
  }
}

class RandomGraph {
  constructor(size) {
    ...
  }

  print() {
    ...
  }

  isConnected() {
    const visitedNodes = new Set();

    function* traverse(nodes) {
      for (const node of nodes) {
        if (!visitedNodes.has(node)) {
          yield node;
          yield* traverse(node.neighbors);
        }
      }
    }

    // Grab first node in the Set
    const firstNode = this.nodes[Symbol.iterator]().next().value;

    // Use the recursive generator to iterate every node
    for (const node of traverse([firstNode])) {
      visitedNodes.add(node);
    }

    return visitedNodes.size === this.nodes.size;
  }
}
```

Using a Generator as the Default Iterator

Because generator objects implement the Iterable interface, and because both generator functions and the default iterator are invoked to produce an iterator, generators are exceptionally well suited to be used as default iterators. The following is a simple example where the default iterator can yield the class's contents in a single line:

```
class Foo {
  constructor() {
    this.values = [1, 2, 3];
  }
  * [Symbol.iterator]() {
    yield* this.values;
  }
}

const f = new Foo();

for (const x of f) {
  console.log(x);
}
// 1
// 2
// 3
```

Here, the for...of loop invokes the default iterator—which happens to be a generator function—and produces a generator object. The generator object is an iterable and therefore compatible for use in iteration.

Early Termination of Generators

Like iterators, generators also support the concept of being "closable." For an object to implement the Iterator interface, it must have a next() and, optionally, a return() method for when the iterator is terminated early. A generator object has both of these methods and an additional third method, throw().

```
function* generatorFn() {}

const g = generatorFn();

console.log(g);          // generatorFn {<suspended>}
console.log(g.next);     // f next() { [native code] }
console.log(g.return);   // f return() { [native code] }
console.log(g.throw);    // f throw() { [native code] }
```

The return() and throw() methods are two methods that can be used to coerce the generator into a closed state.

The *return()* Method

The `return()` method will force the generator into a closed state, and the value provided to `return()` will be the value provided in the terminal iterator object:

```
function* generatorFn() {
  for (const x of [1, 2, 3]) {
    yield x;
  }
}

const g = generatorFn();

console.log(g);              // generatorFn {<suspended>}
console.log(g.return(4));    // { done: true, value: 4 }
console.log(g);              // generatorFn {<closed>}
```

Unlike iterators, all generator objects have a `return()` method that forces it into a closed state that it cannot exit once reached. Subsequent invoking of `next()` will disclose the `done:true` state, but any provided return value is not stored or propagated:

```
function* generatorFn() {
  for (const x of [1, 2, 3]) {
    yield x;
  }
}

const g = generatorFn();

console.log(g.next());       // { done: false, value: 1 }
console.log(g.return(4));    // { done: true, value: 4 }
console.log(g.next());       // { done: true, value: undefined }
console.log(g.next());       // { done: true, value: undefined }
console.log(g.next());       // { done: true, value: undefined }
```

Built-in language constructs such as the `for...of` loop will sensibly ignore any values returned inside the `done:true` IteratorObject.

```
function* generatorFn() {
  for (const x of [1, 2, 3]) {
    yield x;
  }
}

const g = generatorFn();

for (const x of g) {
  if (x> 1) {
    g.return(4);
  }
  console.log(x);
}
// 1
// 2
```

The *throw()* Method

The `throw()` method will inject a provided error into the generator object at the point it is suspended. If the error is unhandled, the generator will close:

```
function* generatorFn() {
  for (const x of [1, 2, 3]) {
    yield x;
  }
}

const g = generatorFn();

console.log(g);     // generatorFn {<suspended>}
try {
  g.throw('foo');
} catch (e) {
  console.log(e);   // foo
}
console.log(g);     // generatorFn {<closed>}
```

If, however, the error is handled *inside* the generator function, then it will not close and can resume execution. The error handling will skip over that yield, so in this example you will see it skip a value. Consider the following example:

```
function* generatorFn() {
  for (const x of [1, 2, 3]) {
    try {
      yield x;
    } catch(e) {}
  }
}

const g = generatorFn();

console.log(g.next());  // { done: false, value: 1 }
g.throw('foo');
console.log(g.next());  // { done: false, value: 3 }
```

In this example, the generator suspends execution at a `yield` keyword inside a try/catch block. While it is suspended, `throw()` injects the `foo` error, which is thrown by the `yield` keyword. Because this error is thrown inside the generator's try/catch block, it is subsequently caught while still inside the generator. However, because `yield` threw that error, that value of 2 will not be produced by the generator. Instead, the generator function continues execution, proceeding on to the next loop iteration where it encounters the `yield` keyword yet again—this time, yielding the value 3.

> **NOTE** *If the generator object has not yet begun execution, calling* `throw()` *cannot be caught inside the function because the error is thrown from outside the function block.*

ASYNCHRONOUS ITERATION

Asynchronous execution involves releasing control of the execution thread to allow slow operations to finish before regaining control, and the iterator protocol involves defining a canonical ordering for arbitrary objects. Asynchronous iteration is merely the logical assimilation of these two concepts.

A synchronous iterator provides you with a { value, done } pair each time next() is invoked. Of course, this requires that the computation and resource fetching needed to determine the contents of this pair be completed by the time the next() invocation exits—otherwise, these values are indeterminate. When using a *synchronous* iterator to iterate over values that are determined *asynchronously*, the main execution thread will be blocked while waiting for the asynchronous operation to complete.

With asynchronous iterators, this problem is totally solved. An asynchronous iterator provides you with a promise that resolves to a { value, done } pair each time next() is invoked. This way, the thread of execution can be released and perform work elsewhere while the current loop iteration is being resolved.

Creating and Using an Async Iterator

Async iterators are best understood through comparison with a traditional synchronous iterator. The following is a simple Emitter class, which contains a synchronous generator function that produces a synchronous iterator that will count from 0 to 4:

```
class Emitter {
  constructor(max) {
    this.max = max;
    this.syncIdx = 0;
  }

  *[Symbol.iterator]() {
    while(this.syncIdx < this.max) {
      yield this.syncIdx++;
    }
  }
}

const emitter = new Emitter(5);

function syncCount() {
  const syncCounter = emitter[Symbol.iterator]();

  for (const x of syncCounter) {
    console.log(x);
  }
}

syncCount();
// 0
// 1
// 2
// 3
// 4
```

The previous example only works because in each iteration, the next value is immediately able to be yielded. If instead you did not want to block the main thread of execution while determining the next value to yield, you can also define an asynchronous generator function that will yield Promise-wrapped values.

This can be accomplished using async-flavored versions of iterators and generators. ECMAScript defines `Symbol.asyncIterator`, which allows you to define and invoke Promise-yielding generator functions. The specification also defines an asynchronous `for` loop iterator, the `for-await-of` loop, intended to consume this async iterator. Using these, the previous example can be extended to support both synchronous and asynchronous iteration:

```
class Emitter {
  constructor(max) {
    this.max = max;
    this.syncIdx = 0;
    this.asyncIdx = 0;
  }

  *[Symbol.iterator]() {
    while(this.syncIdx < this.max) {
      yield this.syncIdx++;
    }
  }   async *[Symbol.asyncIterator]() {
  *[Symbol.asyncIterator]() {
    while(this.asyncIdx < this.max) {
      yield new Promise((resolve) => resolve(this.asyncIdx++;
    }
  }
}

const emitter = new Emitter(5);

function syncCount() {
  const syncCounter = emitter[Symbol.iterator]();

  for (const x of syncCounter) {
    console.log(x);
  }
}

async function asyncCount() {
  const asyncCounter = emitter[Symbol.asyncIterator]();

  for await(const x of asyncCounter) {
    console.log(x);
  }
}

syncCount();
// 0
// 1
// 2
// 3
```

```
// 4

asyncCount();
// 0
// 1
// 2
// 3
// 4
```

To further your understanding, swap out the above example so that the *synchronous* generator is passed to a `for-await-of` loop:

```
const emitter = new Emitter(5);

async function asyncIteratorSyncCount() {
  const syncCounter = emitter[Symbol.iterator]();

  for await(const x of syncCounter) {
    console.log(x);
  }
}

asyncIteratorSyncCount();
// 0
// 1
// 2
// 3
// 4
```

Even though the sync counter iterates through primitive values, the `for-await-of` loop will handle the values as if they were returned wrapped in promises. This demonstrates the power of the `for-await-of` loop, which allows it to fluently handle both synchronous and asynchronous iterables. This is not true for a normal `for` loop, which cannot handle an asynchronous iterator:

```
function syncIteratorAsyncCount() {
  const asyncCounter = emitter[Symbol.asyncIterator]();

  for (const x of asyncCounter) {
    console.log(x);
  }
}

syncIteratorAsyncCount();
// TypeError: asyncCounter is not iterable
```

One of the most important concepts to understand about async iterators is that the `Symbol.asyncIterator` designation doesn't alter the behavior of the generator function or how the generator is consumed. Note that the generator function is defined as an async function and designated as a generator using an asterisk. `Symbol.asyncIterator` merely suggests to an external construct such as a `for-await-of` loop that the associated iterator will return a sequence of promise objects.

Understanding the Async Iterator Queue

Of course, the previous example is quite contrived, as the promises returned from the iterator are instantaneously resolved, and therefore it is little more than a thinly wrapped synchronous iterator. Suppose instead that the yielded promises resolved after an indeterminate period of time; what's more, suppose they return out of order. An asynchronous iterator should emulate a synchronous iterator in every way possible, including in-order execution of code associated with each iteration. To address this, asynchronous iterators maintain a queue of callbacks to ensure that the iterator handler for an earlier value will always complete execution before proceeding to a later value, even if the later value resolves before the earlier value.

To prove this, the async iterator in the following example returns promises which resolve after a random period of time—behavior that emulates multiple network requests. The async iteration queue ensures that the promise resolution order does not interfere with the order of iteration. As a result, the integers will be printed in order (at random intervals):

```
class Emitter {
  constructor(max) {
    this.max = max;
    this.syncIdx = 0;
    this.asyncIdx = 0;
  }

  *[Symbol.iterator]() {
    while(this.syncIdx < this.max) {
      yield this.syncIdx++;
    }
  }
  async *[Symbol.asyncIterator]() {
    while(this.asyncIdx < this.max) {
      yield new Promise((resolve) => {
        setTimeout(() => {
          resolve(this.asyncIdx++);
        }, Math.floor(Math.random() * 1000));
      });
    }
  }
}

const emitter = new Emitter(5);

function syncCount() {
  const syncCounter = emitter[Symbol.iterator]();

  for (const x of syncCounter) {
    console.log(x);
  }
}

async function asyncCount() {
  const asyncCounter = emitter[Symbol.asyncIterator]();

  for await(const x of asyncCounter) {
    console.log(x);
  }
}
```

```
    }

syncCount();
// 0
// 1
// 2
// 3
// 4

asyncCount();
// 0
// 1
// 2
// 3
// 4
```

Async Iterator *reject()* Handling

Because the composition of asynchronous iterators consists of promises, one must consider the possibility that one of the promises produced by the iterator will reject. Because the design of asynchronous iteration insists on in-order completion, it would not make sense to proceed past a rejected promise through the loop; therefore, a rejected promise will force the iterator to exit:

```
class Emitter {
  constructor(max) {
    this.max = max;
    this.asyncIdx = 0;
  }

  async *[Symbol.asyncIterator]() {
    while (this.asyncIdx < this.max) {
      if (this.asyncIdx < 3) {
        yield this.asyncIdx++;
      } else {
        throw 'Exited loop';
      }
    }
  }
}

const emitter = new Emitter(5);

async function asyncCount() {
  const asyncCounter = emitter[Symbol.asyncIterator]();

  for await (const x of asyncCounter) {
    console.log(x);
  }
}

asyncCount();
// 0
// 1
// 2
// Uncaught (in promise) Exited loop
```

Manual Async Iteration Using *next()*

The `for-await-of` loop offers two useful features: it makes use of the async iterator queue to ensure in-order execution, and it hides the promise structure of the async iterator. However, using such a loop conceals much of the underlying behavior.

Because the async iterator still follows the iterator protocol, you can just as easily progress through the async iterable using `next()`. As described earlier, `next()` contains a promise that will resolve to `{ value, done }`. This means that you must use the Promise API to retrieve methods, but it also means that you are not forced to use the async iterator queue.

```
const emitter = new Emitter(5);

const asyncCounter = emitter[Symbol.asyncIterator]();

console.log(asyncCounter.next());
// { value: Promise, done: false }
```

Top-Level Async Loops

As a rule, async behavior—including `for-await-of` loops—cannot exist outside of an async function. However, you may find it necessary on occasion to make use of async behavior in such a context. This can be accomplished by creating an async IIFE:

```
class Emitter {
  constructor(max) {
    this.max = max;
    this.asyncIdx = 0;
  }

  async *[Symbol.asyncIterator]() {
    while(this.asyncIdx < this.max) {
      yield new Promise((resolve) => resolve(this.asyncIdx++));
    }
  }
}

const emitter = new Emitter(5);

(async function() {
  const asyncCounter = emitter[Symbol.asyncIterator]();

  for await(const x of asyncCounter) {
    console.log(x);
  }
})();
// 0
// 1
// 2
// 3
// 4
```

Implementing Observables

Because asynchronous iterators will patiently wait for the next iteration without incurring computational cost, an entirely new avenue for implementing an observable interface opens up. At a high level, this will take the form of capturing events, wrapping them in promises, and then feeding these events through the iterator to allow for the listener to hook into the asynchronous iterator. When an event is fired, the next promise in the async iterator will resolve with that event.

> **NOTE** *The topic of observables is outside the scope of this book because they are largely implemented as third-party libraries. For further reading, look into the popular RxJS library (*`http://reactivex.io/rxjs`*).*

A simplistic example of this would be to capture an observable stream of browser events. This requires a queue of promises, each of which corresponds to a single event. The queue will also preserve the order in which events are generated, which is a desirable feature for this sort of problem.

```
class Observable {
  constructor() {
    this.promiseQueue = [];

    // Holds the resolver for the next promise in the queue
    this.resolve = null;

    // Pushes the initial promise on the queue which will
    // resolve with the first observed event
    this.enqueue();
  }

  // Create a new promise, save its resolve method, and
  // store it on the queue
  enqueue() {
    this.promiseQueue.push(
      new Promise((resolve) => this.resolve = resolve));
  }

  // Remove the promise at the front of the queue and
  // return it
  dequeue() {
    return this.promiseQueue.shift();
  }
}
```

To make use of this promise queue, define an asynchronous generator method on this class. This generator should work for any event type:

```
class Observable {
  constructor() {
```

```
      this.promiseQueue = [];

      // Holds the resolver for the next promise in the queue
      this.resolve = null;

      // Pushes the initial promise on the queue which will
      // resolve with the first observed event
      this.enqueue();
    }

    // Create a new promise, save its resolve method, and
    // store it on the queue
    enqueue() {
      this.promiseQueue.push(
        new Promise((resolve) => this.resolve = resolve));
    }

    // Remove the promise at the front of the queue and
    // return it
    dequeue() {
      return this.promiseQueue.shift();
    }

    async *fromEvent (element, eventType) {
      // Whenever an event is generated, resolve the promise
      // at the front of the queue with the event object and
      // enqueue another promise.
      element.addEventListener(eventType, (event) => {
        this.resolve(event);
        this.enqueue();
      });

      // Each resolved promise at the front of the queue will
      // yield the event object to the async iterator
      while (1) {
        yield await this.dequeue();
      }
    }
  }
```

With this fully defined class, it is now trivial to define an observable on DOM elements. Suppose the page has a <button> inside it; you could capture a stream of click events on this button and log each of them to the console as follows:

```
class Observable {
  constructor() {
    this.promiseQueue = [];

    // Holds the resolver for the next promise in the queue
    this.resolve = null;

    // Pushes the initial promise on the queue which will
    // resolve with the first observed event
    this.enqueue();
```

```
    }

    // Create a new promise, save its resolve method, and
    // store it on the queue
    enqueue() {
      this.promiseQueue.push(
        new Promise((resolve) => this.resolve = resolve));
    }

    // Remove the promise at the front of the queue and
    // return it
    dequeue() {
      return this.promiseQueue.shift();
    }

    async *fromEvent(element, eventType) {
      // Whenever an event is generated, resolve the promise
      // at the front of the queue with the event object and
      // enqueue another promise.
      element.addEventListener(eventType, (event) => {
        this.resolve(event);
        this.enqueue();
      });

      // Each resolved promise at the front of the queue will
      // yield the event object to the async iterator
      while (1) {
        yield await this.dequeue();
      }
    }
  }


  (async function() {
    const observable = new Observable();

    const button = document.querySelector('button');
    const mouseClickIterator = observable.fromEvent(button, 'click');

    for await (const clickEvent of mouseClickIterator) {
      console.log(clickEvent);
    }
  })();
```

SUMMARY

Iteration is a pattern that is encountered in essentially every programming language. The ECMAScript specification formally embraces the concept of iteration by introducing two formal concepts in the language, iterators and generators.

An iterator is an interface that can be implemented by any object and allows for successive visitation of values that it produces. Anything that implements the Iterable interface features a `Symbol.iterator` property, which references the default iterator. The default iterator behaves as an iterator factory: a function which, when invoked, produces an object that implements the Iterator interface.

Successive values are coerced from an iterator via its `next()` method, which returns an IteratorObject. This object contains a `done` property, a Boolean indicating if there are more values available, and a `value` property, which contains the present value provided from the iterator. This interface can be manually consumed by invoking `next()` repeatedly, or automatically consumed by native iterable consumers such as the `for...of` loop.

Generators are a special type of function that, when invoked, produces a generator object. This generator object implements the Iterable interface, and therefore can be used anywhere an iterable is expected. Generators are unique in that they support the `yield` keyword, which is used to pause execution of the generator function. The yield keyword can also be used to accept input and output through the `next()` method. When accompanied by an asterisk, the yield keyword will serve to serialize an iterable it is paired with.

Async iteration allows you to write JavaScript that can use iterator and async concepts simultaneously. Like synchronous iteration, anything that implements the Iterable interface features a `Symbol.asyncIterator` property, which references the default async iterator. Constructs such as the `for-await-of` loop are capable of iterating and serializing asynchronous operations that may not resolve in their order of iteration but will nevertheless be iterated in that order all the same. This is especially useful when dealing with sequential network requests.

8

Objects, Classes, and Object-Oriented Programming

WHAT'S IN THIS CHAPTER?

➤ JavaScript objects

➤ Object creation and inheritance

➤ JavaScript classes

ECMA-262 defines an object as an unordered collection of properties. Strictly speaking, this means that an object is an array of values in no particular order. Each property or method is identified by a name that is mapped to a value. For this reason (and others yet to be discussed), it helps to think of ECMAScript objects as hash tables: nothing more than a grouping of name-value pairs where the value may be data or a function.

UNDERSTANDING OBJECTS

The canonical way of creating a custom object is to create a new instance of `Object` and add properties and methods to it, as in this example:

```
let person = new Object();
person.name = "Alice";
person.age = 29;
```

```
person.job = "Software Engineer";

person.sayName = function() {
  console.log(this.name);
};
```

This example creates an object called `person` that has three properties (`name`, `age`, and `job`) and one method (`sayName()`). The `sayName()` method displays the value of `this.name`, which resolves to `person.name`. Early JavaScript developers used this pattern frequently to create new objects. A few years later, object literals became the preferred pattern for creating such objects. The previous example can be rewritten using object literal notation as follows:

```
let person = {
  name: "Alice",
  age: 29,
  job: "Software Engineer",
  sayName() {
    console.log(this.name);
  }
};
```

The `person` object in this example is equivalent to the person object in the prior example, with all the same properties and methods. These properties are all created with certain characteristics that define their behavior in JavaScript.

Types of Properties

ECMA-262 describes characteristics of properties using internal-only attributes. These attributes are defined in the ECMAScript specification and implemented in JavaScript engines, but they are not directly accessible in JavaScript. To indicate that an attribute is internal, surround the attribute name with two pairs of square brackets, such as `[[Enumerable]]`.

There are two types of properties: data properties and accessor properties.

Data Properties

Data properties contain a single location for a data value. Values are read from and written to this location. Data properties have four attributes describing their behavior:

➤ `[[Configurable]]`—Indicates if the property may be redefined by removing the property via `delete`, changing the property's attributes, or changing the property into an accessor property. By default, this is `true` for all properties defined directly on an object, as in the previous example.

➤ `[[Enumerable]]`—Indicates if the property will be returned in a `for-in` loop. By default, this is `true` for all properties defined directly on an object, as in the previous example.

➤ `[[Writable]]`—Indicates if the property's value can be changed. By default, this is `true` for all properties defined directly on an object, as in the previous example.

➤ `[[Value]]`—Contains the actual data value for the property. This is the location from which the property's value is read and the location to which new values are saved. The default value for this attribute is `undefined`.

When a property is explicitly added to an object as in the previous examples, `[[Configurable]]`, `[[Enumerable]]`, and `[[Writable]]` are all set to `true` while the `[[Value]]` attribute is set to the assigned value. For example:

```
let person = {
    name: "Alice"
};
```

Here, the property called name is created and a value of `"Alice"` is assigned. That means `[[Value]]` is set to `"Alice"`, and any changes to that value are stored in this location.

To change any of the default property attributes, you must use the `Object.defineProperty()` method. This method accepts three arguments: the object on which the property should be added or modified, the name of the property, and a descriptor object. The properties on the descriptor object match the attribute names: `configurable`, `enumerable`, `writable`, and `value`. You can use any number of these values to change the corresponding attribute values. For example:

```
let person = {};
Object.defineProperty(person, "name", {
    writable: false,
    value: "Alice"
});
console.log(person.name);    // "Alice"
person.name = "Greg";
console.log(person.name);    // "Alice"
```

This example creates a property called name with a value of `"Alice"` that is read-only. The value of this property can't be changed, and any attempts to assign a new value are ignored in nonstrict mode. In strict mode, an error is thrown when an attempt is made to change the value of a read-only property.

Similar rules apply to creating a nonconfigurable property. For example:

```
let person = {};
Object.defineProperty(person, "name", {
    configurable: false,
    value: "Alice"
});
console.log(person.name);    // "Alice"
delete person.name;
console.log(person.name);    // "Alice"
```

Here, setting `configurable` to `false` means that the property cannot be removed from the object. Calling `delete` on the property has no effect in nonstrict mode and throws an error in strict mode. Additionally, once a property has been defined as nonconfigurable, it cannot become configurable again. Any attempt to call `Object.defineProperty()` and change any attribute other than `writable` causes an error:

```
let person = {};
Object.defineProperty(person, "name", {
    configurable: false,
```

```
    value: "Alice"
});

// Throws an error
Object.defineProperty(person, "name", {
  configurable: true,
  value: "Alice"
});
```

Although you can call `Object.defineProperty()` multiple times for the same property, there are limits once configurable has been set to `false`.

When you are using `Object.defineProperty()`, the values for `configurable`, `enumerable`, and `writable` default to `false` unless otherwise specified. In most cases, you likely won't need the powerful options provided by `Object.defineProperty()`, but it's important to understand the concepts to have a good understanding of JavaScript objects.

Accessor Properties

Accessor properties do not contain a data value. Instead, they contain a combination of a *getter* function and a *setter* function (though both are not necessary). When an accessor property is read, the getter function is called, and it's the function's responsibility to return a valid value; when an accessor property is written, a function is called with the new value, and that function must decide how to react to the data. Accessor properties have four attributes:

➤ `[[Configurable]]`—Indicates if the property may be redefined by removing the property via `delete`, changing the property's attributes, or changing the property into a data property. By default, this is `true` for all properties defined directly on an object.

➤ `[[Enumerable]]`—Indicates if the property will be returned in a `for-in` loop. By default, this is `true` for all properties defined directly on an object.

➤ `[[Get]]`—The function to call when the property is read from. The default value is `undefined`.

➤ `[[Set]]`—The function to call when the property is written to. The default value is `undefined`.

It is not possible to define an accessor property explicitly; you must use `Object.defineProperty()`. Here's a simple example:

```
// Define object with pseudo-private member 'year_'
// and public member 'edition'
let book = {
  year_: 2023,
  edition: 1
};

Object.defineProperty(book, "year", {
  get() {
    return this.year_;
  },
```

```
    set(newValue) {
      if (newValue> 2023) {
        this.year_ = newValue;
        this.edition += newValue - 2023;
      }
    }
  });
  book.year = 2024;
  console.log(book.edition);   // 2
```

In this code, an object book is created with two default properties: `year_` and `edition`. The underscore on `year_` is a common notation to indicate that a property is not intended to be accessed from outside of the object's methods. The `year` property is defined to be an accessor property where the getter function simply returns the value of `year_` and the setter does some calculation to determine the correct edition. So changing the year property to 2024 results in both `year_` and edition changing to 2. This is a typical use case for accessor properties, when setting a property value results in some other changes to occur.

It's not necessary to assign both a getter and a setter. Assigning just a getter means that the property cannot be written to and attempts to do so will be ignored. In strict mode, trying to write to a property with only a getter throws an error. Likewise, a property with only a setter cannot be read and will return the value `undefined` in nonstrict mode, while doing so throws an error in strict mode.

There is no way to modify `[[Configurable]]` or `[[Enumerable]]` in browsers that don't support `Object.defineProperty()`.

Accessing Object Properties

To read an object property, you can use the dot notation or square bracket notation. The dot notation is the most common and straightforward approach. It involves specifying the object followed by a dot (.) and then the property name:

```
const person = {
  name: "Alice",
  age: 30
};

console.log(person.name);   // Alice
console.log(person.age);    // 30
```

Alternatively, you can use square brackets and pass the property name as a string:

```
console.log(person["name"]);   // Alice
console.log(person["age"]);    // 30
```

Both approaches yield the same result, but the square bracket notation is useful when the property name needs to be dynamically determined or when it contains special characters or spaces. However, note that static code analysis tools may not always be able to identify that person.name and person["name"] are the same, so I prefer to use the dot notation wherever possible.

Chaining Properties

Nesting objects inside other objects is common practice in JavaScript. From a parent object, accessing child object properties is as simple as recursively using a property access pattern called *property chaining*. Consider the following example:

```
const person = {
  name: "Alice",
  address: {
    city: "Chicago",
    street: "1060 W Addison St"
  }
};

console.log(person.address.city);        // Chicago
console.log(person.address.postalCode);  // undefined

console.log(person.address.postalCode.length);
// TypeError: Cannot read property 'length' of undefined
```

In this example, we can safely access properties of the child `address` object via chained property access operations. This is equivalent to doing the following:

```
const person = { ... };
const address = person.address;
console.log(address.city);  // Chicago
```

Chaining property access is fine in situations where the nested object structure is well-defined, but this starts to fall apart where an intermediate object does not exist, as shown in the final line of the example, where a `TypeError` is thrown. To prevent this, you would need to check the existence of every nested object in the chain—something that can be quite tedious:

```
const person = { ... };
if (person.address) {
  if (person.address.postalCode) {
    console.log(person.address.postalCode.length);
  }
}
```

To avoid doing this, you can use the *optional chaining operator* by appending the question mark (`?.`) to the property or method you want to access that may or may not be defined. It short-circuits the evaluation and returns `undefined` if that portion of the chain is `undefined` or `null`:

```
console.log(person.address?.postalCode?.length);        // undefined

// Once the optional chaining short-circuits, it will not evaluate
// anything to the right of the operator
console.log(person.address?.postalCode?.foo.bar.baz);   // undefined
```

Importantly, that operator will only short-circuit the chain for that specific property:

```
console.log(person.address.postalCode?.length);
// undefined

console.log(person.address?.postalCode.length);
// TypeError: Cannot read property 'length' of undefined
```

Object Static Methods

The `Object` class includes a hefty number of static methods used for inspecting and manipulating objects. Since all non-primitives in JavaScript inherit from `Object`, these can be used on any object. The following table lists each available method with a brief description of its behavior:

KEY-VALUE	DESCRIPTION
`Object.assign()`	Copies the values of all enumerable properties from one or more source objects to a target object.
`Object.create()`	Creates a new object with the specified prototype object and properties.
`Object.defineProperties()`	Defines new or modifies existing properties of an object, with descriptors for each property.
`Object.defineProperty()`	Defines a new property or modifies an existing property of an object, with a descriptor for the property.
`Object.entries()`	Returns an array of a given object's own enumerable string-keyed property [key-value] pairs.
`Object.freeze()`	Freezes an object, preventing new properties from being added to it and existing properties from being modified or removed.
`Object.fromEntries()`	Returns a new object from an iterable (such as an array or map) of key-value pairs.
`Object.getOwnPropertyDescriptor()`	Returns an object describing the configuration of a specific property on an object.
`Object.getOwnPropertyDescriptors()`	Returns an object containing all own property descriptors of an object.
`Object.getOwnPropertyNames()`	Returns an array of all property names (including non-enumerable properties) found directly on an object.
`Object.getOwnPropertySymbols()`	Returns an array of all symbol properties (including non-enumerable properties) found directly on an object.
`Object.getPrototypeOf()`	Returns the prototype (i.e., the internal `[[Prototype]]` property) of the specified object.
`Object.hasOwn()`	Determines if the specified object has the indicated property as its own property.

continues

(continued)

KEY-VALUE	DESCRIPTION
`Object.is()`	Determines whether two values are the same value, considering edge cases like `NaN` and -0.
`Object.isExtensible()`	Determines if an object is extensible, i.e., if new properties can be added to it.
`Object.isFrozen()`	Determines if an object is frozen, i.e., if it is not extensible and all its properties are non-configurable.
`Object.isSealed()`	Determines if an object is sealed, i.e., if it is not extensible and all its properties are non-configurable.
`Object.keys()`	Returns an array of a given object's own enumerable property names.
`Object.preventExtensions()`	Prevents new properties from being added to an object, making it non-extensible.
`Object.seal()`	Seals an object, preventing new properties from being added and existing properties from being deleted or configured.
`Object.setPrototypeOf()`	Sets the prototype (i.e., the internal `[[Prototype]]` property) of a specified object to another object or `null`.
`Object.values()`	Returns an array of a given object's own enumerable property values.

Controlling Object Mutability

`Object` includes static methods to manipulate and control the mutability of objects. Developers can freeze objects to make them completely immutable, determine if an object can have new properties added, seal objects to prevent addition or deletion of properties while allowing property modification, and more.

Freezing Objects

The `Object.freeze()` method is primarily used to *freeze* an object and make it object immutable. The frozen object becomes non-extensible and all its existing properties become non-configurable. Once an object is frozen, new properties cannot be added, existing properties cannot be modified or deleted, and the object's prototype cannot be changed. Any attempt to modify a frozen object or its properties will result in an error or failure. You can detect if an object was frozen with `Object.isFrozen()`.

```
const person = {
  name: "Alice",
  age: 30
};

console.log(Object.isFrozen(person));   // false
Object.freeze(person);
console.log(Object.isFrozen(person));   // true


person.name = "Bob";
// Ignored in non-strict mode
// Throws error in strict mode
```

Freezing cannot be undone; it is intended to be a permanent operation.

> **NOTE** *Freezing only applies to immediate properties of the frozen object. If the value of any of those properties is an object itself, then the properties of those objects remain mutable. To "deep freeze" a nested object, we must recursively freeze all non-primitive properties.*

Sealing Objects

The `Object.seal()` method provides a way to *seal* an object, making it non-extensible and marking all its existing properties as non-configurable. Sealing an object prevents the addition and deletion of properties while still allowing the modification of existing property values. Once an object is sealed, new properties cannot be added, but existing properties can be modified. The `Object.isSealed()` method can be used to determine if an object is sealed.

```
const person = {
  name: "Alice",
  age: 30
};

console.log(Object.isSealed(person));   // false
Object.seal(person);
console.log(Object.isSealed(person));   // true

person.name = "Bob";   // Modifying existing property is allowed
person.height = "6 feet";
// Ignored in non-strict mode
// Error in strict mode

delete person.age;
// Ignored in non-strict mode
// Error in strict mode
```

Sealing an object does not prevent modifications to existing properties, but it prevents new properties from being added and existing properties from being deleted. It is a less strict form of immutability compared to `Object.freeze()`.

Controlling Extensibility

The `Object.preventExtensions()` method is used to make an object non-extensible, meaning that new properties cannot be added to it. By default, JavaScript objects are extensible, meaning new properties can be added to them. The `Object.isExtensible()` method can be used to check if an object is extensible or not.

```
const person = {
  name: "Alice",
  age: 30
};

console.log(Object.isExtensible(person));  // true
Object.preventExtensions(person);
console.log(Object.isExtensible(person));  // false

person.name = "Bob";  // Modifying existing property is allowed
person.gender = "Female";
// Ignored in non-strict mode
// Error in strict mode

delete person.age;
// Ignored in non-strict mode
// Error in strict mode
```

The `Object.preventExtensions()` method makes an object non-extensible, preventing the addition of new properties while allowing modifications and deletions to existing properties. It differs from `Object.seal()` as it does not mark existing properties as non-configurable, thus allowing their modification.

Defining Multiple Properties

To define more than one property on an object at once, ECMAScript provides the `Object.defineProperties()` method. This method allows you to define multiple properties using descriptors at once. There are two arguments: the object on which to add or modify the properties and an object whose property names correspond to the properties' names to add or modify. For example:

```
let book = {};
Object.defineProperties(book, {
  year_: {
    value: 2023
  },

  edition: {
    value: 1
  },

  year: {
    get() {
      return this.year_;
```

```
    },

    set(newValue) {
      if (newValue> 2023) {
        this.year_ = newValue;
        this.edition += newValue - 2023;
      }
    }
  }
});
```

This code defines two data properties, `year_` and `edition`, and an accessor property called `year` on the book object. The resulting object is identical to the example in the previous section.

Reading Property Attributes

It's also possible to retrieve the property descriptor for a given property by using the `Object` `.getOwnPropertyDescriptor()` method. This method accepts two arguments: the object on which the property resides and the `name` of the property whose descriptor should be retrieved. The return value is an object with properties for `configurable`, `enumerable`, `get`, and `set` for accessor properties or `configurable`, `enumerable`, `writable`, and `value` for data properties. For example:

```
let book = {};
Object.defineProperties(book, {
  year_: {
    value: 2023
  },

  edition: {
    value: 1
  },

  year: {
    get: function() {
      return this.year_;
    },

    set: function(newValue){
      if (newValue> 2023) {
        this.year_ = newValue;
        this.edition += newValue - 2023;
      }
    }
  }
});

let descriptor = Object.getOwnPropertyDescriptor(book, "year_");
console.log(descriptor.value);         // 2023
console.log(descriptor.configurable);  // false
console.log(typeof descriptor.get);    // "undefined"
let descriptor = Object.getOwnPropertyDescriptor(book, "year");
console.log(descriptor.value);         // undefined
console.log(descriptor.enumerable);    // false
console.log(typeof descriptor.get);    // "function"
```

For the data property year_, value is equal to the original value, configurable is false, and get is undefined. For the accessor property year, value is undefined, enumerable is false, and get is a pointer to the specified getter function.

The Object.getOwnPropertyDescriptors() static method calls Object .getOwnPropertyDescriptor() for all *own properties* and returns them in a new object. *Own properties* refers to the properties that are directly defined on an object, as opposed to properties inherited from its prototype chain.

For the previous example, using this static method would return the following object:

```
let book = {};
Object.defineProperties(book, {
  year_: {
    value: 2023
  },

  edition: {
    value: 1
  },

  year: {
    get: function() {
      return this.year_;
    },

    set: function(newValue){
      if (newValue> 2023) {
        this.year_ = newValue;
        this.edition += newValue - 2023;
      }
    }
  }
});

console.log(Object.getOwnPropertyDescriptors(book));
// {
//   edition: {
//     configurable: false,
//     enumerable: false,
//     value: 1,
//     writable: false
//   },
//   year: {
//     configurable: false,
//     enumerable: false,
//     get: f(),
//     set: f(newValue),
//   },
//   year_: {
//     configurable: false,
//     enumerable: false,
```

```
//      value: 2019,
//      writable: false
//   }
// }
```

Merging Objects

JavaScript developers will often find that it is useful to be able to perform a "merge" of two objects. More specifically, this merge will take the form of folding all the local properties of one source object into a destination object, with the source object's properties taking priority in the event of any property collisions.

The `Object.assign()` method accepts one destination object, and one or many source objects, and for each source object copies the `enumerable` (`Object.propertyIsEnumerable` returns `true`) and own (`Object.hasOwnProperty` returns `true`) properties onto the destination object. Properties keyed with strings and symbols will be copied. For each suitable property, the method will use `[[Get]]` to retrieve a value from the source object and `[[Set]]` on the destination object to assign the value.

```
let dest, src, result;

/**
 * Simple copy
 */
dest = {};
src = { id: 'src' };

result = Object.assign(dest, src);

// Object.assign mutates the destination object
// and also returns that object after exiting.
console.log(dest === result);  // true
console.log(dest !== src);     // true
console.log(result);           // { id: src }
console.log(dest);             // { id: src }


/**
 * Multiple source objects
 */
dest = {};

result = Object.assign(dest, { a: 'foo' }, { b: 'bar' });

console.log(result);  // { a: foo, b: bar }


/**
 * Getters and setters
 */
dest = {
  set a(val) {
    console.log('Invoked dest setter with param ${val}');
  }
```

```
};
src = {
  get a() {
    console.log('Invoked src getter');
    return 'foo';
  }
};

Object.assign(dest, src);
// Invoked src getter
// Invoked dest setter with param foo

// Since the setter does not perform an assignment,
// no value is actually transferred
console.log(dest);  // { set a(val) {...} }
```

Object.assign() is effectively performing a shallow copy from each source object. If multiple source objects have the same property defined, the last one to be copied will be the ultimate value. Furthermore, any value retrieved from accessor properties, such as a getter, on a source object will be assigned as a static value on the destination object—there is no ability to transfer getters and setters between objects.

```
let dest, src, result;

/**
 * Overwritten properties
 */
dest = { id: 'dest' };

result = Object.assign(dest, { id: 'src1', a: 'foo' }, { id: 'src2', b: 'bar' });

// Object.assign will overwrite duplicate properties.
console.log(result);  // { id: src2, a: foo, b: bar }

// This can be observed by using a setter on the destination object:
dest = {
  set id(x) {
    console.log(x);
  }
};

Object.assign(dest, { id: 'first' }, { id: 'second' }, { id: 'third' });
// first
// second
// third


/**
 * Object references
 */

dest = {};
```

```
src = { a: {} };

Object.assign(dest, src);

// Shallow property copies means only object references copied.
console.log(dest);                // { a :{} }
console.log(dest.a === src.a);   // true
```

If an error is thrown during the assignment, it will discontinue and exit with the thrown error. `Object.assign()` has no concept of "rolling back" earlier assignments so it is a best-effort method that may only partially complete.

```
let dest, src, result;

/**
 * Error handling
 */
dest = {};
src = {
  a: 'foo',
  get b() {
    // Error will be thrown when Object.assign()
    // invokes this getter.
    throw new Error();
  },
  c: 'bar'
};

try {
  Object.assign(dest, src);
} catch(e) {}

// Object.assign() has no way of rolling back already performed changes,
// so set operations already performed on the destination object before
// the error is thrown remain:
console.log(dest);  // { a: foo }
```

Object Identity and Equality

There are several tricky corner cases where the `===` operator exhibits unexpected behavior:

```
// These are cases where === behaves as expected:
console.log(true === 1);     // false
console.log({} === {});      // false
console.log("2" === 2);      // false

// These have different representations in the JS engine
// and yet are treated as equal
console.log(+0 === -0);      // true
console.log(+0 === 0);       // true
console.log(-0 === 0);       // true

// To determine NaN equivalence, the profoundly annoying isNaN() is required
console.log(NaN === NaN);    // false
console.log(isNaN(NaN));     // true
```

To address this, the ECMAScript defines `Object.is()`, which behaves mostly as `===` does but also accounts for the corner cases listed previously. The method accepts exactly two arguments:

```
console.log(Object.is(true, 1));    // false
console.log(Object.is({}, {}));     // false
console.log(Object.is("2", 2));     // false

// Correct 0, -0, +0 equivalence/nonequivalence:
console.log(Object.is(+0, -0));     // false
console.log(Object.is(+0, 0));      // true
console.log(Object.is(-0, 0));      // false

// Correct NaN equivalence:
console.log(Object.is(NaN, NaN));   // true
```

To check more than two objects, it is trivial to recursively use transitive equality:

```
function recursivelyCheckEqual(x, ...rest) {
  return Object.is(x, rest[0]) &&
         (rest.length < 2 || recursivelyCheckEqual(...rest));
}
```

Enhanced Object Syntax

ECMAScript features a handful of extremely useful syntactical tools for defining and interacting with objects. None of them meaningfully change existing engine behavior, but they enormously enhance the convenience of dealing with objects.

All object syntax conventions introduced in this section are also applicable to ECMAScript classes, defined later in this chapter.

> **NOTE** *The enhanced object syntax described in this section is more concise and expressive; therefore, you will find that it is used by default here in this chapter as well as elsewhere in the book.*

Property Value Shorthand

Developers frequently find that, when adding a variable to an object, the property name used to key that variable often will match the variable name itself. For example:

```
let name = 'Matt';

let person = {
  name: name
};

console.log(person);  // { name: 'Matt' }
```

Thus, the *property value shorthand* convention was introduced. This allows you to simply use the variable itself without the colon notation, and the interpreter will automatically use the variable name as the property key. If the variable name is not found, a `ReferenceError` will be thrown.

The following code uses this shorthand:

```
let name = 'Matt';

let person = {
  name
};

console.log(person);  // { name: 'Matt' }
```

Minifiers are intelligent enough to preserve property names between scopes to prevent breaking references. Take the following code snippet for example:

```
function makePerson(name) {
  return {
    name
  };
}

let person = makePerson('Matt');

console.log(person.name);  // Matt
```

Compilers are careful to preserve the initial name string identifier inside the function definition even though the parameter identifier is restricted to the function scope. For example, when this is compiled using the Google Closure compiler, the function parameter name will be shortened, but the property name will remain:

```
function makePerson(a) {
  return {
    name: a
  };
}

var person = makePerson("Matt");

console.log(person.name);  // Matt
```

Computed Property Keys

Prior to the introduction of computed property keys, there was no way to dynamically assign property keys in an object literal without declaring the object and then individually using the square bracket notation for property assignment. For example:

```
const nameKey = 'name';
const ageKey = 'age';
const jobKey = 'job';

let person = {};
person[nameKey] = 'Matt';
person[ageKey] = 27;
person[jobKey] = 'Software engineer';

console.log(person);  // { name: 'Matt', age: 27, job: 'Software engineer' }
```

With computed properties, the property assignment can occur inside the object literal's initial definition. Square brackets around the object property key instruct the runtime to evaluate its contents as a JavaScript expression instead of a string:

```
const nameKey = 'name';
const ageKey = 'age';
const jobKey = 'job';

let person = {
  [nameKey]: 'Matt',
  [ageKey]: 27,
  [jobKey]: 'Software engineer'
};

console.log(person);  // { name: 'Matt', age: 27, job: 'Software engineer' }
```

Because the contents are evaluated as a JavaScript expression, it is possible to make the contents of the computed property complex expressions to be evaluated upon instantiation:

```
const nameKey = 'name';
const ageKey = 'age';
const jobKey = 'job';
let uniqueToken = 0;

function getUniqueKey(key) {
  return '${key}_${uniqueToken++}';
}

let person = {
  [getUniqueKey(nameKey)]: 'Matt',
  [getUniqueKey(ageKey)]: 27,
  [getUniqueKey(jobKey)]: 'Software engineer'
};

console.log(person);  // { name_0: 'Matt', age_1: 27, job_2: 'Software engineer' }
```

> **NOTE** *Any errors thrown in a computed property key expression will abort the creation of the object. Be careful when the expressions computing a property key have side effects, as an error thrown in an expression will not roll back earlier computation.*

Concise Method Syntax

When defining function properties of an object, the format almost always takes the form of a property key referencing an anonymous function expression, as follows:

```
let person = {
  sayName: function(name) {
    console.log('My name is ${name}');
  }
};

person.sayName('Matt');  // My name is Matt
```

The new shorthand method syntax follows this pattern and allows the developer to give up the capability to name the function expression—which, most of the time, is not useful anyway—and in exchange dramatically shorten how a function property can be expressed.

The following code uses this shorthand syntax:

```
let person = {
  sayName(name) {
    console.log('My name is ${name}');
  }
};

person.sayName('Matt');  // My name is Matt
```

This is also applicable to the getter and setter object conventions:

```
let person = {
  name_: '',
  get name() {
    return this.name_;
  },
  set name(name) {
    this.name_ = name;
  },
  sayName() {
    console.log('My name is ${this.name_}');
  }
};

person.name = 'Matt';
person.sayName();  // My name is Matt
```

Shorthand method syntax and computed property keys can be used together:

```
const methodKey = 'sayName';

let person = {
  [methodKey](name) {
    console.log('My name is ${name}');
  }
}

person.sayName('Matt');  // My name is Matt
```

Object Destructuring

Object destructuring allows you to perform one or many operations using nested data within a single statement. With respect to objects, this gives you the ability to perform assignments from object properties using syntax that matches the structure of an object.

The following is an example of two equivalent code snippets, first without object destructuring:

```
// Without object destructuring
let person = {
  name: 'Matt',
```

```
    age: 27
};

let personName = person.name,
    personAge = person.age;

console.log(personName);   // Matt
console.log(personAge);    // 27
```

Second, with object destructuring:

```
// With object destructuring
let person = {
  name: 'Matt',
  age: 27
};

let { name: personName, age: personAge } = person;

console.log(personName);   // Matt
console.log(personAge);    // 27
```

Destructuring allows you to declare multiple variables and simultaneously perform multiple assignments all at once. If you want to reuse the property name as a local variable name, you can use a shorthand syntax, as follows:

```
let person = {
  name: 'Matt',
  age: 27
};

let { name, age } = person;

console.log(name);   // Matt
console.log(age);    // 27
```

Destructuring assignments do not have to match what is inside the object. You can ignore properties when performing an assignment; conversely, if you reference a property that does not exist, undefined will be assigned:

```
let person = {
  name: 'Matt',
  age: 27
};

let { name, job } = person;

console.log(name);   // Matt
console.log(job);    // undefined
```

It is also possible to define default values, which will be applied if a property does not exist in the source object:

```
let person = {
  name: 'Matt',
  age: 27
```

```
};

let { name, job='Software engineer' } = person;

console.log(name);   // Matt
console.log(job);    // Software engineer
```

Destructuring uses the internal function ToObject() (which is not directly accessible in the runtime) to coerce a source into an object. This means that primitive values will be treated as objects when used in a destructuring operation; this also means that null and undefined cannot be destructured and will throw an error.

```
let { length } = 'foobar';
console.log(length);        // 6

let { constructor: c } = 4;
console.log(c === Number);  // true

let { _ } = null;           // TypeError

let { _ } = undefined;      // TypeError
```

Destructuring does not demand that variable declarations occur inside the destructuring expression. However, doing so requires the assignment expression to be contained inside parentheses:

```
let personName, personAge;

let person = {
  name: 'Matt',
  age: 27
};

({name: personName, age: personAge} = person);

console.log(personName, personAge);  // Matt, 27
```

Nested Destructuring

There are no restrictions on referencing nested properties or assignment targets. This allows you to do things like perform copies of object properties:

```
let person = {
  name: 'Matt',
  age: 27,
  job: {
    title: 'Software engineer'
  }
};
let personCopy = {};


({
  name: personCopy.name,
  age: personCopy.age,
  job: personCopy.job
```

```
    } = person);

    // Because an object reference was assigned into personCopy, changing a property
    // inside the person.job object will be propagated to personCopy:
    person.job.title = 'Hacker'

    console.log(person);
    // { name: 'Matt', age: 27, job: { title: 'Hacker' } }

    console.log(personCopy);
    // { name: 'Matt', age: 27, job: { title: 'Hacker' } }
```

Destructuring assignments can be nested to match nested property references:

```
    let person = {
      name: 'Matt',
      age: 27,
      job: {
        title: 'Software engineer'
      }
    };

    // Declares 'title' variable and assigns person.job.title as its value
    let { job: { title }} = person;

    console.log(title);  // Software engineer
```

You cannot use nested property references when an outer property is undefined. This is true for both source objects and destination objects:

```
    let person = {
      job: {
        title: 'Software engineer'
      }
    };
    let personCopy = {};

    // 'foo' is undefined on the source object
    ({
      foo: {
        bar: personCopy.bar
      }
    } = person);
    // TypeError: Cannot destructure property 'bar' of 'undefined' or 'null'.

    // 'job' is undefined on the destination object
    ({
      job: {
        title: personCopy.job.title
      }
    } = person);
    // TypeError: Cannot set property 'title' of undefined
```

Partial Destructuring Completion

It's important to note that a destructured assignment involving multiple properties is a sequential operation with independent outcomes. If, within a single destructured expression with multiple assignments, the initial assignments succeed but a later one throws an error, the destructured assignment will exit having only partially completed:

```
let person = {
  name: 'Matt',
  age: 27
};

let personName, personBar, personAge;

try {
  // person.foo is undefined, so this will throw an error
  ({name: personName, foo: { bar: personBar }, age: personAge} = person);
} catch(e) {}

console.log(personName, personBar, personAge);
// Matt, undefined, undefined
```

Parameter Context Matching

It is also possible to perform a destructured assignment inside a function parameter list. It does not affect the arguments object, but it allows you to declare variables inside the function signature that are immediately available inside the function body:

```
let person = {
  name: 'Matt',
  age: 27
};

function printPerson(foo, {name, age}, bar) {
  console.log(arguments);
  console.log(name, age);
}

function printPerson2(foo, {name: personName, age: personAge}, bar) {
  console.log(arguments);
  console.log(personName, personAge);
}

printPerson('1st', person, '2nd');
// ['1st', { name: 'Matt', age: 27 }, '2nd']
// 'Matt', 27

printPerson2('1st', person, '2nd');
// ['1st', { name: 'Matt', age: 27 }, '2nd']
// 'Matt', 27
```

Rest Operator

When restructuring an object, you can use the rest operator to collect all remaining unspecified enumerable properties into a single object. This can be done as follows:

```
const person = { name: 'Matt', age: 27, job: 'Engineer' };
const { name, ...remainingData } = person;

console.log(name);  // Matt
console.log(remainingData);  // { age: 27, job: 'Engineer' }
```

The rest operator can be used at most once per object literal and must be listed last. Because there can be only a single rest operator per object literal, it is possible to nest the rest operators. When nesting, because there is no ambiguity about which elements of the property subtree are allocated to any given rest operator, the resulting objects will never overlap with respect to their contents:

```
const person = { name: 'Matt', age: 27, job: { title: 'Engineer', level: 10 } };

const { name, job: { title, ...remainingJobData }, ...remainingPersonData } = person;

console.log(name);              // Matt
console.log(title);             // Engineer
console.log(remainingPersonData);  // { age: 27 }
console.log(remainingJobData);     // { level: 10 }

const { ...a, job } = person;
// SyntaxError: Rest element must be last element
```

The rest operator performs a shallow copy between objects, so object references will be copied instead of creating entire object clones:

```
const person = { name: 'Matt', age: 27, job: { title: 'Engineer', level: 10 } };

const { ...remainingData } = person;

console.log(person === remainingData);          // false
console.log(person.job === remainingData.job);  // true
```

The rest operator will copy all enumerable own properties, including symbols:

```
const s = Symbol();
const foo = { a: 1, [s]: 2, b: 3 }

const {a, ...remainingData} = foo;

console.log(remainingData);
// { b: 3, Symbol(): 2 }
```

Spread Operator

The spread operator allows you to join two objects together in a fashion similar to array concatenation. The spread operator applied to an inner object will perform a shallow copy of all enumerable own properties, including symbols, into the outer object:

```
const s = Symbol();
const foo = { a: 1 };
```

```
const bar = { [s]: 2 };

const foobar = {...foo, c: 3, ...bar};

console.log(foobar);
// { a: 1, c: 3 Symbol(): 2 }
```

The order in which the spread objects are listed matters for two reasons:

1. Objects track insertion order. The properties copied from spread objects will be performed in the order they are listed inside the object literal.

2. Objects will overwrite properties as duplicates are encountered. The last property encountered will be the one that assumes the value.

These ordering conventions are demonstrated here:

```
const foo = { a: 1 };
const bar = { b: 2 };

const foobar = {c: 3, ...bar, ...foo};

console.log(foobar);
// { c: 3, b: 2, a: 1}

const baz = { c: 4 };

const foobarbaz = {...foo, ...bar, c: 3, ...baz };

console.log(foobarbaz);
// { a: 1, b: 2, c: 4 }
```

As with the rest operator, all copies performed are shallow:

```
const foo = { a: 1 };
const bar = { b: 2, c: { d: 3 } };

const foobar = {...foo, ...bar};

console.log(foobar.c === bar.c);  // true
```

OBJECT CREATION

Although using the Object constructor or an object literal are convenient ways to create single objects, there is an obvious downside: creating multiple objects with the same interface requires a lot of code duplication.

Overview

Through successive specifications, the available features of ECMAScript followed a highly unusual pattern. Through the ECMAScript 5.1 specification, there was no formal support for object-oriented constructs such as classes or inheritance. However, as you will see in the following sections, clever application of prototypal inheritance allowed JavaScript developers to emulate this behavior—quite successfully.

With the ECMAScript 6 specification, formal support for classes and inheritance was introduced. These ECMAScript classes are intended to completely subsume the prototype-based class solutions designed in previous specifications. However, their implementation is, in many ways, merely a syntactical abstraction for ES5.1-style constructor functions and prototypal inheritance.

> **NOTE** *A JavaScript codebase built upon object-oriented patterns should almost always use ECMAScript classes. That said, it is instructive to learn about the conventions that existed prior to ES6, especially since the ECMAScript class definition can be imagined as a thin wrapper around existing constructs. Therefore, before the classes section, the following sections will progressively introduce the underlying concepts that are replaced by classes.*

The Function Constructor Pattern

As mentioned in previous chapters, constructors in ECMAScript are used to create specific types of objects. There are native constructors, such as `Object` and `Array`, which are available automatically in the execution environment at runtime. It is also possible to define custom constructors, in the form of a function, that define properties and methods for your own type of object.

Consider the following example that uses the function constructor pattern:

```
function Person(name, age, job){
  this.name = name;
  this.age = age;
  this.job = job;
  this.sayName = function() {
    console.log(this.name);
  };
}

let person1 = new Person("Alice", 29, "Software Engineer");
let person2 = new Person("Greg", 27, "Doctor");

person1.sayName();  // Alice
person2.sayName();  // Greg
```

Note that:

➤ There is no object being created explicitly.

➤ The properties and method are assigned directly onto the `this` object.

➤ There is no `return` statement.

Also note the name of the function is `Person` with an uppercase *P*. By convention, constructor functions always begin with an uppercase letter, whereas nonconstructor functions begin with a lowercase letter. This convention is borrowed from other object-oriented languages and helps to distinguish function use in ECMAScript because constructors are simply functions that create objects.

To create a new instance of `Person`, use the `new` operator. Calling a constructor in this manner will do the following:

1. A new object is created in memory.

2. The new object's internal `[[Prototype]]` pointer is assigned to the constructor's prototype property.

3. The `this` value of the constructor is assigned to the new object (so this points to the new object).

4. The code inside the constructor is executed (adds properties to the new object).

5. If the constructor function returns a non-`null` value, that object is returned. Otherwise, the new object that was just created is returned.

At the end of the preceding example, `person1` and `person2` are each filled with a different instance of `Person`. Each of these objects has a constructor property that points back to `Person`, as follows:

```
console.log(person1.constructor == Person);  // true
console.log(person2.constructor == Person);  // true
```

The `constructor` property was originally intended for use in identifying the object type. However, the `instanceof` operator is a safer way of determining type. Each of the objects in this example is both an instance of `Object` and an instance of `Person`, as indicated by using the `instanceof` operator like this:

```
console.log(person1 instanceof Object);  // true
console.log(person1 instanceof Person);  // true
console.log(person2 instanceof Object);  // true
console.log(person2 instanceof Person);  // true
```

Defining your own constructors ensures that instances can be identified as a particular. In this example, `person1` and `person2` are considered to be instances of `Object` because all custom objects inherit from `Object` (the specifics of this are discussed later).

Constructor functions do not have to be expressed as a function declaration. A function expression assigned to a variable behaves identically:

```
let Person = function(name, age, job) {
  this.name = name;
  this.age = age;
  this.job = job;
  this.sayName = function() {
    console.log(this.name);
  };
};

let person1 = new Person("Alice", 29, "Software Engineer");
```

```
    let person2 = new Person("Greg", 27, "Doctor");

    person1.sayName();   // Alice
    person2.sayName();   // Greg

    console.log(person1 instanceof Object);   // true
    console.log(person1 instanceof Person);   // true
    console.log(person2 instanceof Object);   // true
    console.log(person2 instanceof Person);   // true
```

When instantiating, the parentheses after the constructor function are optional if you do not wish to pass any arguments—the new operator will invoke the constructor function no matter what:

```
function Person() {
  this.name = "Jake";
  this.sayName = function() {
    console.log(this.name);
  };
}

let person1 = new Person();
let person2 = new Person;

person1.sayName();   // Jake
person2.sayName();   // Jake

console.log(person1 instanceof Object);   // true
console.log(person1 instanceof Person);   // true
console.log(person2 instanceof Object);   // true
console.log(person2 instanceof Person);   // true
```

Constructors as Functions

The only difference between constructor functions and other functions is the way in which they are called. Constructors are, after all, just functions; there's no special syntax to define a constructor that automatically makes it behave as such. Any function that is called with the new operator acts as a constructor, whereas any function called without it acts just as you would expect a normal function call to act. For instance, the Person() function from the previous example may be called in any of the following ways:

```
// use as a constructor
let person = new Person("Alice", 29, "Software Engineer");
person.sayName();   // "Alice"

// call as a function
Person("Greg", 27, "Doctor");   // adds to window
window.sayName();   // "Greg"

// call in the scope of another object
let o = new Object();
Person.call(o, "Kristen", 25, "Nurse");
o.sayName();   // "Kristen"
```

The first part of this example shows the typical use of a constructor—to create a new object via the new operator. The second part shows what happens when the Person() function is called without the new operator: The properties and methods get added to the window object. Remember that the this object always points to the Global object (window in web browsers) when a function is called without an explicitly set this value (by being an object method or through call()/apply()). After the function is called, the sayName() method can be called on the window object, and it will return "Greg". The Person() function can also be called within the scope of a particular object using call() (or apply()). In this case, it's called with a this value of the object o, which then gets assigned all of the properties and the sayName() method.

Problems with Constructors

Though the constructor paradigm is useful, it is not without its faults. The major downside to constructors is that methods are created once for each instance. So, in the previous example, both person1 and person2 have a method called sayName(), but those methods are not the same instance of Function. Remember that all functions are objects in ECMAScript, so every time a function is defined, it's an object being instantiated. Logically, the constructor might look like this:

```
function Person(name, age, job){
    this.name = name;
    this.age = age;
    this.job = job;
    this.sayName = new Function("console.log(this.name)");  // logical equivalent
}
```

Thinking about the constructor in this manner makes it clear that each instance of Person gets its own instance of Function that happens to display the name property. To be clear, creating a function in this manner is different with regard to scope chains and identifier resolution, but the mechanics of creating a new instance of Function remain the same. So, functions of the same name on different instances are not equivalent, as the following code proves:

```
console.log(person1.sayName == person2.sayName);  // false
```

It doesn't make sense to have two instances of Function that do the same thing, especially when the this object makes it possible to avoid binding functions to particular objects until runtime.

It's possible to work around this limitation by moving the function definition outside of the constructor, as follows:

```
function Person(name, age, job){
    this.name = name;
    this.age = age;
    this.job = job;
    this.sayName = sayName;
}

function sayName() {
    console.log(this.name);
}

let person1 = new Person("Alice", 29, "Software Engineer");
let person2 = new Person("Greg", 27, "Doctor");

person1.sayName();  // Alice
person2.sayName();  // Greg
```

In this example, the `sayName()` function is defined outside the constructor. Inside the constructor, ·
the `sayName` property is set equal to the global `sayName()` function. Because the `sayName` property
now contains just a pointer to a function, both `person1` and `person2` end up sharing the `sayName()`
function that is defined in the global scope. This solves the problem of having duplicate functions that
do the same thing but also creates some clutter in the global scope by introducing a function that can
realistically be used only in relation to an object. If the object needed multiple methods, that would
mean multiple global functions, and all of a sudden the custom reference type definition is no longer
nicely grouped in the code. These problems are addressed by using the prototype pattern.

The Prototype Pattern

Each function is created with a `prototype` property, which is an object containing properties and
methods that should be available to instances of a particular reference type. This object is literally a prototype for the object to be created once the constructor is called. The benefit of using the
prototype is that all of its properties and methods are shared among object instances. Instead of
assigning object information in the constructor, they can be assigned directly to the prototype, as in
this example:

```
function Person() {}

Person.prototype.name = "Alice";
Person.prototype.age = 29;
Person.prototype.job = "Software Engineer";
Person.prototype.sayName = function() {
  console.log(this.name);
};

let person1 = new Person();
person1.sayName();    // "Alice"

let person2 = new Person();
person2.sayName();    // "Alice"

console.log(person1.sayName == person2.sayName);   // true
```

Using a function expression is also suitable:

```
let Person = function() {};

Person.prototype.name = "Alice";
Person.prototype.age = 29;
Person.prototype.job = "Software Engineer";
Person.prototype.sayName = function() {
  console.log(this.name);
};

let person1 = new Person();
```

```
person1.sayName();    // "Alice"

let person2 = new Person();
person2.sayName();    // "Alice"

console.log(person1.sayName == person2.sayName);   // true
```

Here, the properties and the `sayName()` method are added directly to the prototype property of `Person`, leaving the constructor empty. However, it's still possible to call the constructor to create a new object and have the properties and methods present. Unlike the constructor pattern, the properties and methods are all shared among instances, so `person1` and `person2` are both accessing the same set of properties and the same `sayName()` function. To understand how this works, you must understand the nature of prototypes in ECMAScript.

How Prototypes Work

Whenever a function is created, its `prototype` property is also created according to a specific set of rules. By default, all prototypes automatically get a property called `constructor` that points back to the function on which it is a property. In the previous example, for instance, `Person.prototype` `.constructor` points back to `Person`. Then, depending on the constructor, other properties and methods may be added to the prototype.

When defining a custom constructor, the prototype gets the `constructor` property only by default; all other methods are inherited from `Object`. Each time the constructor is called to create a new instance, that instance has an internal pointer to the constructor's prototype. In ECMA-262, this is called `[[Prototype]]`. There is no standardized way to access `[[Prototype]]` from script, but modern browsers support a property on every object called `__proto__`. The important thing to understand is that a direct link exists between the instance and the constructor's prototype, but not between the instance and the constructor.

This relationship can be difficult to visualize, so refer to the following table of code snippets demonstrating the various relationships between constructors, prototypes, and instances.

CONCEPT	EXAMPLE SNIPPET
`constructor` function declaration and function expression	`function Person() {}` `let Person = function() {}`

Constructor function's `prototype` object	`console.log(typeof Person.prototype);`
	`console.log(Person.prototype);`
	`// {`
	`//    constructor: f Person(),`
	`//    __proto__: Object`
	`// }`

Cyclical references between `constructor` function and `prototype` object	`console.log(Person.prototype`
	`.constructor ===`
	`Person);`
	`// true`

continues

(continued)

| Prototype chain termination at the `Object` prototype | ```
console.log(Person.prototype.__proto__
=== Object.prototype);
// true

console.log(Person.prototype.__proto__
.constructor === Object);
// true

console.log(Person.prototype.__proto__.__
proto__ === null);
// true

console.log(Person.prototype.__proto__);
// {
//   constructor: f Object(),
//   toString: ...
//   hasOwnProperty: ...
//   isPrototypeOf: ...
//   ...
// }
``` |
|---|---|
| Creating instances of the `constructor` function | ```
let person1 = new Person(),
    person2 = new Person();
``` |
| Distinct objects in constructor, `prototype` object, and instance | ```
console.log(person1 !== Person);
// true

console.log(person1 !== Person.prototype);
// true

console.log(Person.prototype !== Person);
// true
``` |
| Instance, `constructor`, and `prototype` relationships | ```
Console.log(person1.__proto__
=== Person.prototype);
// true

conosle.log(person1.__proto__
.constructor === Person);
// true
``` |
| Instances sharing the same `prototype` | ```
console.log(person1.__proto__ ===
person2.__proto__);
// true
``` |
| `instanceof` operator usage | ```
console.log(person1 instanceof Person);
// true

console.log(person1 instanceof Object);
// true

console.log(Person.prototype instanceof
Object);
// true
``` |

Consider the original example using the `Person` constructor and `Person.prototype`. The relationship between the objects in the example is shown in Figure 8.1.

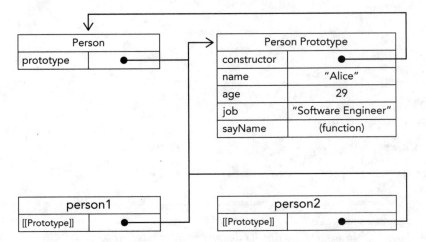

FIGURE 8.1: Diagram showing the relationship between `constructor`, `prototype`, and instances

Figure 8.1 shows the relationship between the `Person` constructor, the `Person` prototype, and the two instances of `Person` that exist. Note that `Person.prototype` points to the `prototype` object, but `Person.prototype.constructor` points back to `Person`. The prototype contains the `constructor` property and the other properties that were added. Each instance of `Person`, `person1`, and `person2` has internal properties that point back to `Person.prototype` only; each has no direct relationship with the `constructor`. Also note that even though neither of these instances have properties or methods, `person1.sayName()` works. This is due to the lookup procedure for object properties.

Even though `[[Prototype]]` is not accessible in all implementations, the `isPrototypeOf()` method can be used to determine if this relationship exists between objects. Essentially, `isPrototypeOf()` returns `true` if `[[Prototype]]` points to the `prototype` on which the method is being called, as shown here:

```
console.log(Person.prototype.isPrototypeOf(person1));   // true
console.log(Person.prototype.isPrototypeOf(person2));   // true
```

In this code, the `prototype.isPrototypeOf()` method is called on both `person1` and `person2`. Because both instances have a link to `Person.prototype`, it returns `true`.

The ECMAScript `Object` type has a method called `Object.getPrototypeOf()`, which returns the value of `[[Prototype]]`. For example:

```
console.log(Object.getPrototypeOf(person1) == Person.prototype);   // true
console.log(Object.getPrototypeOf(person1).name);                  // "Alice"
```

The first line of this code simply confirms that the object returned from `Object.getPrototypeOf()` is actually the `prototype` of the object. The second line retrieves the value of the `name` property on the prototype, which is `"Alice"`. Using `Object.getPrototypeOf()`, you can retrieve an object's prototype easily, which becomes important once you want to implement inheritance using the prototype (discussed later in this chapter).

The `Object` type also features a `setPrototypeOf()` method, which writes a new value into the `[[Prototype]]` of the instance. This allows you to overwrite the `prototype` hierarchy of an already-instantiated object:

```
let biped = {
  numLegs: 2
};
let person = {
  name: 'Matt'
};

Object.setPrototypeOf(person, biped);

console.log(person.name);                              // Matt
console.log(person.numLegs);                           // 2
console.log(Object.getPrototypeOf(person) === biped);  // true
```

> **NOTE** *The* `Object.setPrototypeOf()` *operation will likely cause severe performance slowdowns when used. The Mozilla documentation has this to say: "In every browser and JavaScript engine, the effects on performance of altering inheritance are subtle and far-flung, and are not limited to simply the time spent in* `Object.setPrototypeOf()` *statements, but may extend to any code that has access to any object whose* `[[Prototype]]` *has been altered."*

To avoid these slowdowns, prefer to just create a new object and specify its prototype with `Object.create()`:

```
let biped = {
  numLegs: 2
};
let person = Object.create(biped);
person.name = 'Matt';

console.log(person.name);                              // Matt
console.log(person.numLegs);                           // 2
console.log(Object.getPrototypeOf(person) === biped);  // true
```

Understanding the Prototype Hierarchy

Whenever a property is accessed for reading on an object, a search is started to find a property with that name. The search begins on the object instance itself. If a property with the given name is found on the instance, then that value is returned; if the property is not found, then the search continues up the pointer to the prototype, and the prototype is searched for a property with the same name. If the property is found on the prototype, then that value is returned.

When `person1.sayName()` is called, a two-step process happens. First, the JavaScript engine checks, "Does the instance `person1` have a property called `sayName`?" The answer is no, so it continues the search and checks, "Does the `person1` prototype have a property called `sayName`?" The answer is yes, so the function stored on the prototype is accessed. When `person2.sayName()` is called, the same search executes, ending with the same result.

This is how prototypes are used to share properties and methods among multiple object instances.

> **NOTE** *The* constructor *property mentioned earlier exists only on the* prototype *and so is accessible from object instances.*

Although it's possible to read values on the prototype from object instances, it is not possible to overwrite them. If you add a property to an instance that has the same name as a property on the prototype, you create the property on the instance, which then masks the property on the prototype. Here's an example:

```
function Person() {}

Person.prototype.name = "Alice";
Person.prototype.age = 29;
Person.prototype.job = "Software Engineer";
Person.prototype.sayName = function() {
    console.log(this.name);
};

let person1 = new Person();
let person2 = new Person();

person1.name = "Greg";
console.log(person1.name);    // "Greg" - from instance
console.log(person2.name);    // "Alice" - from prototype
```

In this example, the `name` property of `person1` is shadowed by a new value. Both `person1.name` and `person2.name` still function appropriately, returning `"Greg"` (from the object instance) and `"Alice"` (from the `prototype`), respectively. When `person1.name` is accessed, the search began for a property called `name` on the instance. Because the property exists, it is used without searching the prototype. When `person2.name` is accessed the same way, the search doesn't find the property on the instance, so it continues to search on the prototype where the name property is found.

Once a property is added to the object instance, it *shadows* any properties of the same name on the prototype, which means that it blocks access to the property on the prototype without altering it. Even setting the property to `null` only sets the property on the instance and doesn't restore the link to the prototype. The `delete` operator, however, completely removes the instance property and allows the prototype property to be accessed again as follows:

```
function Person() {}

Person.prototype.name = "Alice";
Person.prototype.age = 29;
Person.prototype.job = "Software Engineer";
Person.prototype.sayName = function() {
    console.log(this.name);
```

```
};

let person1 = new Person();
let person2 = new Person();

person1.name = "Greg";
console.log(person1.name);    // "Greg" - from instance
console.log(person2.name);    // "Alice" - from prototype

delete person1.name;
console.log(person1.name);    // "Alice" - from the prototype
```

In this modified example, `delete` is called on `person1.name`, which previously had been shadowed with the value `"Greg"`. This restores the link to the prototype's `name` property, so the next time `person1.name` is accessed, it's the `prototype` property's value that is returned.

The `hasOwnProperty()` method determines if a property exists on the instance or on the prototype. This method, which is inherited from `Object`, returns `true` only if a property of the given name exists on the object instance, as in this example:

```
function Person() {}

Person.prototype.name = "Alice";
Person.prototype.age = 29;
Person.prototype.job = "Software Engineer";
Person.prototype.sayName = function() {
  console.log(this.name);
};

let person1 = new Person();
let person2 = new Person();

console.log(person1.hasOwnProperty("name"));    // false

person1.name = "Greg";
console.log(person1.name);    // "Greg" - from instance
console.log(person1.hasOwnProperty("name"));    // true

console.log(person2.name);    // "Alice" - from prototype
console.log(person2.hasOwnProperty("name"));    // false

delete person1.name;
console.log(person1.name);    // "Alice" - from the prototype
console.log(person1.hasOwnProperty("name"));    // false
```

By injecting calls to `hasOwnProperty()` in this example, it becomes clear when the instance's property is being accessed and when the `prototype`'s property is being accessed. Calling `person1.hasOwnProperty("name")` returns `true` only after `name` has been overwritten on `person1`, indicating that it now has an instance property instead of a `prototype` property. Figure 8.2 illustrates the various steps being taken in this example. (For simplicity, the relationship to the `Person` constructor has been omitted.)

The `Object.hasOwn()` method is an alternative shorthand notation for `Object.prototype.hasOwnProperty()`. The following lines are equivalent:

```
person.hasOwnProperty("name");
Object.hasOwn(person, "name");
```

Initially

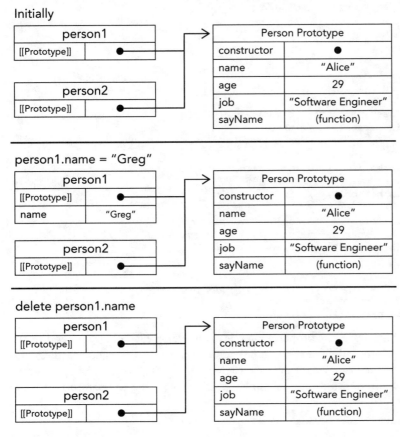

FIGURE 8.2: Diagram showing the effects of assignment and `delete` operations

> **NOTE** *The ECMAScript* `Object.getOwnPropertyDescriptor()` *method works only on instance properties; to retrieve the descriptor of a* `prototype` *property, you must call* `Object.getOwnPropertyDescriptor()` *on the* `prototype` *object directly.*

Prototypes and the *in* Operator

There are two ways to use the `in` operator: on its own or as a `for-in` loop. When used on its own, the in operator returns `true` when a property of the given name is accessible by the object, which is to say that the property may exist on the instance *or* on the `prototype`. Consider the following example:

```
function Person() {}

Person.prototype.name = "Alice";
Person.prototype.age = 29;
```

```
Person.prototype.job = "Software Engineer";
Person.prototype.sayName = function() {
  console.log(this.name);
};

let person1 = new Person();
let person2 = new Person();

console.log(person1.hasOwnProperty("name"));  // false
console.log("name" in person1);  // true

person1.name = "Greg";
console.log(person1.name);   // "Greg" - from instance
console.log(person1.hasOwnProperty("name"));  // true
console.log("name" in person1);  // true

console.log(person2.name);   // "Alice" - from prototype
console.log(person2.hasOwnProperty("name"));  // false
console.log("name" in person2);  // true

delete person1.name;
console.log(person1.name);   // "Alice" - from the prototype
console.log(person1.hasOwnProperty("name"));  // false
console.log("name" in person1);  // true
```

Throughout the execution of this code, the property name is available on each object either directly or from the prototype. Therefore, calling "name" on person1 always returns true, regardless of whether the property exists on the instance. It's possible to determine if the property of an object exists on the prototype by combining a call to hasOwnProperty() with the in operator:

```
function hasPrototypeProperty(object, name){
  return !object.hasOwnProperty(name) && (name in object);
}
```

Because the in operator always returns true as long as the property is accessible by the object, and hasOwnProperty() returns true only if the property exists on the instance, a prototype property can be determined if the in operator returns true but hasOwnProperty() returns false. Consider the following example:

```
function Person() {}

Person.prototype.name = "Alice";
Person.prototype.age = 29;
Person.prototype.job = "Software Engineer";
Person.prototype.sayName = function() {
  console.log(this.name);
};

let person = new Person();
console.log(hasPrototypeProperty(person, "name"));  // true

person.name = "Greg";
console.log(hasPrototypeProperty(person, "name"));  // false
```

In this code, the name property first exists on the `prototype`, so `hasPrototypeProperty()` returns `true`. Once the `name` property is overwritten, it exists on the instance, so `hasPrototypeProperty()` returns `false`. Even though the `name` property still exists on the prototype, it is no longer used because the instance property now exists.

When using a `for-in` loop, all properties that are accessible by the object and can be enumerated will be returned, which includes properties both on the instance and on the `prototype`. Instance properties that shadow a non-enumerable prototype property (a property that has `[[Enumerable]]` set to `false`) will be returned in the `for-in` loop because all manually defined properties are enumerable by default.

To retrieve a list of all enumerable instance properties on an object, you can use the `Object.keys()` method, which accepts an object as its argument and returns an array of strings containing the names of all enumerable properties. For example:

```
function Person() {}

Person.prototype.name = "Alice";
Person.prototype.age = 29;
Person.prototype.job = "Software Engineer";
Person.prototype.sayName = function() {
  console.log(this.name);
};

let keys = Object.keys(Person.prototype);
console.log(keys);     // "name,age,job,sayName"
let p1 = new Person();
p1.name = "Rob";
p1.age = 31;
let p1keys = Object.keys(p1);
console.log(p1keys);   // "name,age"
```

Here, the keys variable is filled with an array containing `"name"`, `"age"`, `"job"`, and `"sayName"`. This is the order in which they would normally appear using `for-in`. When called on an instance of `Person`, `Object.keys()` returns an array of `"name"` and `"age"`, the only two instance properties.

If you'd like a list of all instance properties (including non-enumerable), you can use `Object.getOwnPropertyNames()` in the same way:

```
let keys = Object.getOwnPropertyNames(Person.prototype);
console.log(keys);    // "constructor,name,age,job,sayName"
```

Note the inclusion of the non-enumerable `constructor` property in the list of results. Both `Object.keys()` and `Object.getOwnPropertyNames()` may be suitable replacements for using `for-in`.

Because symbol-keyed properties do not have a concept of a "name," a sibling method to `Object.getOwnPropertyNames()` is needed. `Object.getOwnPropertySymbols()` offers the same behavior as `Object.getOwnPropertyNames()` but with respect to symbols:

```
let k1 = Symbol('k1'),
```

```
    k2 = Symbol('k2');

let o = {
  [k1]: 'k1',
  [k2]: 'k2'
};

console.log(Object.getOwnPropertySymbols(o));
// [Symbol(k1), Symbol(k2)]
```

Property Enumeration Order

for-in loops, Object.keys(), Object.getOwnPropertyNames, Object
.getOwnPropertySymbols(), and Object.assign() have an important distinction when it comes to property enumeration order. for-in loops and Object.keys() do not have a deterministic order of enumeration—these are determined by the JavaScript engine and may vary by browser.

Object.getOwnPropertyNames(), Object.getOwnPropertySymbols(), and Object.assign() *do* have a deterministic enumeration order. Number keys will first be enumerated in ascending order, then string and symbol keys enumerated in insertion order. Keys defined inline in an object literal will be inserted in their comma delimited order.

```
let k1 = Symbol('k1'),
    k2 = Symbol('k2');

let o = {
  1: 1,
  first: 'first',
  [k1]: 'sym2',
  second: 'second',
  0: 0
};

o[k2] = 'sym2';
o[3] = 3;
o.third = 'third';
0[2] = 2;

console.log(Object.getOwnPropertyNames(o));
// ["0", "1", "3", "first", "second", "third"]

console.log(Object.getOwnPropertySymbols(o));
// [Symbol(k1), Symbol(k2)]
```

Object Iteration

The static methods, Object.values() and Object.entries(), can be used for converting an object's contents into a serialized and iterable format. These methods accept an object and return its contents in an array. Object.values() returns an array of the object's values, and Object.entries() returns an array of array pairs, each representing a key-value pair in the object.

These methods are demonstrated here:

```
const o = {
  foo: 'bar',
  baz: 1,
```

```
    qux: {}
};

console.log(Object.values(o));
// ["bar", 1, {}]

console.log(Object.entries((o)));
// [["foo", "bar"], ["baz", 1], ["qux", {}]]
```

Note that non-string properties are converted to strings in the output array. Furthermore, the method performs a shallow copy of the object:

```
const o = {
    qux: {}
};

console.log(Object.values(o)[0] === o.qux);
// true

console.log(Object.entries(o)[0][1] === o.qux);
// true
Symbol-keyed properties are ignored:
const sym = Symbol();
const o = {
    [sym]: 'foo'
};

console.log(Object.values(o));
// []

console.log(Object.entries((o)));
// []
```

ECMAScript also features the static method `Object.fromEntries()`, which builds an object from a collection of key-value array pairs. This method performs the inverse operation of `Object.entries()` and is demonstrated here:

```
const obj = {
    foo: 'bar',
    baz: 'qux'
};

const objEntries = Object.entries(obj);

console.log(objEntries);
// [["foo", "bar"], ["baz", "qux"]]

console.log(Object.fromEntries(objEntries));
// { foo: "bar", baz: "qux" }
```

The static method expects an iterable object containing any number of iterable objects of size 2. This is especially useful in cases where you wish to convert a `Map` instance to an `Object` instance, as the `Map` iterator's output exactly matches the signature that `fromEntries()` ingests:

```
const map = new Map().set('foo', 'bar');

console.log(Object.fromEntries(map));
// { foo: "bar" }
```

Dynamic Nature of Prototypes

Because the process of looking up values on a prototype is a search, changes made to the prototype at any point are immediately reflected on instances, even the instances that existed before the change was made. Here's an example:

```
let friend = new Person();

Person.prototype.sayHi = function() {
  console.log("hi");
};

friend.sayHi();  // "hi" - works!
```

In this code, an instance of Person is created and stored in friend. The next statement adds a method called sayHi() to Person.prototype. Even though the friend instance was created prior to this change, it still has access to the new method. This happens because of the loose link between the instance and the prototype. When friend.sayHi() is called, the instance is first searched for a property named sayHi; when it's not found, the search continues to the prototype. Because the link between the instance and the prototype is simply a pointer, not a copy, the search finds the new sayHi property on the prototype and returns the function stored there.

Although properties and methods may be added to the prototype at any time, and they are reflected instantly by all object instances, you cannot overwrite the entire prototype and expect the same behavior. The [[Prototype]] pointer is assigned when the constructor is called, so changing the prototype to a different object severs the tie between the constructor and the original prototype. Remember that the instance has a pointer to only the prototype, not to the constructor. Consider the following:

```
function Person() {}

let friend = new Person();

Person.prototype = {
  constructor: Person,
  name: "Alice",
  age: 29,
  job: "Software Engineer",
  sayName() {
    console.log(this.name);
  }
};

friend.sayName();   // error
```

In this example, a new instance of Person is created before the prototype object is overwritten. When friend.sayName() is called, it causes an error, because the prototype that friend points to doesn't contain a property of that name. Figure 8.3 illustrates why this happens.

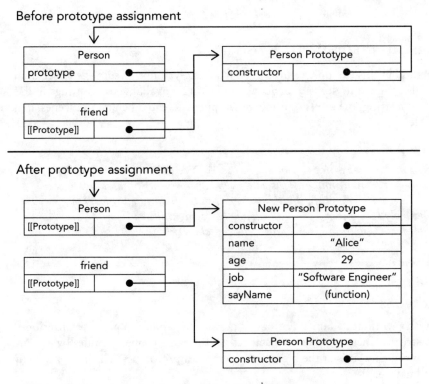

FIGURE 8.3: Diagram demonstrating effects of prototype assignment

Overwriting the prototype on the constructor means that new instances will reference the new prototype while any previously existing object instances still reference the old prototype.

Native Object Prototypes

The prototype pattern is important not just for defining custom types but also because it is the pattern used to implement all of the native reference types. Each of these (including `Object`, `Array`, `String`, and so on) has its methods defined on the constructor's prototype. For instance, the `sort()` method can be found on `Array.prototype`, and `substring()` can be found on `String.prototype`, as shown here:

```
console.log(typeof Array.prototype.sort);       // "function"
console.log(typeof String.prototype.substring);  // "function"
```

Through native object prototypes, it's possible to get references to all the default methods and to define new methods. Native object prototypes can be modified just like custom object prototypes, so methods can be added at any time. For example, the following code adds a method called `startsWith()` to the `String` primitive wrapper:

```
String.prototype.startsWith = function (text) {
    return this.indexOf(text) === 0;
```

```
};

let msg = "Hello world!";
console.log(msg.startsWith("Hello"));   // true
```

The `startsWith()` method in this example returns `true` if some given text occurs at the beginning of a string. The method is assigned to `String.prototype`, making it available to all strings in the environment. Since `msg` is a string, the `String` primitive wrapper is created behind the scenes, making `startsWith()` accessible.

> **NOTE** *Although possible, it is not recommended to modify native object prototypes in a production environment. This can often cause confusion and create possible name collisions if a method that didn't exist natively in one browser is implemented natively in another. It's also possible to accidentally overwrite native methods. The preferred method is to create a custom class that inherits from the native type.*

Problems with Prototypes

The prototype pattern isn't without its faults. For one, it negates the ability to pass initialization arguments into the constructor, meaning that all instances get the same property values by default. Although this is an inconvenience, it isn't the biggest problem with prototypes. The main problem comes with their shared nature.

All properties on the prototype are shared among instances, which is ideal for functions. Properties that contain primitive values also tend to work well, as shown in the previous example, where it's possible to hide the prototype property by assigning a property of the same name to the instance. The real problem occurs when a property contains a reference value. Consider the following example:

```
function Person() {}

Person.prototype = {
  constructor: Person,
  name: "Alice",
  age: 29,
  job: "Software Engineer",
  friends: ["Shelby", "Court"],
  sayName() {
    console.log(this.name);
  }
};

let person1 = new Person();
let person2 = new Person();

person1.friends.push("Van");

console.log(person1.friends);  // "Shelby,Court,Van"
console.log(person2.friends);  // "Shelby,Court,Van"
console.log(person1.friends === person2.friends);  // true
```

Here, the `Person.prototype` object has a property called friends that contains an array of strings. Two instances of `Person` are then created. The `person1.friends` array is altered by adding another string. Because the `friends` array exists on `Person.prototype`, not on `person1`, the changes made are also reflected on `person2.friends` (which points to the same array). If the intention is to have an array shared by all instances, then this outcome is okay. Typically, though, instances want to have their own copies of all properties. This is why the prototype pattern is rarely used on its own.

Prototype Inheritance

The concept most often discussed in relation to object-oriented programming is inheritance. Many object-oriented languages support two types of inheritance: interface inheritance, where only the method signatures are inherited, and implementation inheritance, where actual methods are inherited. Interface inheritance is not possible in ECMAScript because functions do not have signatures. Implementation inheritance is the only type of inheritance supported by ECMAScript, and this is done primarily with prototype chaining.

Prototype Chaining

ECMA-262 describes *prototype chaining* as the primary method of inheritance in ECMAScript. The basic idea is to use the concept of prototypes to inherit properties and methods between two reference types. Recall the relationship between constructors, prototypes, and instances: each constructor has a prototype object that points back to the constructor, and instances have an internal pointer to the prototype. What if the prototype were an instance of another type? That would mean the prototype itself would have a pointer to a different prototype that, in turn, would have a pointer to another constructor. If that prototype were also an instance of another type, then the pattern would continue, forming a chain between instances and prototypes. This is the basic idea behind prototype chaining.

Implementing prototype chaining involves the following code pattern:

```
function SuperType() {
  this.property = true;
}

SuperType.prototype.getSuperValue = function() {
  return this.property;
};

function SubType() {
  this.subproperty = false;
}

// inherit from SuperType
SubType.prototype = new SuperType();

SubType.prototype.getSubValue = function () {
  return this.subproperty;
};

let instance = new SubType();
console.log(instance.getSuperValue());  // true
```

This code defines two types: SuperType and SubType. Each type has a single property and a single method. The main difference between the two is that SubType inherits from SuperType by creating a new instance of SuperType and assigning it to SubType.prototype. This overwrites the original prototype and replaces it with a new object, which means that all properties and methods that typically exist on an instance of SuperType now also exist on SubType.prototype. After the inheritance takes place, a method is assigned to SubType.prototype, adding a new method on top of what was inherited from SuperType. The relationship between the instance and both constructors and prototypes is displayed in Figure 8.4.

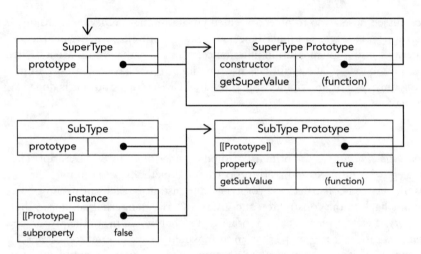

FIGURE 8.4: Diagram demonstrating the relationship between instances, constructors, and prototypes

Instead of using the default prototype of SubType, a new prototype is assigned. That new prototype happens to be an instance of SuperType, so it not only gets the properties and methods of a SuperType instance but also points back to the SuperType's prototype. So instance points to SubType.prototype and SubType.prototype points to SuperType.prototype. Note that the getSuperValue() method remains on the SuperType.prototype object, but property ends up on SubType.prototype. That's because getSuperValue() is a prototype method, and property is an instance property. SubType.prototype is now an instance of SuperType, so property is stored there. Also note that instance.constructor points to SuperType because the constructor property on the SubType.prototype was overwritten.

Prototype chaining extends to the prototype search mechanism described earlier. As you may recall, when a property is accessed in read mode on an instance, the property is first searched for on the instance. If the property is not found, then the search continues to the prototype. When inheritance has been implemented via prototype chaining, that search can continue up the prototype chain. In the previous example, for instance, a call to instance.getSuperValue() results in a three-step search: the instance, SubType.prototype, and SuperType.prototype, where the method is found. The search for properties and methods always continues until the end of the prototype chain is reached.

Default Prototypes

Up until this point, we've ignored the final step in the prototype chain. All reference types inherit from Object by default, which is accomplished through prototype chaining. The default prototype for any function is an instance of `Object`, meaning that its internal prototype pointer points to `Object.prototype`. This is how custom types inherit all of the default methods such as `toString()` and `valueOf()`. The previous example has an extra layer of inheritance. Figure 8.5 shows the complete prototype chain.

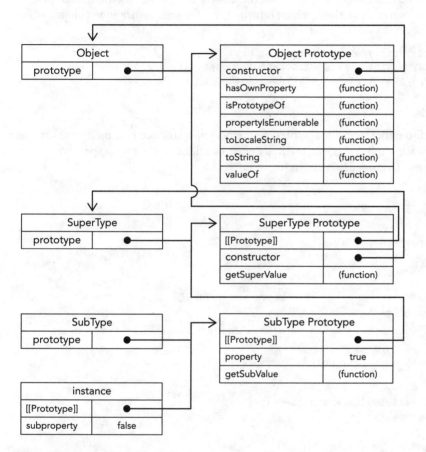

FIGURE 8.5: Diagram demonstrating the path of a prototype chain

`SubType` inherits from `SuperType`, and `SuperType` inherits from `Object`. When `instance.toString()` is called, the method being called actually exists on `Object.prototype`.

Prototype and Instance Relationships

The relationship between prototypes and instances is discernible in two ways. The first way is to use the `instanceof` operator, which returns true whenever an instance is used with a constructor that appears in its prototype chain, as in this example:

```
console.log(instance instanceof Object);    // true
console.log(instance instanceof SuperType); // true
console.log(instance instanceof SubType);   // true
```

Here, the instance object is technically an instance of `Object`, `SuperType`, and `SubType` because of the prototype chain relationship. The result is that `instanceof` returns true for all of these constructors.

The second way to determine this relationship is to use the `isPrototypeOf()` method. Each prototype in the chain has access to this method, which returns `true` for an instance in the chain, as in this example:

```
console.log(Object.prototype.isPrototypeOf(instance));      // true
console.log(SuperType.prototype.isPrototypeOf(instance));   // true
console.log(SubType.prototype.isPrototypeOf(instance));     // true
```

Working with Methods

Often a subtype will need to either override a supertype method or introduce new methods that don't exist on the supertype. To accomplish this, the methods must be added to the prototype after the prototype has been assigned. Consider this example:

```
function SuperType() {
  this.property = true;
}

SuperType.prototype.getSuperValue = function() {
  return this.property;
};

function SubType() {
  this.subproperty = false;
}

// inherit from SuperType
SubType.prototype = new SuperType();

// new method
SubType.prototype.getSubValue = function () {
  return this.subproperty;
};

// override existing method
SubType.prototype.getSuperValue = function () {
  return false;
};

let instance = new SubType();
console.log(instance.getSuperValue());   // false
```

In this code, the highlighted area shows two methods. The first is `getSubValue()`, which is a new method on the `SubType`. The second is `getSuperValue()`, which already exists in the prototype chain but is being shadowed here. When `getSuperValue()` is called on an instance of `SubType`, it will call this one, but instances of `SuperType` will still call the original. The important thing to note is that both of the methods are defined after the prototype has been assigned as an instance of `SuperType`.

Problems with Prototype Chaining

Even though prototype chaining is a powerful tool for inheritance, it is not without its issues. The major issue revolves around prototypes that contain reference values. Recall from earlier that prototype properties containing reference values are shared with all instances; this is why properties are typically defined within the constructor instead of on the prototype. When implementing inheritance using prototypes, the prototype actually becomes an instance of another type, meaning that what once were instance properties are now prototype properties. The issue is highlighted by the following example:

```
function SuperType() {
    this.colors = ["red", "blue", "green"];
}

function SubType() {}

// inherit from SuperType
SubType.prototype = new SuperType();

let instance1 = new SubType();
instance1.colors.push("black");
console.log(instance1.colors);  // "red,blue,green,black"

let instance2 = new SubType();
console.log(instance2.colors);  // "red,blue,green,black"
```

In this example, the SuperType constructor defines a property, colors, that contains an array (a reference value). Each instance of SuperType has its own colors property containing its own array. When SubType inherits from SuperType via prototype chaining, SubType.prototype becomes an instance of SuperType, and so it gets its own colors property, which is akin to specifically creating SubType.prototype.colors. The end result: all instances of SubType share a colors property. This is indicated as the changes made to instance1.colors are reflected on instance2.colors.

A second issue with prototype chaining is that you cannot pass arguments into the supertype constructor when the subtype instance is being created. In fact, there is no way to pass arguments into the supertype constructor without affecting all of the object instances. Because of this and the aforementioned issue with reference values on the prototype, prototype chaining is rarely used alone.

CLASSES

The previous sections are an in-depth overview of how it was possible to emulate class-like behavior using only features available in ECMAScript 5. It is not difficult to conclude that the strategies shown presented various problems and tradeoffs. On top of this, the syntax was inarguably excessively verbose and messy.

To address these problems, ECMAScript added the ability to formally define classes using the class keyword. Although ECMAScript classes appear to feature canonical object-oriented programming, they still uses prototype and constructor concepts under the hood.

Class Definition Basics

Similar to the `function` type, there are two primary ways of defining a class: *class declarations* and *class expressions*. Both use the `class` keyword and curly braces:

```
// class declaration
class Person {}

// class expression
const Animal = class {};
```

Like function expressions, class expressions cannot be referenced until they are evaluated in execution. However, an important departure from the parallel behavior of function definition is that, while function declarations are hoisted, class declarations are not:

```
console.log(FunctionExpression);   // undefined
var FunctionExpression = function() {};
console.log(FunctionExpression);   // function() {}


console.log(FunctionDeclaration); // FunctionDeclaration() {}
function FunctionDeclaration() {}
console.log(FunctionDeclaration); // FunctionDeclaration() {}


console.log(ClassExpression);      // undefined
var ClassExpression = class {};
console.log(ClassExpression);      // class {}


console.log(ClassDeclaration);     // ReferenceError: ClassDeclaration is
                                   // not defined
class ClassDeclaration {}
console.log(ClassDeclaration);     // class ClassDeclaration {}
```

Whereas function declarations are function scoped, class declarations are block scoped:

```
{
  function FunctionDeclaration() {}
  class ClassDeclaration {}
}

console.log(FunctionDeclaration); // FunctionDeclaration() {}
console.log(ClassDeclaration);    // ReferenceError: ClassDeclaration is
                                  // not defined
```

Class Composition

A class can be composed of the class's constructor method, instance methods, getters, setters, and static class methods. None of these are explicitly required; an empty class definition is valid syntax. By default, everything inside a class definition executes in strict mode.

As with function constructors, most style guides will direct you to capitalize the class name to distinguish it from instances that are created from it (for example, `class Foo {}` might create an instance `foo`):

```
// Valid empty class definition
class Foo {}

// Valid class definition with constructor
class Bar {
  constructor() {}
}

// Valid class definition with getter
class Baz {
  get myBaz() {}
}

// Valid class definition with static method
class Qux {
  static myQux() {}
}
```

Class expressions may be optionally named. When the expression is assigned to a variable, the name property may be used to retrieve the class expression name string, but the identifier itself is not accessible outside the class expression scope.

```
let Person = class PersonName {
  identify() {
    console.log(Person.name, PersonName.name);
  }
}

let p = new Person();

p.identify();              // PersonName, PersonName

console.log(Person.name);   // PersonName
console.log(PersonName);    // ReferenceError: PersonName is not defined
```

> **NOTE** *Most codebases will prefer class declarations over class expressions; the syntax is more natural to write and use.*

The Class Constructor

The `constructor` keyword is used inside the class definition block to signal the definition of the class's constructor function. Using the method name `constructor` will signal to the interpreter that this particular function should be invoked to create a fresh instance using the `new` operator. Definition of the constructor is optional; electing not to define the class constructor is the same as defining the constructor as an empty function.

Instantiation

Instantiating a `Person` using the `new` operator operates identically to using `new` with a function constructor. The only perceptible difference is that the JavaScript interpreter understands that using `new` with a class means the `constructor` function should be used for instantiation.

Calling a class constructor using new will do the following:

1. A new object is created in memory.

2. The new object's internal `[[Prototype]]` pointer is assigned to be the constructor's `prototype` property.

3. The `this` value of the constructor is assigned to the new object (so this points to the new object when referenced inside the `constructor` function).

4. The code inside the `constructor` function is executed (adds properties to the new object).

5. If the `constructor` function returns an object, that object is returned. Otherwise, the new object that was just created is returned.

```
class Animal {}

class Person {
  constructor() {
    console.log('person ctor');
  }
}

class Vegetable {
  constructor() {
    this.color = 'orange';
  }
}

let a = new Animal();

let p = new Person();  // person ctor

let v = new Vegetable();
console.log(v.color);  // orange
```

Parameters provided when instantiating the class are used as parameters to the `constructor` function. If you do not require the use of parameters, empty parentheses following the class name are optional:

```
class Person {
  constructor(name) {
    console.log(arguments.length);
    this.name = name || null;
  }
```

```
}
let p1 = new Person;            // 0
console.log(p1.name);           // null

let p2 = new Person();          // 0
console.log(p2.name);           // null

let p3 = new Person('Jake');    // 1
console.log(p3.name);           // Jake
```

By default, the `constructor` function will return the `this` object after execution. If an object is returned from the constructor function, that value will be used as the instantiated object and the newly created this object will be discarded if a reference to it is not preserved. However, if a different object is returned, the returned object will not be associated with the class via `instanceof` because its `prototype` pointer was never modified.

```
class Person {
  constructor(override) {
    this.foo = 'foo';
    if (override) {
      return {
        bar: 'bar'
      };
    }
  }
}

let p1 = new Person(),
    p2 = new Person(true);

console.log(p1);                      // Person{ foo: 'foo' }
console.log(p1 instanceof Person);    // true

console.log(p2);                      // { bar: 'bar' }
console.log(p2 instanceof Person);    // false
```

One major departure from function constructors is that the use of the new operator with class constructors is *mandatory*. With function constructors, when electing not to use the new operator, the constructor would use the global `this` value—typically the `window` object—inside the constructor. With class constructors, neglecting to use the new operator will throw an error:

```
function Person() {}

class Animal {}

// Constructs instance using window as 'this'
let p = Person();

let a = Animal();
// TypeError: class constructor Animal cannot be invoked without 'new'
```

The class constructor method is not special and, after instantiation, behaves as a regular instance method (with the same constructor restrictions). Because of this, you can reference and use it post-instantiation:

```
class Person {}

// Create a new instance using the class
let p1 = new Person();

p1.constructor();
// TypeError: Class constructor Person cannot be invoked without 'new'

// Create a new instance using the reference to the class constructor
let p2 = new p1.constructor();
```

Understanding Classes as Special Functions

There is no formal "Class" type in the ECMAScript specification, and in many ways ECMAScript classes behave like special functions. Once declared, the class identifier identifies as a function when checked with the typeof operator:

```
class Person {}

console.log(Person);          // class Person {}
console.log(typeof Person);   // function
```

The class identifier has a prototype property, and the prototype has a constructor property that refers back to the class itself:

```
class Person{}

console.log(Person.prototype);                         // { constructor: f() }
console.log(Person === Person.prototype.constructor);  // true
```

As with function constructors, you can use the instanceof operator to test if the constructor prototype appears in the prototype chain of an instance:

```
class Person {}

let p = new Person();

console.log(p instanceof Person);  // true
```

You have likely come to understand that the instanceof operator checks an instance's prototype chain against a constructor function, which in this example would be checking the instance p against the constructor function Person, which appears to be a class.

As shown earlier, the class behaves in the same way as a constructor function, and in the context of classes, the class itself is considered the constructor when new is applied to it. Importantly, the constructor method inside the class definition is *not* considered to be the constructor and will return false when used with instanceof. If the constructor method is invoked directly, this is the same as using a non-class function constructor, and the instanceof convention will reverse:

```
class Person {}

let p1 = new Person();

console.log(p1.constructor === Person);       // true
```

```
console.log(p1 instanceof Person);              // true
console.log(p1 instanceof Person.constructor);  // false

let p2 = new Person.constructor();

console.log(p2.constructor === Person);         // false
console.log(p2 instanceof Person);              // false
console.log(p2 instanceof Person.constructor);  // true
```

Classes are first-class citizens in JavaScript, meaning they can be passed around as you would any other object or function reference:

```
// Classes may be defined anywhere a function would, such as inside an array:
let classList = [
  class {
    constructor(id) {
      this.id_ = id;
      console.log('instance ${this.id_}');
    }
  }
];

function createInstance(classDefinition, id) {
  return new classDefinition(id);
}

let foo = createInstance(classList[0], 3141);  // instance 3141
```

Similar to an immediately invoked function expression, a class can also be immediately instantiated:

```
// Because it is a class expression, the class name is optional
let p = new class Foo {
  constructor(x) {
    console.log(x);
  }
}('bar');           // bar

console.log(p);  // Foo {}
```

Instance, Prototype, and Class Members

The class definition syntax allows you to neatly define members that should exist on an object instance, members that should exist on the object prototype, and members that should exist on the class itself.

Instance Members

Each time new <classname> is invoked, the constructor function will execute. Inside this function, you are able to populate the freshly created instance (the this object) with "own" properties. There are no restrictions to what may be added to the new instance and no restrictions on members added after the constructor exits.

Each instance is assigned unique member objects, meaning nothing is shared on the prototype:

```
class Person {
  constructor() {
    // For this example, define a string with object wrapper
    // as to check object equality between instances below
    this.name = new String('Jack');

    this.sayName = () => console.log(this.name);

    this.nicknames = ['Jake', 'J-Dog']
  }
}

let p1 = new Person(),
    p2 = new Person();

p1.sayName();  // Jack
p2.sayName();  // Jack

console.log(p1.name === p2.name);            // false
console.log(p1.sayName === p2.sayName);      // false
console.log(p1.nicknames === p2.nicknames);  // false

p1.name = p1.nicknames[0];
p2.name = p2.nicknames[1];

p1.sayName();  // Jake
p2.sayName();  // J-Dog
```

Class Field Declarations

Assigning initial member values for each instance inside the constructor is such a common pattern that the *class field declaration* was introduced as shorthand. This allows for members to be initialized inside the class body itself instead of inside the constructor. The following two patterns are identical:

```
class PersonWithConstructor {
  constructor() {
    this.friendCount = 0;
  }
}

class PersonWithClassFields {
  friendCount = 0;
}
```

If you define a constructor function, the class field declarations will be available inside the constructor:

```
class Person {
  friendCount = 0;

  constructor() {
    console.log(this.friendCount);  // 0
  }
}
```

Members can be declared but not initialized. They will be treated as having a value of undefined:

```
class Person {
  friendCount;

  constructor() {
    console.log(this.friendCount);  // undefined
  }
}
```

Prototype Methods and Accessors

To allow for sharing of methods between instances, the class definition syntax allows for definition of methods on the prototype object inside the class body.

```
class Person {
  constructor() {
    // Everything added to 'this' will exist on each individual instance
    this.locate = () => console.log('instance');
  }

  // Everything defined in the class body is defined on the class prototype object
  locate() {
    console.log('prototype');
  }
}

let p = new Person();

p.locate();                    // instance
Person.prototype.locate();  // prototype
```

Methods can be defined in either location, but member data such as primitives and objects cannot be added to the prototype inside the class body:

```
class Person {
  name: 'Jake'
}
// Uncaught SyntaxError: Unexpected token :
```

Class methods behave identically to object properties, meaning they can be keyed with strings, symbols, or computed values:

```
const symbolKey = Symbol('symbolKey');

class Person {
  stringKey() {
    console.log('invoked stringKey');
  }
  [symbolKey]() {
    console.log('invoked symbolKey');
  }
  ['computed' + 'Key']() {
    console.log('invoked computedKey');
  }
```

```
  }

  let p = new Person();

  p.stringKey();      // invoked stringKey
  p[symbolKey]();     // invoked symbolKey
  p.computedKey();    // invoked computedKey
```

Class definitions also support getters and setter accessors. The syntax and behavior are identical to that of regular objects:

```
  class Person {
    set name(newName) {
      this.name_ = newName;
    }

    get name() {
      return this.name_;
    }
  }

  let p = new Person();
  p.name = 'Jake';
  console.log(p.name);   // Jake
```

Private Class Members

Private class members in JavaScript allow you to define properties and methods that are only accessible within the class itself. They provide encapsulation and information hiding, preventing direct access and modification from outside the class. To declare a private class member, prefix the member name with #. Here's an example that contrasts public and private class members:

```
  class Person {
    #name = "Alice";
    age = 30;

    getName() {
      return this.#name;
    }
  }

  const person = new Person();
  console.log(person.age);        // 30
  console.log(person.getName());  // Alice
```

In this example, a public variable age and a private variable #name are declared. A public method getName() is used to access the private member, which is a common pattern that protects the #name value by only offering indirect access.

To verify this member is indeed private, the following code attempts to retrieve the private variable in several different ways. Note that both attempts to retrieve the value fail.

```
  console.log(person.#name);
  // SyntaxError: Private field '#name' must be declared in an enclosing class

  console.log(person['age']);    // 30
  console.log(person['#name']);  // undefined
```

The # property prefix imparts special behavior, as JavaScript performs a compile-time check for this character and applies special rules to matching properties:

➤ Private members are only accessible from within the class where they are defined. They cannot be accessed or modified from outside the class.

➤ Private members are not inherited by subclasses. They are specific to the class in which they are defined.

➤ Private members cannot be accessed or overridden by methods or properties with the same name in derived classes.

➤ Constructors cannot be private.

➤ Private members must be declared in the class body; they cannot be added during or after the constructor has been called.

The following example demonstrates some possibly unexpected behavior of private members:

```
class Person {
  #age;

  constructor() {
    this.#age = 30;

    // Private members cannot be deleted
    delete this.#age; // SyntaxError

    // You must declare all private members in the class body
    this.#name = "Alice"; // SyntaxError
  }
}

new Person();
```

Fields, methods, getters, setters, async functions, and static members can all be private. The following example gives some examples of the various forms private members can take:

```
class Person {
  #name;
  #age;
  static #counter = 0;

  constructor(name, age) {
    this.#name = name;
    this.#age = age;
    Person.#incrementCounter();
  }

  // Private method
  #getNameInUpperCase() {
    return this.#name.toUpperCase();
```

```
      }

      // Private getter
      get #capitalizedName() {
        return this.#getNameInUpperCase();
      }

      // Public getter
      get name() {
        return this.#name;
      }

      // Public getter to access private getter
      get capitalizedName() {
        return this.#capitalizedName;
      }

      // Static method
      static getCounter() {
        return Person.#counter;
      }

      // Private static method
      static #incrementCounter() {
        Person.#counter += 1;
      }
    }

    let p = new Person("Alice", 30);
    console.log(p.name);                 // Alice
    console.log(p.capitalizedName);      // ALICE
    console.log(Person.getCounter());    // 1
```

Static Class Methods and Accessors

It is also possible to define members on the `class` itself. These are intended to be used in situations where a piece of data or function is used in a way that is not centered on a specific instance and does not require a class instance to exist. Like prototype members, these are only ever created once per class.

A *static class member* is designated using the `static` keyword as a prefix inside the class definition. Inside static methods, this refers to the `class` itself. All other conventions are identical to prototype members:

```
    class Person {
      // defined on the class
      static species = "sapiens";

      constructor() {
        // Everything added to 'this' will exist on each individual instance
        this.locate = () => console.log('instance', this);
      }

      // Defined on the class prototype object
      locate() {
        console.log('prototype', this);
```

```
  }

  // Defined on the class
  static locate() {
    console.log('class', this);
  }
}

let p = new Person();

console.log(Person.species);   // sapiens

p.locate();                    // instance, Person {}
Person.prototype.locate();     // prototype, {constructor: ... }
Person.locate();               // class, class Person {}
```

Static class methods can be useful as instance factories:

```
class Person {
  constructor(age) {
    this.age_ = age;
  }

  sayAge() {
    console.log(this.age_);
  }

  static create() {
    // Create and return a person instance with a random age
    return new Person(Math.floor(Math.random()*100));
  }
}

console.log(Person.create());  // Person { age_:... }
```

Static Initialization Blocks

In cases where static initialization is nontrivial, classes support *static initialization blocks* for writing complex code to initialize static members. A simple example is as follows:

```
class Person {
  static name = "Alice";
  static age;
  static {
    this.age = 30;
  }
}
```

Static initialization blocks provide a way to declare and execute arbitrary initialization logic within a class during its evaluation. The initialization block is useful when you must compute complex static values or inspect existing static values. When reaching for static initialization blocks, keep the following in mind:

➤   Any number of blocks can be used in a class. Blocks will be evaluated in the order they appear.

➤   The blocks must be evaluated synchronously.

➤ The initialization block scope is treated as normal lexical scope.

➤ The this inside a static block refers to the constructor object of the class.

Iterator and Generator Methods

The class definition syntax allows for definition of generator methods on both the prototype and the class itself:

```
class Person {
  // define generator on prototype
  *createNicknameIterator() {
    yield 'Jack';
    yield 'Jake';
    yield 'J-Dog';
  }

  // define generator on class
  static *createJobIterator() {
    yield 'Butcher';
    yield 'Baker';
    yield 'Candlestick maker';
  }
}

let jobIter = Person.createJobIterator();
console.log(jobIter.next().value);  // Butcher
console.log(jobIter.next().value);  // Baker
console.log(jobIter.next().value);  // Candlestick maker

let p = new Person();
let nicknameIter = p.createNicknameIterator();
console.log(nicknameIter.next().value);  // Jack
console.log(nicknameIter.next().value);  // Jake
console.log(nicknameIter.next().value);  // J-Dog
```

Because generator methods are supported, it is possible to make a class instance iterable by adding a default iterator:

```
class Person {
  constructor() {
    this.nicknames = ['Jack', 'Jake', 'J-Dog'];
  }

  *[Symbol.iterator]() {
    yield *this.nicknames.entries();
  }
}

let p = new Person();
for (let [idx, nickname] of p) {
  console.log(nickname);
}
// Jack
// Jake
// J-Dog
```

Alternately, to merely return the iterator instance:

```
class Person {
  constructor() {
    this.nicknames = ['Jack', 'Jake', 'J-Dog'];
  }

  [Symbol.iterator]() {
    return this.nicknames.entries();
  }
}

let p = new Person();
for (let [idx, nickname] of p) {
  console.log(nickname);
}
// Jack
// Jake
// J-Dog
```

Class Inheritance

Earlier in the chapter, we covered the laborious details of implementing inheritance using ES5 mechanisms. ECMAScript classes support a native inheritance mechanism. Class inheritance still uses the prototype chain under the hood.

Inheritance Basics

ECMAScript classes use `single inheritance`, meaning there can only be one parent class. Using the `extends` keyword, you can inherit from anything that has a `[[Construct]]` property and a `prototype`. For the most part, this means inheriting from another `class`, but this also allows for backwards compatibility with function constructors:

```
class Vehicle {}

// Inherit from class
class Bus extends Vehicle {}

let b = new Bus();
console.log(b instanceof Bus);      // true
console.log(b instanceof Vehicle);  // true


function Person() {}

// Inherit from function constructor
class Engineer extends Person {}

let e = new Engineer();
console.log(e instanceof Engineer);  // true
console.log(e instanceof Person);    // true
```

Both class and prototype methods are carried down to the derived class. The value of this reflects the class or instance that is invoking the method:

```
class Vehicle {
  identifyPrototype(id) {
    console.log(id, this);
  }

  static identifyClass(id) {
    console.log(id, this);
  }
}

class Bus extends Vehicle {}

let v = new Vehicle();
let b = new Bus();

b.identifyPrototype('bus');          // bus, Bus {}
v.identifyPrototype('vehicle');      // vehicle, Vehicle {}

Bus.identifyClass('bus');            // bus, class Bus {}
Vehicle.identifyClass('vehicle');    // vehicle, class Vehicle {}
```

> **NOTE** *The* extends *keyword is valid inside class expressions, so* `let Bar = class extends Foo {}` *is perfectly valid syntax.*

Constructors, HomeObjects, and *super()*

Derived class methods have a reference to their prototype via the super keyword. This is only available for derived classes inside the constructor, instance methods, and static methods. super is used inside the constructor to control when to invoke the parent class constructor.

```
class Vehicle {
  constructor() {
    this.hasEngine = true;
  }
}

class Bus extends Vehicle {
  constructor() {
    // Cannot reference 'this' before super(), will throw ReferenceError

    super();  // same as super.constructor()

    console.log(this instanceof Vehicle);  // true
    console.log(this);                     // Bus { hasEngine: true }
  }
}

new Bus();
```

super can also be used inside static methods to invoke static methods defined on the inherited class:

```
class Vehicle {
  static identify() {
    console.log('vehicle');
  }
}

class Bus extends Vehicle {
  static identify() {
    super.identify();
  }
}

Bus.identify();  // vehicle
```

> **NOTE** *ECMAScript gives the constructor and static methods a reference to the internal* `[[HomeObject]]`, *which points to the object the method is defined upon. This pointer is assigned automatically and is only accessible internally inside the JavaScript engine.* super *will always be defined as the prototype of* `[[HomeObject]]`.

Things to note when using super:

➤ super can only be used in a derived class constructor or static method.

```
class Vehicle {
  constructor() {
    super();
    // SyntaxError: 'super' keyword unexpected
  }
}
```

➤ The super keyword cannot be referenced by itself; it must be either invoked as a constructor or used to reference a static method.

```
class Vehicle {}

class Bus extends Vehicle {
  constructor() {
    console.log(super);
    // SyntaxError: 'super' keyword unexpected here
  }
}
```

➤ Calling super() will invoke the parent class constructor and assign the resulting instance to this.

```
class Vehicle {}

class Bus extends Vehicle {
  constructor() {
```

```
        super();

        console.log(this instanceof Vehicle);
      }
    }

new Bus();  // true
```

➤ super() behaves like a constructor function; you must manually pass arguments to it to pass them to the parent constructor.

```
class Vehicle {
  constructor(licensePlate) {
    this.licensePlate = licensePlate;
  }
}

class Bus extends Vehicle {
  constructor(licensePlate) {
    super(licensePlate);
  }
}

console.log(new Bus('1337H4X'));  // Bus { licensePlate: '1337H4X' }
```

➤ If you decline to define a constructor function, super() will be implicitly invoked and all arguments passed to the derived class constructor.

```
class Vehicle {
  constructor(licensePlate) {
    this.licensePlate = licensePlate;
  }
}

class Bus extends Vehicle {}

console.log(new Bus('1337H4X'));  // Bus { licensePlate: '1337H4X' }
```

➤ You cannot reference this inside the constructor before invoking super().

```
class Vehicle {}

class Bus extends Vehicle {
  constructor() {
    console.log(this);
  }
}

new Bus();
// ReferenceError: Must call super constructor in derived class
// before accessing 'this' or returning from derived constructor
```

➤ If a class is derived from a parent class and you explicitly define a constructor, you must either invoke `super()` or return an object from the constructor.

```
class Vehicle {}

class Car extends Vehicle {}

class Bus extends Vehicle {
  constructor() {
    super();
  }
}

class Van extends Vehicle {
  constructor() {
    return {};
  }
}

console.log(new Car());  // Car {}
console.log(new Bus());  // Bus {}
console.log(new Van());  // {}
```

Abstract Base Classes

You may find a need to define an *abstract base class*, which is a class that should be inherited from but not directly instantiated. Although ECMAScript does not explicitly support this, it is easy to implement using `new.target`, which informs you what was used in conjunction with the `new` keyword. You can prevent direct instantiation by checking that `new.target` is never the abstract base class:

```
// Abstract base class
class Vehicle {
  constructor() {
    console.log(new.target);
    if (new.target === Vehicle) {
      throw new Error('Vehicle cannot be directly instantiated');
    }
  }
}

// Derived class
class Bus extends Vehicle {}

new Bus();       // class Bus {}
new Vehicle();   // class Vehicle {}
// Error: Vehicle cannot be directly instantiated
```

It is also possible to require that a method be defined on a derived class by checking for it in the abstract base class constructor. Because prototype methods exist before the constructor is invoked, you can check for them on the this keyword:

```
// Abstract base class
class Vehicle {
  constructor() {
    if (new.target === Vehicle) {
      throw new Error('Vehicle cannot be directly instantiated');
    }

    if (!this.foo) {
      throw new Error('Inheriting class must define foo()');
    }

    console.log('success!');
  }
}

// Derived class
class Bus extends Vehicle {
  foo() {}
}

// Derived class
class Van extends Vehicle {}

new Bus();  // success!
new Van();  // Error: Inheriting class must define foo()
```

Inheriting from Built-In Types

ECMAScript classes offer seamless interoperability with existing built-in reference types, allowing you to extend them easily:

```
class SuperArray extends Array {
  shuffle() {
    // Fisher-Yates shuffle
    for (let i = this.length - 1; i> 0; i--) {
      const j = Math.floor(Math.random() * (i + 1));
      [this[i], this[j]] = [this[j], this[i]];
    }
  }
}

let a = new SuperArray(1, 2, 3, 4, 5);

console.log(a instanceof Array);       // true
console.log(a instanceof SuperArray);  // true

console.log(a);  // [1, 2, 3, 4, 5]
a.shuffle();
console.log(a);  // [3, 1, 4, 5, 2]
```

Some built-in types have methods defined in which a new object instance is returned. By default, the type of this object instance will match the type of the original instance:

```
class SuperArray extends Array {}

let a1 = new SuperArray(1, 2, 3, 4, 5);
let a2 = a1.filter(x => !!(x%2))

console.log(a1);  // [1, 2, 3, 4, 5]
console.log(a2);  // [1, 3, 5]
console.log(a1 instanceof SuperArray);  // true
console.log(a2 instanceof SuperArray);  // true
```

If you wish to override this, you can override the `Symbol.species` accessor, which is used to determine the class to be used to create the returned instance:

```
class SuperArray extends Array {
  static get [Symbol.species]() {
    return Array;
  }
}

let a1 = new SuperArray(1, 2, 3, 4, 5);
let a2 = a1.filter(x => !!(x%2))

console.log(a1);  // [1, 2, 3, 4, 5]
console.log(a2);  // [1, 3, 5]
console.log(a1 instanceof SuperArray);  // true
console.log(a2 instanceof SuperArray);  // false
```

Class Mixins

A common pattern in JavaScript is to bundle together behavior from several different classes into a single package. Although ECMAScript classes do not explicitly support inheriting from multiple classes, the feature offers extensibility that can be cleverly wielded to emulate such behavior.

> **NOTE** *The* `Object.assign()` *method is designed to offer mixin behavior from object mixins. Implementing your own mixin expressions is only necessary when your mixins take the form of classes. If you only need to merge properties between multiple objects, prefer to use* `Object.assign()`.

The reference following the `extends` keyword is a JavaScript expression. Any syntax is valid there as long as it resolves to a class or function constructor. The expression is evaluated when the class definition is evaluated:

```
class Vehicle {}

function getParentClass() {
  console.log('evaluated expression');
  return Vehicle;
```

```
    }

    class Bus extends getParentClass() {}
    // evaluated expression
```

A mixin pattern can be achieved by chaining multiple mixin elements inside the expression, which will resolve into a single class that can be inherited from. If a class Person needs to incorporate mixins A, B, and C, you will in some form architect a pattern that configures B to inherit from A, C to inherit from B, and Person to inherit from C—thereby joining all three mixins into the superclass. There are several strategies that can accomplish such a pattern.

One strategy is to define "nestable" functions that accept a superclass as a parameter, define the mixin class as a subclass of the parameter, and return that class. These mixins can be chained inside each other and provided as the superclass expression:

```
    class Vehicle {}

    let FooMixin = (Superclass) => class extends Superclass {
      foo() {
        console.log('foo');
      }
    };
    let BarMixin = (Superclass) => class extends Superclass {
      bar() {
        console.log('bar');
      }
    };
    let BazMixin = (Superclass) => class extends Superclass {
      baz() {
        console.log('baz');
      }
    };

    class Bus extends FooMixin(BarMixin(BazMixin(Vehicle))) {}

    let b = new Bus();
    b.foo();  // foo
    b.bar();  // bar
    b.baz();  // baz
```

It is possible to flatten this nesting using a utility function:

```
    class Vehicle {}

    let FooMixin = (Superclass) => class extends Superclass {
      foo() {
        console.log('foo');
      }
    };
    let BarMixin = (Superclass) => class extends Superclass {
      bar() {
        console.log('bar');
      }
    };
```

```
let BazMixin = (Superclass) => class extends Superclass {
  baz() {
    console.log('baz');
  }
};

function mix(BaseClass, ...Mixins) {
  return Mixins.reduce((accumulator, current) => current(accumulator), BaseClass);
}

class Bus extends mix(Vehicle, FooMixin, BarMixin, BazMixin) {}

let b = new Bus();
b.foo();  // foo
b.bar();  // bar
b.baz();  // baz
```

> **NOTE** *Many JavaScript frameworks, most notably React, are moving away from mixin patterns and toward composition (in the form of extracting methods into separate classes and utilities, and incorporating those piecemeal without the use of inheritance). This reflects the well-known software principle of "composition over inheritance," which is regarded by many to offer superior flexibility and code design.*

SUMMARY

Objects are created and augmented at any point during code execution, making objects into dynamic, rather than strictly defined, entities. The following patterns are used for the creation of objects:

➤ The factory pattern uses a simple function that creates an object, assigns properties and methods, and then returns the object. This pattern fell out of favor when the constructor pattern emerged.

➤ With the constructor pattern, it's possible to define custom reference types that can be created using the new operator in the same way as built-in object instances are created. The constructor pattern does have a downside, however, in that none of its members are reused, including functions. Because functions can be written in a loosely typed manner, there's no reason they cannot be shared by multiple object instances.

➤ The prototype pattern takes this into account, using the constructor's prototype property to assign properties and methods that should be shared. The combination constructor/prototype pattern uses the constructor to define instance properties and the prototype pattern to define shared properties and methods.

Inheritance in JavaScript is implemented primarily using the concept of prototype chaining. Prototype chaining involves assigning a constructor's prototype to be an instance of another type. In doing so, the subtype assumes all of the properties and methods of the supertype in a manner similar to class-based inheritance. The problem with prototype chaining is that all of the inherited properties and methods are shared among object instances, making it ill-suited for use on its own. The constructor stealing pattern avoids these issues, calling the supertype's constructor from inside of the subtype's constructor. This allows each instance to have its own properties but forces the types to be defined using only the constructor pattern. The most popular pattern of inheritance is combination inheritance, which uses prototype chaining to inherit shared properties and methods and uses constructor stealing to inherit instance properties.

ECMAScript classes are a syntactical wrapper for prototype-based concepts. They offer a host of powerful features and have seen continuous enhancements with each ECMAScript version. These classes provide a clean and intuitive syntax for defining objects and for incorporating key features such as constructors, instance methods, static methods, and getters/setters. Furthermore, ECMAScript has introduced additional features like private class fields, public and private class methods, and class fields with initializer expressions.

Proxies and Reflect

WHAT'S IN THIS CHAPTER?

➤   Proxy fundamentals

➤   Proxy traps and reflect methods

➤   Proxy patterns

> **DOWNLOADS FOR THIS CHAPTER**
>
> Please note that all the code examples for this chapter are available as a part of this chapter's code download on the book's website at www.wiley.com/go/projavascript5e.

Proxies and reflection are constructs that afford you the ability to intercept and shim additional behavior into fundamental operations within the language. More specifically, you can define a proxy object associated with a target object, and the proxy object can be used as an abstracted target object within which you can control what happens when various operations are performed before they actually reach the target object.

For developers approaching this subject for the first time, this is a fairly nebulous concept paired with a healthy corpus of new terminology. Working through multiple examples will help to cement your understanding.

> **NOTE** *There is no analogue for proxies in ECMAScript versions prior to ES6. Because it is a fundamentally new language ability, many transpilers are unable to convert proxy behavior into earlier ECMAScript versions because replicating the behavior of a proxy is effectively impossible. Therefore, proxies and reflection are useful only in situations where native support is offered on 100 percent of platforms. It is possible to detect support for proxies and divert to fallback code as necessary, but this would lead to code duplication and is therefore discouraged.*

PROXY FUNDAMENTALS

As mentioned in the chapter introduction, a proxy behaves as an abstraction for a target object. In many ways, it is analogous to a C++ pointer in that it can be wielded as a stand-in for the target object it points to but is, in fact, totally separate from the target object. The target object can either be manipulated directly or through the proxy, but manipulating directly will circumvent the behavior that a proxy enables.

> **NOTE** *There are key differences between ECMAScript proxies and C++ pointers that will be discussed later, but for introductory purposes pointers are a suitable conceptual building block.*

Creating a Passthrough Proxy

In its simplest form, a proxy can exist as nothing more than an abstracted target object. By default, all operations performed on a proxy object will be transparently propagated through to the target object. Therefore, you are able to use a proxy object in all the same ways and places that you would use the target object that the proxy object is associated with.

A proxy is created using the Proxy constructor. It requires you to provide both a target object and a handler object, without which a `TypeError` is thrown. For a simple passthrough proxy, using a simple object literal for the handler object will allow all operations to reach the target object unimpeded.

As shown here, all operations performed on the proxy will effectively be applied to the target object instead. The only perceptible difference is the identity of the proxy object.

```
const target = {
  id: 'target'
};

const handler = {};

const proxy = new Proxy(target, handler);

// The 'id' property will access the same value
console.log(target.id);  // target
```

```
console.log(proxy.id);    // target

// Assignment to a target property changes both since
// both are accessing the same value.
target.id = 'foo';
console.log(target.id);   // foo
console.log(proxy.id);    // foo

// Assignment to a proxy property changes both since
// this assignment is conferred to the target object.
proxy.id = 'bar';
console.log(target.id);   // bar
console.log(proxy.id);    // bar

// The hasOwnProperty() method is effectively applied
// to the target in both cases.
console.log(target.hasOwnProperty('id'));   // true
console.log(proxy.hasOwnProperty('id'));    // true

// Strict object equality can still be used to
// differentiate proxy from target.
console.log(target === proxy);  // false
```

Defining Traps

The primary purpose of a proxy is to allow you to define *traps*, which behave as "fundamental operation interceptors" inside the handler object. Each handler object is made up of zero, one, or many traps, and each trap corresponds to a fundamental operation that can be directly or indirectly called on the proxy. When these fundamental operations are called on the proxy object, before being invoked on the target object, the proxy will invoke the trap function instead, allowing you to intercept and modify its behavior.

> **NOTE** *The term "trap" is borrowed from the world of operating systems, where a trap is a synchronous interrupt in program flow that diverts processor execution to execute a subroutine before returning to the original program flow.*

For example, you are able to define a `get()` trap that is triggered each time any ECMAScript operation performs a `get()` in one form or another. Such a trap can be defined as follows:

```
const target = {
  foo: 'bar'
};

const handler = {
  // Traps are keyed by method name inside the handler object
  get() {
    return 'handler override';
  }
};

const proxy = new Proxy(target, handler);
```

When a `get()` operation is called on this proxy object, the trap function that is defined for `get()` will be invoked instead. Of course, `get()` is not a usable method on ECMAScript objects. The `get()` operation that is being trapped is shared between multiple operations that can be found in actual JavaScript code. Operations of the form `proxy[property]`, `proxy.property`, or `Object.create(proxy)[property]` will all use the fundamental operation `get()` to retrieve the property, and therefore all of these will invoke the trap function instead when they are used on the proxy. Only the proxy will use the trap handler functions; these operations will behave normally when used with the target object.

```
const target = {
  foo: 'bar'
};

const handler = {
  // Traps are keyed by method name inside the handler object
  get() {
    return 'handler override';
  }
};

const proxy = new Proxy(target, handler);

console.log(target.foo);                      // bar
console.log(proxy.foo);                       // handler override

console.log(target['foo']);                   // bar
console.log(proxy['foo']);                    // handler override

console.log(Object.create(target)['foo']);    // bar
console.log(Object.create(proxy)['foo']);     // handler override
```

Trap Parameters and the Reflect API

All traps have access to parameters that will allow you to fully re-create the original behavior of the trapped method. For example, the `get()` method receives a reference to the target object, the property being looked up, and a reference to the proxy object.

```
const target = {
  foo: 'bar'
};

const handler = {
  get(trapTarget, property, receiver) {
    console.log(trapTarget === target);
    console.log(property);
    console.log(receiver === proxy);
  }
};

const proxy = new Proxy(target, handler);

proxy.foo;
// true
// foo
// true
```

Thus, it is possible to define a trap handler that wholly re-creates the behavior of the method being trapped:

```
const target = {
  foo: 'bar'
};

const handler = {
  get(trapTarget, property, receiver) {
    return trapTarget[property];
  }
};

const proxy = new Proxy(target, handler);

console.log(proxy.foo);    // bar
console.log(target.foo);   // bar
```

Such a tactic can be implemented for all traps, but not all trap behavior is as simple to re-create as get(); therefore, this is an impractical strategy. Instead of manually implementing the contents of the trapped method, the original behavior of the trapped method is wrapped inside an identically named method on the global Reflect object.

Every method that can be trapped inside a handler object has a corresponding Reflect API method. This method has an identical name and function signature, and performs the exact behavior that the trapped method is intercepting. Therefore, it is possible to define a passthrough proxy using only the Reflect API:

```
const target = {
  foo: 'bar'
};

const handler = {
  get() {
    return Reflect.get(...arguments);
  }
};

const proxy = new Proxy(target, handler);

console.log(proxy.foo);    // bar
console.log(target.foo);   // bar
```

Alternately, in a more succinct format:

```
const target = {
  foo: 'bar'
};

const handler = {
  get: Reflect.get
};

const proxy = new Proxy(target, handler);

console.log(proxy.foo);    // bar
console.log(target.foo);   // bar
```

If you wish to create a true passthrough proxy that traps every available method and forwards each one to its corresponding Reflect API function, defining an explicit handler object is not required:

```
const target = {
  foo: 'bar'
};

const proxy = new Proxy(target, Reflect);

console.log(proxy.foo);    // bar
console.log(target.foo);   // bar
```

The Reflect API allows you to modify the trapped method with minimal boilerplate code. For example, the following decorates the return value whenever a certain property is accessed:

```
const target = {
  foo: 'bar',
  baz: 'qux'
};

const handler = {
  get(trapTarget, property, receiver) {
    let decoration = '';
    if (property === 'foo') {
      decoration = '!!!';
    }

    return Reflect.get(...arguments) + decoration;
  }
};

const proxy = new Proxy(target, handler);

console.log(proxy.foo);    // bar!!!
console.log(target.foo);   // bar

console.log(proxy.baz);    // qux
console.log(target.baz);   // qux
```

Trap Invariants

Traps give you a broad ability to change how nearly any fundamental method behaves, but they are not without restriction. Each trapped method is aware of the target object context and trap function signature, and the behavior of the trap handler function must obey the "trap invariants" as specified in the ECMAScript specification. Trap invariants vary by method, but in general they will prevent the trap definition from exhibiting any grossly unexpected behavior.

For example, if a target object has a non-configurable and non-writable data property, a `TypeError` will be thrown if you attempt to return a value from the trap that is different from the target object's property:

```
const target = {};
Object.defineProperty(target, 'foo', {
  configurable: false,
```

```
    writable: false,
    value: 'bar'
});

const handler = {
  get() {
    return 'qux';
  }
};

const proxy = new Proxy(target, handler);

console.log(proxy.foo);
// TypeError
```

Revocable Proxies

You may find a need for disabling the association between the proxy object and the target object. For a normal proxy created with new Proxy(), this association lasts the lifetime of the proxy object.

Proxy also exposes a revocable() method, which provides you with an additional revoke function that can be called to disassociate the proxy object from the target object. Revoking the proxy is irreversible. Furthermore, the revoke function is idempotent and will not have a further effect if called multiple times. Any method called on a proxy after it is revoked will throw a TypeError.

The revoke function can be captured upon proxy instantiation:

```
const target = {
  foo: 'bar'
};

const handler = {
  get() {
    return 'intercepted';
  }
};

const { proxy, revoke } = Proxy.revocable(target, handler);

console.log(proxy.foo);    // intercepted
console.log(target.foo);   // bar

revoke();

console.log(proxy.foo);    // TypeError
```

Utility of the Reflect API

There are a handful of reasons to favor the Reflect API in certain situations.

Reflect API vs. Object API

When diving into the Reflect API, remember:

1. The Reflect API is not limited to trap handler.

2. Most Reflect API methods have an analogue on the Object type.

In general, the Object methods are geared for general application use, and the Reflect methods are geared for fine-tuned object control and manipulation.

Status Flags

Many Reflect methods return a Boolean, indicating if the operation they intend to perform will be successful or not. In certain situations, this is more useful than how other Reflect API methods behave, which will either return the modified object or throw an error (depending on the method). For example, you can use the Reflect API to perform the following refactor:

```
// Initial code

const o = {};

try {
  Object.defineProperty(o, 'foo', 'bar');
  console.log('success');
} catch(e) {
  console.log('failure');
}
```

In the event of a problem with defining the new property, `Reflect.defineProperty` will return `false` instead of throwing an error, enabling you to do the following:

```
// Refactored code

const o = {};

if(Reflect.defineProperty(o, 'foo', {value: 'bar'})) {
  console.log('success');
} else {
  console.log('failure');
}
```

The following `Reflect` methods provide you with status flags:

➤ `Reflect.defineProperty`

➤ `Reflect.preventExtensions`

➤ `Reflect.setPrototypeOf`

➤ `Reflect.set`

➤ `Reflect.deleteProperty`

Supplanting Operators with First-Class Functions

Several `Reflect` methods offer behavior that is available only via operators:

➤ `Reflect.get()` accesses behavior that is only available otherwise via object property access.

➤ `Reflect.set()` accesses behavior that is only available otherwise via the `=` assignment operator.

➤ `Reflect.has()` accesses behavior that is only available otherwise via the `in` operator or `with()`.

➤ `Reflect.deleteProperty()` accesses behavior that is only available otherwise via the `delete` operator.

➤ `Reflect.construct()` accesses behavior that is only available otherwise via the `new` operator.

Safe Function Application

When invoking a function using the `apply` method, there is a small possibility that the function being called defines its own `apply` property. To circumvent this, it is possible to pluck the `apply` method off the Function prototype, as follows:

```
Function.prototype.apply.call(myFunc, thisVal, argumentList);
```

This nightmarish line of code can be avoided and fully replicated using `Reflect.apply`:

```
Reflect.apply(myFunc, thisVal, argumentsList);
```

Proxying a Proxy

Proxies are capable of intercepting Reflect API operations, and this means that it is entirely possible to create a proxy of a proxy. This allows you to build multiple layers of indirection on top of a singular target object:

```
const target = {
  foo: 'bar'
};

const firstProxy = new Proxy(target, {
  get() {
    console.log('first proxy');
    return Reflect.get(...arguments);
  }
});

const secondProxy = new Proxy(firstProxy, {
  get() {
    console.log('second proxy');
    return Reflect.get(...arguments);
  }
```

```
});

console.log(secondProxy.foo);
// second proxy
// first proxy
// bar
```

Proxy Considerations and Shortcomings

Proxies are an API built upon existing ECMAScript infrastructure, and therefore their implementation was best-effort. For the most part, proxies work very well as a virtualization layer for objects. Nevertheless, proxies cannot always seamlessly integrate with existing ECMAScript constructs in certain scenarios.

this Inside a Proxy

One potential source of trouble with proxies is the value of this. As you might expect, the this value inside a method will respect the object upon which it was called:

```
const target = {
  thisValEqualsProxy() {
    return this === proxy;
  }
}

const proxy = new Proxy(target, {});

console.log(target.thisValEqualsProxy());  // false
console.log(proxy.thisValEqualsProxy());   // true
```

Intuitively, this should make perfect sense: Any method called on a proxy, proxy.outerMethod(), which in turn calls another method inside its function body, this.innerMethod(), should effectively be invoking proxy.innerMethod(). In most cases, this is certainly the expected behavior; however, if your target relies on object identity, you may encounter unexpected issues.

Recall the WeakMap private variable implementation from Chapter 6, "Advanced Reference Types," an abridged version of which is displayed here:

```
const wm = new WeakMap();

class User {
  constructor(userId) {
    wm.set(this, userId);
  }

  set id(userId) {
    wm.set(this, userId);
  }

  get id() {
    return wm.get(this);
  }
}
```

Because this implementation relies on the object identity of the User instance, it will encounter problems when that instance is proxied:

```
const user = new User(123);
console.log(user.id);  // 123

const userInstanceProxy = new Proxy(user, {});
console.log(userInstanceProxy.id);  // undefined
```

The user instance is initially being keyed in the weak map with the target object, but the proxy is attempting to retrieve that instance with the *proxy* object. The solution to such a problem is to reconfigure the proxying such that the initial key insertion is done with a proxy instance—a feat that can be accomplished by proxying the User class itself, and instantiating a proxy of the class:

```
const UserClassProxy = new Proxy(User, {});
const proxyUser = new UserClassProxy(456);
console.log(proxyUser.id);
```

Proxies and Internal Slots

Often, you will find that instances of built-in reference types can work alongside proxies seamlessly, as is the case with Array. However, some ECMAScript built-in types can rely on mechanisms that proxies cannot control. The result of this is that some methods on a wrapped instance will flat out not work properly.

The canonical example of this is the Date type. Per the ECMAScript specification, Date types rely on the existence of an "internal slot" named [[NumberData]] on the this value when executing methods. Because the internal slot does not exist on the proxy, and because these internal slot values are not accessed via the normal get and set operations that a proxy could otherwise intercept and redirect to the target, the method will throw a TypeError:

```
const target = new Date();
const proxy = new Proxy(target, {});

console.log(proxy instanceof Date);  // true

proxy.getDate();  // TypeError: 'this' is not a Date object
```

PROXY TRAPS AND REFLECT METHODS

Proxies are able to trap thirteen different fundamental operations. Each has its own entry in the Reflect API, parameters, associated ECMAScript operations, and invariants.

As demonstrated earlier, several different JavaScript operations may invoke the same trap handler. However, for any single operation that is performed on a proxy object, only one trap handler will ever be called; there is no overlap of trap coverage.

All traps will also intercept their corresponding Reflect API operations if they are invoked on the proxy.

get()

The get() trap is called inside operations that retrieve a property value. Its corresponding Reflect API method is Reflect.get().

```
const myTarget = {};

const proxy = new Proxy(myTarget, {
  get(target, property, receiver) {
    console.log('get()');
    return Reflect.get(...arguments)
  }
});

proxy.foo;
// get()
```

This trap exhibits the following behavior:

Return value	The return value is unrestricted.
Intercepted operations	➤ proxy.property
	➤ proxy[property]
	➤ Object.create(proxy)[property]
	➤ Reflect.get(proxy, property, receiver)
Trap handler parameters	➤ **target**—Target object
	➤ **property**—String key property being referenced on target object
	➤ **receiver**—Proxy object or object that inherits from proxy object
Trap invariants	➤ If target.property is non-writable and non-configurable, the handler return value must match target.property.
	➤ If target.property is non-configurable and has undefined as its [[Get]] attribute, the handler return value must also be undefined.

set()

The set() trap is called inside operations that assign a property value. Its corresponding Reflect API method is Reflect.set().

```
const myTarget = {};

const proxy = new Proxy(myTarget, {
  set(target, property, value, receiver) {
    console.log('set()');
    return Reflect.set(...arguments)
  }
```

```
  });

  proxy.foo = 'bar';
  // set()
```

This trap exhibits the following behavior:

Return value	A return value of `true` indicates success; a return value of `false` indicates failure and in strict mode will throw a `TypeError`.
Intercepted operations	➤ `proxy.property = value` ➤ `proxy[property] = value` ➤ `Object.create(proxy)[property] = value` ➤ `Reflect.set(proxy, property, value, receiver)`
Trap handler parameters	➤ **target**—Target object ➤ **property**—String key property being referenced on target object ➤ **value**—The value being assigned to `property` ➤ **receiver**—The original assignment recipient object
Trap invariants	➤ If `target.property` is non-writable and non-configurable, the target property value cannot be altered. ➤ If `target.property` is non-configurable and has undefined as its `[[Set]]` attribute, the target property value cannot be altered. ➤ Returning `false` from the handler will throw a `TypeError` in strict mode.

has()

The `has()` trap is called inside the `in` operator. Its corresponding Reflect API method is `Reflect.has()`.

```
const myTarget = {};

const proxy = new Proxy(myTarget, {
  has(target, property) {
    console.log('has()');
    return Reflect.has(...arguments)
  }
});

'foo' in proxy;
// has()
```

This trap exhibits the following behavior:

Return value	`has()` must return a Boolean indicating if the property is present or not. Non-Boolean return values will be coerced into a Boolean.
Intercepted operations	➤ `property in proxy` ➤ `property in Object.create(proxy)` ➤ `with(proxy) {(property);}` ➤ `Reflect.has(proxy, property)`
Trap handler parameters	➤ **target**—Target object ➤ **property**—String key property being referenced on target object
Trap invariants	➤ If an own `target.property` exists and is non-configurable, the handler must return `true`. ➤ If an own `target.property` exists and the target object is non-extensible, the handler must return `true`.

defineProperty()

The `defineProperty()` trap is called inside `Object.defineProperty()`. Its corresponding Reflect API method is `Reflect.defineProperty()`.

```
const myTarget = {};

const proxy = new Proxy(myTarget, {
  defineProperty(target, property, descriptor) {
    console.log('defineProperty()');
    return Reflect.defineProperty(...arguments)
  }
});

Object.defineProperty(proxy, 'foo', { value: 'bar' });
// defineProperty()
```

This trap exhibits the following behavior:

Return value	`defineProperty()` must return a Boolean indicating if the property was successfully defined or not. Non-Boolean return values will be coerced into a Boolean.
Intercepted operations	➤ `Object.defineProperty(proxy, property, descriptor)` ➤ `Reflect.defineProperty(proxy, property, descriptor)`

Trap handler parameters	➤ **target**—Target object
	➤ **property**—String key property being referenced on target object
	➤ **descriptor**—Object containing optional definitions for enumerable, configurable, writable, value, get, or set
Trap invariants	➤ If the target object is non-extensible, properties cannot be added.
	➤ If the target object has a configurable property, a non-configurable property of the same key cannot be added.
	➤ If the target object has a non-configurable property, a configurable property of the same key cannot be added.

getOwnPropertyDescriptor()

The `getOwnPropertyDescriptor()` trap is called inside `Object.getOwnPropertyDescriptor()`. Its corresponding Reflect API method is `Reflect.getOwnPropertyDescriptor()`.

```
const myTarget = {};

const proxy = new Proxy(myTarget, {
  getOwnPropertyDescriptor(target, property) {
    console.log('getOwnPropertyDescriptor()');
    return Reflect.getOwnPropertyDescriptor(...arguments)
  }
});

Object.getOwnPropertyDescriptor(proxy, 'foo');
// getOwnPropertyDescriptor()
```

This trap exhibits the following behavior:

Return value	`getOwnPropertyDescriptor()` must return an object or `undefined` if the property does not exist.
Intercepted operations	➤ `Object.getOwnPropertyDescriptor(proxy, property)`
	➤ `Reflect.getOwnPropertyDescriptor(proxy, property)`
Trap handler parameters	➤ **target**—Target object
	➤ **property**—String key property being referenced on target object

Trap invariants	➤	If an own `target.property` exists and is non-configurable, the handler must return an object to indicate that the property exists.
	➤	If an own `target.property` exists and is configurable, the handler cannot return an object indicating that the property is configurable.
	➤	If an own `target.property` exists and `target` is non-extensible, the handler must return an object to indicate that the property exists.
	➤	If `target.property` does not exist and `target` is non-extensible, the handler must return undefined to indicate that the property does not exist.
	➤	If `target.property` does not exist, the handler cannot return an object indicating that the property is configurable.

deleteProperty()

The `deleteProperty()` trap is called inside the `delete` operator. Its corresponding Reflect API method is `Reflect.deleteProperty()`.

```
const myTarget = {};

const proxy = new Proxy(myTarget, {
  deleteProperty(target, property) {
    console.log('deleteProperty()');
    return Reflect.deleteProperty(...arguments)
  }
});

delete proxy.foo
// deleteProperty()
```

This trap exhibits the following behavior:

Return value	`deleteProperty()` must return a Boolean indicating if the property was successfully deleted or not. Non-Boolean return values will be coerced into a Boolean.
Intercepted operations	➤ `delete proxy.property`
	➤ `delete proxy[property]`
	➤ `Reflect.deleteProperty(proxy, property)`
Trap handler parameters	➤ **target**—Target object
	➤ **property**—String key property being referenced on target object
Trap invariants	➤ If an own `target.property` exists and is non-configurable, the handler cannot delete the property.

ownKeys()

The `ownKeys()` trap is called inside `Object.keys()` and similar methods. Its corresponding Reflect API method is `Reflect.ownKeys()`.

```
const myTarget = {};

const proxy = new Proxy(myTarget, {
  ownKeys(target) {
    console.log('ownKeys()');
    return Reflect.ownKeys(...arguments)
  }
});

Object.keys(proxy);
// ownKeys()
```

This trap exhibits the following behavior:

Return value	`ownKeys()` must return an enumerable object that contains either strings or symbols.
Intercepted operations	➤ `Object.getOwnPropertyNames(proxy)` ➤ `Object.getOwnPropertySymbols(proxy)` ➤ `Object.keys(proxy)` ➤ `Reflect.ownKeys(proxy)`
Trap handler parameters	➤ **target**—Target object
Trap invariants	➤ The returned enumerable object must contain all non-configurable own properties of target. ➤ If target is non-extensible, the returned enumerable object must exactly contain the own property keys of target.

getPrototypeOf()

The `getPrototypeOf()` trap is called inside `Object.getPrototypeOf()`. Its corresponding Reflect API method is `Reflect.getPrototypeOf()`.

```
const myTarget = {};

const proxy = new Proxy(myTarget, {
  getPrototypeOf(target) {
    console.log('getPrototypeOf()');
    return Reflect.getPrototypeOf(...arguments)
  }
```

```
  });

  Object.getPrototypeOf(proxy);
  // getPrototypeOf()
```

This trap exhibits the following behavior:

Return value	`getPrototypeOf()` must return an object or `null`.
Intercepted operations	➤ `Object.getPrototypeOf(proxy)` ➤ `Reflect.getPrototypeOf(proxy)` ➤ `proxy.__proto__` ➤ `Object.prototype.isPrototypeOf(proxy)` ➤ `proxy instanceof Object`
Trap handler parameters	➤ **target**—Target object
Trap invariants	➤ If target is non-extensible, the only valid return value of `Object.getPrototypeOf(proxy)` is the value returned from `Object.getPrototypeOf(target)`.

setPrototypeOf()

The `setPrototypeOf()` trap is called inside `Object.setPrototypeOf()`. Its corresponding Reflect API method is `Reflect.setPrototypeOf()`.

```
  const myTarget = {};

  const proxy = new Proxy(myTarget, {
    setPrototypeOf(target, prototype) {
      console.log('setPrototypeOf()');
      return Reflect.setPrototypeOf(...arguments)
    }
  });

  Object.setPrototypeOf(proxy, Object);
  // setPrototypeOf()
```

This trap exhibits the following behavior:

Return value	`setPrototypeOf()` must return a Boolean indicating if the prototype assignment was successful or not. Non-Boolean return values will be coerced into a Boolean.
Intercepted operations	➤ `Object.setPrototypeOf(proxy)` ➤ `Reflect.setPrototypeOf(proxy)`

Trap handler parameters	➤ **target**—Target object
	➤ **prototype**—The intended replacement prototype for target, or `null` if this is to be a top-level prototype
Trap invariants	➤ If `target` is non-extensible, the only valid prototype parameter is the value returned from `Object.getPrototypeOf(target)`.

isExtensible()

The `isExtensible()` trap is called inside `Object.isExtensible()`. Its corresponding Reflect API method is `Reflect.isExtensible()`.

```
const myTarget = {};

const proxy = new Proxy(myTarget, {
  isExtensible(target) {
    console.log('isExtensible()');
    return Reflect.isExtensible(...arguments)
  }
});

Object.isExtensible(proxy);
// isExtensible()
```

This trap exhibits the following behavior:

Return value	➤ `isExtensible()` must return a Boolean indicating if the prototype assignment was successful or not. Non-Boolean return values will be coerced into a Boolean.
Intercepted operations	➤ `Object.isExtensible(proxy)`
	➤ `Reflect.isExtensible(proxy)`
Trap handler parameters	➤ **target**—Target object
Trap invariants	➤ If target is extensible, the handler must return `true`.
	➤ If target is non-extensible, the handler must return `false`.

preventExtensions()

The `preventExtensions()` trap is called inside `Object.preventExtensions()`. Its corresponding Reflect API method is `Reflect.preventExtensions()`.

```
Const myTarget = {};

const proxy = new Proxy(myTarget, {
  preventExtensions(target) {
```

```
        console.log('preventExtensions()');
        return Reflect.preventExtensions(...arguments)
    }
});

Object.preventExtensions(proxy);
// preventExtensions()
```

This trap exhibits the following behavior:

Return value	➤ preventExtensions() must return a Boolean indicating if target is already non-extensible. Non-Boolean return values will be coerced into a Boolean.
Intercepted operations	➤ Object.preventExtensions(proxy)
	➤ Reflect.preventExtensions(proxy)
Trap handler parameters	➤ **target**—Target object
Trap invariants	➤ If Object.isExtensible(proxy) is false, the handler must return true.

apply()

The apply() trap is called on function calls. Its corresponding Reflect API method is Reflect.apply().

```
const myTarget = () => {};

const proxy = new Proxy(myTarget, {
  apply(target, thisArg, ...argumentsList) {
    console.log('apply()');
    return Reflect.apply(...arguments)
  }
});

proxy();
// apply()
```

This trap exhibits the following behavior:

Return value	The return value is unrestricted.
Intercepted operations	➤ proxy(...argumentsList)
	➤ Function.prototype.apply(thisArg, argumentsList)
	➤ Function.prototype.call(thisArg, ...argumentsList)
	➤ Reflect.apply(target, thisArgument, argumentsList)

Trap handler parameters	➤ **target**—Target object
	➤ **thisArg**—`this` argument for the function call
	➤ **argumentsList**—List of arguments for the function call
Trap invariants	➤ `target` must be a function object.

construct()

The `construct()` trap is called inside the `new` operator. Its corresponding Reflect API method is `Reflect.construct()`.

```
Const myTarget = function() {};

const proxy = new Proxy(myTarget, {
  construct(target, argumentsList, newTarget) {
    console.log('construct()');
    return Reflect.construct(...arguments)
  }
});

new proxy;
// construct()
```

This trap exhibits the following behavior:

Return value	`construct()` must return an object.
Intercepted operations	➤ `new proxy(...argumentsList)`
	➤ `Reflect.construct(target, argumentsList, newTarget)`
Trap handler parameters	➤ **target**—Target constructor
	➤ **argumentsList**—List of arguments passed to the target constructor
	➤ **newTarget**—The originally called constructor
Trap invariants	➤ `target` must be able to be used as a constructor.

PROXY PATTERNS

The Proxy API allows you to introduce some incredibly useful patterns into your code.

Tracking Property Access

The nature of `get`, `set`, and `has` affords you total insight into when object properties are being accessed and inspected. If you provide a trapped proxy to an object throughout your application, you will be able to see exactly when and where this object is accessed:

```
const user = {
  name: 'Jake'
};

const proxy = new Proxy(user, {
  get(target, property, receiver) {
    console.log('Getting ${property}');

    return Reflect.get(...arguments);
  },
  set(target, property, value, receiver) {
    console.log('Setting ${property}=${value}');

    return Reflect.set(...arguments);
  }
});

proxy.name;        // Getting name
proxy.age = 27;    // Setting age=27
```

Hidden Properties

The innards of proxies are totally hidden to remote code so it is very easy to conceal the existence of properties on the target object. For example:

```
const hiddenProperties = ['foo', 'bar'];
const targetObject = {
  foo: 1,
  bar: 2,
  baz: 3
};
const proxy = new Proxy(targetObject, {
  get(target, property) {
    if (hiddenProperties.includes(property)) {
      return undefined;
    } else {
      return Reflect.get(...arguments);
    }
  },
  has(target, property) {
    if (hiddenProperties.includes(property)) {
      return false;
    } else {
      return Reflect.has(...arguments);
    }
  }
}
```

```
  });

  // get()
  console.log(proxy.foo);  // undefined
  console.log(proxy.bar);  // undefined
  console.log(proxy.baz);  // 3

  // has()
  console.log('foo' in proxy);  // false
  console.log('bar' in proxy);  // false
  console.log('baz' in proxy);  // true
```

Property Validation

Because all assignments must go through the set() trap, you can allow or reject assignments based on the content of the intended value:

```
  const target = {
    onlyNumbersGoHere: 0
  };

  const proxy = new Proxy(target, {
    set(target, property, value) {
      if (typeof value !== 'Number') {
        return false;
      } else {
        return Reflect.set(...arguments);
      }
    }
  });

  proxy.onlyNumbersGoHere = 1;
  console.log(proxy.onlyNumbersGoHere);  // 1
  proxy.onlyNumbersGoHere = '2';
  console.log(proxy.onlyNumbersGoHere);  // 1
```

Function and Constructor Parameter Validation

In the same way that object properties can be validated and protected, function and constructor parameters are also available for vetting. For example, a function can ensure that it is only provided values of a certain type:

```
  function median(...nums) {
    return nums.sort()[Math.floor(nums.length / 2)];
  }

  const proxy = new Proxy(median, {
    apply(target, thisArg, ...argumentsList) {
      for (const arg of argumentsList) {
        if (typeof arg !== 'number') {
          throw 'Non-number argument provided';
        }
      }
```

```
      return Reflect.apply(...arguments);
    }
});

console.log(proxy(4, 7, 1));     // 4
console.log(proxy(4, '7', 1));
// Error: Non-number argument provided
```

Similarly, a constructor can enforce the presence of constructor parameters:

```
class User {
  constructor(id) {
    this.id_ = id;
  }
}

const proxy = new Proxy(User, {
  construct(target, argumentsList, newTarget) {
    if (argumentsList[0] === undefined) {
      throw 'User cannot be instantiated without id';
    } else {
      return Reflect.construct(...arguments);
    }
  }
});

new proxy(1);

new proxy();
// Error: User cannot be instantiated without id
```

Data Binding and Observables

Proxying allows you to intertwine the existence of various parts of the runtime that would otherwise be disparate. This allows for a wide variety of patterns that enable different bits of code to interact with one another.

For example, a proxied class can be bound to a global collection of instances so that every created instance is added to that collection:

```
const userList = [];

class User {
  constructor(name) {
    this.name_ = name;
  }
}

const proxy = new Proxy(User, {
  construct() {
    const newUser = Reflect.construct(...arguments);
    userList.push(newUser);
    return newUser;
  }
});
```

```
new proxy('John');
new proxy('Jacob');
new proxy('Jingleheimerschmidt');

console.log(userList); // [User {}, User {}, User{}]
```

Alternately, a collection can be bound to an emitter, which will fire each time a new instance is inserted:

```
const userList = [];

function emit(newValue) {
  console.log(newValue);
}

const proxy = new Proxy(userList, {
  set(target, property, value, receiver) {
    const result = Reflect.set(...arguments);
    if (result) {
      emit(Reflect.get(target, property, receiver));
    }
    return result;
  }
});

proxy.push('John');
// John
proxy.push('Jacob');
// Jacob
```

SUMMARY

Proxies are one of the more exciting and dynamic additions in the ECMAScript specification. Although they have no backwards compilation support, they enable an entirely new field of metaprogramming and abstraction that was not previously available.

At a high level, proxies are a transparent virtualization of a real JavaScript object. When a proxy is created, you are able to define a handler object containing *traps*, which are points of interception that will be encountered by nearly every fundamental JavaScript operator and method. These trap handlers allow you to modify how these fundamental methods operate, although they are bound by *trap invariants*.

Alongside proxies is the Reflect API, which offers a suite of methods that identically encapsulate the behavior each trap is intercepting. The Reflect API can be thought of as a collection of fundamental operations that are the building blocks of nearly all JavaScript object APIs.

The utility of proxies is nearly unbounded, and it allows the developer to wield elegant new patterns such as (but certainly not limited to) tracking property access, hiding properties, preventing modification or deletion of properties, function parameter validation, constructor parameter validation, data binding, and observables.

10

Functions

WHAT'S IN THIS CHAPTER?

➤ Function expressions, function declarations, and arrow functions

➤ Default parameters and spread operators

➤ Recursion with functions

➤ Private variables using closures

Some of the most interesting parts of ECMAScript are its functions, primarily because functions actually are objects. Each function is an instance of the `Function` type that has properties and methods just like any other reference type. Because functions are objects, function names are simply pointers to function objects and are not necessarily tied to the function itself. Functions are typically defined using *function-declaration* syntax, as in this example:

```
function sum (num1, num2) {
    return num1 + num2;
}
```

In this code, a variable `sum` is defined and initialized to be a function. Note that there is no name included after the `function` keyword because it's not needed—the function can be referenced by the variable `sum`. Also note that there is no semicolon after the end of the function definition.

The function-declaration syntax is almost exactly equivalent to using a *function expression*, such as this:

```
let sum = function(num1, num2) {
  return num1 + num2;
};
```

Note that there is a semicolon after the end of the function, just as there would be after any variable initialization.

Another way to define a function that is quite similar to a function expression is to use the *arrow function* syntax, such as this:

```
let sum = (num1, num2) => {
  return num1 + num2;
};
```

The final way to define functions is to use the `Function` constructor, which accepts any number of arguments. The last argument is always considered to be the function body, and the previous arguments enumerate the new function's arguments. Consider this example:

```
let sum = new Function("num1", "num2", "return num1 + num2");   // not recommended
```

This syntax is not recommended because it causes a double interpretation of the code (once for the regular ECMAScript code and once for the strings that are passed into the constructor) and thus can affect performance. However, it's important to think of functions as objects and function names as pointers—this syntax is great at representing that concept.

> **NOTE** *There are subtle but important differences between these different ways to instantiate a function object that will be discussed later in the chapter. Nevertheless, all of them are invoked in an identical way.*

ARROW FUNCTIONS

Function expressions can be defined using the fat-arrow syntax. For the most part, arrow functions instantiate function objects that behave in the same manner as their formal function expression counterparts. Anywhere a function expression can be used, an arrow function can also be used:

```
let arrowSum = (a, b) => {
  return a + b;
};

let functionExpressionSum = function(a, b) {
  return a + b;
};

console.log(arrowSum(5, 8));  // 13
console.log(functionExpressionSum(5, 8));  // 13
```

Arrow functions are exceptionally useful in inline situations where they offer a more succinct syntax:

```
let ints = [1, 2, 3];

console.log(ints.map(function(i) { return i + 1; }));  // [2, 3, 4]
console.log(ints.map((i) => { return i + 1 }));        // [2, 3, 4]
```

Arrow functions do not require the parentheses if you only want to use a single parameter. If you want to have zero parameters, or more than one parameter, parentheses are required:

```
// Both are valid
let double = (x) => { return 2 * x; };
let triple = x => { return 3 * x; };

// Zero parameters require an empty pair of parentheses
let getRandom = () => { return Math.random(); };

// Multiple parameters require parentheses
let sum = (a, b) => { return a + b; };

// Invalid syntax:
let multiply = a, b => { return a * b; };
```

Arrow functions also do not require curly braces, but choosing to not use them changes the behavior of the function. Using the curly braces is called the *block body* syntax and behaves in the same way as a normal function expression in that multiple lines of code can exist inside the arrow function as they would for a normal function expression. If you omit the curly braces, you are using the *concise body* syntax and are limited to a single line of code, such as an assignment or expression. The value of this line will implicitly return, as demonstrated here:

```
// Both are valid and will return the value
let double = (x) => { return 2 * x; };
let triple = (x) => 3 * x;

// Assignment is allowed
let value = {};
let setName = (x) => x.name = "Matt";
setName(value);
console.log(value.name);  // "Matt"

// Invalid syntax:
let multiply = (a, b) => return a * b;
```

Arrow functions, although syntactically succinct, are not suited in several situations. They do not allow the use of `arguments`, `super`, or `new.target`, and cannot be used as a constructor. Additionally, function objects created with the arrow syntax do not have a `prototype` defined.

FUNCTION NAMES

Because function names are simply pointers to functions, they act like any other variable containing a pointer to an object. This means it's possible to have multiple names for a single function, as in this example:

```
function sum(num1, num2) {
  return num1 + num2;
```

```
    }

    console.log(sum(10, 10));            // 20

    let anotherSum = sum;
    console.log(anotherSum(10, 10));   // 20

    sum = null;
    console.log(anotherSum(10, 10));   // 20
```

This code defines a function named sum() that adds two numbers together. A variable, anotherSum, is declared and set equal to sum. Note that using the function name without parentheses accesses the function pointer instead of executing the function. At this point, both anotherSum and sum point to the same function, meaning that anotherSum() can be called and a result returned. When sum is set to null, it severs its relationship with the function, although anotherSum() can still be called without any problems.

All function objects expose a read-only name property that describes the function. In many cases, this will just be the function identifier, or the stringified variable name that references the function. If a function is unnamed, it will be reported as such. If it is created using the function constructor, it will be identified as "anonymous":

```
    function foo() {}
    let bar = function() {};
    let baz = () => {};

    console.log(foo.name);              // foo
    console.log(bar.name);              // bar
    console.log(baz.name);              // baz
    console.log((() => {}).name);       // (empty string)
    console.log((new Function()).name); // anonymous
```

If a function is a getter, a setter, or instantiated using bind(), a prefix will be prepended to identify it as such:

```
    function foo() {}

    console.log(foo.bind(null).name);       // bound foo

    let dog = {
      years: 1,
      get age() {
        return this.years;
      },
      set age(newAge) {
        this.years = newAge;
      }
    }

    let propertyDescriptor = Object.getOwnPropertyDescriptor(dog, 'age');
    console.log(propertyDescriptor.get.name);   // get age
    console.log(propertyDescriptor.set.name);   // set age
```

UNDERSTANDING ARGUMENTS

Function arguments in ECMAScript don't behave in the same way as function arguments in most other languages. An ECMAScript function doesn't care how many arguments are passed in, nor does it care about the data types of those arguments. Just because you define a function to accept two arguments doesn't mean you can pass in only two arguments. You could pass in one or three or none, and the interpreter won't complain.

This indifference happens because arguments in ECMAScript are represented as an array internally. The array is always passed to the function, but the function doesn't care what (if anything) is in the array. If the array arrives with zero items, that's fine; if it arrives with more, that's okay, too. In fact, when a function is defined using the `function` keyword (meaning a non-arrow function), there actually is an `arguments` object that can be accessed while inside a function to retrieve the values of each argument that was passed in.

The `arguments` object acts like an array (though it isn't an instance of `Array`) in that you can access each argument using bracket notation (the first argument is `arguments[0]`, the second is `arguments[1]`, and so on) and determine how many arguments were passed in by using the length property.

In the following example, the `sayHi()` function's first argument is named name.

```
function sayHi(name, message) {
  console.log("Hello " + name + ", " + message);
}
```

The same value can be accessed by referencing `arguments[0]`. Therefore, the function can be rewritten without naming the arguments explicitly, like this:

```
function sayHi() {
  console.log("Hello " + arguments[0] + ", " + arguments[1]);
}
```

In this rewritten version, there are no named `arguments`. The name and message arguments have been removed, yet the function will behave appropriately. This illustrates an important point about functions in ECMAScript: named arguments are a convenience, not a necessity. Unlike in other languages, naming your arguments in ECMAScript does not create a function signature that must be matched later on; there is no validation against named arguments.

The `arguments` object can also be used to check the number of arguments passed into the function via the `length` property. The following example outputs the number of arguments passed into the function each time it is called:

```
function howManyArgs() {
  console.log(arguments.length);
}

howManyArgs("string", 45);    // 2
howManyArgs();                // 0
howManyArgs(12);              // 1
```

This example shows alerts displaying 2, 0, and 1 (in that order). In this way, developers have the freedom to let functions accept any number of arguments and behave appropriately. Consider the following:

```
function doAdd() {
  if (arguments.length === 1) {
    console.log(arguments[0] + 10);
  } else if (arguments.length === 2) {
    console.log(arguments[0] + arguments[1]);
  }
}
```

```
doAdd(10);        // 20
doAdd(30, 20);    // 50
```

The function doAdd() adds 10 to a number only if there is one argument; if there are two arguments, they are simply added together and returned. So doAdd(10) returns 20, whereas doAdd(30,20) returns 50. It's not quite as good as overloading, but it is a sufficient workaround for this ECMAScript limitation.

Another important thing to understand about arguments is that the arguments object can be used in conjunction with named arguments, such as the following:

```
function doAdd(num1, num2) {
  if (arguments.length === 1) {
    console.log(num1 + 10);
  } else if (arguments.length === 2) {
    console.log(arguments[0] + num2);
  }
}
```

In this rewrite of the doAdd() function, two-named arguments are used in conjunction with the arguments object. The named argument num1 holds the same value as arguments[0], so they can be used interchangeably (the same is true for num2 and arguments[1]).

Another interesting behavior of arguments is that its values always stay in sync with the values of the corresponding named parameters. For example:

```
function doAdd(num1, num2) {
  arguments[1] = 10;
  console.log(arguments[0] + num2);
}
```

This version of doAdd() always overwrites the second argument with a value of 10. Because values in the arguments object are automatically reflected by the corresponding named arguments, the change to arguments[1] also changes the value of num2, so both have a value of 10. This doesn't mean that both access the same memory space, however; their memory spaces are separate but happen to be kept in sync. This effect goes only one way: changing the named argument does *not* result in a change to the corresponding value in arguments. Another thing to keep in mind: if only one argument is passed in, then setting arguments[1] to a value will not be reflected by the named argument because the length of the arguments object is set based on the number of arguments passed in, not the number of named arguments listed for the function.

Any named argument that is not passed into the function is automatically assigned the value `undefined`. This is akin to defining a variable without initializing it. For example, if only one argument is passed into the `doAdd()` function, then `num2` has a value of `undefined`.

Strict mode makes several changes to how the `arguments` object can be used. First, assignment, as in the previous example, no longer works. The value of `num2` remains undefined even though `arguments[1]` has been assigned to 10. Second, trying to overwrite the value of `arguments` is a syntax error. (The code will not execute.)

Arguments in Arrow Functions

When a function is defined using the arrow notation, the arguments passed to the function cannot be accessed using the `arguments` keyword; they can only be accessed using their named token in the function definition.

```
function foo() {
  console.log(arguments[0]);
}
foo(5);  // 5

let bar = () => {
  console.log(arguments[0]);
};
bar(5);  // ReferenceError: arguments is not defined
```

Although the arrow function arguments may not be available, be aware that it is possible that the `arguments` keyword is provided to the arrow function scope from the scope of a wrapping function being invoked:

```
function foo() {
  let bar = () => {
    console.log(arguments[0]);  // 5
  };
  bar();
}

foo(5);
```

> **NOTE** *All arguments in ECMAScript are passed by value. It is not possible to pass arguments by reference. If an object is passed as an argument, the value is just a reference to the object.*

NO OVERLOADING

ECMAScript functions cannot be overloaded in the traditional sense. In other languages, such as Java, it is possible to write two definitions of a function as long as their signatures (the type and number of arguments accepted) are different. As just discussed, functions in ECMAScript don't have signatures because the arguments are represented as an array containing zero or more values. Without function signatures, true overloading is not possible.

If two functions are defined to have the same name in ECMAScript, it is the last function that becomes the owner of that name. Consider the following example:

```
function addSomeNumber(num) {
  return num + 100;
}

function addSomeNumber(num) {
  return num + 200;
}

let result = addSomeNumber(100);   // 300
```

Here, the function `addSomeNumber()` is defined twice. The first version of the function adds 100 to the argument, and the second adds 200. When the last line is called, it returns 300 because the second function has overwritten the first.

As mentioned previously, it's possible to simulate overloading of methods by checking the type and number of arguments that have been passed into a function and then reacting accordingly.

Thinking of function names as pointers also explains why there can be no function overloading in ECMAScript. In the previous example, it's clear that declaring two functions with the same name always results in the last function overwriting the previous one. This code is almost exactly equivalent to the following:

```
let addSomeNumber = function(num) {
    return num + 100;
};

addSomeNumber = function(num) {
    return num + 200;
};

let result = addSomeNumber(100);    // 300
```

In this rewritten code, it's much easier to see exactly what is going on. The variable `addSomeNumber` is simply being overwritten when the second function is created.

DEFAULT PARAMETER VALUES

In old ECMAScript versions, a common strategy for implementing default parameter values was to determine if a parameter was not provided to the function invocation by checking if it was `undefined`, and assigning a value to the parameter if that was the case:

```
function makeKing(name) {
  name = (typeof name !== 'undefined') ? name : 'Henry';
  return `King ${name} VIII`;
}

console.log(makeKing());         // 'King Henry VIII'
console.log(makeKing('Louis'));  // 'King Louis VIII'
```

This is no longer required; it is possible to explicitly define values for parameters if they are not provided when the function is invoked. The equivalent of the previous function default parameters is done using the = operator directly inside the function signature:

```
function makeKing(name = 'Henry') {
  return `King ${name} VIII`;
}

console.log(makeKing('Louis'));   // 'King Louis VIII'
console.log(makeKing());          // 'King Henry VIII'
```

Passing undefined as an argument is treated the same as not passing any argument, which allows for multiple independent default variables:

```
function makeKing(name = 'Henry', numerals = 'VIII') {
  return `King ${name} ${numerals}`;
}

console.log(makeKing());                     // 'King Henry VIII'
console.log(makeKing('Louis'));              // 'King Louis VIII'
console.log(makeKing(undefined, 'VI'));      // 'King Henry VI'
```

When using default parameters, the arguments object's value does not reflect the default value of a parameter, but rather the argument passed to the function. This mirrors strict mode behavior and is valuable because it preserves the values as they were passed when the function was invoked:

```
function makeKing(name = 'Henry') {
  name = 'Louis';
  return `King ${arguments[0]}`;
}

console.log(makeKing());          // 'King undefined'
console.log(makeKing('Louis'));   // 'King Louis'
```

Default parameter values are not limited to primitives or object types, you can also calculate a value from an invoked function:

```
let romanNumerals = ['I', 'II', 'III', 'IV', 'V', 'VI'];
let ordinality = 0;

function getNumerals() {
  // Increment the ordinality after using it to index into the numerals array
  return romanNumerals[ordinality++];
}

function makeKing(name = 'Henry', numerals = getNumerals()) {
  return `King ${name} ${numerals}`;
}

console.log(makeKing());                     // 'King Henry I'
console.log(makeKing('Louis', 'XVI'));       // 'King Louis XVI'
console.log(makeKing());                     // 'King Henry II'
console.log(makeKing());                     // 'King Henry III'
```

The function default parameter is only invoked when the function itself is invoked, not when the function is defined. Note that the method that calculates the default value is only invoked when the argument is not provided.

Arrow functions are also capable of utilizing default parameters in the same way, although it means parentheses around a single argument is no longer optional when a default value is specified:

```
let makeKing = (name = 'Henry') => `King ${name}`;

console.log(makeKing());  // King Henry
```

Default Parameter Scope and Temporal Dead Zone

Because you can define objects and invoke functions on the fly when evaluating default parameter values, there is an execution scope for function parameters.

Defining multiple parameters with default values operates in effectively the same way as declaring variables sequentially using the `let` keyword. Consider the following function:

```
function makeKing(name = 'Henry', numerals = 'VIII') {
  return `King ${name} ${numerals}`;
}

console.log(makeKing());  // King Henry VIII
```

The default parameter values are initialized in the order in which they are listed in the list of parameters. You can think of it as behaving similar to the following:

```
function makeKing() {
  let name = 'Henry';
  let numerals = 'VIII';

  return `King ${name} ${numerals}`;
}
```

Because the parameters are initialized in order, parameters that have their default value defined later can reference an earlier parameter. The following silly example does exactly this:

```
function makeKing(name = 'Henry', numerals = name) {
  return `King ${name} ${numerals}`;
}

console.log(makeKing());  // King Henry Henry
```

The order of parameter initialization follows the same Temporal Dead Zone rules specifying that parameter values cannot reference other parameter values that are defined later. This would throw an error:

```
// Error
function makeKing(name = numerals, numerals = 'VIII') {
  return `King ${name} ${numerals}`;
}
```

Parameters also exist inside their own scope, and therefore cannot reference the scope of the function body. This would throw an error:

```
// Error
function makeKing(name = 'Henry', numerals = defaultNumeral) {
  let defaultNumeral = 'VIII';
  return `King ${name} ${numerals}`;
}
```

SPREAD ARGUMENTS AND REST PARAMETERS

The spread operator (...) allows for a very elegant way of managing and grouping collections. One of its most useful applications is in the domain of function signatures where it shines especially brightly in the domain of weak typing and variable length arguments. The spread operator is useful both when invoking a function, as well as when defining a function's parameters.

Spread Arguments

Instead of passing an array as a single function argument, it is often useful to be able to break apart an array of values and individually pass each value as a separate argument.

Suppose you have the following function defined, which sums all the values passed as arguments:

```
let values = [1, 2, 3, 4];

function getSum() {
  let sum = 0;
  for (let i = 0; i < arguments.length; ++i) {
    sum += arguments[i];
  }
  return sum;
}
```

This function expects each of its arguments to be an individual number that will be iterated through to find the sum. An array outside the function containing all the values you want to sum is a logical format, but before spread arguments, the most prudent way to flatten this array into separate parameters was to inelegantly utilize .apply():

```
console.log(getSum.apply(null, values));  // 10
```

With spread arguments, you are now able to perform this action more succinctly using the spread operator. Applying the spread operator to an iterable object and passing that as a single argument to a function will break apart that iterable object of size N and pass it to the function as N separate arguments.

With the spread operator, you can unpack the outer array into individual arguments directly inside the function invocation:

```
console.log(getSum(...values));  // 10
```

Because the size of the array is known, there are no restrictions on other parameters appearing before or after the spread operator, including other spread operators:

```
console.log(getSum(-1, ...values));        // 9
console.log(getSum(...values, 5));         // 15
console.log(getSum(-1, ...values, 5));     // 14
console.log(getSum(...values, ...[5,6,7])); // 28
```

The presence of the spread operator is totally unknown to the arguments object; it will treat the value being broken apart as separate pieces because that is how they are passed to the function:

```
let values = [1,2,3,4]

function countArguments() {
```

```
    console.log(arguments.length);
}

countArguments(-1, ...values);          // 5
countArguments(...values, 5);           // 5
countArguments(-1, ...values, 5);       // 6
countArguments(...values, ...[5,6,7]);  // 7
```

The `arguments` object is only one way to consume spread arguments. Spread arguments can be used as named parameters in both standard functions and arrow functions, as well as alongside default arguments:

```
function getProduct(a, b, c = 1) {
    return a * b * c;
}

let getSum = (a, b, c = 0) => {
    return a + b + c;
}

console.log(getProduct(...[1,2]));       // 2
console.log(getProduct(...[1,2,3]));     // 6
console.log(getProduct(...[1,2,3,4]));   // 6

console.log(getSum(...[0,1]));           // 1
console.log(getSum(...[0,1,2]));         // 3
console.log(getSum(...[0,1,2,3]));       // 3
```

Rest Parameter

When composing a function definition, instead of handling parameters individually, it is possible to use the spread operator to combine ranges of parameters of variable length into a single array. In many ways, this is very similar to how the `arguments` object works, but in this case the rest parameter becomes a formal `Array` object.

```
function getSum(...values) {
    // Sequentially sum all elements in 'values'
    // Initial total = 0
    return values.reduce((x, y) => x + y, 0);
}

console.log(getSum(1,2,3));   // 6
```

If there are named parameters preceding the rest parameter, it will assume the size of the remaining parameters that remain unnamed, or an empty array if there are none. Because the rest parameter is variable in size, you are only able to use it as the last formal parameter:

```
// Error
function getProduct(...values, lastValue) {}

// OK
function ignoreFirst(firstValue, ...values) {
    console.log(values);
```

```
   }

   ignoreFirst();        // []
   ignoreFirst(1);       // []
   ignoreFirst(1,2);     // [2]
   ignoreFirst(1,2,3);   // [2, 3]
```

Although arrow functions do not support the `arguments` object, they do support rest parameters, which affords you behavior that is extremely similar to arguments:

```
   let getSum = (...values) => {
     return values.reduce((x, y) => x + y, 0);
   }

   console.log(getSum(1,2,3));  // 6
```

As you might expect, using a rest parameter does not affect the `arguments` object—it will still exactly reflect what was passed to the function:

```
   function getSum(...values) {
     console.log(arguments.length);  // 3
     console.log(arguments);         // [1, 2, 3]
     console.log(values);            // [1, 2, 3]
   }

   console.log(getSum(1,2,3));
```

FUNCTION DECLARATIONS VERSUS FUNCTION EXPRESSIONS

There are two ways to define a function: by *function declaration* and by *function expression*. The first, function declaration, has the following form:

```
   function functionName(arg0, arg1, arg2) {
     // function body
   }
```

One of the key characteristics of function declarations is *function declaration hoisting*, whereby function declarations are read before the code executes. That means a function declaration may appear after code that calls it and still work:

```
   sayHi();
   function sayHi() {
     console.log("Hi!");
   }
```

This example doesn't throw an error because the function declaration is read first before the code begins to execute.

The second way to create a function is by using a function expression. Function expressions have several forms. The most common is as follows:

```
   let functionName = function(arg0, arg1, arg2) {
     // function body
   };
```

This pattern of function expression looks like a normal variable assignment. A function is created and assigned to the variable `functionName`. The created function is considered to be an *anonymous function*, because it has no identifier after the `function` keyword. (Anonymous functions are also sometimes called *lambda functions*.) This means the name property is the empty string.

Function expressions act like other expressions and, therefore, must be assigned before usage. The following causes an error:

```
sayHi();  // Error! function doesn't exist yet
let sayHi = function() {
  console.log("Hi!");
};
```

Understanding function hoisting is key to understanding the differences between function declarations and function expressions. For instance, the result of the following code may be surprising:

```
// Never do this!
if (condition) {
  function sayHi() {
    console.log('Hi!');
  }
} else {
  function sayHi() {
    console.log('Yo!');
  }
}
```

The code seems to indicate that if `condition` is `true`, use one definition for `sayHi()`, otherwise use a different definition. In fact, this is not valid syntax in ECMAScript, so JavaScript engines try to error correct into an appropriate state. The problem is that browsers don't consistently error correct in this case. This pattern is dangerous and should not be used. It is perfectly fine, however, to use function expressions in this way:

```
// OK
let sayHi;
if (condition) {
  sayHi = function() {
    console.log("Hi!");
  };
} else {
  sayHi = function() {
    console.log("Yo!");
  };
}
```

This example behaves the way you would expect, assigning the correct function expression to the variable `sayHi` based on condition.

The ability to create functions for assignment to variables also allows you to return functions as the value of other functions.

```
function createComparisonFunction(propertyName) {
  return function(object1, object2) {
    let value1 = object1[propertyName];
```

```
      let value2 = object2[propertyName];

      if (value1 < value2) {
        return -1;
      } else if (value1> value2) {
        return 1;
      } else {
        return 0;
      }
    };
  }
```

`createComparisonFunction()` returns an anonymous function. The returned function will, presumably, be either assigned to a variable or otherwise called, but within `createComparisonFunction()` it is anonymous. Anytime a function is being used as a value, it is a function expression. However, these are not the only uses for function expressions, as the rest of this chapter will show.

FUNCTIONS AS VALUES

Because function names in ECMAScript are nothing more than variables, functions can be used anywhere variables can be used. This means it's possible not only to pass a function into another function as an argument, but also to return a function as the result of another function. Consider the following function:

```
function callSomeFunction(someFunction, someArgument) {
  return someFunction(someArgument);
}
```

This function accepts two arguments. The first argument should be a function, and the second argument should be a value to pass to that function. Any function can then be passed in as follows:

```
function add10(num) {
  return num + 10;
}

let result1 = callSomeFunction(add10, 10);
console.log(result1);   // 20

function getGreeting(name) {
  return "Hello, " + name;
}

let result2 = callSomeFunction(getGreeting, "Alice");
console.log(result2);    // "Hello, Alice"
```

The `callSomeFunction()` function is generic, so it doesn't matter what function is passed in as the first argument—the result will always be returned from the first argument being executed. Remember that to access a function pointer instead of executing the function, you must leave off the parentheses, so the variables `add10` and `getGreeting` are passed into `callSomeFunction()` instead of their results being passed in.

Returning a function from a function is also possible and can be quite useful. For instance, suppose that you have an array of objects and want to sort the array on an arbitrary object property. A comparison function for the array's `sort()` method accepts only two arguments, which are the values to compare, but really you need a way to indicate which property to sort by. This problem can be addressed by defining a function to create a comparison function based on a property name, as in the following example:

```
function createComparisonFunction(propertyName) {
    return function(object1, object2) {
        let value1 = object1[propertyName];
        let value2 = object2[propertyName];

        if (value1 < value2) {
            return -1;
        } else if (value1> value2) {
            return 1;
        } else {
            return 0;
        }
    };
}
```

This function's syntax may look complicated, but it's just a function inside of a function, preceded by the `return` operator. The `propertyName` argument is accessible from the inner function and is used with bracket notation to retrieve the value of the given property. Once the property values are retrieved, a simple comparison can be done. This function can be used as in the following example:

```
let data = [
    {name: "Bob", age: 28},
    {name: "Alice", age: 29}
];

data.sort(createComparisonFunction("name"));
console.log(data[0].name);   // Alice

data.sort(createComparisonFunction("age"));
console.log(data[0].name);   // Bob
```

In this code, an array called data is created with two objects. Each object has a name and age property. By default, the `sort()` method would call `toString()` on each object to determine the sort order, which wouldn't give logical results in this case. Calling `createComparisonFunction("name")` creates a comparison function that sorts based on the name property, which means the first item will have the name `"Alice"` and an age of 29. When `createComparisonFunction("age")` is called, it creates a comparison function that sorts based on the age property, meaning the first item will be the one with its name equal to `"Bob"` and age equal to 28.

FUNCTION INTERNALS

In ECMAScript, three special objects exist inside a function: `arguments`, `this`, and `new.target`.

arguments

The `arguments` object, as discussed previously, is an array-like object that contains all of the arguments that were passed into the function. It is only available when a function is declared using the function keyword (as opposed to arrow function declaration). Though its primary use is to represent function arguments, the `arguments` object also has a property named `callee`, which is a pointer to the function that owns the `arguments` object. Consider the following classic factorial function:

```
function factorial(num) {
  if (num <= 1) {
    return 1;
  } else {
    return num * factorial(num - 1);
  }
}
```

This factorial computation is recursive, which works fine when the name of the function is set and won't be changed. However, the proper execution of this function is tightly coupled with the function name `"factorial"`. It can be decoupled by using `arguments.callee` as follows:

```
function factorial(num) {
  if (num <= 1) {
    return 1;
  } else {
    return num * arguments.callee(num - 1);
  }
}
```

In this rewritten version of the `factorial()` function, there is no longer a reference to the name `factorial` in the function body, which ensures that the recursive call will happen on the correct function no matter how the function is referenced. Consider the following:

```
let trueFactorial = factorial;

factorial = function() {
  return 0;
};

console.log(trueFactorial(5));  // 120
console.log(factorial(5));       // 0
```

Here, the variable `trueFactorial` is assigned the value of factorial, effectively storing the function pointer in a second location. The factorial variable is then reassigned to a function that simply returns 0. Without using `arguments.callee` in the original `factorial()` function's body, the call to `trueFactorial()` would return 0. However, with the function decoupled from the function name, `trueFactorial()` correctly calculates the factorial, and `factorial()` is the only function that returns 0.

this

The next special object is called `this`, which behaves differently when used inside a standard function and an arrow function.

Inside a standard function, it is a reference to the context object that the function is operating on—often called the *this value* (when a function is called in the global scope of a web page, the `this` object points to `window`). Consider the following:

```
window.color = 'red';
```

```
let o = {
  color: 'blue'
};

function sayColor() {
  console.log(this.color);
}

sayColor();      // 'red'

o.sayColor = sayColor;
o.sayColor();    // 'blue'
```

The function `sayColor()` is defined globally but references the `this` object. The value of `this` is not determined until the function is called, so its value may not be consistent throughout the code execution. When `sayColor()` is called in the global scope, it outputs "red" because `this` is pointing to `window`, which means `this.color` evaluates to `window.color`. By assigning the function to the object `o` and then calling `o.sayColor()`, the `this` object points to `o`, so `this.color` evaluates to `o.color` and "blue" is displayed.

Inside an arrow function, `this` references the context in which the arrow function expression is *defined*. This is demonstrated in the following example, where two different invocations of `sayColor` both reference the property of the `window` object, which is the context inside which the arrow function was initially defined:

```
window.color = 'red';
let o = {
  color: 'blue'
};

let sayColor = () => console.log(this.color);

sayColor();      // 'red'

o.sayColor = sayColor;
o.sayColor();    // 'red'
```

This behavior is especially useful in situations where events or timeouts will invoke a function inside a callback where the invoking object is not the intended object. When an arrow function is used in these situations, the context referenced by this is preserved:

```
function King() {
  this.royaltyName = 'Henry';

  // 'this' will be the King instance
  setTimeout(() => console.log(this.royaltyName), 1000);
}

function Queen() {
  this.royaltyName = 'Elizabeth';

  // 'this' will be the window object
  setTimeout(function() { console.log(this.royaltyName); }, 1000);
```

```
}

new King();    // Henry
new Queen();   // undefined
```

> **NOTE** *Remember that function names are simply variables containing pointers, so the global* sayColor() *function and* o.sayColor() *point to the same function even though they execute in different contexts.*

caller

ECMAScript also formalizes an additional property on a function object: caller. This property contains a reference to the function that called this function or null if the function was called from the global scope. For example:

```
function outer() {
  inner();
}
function inner() {
  console.log(inner.caller);
}
outer();
```

This code displays an alert with the source text of the outer() function. Because outer() calls inner(), inner.caller points back to outer(). For looser coupling, you can also access the same information via arguments.callee.caller:

```
function outer() {
  inner();
}

function inner() {
  console.log(arguments.callee.caller);
}

outer();
```

When function code executes in strict mode, attempting to access arguments.callee results in an error. ECMAScript also defines arguments.caller, which also results in an error in strict mode and is always undefined outside of strict mode. This is to clear up confusion between arguments.caller and the caller property of functions. These changes were made as security additions to the language, so third-party code could not inspect other code running in the same context.

Strict mode places one additional restriction: you cannot assign a value to the caller property of a function. Doing so results in an error.

new.target

Functions have always been able to behave as both a constructor to instantiate a new object and as a normal callable function. To address this, ECMAScript supports the ability to determine if a function was invoked with the new keyword using new.target. Suppose we have this simple function:

```
function foo() {}
```

If this function is called using foo(), new.target will be undefined. If this function is called using new foo, new.target will reference the constructor or function.

```
function King() {
  if (!new.target) {
    throw 'King must be instantiated using "new"'
  }
  console.log('King instantiated using "new"';
}

new King();  // King instantiated using "new"
King();      // Error: King must be instantiated using "new"
```

FUNCTION PROPERTIES AND METHODS

Functions are objects in ECMAScript and, as mentioned previously, therefore have properties and methods. Each function has two properties: length and prototype. The length property indicates the number of named arguments that the function expects, as in this example:

```
function sayName(name) {
  console.log(name);
}

function sum(num1, num2) {
  return num1 + num2;
}

function sayHi() {
  console.log("hi");
}

console.log(sayName.length);  // 1
console.log(sum.length);      // 2
console.log(sayHi.length);    // 0
```

This code defines three functions, each with a different number of named arguments. The sayName() function specifies one argument, so its length property is set to 1. Similarly, the sum() function specifies two arguments, so its length property is 2, and sayHi() has no named arguments, so its length is 0.

The prototype property is perhaps the most interesting part of the ECMAScript core. prototype is the actual location of all instance methods for reference types, meaning methods such as toString() and valueOf() actually exist on the prototype and are then accessed from the object instances. This property is very important in terms of defining your own reference types and inheritance. (These topics are covered in Chapter 8, "Objects, Classes, and Object-Oriented Programming.") The prototype property is not enumerable and so will not be found using for-in.

Using *apply()*, *call()*, and *bind()*

There are three additional methods for functions: `apply()`, `call()`, and `bind()`. These methods use different strategies to call the function with a specific `this` value, effectively setting the value of the `this` object inside the function body. The `apply()` method accepts two arguments: the value of `this` inside the function and an array of arguments. This second argument may be an instance of `Array`, but it can also be the `arguments` object. Consider the following:

```
function sum(num1, num2) {
    return num1 + num2;
}

function callSum1(num1, num2) {
    return sum.apply(this, arguments);   // passing in arguments object
}

function callSum2(num1, num2) {
    return sum.apply(this, [num1, num2]);   // passing in array
}

console.log(callSum1(10, 10));   // 20
console.log(callSum2(10, 10));   // 20
```

In this example, `callSum1()` executes the `sum()` method, passing in `this` as the `this` value (which is equal to `window` because it's being called in the global scope) and also passing in the `arguments` object. The `callSum2()` method also calls `sum()`, but it passes in an array of the arguments instead. Both functions will execute and return the correct result.

> **NOTE** *In strict mode, the* `this` *value of a function called without a context object is not coerced to* `window`. *Instead,* `this` *becomes* `undefined` *unless explicitly set by either attaching the function to an object or using* `apply()` *or* `call()`.

The `call()` method exhibits the same behavior as `apply()`, but arguments are passed to it differently. The first argument is the `this` value, but the remaining arguments are passed directly into the function. Using `call()` arguments must be enumerated specifically, as in this example:

```
function sum(num1, num2) {
    return num1 + num2;
}

function callSum(num1, num2) {
    return sum.call(this, num1, num2);
}

console.log(callSum(10, 10));   // 20
```

The `callSum()` method must pass in each of its arguments explicitly into the `call()` method. The result is the same as using `apply()`. The decision to use either `apply()` or `call()` depends solely on the easiest way for you to pass arguments into the function. If you intend to pass in the arguments object directly or if you already have an array of data to pass in, then `apply()` is the better choice; otherwise, `call()` may be a more appropriate choice. (If there are no arguments to pass in, these methods are identical.)

The true power of `apply()` and `call()` lies not in their ability to pass arguments but rather in their ability to augment the `this` value inside of the function. Consider the following example:

```
window.color = 'red';
let o = {
  color: 'blue'
};

function sayColor() {
  console.log(this.color);
}

sayColor();                // red

sayColor.call(this);       // red
sayColor.call(window);     // red
sayColor.call(o);          // blue
```

This example is a modified version of the one used to illustrate the `this` object. Once again, `sayColor()` is defined as a global function, and when it's called in the global scope, it displays `"red"` because `this.color` evaluates to `window.color`. You can then call the function explicitly in the global scope by using `sayColor.call(this)` and `sayColor.call(window)`, which both display `"red"`. Running `sayColor.call(o)` switches the context of the function such that `this` points to `o`, resulting in a display of `"blue"`.

The advantage of using `call()` (or `apply()`) to augment the scope is that the object doesn't need to know anything about the method. In the first version of this example, the `sayColor()` function was placed directly on the object `o` before it was called; in the updated example, that step is no longer necessary.

The `bind()` method creates a new function instance whose `this` value is *bound* to the value that was passed into `bind()`. For example:

```
window.color = 'red';
var o = {
  color: 'blue'
};

function sayColor() {
  console.log(this.color);
}
let objectSayColor = sayColor.bind(o);
objectSayColor();  // blue
```

Here, a new function called `objectSayColor()` is created from `sayColor()` by calling `bind()` and passing in the object `o`. The `objectSayColor()` function has a `this` value equivalent to `o`, so calling the function, even as a global call, results in the string `"blue"` being displayed.

> **NOTE** *More recent additions to ECMAScript, such as arrow functions and new* `Array` *methods, have narrowed the utility of* `apply()`, `call()`, *and* `bind()`. *They are still needed in some situations, but their appearance in modern JavaScript codebases is markedly attenuated.*

Serializing Functions

The inherited methods `toLocaleString()` and `toString()` always return the function's code as long, as it was defined in ECMAScript. Native functions will return a placeholder. The following example demonstrates this distinction:

```
function foo(value = "foo") { return value; }
console.log(foo.toString());
// function foo(value = "foo") { return value; }

const bar = (value = "bar") => value;
console.log(bar.toString());
// (value = "bar") => value

console.log(alert);
// function alert() { [native code] }
```

The exact format of this code varies from browser to browser—some return your code exactly as it appeared in the source code, including comments, whereas others return the internal representation of your code, which has comments removed and possibly some code changes that the interpreter made. Because of these differences, you can't rely on what is returned for any important functionality, though this information may be useful for debugging purposes. The inherited method `valueOf()` simply returns the function itself.

RECURSION

A *recursive function* typically is formed when a function calls itself by name, as in the following example:

```
function factorial(num) {
  if (num <= 1) {
    return 1;
  } else {
    return num * factorial(num - 1);
  }
}
```

This is the classic recursive factorial function. Although this works initially, it's possible to prevent it from functioning by running the following code immediately after it:

```
let anotherFactorial = factorial;
factorial = null;
console.log(anotherFactorial(4));  // error!
```

Here, the `factorial()` function is stored in a variable called `anotherFactorial`. The `factorial` variable is then set to `null`, so only one reference to the original function remains. When `anotherFactorial()` is called, it will cause an error because it will try to execute `factorial()`, which is no longer a function. Using `arguments.callee` can alleviate this problem.

Recall that `arguments.callee` is a pointer to the function being executed and, as such, can be used to call the function recursively, as shown here:

```
function factorial(num) {
  if (num <= 1) {
    return 1;
  } else {
    return num * arguments.callee(num - 1);
  }
}
```

Changing the highlighted line to use `arguments.callee` instead of the function name ensures that this function will work regardless of how it is accessed. It's advisable to always use `arguments.callee` of the function name whenever you're writing recursive functions.

The value of `arguments.callee` is not accessible to a script running in strict mode and will cause an error when attempts are made to read it. Instead, you can use *named function expressions* to achieve the same result. For example:

```
const factorial = (function f(num) {
  if (num <= 1) {
    return 1;
  } else {
    return num * f(num - 1);
  }
});
```

In this code, a named function expression `f()` is created and assigned to the variable factorial. The name `f` remains the same even if the function is assigned to another variable, so the recursive call will always execute correctly. This pattern works in both nonstrict mode and strict mode.

TAIL CALL OPTIMIZATION

The JavaScript engine will optimize memory management by reusing stack frames when certain conditions are met. Specifically, this optimization pertains to *tail calls*, where the return value of an outer function is the returned value of an inner function, as follows:

```
function outerFunction() {
  return innerFunction();  // tail call
}
```

Without the optimization, executing this example would have the following effect in memory:

1. Execution reaches `outerFunction` body, first stack frame is pushed onto stack.

2. Body of `outerFunction` executes, `return` statement is reached. To evaluate the `return` statement, `innerFunction` must be evaluated.

3. Execution reaches `innerFunction` body, second stack frame is pushed onto stack.

4. Body of innerFunction executes, and its returned value is evaluated.

5. Return value is passed back to outerFunction, which in turn can return that value.

6. Stack frames are popped off the stack.

With the tail call optimization, executing this example would have the following effect in memory:

1. Execution reaches outerFunction body, first stack frame is pushed onto stack.

2. Body of outerFunction executes, return statement is reached. To evaluate the return statement, innerFunction must be evaluated.

3. Engine recognizes that first stack frame can safely be popped off the stack since the return value of innerFunction is also the return value of outerFunction.

4. outerFunction stack frame is popped off the stack.

5. Execution reaches innerFunction body, stack frame is pushed onto stack.

6. Body of innerFunction executes, and its returned value is evaluated.

7. innerFunction stack frame is popped off the stack.

The difference here is that the first implementation will incur an additional stack frame for every successive nested function call, whereas the second implementation will incur a single stack frame for the entire length of execution. This is the core of the tail call optimization: if the function is structured in a way that allows it to be safely discarded upon the tail call, the engine will do so.

> **NOTE** *There is no ability to directly measure if the tail call optimization is occurring, but modern browsers are guaranteed to apply the optimization if your code satisfies the requirements.*

Tail Call Optimization Requirements

The engine is only capable of performing such an optimization when it is sure that the outer stack frame is truly not needed any longer. This demands the following conditions:

➤ The code is executing in strict mode.

➤ The return value of the outer function is the invoked tail call function.

➤ There is no further execution required after the tail call function returns.

➤ The tail call function is not a closure that refers to variables in the outer function's scope.

The following are a few examples that violate these conditions and therefore are not subject to the tail call optimization:

```
"use strict";

// No optimization: tail call is not returned
```

```
function outerFunction() {
  innerFunction();
}

// No optimization: tail call is not directly returned
function outerFunction() {
  let innerFunctionResult = innerFunction();
  return innerFunctionResult;
}

// No optimization: tail call must be cast as a string after return
function outerFunction() {
  return innerFunction().toString();
}

// No optimization: tail call is a closure
function outerFunction() {
  let foo = 'bar';
  function innerFunction() { return foo; }

  return innerFunction();
}
```

The following are a few examples which do not violate these conditions, and therefore will be optimized:

```
"use strict";

// Optimization used: argument computation occurrs before stack frame is discarded
function outerFunction(a, b) {
  return innerFunction(a + b);
}

// Optimization used: initial return values do not have stack frame implications
function outerFunction(a, b) {
  if (a < b) {
    return a;
  }
  return innerFunction(a + b);
}

// Optimization used: both inner functions are considered to be in a tail position
function outerFunction(condition) {
  return condition ? innerFunctionA() : innerFunctionB();
}
```

A common source of confusion is the nature of differentiating tail calls and recursive calls. The optimization will be applied to recursive or non-recursive tail calls; the engine makes no distinction if the function is calling itself or a different function in the tail call. However, your code will stand to see the most benefit from this optimization in recursive situations, as this code is the form factor which tends to swamp the stack with stack frames.

> **NOTE** *The reason for requiring strict mode is that non-strict mode function invocation allows the use of* `f.arguments` *and* `f.caller`, *which are references to the outer function's stack frame. Obviously, this means the optimization would not be possible, and therefore the strict mode requirement exists to prevent these properties from existing.*

Coding for Tail Call Optimization

It's instructive to convert a naïve recursive function into one which will be optimized. Take the following simple Fibonacci example:

```
function fib(n) {
  if (n < 2) {
    return n;
  }

  return fib(n - 1) + fib(n - 2);
}

console.log(fib(0));   // 0
console.log(fib(1));   // 1
console.log(fib(2));   // 1
console.log(fib(3));   // 2
console.log(fib(4));   // 3
console.log(fib(5));   // 5
console.log(fib(6));   // 8
```

It's easy to see that this function is not subject to tail call optimization since there is a disqualifying add operation occurring in the return statement. As a result, the number of stack frames for `fib(n)` will have a memory complexity of $O(2^n)$. Therefore, it's very simple to swamp your browser with something as simple as:

```
fib(1000);
```

Of course, there are techniques which solve this problem differently such as memoization or flattening into an iterative loop, but you can keep this implementation recursive and refactor it into an optimization-compatible form. An excellent strategy is to nest two functions: the outer one acting as the base case, and the inner one acting as the recursive case:

```
"use strict";

// base case
function fib(n) {
  return fibImpl(0, 1, n);
}

// recursive case
function fibImpl(a, b, n) {
  if (n === 0) {
    return a;
  }
  return fibImpl(b, a + b, n - 1);
}
```

With this implementation, all tail call optimization requirements are satisfied, and your browser will have no problems with `fib(1000)`.

CLOSURES

The terms *anonymous functions* and *closures* are often incorrectly used interchangeably. Closures are functions that have access to variables from another function's scope. This is often accomplished by creating a function inside a function, as in the following highlighted lines from the previous `createComparisonFunction()` example:

```
function createComparisonFunction(propertyName) {
  return function(object1, object2) {
    let value1 = object1[propertyName];
    let value2 = object2[propertyName];

    if (value1 < value2) {
      return -1;
    } else if (value1> value2) {
      return 1;
    } else {
      return 0;
    }
  };
}
```

The highlighted lines in this example are part of the inner function (an anonymous function) that is accessing a variable (`propertyName`) from the outer function. Even after the inner function has been returned and is being used elsewhere, it has access to that variable. This occurs because the inner function's scope chain includes the scope of `createComparisonFunction()`. To understand why this is possible, consider what happens when a function is first called.

Chapter 4, "Variables, Scope, and Memory," introduced the concept of a scope chain. The details of how scope chains are created and used are important for a good understanding of closures. When a function is called, an execution context is created, and its scope chain is created. The activation object for the function is initialized with values for arguments and any named arguments. The outer function's activation object is the second object in the scope chain. This process continues for all containing functions until the scope chain terminates with the global execution context.

As the function executes, variables are looked up in the scope chain for the reading and writing of values. Consider the following:

```
function compare(value1, value2) {
  if (value1 < value2) {
    return -1;
  } else if (value1> value2) {
    return 1;
  } else {
    return 0;
  }
}

let result = compare(5, 10);
```

This code defines a function named `compare()` that is called in the global execution context. When `compare()` is called for the first time, a new activation object is created that contains arguments, `value1`, and `value2`. The global execution context's variable object is next in the `compare()` execution context's scope chain, which contains this, result, and compare. Figure 10.1 illustrates this relationship.

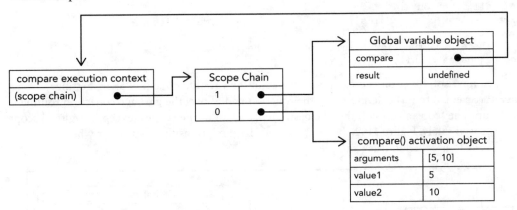

FIGURE 10.1: An execution context's scope chain

Behind the scenes, an object represents the variables in each execution context. The global context's variable object always exists, whereas local context variable objects, such as the one for `compare()`, exist only while the function is being executed. When `compare()` is defined, its scope chain is created, preloaded with the global variable object, and saved to the internal [[Scope]] property. When the function is called, an execution context is created and its scope chain is built up by copying the objects in the function's [[Scope]] property. After that, an activation object (which also acts as a variable object) is created and pushed to the front of the context's scope chain. In this example, that means the `compare()` function's execution context has two variable objects in its scope chain: the local activation object and the global variable object. Note that the scope chain is essentially a list of pointers to variable objects and does not physically contain the objects.

Whenever a variable is accessed inside a function, the scope chain is searched for a variable with the given name. Once the function has completed, the local activation object is destroyed, leaving only the global scope in memory. Closures, however, behave differently.

A function that is defined inside another function adds the containing function's activation object into its scope chain. So, in `createComparisonFunction()`, the anonymous function's scope chain actually contains a reference to the activation object for `createComparisonFunction()`. Figure 10.2 illustrates this relationship when the following code is executed:

```
let compare = createComparisonFunction('name');
let result = compare({ name: 'Alice' }, { name: 'Matt' });
```

When the anonymous function is returned from `createComparisonFunction()`, its scope chain has been initialized to contain the activation object from `createComparisonFunction()` and the global variable object. This gives the anonymous function access to all of the variables from `createComparisonFunction()`. Another interesting side effect is that the activation object from `createComparisonFunction()` cannot be destroyed once the function finishes executing, because a reference still exists in the anonymous function's scope chain. After `createComparisonFunction()`

completes, the scope chain for its execution context is destroyed, but its activation object will remain in memory until the anonymous function is destroyed, as in the following:

```
// create function
let compareNames = createComparisonFunction('name');

// call function
let result = compareNames({ name: 'Alice' }, { name: 'Matt' });

// dereference function - memory can now be reclaimed
compareNames = null;
```

Here, the comparison function is created and stored in the variable compareNames. Setting compareNames equal to null dereferences the function and allows the garbage collection routine to clean it up. The scope chain will then be destroyed, and all of the scopes (except the global scope) can be destroyed safely. Figure 10.2 shows the scope-chain relationships that occur when compareNames() is called in this example.

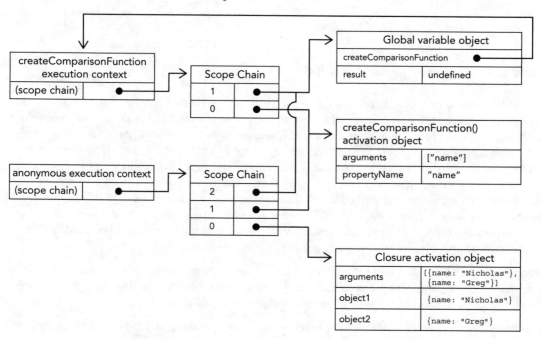

FIGURE 10.2: Closure scope chain

> **NOTE** *Because closures carry with them the containing function's scope, they take up more memory than other functions. Overuse of closures can lead to excess memory consumption, so it's recommended you use them only when absolutely necessary. Optimizing JavaScript engines, such as V8, make attempts to reclaim memory that is trapped because of closures, but it's still recommended to be careful when using closures.*

The *this* Object

Using the `this` object inside closures introduces some complex behaviors. When a function is not defined using the arrow syntax, the `this` object is bound at runtime based on the context in which a function is executed: when used inside global functions, this is equal to `window` in nonstrict mode and `undefined` in strict mode, whereas this is equal to the object when called as an object method. Anonymous functions are not bound to an object in this context, meaning the `this` object points to `window` unless executing in strict mode (where `this` is `undefined`). Because of the way closures are written, however, this fact is not always obvious. Consider the following:

```
window.identity = 'The Window';

let object = {
  identity: 'My Object',
  getIdentityFunc() {
    return function() {
      return this.identity;
    };
  }
};

console.log(object.getIdentityFunc()());  // 'The Window'
```

Here, a global variable called `name` is created along with an object that also contains a property called `name`. The object contains a method, `getNameFunc()`, that returns an anonymous function, which returns `this.identity`. Because `getIdentityFunc()` returns a function, calling `object.getIdentityFunc()()` immediately calls the function that is returned, which returns a string. In this case, however, it returns `'The Window'`, which is the value of the global identity variable. Why didn't the anonymous function pick up the containing scope's `this` object?

Remember that each function automatically gets two special variables as soon as the function is called: `this` and `arguments`. An inner function can never access these variables directly from an outer function. It is possible to allow a closure access to a different `this` object by storing it in another variable that the closure can access, as in this example:

```
window.identity = 'The Window';

let object = {
  identity: 'My Object',
  getIdentityFunc() {
    let that = this;
    return function() {
      return that.identity;
    };
  }
};

console.log(object.getIdentityFunc()());  // 'My Object'
```

The two highlighted lines show the difference between this example and the previous one. Before defining the anonymous function, a variable named `that` is assigned equal to the `this` object. When the closure is defined, it has access to `that` because it is a uniquely named variable in the containing function. Even after the function is returned, `that` is still bound to object, so calling `object.getIdentityFunc()()` returns `'My Object'`.

> **NOTE** *Both* this *and* `arguments` *behave in this way. If you want access to a containing scope's* `arguments` *object, you'll need to save a reference into another variable that the closure can access.*

There are a few special cases where the value of `this` may not end up as the value you expect. Consider the following modification to the previous example:

```
window.identity = 'The Window';
let object = {
  identity: 'My Object',
  getIdentity () {
    return this.identity;
  }
};
```

The `getIdentity()` method simply returns the value of `this.identity`. Here are various ways to call `object.getName()` and the results:

```
object.getIdentity();                              // 'My Object'
(object.getIdentity)();                            // 'My Object'
(object.getIdentity = object.getIdentity)();       // 'The Window'
```

The first line calls `object.getIdentity()` in the way you normally would and so returns `'My Object'`, as `this.identity` is the same as `object.identity`. The second line places parentheses around `object.getIdentity` before calling it. While this might seem to be a reference just to the function, the `this` value is maintained because `object.getIdentity` and `(object.getIdentity)` are defined to be equivalent. The third line performs an assignment and then calls the result. Because the value of this assignment expression is the function itself, the `this` value is not maintained, and so `'The Window'` is returned.

It's unlikely that you'll intentionally use the patterns in lines two or three, but it is helpful to know that the value of `this` can change in unexpected ways when syntax is changed slightly.

Memory Leaks

When used incorrectly, closures can lead to memory leaks in your application. A memory leak occurs when your program continues to allocate memory without releasing it, which can cause your application to slow down or even crash. Function closures can contribute to memory leaks because they allow variables to persist beyond their intended lifetime. Here's an example of a function closure that can cause a memory leak:

```
function createArrayAppender() {
  const arr = [];
  return function appendTo(num) {
    arr.push(num);
  };
```

```
  }

  const appendToLargeArray = createArrayAppender();
  for (let i = 0; i < 1e8; i++) {
    appendToLargeArray(i);
  }
```

In this code, the `createArrayAppender` function returns a closure that references the `arr` variable in its parent scope. Each time the `appendTo` function is called, it pushes a number into the array.

The problem is that the `arr` variable is never released from memory, even though it is no longer needed outside of the closure. This is because the closure maintains a reference to the array, which prevents it from being garbage collected even after the `createArrayAppender` function has finished executing. As a result, when we call the `appendToLargeArray` function in a loop, it keeps pushing numbers into the same array over and over again, causing the array to grow larger and larger in memory. In testing, the memory footprint of a web page running only this code idles at an eye-watering 1087MB.

To resolve this, this code can be refactored to allow the garbage collector to reclaim the array memory when we're done with it:

```
  function appendToArray(arr, num) {
    arr.push(num);
  }

  const largeArray = [];
  for (let i = 0; i < 1e8; i++) {
    appendToArray(largeArray, i);
  }
```

IMMEDIATELY INVOKED FUNCTION EXPRESSIONS

An anonymous function that is called immediately is most often called an *immediately invoked function expression (IIFE)*. It might also be referred to as a *self-executing anonymous function*. It resembles a function declaration, but because it is enclosed in parentheses, it is interpreted as a function expression. This function is then called via the second set of parentheses at the end. The basic syntax is as follows:

```
  (function() {
    // block code here
  })();
```

If you're writing a library or plug-in, you may want to encapsulate your code to avoid conflicts with other libraries that may be loaded on the same page. An IIFE can be used to create a private scope for your code, which helps prevent naming collisions.

```
  (function($) {
    // code that uses jQuery
  })(jQuery);
```

In this example, we pass in `jQuery` as an argument and then use the `$` variable to refer to it within the function. This ensures that the `$` variable is always referencing the correct version of `jQuery`, even if another library has defined its own `$` variable.

Another common use case for async IIFEs is when you need to perform some asynchronous setup logic. For example, you might want to fetch some data from an API and store it in a local variable before your app starts rendering, or you might want to use async/await syntax inside a function that is *not* an async function. An async IIFE allows you to execute asynchronous code immediately and in a local scope. Here's an example:

```
(async function() {
  const data = await fetch('/api/data');
  const result = await data.json();
  // do something with the result
})();
```

SUMMARY

Functions are useful and versatile tools in JavaScript programming. They provide powerful syntax allowing you to wield them even more effectively.

➤ Function expressions are different from function declarations. Function declarations require names, while function expressions do not. A function expression without a name is also called an anonymous function.

➤ Arrow functions are similar to function expressions, but with some important differences.

➤ Arguments and parameters in JavaScript functions are highly flexible. The arguments object, along with the spread operator, allows for totally dynamic definition and invocation.

➤ Internally, functions expose a handful of objects and references that provide you information on how the function was invoked, where it was invoked, and what was originally passed to it.

➤ Engines will optimize functions with tail calls to preserve stack space.

➤ Behind the scenes, the closure's scope chain contains a variable object for itself, the containing function, and the global context.

➤ Typically, a function's scope and all of its variables are destroyed when the function has finished executing.

➤ When a closure is returned from that function, its scope remains in memory until the closure no longer exists.

➤ A function can be created and called immediately, executing the code within it but never leaving a reference to the function.

➤ This results in all of the variables inside the function being destroyed unless they are specifically set to a variable in the containing scope.

11

Promises and Async/Await

DOWNLOADS FOR THIS CHAPTER

Please note that all the code examples for this chapter are available as a part of this chapter's code download on the book's website at www.wiley.com/go/projavascript5e.

Promises and async/await are two of the most important features in JavaScript, offering developers elegant and efficient ways to handle asynchronous operations. Promises offer a powerful abstraction over callbacks, allowing developers to write cleaner and more maintainable code. Async/await enhances the simplicity of promises by providing a more natural syntax that looks synchronous but runs asynchronously, making it easier to reason about asynchronous code.

> **NOTE** *Throughout this chapter, examples make extensive use of the asynchronous logging function* `console.asyncLog()` *to log the state of promise instances. This function is not native to the browser, but it can easily be defined as follows:*
>
> ```
> console.asyncLog = (...args) => setTimeout(console.log, 0, ...args)
> ```
>
> *The log output will be shown in the chapter as though it is printed synchronously when, in fact, it is printed asynchronously. This is done to allow for values such as promises to assume their final state. Head to the "Promises and the Microtask Queue" section to understand why this is necessary.*
>
> *Additionally, a browser's console output will often print information about objects that is not otherwise available to the JavaScript runtime (such as the state of a promise). This feature is used extensively in examples throughout the chapter to aid in broadening the reader's understanding.*

INTRODUCTION TO ASYNCHRONOUS PROGRAMMING

The duality between synchronous and asynchronous behavior is a fundamental concept in computer science—especially in a single-threaded event loop model such as JavaScript. Asynchronous behavior is borne out of the need to optimize for higher computational throughput in the face of high-latency operations. If it is feasible to run other instructions while a computation is completing and still maintain a stable system, then it is pragmatic to do so.

Importantly, an asynchronous operation is not necessarily a computationally intensive or high-latency operation. It can be used anywhere it doesn't make sense to block a thread of execution to wait for the asynchronous behavior to occur.

Synchronous vs. Asynchronous JavaScript

Synchronous behavior is analogous to sequential processor instructions in memory. Each instruction is executed strictly in the order in which it appears, and each is also capable of immediately retrieving information that is stored locally within the system (for example: in a processor register or in system memory). As a result, it is easy to reason about the program state (for example, the value of a variable) at any given point in code.

A trivial example of this would be performing a simple arithmetic operation:

```
let x = 3;
x = x + 4;
```

At each step in this program, it is possible to reason about the state of the program because execution will not proceed until the previous instruction is completed. When the last instruction completes, the computed value of x is immediately available for use.

This JavaScript snippet is easy to reason about because it is not difficult to anticipate what low-level instructions this will be compiled to (from JavaScript to x86, for example). Presumably, the operating system will allocate some memory for a floating point number on the stack, perform an arithmetic operation on that value, and write the result to that allocated memory. All of these instructions exist serially inside a single thread of execution. At each point in the compiled low-level program, you are well-equipped to assert what can and cannot be known about the state of the system.

Conversely, *asynchronous behavior* is analogous to interrupts, where an entity external to the current process is able to trigger code execution. An asynchronous operation is often required because it is infeasible to force the process to wait a long time for an operation to complete (which is the case with a synchronous operation). This long wait might occur because the code is accessing a high-latency resource, such as sending a request to a remote server and awaiting a response.

A trivial JavaScript example of this would be performing an arithmetic operation inside a timeout:

```
let x = 3;
setTimeout(() => x = x + 4, 1000);
```

This program eventually performs the same work as the synchronous one—adding two numbers together—but this thread of execution cannot know exactly when the value of x will change because that depends on when the callback is dequeued from the message queue and executed.

This code is not as easy to reason about. Although the low-level instructions used in this example ultimately do the same work as the previous example, the second chunk of instructions (the addition operation and assignment) are triggered by a system timer, which will generate an interrupt to enqueue execution. Precisely when this interrupt will be triggered is a black box to the JavaScript runtime, so it effectively cannot be known exactly when the interrupt will occur (although it is guaranteed to be *after* the current thread of synchronous execution completes, since the callback will not yet have had an opportunity to be dequeued and executed). Nevertheless, you are generally unable to assert when the system state will change after the callback is scheduled.

For the value of x to become useful, this asynchronously executed function would need to signal to the rest of the program that it has updated the value of x. However, if the program does not need this value, then it is free to proceed and do other work instead of waiting for the result.

Designing a system to know when the value of x can be read is surprisingly tricky. Implementations of such a system within the JavaScript have undergone several iterations.

Legacy Asynchronous Programming Patterns

Asynchronous behavior has long been an important cornerstone of JavaScript. In early versions of the language, an asynchronous operation only supported definition of a callback function to indicate that the asynchronous operation had completed. Serializing asynchronous behavior was a common problem, usually solved by a codebase full of nested callback functions—colloquially referred to as "callback hell."

Suppose you were working with the following asynchronous function, which uses setTimeout to perform some behavior after one second:

```
function double(value) {
  setTimeout(() => console.asyncLog(value * 2), 1000);
}

double(3);
// 6 (printed after roughly 1000ms)
```

There's nothing mysterious occurring here, but it is important to understand exactly why this is an asynchronous function. setTimeout allows for the definition of a callback that is scheduled to execute after a specified amount of time. After 1000ms, the JavaScript runtime will schedule the callback for execution by pushing it onto JavaScript's message queue. This callback is dequeued and executed in a manner that is totally invisible to JavaScript code. What's more, the double() function exits immediately after the setTimeout scheduling operation is successful.

Returning Asynchronous Values

Suppose the setTimeout operation returned a useful value. What's the best way to transport the value back to where it is needed? The widely accepted strategy is to provide a callback to the asynchronous operation, where the callback contained the code that needs access to the calculated value (provided as a parameter). This looks like the following:

```
function double(value, callback) {
  setTimeout(() => callback(value * 2), 1000);
}

double(3, (x) => console.log(`I was given: ${x}`));
// I was given: 6 (printed after roughly 1000ms)
```

Here, the setTimeout invocation is instructed to push a function onto the message queue after 1000ms have elapsed. This function will be dequeued and asynchronously evaluated by the runtime. The callback function and its parameters are still available in the asynchronous execution through a function closure.

Handling Failure

The possibility of failure needs to be incorporated into this callback model as well, so this typically took the form of a success and failure callback:

```
function double(value, success, failure) {
  setTimeout(() => {
    try {
      if (typeof value !== 'number') {
        throw 'Must provide number as first argument';
      }
      success(2 * value);
    } catch (e) {
      failure(e);
    }
  }, 1000);
}

const successCallback = (x) => console.log(`Success: ${x}`);
const failureCallback = (e) => console.log(`Failure: ${e}`);

double(3, successCallback, failureCallback);
double('b', successCallback, failureCallback);

// Success: 6 (printed after roughly 1000ms)
// Failure: Must provide number as first argument (printed after roughly 1000ms)
```

This format is already undesirable, as the callbacks must be defined when the asynchronous operation is initialized. The value returned from the asynchronous function is transient, and so only callbacks that are prepared to accept this transient value as a parameter are capable of accessing it.

Nesting Asynchronous Callbacks

The callback situation is further complicated when access to the asynchronous values have dependencies on other asynchronous values. In the world of callbacks, this necessitates nesting the callbacks:

```
function double(value, success, failure) {
  setTimeout(() => {
    try {
      if (typeof value !== 'number') {
        throw 'Must provide number as first argument';
      }
      success(2 * value);
    } catch (e) {
      failure(e);
    }
  }, 1000);
}

const successCallback = (x) => {
  double(x, (y) => console.log(`Success: ${y}`));
};
const failureCallback = (e) => console.log(`Failure: ${e}`);

double(3, successCallback, failureCallback);

// Success: 12 (printed after roughly 2000ms)
```

It should come as no surprise that this callback strategy does not scale well as code complexity grows. The "callback hell" colloquialism is well-deserved, as JavaScript codebases that were afflicted with such a structure became nearly unmaintainable.

PROMISES

A "promise" is a surrogate entity that acts as a stand-in for a result that does not yet exist. The term "promise" was first proposed by Daniel Friedman and David Wise in their 1976 paper, *The Impact of Applicative Programming on Multiprocessing*, but the conceptual behavior of a promise would not be formalized until a decade later by Barbara Liskov and Liuba Shrira in their 1988 paper, *Promises: Linguistic Support for Efficient Asynchronous Procedure Calls in Distributed Systems*. Contemporary computer scientists described similar concepts such as an "eventual," "future," "delay," or "deferred"; all of these described in one form or another a programming tool for synchronizing program execution.

The Promises/A+ Specification

Early forms of promises appeared in jQuery and Dojo's Deferred API, and in 2010, growing popularity led to the Promises/A specification inside the CommonJS project. Third-party JavaScript promise libraries such as Q and Bluebird continued to gain adoption, yet each implementation was slightly different. To address the rifts in the promise space, in 2012 the Promises/A+ organization forked the CommonJS "Promises/A" proposal and created the eponymous Promises/A+ Promise Specification (`https://promisesaplus.com`). This specification would eventually govern how promises were implemented in the ECMAScript 6 specification.

ECMAScript 6 introduced a first-class implementation of a Promises/A+–compliant `Promise` type. In the time since its introduction, promises have enjoyed an overwhelmingly robust rate of adoption. All modern browsers fully support the `Promise` type, and multiple browser APIs such as `fetch()` use it exclusively.

Promise Basics

A `Promise` instance can be instantiated with the `new` operator. Doing so requires passing an executor function parameter (covered in an upcoming section), which here is an empty function object to please the interpreter:

```
let p = new Promise(() => {});
console.asyncLog(p);  // Promise <pending>
```

If an executor function is not provided, a `SyntaxError` will be thrown.

The Promise State Machine

When passing a promise instance to `console.asyncLog`, the console output (which may vary between browsers) indicates that this promise instance is *pending*. As mentioned previously, a promise is a stateful object that can exist in one of three states:

➤ *Pending*

➤ *Fulfilled* (sometimes also referred to as *resolved*)

➤ *Rejected*

A *pending* state is the initial state a promise begins in. From a pending state, a promise can become *settled* by transitioning to either a *fulfilled* state to indicate success or a *rejected* state to indicate failure. This transition to a *settled* state is irreversible; once a transition to either *fulfilled* or *rejected* occurs, the state of the promise can never change. Furthermore, it is not guaranteed that a promise will ever leave the *pending* state. Therefore, well-structured code should behave properly if the promise successfully resolves, if the promise rejects, or if it never exits the pending state.

Importantly, the state of a promise is private and cannot be directly inspected in JavaScript. The reason for this is primarily to prevent synchronous programmatic handling of a promise object based on its state when it is read. Furthermore, the state of a promise cannot be mutated by external JavaScript. This is for the same reason the state cannot be read: The promise intentionally encapsulates a block of asynchronous behavior, and external code performing synchronous definition of its state would be antithetical to its purpose.

Fulfilled Values, Rejection Reasons, and Utility of Promises

There are two primary reasons the promise construct is useful. The first is to abstractly represent a block of asynchronous execution. The state of the promise is indicative of whether or not the promise has yet to complete execution. The *pending* state indicates that execution has not yet begun or is still in progress. The *fulfilled* state is a nonspecific indicator that the execution has completed successfully. The *rejected* state is a nonspecific indicator that the execution did not complete successfully.

In some cases, the internal state machine is all the utility a promise needs to provide: the mere knowledge that a piece of asynchronous code has completed is sufficient for informing program flow. For example, suppose a promise is dispatching an HTTP request to a server. The request returning with a status of 200–299 might be sufficient to transition the promise state to *fulfilled*. Similarly, the request returning with a status that is *not* 200-299 would transition the promise state to *rejected*.

In other cases, the asynchronous execution that the promise is wrapping is actually generating a value, and the program flow will expect this value to be available when the promise changes state. Alternately, if the promise rejects, the program flow will expect the reason for rejection when the promise changes state. For example, suppose a promise is dispatching an HTTP request to a server and expecting it to return JSON. The request returning with a status of 200–299 might be sufficient to transition the promise to *fulfilled*, and the JSON string will be available inside the promise. Similarly, the request returning with a status that is *not* 200–299 would transition the promise state to *rejected*, and the reason for rejection might be an Error object containing the text accompanying the HTTP status code.

To support these two use cases, every promise that transitions to a *fulfilled* state has a private internal *value*. Similarly, every promise that transitions to a *rejected* state has a private internal *reason*. Both *value* and *reason* are an immutable reference to a primitive or object. Both are optional and will default to `undefined`. Asynchronous code that is scheduled to execute after a promise reaches a certain *settled* state is always provided with the *value* or *reason*.

Controlling Promise State with the Executor

Because the state of a promise is private, it can only be manipulated internally. This internal manipulation is performed inside the promise's *executor function*. The executor function has two primary duties: initializing the asynchronous behavior of the promise, and controlling any eventual state transition. Control of the state transition is accomplished by invoking one of its two function parameters, typically named `resolve` and `reject`. Calling `resolve()` will change the state to *fulfilled*; calling `reject()` will change the state to *rejected* and throw an error (this error behavior is covered more later in the chapter).

```
let p1 = new Promise((resolve, reject) => resolve());
console.asyncLog(p1);   // Promise <fulfilled>

let p2 = new Promise((resolve, reject) => reject());
console.asyncLog(p2);   // Promise <rejected>
// Uncaught error (in promise)
```

In the preceding example, there isn't really any asynchronous behavior occurring because the state of each promise is already changed by the time the executor function exits. Importantly, the executor function will execute *synchronously*, as it acts as the initializer for the promise. This order of execution is demonstrated here:

```
new Promise(() => console.asyncLog('executor'));
console.asyncLog('promise initialized');

// executor
// promise initialized
```

You can delay the state transition by adding a `setTimeout`:

```
let p = new Promise((resolve, reject) => setTimeout(resolve, 1000));

// When this console.asyncLog executes, the timeout callback has not yet executed:
console.asyncLog(p);  // Promise <pending>
```

Once either resolve or reject is invoked, the state transition cannot be undone. Attempts to further mutate the state will silently be ignored. This is demonstrated here:

```
let p = new Promise((resolve, reject) => {
  resolve();
  reject();  // No effect
});

console.asyncLog(p);  // Promise <fulfilled>
```

You can avoid promises getting stuck in a pending state by adding timed exit behavior. For example, you can set a timeout to reject the promise after 10 seconds:

```
let p = new Promise((resolve, reject) => {
  setTimeout(reject, 10000);  // After 10 seconds, invoke reject()

  // Do executor things
});

console.asyncLog(p);        // Promise <pending>
setTimeout(console.log, 11000, p);  // Check state after 11 seconds

// (After 10 seconds) Uncaught error
// (After 11 seconds) Promise <rejected>
```

Because a promise can only change state a single time, this timeout behavior allows you to safely set a maximum on the amount of time a promise can remain in the pending state. If the code inside the executor were to resolve or reject prior to the timeout, the timeout handler's attempt to reject the promise will be silently ignored.

Promise Casting with *Promise.resolve()*

A promise does not necessarily need to begin in a pending state and utilize an executor function to reach a settled state. It is possible to instantiate a promise in the "fulfilled" state by invoking the `Promise.resolve()` static method. The following two promise instantiations are effectively equivalent:

```
let p1 = new Promise((resolve, reject) => resolve());
let p2 = Promise.resolve();
```

The value of this fulfilled promise will become the first argument passed to `Promise.resolve()`. This effectively allows you to "cast" any value into a promise:

```
console.asyncLog(Promise.resolve());
// Promise <fulfilled>: undefined

console.asyncLog(Promise.resolve(3));
// Promise <fulfilled>: 3

// Additional arguments are ignored
console.asyncLog (Promise.resolve(4, 5, 6));
// Promise <fulfilled>: 4
```

Perhaps the most important aspect of this static method is its ability to act as a passthrough when the argument is already a promise. As a result, `Promise.resolve()` is an idempotent method, as demonstrated here:

```
let p = Promise.resolve(7);

console.log(p === Promise.resolve(p));  // true
console.log(p === Promise.resolve(Promise.resolve(p)));  // true
```

This idempotence will respect the state of the promise passed to it:

```
let p = new Promise(() => {});

console.asyncLog(p);                       // Promise <pending>
console.asyncLog(Promise.resolve(p));      // Promise <pending>

console.asyncLog(p === Promise.resolve(p));  // true
```

Be aware that this static method will happily wrap any non-promise, including an error object, as a fulfilled promise, which might lead to unintended behavior:

```
let p = Promise.resolve(new Error('foo'));

console.asyncLog(p);  // Promise <fulfilled>: Error: foo
```

Promise Rejection with *Promise.reject()*

Similar in concept to `Promise.resolve()`, `Promise.reject()` instantiates a rejected promise and throws an asynchronous error (which will not be caught by try/catch and can only be caught by a rejection handler). The following two promise instantiations are effectively equivalent:

```
let p1 = new Promise((resolve, reject) => reject());
let p2 = Promise.reject();
```

The "reason" field of this fulfilled promise will be the first argument passed to `Promise.reject()`. This will also be the error passed to the reject handler:

```
let p = Promise.reject(3);
console.asyncLog(p);  // Promise <rejected>: 3

p.then(undefined, (e) => console.asyncLog(e));  // 3
```

Importantly, `Promise.reject()` does not mirror the behavior of `Promise.resolve()` with respect to idempotence. If passed a promise object, it will happily use that promise as the "reason" field of the rejected promise:

```
console.asyncLog(Promise.reject(Promise.resolve()));
// Promise <rejected>: Promise <fulfilled>
```

Synchronous/Asynchronous Execution Duality

Much of the design of the promise construct is to engender a totally separate mode of computation in JavaScript. This is neatly encapsulated in the following example, which throws errors in two different ways:

```
try {
  throw new Error('foo');
} catch(e) {
  console.log(e);  // Error: foo
}

try {
  Promise.reject(new Error('bar'));
} catch(e) {
  console.log(e);
}
// Uncaught (in promise) Error: bar
```

The first `try/catch` block throws an error and then proceeds to catch it, but the second `try/catch` block throws an error that is *not* caught. This might seem counterintuitive because the code appears to be synchronously creating a rejected promise instance, which then throws an error upon rejection. However, the reason the second promise is not caught is that the code is not attempting to catch the error in the appropriate "asynchronous mode." Such behavior underscores how promises actually behave: they are synchronous objects—used inside a synchronous mode of execution—acting as a bridge to an *asynchronous* mode of execution.

In the preceding example, the error from the rejected promise is not being thrown inside the synchronous execution thread, but instead from the asynchronous handler execution. Therefore, the encapsulating `try/catch` block will not suffice to catch this error. Once code starts to execute in this asynchronous mode, the only way to interact with it is to use asynchronous mode constructs—more specifically, promise methods.

Promise Instance Methods

The methods exposed on a promise instance serve to bridge the gap between the synchronous external code path and the asynchronous internal code path. These methods can be used to access data returned from an asynchronous operation, handle success and failure outcomes of the promise, serially evaluate promises, or add functions that only execute once the promise enters a terminal state.

Implementing the thenable Interface

For the purposes of ECMAScript asynchronous constructs, any object that exposes a then() method is considered to implement the thenable interface. The following is an example of the simplest possible class that implements this interface:

```
class MyThenable {
  then() {}
}
```

The ECMAScript Promise type implements the *thenable interface*. This simplistic interface is not to be confused with other interfaces or type definitions in packages like TypeScript, which lay out a much more specific form of a thenable interface.

> **NOTE** *The utility and purpose of the thenable interface is revisited later in the chapter in the "Async Functions" section.*

Using *Promise.prototype.then()*

The method Promise.prototype.then() is the primary method that is used to attach handlers to a promise instance. The then() method accepts up to two arguments: an optional onFulfilled handler function, and an optional onRejected handler function. Each will execute only when the promise upon which they are defined reaches its respective fulfilled or rejected state.

```
function onFulfilled(id) {
  console.asyncLog(id, 'fulfilled');
}
function onRejected(id) {
  console.asyncLog(id, 'rejected');
}

let p1 = new Promise((resolve, reject) => setTimeout(resolve, 3000));
let p2 = new Promise((resolve, reject) => setTimeout(reject, 3000));

p1.then(() => onFulfilled('p1'),
        () => onRejected('p1'));
p2.then(() => onFulfilled('p2'),
        () => onRejected('p2'));

// (after 3s)
// p1 fulfilled
// p2 rejected
```

Because a promise can only transition to a final state a single time, you are guaranteed that execution of these handlers is mutually exclusive.

As described earlier, both handler arguments are completely optional. Any non-function type provided as an argument to `then()` will be silently ignored. If you wish to explicitly provide only an `onRejected` handler, providing `null` or `undefined` as the `onFulfilled` argument is ideal. This allows you to avoid creating a temporary object in memory just to be ignored by the interpreter, and it will also please type systems that expect an optional function object as an argument.

```
function onFulfilled(id) {
  console.asyncLog(id, 'fulfilled');
}
function onRejected(id) {
  console.asyncLog(id, 'rejected');
}

let p1 = new Promise((resolve, reject) => setTimeout(resolve, 3000));
let p2 = new Promise((resolve, reject) => setTimeout(reject, 3000));

// Non-function handlers are silently ignored, not recommended
p1.then('gobbeltygook');

// Canonical form of explicit onFulfilled handler skipping
p2.then(null, () => onRejected('p2'));

// p2 rejected (after 3s)
```

The `Promise.prototype.then()` method returns a new promise instance:

```
let p1 = new Promise(() => {});
let p2 = p1.then();
console.asyncLog(p1);        // Promise <pending>
console.asyncLog(p2);        // Promise <pending>
console.asyncLog(p1 === p2); // false
```

This new promise instance is derived from the return value of the onFulfilled handler. The return value of the handler is wrapped in `Promise.resolve()` to generate a new promise. If no handler function is provided, the method acts as a passthrough for the initial promise's fulfilled value. If there is no explicit return statement, the default return value is `undefined` and wrapped in a `Promise` `.resolve()`.

```
let p1 = Promise.resolve('foo');

// Calling then() with no handler function acts as a passthrough
let p2 = p1.then();

console.asyncLog(p2);  // Promise <fulfilled>: foo

// These are equivalent
let p3 = p1.then(() => undefined);
let p4 = p1.then(() => {});
let p5 = p1.then(() => Promise.resolve());

console.asyncLog(p3);  // Promise <fulfilled>: undefined
console.asyncLog(p4);  // Promise <fulfilled>: undefined
console.asyncLog(p5);  // Promise <fulfilled>: undefined
```

Explicit return values are wrapped in `Promise.resolve()`:

```
...

// These are equivalent:
let p6 = p1.then(() => 'bar');
let p7 = p1.then(() => Promise.resolve('bar'));

console.asyncLog(p6);  // Promise <fulfilled>: bar
console.asyncLog(p7);  // Promise <fulfilled>: bar

// Promise.resolve() preserves the returned promise
let p8 = p1.then(() => new Promise(() => {}));
let p9 = p1.then(() => Promise.reject());
// Uncaught (in promise): undefined

console.asyncLog(p8);  // Promise <pending>
console.asyncLog(p9);  // Promise <rejected>: undefined
```

Throwing an exception will return a rejected promise:

```
...

let p10 = p1.then(() => { throw 'baz'; });
// Uncaught (in promise) baz

console.asyncLog(p10);  // Promise <rejected> baz
```

Importantly, returning an error will not trigger the same rejection behavior, and will instead wrap the error object in a fulfilled promise:

```
...

let p11 = p1.then(() => Error('qux'));

console.asyncLog(p11);  // Promise <fulfilled>: Error: qux
```

The `onRejected` handler behaves in the same way: values returned from the `onRejected` handler are wrapped in `Promise.resolve()`. This might seem counterintuitive at first, but the `onRejected` handler is doing its job to catch an asynchronous error. Therefore, this rejection handler completing execution without throwing an additional error should be considered expected promise behavior and therefore return a fulfilled promise.

The following code snippet is the `Promise.reject()` analog of the previous examples using `Promise.resolve()`:

```
let p1 = Promise.reject('foo');

// Calling then() with no handler function acts as a passthrough
let p2 = p1.then();
// Uncaught (in promise) foo

console.asyncLog(p2);  // Promise <rejected>: foo

// These are equivalent
let p3 = p1.then(null, () => undefined);
```

```
let p4 = p1.then(null, () => {});
let p5 = p1.then(null, () => Promise.resolve());

console.asyncLog(p3);  // Promise <fulfilled>: undefined
console.asyncLog(p4);  // Promise <fulfilled>: undefined
console.asyncLog(p5);  // Promise <fulfilled>: undefined


// These are equivalent
let p6 = p1.then(null, () => 'bar');
let p7 = p1.then(null, () => Promise.resolve('bar'));

console.asyncLog(p6);  // Promise <fulfilled>: bar
console.asyncLog(p7);  // Promise <fulfilled>: bar

// Promise.resolve() preserves the returned promise
let p8 = p1.then(null, () => new Promise(() => {}));
let p9 = p1.then(null, () => Promise.reject());
// Uncaught (in promise): undefined

console.asyncLog(p8);  // Promise <pending>
console.asyncLog(p9);  // Promise <rejected>: undefined


let p10 = p1.then(null, () => { throw 'baz'; });
// Uncaught (in promise) baz

console.asyncLog(p10);  // Promise <rejected>: baz


let p11 = p1.then(null, () => Error('qux'));

console.asyncLog(p11);  // Promise <fulfilled>: Error: qux
```

Using *Promise.prototype.catch()*

The `Promise.prototype.catch()` method can be used to attach only a reject handler to a promise. It takes a single argument, the `onRejected` handler function. The method behaves identically to `Promise.prototype.then(null, onRejected)`.

The following code demonstrates this equivalence:

```
let p = Promise.reject();
let onRejected = function(e) {
  console.asyncLog('rejected');
};

// These two reject handlers behave identically:
p.then(null, onRejected);  // rejected
p.catch(onRejected);       // rejected
```

The `Promise.prototype.catch()` method returns a new promise instance:

```
let p1 = new Promise(() => {});
let p2 = p1.catch();
console.asyncLog(p1);          // Promise <pending>
console.asyncLog(p2);          // Promise <pending>
console.asyncLog(p1 === p2);   // false
```

With respect to creation of the new promise instance, `Promise.prototype.catch()` behaves identically to the `onRejected` handler of `Promise.prototype.then()`.

Using *Promise.prototype.finally()*

The `Promise.prototype.finally()` method can be used to attach an `onFinally` handler, which executes when the promise reaches either a fulfilled *or* a rejected state. Importantly, the handler does not have any way of determining if the promise was fulfilled or rejected, so this method is designed to be used for things like cleanup or avoiding code duplication between `onFulfilled` and `onRejected` handlers.

```
let p1 = Promise.resolve();
let p2 = Promise.reject();
let onFinally = function() {
  console.asyncLog('Finally!')
}

p1.finally(onFinally);  // Finally
p2.finally(onFinally);  // Finally
```

The `Promise.prototype.finally()` method returns a new promise instance:

```
let p1 = new Promise(() => {});
let p2 = p1.finally();
console.asyncLog(p1);          // Promise <pending>
console.asyncLog(p2);          // Promise <pending>
console.asyncLog(p1 === p2);   // false
```

This new promise instance is derived in a different manner than `then()` or `catch()`. Because `onFinally` is intended to be a state-agnostic method, in most cases it will behave as a passthrough for the parent promise. This is true for both the fulfilled and rejected states.

```
let p1 = Promise.resolve('foo');

// These all act as a passthrough
let p2 = p1.finally();
let p3 = p1.finally(() => undefined);
let p4 = p1.finally(() => {});
let p5 = p1.finally(() => Promise.resolve());
let p6 = p1.finally(() => 'bar');
let p7 = p1.finally(() => Promise.resolve('bar'));
let p8 = p1.finally(() => Error('qux'));

console.asyncLog(p2);  // Promise <fulfilled>: foo
console.asyncLog(p3);  // Promise <fulfilled>: foo
console.asyncLog(p4);  // Promise <fulfilled>: foo
```

```
console.asyncLog(p5);   // Promise <fulfilled>: foo
console.asyncLog(p6);   // Promise <fulfilled>: foo
console.asyncLog(p7);   // Promise <fulfilled>: foo
console.asyncLog(p8);   // Promise <fulfilled>: foo
```

The only exceptions to this are when it returns a pending promise, or an error is thrown (via an explicit throw or returning a rejected promise). In these cases, the corresponding promise is returned (pending or rejected), as shown here:

```
...

// Promise.resolve() preserves the returned promise
let p9 = p1.finally(() => new Promise(() => {}));
let p10 = p1.finally(() => Promise.reject());
// Uncaught (in promise): undefined

console.asyncLog(p9);    // Promise <pending>
console.asyncLog(p10);   // Promise <rejected>: undefined

let p11 = p1.finally(() => { throw 'baz';});
// Uncaught (in promise) baz

console.asyncLog(p11);   // Promise <rejected>: baz
```

Returning a pending promise is an unusual case, as once the promise resolves, the new promise will still behave as a passthrough for the initial promise:

```
let p1 = Promise.resolve('foo');

// The fulfilled value is ignored
let p2 = p1.finally(
    () => new Promise((resolve, reject) => setTimeout(() => resolve('bar'), 100)));

console.asyncLog(p2);   // Promise <pending>

setTimeout(() => console.asyncLog(p2), 200);

// After 200ms:
// Promise <fulfilled>: foo
```

Non-Reentrant Promise Methods

When a promise reaches a settled state, execution of handlers associated with that state are merely *scheduled* rather than immediately executed. Synchronous code following the attachment of the handler is guaranteed to execute before the handler is invoked. This remains true even if the promise already exists in the state the newly attached handler is associated with. This property, called *non-reentrancy*, is guaranteed by the JavaScript runtime. The following simple example demonstrates this property:

```
// Create a fulfilled promise
```

```
let p = Promise.resolve();

// Attach an onFulfulled handler to the already fulfilled promise.
// Intuitively, this would execute as soon as possible
// because p is already fulfilled.
p.then(() => console.asyncLog("onFulfilled handler"));

// Synchronously log to indicate that then() has returned
console.log("then() returns");

// Actual output:
// then() returns
// onFulfilled handler
```

In this example, calling then() on a fulfilled promise will schedule the onFulfilled handler to execute. This handler will not be executed until *after* the current thread of execution completes. Therefore, synchronous code immediately following then() is guaranteed to execute prior to the handler.

The inverse of this scenario yields the same result. If handlers are already attached to a promise that later synchronously changes state, the handler execution is non-reentrant upon that state change. The following example demonstrates how, even with an onFulfilled handler already attached, synchronously invoking resolve() will still exhibit non-reentrant behavior:

```
let synchronousResolve;

// Create a promise and capture the resolve function in a local variable
let p = new Promise((resolve) => {
  synchronousResolve = function() {
    console.log('1: invoking resolve()');
    resolve();
    console.log('2: resolve() returns');
  };
});

p.then(() => console.log('4: then() handler executes'));

synchronousResolve();
console.log('3: synchronousResolve() returns');

// Actual output:
// 1: invoking resolve()
// 2: resolve() returns
// 3: synchronousResolve() returns
// 4: then() handler executes
```

In this example, even though the promise state changes synchronously with handlers attached to that state, the handler execution will still occur asynchronously.

> **NOTE** *Non-reentrancy is guaranteed for both* onFulfilled *and* onRejected *handlers,* catch() *handlers, and* finally() *handlers.*

Sibling Handler Order of Execution

If multiple handlers are attached to a promise, when the promise transitions to a settled state, the associated handlers will execute in the order in which they were attached. This is true for then(), catch(), and finally():

```
let p1 = Promise.resolve();
let p2 = Promise.reject();

p1.then(() => console.asyncLog(1));
p1.then(() => console.asyncLog(2));
// 1
// 2

p2.then(null, () => console.asyncLog(3));
p2.then(null, () => console.asyncLog(4));
// 3
// 4

p2.catch(() => console.asyncLog(5));
p2.catch(() => console.asyncLog(6));
// 5
// 6

p1.finally(() => console.asyncLog(7));
p1.finally(() => console.asyncLog(8));
// 7
// 8
```

Fulfilled Value and Rejected Reason Passing

When reaching a settled state, a promise will provide its fulfilled value (if it is fulfilled) or its rejection reason (if it is rejected) to any handlers that are attached to that state. This is especially useful in cases where successive blocks of serial computation are required. For example, if the JSON response of one network request is required to perform a second network request, the response from the first request can be passed as the fulfilled value to the onFulfilled handler. Alternately, a failed network request can pass the HTTP status code to the onRejected handler.

Fulfilled values and rejected reasons are assigned from inside the executor as the first argument to the resolve() or reject() functions. These values are provided to their respective onFulfilled or onRejected handler as the sole parameter. This handoff is demonstrated here:

```
let p1 = new Promise((resolve, reject) => resolve('foo'));
p1.then((value) => console.log(value));      // foo

let p2 = new Promise((resolve, reject) => reject('bar'));
p2.catch((reason) => console.log(reason));   // bar
```

Promise.resolve() and Promise.reject() accept the value/reason argument when calling the static method. The onFulfilled and onRejected handlers are provided the value or reason in the same way as if it were passed from the executor:

```
let p1 = Promise.resolve('foo');
```

```
p1.then((value) => console.log(value));      // foo

let p2 = Promise.reject('bar');
p2.catch((reason) => console.log(reason));   // bar
```

Rejecting Promises and Rejection Error Handling

Rejecting a promise is analogous to a throw expression in that they both represent a program state that should force a discontinuation of any subsequent operations. Throwing an error inside a promise executor or handler will cause it to reject; the corresponding error object will be the rejection reason. Therefore, these promises all will reject with an error object:

```
let p1 = new Promise((resolve, reject) => reject(Error('foo')));
let p2 = new Promise((resolve, reject) => { throw Error('foo'); });
let p3 = Promise.resolve().then(() => { throw Error('foo'); });
let p4 = Promise.reject(Error('foo'));

console.asyncLog(p1);  // Promise <rejected>: Error: foo
console.asyncLog(p2);  // Promise <rejected>: Error: foo
console.asyncLog(p3);  // Promise <rejected>: Error: foo
console.asyncLog(p4);  // Promise <rejected>: Error: foo


// Also throws four uncaught errors
```

Promises can be rejected with any value including undefined, but it is strongly recommended that you consistently use error object. The primary reason for this is that constructing an error object allows the browser to capture the stack trace inside the error object, which is immensely useful in debugging. For example, the stack trace for the three errors in the preceding code should appear something like the following:

```
Uncaught (in promise) Error: foo
    at Promise (test.html:5)
    at new Promise (<anonymous>)
    at test.html:5
Uncaught (in promise) Error: foo
    at Promise (test.html:6)
    at new Promise (<anonymous>)
    at test.html:6
Uncaught (in promise) Error: foo
    at test.html:8
Uncaught (in promise) Error: foo
    at Promise.resolve.then (test.html:7)
```

All errors are asynchronously thrown and unhandled, and the stack trace captured by the error objects show the path that the error object took. Also note here the order of errors: The Promise .resolve().then() error executes last because it is creating one *additional* promise prior to ultimately throwing the uncaught error.

This example also uncovers an interesting side effect of asynchronous errors. Normally, when throwing an error using the throw keyword, the JavaScript runtime's error handling behavior will decline to execute any instructions following the thrown error.

```
throw Error('foo');
console.log('bar');  // This will never print

// Uncaught Error: foo
```

However, when an error is thrown inside a promise, because the error is actually being thrown asynchronously, it will not prevent the runtime from continuing to execute synchronous instructions:

```
Promise.reject(Error('foo'));
console.log('bar');
// bar

// Uncaught (in promise) Error: foo
```

As demonstrated earlier in this chapter with `Promise.reject()`, an asynchronous error can be caught only with an asynchronous `onRejected` handler.

```
// Correct
Promise.reject(Error('foo')).catch((e) => {});

// Incorrect
try {
  Promise.reject(Error('foo'));
} catch(e) {}
```

This does not apply to catching the error while still inside the executor, where `try/catch` will still suffice to catch the error before it rejects the promise:

```
let p = new Promise((resolve, reject) => {
  try {
    throw Error('foo');
  } catch(e) {}

  resolve('bar');
});

console.asyncLog(p);  // Promise <fulfilled>: bar
```

The `onRejected` handler for `then()` and `catch()` is analogous to the semantics of `try/catch` in that catching an error should effectively neutralize it and allow for normal computation to continue. Therefore, it should make sense that an `onRejected` handler tasked with catching an asynchronous error will in fact return a *fulfilled promise*. The synchronous/*asynchronous* comparison is demonstrated in the following example:

```
console.log('begin synchronous execution');
try {
  throw Error('foo');
} catch(e) {
  console.log('caught error', e);
}
console.log('continue synchronous execution');

// begin synchronous execution
// caught error: foo
// continue synchronous execution
```

```
new Promise((resolve, reject) => {
  console.log('begin asynchronous execution');
  reject(Error('bar'));
}).catch((e) => {
  console.log('caught error', e);
}).then(() => {
  console.log('continue asynchronous execution');
});

// begin asynchronous execution
// caught error: bar
// continue asynchronous execution
```

Promise Chaining and Composition

Combining multiple promises together enables some powerful code patterns. Such behavior is possible in two primary ways: promise chaining, which involves strictly sequencing multiple promises, and promise composition, which involves combining multiple promises into a single promise.

Promise Chaining

One of the more useful aspects of ECMAScript promises is their ability to be strictly sequenced. This is enabled through the Promise API's structure: Each of the promise instance's methods—then(), catch(), and finally()—returns a new promise instance, which in turn can have another instance method called upon it. Successively invoking methods in such a manner is referred to as *promise chaining*. The following is a trivial example of this:

```
let p = new Promise((resolve, reject) => {
  console.log('first');
  resolve();
});
p.then(() => console.log('second'))
 .then(() => console.log('third'))
 .then(() => console.log('fourth'));

// first
// second
// third
// fourth
```

This implementation is ultimately executing chained *synchronous* tasks. Because of this, the work performed isn't very useful or interesting because it is approximately the same as successively invoking four functions in sequence:

```
(() => console.log('first'))();
(() => console.log('second'))();
(() => console.log('third'))();
(() => console.log('fourth'))();
```

To chain asynchronous tasks, this example can be retooled so that each executor returns a promise instance. Because each successive promise will await the resolution of its predecessor, such a strategy can be used to serialize asynchronous tasks. For example, this can be used to execute multiple promises in series that resolve after a timeout:

```
let p1 = new Promise((resolve, reject) => {
  console.log('p1 executor');
```

```
    setTimeout(resolve, 1000);
});

p1.then(() => new Promise((resolve, reject) => {
    console.log('p2 executor');
    setTimeout(resolve, 1000);
}))
    .then(() => new Promise((resolve, reject) => {
    console.log('p3 executor');
    setTimeout(resolve, 1000);
}))
    .then(() => new Promise((resolve, reject) => {
    console.log('p4 executor');
    setTimeout(resolve, 1000);
}));

// p1 executor (after 1s)
// p2 executor (after 2s)
// p3 executor (after 3s)
// p4 executor (after 4s)
```

Combining the promise generation into a single factory function yields the following:

```
function delayedResolve(str) {
  return new Promise((resolve, reject) => {
    console.log(str);
    setTimeout(resolve, 1000);
  });
}

delayedResolve('p1 executor')
  .then(() => delayedResolve('p2 executor'))
  .then(() => delayedResolve('p3 executor'))
  .then(() => delayedResolve('p4 executor'))

// p1 executor (after 1s)
// p2 executor (after 2s)
// p3 executor (after 3s)
// p4 executor (after 4s)
```

Each successive handler waits for its predecessor to resolve, instantiates a new promise instance, and returns it. Such a structure can neatly serialize asynchronous code without forcing the use of callbacks. Without the use of promises, the preceding code would look something like this:

```
function delayedExecute(str, callback = null) {
  setTimeout(() => {
    console.log(str);
    callback && callback();
  }, 1000)
}

delayedExecute('p1 callback', () => {
  delayedExecute('p2 callback', () => {
    delayedExecute('p3 callback', () => {
      delayedExecute('p4 callback');
```

```
    });
  });
});

// p1 callback (after 1s)
// p2 callback (after 2s)
// p3 callback (after 3s)
// p4 callback (after 4s)
```

This effectively reintroduces the callback hell that promises are designed to circumvent.

Because then(), catch(), and finally() all return a promise, chaining them together is straightforward. The following example incorporates all three:

```
let p = new Promise((resolve, reject) => {
  console.log('initial promise rejects');
  reject();
});

p.catch(() => console.log('reject handler'))
  .then(() => console.log('resolve handler'))
  .finally(() => console.log('finally handler'));

// initial promise rejects
// reject handler
// resolve handler
// finally handler
```

Using *Promise.all()*

The Promise.all() static method creates an all-or-nothing promise that resolves only once every promise in a collection of promises resolves. For instance, when fetching data from multiple APIs or executing multiple database queries, you would need to wait for all of the requests to complete before processing the results. The static method accepts an iterable and returns a new promise:

```
let p1 = Promise.all([
  Promise.resolve(),
  Promise.resolve()
]);

// Elements in the iterable are coerced into a promise using Promise.resolve()
let p2 = Promise.all([3, 4]);

// Empty iterable is equivalent to Promise.resolve()
let p3 = Promise.all([]);

// Invalid syntax
let p4 = Promise.all();
// TypeError: cannot read Symbol.iterator of undefined
```

The composed promise will only resolve once every contained promise is fulfilled:

```
let p = Promise.all([
  Promise.resolve(),
  new Promise((resolve, reject) => setTimeout(resolve, 1000))
```

```
]);
console.asyncLog(p);  // Promise <pending>

p.then(() => console.asyncLog('all() fulfilled!'));

// all() fulfilled! (After &#x0007E;1000ms)
```

If at least one contained promise remains pending, the composed promise also will remain pending. If one contained promise rejects, the composed promise will reject:

```
// Will forever remain pending
let p1 = Promise.all([new Promise(() => {})]);
console.asyncLog(p1);  // Promise <pending>

// Single rejection causes rejection of composed promise
let p2 = Promise.all([
  Promise.resolve(),
  Promise.reject(),
  Promise.resolve()
]);
console.asyncLog(p2);  // Promise <rejected>

// Uncaught (in promise) undefined
```

If all promises successfully resolve, the fulfilled value of the composed promise will be an array of all of the fulfilled values of the contained promises, in iterator order:

```
let p = Promise.all([
  Promise.resolve(3),
  Promise.resolve(),
  Promise.resolve(4)
]);

p.then((values) => console.asyncLog(values));  // [3, undefined, 4]
```

If one of the promises rejects, whichever is the first to reject will set the rejection reason for the composed promise. Subsequent rejections will not affect the rejection reason; however, the normal rejection behavior of those contained promise instances is not affected. Importantly, the composed promise will silently handle the rejection of all contained promises, as demonstrated here:

```
// Although only the first rejection reason will be provided in
// the rejection handler, the second rejection will be silently
// handled and no error will escape
let p = Promise.all([
  Promise.reject(3),
  new Promise((resolve, reject) => setTimeout(reject, 1000))
]);

p.catch((reason) => console.asyncLog(reason));  // 3

// No unhandled errors
```

Using *Promise.allSettled()*

The `Promise.allSettled()` static method allows you to wait for all promises in a collection to be settled, regardless of whether they resolve or reject. This method is useful when you need to handle the results of multiple asynchronous operations without the requirement that all of them succeed. Just like `Promise.all()`, the static method accepts an iterable and returns a new promise:

```
let p1 = Promise.allSettled([
  Promise.resolve(),
  Promise.reject()
]);

// Elements in the iterable are coerced into a promise using Promise.resolve()
let p2 = Promise.allSettled([3, 4]);

// Empty iterable is equivalent to Promise.resolve()
let p3 = Promise.allSettled([]);

// Invalid syntax
let p4 = Promise.allSettled();
// TypeError: cannot read Symbol.iterator of undefined
```

The composed promise will resolve once every contained promise is settled, either fulfilled or rejected:

```
let p = Promise.allSettled([
  Promise.resolve(),
  new Promise((resolve, reject) => setTimeout(reject, 1000))
]);
console.asyncLog(p);  // Promise <pending>

p.then(() => console.asyncLog('allSettled() resolved!'));

// allSettled() resolved! (After ~1000ms)
```

When all the promises are settled, the fulfilled value of the composed promise will be an array of objects that describe the outcome of each promise in the iterable. Each object will have a `status` property set to either `'fulfilled'` or `'rejected'`, and a `value` or `reason` property, depending on the status:

```
let p = Promise.allSettled([
  Promise.resolve(3),
  Promise.reject(4),
  Promise.resolve(5)
]);

p.then((results) => console.asyncLog(results));
// [
//   { status: 'fulfilled', value: 3 },
//   { status: 'rejected', reason: 4 },
//   { status: 'fulfilled', value: 5 }
// ]
```

This allows you to easily process the results of each contained promise without the need to add individual error handlers. You can use the `status` property of each result object to determine the appropriate action for each promise's outcome:

```
Promise.allSettled([
  fetchDataFromAPI1(),
  fetchDataFromAPI2(),
  fetchDataFromAPI3()
]).then((results) => {
  results.map((result, i) => {
    if (result.status === 'fulfilled') {
      console.asyncLog(`API ${i} data:`, result.value);
    } else {
      console.asyncLog(`API ${i} error:`, result.reason);
    }
  });
});
```

Using *Promise.race()*

The `Promise.race()` static method creates a promise that will mirror whichever promise inside a collection of promises reaches a fulfilled or rejected state first. The static method accepts an iterable and returns a new promise:

```
let p1 = Promise.race([
  Promise.resolve(),
  Promise.resolve()
]);

// Elements in the iterable are coerced into a promise using Promise.resolve()
let p2 = Promise.race([3, 4]);

// Empty iterable is equivalent to new Promise(() => {})
let p3 = Promise.race([]);

// Invalid syntax
let p4 = Promise.race();
// TypeError: cannot read Symbol.iterator of undefined
```

The `Promise.race()` method does not give preferential treatment to a fulfilled or a rejected promise. The composed promise will pass through the status and value/reason of the first settled promise, as shown here:

```
// Resolve occurs first, reject in timeout ignored
let p1 = Promise.race([
  Promise.resolve(3),
  new Promise((resolve, reject) => setTimeout(reject, 1000))
]);
console.asyncLog(p1);  // Promise <fulfilled>: 3

// Reject occurs first, resolve in timeout ignored
let p2 = Promise.race([
  Promise.reject(4),
  new Promise((resolve, reject) => setTimeout(resolve, 1000))
```

```
]);
console.asyncLog(p2);  // Promise <rejected>: 4

// Iterator order is the tiebreaker for settling order
let p3 = Promise.race([
  Promise.resolve(5),
  Promise.resolve(6),
  Promise.resolve(7)
]);
console.asyncLog(p3);  // Promise <fulfilled>: 5
```

If one of the promises rejects, whichever is the first to reject will set the rejection reason for the composed promise. Subsequent rejections will not affect the rejection reason; however, the normal rejection behavior of those contained promise instances is not affected. As is the case with `Promise`
`.all()`, the composed promise *will* silently handle the rejection of all contained promises, as demonstrated here:

```
// Although only the first rejection reason will be provided in
// the rejection handler, the second rejection will be silently
// handled and no error will escape
let p = Promise.race([
  Promise.reject(3),
  new Promise((resolve, reject) => setTimeout(reject, 1000))
]);

p.catch((reason) => console.asyncLog(reason));  // 3

// No unhandled errors
```

Using *Promise.any()*

The `Promise.any()` static method allows you to wait for the first fulfilled promise in a collection of promises, effectively short-circuiting the operation once a single promise is resolved. This method is particularly useful when you have multiple sources of data or when you are looking for the fastest response among several competing tasks. Like `Promise.all()` and `Promise.allSettled()`, the static method accepts an iterable and returns a new promise:

```
let p1 = Promise.any([
  Promise.resolve(),
  Promise.reject()
]);

// Elements in the iterable are coerced into a promise using Promise.resolve()
let p2 = Promise.any([3, 4]);

// Empty iterable is equivalent to Promise.reject()
let p3 = Promise.any([]);
// Uncaught (in promise) AggregateError: All promises were rejected

// Invalid syntax
let p4 = Promise.any();
// TypeError: cannot read Symbol.iterator of undefined
```

The composed promise will resolve as soon as any contained promise is fulfilled:

```
let p = Promise.any([
  new Promise((resolve, reject) => setTimeout(resolve, 1000, 'first')),
  new Promise((resolve, reject) => setTimeout(resolve, 2000, 'second'))
]);
console.asyncLog(p);  // Promise <pending>

p.then((value) => console.asyncLog('any() resolved:', value));

// any() resolved: first (After &#x0007E;1000ms)
```

If all contained promises reject, the composed promise will also reject. The rejection reason will be an `AggregateError` instance that contains all rejection reasons:

```
let p = Promise.any([
  Promise.reject("error1"),
  Promise.reject("error2")
]);
console.asyncLog(p);  // Promise <rejected>

// Uncaught (in promise) AggregateError: All promises were rejected
```

You can catch the `AggregateError` and process the rejection reasons if necessary:

```
Promise.any([
  fetchDataFromAPI1(),
  fetchDataFromAPI2(),
  fetchDataFromAPI3()
]).then((data) => {
  console.asyncLog('Fastest data:', data);
}).catch((error) => {
  if (error instanceof AggregateError) {
    console.asyncLog('All promises rejected. Errors:', error.errors);
  } else {
    console.asyncLog('Unknown error:', error);
  }
});
```

Serial Promise Composition

The discussion of promise chaining thus far has focused on serialization of execution and largely ignored a core feature of promises: their ability to asynchronously produce a value and provide it to handlers. Chaining promises together with the intention of each successive promise using the value of its predecessor is a fundamental feature of promises. This is in many ways analogous to *function composition*, where multiple functions are composed together into a new function, demonstrated here:

```
function addTwo(x) {return x + 2;}
function addThree(x) {return x + 3;}
function addFive(x) {return x + 5;}

function addTen(x) {
  return addFive(addTwo(addThree(x)));
}

console.log(addTen(7));  // 17
```

In this example, function composition is used to combine these three functions together to operate on a single value. Similarly, promises can be composed together to progressively consume a value and produce a single promise containing the result. Doing so explicitly would appear as follows:

```
function addTwo(x) {return x + 2;}
function addThree(x) {return x + 3;}
function addFive(x) {return x + 5;}

function addTen(x) {
  return Promise.resolve(x)
    .then(addTwo)
    .then(addThree)
    .then(addFive);
}

addTen(8).then(console.log);   // 18
```

This can be fashioned into a more succinct form using `Array.prototype.reduce()`:

```
function addTwo(x) {return x + 2;}
function addThree(x) {return x + 3;}
function addFive(x) {return x + 5;}

function addTen(x) {
  return [addTwo, addThree, addFive]
      .reduce((promise, fn) => promise.then(fn), Promise.resolve(x));
}

addTen(8).then(console.log);   // 18
```

Such a strategy for composing promises can be generalized into a function that can compose any number of functions into a value-passing promise chain. This generalized composition function can be implemented as follows:

```
function addTwo(x) {return x + 2;}
function addThree(x) {return x + 3;}
function addFive(x) {return x + 5;}

function compose(...fns) {
  return (x) => fns.reduce((promise, fn) => promise.then(fn), Promise.resolve(x))
}

let addTen = compose(addTwo, addThree, addFive);

addTen(8).then(console.log);   // 18
```

> **NOTE** *This concept is revisited in the "Async Functions" section later in the chapter.*

Promises and the Microtask Queue

When a promise is settled, any functions that were waiting for its result are added to a queue called the *microtask queue*. The microtask queue is used to store all of the functions that need to be executed after the current synchronous code has finished running. This means that any functions added to the microtask queue will be executed before the next block of synchronous code is run.

Here's an example to help illustrate how promises and the microtask queue work together. The number 1 through 4 will be printed in order:

```
console.log('1');
setTimeout(console.log, 0, '4');
Promise.resolve('3').then(console.log);
console.log('2');

// 1
// 2
// 3
// 4
```

The execution is as follows:

1. "1" is logged to the console.

2. `setTimeout()` schedules a function to log "4" to the console after a delay of 0 milliseconds. This function will be added to the message queue and executed as soon as the current block of synchronous code has finished running.

3. A resolved promise is created using `Promise.resolve()` with an `onResolved` handler that will log "3" to the console. Because the promise is immediately resolved, the `onResolved` handler is added to the microtask queue.

4. "2" is logged to the console.

5. The current block of synchronous code has finished running, so the JavaScript engine checks the microtask queue to see if there are any functions waiting to be executed. It finds the `.then()` function we added to the promise chain, so it executes that function and "3" is logged to the console.

6. This turn of the event loop has completed, and the microtask queue has been emptied, so the browser evaluates the message queue and "4" is logged to the console.

Avoiding Unhandled Rejections

Promise rejection behavior is not intuitive. You should internalize the following two properties of promise rejections:

➤ An unhandled promise rejection will always throw an "unhandled rejection" error at the top level.

➤ A rejection can be handled as long as any part of the code either explicitly or implicitly adds an `onRejected` handler.

Let's begin with a simple rejected promise:

```
Promise.reject('foo')
// Uncaught (in promise) foo
```

This error is being thrown at the page level. If you don't add an `onRejected` handler before the microtask queue executes, there is only one way to programmatically detect this promise error, via the `unhandledrejection` event:

```
window.addEventListener('unhandledrejection', () => console.log("UNHANDLED"));

Promise.reject('foo')
// UNHANDLED
// Uncaught (in promise) foo
```

One way to prevent unhandled rejections is to explicitly add an `onRejected` handler via `then()` or `catch()`:

```
window.addEventListener('unhandledrejection', () => console.log("UNHANDLED"));

Promise.reject().catch( () => {})
Promise.reject().then(null, () => {})

// No console output
```

The other way is to implicitly add an `onRejected` handler via `Promise.allSettled()`:

```
window.addEventListener('unhandledrejection', () => console.log("UNHANDLED"));

Promise.allSettled([Promise.reject()]);

// No console output
```

To detect a late handling of a rejection (meaning adding `onRejected` after the promise has already settled), use the `rejectionhandled` event:

```
window.addEventListener('rejectionhandled', () => console.log("HANDLED LATE"));

const p = Promise.reject();

setTimeout(() => p.catch(() => {}), 1000);

// (after 1000ms): HANDLED LATE
```

Avoid having unhandled rejections in your code whenever possible. Errors bubbling up to the top level where they are visible to the user are typically indicative of a code smell.

Promise Extensions

The ECMAScript promise implementation is robust, but as is the case with any piece of software, there will be shortcomings. Two offerings available in some third-party promise implementations but lacking in the formal ECMAScript specification are promise canceling and progress tracking.

Promise Canceling

Often, a promise will be in progress but the program will no longer care about the result. The ability to "cancel" a promise would be useful in such a situation. Some third-party promise libraries such as Bluebird offer such a feature, and even ECMAScript was slated to offer such a feature before it was ultimately withdrawn (`https://github.com/tc39/proposal-cancelable-promises`). As a result, ECMAScript promises are considered "eager": once the promise's encapsulated function is underway, there is no way to prevent this process from completing.

It is still possible to implement an ad-hoc implementation that is a facsimile of the original design. Such an implementation makes use of a "cancel token," a concept fleshed out in Kevin Smith's design sketch (`https://github.com/zenparsing/es-cancel-token`). A generated cancel token provides an interface through which to cancel a promise, as well as a promise hook with which to trigger cancellation behavior and evaluate the cancellation state.

A basic implementation of a `CancelToken` class might appear as follows:

```
class CancelToken {
  constructor(cancelFn) {
    this.promise = new Promise((resolve, reject) => {
      cancelFn(resolve);
    });
  }
}
```

This class wraps a promise that exposes the resolve method to a `cancelFn` parameter. An external entity will then be able to provide a function to the constructor, allowing that entity to control exactly when the token should be canceled. This promise is a public member of the token class, and therefore it is possible to add listeners to the cancellation promise.

A rough example of how this class could be used is shown here:

```
<button id="start">Start</button>
<button id="cancel">Cancel</button>

<script>
class CancelToken {
  constructor(cancelFn) {
    this.promise = new Promise((resolve, reject) => {
      cancelFn(() => {
        console.asyncLog("delay cancelled");
        resolve();
      });
    });
  }
}

const startButton = document.querySelector('#start');
const cancelButton = document.querySelector('#cancel');

function cancellableDelayedResolve(delay) {
```

```
    console.asyncLog("set delay");

    return new Promise((resolve, reject) => {
      const id = setTimeout((() => {
        console.asyncLog("delayed resolve");
        resolve();
      }), delay);

      const cancelToken = new CancelToken((cancelCallback) =>
          cancelButton.addEventListener("click", cancelCallback));

      cancelToken.promise.then(() => clearTimeout(id));
    });
  }

  startButton.addEventListener("click", () => cancellableDelayedResolve(1000));
</script>
```

Each click on the Start button begins a timeout and instantiates a new `CancelToken` instance. The Cancel button is configured so that a click will trigger the token's promise to resolve. Upon resolving, the timeout initially set by the Start button click will be canceled.

Promise Progress Notifications

An in-progress promise might have several discrete stages that it will progress through before actually resolving. In some situations, it can be useful to allow a program to watch for a promise to reach these checkpoints. ECMAScript promises do not support this concept, but it is still possible to emulate this behavior by extending a promise.

One potential implementation is to extend the `Promise` class with a `notify()` method, as shown here:

```
class TrackablePromise extends Promise {
  constructor(executor) {
    const notifyHandlers = [];

    super((resolve, reject) => {
      return executor(resolve, reject, (status) => {
        notifyHandlers.map((handler) => handler(status));
      });
    });

    this.notifyHandlers = notifyHandlers;
  }

  notify(notifyHandler) {
    this.notifyHandlers.push(notifyHandler);
    return this;
  }
}
```

A `TrackablePromise` would then be able to use the `notify()` function inside the executor. A promise instantiation could use this function as follows:

```
let p = new TrackablePromise((resolve, reject, notify) => {
  function countdown(x) {
```

```
          if (x> 0) {
              notify(`${20 * x}% remaining`);
              setTimeout(() => countdown(x - 1), 1000);
          } else {
            resolve();
          }
        }

      countdown(5);
    });
```

This promise will recursively set a 1000ms timeout five consecutive times before resolving. Each timeout handler will invoke `notify()` and pass a status. Providing a notification handler could be done as follows:

```
  ...

  let p = new TrackablePromise((resolve, reject, notify) => {
    function countdown(x) {
        if (x> 0) {
            notify(`${20 * x}% remaining`);
            setTimeout(() => countdown(x - 1), 1000);
        } else {
          resolve();
        }
      }

    countdown(5);
  });

  p.notify((x) => console.asyncLog('progress:', x));

  p.then(() => console.asyncLog('completed'));

  // (after 1s) 80% remaining
  // (after 2s) 60% remaining
  // (after 3s) 40% remaining
  // (after 4s) 20% remaining
  // (after 5s) completed
```

This `notify()` method is designed to be chainable by returning itself, and handler execution will be preserved on a per-notification basis, as shown here:

```
  ...

  p.notify((x) => console.asyncLog('a:', x))
    .notify((x) => console.asyncLog('b:', x));

  p.then(() => console.asyncLog('completed'));

  // (after 1s) a: 80% remaining
  // (after 1s) b: 80% remaining
  // (after 2s) a: 60% remaining
  // (after 2s) b: 60% remaining
```

```
// (after 3s) a: 40% remaining
// (after 3s) b: 40% remaining
// (after 4s) a: 20% remaining
// (after 4s) b: 20% remaining
// (after 5s) completed
```

Overall, this is a relatively crude implementation, but it should demonstrate how such a notification feature could be useful.

> **NOTE** *One of the primary reasons that promises do not feature cancellation or notification features is that it greatly complicates promise chaining and composition. It isn't entirely clear what is expected to happen in scenarios where cancelations or notifications occur in promises with other promise dependencies, such as in a promise chain. Rhetorically speaking, what is sensible behavior when a promise inside* Promise.all() *cancels, or when a notification is sent from a preceding promise inside a promise chain?*

ASYNC FUNCTIONS

Async functions, also referred to by the operative keyword pair *async/await*, are the application of the promise paradigm to ECMAScript functions. It is both a behavioral and syntactical enhancement to the specification that allows for JavaScript code which is written in a synchronous fashion, but actually is able to behave asynchronously. The simplest example of this begins with a promise, which resolves with a value after a timeout:

```
let p = new Promise((resolve, reject) => setTimeout(resolve, 1000, 3));
```

This promise will resolve with a value of 3 after 1000ms. For other parts of the program to access this value once it is ready, it will need to exist inside a fulfilled handler:

```
let p = new Promise((resolve, reject) => setTimeout(resolve, 1000, 3));

p.then((x) => console.log(x));   // 3
```

This is fairly inconvenient, as the rest of the program now needs to be shoehorned into the promise handler. It is possible to move the handler into a function definition:

```
function handler(x) { console.log(x); }

let p = new Promise((resolve, reject) => setTimeout(resolve, 1000, 3));

p.then(handler);   // 3
```

This isn't much of an improvement. Any subsequent code that wishes to access the value produced by the promise needs to be fed that value through a handler, which means being shoved into a handler function. Using an *async function* and *awaiting* a value, also known as *async/await*, is an elegant solution to this problem.

Async Function Basics

Async/await is intended to directly address the issue of organizing code which makes use of asynchronous constructs. It introduces a logical extension of asynchronous behavior into the domain of JavaScript functions by introducing two new keywords, `async` and `await`.

The *async* keyword

An *async function* can be declared by prepending the `async` keyword to the function definition. This keyword can be used on function declarations, function expressions, arrow functions, and methods:

```
async function foo() {}

let bar = async function() {};

let baz = async () => {};

class Qux {
    async qux() {}
}
```

Using the `async` keyword will create a function that exhibits some asynchronous characteristics but overall is still synchronously evaluated. In all other respects such as arguments and closures, it still exhibits all the normal behavior of a JavaScript function. Consider this simple demonstration here, which shows the `foo()` function is still evaluated before proceeding to subsequent instructions:

```
async function foo() {
    console.log(1);
}

foo();
console.log(2);

// 1
// 2
```

In an async function, whatever value is returned with the `return` keyword (or `undefined` if there is no return) will be effectively converted into a promise object with `Promise.resolve()`. An async function will always return a promise object. Outside the function, the evaluated function will be this promise object:

```
async function foo() {
    console.log(1);
    return 3;
}

// Attach a fulfilled handler to the returned promise
foo().then(console.log);

console.log(2);

// 1
// 2
// 3
```

Of course, this means returning a promise object affords identical behavior:

```
async function foo() {
  console.log(1);
  return Promise.resolve(3);
}

// Attach a fulfilled handler to the returned promise
foo().then(console.log);

console.log(2);

// 1
// 2
// 3
```

The return value of an async function anticipates, but does not actually require, a thenable object: It will also work with regular values. A thenable object will be "unwrapped" via the first argument provided to the then() callback. A non-thenable object will be passed through as if it were an already fulfilled promise. These various scenarios are demonstrated here:

```
// Return a primitive
async function foo() {
  return 'foo';
}
foo().then(console.log);
// foo

// Return a non-thenable object
async function bar() {
  return ['bar'];
}
bar().then(console.log);
// ['bar']

// Return a thenable non-promise object
async function baz() {
  const thenable = {
    then(callback) { callback('baz'); }
  };
  return thenable;
}
baz().then(console.log);
// baz

// Return a promise
async function qux() {
  return Promise.resolve('qux');
}
qux().then(console.log);
// qux
```

As with promise handler functions, throwing an error value will instead return a rejected promise:

```
async function foo() {
  console.log(1);
  throw 3;
}

// Attach a rejected handler to the returned promise
foo().catch(console.log);
console.log(2);

// 1
// 2
// 3
```

However, promise rejection errors will *not* be captured by the async function:

```
async function foo() {
  console.log(1);
  Promise.reject(3);
}

// Attach a rejected handler to the returned promise
foo().catch(console.log);
console.log(2);

// 1
// 2
// Uncaught (in promise): 3
```

The *await* keyword

Because an async function indicates to code invoking it that there is no expectation of timely completion, the logical extension of this behavior is the ability to pause and resume execution. This exact feature is possible using the await keyword, which is used to pause execution while waiting for a promise to resolve. Consider the example from the beginning of the chapter, shown here:

```
let p = new Promise((resolve, reject) => setTimeout(resolve, 1000, 3));

p.then((x) => console.log(x));  // 3
```

This can be rewritten using async/await as follows:

```
async function foo() {
  let p = new Promise((resolve, reject) => setTimeout(resolve, 1000, 3));
  console.log(await p);
}

foo();
// 3
```

The await keyword will pause execution of the async function, releasing the JavaScript runtime's thread of execution. This behavior is not unlike that of the yield keyword in a generator function. The await keyword will attempt to "unwrap" the object's value, pass the value through to the expression, and asynchronously resume execution of the async function.

The `await` keyword is used in the same way as a JavaScript unary operator. It can be used standalone or inside an expression, as shown in the following examples:

```javascript
// Asynchronously print "foo"
async function foo() {
  console.log(await Promise.resolve('foo'));
}
foo();
// foo


// Asynchronously print "bar"
async function bar() {
  return await Promise.resolve('bar');
}
bar().then(console.log);
// bar

// Asynchronously print "baz" after 1000ms
async function baz() {
  await new Promise((resolve, reject) => setTimeout(resolve, 1000));
  console.log('baz');
}
baz();
// baz <after 1000ms>
```

The `await` keyword anticipates, but does not actually require, a thenable object: It will also work with regular values. A thenable object will be "unwrapped" via the first argument provided to the `then()` callback. A non-thenable object will be passed through as if it were an already fulfilled promise. These various scenarios are demonstrated here:

```javascript
// Await a primitive
async function foo() {
  console.log(await 'foo');
}
foo();
// foo

// Await a non-thenable object
async function bar() {
  console.log(await ['bar']);
}
bar();
// ['bar']

// Await a thenable non-promise object
async function baz() {
  const thenable = {
    then(callback) { callback('baz'); }
  };
  console.log(await thenable);
}
baz();
```

```
// baz

// Await a promise
async function qux() {
  console.log(await Promise.resolve('qux'));
}
qux();
// qux
```

Awaiting a synchronous operation that throws an error will instead return a rejected promise:

```
async function foo() {
  console.log(1);
  await (() => { throw 3; })();
}

// Attach a rejected handler to the returned promise
foo().catch(console.log);
console.log(2);

// 1
// 2
// 3
```

As shown earlier, a standalone `Promise.reject()` will not be captured by an async function and will throw as an unhandled error. However, using `await` on a promise that rejects will unwrap the error value:

```
async function foo() {
  console.log(1);
  await Promise.reject(3);
  console.log(4);  // never prints
}

// Attach a rejected handler to the returned promise
foo().catch(console.log);
console.log(2);

// 1
// 2
// 3
```

Restrictions on *await*

The `await` keyword can be used inside an async function *or* in a top-level context of a module. If you need to use `await` inside a non-async function, you can use an immediately invoked async function expression. The following two code snippets are effectively identical:

```
async function foo() {
  console.log(await Promise.resolve(3));
}
foo();
```

```
// 3

// Immediately invoked async function expression
(async function() {
  console.log(await Promise.resolve(3));
})();
// 3
```

Furthermore, the async nature of a function does not extend to nested functions. Therefore, the `await` keyword can also only appear directly inside an async function definition; attempting to use `await` inside a synchronous function will throw a `SyntaxError`.

Shown below are a few disallowed examples:

```
// Not allowed: 'await' inside arrow function
function foo() {
  const syncFn = () => {
    return await Promise.resolve('foo');
  };
  console.log(syncFn());
}

// Not allowed: 'await' inside function declaration
function bar() {
  function syncFn() {
    return await Promise.resolve('bar');
  }
  console.log(syncFn());
}

// Not allowed: 'await' inside function expression
function baz() {
  const syncFn = function() {
  return await Promise.resolve('baz');
  };
  console.log(syncFn());
}

// Not allowed: IIFE using function expression or arrow function
function qux() {
  (function () { console.log(await Promise.resolve('qux')); })();
  (() => console.log(await Promise.resolve('qux')))();
}
```

The `for-await-of` loop provides a convenient and concise way of iterating over asynchronous data streams in JavaScript. It is similar to the traditional `for-of` loop, but instead of synchronously iterating over an array or iterable object, it waits for asynchronous operations to complete before iterating over the next item. The syntax for the `for-await-of` loop is as follows:

```
for await (let variable of iterable) {
  // code to be executed
}
```

In this syntax, the iterable can be any asynchronous iterable, such as a promise, an asynchronous function, or an object that has a `Symbol.asyncIterator` method.

Asynchronous functions are another type of iterable that can be used with the `for-await-of` loop. Let's take an example of using the `for-await-of` loop with an asynchronous function. Suppose we have an asynchronous function that returns promises that resolve to random numbers. We can use the `for-await-of` loop to wait for the promises to resolve and iterate over the resulting numbers:

```
async function getRandomNumber(i) {
  return new Promise(resolve => {
    console.log(i);
    setTimeout(resolve, 1000, Math.random());
  });
}

async function printRandomNumbers() {
  for await (const x of Array.from(Array(5).keys()).map(getRandomNumber)) {
    console.log(x);
  }
  console.log("loop has exited");
}

printRandomNumbers();

// Printed immediately:
// 0
// 1
// 2
// 3
// 4

// Printed after 1000ms:
// 0.8748458184008716
// ...
// loop has exited
```

In this example, we define an asynchronous function `getRandomNumber` that returns a promise that resolves to a random number after 1000ms. `printRandomNumbers()` uses the `for-await-of` loop to iterate over the promises returned by `getRandomNumber` and log the resulting numbers to the console.

If you were to remove the `async` keyword in the preceding code and use a regular `for` loop, you would see the following console output:

```
// Printed immediately:
// 0
// 1
// 2
// 3
// 4
// Promise<pending>
// ...
// loop has exited
```

The `for-await-of` loop can handle both normal iterables and async iterables:

```
const myArray = [1, 2, 3];

for await (const item of myArray) {
  console.log(item);
}


// Printed immediately:
// 1
// 2
// 3
```

Now let's refactor this so that the `for-await-of` loop is consuming values produced by an async iterator:

```
async function* asyncIterable(array) {
  for (const item of array) {
    yield item;
  }
}

const myArray = [1, 2, 3];

for await (const item of asyncIterable(myArray)) {
  console.log(item);
}

// Printed immediately:
// 1
// 2
// 3
```

To observe the `for-await-of` loop consuming sequential asynchronous values, let's rework the async generator with a delay:

```
async function* asyncIterable(array) {
  for (const item of array) {
    // 1000ms delay
    await new Promise(resolve => setTimeout(resolve, 1000));
    yield item;
  }
}

const myArray = [1, 2, 3];

for await (const item of asyncIterable(myArray)) {
  console.log(item);
}

// Printed after 1000ms:
```

```
// 1

// Printed after 2000ms:
// 2

// Printed after 3000ms:
// 3
```

> **NOTE** *Refer to Chapter 7, "Iterators and Generators," for details on generator functions.*

Strategies for Async Functions

Because of their convenience and utility, async functions are increasingly a ubiquitous pillar of JavaScript codebases. Even so, when wielding async functions, keep certain considerations in mind.

Implementing *Sleep()*

When learning JavaScript for the first time, many developers will reach for a construct similar to Java's `Thread.sleep()` in an attempt to introduce a non-blocking delay into their program. With async functions, it is trivial to build a utility that allows a function to `sleep()` for a variable number of milliseconds:

```
async function sleep(delay) {
  return new Promise((resolve) => setTimeout(resolve, delay));
}

async function foo() {
  const t0 = Date.now();
  await sleep(1500);   // sleep for ~1500ms
  console.log(Date.now() - t0);
}
foo();
// 1502
```

Maximizing Parallelization

If the `await` keyword is not used carefully, your program may be missing out on possible parallelization speedups. Consider the following example, which awaits five random timeouts sequentially:

```
async function randomDelay(id) {
  // Delay between 0 and 1000 ms
  const delay = Math.random() * 1000;
  return new Promise((resolve) => setTimeout(() => {
    console.log(`${id} finished`);
    resolve();
  }, delay));
}

async function foo() {
  const t0 = Date.now();
  await randomDelay(0);
```

```
    await randomDelay(1);
    await randomDelay(2);
    await randomDelay(3);
    await randomDelay(4);
    console.log(`${Date.now() - t0}ms elapsed`);
}
foo();

// 0 finished
// 1 finished
// 2 finished
// 3 finished
// 4 finished
// 2219ms elapsed
```

Rolling up into a for loop yields the following:

```
async function randomDelay(id) {
  // Delay between 0 and 1000 ms
  const delay = Math.random() * 1000;
  return new Promise((resolve) => setTimeout(() => {
    console.log(`${id} finished`);
    resolve();
  }, delay));
}

async function foo() {
  const t0 = Date.now();
  for (let i = 0; i < 5; ++i) {
    await randomDelay(i);
  }
  console.log(`${Date.now() - t0}ms elapsed`);
}
foo();

// 0 finished
// 1 finished
// 2 finished
// 3 finished
// 4 finished
// 2219ms elapsed
```

Even though there is no interdependence between the promises, this async function will pause and wait for each to complete before beginning the next. Doing so guarantees in-order execution, but at the expense of total execution time.

If in-order execution is not required, it is better to initialize the promises all at once and await the results as they become available. This can be done as follows:

```
async function randomDelay(id) {
  // Delay between 0 and 1000 ms
  const delay = Math.random() * 1000;
  return new Promise((resolve) => setTimeout(() => {
    console.asyncLog(`${id} finished`);
    resolve();
```

```
    }, delay));
}

async function foo() {
  const t0 = Date.now();

  const p0 = randomDelay(0);
  const p1 = randomDelay(1);
  const p2 = randomDelay(2);
  const p3 = randomDelay(3);
  const p4 = randomDelay(4);

  await p0;
  await p1;
  await p2;
  await p3;
  await p4;

  console.asyncLog(`${Date.now() - t0}ms elapsed`);
}
foo();

// 1 finished
// 4 finished
// 3 finished
// 0 finished
// 2 finished
// 2219ms elapsed
```

Rolling up into an array and `for` loop yields the following:

```
async function randomDelay(id) {
  // Delay between 0 and 1000 ms
  const delay = Math.random() * 1000;
  return new Promise((resolve) => setTimeout(() => {
    console.log(`${id} finished`);
    resolve();
  }, delay));
}

async function foo() {
  const t0 = Date.now();

  const promises = Array(5).fill(null).map((_, i) => randomDelay(i));

  for (const p of promises) {
    await p;
  }

  console.log(`${Date.now() - t0}ms elapsed`);
}
foo();

// 4 finished
// 2 finished
```

```
// 1 finished
// 0 finished
// 3 finished
// 877ms elapsed
```

Note that, although the execution of the promises is out of order, the `await` statements are provided to the fulfilled values *in* order:

```
async function randomDelay(id) {
  // Delay between 0 and 1000 ms
  const delay = Math.random() * 1000;
  return new Promise((resolve) => setTimeout(() => {
    console.log(`${id} finished`);
    resolve(id);
  }, delay));
}

async function foo() {
  const t0 = Date.now();

  const promises = Array(5).fill(null).map((_, i) => randomDelay(i));

  for (const p of promises) {
    console.log(`awaited ${await p}`);
  }

  console.log(`${Date.now() - t0}ms elapsed`);
}
foo();

// 1 finished
// 2 finished
// 4 finished
// 3 finished
// 0 finished
// awaited 0
// awaited 1
// awaited 2
// awaited 3
// awaited 4
// 645ms elapsed
```

Serial Promise Execution

In the "Promises" section of this chapter, there is a discussion on how to compose promises that serially execute and pass values to the subsequent promise. With async/await, chaining promises becomes trivial:

```
function addTwo(x) {return x + 2;}
function addThree(x) {return x + 3;}
function addFive(x) {return x + 5;}

async function addTen(x) {
  for (const fn of [addTwo, addThree, addFive]) {
    x = await fn(x);
```

```
    }
    return x;
  }
```

```
  addTen(9).then(console.log);   // 19
```

Here, `await` is directly passed the return value of each function and the result is iteratively derived. The preceding example does not actually deal in promises, but it can be reconfigured to use async functions—and therefore promises—instead:

```
  async function addTwo(x) {return x + 2;}
  async function addThree(x) {return x + 3;}
  async function addFive(x) {return x + 5;}

  async function addTen(x) {
    for (const fn of [addTwo, addThree, addFive]) {
      x = await fn(x);
    }
    return x;
  }

  addTen(9).then(console.log);   // 19
```

Stack Traces and Memory Management

Promises and async functions have a considerable degree of overlap in terms of functionality they provide, but they diverge considerably when it comes to how they are represented in memory. Consider the following example, which shows the stack trace readout for a rejected promise:

```
  function fooPromiseExecutor(resolve, reject) {
    setTimeout(reject, 1000, 'bar');
  }

  function foo() {
    new Promise(fooPromiseExecutor);
  }

  foo();
  // Uncaught (in promise) bar
  //     setTimeout
  //     setTimeout (async)
  //     fooPromiseExecutor
  //     foo
```

Based on your understanding of promises, this stack trace readout should puzzle you a bit. The stack trace should, quite literally, represent the nested nature of function calls that exists currently in the JavaScript engine's memory stack. When the timeout handler executes and rejects the promise, the error readout shown identifies the nested functions that were invoked to create the promise instance originally. However, it is known that these functions have *already returned* and therefore wouldn't be found in a stack trace.

The answer is simply that the JavaScript engine does extra work to preserve the call stack while it can when creating the promise structure. When an error is thrown, this call stack is retrievable by the runtime's error handling logic and therefore is available in the stack trace. This, of course, means it must preserve the stack trace in memory, which comes at a computational and storage cost.

Consider the previous example if it were reworked with async functions, as demonstrated here:

```
function fooPromiseExecutor(resolve, reject) {
  setTimeout(reject, 1000, 'bar');
}

async function foo() {
  await new Promise(fooPromiseExecutor);
}
foo();

// Uncaught (in promise) bar
//    foo
//    async function (async)
//    foo
```

With this structure, the stack trace is accurately representing the current call stack because fooPromiseExecutor has returned and is no longer on the stack, but foo is suspended and has not yet exited. The JavaScript runtime can merely store a pointer from a nested function to its container function, as it would with a synchronous function call stack. This pointer is efficiently stored in memory and can be used to generate the stack trace in the event of an error. Such a strategy does not incur extra overhead as is the case with the previous example, and therefore should be preferred if performance is critical to your application.

Rejection-Safe Parallelization

Async/await gets a bit sticky when it comes to batches of unreliable promises. Let's consider a scenario where you wish to dispatch a sequence of network requests to load data from an imaginary API. We can assume that each imaginary page will be an array of arbitrary data and that consecutive pages should be stitched together ordinally.

The following code is a simplistic implementation:

```
async function getApiPages(pageCount) {
  const data = [];
  const pageUrls = Array.from(Array(pageCount).keys())
    .map(i => `https://foo.com/api?page=${i}`);

  for (const url of pageUrls) {
    const response = await fetch(url);
    const pageData = await response.json();
    data.push(data);
  }

  return data.flat();
}
```

The implementation returns the page data in order, but it has some undesirable properties:

➤ The network requests are serially executed, which is slow.

➤ Any rejected `fetch()` will throw an unhandled rejection.

To parallelize the requests but still preserve order and handle any rejections, we can refactor this as follows:

```
async function getApiPages(pageCount) {
  const data = [];
  const pageUrls = Array.from(Array(pageCount).keys())
    .map(i => `https://foo.com/api?page=${i}`);

  // Fire off the requests in parallel and combine the
  // fetch promises into an array
  const pagePromises = pageUrls.map(async (url) => {
    const response = await fetch(url);
    return response.json();
  });

  // Implicitly adds silent rejection handlers to all promises
  Promise.allSettled(pagePromises);

  // Record data at its proper page index
  for await (const [i, pageData] of pagePromises.entries()) {
    data[i] = pageData;
  }

  return data.flat();
}
```

Of course, this implementation is a bit silly, because we are silently ignoring when some of the data pages don't load. If you wished to add rejection handling to the promises, it can be supplementally added without interfering with the overall behavior. The use of `Promise.allSettled()` simply silences any unhandled rejections that would otherwise escape; if you wished to add handling for a failed page load, you could add *additional* `onRejected` handlers without issue.

> **NOTE** *This example was inspired by Jake Archibald's excellent blog post, "The gotcha of unhandled promise rejections"* (`https://jakearchibald.com/2023/unhandled-rejections`).

SUMMARY

Mastering asynchronous behavior inside the single-threaded JavaScript runtime has long been an imposing task. With the introduction of promises and async/await, asynchronous constructs in ECMAScript have been greatly enhanced. Not only do promises and async/await enable patterns that were previously difficult or impossible to implement, but they engender an entirely new way of writing JavaScript that is cleaner, shorter, and easier to understand and debug.

Promises are built to offer a clean abstraction around asynchronous code. They can represent an asynchronously executed block of code, but they can also represent an asynchronously calculated value. They are especially useful in a situation where the need to serialize asynchronous code blocks arises. Promises are a delightfully malleable construct: They can be serialized, chained, composed, extended, and recombined.

Async functions are the result of applying the promise paradigm to JavaScript functions. They introduce the ability to suspend execution of a function without blocking the main thread of execution. They are tremendously useful both in writing readable promise-centric code as well as in managing serialization and parallelization of asynchronous code. They are one of the most important tools in the modern JavaScript toolkit.

12

The Browser Object Model

WHAT'S IN THIS CHAPTER?

➤ Understanding the window object, the core of the BOM

➤ Controlling windows and pop-ups

➤ Page information from the location object

➤ Using the navigator object to learn about the browser

➤ Manipulating the browser history stack with the history object

DOWNLOADS FOR THIS CHAPTER

Please note that all the code examples for this chapter are available as a part of this chapter's code download on the book's website at www.wiley.com/go/projavascript5e.

Though ECMAScript describes it as the core of JavaScript, the Browser Object Model (BOM) is really the core of using JavaScript on the web. The BOM provides objects that expose browser functionality independent of any web page content. For years, a lack of any real specification made the BOM both interesting and problematic because browser vendors were free to augment it as they saw fit. The commonalities between browsers became de facto standards that have survived browser development mostly for the purpose of interoperability. Part of the HTML5 specification now covers the major aspects of the BOM, standardizing one of the most fundamental parts of JavaScript in the browser.

THE WINDOW OBJECT

At the core of the BOM is the window object, which represents an instance of the browser. The window object serves a dual purpose in browsers, acting as the JavaScript interface to the browser window and the ECMAScript Global object. This means that every object, variable, and function defined in a web page uses window as its Global object and has access to methods like parseInt().

> **NOTE** *Because window object properties are available in the global scope, many browser APIs and associated constructors use a window object property as an access point. These APIs are covered elsewhere in the book, predominantly in the Chapter 18, "JavaScript APIs."*

The Global Scope

Because the window object doubles as the ECMAScript Global object, all variables and functions declared globally with var become properties and methods of the window object. Consider this example:

```
var age = 29;
var sayAge = () => alert(this.age);

alert(window.age);    // 29
sayAge();             // 29
window.sayAge();      // 29
```

Here, a variable named age and a function named sayAge() are defined in the global scope, which automatically places them on the window object. Thus, the variable age is also accessible as window.age, and the function sayAge() is also accessible via window.sayAge(). Because sayAge() exists in the global scope, this.age maps to window.age, and the correct result is displayed.

If, instead, let or const is substituted for var, the default attachment to the global object does not occur:

```
let age = 29;
const sayAge = () => alert(this.age);

alert(window.age);    // undefined
sayAge();             // undefined
window.sayAge();      // TypeError: window.sayAge is not a function
```

Another thing to keep in mind: attempting to access an undeclared variable throws an error, but it is possible to check for the existence of a potentially undeclared variable by looking on the window object. For example:

```
// this throws an error because oldValue is undeclared
var newValue = oldValue;
// this doesn't throw an error, because it's a property lookup
// newValue is set to undefined
var newValue = window.oldValue;
```

Keeping this in mind, there are many objects in JavaScript that are considered to be global, such as `location` and `navigator` (both discussed later in the chapter), but are actually properties of the `window` object.

The *globalThis* property

Depending on where some JavaScript is executing, the global object takes on different forms:

➤ In a web page script, the global object is `window`, `self`, or `frames`.

➤ Inside a web worker script, the global object is `self`.

➤ In Node.js, the global object is `global`.

➤ In the top level of a script, `this` usually refers to the global object, but strict mode and arrow functions complicate this.

To address this disparity, ECMAScript defines a `globalThis` property that accomplishes two goals:

1. `globalThis` standardizes access to the global `this` object across environments: in a web page, `globalThis===window`, and in a web worker, `globalThis===self`.

2. `globalThis` is a configurable and writable indirect reference to the global object, allowing for scripts to modify and control the properties and behavior of `globalThis`.

In non-browser engines, the `globalThis` property will directly reference the global object, but in browser engines, it indirectly references the global object via a proxy instance.

The `globalThis` property should be used when a script needs to access the global object but could potentially be shared between unalike JavaScript environments. If you are certain that a script will only be used in a single context, there is less of a need for `globalThis`.

Window Relationships

The `top` object always points to the very top (outermost) window, which is the browser window itself. Another window object is called `parent`. The `parent` object always points to the current window's immediate parent window. For the topmost browser window, `parent` is equal to `top` (and both are equal to `window`). The topmost window will never have a value set for `name` unless the window was opened using `window.open()`, as discussed later in this chapter.

There is one final `window` property, called `self`, which always points to `window`. The two can, in fact, be used interchangeably. Even though it has no separate value, `self` is included for consistency with the `top` and `parent` objects.

Each of these objects is a property of the `window` object, accessible via `window.parent`, `window.top`, and so on. This means it's possible to chain window objects together, such as `window.parent.parent`.

Window Position and Pixel Ratio

The position of a window object may be determined and changed using various properties and methods. Modern browsers all provide `screenLeft` and `screenTop` properties that indicate the window's location in relation to the left and top of the screen, respectively, in CSS pixels.

It is also possible to move the window to a new position using the `moveTo()` and `moveBy()` methods. `moveTo()` expects the x and y coordinates to move to an absolute coordinate, and `moveBy()` expects the number of pixels to move relative to the current coordinate. These methods are demonstrated here:

```
// move the window to the upper-left coordinate
window.moveTo(0,0);

// move the window down by 100 pixels
window.moveBy(0, 100);

// move the window to position (200, 300)
window.moveTo(200, 300);

// move the window left by 50 pixels
window.moveBy(-50, 0);
```

Depending on the browser, these methods may be conditionally or completely disabled.

Pixel Ratios

A "CSS pixel" is the denomination of the pixel used universally in web development. It is defined as an angular measurement: 0.0213°, approximately 1/96 of an inch on a device held at arm's length. The purpose of this definition is to give the pixel size a uniform meaning across devices: for example, 12px font (measured in CSS pixels) on a low-resolution tablet should appear to be the same size as a 12px (measured in CSS pixels) font on a high-resolution 4k monitor. Therein lies a problem: such a system requires an inherent scaling factor required to convert from physical pixels (the actual resolution of the display) to CSS pixels (the virtual resolution reported to the web browser).

For example, a phone screen might have a *physical* resolution of 1920x1080, but because these pixels are incredibly small the web browser will scale this resolution down to a smaller *logical* resolution, such as 640x360. This scaling factor is provided to the browser as `window.devicePixelRatio`. For a device converting from 1920x1080 to 640x360, the `devicePixelRatio` would be reported as 3. In this way, a 12px font in *physical* pixels would really be a 36px font in *logical* pixels (or CSS pixels).

This `devicePixelRatio` is effectively an analogue of DPI (dots per inch). DPI is effectively recording the same information, but `devicePixelRatio` offers it as a unitless ratio.

Window Size

Determining the size of a window cross-browser is not straightforward. All modern browsers provide four properties: `innerWidth`, `innerHeight`, `outerWidth`, and `outerHeight`. `outerWidth` and `outerHeight` return the dimensions of the browser window itself (regardless of whether it's used on the topmost window object or on a frame). The `innerWidth` and `innerHeight` properties indicate the size of the page viewport inside the browser window (minus borders and toolbars). Additionally, the `document.documentElement.clientWidth` and `document.documentElement.clientHeight` properties provide the width and height of the page viewport.

For mobile devices, `window.innerWidth` and `window.innerHeight` are the dimensions of the visual viewport, which is the visible area of the page on the screen. These values change as you zoom in or out of a page. The measurements of `document.documentElement` provide measurements for the layout viewport, which are the actual dimensions of the rendered page (as opposed to the visual viewport, which is only a small portion of the entire page). These values do not change as you zoom in and out.

Because of these differences from desktop browsers, you may need to first determine if the user is on a mobile device before deciding which measurements to use and honor.

The browser window can be resized using the `resizeTo()` and `resizeBy()` methods. Each method accepts two arguments: `resizeTo()` expects a new width and height, and `resizeBy()` expects the differences in each dimension. Here's an example:

```
// resize to 100 x 100
window.resizeTo(100, 100);

// resize to 200 x 150
window.resizeBy(100, 50);

// resize to 300 x 300
window.resizeTo(300, 300);
```

As with the window-movement methods, the resize methods may be disabled by the browser and are disabled by default in some browsers. Also like the movement methods, these methods apply only to the topmost `window` object.

Window Viewport Position

Because the browser window is usually not large enough to display the entire rendered document at once, the user is given the ability to scroll around the document with a limited viewport. The CSS pixel offset of the current viewport is available as an X and Y pair, representing the number of pixels the viewport is currently scrolled in that direction. The X and Y offsets are each accessible via two properties, which return identical values: `window.pageXoffset` / `window.scrollX`, and `window.pageYoffset` / `window.scrollY`.

It is also possible to explicitly scroll the page by a certain amount using several different window methods. These methods are passed two coordinates indicating how far in the X and Y direction the viewport should scroll. `window.scroll(x, y)` will scroll the viewport by a relative amount. (`window.scrollBy(x, y)` behaves identically). `window.scrollTo(x, y)` scrolls the viewport to an absolute offset.

```
// Scroll down 100px relative to the current viewport
window.scroll(0, 100);

// Scroll right 40px relative to the current viewport
Window.scroll(40, 0);
```

```
// Scroll to the top left corner of the page
// window.scrollTo(0, 0);

// Scroll to 100px from the top and left of the page
// window.scrollTo(100, 100);
```

These methods also accept a `ScrollToOptions` dictionary, which in addition to holding the offset values can instruct the browser to smooth the scroll via the `behavior` property.

```
// normal scroll
window.scrollTo({
  left: 100,
  top: 100,
  behavior: 'auto'
});

// smooth scroll
window.scrollTo({
  left: 100,
  top: 100,
  behavior: 'smooth'
});
```

Navigating and Opening Windows

The `window.open()` method can be used both to navigate to a particular URL and to open a new browser window. This method accepts four arguments: the URL to load, the window target, a string of features, and a Boolean value indicating that the new page should take the place of the currently loaded page in the browser history. Typically only the first three arguments are used; the last argument applies only when not opening a new window.

If the second argument passed to `window.open()` is the name of a window or frame that already exists, then the URL is loaded into the window or frame with that name. Here's an example:

```
// same as <a href="http://www.wiley.com" target="topFrame"/>
window.open("http://www.wiley.com/", "topFrame");
```

This line of code acts as if the user clicked a link with the `href` attribute set to `"http://www.wiley.com"` and the target attribute set to `"topFrame"`. If there is a window named `"topFrame"`, then the URL will be loaded there; otherwise, a new window is created and given the name `"topFrame"`. The second argument may also be any of the special window names: `_self`, `_parent`, `_top`, or `_blank`.

Popping Up Windows

When the second argument doesn't identify an existing window, a new window or tab is created based on a string passed in as the third argument. If the third argument is missing, a new browser window (or tab, based on browser settings) is opened with all of the default browser window settings. (Toolbars, the location bar, and the status bar are all set based on the browser's default settings.) The third argument is ignored when not opening a new window.

The third argument is a comma-delimited string of settings indicating display information for the new window. The following table describes the various options.

SETTING	VALUE(S)	DESCRIPTION
height	Number	The initial height of the new window. This cannot be less than 100.
left	Number	The initial left coordinate of the new window. This cannot be a negative number.
location	"yes" or "no"	Indicates if the location bar should be displayed. The default varies based on the browser. When set to "no", the location bar may be either hidden or disabled (browser-dependent).
menubar	"yes" or "no"	Indicates if the menu bar should be displayed. The default is "no".
resizable	"yes" or "no"	Indicates if the new window can be resized by dragging its border. The default is "no".
scrollbars	"yes" or "no"	Indicates if the new window allows scrolling if the content cannot fit in the viewport. The default is "no".
status	"yes" or "no"	Indicates if the status bar should be displayed. The default varies based on the browser.
toolbar	"yes" or "no"	Indicates if the toolbar should be displayed. The default is "no".
top	Number	The initial top coordinate of the new window. This cannot be a negative number.
width	Number	The initial width of the new window. This cannot be less than 100.

> **NOTE** *Some of these options (e.g., toolbar, scrollbars) are not universally supported across modern browsers like Firefox and Chrome.*

Any or all of these settings may be specified as a comma-delimited set of name-value pairs. The name-value pairs are indicated by an equal sign. (No white space is allowed in the feature string.) Consider the following example:

```
window.open("http://www.wiley.com/",
            "wileyWindow",
            "height=400,width=400,top=10,left=10,resizable=yes");
```

This code opens a new resizable window that's 400x400 and positioned 10 pixels from the top and left of the screen.

The window.open() method returns a reference to the newly created window. This object is the same as any other window object except that you typically have more control over it. For instance, some browsers that don't allow you to resize or move the main browser window by default may allow you to resize or move windows that you've created using `window.open()`. This object can be used to manipulate the newly opened window in the same way as any other window, as shown in this example:

```
let wileyWin = window.open("http://www.wiley.com/",
                "wileyWindow",
                "height=400,width=400,top=10,left=10,resizable=yes");

// resize it
wileyWin.resizeTo(500, 500);

// move it
wileyWin.moveTo(100, 100);
```

It's possible to close the newly opened window by calling the `close()` method as follows:

```
wileyWin.close();
```

This method works only for pop-up windows created by `window.open()`. It's not possible to close the main browser window without confirmation from the user. It is possible, however, for the pop-up window to close itself without user confirmation by calling `top.close()`. Once the window has been closed, the `window` reference still exists but cannot be used other than to check the closed property, as shown here:

```
wileyWin.close();
alert(wileyWin.closed);  // true
```

The newly created `window` object has a reference back to the window that opened it via the `opener` property. This property is defined only on the topmost `window` object (`top`) of the pop-up window and is a pointer to the window or frame that called `window.open()`. For example:

```
let wileyWin = window.open("http://www.wiley.com/",
                "wileyWindow",
                "height=400,width=400,top=10,left=10,resizable=yes");

alert(wileyWin.opener === window);  // true
```

Even though there is a pointer from the pop-up window back to the window that opened it, there is no reverse relationship. Windows do not keep track of the pop-ups that they spawn, so it's up to you to keep track if necessary.

Some browsers, try to run each tab in the browser as a separate process. When one tab opens another, the window objects need to be able to communicate with one another, so the tabs cannot run in separate processes. These browsers allow you to indicate that the newly created tab should be run in a separate process by setting the opener property to `null`, as in the following example:

```
let wileyWin = window.open("http://www.wiley.com/",
                "wileyWindow",
                "height=400,width=400,top=10,left=10,resizable=yes");

wileyWin.opener = null;
```

Setting `opener` to `null` indicates to the browser that the newly created tab doesn't need to communicate with the tab that opened it, so it may be run in a separate process. Once this connection has been severed, there is no way to recover it.

Security Restrictions

Pop-up windows went through a period of overuse by advertisers online. Pop-ups were often disguised as system dialogs to get the user to click on an advertisement. Because these pop-up web pages were styled to look like system dialogs, it was unclear to the user whether the dialog was legitimate. To aid in this determination, browsers began putting limits on the configuration of pop-up windows.

Additionally, browsers will allow the creation of pop-up windows only after a user action. A call to window.open() while a page is still being loaded, for instance, will not be executed and may cause an error to be displayed to the user. Pop-up windows may be opened based only on a click or a key press.

Pop-Up Blockers

All modern browsers have pop-up–blocking software built in. The result is that most unexpected pop-ups are blocked. When a pop-up is blocked, one of two things happens. If the browser's built-in pop-up blocker stopped the pop-up, then window.open() will most likely return null. In that case, you can tell if a pop-up was blocked by checking the return value, as shown in the following example:

```
let wileyWin = window.open("http://www.wiley.com", "_blank");
if (wileyWin == null){
  alert("The popup was blocked!");
}
```

When a browser add-on or other program blocks a pop-up, window.open() typically throws an error. So to accurately detect when a pop-up has been blocked, you must check the return value and wrap the call to window.open() in a try-catch block, as in this example:

```
let blocked = false;

try {
  let wileyWin = window.open("http://www.wiley.com", "_blank");
  if (wileyWin == null){
    blocked = true;
  }
} catch (ex){
  blocked = true;
}

if (blocked){
  alert("The popup was blocked!");
}
```

This code accurately detects if a pop-up blocker has blocked the call to window.open(), regardless of the method being used.

> **NOTE** *Detecting if a pop-up was blocked does not stop the browser from displaying its own message about a pop-up being blocked.*

Intervals and Timeouts

JavaScript execution in a browser is single-threaded but does allow for the scheduling of code to run at specific points in time through the use of timeouts and intervals. Timeouts execute some code after a specified amount of time, whereas intervals execute code repeatedly, waiting a specific amount of time in between each execution.

You set a timeout using the window's `setTimeout()` method, which accepts two arguments: the code to execute and the time (in milliseconds) to wait before scheduling the callback function to be executed. The first argument can be either a string containing JavaScript code (as would be used with `eval()`) or a function. For example:

```
// schedules an alert to show after 1 second
setTimeout(() => alert("Hello world!"), 1000);
```

The second argument, the number of milliseconds to wait, is not necessarily when the specified code will execute. JavaScript is single-threaded and, as such, can execute only one piece of code at a time. To manage execution, there is a queue of JavaScript tasks to execute. The tasks are executed in the order in which they were added to the queue. The second argument of `setTimeout()` tells the Java-Script engine to add this task onto the queue after a set number of milliseconds. If the queue is empty, then that code is executed immediately; if the queue is not empty, the code must wait its turn.

When `setTimeout()` is called, it returns a numeric ID for the timeout. The timeout ID is a unique identifier for the scheduled code that can be used to cancel the timeout. To cancel a pending timeout, use the `clearTimeout()` method and pass in the timeout ID, as in the following example:

```
// set the timeout
let timeoutId = setTimeout(() => alert("Hello world!"), 1000);

// cancel it
clearTimeout(timeoutId);
```

As long as `clearTimeout()` is called before the specified amount of time has passed, a timeout can be canceled completely. Calling `clearTimeout()` after the code has been executed has no effect.

> **NOTE** *All code executed by a timeout using a conventional anonymous function runs in the global scope, so the value of* this *inside the function will always point to* window *when running in nonstrict mode and* undefined *when running in strict mode. When* setTimeout *is instead provided an arrow function, this preserves the lexical scope in which it was defined.*

Intervals work in the same way as timeouts except that they schedule the code for execution repeatedly at specific time intervals until the interval is canceled or the page is unloaded. The `setInterval()` method lets you set up intervals, and it accepts the same arguments as `setTimeout()`: the code to execute (string or function) and the milliseconds to wait between addition of the callback function to the execution queue. Here's an example:

```
setInterval(() => alert("Hello world!"), 10000);
```

> **NOTE** *Importantly, the time interval specified with the second argument represents the amount of time the browser will wait in between adding a new callback execution onto the queue. For example, suppose you invoked* `setInterval()` *at exactly 01:00:00 with a 3000ms interval. This means that at 01:00:03 the browser would schedule the callback. The browser doesn't care when the callback executes or how long it takes; it will schedule another one at 01:00:06. It follows that short and non-blocking callback functions are ideal for* `setInterval`.

The `setInterval()` method also returns an interval ID that can be used to cancel the interval at some point in the future. The `clearInterval()` method can be used with this ID to cancel all pending intervals. This ability is more important for intervals than timeouts since, if left unchecked, they continue to execute until the page is unloaded. Here is a common example of interval usage:

```
let num = 0, intervalId = null;
let max = 10;

let incrementNumber = function() {
  num++;

  // if the max has been reached, cancel all pending executions
  if (num == max) {
    clearInterval(intervalId);
    alert("Done");
  }
}

intervalId = setInterval(incrementNumber, 500);
```

In this example, the variable num is incremented every half second until it finally reaches the maximum number, at which point the interval is canceled. This pattern can also be implemented using timeouts, as shown here:

```
let num = 0;
let max = 10;

let incrementNumber = function() {
  num++;

  //if the max has not been reached, set another timeout
  if (num < max) {
    setTimeout(incrementNumber, 500);
```

```
      } else {
        alert("Done");
      }
    }

    setTimeout(incrementNumber, 500);
```

Note that when you're using timeouts, it is unnecessary to track the timeout ID because the execution will stop on its own and continue only if another timeout is set. This pattern is considered a best practice for setting intervals without actually using intervals. True intervals are rarely used in production environments because the time between the end of one interval and the beginning of the next is not necessarily guaranteed, and some intervals may be skipped. Using timeouts, as in the preceding example, ensures that can't happen. Generally speaking, it's best to avoid intervals.

System Dialogs

The browser is capable of invoking system dialogs to display to the user through the alert(), confirm(), and prompt() methods. These dialogs are not related to the web page being displayed in the browser and do not contain HTML. Their appearance is determined by operating system and/or browser settings rather than CSS. Additionally, each of these dialogs is synchronous and modal, meaning code execution stops when a dialog is displayed, and resumes after it has been dismissed.

The alert() method has been used throughout this book. It simply accepts a string to display to the user. Unlike console.log, which can accept a variable number of arguments and display them all at once, alert expects only one argument. When alert() is called, a system message box displays the specified text to the user, followed by a single OK button. If alert() is passed an argument that is not a string primitive, it will coerce the argument into a string.

Alert dialogs are typically used when users must be made aware of something that they have no control over, such as an error. A user's only choice is to dismiss the dialog after reading the message. As shown in Figure 12.1.

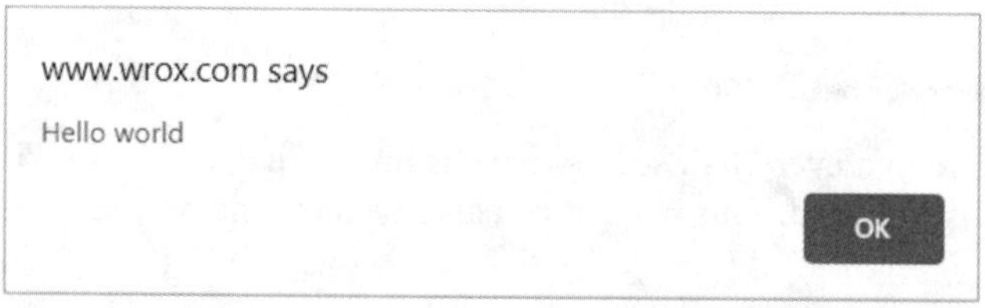

FIGURE 12.1: The alert() **dialog**

The second type of dialog is invoked by calling confirm(). A confirm dialog looks similar to an alert dialog in that it displays a message to the user. The main difference between the two is the presence of a Cancel button along with the OK button, which allows the user to indicate if a given action should be taken. For example, confirm("Are you sure?") displays the confirm dialog box shown in Figure 12.2.

FIGURE 12.2: The `confirm()` dialog

To determine if the user clicked OK or Cancel, the `confirm()` method returns a Boolean value: `true` if OK was clicked, or `false` if Cancel was clicked or the dialog box was closed by clicking the X in the corner. Typical usage of a confirm dialog looks like this:

```
if (confirm("Are you sure?")) {
  alert("I'm so glad you're sure!");
} else {
    alert("I'm sorry to hear you're not sure.");
}
```

In this example, the confirm dialog is displayed to the user in the first line, which is a condition of the if statement. If the user clicks OK, an alert is displayed saying, "I'm so glad you're sure!" If, however, the Cancel button is clicked, an alert is displayed saying, "I'm sorry to hear you're not sure." This type of pattern can be employed when the user tries to delete something, such as an e-mail message. Because the dialog will totally disrupt the user's experience on the page, this should be reserved for only actions that have dire consequences.

The final type of dialog is displayed by calling `prompt()`, which prompts the user for input. Along with OK and Cancel buttons, this dialog has a text box where the user may enter some data. The `prompt()` method accepts two arguments: the text to display to the user, and the default value for the text box (which can be an empty string). Calling `prompt("What is your name?", "Jake")` results in the dialog box shown in Figure 12.3.

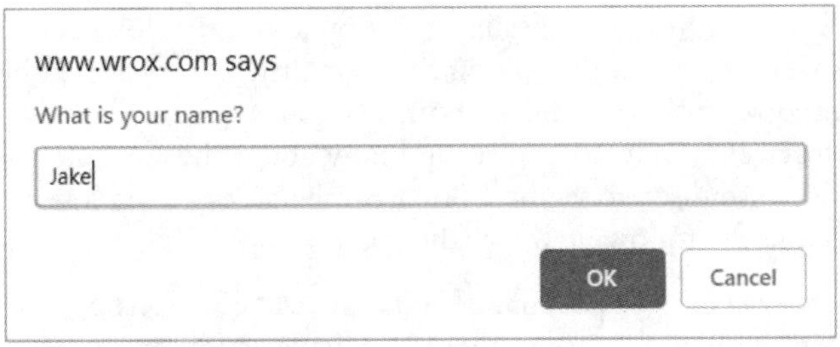

FIGURE 12.3: The `prompt()` dialog

If the OK button is clicked, `prompt()` returns the value in the text box; if Cancel is clicked or the dialog is otherwise closed without clicking OK, the function returns `null`. Here's an example:

```
let result = prompt("What is your name? ", "");
if (result !== null) {
  alert("Welcome, " + result);
}
```

These system dialogs can be helpful for displaying information to the user and asking for confirmation of decisions. Because they require no HTML or CSS, they are fast and easy ways to enhance a web application.

Many browsers have introduced a special feature regarding these system dialogs. If the actively running script produces two or more system dialogs during its execution, each subsequent dialog after the first displays a check box that allows the user to disable any further dialogs until the page reloads.

When the check box is checked and the dialog box is dismissed, all further system dialogs (alerts, confirms, and prompts) are blocked until the page is reloaded. The developer is given no indication as to whether the dialog was displayed. The dialog counter resets whenever the browser is idle, so if two separate user actions produce an alert, the check box will not be displayed in either; if a single user action produces two alerts in a row, the second will contain the check box.

Two other types of dialogs can be displayed from JavaScript: find and print. Both of these dialogs are displayed asynchronously, returning control to the script immediately. The dialogs are the same as the ones the browser employs when the user selects either Find or Print from the browser's menu. These are displayed using the `find()` and `print()` methods on the `window` object as follows:

```
// display print dialog
window.print();

// display find dialog
window.find();
```

These two methods give no indication as to whether the user has done anything with the dialog, so it is difficult to make good use of them. Furthermore, because they are asynchronous, they don't contribute to the browser's dialog counter and won't be affected by the user opting to disallow further dialogs.

THE LOCATION OBJECT

One of the most useful BOM objects is location, which provides information about the document that is currently loaded in the window, as well as general navigation functionality. The location object is unique in that it is a property of both `window` and `document`, so both `window.location` and `document.location` point to the same object. Not only does location know about the currently loaded document, but it also parses the URL into discrete segments that can be accessed via a series of properties. These properties are enumerated in the following table (the location prefix is assumed).

If the browser was currently located at `http://foouser:barpassword@www.wiley.com:80/WileyCDA/?q=javascript#contents`, then the `location` object would behave as follows:

PROPERTY NAME	RETURN VALUE	DESCRIPTION
`location.hash`	`"#contents"`	The URL hash (the pound sign followed by zero or more characters), or an empty string if the URL doesn't have a hash.

continues

(continued)

PROPERTY NAME	RETURN VALUE	DESCRIPTION
`location.host`	`"www.wiley.com:80"`	The name of the server and port number if present.
`location.hostname`	`"www.wiley.com"`	The name of the server without the port number.
`location.href`	`"http://www.wiley.com:80/WileyCDA/?q=javascript#contents"`	The full URL of the currently loaded page. The `toString()` method of `location` returns this value.
`location.pathname`	`"/WileyCDA/"`	The directory and/or filename of the URL.
`location.port`	`"80"`	The port of the request if specified in the URL. If a URL does not contain a port, then this property returns an empty string.
`location.protocol`	`"http:"`	The protocol used by the page. Typically `"http:"` or `"https:"`.
`location.search`	`"?q=javascript"`	The query string of the URL. It returns a string beginning with a question mark.
`location.username`	`"foouser"`	The username specified before the domain name.
`location.password`	`"barpassword"`	The password specified before the domain name.
`location.origin`	`"http:// www.wiley.com"`	The origin of the URL. Read only.

> **NOTE** *The URL API and URLSearchParams API are very useful when dealing with the* `location` *object. Refer to Chapter 18 for details.*

Manipulating the Location

The browser location can be changed in a number of ways using the location object. The first, and most common, way is to use the `assign()` method and pass in a URL, as in the following example:

```
location.assign("http://www.wiley.com");
```

This immediately starts the process of navigating to the new URL and makes an entry in the browser's history stack. If `location.href` or `window.location` is set to a URL, the `assign()` method is called with the value. For example, both of the following perform the same behavior as calling `assign()` explicitly:

```
window.location = "http://www.wiley.com";
location.href = "http://www.wiley.com";
```

Of these three approaches to changing the browser location, setting `location.href` is most often seen in code.

Changing various properties on the location object can also modify the currently loaded page. The `hash`, `search`, `hostname`, `pathname`, and `port` properties can be set with new values that alter the current URL, as in this example:

```
// assume starting at http://www.wiley.com/WileyCDA/

// changes URL to "http://www.wiley.com/WileyCDA/#section1"
location.hash = "#section1";

// changes URL to "http://www.wiley.com/WileyCDA/?q=javascript"
location.search = "?q=javascript";

// changes URL to "http://www.yahoo.com/WileyCDA/"
location.hostname = "www.yahoo.com";

// changes URL to "http://www.yahoo.com/mydir/"
location.pathname = "mydir";

// changes URL to "http://www.yahoo.com:8080/WileyCDA/"
Location.port = 8080;
```

Each time a property on location is changed, with the exception of hash, the page reloads with the new URL.

> **NOTE** *Changing the value of hash causes a new entry in the browser's history to be recorded.*

When the URL is changed using one of the previously mentioned approaches, an entry is made in the browser's history stack so the user may click the Back button to navigate to the previous page. It is possible to disallow this behavior by using the `replace()` method. This method accepts a single argument, the URL to navigate to, but does not make an entry in the history stack. After calling `replace()`, the user cannot go back to the previous page. Consider this example:

```
<!DOCTYPE html>
<html>
<head>
  <title>You won't be able to get back here</title>
</head>
```

```
<!--<ce:anchor id="pp:453 np:454" role="page-break"/>--><body>
<p>Enjoy this page for a second, because you won't be coming back here.</p>
<script>
    setTimeout(() => location.replace("http://www.wiley.com/"), 1000);
</script>
</body>
</html>
```

If this page is loaded into a web browser, it will redirect to `www.wiley.com` after a second. At that point, the Back button will be disabled, and you won't be able to navigate back to this example page without typing in the complete URL again.

The last method of location is `reload()`, which reloads the currently displayed page. When `reload()` is called with no argument, the page is reloaded in the most efficient way possible, which is to say that the page may be reloaded from the browser cache if it hasn't changed since the last request. To force a reload from the server, pass in `true` as an argument like this:

```
location.reload();      // reload - possibly from cache
location.reload(true);  // reload - go back to the server
```

Any code located after a `reload()` call may or may not be executed, depending on factors such as network latency and system resources. For this reason, it is best to have `reload()` as the last line of code.

THE NAVIGATOR OBJECT

Originally introduced in Netscape Navigator 2, the navigator object is the standard for browser identification on the client. The navigator object is common among all JavaScript-enabled web browsers. As with other BOM objects, each browser supports its own set of properties.

The following table lists each available property and method:

PROPERTY/METHOD	DESCRIPTION
`activeVrDisplays`	Returns an array of every `VRDisplay` instance with its `ispresenting` property set to `true`.
`appCodeName`	Returns "Mozilla" even in non-Mozilla browsers.
`appName`	Full browser name.
`appVersion`	Browser version. Typically does not correspond to the actual browser version.
`battery`	Returns a `BatteryManager` object to interact with the Battery Status API.
`buildId`	Build number for the browser.

continues

(continued)

PROPERTY/METHOD	DESCRIPTION
connection	Returns a `NetworkInformation` object to interact with the Network Information API.
cookieEnabled	Indicates if cookies are enabled.
credentials	A `CredentialsContainer` to interact with the Credentials Management API.
deviceMemory	The amount of device memory in gigabytes.
doNotTrack	The user's do-not-track preference.
geolocation	A `Geolocation` object to interact with the Geolocation API.
getVRDisplays()	Returns an array of every `VRDisplay` instance available.
getUserMedia()	Returns the stream associated with the available media device hardware.
hardwareConcurrency	The device's number of processor cores.
javaEnabled	Indicates if Java is enabled in the browser.
language	The browser's primary language.
languages	An array of all the browser's preferred languages.
locks	A `LockManager` object to interact with the Web Locks API.
mediaCapabilities	A `MediaCapabilities` object to interact with the Media Capabilities API.
mediaDevices	The available media devices.
maxTouchPoints	The maximum number of supported touch points for the device's touchscreen.
mimeTypes	Array of MIME types registered with the browser.
onLine	Indicates if the browser is connected to the Internet.
oscpu	The operating system and/or CPU on which the browser is running.
permissions	A `Permissions` object to interact with the Permissions API.
platform	The system platform on which the browser is running.
plugins	Array of plug-ins installed on the browser.

(continued)

PROPERTY/METHOD	DESCRIPTION
product	The name of the product (typically "Gecko").
productSub	Extra information about the product (typically Gecko version information).
registerProtocolHandler()	Registers a website as a handler for a particular protocol.
requestMediaKeySystemAccess()	Returns a Promise which resolves to a `MediaKeySystemAccess` object.
sendBeacon()	Asynchronously transmits a small payload.
serviceWorker	The `ServiceWorkerContainer` used to interact with `ServiceWorker` objects.
share()	If available, invokes the current platform's native sharing mechanism.
storage	Returns the `StorageManager` object to interact with the Storage API.
userAgent	The user-agent string for the browser.
vendor	The brand name of the browser.
vendorSub	Extra information about the vendor.
vibrate()	Triggers the device to vibrate if vibration is supported.
webdriver	Indicates if the browser is controlled by automation.

The navigator object's properties are typically used to determine the type of browser that is running a web page.

Registering Handlers

The registerProtocolHandler() method allows a website to indicate that it can handle specific types of information. This is a way for applications like online RSS readers and online e-mail clients to be used by default just as desktop applications are used.

A call can be made for protocols by using registerProtocolHandler(), which accepts three arguments: the protocol to handle (i.e., "mailto" or "ftp"), the URL of the page that handles the protocol, and the name of the application. For example, to register a web application as the default mail client, you can use the following:

```
navigator.registerProtocolHandler("mailto",
  "http://www.somemailclient.com?cmd=%s",
  "Some Mail Client");
```

In this example, a handler is registered for the mailto protocol, which will now point to a web-based e-mail client. Once again, the second argument is the URL that should handle the request, and `%s` represents the original request.

THE SCREEN OBJECT

The `screen` object (also a property of `window`) is one of the few JavaScript objects that have little to no programmatic use; it is used purely as an indication of client capabilities. This object provides information about the client's display outside the browser window, including information such as pixel width and height. Each browser provides different properties on the `screen` object. The following table describes each of the properties.

PROPERTY	DESCRIPTION
availHeight	The pixel height of the screen minus system elements such as Windows (read only).
availLeft	The first pixel from the left that is not taken up by system elements (read only).
availTop	The first pixel from the top that is not taken up by system elements (read only).
availWidth	The pixel width of the screen minus system elements (read only).
colorDepth	The number of bits used to represent colors; for most systems, 32 (read only).
height	The pixel height of the screen.
left	The pixel distance of the current screen's left side.
pixelDepth	The bit depth of the screen (read only).
top	The pixel distance of the current screen's top.
width	The pixel width of the screen.
orientation	Returns the screen orientation as specified in the Screen Orientation API.

THE HISTORY OBJECT

The `history` object represents the user's navigation history since the given window was first used. Because `history` is a property of `window`, each browser window object has its own `history` object relating specifically to that instance. For security reasons, it's not possible to determine the URLs that the user has visited. It is possible, however, to navigate backwards and forwards through the list of places the user has been without knowing the exact URL.

Navigation

The `go()` method navigates through the user's history in either direction, backward or forward. This method accepts a single argument, which is an integer representing the number of pages to go backward or forward. A negative number moves backward in history (similar to clicking the browser's Back button), and a positive number moves forward (similar to clicking the browser's Forward button). Here's an example:

```
// go back one page
history.go(-1);

// go forward one page
history.go(1);

// go forward two pages
history.go(2);
```

The `go()` method argument can also be a string, in which case the browser navigates to the first location in history that contains the given string. The closest location may be either backward or forward. If there's no entry in history matching the string, then the method does nothing, as in this example:

```
// go to nearest wiley.com page
history.go("wiley.com");

// go to nearest nczonline.net page
history.go("nczonline.net");
```

Two shortcut methods, `back()` and `forward()`, may be used in place of `go()`. As you might expect, these mimic the browser Back and Forward buttons as follows:

```
// go back one page
history.back();

// go forward one page
history.forward();
```

The `history` object also has a property, `length`, which indicates how many items are in the history stack. This property reflects all items in the history stack, both those going backward and those going forward. For the first page loaded into a window or tab, `history.length` is equal to 0. By testing for this value as shown here, it's possible to determine if the user's start point was your page:

```
if (history.length == 0){
  //this is the first page in the user's window
}
```

The `history` object typically is used to create custom Back and Forward buttons and to determine if the page is the first in the user's history.

> **NOTE** *Entries are made in the history stack whenever the page's URL changes. This includes changes to the URL hash (thus, setting* `location.hash` *causes a new entry to be inserted into the history stack for these browsers). This behavior is commonly used by single-page application frameworks, which wish to simulate Back and Forward button functionality without causing full page reloads upon each navigation event.*

History State Management

One of the most difficult aspects of modern web application programming is history management. Gone are the days where every action takes a user to a completely new page, which also means that the Back and Forward buttons have been taken away from users as a familiar way to say "get me to a different state." The first step to solving that problem was the hashchange event (discussed in Chapter 15, "Events,"). HTML5 updates the history object to provide easy state management.

Where the hashchange event simply lets you know when the URL hash changed and expected you to act accordingly, the state management API actually lets you change the browser URL without loading a new page. To do so, use the history.pushState() method. This method accepts three arguments: a data object, the title of the new state, and an optional relative URL. For example:

```
let stateObject = {foo:"bar"};

history.pushState(stateObject, "My title", "baz.html");
```

As soon as pushState() executes, the state information is pushed onto the history stack and the browser's address bar changes to reflect the new relative URL. Despite this change, the browser does not make a request to the server, even though querying location.href will return exactly what's in the address bar. The second argument isn't currently used by any implementations and so it is safe to either leave it as an empty string or provide a short title. The first argument should contain all of the information necessary to correctly initialize this page state when necessary. To prevent abuse, the size of the state object is limited, typically to less than 500MB–1MB.

Since pushState() creates a new history entry, you'll notice that the Back button is enabled. When the Back button is pressed, the popstate event fires on the window object. The event object for popstate has a property called state, which contains the object that was passed into pushState() as the first argument:

```
window.addEventListener("popstate", (event) => {
  let state = event.state;
  if (state) {   // state is null when at first page load
    processState(state);
  }
});
```

Using this state, you must then reset the page into the state represented by the data in the state object (as the browser doesn't do this automatically for you). Keep in mind that when a page is first loaded, there is no state, so hitting the Back button until you get to the original page state will result in event.state being null.

You can access the current state object by using history.state. You can also update the current state information by using replaceState() and passing in the same first two arguments as pushState(). Doing so does not create a new entry in history, it just overwrites the current state:

```
history.replaceState({newFoo: "newBar"}, "New title");
```

The state object passed into pushState() or replaceState() should only contain information that can be serialized. Therefore, things like DOM elements are inappropriate for use in the state object.

> **NOTE** *When using HTML5 history state management, make sure that any "fake" URL you create using* pushState() *is backed up by a real, physical URL on the web server. Otherwise, hitting the Refresh button will result in a 404. All single-page application (SPA) frameworks must address this problem in some way via configuration on the server or client.*

SUMMARY

The Browser Object Model (BOM) is based on the window object, which represents the browser window and the viewable page area. The window object doubles as the ECMAScript Global object, so all global variables and functions become properties on it, and all native constructors and functions exist on it initially. This chapter discussed the following elements of the BOM:

➤ To reference other window objects, there are several window pointers.

➤ The location object allows programmatic access to the browser's navigation system. By setting properties, it's possible to change the browser's URL piece by piece or altogether.

➤ The replace() method allows for navigating to a new URL and replacing the currently displayed page in the browser's history.

➤ The navigator object provides information about the browser. The type of information provided depends largely on the browser being used, though some common properties, such as userAgent, are available in all browsers.

Two other objects available in the BOM perform very limited functions. The screen object provides information about the client display. This information is typically used in metrics gathering for websites. The history object offers a limited peek into the browser's history stack, allowing developers to determine how many sites are in the history stack and giving them the ability to go back or forward to any page in the history, as well as modify the history stack.

13

The Document Object Model

WHAT'S IN THIS CHAPTER?

➤   Understanding the DOM as a hierarchy of nodes

➤   Working with the various node types

➤   Using supplemental APIs such as selectors, element traversal, and HTML5

The Document Object Model (DOM) is an application programming interface (API) for HTML and XML documents. The DOM represents a document as a hierarchical tree of nodes, allowing developers to add, remove, and modify individual parts of the page. Evolving out of early Dynamic HTML (DHTML) innovations from Netscape and Microsoft, the DOM is now a truly cross-platform, language-independent way of representing and manipulating pages for markup.

DOM Level 1 became a W3C recommendation in October 1998, providing interfaces for basic document structure and querying. This chapter focuses on the features and uses of the DOM as it relates to HTML pages in the browser and the DOM JavaScript API.

HIERARCHY OF NODES

Any HTML or XML document can be represented as a hierarchy of nodes using the DOM. There are several node types, each representing different information and/or markup in the document. Each node type has different characteristics, data, and methods, and each may have relationships with other nodes. These relationships create a hierarchy that allows markup to be represented as a tree, rooted at a particular node. For instance, consider the following HTML:

```html
<html>
  <head>
    <title>Sample Page</title>
  </head>
  <body>
    <p>Hello World!</p>
  </body>
</html>
```

This simple HTML document can be represented in a hierarchy, as illustrated in Figure 13.1.

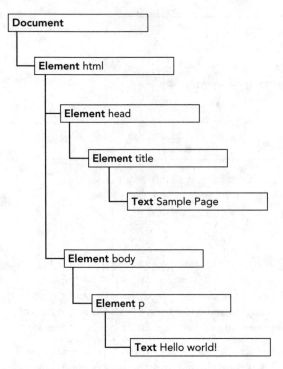

FIGURE 13.1: An HTML document hierarchy

A document node represents every document as the root. In this example, the only child of the document node is the `<html>` element, which is called the *document element*. The document element is the outermost element in the document within which all other elements exist. There can be only one document element per document. In HTML pages, the document element is always the `<html>` element. In XML, where there are no predefined elements, any element may be the document element.

Every piece of markup can be represented by a node in the tree: HTML elements are represented by element nodes, attributes are represented by attribute nodes, the document type is represented by a document type node, and comments are represented by comment nodes. In total, there are 12 node types, all of which inherit from a base type.

The Node Type

DOM Level 1 describes an interface called Node that is to be implemented by all node types in the DOM. The `Node` interface is implemented in JavaScript as the `Node` type. All node types inherit from `Node` in JavaScript, so all node types share the same basic properties and methods.

Every node has a `nodeType` property that indicates the type of node that it is. `Node` types are represented by one of the following 12 numeric constants on the `Node` type:

➤ `Node.ELEMENT_NODE` (1)

➤ `Node.ATTRIBUTE_NODE` (2)

➤ `Node.TEXT_NODE` (3)

➤ `Node.CDATA_SECTION_NODE` (4)

➤ `Node.ENTITY_REFERENCE_NODE` (5)

➤ `Node.ENTITY_NODE` (6)

➤ `Node.PROCESSING_INSTRUCTION_NODE` (7)

➤ `Node.COMMENT_NODE` (8)

➤ `Node.DOCUMENT_NODE` (9)

➤ `Node.DOCUMENT_TYPE_NODE` (10)

➤ `Node.DOCUMENT_FRAGMENT_NODE` (11)

➤ `Node.NOTATION_NODE` (12)

A node's type is easy to determine by comparing against one of these constants, as shown here:

```
if (someNode.nodeType == Node.ELEMENT_NODE){
    alert("Node is an element.");
}
```

This example compares the `someNode.nodeType` to the `Node.ELEMENT_NODE` constant. If they're equal, it means `someNode` is actually an element.

Not all node types are supported in web browsers. Developers most often work with element and text nodes. The support level and usage of each node type is discussed later in the chapter.

The *nodeName* and *nodeValue* Properties

Two properties, `nodeName` and `nodeValue`, give specific information about the node. The values of these properties are completely dependent on the node type. It's always best to test the node type before using one of these values, as the following code shows:

```
if (someNode.nodeType == 1){
  value = someNode.nodeName;    // will be the element's tag name
}
```

In this example, the node type is checked to see if the node is an element. If so, the `nodeName` value is assigned to a variable. For elements, `nodeName` is always equal to the element's tag name, and `nodeValue` is always `null`.

Node Relationships

All nodes in a document have relationships to other nodes. These relationships are described in terms of traditional family relationships as if the document tree were a family tree. In HTML, the `<body>` element is considered a child of the `<html>` element; likewise the `<html>` element is considered the parent of the `<body>` element. The `<head>` element is considered a sibling of the `<body>` element, because they both share the same immediate parent, the `<html>` element.

Each node has a `childNodes` property containing a `NodeList`. A `NodeList` is an array-like object used to store an ordered list of nodes that are accessible by position. Keep in mind that a `NodeList` is not an instance of Array even though its values can be accessed using bracket notation and the length property is present. `NodeList` objects are unique in that they are actually queries being run against the DOM structure, so changes will be reflected in `NodeList` objects automatically. It is often said that a `NodeList` is a living, breathing object rather than a snapshot of what happened at the time it was first accessed.

The following example shows how nodes stored in a `NodeList` may be accessed via bracket notation or by using the `item()` method:

```
let firstChild = someNode.childNodes[0];
let secondChild = someNode.childNodes.item(1);
let count = someNode.childNodes.length;
```

Note that using bracket notation and using the `item()` method are both acceptable practices, although most developers use bracket notation because of its similarity to arrays. Also note that the `length` property indicates the number of nodes in the `NodeList` at that time. It's possible to convert `NodeList` objects into arrays using destructuring or `Array.prototype.slice`. Consider the following example:

```
let arrayOfNodes = Array.prototype.slice.call(someNode.childNodes,0);
```

Each node has a `parentNode` property pointing to its parent in the document tree. All nodes contained within a `childNodes` list have the same parent, so each of their `parentNode` properties points to the same node. Additionally, each node within a `childNodes` list is considered to be a sibling of the other nodes in the same list. It's possible to navigate from one node in the list to another by using the `previousSibling` and `nextSibling` properties. The first node in the list has `null` for the value of its previousSibling property, and the last node in the list has null for the value of its nextSibling property, as shown in the following example:

```
if (someNode.nextSibling === null){
  alert("Last node in the parent's childNodes list.");
} else if (someNode.previousSibling === null){
  alert("First node in the parent's childNodes list.");
}
```

Note that if there's only one child node, both nextSibling and previousSibling will be null.

Another relationship exists between a parent node and its first and last child nodes. The firstChild and lastChild properties point to the first and last node in the childNodes list, respectively. The value of someNode.firstChild is always equal to someNode.childNodes[0], and the value of someNode.lastChild is always equal to someNode.childNodes[someNode.childNodes.length-1]. If there is only one child node, firstChild and lastChild point to the same node; if there are no children, then firstChild and lastChild are both null. All of these relationships help to navigate easily between nodes in a document structure. Figure 13.2 illustrates these relationships.

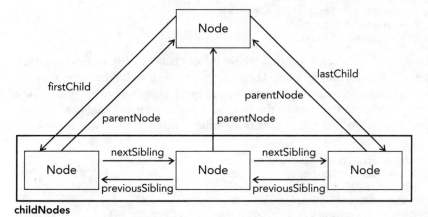

FIGURE 13.2: A diagram of the parent, child, and sibling relationships

With all of these relationships, the childNodes property is really more of a convenience than a necessity because it's possible to reach any node in a document tree by simply using the relationship pointers. Another convenience method is hasChildNodes(), which returns true if the node has one or more child nodes and is more efficient than querying the length of the childNodes list.

One final relationship is shared by every node. The ownerDocument property is a pointer to the document node that represents the entire document. Nodes are considered to be owned by the document in which they were created (typically the same in which they reside), because nodes cannot exist simultaneously in two or more documents. This property provides a quick way to access the document node without needing to traverse the node hierarchy back up to the top.

> **NOTE** *Not all node types can have child nodes even though all node types inherit from Node. The differences among node types are discussed later in this chapter.*

Manipulating Nodes

Because all relationship pointers are read-only, several methods are available to manipulate nodes. The most-often-used method is `appendChild()`, which adds a node to the end of the `childNodes` list. Doing so updates all of the relationship pointers in the newly added node, the parent node, and the previous last child in the `childNodes` list. When complete, `appendChild()` returns the newly added node. Here is an example:

```
let returnedNode = someNode.appendChild(newNode);
alert(returnedNode == newNode);          // true
alert(someNode.lastChild == newNode);    // true
```

If the node passed into `appendChild()` is already part of the document, it is removed from its previous location and placed at the new location. Even though the DOM tree is connected by a series of pointers, no DOM node may exist in more than one location in a document. So if you call `appendChild()` and pass in the first child of a parent, as the following example shows, it will end up as the last child:

```
// assume multiple children for someNode
let returnedNode = someNode.appendChild(someNode.firstChild);
alert(returnedNode == someNode.firstChild);  // false
alert(returnedNode == someNode.lastChild);   // true
```

When a node needs to be placed in a specific location within the `childNodes` list, instead of just at the end, the `insertBefore()` method may be used. The `insertBefore()` method accepts two arguments: the node to insert and a reference node. The node to insert becomes the previous sibling of the reference node and is ultimately returned by the method. If the reference node is `null`, then `insertBefore()` acts the same as `appendChild()`, as this example shows:

```
// insert as last child
returnedNode = someNode.insertBefore(newNode, null);
alert(newNode == someNode.lastChild);    // true

// insert as the new first child
returnedNode = someNode.insertBefore(newNode, someNode.firstChild);
alert(returnedNode == newNode);          // true
alert(newNode == someNode.firstChild);   // true

// insert before last child
returnedNode = someNode.insertBefore(newNode, someNode.lastChild);
alert(newNode == someNode.childNodes[someNode.childNodes.length - 2]);  // true
```

Both `appendChild()` and `insertBefore()` insert nodes without removing any. The `replaceChild()` method accepts two arguments: the node to insert and the node to replace. The node to replace is returned by the function and is removed from the document tree completely while the inserted node takes its place. Here is an example:

```
// replace first child
let returnedNode = someNode.replaceChild(newNode, someNode.firstChild);

// replace last child
returnedNode = someNode.replaceChild(newNode, someNode.lastChild);
```

When a node is inserted using `replaceChild()`, all of its relationship pointers are duplicated from the node it is replacing. Even though the replaced node is technically still owned by the same document, it no longer has a specific location in the document.

To remove a node without replacing it, you can use the `removeChild()` method. This method accepts a single argument, which is the node to remove. The removed node is then returned as the function value, as this example shows:

```
// remove first child
let formerFirstChild = someNode.removeChild(someNode.firstChild);

// remove last child
let formerLastChild = someNode.removeChild(someNode.lastChild);
```

As with `replaceChild()`, a node removed via `removeChild()` is still owned by the document but doesn't have a specific location in the document.

All four of these methods work on the immediate children of a specific node, meaning that to use them you must know the immediate parent node (which is accessible via the previously mentioned `parentNode` property). Not all node types can have child nodes, and these methods will throw errors if you attempt to use them on nodes that don't support children.

Other Methods

Two other methods are shared by all node types. The first is `cloneNode()`, which creates an exact clone of the node on which it's called. The `cloneNode()` method accepts a single Boolean argument indicating whether to do a deep copy. When the argument is `true`, a deep copy is used, cloning the node and its entire subtree; when `false`, only the initial node is cloned. The cloned node that is returned is owned by the document but has no parent node assigned. As such, the cloned node is an orphan and doesn't exist in the document until added via `appendChild()`, `insertBefore()`, or `replaceChild()`. For example, consider the following HTML:

```
<ul>
  <li>item 1</li>
  <li>item 2</li>
  <li>item 3</li>
</ul>
```

If a reference to this `<ul>` element is stored in a variable named `myList`, the following code shows the two modes of the `cloneNode()` method:

```
let deepList = myList.cloneNode(true);
alert(deepList.childNodes.length);      // 3 (IE < 9) or 7 (others)

let shallowList = myList.cloneNode(false);
alert(shallowList.childNodes.length);   // 0
```

In this example, `deepList` is filled with a deep copy of `myList`. This means `deepList` has three list items, each of which contains text. The variable `shallowList` contains a shallow copy of `myList`, so it has no child nodes.

> **NOTE** *The* `cloneNode()` *method doesn't copy JavaScript properties that you add to DOM nodes, such as event handlers. This method copies only attributes and, optionally, child nodes. Everything else is lost.*

The last remaining method is `normalize()`. Its sole job is to deal with text nodes in a document subtree. Because of parser implementations or DOM manipulations, it's possible to end up with text nodes that contain no text or text nodes that are siblings. When `normalize()` is called on a node, that node's descendants are searched for both of these circumstances. If an empty text node is found, it is removed; if text nodes are immediate siblings, they are joined into a single text node. This method is discussed further later on in this chapter.

The Document Type

JavaScript represents document nodes via the `Document` type. In browsers, the document object is an instance of `HTMLDocument` (which inherits from `Document`) and represents the entire HTML page. The document object is a property of `window` and so is accessible globally. A `Document` node has the following characteristics:

- ➤ `nodeType` is 9.

- ➤ `nodeName` is `"#document"`.

- ➤ `nodeValue` is null.

- ➤ `parentNode` is null.

- ➤ `ownerDocument` is null.

- ➤ Child nodes may be a DocumentType (maximum of one), Element (maximum of one), ProcessingInstruction, or Comment.

The `Document` type can represent HTML pages or other XML-based documents, though the most common use is through an instance of `HTMLDocument` through the `document` object. The `document` object can be used to get information about the page and to manipulate both its appearance and the underlying structure.

Document Children

Though the DOM specification states that the children of a `Document` node can be a `DocumentType`, `Element`, `ProcessingInstruction`, or Comment, there are two built-in shortcuts to child nodes. The first is the `documentElement` property, which always points to the `<html>` element in an HTML page. The document element is always represented in the `childNodes` list as well, but the `documentElement` property gives faster and more direct access to that element. Consider the following simple page:

```
<html>
  <body>

  </body>
</html>
```

When this page is parsed by a browser, the document has only one child node, which is the `<html>` element. This element is accessible from both `documentElement` and the `childNodes` list, as shown here:

```
let html = document.documentElement;       // get reference to <html>
alert(html === document.childNodes[0]);    // true
alert(html === document.firstChild);       // true
```

This example shows that the values of `documentElement`, `firstChild`, and `childNodes[0]` are all the same—all three point to the `<html>` element.

As an instance of HTMLDocument, the document object also has a body property that points to the `<body>` element directly. Because this is the element most often used by developers, `document.body` tends to be used quite frequently in JavaScript, as this example shows:

```
let body = document.body;  // get reference to <body>
```

Both `document.documentElement` and `document.body` are supported in all major browsers.

Another possible child node of a `Document` is a `DocumentType`. The `<!DOCTYPE>` tag is considered to be a separate entity from other parts of the document, and its information is accessible through the doctype property (`document.doctype` in browsers), as shown here:

```
let doctype = document.doctype;    // get reference to <!DOCTYPE>
```

Comments that appear outside of the `<html>` element are, technically, child nodes of the document. Once again, browser support varies greatly as to whether these comments will be recognized and represented appropriately. Consider the following HTML page:

```
<!-- first comment -->
<html>
  <body>

  </body>
</html>
<!-- second comment -->
```

This page seems to have three child nodes: a comment, the `<html>` element, and another comment. Logically, you would expect `document.childNodes` to have three items corresponding to what appears in the code. In practice, however, browsers handle comments outside of the `<html>` element in different ways with respect to ignoring one or both of the comment nodes.

For the most part, the `appendChild()`, `removeChild()`, and `replaceChild()` methods aren't used on document because the document type (if present) is read-only and there can be only one element child node (which is already present).

Document Information

The document object, as an instance of HTMLDocument, has several additional properties that standard Document objects do not have. These properties provide information about the web page that is loaded. The first such property is `title`, which contains the text in the `<title>` element and is displayed in the title bar or tab of the browser window. This property can be used to retrieve the current page title and to change the page title such that the changes are reflected in the browser title bar. Changing the value of the title property does not change the `<title>` element at all. Here is an example:

```
// get the document title
let originalTitle = document.title;

// set the document title
document.title = "New page title";
```

The next three properties are all related to the request for the web page: URL, domain, and referrer. The URL property contains the complete URL of the page (the URL in the address bar), the domain property contains just the domain name of the page, and the referrer property gives the URL of the page that linked to this page. The referrer property may be an empty string if there is no referrer to the page. All of this information is available in the HTTP header of the request and is simply made available in JavaScript via these properties, as shown in the following example:

```
// get the complete URL
let url = document.URL;

// get the domain
let domain = document.domain;

// get the referrer
let referrer = document.referrer;
```

The URL and domain properties are related. For example, if document.URL is http://www.wrox .com/WileyCDA/, then document.domain will be www.wrox.com.

Of these three properties, the domain property is the only one that can be set. There are some restrictions as to what the value of domain can be set to because of security issues. If the URL contains a subdomain, such as p2p.wrox.com, the domain may be set only to "wrox.com" (the same is true when the URL contains "www" such as www.wrox.com). The property can never be set to a domain that the URL doesn't contain, as this example demonstrates:

```
// page from p2p.wrox.com

document.domain = "wrox.com";        // succeeds

document.domain = "nczonline.net";   // error!
```

The ability to set document.domain is useful when there is a frame or iframe on the page from a different subdomain. Pages from different subdomains can't communicate with one another via JavaScript because of cross-domain security restrictions. By setting document.domain in each page to the same value, the pages can access JavaScript objects from each other. For example, if a page is loaded from www.wrox.com and it has an iframe with a page loaded from p2p.wrox.com, each page's document.domain string will be different, and the outer page and the inner page are restricted from accessing each other's JavaScript objects. If the document.domain value in each page is set to "wrox .com", the pages can then communicate.

A further restriction in the browser disallows tightening of the domain property once it has been loosened. This means you cannot set `document.domain` to `"wrox.com"` and then try to set it back to `"p2p.wrox.com"` because the latter would cause an error, as shown here:

```
// page from p2p.wrox.com

document.domain = "wrox.com";        // loosen - succeeds

document.domain = "p2p.wrox.com";    // tighten - error!
```

Locating Elements

Perhaps the most common DOM activity is to retrieve references to a specific element or sets of elements to perform certain operations. This capability is provided via a number of methods on the document object. The `Document` type provides two methods to this end: `getElementById()` and `getElementsByTagName()`.

The `getElementById()` method accepts a single argument—the ID of an element to retrieve—and returns the element if found, or `null` if an element with that ID doesn't exist. The ID must be an exact match, including character case, to the id attribute of an element on the page. Consider the following element:

```
<div id="myDiv">Some text</div>
```

This element can be retrieved using the following code:

```
let div = document.getElementById("myDiv");  // retrieve reference to the <div>
```

The following code, however, would return `null`:

```
let div = document.getElementById("mydiv");  // null
```

If more than one element with the same ID are in a page, `getElementById()` returns the element that appears first in the document.

The `getElementsByTagName()` method is another commonly used method for retrieving element references. It accepts a single argument—the tag name of the elements to retrieve—and returns a `NodeList` containing zero or more elements. In HTML documents, this method returns an `HTMLCollection` object, which is very similar to a `NodeList` in that it is considered a "live" collection. For example, the following code retrieves all `<img>` elements in the page and returns an `HTMLCollection`:

```
let images = document.getElementsByTagName("img");
```

This code stores an `HTMLCollection` object in the `images` variable. As with `NodeList` objects, items in `HTMLCollection` objects can be accessed using bracket notation or the `item()` method. The number of elements in the object can be retrieved via the `length` property, as this example demonstrates:

```
alert(images.length);         // output the number of images
alert(images[0].src);         // output the src attribute of the first image
alert(images.item(0).src);    // output the src attribute of the first image
```

The `HTMLCollection` object has an additional method, `namedItem()`, that lets you reference an item in the collection via its `name` attribute. For example, suppose you had the following `<img>` element in a page:

```
<img src="myimage.gif" name="myImage">
```

A reference to this `<img>` element can be retrieved from the `images` variable like this:

```
let myImage = images.namedItem("myImage");
```

In this way, an `HTMLCollection` gives you access to named items in addition to indexed items, making it easier to get exactly the elements you want. You can also access named items by using bracket notation, as shown in the following example:

```
let myImage = images["myImage"];
```

For `HTMLCollection` objects, bracket notation can be used with either numeric or string indices. Behind the scenes, a numeric index calls `item()` and a string index calls `namedItem()`.

To retrieve all elements in the document, pass in `*` to `getElementsByTagName()`. The asterisk is generally understood to mean "all" in JavaScript and Cascading Style Sheets (CSS). Here's an example:

```
let allElements = document.getElementsByTagName("*");
```

This single line of code returns an `HTMLCollection` containing all of the elements in the order in which they appear. So the first item is the `<html>` element, the second is the `<head>` element, and so on.

> **NOTE** *Even though the specification states that tag names are case-sensitive, the* `getElementsByTagName()` *method is case-insensitive for maximum compatibility with existing HTML pages. When used in XML pages, including XHTML,* `getElementsByTagName()` *switches to case-sensitive mode.*

A third method, which is defined on the `HTMLDocument` type only, is `getElementsByName()`. As its name suggests, this method returns all elements that have a given name attribute. The `getElementsByName()` method is most often used with radio buttons, all of which must have the same name to ensure the correct value gets sent to the server, as the following example shows:

```
<fieldset>
  <legend>Which color do you prefer?</legend>
  <ul>
    <li>
      <input type="radio" value="red" name="color" id="colorRed">
      <label for="colorRed">Red</label>
    </li>
    <li>
      <input type="radio" value="green" name="color" id="colorGreen">
      <label for="colorGreen">Green</label>
    </li>
    <li>
      <input type="radio" value="blue" name="color" id="colorBlue">
      <label for="colorBlue">Blue</label>
```

```
    </li>
  </ul>
</fieldset>
```

In this code, the radio buttons all have a name attribute of "color" even though their IDs are different. The IDs allow the `<label>` elements to be applied to the radio buttons, and the name attribute ensures that only one of the three values will be sent to the server. These radio buttons can all then be retrieved using the following line of code:

```
let radios = document.getElementsByName("color");
```

As with `getElementsByTagName()`, the `getElementsByName()` method returns an `HTMLCollection`. In this context, however, the `namedItem()` method always retrieves the first item (since all items have the same name).

Special Collections

The `document` object has several special collections. Each of these collections is an `HTMLCollection` object and provides faster access to common parts of the document, as described here:

➤ `document.anchors`—Contains all `<a>` elements with a name attribute in the document.

➤ `document.applets`—Contains all `<applet>` elements in the document. This collection is deprecated because the `<applet>` element is no longer recommended for use.

➤ `document.forms`—Contains all `<form>` elements in the document. The same as `document.getElementsByTagName("form")`.

➤ `document.images`—Contains all `<img>` elements in the document. The same as `document.getElementsByTagName("img")`.

➤ `document.links`—Contains all `<a>` elements with an `href` attribute in the document.

These special collections are always available on `HTMLDocument` objects and, like all `HTMLCollection` objects, are constantly updated to match the contents of the current document.

Document Writing

One of the older capabilities of the document object is the ability to write to the output stream of a web page. This capability comes in the form of four methods: `write()`, `writeln()`, `open()`, and `close()`. The `write()` and `writeln()` methods each accept a string argument to write to the output stream. `write()` simply adds the text as is, whereas `writeln()` appends a new-line character (`\n`) to the end of the string. These two methods can be used as a page is being loaded to dynamically add content to the page, as shown in the following example:

```
<html>
<head>
  <title>document.write() Example</title>
</head>
<body>
  <p>The current date and time is:
  <script type="text/javascript">
```

```
      document.write("<strong>" + (new Date()).toString() + "</strong>");
    </script>
  </p>
  </body>
  </html>
```

This example outputs the current date and time as the page is being loaded. The date is enclosed by a `<strong>` element, which is treated the same as if it were included in the HTML portion of the page, meaning that a DOM element is created and can later be accessed. Any HTML that is output via `write()` or `writeln()` is treated this way.

The `write()` and `writeln()` methods are often used to dynamically include external resources such as JavaScript files. When including JavaScript files, you must be sure not to include the string `"</script>"` directly, as the following example demonstrates, because it will be interpreted as the end of a script block and the rest of the code won't execute.

```
<html>
<head>
  <title>document.write() Example</title>
</head>
<body>
  <script type="text/javascript">
    document.write("<script type=\"text/javascript\" src=\"file.js\">" +
      "</script>");
  </script>
</body>
</html>
```

Even though this file looks correct, the closing `"</script>"` string is interpreted as matching the outermost `<script>` tag, meaning that the text `");` will appear on the page. To avoid this, you simply need to change the string, as shown here:

```
<html>
<head>
  <title>document.write() Example</title>
</head>
<body>
  <script type="text/javascript">
    document.write("<script type=\"text/javascript\" src=\"file.js\">" +
      "<\/script>");
  </script>
</body>
</html>
```

The string `"<\/script>"` no longer registers as a closing tag for the outermost `<script>` tag, so there is no extra content output to the page.

The previous examples use `document.write()` to output content directly into the page as it's being rendered. If `document.write()` is called after the page has been completely loaded, the content overwrites the entire page, as shown in the following example:

```
<html>
<head>
  <title>document.write() Example</title>
</head>
```

```
<body>
  <p>This is some content that you won't get to see because it will be
  overwritten.</p>
  <script type="text/javascript">
    window.onload = function(){
      document.write("Hello world!");
    };
  </script>
</body>
</html>
```

In this example, the `window.onload` event handler is used to delay the execution of the function until the page is completely loaded. When that happens, the string `"Hello world!"` overwrites the entire page content.

The `open()` and `close()` methods are used to open and close the web page output stream, respectively. Neither method is required to be used when `write()` or `writeln()` is used during the course of page loading.

The Element Type

Next to the `Document` type, the `Element` type is most often used in web programming. The `Element` type represents an XML or HTML element, providing access to information such as its tag name, children, and attributes. An `Element` node has the following characteristics:

➤ `nodeType` is 1.

➤ `nodeName` is the element's tag name.

➤ `nodeValue` is `null`.

➤ `parentNode` may be a `Document` or `Element`.

➤ Child nodes may be `Element`, `Text`, `Comment`, `ProcessingInstruction`, `CDATASection`, or `EntityReference`.

An element's tag name is accessed via the `nodeName` property or by using the `tagName` property; both properties return the same value (the latter is typically used for clarity). Consider the following element:

```
<div id="myDiv"></div>
```

This element can be retrieved and its tag name accessed in the following way:

```
let div = document.getElementById("myDiv");
alert(div.tagName);  // "DIV"
alert(div.tagName == div.nodeName);    // true
```

The element in question has a tag name of div and an ID of `"myDiv"`. Note, however, that div `.tagName` actually outputs "DIV" instead of `"div"`. When used with HTML, the tag name is always represented in all uppercase; when used with XML (including XHTML), the tag name always matches the case of the source code. If you aren't sure whether your script will be on an HTML or XML document, it's best to convert tag names to a common case before comparison.

HTML Elements

All HTML elements are represented by the `HTMLElement` type, either directly or through subtyping. The `HTMLElement` inherits directly from Element and adds several properties. Each property represents one of the following standard attributes that are available on every HTML element:

➤ `id`—A unique identifier for the element in the document.

➤ `title`—Additional information about the element, typically represented as a tooltip.

➤ `lang`—The language code for the contents of the element (rarely used).

➤ `dir`—The direction of the language, "ltr" (left-to-right) or "rtl" (right-to-left); also rarely used.

➤ `className`—The equivalent of the class attribute, which is used to specify CSS classes on an element. The property could not be named class because class is an ECMAScript reserved word.

Each of these properties can be used both to retrieve the corresponding attribute value and to change the value. Consider the following HTML element:

```
<div id="myDiv" class="bd" title="Body text" lang="en" dir="ltr"></div>
```

All of the information specified by this element may be retrieved using the following JavaScript code:

```
let div = document.getElementById("myDiv");
alert(div.id);          // "myDiv"
alert(div.className);   // "bd"
alert(div.title);       // "Body text"
alert(div.lang);        // "en"
alert(div.dir);         // "ltr"
```

It's also possible to use the following code to change each of the attributes by assigning new values to the properties:

```
div.id = "someOtherId";
div.className = "ft";
div.title = "Some other text";
div.lang = "fr";
div.dir ="rtl";
```

Not all of the properties affect the page when overwritten. Changes to id or lang will be transparent to the user (assuming no CSS styles are based on these values), whereas changes to title will be apparent only when the mouse is moved over the element. Changes to `dir` will cause the text on the page to be aligned to either the left or the right as soon as the property is written. Changes to `className` may appear immediately if the class has different CSS style information than the previous one.

Getting Attributes

Each element may have zero or more attributes, which are typically used to give extra information about the particular element or its contents. The three primary DOM methods for working with attributes are `getAttribute()`, `setAttribute()`, and `removeAttribute()`. These methods are intended to work on any attribute, including those defined as properties on the HTMLElement type. Here's an example:

```
let div = document.getElementById("myDiv");
alert(div.getAttribute("id"));      // "myDiv"
alert(div.getAttribute("class"));   // "bd"
alert(div.getAttribute("title"));   // "Body text"
alert(div.getAttribute("lang"));    // "en"
alert(div.getAttribute("dir"));     // "ltr"
```

Note that the attribute name passed into getAttribute() is exactly the same as the actual attribute name, so you pass in "class" to get the value of the class attribute (not className, which is necessary when the attribute is accessed as an object property). If the attribute with the given name doesn't exist, getAttribute() always returns null.

The getAttribute() method can also retrieve the value of custom attributes that aren't part of the formal HTML language. Consider the following element:

```
<div id="myDiv" my_special_attribute="hello!"></div>
```

In this element, a custom attribute named my_special_attribute is defined to have a value of "hello!". This value can be retrieved using getAttribute() just like any other attribute, as shown here:

```
let value = div.getAttribute("my_special_attribute");
```

Note that attribute names are case-insensitive, so "ID" and "id" are considered the same attribute. Also note that, according to HTML5, custom attributes should be prepended with data- in order to validate.

All attributes on an element are also accessible as properties of the DOM element object itself. There are, of course, the five properties defined on HTMLElement that map directly to corresponding attributes, but all recognized (noncustom) attributes get added to the object as properties. Consider the following element:

```
<div id="myDiv" align="left" my_special_attribute="hello"></div>
```

Because id and align are recognized attributes for the <div> element in HTML, they will be represented by properties on the element object. The my_special_attribute attribute is custom and so won't show up as a property on the element.

Two types of attributes have property names that don't map directly to the same value returned by getAttribute(). The first attribute is style, which is used to specify stylistic information about the element using CSS. When accessed via getAttribute(), the style attribute contains CSS text while accessing it via a property that returns an object. The style property is used to programmatically access the styling of the element and so does not map directly to the style attribute.

The second category of attribute that behaves differently is event-handler attributes such as onclick. When used on an element, the onclick attribute contains JavaScript code, and that code string is returned when using getAttribute(). When the onclick property is accessed, however, it returns a JavaScript function (or null if the attribute isn't specified). This is because onclick and other event-handling properties are provided such that functions can be assigned to them.

Because of these differences, developers tend to forego `getAttribute()` when programming the DOM in JavaScript and instead use the object properties exclusively. The `getAttribute()` method is used primarily to retrieve the value of a custom attribute.

Setting Attributes

The sibling method to `getAttribute()` is `setAttribute()`, which accepts two arguments: the name of the attribute to set and the value to set it to. If the attribute already exists, `setAttribute()` replaces its value with the one specified; if the attribute doesn't exist, `setAttribute()` creates it and sets its value. Here is an example:

```
div.setAttribute("id", "someOtherId");
div.setAttribute("class", "ft");
div.setAttribute("title", "Some other text");
div.setAttribute("lang","fr");
div.setAttribute("dir", "rtl");
```

The `setAttribute()` method works with both HTML attributes and custom attributes in the same way. Attribute names get normalized to lowercase when set using this method, so `"ID"` ends up as `"id"`.

Because all attributes are properties, assigning directly to the property can set the attribute values, as shown here:

```
div.id = "someOtherId";
div.align = "left";
```

Note that adding a custom property to a DOM element, as the following example shows, does not automatically make it an attribute of the element:

```
div.mycolor = "red";
alert(div.getAttribute("mycolor"));    // null
```

This example adds a custom property named `mycolor` and sets its value to `"red"`. In most browsers, this property does not automatically become an attribute on the element, so calling `getAttribute()` to retrieve an attribute with the same name returns `null`.

The last method is `removeAttribute()`, which removes the attribute from the element altogether. This does more than just clear the attribute's value; it completely removes the attribute from the element, as shown here:

```
div.removeAttribute("class");
```

This method isn't used very frequently, but it can be useful for specifying exactly which attributes to include when serializing a DOM element.

The *attributes* Property

The `Element` type is the only DOM node type that uses the attributes property. The attributes property contains a `NamedNodeMap`, which is a "live" collection similar to a `NodeList`. Every attribute on an element is represented by an `Attr` node, each of which is stored in the `NamedNodeMap` object. A `NamedNodeMap` object has the following methods:

➤ `getNamedItem(name)`—Returns the node whose `nodeName` property is equal to `name`.

➤ `removeNamedItem(name)`—Removes the node whose `nodeName` property is equal to `name` from the list.

➤ `setNamedItem(node)`—Adds the node to the list, indexing it by its `nodeName` property.

➤ `item(pos)`—Returns the node in the numerical position `pos`.

Each node in the `attributes` property is a node whose `nodeName` is the attribute name and whose `nodeValue` is the attribute's value. To retrieve the `id` attribute of an element, you can use the following code:

```
let id = element.attributes.getNamedItem("id").nodeValue;
```

Following is a shorthand notation for accessing attributes by name using bracket notation:

```
let id = element.attributes["id"].nodeValue;
```

It's possible to use this notation to set attribute values as well, retrieving the attribute node and then setting the `nodeValue` to a new value, as this example shows:

```
element.attributes["id"].nodeValue = "someOtherId";
```

The `removeNamedItem()` method functions the same as the `removeAttribute()` method on the element—it simply removes the attribute with the given name. The following example shows how the sole difference is that `removeNamedItem()` returns the `Attr` node that represented the attribute:

```
let oldAttr = element.attributes.removeNamedItem("id");
```

The `setNamedItem()` is a rarely used method that allows you to add a new attribute to the element by passing in an attribute node, as shown in this example:

```
element.attributes.setNamedItem(newAttr);
```

Generally speaking, because of their simplicity, the `getAttribute()`, `removeAttribute()`, and `setAttribute()` methods are preferred to using any of the preceding attribute methods.

The one area where the attributes property is useful is to iterate over the attributes on an element. This is done most often when serializing a DOM structure into an XML or HTML string. The following code iterates over each attribute on an element and constructs a string in the format *attribute1="value1" attribute2="value2"*:

```
function outputAttributes(element) {
  let pairs = [];

  for (let i = 0, len = element.attributes.length; i < len; ++i) {
    const attribute = element.attributes[i];
    pairs.push(`${attribute.nodeName}="${attribute.nodeValue}"`);
  }

  return pairs.join(" ");
}
```

This function uses an array to store the name-value pairs until the end, concatenating them with a space in between. (This technique is frequently used when serializing into long strings.) Using the `attributes.length` property, the `for` loop iterates over each attribute, outputting the name and value into a string. Browsers differ on the order in which they return attributes in the attributes object. The order in which the attributes appear in the HTML or XML code may not necessarily be the order in which they appear in the attributes object.

Creating Elements

New elements can be created by using the `document.createElement()` method. This method accepts a single argument, which is the tag name of the element to create. In HTML documents, the tag name is case-insensitive, whereas it is case-sensitive in XML documents (including XHTML). To create a `<div>` element, the following code can be used:

```
let div = document.createElement("div");
```

Using the `createElement()` method creates a new element and sets its `ownerDocument` property. At this point, you can manipulate the element's attributes, add more children to it, and so on. Consider the following example:

```
div.id = "myNewDiv";
div.className = "box";
```

Setting these attributes on the new element assigns information only. Because the element is not part of the document tree, it doesn't affect the browser's display. The element can be added to the document tree using `appendChild()`, `insertBefore()`, or `replaceChild()`. The following code adds the newly created element to the document's `<body>` element:

```
document.body.appendChild(div);
```

Once the element has been added to the document tree, the browser renders it immediately. Any changes to the element after this point are immediately reflected by the browser.

Element Children

Elements may have any number of children and descendants because elements may be children of elements. The `childNodes` property contains all of the immediate children of the element, which may be other elements, text nodes, comments, or processing instructions. There is a significant difference between browsers regarding the identification of these nodes. For example, consider the following code:

```
<ul id="myList">
  <li>Item 1</li>
  <li>Item 2</li>
  <li>Item 3</li>
</ul>
```

When this code is parsed, the `<ul>` element will have seven elements: three `<li>` elements and four text nodes representing the white space between `<li>` elements. If the white space between elements is removed, as the following example demonstrates, all browsers return the same number of child nodes:

```
<ul id="myList"><li>Item 1</li><li>Item 2</li><li>Item 3</li></ul>
```

Using this code, browsers return three child nodes for the `<ul>` element. Oftentimes, it's necessary to check the `nodeType` before performing an action, as the following example shows:

```
for (let i = 0, len = element.childNodes.length; i < len; ++i) {
  if (element.childNodes[i].nodeType == 1) {
    // do processing
  }
}
```

This code loops through each child node of a particular element and performs an operation only if `nodeType` is equal to 1 (the element node type identified).

To get child nodes and other descendants with a particular tag name, elements also support the `getElementsByTagName()` method. When used on an element, this method works exactly the same as the document version except that the search is rooted on the element, so only descendants of that element are returned. In the `<ul>` code earlier in this section, all `<li>` elements can be retrieved using the following code:

```
let ul = document.getElementById("myList");
let items = ul.getElementsByTagName("li");
```

Keep in mind that this works because the `<ul>` element has only one level of descendants. If there were more levels, all `<li>` elements contained in all levels would be returned.

The Text Type

Text nodes are represented by the `Text` type and contain plain text that is interpreted literally and may contain escaped HTML characters but no HTML code. A Text node has the following characteristics:

➤ `nodeType` is 3.

➤ `nodeName` is `"#text"`.

➤ `nodeValue` is text contained in the node.

➤ `parentNode` is an `Element`.

➤ Child nodes are not supported.

The text contained in a `Text` node may be accessed via either the `nodeValue` property or the `data` property, both of which contain the same value. Changes to either `nodeValue` or `data` are reflected in the other as well. The following methods allow for manipulation of the text in the node:

➤ `appendData(text)`—Appends `text` to the end of the node.

➤ `deleteData(offset, count)`—Deletes `count` number of characters starting at position `offset`.

➤ `insertData(offset, text)`—Inserts `text` at position `offset`.

➤ `replaceData(offset, count, text)`—Replaces the text starting at `offset` through `offset + count` with `text`.

➤ `splitText(offset)`—Splits the text node into two text nodes separated at position `offset`.

➤ `substringData(offset, count)`—Extracts a string from the text beginning at position `offset` and continuing until `offset + count`.

In addition to these methods, the length property returns the number of characters in the node. This value is the same as using `nodeValue.length` or `data.length`.

By default, every element that may contain content will have at most one text node when content is present. Here is an example:

```
<!-- no content, so no text node -->
<div></div>

<!-- white space content, so one text node -->
<div> </div>

<!-- content, so one text node -->
<div>Hello World!</div>
```

The first `<div>` element in this code has no content, so there is no text node. Any content between the opening and closing tags means that a text node must be created, so the second `<div>` element has a single text node as a child even though its content is white space. The text node's `nodeValue` is a single space. The third `<div>` also has a single text node whose `nodeValue` is `"Hello World!"`. The following code lets you access this node:

```
let textNode = div.firstChild;  // or div.childNodes[0]
```

Once a reference to the text node is retrieved, it can be changed like this:

```
div.firstChild.nodeValue = "Some other message";
```

As long as the node is currently in the document tree, the changes to the text node will be reflected immediately. Another note about changing the value of a text node is that the string is HTML- or XML-encoded (depending on the type of document), meaning that any less-than symbols, greater-than symbols, or quotation marks are escaped, as shown in this example:

```
// outputs as "Some <strong>other</strong> message"
div.firstChild.nodeValue = "Some <strong>other</strong> message";
```

This is an effective way of HTML-encoding a string before inserting it into the DOM document.

Creating Text Nodes

New text nodes can be created using the `document.createTextNode()` method, which accepts a single argument—the text to be inserted into the node. As with setting the value of an existing text node, the text will be HTML- or XML-encoded, as shown in this example:

```
let textNode = document.createTextNode("<strong>Hello</strong> world!");
```

When a new text node is created, its `ownerDocument` property is set, but it does not appear in the browser window until it is added to a node in the document tree. The following code creates a new `<div>` element and adds a message to it:

```
let element = document.createElement("div");
element.className = "message";

let textNode = document.createTextNode("Hello world!");
element.appendChild(textNode);

document.body.appendChild(element);
```

This example creates a new `<div>` element and assigns it a class of `"message"`. Then a text node is created and added to that element. The last step is to add the element to the document's body, which makes both the element and the text node appear in the browser.

Typically, elements have only one text node as a child. However, it is possible to have multiple text nodes as children, as this example demonstrates:

```
let element = document.createElement("div");
element.className = "message";

let textNode = document.createTextNode("Hello world!");
element.appendChild(textNode);

let anotherTextNode = document.createTextNode("Yippee!");
element.appendChild(anotherTextNode);

document.body.appendChild(element);
```

When a text node is added as a sibling of another text node, the text in those nodes is displayed without any space between them.

Normalizing Text Nodes

Sibling text nodes can be confusing in DOM documents because there is no simple text string that can't be represented in a single text node. Still, it is not uncommon to come across sibling text nodes in DOM documents, so there is a method to join sibling text nodes together. This method is called `normalize()`, and it exists on the `Node` type (and thus is available on all node types). When `normalize()` is called on a parent of two or more text nodes, those nodes are merged into one text node whose `nodeValue` is equal to the concatenation of the `nodeValue` properties of each text node. Here's an example:

```
let element = document.createElement("div");
element.className = "message";

let textNode = document.createTextNode("Hello world!");
element.appendChild(textNode);

let anotherTextNode = document.createTextNode("Yippee!");
```

```
element.appendChild(anotherTextNode);

document.body.appendChild(element);

alert(element.childNodes.length);      // 2

element.normalize();
alert(element.childNodes.length);      // 1
alert(element.firstChild.nodeValue);   // "Hello world!Yippee!"
```

When the browser parses a document, it will never create sibling text nodes. Sibling text nodes can appear only by programmatic DOM manipulation.

Splitting Text Nodes

The Text type has a method that does the opposite of normalize(): the splitText() method splits a text node into two text nodes, separating the nodeValue at a given offset. The original text node contains the text up to the specified offset, and the new text node contains the rest of the text. The method returns the new text node, which has the same parentNode as the original. Consider the following example:

```
let element = document.createElement("div");
element.className = "message";

let textNode = document.createTextNode("Hello world!");
element.appendChild(textNode);

document.body.appendChild(element);

let newNode = element.firstChild.splitText(5);
alert(element.firstChild.nodeValue);   // "Hello"
alert(newNode.nodeValue);              // " world!"
alert(element.childNodes.length);      // 2
```

In this example, the text node containing the text "Hello world!" is split into two text nodes at position 5. Position 5 contains the space between "Hello" and "world!", so the original text node has the string "Hello" and the new one has the text " world!" (including the space).

Splitting text nodes is used most often with DOM parsing techniques for extracting data from text nodes.

The Comment Type

Comments are represented in the DOM by the Comment type. A Comment node has the following characteristics:

➤   nodeType is 8.

➤   nodeName is "#comment".

➤   nodeValue is the content of the comment.

➤   parentNode is a Document or Element.

➤   Child nodes are not supported.

The Comment type inherits from the same base as the Text type, so it has all of the same string-manipulation methods except splitText(). Also similar to the Text type, the actual content of the comment may be retrieved using either nodeValue or the data property.

A comment node can be accessed as a child node from its parent. Consider the following HTML code:

```
<div id="myDiv"><!-- A comment --></div>
```

In this case, the comment is a child node of the <div> element, which means it can be accessed like this:

```
let div = document.getElementById("myDiv");
let comment = div.firstChild;
alert(comment.data);  // "A comment"
```

Comment nodes can also be created using the document.createComment() method and passing in the comment text, as shown in the following code:

```
let comment = document.createComment("A comment");
```

Not surprisingly, comment nodes are rarely accessed or created, because they serve very little purpose algorithmically. Additionally, browsers don't recognize comments that exist after the closing </html> tag. If you need to access comment nodes, make sure they appear as descendants of the <html> element.

The CDATASection Type

CDATA sections are specific to XML-based documents and are represented by the CDATASection type. Similar to Comment, the CDATASection type inherits from the base Text type, so it has all of the same string manipulation methods except for splitText(). A CDATASection node has the following characteristics:

➤ nodeType is 4.

➤ nodeName is "#cdata-section".

➤ nodeValue is the contents of the CDATA section.

➤ parentNode is a Document or Element.

➤ Child nodes are not supported.

CDATA sections are valid only in XML documents, so most browsers will incorrectly parse a CDATA section into either a Comment or an Element. Consider the following:

```
<div id="myDiv"><![CDATA[This is some content.]]></div>
```

In this example, a CDATASection node should exist as the first child of the <div>; however, none of the four major browsers interpret it as such. Even in valid XHTML pages, the browsers don't properly support embedded CDATA sections.

True XML documents allow the creation of CDATA sections using document.createCDataSection() and pass in the node's content.

The DocumentType Type

A DocumentType object contains all of the information about the document's doctype and has the following characteristics:

➤ nodeType is 10.

➤ nodeName is the name of the doctype.

➤ nodeValue is null.

➤ parentNode is a Document.

➤ Child nodes are not supported.

DocumentType objects cannot be created dynamically in DOM Level 1; they are created only as the document's code is being parsed. For browsers that support it, the DocumentType object is stored in document.doctype. DOM Level 1 describes three properties for DocumentType objects: name, which is the name of the doctype; entities, which is a NamedNodeMap of entities described by the doctype; and notations, which is a NamedNodeMap of notations described by the doctype. Because documents in browsers typically use an HTML or XHTML doctype, the entities and notations lists are typically empty. (They are filled only with inline doctypes.) For all intents and purposes, the name property is the only useful one available. This property is filled with the name of the doctype, which is the text that appears immediately after <!DOCTYPE. Consider the following HTML 4.01 strict doctype:

```
<!DOCTYPE HTML PUBLIC "-// W3C// DTD HTML 4.01// EN"
    "http:// www.w3.org/TR/html4/strict.dtd">
```

For this doctype, the name property is "HTML":

```
alert(document.doctype.name); // "HTML"
```

The DocumentFragment Type

Of all the node types, the DocumentFragment type is the only one that has no representation in markup. The DOM defines a document fragment as a "lightweight" document, capable of containing and manipulating nodes without all of the additional overhead of a complete document. DocumentFragment nodes have the following characteristics:

➤ nodeType is 11.

➤ nodeName is "#document-fragment".

➤ nodeValue is null.

➤ parentNode is null.

➤ Child nodes may be Element, ProcessingInstruction, Comment, Text, CDATASection, or EntityReference.

A document fragment cannot be added to a document directly. Instead, it acts as a repository for other nodes that may need to be added to the document. Document fragments are created using the `document.createDocumentFragment()` method, shown here:

```
let fragment = document.createDocumentFragment();
```

Document fragments inherit all methods from Node and are typically used to perform DOM manipulations that are to be applied to a document. If a node from the document is added to a document fragment, that node is removed from the document tree and won't be rendered by the browser. New nodes that are added to a document fragment are also not part of the document tree. The contents of a document fragment can be added to a document via `appendChild()` or `insertBefore()`. When a document fragment is passed in as an argument to either of these methods, all of the document fragment's child nodes are added in that spot; the document fragment itself is never added to the document tree. For example, consider the following HTML:

```
<ul id="myList"></ul>
```

Suppose you would like to add three list items to this `<ul>` element. Adding each item directly to the element causes the browser to rerender the page with the new information. To avoid this, the following code example uses a document fragment to create the list items and then add them all at the same time:

```
let fragment = document.createDocumentFragment();
let ul = document.getElementById("myList");

for (let i = 0; i < 3; ++i) {
  let li = document.createElement("li");
  li.appendChild(document.createTextNode(`Item ${i + 1}`));
  fragment.appendChild(li);
}

ul.appendChild(fragment);
```

This example begins by creating a document fragment and retrieving a reference to the `<ul>` element. The `for` loop creates three list items, each with text indicating which item they are. To do this, an `<li>` element is created and then a text node is created and added to that element. The `<li>` element is then added to the document fragment using `appendChild()`. When the loop is complete, all of the items are added to the `<ul>` element by calling `appendChild()` and passing in the document fragment. At that point, the document fragment's child nodes are all removed and placed onto the `<ul>` element.

The Attr Type

Element attributes are represented by the `Attr` type in the DOM. The `Attr` type constructor and prototype are accessible in all browsers. Technically, attributes are nodes that exist in an element's attributes property. Attribute nodes have the following characteristics:

➤ `nodeType` is 11.

➤ `nodeName` is the attribute name.

➤ `nodeValue` is the attribute value.

➤ `parentNode` is `null`.

➤ Child nodes are not supported in HTML.

➤ Child nodes may be `Text` or `EntityReference` in XML.

Even though they are nodes, attributes are not considered part of the DOM document tree. Attribute nodes are rarely referenced directly, with most developers favoring the use of `getAttribute()`, `setAttribute()`, and `removeAttribute()`.

There are three properties on an `Attr` object: `name`, which is the attribute name (same as `nodeName`); `value`, which is the attribute value (same as `nodeValue`); and `specified`, which is a Boolean value indicating if the attribute was specified in code or if it is a default value.

New attribute nodes can be created by using `document.createAttribute()` and passing in the name of the attribute. For example, to add an align attribute to an element, the following code can be used:

```
let attr = document.createAttribute("align");
attr.value = "left";
element.setAttributeNode(attr);

alert(element.attributes["align"].value);        // "left"
alert(element.getAttributeNode("align").value);  // "left"
alert(element.getAttribute("align"));            // "left"
```

In this example, a new attribute node is created. The name property is assigned by the call to `createAttribute()`, so there is no need to assign it directly afterward. The value property is then assigned to `"left"`. To add the newly created attribute to an element, you can use the element's `setAttributeNode()` method. Once the attribute is added, it can be accessed in any number of ways: via the attributes property, using `getAttributeNode()`, or using `getAttribute()`. Both attributes and `getAttributeNode()` return the actual `Attr` node for the attribute, whereas `getAttribute()` returns only the attribute value.

> **NOTE** *There is really not a good reason to access attribute nodes directly. The get* `Attribute()`, `setAttribute()`, *and* `removeAttribute()` *methods are preferable over manipulating attribute nodes.*

WORKING WITH THE DOM

In many cases, working with the DOM is fairly straightforward, making it easy to re-create with JavaScript what normally would be created using HTML code. There are, however, times when using the DOM is not as simple as it may appear. Browsers are filled with hidden gotchas and incompatibilities that make coding certain parts of the DOM more complicated than coding its other parts.

Dynamic Scripts

The `<script>` element is used to insert JavaScript code into the page, either by using the `src` attribute to include an external file or by including text inside the element itself. Dynamic scripts are those that don't exist when the page is loaded but are included later by using the DOM. As with the HTML element, there are two ways to do this: pulling in an external file or inserting text directly.

Dynamically loading an external JavaScript file works as you would expect. Consider the following `<script>` element:

```
<script src="foo.js"></script>
```

The DOM code to create this node is as follows:

```
let script = document.createElement("script");
script.src = "foo.js";
document.body.appendChild(script);
```

As you can see, the DOM code exactly mirrors the HTML code that it represents. Note that the external file is not downloaded until the `<script>` element is added to the page on the last line. The element could be added to the `<head>` element as well, though this has the same effect. This process can be generalized into the following function:

```
function loadScript(url) {
  let script = document.createElement("script");
  script.src = url;
  document.body.appendChild(script);
}
```

This function can now be used to load external JavaScript files via the following call:

```
loadScript("client.js");
```

Once loaded, the script is fully available to the rest of the page. This leaves only one problem: how do you know when the script has been fully loaded? Unfortunately, there is no standard way to handle this. Some events are available depending on the browser being used, as discussed in the Chapter 15, "Events."

The other way to specify JavaScript code is inline, as in this example:

```
<script>
  function sayHi() {
    alert("hi");
  }
</script>
```

Importantly, all `<script>` elements created with `innerHTML` will never execute. The browser will dutifully create the `<script>` element and the script text inside it, but the parser will flag the `<script>` element as one that should never execute. Once created using `innerHTML`, there is no way to force the script to run later.

Dynamic Styles

CSS styles are included in HTML pages using one of two elements. The `<link>` element is used to include CSS from an external file, whereas the `<style>` element is used to specify inline styles. Similar to dynamic scripts, dynamic styles don't exist on the page when it is loaded initially; rather, they are added after the page has been loaded.

Consider this typical `<link>` element:

```
<link rel="stylesheet" type="text/css" href="styles.css">
```

This element can just as easily be created using the following DOM code:

```
let link = document.createElement("link");
link.rel = "stylesheet";
link.type = "text/css";
link.href = "styles.css";
let head = document.getElementsByTagName("head")[0];
head.appendChild(link);
```

This code works in all major browsers without any issue. Note that `<link>` elements should be added to the `<head>` instead of the body for this to work properly in all browsers. The technique can be generalized into the following function:

```
function loadStyles(url){
    let link = document.createElement("link");
    link.rel = "stylesheet";
    link.type = "text/css";
    link.href = url;
    let head = document.getElementsByTagName("head")[0];
    head.appendChild(link);
}
```

The `loadStyles()` function can then be called like this:

```
loadStyles("styles.css");
```

Loading styles via an external file is asynchronous, so the styles will load out of order with the JavaScript code being executed. Typically, it's not necessary to know when the styles have been fully loaded.

The other way to define styles is using the `<style>` element and including inline CSS, such as this:

```
<style type="text/css">
body {
    background-color: red;
}
</style>
```

Using NodeLists

Understanding a `NodeList` object and its relatives, `NamedNodeMap` and `HTMLCollection`, is critical to a good understanding of the DOM as a whole. Each of these collections is considered "live," which is to say that they are updated when the document structure changes such that they are always current with the most accurate information. In reality, all `NodeList` objects are queries that are run against the DOM document whenever they are accessed. For instance, the following results in an infinite loop:

```
let divs = document.getElementsByTagName("div");

for (let i = 0; i < divs.length; ++i){
    let div = document.createElement("div");
    document.body.appendChild(div);
}
```

The first part of this code gets an HTMLCollection of all <div> elements in the document. Because that collection is "live," any time a new <div> element is added to the page, it gets added into the collection. Because the browser doesn't want to keep a list of all the collections that were created, the collection is updated only when it is accessed again. This creates an interesting problem in terms of a loop such as the one in this example. Each time through the loop, the condition i < divs.length is being evaluated. That means the query to get all <div> elements is being run. Because the body of the loop creates a new <div> element and adds it to the document, the value of divs.length increments each time through the loop; thus i will never equal divs.length because both are being incremented.

Using an iterator doesn't fix the situation because an ever-growing live collection remains the subject of iteration. This will still result in an infinite loop:

```
for (let div of document.getElementsByTagName("div")){
    let newDiv = document.createElement("div");
    document.body.appendChild(newDiv);
}
```

Any time you want to iterate over a NodeList, it's best to initialize a second variable with the length and then compare the iterator to that variable, as shown in the following example:

```
let divs = document.getElementsByTagName("div");

for (let i = 0, len = divs.length; i < len; ++i) {
    let div = document.createElement("div");
    document.body.appendChild(div);
}
```

In this example, a second variable, len, is initialized. Because len contains a snapshot of divs.length at the time the loop began, it prevents the infinite loop that was experienced in the previous example. This technique has been used through this chapter to demonstrate the preferred way of iterating over NodeList objects.

Alternately, if you want to avoid having the second variable, you can also iterate the list in reverse:

```
let divs = document.getElementsByTagName("div");

for (let i = divs.length - 1; i >= 0; --i) {
    let div = document.createElement("div");
    document.body.appendChild(div);
}
```

Generally speaking, it is best to limit the number of times you interact with a NodeList. Because a query is run against the document each time, try to cache frequently used values retrieved from a NodeList.

SELECTORS API

One of the most popular capabilities of JavaScript libraries is the ability to retrieve a number of DOM elements matching a pattern specified using CSS selectors. Indeed, the library jQuery (www .jquery.com) is built completely around the CSS selector queries of a DOM document in order to retrieve references to elements instead of using getElementById() and getElementsByTagName().

The Selectors API (www.w3.org/TR/selectors-api) was started by the W3C to specify native support for CSS queries in browsers. All JavaScript libraries implementing this feature had to do so by writing a rudimentary CSS parser and then using existing DOM methods to navigate the document and identify matching nodes. Although library developers worked tirelessly to speed up the performance of such processing, there was only so much that could be done while the code ran in JavaScript. By making this a native API, the parsing and tree navigating can be done at the browser level in a compiled language and thus tremendously increase the performance of such functionality.

At the core of Selectors API Level 1 are two methods: querySelector() and querySelectorAll(). On a conforming browser, these methods are available on the Document type and on the Element type.

The Selectors API Level 2 specification (www.w3.org/TR/selectors-api2) introduces more methods, matches(), find(), and findAll(), on the Element type, although no browsers currently have or have stated an intention to support find() or findAll().

The *querySelector()* Method

The querySelector() method accepts a CSS query and returns the first descendant element that matches the pattern or null if there is no matching element. Here is an example:

```
// Get the body element
let body = document.querySelector("body");

// Get the element with the ID "myDiv"
let myDiv = document.querySelector("#myDiv");

// Get first element with a class of "selected"
let selected = document.querySelector(".selected");

// Get first image with class of "button"
let img = document.body.querySelector("img.button");
```

When the querySelector() method is used on the Document type, it starts trying to match the pattern from the document element; when used on an Element type, the query attempts to make a match from the descendants of the element only.

The CSS query may be as complex or as simple as necessary. If there's a syntax error or an unsupported selector in the query, then querySelector() throws an error.

The *querySelectorAll()* Method

The querySelectorAll() method accepts the same single argument as querySelector()—the CSS query—but returns all matching nodes instead of just one. This method returns a static instance of NodeList.

To clarify, the return value is actually a NodeList with all of the expected properties and methods, but its underlying implementation acts as a snapshot of elements rather than a dynamic query that is constantly re-executed against a document. This implementation eliminates most of the performance overhead associated with the use of NodeList objects.

Any call to querySelectorAll() with a valid CSS query will return a NodeList object regardless of the number of matching elements; if there are no matches, the NodeList is empty.

As with querySelector(), the querySelectorAll() method is available on the Document, DocumentFragment, and Element types. Here are some examples:

```
// Get all <em> elements in a <div> (similar to getElementsByTagName("em"))
let ems = document.getElementById("myDiv").querySelectorAll("em");

// Get all elements that have "selected" as a class
let selecteds = document.querySelectorAll(".selected");

// Get all <strong> elements inside of <p> elements
let strongs = document.querySelectorAll("p strong");
```

The resulting NodeList object may be iterated over using iteration hooks, item(), or bracket notation to retrieve individual elements. Here's an example:

```
let strongElements = document.querySelectorAll("p strong");
// All three of the following loops will have the same effect:
for (let strong of strongElements) {
  strong.className = "important";
}
for (let i = 0; i < strongElements.length; ++i) {
  strongElements.item(i).className = "important";
}
for (let i = 0; i < strongElements.length; ++i) {
  strongElements [i].className = "important";
}
```

As with querySelector(), querySelectorAll() throws an error when the CSS selector is not supported by the browser or if there's a syntax error in the selector.

The *matches()* Method

matches() was formerly referred to as matchesSelector() in the specification draft. This method accepts a single argument, a CSS selector, and returns true if the given element matches the selector or false if not. For example:

```
if (document.body.matches ("body.page1")){
  // true
}
```

This method allows you to easily check if an element would be returned by `querySelector()` or `querySelectorAll()` when you already have the element reference.

ELEMENT TRAVERSAL

The Element Traversal API defines five properties on DOM elements:

1. `childElementCount`—Returns the number of child elements (excludes text nodes and comments).

2. `firstElementChild`—Points to the first child that is an element. Element-only version of `firstChild`.

3. `lastElementChild`—Points to the last child that is an element. Element-only version of `lastChild`.

4. `previousElementSibling`—Points to the previous sibling that is an element. Element-only version of `previousSibling`.

5. `nextElementSibling`—Points to the next sibling that is an element. Element-only version of `nextSibling`.

Supporting browsers add these properties to all DOM elements to allow for easier traversal of DOM elements without the need to worry about white space text nodes.

For example, iterating over all child elements of a particular element in a traditional cross-browser way looks like this:

```
let parentElement = document.getElementById('parent');
let currentChildNode = parentElement.firstChild;
// For zero children, firstChild returns null and the loop is skipped
while (currentChildNode) {
  if (currentChildNode.nodeType === 1) {
    // If this is an ELEMENT_NODE, do whatever work is needed in here
    processChild(currentChildNode);
  }
  if (currentChildNode === parentElement.lastChild) {
    break;
  }
  currentChildNode = currentChildNode.nextSibling;
}
```

Using the Element Traversal properties allows a simplification of the code:

```
let parentElement = document.getElementById('parent');
let currentChildElement = parentElement.firstElementChild;
// For zero children, firstElementChild returns null and the loop is skipped
while (currentChildElement) {
  // You already know this is an ELEMENT_NODE, do whatever work is needed here
  processChild(currentChildElement);
```

```
    if (currentChildElement === parentElement.lastElementChild) {
      break;
    }
    currentChildElement = currentChildElement.nextElementSibling;
  }
```

HTML5

HTML5 represents a radical departure from the tradition of HTML. In all previous HTML specifications, the descriptions stopped short of describing any JavaScript interfaces, instead focusing purely on the markup of the language and deferring JavaScript bindings to the DOM specification.

The HTML5 specification, on the other hand, contains a large amount of JavaScript APIs designed for use with the markup additions. Part of these APIs overlap with the DOM and define DOM extensions that browsers should provide.

Although all browser vendors understand the importance of adherence to standards, they all have a history of adding proprietary extensions to the DOM in order to fill perceived gaps in functionality. Though this may seem like a bad thing on the surface, proprietary extensions have given the web development community many important features that were later codified into standards such as HTML5.

> **NOTE** *Because the scope of HTML5 is vast, the following sections focus only on the parts that affect all DOM nodes. Other parts of HTML5 are discussed with their related topics throughout the book.*

Class-Related Additions

One of the major changes in web development since the time HTML4 was adopted is the increased usage of the class attribute to indicate both stylistic and semantic information about elements. This caused a lot of JavaScript interaction with CSS classes, including the dynamic changing of classes and querying the document to find elements with a given class or set of classes. To adapt to developers and their newfound appreciation of the class attribute, HTML5 introduces a number of changes to make CSS class usage easier.

The *getElementsByClassName()* Method

One of HTML5's most popular additions is getElementsByClassName(), which is available on the document object and on all HTML elements. This method evolved out of JavaScript libraries that implemented it using existing DOM features and is provided as a native implementation for performance reasons.

The getElementsByClassName() method accepts a single argument, which is a string containing one or more class names, and returns a NodeList containing all elements that have all of the specified classes applied. If multiple class names are specified, then the order is considered unimportant. Here are some examples:

```
// Get all elements with a class containing "username" and "current"
// It does not matter if one is declared before the other
let allCurrentUsernames = document.getElementsByClassName("username current");

// Get all elements with a class of "selected" that exist in myDiv's subtree
let selected = document.getElementById("myDiv").getElementsByClassName("selected");
```

When this method is called, it will return only elements in the subtree of the root from which it was called. Calling `getElementsByClassName()` on a document always returns all elements with matching class names, whereas calling it on an element will return only descendant elements.

This method is useful for attaching events to classes of elements rather than using IDs or tag names. Keep in mind that since the returned value is a `NodeList`, there are the same performance issues as when you're using `getElementsByTagName()` and other DOM methods that return `NodeList` objects.

The *classList* Property

In class name manipulation, the `className` property is used to add, remove, and replace class names. Because `className` contains a single string, it's necessary to set its value every time a change needs to take place, even if there are parts of the string that should be unaffected. For example, consider the following HTML code:

```
<div class="bd user disabled"> ... </div>
```

This `<div>` element has three classes assigned. To remove one of these classes, you need to split the class attribute into individual classes, remove the unwanted class, and then create a string containing the remaining classes. Here is an example:

```
// Remove the "user" class
let targetClass = "user";

// First, get list of class names
let classNames = div.className.split(/\s+/);

// Find the class name to remove
let idx = classNames.indexOf(targetClass);

// Remove the class name if found
if (idx> -1) {
  classNames.splice(i,1);
}

// Set back the class name
div.className = classNames.join(" ");
```

All of this code is necessary to remove the `"user"` class from the `<div>` element's class attribute. A similar algorithm must be used for replacing class names and detecting if a class name is applied to an element. Adding class names can be done by using string concatenation, but checks must be done to ensure that you're not applying the same class more than one time. Many JavaScript libraries implement methods to aid in these behaviors.

HTML5 introduces a way to manipulate class names in a much simpler and safer manner through the addition of the `classList` property for all elements. The `classList` property is an instance of a new type of collection named `DOMTokenList`. As with other DOM collections, `DOMTokenList` has a length property to indicate how many items it contains, and individual items may be retrieved via the `item()` method or using bracket notation. It also has the following additional methods:

1. `add(value)`—Adds the given string value to the list. If the value already exists, it will not be added.

2. `contains(value)`—Indicates if the given value exists in the list (`true` if so; `false` if not).

3. `remove(value)`—Removes the given string value from the list.

4. `toggle(value)`—If the value already exists in the list, it is removed. If the value doesn't exist, then it's added.

The entire block of code in the previous example can quite simply be replaced with the following:

```
div.classList.remove("user");
```

Using this code ensures that the rest of the class names will be unaffected by the change. The other methods also greatly reduce the complexity of the basic operations, as shown in these examples:

```
// Remove the "disabled" class
div.classList.remove("disabled");

// Add the "current" class
div.classList.add("current");

// Toggle the "user" class
div.classList.toggle("user");

// Figure out what's on the element now
if (div.classList.contains("bd") && !div.classList.contains("disabled")){
  // Do stuff
)

// Iterate over the class names
for (let class of div.classList){
  doStuff(class);
}
```

The addition of the `classList` property makes it unnecessary to access the `className` property unless you intend to completely remove or completely overwrite the element's class attribute.

Focus Management

HTML5 adds functionality to aid with focus management in the DOM. The first is `document .activeElement`, which always contains a pointer to the DOM element that currently has focus. An element can receive focus automatically as the page is loading, via user input (typically using the Tab key), or programmatically using the `focus()` method. For example:

```
let button = document.getElementById("myButton");
button.focus();
console.log(document.activeElement === button);  // true
```

By default, `document.activeElement` is set to `document.body` when the document is first loaded. Before the document is fully loaded, `document.activeElement` is `null`.

The second addition is `document.hasFocus()`, which returns a Boolean value indicating if the document has focus:

```
let button = document.getElementById("myButton");
button.focus();
console.log(document.hasFocus());  // true
```

Determining if the document has focus allows you to determine if the user is interacting with the page.

This combination of being able to query the document to determine which element has focus and being able to ask the document if it has focus is of the utmost importance for web application accessibility. One of the key components of accessible web applications is proper focus management, and being able to determine which elements currently have focus is a major improvement over the guess-work of the past.

Changes to HTMLDocument

HTML5 extends the `HTMLDocument` type to include more functionality. As with other DOM extensions specified in HTML5, the changes are based on proprietary extensions that are well supported across browsers. As such, even though the standardization of the extensions is relatively new, some browsers have supported the functionality for a while.

The *readyState* Property

The `readyState` property for `document` has two possible values:

1. `loading`—The document is loading.
2. `complete`—The document is completely loaded.

The best way to use the `document.readyState` property is as an indicator that the document has loaded. Before this property was widely available, you would need to add an `onload` event handler to set a flag indicating that the document was loaded. Basic usage:

```
if (document.readyState == "complete"){
  // Do stuff
}
```

Compatibility Mode

With the introduction of Internet Explorer 6 and the ability to render a document in either standards or quirks mode, it became necessary to determine in which mode the browser was rendering the page. To address this need, Internet Explorer added a property on the document named `compatMode` whose sole job is to indicate what rendering mode the browser is in. As shown in the following example, when in standards mode, `document.compatMode` is equal to "CSS1Compat"; when in quirks mode, `document.compatMode` is "BackCompat":

```
if (document.compatMode == "CSS1Compat"){
  console.log("Standards mode");
```

```
  } else {
    console.log("Quirks mode");
  }
```

The `compatMode` property was added to HTML5 to formalize its implementation. Unless you need to target extremely old browsers, it is unlikely you will need this property.

The *head* Property

HTML5 introduces `document.head` to point to the `<head>` element of a document to complement `document.body`, which points to the `<body>` element of the document. You can retrieve a reference to the `<head>` element using this property:

```
let head = document.head;
```

Character Set Properties

HTML5 describes several new properties dealing with the character set of the document. The `characterSet` property indicates the actual character set being used by the document and can also be used to specify a new character set. By default, this value is `"UTF-16"`, although it may be changed by using `<meta>` elements or response headers or through setting the `characterSet` property directly. Here's an example:

```
console.log(document.characterSet);    // "UTF-16"
document.characterSet = "UTF-8";
```

Custom Data Attributes

HTML5 allows elements to be specified with nonstandard attributes prefixed with `data-` in order to provide information that isn't necessary to the rendering or semantic value of the element. These attributes can be added as desired and named anything, provided that the name begins with `data-`. Here is an example:

```
<div id="myDiv" data-appId="12345" data-myname="Matt"></div>
```

When a custom data attribute is defined, it can be accessed via the `dataset` property of the element. The `dataset` property contains an instance of `DOMStringMap` that is a mapping of name-value pairs. Each attribute of the format `data-name` is represented by a property with a name equivalent to the attribute but without the `data-` prefix (for example, attribute `data-myname` is represented by a property called `myname`). The following is an example of how to use custom data attributes:

```
// Methods used in this example are for illustrative purposes only

let div = document.getElementById("myDiv");

// Get the values
let appId = div.dataset.appId;
let myName = div.dataset.myname;

// Set the value
div.dataset.appId = 23456;
```

```
div.dataset.myname = "Michael";

// Is there a "myname" value?
if (div.dataset.myname){
  console.log('Hello, ${div.dataset.myname}');
}
```

Custom data attributes are useful when nonvisual data needs to be tied to an element for some other form of processing. This is a common technique to use for link tracking and mashups in order to better identify parts of a page. It is also extensively utilized in numerous single-page application frameworks.

Markup Insertion

Although the DOM provides fine-grained control over nodes in a document, it can be cumbersome when attempting to inject a large amount of new HTML into the document. Instead of creating a series of DOM nodes and connecting them in the correct order, it's much easier (and faster) to use one of the markup insertion capabilities to inject a string of HTML. The following DOM extensions have been standardized in HTML5 for this purpose.

The *innerHTML* Property

When used in read mode, innerHTML returns the HTML representing all of the child nodes, including elements, comments, and text nodes. When used in write mode, innerHTML completely replaces all of the child nodes in the element with a new DOM subtree based on the specified value. Consider the following HTML code:

```
<div id="content">
  <p>This is a <strong>paragraph</strong> with a list following it.</p>
  <ul>
    <li>Item 1</li>
    <li>Item 2</li>
    <li>Item 3</li>
  </ul>
</div>
```

For the `<div>` element in this example, the innerHTML property returns the following string:

```
<p>This is a <strong>paragraph</strong> with a list following it.</p>
<ul>
  <li>Item 1</li>
  <li>Item 2</li>
  <li>Item 3</li>
</ul>
```

The exact text returned from innerHTML differs from browser to browser. Browsers will vary in the way it is specified in the document, including white space and indentation. You cannot depend on the returned value of innerHTML being exactly the same from browser to browser.

When used in write mode, innerHTML parses the given string into a DOM subtree and replaces all of the existing child nodes with it. Because the string is considered to be HTML, all tags are converted into elements in the standard way that the browser handles HTML (again, this differs from browser to browser). Setting simple text without any HTML tags, as shown here, sets the plain text:

```
div.innerHTML = "Hello world!";
```

Setting `innerHTML` to a string containing HTML behaves quite differently as `innerHTML` parses them. Consider the following example:

```
div.innerHTML = "Hello & welcome, <b>\"reader\"!</b>";
```

The result of this operation is as follows:

```
<div id="content">Hello & welcome, <b>"reader"!</b></div>
```

After setting `innerHTML`, you can access the newly created nodes as you would any other nodes in the document.

> **NOTE** *Setting* `innerHTML` *causes the HTML string to be parsed by the browser into an appropriate DOM tree. This means that setting* `innerHTML` *and then reading it back typically results in a different string being returned. This is because the returned string is the result of serializing the DOM subtree that was created for the original HTML string.*

The *outerHTML* Property

When `outerHTML` is called in read mode, it returns the HTML of the element on which it is called, as well as its child nodes. When called in write mode, `outerHTML` replaces the node on which it is called with the DOM subtree created from parsing the given HTML string. Consider the following HTML code:

```
<div id="content">
  <p>This is a <strong>paragraph</strong> with a list following it.</p>
  <ul>
    <li>Item 1</li>
    <li>Item 2</li>
    <li>Item 3</li>
  </ul>
</div>
```

When `outerHTML` is called on the `<div>` in this example, the same code is returned, including the code for the `<div>`. Note that there may be differences based on how the browser parses and interprets the HTML code. (These are the same types of differences you'll notice when using `innerHTML`.)

Use `outerHTML` to set a value in the following manner:

```
div.outerHTML = "<p>This is a paragraph.</p>";
```

The preceding code performs the same operation as the following DOM code:

```
let p = document.createElement("p");
p.appendChild(document.createTextNode("This is a paragraph."));
div.parentNode.replaceChild(p, div);
```

The new `<p>` element replaces the original `<div>` element in the DOM tree.

The *insertAdjacentHTML()* and *insertAdjacentText()* Methods

The last addition for markup insertion are the `insertAdjacentHTML()` and `insertAdjacentText()` methods. These methods accept two arguments: the position in which to insert and the HTML or text to insert. The first argument must be one of the following values:

1. `"beforebegin"`—Insert just before the element as a previous sibling.

2. `"afterbegin"`—Insert just inside of the element as a new child or series of children before the first child.

3. `"beforeend"`—Insert just inside of the element as a new child or series of children after the last child.

4. `"afterend"`—Insert just after the element as a next sibling.

Note that each of these values is case insensitive. The second argument is parsed as an HTML string (the same as with `innerHTML`/`outerHTML`) or as a raw string (the same as with `innerText`/`outerText`) and in the case of HTML, will throw an error if the value cannot be properly parsed. Basic usage is as follows:

```
// Insert as previous sibling
element.insertAdjacentHTML("beforebegin", "<p>Hello world!</p>");
element.insertAdjacentText("beforebegin", "Hello world!");
// Insert as first child
element.insertAdjacentHTML("afterbegin", "<p>Hello world!</p>");
element.insertAdjacentText("afterbegin", "Hello world!");
// Insert as last child
element.insertAdjacentHTML("beforeend", "<p>Hello world!</p>");
element.insertAdjacentText("beforeend", "Hello world!");
// Insert as next sibling
element.insertAdjacentHTML("afterend", "<p>Hello world!</p>"); element
.insertAdjacentText("afterend", "Hello world!");
```

Memory and Performance Issues

Replacing child nodes using the methods in this section may cause memory problems in the browser. The problem occurs when event handlers or other JavaScript objects are assigned to subtree elements that are removed. If an element has an event handler (or a JavaScript object as a property), and one of these properties is used in such a way that the element is removed from the document tree, the binding between the element and the event handler remains in memory. If this is repeated frequently, memory usage increases for the page. When using `innerHTML`, `outerHTML`, and `insertAdjacentHTML()`, it's best to manually remove all event handlers and JavaScript object properties on elements that are going to be removed.

Using these properties does have an upside, especially when using `innerHTML`. Generally speaking, inserting a large amount of new HTML is more efficient through `innerHTML` than through multiple DOM operations to create nodes and assign relationships between them. This is because an HTML parser is created whenever a value is set to `innerHTML` (or `outerHTML`). This parser runs in browser-level code (often written in C++), which is must faster than JavaScript. That being said, the creation and destruction of the HTML parser does have some overhead, so it's best to limit the number of times you set `innerHTML` or `outerHTML`. For example, the following creates a number of list items using `innerHTML`:

```
for (let value of values){
    ul.innerHTML += '<li>${value}</li>';  // avoid!!
}
```

This code is inefficient because it sets `innerHTML` once each time through the loop. Furthermore, this code is reading `innerHTML` each time through the loop, meaning that `innerHTML` is being accessed twice each time through the loop. It's best to build up the string separately and assign it using `innerHTML` just once at the end, like this:

```
let itemsHtml = "";
for (let value of values){
    itemsHtml += '<li>${value}</li>';
}
ul.innerHTML = itemsHtml;
```

This example is more efficient, limiting the use of `innerHTML` to one assignment. Of course, if you wanted to condense it to a single line:

```
ul.innerHTML = values.map(value => '<li>${value}</li>').join('');
```

Cross-Site Scripting Considerations

Although `innerHTML` does not execute script tags that it creates, it still provides an extremely broad attack surface for malicious actors looking to compromise a web page because it so readily creates elements and executable attributes such as `onclick`.

Anywhere you are interpolating user-provided information into the page, it is nearly always inadvisable to do so using `innerHTML`. The headaches of preventing XSS vulnerabilities far outweigh any convenience benefits gained from using `innerHTML`. Compartmentalize interpolated data, and don't hesitate to use libraries that escape interpolated data before inserting them into the page.

The *scrollIntoView()* Method

One of the issues not addressed by the DOM specification is how to scroll areas of a page. To fill this gap, browsers implemented several methods that control scrolling in different ways. Of the various proprietary methods, only `scrollIntoView()` was selected for inclusion in HTML5.

The `scrollIntoView()` method exists on all HTML elements and scrolls the browser window or container element so the element is visible in the viewport.

1. If an argument of `true` is supplied, it specifies `alignToTop`: the window scrolls so that the top of the element is at the top of the viewport.

2. If an argument of `false` is supplied, it specifies `alignToTop`: the window scrolls so that the bottom of the element is at the top of the viewport.

3. If an object argument is supplied, the user can provide values for the behavior property, which specifies how the scroll should occur: "auto", "instant", or "smooth", and the block property is the same as `alignToTop`.

4. If no argument is supplied, the element is scrolled so that it is fully visible in the viewport but may not be aligned at the top. For example:

```
// Ensures this element is visible
document.forms[0].scrollIntoView();
// These behave identically
document.forms[0].scrollIntoView(true);
document.forms[0].scrollIntoView({block: true});
// This attempts to scroll the element smoothly into view:
document.forms[0].scrollIntoView({behavior: 'smooth', block: true});
```

This method is most useful for getting the user's attention when something has happened on the page. Note that setting focus to an element also causes the browser to scroll the element into view so that the focus can properly be displayed.

The *children* Property

The `children` property is an `HTMLCollection` that contains only an element's child nodes that are also elements. Otherwise, the `children` property is the same as `childNodes` and may contain the same items when an element has only elements as children. The `children` property is accessed as follows:

```
let childCount = element.children.length;
let firstChild = element.children[0];
```

The *contains()* Method

It's often necessary to determine if a given node is a descendant of another. The `contains()` method is called on the ancestor node from which the search should begin and accepts a single argument, which is the suspected descendant node. If the node exists as a descendant of the root node, the method returns `true`; otherwise it returns `false`. Here is an example:

```
console.log(document.documentElement.contains(document.body));  // true
```

This example tests to see if the `<body>` element is a descendant of the `<html>` element, which returns `true` in all well-formed HTML pages.

There is another way of determining node relationships, by using the DOM Level 3 `compareDocumentPosition()` method. This method determines the relationship between two nodes and returns a bitmask indicating the relationship. The values for the bitmask are as shown in the following table.

MASK	RELATIONSHIP BETWEEN NODES
0x1	Disconnected (The passed-in node is not in the document.)
0x2	Precedes (The passed-in node appears in the DOM tree prior to the reference node.)
0x4	Follows (The passed-in node appears in the DOM tree after the reference node.)
0x8	Contains (The passed-in node is an ancestor of the reference node.)
0x10	Is contained by (The passed-in node is a descendant of the reference node.)

To mimic the `contains()` method, you will be interested in the 16 mask. The result of `compareDocumentPosition()` can be bitwise ANDed to determine if the reference node contains the given node. Here is an example:

```
let result = document.documentElement.compareDocumentPosition(document.body);
console.log(!!(result & 0x10));
```

When this code is executed, the result becomes 20, or 0x14 (0x4 for "follows" plus 0x10 for "is contained by"). Applying a bitwise mask of 0x10 to the result returns a nonzero number, and the two NOT bang operators convert that value into a Boolean.

Markup Insertion

While the `innerHTML` and `outerHTML` markup insertion properties were adopted by HTML5, there are two others that were not. The two remaining properties that are left out of HTML5 are `innerText` and `outerText`.

The *innerText* Property

The `innerText` property works with all text content contained within an element, regardless of how deep in the subtree the text exists. When used to read the value, `innerText` concatenates the values of all text nodes in the subtree in depth-first order. When used to write the value, `innerText` removes all children of the element and inserts a text node containing the given value. Consider the following HTML code:

```
<div id="content">
  <p>This is a <strong>paragraph</strong> with a list following it.</p>
  <ul>
    <li>Item 1</li>
    <li>Item 2</li>
    <li>Item 3</li>
  </ul>
</div>
```

For the `<div>` element in this example, the `innerText` property returns the following string:

```
This is a paragraph with a list following it.
Item 1
Item 2
Item 3
```

Note that different browsers treat white space in different ways, so the formatting may or may not include the indentation in the original HTML code.

Using the `innerText` property to set the contents of the `<div>` element is as simple as this single line of code:

```
div.innerText = "Hello world!";
```

After executing this line of code, the HTML of the page is effectively changed to the following:

```
<div id="content">Hello world!</div>
```

Setting `innerText` removes all of the child nodes that existed before, completely changing the DOM subtree. Additionally, setting `innerText` encodes all HTML syntax characters (less-than, greater-than, quotation marks, and ampersands) that may appear in the text. Here is an example:

```
div.innerText = "Hello & welcome, <b>\"reader\"!</b>";
```

The result of this operation is as follows:

```
<div id="content">Hello & welcome, <b>"reader"!</b></div>
```

Setting `innerText` can never result in anything other than a single text node as the child of the container, so the HTML encoding of the text must take place in order to keep to that single text node. The `innerText` property is also useful for stripping out HTML tags. By setting the `innerText` equal to the `innerText`, as shown here, all HTML tags are removed:

```
div.innerText = div.innerText;
```

Executing this code replaces the contents of the container with just the text that exists already.

> **NOTE** *While* `innerText` *skips over inline style and script blocks,* `textContent` *returns any inline style or script code along with other text.* `innerText` *is now supported across all browsers and should be the primary tool for getting and setting text content.*

The *outerText* Property

The `outerText` property works in the same way as `innerText` except that it includes the node on which it's called. For reading text values, `outerText` and `innerText` essentially behave in the exact same way. In writing mode, however, `outerText` behaves very differently. Instead of replacing just the child nodes of the element on which it's used, `outerText` actually replaces the entire element, including its child nodes. Consider the following:

```
div.outerText = "Hello world!";
```

This single line of code is equivalent to the following two lines:

```
let text = document.createTextNode("Hello world!");
div.parentNode.replaceChild(text, div);
```

Essentially, the new text node completely replaces the element on which `outerText` was set. After that point in time, the element is no longer in the document and cannot be accessed.

SUMMARY

The Document Object Model (DOM) is a language-independent API for accessing and manipulating HTML and XML documents. DOM Level 1 deals with representing HTML and XML documents as a hierarchy of nodes that can be manipulated to change the appearance and structure of the underlying documents using JavaScript.

The DOM is made up of a series of node types, as described here:

➤ The base node type is Node, which is an abstract representation of an individual part of a document; all other types inherit from Node.

➤ The Document type represents an entire document and is the root node of a hierarchy. In JavaScript, the document object is an instance of Document, which allows for querying and retrieval of nodes in a number of different ways.

➤ An Element node represents all HTML or XML elements in a document and can be used to manipulate their contents and attributes.

➤ Other node types exist for text contents, comments, document types, the CDATA section, and document fragments.

DOM access works as expected in most cases, although there are often complications when working with <script> and <style> elements. Because these elements contain scripting and stylistic information, respectively, they are often treated differently in browsers than other elements.

Perhaps the most important thing to understand about the DOM is how it affects overall performance. DOM manipulations are some of the most expensive operations that can be done in JavaScript, with NodeList objects being particularly troublesome. NodeList objects are "live," meaning that a query is run every time the object is accessed. Because of these issues, it is best to minimize the number of DOM manipulations.

Three additional specifications were also covered in this chapter:

1. **Selectors API**, which defines three methods for retrieving DOM elements based on CSS selectors: querySelector(), querySelectorAll(), and matches().

2. **Element Traversal**, which defines additional properties on DOM elements to allow easy traversal to the next related DOM element. The need for this arose because of the handling of white space in the DOM that creates text nodes between elements.

3. **HTML5**, which provides a large number of extensions to the standard DOM. These include standardization of de facto standards such as innerHTML as well as additional functionality for dealing with focus management, character sets, scrolling, and more.

14

DOM Extensions

WHAT'S IN THIS CHAPTER?

➤ The DOM API for manipulating styles

➤ Working with DOM traversal and ranges

➤ Using Observer APIs

> **DOWNLOADS FOR THIS CHAPTER**
>
> Please note that all the code examples for this chapter are available as a part of this chapter's code download on the book's website at www.wiley.com/go/projavascript5e.

Even though the Document Object Model is a fairly well-defined API, it is also frequently augmented with both standards-based and proprietary extensions to provide additional functionality. Prior to 2008, almost all of the DOM extensions found in browsers were proprietary. After that point, the W3C went to work to codify some of the proprietary extensions that had become de facto standards into formal specifications.

The first level of the DOM focuses on defining the underlying structure of HTML documents. DOM Levels 2 and 3 build on this structure to introduce more interactivity and support for more advanced features.

There are also three types of observer APIs that allow you to define listeners that will fire upon various changes happening in the browser. These observer APIs are defined in different specifications, but they share a common interface:

➤ **Mutation Observers**—Detect changes to a full or partial DOM tree

➤ **Intersection Observers**—Detect if elements are overlapping and by how much

➤ **Resize Observers**—Detect if an element's dimensions change

STYLES

Styles are defined in HTML in three ways: including an external style sheet via the `<link>` element, defining inline styles using the `<style>` element, and defining element-specific styles using the style attribute. DOM Level 2 Styles provide an API around all three of these styling mechanisms.

Accessing Element Styles

Any HTML element that supports the `style` attribute also has a `style` property exposed in JavaScript. The `style` object is an instance of CSSStyleDeclaration and contains all stylistic information specified by the HTML style attribute but no information about styles that have cascaded from either included or inline style sheets. Any CSS properties specified in the `style` attribute are represented as properties on the `style` object. Because CSS property names use dash case (using dashes to separate words, such as `background-image`), the names must be converted into camel case in order to be used in JavaScript. The following table lists some common CSS properties and the equivalent property names on the style object.

CSS PROPERTY	JAVASCRIPT PROPERTY
background-image	style.backgroundImage
color	style.color
display	style.display
font-family	style.fontFamily

For the most part, you change a property name directly simply by changing the format of its name. The one CSS property that doesn't translate directly is `float`. Because `float` is a reserved word in JavaScript, it can't be used as a property name. The DOM Level 2 Style specification states that the corresponding property on the style object should be `cssFloat`.

Styles can be set using JavaScript at any time as long as a valid DOM element reference is available. Here are some examples:

```
let myDiv = document.getElementById("myDiv");

// set the background color
```

```
myDiv.style.backgroundColor = "red";

// change the dimensions
myDiv.style.width = "100px";
myDiv.style.height = "200px";

// assign a border
myDiv.style.border = "1px solid black";
```

When styles are changed in this manner, the display of the element is automatically updated.

> **NOTE** *All measurements have to include a unit of measure. Setting* `style.width` *to* `"20"` *will be ignored because it has no unit of measure. Always include the unit of measurement.*

Styles specified in the `style` attribute can also be retrieved using the style object. Consider the following HTML:

```
<div id="myDiv"
     style="background-color: blue; width: 10px; height: 25px"></div>
```

The information from this element's `style` attribute can be retrieved via the following code:

```
console.log(myDiv.style.backgroundColor);    // "blue"
console.log(myDiv.style.width);              // "10px"
console.log(myDiv.style.height);             // "25px"
```

If no style attribute is specified on an element, the `style` object will contain empty values for all possible CSS properties.

DOM Style Properties and Methods

The DOM Level 2 Style specification also defines several properties and methods on the `style` object. These properties and methods provide information about the contents of the element's style attribute and enabling changes. They are as follows:

➤ `cssText`—As described previously, `cssText` provides access to the CSS code of the style attribute.

➤ `length`—The number of CSS properties applied to the element.

➤ `parentRule`—The CSSRule object representing the CSS information. The CSSRule type is discussed in a later section.

➤ `getPropertyCSSValue(propertyName)`—Returns a CSSValue object containing the value of the given property.

➤ `getPropertyPriority(propertyName)`—Returns "important" if the given property is set using `!important`; otherwise, it returns an empty string.

➤ `getPropertyValue(propertyName)`—Returns the string value of the given property.

➤ `item(index)`—Returns the name of the CSS property at the given position.

➤ `removeProperty(propertyName)`—Removes the given property from the style.

➤ `setProperty(propertyName, value, priority)`—Sets the given property to the given value with a priority (either "important" or an empty string).

The `cssText` property allows access to the CSS code of the style. When used in read mode, `cssText` returns the browser's internal representation of the CSS code in the style attribute. When used in write mode, the value assigned to `cssText` overwrites the *entire* value of the style attribute, meaning that all previous style information specified using the attribute is lost. For instance, if the element has a border specified via the `style` attribute and you overwrite `cssText` with rules that don't include the border, it is removed from the element. The `cssText` property is used as follows:

```
myDiv.style.cssText = "width: 25px; height: 100px; background-color: green";
console.log(myDiv.style.cssText);
```

Setting the `cssText` property is the fastest way to make multiple changes to an element's style because all of the changes are applied at once.

The length property is designed for use in conjunction with the `item()` method for iterating over the CSS properties defined on an element. With these, the `style` object effectively becomes a collection, and bracket notation can be used in place of `item()` to retrieve the CSS property name in the given position, as shown in the following example:

```
for (let i = 0, len = myDiv.style.length; i < len; i++) {
  console.log(myDiv.style[i]);    // alternately, myDiv.style.item(i)
}
```

Using either bracket notation or `item()`, you can retrieve the CSS property name (`"background-color"`, not `"backgroundColor"`). This property name can then be used in `get PropertyValue()` to retrieve the actual value of the property, as shown in the following example:

```
let prop, value, i, len;
for (i = 0, len = myDiv.style.length; i < len; i++) {
  prop = myDiv.style[i];    // alternately, myDiv.style.item(i)
  value = myDiv.style.getPropertyValue(prop);
  console.log('prop: ${value}');
}
```

The `getPropertyValue()` method always retrieves the string representation of the CSS property value. If you need more information, `getPropertyCSSValue()` returns a CSSValue object that has two properties: `cssText` and `cssValueType`. The `cssText` property is the same as the value returned from `getPropertyValue()`. The `cssValueType` property is a numeric constant indicating the type of value being represented: 0 for an inherited value, 1 for a primitive value, 2 for a list, or 3 for a custom value. The following code outputs the CSS property value and the value type:

```
let prop, value, i, len;
for (i = 0, len = myDiv.style.length; i < len; i++) {
  prop = myDiv.style[i];    // alternately, myDiv.style.item(i)
  value = myDiv.style.getPropertyCSSValue(prop);
  console.log('prop: ${value.cssText} (${value.cssValueType})');
}
```

The `removeProperty()` method is used to remove a specific CSS property from the element's styling. Removing a property using this method means that any default styling for that property (cascading from other style sheets) will be applied. For instance, to remove a border property that was set in the `style` attribute, you can use the following code:

```
myDiv.style.removeProperty("border");
```

This method is helpful when you're not sure what the default value for a given CSS property is. Simply removing the property allows the default value to be used.

Computed Styles

The `style` object offers information about the style attribute on any element that supports it but contains no information about the styles that have cascaded from style sheets and affect the element. DOM Level 2 Style augments `document.defaultView` to provide a method called `getComputedStyle()`. This method accepts two arguments: the element to get the computed style for and a pseudo-element string (such as `":after"`). The second argument can be `null` if no pseudo-element information is necessary. The `getComputedStyle()` method returns a CSSStyleDeclaration object (the same type as the style property) containing all computed styles for the element. Consider the following HTML page:

```
<!DOCTYPE html>
<html>
<head>
  <title>Computed Styles Example</title>
  <style type="text/css">
    #myDiv {
      background-color: blue;
      width: 100px;
      height: 200px;
    }
  </style>
</head>
<body>
  <div id="myDiv" style="background-color: red; border: 1px solid black"></div>
</body>
</html>
```

In this example, the `<div>` element has styles applied to it both from an inline style sheet (the `<style>` element) and from the style attribute. The style object has values for `backgroundColor` and `border`, but nothing for `width` and `height`, which are applied through a style sheet rule. The following code retrieves the computed style for the element:

```
let myDiv = document.getElementById("myDiv");
let computedStyle = document.defaultView.getComputedStyle(myDiv, null);

console.log(computedStyle.backgroundColor);  // "red"
console.log(computedStyle.width);            // "100px"
console.log(computedStyle.height);           // "200px"
console.log(computedStyle.border);           // "1px solid black" in some browsers
```

The computed style of this element reports the background color as `"red"`, the width as `"100px"`, and the height as `"200px"`. Note that the background color is not `"blue"` because that style is overridden on the element itself. The `border` property may or may not return the exact border rule from the style sheet. This inconsistency is due to the way that browsers interpret rollup properties, such as `border`, that actually set a number of other properties. When you set border, you're actually setting rules for the border width, color, and style on all four borders (border-left-width, border-top-color, border-bottom-style, and so on). So even though `computedStyle.border` may not return a value in all browsers, `computedStyle.borderLeftWidth` does.

The important thing to remember about computed styles in all browsers is that they are read-only; you cannot change CSS properties on a computed style object. Also, the computed style contains styling information that is part of the browser's internal style sheet, so any CSS property that has a default value will be represented in the computed style. For instance, the `visibility` property always has a default value in all browsers, but this value differs per implementation. Some browsers set the `visibility` property to `"visible"` by default, whereas others have it as `"inherit"`. You cannot depend on the default value of a CSS property to be the same across browsers. If you need elements to have a specific default value, you should manually specify it in a style sheet.

Working with Style Sheets

The `CSSStyleSheet` type represents a CSS style sheet as included using a `<link>` element or defined in a `<style>` element. Note that the elements themselves are represented by the `HTMLLinkElement` and `HTMLStyleElement` types, respectively. The `CSSStyleSheet` type is generic enough to represent a style sheet no matter how it is defined in HTML. Furthermore, the element-specific types allow for modification of HTML attributes, whereas a `CSSStyleSheet` object is, with the exception of one property, a read-only interface.

The `CSSStyleSheet` type inherits from `StyleSheet`, which can be used as a base to define non-CSS style sheets. The following properties are inherited from `StyleSheet`:

➤ `disabled`—A Boolean value indicating if the style sheet is disabled. This property is read/write, so setting its value to `true` will disable a style sheet.

➤ `href`—The URL of the style sheet if it is included using `<link>`; otherwise, this is `null`.

➤ `media`—A collection of media types supported by this style sheet. The collection has a length property and `item()` method, as with all DOM collections. As with other DOM collections, you can use bracket notation to access specific items in the collection. An empty list indicates that the style sheet should be used for all media.

➤ `ownerNode`—Pointer to the node that owns the style sheet, which is either a `<link>` or a `<style>` element. This property is `null` if a style sheet is included in another style sheet using `@import`.

➤ `parentStyleSheet`—When a style sheet is included via `@import`, this is a pointer to the style sheet that imported it.

➤ `title`—The value of the title attribute on the `ownerNode`.

➤ `type`—A string indicating the type of style sheet. For CSS style sheets, this is `"text/css"`.

With the exception of `disabled`, the rest of these properties are read-only. The CSSStyleSheet type supports all of these properties and the following properties and methods:

➤ `cssRules`—A collection of rules contained in the style sheet.

➤ `ownerRule`—If the style sheet was included using `@import`, this is a pointer to the rule representing the import; otherwise, this is `null`.

➤ `deleteRule(index)`—Deletes the rule at the given location in the `cssRules` collection.

➤ `insertRule(rule, index)`—Inserts the given string rule at the position specified in the `cssRules` collection.

The list of style sheets available on the document is represented by the `document.styleSheets` collection. The number of style sheets on the document can be retrieved using the `length` property, and each individual style sheet can be accessed using either the `item()` method or bracket notation. Here is an example:

```
let sheet = null;
for (let i = 0, len = document.styleSheets.length; i < len; i++) {
  sheet = document.styleSheets[i];
  console.log(sheet.href);
}
```

This code outputs the `href` property of each style sheet used in the document (`<style>` elements have no `href`).

The style sheets returned in `document.styleSheets` vary from browser to browser. All browsers include `<style>` elements and `<link>` elements with rel set to "stylesheet."

It's also possible to retrieve the `CSSStyleSheet` object directly from the `<link>` or `<style>` element. The DOM specifies a property called sheet that contains the `CSSStyleSheet` object.

CSS Rules

A `CSSRule` object represents each rule in a style sheet. The `CSSRule` type is actually a base type from which several other types inherit, but the most often used is `CSSStyleRule`, which represents styling information (other rules include `@import`, `@font-face`, `@page`, and `@charset`, although these rules rarely need to be accessed from script). The following properties are available on a `CSSStyleRule` object:

➤ `cssText`—Returns the text for the entire rule. This text may be different from the actual text in the style sheet because of the way that browsers handle style sheets internally.

➤ `parentRule`—If this rule is imported, this is the import rule; otherwise, this is `null`.

➤ `parentStyleSheet`—The style sheet that this rule is a part of.

➤ `selectorText`—Returns the selector text for the rule. This text may be different from the actual text in the style sheet because of the way that browsers handle style sheets internally.

➤ `style`—A `CSSStyleDeclaration` object that allows the setting and getting of specific style values for the rule.

➤ `type`—A constant indicating the type of rule. For style rules, this is always 1.

The three most frequently used properties are `cssText`, `selectorText`, and `style`. The `cssText` property is similar to the `style.cssText` property but not exactly the same. The former includes the selector text and the braces around the style information; the latter contains only the style information (similar to `style.cssText` on an element). Also, `cssText` is read-only, whereas `style.cssText` may be overwritten.

Most of the time, the `style` property is all that is required to manipulate style rules. This object can be used just like the one on each element to read or change the style information for a rule. Consider the following CSS rule:

```css
div.box {
    background-color: blue;
    width: 100px;
    height: 200px;
}
```

Assuming that this rule is in the first style sheet on the page and is the only style in that style sheet, the following code can be used to retrieve all of its information:

```js
let sheet = document.styleSheets[0];
let rules = sheet.cssRules || sheet.rules;   // get rules list
let rule = rules[0];                         // get first rule

console.log(rule.selectorText);              // "div.box"
console.log(rule.style.cssText);             // complete CSS code
console.log(rule.style.backgroundColor);     // "blue"
console.log(rule.style.width);               // "100px"
console.log(rule.style.height);              // "200px"
```

Using this technique, it's possible to determine the style information related to a rule in the same way you can determine the inline style information for an element. As with elements, it's also possible to change the style information, as shown in the following example:

```js
let sheet = document.styleSheets[0];
let rules = sheet.cssRules || sheet.rules;   // get rules list
let rule = rules[0];                         // get first rule
rule.style.backgroundColor = "red"
```

Note that changing a rule in this way affects all elements on the page for which the rule applies. If there are two `<div>` elements that have the box class, they will both be affected by this change.

Creating Rules

The DOM states that new rules are added to existing style sheets using the `insertRule()` method. This method expects two arguments: the text of the rule and the index at which to insert the rule. Here is an example:

```js
sheet.insertRule("body { background-color: silver }", 0);  // DOM method
```

This example inserts a rule that changes the document's background color. The rule is inserted as the first rule in the style sheet (position 0)—the order is important in determining how the rule cascades into the document.

Although adding rules in this way is possible, it quickly becomes burdensome when the number of rules to add is large. In that case, it's better to use the dynamic style loading technique discussed in Chapter 13, "The Document Object Model."

Deleting Rules

The DOM method for deleting rules from a style sheet is `deleteRule()`, which accepts a single argument: the index of the rule to remove. To remove the first rule in a style sheet, you can use the following code:

```
sheet.deleteRule(0);  // DOM method
```

As with adding rules, deleting rules is not a common practice in web development and should be used carefully.

Element Dimensions

The following properties and methods are not part of the DOM Level 2 Style specification but are nonetheless related to styles on HTML elements. The DOM stops short of describing ways to determine the actual dimensions of elements on a page.

Offset Dimensions

The first set of properties deals with *offset dimensions*, which incorporate all of the visual space that an element takes up on the screen. An element's visual space on the page is made up of its height and width, including all padding, scrollbars, and borders (but not including margins). The following four properties are used to retrieve offset dimensions:

➤ `offsetHeight`—The amount of vertical space, in pixels, taken up by the element, including its height, the height of a horizontal scrollbar (if visible), the top border height, and the bottom border height.

➤ `offsetLeft`—The number of pixels between the element's outside left border and the containing element's inside left border.

➤ `offsetTop`—The number of pixels between the element's outside top border and the containing element's inside top border.

➤ `offsetWidth`—The amount of horizontal space taken up by the element, including its width, the width of a vertical scrollbar (if visible), the left border width, and the right border width.

The `offsetLeft` and `offsetTop` properties are in relation to the containing element, which is stored in the `offsetParent` property. The `offsetParent` may not necessarily be the same as the `parentNode`. For example, the `offsetParent` of a `<td>` element is the `<table>` element that it's an ancestor of, because the `<table>` is the first element in the hierarchy that provides dimensions. Figure 14.1 illustrates the various dimensions these properties represent.

offsetParent

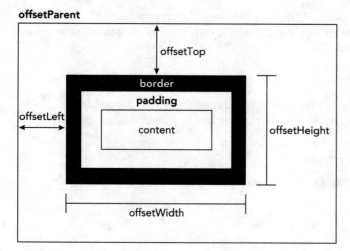

FIGURE 14.1: Illustration of various offset dimensions

The offset of an element on the page can roughly be determined by taking the offsetLeft and offsetTop properties and adding them to the same properties of the offsetParent, continuing up the hierarchy until you reach the root element. Here is an example:

```
function getElementLeft(element) {
  let actualLeft = element.offsetLeft;
  let current = element.offsetParent;

  while (current !== null) {
    actualLeft += current.offsetLeft;
    current = current.offsetParent;
  }

  return actualLeft;
}

function getElementTop(element) {
  let actualTop = element.offsetTop;
  let current = element.offsetParent;

  while (current !== null) {
    actualTop += current.offsetTop;
    current = current.offsetParent;
  }

  return actualTop;
}
```

These two functions climb through the DOM hierarchy using the offsetParent property, adding up the offset properties at each level. For simple page layouts using CSS-based layouts, these functions are very accurate. For page layouts using tables and iframes, the values returned are less accurate on a cross-browser basis because of the different ways that these elements are implemented. Generally, all elements that are contained solely within `<div>` elements have `<body>` as their `offsetParent`, so `getElementLeft()` and `getElementTop()` will return the same values as `offsetLeft` and `offsetTop`.

> **NOTE** *All of the offset dimension properties are read-only and incur an expensive calculation each time they are accessed. Therefore, you should try to avoid making multiple calls to any of these properties; instead, store the values you need in local variables to avoid incurring a performance penalty.*

Client Dimensions

The *client dimensions* of an element comprise the space occupied by the element's content and its padding. There are only two properties related to client dimensions: `clientWidth` and `clientHeight`. The `clientWidth` property is the width of the content area plus the width of both the left and the right padding. The `clientHeight` property is the height of the content area plus the height of both the top and the bottom padding. Figure 14.2 illustrates these properties.

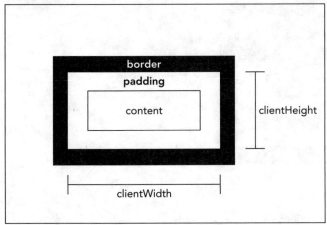

FIGURE 14.2: Illustration of various client dimensions

The client dimensions are literally the amount of space inside of the element, so the space taken up by scrollbars is not counted. The most common use of these properties is to determine the browser viewport size. This is done by using the `clientWidth` and `clientHeight` of `document .documentElement`. These properties represent the dimensions of the viewport (the `<html>` or `<body>` elements).

> **NOTE** *As with offset dimensions, client dimensions are read-only and are calculated each time they are accessed.*

Scroll Dimensions

The last set of dimensions is *scroll dimensions*, which provide information about an element whose content is scrolling. Some elements, such as the `<html>` element, scroll automatically without needing any additional code, whereas other elements can be made to scroll by using the CSS overflow property. The four scroll dimension properties are as follows:

➤ `scrollHeight`—The total height of the content if there were no scrollbars present.

➤ `scrollLeft`—The number of pixels that are hidden to the left of the content area. This property can be set to change the scroll position of the element.

➤ `scrollTop`—The number of pixels that are hidden in the top of the content area. This property can be set to change the scroll position of the element.

➤ `scrollWidth`—The total width of the content if there were no scrollbars present.

Figure 14.3 illustrates these properties.

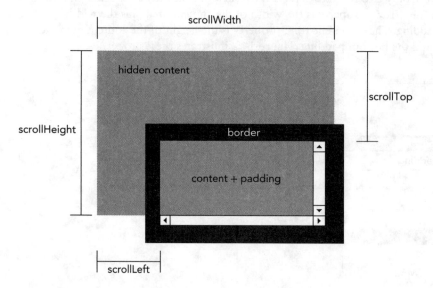

FIGURE 14.3: Illustration of various scroll dimensions

The `scrollWidth` and `scrollHeight` properties are useful for determining the actual dimensions of the content in a given element. For example, the `<html>` element is considered the element that scrolls the viewport in a web browser. Therefore, the height of an entire page that has a vertical scrollbar is `document.documentElement.scrollHeight`.

When trying to determine the total height of a document, including the minimum height based on the viewport, you must take the maximum value of `scrollWidth`/`clientWidth` and `scrollHeight`/`clientHeight` to guarantee accurate results across browsers. Here is an example:

```
let docHeight = Math.max(document.documentElement.scrollHeight,
```

```
                        document.documentElement.clientHeight);

    let docWidth = Math.max(document.documentElement.scrollWidth,
                        document.documentElement.clientWidth);
```

The `scrollLeft` and `scrollTop` properties can be used either to determine the current scroll settings on an element or to set them. When an element hasn't been scrolled, both properties are equal to 0. If the element has been scrolled vertically, `scrollTop` is greater than 0, indicating the amount of content that is not visible at the top of the element. If the element has been scrolled horizontally, `scrollLeft` is greater than 0, indicating the number of pixels that are not visible on the left. Because each property can also be set, you can reset the element's scroll position by setting both `scrollLeft` and `scrollTop` to 0. The following function checks to see if the element is at the top, and if not, it scrolls it back to the top:

```
function scrollToTop(element) {
  if (element.scrollTop != 0) {
    element.scrollTop = 0;
  }
}
```

This function uses `scrollTop` both for retrieving the value and for setting it.

Determining Element Dimensions

Browsers offer a method called `getBoundingClientRect()` on each element, which returns a DOMRect object that has six properties: `left`, `top`, `right`, `bottom`, `height`, and `width`. These properties give the location of the element on the page relative to the viewport.

TRAVERSALS

The DOM Level 2 Traversal and Range module defines two types that aid in sequential traversal of a DOM structure. These types, NodeIterator and TreeWalker, perform depth-first traversals of a DOM structure given a certain starting point.

As stated previously, DOM traversals are a depth-first traversal of the DOM structure that allows movement in at least two directions (depending on the type being used). A traversal is rooted at a given node, and it cannot go any further up the DOM tree than that root. Consider the following HTML page:

```
<!DOCTYPE html>
<html>
  <head>
    <title>Example</title>
  </head>
  <body>
    <p><b>Hello</b> world!</p>
  </body>
</html>
```

This page evaluates to the DOM tree represented in Figure 14.4.

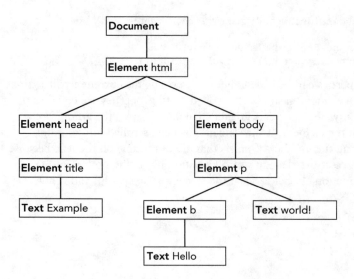

FIGURE 14.4: Visual representation of DOM tree

Any node can be the root of the traversals. Suppose, for example, that the `<body>` element is the traversal root. The traversal can then visit the `<p>` element, the `<b>` element, and the two text nodes that are descendants of `<body>`; however, the traversal can never reach the `<html>` element, the `<head>` element, or any other node that isn't in the `<body>` element's subtree. A traversal that has its root at document, on the other hand, can access all of the nodes in document. Figure 14.5 depicts a depth-first traversal of a DOM tree rooted at document.

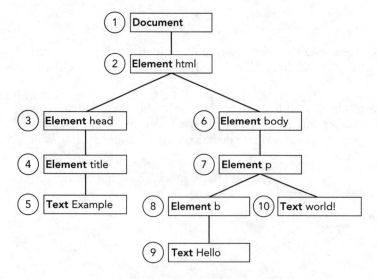

FIGURE 14.5: Illustrated order of depth-first traversal

Starting at document and moving sequentially, the first node visited is document, and the last node visited is the text node containing " world!". From the very last text node at the end of the document, the traversal can be reversed to go back up the tree. In that case, the first node visited is the text node containing " world!", and the last one visited is the document node itself. Both NodeIterator and TreeWalker perform traversals in this manner.

NodeIterator

The NodeIterator type is the simpler of the two, and a new instance can be created using the document.createNodeIterator() method. This method accepts the following four arguments:

➤ root—The node in the tree that you want to start searching from.

➤ whatToShow—A numerical code indicating which nodes should be visited.

➤ filter—A NodeFilter object or a function indicating whether a particular node should be accepted or rejected.

➤ entityReferenceExpansion—A Boolean value indicating whether entity references should be expanded. This has no effect in HTML pages because entity references are never expanded.

The whatToShow argument is a bitmask that determines which nodes to visit by applying one or more filters. Possible values for this argument are included as constants on the NodeFilter type as follows:

➤ NodeFilter.SHOW_ALL—Show all node types.

➤ NodeFilter.SHOW_ELEMENT—Show element nodes.

➤ NodeFilter.SHOW_ATTRIBUTE—Show attribute nodes. This can't actually be used because of the DOM structure.

➤ NodeFilter.SHOW_TEXT—Show text nodes.

➤ NodeFilter.SHOW_CDATA_SECTION—Show CData section nodes. This is not used in HTML pages.

➤ NodeFilter.SHOW_ENTITY_REFERENCE—Show entity reference nodes. This is not used in HTML pages.

➤ NodeFilter.SHOW_ENTITY—Show entity nodes. This is not used in HTML pages.

➤ NodeFilter.SHOW_PROCESSING_INSTRUCTION—Show PI nodes. This is not used in HTML pages.

➤ NodeFilter.SHOW_COMMENT—Show comment nodes.

➤ NodeFilter.SHOW_DOCUMENT—Show document nodes.

➤ NodeFilter.SHOW_DOCUMENT_TYPE—Show document type nodes.

➤ NodeFilter.SHOW_DOCUMENT_FRAGMENT—Show document fragment nodes. This is not used in HTML pages.

➤ NodeFilter.SHOW_NOTATION—Show notation nodes. This is not used in HTML pages.

With the exception of `NodeFilter.SHOW_ALL`, you can combine multiple options using the bitwise OR operator, as shown in the following example:

```
let whatToShow = NodeFilter.SHOW_ELEMENT | NodeFilter.SHOW_TEXT;
```

The filter argument of `createNodeIterator()` can be used to specify a custom NodeFilter object or a function that acts as a node filter. A NodeFilter object has only one method, `acceptNode()`, which returns `NodeFilter.FILTER_ACCEPT` if the given node should be visited or `NodeFilter.FILTER_SKIP` if the given node should not be visited. Because NodeFilter is an abstract type, it's not possible to create an instance of it. Instead, just create an object with an `acceptNode()` method and pass the object into `createNodeIterator()`. The following code accepts only `<p>` elements:

```
let filter = {
  acceptNode(node) {
    return node.tagName.toLowerCase() == "p" ?
        NodeFilter.FILTER_ACCEPT :
        NodeFilter.FILTER_SKIP;
  }
};

let iterator = document.createNodeIterator(root, NodeFilter.SHOW_ELEMENT,
                                           filter, false);
```

The third argument can also be a function that takes the form of the `acceptNode()` method, as shown in this example:

```
let filter = function(node) {
    return node.tagName.toLowerCase() == "p" ?
        NodeFilter.FILTER_ACCEPT :
        NodeFilter.FILTER_SKIP;
};

let iterator = document.createNodeIterator(root, NodeFilter.SHOW_ELEMENT,
                                           filter, false);
```

Typically, this is the form that is used in JavaScript because it is simpler and works more like the rest of JavaScript. If no filter is required, the third argument should be set to `null`.

To create a simple `NodeIterator` that visits all node types, use the following code:

```
let iterator = document.createNodeIterator(document, NodeFilter.SHOW_ALL,
                                           null, false);
```

The two primary methods of `NodeIterator` are `nextNode()` and `previousNode()`. The `nextNode()` method moves one step forward in the depth-first traversal of the DOM subtree, and `previousNode()` moves one step backward in the traversal. When the NodeIterator is first created, an internal pointer points to the root, so the first call to `nextNode()` returns the root. When the traversal has reached the last node in the DOM subtree, `nextNode()` returns `null`. The `previousNode()` method works in a similar way. When the traversal has reached the last node in the DOM subtree, after `previousNode()` has returned the root of the traversal, it will return `null`.

Consider the following HTML fragment:

```
<div id="div1">
  <p><b>Hello</b> world!</p>
```

```
  <ul>
    <li>List item 1</li>
    <li>List item 2</li>
    <li>List item 3</li>
  </ul>
</div>
```

Suppose that you would like to traverse all elements inside of the `<div>` element. This can be accomplished using the following code:

```
let div = document.getElementById("div1");
let iterator = document.createNodeIterator(div, NodeFilter.SHOW_ELEMENT,
                                  null, false);

let node = iterator.nextNode();
while (node !== null) {
  console.log(node.tagName);      // output the tag name
  node = iterator.nextNode();
}
```

The first call to `nextNode()` in this example returns the `<p>` element. Because `nextNode()` returns null when it has reached the end of the DOM subtree, a `while` loop checks to see when `null` has been returned as it calls `nextNode()` each time through. When this code is executed, logs are displayed with the following tag names:

```
DIV
P
B
UL
LI
LI
LI
```

Perhaps this is too much information and you really only want to return the `<li>` elements that occur in the traversal. This can be accomplished by using a filter, as shown in the following example:

```
let div = document.getElementById("div1");
let filter = function(node) {
  return node.tagName.toLowerCase() == "li" ?
    NodeFilter.FILTER_ACCEPT :
    NodeFilter.FILTER_SKIP;
};

let iterator = document.createNodeIterator(div, NodeFilter.SHOW_ELEMENT,
      filter, false);

let node = iterator.nextNode();
while (node !== null) {
  console.log(node.tagName);      // output the tag name
  node = iterator.nextNode();
}
```

In this example, only `<li>` elements will be returned from the iterator.

The `nextNode()` and `previousNode()` methods work with NodeIterator's internal pointer in the DOM structure, so changes to the structure are represented appropriately in the traversal.

TreeWalker

`TreeWalker` is a more advanced version of `NodeIterator`. It has the same functionality, including `nextNode()` and `previousNode()`, and adds the following methods to traverse a DOM structure in different directions:

➤ `parentNode()`—Travels to the current node's parent.

➤ `firstChild()`—Travels to the first child of the current node.

➤ `lastChild()`—Travels to the last child of the current node.

➤ `nextSibling()`—Travels to the next sibling of the current node.

➤ `previousSibling()`—Travels to the previous sibling of the current node.

A `TreeWalker` object is created using the `document.createTreeWalker()` method, which accepts the same arguments as `document.createNodeIterator()`: the root to traverse from, which node types to show, a filter, and a Boolean value indicating if entity references should be expanded. Because of these similarities, `TreeWalker` can always be used in place of `NodeIterator`, as in this example:

```
let div = document.getElementById("div1");
let filter = function(node) {
  return node.tagName.toLowerCase() == "li" ?
    NodeFilter.FILTER_ACCEPT :
    NodeFilter.FILTER_SKIP;
};

let walker = document.createTreeWalker(div, NodeFilter.SHOW_ELEMENT,
                                       filter, false);

let node = iterator.nextNode();
while (node !== null) {
  console.log(node.tagName);      // output the tag name
  node = iterator.nextNode();
}
```

One difference is in the values that the filter can return. In addition to `NodeFilter.FILTER_ACCEPT` and `NodeFilter.FILTER_SKIP`, there is `NodeFilter.FILTER_REJECT`. When used with a `NodeIterator` object, `NodeFilter.FILTER_SKIP` and `NodeFilter.FILTER_REJECT` do the same thing: they skip over the node. When used with a `TreeWalker` object, `NodeFilter.FILTER_SKIP` skips over the node and goes on to the next node in the subtree, whereas `NodeFilter.FILTER_REJECT` skips over that node and that node's entire subtree. For instance, changing the filter in the previous example to return `NodeFilter.FILTER_REJECT` instead of `NodeFilter.FILTER_SKIP` will result in no nodes being visited. This is because the first element returned is `<div>`, which does not have a tag name of "li", so `NodeFilter.FILTER_REJECT` is returned, indicating that the entire subtree should be skipped. Because the `<div>` element is the traversal root, this means that the traversal stops.

Of course, the true power of `TreeWalker` is its ability to move around the DOM structure. Instead of specifying a filter, it's possible to get at the `<li>` elements by navigating through the DOM tree using `TreeWalker`, as shown here:

```
let div = document.getElementById("div1");
```

```
let walker = document.createTreeWalker(div, NodeFilter.SHOW_ELEMENT, null, false);

walker.firstChild();    // go to <p>
walker.nextSibling();   // go to <ul>

let node = walker.firstChild();  // go to first <li>
while (node !== null) {
  console.log(node.tagName);
  node = walker.nextSibling();
}
```

Because you know where the `<li>` elements are located in the document structure, it's possible to navigate there, using `firstChild()` to get to the `<p>` element, `nextSibling()` to get to the `<ul>` element, and then `firstChild()` to get to the first `<li>` element. Keep in mind that TreeWalker is returning only elements (because of the second argument passed in to `createTreeWalker()`). Then, `nextSibling()` can be used to visit each `<li>` until there are no more, at which point the method returns `null`.

The `TreeWalker` type also has a property called `currentNode` that indicates the node that was last returned from the traversal via any of the traversal methods. This property can also be set to change where the traversal continues from when it resumes, as shown in this example:

```
let node = walker.nextNode();
console.log(node === walker.currentNode);  // true
walker.currentNode = document.body;        // change where to start from
```

Compared to `NodeIterator`, the `TreeWalker` type allows greater flexibility when traversing the DOM.

RANGES

To allow an even greater measure of control over a page, the DOM Level 2 Traversal and Range module defines an interface called a range. A range can be used to select a section of a document regardless of node boundaries. (This selection occurs behind the scenes and cannot be seen by the user.) Ranges are helpful when regular DOM manipulation isn't specific enough to change a document.

Ranges in the DOM

DOM Level 2 defines a method on the `Document` type called `createRange()`, which belongs to the document object. A DOM range can be created using `createRange()`, as shown here:

```
let range = document.createRange();
```

Similar to nodes, the newly created range is tied directly to the document on which it was created and cannot be used on other documents. This range can then be used to select specific parts of the document behind the scenes. Once a range has been created and its position set, several different operations can be performed on the contents of the range, allowing more fine-grained manipulation of the underlying DOM tree.

Each range is represented by an instance of the `Range` type, which has several properties and methods. The following properties provide information about where the range is located in the document:

➤ `startContainer`—The node within which the range starts (the parent of the first node in the selection).

➤ `startOffset`—The offset within the `startContainer` where the range starts. If `startContainer` is a text node, comment node, or CData node, the `startOffset` is the number of characters skipped before the range starts; otherwise, the offset is the index of the first child node in the range.

➤ `endContainer`—The node within which the range ends (the parent of the last node in the selection).

➤ `endOffset`—The offset within the `endContainer` where the range ends (follows the same rules as `startOffset`).

➤ `commonAncestorContainer`—The deepest node in the document that has both `startContainer` and `endContainer` as descendants.

These properties are filled when the range is placed into a specific position in the document.

Simple Selection in DOM Ranges

The simplest way to select a part of the document using a range is to use either `selectNode()` or `selectNodeContents()`. These methods each accept one argument, a DOM node, and fill a range with information from that node. The `selectNode()` method selects the entire node, including its children, whereas `selectNodeContents()` selects only the node's children. For example, consider the following HTML:

```
<!DOCTYPE html>
<html>
  <body>
    <p id="p1"><b>Hello</b> world!</p>
  </body>
</html>
```

This code can be accessed using the following JavaScript:

```
let range1 = document.createRange(),
    range2 = document.createRange(),
    p1 = document.getElementById("p1");
range1.selectNode(p1);
range2.selectNodeContents(p1);
```

The two ranges in this example contain different sections of the document: `range1` contains the `<p>` element and all its children, whereas `range2` contains the `<b>` element, the text node `"Hello"`, and the text node `" world!"`, as seen in Figure 14.6.

When `selectNode()` is called, `startContainer`, `endContainer`, and `commonAncestorContainer` are all equal to the parent node of the node that was passed in; in this example, these would all be equal to `document.body`. The `startOffset` property is equal to the index of the given node within the parent's `childNodes` collection (which is 1 in this example—remember DOM-compliant browsers count white space as text nodes), whereas endOffset is equal to the startOffset plus one (because only one node is selected).

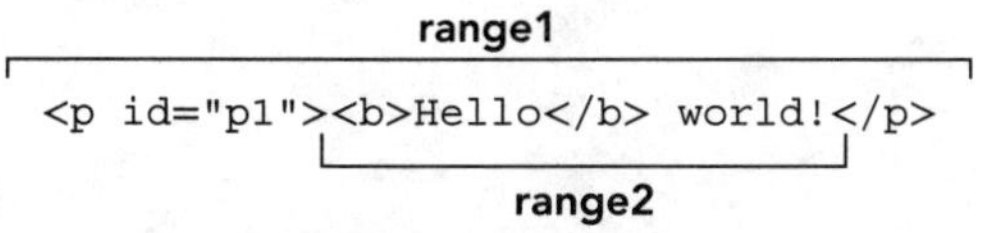

range1

`<p id="p1"><b>Hello</b> world!</p>`

range2

FIGURE 14.6: Illustration of two different ranges

When selectNodeContents() is called, startContainer, endContainer, and commonAncestorContainer are equal to the node that was passed in, which is the `<p>` element in this example.

The startOffset property is always equal to 0, because the range begins with the first child of the given node, whereas endOffset is equal to the number of child nodes (node.childNodes.length), which is 2 in this example.

It's possible to get more fine-grained control over which nodes are included in the selection by using the following range methods:

➤ setStartBefore(refNode)—Sets the starting point of the range to begin before refNode, so refNode is the first node in the selection. The startContainer property is set to refNode.parentNode, and the startOffset property is set to the index of refNode within its parent's childNodes collection.

➤ setStartAfter(refNode)—Sets the starting point of the range to begin after refNode, so refNode is not part of the selection; rather, its next sibling is the first node in the selection. The startContainer property is set to refNode.parentNode, and the startOffset property is set to the index of refNode within its parent's childNodes collection plus one.

➤ setEndBefore(refNode)—Sets the ending point of the range to begin before refNode, so refNode is not part of the selection; its previous sibling is the last node in the selection. The endContainer property is set to refNode.parentNode, and the endOffset property is set to the index of refNode within its parent's childNodes collection.

➤ setEndAfter(refNode)—Sets the ending point of the range to begin before refNode, so refNode is the last node in the selection. The endContainer property is set to refNode.parentNode, and the endOffset property is set to the index of refNode within its parent's childNodes collection plus one.

When you use any of these methods, all properties are assigned for you. However, it is possible to assign these values directly in order to make complex range selections.

Complex Selection in DOM Ranges

Creating complex ranges requires the use of the setStart() and setEnd() methods. Both methods accept two arguments: a reference node and an offset. For setStart(), the reference node becomes the startContainer, and the offset becomes the startOffset. For setEnd(), the reference node becomes the endContainer, and the offset becomes the endOffset.

With these methods, it is possible to mimic selectNode() and selectNodeContents(). Here is an example:

```
let range1 = document.createRange(),
    range2 = document.createRange(),
    p1 = document.getElementById("p1"),
    p1Index = -1,
    i,
    len;
for (i = 0, len = p1.parentNode.childNodes.length; i < len; i++) {
  if (p1.parentNode.childNodes[i] === p1) {
    p1Index = i;
    break;
  }
}

range1.setStart(p1.parentNode, p1Index);
range1.setEnd(p1.parentNode, p1Index + 1);
range2.setStart(p1, 0);
range2.setEnd(p1, p1.childNodes.length);
```

Note that to select the node (using range1), you must first determine the index of the given node (p1) in its parent node's childNodes collection. To select the node contents (using range2), you do not need calculations; setStart() and setEnd() can be set with default values. Although mimicking selectNode() and selectNodeContents() is possible, the real power of setStart() and setEnd() is in the partial selection of nodes.

Suppose that you want to select only from the "llo" in "Hello" to the "o" in " world!" in the previous HTML code. This is quite easy to accomplish. The first step is to get references to all of the relevant nodes, as shown in the following example:

```
let p1 = document.getElementById("p1"),
    helloNode = p1.firstChild.firstChild,
    worldNode = p1.lastChild;
```

The "Hello" text node is actually a grandchild of <p> because it's a child of <b>, so you can use p1.firstChild to get <b> and p1.firstChild.firstChild to get the text node. The " world!" text node is the second (and the last) child of <p>, so you can use p1.lastChild to retrieve it. Next, the range must be created and its boundaries defined, as shown in the following example:

```
let range = document.createRange();
range.setStart(helloNode, 2);
range.setEnd(worldNode, 3);
```

Because the selection should start after the "e" in "Hello", helloNode is passed into setStart() with an offset of 2 (the position after the "e" where "H" is in position 0). To set the end of the selection, pass worldNode into setEnd() with an offset of 3, indicating the first character that should not be selected, which is "r" in position 3 (there is actually a space in position 0). You'll see this illustrated in Figure 14.7.

Because both helloNode and worldNode are text nodes, they become the startContainer and endContainer for the range so that the startOffset and endOffset accurately look at the text contained within each node rather than looking for child nodes (which is what happens when an element is passed in). The commonAncestorContainer is the <p> element, which is the first ancestor that contains both nodes.

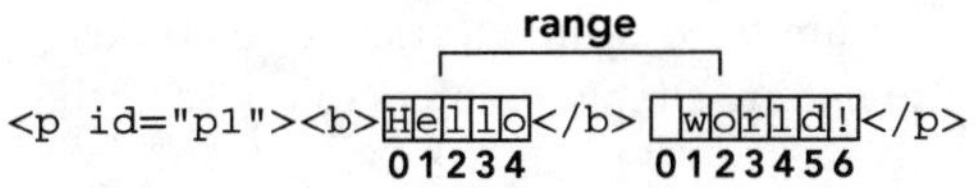

```
                         range
                    ┌──────────────┐
<p id="p1"><b>He│llo</b> │wo│rld!│</p>
                01234      0123456
```

FIGURE 14.7: Illustration of range character selection

Of course, just selecting sections of the document isn't very useful unless you can interact with the selection.

Interacting with DOM Range Content

When a range is created, internally it creates a document fragment node onto which all of the nodes in the selection are attached. The range contents must be well formed in order for this process to take place. In the previous example, the range does not represent a well-formed DOM structure because the selection begins inside one text node and ends in another, which cannot be represented in the DOM. Ranges, however, recognize missing opening and closing tags and are, therefore, able to reconstruct a valid DOM structure to operate on.

In the previous example, the range calculates that a `<b>` start tag is missing inside the selection, so the range dynamically adds it behind the scenes, along with a new `</b>` end tag to enclose `"He"`, thus altering the DOM to the following:

```
<p><b>He</b><b>llo</b> world!</p>
```

Additionally, the `" world!"` text node is split into two text nodes, one containing `" wo"` and the other containing `"rld!"`. The resulting DOM tree is shown in Figure 14.8, along with the contents of the document fragment for the range.

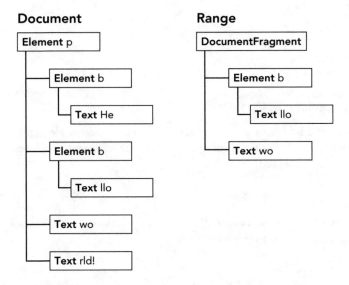

FIGURE 14.8: Comparing a DOM tree and a range document fragment

With the range created, the contents of the range can be manipulated using a variety of methods. (Note that all nodes in the range's internal document fragment are simply pointers to nodes in the document.)

The first method is the simplest to understand and use: deleteContents(). This method simply deletes the contents of the range from the document. Here is an example:

```
let p1 = document.getElementById("p1"),
    helloNode = p1.firstChild.firstChild,
    worldNode = p1.lastChild,
    range = document.createRange();

range.setStart(helloNode, 2);
range.setEnd(worldNode, 3);

range.deleteContents();
```

Executing this code results in the following HTML being shown on the page:

```
<p><b>He</b>rld!</p>
```

Because the range selection process altered the underlying DOM structure to remain well formed, the resulting DOM structure is well formed even after the contents are removed.

extractContents() is similar to deleteContents() in that it also removes the range selection from the document. The difference is that extractContents() returns the range's document fragment as the function value. This allows you to insert the contents of the range somewhere else. Here is an example:

```
let p1 = document.getElementById("p1"),
    helloNode = p1.firstChild.firstChild,
    worldNode = p1.lastChild,
    range = document.createRange();

range.setStart(helloNode, 2);
range.setEnd(worldNode, 3);

let fragment = range.extractContents();
p1.parentNode.appendChild(fragment);
```

In this example, the fragment is extracted and added to the end of the document's <body> element. (Remember, when a document fragment is passed into appendChild(), only the fragment's children are added, not the fragment itself.) The resulting HTML is as follows:

```
<p><b>He</b>rld!</p>
<b>llo</b> wo
```

Another option is to leave the range in place but create a clone of it that can be inserted elsewhere in the document by using cloneContents(), as shown in this example:

```
let p1 = document.getElementById("p1"),
    helloNode = p1.firstChild.firstChild,
    worldNode = p1.lastChild,
```

```
        range = document.createRange();

range.setStart(helloNode, 2);
range.setEnd(worldNode, 3);

let fragment = range.cloneContents();
p1.parentNode.appendChild(fragment);
```

This method is very similar to extractContents() because both return a document fragment. The main difference is that the document fragment returned by cloneContents() contains clones of the nodes contained in the range instead of the actual nodes. With this operation, the HTML in the page is as follows:

```
<p><b>Hello</b> world!</p>
<b>llo</b> wo
```

It's important to note that the splitting of nodes ensures that a well-formed document isn't produced until one of these methods is called. The original HTML remains intact right up until the point that the DOM is modified.

Inserting DOM Range Content

Ranges can be used to remove or clone content, as you saw in the previous section, and to manipulate the contents inside of the range. The insertNode() method enables you to insert a node at the beginning of the range selection. For example, suppose that you want to insert the following HTML prior to the HTML used in the previous example:

```
<span style="color: red">Inserted text</span>
```

The following code accomplishes this:

```
let p1 = document.getElementById("p1"),
    helloNode = p1.firstChild.firstChild,
    worldNode = p1.lastChild,
    range = document.createRange();

range.setStart(helloNode, 2);
range.setEnd(worldNode, 3);

let span = document.createElement("span");
span.style.color = "red";
span.appendChild(document.createTextNode("Inserted text"));
range.insertNode(span);
```

Running this JavaScript effectively creates the following HTML code:

```
<p id="p1"><b>He<span style="color: red">Inserted text</span>llo</b> world</p>
```

Note that <span> is inserted just before the "llo" in "Hello", which is the first part of the range selection. Also note that the original HTML didn't add or remove <b> elements because none of the methods introduced in the previous section were used. You can use this technique to insert helpful information, such as an image next to links that open in a new window.

Along with inserting content into the range, it is possible to insert content surrounding the range by using the surroundContents() method. This method accepts one argument, which is the node that surrounds the range contents. Behind the scenes, the following steps are taken:

1. The contents of the range are extracted.

2. The given node is inserted into the position in the original document where the range was.

3. The contents of the document fragment are added to the given node.

This sort of functionality is useful online to highlight certain words in a web page, as shown here:

```
let p1 = document.getElementById("p1"),
    helloNode = p1.firstChild.firstChild,
    worldNode = p1.lastChild,
    range = document.createRange();

range.selectNode(helloNode);
let span = document.createElement("span");
span.style.backgroundColor = "yellow";
range.surroundContents(span);
```

This code highlights the range selection with a yellow background. The resulting HTML is as follows:

```
<p><b><span style="background-color:yellow">Hello</span></b> world!</p>
```

In order to insert the <span>, the range has to contain a whole DOM selection. (It can't have only partially selected DOM nodes.)

Collapsing a DOM Range

When a range isn't selecting any part of a document, it is said to be *collapsed*. Collapsing a range resembles the behavior of a text box. When you have text in a text box, you can highlight an entire word using the mouse. However, if you left-click the mouse again, the selection is removed and the cursor is located between two letters. When you collapse a range, its location is set between parts of a document, either at the beginning of the range selection or at the end. Figure 14.9 illustrates what happens when a range is collapsed.

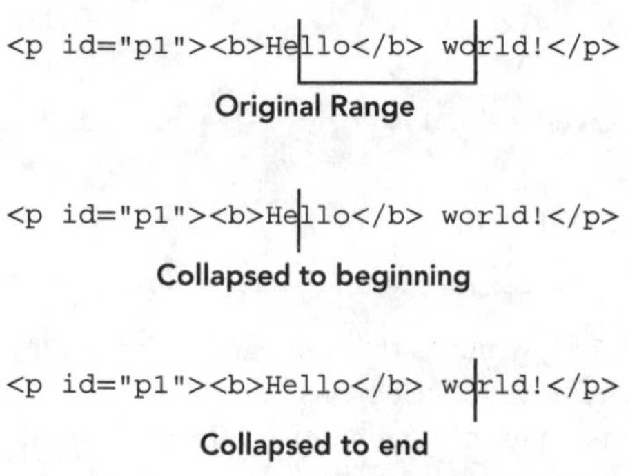

```
<p id="p1"><b>Hello</b> world!</p>
```
Original Range

```
<p id="p1"><b>Hello</b> world!</p>
```
Collapsed to beginning

```
<p id="p1"><b>Hello</b> world!</p>
```
Collapsed to end

FIGURE 14.9: Illustration of range collapse

You can collapse a range by using the `collapse()` method, which accepts a single argument: a Boolean value indicating which end of the range to collapse to. If the argument is `true`, then the range is collapsed to its starting point; if it is `false`, the range is collapsed to its ending point. To determine if a range is already collapsed, you can use the collapsed property as follows:

```
range.collapse(true);      // collapse to the starting point
console.log(range.collapsed);  // outputs "true"
```

Testing whether a range is collapsed is helpful if you aren't sure if two nodes in the range are next to each other. For example, consider this HTML code:

```
<p id="p1">Paragraph 1</p><p id="p2">Paragraph 2</p>
```

If you don't know the exact makeup of this code (for example, if it is automatically generated), you might try creating a range like this:

```
let p1 = document.getElementById("p1"),
    p2 = document.getElementById("p2"),
    range = document.createRange();
range.setStartAfter(p1);
range.setStartBefore(p2);
console.log(range.collapsed);  // true
```

In this case, the created range is collapsed because there is nothing between the end of `p1` and the beginning of `p2`.

Comparing DOM Ranges

If you have more than one range, you can use the `compareBoundaryPoints()` method to determine if the ranges have any boundaries (start or end) in common. The method accepts two arguments: the range to compare to and how to compare. It is one of the following constant values:

➤ `Range.START_TO_START` (0)—Compares the starting point of the first range to the starting point of the second.

➤ `Range.START_TO_END` (1)—Compares the starting point of the first range to the end point of the second.

➤ `Range.END_TO_END` (2)—Compares the end point of the first range to the end point of the second.

➤ `Range.END_TO_START` (3)—Compares the end point of the first range to the starting point of the second.

The `compareBoundaryPoints()` method returns –1 if the point from the first range comes before the point from the second range, 0 if the points are equal, or 1 if the point from the first range comes after the point from the second range. Consider the following example:

```
let range1 = document.createRange();
let range2 = document.createRange();
```

```
let p1 = document.getElementById("p1");

range1.selectNodeContents(p1);
range2.selectNodeContents(p1);
range2.setEndBefore(p1.lastChild);

console.log(range1.
compareBoundaryPoints(Range.START_TO_START,
range2));  // 0
console.log(range1.
compareBoundaryPoints(Range.END_TO_END,
range2));      // 1
```

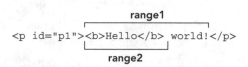

FIGURE 14.10: Illustration of the effect of `setEndBefore()`

In this code, the starting points of the two ranges are exactly the same because both use the default value from `selectNodeContents()`; therefore, the method returns 0. For `range2`, however, the end point is changed using `setEndBefore()`, making the end point of `range1` come after the end point of `range2` (see Figure 14.10), so the method returns 1.

Cloning DOM Ranges

Ranges can be cloned by calling the `cloneRange()` method. This method creates an exact duplicate of the range on which it is called:

```
let newRange = range.cloneRange();
```

The new range contains all of the same properties as the original, and its end points can be modified without affecting the original in any way.

Cleanup

When you are done using a range, it is best to call the `detach()` method, which detaches the range from the document on which it was created. After `detach()` is called, the range can be safely dereferenced, so the memory can be reclaimed through garbage collection. Here is an example:

```
range.detach();  // detach from document
range = null;    //  dereferenced
```

Following these two steps is the most appropriate way to finish using a range. Once it is detached, a range can no longer be used.

OBSERVER APIS

The Observer APIs allow you to track changes to different aspects of a web page and execute a callback function in response. There are several observer APIs available in modern web browsers, including Mutation Observer, Resize Observer, and Intersection Observer.

➤ The Mutation Observer API is defined in the DOM standard.

➤ The Resize Observer API is defined in the Resize Observer specification from the W3C CSS Working Group.

➤ The Intersection Observer API is defined in the Intersection Observer specification from the W3C Web Applications Working Group.

Though there is no unifying specification that governs these APIs; at a high level, the way they are used is more or less identical.

Observer API Methods

The Observer APIs are initialized and managed using slight variations of the same structure. For this section, we'll use a fake observer class, `FakeObserver`, to demonstrate the shared API features.

Initialization

An observer instance is created by calling the constructor with `new`. The constructor will always be passed a callback function that executes each time the relevant event is "observed." An instance of a `FakeObserver` can be created as follows:

```
let fakeCallback = () =>{};

let fakeObserver = new FakeObserver(fakeCallback);
```

This creates an observer instance that executes the empty arrow function each time a "fake event" is detected. You won't see any callbacks execute yet because this observer *isn't observing anything*. Read on to learn how to observe elements.

Callback Execution

An observer will execute the callback each time it detects that an observed object changed in a relevant way. (A `ResizeObserver` tracks resize events, an `IntersectionObserver` tracks intersection events, etc.)

```
let fakeCallback = (fakeEventContext, observer) => console.log("Fake event
happened!");

let fakeObserver = new FakeObserver(fakeCallback);
```

Inside the callback, `fakeEventContext` will contain information about what events triggered the callback. For some of the APIs, this will be an object with different properties describing different events; for other APIs, this will be an array of entries that describe one or more fake events. The callback will also be passed a reference to the observer as the second argument.

The frequency of the callback execution will depend on the API. Some callbacks will execute during the rendering process, and others will execute asynchronously as a microtask.

The *observe()* method

An observer instance will only start executing callbacks once it has been assigned an element to observe; this is accomplished with the `observe()` method. The arguments to this method will vary between the APIs, but in all cases, you will need to pass in the element to be observed. For example, the following code will instruct a fake observer to begin observing the document body for fake events:

```
fakeObserver.observe(document.body);
```

The `observe()` method can be called any number of times to watch multiple elements, as shown here:

```
for (const div of document.querySelectorAll("div")) {
  fakeObserver.observe(div);
}
```

Inside the callback, multiple changed elements will be distinguishable from the entries passed to the callback.

> **NOTE** `ResizeObserver` *will always trigger a callback immediately after* `observe()` *is called.*

The *unobserve()* and *disconnect()* methods

Use the `unobserve()` method to stop observing a single element and the `disconnect()` method to stop observing all elements. These methods are idempotent; calling them on an unobserved element or multiple times will cause them to behave as a NOOP. Elements can be added and removed from an observer at will.

```
// Stop observing one element
fakeObserver.unobserve(document.body);

// Stop observing all elements
fakeObserver.disconnect();
```

Importantly, calling one of these methods while a callback is still enqueued will cancel the execution of that callback.

> **NOTE** `MutationObserver` *does not implement the* `unobserve()` *method.*

Async Callbacks and the Record Queue

The observer specification is designed for performance, and at the core of its design is the asynchronous callback and record queue model. To allow for a large number of intersections to be registered without degrading performance, information about each qualifying event (determined by the observer instance) is captured in a record and then enqueued on a *record queue*. This queue is unique to each observer instance and represents an in-order record of each event.

Each time a record is added to a record queue, the observer callback (initially provided to the constructor) is scheduled as a microtask only if there is no callback microtask already scheduled—for example, the queue length is > 0. This ensures there is no dual-callback processing of the record queue's contents.

It is possible that, by the time the callback's microtask asynchronously executes, more events have occurred than the one that initially scheduled the callback microtask. The invoked callback is passed an array of record instances as they appear in the record queue. The callback is responsible for fully handling each instance in the array, as they will not persist after the function exits. Following the callback execution, it is expected that each record is no longer needed, so the record queue is emptied and its contents discarded.

> **NOTE** `ResizeObserver` *does not use a record queue and does not implement the* `takeRecords()` *method.*

The *takeRecords()* method

Normally, records will be automatically dequeued and passed to your callback. If instead you wish to manually process the queue, you can call `observer.takeRecords()` to get all the pending event records that have not yet been handled in a callback. To prevent double-handling, this will also empty the queue.

```
console.logfakeObserver.takeRecords();
// [FakeObserverRecord, FakeObserverRecord, ...]
```

This is especially useful when you would like to call `disconnect()` but wish to handle all pending record instances in the queue before they are discarded when calling `disconnect()`.

Observer References

The reference relationship between an observer and the node (or nodes) it observes is asymmetric. An observer has a weak reference to the target node it is observing. Because this reference is weak, it will not prevent the target node from being garbage collected.

However, a node has a strong reference to its observer. If the target node is removed from the DOM and subsequently garbage collected, the associated observer is also garbage collected.

Resize Observers

The `ResizeObserver` API allows you to track changes to the size of DOM elements. With a `ResizeObserver`, you can asynchronously execute a callback function whenever an observed element's dimensions change, including both its width and height. This API is useful when dealing with responsive web design or dynamic layout updates. `ResizeObserver` also enables you to observe changes to the size of an element's content or padding box, making it a versatile tool for monitoring and responding to changes in your web application's layout.

A `ResizeObserver` instance is created by calling the `ResizeObserver` constructor and passing a callback function:

```
let observer = new ResizeObserver(() => console.log("Resized!"));
```

The `ResizeObserver` `observe()` method accepts two arguments: the target DOM node to be observed for changes, and an optional `options` object. The following example creates an observer and configures it to watch for resizes of the body element:

```
let observer = new ResizeObserver(() => console.log('<body> size changed'));

observer.observe(document.body);

// <body> size changed!
```

After calling `observe()`, any changes to the `<body>` element's dimensions will be detected by the `ResizeObserver` instance, and the callback will asynchronously execute. Note that the initial call to `observe()` will trigger a single callback execution. This allows you a chance to perform initialization with the starting dimensions.

The following example demonstrates the resize callback firing initially and after a subsequent resize:

```
let observer = new ResizeObserver(() => console.log('<body> was resized'));

observer.observe(document.body);

// ResizeObserver will always fire the callback once when observe() is called
// <body> was resized

setTimeout(() => {
  document.body.style.width = "100px";
}, 1000);

// (After 1000ms):
// <body> was resized
```

Resizes of child elements will not generate a callback unless they cause the observed element to change in size.

Calling `unobserve()` or `disconnect()` stops resize events from triggering callbacks. Importantly, these will cause enqueued callbacks to be cancelled.

```
let observer = new ResizeObserver(() => console.log("<body> was resized"));

observer.observe(document.body);

// ResizeObserver will always fire the callback once when observe() is called
// <body> was resized

setTimeout(() => {
  document.body.style.width = "100px";
  observer.unobserve(document.body);
}, 1000);

// nothing logged
```

Box Model Configuration

The `options` object is used to control what box model should be used to calculate the size of the target node. This can be done by setting its `box` property to one of three options:

➤ `content-box` uses the content dimensions. This is the default.

➤ `border-box` uses the border dimensions.

➤ `device-pixel-content-box` uses the content dimensions prior to applying any CSS transforms.

```
observer.observe(document.body, { box: "device-pixel-content-box" });
```

Callback Scheduling and Execution

A `ResizeObserver` will process resize events during the rendering process: all the action occurs *after* layout but *before* paint. This should make sense: the browser waits as long as possible to measure the elements and determine if a resize occurred but runs the callback before performing a paint in case the callback further modifies the layout.

```
let observer = new ResizeObserver(() => console.log('<body> was resized'));

observer.observe(document.body);

// ResizeObserver will always fire the callback once when observe() is called
// <body> was resized

setTimeout(() => {
  document.body.style.width = "100px";
  console.log("Changed body width");
}, 1000);

// (After 1000ms):
// Changed body width
// <body> was resized
```

Note that the callback `console.log` executes *second*, indicating that the callback does not synchronously execute when `style.width` is assigned a new value.

In practice, resizes often do not happen all at once: the user dragging to resize a window, an animation that modifies element size, or progressive content rendering will incur a veritable firehose of resize events. Your callbacks will need to take this into account.

ResizeObserverEntry

Each callback is passed two arguments: an array of `ResizeObserverEntry` objects that represents each resize event that was tracked and the observer instance. This allows you to make alterations to the page based on the resize dimensions as well as use the observer reference to unobserve an element if needed.

The `ResizeObserverEntry` object is a dictionary that includes the following read-only values:

➤ `borderBoxSize` contains the new border box size.

➤ `contentBoxSize` contains the new content box size.

➤ `devicePixelContentBoxSize` contains the new content box size in device pixels.

➤ `contentRect` contains the new element size as a `DOMRect` object. It is a holdover from a previous API specification.

➤ `target` is a reference to the element.

The `*-BoxSize` properties have an array of objects with two properties: `blockSize`, the length of the element's box in the block dimension, and `inlineSize`, the length of the element's box in the inline dimension. An array is needed because elements may have multiple fragments in multi-column scenarios, but you will usually be dealing with an array of length 1.

The following example shows a sample `ResizeObserverEntry` array logged to the console:

```
let observer = new ResizeObserver((entries, observer) => console.log(entries));
observer.observe(document.body);

// [
//   {
//     borderBoxSize: [
//       {
//         inlineSize: 323,
//         blockSize: 51
//       }
//     ],
//     contentBoxSize: [
//       {
//         inlineSize: 323,
//         blockSize: 51
//       }
//     ],
//     devicePixelContentBoxSize: [
//       {
//         inlineSize: 323,
//         blockSize: 51
//       }
//     ],
//     contentRect: {
//       top: 0,
//       right: 323,
//       bottom: 51,
//       left: 0,
//       height: 51,
//       width: 323,
//       x: 0,
//       y: 0
//     },
//     target: body
//   }
// ]
```

The Resize Observer API does not use a record queue system because the interval at which callbacks are fired is strictly defined: if the browser detects a resize has occurred following the layout rendering phase, it will fire a single callback with a single `ResizeObserverEntry` that captures the current state of the resized target. The next time an event can be fired is the subsequent layout phase. As a result, there is no scenario where two resize events would fire for the same event—and therefore, no queue is required.

Intersection Observers

The Intersection Observer API allows you to track the visibility and position of DOM elements relative to a specified viewport or container element. By using an `IntersectionObserver`, you can execute a callback function asynchronously whenever an observed element intersects with or leaves the intersection area, known as the "viewport." This API is particularly useful for implementing scroll-based animations or performance optimizations like lazy loading of images or infinite scrolling. `IntersectionObserver` also offers various options for fine-tuning your observation, such as controlling the threshold for triggering an intersection, observing multiple elements simultaneously, or adjusting the root element of the intersection area.

An `IntersectionObserver` instance is created by calling the `IntersectionObserver` constructor and passing a callback function and an optional `options` object:

```
let observer = new IntersectionObserver(() => console.log("Intersection!"));
```

When `options` are not provided, the default behavior of the observer is as follows:

➤ The default viewport is the document's viewport, effectively the entire screen.

➤ The default threshold is 0, meaning that a single pixel of the target element overlapping the viewport will fire the callback.

Consider the following example that uses the defaults:

```
document.body.innerHTML = `
  <div style="margin-top:150vh; height: 100px;"></div>
`;

let observer = new IntersectionObserver(() => console.log("Intersection!"));

observer.observe(document.querySelector("div"));
```

The initial state of the page is a `<div>` that is fully below the viewport. An `IntersectionObserver` callback fires when the threshold is reached in either direction: going from totally occluded to partially visible and also from partially visible to totally occluded. When the user scrolls down, as soon as the top of the `<div>` intersects the document viewport, the callback will fire. When they scroll up and the `<div>` becomes hidden again, the callback will fire once more.

Intersection Configuration

The `options` object can configure what the observer treats as an intersection event using the following properties:

➤ `root` indicates what element should be treated as the viewport. This defaults to the document viewport. You'll rarely find the need to set this value, since elements entering the device viewport are overwhelmingly how intersection observers are used.

➤ rootMargin allows you to artificially modify the bounding box of the viewport, growing or shrinking it to modulate what is considered as part of the viewport. This property should be used identically to the CSS margin style, and it defaults to 0px 0px 0px 0px.

➤ threshold is a float or array of floats between 0.0 and 0.1. These define the percentage (or percentages) that will trigger an intersection observer callback.

➤ trackVisibility is a Boolean indicating if the observer should track changes in a target element's visibility. If true, a delay value is also required.

➤ delay is only required when trackVisibility is true and indicates the minimum delay in milliseconds between notifications from the observer for a given target. Minimum value is 100.

The following example modifies the previous one to fire every time the visibility reaches 0%, 50%, and 100%:

```
document.body.innerHTML = `
  <div style="margin-top:150vh; height: 100px;"></div>
`;

let observer = new IntersectionObserver(
  () => console.log("Intersection!"),
  {
    threshold: [0, 0.5, 1]
  }
);

observer.observe(document.querySelector("div"));
```

Scrolling the <div> fully into view and then fully out of view will fire the callback six times: once for each threshold while scrolling fully into view and once for each threshold while scrolling completely out of view.

trackVisibility and delay were introduced in the IntersectionObserver v2 specification, which is currently only supported in Chromium browsers. With v1, the intersection coordinates indicate if a target element overlaps the viewport, but this does not mean the user can actually see the element: CSS rules like transform, filter, opacity, z-index, and visibility can make an element effectively invisible to the user. The v2 additions serve to address this problem by optionally calculating the isVisible Boolean, which indicates if there is overlap *and* if there are real pixels rendered on the screen that the user can see. The following example creates an observer that checks for actual visibility for two <div> elements:

```
document.body.innerHTML = `
  <div style="height: 100px; width: 100px; ">Foo</div>
  <div style="height: 100px; width: 100px; opacity: 0;">Bar</div>
`;

let observer = new IntersectionObserver(
  (entries) => console.log(`isVisible: ${entries.map((x) => x.isVisible)}`),
  {
    trackVisibility: true,
    delay: 1000
```

```
  }
);
[...document.querySelectorAll("div")].map((el) => observer.observe(el));
```

// isVisible: [true,false]

Calculating effective visibility is *extremely* expensive compared to cartesian intersection. The `delay` value is used so that the browser has to perform this calculation as infrequently as possible, and it should be set to the maximum amount that your application can tolerate.

> **NOTE** *The browser's visibility calculation will bias toward false negatives. It might return* `isVisible:false` *when the target element in fact is visible, but it will never return* `isVisible:true` *when the target is invisible.*

Working with Callbacks and IntersectionObserverEntry

When a callback is fired, the callback is passed an array of `IntersectionObserverEntry` objects. Each of these corresponds to an observed element, and the entry indicates the current intersection state of that element when a threshold triggered the callback. It contains the following read-only properties:

➤ `boundingClientRect` is the DOMRect bounding rectangle of the observed element, relative to the viewport.

➤ `intersectionRatio` is the decimal ratio of the observed element's intersection area to its total area. This value is a number between 0 and 1. Importantly, this value may not match the threshold that triggered the callback.

➤ `isIntersection` is a Boolean indicating if this target element intersects the viewport by any amount.

➤ `rootBounds` is the DOMRect bounding rectangle of the root.

➤ `target` is a reference to the observed element.

➤ `isVisible` is a Boolean indicating if the element was determined to be visible. It is only used when `trackVisibility` and `delay` are set. Defaults to `false`.

➤ `time` is a DOMHighResTimeStamp indicating when the intersection was recorded.

The following example logs a sample entry for a simple <div>:

```
document.body.innerHTML = `
  <div style="height: 100px; width: 100px; margin-top: -50px;"></div>
`;

let observer = new IntersectionObserver((entries) =>
  console.log({ entries })
);
```

```
observer.observe(document.querySelector("div"));

// {
//   entries: [
//     {
//       boundingClientRect: {
//         x: 8,
//         y: -42,
//         width: 100,
//         height: 100,
//         top: -42,
//         right: 108,
//         bottom: 58,
//         left: 8
//       },
//       intersectionRatio: 0.5799999833106995,
//       intersectionRect: {
//         x: 8,
//         y: 0,
//         width: 100,
//         height: 58,
//         top: 0,
//         right: 108,
//         bottom: 58,
//         left: 8
//       },
//       isIntersecting: true,
//       isVisible: false,
//       rootBounds: null,
//       target: <div>,
//       time: 1794.5
//     }
//   ]
// }
```

The isIntersecting boolean is particularly useful, as it allows for conditionally applying logic based on the most recent state inside the callback. Consider the following example:

```
// Generate a vertical column of 30 divs
document.body.innerHTML = `
  <div style="height: 100px; width: 100px;"></div>
`.repeat(30);

let observer = new IntersectionObserver(
  (entries) => {
    entries.map((entry) => {
      // Change between blue and red based on visibility
      entry.target.style.backgroundColor = entry.isIntersecting
        ? "blue"
        : "red";
    });
  },
  // Only fire a callback when a <div> crosses half visible
  { threshold: 0.5 }
);
[...document.querySelectorAll("div")].map((el) => observer.observe(el));
```

In this example, a single observer is observing a collection of `<div>` elements, but we only want to set visible elements to blue. Each time the callback fires, we won't know how many `IntersectionObserverEntry` objects to expect. It might be one, it might be all 30, it might be somewhere in between. Furthermore, some of the entries might be indicating a target element has become *visible*, and others might be indicating a target element has become *invisible*. To account for this, the preceding example demonstrates a common pattern that processes the entire collection at once, using `isIntersecting` to bifurcate its handling of the entries.

Mutation Observers

The Mutation Observer API allows you to asynchronously execute a callback when the DOM is modified. With a `MutationObserver`, you are able to observe an entire document, a DOM subtree, or just a single element. Furthermore, you are also able to observe changes to element attributes, child nodes, text, or any combination of the three.

> **NOTE** *Mutation observers were introduced to replace the abandoned Mutation Events feature.*

A `MutationObserver` instance is created by calling the `MutationObserver` constructor and passing a callback function:

```
let observer = new MutationObserver(() => console.log('DOM was mutated!'));
```

This instance begins unassociated with any part of the DOM. To link this observer with the DOM, the `observe()` method is used. This method accepts two required arguments: the target DOM node that is observed for changes, and the `MutationObserverInit` object.

The `MutationObserverInit` object is used to control what changes the observer should watch for. It takes the form of a dictionary of key-value configuration options. For example, the following code creates an observer and configures it to watch for attribute changes on the body element:

```
let observer = new MutationObserver(
    () => console.log('<body> attributes changed'));

observer.observe(document.body, { attributes: true });
```

At this point, any attribute changes to the `<body>` element will be detected by the `MutationObserver` instance, and the callback will asynchronously execute. Modifications to children or other non-attribute DOM mutations will not schedule a callback. This behavior is demonstrated here:

```
let observer = new MutationObserver(
    () => console.log('<body> attributes changed'));

observer.observe(document.body, { attributes: true });

document.body.className = 'foo';
console.log('Changed body class');

// Changed body class
// <body> attributes changed
```

Note that the callback `console.log` executes second, indicating that the callback does not synchronously execute with the actual DOM mutation.

Working with Callbacks and MutationRecords

Each callback is passed an array of `MutationRecord` instances. Each instance contains information about what kind of mutation occurred and what part of the DOM was affected. Because it is possible that multiple qualifying mutations occurred before a callback is executed, each callback invocation is passed the queued backup of `MutationRecord` instances.

The `MutationRecord` array for a single attribute mutation is shown here:

```
let observer = new MutationObserver(
    (mutationRecords) => console.log(mutationRecords));

observer.observe(document.body, { attributes: true });

document.body.setAttribute('foo', 'bar');

// [
//   {
//       addedNodes: NodeList [],
//       attributeName: "foo",
//       attributeNamespace: null,
//       nextSibling: null,
//       oldValue: null,
//       previousSibling: null
//       removedNodes: NodeList [],
//       target: body
//       type: "attributes"
//   }
// ]
```

A similar mutation involving a namespace is shown here:

```
let observer = new MutationObserver(
    (mutationRecords) => console.log(mutationRecords));

observer.observe(document.body, { attributes: true });

document.body.setAttributeNS('baz', 'foo', 'bar');

// [
//   {
//       addedNodes: NodeList [],
//       attributeName: "foo",
//       attributeNamespace: "baz",
//       nextSibling: null,
//       oldValue: null,
//       previousSibling: null
//       removedNodes: NodeList [],
//       target: body
//       type: "attributes"
//   }
// ]
```

Sequential modifications will generate multiple `MutationRecord` instances, and the next callback invocation will be passed all the pending instances in the order they were enqueued:

```
let observer = new MutationObserver(
    (mutationRecords) => console.log(mutationRecords));

observer.observe(document.body, { attributes: true });

document.body.className = 'foo';
document.body.className = 'bar';
document.body.className = 'baz';

// [MutationRecord, MutationRecord, MutationRecord]
```

A `MutationRecord` instance will have the following properties:

KEY	VALUE
target	The node that was affected by the mutation.
type	A string indicating what type of mutation occurred. Can be "attributes", "characterData", or "childList".
oldValue	When enabled in the `MutationObserverInit` object, attributes or character data mutations will set this field to the value that was replaced. This value is only provided when `attributeOldValue` or `characterDataOldValue` is `true`, otherwise this value is `null`. A `childList` mutation will always set this field to `null`.
attributeName	For attributes mutations, the string name of the attribute that was modified. For all other mutations, this field is set to `null`.
attributeNamespace	For attributes mutations that make use of namespaces, the string namespace of the attribute that was modified. For all other mutations, this field is set to `null`.
addedNodes	For `childList` mutations, returns a `NodeList` of nodes added in the mutation. Defaults to an empty `NodeList`.
removedNodes	For `childList` mutations, returns a `NodeList` of nodes removed in the mutation. Defaults to an empty `NodeList`.
previousSibling	For `childList` mutations, returns the previous sibling node of the mutated node. Defaults to `null`.
nextSibling	For `childList` mutations, returns the next sibling node of the mutated node. Defaults to `null`.

The second argument to the callback is the `MutationObserver` instance that detected the mutation, demonstrated here:

```
let observer = new MutationObserver(
    (mutationRecords, mutationObserver) => console.log(mutationRecords,
    mutationObserver));

observer.observe(document.body, { attributes: true });

document.body.className = 'foo';

// [MutationRecord], MutationObserver
```

Controlling the Observer Scope with MutationObserverInit

The `MutationObserverInit` object is used to control which elements the observer should care about and what kinds of changes to those elements it should care about. Broadly speaking, the observer can watch for attribute changes, text changes, or child node changes.

The following are the expected properties in the `MutationObserverInit` object:

KEY	VALUE
subtree	Boolean indicating if the target element's node subtree should be watched in addition to the target element. When `false`, only the target element will be observed for designated mutations. When `true`, the target element and its entire node subtree will be watched for designated mutations. Defaults to `false`.
attributes	Boolean indicating if modifications to node attributes should register as a mutation. Defaults to `false`.
attributeFilter	Array of string values indicating which specific attributes should be observed for mutations. Setting this value to `true` will also coerce the value of attributes to `true`. Defaults to observing all attributes.
attributeOldValue	Boolean indicating if the character data prior to mutation should be recorded in the `MutationRecord`. Setting this value to an array will also coerce the value of attributes to `true`. Defaults to `false`.

continues

(continued)

KEY	VALUE
characterData	Boolean indicating if modifications to character data should register as a mutation. Defaults to `false`.
characterDataOldValue	Boolean indicating if the character data prior to mutation should be recorded in the `MutationRecord`. Setting this value to `true` will also coerce the value of `characterData` to `true`. Defaults to `false`.
childList	Boolean indicating if modifications to the target node's child nodes should register as a mutation. Defaults to `false`.

> **NOTE** *When* `observe()` *is called, the* `MutationObserverInit` *object must specify at least one of* `attributes`, `characterData`, *or* `childList` *to be* `true` *(either explicitly or implicitly via an associated property such as* `attribute OldValue`*). Otherwise, an error will be thrown since there is no mutation that will trigger a callback to be invoked.*

Observing Attribute Mutations

A `MutationObserver` is capable of registering when a node attribute is added, removed, or changed. Registering a callback is accomplished by setting the attributes property inside the `MutationObserverInit` object to `true`, as demonstrated here:

```
let observer = new MutationObserver(
    (mutationRecords) => console.log(mutationRecords));

observer.observe(document.body, { attributes: true });

// Add attribute
document.body.setAttribute('foo', 'bar');

// Modify existing attribute
document.body.setAttribute('foo', 'baz');

// Remove attribute
document.body.removeAttribute('foo');

// All three are recorded as mutations
// [MutationRecord, MutationRecord, MutationRecord]
```

The default behavior is to observe all attribute changes and to not record the old value inside the `MutationRecord`. If you desire to observe a subset of attributes, the `attributeFilter` property can be used as a whitelist of attribute names:

```
let observer = new MutationObserver(
    (mutationRecords) => console.log(mutationRecords));

observer.observe(document.body, { attributeFilter: ['foo'] });

// Add whitelisted attribute
document.body.setAttribute('foo', 'bar');

// Add excluded attribute
document.body.setAttribute('baz', 'qux');

// Only a single mutation record is created for the 'foo' attribute mutation
// [MutationRecord]
```

If you desire to preserve the old value inside the mutation record, the `attributeOldValue` can be set to true:

```
let observer = new MutationObserver(
    (mutationRecords) => console.log(mutationRecords.map((x) => x.oldValue)));

observer.observe(document.body, { attributeOldValue: true });

document.body.setAttribute('foo', 'bar');
document.body.setAttribute('foo', 'baz');
document.body.setAttribute('foo', 'qux');

// Each mutation records the previous value
// [null, 'bar', 'baz']
```

Observing Character Data Mutations

A `MutationObserver` is capable of registering when a textual node (such as `Text`, `Comment`, or `ProcessingInstruction` nodes) has its character data added, removed, or changed. This is accomplished by setting the `characterData` property inside the `MutationObserverInit` object to true, as demonstrated here:

```
let observer = new MutationObserver(
    (mutationRecords) => console.log(mutationRecords));

// Create an initial text node to observe
document.body.innerText = 'foo';

observer.observe(document.body.firstChild, { characterData: true });

// Identical string assignment
document.body.innerText = 'foo';

// New string assignment
```

```
document.body.innerText = 'bar';

// Node setter assignment
document.body.firstChild.textContent = 'baz';

// All three are recorded as mutations
// [MutationRecord, MutationRecord, MutationRecord]
```

The default behavior is to not record the old value inside the `MutationRecord`. If you desired to preserve the old value inside the mutation record, the `attributeOldValue` can be set to `true`:

```
let observer = new MutationObserver(
    (mutationRecords) => console.log(mutationRecords.map((x) => x.oldValue)));
document.body.innerText = 'foo';

observer.observe(document.body.firstChild, { characterDataOldValue: true });

document.body.innerText = 'foo';
document.body.innerText = 'bar';
document.body.firstChild.textContent = 'baz';

// Each mutation records the previous value
// ["foo", "foo", "bar"]
```

Observing Child Mutations

A `MutationObserver` is capable of registering when an element has a child node added or removed. This is accomplished by setting the `childList` property inside the `MutationObserverInit` object to `true`.

A child node addition is demonstrated here:

```
// clear body
document.body.innerHTML = '';

let observer = new MutationObserver(
    (mutationRecords) => console.log(mutationRecords));

observer.observe(document.body, { childList: true });

document.body.appendChild(document.createElement('div'));

// [
//   {
//     addedNodes: NodeList[div],
//     attributeName: null,
//     attributeNamespace: null,
//     oldValue: null,
//     nextSibling: null,
//     previousSibling: null,
//     removedNodes: NodeList[],
//     target: body,
//     type: "childList",
//   }
// ]
```

A child node removal is demonstrated here:

```
// clear body
document.body.innerHTML = '';

let observer = new MutationObserver(
    (mutationRecords) => console.log(mutationRecords));

observer.observe(document.body, { childList: true });

document.body.appendChild(document.createElement('div'));

// [
//   {
//     addedNodes: NodeList[],
//     attributeName: null,
//     attributeNamespace: null,
//     oldValue: null,
//     nextSibling: null,
//     previousSibling: null,
//     removedNodes: NodeList[div],
//     target: body,
//     type: "childList",
//   }
// ]
```

A child *reordering*, although it can be performed with a single method, will register as two separate mutations since it is technically a node removal and subsequent re-addition:

```
// clear body
document.body.innerHTML = '';

let observer = new MutationObserver(
    (mutationRecords) => console.log(mutationRecords));

// Create two initial children
document.body.appendChild(document.createElement('div'));
document.body.appendChild(document.createElement('span'));

observer.observe(document.body, { childList: true });

// Reorder children
document.body.insertBefore(document.body.lastChild, document.body.firstChild);

// Two mutations are registered:
// 0-index record is removal, 1-index record is addition
// [
//   {
//     addedNodes: NodeList[],
//     attributeName: null,
//     attributeNamespace: null,
//     oldValue: null,
//     nextSibling: null,
//     previousSibling: div,
//     removedNodes: NodeList[span],
```

```
//      target: body,
//      type: childList,
//    },
//    {
//      addedNodes: NodeList[span],
//      attributeName: null,
//      attributeNamespace: null,
//      oldValue: null,
//      nextSibling: div,
//      previousSibling: null,
//      removedNodes: NodeList[],
//      target: body,
//      type: "childList",
//    }
//  ]
```

Observing Subtree Mutations

By default, the `MutationObserver` is scoped to only observe modifications to a single element and its child node list. This scope can be expanded to the entirety of its DOM subtree by setting the subtree property inside the `MutationObserverInit` object to `true`.

Watching a subtree for attribute mutations can be accomplished in the following fashion:

```
// clear body
document.body.innerHTML = '';

let observer = new MutationObserver(
    (mutationRecords) => console.log(mutationRecords));

// Create initial element
document.body.appendChild(document.createElement('div'));

// Observe the <body> subtree
observer.observe(document.body, { attributes: true, subtree: true });

// Modify <body> subtree
document.body.firstChild.setAttribute('foo', 'bar');

// Subtree modification registers as mutation
// [
//    {
//      addedNodes: NodeList[],
//      attributeName: "foo",
//      attributeNamespace: null,
//      oldValue: null,
//      nextSibling: null,
//      previousSibling: null,
//      removedNodes: NodeList[],
//      target: div,
//      type: "attributes",
//    }
//  ]
```

Interestingly, the subtree designation of a node will persist even when that node is moved out of the observed tree. This means that after a subtree node leaves that specific subtree, mutations that are now technically outside the observed subtree will still register as qualified mutations.

This behavior is demonstrated here:

```
// clear body
document.body.innerHTML = '';

let observer = new MutationObserver(
    (mutationRecords) => console.log(mutationRecords));

let subtreeRoot = document.createElement('div'),
    subtreeLeaf = document.createElement('span');

// Create initial subtree of height 2
document.body.appendChild(subtreeRoot);
subtreeRoot.appendChild(subtreeLeaf);

// Observe the subtree
observer.observe(subtreeRoot, { attributes: true, subtree: true });

// Move node in subtree outside of observed subtree
document.body.insertBefore(subtreeLeaf, subtreeRoot);

subtreeLeaf.setAttribute('foo', 'bar');

// subtree modification still registers as mutation
// [MutationRecord]
```

OBSERVER PERFORMANCE

Managing callback performance is crucial when using observer APIs. These APIs have the potential to execute callbacks with staggering frequency and cause a significant degradation in page performance. For example, a single resize observer on <body> can fire hundreds of times with just a single window resize drag. Furthermore, computation by observers can add a uniform slowdown on a page. Whereas a slow click handler will cause a temporary page slowdown following a click, an inefficient observer might be firing almost constantly—thereby slowing down the web page for the duration of the user's visit.

One way to optimize observer performance is to debounce the callback function. Debouncing delays the execution of the callback function until a set time has passed since the last trigger event while still ensuring that the final event in a sequence will be handled. This is important in the context of observers, where it's important to understand the final state of an element.

The following example will only execute the callback at most once per second:

```
let timeoutId = null;
let observer = new ResizeObserver(() => {
  clearTimeout(timeoutId);
  timeoutId = setTimeout(() => console.log("<body> size changed"), 1000);
});

observer.observe(document.body);
```

Another simple but important optimization strategy is to remove observers when they are no longer needed. Eagerly call `unobserve()` and `disconnect()` when elements no longer require an observer.

Finally, prefer to use asynchronous callbacks whenever possible. For example, because the `ResizeObserver` anticipates that the callback might cause further layout changes, it will run the callback synchronously and delay the rendering paint until the callback completes. If you do not have a need for this, define the callback as an *asynchronous* function; this will defer the callback execution and allow the paint to occur sooner.

SUMMARY

While the DOM specifies the core API for interacting with HTML documents, there are several specifications that provide extensions to the standard DOM. Many of the extensions are based on proprietary extensions that later became de facto standards as other browsers began to mimic their functionality.

The DOM Level 2 specifications define several modules that augment the functionality of DOM Level 1. The DOM Level 2 Style module specifies how to interact with stylistic information about elements as follows:

➤ Every element has a style object associated with it that can be used to determine and change inline styles.

➤ To determine the computed style of an element, including all CSS rules that apply to it, you can use a method called `getComputedStyle()`.

➤ It's also possible to access style sheets via the `document.styleSheets` collection.

The DOM Level 2 Traversals and Range module specifies different ways to interact with a DOM structure as follows:

➤ Traversals are handled using either `NodeIterator` or `TreeWalker` to perform depth-first traversals of a DOM tree.

➤ The `NodeIterator` interface is simple, allowing only forward and backward movement in one-step increments. The `TreeWalker` interface supports the same behavior and moves across the DOM structure in all other directions, including parents, siblings, and children.

➤ Ranges are a way to select specific portions of a DOM structure to augment it in some fashion.

➤ Selections of ranges can be used to remove portions of a document while retaining a well-formed document structure or for cloning portions of a document.

The Observer APIs are a powerful set of JavaScript interfaces that allow you to monitor changes in the DOM and respond to them in various ways. The `IntersectionObserver` allows you to track the visibility and position of DOM elements relative to a specified viewport or container element. By using an `IntersectionObserver`, you can execute a callback function asynchronously whenever an observed element intersects with or leaves the intersection area. This API is particularly useful for implementing scroll-based animations or performance optimizations like lazy loading of images or infinite scrolling.

Another useful observer is the `ResizeObserver`, which allows you to detect changes in the size of an element or its children. This observer can be useful for implementing responsive designs or layout algorithms that need to adapt to changes in the size of the viewport or the content.

The `MutationObserver` allows you to monitor changes in the DOM tree and execute a callback function whenever a specified type of mutation occurs. This can be useful for implementing reactive user interfaces or for detecting changes in third-party widgets or scripts that modify the DOM dynamically.

15

Events

WHAT'S IN THIS CHAPTER?

➤ Understanding event flow

➤ Working with event handlers

➤ Examining the different types of events

DOWNLOADS FOR THIS CHAPTER

Please note that all the code examples for this chapter are available as a part of this chapter's code download on the book's website at www.wiley .com/go/projavascript5e.

JavaScript's interaction with HTML is handled through *events*, which indicate when particular moments of interest occur in the document or browser window. Events can be subscribed to using *listeners* (also called handlers) that execute only when an event occurs. This model, called the "observer pattern" in traditional software engineering, allows a loose coupling between the behavior of a page (defined in JavaScript) and the appearance of the page (defined in HTML and CSS).

Events first appeared in Internet Explorer 3 and Netscape Navigator 2 as a way to offload some form processing from the server onto the browser. By the time Internet Explorer 4 and Netscape 4 were released, each browser delivered similar but different APIs that continued for several generations. DOM Level 2 was the first attempt to standardize the DOM events API in a logical way. All modern browsers have implemented the core parts of DOM Level 2 Events. Internet Explorer 8 was the last major browser to use a purely proprietary event system.

The browser event system is a complex one. Even though all major browsers have implemented DOM Level 2 Events, the specification doesn't cover all event types. The BOM also supports events, and the relationship between these and the DOM events is often confusing because of a longtime lack of documentation (something that HTML5 has tried to clarify). Further complicating matters is the augmentation of the DOM events API by DOM Level 3. Working with events can be relatively simple or very complex, depending on your requirements. Still, there are some core concepts that are important to understand.

EVENT FLOW

When development for the fourth generation of web browsers began (Internet Explorer 4 and Netscape Communicator 4), the browser development teams were met with an interesting question: What part of a page owns a specific event? To understand the issue, consider a series of concentric circles on a piece of paper. When you place your finger at the center, it is inside of not just one circle but all of the circles on the paper. Both development teams looked at browser events in the same way. When you click on a button, they concluded, you're clicking not just on the button but also on its container and on the page as a whole.

Event flow describes the order in which events are received on the page, and interestingly, the Internet Explorer and Netscape development teams came up with an almost exactly opposite concept of event flow. Internet Explorer would support an event bubbling flow, whereas Netscape Communicator would support an event capturing flow.

Event Bubbling

The universally adopted event flow model is called *event bubbling* because an event is said to start at the most specific element (the deepest possible point in the document tree) and then flow upward toward the least specific node (the document). Consider the following HTML page:

```
<!DOCTYPE html>
<html>
<head>
  <title>Event Bubbling Example</title>
</head>
<body>
  <div id="myDiv">Click Me</div>
</body>
</html>
```

When you click the `<div>` element in the page, the click event occurs in the following order:

1. `<div>`
2. `<body>`
3. `<html>`
4. `document`
5. `window`

The click event is first fired on the `<div>`, which is the element that was clicked. Then the click event goes up the DOM tree, firing on each node along its way until it reaches the `window` object. Figure 15.1 illustrates this effect.

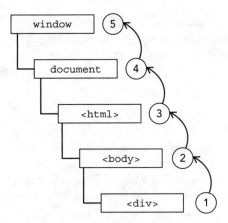

FIGURE 15.1: Illustration of event bubbling

DOM Event Flow

The event flow specified by DOM Level 2 Events has three phases: the event capturing phase, at the target, and the event bubbling phase. Event capturing occurs first, providing the opportunity to intercept events if necessary. Next, the actual target receives the event. The final phase is bubbling, which allows a final response to the event. Considering the simple HTML example used previously, clicking the <div> fires the event in the order indicated in Figure 15.2.

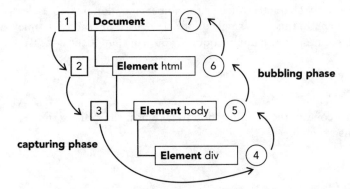

FIGURE 15.2: Illustration of event capturing

In the DOM event flow, the actual target (the <div> element) does not receive the event during the capturing phase. This means that the capturing phase moves from document to <html> to <body> and stops. The next phase is "at target," which fires on the <div> and is considered to be part of the bubbling phase in terms of event handling (discussed later). Then, the bubbling phase occurs and the event travels back up to the document.

Most of the browsers that support DOM event flow have implemented a quirk. Even though the DOM Level 2 Events specification indicates that the capturing phase doesn't hit the event target, modern browsers all fire an event during the capturing phase on the event target. The end result is that there are two opportunities to work with the event on the target.

EVENT HANDLERS

Events are certain actions performed either by the user or by the browser itself. These events have names like click, load, and mouseover. A function that is called in response to an event is called an *event handler* (or an *event listener*). Event handlers have names beginning with "on," so an event handler for the click event is called onclick and an event handler for the load event is called onload. Assigning event handlers can be accomplished in a number of different ways.

HTML Event Handlers

Each event supported by a particular element can be assigned using an HTML attribute with the name of the event handler. The value of the attribute should be some JavaScript code to execute. For example, to execute some JavaScript when a button is clicked, you can use the following:

```
<input type="button" value="Click Me" onclick="console.log('Clicked')"/>
```

When this button is clicked, a message is logged. This interaction is defined by specifying the onclick attribute and assigning some JavaScript code as the value. Note that because the JavaScript code is an attribute value, you cannot use HTML syntax characters such as the ampersand, double quotes, less-than, or greater-than without escaping them. In this case, single quotes were used instead of double quotes to avoid the need to use HTML entities. To use double quotes, you will change the code to the following:

```
<input type="button" value="Click Me"
        onclick="console.log("Clicked")"/>
```

An event handler defined in HTML may contain the precise action to take or it can call a script defined elsewhere on the page, as in this example:

```
<script>
  function showMessage() {
    console.log("Hello world!");
  }
</script>
<input type="button" value="Click Me" onclick="showMessage()"/>
```

In this code, the button calls showMessage() when it is clicked. The showMessage() function is defined in a separate <script> element and could also be included in an external file. Code executing as an event handler has access to everything in the global scope.

Event handlers assigned in this way have some unique aspects. First, a function is created that wraps the attribute value. That function has a special local variable called event, which is the event object (discussed later in this chapter):

```
<!-- outputs "click" -->
<input type="button" value="Click Me" onclick="console.log(event.type)">
```

This gives you access to the event object without needing to define it yourself and without needing to pull it from the enclosing function's argument list.

The `this` value inside of the function is equivalent to the event's target element, as shown in this example:

```
<!-- outputs "Click Me" -->
<input type="button" value="Click Me" onclick="console.log(this.value)">
```

Another interesting aspect of this dynamically created function is how it augments the scope chain. Within the function, members of both document and the element itself can be accessed as if they were local variables. The function accomplishes this via scope chain augmentation using with:

```
function() {
  with(document) {
    with(this) {
      // attribute value
    }
  }
}
```

This means that an event handler can access its own properties easily. The following is functionally the same as the previous example:

```
<!-- outputs "Click Me" -->
<input type="button" value="Click Me" onclick="console.log(value)">
```

If the element is a form input element, then the scope chain also contains an entry for the parent form element, making the function the equivalent to the following:

```
function() {
  with(document) {
    with(this.form) {
      with(this) {
        // attribute value
      }
    }
  }
}
```

Basically, this augmentation allows the event handler code to access other members of the same form without referencing the form element itself. This pattern of member access is demonstrated in the following example:

```
<form method="post">
  <input type="text" name="username" value="">
  <input type="button" value="Echo Username"
         onclick="console.log(username.value)">
</form>
```

Clicking the button in this example results in the text from the text box being displayed. Note that it just references username directly.

There are a few downsides to assigning event handlers in HTML. The first is a timing issue: It's possible that the HTML element appears on the page and is interacted with by the user before the event handler code is ready. In the previous example, imagine a scenario where the showMessage()

function isn't defined until later on the page, after the code for the button. If the user were to click the button before `showMessage()` was defined, an error would occur. For this reason, most HTML event handlers are enclosed in `try-catch` blocks so that they quietly fail, as in the following example:

```
<input type="button" value="Click Me" onclick="try{showMessage();}catch(ex) {}">
```

If this button is clicked before the `showMessage()` function is defined, no JavaScript error occurs because the error is caught before the browser can handle it.

Another downside is that the scope chain augmentation in the event handler function can lead to different results in different browsers. The rules being followed for identifier resolution are slightly different amongst JavaScript engines, and so the result of accessing unqualified object members may cause errors.

The last downside to assigning event handlers using HTML is that it tightly couples the HTML to the JavaScript. If the event handler needs to be changed, you may need to change code in two places: in the HTML and in the JavaScript. This is the primary reason that many developers avoid HTML event handlers in favor of using JavaScript to assign event handlers.

DOM Level 0 Event Handlers

The traditional way of assigning event handlers in JavaScript is to assign a function to an event handler property. This was the event handler assignment method introduced in the fourth generation of web browsers, and it still remains in all modern browsers because of its simplicity and cross-browser support. To assign an event handler using JavaScript, you must first retrieve a reference to the object to act on.

Each element (as well as window and document) has event handler properties that are typically all lowercase, such as `onclick`. An event handler is assigned by setting the property equal to a function, as in this example:

```
let btn = document.getElementById("myBtn");
btn.onclick = function() {
  console.log("Clicked");
};
```

Here, a button is retrieved from the document and an `onclick` event handler is assigned. Note that the event handler isn't assigned until this code is run, so if the code appears after the code for the button in the page, there may be an amount of time during which the button will do nothing when clicked.

When assigning event handlers using the DOM Level 0 method, the event handler is considered to be a method of the element. The event handler, therefore, is run within the scope of the element, meaning that this is equivalent to the element. The value of this is demonstrated in the following example:

```
let btn = document.getElementById("myBtn");
btn.onclick = function() {
  console.log(this.id);   // "myBtn"
};
```

This code displays the element's ID when the button is clicked. The ID is retrieved using `this.id`. It's possible to use this to access any of the element's properties or methods from within the event handlers. Event handlers added in this way are intended for the bubbling phase of the event flow.

You can remove an event handler assigned via the DOM Level 0 approach by setting the value of the event handler property to `null`, as in the following example:

```
btn.onclick = null;  // remove event handler
```

Once the event handler is set to `null`, the button no longer has any action to take when it is clicked.

> **NOTE** *If you've assigned an event handler using HTML, the value on the `onclick` property is a function containing the code specified in the HTML attribute. These event handlers can also be removed by setting the property to `null`.*

DOM Level 2 Event Handlers

DOM Level 2 Events define two methods to deal with the assignment and removal of event handlers: `addEventListener()` and `removeEventListener()`. These methods exist on all DOM nodes and accept three arguments: the event name to handle, the event handler function, and a Boolean value indicating whether to call the event handler during the capture phase (`true`) or during the bubble phase (`false`).

To add an event handler for the click event on a button, you can use the following code:

```
let btn = document.getElementById("myBtn");
btn.addEventListener("click", () => {
  console.log(this.id);
}, false);
```

This code adds an onclick event handler to a button that will be fired in the bubbling phase (since the last argument is false). As with the DOM Level 0 approach, the event handler runs in the scope of the element on which it is attached. The major advantage to using the DOM Level 2 method for adding event handlers is that multiple event handlers can be added. Consider the following example:

```
let btn = document.getElementById("myBtn");
btn.addEventListener("click", () => {
  console.log(this.id);
}, false);
btn.addEventListener("click", () => {
  console.log("Hello world!");
}, false);
```

Here, two event handlers are added to the button. The event handlers fire in the order in which they were added, so the first log displays the element's ID and the second displays the message `"Hello world!"`.

Event handlers added via `addEventListener()` can be removed only by using `removeEventListener()` and passing in the same arguments as were used when the handler was added. This means that anonymous functions added using `addEventListener()` cannot be removed, as shown in this example:

```
let btn = document.getElementById("myBtn");
btn.addEventListener("click", () => {
```

```
      console.log(this.id);
}, false);

// other code here

btn.removeEventListener("click", function() {    // won't work!
   console.log(this.id);
}, false);
```

In this example, an anonymous function is added as an event handler using addEventListener(). The call to removeEventListener() looks like it's using the same arguments, but in reality, the second argument is a completely different function than the one used in addEventListener(). The event handler function passed into removeEventListener() must be the same one that was used in addEventListener(), as in this example:

```
let btn = document.getElementById("myBtn");
let handler = function() {
   console.log(this.id);
};
btn.addEventListener("click", handler, false);

// other code here

btn.removeEventListener("click", handler, false);   // works!
```

This rewritten example works as expected because the same function is used for both addEventListener() and removeEventListener().

In most cases, event handlers are added to the bubbling phase of the event flow because this offers the broadest possible cross-browser support. Attaching an event handler in the capture phase is best done if you need to intercept events before they reach their intended target. If this is not necessary, it's advisable to avoid event capturing.

THE EVENT OBJECT

When an event related to the DOM is fired, all of the relevant information is gathered and stored on an object called event. This object contains basic information such as the element that caused the event, the type of event that occurred, and any other data that may be relevant to the particular event. For example, an event caused by a mouse action generates information about the mouse's position, whereas an event caused by a keyboard action generates information about the keys that were pressed. All browsers support the event object, though not in the same way.

The DOM Event Object

In DOM-compliant browsers, the event object is passed in as the sole argument to an event handler. Regardless of the method used to assign the event handler, DOM Level 0 or DOM Level 2, the event object is passed in. Here is an example which references the event object inside the handler both ways:

```
let btn = document.getElementById("myBtn");
btn.onclick = function(event) {
```

```
    console.log(event.type);  // "click"
};

btn.addEventListener("click", (event) => {
    console.log(event.type);  // "click"
}, false);
```

Both event handlers in this example log a message indicating the type of event being fired by using the event.type property. This property always contains the type of event that was fired, such as "click" (it is the same value that you pass into addEventListener() and removeEventListener()).

When an event handler is assigned using HTML attributes, the event object is available as a variable called event. This example demonstrates how to use this variable:

```
<input type="button" value="Click Me" onclick="console.log(event.type)">
```

Providing the event object in this way allows HTML attribute event handlers to perform the same as JavaScript functions.

The event object contains properties and methods related to the specific event that caused its creation. The available properties and methods differ based on the type of event that was fired, but all events have the members listed in the following table.

PROPERTY/METHOD	TYPE	READ/WRITE	DESCRIPTION
bubbles	Boolean	Read only	Indicates if the event bubbles.
cancelable	Boolean	Read only	Indicates if the default behavior of the event can be canceled.
currentTarget	Element	Read only	The element whose event handler is currently handling the event.
defaultPrevented	Boolean	Read only	When true, indicates that preventDefault() has been called (added in DOM Level 3 Events).
detail	Integer	Read only	Extra information related to the event.
eventPhase	Integer	Read only	The phase during which the event handler is being called: 1 for the capturing phase, 2 for "at target," and 3 for bubbling.
preventDefault()	Function	Read only	Cancels the default behavior for the event. If cancelable is true, this method can be used.

continues

(continued)

PROPERTY/METHOD	TYPE	READ/WRITE	DESCRIPTION
stopImmediatePropagation()	Function	Read only	Cancels any further event capturing or event bubbling and prevents any other event handlers from being called. (Added in DOM Level 3 Events.)
stopPropagation()	Function	Read only	Cancels any further event capturing or event bubbling. If bubbles is true, this method can be used.
target	Element	Read only	The target of the event.
trusted	Boolean	Read only	When true, indicates if the event was generated by the browser. When false, indicates the event was created using JavaScript by the developer. (Added in DOM Level 3 Events.)
type	String	Read only	The type of event that was fired.
View	Abstract View	Read only	The abstract view associated with the event. This is equal to the window object in which the event occurred.

Inside an event handler, the this object is always equal to the value of currentTarget, whereas target contains only the actual target of the event. If the event handler is assigned directly onto the intended target, then this, currentTarget, and target all have the same value. Here is an example demonstrating where the two properties are equivalent to this:

```
let btn = document.getElementById("myBtn");
btn.onclick = function(event) {
  console.log(event.currentTarget === this);  // true
  console.log(event.target === this);          // true
};
```

This code examines the values of currentTarget and target relative to this. Because the target of the click event is the button, all three are equal. If the event handler existed on a parent node of the button, such as document.body, the values would be different. Consider the following example, where a click handler is set on document.body:

```
document.body.onclick = function(event) {
  console.log(event.currentTarget === document.body);              // true
  console.log(this === document.body);                             // true
  console.log(event.target === document.getElementById("myBtn"));  // true
};
```

When the button is clicked in this example, both this and `currentTarget` are equal to `document .body` because that's where the event handler was registered. The `target` property, however, is equal to the button element itself, because that's the true target of the click event. Because the button itself doesn't have an event handler assigned, the click event bubbles up to `document.body`, where the event is handled.

The `type` property is useful when you want to assign a single function to handle multiple events. Here is an example which uses `event.type`:

```
let btn = document.getElementById("myBtn");
let handler = function(event) {
  switch(event.type) {
    case "click":
      console.log("Clicked");
      break;
    case "mouseover":
      event.target.style.backgroundColor = "red";
      break;
    case "mouseout":
      event.target.style.backgroundColor = "";
      break;
  }
};

btn.onclick = handler;
btn.onmouseover = handler;
btn.onmouseout = handler;
```

In this example, a single function called `handler` is defined to handle three different events: `click`, `mouseover`, and `mouseout`. When the button is clicked, it should log a message, as in the previous examples. When the mouse is moved over the button, the background color should change to red, and when the mouse is moved away from the button, the background color should revert to its default. Using the `event.type` property, the function is able to determine which event occurred and then react appropriately.

The `preventDefault()` method is used to prevent the default action of a particular event. The default behavior of a link, for example, is to navigate to the URL specified in its `href` attribute when clicked. If you want to prevent that navigation from occurring, an onclick event handler can cancel that behavior, as in the following example:

```
let link = document.getElementById("myLink");
link.onclick = function(event) {
  event.preventDefault();
};
```

Any event that can be canceled using `preventDefault()` will have its cancelable property set to true.

The `stopPropagation()` method stops the flow of an event through the DOM structure immediately, canceling any further event capturing or bubbling before it occurs. For example, an event handler added directly to a button can call `stopPropagation()` to prevent an event handler on `document.body` from being fired, as shown in the following example:

```
let btn = document.getElementById("myBtn");
btn.onclick = function(event) {
```

```
        console.log("Clicked");
        event.stopPropagation();
    };

    document.body.onclick = function(event) {
        console.log("Body clicked");
    };
```

Without the call to stopPropagation() in this example, two messages would be logged when the button is clicked. However, the click event never reaches document.body, so the onclick event handler is never executed.

The eventPhase property aids in determining what phase of event flow is currently active. If the event handler is called during the capture phase, eventPhase is 1; if the event handler is at the target, eventPhase is 2; if the event handler is during the bubble phase, eventPhase is 3. Note that even though "at target" occurs during the bubbling phase, eventPhase is always 2. Here is an example showing the various eventPhase values:

```
    let btn = document.getElementById("myBtn");
    btn.onclick = function(event) {
        console.log(event.eventPhase);    // 2
    };

    document.body.addEventListener("click", (event) => {
        console.log(event.eventPhase);    // 1
    }, true);

    document.body.onclick = (event) => {
        console.log(event.eventPhase);    // 3
    };
```

When the button in this example is clicked, the first event handler to fire is the one on document .body in the capturing phase, which logs a message that displays 1 as the eventPhase. Next, the event handler on the button itself is fired, at which point the eventPhase is 2. The last event handler to fire is during the bubbling phase on document.body when eventPhase is 3. Whenever eventPhase is 2, this, target, and currentTarget are always equal.

> **NOTE** *The event object exists only while event handlers are still being executed; once all event handlers have been executed, the event object is destroyed.*

EVENT TYPES

There are numerous categories of events that can occur in a web browser. As mentioned previously, the type of event being fired determines the information that is available about the event. DOM Level 3 Events specifies the following event groups:

> ➤ **User interface (UI) events** are general browser events that may have some interaction with the BOM.

> ➤ **Focus events** are fired when an element gains or loses focus.

➤ **Mouse events** are fired when the mouse is used to perform an action on the page.

➤ **Wheel events** are fired when a mouse wheel (or similar device) is used.

➤ **Text events** are fired when text is input into the document.

➤ **Keyboard events** are fired when the keyboard is used to perform an action on the page.

➤ **Composition events** are fired when inputting characters for an Input Method Editor (IME).

In addition to these categories, HTML5 defines another set of events, and browsers often implement proprietary events both on the DOM and on the BOM. These proprietary events are typically driven by developer demand rather than specifications and so may be implemented differently across browsers.

DOM Level 3 Events redefines the event groupings from DOM Level 2 Events and adds additional event definitions. All major browsers support DOM Level 2 and 3 Events.

UI Events

UI events are those events that aren't necessarily related to user actions. These events existed in some form or another prior to the DOM specification and were retained for backwards compatibility. The UI events are as follows:

➤ `load`—Fires on a window when the page has been completely loaded, on a frameset when all frames have been completely loaded, on an `<img>` element when it has been completely loaded, or on an `<object>` element when it has been completely loaded.

➤ `unload`—Fires on a window when the page has been completely unloaded, on a frameset when all frames have been completely unloaded, or on an `<object>` element when it has been completely unloaded.

➤ `abort`—Fires on an `<object>` element if it is not fully loaded before the user stops the download process.

➤ `error`—Fires on a window when a JavaScript error occurs, on an `<img>` element if the image specified cannot be loaded, on an `<object>` element if it cannot be loaded, or on a frameset if one or more frames cannot be loaded..

➤ `select`—Fires when the user selects one or more characters in a text box (either `<input>` or `<textarea>`).

➤ `resize`—Fires on a window or frame when it is resized.

➤ `scroll`—Fires on any element with a scrollbar when the user scrolls it. The `<body>` element contains the scrollbar for a loaded page.

Most of the HTML events are related either to the window object or to form controls.

These events were part of the HTML Events group in DOM Level 2 Events. Note that browsers should return `true` for this only if they implement these events according to the DOM Level 2 Events. Browsers may support these events in nonstandard ways and thus return `false`.

> **NOTE** `DOMActivate` *fires when an element has been activated by some user action, by either mouse or keyboard (more generic than* `click` *or* `keydown`*). This event is deprecated in DOM Level 3 Events. Because of cross-browser implementation differences, avoid using this event.*

The *load* Event

The `load` event is perhaps the most often used event in JavaScript. For the window object, the `load` event fires when the entire page has been loaded, including all external resources such as images, JavaScript files, and CSS files. You can define an `onload` event handler on the window object:

```
window.addEventListener("load", (event) => {
  console.log("Loaded!");
});
```

The event object is passed into the event handler. The event object doesn't provide any extra information for this type of event.

The `load` event also fires on images, both those that are in the DOM and those that are not. You can assign an `onload` event handler directly using HTML on any images in the document, using code such as this:

```
<img src="smile.gif" onload="console.log('Image loaded.')">
```

This example logs a message when the given image has been loaded. This can also be done using JavaScript, as follows:

```
let image = document.getElementById("myImage");
image.addEventListener("load", (event) => {
  console.log(event.target.src);
});
```

Here, the `onload` event handler is assigned using JavaScript. The event object is passed in, though it doesn't have much useful information. The target of the event is the `<img>` element, so its `src` property can be accessed and displayed.

When creating a new `<img>` element, an event handler can be assigned to indicate when the image has been loaded. In this case, it's important to assign the event before assigning the `src` property, as in the following example:

```
window.addEventListener("load", () => {
  let image = document.createElement("img");
  image.addEventListener("load", (event) => {
    console.log(event.target.src);
  });
  document.body.appendChild(image);
  image.src = "smile.gif";
});
```

The first part of this example is to assign an `onload` event handler for the window. Because the example involves adding a new element to the DOM, you must be certain that the page is loaded, because trying to manipulate `document.body` prior to its being fully loaded can cause errors. A new image element is created and its `onload` event handler is set. Then, the image is added to the page and its `src` is assigned. Note that the element need not be added to the document for the image download to begin; it begins as soon as the `src` property is set.

This same technique can be used with the DOM Level 0 Image object. Prior to the DOM, the Image object was used to preload images on the client. It can be used the same way as an `<img>` element with the exception that it cannot be added into the DOM tree. Consider the following example which instantiates a new Image object:

```
window.addEventListener("load", () => {
  let image = new Image();
  image.addEventListener("load", (event) => {
    console.log("Image loaded!");
  });
  image.src = "smile.gif";
});
```

Here, the Image constructor is used to create a new image and the event handler is assigned. Some browsers implement the Image object as an `<img>` element, but not all, so it's best to treat them as separate.

There are other elements that also support the `load` event in nonstandard ways. The `<script>` element fires a `load` event, allowing you to determine when dynamically loaded JavaScript files have been completely loaded. Unlike images, JavaScript files start downloading only after the `src` property has been assigned and the element has been added into the document, so the order in which the event handler and the `src` property are assigned is insignificant. The following illustrates how to assign an event handler for a `<script>` element:

```
window.addEventListener("load", () => {
  let script = document.createElement("script");
  script.addEventListener("load", (event) => {
    console.log("Loaded");
  });
  script.src = "example.js";
  document.body.appendChild(script);
});
```

The event object's target is the `<script>` node in most browsers. As with the `<script>` node, a style sheet does not begin downloading until the `href` property has been assigned and the `<link>` element has been added to the document.

The *unload* Event

A companion to the `load` event, the `unload` event fires when a document has completely unloaded. The `unload` event typically fires when navigating from one page to another and is most often used to clean up references to avoid memory leaks. Similar to the `load` event, an `onunload` event handler can be assigned to the window:

```
window.addEventListener("unload", (event) => {
  console.log("Unloaded!");
});
```

The event object is generated for this event but contains nothing more than the target (set to document) in DOM-compliant browsers.

Be careful with the code that executes inside of an `onunload` event handler. Because the `unload` event fires after everything is unloaded, not all objects that were available when the page was loaded are still available. Trying to manipulate the location of a DOM node or its appearance can result in errors.

The *resize* Event

When the browser window is resized to a new height or width, the `resize` event fires. This event fires on window, so an event handler can be assigned either via JavaScript or by using the `onresize` attribute on the `<body>` element. Prefer to use the JavaScript approach, as shown here:

```
window.addEventListener("resize", (event) => {
    console.log("Resized");
});
```

Similar to other events that occur on the window, the event object is created and its target is document in modern browsers.

You should avoid computation-heavy code in the event handler for this event because it will be executed frequently and cause a noticeable slowdown in the browser.

> **NOTE** *The* `resize` *event also fires when the browser window is minimized or maximized.*

The *scroll* Event

Even though the `scroll` event occurs on the window, it actually refers to changes in the appropriate page-level element. The following example shows how to properly handle this:

```
window.addEventListener("scroll", (event) => {
    console.log(document.body.scrollTop);
});
```

This code assigns an event handler that outputs the vertical scroll position of the page.

Similar to resize, the `scroll` event occurs repeatedly as the document is being scrolled, so it's best to keep the event handlers as simple as possible.

Focus Events

Focus events are fired when elements of a page receive or lose focus. These events work in concert with the `document.hasFocus()` and `document.activeElement` properties to give insight as to how the user is navigating the page. There are six focus events:

➤   `blur`—Fires when an element has lost focus. This event does not bubble and is supported in all browsers.

➤ DOMFocusIn—Fires when an element has received focus. This is a bubbling version of the focus HTML event. DOM Level 3 Events deprecates DOMFocusIn in favor of focusin.

➤ DOMFocusOut—Fires when an element has lost focus. This is a generic version of the blur HTML event. DOM Level 3 Events deprecates DOMFocusOut in favor of focusout.

➤ focus—Fires when an element has received focus. This event does not bubble and is supported in all browsers.

➤ focusin—Fires when an element has received focus. This is a bubbling version of the focus HTML event.

➤ focusout—Fires when an element has lost focus. This is a generic version of the blur HTML event.

The two primary events of this group are focus and blur, both of which have been supported in browsers since the early days of JavaScript. One of the biggest issues with these events is that they don't bubble. This led to the inclusion of focusin and focusout that has been standardized in DOM Level 3 Events.

When focus is moved from one element to another on the page, the order of events is as follows:

1. focusout fires on the element losing focus.

2. focusin fires on the element receiving focus.

3. blur fires on the element losing focus.

4. DOMFocusOut fires on the element losing focus.

5. focus fires on the element receiving focus.

6. DOMFocusIn fires on the element receiving focus.

The event target for blur, DOMFocusOut, and focusout is the element losing focus while the event target for focus, DOMFocusIn, and focusin is the element receiving focus.

Mouse and Wheel Events

Mouse events are the most commonly used group of events on the web, because the mouse is the primary navigation device used. There are nine mouse events defined in DOM Level 3 Events. They are as follows:

➤ click—Fires when the user clicks the primary mouse button (typically the left button) or when the user presses the Enter key. This is an important fact for accessibility purposes, because onclick event handlers can be executed using the keyboard and the mouse.

➤ dblclick—Fires when the user double-clicks the primary mouse button (typically the left button).

➤ mousedown—Fires when the user pushes any mouse button down. This event cannot be fired via the keyboard.

➤ mouseenter—Fires when the mouse cursor is outside of an element and then the user first moves it inside of the boundaries of the element. This event does not bubble and does not fire when the cursor moves over descendant elements.

➤ mouseleave—Fires when the mouse cursor is over an element and then the user moves it outside of that element's boundaries. This event does not bubble and does not fire when the cursor moves over descendant elements.

➤ mousemove—Fires repeatedly as the cursor is being moved around an element. This event cannot be fired via the keyboard.

➤ mouseout—Fires when the mouse cursor is over an element and then the user moves it over another element. The element moved to may be outside of the bounds of the original element or a child of the original element. This event cannot be fired via the keyboard.

➤ mouseover—Fires when the mouse cursor is outside of an element and then the user first moves it inside of the boundaries of the element. This event cannot be fired via the keyboard.

➤ mouseup—Fires when the user releases a mouse button. This event cannot be fired via the keyboard.

All elements on a page support mouse events. All mouse events bubble except mouseenter and mouseleave, and they can all be canceled, which affects the default behavior of the browser.

Canceling the default behavior of mouse events can affect other events as well because of the relationship that exists amongst the events.

A click event can be fired only if a mousedown event is fired and followed by a mouseup event on the same element; if either mousedown or mouseup is canceled, then the click event will not fire. Similarly, it takes two click events to cause the dblclick event to fire. If anything prevents these two click events from firing (either canceling one of the click events or canceling either mousedown or mouseup), the dblclick event will not fire. These four mouse events always fire in the following order:

1. mousedown
2. mouseup
3. click
4. mousedown
5. mouseup
6. click
7. dblclick

Both click and dblclick rely on other events to fire before they can fire, whereas mousedown and mouseup are not affected by other events.

Note that the DOM Level 3 feature name is just "MouseEvent" instead of "MouseEvents".

There is also a subgroup of mouse events called *wheel events*. Wheel events are really just a single event, `mousewheel`, which monitors interactions of a mouse wheel or a similar device such as the Mac trackpad.

Client Coordinates

Mouse events all occur at a particular location within the browser viewport. This information is stored in the `clientX` and `clientY` properties of the event object. These properties indicate the location of the mouse cursor within the viewport at the time of the event and are supported in all browsers. Figure 15.3 illustrates the *client coordinates* in a viewport.

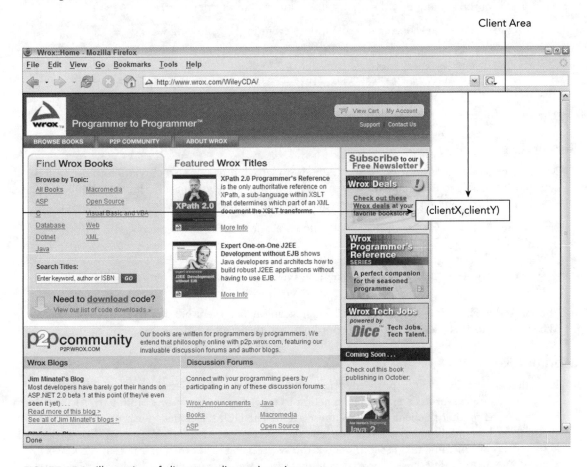

FIGURE 15.3: Illustration of client coordinates in a viewport

You can retrieve the client coordinates of a mouse event in the following way:

```
let div = document.getElementById("myDiv");
div.addEventListener("click", (event) => {
  console.log(`Client coordinates: ${event.clientX}, ${event.clientY}`);
});
```

This example assigns an `onclick` event handler to a `<div>` element. When the element is clicked, the client coordinates of the event are displayed. Keep in mind that these coordinates do not take into account the scroll position of the page, so these numbers do not indicate the location of the cursor on the page.

Page Coordinates

Where client coordinates give you information about where an event occurred in the viewport, *page coordinates* tell you where on the page the event occurred via the `pageX` and `pageY` properties of the event object. These properties indicate the location of the mouse cursor on the page, so the coordinates are from the left and top of the page itself rather than the viewport.

You can retrieve the page coordinates of a mouse event in the following way:

```
let div = document.getElementById("myDiv");
div.addEventListener("click", (event) => {
  console.log(`Page coordinates: ${event.pageX}, ${event.pageY}`);
});
```

The values for `pageX` and `pageY` are the same as `clientX` and `clientY` when the page is not scrolled.

Screen Coordinates

Mouse events occur not only in relation to the browser window but also in relation to the entire screen. It's possible to determine the location of the mouse in relation to the entire screen by using the `screenX` and `screenY` properties. Figure 15.4 illustrates the *screen coordinates* in a browser.

You can retrieve the screen coordinates of a mouse event in the following way:

```
let div = document.getElementById("myDiv");
div.addEventListener("click", (event) => {
  console.log(`Screen coordinates: ${event.screenX}, ${event.screenY}`);
});
```

Similar to the previous examples, this code assigns an onclick event handler to a `<div>` element. When the element is clicked, the screen coordinates of the event are displayed.

Modifier Keys

Even though a mouse event is primarily triggered by using the mouse, the state of certain keyboard keys may be important in determining the action to take. The *modifier keys* Shift, Ctrl, Alt, and Meta are often used to alter the behavior of a mouse event. The DOM specifies four properties to indicate the state of these modifier keys: `shiftKey`, `ctrlKey`, `altKey`, and `metaKey`. Each of these properties contains a Boolean value that is set to `true` if the key is being held down or `false` if the key is not pressed. When a mouse event occurs, you can determine the state of the various keys by inspecting these properties. Consider the following example, which checks for modifier key state when a `click` event is fired:

```
let div = document.getElementById("myDiv");
div.addEventListener("click", (event) => {
```

```
      let keys = new Array();

      if (event.shiftKey) {
        keys.push("shift");
      }

      if (event.ctrlKey) {
        keys.push("ctrl");
      }

      if (event.altKey) {
        keys.push("alt");
      }

      if (event.metaKey) {
        keys.push("meta");
      }

      console.log("Keys: " + keys.join(","));

    });
```

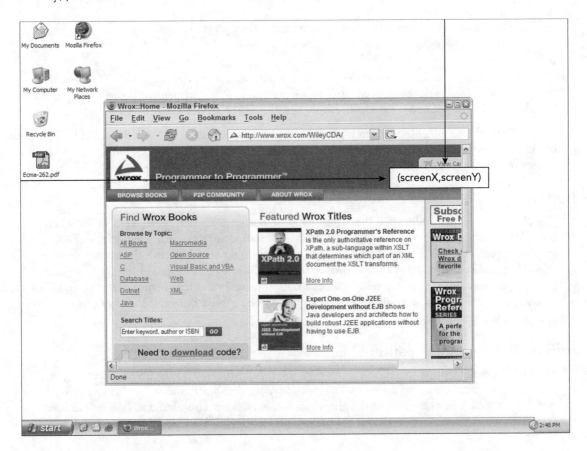

FIGURE 15.4: Illustration of screen coordinates in a browser

In this example, an `onclick` event handler checks the state of the various modifier keys. The `keys` array contains the names of the modifier keys that are being held down. For each property that is `true`, the name of the key is added to `keys`. At the end of the event handler, the keys are displayed in a log message.

Related Elements

For the `mouseover` and `mouseout` events, there are other elements related to the event. Both of these events involve moving the mouse cursor from within the boundaries of one element to within the boundaries of another element. For the mouseover event, the primary target of the event is the element that is gaining the cursor, and the related element is the one that is losing the cursor. Likewise, for `mouseout`, the primary target is the element that is losing the cursor, and the related element is the one that is gaining the cursor. Consider the following example:

```
<!DOCTYPE html>
<html>
<head>
  <title>Related Elements Example</title>
</head>
<body>
  <div id="myDiv"
       style="background-color:red;height:100px;width:100px;"></div>
</body>
</html>
```

This page renders a single `<div>` on the page. If the mouse cursor starts over the `<div>` and then moves outside of it, a `mouseout` event fires on `<div>` and the related element is the `<body>` element. Simultaneously, the `mouseover` event fires on `<body>` and the related element is the `<div>`.

The DOM provides information about related elements via the `relatedTarget` property on the event object. This property contains a value only for the `mouseover` and `mouseout` events; it is `null` for all other events.

Buttons

The click event is fired only when the primary mouse button is clicked on an element (or when the Enter key is pressed on the keyboard), so button information isn't necessary. For the `mousedown` and `mouseup` events, there is a button property on the event object that indicates the button that was pressed or released. The DOM button property has the following three possible values: 0 for the primary mouse button, 1 for the middle mouse button (usually the scroll wheel button), and 2 for the secondary mouse button. In traditional setups, the primary mouse button is the left button and the secondary button is the right one.

Additional Event Information

The DOM Level 2 Events specification provides the detail property on the event object to give additional information about an event. For mouse events, detail contains a number indicating how many times a click has occurred at the given location. Clicks are considered to be a `mousedown` event followed by a `mouseup` event at the same pixel location. The value of detail starts at 1 and is incremented every time a click occurs. If the mouse is moved between mousedown and mouseup, then detail is set back to 0.

The *mousewheel* Event

The mousewheel event fires when the user interacts with the mouse wheel, rolling it vertically in either direction. This event fires on each element and bubbles up to the window. The event object for the mousewheel event contains all standard information about mouse events and an additional property called wheelDelta. When the mouse wheel is rolled toward the front of the mouse, wheelDelta is a positive multiple of 120; when the mouse wheel is rolled toward the rear of the mouse, wheelDelta is a negative multiple of 120. See Figure 15.5.

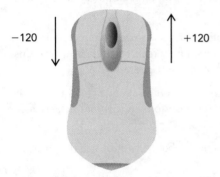

−120   +120

FIGURE 15.5: Illustration of mousewheel events

An onmousewheel event handler can be assigned to any element on the page or to the document to handle all mouse wheel interactions. Here's an example:

```
document.addEventListener("mousewheel", (event) => {
  console.log(event.wheelDelta);
});
```

This example simply displays the wheelDelta value when the event is fired. In most cases, you need only know which direction the mouse wheel was turned, which can easily be determined by the sign of the wheelDelta value.

Touch Device Support

Touch devices have interesting implementations because, of course, there is no mouse to interact with. When developing for touch devices, keep the following in mind:

➤ The dblclick event is not supported at all. Double-clicking on the browser window zooms in, and there is no way to override that behavior.

➤ Tapping on a clickable element causes the mousemove event to fire. If content changes as a result of this action, no further events are fired; if there are no changes to the screen, then the mousedown, mouseup, and click events fire in order. No events are fired when tapping on a nonclickable element. Clickable elements are defined as those that have a default action when clicked (such as links) or elements that have an onclick event handler assigned.

➤ The mousemove event also fires mouseover and mouseout events.

➤ The mousewheel and scroll events fire when two fingers are on the screen and the page is scrolled as the result of finger movement.

Accessibility Issues

If your web application or website must be accessible to users with disabilities, specifically those who are using screen readers, you should be careful when using mouse events. As mentioned previously, the click event can be fired using the Enter key on the keyboard, but other mouse events have no keyboard support. It's advisable not to use mouse events other than click to show functionality or cause code execution, as this will severely limit the usability for blind or sight-impaired users. Here are some tips for accessibility using mouse events:

➤ Use click to execute code. Some suggest that an application feels faster when code is executed using onmousedown, which is true for sighted users. For screen readers, however, this code is not accessible, because the mousedown event cannot be triggered.

➤ Avoid using onmouseover to display new options to the user. Once again, screen readers have no way to trigger this event. If you really must display new options in this manner, consider adding keyboard shortcuts to display the same information.

➤ Avoid using dblclick to execute important actions. The keyboard cannot fire this event.

Following these simple hints can greatly increase the accessibility of your web application or website to those with disabilities.

> **NOTE** *To learn more about accessibility on web pages, please visit* www.webaim .org.

Keyboard and Text Events

Keyboard events are fired when the user interacts with the keyboard. DOM Level 2 Events originally specified keyboard events, but that section was removed before the specification became final. As a result, keyboard events are largely supported based on the original DOM Level 0 implementations.

DOM Level 3 Events provide a specification for keyboard events. There are three keyboard events, as described here:

➤ keydown—Fires when the user presses a key on the keyboard and fires repeatedly while the key is being held down.

➤ keypress—Fires when the user presses a key on the keyboard that results in a character and fires repeatedly while the key is being held down. This event also fires for the Esc key. DOM Level 3 Events deprecate the keypress event in favor of the textInput event.

➤ keyup—Fires when the user releases a key on the keyboard.

These events are most easily seen as the user types in a text box, though all elements support them.

There is only one text event and it is called textInput. This event is an augmentation of keypress intended to make it easier to intercept text input before being displayed to the user. The textInput event fires just before text is inserted into a text box.

When the user presses a character key once on the keyboard, the keydown event is fired first, followed by the keypress event, followed by the keyup event. Note that both keydown and keypress are fired before any change has been made to the text box, whereas the keyup event fires after changes have been made to the text box. If a character key is pressed and held down, keydown and keypress are fired repeatedly and don't stop until the key is released.

For noncharacter keys, a single key press on the keyboard results in the keydown event being fired followed by the keyup event. If a noncharacter key is held down, the keydown event fires repeatedly until the key is released, at which point the keyup event fires.

> **NOTE** *Keyboard events support the same set of modifier keys as mouse events. The* shiftKey, ctrlKey, altKey, *and* metaKey *properties are all available for keyboard events.*

Key Codes

For keydown and keyup events, the event object's keyCode property is filled in with a code that maps to a specific key on the keyboard. For alphanumeric keys, the keyCode is the same as the ASCII value for the lowercase letter or number on that key, so the 7 key has a keyCode of 55 and the A key has a keyCode of 65, regardless of the state of the Shift key. Here's an example demonstrating inspection of the keyCode property:

```
let textbox = document.getElementById("myText");
textbox.addEventListener("keyup", (event) => {
  console.log(event.keyCode);
});
```

In this example, the keyCode is displayed every time a keyup event is fired. When a keypress event occurs, this means that the key affects the display of text on the screen. All browsers fire the keypress event for keys that insert or remove a character; other keys are browser-dependent. Because the DOM Level 3 Events specification has only started being implemented, there are significant implementation differences across browsers.

Browsers support a property on the event object called charCode, which is filled in only for the keypress event and contains the ASCII code for the character related to the key that was pressed. In this case, the keyCode is typically equal to 0 or may also be equal to the key code for the key that was pressed. Once you have the character code, it's possible to convert it to the actual character using the String.fromCharCode() method.

DOM Level 3 Changes

Although all browsers implement some form of keyboard events, DOM Level 3 Events make several changes. The charCode property, for instance, isn't part of the DOM Level 3 Events specification for keyboard events. Instead, the specification defines two additional properties: key and char.

The key property is intended as a replacement for keyCode and contains a string. When a character key is pressed, the value of key is equal to the text character (for example, "k" or "M"); when a noncharacter key is pressed, the value of key is the name of the key (for example, "Shift" or "Down"). The char property behaves the same as key when a character key is pressed and is set to null when a noncharacter key is pressed.

DOM Level 3 Events also adds a property called location, which is a numeric value indicating where the key was pressed. Possible values are 0 for default keyboard, 1 for left location (such as the left Alt key), 2 for the right location (such as the right Shift key), 3 for the numeric keypad, 4 for mobile (indicating a virtual keypad), or 5 for joystick.

```
let textbox = document.getElementById("myText");
textbox.addEventListener("keypress", (event) => {
  let loc = event.location || event.keyLocation;
  if (loc) {
    console.log(loc);
  }
});
```

As with the key property, the location property isn't widely supported and so isn't recommended for cross-browser development.

The last addition to the event object is the getModifierState() method. This method accepts a single argument, a string equal to Shift, Control, Alt, AltGraph, or Meta, which indicates the modifier key to check. The method returns true if the given modifier is active (the key is being held down) or false if not:

```
let textbox = document.getElementById("myText");
textbox.addEventListener("keypress", (event) => {
  if (event.getModifierState) {
    console.log(event.getModifierState("Shift"));
  }
});
```

You can retrieve some of this information already using the shiftKey, altKey, ctrlKey, and metaKey properties on the event object.

The *textInput* Event

The DOM Level 3 Events specification introduced an event called textInput that fires when a character is input to an editable area. Designed as a replacement for keypress, a textInput event behaves somewhat differently. One difference is that keypress fires on any element that can have focus, but textInput fires only on editable areas. Another difference is that textInput fires only for keys that result in a new character being inserted, whereas keypress fires for keys that affect text in any way (including Backspace).

Because the textInput event is interested primarily in characters, it provides a data property on the event object that contains the character that was inserted (not the character code). The value of data is always the exact character that was inserted, so if the S key is pressed without Shift, data is `"s"`, but if the same key is pressed holding Shift down, then data is `"S"`.

The textInput event can be used as follows:

```
let textbox = document.getElementById("myText");
textbox.addEventListener("textInput", (event) => {
  console.log(event.data);
});
```

In this example, the character that was inserted into the text box is displayed in a log message.

There is another property, on the event object, called inputMethod that indicates how the text was input into the control. The possible values are:

➤ 0 indicates the browser couldn't determine how the input was entered.

➤ 1 indicates a keyboard was used.

➤ 2 indicates the text was pasted in.

➤ 3 indicates the text was dropped in as part of a drag operation.

➤ 4 indicates the text was input using an IME.

➤ 5 indicates the text was input by selecting an option in a form.

➤ 6 indicates the text was input by handwriting (such as with a stylus).

➤ 7 indicates the text was input by voice command.

➤ 8 indicates the text was input by a combination of methods.

➤ 9 indicates the text was input by script.

Using this property, you can determine how text was input into a control in order to verify its validity.

Composition Events

Composition events were first introduced in DOM Level 3 Events to handle complex input sequences typically found on IMEs. IMEs allow users to input characters not found on the physical keyboard. For example, those using a Latin keyboard can still enter Japanese characters into the computer. IMEs often require multiple keys to be pressed at once while resulting in only a single character being entered. Composition events help to detect and work with such input. There are three composition events:

➤ compositionstart—Fires when the text composition system of the IME is opened, indicating that input is about to commence.

➤ compositionupdate—Fires when a new character has been inserted into the input field.

➤ compositionend—Fires when the text composition system is closed, indicating a return to normal keyboard input.

Composition events are similar to text events in many ways. When a composition event fires, the target is the input field receiving the text. The only additional event property is data, which contains one of the following:

➤ When accessed during `compositionstart`, contains the text being edited (for instance, if text has been selected and will now be replaced).

➤ When accessed during `compositionupdate`, contains the new character being inserted.

➤ When accessed during `compositionend`, contains all of the input entered during this composition session.

As with text events, composition events can be used to filter input where necessary. These events can be used as follows:

```
let textbox = document.getElementById("myText");
textbox.addEventListener("compositionstart", (event) => {
  console.log(event.data);
});
textbox.addEventListener("compositionupdate", (event) => {
  console.log(event.data);
});
textbox.addEventListener("compositionend", (event) => {
  console.log(event.data);
});
```

Mutation Events

The DOM Level 2 *mutation events* were designed to provide notification when a part of the DOM has been changed.

> **NOTE** *These events are deprecated, and support is gradually being phased out. This feature is replaced by Mutation Observers, which is covered in Chapter 13, "The Document Object Model."*

HTML5 Events

The DOM specification doesn't cover all events that are supported by all browsers. Many browsers have implemented custom events for various purposes based on either user need or a specific use case. HTML5 has an exhaustive list of all events that should be supported by browsers. This section discusses several events in HTML5 that are well supported by browsers. Note that this is not an exhaustive list of all events the browser supports. (Other events will be discussed throughout this book.)

The *contextmenu* Event

Windows 95 introduced the concept of context menus to PC users via a right mouse click. Soon, that paradigm was being mimicked on the web. The problem developers were facing was how to detect that a context menu should be displayed (in Windows, it's a right click; on a Mac, it's a Ctrl+click) and then how to avoid the default context menu for the action. This resulted in the introduction of the `contextmenu` event to specifically indicate when a context menu is about to be displayed, allowing developers to cancel the default context menu and provide their own.

The `contextmenu` event bubbles, so a single event handler can be assigned to a document that handles all such events for the page. The target of the event is the element that was acted on. This event can be canceled in all browsers, using `event.preventDefault()`. The `contextmenu` event is considered a mouse event and so has all of the properties related to the cursor position. Typically, a custom context menu is displayed using an `oncontextmenu` event handler and hidden again using the `onclick` event handler. Consider the following HTML page:

```html
<!DOCTYPE html>
<html>
<head>
  <title>ContextMenu Event Example</title>
</head>
<body>
  <div id="myDiv">Right click or Ctrl+click me to get a custom context menu.
    Click anywhere else to get the default context menu.</div>
  <ul id="myMenu" style="position:absolute;visibility:hidden;background-color:
    silver">
    <li><a href="http://www.mattfriz.com">Matt's site</a></li>
    <li><a href="http://www.wiley.com">Wiley site</a></li>
  </ul>
</body>
</html>
```

In this code, a `<div>` is created that has a custom context menu. The `<ul>` element serves as the custom context menu and is initially hidden. The JavaScript to make this example work is as follows:

```javascript
window.addEventListener("load", (event) => {
  let div = document.getElementById("myDiv");

  div.addEventListener("contextmenu", (event) => {
    event.preventDefault();

    let menu = document.getElementById("myMenu");
    menu.style.left = event.clientX + "px";
    menu.style.top = event.clientY + "px";
    menu.style.visibility = "visible";
  });

  document.addEventListener("click", (event) => {
    document.getElementById("myMenu").style.visibility = "hidden";
  });
});
```

Here, an `oncontextmenu` event handler is defined for the `<div>`. The event handler begins by canceling the default behavior, ensuring that the browser's context menu won't be displayed. Next, the `<ul>` element is placed into position based on the `clientX` and `clientY` properties of the event object. The last step is to show the menu by setting its visibility to "visible." An `onclick` event handler is then added to the document to hide the menu whenever a click occurs (which is the behavior of system context menus).

Though this example is very basic, it is the basis for all custom context menus on the web. Applying some additional CSS to the context menu in this example can yield great results.

The *beforeunload* Event

The `beforeunload` event fires on the window and is intended to give developers a way to prevent the page from being unloaded. This event fires before the page starts to unload from the browser, allowing continued use of the page should it ultimately not be unloaded. You cannot cancel this event outright because that would be the equivalent of holding the user hostage on a page. Instead, the event gives you the ability to display a message to the user in a dialog box similar to a `confirm()` dialog. The message indicates that the page is about to be unloaded and asks if the user would like to continue to close the page or remain on the page (see Figure 15.6). If the user selects Cancel, they will remain on the page.

FIGURE 15.6: Example of a confirm dialog

It was previously the case that you could control the content of this message, but this ability was exploited by malicious websites to confuse the user with misleading dialog text when they tried to leave. In all modern browsers, you no longer have the ability to control the text content; it will always show a uniform message that varies depending on the browser vendor. Safari shows "Are you sure you want to leave this page?" whereas Chrome shows "Leave site? Changes you made may not be saved."

To trigger this behavior, you need only set a `beforeunload` handler on the window object that returns an empty string. Either of the following will work:

```
window.onbeforeunload = () => "";

window.addEventListener("beforeunload", (event) => "");
```

The *DOMContentLoaded* Event

The window's `load` event fires when everything on the page has been completely loaded, which may take some time for pages with lots of external resources. The `DOMContentLoaded` event fires as soon as the DOM tree is completely formed and without regard to images, JavaScript files, CSS files, or other such resources. As compared to the load event, `DOMContentLoaded` allows event handlers to be attached earlier in the page download process, which means a faster time to interactivity for users.

To handle the DOMContentLoaded event, you can attach an event handler either on the document or on the window (the target for the event actually is document, although it bubbles up to window). Here's an example which listens for the event on document:

```
document.addEventListener("DOMContentLoaded", (event) => {
  console.log("Content loaded");
});
```

The event object for DOMContentLoaded doesn't provide any additional information (target is document).

The DOMContentLoaded event is typically used to attach event handlers or perform other DOM manipulations. This event always fires before the load event.

For browsers that don't support DOMContentLoaded, it has been suggested that a timeout should be set during page loading with a millisecond delay of 0, as in this example:

```
setTimeout(() => {
  // attach event handlers here
}, 0);
```

This code essentially says, "Run this function as soon as the current JavaScript process is complete." There is a single JavaScript process running as the page is being downloaded and constructed, so the timeout will fire after that. Whether or not this coincides directly with the timing of DOMContentLoaded relates to both the browser being used and other code on the page. To work properly, this must be the first timeout set on the page, and even then, it is not guaranteed that the timeout will run prior to the load event in all circumstances.

The *readystatechange* Event

Internet Explorer first defined an event called readystatechange on several parts of a DOM document. This somewhat mysterious event is intended to provide information about the loading state of the document or of an element, though its behavior is often erratic. Each object that supports the readystatechange event has a readyState property that can have one of the following five possible string values:

➤ uninitialized—The object exists but has not been initialized.

➤ loading—The object is loading data.

➤ loaded—The object has finished loading its data.

➤ interactive—The object can be interacted with but it's not fully loaded.

➤ complete—The object is completely loaded.

Even though this seems straightforward, not all objects go through all readystate phases. The documentation indicates that objects may completely skip a phase if it doesn't apply but doesn't indicate which phases apply to which objects. This means that the readystatechange event often fires fewer than four times and the readyState value doesn't always follow the same progression.

When used on document, a `readyState` of "interactive" fires the `readystatechange` event at a time similar to `DOMContentLoaded`. The interactive phase occurs when the entire DOM tree has been loaded and thus is safe to interact with. Images and other external resources may or may not be available at that point in time. The `readystatechange` event can be handled like this:

```
document.addEventListener("readystatechange", (event) => {
    if (document.readyState == "interactive") {
        console.log("Content loaded");
    }
});
```

The event object for this event doesn't provide any additional information and has no target set.

When used in conjunction with the `load` event, the order in which these events fire is not guaranteed. In pages with numerous or large external resources, the `interactive` phase is reached well before the `load` event fires; in smaller pages with few or small external resources, the `readystatechange` event may not fire until after the `load` event.

To make matters even more confusing, the `interactive` phase may come either before or after the `complete` phase; the order is not constant. In pages with more external resources, it is more likely that the `interactive` phase will occur before the `complete` phase, whereas in pages with fewer resources, it is more likely that the `complete` phase will occur before the `interactive` phase. So, to ensure that you are getting the earliest possible moment, it's necessary to check for both the interactive and the complete phases, as in this example:

```
document.addEventListener("readystatechange", function (event) {
    if (document.readyState == "interactive" ||
        document.readyState == "complete") {
        document.removeEventListener("readystatechange", arguments.callee);
        console.log("Content loaded");
    }
});
```

When the `readystatechange` event fires in this code, the `document.readyState` property is checked to see if it's either the `interactive` or the `complete` phase. If so, the event handler is removed to ensure that it won't be executed for another phase. Note that because the event handler is an anonymous function, `arguments.callee` is used as the pointer to the function. After that, the message is logged indicating that the content is loaded. This construct allows you to get as close as possible to the `DOMContentLoaded` event.

> **NOTE** *Even though you can get close to mimicking* `DOMContentLoaded` *using* `readystatechange`, *they are not exactly the same. The order in which the load event and* `readystatechange` *events are fired is not consistent from page to page.*

The *pageshow* and *pagehide* Events

The *back-forward cache* (bfcache) is designed to speed up page transitions when using the browser's Back and Forward buttons. The cache stores not only page data but also the DOM and JavaScript state, effectively keeping the entire page in memory. If a page is in the bfcache, the `load` event will not fire when the page is navigated to. This usually doesn't cause an issue because the entire page state is stored, but some events can give visibility to the bfcache behavior.

The first event is pageshow, which fires whenever a page is displayed, whether from the bfcache or not. On a newly loaded page, pageshow fires after the load event; on a page in the bfcache, pageshow fires as soon as the page's state has been completely restored. Note that even though the target of this event is document, the event handler must be attached to window. Consider the following example which tracks these events:

```
(function() {
  let showCount = 0;

  window.addEventListener("load", () => {
    console.log("Load fired");
  });

  window.addEventListener("pageshow", () => {
    showCount++;
    console.log(`Show has been fired ${showCount} times.`);
  });
})();
```

This example uses a private scope to protect the showCount variable from being introduced into the global scope. When the page is first loaded, showCount has a value of 0. Every time the pageshow event fires, showCount is incremented and a message is logged. If you navigate away from the page containing this code and then click the Back button to restore it, you will see that the value of showCount is incremented each time. That's because the variable state, along with the entire page state, is stored in memory and then retrieved when you navigate back to the page. If you were to click the Reload button on the browser, the value of showCount would be reset to 0 because the page would be completely reloaded.

Besides the usual properties, the event object for pageshow includes a property called persisted. This is a Boolean value that is set to true if the page is stored in the bfcache or false if the page is not. The property can be checked in the event handler as follows:

```
(function() {
  let showCount = 0;

  window.addEventListener("load", () => {
    console.log("Load fired");
  });

  window.addEventListener("pageshow", (event) => {
    showCount++;
    console.log(`Show has been fired ${showCount} times.`,
                `Persisted? ${event.persisted}`);
  });
})();
```

The persisted property lets you determine if a different action must be taken depending on the state of the page in the bfcache.

The `pagehide` event is a companion to `pageshow` and fires whenever a page is unloaded from the browser, firing immediately before the `unload` event. As with the `pageshow` event, `pagehide` fires on the document even though the event handler must be attached to the window. The event object also includes the persisted property, though there is a slight difference in its usage. Consider the following example which checks the `event.persisted` property:

```
window.addEventListener("pagehide", (event) => {
    console.log("Hiding. Persisted? " + event.persisted);
});
```

You may decide to take a different action based on the value of persisted when `pagehide` fires. For the `pageshow` event, persisted is set to `true` if the page has been loaded from the bfcache; for the `pagehide` event, persisted is set to `true` if the page will be stored in the bfcache once unloaded. So the first time `pageshow` is fired, persisted is always `false`, whereas the first time `pagehide` is fired, persisted will be `true` (unless the page won't be stored in the bfcache).

> **NOTE** *Pages that have an* `onunload` *event handler assigned are automatically excluded from the bfcache, even if the event handler is empty. The reasoning is that* `onunload` *is typically used to undo what was done using* `onload`, *and so skipping* `onload` *the next time the page is displayed could cause it to break.*

The *hashchange* Event

The `hashchange` event indicates when the URL hash (everything following a pound sign (#) in a URL) changed. This came about as developers frequently used the URL hash to store state information or navigational information in Ajax applications.

The `onhashchange` event handler must be attached to the window, and it is called whenever the URL hash changes. The event object should have two additional properties: `oldURL` and `newURL`. These properties hold the complete URL including the hash before the change and after the change. The contrasting URLs are tracked in the following example:

```
window.addEventListener("hashchange", (event) => {
    console.log(`Old URL: ${event.oldURL}, New URL: ${event.newURL}`);
});
```

It's best to use the location object to determine the current hash:

```
window.addEventListener("hashchange", (event) => {
    console.log(`Current hash: ${location.hash}`);
});
```

Device Events

With the introduction of smartphones and tablet devices came a new set of ways for users to interact with a browser. As such, a new class of events was invented. *Device events* allow you to determine how a device is being used.

The *orientationchange* Event

The `orientationchange` event indicates when the user switched the device from landscape to portrait mode. There is a `window.orientation` property that contains one of three values: 0 for portrait mode, 90 for landscape mode when rotated to the left (the bottom of the device on the right), and −90 for landscape mode when rotated to the right (the bottom of the device on the left). The documentation also mentions a value of 180 if the device is upside down, but that configuration is not supported to date. Figure 15.7 illustrates the various values for `window.orientation`.

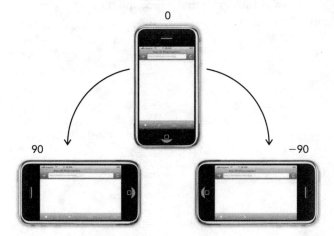

FIGURE 15.7: Illustration of orientation change events

Whenever the user changes from one mode to another, the `orientationchange` event fires. The event object doesn't contain any useful information because the only relevant information is accessible via `window.orientation`. Typical usage of this event is as follows:

```
window.addEventListener("load", (event) => {
    let div = document.getElementById("myDiv");
    div.innerHTML = "Current orientation is " + window.orientation;

    window.addEventListener("orientationchange", (event) => {) {
        div.innerHTML = "Current orientation is " + window.orientation;
    });
});
```

In this example, the initial orientation is displayed when the load event fires. Then, the event handler for `orientationchange` is assigned. Whenever the event fires, the message on the page is updated to indicate the new orientation.

> **NOTE** *Because* `orientationchange` *is considered a window event, you can also assign an event handler by adding the* `onorientationchange` *attribute to the* `<body>` *element.*

The *deviceorientation* Event

The `deviceorientation` event is defined in the DeviceOrientationEvent specification. The event is fired on `window` when accelerometer information is available and changes. Keep in mind that the purpose of `deviceorientation` is to inform you of how the device is oriented in space and not of movement.

A device is said to exist in three-dimensional space along an x-axis, a y-axis, and a z-axis. These all start at zero when the device is at rest on a horizontal surface. The x-axis goes from the left of the device to the right, the y-axis goes from the bottom of the device to the top, and the z-axis goes from the back of the device to the front (see Figure 15.8).

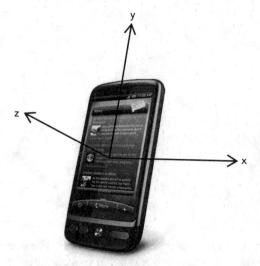

FIGURE 15.8: Illustration of device axes
Caroline et Louis VOLANT / Flickr / CC BY-NC-SA 2.0.

When `deviceorientation` fires, it returns information about how the values of each axis have changed relative to the device at rest. The event object has five properties:

➤ `alpha`—The difference in y-axis degrees as you rotate around the z-axis (side-to-side tilt); a floating point number between 0 and 360.

➤ `beta`—The difference in z-axis degrees as you rotate around the x-axis (front-to-back tilt); a floating point number between –180 and 180.

➤ `gamma`—The difference in the z-axis degrees as you rotate around the y-axis (twisting tilt); a floating point number between –90 and 90.

➤ `absolute`—A Boolean value indicating if the device is returning absolute values or not.

➤ `compassCalibrated`—A Boolean value indicating if the device's compass is properly calibrated or not.

Figure 15.9 shows how the values of alpha, beta, and gamma are calculated.

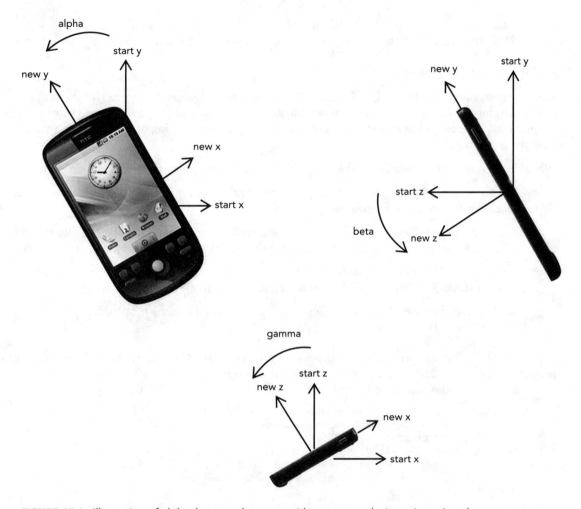

FIGURE 15.9: Illustration of alpha, beta, and gamma with respect to device orientation changes

Here's a simple example that outputs the values for alpha, beta, and gamma:

```
window.addEventListener("deviceorientation", (event) => {
  let output = document.getElementById("output");
  output.innerHTML =
    `Alpha=${event.alpha}, Beta=${event.beta], Gamma=${event.gamma$}<br>`;
});
```

You can use this information to rearrange or otherwise alter elements on the screen in reaction to the device changing its orientation. For example, this code rotates an element in reaction to the device orientation:

```
window.addEventListener("deviceorientation", (event) => {
  let arrow = document.getElementById("arrow");
  arrow.style.transform = `rotate(${Math.round(event.alpha)}deg)`;
});
```

The element "arrow" is rotated along with the value of `event.alpha`, giving it a compass-like feel. The CSS3 rotation transformation is used with a rounded version of the value to ensure smoothness.

The *devicemotion* Event

The `DeviceOrientationEvent` specification also includes a `devicemotion` event. This event is designed to inform you when the device is actually moving, not just when it has changed orientation. For instance, `devicemotion` is useful to determine that the device is falling or is being held by someone who is walking.

When the `devicemotion` event fires, the event object contains the following additional properties:

➤ `acceleration`—An object containing x, y, and z properties that tells you the acceleration in each dimension without considering gravity.

➤ `accelerationIncludingGravity`—An object containing x, y, and z properties that tells you the acceleration in each dimension, including the natural acceleration of gravity in the z-axis.

➤ `interval`—The amount of time, in milliseconds, that will pass before another `devicemotion` event is fired. This value should be constant from event to event.

➤ `rotationRate`—An object containing the alpha, beta, and gamma properties that indicate device orientation.

If `acceleration`, `accelerationIncludingGravity`, or `rotationRate` cannot be provided, then the property value is `null`. Because of that, you should always check that the value is not `null` before using any of these properties. For example:

```
window.addEventListener("devicemotion", (event) => {
    let output = document.getElementById("output");
    if (event.rotationRate !== null) {
      output.innerHTML += `Alpha=${event.rotationRate.alpha}` +
                          `Beta=${event.rotationRate.beta}` +
                          `Gamma=${event.rotationRate.gamma}`;
    }
});
```

Touch and Gesture Events

Because mobile devices are mouseless and keyboardless, the regular mouse and keyboard events simply aren't enough to create a completely interactive web page designed with mobile browsers in mind. With the introduction of WebKit for Android, many of the proprietary events became de facto standards and led to the beginning of a Touch Events specification from the W3C. The following events work only on touch-based devices.

Touch Events

Touch events are fired when a finger is placed on the screen, dragged across the screen, or removed from the screen. The touch events are as follows:

➤ `touchstart`—Fires when a finger touches the screen even if another finger is already touching the screen.

➤ touchmove—Fires continuously as a finger is moved across the screen. Calling preventDefault() during this event prevents scrolling.

➤ touchend—Fires when a finger is removed from the screen.

➤ touchcancel—Fires when the system has stopped tracking the touch.

Each of these events bubbles and can be canceled. Even though touch events aren't part of the DOM specification, they are implemented in a DOM-compatible way. Thus, the event object for each touch event provides properties that are common to mouse events: bubbles, cancelable, view, clientX, clientY, etc.

In addition to these common DOM properties, touch events have the following three properties to track touches:

➤ touches—An array of Touch objects that indicate the currently tracked touches.

➤ targetTouches—An array of Touch objects specific to the event's target.

➤ changedTouches—An array of Touch objects that have been changed in the last user action.

Each Touch object, in turn, has the following properties:

➤ clientX—The x-coordinate of the touch target in the viewport.

➤ clientY—The y-coordinate of the touch target in the viewport.

➤ identifier—A unique ID for the touch.

➤ pageX—The x-coordinate of the touch target on the page.

➤ pageY—The y-coordinate of the touch target on the page.

➤ screenX—The x-coordinate of the touch target on the screen.

➤ screenY—The y-coordinate of the touch target on the screen.

➤ target—The DOM node target for the touch.

These properties can be used to track the touch around the screen. For example:

```
function handleTouchEvent(event) {
  // only for one touch
  if (event.touches.length == 1) {
    let output = document.getElementById("output");
    switch(event.type) {
      case "touchstart":
        output.innerHTML += `<br>Touch started:` +
                            `(${event.touches[0].clientX}` +
                            ` ${event.touches[0].clientY})`;
        break;
      case "touchend":
        output.innerHTML += `<br>Touch ended:` +
                            `(${event.changedTouches[0].clientX}` +
                            ` ${event.changedTouches[0].clientY})`;
```

```
                break;
            case "touchmove":
                event.preventDefault();  // prevent scrolling
                output.innerHTML += `<br>Touch moved:` +
                                    `(${event.changedTouches[0].clientX}` +
                                    ` ${event.changedTouches[0].clientY})`;
                break;
        }
    }
}

document.addEventListener("touchstart", handleTouchEvent);
document.addEventListener("touchend", handleTouchEvent);
document.addEventListener("touchmove", handleTouchEvent);
```

This code tracks a single touch around the screen. To keep things simple, it outputs information only when there's a single active touch. When the `touchstart` event occurs, it outputs the location of the touch into a `<div>`. When a `touchmove` event fires, its default behavior is canceled to prevent scrolling (moving touches typically scroll the page), and then it outputs information about the changed touch. The `touchend` event outputs the last information about the touch. Note that there is nothing in the touches collection during the `touchend` event, because there is no longer an active touch; the `changedTouches` collection must be used instead.

These events fire on all elements of the document, so you can manipulate different parts of the page individually. The order of events (including mouse events) when you tap on an element are:

1. `touchstart`

2. `mouseover`

3. `mousemove` (once)

4. `mousedown`

5. `mouseup`

6. `click`

7. `touchend`

Gesture Events

A *gesture* occurs when two fingers are touching the screen and typically causes a change in the scale of the displayed item or the rotation. There are three gesture events, as described here:

➤ `gesturestart`—Fires when a finger is already on the screen and another finger is placed on the screen.

➤ `gesturechange`—Fires when the position of either finger on the screen has changed.

➤ `gestureend`—Fires when one of the fingers has been removed from the screen.

These events fire only if the two fingers are touching the recipient of the event. Setting event handlers on a single element means that both fingers must be within the bounds of the element in order for gesture events to fire (this will be the target). Because these events bubble, you can also place event handlers at the document level to handle all gesture events. When you are using this approach, the target of the event will be the element that has both fingers within its boundaries.

There is a relationship between the touch and the gesture events. When a finger is placed on the screen, the touchstart event fires. When another finger is placed on the screen, the gesturestart event fires first and is followed by the touchstart event for that finger. If one or both of the fingers are moved, a gesturechange event is fired. As soon as one of the fingers is removed, the gestureend event fires, followed by touchend for that finger.

As with touch events, each gesture event object contains all of the standard mouse event properties: bubbles, cancelable, view, clientX, clientY, etc. The two additions to the event object are rotation and scale. The rotation property indicates the degrees of rotation that the fingers have changed, where negative numbers indicate a counterclockwise rotation and positive numbers indicate clockwise rotation (the value begins as 0). The scale property indicates how much of a change in distance occurred between the fingers (making a pinch motion). This starts out as 1 and will either increase as the distance increases or decrease as the distance decreases.

These events can be used as follows:

```
function handleGestureEvent(event) {
  let output = document.getElementById("output");
  switch(event.type) {
    case "gesturestart":
      output.innerHTML += `Gesture started: ` +
                          `rotation=${event.rotation},` +
                          `scale=${event.scale}`;
      break;
    case "gestureend":
      output.innerHTML += `Gesture ended: ` +
                          `rotation=${event.rotation},` +
                          `scale=${event.scale}`;
      break;
    case "gesturechange":
      output.innerHTML += `Gesture changed: ` +
                          `rotation=${event.rotation},` +
                          `scale=${event.scale}`;
      break;
  }
}

document.addEventListener("gesturestart", handleGestureEvent, false);
document.addEventListener("gestureend", handleGestureEvent, false);
document.addEventListener("gesturechange", handleGestureEvent, false);
```

As with the touch events example, this code simply wires up each event to a single function and then outputs information about each event.

> **NOTE** *Touch events also return* rotation *and* scale *properties, but they change only when two fingers are in contact with the screen. Generally, it is easier to use gesture events with two fingers than to manage all interactions with touch events.*

Event Reference

MDN publishes a list of all available browser events defined in a DOM specification, the HTML5 specification, and any other currently published specifications which outline event behavior. They are categorized by API and/or the specification in which they appear. The list can be found at `https://developer.mozilla.org/en-US/docs/Web/Events#event_listing`.

MEMORY AND PERFORMANCE

Because event handlers provide the interaction on modern web applications, many developers mistakenly add a large number of them to the page. In languages that create GUIs, such as C#, it's customary to add an onclick event handler to each button in the GUI, and there is no real penalty for doing so. In JavaScript, the number of event handlers on the page directly relates to the overall performance of the page. This happens for a number of reasons. The first is that each function is an object and takes up memory; the more objects in memory, the slower the performance. Second, the amount of DOM access needed to assign all of the event handlers up front delays the interactivity of the entire page. There are a number of ways that you can improve performance by minding your use of event handlers.

Event Delegation

The solution to the "too many event handlers" issue is called *event delegation*. Event delegation takes advantage of event bubbling to assign a single event handler to manage all events of a particular type. The click event, for example, bubbles all the way up to the document level. This means that it's possible to assign one onclick event handler for an entire page instead of one for each clickable element. Consider the following HTML:

```
<ul id="myLinks">
  <li id="goSomewhere">Go somewhere</li>
  <li id="doSomething">Do something</li>
  <li id="sayHi">Say hi</li>
</ul>
```

The HTML in this example contains three items that should perform actions when clicked. Traditional thinking simply attaches three event handlers like this:

```
let item1 = document.getElementById("goSomewhere");
let item2 = document.getElementById("doSomething");
let item3 = document.getElementById("sayHi");

item1.addEventListener("click", (event) => {
  location.href = "http:// www.wiley.com";
});

item2.addEventListener("click", (event) => {
  document.title = "I changed the document's title";
});

item3.addEventListener("click", (event) => {
  console.log("hi");
});
```

If this scenario is repeated for all of the clickable elements in a complex web application, the result is an incredibly long section of code that simply attaches event handlers. Event delegation approaches this problem by attaching a single event handler to the highest possible point in the DOM tree, as in this example:

```
let list = document.getElementById("myLinks");

list.addEventListener("click", (event) => {
  let target = event.target;

  switch(target.id) {
    case "doSomething":
      document.title = "I changed the document's title";
      break;

    case "goSomewhere":
      location.href = "http:// www.wiley.com";
      break;

    case "sayHi":
      console.log("hi");
      break;
  }
});
```

In this code, event delegation is used to attach a single onclick event handler to the `<ul>` element. Because all of the list items are children of this element, their events bubble up and are handled by this function. The event target is the list item that was clicked so you can check the id property to determine the appropriate action. In comparison with the previous code that didn't use event delegation, this code has less of an up-front cost because it just retrieves one DOM element and attaches one event handler. The end result is the same for the user, but this approach requires much less memory. All events that use buttons (most mouse events and keyboard events) are candidates for this technique.

If it's practical, you may want to consider attaching a single event handler on document that can handle all of the page events of a particular type. This has the following advantages compared to traditional techniques:

➤ The document object is immediately available and can have event handlers assigned at any point during the page's lifecycle (no need to wait for DOMContentLoaded or load events). This means that as soon as a clickable element is rendered, it can function appropriately without delay.

➤ Less time is spent setting up event handlers on the page. Assigning one event handler takes fewer DOM references and less time.

➤ Lower memory usage is required for the entire page, improving overall performance.

The best candidates for event delegation are click, mousedown, mouseup, keydown, keyup, and keypress. The mouseover and mouseout events bubble but are complicated to handle properly and often require calculating element position to appropriately handle (because mouseout fires when moving from an element to one of its child nodes and when moving outside of the element).

Removing Event Handlers

When event handlers are assigned to elements, a connection is formed between code that is running the browser and JavaScript code interacting with the page. The more of these connections that exist, the slower a page performs. One way to handle this issue is through event delegation to limit the number of connections that are set up. Another way to manage the issue is to remove event handlers when they are no longer needed. Dangling event handlers, those that remain in memory after they are necessary, are a major source of memory and performance issues in web applications.

This problem occurs at two specific points during a page's lifecycle. The first is when an element is removed from the document while it has event handlers attached. This can be due to a true DOM manipulation involving `removeChild()` or `replaceChild()`, but it happens most often when using `innerHTML` to replace a section of the page. Any event handlers assigned to an element that was eliminated by the call to `innerHTML` may not be properly garbage collected. Consider the following example:

```
<div id="myDiv">
  <input type="button" value="Click Me" id="myBtn">
</div>
<script type="text/javascript">
  let btn = document.getElementById("myBtn");
  btn.onclick = function() {

    // do something

    document.getElementById("myDiv").innerHTML = "Processing...";
    // Bad!!!
  };
</script>
```

Here, a button exists inside of a `<div>` element. When the button is clicked, it is removed and replaced with a message to prevent double-clicking, which is a very common paradigm on websites. The issue is that the button still had an event handler attached when it was removed from the page. Setting `innerHTML` on the `<div>` removed the button completely, but the event handler remains attached. If you know that a given element is going to be removed, it's best to manually remove the event handlers yourself, as in this example:

```
<div id="myDiv">
  <input type="button" value="Click Me" id="myBtn">
</div>
<script type="text/javascript">
  let btn = document.getElementById("myBtn");
  btn.onclick = function() {

    // do something

    btn.onclick = null;    // remove event handler

    document.getElementById("myDiv").innerHTML = "Processing&hellip;";
  };
</script>
```

In this rewritten code, the button's event handler is removed before setting the `<div>` element's `innerHTML`. This ensures that the memory will be reclaimed and the button can safely be removed from the DOM.

Note also that removing the button in the event handler prevents bubbling of the event. An event will bubble only if its target is still present in the document.

> **NOTE** *Event delegation also helps solve this problem. If you know that a particular part of the page is going to be replaced using* `innerHTML`, *do not attach event handlers directly to elements within that part. Instead, attach event handlers at a higher level that can handle events in that area.*

SIMULATING EVENTS

Events are designed to indicate particular moments of interest in a web page. These events are often fired based on user interaction or other browser functionality. It's a little-known fact that JavaScript can be used to fire specific events at any time, and those events are treated the same as events that are created by the browser. This means that the events bubble appropriately and cause the browser to execute event handlers assigned to deal with the event. This capability can be extremely useful in testing web applications. The DOM Level 3 specification indicates ways to simulate specific types of events.

DOM Event Simulation

An event object can be created at any time by using the `createEvent()` method on `document`. This method accepts a single argument, which is a string indicating the type of event to create. In DOM Level 2, all of these strings were plural, while DOM Level 3 changed them to singular. The string may be one of the following:

➤   **UIEvents**—Generic UI event. Mouse events and keyboard events inherit from UI events. For DOM Level 3, use UIEvent.

➤   **MouseEvents**—Generic mouse event. For DOM Level 3, use MouseEvent.

➤   **HTMLEvents**—Generic HTML event. There is no equivalent DOM Level 3 Event. (HTML events were dispersed into other groupings.)

Note that keyboard events are not specifically described in DOM Level 2 Events and were only later introduced in DOM Level 3 Events.

Once an event object is created, it needs to be initialized with information about the event. Each type of event object has a specific method that is used to initialize it with the appropriate data. The name of the method is different, depending on the argument that was used with `createEvent()`.

The final step in event simulation is to fire the event. This is done by using the `dispatchEvent()` method that is present on all DOM nodes that support events. The `dispatchEvent()` method accepts a single argument, which is the event object representing the event to fire. After that point, the event becomes "official," bubbling and causing event handlers to execute.

Simulating Mouse Events

Mouse events can be simulated by creating a new mouse event object and assigning the necessary information. A mouse event object is created by passing "MouseEvents" into the `createEvent()` method. The returned object has a method called `initMouseEvent()` that is used to assign mouse-related information. This method accepts 15 arguments, one for each property typically available on a mouse event. The arguments are as follows:

➤ `type` (string)—The type of event to fire, such as "click."

➤ `bubbles` (Boolean)—Indicates if the event should bubble. This should be set to `true` for accurate mouse event simulation.

➤ `cancelable` (Boolean)—Indicates if the event can be canceled. This should be set to `true` for accurate mouse event simulation.

➤ `view` (AbstractView)—The view associated with the event. This is almost always `document` `.defaultView`.

➤ `detail` (integer)—Additional information for the event. This is used only by event handlers, though it's typically set to 0.

➤ `screenX` (integer)—The x-coordinate of the event relative to the screen.

➤ `screenY` (integer)—The y-coordinate of the event relative to the screen.

➤ `clientX` (integer)—The x-coordinate of the event relative to the viewport.

➤ `clientY` (integer)—The y-coordinate of the event relative to the viewport.

➤ `ctrlKey` (Boolean)—Indicates if the Ctrl key is pressed. The default is `false`.

➤ `altKey` (Boolean)—Indicates if the Alt key is pressed. The default is `false`.

➤ `shiftKey` (Boolean)—Indicates if the Shift key is pressed. The default is `false`.

➤ `metaKey` (Boolean)—Indicates if the Meta key is pressed. The default is `false`.

➤ `button` (integer)—Indicates the button that was pressed. The default is 0.

➤ `relatedTarget` (object)—An object related to the event. This is used only when simulating `mouseover` or `mouseout`.

As should be obvious, the arguments for `initMouseEvent()` map directly to the event object properties for a mouse event. The first four arguments are the only ones that are critical for the proper execution of the event because they are used by the browser; only event handlers use the other arguments. The `target` property of the event object is set automatically when it is passed into the `dispatchEvent()` method. As an example, the following simulates a click on a button using default values:

```
let btn = document.getElementById("myBtn");

// create event object
let event = document.createEvent("MouseEvents");

// initialize the event object
event.initMouseEvent("click", true, true, document.defaultView,
                    0, 0, 0, 0, 0, false, false, false, false, 0, null);

// fire the event
btn.dispatchEvent(event);
```

All other mouse events, including `dblclick`, can be simulated using this same technique in DOM-compliant browsers.

Simulating Keyboard Events

As mentioned previously, keyboard events were left out of DOM Level 2 Events, so simulating keyboard events is not straightforward. Keyboard events were included in draft versions of DOM Level 2 Events and were removed before finalization. It's worth noting that keyboard events in DOM Level 3 are drastically different from the draft version originally included in DOM Level 2.

The DOM Level 3 way to create a keyboard event is to pass `"KeyboardEvent"` into the `createEvent()` method. Doing so creates an event object with a method called `initKeyboardEvent()`. This method has the following parameters:

- ➤ `type` (string)—The type of event to fire, such as `"keydown"`.

- ➤ `bubbles` (Boolean)—Indicates if the event should bubble. This should be set to `true` for accurate mouse event simulation.

- ➤ `cancelable` (Boolean)—Indicates if the event can be canceled. This should be set to true for accurate mouse event simulation.

- ➤ `view` (AbstractView)—The view associated with the event. This is almost always `document.defaultView`.

- ➤ `key` (string)—String code for the key that was pressed.

- ➤ `location` (integer)—The location of the key that was pressed. 0 for the default keyboard, 1 for the left location, 2 for the right location, 3 for the numeric keypad, 4 for mobile (indicating a virtual keypad), or 5 for joystick.

- ➤ `modifiers` (string)—A space-separated list of modifiers such as "Shift."

- ➤ `repeat` (integer)—The number of times this key has been pressed in a row.

Keep in mind that DOM Level 3 Events deprecate the keypress event, so you can simulate only the keydown and keyup events using this technique:

```
let textbox = document.getElementById("myTextbox"),
    event;

// create event object the DOM Level 3 way
if (document.implementation.hasFeature("KeyboardEvents", "3.0")) {
  event = document.createEvent("KeyboardEvent");

  // initialize the event object
  event.initKeyboardEvent("keydown", true, true, document.defaultView, "a",
                          0, "Shift", 0);
}
// fire the event
textbox.dispatchEvent(event);
```

This example simulates keydown of the A key while Shift is being held. You should always check for DOM Level 3 keyboard event support before attempting to use document .createEvent("KeyboardEvent"); other browsers return a nonstandard KeyboardEvent object.

Firefox allows you to create a keyboard event by passing "KeyEvents" into the createEvent() method. This returns an event object with a method called initKeyEvent(), which accepts the following 10 arguments:

➤ type (string)—The type of event to fire, such as "keydown".

➤ bubbles (Boolean)—Indicates if the event should bubble. This should be set to true for accurate mouse event simulation.

➤ cancelable (Boolean)—Indicates if the event can be canceled. This should be set to true for accurate mouse event simulation.

➤ view (AbstractView)—The view associated with the event. This is almost always document .defaultView.

➤ ctrlKey (Boolean)—Indicates if the Ctrl key is pressed. The default is false.

➤ altKey (Boolean)—Indicates if the Alt key is pressed. The default is false.

➤ shiftKey (Boolean)—Indicates if the Shift key is pressed. The default is false.

➤ metaKey (Boolean)—Indicates if the Meta key is pressed. The default is false.

➤ keyCode (integer)—The key code of the key that was pressed or released. This is used for keydown and keyup. The default is 0.

➤ charCode (integer)—The ASCII code of the character generated from the keypress. This is used for keypress. The default is 0.

A keyboard event can then be fired by passing this event object to dispatchEvent(), as in this example:

```
// for Firefox only
```

```
let textbox = document.getElementById("myTextbox");

// create event object
let event = document.createEvent("KeyEvents");

// initialize the event object
event.initKeyEvent("keydown", true, true, document.defaultView, false,
                   false, true, false, 65, 65);

// fire the event
textbox.dispatchEvent(event);
```

This example simulates `keydown` for the A key with the Shift key held down. You can also simulate `keyup` and `keypress` events using this technique.

For other browsers, you'll need to create a generic event and assign keyboard-specific information to it, as shown in this example:

```
let textbox = document.getElementById("myTextbox");

// create event object
let event = document.createEvent("Events");

// initialize the event object
event.initEvent(type, bubbles, cancelable);
event.view = document.defaultView;
event.altKey = false;
event.ctrlKey = false;
event.shiftKey = false;
event.metaKey = false;
event.keyCode = 65;
event.charCode = 65;

// fire the event
textbox.dispatchEvent(event);
```

This code creates a generic event, initializes it by using `initEvent()`, and then assigns keyboard event information. It's necessary to use a generic event instead of a UI event because the UI event prevents new properties from being added to the event object. Simulating an event in this way causes the keyboard event to fire, but no text will be placed into the text box because this doesn't accurately simulate a keyboard event.

Simulating Other Events

Mouse events and keyboard events are the ones most often simulated in the browser, though it is possible to simulate HTML events as well. HTML events are simulated by creating an event object, using `createEvent("HTMLEvents")`, and then initializing the event object using `initEvent()` as shown in this example:

```
let event = document.createEvent("HTMLEvents");
event.initEvent("focus", true, false);
target.dispatchEvent(event);
```

This example fires the focus event on a given target. Other HTML events may be simulated the same way.

> **NOTE** *HTML events are rarely used in browsers because they are of limited utility.*

Custom DOM Events

DOM Level 3 specifies a class of events called *custom events*. Custom events don't get fired natively by the DOM but are provided so that developers can create their own events. You create a new custom event by calling `createEvent("CustomEvent")`. The returned object has a method called `initCustomEvent()`, which takes four arguments:

➤ `type` (string)—The type of event to fire, such as `"keydown"`.

➤ `bubbles` (Boolean)—Indicates if the event should bubble.

➤ `cancelable` (Boolean)—Indicates if the event can be canceled.

➤ `detail` (object)—Any value. This fills in the detail property of the event object.

The created event can then be dispatched in the DOM just like any other event, shown here:

```
let div = document.getElementById("myDiv"),
    event;

div.addEventListener("myevent", (event) => {
  console.log("DIV: " + event.detail);
});

document.addEventListener("myevent", (event) => {
  console.log("DOCUMENT: " + event.detail);
});

if (document.implementation.hasFeature("CustomEvents", "3.0")) {
  event = document.createEvent("CustomEvent");
  event.initCustomEvent("myevent", true, false, "Hello world!");
  div.dispatchEvent(event);
}
```

This example creates a bubbling event called `"myevent"`. The value of `event.detail` is set to a simple string and is then listened for both on a `<div>` element and at the document level. Because the event is specified as bubbling using `initCustomEvent()`, the browser takes care of bubbling the event up to the document.

SUMMARY

Events are the primary way that JavaScript is tied to web pages. Most common events are defined in the DOM Level 3 Events specification or in HTML5. Even though there is a specification for basic events, many browsers have gone beyond the specification and implemented proprietary events to give developers greater insight into user interactions. Some proprietary events are directly related to specific devices.

There are some memory and performance considerations surrounding events. For example:

➤   It's best to limit the number of event handlers on a page because they can take up more memory and make the page feel less responsive to the user.

➤   Event delegation can be used to limit the number of event handlers by taking advantage of event bubbling.

➤   It's a good idea to remove all event handlers that were added before the page is unloaded.

It's possible to simulate events in the browser using JavaScript. The DOM Level 2 and 3 Events specifications provide for the simulation of all events, making it easy to simulate all defined events. It's also possible to simulate keyboard events to a point by using a combination of other techniques.

Events are one of the most important topics in JavaScript, and a good understanding of how they work and their performance implications is critical.

16

Animation and Graphics with Canvas

WHAT'S IN THIS CHAPTER?

➤ Using requestAnimationFrame

➤ Understanding the <canvas> element

➤ Drawing simple 2D graphics

➤ 3D drawing with WebGL

Graphics and animation in the browser are an increasingly essential component of the modern web, but they are also extremely difficult to do well. Visually complicated features require performance tuning and hardware acceleration so that they don't slow down the browser. An increasingly robust suite of APIs and tools allows for development of such features.

Arguably, HTML5's most popular addition is the <canvas> element. This element designates an area of the page where graphics can be created, on the fly, using JavaScript. Originally proposed by Apple for use with its Dashboard widgets, <canvas> quickly was added into HTML5 and found a very fast adoption rate by browsers.

Similar to the other parts of the browser environment, <canvas> is made up of a few API sets. There is a 2D context with basic drawing capabilities and a 3D context called WebGL.

USING REQUESTANIMATIONFRAME

For a long time, timers and intervals have been the state of the art for JavaScript-based animations. While CSS transitions and animations make some animations easy for web developers, little has changed in the world of JavaScript-based animation over the years. Firefox 4 was the first browser to include a new API for JavaScript animations called `mozRequestAnimationFrame()`. This method indicates to the browser that an animation is taking place so that the browser can, in turn, determine the best way to schedule a redraw. Since its introduction, the API gained widespread adoption and is now available across all major browsers as `requestAnimationFrame()`.

Early Animation Loops

The typical way to create animations in JavaScript is to use `setInterval()` to manage all animations. A basic animation loop using `setInterval()` looks like this:

```
(function() {
  function updateAnimations() {
  doAnimation1();
  doAnimation2();
  //etc.
  }
  setInterval(updateAnimations, 100);
})();
```

To build out a small animation library, the `updateAnimations()` method would cycle through the running animations and make the appropriate changes to each one (for example, both a news ticker and a progress bar running together). If there are no animations to update, the method can exit without doing anything and perhaps even stop the animation loop until more animations are ready for updating.

The tricky part about this animation loop is knowing what the delay should be. The interval has to be short enough to handle a variety of different animation types smoothly but long enough so as to produce changes the browser can actually render. Most computer monitors refresh at a rate of 60 Hz, which basically means there's a repaint 60 times per second. Most browsers cap their repaints so they do not attempt to repaint any more frequently than that, knowing that the end user gets no improvement in experience.

Therefore, the best interval for the smoothest animation is 1000ms/60, or about 17ms. You'll see the smoothest animation at this rate because you're more closely mirroring what the browser is capable of doing. Multiple animations may need to be throttled so they don't complete too quickly when using an animation loop with a 17ms interval.

Even though `setInterval()`-based animation loops are more efficient than having multiple sets of `setTimeout()`-based loops, there are still problems. Neither `setInterval()` nor `setTimeout()` are intended to be precise. The delay you specify as the second argument is only an indication of when the code is added in the browser's UI thread queue for possible execution. If there are other jobs in the queue ahead of it, then that code waits to be executed. In short, the millisecond delay is not an indication of when the code will be executed, only an indication of when the job will be queued. If the UI thread is busy, perhaps dealing with user actions, then that code will not execute immediately.

Problems with Intervals

Understanding when the next frame will be drawn is key to smooth animations, and until recently, there was no way to guarantee when the next frame would be drawn in a browser. As <canvas> became popular and new browser-based games emerged, developers became increasingly frustrated with the inaccuracy of setInterval() and setTimeout().

Exacerbating these problems is the timer resolution of the browser. Timers are not accurate to the millisecond. Complicating matters more is that browsers have started to throttle timers for tabs that are in the background or inactive. So even if you set your interval for optimum display, you're still only getting close to the timing you want.

requestAnimationFrame

Robert O'Callahan of Mozilla was thinking about this problem and came up with a unique solution. He pointed out that CSS transitions and animations benefit from the browser knowing that some animation should be happening, and so figured out the correct interval at which to refresh the UI. With JavaScript animations, the browser has no idea that an animation is taking place. His solution was to create a new method, called mozRequestAnimationFrame(), that indicates to the browser that some JavaScript code is performing an animation. This allows the browser to optimize appropriately after running some code. All browsers have converged on a prefix-less version of this method, requestAnimationFrame().

The requestAnimationFrame() method accepts a single argument, which is a function to call prior to repainting the screen. This function is where you make appropriate changes to DOM styles that will be reflected with the next repaint. In order to create an animation loop, you can chain multiple calls to requestAnimationFrame() together in the same way previously done with setTimeout(). For example:

```
function updateProgress() {
  var div = document.getElementById("status");
  div.style.width = (parseInt(div.style.width, 10) + 5) + "%";
  if (div.style.left != "100%") {
  requestAnimationFrame(updateProgress);
  }
}
requestAnimationFrame(updateProgress);
```

Because requestAnimationFrame() runs the given function only once, you need to call it again manually the next time you want to make a UI change for the animation. You also need to manage when to stop the animation in the same way. The result is a very smooth animation.

So far, requestAnimationFrame() has solved the problem of browsers not knowing when a JavaScript animation is happening and the problem of not knowing the best interval, but what about the problem of not knowing when your code will actually execute? That's also covered with the same solution.

The function you pass into requestAnimationFrame() receives an argument, which is a DOMHighResTimeStamp time code (such as the value returned from performance.now()) for when the next repaint will actually occur. This is a very important point: requestAnimationFrame() schedules a repaint for some known point in the future and can tell you when that is. You're then able to determine how best to adjust your animation.

cancelAnimationFrame

Similar to `setTimeout()`, `requestAnimationFrame()` returns a request ID which can be used to cancel the request via `cancelAnimationFrame()`. In the following example, the request callback is enqueued but immediately cancelled:

```
let requestID = window.requestAnimationFrame(() => {
  console.log('Repaint!');
});
window.cancelAnimationFrame(requestID);
```

Performance Throttling with *requestAnimationFrame*

The name of `requestAnimationFrame` is somewhat misleading. Browsers that support this method are effectively exposing a hook callback queue. The hook is the point just before the browser performs the next repaint. The callback queue is a mutable list of functions, which should be invoked before performing that repaint. Invoking `requestAnimationFrame()` pushes a callback function onto that queue, and there is no limit to the length of the queue.

The behavior of the queued callback does not need to involve animation. However, recursively enqueuing callback functions with `requestAnimationFrame()` ensures that the callback will be invoked at most once per repaint, which is an excellent rate limiting tool. This is especially useful when dealing with frequently invoked code that affects the visual appearance of the page, such as scroll event listeners.

Consider the following naïve implementation, which will invoke the pseudo-expensive operation upon a scroll event being fired from the window object. When scrolling down a web page, this event can be fired hundreds or thousands of times very quickly:

```
function expensiveOperation() {
  console.log('Invoked at', Date.now());
}

window.addEventListener('scroll', () => {
  expensiveOperation();
});
```

If you wanted to restrict the callback to only occur just before a repaint, you could wrap it inside a requestAnimationFrame:

```
function expensiveOperation() {
  console.log('Invoked at', Date.now());
}

window.addEventListener('scroll', () => {
  window.requestAnimationFrame(expensiveOperation);
});
```

This will condense all the callback execution into the repaint hook, but it won't prevent redundant execution per repaint. You can prevent redundant repaint execution by introducing a flag that is set and unset by the callback:

```
let enqueued = false;

function expensiveOperation() {
```

```
      console.log('Invoked at', Date.now());
      enqueued = false;
}


window.addEventListener('scroll', () => {
  if (!enqueued) {
    enqueued = true;
    window.requestAnimationFrame(expensiveOperation);
  }
});
```

Because repaints are a very frequent operation, this isn't much of a throttle. Far better is to combine this with a timer, which will throttle the frequency with which this operation can occur. This way, the timer can restrict the real-world time interval at which the operation occurs, and `requestAnimationFrame` controls when in the browser rendering cycle the execution occurs. The following example will prevent the callback from executing more than once every 50ms:

```
let enabled = true;

function expensiveOperation() {
  console.log('Invoked at', Date.now());
}

window.addEventListener('scroll', () => {
  if (enabled) {
    enabled = false;
    window.requestAnimationFrame(expensiveOperation);
    window.setTimeout(() => enabled = true, 50);
  }
});
```

BASIC CANVAS USAGE

The `<canvas>` element requires at least its `width` and `height` attributes to be set in order to indicate the size of the drawing to be created. Any content appearing between the opening and closing tags is fallback data that is displayed only if the `<canvas>` element isn't supported. For example:

```
<canvas id="drawing" width="200" height="200">A drawing of something.</canvas>
```

As with other elements, the width and height attributes are also available as properties on the DOM element object and may be changed at any time. The entire element may be styled using CSS as well, and the element is invisible until it is styled or drawn upon.

To begin drawing on a canvas, you need to retrieve a drawing context. A reference to a drawing context is retrieved using the `getContext()` method and passing in the name of the context. For example, passing "2d" retrieves a 2D context object:

```
let drawing = document.getElementById("drawing");

let context = drawing.getContext("2d");
```

Images created on a `<canvas>` element can be exported using the `toDataURL()` method. This method accepts a single argument, the MIME type format of the image to produce, and is applicable regardless of the context used to create the image. For example, to return a PNG-formatted image from a canvas, use the following:

```
let drawing = document.getElementById("drawing");

// get data URI of the image
let imgURI = drawing.toDataURL("image/png");

// display the image
let image = document.createElement("img");
image.src = imgURI;
document.body.appendChild(image);
```

By default, browsers encode the image as PNG unless otherwise specified.

> **NOTE** *The* `toDataURL()` *method throws an error if an image from a different domain is drawn onto a canvas. More details are available later in this chapter.*

THE 2D CONTEXT

The 2D drawing context provides methods for drawing simple 2D shapes such as rectangles, arcs, and paths. The coordinates in a 2D context begin at the upper-left of the `<canvas>` element, which is considered point (0, 0). All coordinate values are calculated in relation to that point, with x increasing to the right and y increasing toward the bottom. By default, the width and height indicate how many pixels are available in each direction.

Fills and Strokes

There are two basic drawing operations on the 2D context: fill and stroke. Fill automatically fills in the shape with a specific style (color, gradient, or image) while stroke colors only the edges. Most of the 2D context operations have both fill and stroke variants, and how they are displayed is based on a couple of properties: `fillStyle` and `strokeStyle`.

Both properties can be set to a string, a gradient object, or a pattern object, and both default to a value of `"#000000"`. A string value indicates a color defined using one of the various CSS color formats: name, hex code, rgb, rgba, hsl, or hsla. For example:

```
let drawing = document.getElementById("drawing");

let context = drawing.getContext("2d");
context.strokeStyle = "red";
context.fillStyle = "#0000ff";
```

This code sets the `strokeStyle` to "red" (a named CSS color) and `fillStyle` to "#0000ff" (also known as blue). All drawing operations involving stroke and fill will use these styles until the properties are changed again. These properties can also be set to a gradient or a pattern, both of which are discussed later in this chapter.

Drawing Rectangles

The only shape that can be drawn directly on the 2D drawing context is the rectangle. There are three methods for working with rectangles: `fillRect()`, `strokeRect()`, and `clearRect()`. Each of these methods accepts four arguments: the x-coordinate of the rectangle, the y-coordinate of the rectangle, the width of the rectangle, and the height of the rectangle. Each of these arguments is considered to be in pixels.

The `fillRect()` method is used to draw a rectangle that is filled with a specific color onto the canvas. The fill color is specified using the `fillStyle` property. Consider the following example:

```
let drawing = document.getElementById("drawing");

let context = drawing.getContext("2d");

// draw a red rectangle
context.fillStyle = "#ff0000";
context.fillRect(10, 10, 50, 50);

// draw a blue rectangle that's semi-transparent
context.fillStyle = "rgba(0,0,255,0.5)";
context.fillRect(30, 30, 50, 50);
```

This code first sets the `fillStyle` to red and draws a rectangle located at (10, 10) that's 50 pixels tall and wide. Next, it sets the `fillStyle` to a semitransparent blue color using `rgba()` format and draws another rectangle that overlaps the first. The result is that you can see the red rectangle through the blue rectangle (see Figure 16.1).

FIGURE 16.1: Overlapping semi-transparent rectangles drawn with `fillRect()`

The `strokeRect()` method draws a rectangle outline using the color specified with the `strokeStyle` property. Here is an example:

```
let drawing = document.getElementById("drawing");

let context = drawing.getContext("2d");

// draw a red outlined rectangle
context.strokeStyle = "#ff0000";
context.strokeRect(10, 10, 50, 50);

// draw a blue outlined rectangle that's semi-transparent
context.strokeStyle = "rgba(0,0,255,0.5)";
context.strokeRect(30, 30, 50, 50);
```

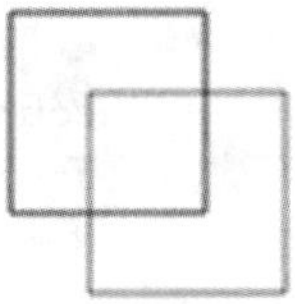

This code also draws two rectangles that overlap; however, they are just outlines rather than filled rectangles (see Figure 16.2).

FIGURE 16.2: Overlapping rectangle outlines drawn with `strokeRect()`

> **NOTE** *The size of the stroke is controlled by the* `lineWidth` *property, which can be set to any whole number. Likewise, a* `lineCap` *property describes the shape that should be used at the end of lines (*"butt"*,* "round"*, or* "square"*) and* `lineJoin` *indicates how lines should be joined (*"round"*,* "bevel"*, or* "miter"*).*

You can erase an area of the canvas by using the `clearRect()` method. This method is used to make an area of the drawing context transparent. By drawing shapes and then clearing specific areas, you are able to create interesting effects, such as cutting out a section of another shape. Consider the following example:

```
let drawing = document.getElementById("drawing");

let context = drawing.getContext("2d");

// draw a red rectangle
context.fillStyle = "#ff0000";
context.fillRect(10, 10, 50, 50);

// draw a blue rectangle that's semi-transparent
context.fillStyle = "rgba(0,0,255,0.5)";
context.fillRect(30, 30, 50, 50);

// clear a rectangle that overlaps both of the previous rectangles
context.clearRect(40, 40, 10, 10);
```

Here, two filled rectangles overlap one another and then a small rectangle is cleared inside of that overlapping area. Figure 16.3 shows the result.

Drawing Paths

The 2D drawing context supports a number of methods for drawing paths on a canvas. Paths allow you to create complex shapes and lines. To start creating a path, you must first call `beginPath()` to indicate that a new path has begun. After that, the following methods can be called to create the path:

FIGURE 16.3:
Removing content with `clearRect()`

➤ `arc(x, y, radius, startAngle, endAngle, counterclockwise)`—Draws an arc centered at point (x, y) with a given radius and between `startAngle` and `endAngle` (expressed in radians). The last argument is a Boolean indicating if `startAngle` and `endAngle` should be calculated counterclockwise instead of clockwise.

➤ `arcTo(x1, y1, x2, y2, radius)`—Draws an arc from the last point to (x2, y2), passing through (x1,y1) with the given radius.

➤ `bezierCurveTo(c1x, c1y, c2x, c2y, x, y)`—Draws a curve from the last point to the point (x,y) using the control points (c1x,c1y) and (c2x, c2y).

➤ `lineTo(x, y)`—Draws a line from the last point to the point (x, y).

➤ `moveTo(x, y)`—Moves the drawing cursor to the point (x, y) without drawing a line.

➤ quadraticCurveTo(cx, cy, x, y)—Draws a quadratic curve from the last point to the point (x, y) using a control point of (cx, cy).

➤ rect(x, y, width, height)—Draws a rectangle at point (x, y) with the given width and height. This is different from strokeRect() and fillRect() in that it creates a path rather than a separate shape.

Once the path has been created, you have several options. To draw a line back to the origin of the path, you can call closePath(). If the path is already completed and you want to fill it with fillStyle, call the fill() method. Another option is to stroke the path by calling the stroke() method, which uses strokeStyle. The last option is to call clip(), which creates a new clipping region based on the path.

As an example, consider the following code for drawing the face of a clock without the numbers:

```
let drawing = document.getElementById("drawing");

let context = drawing.getContext("2d");

// start the path
context.beginPath();

// draw outer circle
context.arc(100, 100, 99, 0, 2 * Math.PI, false);

// draw inner circle
context.moveTo(194, 100);
context.arc(100, 100, 94, 0, 2 * Math.PI, false);

// draw minute hand
context.moveTo(100, 100);
context.lineTo(100, 15);

// draw hour hand
context.moveTo(100, 100);
context.lineTo(35, 100);

// stroke the path
context.stroke();
```

This example draws two circles using arc(): an outer one and an inner one to create a border around the clock. The outer circle has a radius of 99 pixels and is centered at (100, 100), which is the center of the canvas. To draw a complete circle, you must start at an angle of 0 radians and draw all the way around to 2π radians (calculated using Math.PI). Before drawing the inner circle, you must move the path to a point that will be on the circle to avoid an additional line being drawn. The second call to arc() uses a slightly smaller radius for the border effect. After that, combinations of moveTo() and lineTo() are used to draw the hour and minute hands. The last step is to call stroke(), which makes the image appear as shown in Figure 16.4.

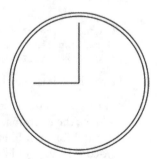

FIGURE 16.4: Drawing with arc() paths

Paths are the primary drawing mechanism for the 2D drawing context because they provide more control over what is drawn. Because paths are used so often, there is also a method called `isPointInPath()`, which accepts an x-coordinate and a y-coordinate as arguments. This method can be called anytime before the path is closed to determine if a point exists on the path, as shown here:

```
if (context.isPointInPath(100, 100)) {
    alert("Point (100, 100) is in the path.");
}
```

The path API for the 2D drawing context is robust enough to create very complex images using multiple fill styles, stroke styles, and more.

Drawing Text

Because it's often necessary to mix text and graphics, the 2D drawing context provides methods to draw text. There are two methods for drawing text, `fillText()` and `strokeText()`, and each takes four arguments: the string to draw, the x-coordinate, the y-coordinate, and an optional maximum pixel width to draw. Both methods base their drawing on the following three properties:

➤ `font`—Indicates the font style, size, and family in the same manner specified in CSS, such as "10px Arial".

➤ `textAlign`—Indicates how the text should be aligned. Possible values are "start", "end", "left", "right", and "center". It's recommended to use "start" and "end" instead of "left" and "right" as these are more indicative of rendering in both left-to-right languages and right-to-left languages.

➤ `textBaseline`—Indicates the baseline of the text. Possible values are "top", "hanging", "middle", "alphabetic", "ideographic", and "bottom".

These properties have a default value, so there's no need to set them each time you want to draw text. The `fillText()` method uses the `fillStyle` property to draw the text, whereas the `strokeText()` method uses the `strokeStyle` property. You will probably use `fillText()` most of the time because this mimics normal text rendering on web pages. For example, the following renders a 12 at the top of the clock created in the previous section:

```
context.font = "bold 14px Arial";
context.textAlign = "center";
context.textBaseline = "middle";
context.fillText("12", 100, 20);
```

The resulting image is displayed in Figure 16.5.

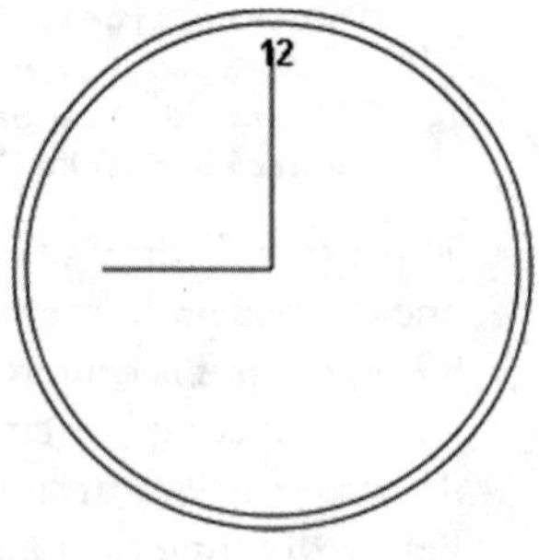

Because `textAlign` is set to "center" and `textBaseline` is set to "middle", the coordinates (100, 80) indicate the horizontal and vertical center and top coordinates for the text. If `textAlign` were "start", then the x-coordinate would represent the left coordinate of the text in a left-to-right language while "end" would make the x-coordinate represent the right coordinate in a left-to-right language. For example:

FIGURE 16.5: Writing text with `fillText()`

```
// normal
context.font = "bold 14px Arial";
```

```
context.textAlign = "center";
context.textBaseline = "middle";
context.fillText("12", 100, 20);
// start-aligned
context.textAlign = "start";
context.fillText("12", 100, 40);
// end-aligned
context.textAlign = "end";
context.fillText("12", 100, 60);
```

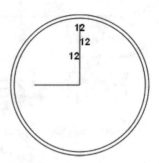

The string "12" is drawn three times, each using the same x-coordinate but with three different textAlign values. The y-coordinate values are also incremented so that the strings don't render on top of one another. The resulting image is shown in Figure 16.6.

FIGURE 16.6:
Demonstration of varying text alignment

The vertical line of the clock is directly at the center so the alignment of the text becomes obvious. You can similarly adjust how the text is aligned vertically by altering textBaseline. Setting to "top" means that the y-coordinate is the top of the text, "bottom" means it's the bottom, and "hanging", "alphabetic", and "ideographic" refer to specific baseline coordinates of a font.

Because drawing text is quite complicated, especially when you want text to render within a specific area, the 2D context provides a little extra help to determine the dimensions of text via the measureText() method. This method accepts a single argument, the text to draw, and returns a TextMetrics object. The returned object currently has only one property, width, but the intent is to provide more metrics in the future.

The measureText() method uses the current values for font, textAlign, and textBaseline to calculate the size of the specified text. For example, suppose you want to fit the text "Hello world!" within a rectangle that is 140 pixels wide. The following code starts with a font size of 100 pixels and decrements until the text fits:

```
let fontSize = 100;
context.font = fontSize + "px Arial";
while(context.measureText("Hello world!").width> 140) {
  fontSize--;
  context.font = fontSize + "px Arial";
}
context.fillText("Hello world!", 10, 10);
context.fillText("Font size is " + fontSize + "px", 10, 50);
```

There is also a fourth argument for both fillText() and strokeText(), which is the maximum width of the text. This argument is optional and hasn't been implemented in all browsers yet (Firefox 4 was the first to implement it). When provided, calling fillText() or strokeText() with a string that will not fit within the maximum width results in the text being drawn with the correct character height, but the characters are scaled horizontally to fit. Figure 16.7 shows this effect.

Text drawing is one of the more complex drawing operations and, as such, not all portions of the API have been implemented in all the browsers that support the <canvas> element.

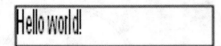

Font size is 26px

FIGURE 16.7: Demonstration of varying font size and width

Transformations

Context transformations allow the manipulation of images drawn onto the canvas. The 2D drawing context supports all of the basic drawing transformations. When the drawing context is created, the transformation matrix is initialized with default values that cause all drawing operations to be applied directly as they are described. Applying transformations to the drawing context causes operations to be applied using a different transformation matrix and thus produces a different result.

The transformation matrix can be augmented by using any of the following methods:

➤ `rotate(angle)`—Rotates the image around the origin by `angle` radians.

➤ `scale(scaleX, scaleY)`—Scales the image by a multiple of `scaleX` in the x dimension and by `scaleY` in the y dimension. The default value for both `scaleX` and `scaleY` is 1.0.

➤ `translate(x, y)`—Moves the origin to the point (x, y). After performing this operation, the coordinates (0, 0) are located at the point previously described as (x, y).

➤ `transform(m1_1, m1_2, m2_1, m2_2, dx, dy)`—Changes the transformation matrix directly by multiplying by the matrix described as this:

```
m1_1 m1_2 dx
m2_1 m2_2 dy
0    0    1
```

➤ `setTransform(m1_1, m1_2, m2_1, m2_2, dx, dy)`—Resets the transformation matrix to its default state and then calls `transform()`.

Transformations can be as simple or as complex as necessary. For example, it may be easier to draw the hands on the clock in the previous example by translating the origin to the center of the clock and then drawing the hands from there. Consider the following:

```
let drawing = document.getElementById("drawing");

let context = drawing.getContext("2d");

// start the path
context.beginPath();

// draw outer circle
context.arc(100, 100, 99, 0, 2 * Math.PI, false);

// draw inner circle
```

```
context.moveTo(194, 100);
context.arc(100, 100, 94, 0, 2 * Math.PI, false);

// translate to center
context.translate(100, 100);

// draw minute hand
context.moveTo(0, 0);
context.lineTo(0, -85);

// draw hour hand
context.moveTo(0, 0);
context.lineTo(-65, 0);

// stroke the path
context.stroke();
```

After translating the origin to (100, 100), the center of the clock face, it's just a matter of simple math to draw the lines in the same direction. All math is now based on (0, 0) instead of (100, 100). You can go further, moving the hands of the clock by using the `rotate()` method as shown here:

```
let drawing = document.getElementById("drawing");

let context = drawing.getContext("2d");

// start the path
context.beginPath();

// draw outer circle
context.arc(100, 100, 99, 0, 2 * Math.PI, false);

// draw inner circle
context.moveTo(194, 100);
context.arc(100, 100, 94, 0, 2 * Math.PI, false);

// translate to center
context.translate(100, 100);

// rotate the hands
context.rotate(1);

// draw minute hand
context.moveTo(0, 0);
context.lineTo(0, -85);

// draw hour hand
context.moveTo(0, 0);
context.lineTo(-65, 0);

// stroke the path
context.stroke();
```

Because the origin has already been translated to the center of the clock, the rotation is applied from that point. This means that the hands are anchored at the center and then rotated around to the right. The result is displayed in Figure 16.8.

FIGURE 16.8: Transforming canvas content with `rotate()`

All of these transformations, as well as properties like `fillStyle` and `strokeStyle`, remain set on the context until explicitly changed. Although there's no way to explicitly reset everything to their default values, there are two methods that can help keep track of changes. Whenever you want to be able to return to a specific set of properties and transformations, call the `save()` method. Once called, this method pushes all of the settings at the moment onto a stack for safekeeping. You can then go on to make other changes to the context. When you want to go back to the previous settings, call the `restore()` method, which pops the settings stack and restores all of the settings. You can keep calling `save()` to store more settings on the stack and then systematically go back through them using `restore()`. Here is an example:

```
context.fillStyle = "#ff0000";
context.save();

context.fillStyle = "#00ff00";
context.translate(100, 100);
context.save();

context.fillStyle = "#0000ff";
context.fillRect(0, 0, 100, 200);    // draws blue rectangle at (100, 100)

context.restore();
context.fillRect(10, 10, 100, 200);   // draws green rectangle at (110, 110)

context.restore();
context.fillRect(0, 0, 100, 200);   // draws red rectangle at (0, 0)
```

In this code, the `fillStyle` is set to red and then `save()` is called. Next, the `fillStyle` is changed to green, and the coordinates are translated to (100, 100). Once again, `save()` is called to save these settings. The `fillStyle` property is then set to blue and a rectangle is drawn. Because the coordinates are translated, the rectangle actually ends up being drawn at (100, 100). When `restore()` is called, `fillStyle` is set back to green, so the next rectangle that's drawn is green. This rectangle is drawn at (110, 110) because the translation is still in effect. When `restore()` is called one more time, the translation is removed and `fillStyle` is set back to red. The last rectangle is drawn at (0, 0).

Note that `save()` saves only the settings and transformations applied to the drawing context but not the contents of the drawing context.

Drawing Images

The 2D drawing context has built-in support for working with images. If you have an existing image that should be drawn on the canvas, you can do so using the `drawImage()` method. This method can be called with three different sets of arguments based on the desired result. The simplest call is to pass in an HTML `<img>` element, as well as the destination x- and y-coordinates, which simply draws the image at the specified location. Consider this example:

```
let image = document.images[0];
context.drawImage(image, 10, 10);
```

This code gets the first image in the document and draws it on the context at position (10, 10). The image is drawn in the same scale as the original. You can change how the image is drawn by adding two more arguments: the destination width and destination height. This scales the drawing without affecting the transformation matrix of the context. Consider this example:

```
context.drawImage(image, 50, 10, 20, 30);
```

When this code is executed, the image is scaled to be 20 pixels wide by 30 pixels tall.

You can also select just a region of the image to be drawn onto the context. This is done by providing nine arguments to `drawImage()`: the image to draw, the source x-coordinate, the source y-coordinate, the source width, the source height, the destination x-coordinate, the destination y-coordinate, the destination width, and the destination height. Using this overload of `drawImage()` gives you the most control. Consider this example:

```
context.drawImage(image, 0, 10, 50, 50, 0, 100, 40, 60);
```

Here, only part of the image is drawn on the canvas. That part of the image begins at point (0, 10) and is 50 pixels wide and 50 pixels tall. The image is drawn to point (0, 100) on the context and scaled to fit in a 40×60 area.

These drawing operations allow you to create interesting effects such as those shown in Figure 16.9.

In addition to passing in an HTML `<img>` element as the first argument, you can also pass in another `<canvas>` element to draw the contents of one canvas onto another.

The `drawImage()` method, in combination with other methods, can easily be used to perform basic image manipulation, the result of which can be retrieved using `toDataURL()`. There is, however, one instance where this won't work: if an image from a different origin than the page is drawn onto the context. In that case, calling `toDataURL()` throws an error. For example, if a page hosted on `www.example.com` draws an image hosted on `www.wrox.com`, the context is considered "dirty" and an error is thrown.

FIGURE 16.9: Drawing images with `drawImage()`

Shadows

The 2D context will automatically draw a shadow along with a shape or path based on the value of several properties:

➤ `shadowColor`—The CSS color in which the shadow should be drawn. The default is black.

➤ `shadowOffsetX`—The x-coordinate offset from the x-coordinate of the shape or path. The default is 0.

➤ `shadowOffsetY`—The y-coordinate offset from the y-coordinate of the shape or path. The default is 0.

➤ `shadowBlur`—The number of pixels to blur. If set to 0, the shadow has no blur. The default is 0.

Each of these properties can be read and written on the context object. You just need to set the values appropriately before drawing and the shadows are drawn automatically. For example:

```
let context = drawing.getContext("2d");
// setup shadow
context.shadowOffsetX = 5;
context.shadowOffsetY = 5;
context.shadowBlur  = 4;
context.shadowColor  = "rgba(0, 0, 0, 0.5)";
// draw a red rectangle
context.fillStyle = "#ff0000";
context.fillRect(10, 10, 50, 50);
// draw a blue rectangle
context.fillStyle = "rgba(0,0,255,1)";
context.fillRect(30, 30, 50, 50);
```

A shadow is drawn using the same styles for both rectangles, resulting in the image displayed in Figure 16.10.

FIGURE 16.10:
Demonstration of canvas shadows

Gradients

Gradients are represented by an instance of CanvasGradient and are very simple to create and modify using the 2D context. To create a new linear gradient, call the `create LinearGradient()` method. This method accepts four arguments: the starting x-coordinate, the starting y-coordinate, the ending x-coordinate, and the ending y-coordinate. Once called, the method creates a new CanvasGradient object of the size you specified and returns the instance.

Once you have the gradient object, the next step is to assign color stops using the `addColorStop()` method. This method accepts two arguments: the location of the color stop and a CSS color. The color stop location is a number between 0 (the first color) and 1 (the last color). For example:

```
let gradient = context.createLinearGradient(30, 30, 70, 70);
gradient.addColorStop(0, "white");
gradient.addColorStop(1, "black");
```

The gradient object now represents a gradient that is drawn from point (30, 30) to point (70, 70) on the canvas. The starting color is white and the stopping color is black. You can now set the `fillStyle` or `strokeStyle` properties to this value to draw a shape using the gradient:

```
// draw a red rectangle
context.fillStyle = "#ff0000";
context.fillRect(10, 10, 50, 50);
// draw a gradient rectangle
context.fillStyle = gradient;
context.fillRect(30, 30, 50, 50);
```

In order for the gradient to be drawn over the entire rectangle and not just part of it, the coordinates need to match up. This code produces the drawing in Figure 16.11.

FIGURE 16.11:
A linear canvas gradient drawn with create LinearGradient()

If the rectangle isn't drawn in exactly this spot, then only part of the gradient is displayed. For example:

```
context.fillStyle = gradient;
context.fillRect(50, 50, 50, 50);
```

This code creates a rectangle with only a small amount of white in the upper-left corner. That's because the rectangle is drawn at the midpoint of the gradient, where the color transition is almost complete. The rectangle is therefore mostly black because gradients do not repeat. Keeping the gradient lined up with your shapes is important, and sometimes using a function to calculate the appropriate coordinates is useful. For example:

```
function createRectLinearGradient(context, x, y, width, height) {
  return context.createLinearGradient(x, y, x+width, y+height);
}
```

This function creates a gradient based on the starting x- and y-coordinates, along with a width and height, so that the same numbers can be used as `fillRect()`:

```
let gradient = createRectLinearGradient(context, 30, 30, 50, 50);
gradient.addColorStop(0, "white");
gradient.addColorStop(1, "black");
// draw a gradient rectangle
context.fillStyle = gradient;
context.fillRect(30, 30, 50, 50);
```

Keeping track of coordinates is an important and tricky aspect of using canvas. Helper functions such as `createRectLinearGradient()` can take some of the pain out of managing coordinates.

Radial gradients are created using the `createRadialGradient()` method. This method accepts six arguments corresponding to the center of a circle and its radius. The first three arguments define the starting circle's center (x and y) and radius, while the last three define the same for the ending circle. When thinking about radial gradients, you will find it helps to think of a long cylinder where you're defining the size of the circle on each end. By making one circle smaller and the other larger, you've effectively made a cone, and you rotate that cone around by moving the center of each circle.

To create a radial gradient that starts in the center of a shape and continues out, you need to set the center of both circles to the same origin. For example, to create a radial gradient in the center of the rectangle in the previous example, both circles must be centered at (55, 55). That's because the rectangle is drawn from point (30, 30) to point (80, 80). Here's the code:

```
let gradient = context.createRadialGradient(55, 55, 10,
55, 55, 30);
gradient.addColorStop(0, "white");
gradient.addColorStop(1, "black");
// draw a red rectangle
context.fillStyle = "#ff0000";
context.fillRect(10, 10, 50, 50);
// draw a gradient rectangle
context.fillStyle = gradient;
context.fillRect(30, 30, 50, 50);
```

FIGURE 16.12:
A radial canvas gradient drawn with `createRadial Gradient()`

Running this code results in the drawing displayed in Figure 16.12.

Radial gradients are a little bit more difficult to work with because of the complexities of their creation, but generally you'll end up using the same center for both starting circle and ending circle and just altering the radii of the circles for most basic effects.

Patterns

Patterns are simply repeating images that may be used to fill or stroke a shape. To create a new pattern, call the `createPattern()` method and pass in two arguments: an HTML `<img>` element and a string indicating how the image should be repeated. The second argument is the same as the values for the CSS background-repeat property: "repeat", "repeat-x", "repeat-y", and "no-repeat". For example:

```
let image = document.images[0],
  pattern = context.createPattern(image, "repeat");
// draw a rectangle
context.fillStyle = pattern;
context.fillRect(10, 10, 150, 150);
```

Keep in mind that, like gradients, a pattern actually starts at point (0, 0) on the canvas. Setting the fill style to a pattern means revealing the pattern in the specified location rather than starting to draw at that position. This code results in a page that looks like Figure 16.13.

FIGURE 16.13: Repeating images drawn with `createPattern()`

The first argument for `createPattern()` can also be a `<video>` element or another `<canvas>` element.

Working with Image Data

One of the more powerful aspects of the 2D context is the ability to retrieve raw image data using the `getImageData()` method. This method accepts four arguments: the left and top position of the first pixel whose data should be retrieved, and the pixel width and the pixel height to retrieve. For instance, to get image data for a 50 by 50 area starting at (10, 5), use the following:

```
let imageData = context.getImageData(10, 5, 50, 50);
```

The returned object is an instance of ImageData. Each ImageData object contains just three proper-ties: `width`, `height`, and `data`. The `data` property is an array that contains the raw pixel informa-tion for the image. Each pixel is actually represented as four items in the data array, one each for red, green, blue, and alpha. So the data for the first pixel is contained in items 0 through 3, such as:

```
let data = imageData.data,
    red = data[0],
    green = data[1],
    blue = data[2],
    alpha = data[3];
```

Each value in the array is a number between 0 and 255, inclusive. Having access to the raw image data allows you to manipulate the image in a variety of ways. For example, a simple grayscale filter can be created by changing the image data:

```
let drawing = document.getElementById("drawing");

let context = drawing.getContext("2d"),
    image = document.images[0],
    imageData, data,
    i, len, average,
    red, green, blue, alpha;

// draw regular size
context.drawImage(image, 0, 0);

// get the image data
imageData = context.getImageData(0, 0, image.width, image.height);
data = imageData.data;

for (i=0, len=data.length; i < len; i+=4) {
    red = data[i];
    green = data[i+1];
    blue = data[i+2];
    alpha = data[i+3];

    // get the average of rgb
    average = Math.floor((red + green + blue) / 3);

    // set the colors, leave alpha alone
    data[i] = average;
    data[i+1] = average;
    data[i+2] = average;
}

// assign back to image data and display
imageData.data = data;
context.putImageData(imageData, 0, 0);
```

This example first draws an image onto the canvas and then retrieves its image data. A `for` loop iterates over each pixel in the image data. Note that each trip through the loop adds 4 to the value of `i`. Once the red, green, and blue values are retrieved, they are averaged together to get a new value.

Then each of the values is set back to that average, effectively washing out the color and leaving only a gray of similar brightness in its place. The data array is then assigned back onto the `imageData` object. After that, the `putImageData()` method is called to draw the image data back to the canvas. The result is a grayscale version of the image.

> **NOTE** *Image data is available only if the canvas isn't dirty from loading a cross-domain resource. Attempting to access image data when the canvas is dirty causes a JavaScript error.*

Compositing

There are two properties that apply to all drawing done on the 2D context: `globalAlpha` and `globalCompositionOperation`. The `globalAlpha` property is a number between 0 and 1, inclusive, that specifies the alpha value for all drawings. The default value is 0. If all of the upcoming drawings should be done with the same alpha, set `globalAlpha` to the appropriate value, perform the drawings, and then set `globalAlpha` back to 0. For example:

```
// draw a red rectangle
context.fillStyle = "#ff0000";
context.fillRect(10, 10, 50, 50);
// change the global alpha
context.globalAlpha = 0.5;
// draw a blue rectangle
context.fillStyle = "rgba(0,0,255,1)";
context.fillRect(30, 30, 50, 50);
// reset
context.globalAlpha = 0;
```

In this example, a blue rectangle is drawn on top of a red rectangle. Because `globalAlpha` is set to 0.5 before drawing the blue rectangle, it becomes partially transparent, allowing the red rectangle to be seen through the blue.

The `globalCompositionOperation` property indicates how newly drawn shapes should merge with the already-existing image on the context. This property is a string value of one of the following:

➤ `"source-over"` (default)—New drawing is drawn on top of the existing image.

➤ `"source-in"`—New drawing is drawn only where it overlaps the existing image. Everything else becomes transparent.

➤ `"source-out"`—New drawing is drawn only where it does not overlap the existing image. Everything else becomes transparent.

➤ `"source-atop"`—New drawing is drawn only where it overlaps the existing image. The existing image is otherwise unaffected.

➤ `"destination-over"`—New drawing is drawn underneath the existing image, visible only through previously transparent pixels.

➤ `"destination-in"`—New drawing is drawn underneath the existing image, and all places where the two images do not overlap become transparent.

➤ `"destination-out"`—New drawing erases the parts of the existing image where they overlap.

➤ `"destination-atop"`—New drawing is drawn behind the existing image. The existing image becomes transparent where there is no overlap with new drawing.

➤ `"lighter"`—New drawing is drawn by combining its values with the existing image values to create a lighter image.

➤ `"copy"`—New drawing erases the existing image and replaces it completely.

➤ `"xor"`—New drawing is drawn by XORing the image data with the existing image.

The descriptions of these composite operations are difficult to represent in words or black-and-white images. Here's a simple example:

```
// draw a red rectangle
context.fillStyle = "#ff0000";
context.fillRect(10, 10, 50, 50);
// set composite operation
context.globalCompositeOperation = "destination-over";
// draw a blue rectangle
context.fillStyle = "rgba(0,0,255,1)";
context.fillRect(30, 30, 50, 50);
```

Even though the blue rectangle would normally be drawn over the red, changing `globalComposite Operation` to "destination-over" means that the red rectangle actually ends up on top of the blue.

WEBGL

WebGL is a 3D context for canvas. Unlike other web technologies, WebGL is not specified by the W3C. Instead, the Khronos Group is developing the specification. According to its website, "The Khronos Group is a not for profit, member-funded consortium focused on the creation of royalty-free open standards for parallel computing, graphics, and dynamic media on a wide variety of platforms and devices." The Khronos Group has also worked on other graphics APIs, such as OpenGL ES 2.0, which is the basis for WebGL in the browser.

3D graphics languages such as OpenGL are complex topics, and it is beyond the scope of this book to cover all concepts. Familiarity with OpenGL ES 2.0 is recommended for using WebGL as many concepts map directly.

This section assumes a working knowledge of OpenGL ES 2.0 concepts and simply attempts to describe how certain parts of OpenGL ES 2.0 have been implemented in WebGL. For more information on OpenGL, please visit `www.opengl.org`, and for an excellent series of WebGL tutorials, please visit `www.learningwebgl.com`.

> **NOTE** *Typed arrays are an important part of performing operations in WebGL. They are covered in depth in the Chapter 6, "Advanced Reference Types."*

The WebGL Context

The WebGL 2.0 context name in fully supporting browsers is "webgl2". The WebGL 1.0 context name in fully supporting browsers is "webgl". If the browser doesn't support WebGL, then attempting to retrieve a WebGL context returns `null`. You should always check the returned value before attempting to use the context:

```
let drawing = document.getElementById("drawing");

let gl = drawing.getContext("webgl");
if (gl) {
  // proceed with WebGL
}
```

The WebGL context object is typically called `gl`. Most WebGL applications and examples use this convention because OpenGL ES 2.0 methods and values typically begin with "gl". Doing so means the JavaScript code reads more closely like an OpenGL program.

WebGL Basics

Once the WebGL context is established, you're ready to start 3D drawing. As mentioned previously, because WebGL is a web version of OpenGL ES 2.0, the concepts discussed in this section are really OpenGL concepts as implemented in JavaScript.

You can specify options for the WebGL context by passing in a second argument to `getContext()`. The argument is an object containing one or more of the following properties:

➤ `alpha`—When set to `true`, creates an alpha channel buffer for the context. Default is `true`.

➤ `depth`—When set to `true`, a 16-bit depth buffer is available. Default is `true`.

➤ `stencil`—When set to `true`, an 8-bit stencil buffer is available. Default is `false`.

➤ `antialias`—When set to `true`, antialiasing will be performed using the default mechanism. Default is `true`.

➤ `premultipliedAlpha`—When set to `true`, the drawing buffer is assumed to have premultiplied alpha values. Default is `true`.

➤ `preserveDrawingBuffer`—When set to `true`, the drawing buffer is preserved after drawing is completed. Default is `false`. Recommended to change only if you know exactly what this does, as there may be performance implications.

The options object is passed in like this:

```
let drawing = document.getElementById("drawing");

let gl = drawing.getContext("webgl", { alpha: false });
if (gl) {
  // proceed with WebGL
}
```

Most of the context options are for advanced use. In many cases, the default values will serve your purpose.

Browsers may throw an error if the WebGL context can't be created via `getContext()`. For that reason, it's best to wrap the call in a try-catch block:

```
let drawing = document.getElementById("drawing"),
  gl;

try {
  gl = drawing.getContext("webgl");
} catch (ex) {
  // noop
}
if (gl) {
  // proceed with WebGL
} else {
  alert("WebGL context could not be created.");
}
```

Constants

If you're familiar with OpenGL, then you're familiar with the large number of constants used for operations. These constants are named in OpenGL with a prefix of `GL_`. In WebGL, each constant is available on the WebGL context object without the `GL_` prefix. For example, the `GL_COLOR_BUFFER_BIT` constant is available as `gl.COLOR_BUFFER_BIT`. WebGL supports most OpenGL constants in this manner (some constants are not available).

Method Naming

Many method names in OpenGL, and so also in WebGL, tend to include information about the type of data to be used with the method. If a method can accept different types and numbers of arguments then it is suffixed to indicate the expected input. The method will indicate the number of arguments (1 through 4) followed by the data type ("f" for float and "i" for int). For example, `gl.uniform4f()` expects four floats to be passed in and `gl.uniform3i()` expects three integers to be passed in.

Many methods also allow an array to be passed in instead of individual arguments. This is indicated by the letter "v," which is short for vector. So `gl.uniform3iv()` accepts an array of integers with three values. Keep this convention in mind throughout the discussion of WebGL.

Getting Ready to Draw

One of the first steps when working on a WebGL context is to clear the `<canvas>` with a solid color to prepare for drawing. To do this, you first must assign the color to use via the `clearColor()` method. This method accepts four arguments: red, green, blue, and alpha. Each argument must be a number between 0 and 1 defining the strength of value as part of a final color. Consider the following example:

```
gl.clearColor(0, 0, 0, 1);  // black
gl.clear(gl.COLOR_BUFFER_BIT);
```

This code sets the clear color buffer value to black and then calls the `clear()` method, which is the equivalent of `glClear()` in OpenGL. Providing the argument `gl.COLOR_BUFFER_BIT` tells WebGL to use the previously defined color to fill the area. Generally speaking, all drawing operations begin with a call to clear the area for drawing.

Viewports and Coordinates

To get started, it's a good idea to define the WebGL viewport. By default, the viewport is set to use the entire `<canvas>` area. To change the viewport, call the `viewport()` method and pass in the x, y, width, and height of the viewport relative to the `<canvas>` element. For example, this call uses the entire `<canvas>` element:

```
gl.viewport(0, 0, drawing.width, drawing.height);
```

The viewport is defined using a different coordinate system than is typically used in a web page. The x- and y-coordinates start with (0, 0) at the bottom-left of the `<canvas>` element and increase toward the top and right, which can be defined as point (width–1, height–1) (see Figure 16.14).

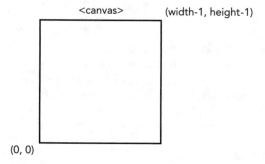

FIGURE 16.14: Diagram of coordinates defining a viewport

Knowing how the viewport is defined allows you to use just a part of the `<canvas>` element for drawing. Consider the following examples:

```
// viewport is a quarter of the <canvas> in the lower-left corner
gl.viewport(0, 0, drawing.width/2, drawing.height/2);
// viewport is a quarter of the <canvas> in the upper-left corner
gl.viewport(0, drawing.height/2, drawing.width/2, drawing.height/2);
// viewport is a quarter of the <canvas> in the lower-right corner
gl.viewport(drawing.width/2, 0, drawing.width/2, drawing.height/2);
```

The coordinate system within a viewport is different than the coordinate system for defining a viewport. Inside of a viewport, the coordinates start with point (0, 0) in the center of the viewport. The lower-left corner is (–1, –1), while the upper-right is (1, 1) (see Figure 16.15).

If a coordinate outside of the viewport is used for a drawing operation then the drawing is clipped along the viewport. For instance, attempting to draw a shape with a vertex at (1, 2) will result in a shape that is cut off on the right side of the viewport.

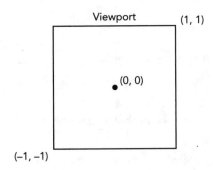

FIGURE 16.15: Diagram of coordinates within a viewport

Buffers

Vertex information is stored in typed arrays in JavaScript and must be converted into WebGL buffers for use. Buffers are created by calling `gl.createBuffer()` and then bound to the WebGL context using `gl.bindBuffer()`. Once that happens, you can fill the buffer with data. For example:

```
let buffer = gl.createBuffer();
gl.bindBuffer(gl.ARRAY_BUFFER, buffer);
gl.bufferData(gl.ARRAY_BUFFER, new Float32Array([0, 0.5, 1]), gl.STATIC_DRAW);
```

The call to `gl.bindBuffer()` sets buffer as the current buffer for the context. After that point, all buffer operations are performed on buffer directly. So the call to `gl.bufferData()` doesn't contain a direct reference to buffer but works on it nonetheless. That last line initializes buffer with information from a Float32Array (you generally will be using Float32Array for all vertex information). You can also use `gl.ELEMENT_ARRAY_BUFFER` if you intend to use `drawElements()` for outputting the buffer content.

The last argument of `gl.bufferData()` indicates how the buffer will be used. This is one of the following constants:

➤   `gl.STATIC_DRAW`—The data will be loaded once and used for drawing multiple times.

➤   `gl.STREAM_DRAW`—The data will be loaded once and used for drawing just a few times.

➤   `gl.DYNAMIC_DRAW`—The data will be modified repeatedly and used for drawing multiple times.

You'll likely use `gl.STATIC_DRAW` for most buffers unless you're an experienced OpenGL programmer.

Buffers stay in memory until the containing page is unloaded. If you no longer need a buffer, then it's best to free its memory by calling `gl.deleteBuffer()`:

```
gl.deleteBuffer(buffer);
```

Errors

One of the differences between most JavaScript and WebGL is that errors are generally not thrown from WebGL operations. Instead, you must call the `gl.getError()` method after invoking a method that may have failed. This method returns a constant value indicating the type of error that has occurred. The constants are as follows:

➤ gl.NO_ERROR—There wasn't an error during the last operation (value of 0).

➤ gl.INVALID_ENUM—An incorrect argument was passed to a method that was expecting one of the WebGL constants.

➤ gl.INVALID_VALUE—A negative number was passed where only an unsigned number is accepted.

➤ gl.INVALID_OPERATION—The operation cannot be completed in the current state.

➤ gl.OUT_OF_MEMORY—There is not enough memory to complete the operation.

➤ gl.CONTEXT_LOST_WEBGL—The WebGL context was lost because of an external event (such as loss of power on a device).

Each call to gl.getError() returns a single error value. After the initial call, the next call to gl .getError() may return another error value. If there are multiple errors, then this process continues until gl.getError() returns gl.NO_ERROR. If you have performed a number of operations, then you'll likely want to call getError() in a loop, such as:

```
let errorCode = gl.getError();
while (errorCode) {
    console.log("Error occurred: " + errorCode);
    errorCode = gl.getError();
}
```

If your WebGL script is not resulting in the correct output, then putting a few calls to gl .getError() into your script may help debug the issue.

Shaders

Shaders are another concept from OpenGL. There are two types of shaders in WebGL: *vertex shaders* and *fragment shaders*. Vertex shaders are used to convert a 3D vertex into a 2D point to be rendered. Fragment shaders are used to compute the correct color for drawing a single pixel. The unique and challenging aspect of WebGL shaders is that they are not written in JavaScript. Shaders are written using *OpenGL Shading Language (GLSL)*, a completely separate language from C or JavaScript.

Writing Shaders

GLSL is a C-like language that is used specifically for defining OpenGL shaders. Because WebGL is an implementation of OpenGL ES 2, the shaders used in OpenGL can be used directly in WebGL, allowing for easy porting of desktop graphics to the web.

Each shader has a method called main() that is executed repeatedly during drawing. There are two ways to pass data into a shader: *attributes* and *uniforms*. Attributes are used to pass vertices into a vertex shader while uniforms are used to pass constant values to either type of shader. Attributes and uniforms are defined outside of `main()` by using the keywords attribute or uniform, respectively. After the value type keyword, the data type is specified followed by a name. Here's a simple example vertex shader:

```
attribute vec2 aVertexPosition;

void main() {
    gl_Position = vec4(aVertexPosition, 0.0, 1.0);
}
```

This vertex shader defines a single attribute called `aVertexPosition`. This attribute is an array of two items (`vec2` data type) representing an x- and y-coordinate. A vertex shader must always result in a four-part vertex being assigned to the special variable `gl_Position` even though only two coordinates were passed. This shader creates a new four-item array (`vec4`) and fills in the missing coordinates, effectively turning a 2D coordinate into a 3D one.

Fragment shaders are similar to vertex shaders except you can pass data only in via uniforms. Here's an example fragment shader:

```
uniform vec4 uColor;

void main() {
    gl_FragColor = uColor;
}
```

Fragment shaders must result in a value being assigned to `gl_FragColor`, which indicates the color to use while drawing. This shader defined a uniform four-part (`vec4`) color named `uColor` to be set. Literally, this shader does nothing but assign the passed-in value to `gl_FragColor`. The value of `uColor` cannot be changed within the shader.

> **NOTE** *OpenGL Shading Language is a more complex language than represented here. There are entire books devoted to explaining the intricacies of the languages, and so this section is just a quick introduction to the language as a way of facilitating WebGL usage.*

Creating Shader Programs

GLSL cannot be natively understood by a browser, so you must have a string of GLSL ready for compilation and linking into a shader program. For ease of use, shaders are typically included in a page using `<script>` elements with a custom `type` attribute. Using an invalid `type` attribute prevents the browser from attempting to interpret the `<script>` contents while allowing you easy access. For example:

```
<script type="x-webgl/x-vertex-shader" id="vertexShader">
attribute vec2 aVertexPosition;

void main() {
    gl_Position = vec4(aVertexPosition, 0.0, 1.0);
}
```

```
</script>
<script type="x-webgl/x-fragment-shader" id="fragmentShader">
uniform vec4 uColor;

void main() {
  gl_FragColor = uColor;
}
</script>
```

You can then extract the contents of the `<script>` element using the text property:

```
let vertexGlsl = document.getElementById("vertexShader").text,
    fragmentGlsl = document.getElementById("fragmentShader").text;
```

More complex WebGL applications may choose to download shaders dynamically. The important aspect is that you need a GLSL string in order to use a shader.

Once you have a GLSL string, the next step is to create a shader object. This is done by calling the `gl.createShader()` method and passing in the type of shader to create (`gl.VERTEX_SHADER` or `gl.FRAGMENT_SHADER`). After that, the source code of the shader is applied using `gl.shaderSource()` and the shader is compiled using `gl.compileShader()`. Here's an example:

```
let vertexShader = gl.createShader(gl.VERTEX_SHADER);
gl.shaderSource(vertexShader, vertexGlsl);
gl.compileShader(vertexShader);
let fragmentShader = gl.createShader(gl.FRAGMENT_SHADER);
gl.shaderSource(fragmentShader, fragmentGlsl);
gl.compileShader(fragmentShader);
```

This code creates two shaders and stores them in `vertexShader` and `fragmentShader`. These two objects can then be linked into a shader program by using the following code:

```
let program = gl.createProgram();
gl.attachShader(program, vertexShader);
gl.attachShader(program, fragmentShader);
gl.linkProgram(program);
```

The first line creates a program and then `attachShader()` is used to include the two shaders. The call to `gl.linkProgram()` encapsulates both shaders together into the variable program. With the program linked, you can instruct the WebGL context to use the program via the `gl.useProgram()` method:

```
gl.useProgram(program);
```

After `gl.useProgram()` has been called, all further drawing operations will use the specified program.

Passing Values to Shaders

Each of the previously defined shaders has a value that must be passed in to complete the shader's job. To pass values into a shader, you must first locate the variable whose value must be filled. For uniform variables, this is done through `gl.getUniformLocation()`, which returns an object representing the location of the uniform variable in memory. You can then use this location to assign data. For example:

```
let uColor = gl.getUniformLocation(program, "uColor");
gl.uniform4fv(uColor, [0, 0, 0, 1]);
```

This example locates the uniform variable uColor in program and returns its memory location. The second line assigns a value into uColor using gl.uniform4fv().

A similar process is followed for attribute variables in vertex shaders. To get the location of an attribute variable, use gl.getAttribLocation(). Once the location is retrieved, it can be used as in this example:

```
let aVertexPosition = gl.getAttribLocation(program, "aVertexPosition");
gl.enableVertexAttribArray(aVertexPosition);
gl.vertexAttribPointer(aVertexPosition, itemSize, gl.FLOAT, false, 0, 0);
```

Here, the location of aVertexPosition is retrieved so that it may be enabled for use via gl.enableVertexAttribArray(). The last line creates a pointer into the last buffer specified using gl.bindBuffer() and stores it in aVertexPosition so that it may be used by the vertex shader.

Debugging Shaders and Programs

As with other operations in WebGL, shader operations may fail and will do so silently. You need to manually ask the WebGL context for information about the shader or program if you think there has been an error.

For shaders, call gl.getShaderParameter() to get the compiled status of the shader after attempting compilation:

```
if (!gl.getShaderParameter(vertexShader, gl.COMPILE_STATUS)) {
    alert(gl.getShaderInfoLog(vertexShader));
}
```

This example checks the compilation status of vertexShader. If the shader compiled successfully, then the call to gl.getShaderParameter() returns true. If the call returns false, then there was an error during compilation and you can retrieve the error by using gl.getShaderInfoLog() and passing in the shader. This method returns a string message indicating the issue. Both gl.getShaderParameter() and gl.getShaderInfoLog() may be used on vertex shaders and fragment shaders.

Programs may also fail and have a similar method, gl.getProgramParameter(), to check status. The most common program failure is during the linking process, for which you would check using the following code:

```
if (!gl.getProgramParameter(program, gl.LINK_STATUS)) {
    alert(gl.getProgramInfoLog(program));
}
```

As with gl.getShaderParameter(), the gl.getProgramParameter() returns either true to indicate that the link succeeded or false to indicate it failed. There is also gl.getProgramInfoLog(), which is used to get information about the program during failures.

These methods are primarily used during development to aid in debugging. As long as there are no external dependencies, it's safe to remove them in production.

Upgrading from GLSL 100 to GLSL 300

One of the primary changes in WebGL2 is the upgrade to the GLSL 3.00 ES shaders. This upgrade exposes a wide range of new shader features such as 3D textures, which are available on devices that support OpenGL ES 3.0. To use the upgraded shader version, the first line of the shaders must be the following:

```
#version 300 es
```

This upgrade requires a few syntactical changes:

➤ Vertex attribute variables are declared using the in keyword instead of attribute.

➤ Variables using the varying keyword for things like vertex or fragment shaders now must use in or out depending on their behavior with respect to the shader.

➤ The gl_FragColor predefined output variable no longer exists; fragment shaders must declare their own out variable for the color output.

➤ Texture lookup functions such as texture2D and textureCube have been unified into a single texture function.

Drawing

WebGL can draw only three types of shapes: points, lines, and triangles. All other shapes must be composed using a combination of these three basic shapes drawn in three-dimensional space. Drawing is executed by using the drawArrays() or drawElements() methods; the former works on array buffers while the latter acts on element array buffers.

The first argument for both gl.drawArrays() and drawElements() is a constant indicating the type of shape to draw. The constants are:

➤ gl.POINTS—Treats each vertex as a single point to be drawn.

➤ gl.LINES—Treats the array as a series of vertices between which to draw lines. Each set of vertices is a start point and an end point, so you must have an even number of vertices in the array for all drawing to take place.

➤ gl.LINE_LOOP—Treats the array as a series of vertices between which to draw lines. The line is drawn from the first vertex to the second, from the second to the third, and so on until the last vertex is reached. A line is then drawn from the last vertex to the first vertex. This effectively creates an outline of a shape.

➤ gl.LINE_STRIP—Same as gl.LINE_LOOP except a line is not drawn from the last vertex back to the first.

➤ gl.TRIANGLES—Treats the array as a series of vertices within which triangles should be drawn. Each triangle is drawn separately from the previous without sharing vertices unless explicitly specified.

➤ `gl.TRIANGLES_STRIP`—Same as `gl.TRIANGLES` except vertices after the first three are treated as the third vertex for a new triangle made with the previous two vertices. For example, if an array contains vertices A, B, C, D, the first triangle is drawn as ABC while the second is drawn as BCD.

➤ `gl.TRIANGLES_FAN`—Same as `gl.TRIANGLES` except vertices after the first three are treated as the third vertex for a triangle made with the previous vertex and the first coordinate. For example, if an array contains vertices A, B, C, D, the first triangle is drawn as ABC while the second is drawn as ACD.

The `gl.drawArrays()` method accepts one of these values as its first argument, the starting index within the array buffer as the second argument, and the number of sets contained in the array buffer as the third argument. The following code uses `gl.drawArrays()` to draw a single triangle across the canvas:

```
// assume viewport is cleared using the shaders from earlier in the section
// define three vertices, x and y for each
let vertices = new Float32Array([ 0, 1, 1, -1, -1, -1 ]),
    buffer = gl.createBuffer(),
    vertexSetSize = 2,
    vertexSetCount = vertices.length/vertexSetSize,
    uColor,
    aVertexPosition;
// put data into the buffer
gl.bindBuffer(gl.ARRAY_BUFFER, buffer);
gl.bufferData(gl.ARRAY_BUFFER, vertices, gl.STATIC_DRAW);
// pass color to fragment shader
uColor = gl.getUniformLocation(program, "uColor");
gl.uniform4fv(uColor, [ 0, 0, 0, 1 ]);
// pass vertex information to shader
aVertexPosition = gl.getAttribLocation(program, "aVertexPosition");
gl.enableVertexAttribArray(aVertexPosition);
gl.vertexAttribPointer(aVertexPosition, vertexSetSize, gl.FLOAT, false, 0, 0);
// draw the triangle
gl.drawArrays(gl.TRIANGLES, 0, vertexSetCount);
```

This example defines a Float32Array containing three sets of two-point vertices. It's important to keep track of the size and number of vertex sets for use in later calculations. The `vertexSetSize` is set to 2 while the `vertexSetCount` is calculated. The vertex information is stored in a buffer. Color information is then passed to the fragment shader.

The vertex shader is passed the size of the vertex set and indicates that the vertex coordinates are floats (`gl.FLOAT`). The fourth argument is a Boolean indicating that the coordinates are not normalized. The fifth is the *stride value*, which indicates how many array items need to be skipped to get the next value. This is 0 unless you really know what you're doing. The last argument is the starting offset, which is 0 to start at the first item.

The last step is to draw the triangle by using `gl.drawArrays()`. By specifying the first argument as `gl.TRIANGLES`, a triangle will be drawn from (0, 1) to (1, −1) to (−1, −1) and filled in with the color passed to the fragment shader. The second argument is the starting offset in the buffer, and the last argument is the total number of vertex sets to read. The result of this drawing operation is displayed in Figure 16.16.

FIGURE 16.16: Drawing with `drawArrays()` and `gl.TRIANGLES`

By changing the first argument to `gl.drawArrays()`, you can change how the triangle is drawn. Figure 16.17 shows some other possible outputs based on changing the first argument.

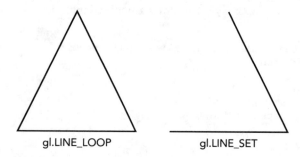

gl.LINE_LOOP   gl.LINE_SET

FIGURE 16.17: Result of passing other arguments to `drawArrays()`

Textures

WebGL textures work together with images from the DOM. You create a new texture using `gl.createTexture()` and then bind an image to that texture. If the image isn't already loaded, then you may create a new instance of Image to dynamically load it. A texture isn't initialized until the image is completely loaded, so texture setup steps must be done after the load event has fired. For example:

```
let image = new Image(),
  texture;
image.src = "smile.gif";
image.onload = function() {
  texture = gl.createTexture();
  gl.bindTexture(gl.TEXTURE_2D, texture);
  gl.pixelStorei(gl.UNPACK_FLIP_Y_WEBGL, true);

  gl.texImage2D(gl.TEXTURE_2D, 0, gl.RGBA, gl.RGBA, gl.UNSIGNED_BYTE, image);
  gl.texParameteri(gl.TEXTURE_2D, gl.TEXTURE_MAG_FILTER, gl.NEAREST);
  gl.texParameteri(gl.TEXTURE_2D, gl.TEXTURE_MIN_FILTER, gl.NEAREST);

  // clear current texture
  gl.bindTexture(gl.TEXTURE_2D, null);
}
```

Aside from using a DOM image, these steps are the same for creating texture in OpenGL. The biggest difference is in setting the pixel storage format with `gl.pixelStorei()`. The constant `gl.UNPACK_FLIP_Y_WEBGL` is unique to WebGL and must be used in most circumstances when loading web-based images. This is because of the different coordinate systems used by GIF, JPEG, and PNG images as compared to the internal coordinate system of WebGL. Without this flag, the image is interpreted upside down.

Images used for textures must be of the same origin as the containing page or else exist on servers that have Cross-Origin Resource Sharing (CORS) enabled for the images.

> **NOTE** *Texture sources may be images, videos loaded into the* `<video>` *element, and even another* `<canvas>` *element. The same restrictions regarding cross-origin resources apply to videos.*

Reading Pixels

As with the 2D context, it's possible to read pixels from the WebGL context. The `readPixels()` method has the same arguments as in OpenGL with the exception that the last argument must be a typed array. Pixel information is read from the frame buffer and placed into the typed array. The arguments for `readPixels()` are x, y, width, height, image format, type, and typed array. The first four arguments specify the location of the pixels to read. The image format argument will almost always be `gl.RGBA`. The `type` argument is the type of data that will be stored in the typed array and has the following restrictions:

➤ If the type is `gl.UNSIGNED_BYTE`, then the typed array must be Uint8Array.

➤ If the type is `gl.UNSIGNED_SHORT_5_6_5`, `gl.UNSIGNED_SHORT_4_4_4_4`, or `gl.UNSIGNED_SHORT_5_5_5_1`, then the typed array must be Uint16Array.

Here's a simple example:

```
let pixels = new Uint8Array(25*25);
gl.readPixels(0, 0, 25, 25, gl.RGBA, gl.UNSIGNED_BYTE, pixels);
```

This code reads a 25 × 25 area of the frame buffer and stores the pixel information in the pixels array. Each pixel color is represented as four array items, one each for red, green, blue, and alpha. The values are numbers 0 through 255, inclusive. Don't forget to initialize the typed array for the amount of data you're expecting back.

Calling `readPixels()` before the browser has drawn the updated WebGL image works as expected. After the paint has occurred, the frame buffer is reverted to its original cleared state and calling `readPixels()` will result in pixel data matching the cleared state. If you want to read pixels after the paint has occurred, then you must initialize the WebGL context with the `preserveDrawingBuffer` option discussed previously:

```
let gl = drawing.getContext("webgl", { preserveDrawingBuffer: true; });
```

Setting this flag forces the frame buffer to stay in its last state until the next draw occurs. This option does have some performance overhead, so it's best to avoid using if possible.

WebGL1 versus WebGL2

Code written for WebGL1 is nearly 100 percent compatible with WebGL2. When using the webgl2 context, the only code modification that is needed to ensure compatibility is treatment of extensions. In WebGL2, many extensions have become default features.

For example, to use draw buffers in WebGL1, you would test for the extension before use, as follows:

```
let ext = gl.getExtension('WEBGL_draw_buffers');

if (!ext) {
    // handle missing extension
} else {
    ext.drawBuffersWEBGL([...])
}
```

In WebGL2, this is no longer required, as the feature is available directly as a context object method:

```
gl.drawBuffers([...]);
```

The following have all become standard features:

➤ `ANGLE_instanced_arrays`

➤ `EXT_blend_minmax`

➤ `EXT_frag_depth`

➤ `EXT_shader_texture_lod`

➤ `OES_element_index_uint`

➤ `OES_standard_derivatives`

➤ `OES_texture_float`

➤ `OES_texture_float_linear`

➤ `OES_vertex_array_object`

➤ `WEBGL_depth_texture`

➤ `WEBGL_draw_buffers`

➤ `Vertex shader texture access`

> **NOTE** *There is an excellent post covering the basics of the WebGL upgrade, which can be found at* `https://webgl2fundamentals.org/webgl/lessons/webgl1-to-webgl2.html`.

SUMMARY

The `requestAnimationFrame` is a simple but elegant tool that allows JavaScript to tap into the rendering cycle of the browser in order to efficiently perform visual manipulation of the page.

The HTML5 `<canvas>` element provides a JavaScript API for creating graphics on the fly. Graphics are created in a specific context, of which there are currently two. The first is a 2D context that allows primitive drawing operations:

- ➤ Setting fill and stroke colors and patterns
- ➤ Drawing rectangles
- ➤ Drawing paths
- ➤ Drawing text
- ➤ Creating gradients and patterns

The second is a 3D context called WebGL. WebGL is a browser port of OpenGL ES 2.0, a language frequently used by game developers for computer graphics. WebGL allows far more powerful graphics processing than the 2D context, providing:

- ➤ Vertex and fragment shaders written in OpenGL Shading Language (GLSL)
- ➤ Typed array support, limiting the type of data contained in an array to specific numeric types
- ➤ Texture creation and manipulation

17

Scripting Forms

WHAT'S IN THIS CHAPTER?

➤ Understanding form basics

➤ Text box validation and interaction

➤ Working with other form controls

> **DOWNLOADS FOR THIS CHAPTER**
>
> Please note that all the code examples for this chapter are available as a part of this chapter's code download on the book's website at www.wiley.com/go/projavascript5e.

One of the original uses of JavaScript was to offload some form-processing responsibilities onto the browser instead of relying on the server to do it all. Although the web and JavaScript have evolved since that time, web forms remain more or less unchanged. The failure of web forms to provide out-of-the-box solutions for common problems led developers to use JavaScript not just for form validation but also to augment the default behavior of standard form controls.

FORM BASICS

Web forms are represented by the `<form>` element in HTML and by the HTMLFormElement type in JavaScript. The HTMLFormElement type inherits from HTMLElement and therefore has all of the same default properties as other HTML elements. However, HTMLFormElement also has the following additional properties and methods:

➤ acceptCharset—The character sets that the server can process; equivalent to the HTML accept-charset attribute.

➤ action—The URL to send the request to; equivalent to the HTML action attribute.

➤ elements—An HTMLCollection of all controls in the form.

➤ enctype—The encoding type of the request; equivalent to the HTML enctype attribute.

➤ length—The number of controls in the form.

➤ method—The type of HTTP request to send, typically "get" or "post"; equivalent to the HTML method attribute.

➤ name—The name of the form; equivalent to the HTML name attribute.

➤ reset()—Resets all form fields to their default values.

➤ submit()—Submits the form.

➤ target—The name of the window to use for sending the request and receiving the response; equivalent to the HTML target attribute.

References to <form> elements can be retrieved in a number of different ways. The most common way is to treat them as any other elements and assign the id attribute, allowing the use of getElementById(), as in the following example:

```
let form = document.getElementById("form1");
```

All forms on the page can also be retrieved from the document.forms collection. Each form can be accessed in this collection by numeric index and by name, as shown in the following examples:

```
// get the first form in the page
let firstForm = document.forms[0];

// get the form with a name of "form2"
let myForm = document.forms["form2"];
```

Note that forms can have both an id and a name and that these values need not be the same.

Submitting Forms

Forms are submitted when a user interacts with a submit button or an image button. Submit buttons are defined using either the <input> element or the <button> element with a type attribute of "submit", and image buttons are defined using the <input> element with a type attribute of "image". All of the following, when clicked, will submit a form in which the button resides:

```
<!-- generic submit button -->
<input type="submit" value="Submit Form">

<!-- custom submit button -->
```

```
<button type="submit">Submit Form</button>

<!-- image button -->
<input type="image" src="graphic.gif">
```

If any one of these types of buttons is within a form that has a submit button, pressing Enter on the keyboard while a form control has focus will also submit the form. (The one exception is a `<textarea>`, within which Enter creates a new line of text.) Note that forms without a submit button will not be submitted when Enter is pressed.

When a form is submitted in this manner, the submit event fires right before the request is sent to the server. This gives you the opportunity to validate the form data and decide whether to allow the form submission to occur. Preventing the event's default behavior cancels the form submission. For example, the following prevents a form from being submitted:

```
let form = document.getElementById("myForm");

form.addEventListener("submit", (event) => {
  // prevent form submission
  event.preventDefault();
});
```

The `preventDefault()` method stops the form from being submitted. Typically, this functionality is used when data in the form is invalid and should not be sent to the server.

It's possible to submit a form programmatically by calling the `submit()` method from JavaScript. This method can be called at any time to submit a form and does not require a submit button to be present in the form to function appropriately. Here's an example:

```
let form = document.getElementById("myForm");

// submit the form
form.submit();
```

When a form is submitted via `submit()`, the submit event does not fire, so be sure to do data validation before calling the method.

One of the biggest issues with form submission is the possibility of submitting the form twice. Users sometimes get impatient when it seems like nothing is happening and may click a submit button multiple times. The results can be annoying (because the server processes duplicate requests) or damaging (if the user is attempting a purchase and ends up placing multiple orders). There are essentially two ways to solve this problem: disable the submit button once the form is submitted, or use the `onsubmit` event handler to cancel any further form submissions.

Resetting Forms

Forms are reset when the user clicks a reset button. Reset buttons are created using either the `<input>` or the `<button>` element with a type attribute of "reset," as in these examples:

```
<!-- generic reset button -->
<input type="reset" value="Reset Form">

<!-- custom reset button -->
```

```
<button type="reset">Reset Form</button>
```

Either of these buttons will reset a form. When a form is reset, all of the form fields are set back to the values they had when the page was first rendered. If a field was originally blank, it becomes blank again, whereas a field with a default value reverts to that value.

When a form is reset by the user clicking a reset button, the reset event fires. This event gives you the opportunity to cancel the reset if necessary. For example, the following prevents a form from being reset:

```
let form = document.getElementById("myForm");

form.addEventListener("reset", (event) => {
  event.preventDefault();
});
```

As with form submission, resetting a form can be accomplished via JavaScript using the reset() method, as in this example:

```
let form = document.getElementById("myForm");

// reset the form
form.reset();
```

Unlike the submit() method's functionality, reset() fires the reset event the same as if a reset button were clicked.

> **NOTE** *Form resetting is typically a frowned-upon approach to web form design. It's often disorienting to the user and, when triggered accidentally, can be quite frustrating. There's almost never a need to reset a form. It's often enough to provide a cancel button that takes the user back to the previous page rather than explicitly revert all values in the form.*

Form Fields

Form elements can be accessed in the same ways as any other elements on the page using native DOM methods. Additionally, all form elements are parts of an elements collection that is a property of each form. The elements collection is an ordered list of references to all form fields in the form and includes all <input>, <textarea>, <button>, <select>, and <fieldset> elements. Each form field appears in the elements collection in the order in which it appears in the markup, indexed by both position and name. Here are some examples:

```
let form = document.getElementById("form1");

// get the first field in the form
let field1 = form.elements[0];

// get the field named "textbox1"
let field2 = form.elements["textbox1"];

// get the number of fields
```

```
        let fieldCount = form.elements.length;
```

If a name is in use by multiple form controls, as is the case with radio buttons, then an HTMLCollection is returned containing all of the elements with the name. For example, consider the following HTML snippet:

```
<form method="post" id="myForm">
  <ul>
    <li><input type="radio" name="color" value="red">Red</li>
    <li><input type="radio" name="color" value="green">Green</li>
    <li><input type="radio" name="color" value="blue">Blue</li>
  </ul>
</form>
```

The form in this HTML has three radio controls that have "color" as their name, which ties the fields together. When accessing `elements["color"]`, a NodeList is returned, containing all three elements; when accessing `elements[0]`, however, only the first element is returned. Consider this example:

```
let form = document.getElementById("myForm");

let colorFields = form.elements["color"];
console.log(colorFields.length);   // 3

let firstColorField = colorFields[0];
let firstFormField = form.elements[0];
console.log(firstColorField === firstFormField);    // true
```

This code shows that the first form field, accessed via `form.elements[0]`, is the same as the first element contained in `form.elements["color"]`.

> **NOTE** *It's possible to access elements as properties of a form as well, such as `form[0]` to get the first form field and `form["color"]` to get a named field. These properties always return the same thing as their equivalent in the elements collection. This approach is provided for backwards compatibility with older browsers and should be avoided when possible in favor of using elements.*

Common Form-Field Properties

With the exception of the `<fieldset>` element, all form fields share a common set of properties. Because the `<input>` type represents many form fields, some properties are used only with certain field types, whereas others are used regardless of the field type. The common form-field properties and methods are as follows:

➤ `disabled`—A Boolean indicating if the field is disabled.

➤ `form`—A pointer to the form that the field belongs to. This property is read-only.

➤ `name`—The name of the field.

➤ `readOnly`—A Boolean indicating if the field is read-only.

➤　　tabIndex—Indicates the tab order for the field.

➤　　type—The type of the field: "checkbox," "radio," and so on.

➤　　value—The value of the field that will be submitted to the server. For file-input fields, this property is read only and simply contains the file's path on the computer.

With the exception of the form property, JavaScript can change all other properties dynamically. Consider this example:

```
let form = document.getElementById("myForm");
let field = form.elements[0];

// change the value
field.value = "Another value";

// check the value of form
console.log(field.form === form);    // true

// set focus to the field
field.focus();

// disable the field
field.disabled = true;

// change the type of field (not recommended, but possible for <input>)
field.type = "checkbox";
```

The ability to change form-field properties dynamically allows you to change the form at any time and in almost any way. For example, a common problem with web forms is the tendency of users to click the submit button twice. This is a major problem when credit-card orders are involved because it may result in duplicate charges. A very common solution to this problem is to disable the submit button once it's been clicked, which is possible by listening for the submit event and disabling the submit button when it occurs. The following code accomplishes this:

```
// Code to prevent multiple form submissions
let form = document.getElementById("myForm");

form.addEventListener("submit", (event) => {
  let target = event.target;

  // get the submit button
  let btn = target.elements["submit-btn"];

  // disable the submit button
  btn.disabled = true;
});
```

This code attaches an event handler on the form for the submit event. When the event fires, the submit button is retrieved and its disabled property is set to true. Note that you cannot attach an onclick event handler to the submit button to do this because of a timing issue across browsers: some browsers fire the click event before the form's submit event, some after. For browsers that fire click first, the button will be disabled before the submission occurs, meaning that the form will never be submitted. Therefore it's better to disable the submit button using the submit event. This approach won't work if you are submitting the form without using a submit button because, as stated before, the submit event is fired only by a submit button.

The type property exists for all form fields except <fieldset>. For <input> elements, this value is equal to the HTML type attribute. For other elements, the value of type is set as described in the following table.

DESCRIPTION	SAMPLE HTML	VALUE OF TYPE
Single-select list	<select>...</select>	"select-one"
Multi-select list	<select multiple>...</select>	"select-multiple"
Custom button	<button>...</button>	"submit"
Custom nonsubmit button	<button type="button">...</button>	"button"
Custom reset button	<button type="reset">...</button>	"reset"
Custom submit button	<button type="submit">...</button>	"submit"

For <input> and <button> elements, the type property can be changed dynamically, whereas the <select> element's type property is read-only.

Common Form-Field Methods

Each form field has two methods in common: focus() and blur(). The focus() method sets the browser's focus to the form field, meaning that the field becomes active and will respond to keyboard events. For example, a text box that receives focus displays its caret and is ready to accept input. The focus() method is most often employed to call the user's attention to some part of the page. It's quite common, for instance, to have the focus moved to the first field in a form when the page is loaded. This can be accomplished by listening for the load event and then calling focus() on the first field, as in the following example:

```
window.addEventListener("load", (event) => {
  document.forms[0].elements[0].focus();
});
```

Note that this code will cause an error if the first form field is an <input> element with a type of "hidden" or if the field is being hidden using the display or visibility CSS property.

HTML5 introduces an autofocus attribute for form fields that causes browsers to automatically set the focus to that element without the use of JavaScript. For example:

```
<input type="text" autofocus>
```

In order for the previous code to work correctly with autofocus, you must first detect if it has been set. If autofocus is set, you should not call focus():

```
window.addEventListener("load", (event) => {
```

```
        let element = document.forms[0].elements[0];

        if (element.autofocus !== true) {
          element.focus();
          console.log("JS focus");
        }
    });
```

Because autofocus is a Boolean attribute, the value of the `autofocus` property will be `true` in supporting browsers. (It will be the empty string in browsers without support.) So this code calls `focus()` only if the autofocus property is not equal to `true`, ensuring forward compatibility.

> **NOTE** *By default, only form elements can have focus set to them. It's possible to allow any element to have focus by setting its* `tabIndex` *property to –1 and then calling* `focus()`.

The opposite of `focus()` is `blur()`, which removes focus from the element. When `blur()` is called, focus isn't moved to any element in particular; it's just removed from the field on which it was called. This method was used early in web development to create read-only fields before the `readonly` attribute was introduced. There's rarely a need to call `blur()`, but it's available if necessary. Here's an example:

```
    document.forms[0].elements[0].blur();
```

Common Form-Field Events

All form fields support the following three events in addition to mouse, keyboard, mutation, and HTML events:

➤   `blur`—Fires when the field loses focus.

➤   `change`—Fires when the field loses focus and the value has changed for `<input>` and `<textarea>` elements; also fires when the selected option changes for `<select>` elements.

➤   `focus`—Fires when the field gets focus.

Both the `blur` and the `focus` events fire because of users manually changing the field's focus, as well as by calling the `blur()` and `focus()` methods, respectively. These two events work the same way for all form fields. The `change` event, however, fires at different times for different controls. For `<input>` and `<textarea>` elements, the `change` event fires when the field loses focus and the value has changed since the time the control got focus. For `<select>` elements, however, the change event fires whenever the user changes the selected option; the control need not lose focus for change to fire.

The `focus` and `blur` events are typically used to change the user interface in some way, to provide either visual cues or additional functionality (such as showing a drop-down menu of options for a text box). The `change` event is typically used to validate data that was entered into a field. For example, consider a text box that expects only numbers to be entered. The `focus` event may be used to change the background color to more clearly indicate that the field has focus, the `blur` event can be used to remove that background color, and the `change` event can change the background color to red if nonnumeric characters are entered. The following code accomplishes this:

```
let textbox = document.forms[0].elements[0];

textbox.addEventListener("focus", (event) => {
  let target = event.target;
  if (target.style.backgroundColor != "red") {
    target.style.backgroundColor = "yellow";
  }
});

textbox.addEventListener("blur", (event) => {
  let target = event.target;
  target.style.backgroundColor = /[^\d]/.test(target.value) ? "red" : "";
});

textbox.addEventListener("change", (event) => {
  let target = event.target;
  target.style.backgroundColor = /[^\d]/.test(target.value) ? "red" : "";
});
```

The onfocus event handler simply changes the background color of the text box to yellow, more clearly indicating that it's the active field. The onblur and onchange event handlers turn the background color red if any nonnumeric character is found. To test for a nonnumeric character, use a simple regular expression against the text box's value. This functionality has to be in both the onblur and onchange event handlers to ensure that the behavior remains consistent regardless of text box changes.

> **NOTE** *The relationship between the* blur *and the* change *events is not strictly defined. In some browsers, the* blur *event fires before change; in others, it's the opposite. You can't depend on the order in which these events fire, so use care whenever they are required.*

SCRIPTING TEXT BOXES

There are two ways to represent text boxes in HTML: a single-line version using the <input> element and a multiline version using <textarea>. These two controls are very similar and behave in similar ways most of the time. There are, however, some important differences.

By default, the <input> element displays a text box, even when the type attribute is omitted (the default value is "text"). The size attribute can then be used to specify how wide the text box should be in terms of visible characters. The value attribute specifies the initial value of the text box, and the maxlength attribute specifies the maximum number of characters allowed in the text box. So to create a text box that can display 25 characters at a time but has a maximum length of 50, you can use the following code:

```
<input type="text" size="25" maxlength="50" value="initial value">
```

The <textarea> element always renders a multiline text box. To specify how large the text box should be, you can use the rows attribute, which specifies the height of the text box in number of characters, and the cols attribute, which specifies the width in number of characters, similar to size for an <input> element. Unlike <input>, the initial value of a <textarea> must be enclosed between <textarea> and </textarea>, as shown here:

```
<textarea rows="25" cols="5">initial value</textarea>
```

Also unlike the <input> element, a <textarea> cannot specify the maximum number of characters allowed using HTML.

Despite the differences in markup, both types of text boxes store their contents in the value property. The value can be used to read the text box value and to set the text box value, as in this example:

```
let textbox = document.forms[0].elements["textbox1"];
console.log(textbox.value);

textbox.value = "Some new value";
```

You should use the value property to read or write text box values rather than to use standard DOM methods. For instance, don't use setAttribute() to set the value attribute on an <input> element, and don't try to modify the first child node of a <textarea> element. Changes to the value property aren't always reflected in the DOM either, so it's best to avoid using DOM methods when dealing with text box values.

Text Selection

Both types of text boxes support a method called select(), which selects all of the text in a text box. Browsers automatically set focus to the text box when the select() method is called. The method accepts no arguments and can be called at any time. Here's an example:

```
let textbox = document.forms[0].elements["textbox1"];
textbox.select();
```

It's quite common to select all of the text in a text box when it gets focus, especially if the text box has a default value. The thinking is that it makes life easier for users when they don't have to delete text separately. This pattern is accomplished with the following code:

```
textbox.addEventListener("focus", (event) => {
  event.target.select();
});
```

With this code applied to a text box, all of the text will be selected as soon as the text box gets focus. This can greatly aid the usability of forms.

The *select* Event

To accompany the select() method, there is a select event. The select event fires when text is selected in the text box. It also fires when the select() method is called. Here's a simple example:

```
let textbox = document.forms[0].elements["textbox1"];

textbox.addEventListener("select", (event) => {
  console.log(`Text selected: ${textbox.value}`);
});
```

Retrieving Selected Text

Although useful for understanding when text is selected, the `select` event provides no information about what text has been selected. HTML5 solved this issue by introducing some extensions to allow for better retrieval of selected text. The specification approach adds two properties to text boxes: `selectionStart` and `selectionEnd`. These properties contain zero-based numbers indicating the text-selection boundaries (the offset of the beginning of text selection and the offset of end of text selection, respectively). So, to get the selected text in a text box, you can use the following code:

```
function getSelectedText(textbox){
    return textbox.value.substring(textbox.selectionStart,
                                   textbox.selectionEnd);
}
```

Because the `substring()` method works on string offsets, the values from `selectionStart` and `selectionEnd` can be passed in directly to retrieve the selected text.

Partial Text Selection

HTML5 also specifies an addition to aid in partially selecting text in a text box. The `setSelectionRange()` method is available on all text boxes in addition to the `select()` method. This method takes two arguments: the index of the first character to select and the index at which to stop the selection (the same as the string's `substring()` method). Here are some examples:

```
textbox.value = "Hello world!"

// select all text
textbox.setSelectionRange(0, textbox.value.length);  // "Hello world!"

// select first three characters
textbox.setSelectionRange(0, 3);    // "Hel"

// select characters 4 through 6
textbox.setSelectionRange(4, 7);   // "o w"
```

To see the selection, you must set focus to the text box either immediately before or after a call to `setSelectionRange()`. Partial text selection is useful for implementing advanced text input boxes such as those that provide autocomplete suggestions.

Input Filtering

It's common for text boxes to expect a certain type of data or data format. Perhaps the data needs to contain certain characters or must match a particular pattern. Because text boxes don't offer much in the way of validation by default, JavaScript must be used to accomplish such *input filtering*. Using a combination of events and other DOM capabilities, you can turn a regular text box into one that understands the data it is dealing with.

Blocking Characters

Certain types of input require that specific characters be present or absent. For example, a text box for the user's phone number should not allow nonnumeric values to be inserted. The `keypress` event is responsible for inserting characters into a text box. Characters can be blocked by preventing this event's default behavior. For example, the following code blocks all key presses:

```
textbox.addEventListener("keypress", (event) => {
  event.preventDefault();
});
```

Running this code causes the text box to effectively become read only, because all key presses are blocked. To block only specific characters, you need to inspect the character code for the event and determine the correct response. For example, the following code allows only numbers:

```
textbox.addEventListener("keypress", (event) => {
  if (!/\d/.test(String.fromCharCode(event.charCode))){
    event.preventDefault();
  }
});
```

In this example, the character code is converted to a string using `String.fromCharCode()`, and the result is tested against the regular expression `/\d/`, which matches all numeric characters. If that test fails, then the event is blocked using `preventDefault()`. This ensures that the text box ignores nonnumeric keys.

Even though the keypress event should be fired only when a character key is pressed, some browsers fire it for other keys as well. This means that simply blocking all characters that aren't numbers isn't good enough because you'll also be blocking these very useful and necessary keys. Fortunately, you can easily detect when one of these keys is pressed. To generalize the case, you don't want to block any character codes lower than 10. The function can then be updated as follows:

```
textbox.addEventListener("keypress", (event) => {
  if (!/\d/.test(String.fromCharCode(event.charCode)) &&
      event.charCode > 9){
    event.preventDefault();
  }
});
```

The event handler now behaves appropriately in all browsers, blocking nonnumeric characters but allowing all basic keys that also fire `keypress`.

There is still one more issue to handle: copying, pasting, and any other functions that involve the Ctrl key. The preceding code disallows the shortcut keystrokes of Ctrl+C, Ctrl+V, and any other combinations using the Ctrl key. The last check, therefore, is to make sure the Ctrl key is not pressed, as shown in the following example:

```
textbox.addEventListener("keypress", (event) => {
  if (!/\d/.test(String.fromCharCode(event.charCode)) &&
      event.charCode > 9 &&
      !event.ctrlKey){
    event.preventDefault();
  }
});
```

This final change ensures that all of the default text box behaviors work. This technique can be customized to allow or disallow any characters in a text box.

Dealing with the Clipboard

Internet Explorer was the first browser to support events related to the clipboard and access to clipboard data from JavaScript. This implementation became a de facto standard as all browsers implemented similar events and clipboard access, and clipboard events were later added to HTML5. The following six events are related to the clipboard:

➤ beforecopy—Fires just before the copy operation takes place.

➤ copy—Fires when the copy operation takes place.

➤ beforecut—Fires just before the cut operation takes place.

➤ cut—Fires when the cut operation takes place.

➤ beforepaste—Fires just before the paste operation takes place.

➤ paste—Fires when the paste operation takes place.

Because this is a fairly new standard governing clipboard access, the behavior of the events and related objects differs from browser to browser. The beforecopy, beforecut, and beforepaste events fire only when the context menu for the text box is displayed (in anticipation of a clipboard event). The copy, cut, and paste events all fire when the selection is made from a context menu and when using keyboard shortcuts.

The beforecopy, beforecut, and beforepaste events give you the opportunity to change the data being sent to or retrieved from the clipboard before the actual event occurs. However, canceling these events does not cancel the clipboard operation—you must cancel the copy, cut, or paste event to prevent the operation from occurring.

Clipboard data is accessible via the clipboardData object that exists on the event object. The clipboardData object is available only during clipboard events to prevent unauthorized clipboard access.

There are three methods on the clipboardData object: getData(), setData(), and clearData(). The getData() method retrieves string data from the clipboard and accepts a single argument, which is the format for the data to retrieve.

The setData() method is similar: its first argument is the data type, and its second argument is the text to place on the clipboard. To prevent the browser overwriting your changes, use preventDefault():

```
document.addEventListener('copy', (e) => {
  e.clipboardData.setData('text/plain', 'foo');
  e.preventDefault(); // default behaviour is to copy any selected text
});
```

Reading text from the clipboard is helpful when you have a text box that expects only certain characters or a certain format of text. For example, if a text box allows only numbers, then pasted values must also be inspected to ensure that the value is valid. In the paste event, you can determine if the text on the clipboard is invalid and, if so, cancel the default behavior, as shown in the following example:

```
textbox.addEventListener("paste", (event) => {
  let text = getClipboardText(event);

  if (!/^\d*$/.test(text)){
    event.preventDefault();
  }
});
```

This onpaste handler ensures that only numeric values can be pasted into the text box. If the clipboard value doesn't match the pattern, then the paste is canceled. Browsers allow access to the getData() method only in an onpaste event handler.

HTML5 Constraint Validation API

HTML5 introduces the ability for browsers to validate data in forms before submitting to the server. This capability enables basic validation even when JavaScript is unavailable or fails to load. The browser itself handles performing the validation based on rules in the code and then displays appropriate error messages on its own (without needing additional JavaScript).

Validation is applied to a form field only under certain conditions. You can use HTML markup to specify constraints on a particular field that will result in the browser automatically performing form validation.

Required Fields

The first condition is when a form field has a required attribute, as in this example:

```
<input type="text" name="username" required>
```

Any field marked as required must have a value in order for the form to be submitted. This attribute applies to <input>, <textarea>, and <select> fields. You can check to see if a form field is required in JavaScript by using the corresponding required property on the element:

```
let isUsernameRequired = document.forms[0].elements["username"].required;
```

You can also test to see if the browser supports the required attribute using this code snippet:

```
let isRequiredSupported = "required" in document.createElement("input");
```

This code uses simple feature detection to determine if the property required exists on a newly created <input> element.

Alternate Input Types

HTML5 specifies several additional values for the type attribute on an <input> element. These type attributes not only provide additional information about the type of data expected but also provide some default validation. The two new input types that are most widely supported are "email" and "url," and each comes with a custom validation that the browser applies. For example:

```
<input type="email" name="email">
<input type="url" name="homepage">
```

The "email" type ensures that the input text matches the pattern for an e-mail address, while the "url" type ensures that the input text matches the pattern for a URL. Note that the browsers as mentioned earlier in this section all have some issues with proper pattern matching. Most notably, the text "-@-" is considered a valid e-mail address. Such issues are still being addressed with browser vendors.

You can detect if a browser supports these new types by creating an element in JavaScript and setting the type property to "email" or "url" and then reading the value back. Older browsers automatically set unknown values back to "text," while supporting browsers echo the correct value back. For example:

```
let input = document.createElement("input");
input.type = "email";
let isEmailSupported = (input.type == "email");
```

Keep in mind that an empty field is also considered valid unless the required attribute is applied. Also, specifying a special input type doesn't prevent the user from entering an invalid value; it only applies some default validation.

Numeric Ranges

In addition to "email" and "url," there are several other new input element types defined in HTML5. These are all numeric types that expect some sort of numbers-based input: "number," "range," "datetime," "datetime-local," "date," "month," "week," and "time".

For each of these numeric types, you can specify a min attribute (the smallest possible value), a max attribute (the largest possible value), and a step attribute (the difference between individual steps along the scale from min to max). For instance, to allow only multiples of 5 between 0 and 100, you could use the following:

```
<input type="number" min="0" max="100" step="5" name="count">
```

Depending on the browser, you may or may not see a spin control (up and down buttons) to automatically increment or decrement the browser.

Each of the attributes have corresponding properties on the element that are accessible (and changeable) using JavaScript. Additionally, there are two methods: stepUp() and stepDown(). These methods each accept an optional argument: the number to either subtract or add from the current value. (By default, they increment or decrement by one.) The methods have not yet been implemented by browsers but will be usable as in this example:

```
input.stepUp();        // increment by 1
input.stepUp(5);       // increment by 5
input.stepDown();      // decrement by 1
input.stepDown(10);    // decrement by 10
```

Input Patterns

The pattern attribute was introduced for text fields in HTML5. This attribute specifies a regular expression with which the input value must match. For example, to allow only numbers in a text field, the following code applies this constraint:

```
<input type="text" pattern="\d+" name="count">
```

Note that ^ and $ are assumed at the beginning and end of the pattern, respectively. That means the input must exactly match the pattern from beginning to end.

As with the alternate input types, specifying a pattern does not prevent the user from entering invalid text. The pattern is applied to the value, and the browser then knows if the value is valid or not. You can read the pattern by accessing the pattern property:

```
let pattern = document.forms[0].elements["count"].pattern;
```

You can also test to see if the browser supports the pattern attribute using this code snippet:

```
let isPatternSupported = "pattern" in document.createElement("input");
```

Checking Validity

You can check if any given field on the form is valid by using the checkValidity() method. This method is provided on all elements and returns true if the field's value is valid or false if not. Whether or not a field is valid is based on the conditions previously mentioned in this section, so a required field without a value is considered invalid, and a field whose value does not match the pattern attribute is considered invalid. For example:

```
if (document.forms[0].elements[0].checkValidity()){
  // field is valid, proceed
} else {
  // field is invalid
}
```

To check if the entire form is valid, you can use the checkValidity() method on the form itself. This method returns true if all form fields are valid and false if even one is not:

```
if(document.forms[0].checkValidity()){
  // form is valid, proceed
} else {
  // form field is invalid
}
```

While checkValidity() simply tells you if a field is valid or not, the validity property indicates exactly why the field is valid or invalid. This object has a series of properties that return a Boolean value:

➤ customError—true if setCustomValidity() was set, false if not.

➤ patternMismatch—true if the value doesn't match the specified pattern attribute.

➤ rangeOverflow—true if the value is larger than the max value.

➤ rangeUnderflow—true if the value is smaller than the min value.

➤ `stepMisMatch`—`true` if the value isn't correct given the step attribute in combination with min and max.

➤ `tooLong`—`true` if the value has more characters than allowed by the `maxlength` property.

➤ `typeMismatch`—value is not in the required format of either "email" or "url".

➤ `valid`—`true` if every other property is `false`. Same value that is required by `checkValidity()`.

➤ `valueMissing`—`true` if the field is marked as required and there is no value.

Therefore, you may wish to check the validity of a form field using validity to get more specific information, as in the following code:

```
if (input.validity && !input.validity.valid){
  if (input.validity.valueMissing){
    console.log("Please specify a value.")
  } else if (input.validity.typeMismatch){
    console.log("Please enter an email address.");
  } else {
    console.log("Value is invalid.");
  }
}
```

Disabling Validation

You can instruct a form not to apply any validation to a form by specifying the `novalidate` attribute:

```
<form method="post" action="/signup" novalidate>
    <!-- form elements here -->
</form>
```

This value can also be retrieved or set by using the JavaScript property `noValidate`, which is set to `true` if the attribute is present and `false` if the attribute is omitted:

```
document.forms[0].noValidate = true;    //turn off validation
```

If there are multiple submit buttons in a form, you can specify that the form not validate when a particular submit button is used by adding the `formnovalidate` attribute to the button itself:

```
<form method="post" action="/foo">
    <!-- form elements here -->
    <input type="submit" value="Regular Submit">
    <input type="submit" formnovalidate name="btnNoValidate"
           value="Non-validating Submit">
</form>
```

In this example, the first submit button will cause the form to validate as usual while the second disables validation when submitting. You can also set this property using JavaScript:

```
// turn off validation
document.forms[0].elements["btnNoValidate"].formNoValidate = true;
```

SCRIPTING SELECT BOXES

Select boxes are created using the <select> and <option> elements. To allow for easier interaction with the control, the HTMLSelectElement type provides the following properties and methods in addition to those that are available on all form fields:

➤ add(newOption, relOption)—Adds a new <option> element to the control before the related option.

➤ multiple—A Boolean value indicating if multiple selections are allowed; equivalent to the HTML multiple attribute.

➤ options—An HTMLCollection of <option> elements in the control.

➤ remove(index)—Removes the option in the given position.

➤ selectedIndex—The zero-based index of the selected option or –1 if no options are selected. For select boxes that allow multiple selections, this is always the first option in the selection.

➤ size—The number of rows visible in the select box; equivalent to the HTML size attribute.

The type property for a select box is either "select-one" or "select-multiple," depending on the absence or presence of the multiple attribute. The option that is currently selected determines a select box's value property according to the following rules:

➤ If there is no option selected, the value of a select box is an empty string.

➤ If an option is selected and it has a value attribute specified, then the select box's value is the value attribute of the selected option. This is true even if the value attribute is an empty string.

➤ If an option is selected and it doesn't have a value attribute specified, then the select box's value is the text of the option.

➤ If multiple options are selected, then the select box's value is taken from the first selected option according to the previous two rules.

Consider the following select box:

```
<select name="location" id="selLocation">
  <option value="Sunnyvale, CA">Sunnyvale</option>
  <option value="Los Angeles, CA">Los Angeles</option>
  <option value="Mountain View, CA">Mountain View</option>
  <option value="">China</option>
  <option>Australia</option>
</select>
```

If the first option in this select box is selected, the value of the field is "Sunnyvale, CA". If the option with the text "China" is selected, then the field's value is an empty string because the value attribute is empty. If the last option is selected, then the value is "Australia" because there is no value attribute specified on the <option>.

Each `<option>` element is represented in the DOM by an `HTMLOptionElement` object. The `HTMLOptionElement` type adds the following properties for easier data access:

➤ `index`—The option's index inside the options collection.

➤ `label`—The option's label; equivalent to the HTML label attribute.

➤ `selected`—A Boolean value used to indicate if the option is selected. Set this property to `true` to select an option.

➤ `text`—The option's text.

➤ `value`—The option's value (equivalent to the HTML value attribute).

Most of the `<option>` properties are used for faster access to the option data. Normal DOM functionality can be used to access this information, but it's quite inefficient, as this example shows:

```
let selectbox = document.forms[0].elements["location"];

// not recommended
let text = selectbox.options[0].firstChild.nodeValue;    // option text
let value = selectbox.options[0].getAttribute("value");   // option value
```

This code gets the text and value of the first option in the select box using standard DOM techniques. Compare this to using the special option properties:

```
let selectbox = document.forms[0].elements["location"];

// preferred
let text = selectbox.options[0].text;    // option text
let value = selectbox.options[0].value;  // option value
```

When dealing with options, it's best to use the option-specific properties because they are well supported across all browsers. The exact interactions of form controls may vary from browser to browser when manipulating DOM nodes. It is not recommended to change the text or values of `<option>` elements by using standard DOM techniques.

As a final note, there is a difference in the way the change event is used for select boxes. As opposed to other form fields, which fire the change event after the value has changed and the field loses focus, the change event fires on select boxes as soon as an option is selected.

Options Selection

For a select box that allows only one option to be selected, the easiest way to access the selected option is by using the select box's `selectedIndex` property to retrieve the option, as shown in the following example:

```
let selectedOption = selectbox.options[selectbox.selectedIndex];
```

This can be used to display all of the information about the selected option, as in this example:

```
let selectedIndex = selectbox.selectedIndex;
let selectedOption = selectbox.options[selectedIndex];
```

```
console.log('Selected index: $[selectedIndex}\n' +
            'Selected text: ${selectedOption.text}\n' +
            'Selected value: ${selectedOption.value}');
```

Here, a log message is displayed showing the selected index along with the text and value of the selected option.

When used in a select box that allows multiple selections, the `selectedIndex` property acts as if only one selection was allowed. Setting `selectedIndex` removes all selections and selects just the single option specified, whereas getting `selectedIndex` returns only the index of the first option that was selected.

Options can also be selected by getting a reference to the option and setting its selected property to `true`. For example, the following selects the first option in a select box:

```
selectbox.options[0].selected = true;
```

Unlike `selectedIndex`, setting the option's selected property does not remove other selections when used in a multiselect select box, allowing you to dynamically select any number of options. If an option's selected property is changed in a single-select select box, then all other selections are removed. It's worth noting that setting the selected property to `false` has no effect in a single-select select box.

The selected property is helpful in determining which options in a select box are selected. To get all of the selected options, you can loop over the options collection and test the selected property. Consider this example:

```
function getSelectedOptions(selectbox) {
    let result = new Array();

    for (let option of selectbox.options) {
      if (option.selected) {
        result.push(option);
      }
    }

    return result;
}
```

This function returns an array of options that are selected in a given select box. First an array to contain the results is created. Then a `for` loop iterates over the options, checking each option's selected property. If the option is selected, it is added to the result array. The last step is to return the array of selected options. The `getSelectedOptions()` function can then be used to get information about the selected options, like this:

```
let selectbox = document.getElementById("selLocation");
let selectedOptions = getSelectedOptions(selectbox);
let message = "";

for (let option of selectedOptions) {
  message += 'Selected index: ${option.index}\n' +
             'Selected text: ${option.text}\n' +
             'Selected value: ${option.value}\n'
}

console.log(message);
```

In this example, the selected options are retrieved from a select box. A `for` loop is used to construct a message containing information about all of the selected options, including each option's index, text, and value. This can be used for select boxes that allow single or multiple selection.

Adding Options

There are several ways to create options dynamically and add them to select boxes using JavaScript. The first way is to use the DOM as follows:

```
let newOption = document.createElement("option");
newOption.appendChild(document.createTextNode("Option text"));
newOption.setAttribute("value", "Option value");

selectbox.appendChild(newOption);
```

This code creates a new <option> element, adds some text using a text node, sets its value attribute, and then adds it to a select box. The new option shows up immediately after being created.

New options can also be created using the `Option` constructor, which is a holdover from pre-DOM browsers. The `Option` constructor accepts two arguments, the text and the value, though the second argument is optional. Even though this constructor is used to create an instance of `Object`, DOM-compliant browsers return an <option> element. This means you can still use `appendChild()` to add the option to the select box. Consider the following:

```
let newOption = new Option("Option text", "Option value");
selectbox.appendChild(newOption);      // problems in IE <= 8
```

Another way to add a new option is to use the select box's `add()` method. The DOM specifies that this method accepts two arguments: the new option to add and the option before which the new option should be inserted. To add an option at the end of the list, the second argument should be `null`.

> **NOTE** *As in HTML, you are not required to assign a value for an option. The* `Option()` *constructor works with just one argument (the option text).*

Removing Options

As with adding options, there are multiple ways to remove options. You can use the DOM `removeChild()` method and pass in the option to remove, as shown here:

```
selectbox.removeChild(selectbox.options[0]);    // remove first option
```

The second way is to use the select box's `remove()` method. This method accepts a single argument, the index of the option to remove, as shown here:

```
selectbox.remove(0);    // remove first option
```

The last way is to simply set the option equal to `null`. This is also a holdover from pre-DOM browsers. Here's an example:

```
selectbox.options[0] = null;      // remove first option
```

To clear a select box of all options, you need to iterate over the options and remove each one, as in this example:

```
function clearSelectbox(selectbox) {
  for (let option of selectbox.options) {
    selectbox.remove(0);
  }
}
```

This function simply removes the first option in a select box repeatedly. Because removing the first option automatically moves all of the options up one spot, this removes all options.

Moving and Reordering Options

Before the DOM, moving options from one select box to another was a rather arduous process that involved removing the option from the first select box, creating a new option with the same name and value, and then adding that new option to the second select box. Using DOM methods, it's possible to literally move an option from the first select box into the second select box by using the appendChild() method. If you pass an element that is already in the document into this method, the element is removed from its parent and put into the position specified. For example, the following code moves the first option from one select box into another select box.

```
let selectbox1 = document.getElementById("selLocations1");
let selectbox2 = document.getElementById("selLocations2");

selectbox2.appendChild(selectbox1.options[0]);
```

Moving options is the same as removing them in that the index property of each option is reset.

Reordering options is very similar, and DOM methods are the best way to accomplish this. To move an option to a particular location in the select box, the insertBefore() method is most appropriate, though the appendChild() method can be used to move any option to the last position. To move an option up one spot in the select box, you can use the following code:

```
let optionToMove = selectbox.options[1];
selectbox.insertBefore(optionToMove,
                       selectbox.options[optionToMove.index-1]);
```

In this code, an option is selected to move and then inserted before the option that is in the previous index. The second line of code is generic enough to work with any option in the select box except the first. The following similar code can be used to move an option down one spot:

```
let optionToMove = selectbox.options[1];
selectbox.insertBefore(optionToMove,
                       selectbox.options[optionToMove.index+2]);
```

This code works for all options in a select box, including the last one.

RICH TEXT EDITING

One of the most requested features for web applications was the ability to edit rich text on a web page (also called *what you see is what you get*, or *WYSIWYG*, editing). Though no specification covers this, a de facto standard has emerged from functionality originally introduced by Internet Explorer. The basic technique is to embed an iframe containing a blank HTML file in the page. Through the `designMode` property, this blank document can be made editable, at which point you're editing the HTML of the page's `<body>` element. The `designMode` property has two possible values: "off" (the default) and "on". When set to "on," an entire document becomes editable (showing a caret), allowing you to edit text as if you were using a word processor complete with keystrokes for making text bold, italic, and so forth.

A very simple, blank HTML page is used as the source of the iframe. Here's an example:

```
<!DOCTYPE html>
<html>
  <head>
    <title>Blank Page for Rich Text Editing</title>
  </head>
  <body>
  </body>
</html>
```

This page is loaded inside an iframe as any other page would be. To allow it to be edited, you must set `designMode` to `"on"`, but this can happen only after the document is fully loaded. In the containing page, you'll need to use the `onload` event handler to indicate the appropriate time to set `designMode`, as shown in the following example:

```
<iframe name="richedit" style="height: 100px; width: 100px"></iframe>

<script>
  window.addEventListener("load", () => {
    frames["richedit"].document.designMode = "on";
  });
</script>
```

Once this code is loaded, you'll see what looks like a text box on the page. The box has the same default styling as any web page, though this can be adjusted by applying CSS to the blank page.

Using *contenteditable*

Another way to interact with rich text is through the use of a special attribute called `contenteditable`. The `contenteditable` attribute can be applied to any element on a page and instantly makes that element editable by the user. This approach has gained favor because it doesn't require the overhead of an iframe, blank page, and JavaScript. Instead, you can just add the attribute to an element:

```
<div class="editable" id="richedit" contenteditable></div>
```

Any text already contained within the element is automatically made editable by the user, making it behave similarly to the `<textarea>` element. You can also toggle the editing mode on or off by setting the `contentEditable` property on an element:

```
let div = document.getElementById("richedit");
richedit.contentEditable = "true";
```

There are three possible values for `contentEditable`: `"true"` to turn on, `"false"` to turn off, or `"inherit"` to inherit the setting from a parent (required because elements can be created/destroyed inside of a `contenteditable` element).

> **NOTE** `contenteditable` *is an extremely versatile attribute. For example, you're able to convert your browser window into a notepad by visiting the pseudo-URL* `data:text/html, <html contenteditable>`. *This creates an ad-hoc DOM with the entire document set to editable.*

Interacting with Rich Text

The primary method of interacting with a rich text editor is through the use of `document.execCommand()`. This method executes named commands on the document and can be used to apply most formatting changes. There are three possible arguments for `document.execCommand()`: the name of the command to execute, a Boolean value indicating if the browser should provide a user interface for the command, and a value necessary for the command to work (or `null` if none is necessary).

> **NOTE** `document.execCommand()` *is considered to be obsolete, but there is currently no alternative. Therefore, most browsers still maintain support.*

Each browser supports a different set of commands. The most commonly supported commands are listed in the following table.

COMMAND	VALUE (THIRD ARGUMENT)	DESCRIPTION
backcolor	A color string	Sets the background color of the document.
bold	null	Toggles bold text for the text selection.
copy	null	Executes a clipboard copy on the text selection.
createlink	A URL string	Turns the current text selection into a link that goes to the given URL.
cut	null	Executes a clipboard cut on the text selection.
delete	null	Deletes the currently selected text.
fontname	The font name	Changes the text selection to use the given font name.

continues

(continued)

COMMAND	VALUE (THIRD ARGUMENT)	DESCRIPTION
`fontsize`	1 through 7	Changes the font size for the text selection.
`forecolor`	A color string	Changes the text color for the text selection.
`formatblock`	The HTML tag to surround the block with; for example, `<h1>`	Formats the entire text box around the selection with a particular HTML tag.
`indent`	`null`	Indents the text.
`inserthorizontalrule`	`null`	Inserts an `<hr>` element at the caret location.
`insertimage`	The image URL	Inserts an image at the caret location.
`insertorderedlist`	`null`	Inserts an `<ol>` element at the caret location.
`insertparagraph`	`null`	Inserts a `<p>` element at the caret location.
`insertunorderedlist`	`null`	Inserts a `<ul>` element at the caret location.
`italic`	`null`	Toggles italic text for the text selection.
`justifycenter`	`null`	Centers the block of text in which the caret is positioned.
`justifyleft`	`null`	Left-aligns the block of text in which the caret is positioned.
`outdent`	`null`	Outdents the text.
`paste`	`null`	Executes a clipboard paste on the text selection.
`removeformat`	`null`	Removes block formatting from the block in which the caret is positioned. This is the opposite of `formatblock`.
`selectall`	`null`	Selects all of the text in the document.
`underline`	`null`	Toggles underlined text for the text selection.
`unlink`	`null`	Removes a text link. This is the opposite of `createlink`.

The clipboard commands are very browser-dependent. Note that even though these commands aren't all available via `document.execCommand()`, they still work with the appropriate keyboard shortcuts.

These commands can be used at any time to modify the appearance of the iframe rich text area, as in this example:

```
// toggle bold text in an iframe
frames["richedit"].document.execCommand("bold", false, null);

// toggle italic text in an iframe
frames["richedit"].document.execCommand("italic", false, null);

// create link to www.wiley.com in an iframe
frames["richedit"].document.execCommand("createlink", false,
                                "http://www.wiley.com");

// format as first-level heading in an iframe
frames["richedit"].document.execCommand("formatblock", false, "<h1>");
```

You can use the same methods to act on a `contenteditable` section of the page; just use the document object of the current window instead of referencing the iframe:

```
// toggle bold text
document.execCommand("bold", false, null);

// toggle italic text
document.execCommand("italic", false, null);

// create link to www.wiley.com
document.execCommand("createlink", false, "http://www.wiley.com");

// format as first-level heading
document.execCommand("formatblock", false, "<h1>");
```

Note that even when commands are supported across all browsers, the HTML that the commands produce is often very different. You cannot rely on consistency in the HTML produced from a rich text editor, because of both command implementation and the transformations done by `innerHTML`.

There are some other methods related to commands. The first is `queryCommandEnabled()`, which determines if a command can be executed given the current text selection or caret position. This method accepts a single argument, the command name to check, and returns `true` if the command is allowed given the state of the editable area or `false` if not. Consider this example:

```
let result = frames["richedit"].document.queryCommandEnabled("bold");
```

This code returns `true` if the `"bold"` command can be executed on the current selection. `queryCommandEnabled()` only indicates if the current selection is appropriate for use with the command.

The `queryCommandState()` method lets you determine if a given command has been applied to the current text selection. For example, to determine if the text in the current selection is bold, you can use the following:

```
let isBold = frames["richedit"].document.queryCommandState("bold");
```

If the `"bold"` command was previously applied to the text selection, then this code returns `true`. This is the method by which full-featured rich text editors are able to update buttons for bold, italic, and so on.

The last method is `queryCommandValue()`, which is intended to return the value with which a command was executed. (The third argument in `execCommand` is in the earlier example.) For instance, a range of text that has the `"fontsize"` command applied with a value of 7 returns "7" from the following:

```
let fontSize = frames["richedit"].document.queryCommandValue("fontsize");
```

This method can be used to determine how a command was applied to the text selection, allowing you to determine whether the next command is appropriate to be executed.

Rich Text Selections

You can determine the exact selection in a rich text editor by using the `getSelection()` method of the iframe. This method is available on both the document object and the window object and returns a Selection object representing the currently selected text. Each Selection object has the following properties:

➤ `anchorNode`—The node in which the selection begins.

➤ `anchorOffset`—The number of characters within the `anchorNode` that are skipped before the selection begins.

➤ `focusNode`—The node in which the selection ends.

➤ `focusOffset`—The number of characters within the `focusNode` that are included in the selection.

➤ `isCollapsed`—Boolean value indicating if the start and end of the selection are the same.

➤ `rangeCount`—The number of DOM ranges in the selection.

The properties for a Selection don't contain a lot of useful information. Fortunately, the following methods provide more information and allow manipulation of the selection:

➤ `addRange(range)`—Adds the given DOM range to the selection.

➤ `collapse(node, offset)`—Collapses the selection to the given text offset within the given node.

➤ `collapseToEnd()`—Collapses the selection to its end.

➤ `collapseToStart()`—Collapses the selection to its start.

➤ `containsNode(node)`—Determines if the given node is contained in the selection.

➤ `deleteFromDocument()`—Deletes the selection text from the document. This is the same as `execCommand("delete", false, null)`.

➤ `extend(node, offset)`—Extends the selection by moving the `focusNode` and `focusOffset` to the values specified.

➤ `getRangeAt(index)`—Returns the DOM range at the given index in the selection.

➤ `removeAllRanges()`—Removes all DOM ranges from the selection. This effectively removes the selection, because there must be at least one range in a selection.

➤ `removeRange(range)`—Removes the specified DOM range from the selection.

➤ `selectAllChildren(node)`—Clears the selection and then selects all child nodes of the given node.

➤ `toString()`—Returns the text content of the selection.

The methods of a Selection object are extremely powerful and make extensive use of DOM ranges to manage the selection. Access to DOM ranges allows you to modify the contents of the rich text editor in even finer-grain detail than is available using `execCommand()` because you can directly manipulate the DOM of the selected text. Consider the following example:

```
let selection = frames["richedit"].getSelection();

// get selected text
let selectedText = selection.toString();

// get the range representing the selection
let range = selection.getRangeAt(0);

// highlight the selected text
let span = frames["richedit"].document.createElement("span");
span.style.backgroundColor = "yellow";
range.surroundContents(span);
```

This code places a yellow highlight around the selected text in a rich text editor. Using the DOM range in the default selection, the `surroundContents()` method surrounds the selection with a `<span>` element whose background color is yellow. The `getSelection()` method was standardized in HTML5.

Rich Text in Forms

Because rich text editing is implemented using an iframe or a `contenteditable` element instead of a form control, a rich text editor is technically not part of a form. That means the HTML will not be submitted to the server unless you extract the HTML manually and submit it yourself. This is typically done by having a hidden form field that is updated with the HTML from the iframe or the `contenteditable` element. Just before the form is submitted, the HTML is extracted from the iframe or element and inserted into the hidden field. For example, the following may be done in the form's `onsubmit` event handler when using an iframe:

```
form.addEventListener("submit", (event) => {
  let target = event.target;

  target.elements["comments"].value =
      frames["richedit"].document.body.innerHTML;
});
```

Here, the HTML is retrieved from the iframe using the `innerHTML` property of the document's body and inserted into a form field named "comments". Doing so ensures that the "comments" field is filled in just before the form is submitted. If you are submitting the form manually using the `submit()` method, take care to perform this operation beforehand. You can perform a similar operation with a `contenteditable` element:

```
form.addEventListener("submit", (event) => {
  let target = event.target;

  target.elements["comments"].value =
      document.getElementById("richedit").innerHTML;
});
```

SUMMARY

Even though HTML and web applications have changed dramatically since their inception, web forms have remained mostly unchanged. JavaScript can be used to augment existing form fields to provide new functionality and usability enhancements. To aid in this, forms and form fields have properties, methods, and events for JavaScript usage. Here are some of the concepts introduced in this chapter:

➤ It's possible to select all of the text in a text box or just part of the text using a variety of standard and nonstandard methods.

➤ All browsers have adopted Firefox's way of interacting with text selection, making it a true standard.

➤ Text boxes can be changed to allow or disallow certain characters by listening for keyboard events and inspecting the characters being inserted.

All browsers support events for the clipboard, including copy, cut, and paste. Clipboard event implementations across the other browsers vary widely between browser vendors.

Hooking into clipboard events is useful for blocking paste events when the contents of a text box must be limited to certain characters.

Select boxes are also frequently controlled using JavaScript. Thanks to the DOM, manipulating select boxes is much easier than it was previously. Options can be added, removed, moved from one select box to another, or reordered using standard DOM techniques.

Rich text editing is handled by using an iframe containing a blank HTML document. By setting the document's `designMode` property to "on," you make the page editable and it acts like a word processor. You can also use an element set as `contenteditable`. By default, you can toggle font styles such as bold and italic and use clipboard actions. JavaScript can access some of this functionality by using the `execCommand()` method and can get information about the text selection by using the `queryCommandEnabled()`, `queryCommandState()`, and `queryCommandValue()` methods. Because building a rich text editor in this manner does not create a form field, it's necessary to copy the HTML from the iframe or `contenteditable` element into a form field if it is to be submitted to the server.

18

JavaScript APIs

WHAT'S IN THIS CHAPTER?

➤ Atomics and SharedArrayBuffer

➤ Cross-context messaging

➤ Clipboard API

➤ Encoding API

➤ File and Blob API

➤ Fullscreen API

➤ Geolocation API

➤ Device APIs

➤ Drag and drop

➤ Notifications API

➤ Page Visibility API

➤ Streams API

➤ Timing APIs

➤ The URL API

➤ Web components

➤ Web Cryptography API

DOWNLOADS FOR THIS CHAPTER

Please note that all the code examples for this chapter are available as a part of this chapter's code download on the book's website at www.wiley.com/go/projavascript5e.

The increasing versatility of web browsers is accompanied by a dizzying increase in complexity. In many ways, the modern web browser has become a Swiss army knife of APIs described in a broad collection of specifications. This browser specification ecosystem is messy and volatile. Some specifications like HTML5 are a bundle of APIs and browser features that enhance an existing standard. Other specifications define an API for a single feature, such as the Web Cryptography API or the Notifications API. Depending on the browser, adoption of these newer APIs can sometimes be partial or nonexistent.

> **NOTE** *The number of web APIs is mind-bogglingly huge (*`https://developer`
> `.mozilla.org/en-US/docs/Web/API`*). This chapter's API coverage is limited to APIs that are relevant to most developers, supported by multiple browser vendors, and not covered elsewhere in this book.*

ATOMICS AND SharedArraybuffer

When a `SharedArrayBuffer` is accessed by multiple contexts, race conditions can occur when operations on the buffer are performed simultaneously. The Atomics API allows multiple contexts to safely read and write to a single `SharedArrayBuffer` by forcing buffer operations to occur only one at a time.

You will notice that the Atomics API in many ways resembles a stripped-down instruction set architecture (ISA)—this is no accident. The nature of atomic operations precludes some optimizations that the operating system or computer hardware would normally perform automatically (such as instruction reordering). Atomic operations also make concurrent memory access impossible, which obviously can slow program execution when improperly applied. Therefore, the Atomics API was designed to enable sophisticated multithreaded JavaScript programs to be architected out of a minimal yet robust collection of atomic behaviors.

SharedArrayBuffer

A `SharedArrayBuffer` features an identical API to an `ArrayBuffer`. The primary difference is that, whereas a reference to an `ArrayBuffer` must be handed off between execution contexts, a reference to a `SharedArrayBuffer` can be used simultaneously by any number of execution contexts.

Sharing memory between multiple execution contexts means that concurrent thread operations become a possibility. Traditional JavaScript operations offer no protection from race conditions resulting from concurrent memory access. The following example demonstrates a race condition between four dedicated workers accessing the same `SharedArrayBuffer`:

```
const workerScript = `
self.onmessage = ({data}) => {
  const view = new Uint32Array(data);

  // Perform 1000000 add operations
  for (let i = 0; i < 1E6; ++i) {
    // Thread-unsafe add operation introduces race condition
    view[0] += 1;
```

```
      }

    self.postMessage(null);
  };
`;

const workerScriptBlobUrl = URL.createObjectURL(new Blob([workerScript]));

// Create worker pool of size 4
const workers = [];
for (let i = 0; i < 4; ++i) {
  workers.push(new Worker(workerScriptBlobUrl));
}

// Log the final value after the last worker completes
let responseCount = 0;
for (const worker of workers) {
  worker.onmessage = () => {
    if (++responseCount == workers.length) {
      console.log(`Final buffer value: ${view[0]}`);
    }
  };
}

// Initialize the SharedArrayBuffer
const sharedArrayBuffer = new SharedArrayBuffer(4);
const view = new Uint32Array(sharedArrayBuffer);
view[0] = 1;

// Send the SharedArrayBuffer to each worker
for (const worker of workers) {
  worker.postMessage(sharedArrayBuffer);
}

// (Expected result is 4000001. Actual output will be something like:)
// Final buffer value: 2145106
```

To address this problem, the Atomics API was introduced to allow for thread-safe JavaScript operations on a SharedArrayBuffer.

> **NOTE** *The* SharedArrayBuffer *API is identical to the* ArrayBuffer *API, which is covered in Chapter 6, "Advanced Reference Types." For details on how to use a* SharedArrayBuffer *across multiple contexts, refer to Chapter 24, "Workers."*

Atomics Basics

The Atomics object exists on all global contexts, and it exposes a suite of static methods for performing thread-safe operations. Most of these methods take a TypedArray instance (referencing a SharedArrayBuffer) as the first argument and the relevant operands as subsequent arguments.

Atomic Arithmetic and Bitwise Methods

The Atomics API offers a simple suite of methods for performing an in-place modification. In the ECMA specification, these methods are defined as `AtomicReadModifyWrite` operations. Under the hood, each of these methods is performing a read from a location in the `SharedArrayBuffer`, an arithmetic or bitwise operation, and a write to the same location. The atomic nature of these operators means that these three operations will be performed in sequence and without interruption by another thread.

All the arithmetic methods are demonstrated here:

```
// Create buffer of size 1
let sharedArrayBuffer = new SharedArrayBuffer(1);

// Create Uint8Array from buffer
let typedArray = new Uint8Array(sharedArrayBuffer);

// All ArrayBuffers are initialized to 0
console.log(typedArray);  // Uint8Array[0]

const index = 0;
const increment = 5;

// Atomic add 5 to value at index 0
Atomics.add(typedArray, index, increment);

console.log(typedArray);  // Uint8Array[5]

// Atomic subtract 5 to value at index 0
Atomics.sub(typedArray, index, increment);

console.log(typedArray);  // Uint8Array[0]
```

All the bitwise methods are demonstrated here:

```
// Create buffer of size 1
let sharedArrayBuffer = new SharedArrayBuffer(1);

// Create Uint8Array from buffer
let typedArray = new Uint8Array(sharedArrayBuffer);

// All ArrayBuffers are initialized to 0
console.log(typedArray);  // Uint8Array[0]

const index = 0;

// Atomic or 0b1111 to value at index 0
Atomics.or(typedArray, index, 0b1111);

console.log(typedArray);  // Uint8Array[15]

// Atomic and 0b1100 to value at index 0
```

```
Atomics.and(typedArray, index, 0b1100);

console.log(typedArray);  // Uint8Array[12]

// Atomic xor 0b1111 to value at index 0
Atomics.xor(typedArray, index, 0b1111);

console.log(typedArray);  // Uint8Array[3]
```

The thread-unsafe example from earlier can be corrected as follows:

```
const workerScript = `
self.onmessage = ({data}) => {
  const view = new Uint32Array(data);

  // Perform 1000000 add operations
  for (let i = 0; i < 1E6; ++i) {
    // Thread-safe add operation
    Atomics.add(view, 0, 1);
  }

  self.postMessage(null);
};
`;

const workerScriptBlobUrl = URL.createObjectURL(new Blob([workerScript]));

// Create worker pool of size 4
const workers = [];
for (let i = 0; i < 4; ++i) {
  workers.push(new Worker(workerScriptBlobUrl));
}

// Log the final value after the last worker completes
let responseCount = 0;
for (const worker of workers) {
  worker.onmessage = () => {
    if (++responseCount == workers.length) {
      console.log(`Final buffer value: ${view[0]}`);
    }
  };
}

// Initialize the SharedArrayBuffer
const sharedArrayBuffer = new SharedArrayBuffer(4);
const view = new Uint32Array(sharedArrayBuffer);
view[0] = 1;

// Send the SharedArrayBuffer to each worker
for (const worker of workers) {
  worker.postMessage(sharedArrayBuffer);
}

// (Expected result is 4000001)
// Final buffer value: 4000001
```

Atomic Reads and Writes

Both the browser's JavaScript compiler and the CPU architecture itself are given license to reorder instructions if they detect it will increase the overall throughput of program execution. Normally, the single-threaded nature of JavaScript means this optimization should be welcomed with open arms. However, instruction reordering across multiple threads can yield race conditions that are extremely difficult to debug.

The Atomics API addresses this problem in two primary ways:

➤ All Atomics instructions are never reordered with respect to one another.

➤ Using an Atomic read or Atomic write guarantees that all instructions (both Atomic and non-Atomic) will never be reordered with respect to that Atomic read/write. This means that all instructions before an Atomic read/write will finish before the Atomic read/write occurs, and all instructions after the Atomic read/write will not begin until the Atomic read/write completes.

In addition to reading and writing values to a buffer, `Atomics.load()` and `Atomics.store()` behave as "code fences." The JavaScript engine guarantees that, although non-Atomic instructions may be *locally* reordered relative to a `load()` or `store()`, the reordering will never violate the Atomic read/write boundary. The following code annotates this behavior:

```
const sharedArrayBuffer = new SharedArrayBuffer(4);
const view = new Uint32Array(sharedArrayBuffer);

// Perform non-Atomic write
view[0] = 1;

// Non-Atomic write is guaranteed to occur before this read,
// so this is guaranteed to read 1
console.log(Atomics.load(view, 0));  // 1

// Perform Atomic write
Atomics.store(view, 0, 2);

// Non-Atomic read is guaranteed to occur after Atomic write,
// so this is guaranteed to read 2
console.log(view[0]);  // 2
```

Atomic Exchanges

The Atomics API offers two types of methods that guarantee a sequential and uninterrupted read-then-write: `exchange()` and `compareExchange()`. `Atomics.exchange()` performs a simple swap, guaranteeing that no other threads will interrupt the value swap:

```
const sharedArrayBuffer = new SharedArrayBuffer(4);
const view = new Uint32Array(sharedArrayBuffer);

// Write 3 to 0-index
```

```
Atomics.store(view, 0, 3);

// Read value out of 0-index and then write 4 to 0-index
console.log(Atomics.exchange(view, 0, 4));  // 3

// Read value at 0-index
console.log(Atomics.load(view, 0));          // 4
```

One thread in a multithreaded program might want to perform a write to a shared buffer *only* if another thread has not modified a specific value since it was last read. If the value has not changed, it can safely write the update value. If the value *has* changed, performing a write would trample the value calculated by another thread. For this task, the Atomics API features the compareExchange() method. This method only performs a write if the value at the intended index matches an expected value. Consider the following example:

```
const sharedArrayBuffer = new SharedArrayBuffer(4);
const view = new Uint32Array(sharedArrayBuffer);

// Write 5 to 0-index
Atomics.store(view, 0, 5);
// Read the value out of the buffer
let initial = Atomics.load(view, 0);

// Perform a non-atomic operation on that value
let result = initial ** 2;

// Write that value back into the buffer only if the buffer has not changed
Atomics.compareExchange(view, 0, initial, result);

// Check that the write succeeded
console.log(Atomics.load(view, 0));  // 25
```

If the value does not match, the compareExchange() call will simply behave as a passthrough:

```
const sharedArrayBuffer = new SharedArrayBuffer(4);
const view = new Uint32Array(sharedArrayBuffer);

// Write 5 to 0-index
Atomics.store(view, 0, 5);
// Read the value out of the buffer
let initial = Atomics.load(view, 0);

// Perform a non-atomic operation on that value
let result = initial ** 2;

// Write that value back into the buffer only if the buffer has not changed
Atomics.compareExchange(view, 0, -1, result);

// Check that the write failed
console.log(Atomics.load(view, 0));  // 5
```

Atomics Futex Operations and Locks

Multithreaded programs wouldn't amount to much without some sort of locking construct. To address this need, the Atomics API offers several methods modeled on the Linux futex (a portmanteau of *fast user-space mutex*). The methods are fairly rudimentary, but they are intended to be used as a fundamental building block for more elaborate locking constructs.

> **NOTE** *All Atomics futex operations only work with an* `Int32Array` *view. Furthermore, they can only be used inside workers.*

`Atomics.wait()` and `Atomics.notify()` are best understood by example. The following rudimentary example spawns four workers to operate on an Int32Array of length 1. The spawned workers will take turns obtaining the lock and performing their add operation:

```
const workerScript = `
self.onmessage = ({data}) => {
  const view = new Int32Array(data);

  console.log('Waiting to obtain lock');

  // Halt when encountering the initial value, timeout at 10000ms
  Atomics.wait(view, 0, 0, 1E5);

  console.log('Obtained lock');

  // Add 1 to data index
  Atomics.add(view, 0, 1);

  console.log('Releasing lock');

  // Allow exactly one worker to continue execution
  Atomics.notify(view, 0, 1);

  self.postMessage(null);
};
`;

const workerScriptBlobUrl = URL.createObjectURL(new Blob([workerScript]));

const workers = [];
for (let i = 0; i < 4; ++i) {
  workers.push(new Worker(workerScriptBlobUrl));
}

// Log the final value after the last worker completes
let responseCount = 0;
for (const worker of workers) {
  worker.onmessage = () => {
    if (++responseCount == workers.length) {
```

```
        console.log(`Final buffer value: ${view[0]}`);
      }
    };
}

// Initialize the SharedArrayBuffer
const sharedArrayBuffer = new SharedArrayBuffer(8);
const view = new Int32Array(sharedArrayBuffer);

// Send the SharedArrayBuffer to each worker
for (const worker of workers) {
  worker.postMessage(sharedArrayBuffer);
}

// Release first lock in 1000ms
setTimeout(() => Atomics.notify(view, 0, 1), 1000);

// Waiting to obtain lock
// Waiting to obtain lock
// Waiting to obtain lock
// Waiting to obtain lock
// Obtained lock
// Releasing lock
// Obtained lock
// Releasing lock
// Obtained lock
// Releasing lock
// Obtained lock
// Releasing lock
// Final buffer value: 4
```

Because the SharedArrayBuffer is initialized with 0s, each worker will arrive at the Atomics .wait() and halt execution. In the halted state, the thread of execution exists inside a *wait queue*, remaining paused until the specified timeout elapses or until Atomics.notify() is invoked for that index. After 1000 milliseconds, the top-level execution context will call Atomics.notify() to release exactly one of the waiting threads. This thread will finish execution and call Atomics.notify() once again, releasing yet another thread. This continues until all the threads have completed execution and transmitted their final postMessage().

The Atomics API also features the Atomics.isLockFree() method. It is almost certain that you will never need to use this method, as it is designed for high-performance algorithms to decide whether or not obtaining a lock is necessary. The specification offers this description:

Atomics.isLockFree() *is an optimization primitive. The intuition is that if the atomic step of an atomic primitive (*compareExchange, load, store, add, sub, and, or, xor, *or* exchange*) on a datum of size n bytes will be performed without the calling agent acquiring a lock outside the n bytes comprising the datum, then* Atomics.isLockFree(n) *will return* true. *High-performance algorithms will use* Atomics.isLockFree *to determine whether to use locks or atomic operations in* *critical sections. If an atomic primitive is not lock-free then it is often more efficient for an algorithm to provide its own locking.*

`Atomics.isLockFree(4)` *always returns* `true` *as that can be supported on all known relevant hardware. Being able to assume this will generally simplify programs.*

CLIPBOARD API

The traditional method of accessing the system clipboard through `document.execCommand()` had limitations: it was synchronous, restricted to reading and writing within the DOM, and was not suited for transferring larger content. Operations like sanitization, image decoding, or loading linked resources caused delays, blocking the page. Additionally, browser permissions were and still are inconsistent and poorly defined for clipboard interactions with `document.execCommand()`.

The Clipboard API aims to replace the old methods and provides a simple way to hook into the common clipboard operations of cut, copy, and paste. There are three interfaces involved in this API:

➤ `Clipboard`–The main interface of the Clipboard API, provides read and write access to the clipboard.

➤ `ClipboardEvent`–Represents events providing clipboard operations.

➤ `ClipboardItem`–Provides a way to represent data that can be copied to the system clipboard. It allows you to store multiple data types (such as text, images, or files) as a single clipboard item.

Unlike its predecessor, the Clipboard API is also asynchronous—so all methods return a promise, and it is accessed from `navigator.clipboard`.

Permissions

Because clipboard information is sensitive, the user must grant permissions before the API can be used. This access pattern is identical to that of notifications or geolocation: the first time the API is accessed, a blocking dialog box will appear asking for access. A user approving or denying access will be remembered by the browser for that domain until the user explicitly updates the permission.

Clipboard permissions are split into two:

➤ `clipboard-read` allows for a page to read the contents of the clipboard. This permission must be explicitly granted by the user.

➤ `clipboard-write` allows for a page to write content *into* the clipboard. This write permission is granted automatically to pages when they are the active tab.

Checking for the read permission can be accomplished as follows:

```
navigator.permissions.query({name: "clipboard-read"}).then(result => {
  if (result.state == "granted") {
    /* clipboard access granted */
  }
});
```

Browsers only allow the Clipboard API to be used if the page is active. If you attempt to read or write the clipboard while the page is not focused, it will throw an error such as DOMException: Document is not focused.

Because programmatic access to the clipboard is a sensitive operation, the clipboard permission options can include an optional allowWithoutGesture Boolean. This controls if the page script may read from or write to the clipboard absent a user "gesture" (any user interaction that generates an event in JavaScript code, such as a click or keystroke). Since programmatic access without a gesture is more invasive, many browsers will default to *only* gesture access. Consider the following Chrome console output on google.com:

```
navigator.permissions.query({
  name: "clipboard-read"
}).then(({state}) => console.log(state));
// granted

navigator.permissions.query({
  name: "clipboard-read",
  allowWithoutGesture: true
}).then(({state}) => console.log(state));
// prompt
```

Adding the allowWithoutGesture option will require the user to explicitly grant permissions for the page script to gain unrestricted programmatic clipboard access.

Text Read and Write

Since textual information is the most common medium to be used in the clipboard, the API has readText() and writeText() to programmatically read and write strings in and out of the clipboard. These can be used as follows:

```
navigator.clipboard.readText().then(
  (clipText) => console.log(clipText)
);

navigator.clipboard.writeText("Put this in the clipboard").then(() => {
  console.log('Writing to clipboard was successful!');
});
```

Clipboard Events

When a user explicitly performs a cut, copy, or paste via keyboard or mouse, you can listen for the cut, copy, or paste events and assign handlers. Since these events will bubble up, document is a logical choice for a global clipboard event handler:

```
document.addEventListener("copy", async () => {
  console.log("Copied text:", await navigator.clipboard.readText());
});
```

Working with Non-Text Data

The Clipboard API also allows you to work with non-text data types, by using the read() and write() methods. These methods are configured to handle generalized data transfer, so you will need to marshal data in and out via ClipboardItem.

The ClipboardItem object has a constructor that takes an array of data objects as its argument. Each data object represents a specific type of data you want to include in the clipboard item. The data object consists of two properties: type and data. The type property represents the MIME type of the data, and the data property holds the actual data value.

> **NOTE** *The* ClipboardItem *object allows for an array of objects to support multiple data types within a single clipboard item. This feature is particularly useful when you want to provide various representations of the same data to accommodate different paste targets or to enhance the user experience. For example, you might include both plain text and HTML representations of the same content in a* ClipboardItem. *This allows users to paste the data as plain text in applications that don't support HTML formatting or as formatted HTML in applications that can interpret HTML.*

The following example creates a dummy image blob, wraps it inside a ClipboardItem, and writes it to the clipboard:

```
// Create empty PNG blob
const blob = await new Promise(
  (resolve) => document.createElement("canvas").toBlob(resolve, "image/png"));

// Generate the ClipboardItem to be stored in the clipboard
const clipboardItem = new ClipboardItem({'image/png': blob});

// Perform the clipboard write
navigator.clipboard.write([myClipboardItem]);
```

To read an object out of the clipboard, you will need to iterate the array of ClipboardItem objects, find a matching MIME type within that ClipboardItem, and access its contents:

```
// clipboard.read() returns an array of ClipboardItem objects
```

```
for (let clipboardItem of await navigator.clipboard.read()) {

  // Iterate the MIME types within this item
  for (let type of clipboardItem.types) {

    // We're looking for a PNG
    if (type === 'image/png') {

      // The clipboard data is accessed via MIME key
      let blob = await clipboardItem.getType(type);

      // Now we can use the blob
    }
  }
}
```

As you have probably noticed, any number of ClipboardItem objects can be written and read with the API. In this example, we write both text and image data in separate objects and then read them all out.

```
// Writing multiple objects to the clipboard
const clipboardItems = [
  new ClipboardItem([
    new ClipboardItemData(textData, 'text/plain')
  ])
  new ClipboardItem([
    new ClipboardItemData(imageData, 'image/png')
  ])
];

await navigator.clipboard.write(clipboardItems);

// Read everything out of the clipboard
navigator.clipboard.read().then((clipboardItems) => {
  for (const clipboardItem of clipboardItems) {
    for (const type of dataItem.types) {
      dataItem.getType(type).then(data => console.log({ type, data }));
    }
  }
});
```

CROSS-CONTEXT MESSAGING

Cross-document messaging, sometimes abbreviated as XDM, is the capability to pass information between different execution contexts, such as web workers or pages from different origins. For example, a page on www.wiley.com wants to communicate with a page from p2p.wiley.com that is contained in an iframe. Prior to XDM, achieving this communication in a secure manner took a lot of work. XDM formalizes this functionality in a way that is both secure and easy to use.

> **NOTE** *Cross-context messaging is used for communication between windows and communication with workers. This section focuses on using* postMessage() *to communicate with other windows. For coverage on worker messaging,* MessageChannel, *and* BroadcastChannel, *refer to Chapter 24.*

At the heart of XDM is the `postMessage()` method. This method name is used in many parts of HTML5 in addition to XDM and is always used for the same purpose: to pass data into another location.

The `postMessage()` method accepts three arguments: a message, a string indicating the intended recipient origin, and an optional array of transferable objects (only relevant to web workers). The second argument is very important for security reasons and restricts where the browser will deliver the message. Consider this example:

```
let iframeWindow = document.getElementById("myframe").contentWindow;
iframeWindow.postMessage("A secret", "http://www.wiley.com");
```

The last line attempts to send a message into the iframe and specifies that the origin must be `"www.wiley.com"`. If the origin matches, then the message will be delivered into the iframe; otherwise, `postMessage()` silently does nothing. This restriction protects your information should the location of the `window` change without your knowledge. It is possible to allow posting to any origin by passing in `"*"` as the second argument to `postMessage()`, but this is not recommended.

A `message` event is fired on window when an XDM message is received. This message is fired asynchronously so there may be a delay between the time at which the message was sent and the time at which the message event is fired in the receiving `window`. The event object that is passed to an `onmessage` event handler has three important pieces of information:

➤ `data`—The string data that was passed as the first argument to `postMessage()`.

➤ `origin`—The origin of the `document` that sent the message, for example, `"www.wiley.com"`.

➤ `source`—A proxy for the `window` object of the `document` that sent the message. This proxy object is used primarily to execute the `postMessage()` method on the `window` that sent the last message. If the sending `window` has the same origin, this may be the actual `window` object.

It's very important when receiving a message to verify the origin of the sending `window`. Just as specifying the second argument to `postMessage()` ensures that data doesn't get passed unintentionally to an unknown page, checking the origin during `onmessage` ensures that the data being passed is coming from the right place. The basic pattern is as follows:

```
window.addEventListener("message", (event) => {
  // ensure the sender is expected
  if (event.origin == "http://www.wiley.com") {
    // do something with the data
    processMessage(event.data);
    // optional: send a message back to the original window
    event.source.postMessage("Received!", "http://p2p.wiley.com");
  }
});
```

Keep in mind that `event.source` is a proxy for a `window` in most cases, not the actual `window` object, so you can't access all of the `window` information. It's best to just use `postMessage()`, which is always present and always callable.

There are a few quirks with XDM. First, the first argument of `postMessage()` was initially implemented as always being a string. The definition of that first argument changed to allow any structured data to be passed in; however, not all browsers have implemented this change. For this reason, it's best to always pass a string using `postMessage()`. If you need to pass structured data, then the best approach is to call `JSON.stringify()` on the data, passing the string to `postMessage()`, and then call `JSON.parse()` in the `onmessage` event handler.

XDM is extremely useful when trying to sandbox content using an iframe to a different domain. The containing page is able to keep itself secure against malicious content by only communicating into an embedded iframe via XDM. XDM can also be used with pages from the same domain.

ENCODING API

The Encoding API allows for converting between strings and typed arrays. The specification introduces four global classes for performing these conversions: `TextEncoder`, `TextEncoderStream`, `TextDecoder`, and `TextDecoderStream`.

> **NOTE** *Support for stream encoding/decoding is much narrower than bulk encoding/decoding.*

Encoding Text

The Encoding API affords two ways of converting a string into its typed array binary equivalent: a *bulk* encoding, and a *stream* encoding. When going from string to typed array, the encoder will always use UTF-8.

Bulk Encoding

The *bulk* designation means that the JavaScript engine will synchronously encode the entire string. For very long strings, this can be a costly operation. Bulk encoding is accomplished using an instance of a `TextEncoder`:

```
const textEncoder = new TextEncoder();
```

This instance exposes an `encode()` method, which accepts a string and returns each character's UTF-8 encoding inside a freshly created `Uint8Array`:

```
const textEncoder = new TextEncoder();
const decodedText = 'foo';
const encodedText = textEncoder.encode(decodedText);

// f encoded in utf-8 is 0x66 (102 in decimal)
// o encoded in utf-8 is 0x6F (111 in decimal)
console.log(encodedText);  // Uint8Array(3) [102, 111, 111]
```

The encoder is equipped to handle characters, which will take up multiple indices in the eventual array, such as emojis:

```
const textEncoder = new TextEncoder();
```

```
const decodedText = '';
const encodedText = textEncoder.encode(decodedText);

//  encoded in UTF-8 is 0xF0 0x9F 0x98 0x8A (240, 159, 152, 138 in decimal)
console.log(encodedText);  // Uint8Array(4) [240, 159, 152, 138]
```

The instance also exposes an encodeInto() method, which accepts a string *and* the destination Uint8Array. This method returns a dictionary containing read and written properties, indicating how many characters were successfully read from the source string and written to the destination array, respectively. If the typed array has insufficient space, the encoding will terminate early and the dictionary will indicate that result:

```
const textEncoder = new TextEncoder();
const fooArr = new Uint8Array(3);
const barArr = new Uint8Array(2);
const fooResult = textEncoder.encodeInto('foo', fooArr);
const barResult = textEncoder.encodeInto('bar', barArr);

console.log(fooArr);      // Uint8Array(3) [102, 111, 111]
console.log(fooResult);   // { read: 3, written: 3 }

console.log(barArr);      // Uint8Array(2) [98, 97]
console.log(barResult);   // { read: 2, written: 2 }
```

encode() must allocate a new Uint8Array, whereas encodeInto() does not. For performance-sensitive applications, this distinction may have significant implications.

> **NOTE** *Text encoding will always utilize the UTF-8 format and must write into a Uint8Array instance. Attempting to use a different typed array when calling* encodeInto() *will throw an error.*

Stream Encoding

A TextEncoderStream is merely a TextEncoder in the form of a TransformStream. Piping a decoded text stream through the stream encoder will yield a stream of encoded text chunks:

```
async function* chars() {
  const decodedText = 'foo';

  for (let char of decodedText) {
    yield await new Promise((resolve) => setTimeout(resolve, 1000, char));
  }
}

const decodedTextStream = new ReadableStream({
  async start(controller) {
    for await (let chunk of chars()) {
      controller.enqueue(chunk);
```

```
      }
      controller.close();
    }
});


const encodedTextStream = decodedTextStream.pipeThrough(new TextEncoderStream());

const readableStreamDefaultReader = encodedTextStream.getReader();

(async function() {
  while(true) {
    const { done, value } = await readableStreamDefaultReader.read();

    if (done) {
      break;
    } else {
      console.log(value);
    }
  }
})();

// Uint8Array[102]
// Uint8Array[111]
// Uint8Array[111]
```

Decoding Text

The Encoding API affords two ways of converting a typed array into its string equivalent: a *bulk* decoding, and a *stream* decoding. Unlike the encoder classes, when going from typed array to string, the decoder supports a large number of string encodings, listed here: https://encoding.spec .whatwg.org/#names-and-labels.

The default character encoding is UTF-8.

Bulk Decoding

The *bulk* designation means that the JavaScript engine will synchronously decode the entire string. For very long strings, this can be a costly operation. Bulk decoding is accomplished using an instance of a DecoderEncoder:

```
const textDecoder = new TextDecoder();
```

This instance exposes a decode() method, which accepts a typed array and returns the decoded string:

```
const textDecoder = new TextDecoder();

// f encoded in utf-8 is 0x66 (102 in decimal)
// o encoded in utf-8 is 0x6F (111 in decimal)
const encodedText = Uint8Array.of(102, 111, 111);
const decodedText = textDecoder.decode(encodedText);

console.log(decodedText);  // foo
```

The decoder does not care which typed array it is passed, so it will dutifully decode the entire binary representation. In this example, 32-bit values only containing 8-bit characters are decoded as UTF-8, yielding extra empty characters:

```
const textDecoder = new TextDecoder();

// f encoded in utf-8 is 0x66 (102 in decimal)
// o encoded in utf-8 is 0x6F (111 in decimal)
const encodedText = Uint32Array.of(102, 111, 111);
const decodedText = textDecoder.decode(encodedText);

console.log(decodedText);  // "f   o      "
```

The decoder is equipped to handle characters that span multiple indices in the typed array, such as emojis:

```
const textDecoder = new TextDecoder();

//  encoded in UTF-8 is 0xF0 0x9F 0x98 0x8A (240, 159, 152, 138 in decimal)
const encodedText = Uint8Array.of(240, 159, 152, 138);
const decodedText = textDecoder.decode(encodedText);

console.log(decodedText);  //
```

Unlike `TextEncoder`, `TextDecoder` is compatible with a wide number of character encodings. Consider the following example, which uses UTF-16 encoding instead of the default UTF-8:

```
const textDecoder = new TextDecoder('utf-16');

// f encoded in utf-8 is 0x0066 (102 in decimal)
// o encoded in utf-8 is 0x006F (111 in decimal)
const encodedText = Uint16Array.of(102, 111, 111);
const decodedText = textDecoder.decode(encodedText);

console.log(decodedText);  // foo
```

Stream Decoding

A `TextDecoderStream` is merely a `TextDecoder` in the form of a `TransformStream`. Piping an encoded text stream through the stream decoder will yield a stream of decoded text chunks:

```
async function* chars() {
  // Each chunk must exist as a typed array
  const encodedText = [102, 111, 111].map((x) => Uint8Array.of(x));

  for (let char of encodedText) {
    yield await new Promise((resolve) => setTimeout(resolve, 1000, char));
  }
}

const encodedTextStream = new ReadableStream({
  async start(controller) {
    for await (let chunk of chars()) {
      controller.enqueue(chunk);
```

```
    }

    controller.close();
  }
});


const decodedTextStream = encodedTextStream.pipeThrough(new TextDecoderStream());

const readableStreamDefaultReader = decodedTextStream.getReader();

(async function() {
  while(true) {
    const { done, value } = await readableStreamDefaultReader.read();

    if (done) {
      break;
    } else {
      console.log(value);
    }
  }
})();

// f
// o
// o
```

Text decoder streams implicitly understand that surrogate pairs may be split between chunks. The decoder stream will retain any fragmented chunks until a complete character is formed. Consider the following example, where the stream decoder will wait for all four chunks to be passed through before the decoded stream emits the single character:

```
async function* chars() {
  //  encoded in UTF-8 is 0xF0 0x9F 0x98 0x8A (240, 159, 152, 138 in decimal)
  const encodedText = [240, 159, 152, 138].map((x) => Uint8Array.of(x));

  for (let char of encodedText) {
    yield await new Promise((resolve) => setTimeout(resolve, 1000, char));
  }
}

const encodedTextStream = new ReadableStream({
  async start(controller) {
    for await (let chunk of chars()) {
      controller.enqueue(chunk);
    }

    controller.close();
  }
});


const decodedTextStream = encodedTextStream.pipeThrough(new TextDecoderStream());

const readableStreamDefaultReader = decodedTextStream.getReader();

(async function() {
```

```
    while(true) {
      const { done, value } = await readableStreamDefaultReader.read();

      if (done) {
        break;
      } else {
        console.log(value);
      }
    }
  }
})();

//
```

Text decoder streams will be most commonly used in conjunction with `fetch()`, as the response body can be processed as a `ReadableStream`. This might take the following form:

```
const response = await fetch(url);
const stream = response.body.pipeThrough(new TextDecoderStream());

for await (let decodedChunk of decodedStream) {
  console.log(decodedChunk);
}
```

BLOB AND FILE APIs

One of the major pain points of web applications has been the inability to interact with files on a user's computer. Since before 2000, the only way to deal with files was to place `<input type="file">` into a form and leave it at that. The Blob and File APIs are designed to give web developers access to files on the client computer in a secure manner that allows for better interaction with those files.

The File Type

The File API is still based around the file input field of a form but adds the ability to access the file information directly. HTML5 adds a files collection to DOM for the file input element. When one or more files are selected in the field, the files collection contains a sequence of File objects that represent each file. Each File object has several read-only properties, including:

➤ name—The file name on the local system.

➤ size—The size of the file in bytes.

➤ type—A string containing the MIME type of the file.

➤ lastModifiedDate—A string representing the last time the file was modified.

For instance, you can retrieve information about each file selected by listening for the change event and then looking at the files collection:

```
let filesList = document.getElementById("files-list");
filesList.addEventListener("change", (event) => {
  let files = event.target.files,
      I = 0,
```

```
        len = files.length;

    while (i < len) {
      const f = files[i];
      console.log('${f.name} (${f.type}, ${f.size} bytes)`);
      i++;
    }
});
```

This example simply outputs the information about each file to the console. This capability alone is a big step forward for web applications, but the File API goes further by allowing you to actually read data from the files via the `FileReader` type.

The FileReader Type

The `FileReader` type represents an asynchronous file-reading mechanism. You can think of `FileReader` as similar to `fetch`, only it is used for reading files from the file system as opposed to reading data from the server. The `FileReader` type offers several methods to read in file data:

➤ `readAsText(file, encoding)`—Reads the file as plain text and stores the text in the result property. The second argument, the encoding type, is optional.

➤ `readAsDataURL(file)`—Reads the file and stores a data URI representing the files in the result property.

➤ `readAsBinaryString(file)`—Reads the file and stores a string where each character represents a byte in the result property.

➤ `readAsArrayBuffer(file)`—Reads the file and stores an `ArrayBuffer` containing the file contents in the result property.

These various ways of reading in a file allow for maximum flexibility in dealing with the file data. For instance, you may wish to read an image as a data URI in order to display it back to the user, or you may wish to read a file as text in order to parse it.

Because the read happens asynchronously, there are several events published by each `FileReader`. The three most useful events are `progress`, `error`, and `load`, which indicate when more data is available, when an error occurred, and when the file is fully read, respectively.

The `progress` event fires roughly every 50 milliseconds and has the following information available: `lengthComputable`, `loaded`, and `total`. Additionally, the `FileReader`'s `result` property is readable during the `progress` event even though it may not contain all of the data yet.

The `error` event fires if the file cannot be read for some reason. When the `error` event fires, the error property of the `FileReader` is filled in. This object has a single property, `code`, which is an error code of 1 (file not found), 2 (security error), 3 (read was aborted), 4 (file isn't readable), or 5 (encoding error).

The `load` event fires when the file has been successfully loaded; it will not fire if the `error` event has fired. Here's an example using all three events:

```
let filesList = document.getElementById("files-list");
filesList.addEventListener("change", (event) => {
```

```
        let info = "",
            output = document.getElementById("output"),
            progress = document.getElementById("progress"),
            files = event.target.files,
            type = "default",
            reader = new FileReader();

    if (/image/.test(files[0].type)) {
      reader.readAsDataURL(files[0]);
      type = "image";
    } else {
      reader.readAsText(files[0]);
      type = "text";
    }

    reader.onerror = function() {
      output.innerHTML = "Could not read file, error code is " +
          reader.error.code;
    };

    reader.onprogress = function(event) {
      if (event.lengthComputable) {
        progress.innerHTML = `${event.loaded}/${event.total}`;
      }
    };

    reader.onload = function() {
      let html = "";

      switch(type) {
        case "image":
          html = `<img src="${reader.result}">`;
          break;
        case "text":
          html = reader.result;
          break;
      }
      output.innerHTML = html;
    };
});
```

This code reads a file from a form field and displays it on the page. If the file has a MIME type indicating it's an image, then a data URI is requested and, upon load, this data URI is inserted as an image into the page. If the file is not an image, then it is read in as a string and output as is into the page. The progress event is used to track and display the bytes of data being read, while the error event watches for any errors.

You can stop a read in progress by calling the abort() method, in which case an abort event is fired. After the firing of load, error, or abort, an event called loadend is fired. The loadend event indicates that all reading has finished for any of the three reasons.

The FileReaderSync Type

The `FileReaderSync` type, as its name suggests, is the *synchronous* version of `FileReader`. This features the same methods as `FileReader` but performs a blocking read of a file, only continuing execution after the entire file has been loaded into memory. `FileReaderSync` is only available inside of web workers, as the extremely slow process of reading an entire file would never be practical to use in the top-level execution environment.

Suppose a worker is sent a `File` object via `postMessage()`. The following code directs the worker to synchronously read the entire file into memory and send back the file's data URL:

```
// worker.js

self.omessage = (messageEvent) => {
  const syncReader = new FileReaderSync();
  console.log(syncReader);  // FileReaderSync {}

  // Blocks worker thread while file is read
  const result = syncReader.readAsDataUrl(messageEvent.data);

  // Example response for PDF file
  console.log(result);  // data:application/pdf;base64,JVBERi0xLjQK...

  // Send URL back up
  self.postMessage(result);
};
```

Blobs and Partial Reads

In some cases, you may want to read only parts of a file instead of the whole file. To that end, the `File` object has a method called `slice()`. The `slice()` method accepts two arguments: the starting byte and the number of bytes to read. This method returns an instance of `Blob`, which is actually the super type of `File`.

A "blob," short for *binary large object*, is a JavaScript wrapper for immutable binary data. `Blob`s can be created from an array containing strings, `ArrayBuffers`, `ArrayBufferViews`, or even other `Blob`s. The `Blob` constructor can optionally be provided a MIME type as part of its `options` parameter:

```
console.log(new Blob(['foo']));
// Blob {size: 3, type: ""}

console.log(new Blob(['{"a": "b"}'], { type: 'application/json' }));
// Blob {size: 10, type: "application/json"}

console.log(new Blob(['<p>Foo</p>','<p>Bar</p>'], { type: 'text/html' }));
// Blob {size: 20, type: "text/html"}
```

A `Blob` also has size and type properties, as well as the `slice()` method for further cutting down the data. You can read from a `Blob` by using a `FileReader` as well. This example reads just the first 32 bytes from a file:

```
let filesList = document.getElementById("files-list");
filesList.addEventListener("change", (event) => {
  let info = "",
    output = document.getElementById("output"),
    progress = document.getElementById("progress"),
    files = event.target.files,
    reader = new FileReader(),
    blob = blobSlice(files[0], 0, 32);
  if (blob) {
    reader.readAsText(blob);

    reader.onerror = function() {
      output.innerHTML = "Could not read file, error code is" +
                  reader.error.code;
    };
    reader.onload = function() {
      output.innerHTML = reader.result;
    };
  } else {
    console.log("Your browser doesn't support slice()");
  }
});
```

Reading just parts of a file can save time, especially when you're just looking for a specific piece of data, such as a file header.

Object URLs and Blobs

Object URLs, also sometimes called *blob URLs*, are URLs that reference data stored in a `File` or `Blob`. The advantage of object URLs is that you don't need to read the file contents into JavaScript in order to use them. Instead, you simply provide the object URL in the appropriate place. To create an object URL, use the `window.URL.createObjectURL()` method and pass in the `File` or `Blob` object. The return value of this function is a string that points to a memory address. Because the string is a URL, it can be used in the DOM. For example, the following displays an image file on the page:

```
let filesList = document.getElementById("files-list");
filesList.addEventListener("change", (event) => {
  let info = "",
    output = document.getElementById("output"),
    progress = document.getElementById("progress"),
    files = event.target.files,
    reader = new FileReader(),
    url = window.URL.createObjectURL(files[0]);
  if (url) {
    if (/image/.test(files[0].type)) {
      output.innerHTML = `<img src="${url}">`;
    } else {
      output.innerHTML = "Not an image";
    }
```

```
    } else {
      output.innerHTML = "Your browser doesn't support object URLs";
    }
  });
```

By feeding the object URL directly into an `<img>` tag, there is no need to read the data into JavaScript first. Instead, the `<img>` tag goes directly to the memory location and reads the data into the page.

Once the data is no longer needed, it's best to free up the memory associated with it. Memory cannot be freed as long as an object URL is in use. You can indicate that the object URL is no longer needed by passing it to `window.URL.revokeObjectURL()`. All object URLs are freed from memory automatically when the page is unloaded. Still, it is best to free each object URL as it is no longer needed to ensure the memory footprint of the page remains as low as possible.

Drag-and-Drop File Reading

Combining the HTML5 Drag-and-Drop API with the File API allows you to create interesting interfaces for the reading of file information. After creating a custom drop target on a page, you can drag files from the desktop and drop them onto the drop target. This fires the drop event just like dragging and dropping an image or link would. The files being dropped are available on `event` `.dataTransfer.files`, which is a list of `File` objects just like those available on a file input field.

The following example prints out information about files that are dropped on a custom drop target in the page:

```
let droptarget = document.getElementById("droptarget");
function handleEvent(event) {
  let info = "",
    output = document.getElementById("output"),
    files, i, len;
  event.preventDefault();

  if (event.type == "drop") {
    files = event.dataTransfer.files;
    i = 0;
    len = files.length;

    while (i < len) {
      info += `${files[i].name} (${files[i].type}, ${files[i].size} bytes)<br>`;
      i++;
    }

    output.innerHTML = info;
  }
}
droptarget.addEventListener("dragenter", handleEvent);
droptarget.addEventListener("dragover", handleEvent);
droptarget.addEventListener("drop", handleEvent);
```

You must cancel the default behavior of `dragenter`, `dragover`, and `drop`. During the `drop` event, the files become available on `event.dataTransfer.files`, and you can read their information at that time.

FULLSCREEN API

The Fullscreen API provides an easy way for web content to be displayed in *fullscreen mode*, offering a more immersive user experience. Fullscreen mode means that an element will be stretched to fill the entire screen, completely covering the browser and operating system. Only one element can be fullscreen at any given time.

To make an element go fullscreen, you use the `requestFullscreen()` method. This method can be called on any HTML element:

```
myDiv.requestFullscreen().catch(err => {
  console.error(`Unable to enter fullscreen mode`);
});
```

The user can exit fullscreen mode manually, or it can also be done programmatically by calling `exitFullscreen()` on the `document` object:

```
document.exitFullscreen().catch(() => {
  console.error(`Unable to exit fullscreen mode`);
});
```

To check whether the page can enter fullscreen mode, you can use the `fullscreenEnabled` property of the `document` object. To check whether the page is currently in fullscreen mode, you can use the `fullscreenElement` property of the `document` object. This property returns the currently fullscreened element or `null` if no element in this `document` is fullscreen.

```
if (document.fullscreenElement) {
  console.log('In fullscreen mode');
} else {
  console.log('Not in fullscreen mode');
}
```

You can listen for changes to the fullscreen state by using the `fullscreenchange` event:

```
document.addEventListener("fullscreenchange", ()=> {
  if (document.fullscreenElement) {
    console.log(`Entered fullscreen mode`);
  } else {
    console.log(`Exited fullscreen mode`);
  }
});
```

GEOLOCATION API

The `navigator.geolocation` property provides access to the GeoLocation API, which allows browser scripts to learn about the current device's location. This API is only available in a secure execution context (scripts that are served via HTTPS).

The API can send out requests to the host system to return the device's location to the best of its ability. Depending on the hardware and configuration of the host system, the accuracy of the results may vary. A cell phone's GPS coordinates will have extremely high accuracy, whereas an IP address will have a much lower accuracy. Per the Geolocation API specification:

Common sources of location information include Global Positioning System (GPS) and location inferred from network signals such as IP address, RFID, Wi-Fi and Bluetooth MAC addresses, and GSM/CDMA cell IDs, as well as user input.

> **NOTE** *Browsers may also make use of tools such as Google Location Services (used by Chrome and Firefox) to determine your location. You will notice that, although your device does not have a GPS radio, the coordinates your browser returns will often be extremely accurate. The browser accomplishes this by collecting the identities of all visible wireless networks in range, both Wi-Fi and cellular towers if possible. These are then checked against a database of networks whose locations are already known. In this manner, these services are able to pinpoint your device's location with exceptionally high accuracy.*

To perform a one-time capture of the browser's current location, use the `getCurrentPosition()` method. It returns a `Coordinates` object, the contents of which may or may not be complete depending on the abilities of the host system:

```
// getCurrentPosition() callback is invoked with
// Position object as only argument
let p;
navigator.geolocation.getCurrentPosition((position) => p = position);
```

The `Position` object contains a `timestamp` representing when the object's contents were obtained and a `Coordinates` object:

```
console.log(p.timestamp);   // 1525364883361
console.log(p.coords);      // Coordinates {...}
```

The `Coordinates` object contains `latitude`/`longitude` in standard degrees format, as well as the accuracy of that pair in meters. The accuracy measurement is provided by the same mechanism that assessed the device location.

```
console.log(p.coords.latitude, p.coords.longitude);  // 37.4854409, -122.2325506
console.log(p.coords.accuracy);                       // 58
```

The Coordinates object contains an `altitude` property, which is defined by the measured distance in meters above the WGS84 (World Geodetic System, 1984) ellipsoid model of Earth. The object also contains an `altitudeAccuracy` property, the accuracy of the measurement in meters. To be filled inside a `Coordinates` object, these values will be directly provided by the device (which means it will need to have access to appropriate measurement hardware, likely a GPS radio or altimeter). Many devices are incapable of measuring altitude, and so one or both of these values are frequently `null`.

```
console.log(p.coords.altitude);          // -8.800000190734863
console.log(p.coords.altitudeAccuracy);  // 200
```

The Coordinates object contains a speed property, which is defined by the measured speed of the device in meters per second. The object also contains a heading property, which is defined by the direction of travel relative to true north in degrees (0 ≤ heading < 360). To be filled inside a Coordinates object, these values will be directly provided by the device (which means it will need to have access to appropriate measurement hardware, likely an accelerometer and compass). Many devices are incapable of measuring speed and heading, so these values are frequently `null`.

> **NOTE** *Devices will not attempt to measure speed and heading using a derived vector of two location measurements. It is possible, however, to manually calculate these values by performing two consecutive measurements and deriving a direction of travel vector. Of course, depending on the accuracy of the two location measurements, the speed and heading you derive may be highly inaccurate!*

Capturing a browser's location is a best-effort operation, and there are a number of reasons the capture could fail. The `getCurrentPosition()` method accepts the failure callback as a second argument, and this method is passed a `PositionError` object. In the event of a failure, this object will contain a code property, and a message property with a short description of the error. The code property will be an integer indicating one of three possible errors:

➤ `PERMISSION_DENIED`—The browser was blocked from accessing the device's location. The first time a page attempts to use the Geolocation API, the browser will prompt the user to allow access (this occurs on a per-domain basis). If this error code is encountered, either the user has denied access to the device's location, or the Geolocation API is being accessed from a non-secure context. The message property can offer additional information.

➤ `POSITION_UNAVAILABLE`—The system was unable to return any location information. This can represent any number of possible points of failure but will be a relatively uncommon error since a networked device can usually resolve an IP address to a low-accuracy coordinate.

➤ `TIMEOUT`—The system was unable to return location information within the timeout period. Configuring the timeout period is discussed in the material that follows.

```
// Browsers will prompt the user to allow access to the Geolocation API.
// This example shows what occurs when the user denies access.
navigator.geolocation.getCurrentPosition(
  () => {},
  (e) => {
    console.log(e.code);     // 1
    console.log(e.message);  // User denied Geolocation
  }
);

// This example shows what occurs when executing in an insecure context.
navigator.geolocation.getCurrentPosition(
  () => {},
  (e) => {
```

```
            console.log(e.code);      // 1
            console.log(e.message);   // Only secure origins are allowed
        }
    );
```

Geolocation API location requests can be configured using a `PositionOptions` object, which is provided as the third argument. This object supports three properties:

➤ `enableHighAccuracy`—A Boolean indicating to the system that, when this property is `true`, the value returned should be as accurate as possible; the default value of the flag is `false`. By default, devices will usually choose to return coordinates in the quickest and most energy-efficient manner possible. This will often mean coordinates are less accurate. For example, on mobile devices, the default location lookup normally takes the form of deriving the device location from only Wi-Fi and cell networks. When `enableHighAccuracy` is `true`, it will also request that the device use the GPS radio to determine the device location, and the returned coordinates will be a hybrid result of these values. Using the GPS radio is a slower and more battery-intensive operation, so weigh the tradeoffs of using the `enableHighAccuracy` flag.

➤ `timeout`—A number indicating the maximum number of milliseconds the API call should wait before invoking the error callback with the `TIMEOUT` status; the default value is `0xFFFFFFFF` ($2^{32} - 1$). A value of 0 will skip the system call entirely and immediately invoke the `TIMEOUT` error callback.

➤ `maximumAge`—A number indicating the maximum age of the returned coordinates in milliseconds; the default value is 0. Because determining a device's location is an expensive operation, systems will often cache coordinates and return the cached value (subject to its location cache expiration policy). The system tracks how old the cached value is, and if the Geolocation API requests coordinates that must be newer than the cached value, the system will perform a fresh location lookup and return that value. A value of 0 will force the system to ignore any cached value and perform a fresh location lookup. A value of `Infinity` will prevent the system from performing a fresh lookup and only use cached values. JavaScript can determine if a cached value is returned by checking for duplicate timestamp properties inside the `Position` object.

DEVICE APIs

Modern browsers offer a suite of information about a page's execution environment, which includes browser information, operating system, hardware, and system peripherals. This information can be accessed through a collection of APIs that are found on the `window.navigator` object.

> **NOTE** *Support for these various APIs will differ by browser.*

Browser and Operating System Identification

The `navigator` and `screen` objects also offer information about the software environment in which the page is currently executing.

> **NOTE** *The properties of* `navigator` *listed in the following sections are deprecated; use caution when relying on them.*

The *navigator.oscpu* Property

The `oscpu` property can provide a string, which is usually the operating system/architecture component of the user-agent. Per the HTML Living Standard:

> *The* `oscpu` *attribute's getter must return either the empty string or a string representing the platform on which the browser is executing—for example, "Windows NT 10.0; Win64; x64," "Linux x86_64."*

For example, in Firefox on Windows 10, the `oscpu` property is reported as follows:

```
console.log(navigator.userAgent);
"Mozilla/5.0 (Windows NT 10.0; Win64; x64; rv:58.0) Gecko/20100101 Firefox/58.0"
console.log(navigator.oscpu);
"Windows NT 10.0; Win64; x64"
```

The *navigator.vendor* Property

The vendor property can provide a string, which is usually the browser vendor. The string returned is a function of the browser's navigator compatibility mode. Per the HTML Living Standard:

> `navigator.vendor` *returns either the empty string, the string "Apple Computer, Inc.," or the string "Google Inc."*

For example, in Chrome, the vendor property is reported as follows:

```
console.log(navigator.vendor);  // "Google Inc."
```

The *navigator.platform* Property

The platform property can provide a string, which is usually indicative of the operating system inside which the browser is executing. Per the HTML Living Standard:

> `navigator.platform` *must return either the empty string or a string representing the platform on which the browser is executing, e.g., "MacIntel," "Win32," "FreeBSD i386," "WebTV OS."*

For example, in Chrome, the platform property is reported as follows:

```
console.log(navigator.platform);  // "Win32"
```

The *screen.colorDepth* and *screen.pixelDepth* Properties

The colorDepth and pixelDepth properties return the same value: the number of color bits that can be represented in the display. Per the CSSOM Specification:

> *The* colorDepth *and* pixelDepth *attributes should return the number of bits allocated to colors for a pixel in the output device, excluding the alpha channel.*

For example, in Chrome, these properties are reported as follows:

```
console.log(screen.colorDepth);  // 24
console.log(screen.pixelDepth);  // 24
```

The *screen.orientation* Property

The orientation property returns a ScreenOrientation object, which contains information about the browser's screen according to the Screen Orientation API. The most interesting properties inside this object are angle, which returns the angle of the screen relative to the default, and type, which returns an orientation type:

portrait-primary

portrait-secondary

landscape-primary

landscape-secondary

For example, in Chrome on a mobile phone, screen.orientation is reported as follows:

```
// Viewed vertically
console.log(screen.orientation.type);   // portrait-primary
console.log(screen.orientation.angle);  // 0

// Rotate phone left
console.log(screen.orientation.type);   // landscape-primary
console.log(screen.orientation.angle);  // 90

// Rotate phone right
console.log(screen.orientation.type);   // landscape-secondary
console.log(screen.orientation.angle);  // 270
```

Per the specification, the initialization of these values is subject to the browser and device so it cannot be assumed that portrait-primary and 0 will always be the initial values. These are best used to assess relative transformations of the browser orientation as the device is rotated.

Connection State and the NetworkInformation API

The browser tracks the network connection state and exposes this information in two ways: connection events and the navigator.onLine property. When the device connects to a network, the browser will become aware of this fact and fire an online event on the window object. In turn, when the device loses a network connection, the browser will fire an `offline` event on the `window` object. At any time, the current browser state can be determined by inspecting the `navigator.onLine` property, which contains a Boolean indicating if the browser is connected.

```
const connectionStateChange = () => console.log(navigator.onLine);

window.addEventListener('online', connectionStateChange);
window.addEventListener('offline', connectionStateChange);

// On device connect:
// true

// On device disconnect:
// false
```

Of course, what determines a network connection is subject to the browser and system implementation. Some browsers will consider a connection to any local area network as `"online"` even though that network might not have proper Internet access.

Also exposed on the navigator object is the NetworkInformation API, which can be found under the `navigator.connection` property. This API offers a handful of read-only properties as well as an event source for attaching callbacks when connection properties change.

The following properties are available:

➤ `downlink`—An integer indicating the current bandwidth of the device in Mbps, rounded to the nearest 25 Kbps. This calculation may be derived from historical network throughput measurements or the capabilities of the connection technology.

➤ `downlinkMax`—An integer indicating the current maximum downlink bandwidth in Mbps as determined by the first network hop. Because the first network hop is not necessarily indicative of end-to-end network performance, this value should only be used as a rough upper bound.

➤ `effectiveType`—A string indicating the general connection speed and quality. The values are designated as cellular data network connections, but these are used to classify wired connections as well. The property will have one of four values:

➤ `"slow-2g"`

➤ Roundtrip time >2000 ms

➤ Downlink bandwidth < 50 Kbps

➤ `"2g"`

➤ 2000 ms > roundtrip time $\geq$ 1400 ms

➤ 70 Kbps > downlink bandwidth $\geq$ 50 Kbps

➤ `"3g"`

➤ 1400 ms > roundtrip time $\geq$ 270 ms

➤ 700 Kbps > downlink bandwidth $\geq$ 70 Kbps

> ➤ "4g"
>
>> ➤ 270 ms > roundtrip time ≥ 0 ms
>>
>> ➤ Downlink bandwidth ≥ 700 Kbps

➤ rtt—An integer indicating the current effective network request roundtrip time in milliseconds, rounded to the nearest 25 ms. This calculation may be derived from historical network throughput measurements or the capabilities of the connection technology.

➤ type—A string indicating the network connection technology. The property will have one of the following values:

> ➤ bluetooth—Indicates a Bluetooth connection.
>
> ➤ cellular—Indicates a cellular network.
>
> ➤ ethernet—Indicates a wired Ethernet connection.
>
> ➤ none—Indicates no network connection. Equivalent to navigator .onLine === false.
>
> ➤ mixed—Indicates multiple simultaneous connection types.
>
> ➤ other—Indicates a connection type that is not listed as a valid value.
>
> ➤ unknown—Indicates a connection type that cannot be determined.
>
> ➤ wifi—Indicates a Wi-Fi connection.
>
> ➤ wimax—Indicates a WiMAX connection.

➤ saveData—A Boolean indicating if the user has enabled the "reduced data mode" on his or her device.

➤ onchange—The property that will emit a change event when any connection status changes. This can be used via either navigator.connection .addEventListener('change', changeHandler) or navigator.connection .onchange = changeHandler.

Battery Status API

The browser is capable of accessing information about the device's battery and charging state. The navigator.getBattery() method returns a promise that resolves to a BatteryManager object.

```
navigator.getBattery().then((b) => console.log(b));
// BatteryManager { ... }
```

The BatteryManager offers four read-only properties that provide information about the device's battery:

➤ charging—A Boolean indicating if the device is currently plugged in and charging. If the device has no battery, returns true.

➤ chargingTime—An integer indicating the estimated number of seconds until the battery is fully charged. Returns 0 if the battery is fully charged or if the device has no battery.

➤ dischargingTime—An integer indicating the estimated number of seconds until the battery is fully depleted. Returns Infinity if the device has no battery.

➤ level—A floating point number indicating the fractional charge of the battery. Returns 0.0 to indicate a fully discharged battery, 1.0 to indicate a fully charged battery. Returns 1.0 if the device has no battery.

The API also offers four event properties that can be used to set callbacks when any of the battery properties change. This can be accomplished either by adding an event listener on the BatteryManager object or assigning the handler to the respective property:

➤ onchargingchange

➤ onchargingtimechange

➤ ondischarcingtimechange

➤ onlevelchange

```
navigator.getBattery().then((battery) => {
  // Assign callback for when the charging state changes:
  const chargingChangeHandler = () => console.log('chargingchange');
  battery.onchargingchange = chargingChangeHandler;
  // OR
  battery.addEventListener('chargingchange', chargingChangeHandler);

  // Assign callback for when the charging time changes:
  const chargingTimeChangeHandler = () => console.log('chargingtimechange');
  battery.onchargingtimechange = chargingTimeChangeHandler;
  // OR
  battery.addEventListener('chargingtimechange', chargingTimeChangeHandler);

  // Assign callback for when the discharging time changes:
  const dischargingChangeHandler = () => console.log('dischargingtimechange');
  battery.ondischargingtimechange = dischargingTimeChangeHandler;
  // OR
  battery.addEventListener('dischargingtimechange', dischargingTimeChangeHandler);

  // Assign callback for when the battery level changes:
  const levelChangeHandler = () => console.log('levelchange');
  battery.onlevelchange = levelChangeHandler;
  // OR
  battery.addEventListener('levelchange', levelChangeHandler);
});
```

Hardware

The ability of the browser to detect the system hardware is quite limited; however, a number of properties on the navigator object can provide basic information.

Processor Cores

It is possible to determine the number of logical processor cores that the browser supports via the `navigator.hardwareConcurrency` property, which contains an integer representing the number of supported cores (or 1 if a determination cannot be made). Importantly, this value indicates the maximum number of concurrent workers that the browser is capable of executing in parallel and not necessarily the number of actual cores the CPU features.

Device Memory

It is possible to determine the approximate amount of system memory on the device via the `navigator.deviceMemory` property, which contains a float representing the number of gigabytes of memory on the device rounded to the nearest power of 2: 512MB would return 0.5; 4GB would return 4.

Maximum Touch Points

It is possible to determine the maximum number of touch contacts supported on a touchscreen via the `navigator.maxTouchPoints` property, which is defined as an integer.

MEDIA ELEMENTS

HTML5 introduces two media-related elements to enable cross-browser audio and video embedding into a browser baseline without any plugins: `<audio>` and `<video>`. Both of these elements allow web developers to easily embed media files into a page, as well as provide JavaScript hooks into common functionality, allowing custom controls to be created for the media. The elements are used as follows:

```
<!-- embed a video -->
<video src="conference.mpg" id="myVideo">Video player not available.</video>
<!-- embed an audio file -->
<audio src="song.mp3" id="myAudio">Audio player not available.</audio>
```

Each of these elements requires, at a minimum, the `src` attribute indicating the media file to load. You can also specify `width` and `height` attributes to indicate the intended dimensions of the video player and a `poster` attribute that is an image URI to display while the video content is being loaded. The controls attribute, if present, indicates that the browser should display a UI enabling the user to interact directly with the media. Any content between the opening and the closing tags is considered alternate content to display if the media player is unavailable.

You may optionally specify multiple different media sources because not all browsers support all media formats. To do so, omit the `src` attribute from the element and instead include one or more `<source>` elements, as in this example:

```
<!-- embed a video -->
<video id="myVideo">
  <source src="conference.webm" type="video/webm; codecs='vp8, vorbis'">
```

```
    <source src="conference.ogv" type="video/ogg; codecs='theora, vorbis'">
    <source src="conference.mpg">
    Video player not available.
</video>
<!-- embed an audio file -->
<audio id="myAudio">
    <source src="song.ogg" type="audio/ogg">
    <source src="song.mp3" type="audio/mpeg">
    Audio player not available.
</audio>
```

It's beyond the scope of this book to discuss the various codecs used with video and audio, but suffice to say that browsers support a varying range of codecs, so multiple source files are typically required.

Properties

The `<video>` and `<audio>` elements provide robust JavaScript interfaces. There are numerous properties shared by both elements that can be evaluated to determine the current state of the media, as described in the following table.

PROPERTY NAME	DATA TYPE	DESCRIPTION
autoplay	Boolean	Gets or sets the `autoplay` flag.
buffered	TimeRanges	An object indicating the buffered time ranges that have already been downloaded.
bufferedBytes	ByteRanges	An object indicating the buffered byte ranges that have already been downloaded.
bufferingRate	Integer	The average number of bits per second received from the download.
bufferingThrottled	Boolean	Indicates if the buffering has been throttled by the browser.
controls	Boolean	Gets or sets the `controls` attribute, which displays or hides the browser's built-in controls.
currentLoop	Integer	The number of loops that the media has played.
currentSrc	String	The URL for the currently playing media.
currentTime	Float	The number of seconds that have been played.
defaultPlaybackRate	Float	Gets or sets the default playback rate. By default, this is 1.0 seconds.
duration	Float	The total number of seconds for the media.
ended	Boolean	Indicates if the media has completely played.

continues

(continued)

PROPERTY NAME	DATA TYPE	DESCRIPTION
loop	Boolean	Gets or sets whether the media should loop back to the start when finished.
muted	Boolean	Gets or sets if the media is muted.
networkState	Integer	Indicates the current state of the network connection for the media: 0 for empty, 1 for loading, 2 for loading meta data, 3 for loaded first frame, and 4 for loaded.
paused	Boolean	Indicates if the player is paused.
playbackRate	Float	Gets or sets the current playback rate. This may be affected by the user causing the media to play faster or slower, unlike defaultPlaybackRate, which remains unchanged unless the developer changes it.
played	TimeRanges	The range of times that have been played thus far.
readyState	Integer	Indicates if the media is ready to be played. Values are 0 if the data is unavailable, 1 if the current frame can be displayed, 2 if the media can begin playing, and 3 if the media can play from beginning to end.
seekable	TimeRanges	The ranges of times that are available for seeking.
seeking	Boolean	Indicates that the player is moving to a new position in the media file.
Src	String	The media file source. This can be rewritten at any time.
start	Float	Gets or sets the location in the media file, in seconds, where playing should begin.
totalBytes	Integer	The total number of bytes needed for the resource (if known).
videoHeight	Integer	Returns the height of the video (not necessarily of the element). Only for <video>.
videoWidth	Integer	Returns the width of the video (not necessarily of the element). Only for <video>.
volume	Float	Gets or sets the current volume as a value between 0.0 and 1.0.

Many of these properties can also be specified as attributes on either the <audio> or the <video> elements.

Events

In addition to the numerous properties, there are also numerous events that fire on these media elements. The events monitor all of the different properties that change because of media playback and user interaction with the player. These events are listed in the following table.

EVENT NAME	FIRES WHEN
abort	Downloading has been aborted.
canplay	Playback can begin; `readyState` is 2.
canplaythrough	Playback can proceed and should be uninterrupted; `readyState` is 3.
canshowcurrentframe	The current frame has been downloaded; `readyState` is 1.
dataunavailable	Playback can't happen because there's no data; `readyState` is 0.
durationchange	The duration property value has changed.
emptied	The network connection has been closed.
empty	An error occurs that prevents the media download.
ended	The media has played completely through and is stopped.
error	A network error occurred during download.
load	All of the media has been loaded. This event is considered deprecated; use `canplaythrough` instead.
loadeddata	The first frame for the media has been loaded.
loadedmetadata	The meta data for the media has been loaded.
loadstart	Downloading has begun.
pause	Playback has been paused.
play	The media has been requested to start playing.
playing	The media has actually started playing.
progress	Downloading is in progress.
ratechange	The speed at which the media is playing has changed.
seeked	Seeking has ended.
seeking	Playback is being moved to a new position.
stalled	The browser is trying to download, but no data is being received.
timeupdate	The `currentTime` is updated in an irregular or unexpected way.

continues

(continued)

EVENT NAME	FIRES WHEN
volumechange	The volume property value or muted property value has changed.
waiting	Playback is paused to download more data.

These events are designed to be as specific as possible to enable web developers to create custom audio/video players using little more than HTML and JavaScript (as opposed to creating a new Flash movie).

Custom Media Players

You can manually control the playback of a media file, using the play() and pause() methods that are available on both <audio> and <video>. Combining the properties, events, and these methods makes it easy to create a custom media player, as shown in this example:

```
<div class="mediaplayer">
  <div class="video">
    <video id="player" src="movie.mov" poster="mymovie.jpg"
           width="300" height="200">
      Video player not available.
    </video>
  </div>
  <div class="controls">
    <input type="button" value="Play" id="video-btn">
    <span id="curtime">0</span>/<span id="duration">0</span>
  </div>
</div>
```

This basic HTML can then be brought to life by using JavaScript to create a simple video player, as shown here:

```
// get references to the elements
let player = document.getElementById("player"),
  btn = document.getElementById("video-btn"),
  curtime = document.getElementById("curtime"),
  duration = document.getElementById("duration");
// update the duration
duration.innerHTML = player.duration;

// attach event handler to button
btn.addEventListener( "click", (event) => {
  if (player.paused) {
    player.play();
    btn.value = "Pause";
  } else {
    player.pause();
    btn.value = "Play";
  }
```

```
      });

      // update the current time periodically
      setInterval(() => {
        curtime.innerHTML = player.currentTime;
      }, 250);
```

The JavaScript code here simply attaches an event handler to the button that either pauses or plays the video, depending on its current state. Then, an event handler is set for the `<video>` element's `load` event so that the duration can be displayed. Last, a repeating timer is set to update the current time display. You can extend the behavior of this custom video player by listening for more events and making use of more properties. The exact same code can also be used with the `<audio>` element to create a custom audio player.

Codec Support Detection

As mentioned previously, not all browsers support all codecs for `<video>` and `<audio>`, which frequently means you must provide more than one media source. There is also a JavaScript API for determining if a given format and codec is supported by the browser. Both media elements have a method called `canPlayType()`, which accepts a format/codec string and returns a string value of `"probably"`, `"maybe"`, or `""` (empty string). The empty string is a false value, which means you can still use `canPlayType()` in an `if` statement like this:

```
      if (audio.canPlayType("audio/mpeg")) {
        // do something
      }
```

Both `"probably"` and `"maybe"` are truthy values and so they get coerced to `true` within the context of an `if` statement.

When just a MIME type is provided to `canPlayType()`, the most likely return values are `"maybe"` and the empty string because a file is really just a container for audio or video data; it is the encoding that really determines if the file can be played. When both a MIME type and a codec are specified, you increase the likelihood of getting `"probably"` as the return value. Some examples:

```
      let audio = document.getElementById("audio-player");
      // most likely "maybe"
      if (audio.canPlayType("audio/mpeg")) {
        // do something
      }
      // could be "probably"
      if (audio.canPlayType("audio/ogg; codecs=\"vorbis\"")) {
        // do something
      }
```

Note that the codecs list must always be enclosed in quotes to work properly. You can also detect video formats using `canPlayType()` on any video element.

The Audio Type

The `<audio>` element also has a native JavaScript constructor called Audio to allow the playing of audio at any point in time. The Audio type is similar to Image in that it is the equivalent of a DOM element but doesn't require insertion into the document to work. Just create a new instance and pass in the audio source file:

```
let audio = new Audio("sound.mp3");
EventUtil.addHandler(audio, "canplaythrough", function(event) {
  audio.play();
});
```

Creating a new instance of `Audio` begins the process of downloading the specified file. Once it's ready, you can call `play()` to start playing the audio.

NOTIFICATIONS API

The Notifications API, as its name suggests, is used to display notifications to the user. In many ways, notifications are similar to `alert()` dialog boxes: both use a JavaScript API to trigger browser behavior outside of the page itself, and both allow the page to handle the various ways in which users interact with the dialog boxes or notification tiles. Notifications, however, offer a far greater degree of customizability.

The Notifications API is especially useful in the context of service workers. It allows a progressive web application (PWA) to behave more like a native app by triggering notifications to show even when a browser page is not active.

Notification Permissions

The Notification API has the potential for abuse, so it enforces two security features by default:

➤ Notifications can be triggered only by code executing in a secure context.

➤ Notifications must be explicitly allowed by the user on a per-origin basis.

The user grants notification permission to an origin inside a browser dialog box. Unless the user declines to explicitly allow or deny permissions, this permission request can only happen a single time per domain: the browser will remember the user's choice, and if denied there is no redress.

The page can ask for notification permission using the `Notification` global object. This object features a `requestPemission()` method that returns a promise, which resolves when the user takes action on the permission dialog box.

```
Notification.requestPermission()
    .then((permission) => {
      console.log('User responded to permission request:', permission);
    });
```

A value of `granted` means the user explicitly granted permission to show notifications. Any other value indicates that attempts to show a notification will silently fail. If a user denies permission, the value will be denied. There is no programmatic redress for this, as it is not possible to re-trigger the permissions prompt.

Showing and Hiding Notification

The Notification constructor is used to create and show notifications. The simplest form of a notification is with only a title string that is passed as the first required parameter to the constructor. When the constructor is called in this way, the notification will display immediately:

```
new Notification('Title text!');
```

Notifications are highly customizable with the options parameter. Settings such as the notification body, images, and vibration are all controllable via this object:

```
new Notification('Title text!', {
  body: 'Body text!',
  image: 'path/to/image.png',
  vibrate: true
});
```

The Notification object returned from the constructor can be used to close an active notification using a close() method. The following example opens a notification and then closes it after 1000 milliseconds:

```
const n = new Notification('I will close in 1000ms');
setTimeout(() => n.close(), 1000);
```

Notification Lifecycle Callbacks

Notifications aren't always just for displaying text strings; they're also designed to be interactive. The Notification API offers four lifecycle hooks for attaching callbacks:

➤ onshow is triggered when the notification is displayed.

➤ onclick is triggered when the notification is clicked.

➤ onclose is triggered when the notification is dismissed or closed via close().

➤ onerror is triggered when an error occurs that prevents the notification from being displayed.

The following notification logs a message upon each lifecycle event:

```
const n = new Notification('foo');

n.onshow = () => console.log('Notification was shown!');
n.onclick = () => console.log('Notification was clicked!');
n.onclose = () => console.log('Notification was closed!');
n.onerror = () => console.log('Notification experienced an error!');
```

PAGE VISIBILITY API

A major pain point for web developers is knowing when users are actually interacting with the page. If a page is minimized or hidden behind another tab, it may not make sense to continue functionality such as polling the server for updates or performing animations. The Page Visibility API aims to give developers information about whether or not the page is visible to the user.

The API itself is very simple, consisting of three parts:

➤ `document.visibilityState`—A string indicating the current page state:

➤ `visible`—The page is currently visible to the user.

➤ `hidden`—The page is currently hidden or minimized.

➤ `prerender`—The page is being prerendered and is not yet visible to the user.

➤ `visibilitychange` event—This event fires when a document changes from hidden to visible, or vice versa.

➤ `document.hidden`—A Boolean value indicating if the page is hidden from view. This may mean the page is in a background tab or that the browser is minimized. This value is supported for backwards compatibility, you should use `document.visibilityState` to assess if the page is visible or not.

To be notified when the page changes from visible to hidden or hidden to visible, you can listen for the `visibilitychange` event.

STREAMS API

The Streams API is the answer to a simple but fundamental question: *How can a web application consume information in sequential chunks rather than in bulk?* This capability is massively useful in two main ways:

➤ **A block of data may not be available all at once.** A perfect example of this is a response to a network request. Network payloads are delivered as a sequence of packets, and stream processing can allow an application to use network-delivered data as it becomes available rather than waiting for the full payload to finish loading.

➤ **A block of data can be processed in small portions.** Video processing, data decompression, image decoding, and JSON parsing are all examples of computation that is localized to a portion of a data block and does not require it to be in memory all at once.

Chapter 21, "Network Requests and Remote Resources," covers how the Streams API is involved with `fetch()`, but the Streams API is totally generalizable. JavaScript libraries that implement Observables share many fundamental concepts with streams.

> **NOTE** *Although the Fetch API is well-supported by major browsers, support for the Streams API lags behind considerably.*

Introduction to Streams

When thinking about streams, imagining the data as a liquid flowing through pipes is an apt mental framework. JavaScript streams borrow heavily from the plumbing lexicon due to their substantial conceptual overlap. Per the Streams specification, "These APIs have been designed to efficiently map to low-level I/O primitives, including specializations for byte streams where appropriate." Two common tasks that the Stream API directly addresses are handling network requests and reading/writing to disk.

The Streams API features three types of streams:

➤ **Readable streams** are streams from which chunks can be read via a public interface. Data enters the stream internally from an *underlying source* and is processed by a *consumer*.

➤ **Writable streams** are streams to which chunks can be written via a public interface. A *producer* writes data into the stream, and that data is passed internally in an *underlying sink*.

➤ **Transform streams** are made up of two streams: a writable stream to accept input data (the *writable side*), and a readable stream to emit output data (the *readable side*). In between these two streams is the *transformer*, which can be used to inspect and modify the stream data as necessary.

Chunks, Internal Queues, and Backpressure

The fundamental unit in streams is the *chunk*. A chunk can be of any data type, but frequently it will take the form of a typed array. Each chunk is a discrete segment of the stream that can be handled in its entirety. Importantly, chunks do *not* have a fixed size or arrive at fixed intervals. In an *ideal* stream, chunks will generally be *approximately* the same size and arrive at *approximately* regular intervals, but any good stream implementation should be prepared to handle edge cases.

For all types of streams, there is a shared concept of an entrance and exit to the stream. There will sometimes be a mismatch between the rate of data entering and exiting the stream. This stream balance can take one of three forms:

➤ **The exit of the stream can process data faster than the data is provided at the entrance.** The stream exit will often be idle (which may indicate potential inefficiencies at the stream entrance), but there is little wasted memory or computation, so this stream imbalance is acceptable.

➤ **The stream entrance and exit are in equilibrium.** This balance is ideal.

➤ **The entrance of the stream can provide data faster than the exit can process it.** This stream imbalance is inherently problematic. There will necessarily be a backlog of data somewhere, and streams must handle this accordingly.

Stream imbalance is a common problem, but streams are tooled to address it. All streams maintain an *internal queue* of chunks that have entered the stream but not yet exited. For a stream in equilibrium, the internal queue will consistently have zero or a small number of enqueued chunks because the stream exit is dequeuing chunks approximately as fast as they can be enqueued. The memory footprint of such a stream's internal queue will remain relatively small.

When chunks are enqueued faster than they can be dequeued, the size of the internal queue will grow. The stream cannot allow its internal queue to grow indefinitely, so it uses *backpressure* to signal the stream entrance to stop sending data until the queue size returns below a predetermined threshold. This threshold is governed by a *queueing strategy* that defines the *high water mark*, the maximum memory footprint of the internal queue.

Readable Streams

Readable streams are a wrapper for an underlying source of data. This underlying source is able to feed its data into the stream and allow that data to be read from the stream's public interface.

Using the ReadableStreamDefaultController

Consider the following generator, which produces an incremented integer every 1000 milliseconds:

```
async function* ints() {
  // yield an incremented integer every 1000ms
  for (let i = 0; i < 5; ++i) {
    yield await new Promise((resolve) => setTimeout(resolve, 1000, i));
  }
}
```

These values can be passed into a readable stream via its controller. The simplest way to access a controller is by creating a new instance of a `ReadableStream`, defining a `start()` method inside the constructor's `underlyingSource` parameter, and using the controller parameter passed to that method. By default, the controller parameter is an instance of `ReadableStreamDefaultController`:

```
const readableStream = new ReadableStream({
  start(controller) {
    console.log(controller);  // ReadableStreamDefaultController {}
  }
});
```

Use the `enqueue()` method to pass values into the controller. Once all the values have been passed, the stream is closed using `close()`:

```
async function* ints() {
  // yield an incremented integer every 1000ms
  for (let i = 0; i < 5; ++i) {
    yield await new Promise((resolve) => setTimeout(resolve, 1000, i));
  }
}

const readableStream = new ReadableStream({
  async start(controller) {
    for await (let chunk of ints()) {
```

```
        controller.enqueue(chunk);
      }

      controller.close();
    }
  });
```

Using the ReadableStreamDefaultReader

This example so far successfully enqueues five values in the stream, but there is nothing reading them out of that queue. To do so, a `ReadableStreamDefaultReader` instance can be acquired from the stream with `getReader()`. This will obtain a lock on the stream, ensuring only this reader can read values from that stream:

```
async function* ints() {
  // yield an incremented integer every 1000ms
  for (let i = 0; i < 5; ++i) {
    yield await new Promise((resolve) => setTimeout(resolve, 1000, i));
  }
}

const readableStream = new ReadableStream({
  async start(controller) {
    for await (let chunk of ints()) {
      controller.enqueue(chunk);
    }

    controller.close();
  }
});

console.log(readableStream.locked);   // false
const readableStreamDefaultReader = readableStream.getReader();
console.log(readableStream.locked);   // true
```

A consumer can get values from this reader instance using its `read()` method:

```
async function* ints() {
  // yield an incremented integer every 1000ms
  for (let i = 0; i < 5; ++i) {
    yield await new Promise((resolve) => setTimeout(resolve, 1000, i));
  }
}

const readableStream = new ReadableStream({
  async start(controller) {
    for await (let chunk of ints()) {
      controller.enqueue(chunk);
    }

    controller.close();
  }
```

```
});

console.log(readableStream.locked);  // false
const readableStreamDefaultReader = readableStream.getReader();
console.log(readableStream.locked);  // true

// Consumer
(async function() {
  while(true) {
    const { done, value } = await readableStreamDefaultReader.read();

    if (done) {
      break;
    } else {
      console.log(value);
    }
  }
})();

// 0
// 1
// 2
// 3
// 4
```

Writable Streams

Writable streams are a wrapper for an underlying sink for data. This underlying sink handles data from the stream's public interface.

Creating a WriteableStream

Consider the following generator, which produces an incremented integer every 1000 milliseconds:

```
async function* ints() {
  // yield an incremented integer every 1000ms
  for (let i = 0; i < 5; ++i) {
    yield await new Promise((resolve) => setTimeout(resolve, 1000, i));
  }
}
```

These values can be written to a writable stream via its public interface. When the public `write()` method is invoked, the `write()` method defined on the `underlyingSink` object passed to the constructor is also called:

```
const readableStream = new ReadableStream({
  write(value) {
    console.log(value);
  }
});
```

Using a WritableStreamDefaultWriter

To write values to this stream, a `WritableStreamDefaultWriter` instance can be acquired from the stream with `getWriter()`. This will obtain a lock on the stream, ensuring only this writer can write values to that stream:

```
async function* ints() {
  // yield an incremented integer every 1000ms
  for (let i = 0; i < 5; ++i) {
    yield await new Promise((resolve) => setTimeout(resolve, 1000, i));
  }
}

const writableStream = new WritableStream({
  write(value) {
    console.log(value);
  }
});

console.log(writableStream.locked);   // false
const writableStreamDefaultWriter = writableStream.getWriter();
console.log(writableStream.locked);   // true
```

Before writing values to the stream, the producer must ensure the writer is capable of accepting values. `WritableStreamDefaultWriter.ready` returns a promise that resolves when the writer is ready for writing values to the stream. Following this, values can be passed with `write()` until the data stream is complete, at which point the stream can be terminated with `close()`:

```
async function* ints() {
  // yield an incremented integer every 1000ms
  for (let i = 0; i < 5; ++i) {
    yield await new Promise((resolve) => setTimeout(resolve, 1000, i));
  }
}

const writableStream = new WritableStream({
  write(value) {
    console.log(value);
  }
});

console.log(writableStream.locked);   // false
const writableStreamDefaultWriter = writableStream.getWriter();
console.log(writableStream.locked);   // true


// Producer
(async function() {
  for await (let chunk of ints()) {
    await writableStreamDefaultWriter.ready;
    writableStreamDefaultWriter.write(chunk);
  }

  writableStreamDefaultWriter.close();
})();
```

Transform Streams

Transform streams combine both a readable stream and a writeable stream. In between the two streams is the `transform()` method, which is the intermediate point at which the chunk transformation occurs.

Consider the following generator, which produces an incremented integer every 1000 milliseconds:

```
async function* ints() {
  // yield an incremented integer every 1000ms
  for (let i = 0; i < 5; ++i) {
    yield await new Promise((resolve) => setTimeout(resolve, 1000, i));
  }
}
```

A `TransformStream`, which doubles the values emitted from this generator, can be defined as follows:

```
async function* ints() {
  // yield an incremented integer every 1000ms
  for (let i = 0; i < 5; ++i) {
    yield await new Promise((resolve) => setTimeout(resolve, 1000, i));
  }
}

const { writable, readable } = new TransformStream({
  transform(chunk, controller) {
    controller.enqueue(chunk * 2);
  }
});
```

Passing data into and pulling data out of the transform stream's component streams can be accomplished identically to the previous readable stream and writable stream sections of this chapter:

```
async function* ints() {
  // yield an incremented integer every 1000ms
  for (let i = 0; i < 5; ++i) {
    yield await new Promise((resolve) => setTimeout(resolve, 1000, i));
  }
}

const { writable, readable } = new TransformStream({
  transform(chunk, controller) {
    controller.enqueue(chunk * 2);
  }
});

const readableStreamDefaultReader = readable.getReader();
const writableStreamDefaultWriter = writable.getWriter();

// Consumer
(async function() {
  while (true) {
```

```
          const { done, value } = await readableStreamDefaultReader.read();

        if (done) {
          break;
        } else {
          console.log(value);
        }
      }
    })();

    // Producer
    (async function() {
      for await (let chunk of ints()) {
        await writableStreamDefaultWriter.ready;
        writableStreamDefaultWriter.write(chunk);
      }

      writableStreamDefaultWriter.close();
    })();
```

Piping Streams

Streams can be piped into one another to form a chain. One common form of this is to pipe a
ReadableStream into a TransformStream using the pipeThrough() method. Internally, the initial
ReadableStream passes its values into the TransformStream's internal WritableStream, the stream
performs the transformation, and the transformed values emerge from the new ReadableStream
endpoint. Consider the following example where a ReadableStream of integers is passed through a
TransformStream that doubles each value:

```
async function* ints() {
  // yield an incremented integer every 1000ms
  for (let i = 0; i < 5; ++i) {
    yield await new Promise((resolve) => setTimeout(resolve, 1000, i));
  }
}

const integerStream = new ReadableStream({
  async start(controller) {
    for await (let chunk of ints()) {
      controller.enqueue(chunk);
    }

    controller.close();
  }
});

const doublingStream = new TransformStream({
  transform(chunk, controller) {
    controller.enqueue(chunk * 2);
  }
});

// Perform stream piping
```

```
const pipedStream = integerStream.pipeThrough(doublingStream);

// Acquire reader on output of piped streams
const pipedStreamDefaultReader = pipedStream.getReader();

// Consumer
(async function() {
  while(true) {
    const { done, value } = await pipedStreamDefaultReader.read();

    if (done) {
      break;
    } else {
      console.log(value);
    }
  }
})();

// 0
// 2
// 4
// 6
// 8
```

It's also possible to pipe a `ReadableStream` to a `WritableStream` using the `pipeTo()` method. This behaves in a similar fashion to `pipeThrough()`:

```
async function* ints() {
  // yield an incremented integer every 1000ms
  for (let i = 0; i < 5; ++i) {
    yield await new Promise((resolve) => setTimeout(resolve, 1000, i));
  }
}

const integerStream = new ReadableStream({
  async start(controller) {
    for await (let chunk of ints()) {
      controller.enqueue(chunk);
    }

    controller.close();
  }
});

const writableStream = new WritableStream({
  write(value) {
    console.log(value);
  }
});

const pipedStream = integerStream.pipeTo(writableStream);

// 0
// 1
// 2
// 3
// 4
```

Notice here that the piping operation is implicitly acquiring a reader from the `ReadableStream` and feeding the produced values into the `WritableStream`.

URL APIs

URL APIs provide a convenient way to create, manipulate, and parse URLs in JavaScript. Prior to these APIs, developers needing to create a URL from its components (e.g., protocol, host, path) or partially modify an existing URL (e.g., update a query param) were forced to messily cobble together regular expressions and string manipulation. Because URL APIs natively understand the URL format, they can expose a collection of properties and methods that make managing URLs effortless.

The URL Object

The `URL()` constructor is used to create a new `URL` object representing a given URL. It accepts two arguments:

➤ `url`—The URL to be represented as a string.

➤ `base` (optional)—A base URL as a string or another URL object, used to resolve relative URLs.

Here's a simple example of creating a URL object:

```
const baseURL = new URL('https://example.com/base/path/');
const relativeURL = new URL('relative/path', baseURL);

console.log(relativeURL.toString());
// https://example.com/base/path/relative/path
```

The `URL` object provides several properties to read and modify different components of a URL:

➤ `href`—The full URL as a string. You can also set a new URL using this property.

➤ `protocol`—The protocol scheme (e.g., `"http:"` or `"https:"`). Include the trailing colon when setting a new protocol.

➤ `username`—The username part of the URL, if present.

➤ `password`—The password part of the URL, if present.

➤ `host`—The combination of the hostname and port, if any (e.g., `"example.com:8080"`).

➤ `hostname`—The domain name or IP address (e.g., `"example.com"`).

➤ `port`—The port number, if present.

➤ `pathname`—The path of the URL (e.g., `"/path/page"`).

➤ `search`—The query string, including the leading `"?"` character.

➤ `hash`—The fragment identifier, including the leading `"#"` character.

➤ `searchParams`—A read-only `URLSearchParams` object that can be used to manipulate the query string.

The following example demonstrates both reading and writing URL properties:

```
// Create a new URL object
const url = new URL(
  "https:// example.com:8080/path/page?q1=val1&q2=val2#fragment");

console.log(url.href);  // (same as url.toString())
// "https://example.com:8080/path/page?q1=val1&q2=val2#fragment"

console.log(url.protocol);  // "https:"
console.log(url.host);      // "example.com:8080"
console.log(url.hostname);  // "example.com"
console.log(url.port);      // "8080"
console.log(url.pathname);  // "/path/page "
console.log(url.search);    // "?q1=val1&q2=val2"
console.log(url.hash);      // "#fragment"

// Manipulate properties
url.host = "newdomain.com:8081";
url.pathname = "/new/path/page";

console.log(url.href);
// "http:// newdomain.com:8081/new/path/page?q1=val1&q2=val2#fragment"
```

The URLSearchParams Object

The URLSearchParams object offers a collection of utility methods which allow you to inspect and modify query parameters using a standardized API. There are two ways developers typically use this type:

➤ A URL instance includes a URLSearchParams object via the searchParams property. Modifying this object will also modify the host URL object.

➤ A standalone URLSearchParams instance can be created with new URLSearchParams() and passing a query string to the constructor.

URLSearchParams has the following methods:

➤ append(name, value) —Appends a new query parameter with the specified name and value.

➤ delete(name) —Removes all query parameters with the specified name.

➤ get(name) —Returns the first value associated with the specified name, or null if the parameter is not found.

➤ getAll(name) —Returns an array of all values associated with the specified name, or an empty array if the parameter is not found.

➤ has(name) —Returns true if there is at least one query parameter with the specified name, or false otherwise.

➤ set(name, value) —Sets or updates the value of a query parameter with the specified name. If the parameter does not exist, it is added.

➤ sort() —Sorts all query parameters by name.

These are demonstrated here:

```
let qs = "?q=javascript&num=10";

let searchParams = new URLSearchParams(qs);

console.log(searchParams.toString());  // "q=javascript&num=10"
searchParams.has("num");               // true
searchParams.get("num");               // 10

searchParams.set("page", "3");
console.log(searchParams.toString());  // "q=javascript&num=10&page=3"

searchParams.delete("q");
console.log(searchParams.toString());  // "num=10&page=3"
```

URLSearchParams also can be iterated:

```
let qs = "?q=javascript&num=10";

let searchParams = new URLSearchParams(qs);

for (let param of searchParams) {
  console.log(param);
}
// ["q", "javascript"]
// ["num", "10"]
```

TIMING APIs

Page performance is always an area of concern for web developers. The Performance interface changes that by exposing internal browser metrics through a JavaScript API, allowing developers to directly access this information and do as they please with it. This interface is available through the `window.performance` object. All metrics related to the page, both those already defined and those in the future, exist on this object.

The performance interface is composed of several APIs; all except the Paint Timing API have two specification levels:

➤ High Resolution Time API

➤ Performance Timeline API

➤ Navigation Timing API

➤ User Timing API

➤ Resource Timing API

➤ Paint Timing API

> **NOTE** *Browsers will generally support the deprecated version 1 and the replacement version 2. This section focuses on the Level 2 specification where applicable.*

High Resolution Time API

The `Date.now()` method is only useful for datetime operations, which do not require precision time-keeping. In the following example, a timestamp is captured before and after `foo()` is invoked:

```
const t0 = Date.now();
foo();
const t1 = Date.now();

const duration = t1 - t0;

console.log(duration);
```

Consider the following scenarios where duration has an unexpected value:

➤ **duration is 0.** `Date.now()` only has millisecond precision, and both timestamps will capture the same value if `foo()` executes quickly enough.

➤ **duration is negative or enormous.** If the system clock is adjusted backwards or forwards while `foo()` executes (such as during daylight saving time), the captured timestamps will not account for this and the difference will incorporate the adjustment.

For these reasons, a different time measurement API must be used to precisely and accurately measure the passage of time. To address these needs, the High Resolution Time API defines `window.performance.now()`, which returns a floating point number with up to microsecond precision. As a result, it is much more unlikely to sequentially capture timestamps and have them be identical. This method also guarantees monotonically increasing timestamps.

```
const t0 = performance.now();
const t1 = performance.now();

console.log(t0);        // 1768.625000026077
console.log(t1);        // 1768.6300000059418

const duration = t1 - t0;

console.log(duration);  // 0.004999979864805937
```

The `performance.now()` timer is a *relative* measurement. It begins counting at 0 when its execution context is spawned: for example, when a page is opened or when a worker is created. Because the timer initialization will be offset between contexts, direct comparison of `performance.now()` values across execution contexts is not possible without a shared reference point. The `performance.timeOrigin` property returns the global system clock's value when the timer initialization occurred.

```
const relativeTimestamp = performance.now();

const absoluteTimestamp = performance.timeOrigin + relativeTimestamp;

console.log(relativeTimestamp);   // 244.43500000052154
console.log(absoluteTimestamp);   // 1561926208892.4001
```

> **NOTE** *Security exploits such as Spectre can perform cache inference attacks by using* performance.now() *to measure the latency delta between the L1 cache and main memory. To address this vulnerability, all major browsers have either reduced the precision of* performance.now() *or incorporated some randomness into the timestamp. The WebKit blog has an excellent article on this topic at* https://webkit.org/blog/8048/what-spectre-and-meltdown-mean-for-webkit.

Performance Timeline API

The Performance Timeline API extends the Performance interface with a suite of tools intended to measure client-side latency. Performance measurements will almost always take the form of calculating the difference between an end and a start time. These start and end times are recorded as DOMHighResTimeStamp values, and the objects that wrap these timestamps are PerformanceEntry instances.

The browser automatically records a variety of different PerformanceEntry objects, and it is also possible to record your own with performance.mark(). All recorded entries recorded in an execution context can be accessed using performance.getEntires():

```
console.log(performance.getEntries());

// [PerformanceNavigationTiming, PerformanceResourceTiming, ... ]
```

This collection represents the browser's *performance timeline*. Every PerformanceEntry object features a name, entryType, startTime, and duration property:

```
const entry = performance.getEntries()[0];

console.log(entry.name);        // "https://foo.com"
console.log(entry.entryType);   // navigation
console.log(entry.startTime);   // 0
console.log(entry.duration);    // 182.36500001512468
```

However, PerformanceEntry is effectively an abstract base class, as recorded entries will always inherit from PerformanceEntry but ultimately exist as one of the following classes:

➤   PerformanceMark

➤   PerformanceMeasure

➤   PerformanceFrameTiming

➤ PerformanceNavigationTiming

➤ PerformanceResourceTiming

➤ PerformancePaintTiming

Each of these types adds a *substantial* number of properties that describe metadata involving what the entry represents. The `name` and `entryType` property for an instance will differ based on its type.

User Timing API

The User Timing API allows you to record and analyze custom performance entries. Recording a custom performance entry is accomplished with `performance.mark()`:

```
performance.mark('foo');

console.log(performance.getEntriesByType('mark')[0]);
// PerformanceMark {
//    name: "foo",
//    entryType: "mark",
//    startTime: 269.8800000362098,
//    duration: 0
// }
```

Creating two performance entries on either side of the computation allows you to calculate the time delta. The newest marks are pushed onto the beginning of the array returned from `getEntriesByType()`:

```
performance.mark('foo');
for (let i = 0; i < 1E6; ++i) {}
performance.mark('bar');

const [endMark, startMark] = performance.getEntriesByType('mark');
console.log(startMark.startTime - endMark.startTime);  // 1.3299999991431832
```

It's also possible to generate a `PerformanceMeasure` entry that corresponds to the duration of time between two marks identified via their `name`. This is accomplished with `performance.measure()`:

```
performance.mark('foo');
for (let i = 0; i < 1E6; ++i) {}
performance.mark('bar');

performance.measure('baz', 'foo', 'bar');

const [differenceMark] = performance.getEntriesByType('measure');

console.log(differenceMark);
// PerformanceMeasure {
//    name: "baz",
//    entryType: "measure",
//    startTime: 298.9800000214018,
//    duration: 1.349999976810068
// }
```

Navigation Timing API

The Navigation Timing API offers high-precision timestamps for metrics covering how quickly the current page loaded. The browser automatically records a `PerformanceNavigationTiming` entry when a navigation event occurs. This object captures a broad range of timestamps describing how and when the page loaded.

The following example calculates the amount of time between the `loadEventStart` and `loadEventEnd` timestamps:

```
const [performanceNavigationTimingEntry] = performance.getEntriesByType(
    'navigation');

console.log(performanceNavigationTimingEntry);
// PerformanceNavigationTiming {
//   connectEnd: 2.259999979287386
//   connectStart: 2.259999979287386
//   decodedBodySize: 122314
//   domComplete: 631.9899999652989
//   ...
// }


console.log(performanceNavigationTimingEntry.loadEventEnd -
            performanceNavigationTimingEntry.loadEventStart);
// 0.805000017862767
```

Resource Timing API

The Resource Timing API offers high-precision timestamps for metrics covering how quickly resources requested for the current page loaded. The browser automatically records a `PerformanceResourceTiming` entry when an asset is loaded. This object captures a broad range of timestamps describing how quickly that resource loaded.

The following example calculates the amount of time it took to load a specific resource:

```
const performanceResourceTimingEntry = performance.getEntriesByType('resource')[0];

console.log(performanceResourceTimingEntry);// PerformanceResourceTiming {
//   connectEnd: 138.11499997973442
//   connectStart: 138.11499997973442
//   decodedBodySize: 33808
//   domainLookupEnd: 138.11499997973442
//   domainLookupStart: 138.11499997973442
//   ...
// }

console.log(performanceResourceTimingEntry.responseEnd -
            performanceResourceTimingEntry.requestStart);
// 493.9600000507198
```

Using the difference between various times can give you a good idea about how a page is being loaded into the browser and where the potential bottlenecks are hiding.

WEB COMPONENTS

The term "web components" refers to a handful of tools designed to enhance DOM behavior: shadow DOM, custom elements, and HTML templates. This collection of browser APIs is particularly messy:

➤ There is no single "Web Components" specification: each web component is defined in a different specification.

➤ Several web components, such as shadow DOM and custom elements, have undergone backwards-incompatible versioning.

➤ Adoption across browser vendors is extremely inconsistent.

Because of these issues, adopting web components often demands a web component library, such as Polymer (`www.polymer-project.org`), to polyfill and emulate missing web components in the browser.

> **NOTE** *This chapter covers only the latest versions of web components.*

HTML Templates

Before web components, there wasn't a particularly good way of writing HTML that would allow the browser to build a DOM subtree from parsed HTML but decline to render that subtree until instructed to do so. One workaround was to use `innerHTML` to convert a markup string into DOM elements, but this strategy has serious security implications. Another workaround was to construct each element using `document.createElement()` and progressively attach them to an orphaned root node (not attached to the DOM), but doing so is quite laborious and circumnavigates using markup at all.

Instead, it would be far better to write special markup in the page that the browser automatically parses into a DOM subtree but skips rendering. This is the core idea of HTML templates, which use the `<template>` tag for precisely this purpose. A simple example of an HTML template is as follows:

```
<template id="foo">
  <p>I'm inside a template!</p>
</template>
```

Using a DocumentFragment

When rendered inside a browser, you will not see this text render on the page. Because the `<template>` content is not considered part of the active document, DOM matching methods such as `document.querySelector()` will be unable to find the `<p>` tag. This is because it exists inside a new Node subclass added as part of HTML templates: the `DocumentFragment`.

The `DocumentFragment` inside a `<template>` is visible when inspecting inside the browser:

```
<template id="foo">
  #document-fragment
    <p>I'm inside a template!</p>
</template>
```

A reference to this `DocumentFragment` can be retrieved via the content property of the `<template>` element:

```
console.log(document.querySelector('#foo').content);  // #document-fragment
```

The `DocumentFragment` behaves as a minimal document object for that subtree. For example, DOM matching methods on a `DocumentFragment` *can* find nodes in its subtree:

```
const fragment = document.querySelector('#foo').content;

console.log(document.querySelector('p'));  // null
console.log(fragment.querySelector('p'));  // <p>...<p>
```

A `DocumentFragment` is also incredibly useful for adding HTML in bulk. Consider a scenario where one wishes to add multiple children to an HTML element as efficiently as possible. Using consecutive `document.appendChild()` calls for each child is painstaking and can potentially incur multiple reflows. Using a `DocumentFragment` allows for you to batch these child additions, guaranteeing at most a single reflow:

```
// Start state:
// <div id="foo"></div>
//
// Desired end state:
// <div id="foo">
//     <p></p>
//     <p></p>
//     <p></p>
// </div>

// Also can use document.createDocumentFragment()
const fragment = new DocumentFragment();

const foo = document.querySelector('#foo');

// Adding children to a DocumentFragment incurs no reflow
fragment.appendChild(document.createElement('p'));
fragment.appendChild(document.createElement('p'));
fragment.appendChild(document.createElement('p'));

console.log(fragment.children.length);  // 3

foo.appendChild(fragment);

console.log(fragment.children.length);  // 0

console.log(document.body.innerHTML);
// <div id="foo">
//     <p></p>
```

```
//    <p></p>
//    <p></p>
// </div>
```

Using *<template>* tags

Notice in the previous example how the child nodes of the DocumentFragment are effectively transferred onto the foo element, leaving the DocumentFragment empty. This same procedure can be replicated using a <template>:

```
const fooElement = document.querySelector('#foo');
const barTemplate = document.querySelector('#bar');
const barFragment = barTemplate.content;

console.log(document.body.innerHTML);
// <div id="foo">
// </div>
// <template id="bar">
//    <p></p>
//    <p></p>
//    <p></p>
// </template>

fooElement.appendChild(barFragment);

console.log(document.body.innerHTML);
// <div id="foo">
//    <p></p>
//    <p></p>
//    <p></p>
// </div>
// <tempate id="bar"></template>
```

If you wish to instead copy the template, a simple importNode() can be used to clone the DocumentFragment:

```
const fooElement = document.querySelector('#foo');
const barTemplate = document.querySelector('#bar');
const barFragment = barTemplate.content;

console.log(document.body.innerHTML);
// <div id="foo">
// </div>
// <template id="bar">
//    <p></p>
//    <p></p>
//    <p></p>
// </template>

fooElement.appendChild(document.importNode(barFragment, true));

console.log(document.body.innerHTML);
// <div id="foo">
//    <p></p>
//    <p></p>
```

```
//    <p></p>
// </div>
// <template id="bar">
//    <p></p>
//    <p></p>
//    <p></p>
// </template>
```

Template Scripts

Script execution will be deferred until the `DocumentFragment` is added to the real DOM tree. This is demonstrated here:

```
// Page HTML:
//
// <div id="foo"></div>
// <template id="bar">
//    <script>console.log('Template script executed');</script>
// </template>

const fooElement = document.querySelector('#foo');
const barTemplate = document.querySelector('#bar');
const barFragment = barTemplate.content;

console.log('About to add template');
fooElement.appendChild(barFragment);
console.log('Added template');

// About to add template
// Template script executed
// Added template
```

This is useful in situations where addition of the new elements requires some initialization.

Shadow DOM

Conceptually, the shadow DOM web component is fairly straightforward: it allows you to attach an entirely separate DOM tree as a node on a parent DOM tree. This allows for DOM encapsulation, meaning that things like CSS styling and CSS selectors can be restricted to a shadow DOM subtree instead of the entire top-level DOM tree.

Shadow DOM is similar to HTML templates in that both are a document-like structure that enables a degree of separation from the top-level DOM. However, shadow DOM is distinct from HTML templates in that shadow DOM content is actually rendered on the page, whereas HTML template content is not.

Introduction to Shadow DOM

Consider a scenario where you have multiple similarly structured DOM subtrees:

```
<div>
  <p>Make me red!</p>
</div>
```

```
<div>
  <p>Make me blue!</p>
</div>
<div>
  <p>Make me green!</p>
</div>
```

As you've likely surmised from the text nodes, each of these three DOM subtrees should be assigned different colors. Normally, in order to apply a style uniquely to each of these without resorting to the style attribute, you'd likely apply a unique class name to each subtree and define the styling inside a corresponding selector:

```
<div class="red-text">
  <p>Make me red!</p>
</div>
<div class="green-text">
  <p>Make me green!</p>
</div>
<div class="blue-text">
  <p>Make me blue!</p>
</div>

<style>
.red-text {
  color: red;
}
.green-text {
  color: green;
}
.blue-text {
  color: blue;
}
</style>
```

Of course, this is a less than ideal solution. This isn't much different than defining variables in a global namespace; this CSS will be applied to the entire DOM even though you know with certainty that these style definitions are not needed anywhere else. You could keep adding CSS selector specificity to prevent these styles from bleeding elsewhere, but this is little more than a half-measure. Ideally, you'd prefer to restrict CSS to only a portion of the DOM: therein lies the raw utility of the shadow DOM.

Creating a Shadow DOM

For reasons involving security or preventing shadow DOM collisions, not all element types can have a shadow DOM attached to them. Attempting to attach a shadow DOM to an invalid element type, or an element with a shadow DOM already attached, will throw an error.

The following is a list of elements capable of hosting a shadow DOM:

➤ Any autonomous custom element with a valid name (as defined in the HTML specification: `https://html.spec.whatwg.org/multipage/custom-elements.html#valid-custom-element-name`)

- ➤ `<article>`
- ➤ `<aside>`
- ➤ `<blockquote>`
- ➤ `<body>`
- ➤ `<div>`
- ➤ `<footer>`
- ➤ `<h1>`
- ➤ `<h2>`
- ➤ `<h3>`
- ➤ `<h4>`
- ➤ `<h5>`
- ➤ `<h6>`
- ➤ `<header>`
- ➤ `<main>`
- ➤ `<nav>`
- ➤ `<p>`
- ➤ `<section>`
- ➤ `<span>`

A shadow DOM is created by attaching it to a valid HTML element using the `attachShadow()` method. The element to which a shadow DOM is attached is referred to as the *shadow host*. The root node of the shadow DOM is referred to as the *shadow root*.

The `attachShadow()` method expects a required `shadowRootInit` object and returns the instance of the shadow DOM. The `shadowRootInit` object must contain a single `mode` property specifying either `"open"` or `"closed"`. A reference to an open shadow DOM can be obtained on an HTML element via the `shadowRoot` property; this is not possible with a closed shadow DOM.

The mode difference is demonstrated here:

```
document.body.innerHTML = `
  <div id="foo"></div>
  <div id="bar"></div>
`;

const foo = document.querySelector('#foo');
const bar = document.querySelector('#bar');

const openShadowDOM = foo.attachShadow({ mode: 'open' });
```

```
const closedShadowDOM = bar.attachShadow({ mode: 'closed' });

console.log(openShadowDOM);      // #shadow-root (open)
console.log(closedShadowDOM);    // #shadow-root (closed)

console.log(foo.shadowRoot);     // #shadow-root (open)
console.log(bar.shadowRoot);     // null
```

In general, there is rarely a situation in which creating a closed shadow DOM is necessary. Although it confers the ability to restrict programmatic access to a shadow DOM from the shadow host, there are plenty of ways for malicious code to circumnavigate this and regain access to the shadow DOM. In short, creating a closed shadow DOM should *not* be used for security purposes.

> **NOTE** *If you wish to protect a separate DOM tree from untrusted code, a shadow DOM is unsuitable for such a requirement. The cross-origin restrictions enforced on an* `<iframe>` *are much more robust.*

Using a Shadow DOM

Once attached to an element, a shadow DOM can be used as a normal DOM. Consider the following example, which re-creates the red/green/blue example shown previously:

```
for (let color of ['red', 'green', 'blue']) {
  const div = document.createElement('div');
  const shadowDOM = div.attachShadow({ mode: 'open' });

  document.body.appendChild(div);

  shadowDOM.innerHTML = `
    <p>Make me ${color}</p>

    <style>
    p {
      color: ${color};
    }
    </style>
  `;
}
```

Although there are three identical selectors applying three different colors, the selectors will only be applied to the shadow DOM in which they are defined. As such, the three `<p>` elements will appear in three different colors.

You can verify that these elements exist inside their own shadow DOM as follows:

```
for (let color of ['red', 'green', 'blue']) {
  const div = document.createElement('div');
  const shadowDOM = div.attachShadow({ mode: 'open' });

  document.body.appendChild(div);

  shadowDOM.innerHTML = `
```

```
    <p>Make me ${color}</p>

    <style>
    p {
      color: ${color};
    }
    </style>
  `;
}

function countP(node) {
  console.log(node.querySelectorAll('p').length);
}

countP(document);  // 0

for (let element of document.querySelectorAll('div')) {
  countP(element.shadowRoot);
}

// 1
// 1
// 1
```

Browser inspector tools will make it clear where a shadow DOM exists. For example, the preceding example will appear as the following in the browser inspector:

```
<body>
<div>
  #shadow-root (open)
    <p>Make me red!</p>

    <style>
    p {
      color: red;
    }
    </style>
</div>
<div>
  #shadow-root (open)
    <p>Make me green!</p>

    <style>
    p {
      color: green;
    }
    </style>
</div>
<div>
  #shadow-root (open)
```

```
    <p>Make me blue!</p>

    <style>
    p {
      color: blue;
    }
    </style>
  </div>
</body>
```

Shadow DOMs are not an impermeable boundary. An HTML element can be moved between DOM trees without restriction:

```
document.body.innerHTML = `
<div></div>
<p id="foo">Move me</p>
`;

const divElement = document.querySelector('div');
const pElement = document.querySelector('p');

const shadowDOM = divElement.attachShadow({ mode: 'open' });

// Remove element from parent DOM
divElement.parentElement.removeChild(pElement);

// Add element to shadow DOM
shadowDOM.appendChild(pElement);

// Check to see that element was moved
console.log(shadowDOM.innerHTML);   // <p id="foo">Move me</p>
```

Composition and Shadow DOM Slots

The shadow DOM is designed to enable customizable components, and this requires the ability to handle nested DOM fragments. Conceptually, this is relatively straightforward: HTML inside a shadow host element needs a way to render inside the shadow DOM without actually being part of the shadow DOM tree.

By default, nested content will be hidden. Consider the following example where the text becomes hidden after 1000 milliseconds:

```
document.body.innerHTML = `
<div>
  <p>Foo</p>
</div>
`;

setTimeout(() => document.querySelector('div').attachShadow({ mode: 'open'
}), 1000);
```

Once the shadow DOM is attached, the browser gives priority to the shadow DOM and will render its contents instead of the text. In this example, the shadow DOM is empty, so the <div> will appear empty in turn.

To show this content, you can use a `<slot>` tag to instruct where the browser should place the HTML. In the code that follows, the previous example is reworked so the text reappears inside the shadow DOM:

```
document.body.innerHTML = `
<div id="foo">
  <p>Foo</p>
</div>
`;

document.querySelector('div')
    .attachShadow({ mode: 'open' })
    .innerHTML = `<div id="bar">
                    <slot></slot>
                  <div>`
```

Now, the projected content will behave as if it exists inside the shadow DOM. Inspecting the page reveals that the content appears to actually replace the `<slot>`:

```
<body>
<div id="foo">
  #shadow-root (open)
    <div id="bar">
      <p>Foo</p>
    </div>
</div>
</body>
```

Note that, despite its appearance in the page inspector, this is only a *projection* of DOM content. The element remains attached to the outer DOM:

```
document.body.innerHTML = `
<div id="foo">
  <p>Foo</p>
</div>
`;

document.querySelector('div')
    .attachShadow({ mode: 'open' })
    .innerHTML = `
      <div id="bar">
        <slot></slot>
      </div>`

console.log(document.querySelector('p').parentElement);
// <div id="foo"></div>
```

The red-green-blue example from before can be reworked to use slots as follows:

```
for (let color of ['red', 'green', 'blue']) {
  const divElement = document.createElement('div');
  divElement.innerText = `Make me ${color}`;
  document.body.appendChild(divElement)

  divElement
    .attachShadow({ mode: 'open' })
```

```
      .innerHTML = `
     <p><slot></slot></p>

     <style>
       p {
         color: ${color};
       }
     </style>
     `;
   }
```

It's also possible to use *named slots* to perform multiple projections. This is accomplished with matching slot/name attribute pairs. The element identified with a `slot="foo"` attribute will be projected into the `<slot>` with `name="foo"`. The following example demonstrates this by switching the rendered order of the shadow host element's children:

```
    document.body.innerHTML = `
   <div>
     <p slot="foo">Foo</p>
     <p slot="bar">Bar</p>
   </div>
   `;

   document.querySelector('div')
       .attachShadow({ mode: 'open' })
       .innerHTML = `
   <slot name="bar"></slot>
   <slot name="foo"></slot>
   `;

   // Renders:
   // Bar
   // Foo
```

Event Retargeting

If a browser event like click occurs inside a shadow DOM, the browser needs a way for the parent DOM to handle the event. However, the implementation must also respect the shadow DOM boundary. To address this, events that escape a shadow DOM and are handled outside undergo *event retargeting*. Once escaped, this event will appear to have been thrown by the shadow host itself instead of the true encapsulated element. This behavior is demonstrated here:

```
   // Create element to be shadow host
   document.body.innerHTML = `
   <div onclick="console.log('Handled outside:', event.target)"></div>
   `;

   // Attach shadow DOM and insert HTML into it
   document.querySelector('div')
     .attachShadow({ mode: 'open' })
     .innerHTML = `
   <button onclick="console.log('Handled inside:', event.target)">Foo</button>
```

```
`;

// When clicking the button:
// Handled inside:  <button onclick="..."></button>
// Handled outside: <div onclick="..."></div>
```

Note that retargeting only occurs for elements that actually exist inside a shadow DOM. Elements projected from outside using a <slot> tag will not have their events retargeted, as they still technically exist outside the shadow DOM.

Custom Elements

If you've used a JavaScript framework, you're likely familiar with the concept of custom elements, as all major frameworks provide this feature in some form. Custom elements introduce an object-oriented programming flavor to HTML elements. With them, it is possible to create custom, complex, and reusable elements and create instances with a simple HTML tag or attribute.

Defining a Custom Element

Browsers already will attempt to incorporate unrecognized elements into the DOM as generic elements. Of course, by default they won't do anything special that a generic HTML element doesn't already do. Consider the following example, where a nonsense HTML tag becomes an instance of an HTMLElement:

```
document.body.innerHTML = `
<x-foo >I'm inside a nonsense element.</x-foo >
`;

console.log(document.querySelector('x-foo') instanceof HTMLElement);  // true
```

Custom elements take this further. They allow you to define complex behavior whenever an <x-foo> tag appears, and also to tap into the element's lifecycle with respect to the DOM. Custom element definition is accomplished using the global customElements property, which returns the CustomElementRegistry object.

```
console.log(customElements);  // CustomElementRegistry {}
```

Defining a custom element is accomplished with the define() method. The following creates a trivial custom element, which inherits from a vanilla HTMLElement:

```
class FooElement extends HTMLElement {}
customElements.define('x-foo', FooElement);

document.body.innerHTML = `
<x-foo>I'm inside a nonsense element.</x-foo>
`;

console.log(document.querySelector('x-foo') instanceof FooElement);  // true
```

> **NOTE** *Custom element names must have at least one hyphen that does not start or end the name string, and the element tag must not self-close.*

The power of custom elements is housed in the class definition. For example, now each instance of this class in the DOM will call the constructor that you control:

```
class FooElement extends HTMLElement {
  constructor() {
    super();
    console.log('x-foo')
  }
}
customElements.define('x-foo', FooElement);

document.body.innerHTML = `
<x-foo></x-foo>
<x-foo></x-foo>
<x-foo></x-foo>
`;

// x-foo
// x-foo
// x-foo
```

> **NOTE** `super()` *must always be called first in the custom element constructor. If the element inherits from* `HTMLElement` *or similar without overriding the constructor, calling* `super()` *is not necessary as the prototype constructor will do it by default. It is very rare to define a custom element that should not inherit from* `HTMLElement`.

If a custom element inherits from an element class, the tag can be specified as an instance of that custom element using the `is` attribute and the `extends` option:

```
class FooElement extends HTMLDivElement {
  constructor() {
    super();
    console.log('x-foo')
  }
}
customElements.define('x-foo', FooElement, { extends: 'div' });

document.body.innerHTML = `
<div is="x-foo"></div>
<div is="x-foo"></div>
<div is="x-foo"></div>
`;

// x-foo
// x-foo
// x-foo
```

Adding Web Component Content

Because the custom element class constructor is called each time the element is added to the DOM, it is easy to automatically populate a custom element with child DOM content. Although you are forbidden from adding DOM children inside the constructor (a DOMException will be thrown), you can attach a shadow DOM and place content inside:

```
class FooElement extends HTMLElement {
  constructor() {
    super();

    // 'this' refers to the web component node
    this.attachShadow({ mode: 'open' });

    this.shadowRoot.innerHTML = `
      <p>I'm inside a custom element!</p>
    `;
  }
}
customElements.define('x-foo', FooElement);

document.body.innerHTML += `<x-foo></x-foo>`;

// Resulting DOM:
// <body>
// <x-foo>
//    #shadow-root (open)
//       <p>I'm inside a custom element!</p>
// <x-foo>
// </body>
```

To avoid the nastiness of string templates and innerHTML, this example can be refactored to use HTML templates and document.createElement():

```
// (Initial HTML)
// <template id="x-foo-tpl">
//    <p>I'm inside a custom element template!</p>
// </template>

const template = document.querySelector('#x-foo-tpl');

class FooElement extends HTMLElement {
  constructor() {
    super();

    this.attachShadow({ mode: 'open' });

    this.shadowRoot.appendChild(template.content.cloneNode(true));
  }
}
customElements.define('x-foo', FooElement);

document.body.innerHTML += `<x-foo></x-foo>`;

// Resulting DOM:
```

```
// <body>
// <template id="x-foo-tpl">
//    <p>I'm inside a custom element template!</p>
// </template>
// <x-foo>
//    #shadow-root (open)
//       <p>I'm inside a custom element template!</p>
// <x-foo>
// </body>
```

This practice allows for a high degree of HTML and code reuse as well as DOM encapsulation inside your custom element. With it, you are free to build reusable widgets without fear of outside CSS trampling your styling.

Using Custom Element Lifecycle Hooks

It is possible to execute code at various points in the lifecycle of a custom element. Instance methods on the custom element class with the corresponding name will be called during that lifecycle phase. There are five available hooks:

➤ `constructor()` is called when an element instance is created, or an existing DOM element is upgraded to a custom element.

➤ `connectedCallback()` is called each time this instance of the custom element is added into the DOM.

➤ `disconnectedCallback()` is called each time this instance of the custom element is removed from the DOM.

➤ `attributeChangedCallback()` is called each time the value of an *observed attribute* is changed. When the element instance is instantiated, definition of the initial value counts as a change.

➤ `adoptedCallback()` is called each time this instance is moved to a new document object with `document.adoptNode()`.

The following example demonstrates the construction, connected, and disconnected callbacks:

```
class FooElement extends HTMLElement {
  constructor() {
    super();
    console.log('ctor');
  }

  connectedCallback() {
    console.log('connected');
  }

  disconnectedCallback() {
    console.log('disconnected');
  }
}
```

```
customElements.define('x-foo', FooElement);

const fooElement = document.createElement('x-foo');
// ctor

document.body.appendChild(fooElement);
// connected

document.body.removeChild(fooElement);
// disconnected
```

Reflecting Custom Element Attributes

Because an element exists as both a DOM entity and a JavaScript object, a common pattern is to reflect changes between the two. In other words, a change to the DOM should reflect a change in the object, and vice versa. To reflect from the object to the DOM, a common strategy is to use getters and setters. The following example reflects the bar property of the object up to the DOM:

```
document.body.innerHTML = `<x-foo></x-foo>`;

class FooElement extends HTMLElement {
  constructor() {
    super();

    this.bar = true;
  }

  get bar() {
    return this.getAttribute('bar');
  }

  set bar(value) {
    this.setAttribute('bar', value)
  }
}
customElements.define('x-foo', FooElement);

console.log(document.body.innerHTML);
// <x-foo bar="true"></x-foo>
```

Reflecting in the reverse direction—from the DOM to the object—requires setting a listener for that attribute. To accomplish this, you can instruct the custom element to call the attributeChangedCallback() each time the attribute's value changes by using the observedAttributes() getter:

```
class FooElement extends HTMLElement {
  static get observedAttributes() {
    // List attributes which should trigger attributeChangedCallback()
    return ['bar'];
  }

  get bar() {
    return this.getAttribute('bar');
```

```
    }

    set bar(value) {
      this.setAttribute('bar', value)
    }

    attributeChangedCallback(name, oldValue, newValue) {
        if (oldValue !== newValue) {
        console.log(`${oldValue} -> ${newValue}`);

        this[name] = newValue;
      }
    }
  }
}
customElements.define('x-foo', FooElement);

document.body.innerHTML = `<x-foo bar="false"></x-foo>`;
// null -> false

document.querySelector('x-foo').setAttribute('bar', true);
// false -> true
```

Upgrading Custom Elements

It's not always possible to define a custom element before the custom element tag appears in the DOM. Web components address this ordering problem by exposing several additional methods on the CustomElementRegistry that allow you to detect when a custom element is eventually defined and upgrade existing elements.

The CustomElementRegistry.get() method returns the custom element class if it was already defined. In a similar vein, the CustomElementRegistry.whenDefined() method returns a promise that resolves when a custom element becomes defined:

```
customElements.whenDefined('x-foo').then(() => console.log('defined!'));

console.log(customElements.get('x-foo'));
// undefined

customElements.define('x-foo', class {});
// defined!

console.log(customElements.get('x-foo'));
// class FooElement {}
```

Elements connected to the DOM will be *automatically* upgraded when the custom element is defined. If you wish to forcibly upgrade an element before it is connected to the DOM, this can be accomplished with CustomElementRegistry.upgrade():

```
// Create HTMLUnknownElement object before custom element definition
const fooElement = document.createElement('x-foo');

// Define custom element
class FooElement extends HTMLElement {}
```

```
customElements.define('x-foo', FooElement);

console.log(fooElement instanceof FooElement);   // false

// Force the upgrade
customElements.upgrade(fooElement);

console.log(fooElement instanceof FooElement);   // true
```

> **NOTE** *There is also an HTML imports web component, but the specification remains a working draft, and no major browsers support it. It remains unclear if any browsers will eventually add support.*

THE WEB CRYPTOGRAPHY API

The Web Cryptography API (www.w3.org/TR/WebCryptoAPI) describes a suite of cryptography tools that standardize how JavaScript can wield cryptographic behavior in a secure and idiomatic fashion. These tools include the ability to generate, use, and apply cryptographic key pairs; encrypt and decrypt messages; and robustly generate random numbers.

> **NOTE** *The organization of the cryptography API is somewhat bizarre, featuring an outer* Crypto *object with an inner* SubtleCrypto *object. Before the Web Cryptography API was standardized, the* window.crypto *property was highly fragmented across browsers. To allow for cross-browser compatibility, the bulk of the API is exposed on the* SubtleCrypto *object.*

Random Number Generation

When tasked with generating random values, most developers reach for Math.random(). This method is implemented in browsers as a *pseudorandom number generator* (PRNG). The "pseudo" designation stems from the nature of the value generation in that it is not truly random. Values emitted from a PRNG only *emulate* properties that are associated with randomness. This appearance of randomness is made possible through some clever engineering. The browser's PRNG doesn't utilize any true sources of randomness—it is purely a fixed algorithm applied to a hermetic internal state. Each time Math.random() is called, the internal state is mutated by an algorithm and the result is converted into a new random value. For example, the V8 engine uses an algorithm called xorshift128+ to perform this mutation.

Because this algorithm is fixed and its input is *only* the previous state, the order of random numbers is deterministic. xorshift128+ uses 128 bits of internal state, and the algorithm is designed such that any initial state will produce a sequence of $2^{128}-1$ pseudorandom values before repeating itself. This looping behavior is called a *permutation cycle*, and the length of this cycle is referred to as the *period*. The implications of this are clear: If an attacker knows the internal state of the PRNG, they are able to predict the pseudorandom values that it will subsequently emit. If an unwitting developer were to use the PRNG to generate a private key for the purposes of encryption, the attacker could use the properties of the PRNG to determine the private key.

Pseudorandom number generators are designed to be able to quickly calculate values that seem to be random. They are, however, unsuitable for the purposes of cryptographic computation. To address this, a *cryptographically secure pseudorandom number generator* (CSPRNG) additionally incorporates a source of entropy as its input, such as measuring hardware timings or other system properties that exhibit unpredictable behavior. Doing so is much slower than a regular PRNG, but values emitted by a CSPRNG are sufficiently unpredictable for cryptographic purposes.

The Web Cryptography API introduces a CSPRNG that can be accessed on the global Crypto object via crypto.getRandomValues(). Unlike Math.random(), which returns a floating point number between 0 and 1, getRandomValues() writes random numbers into the typed array provided as a parameter. The typed array class is not important, as the underlying buffer is being filled with random binary bits.

The following generates five 8-bit random values:

```
const array = new Uint8Array(1);

for (let i=0; i<5; ++i) {
  console.log(crypto.getRandomValues(array));
}

// Uint8Array [41]
// Uint8Array [250]
// Uint8Array [51]
// Uint8Array [129]
// Uint8Array [35]
```

getRandomValues() will generate up to 2^{16} bytes; above that it will throw an error:

```
const fooArray = new Uint8Array(2 ** 16);
console.log(window.crypto.getRandomValues(fooArray));  // Uint32Array(16384) [...]

const barArray = new Uint8Array((2 ** 16) + 1);
console.log(window.crypto.getRandomValues(barArray));  // Error
```

Reimplementing Math.random() using the CSPRNG could be accomplished by generating a single random 32-bit number and dividing this into the maximum possible value, 0xFFFFFFFF. This yields a value between 0 and 1:

```
function randomFloat() {
  // Generate 32 random bits
  const fooArray = new Uint32Array(1);

  // Maximum value is 2^32 - 1
  const maxUint32 = 0xFFFFFFFF;

  // Divide by maximum possible value
  return crypto.getRandomValues(fooArray)[0] / maxUint32;
}

console.log(randomFloat());  // 0.5033651619458955
```

Using the SubtleCrypto Object

The overwhelming majority of the Web Cryptography API resides inside the `SubtleCrypto` object, accessible via `window.crypto.subtle`:

```
console.log(crypto.subtle);  // SubtleCrypto {}
```

This object contains a collection of methods for performing common cryptographic functions such as encryption, hashing, signing, and key generation. Because all cryptographic operations are performed on raw binary data, every `SubtleCrypto` method deals in `ArrayBuffer` and `ArrayBufferView` types. Because strings are so frequently the subject of cryptographic operations, the `TextEncoder` and `TextDecoder` classes will often be used alongside `SubtleCrypto` to convert to and from strings.

> **NOTE** *The* `SubtleCrypto` *object is only accessible in a secure context (https). In an insecure context, the subtle property will be undefined.*

Generating Cryptographic Digests

One extremely common cryptography operation is to calculate a cryptographic digest of data. The specification supports four algorithms for this, SHA-1 and three flavors of SHA-2:

➤ **Secure Hash Algorithm 1 (SHA-1)**—A hash function with an architecture similar to MD5. It takes an input of any size and generates a 160-bit message digest. This algorithm is no longer considered secure as it is vulnerable to collision attacks.

➤ **Secure Hash Algorithm 2 (SHA-2)**—A family of hash functions all built upon the same collision-resistant one-way compression function. The specification supports three members of this family: SHA-256, SHA-384, and SHA-512. The size of the generated message digest can be 256 bits (SHA-256), 384 bits (SHA-384), or 512 bits (SHA-512). This algorithm is considered secure and widely used in many applications and protocols, including TLS, PGP, and cryptocurrencies like Bitcoin.

The `SubtleCrypto.digest()` method is used to generate a message digest. The hash algorithm is specified using a string: SHA-1, SHA-256, SHA-384, or SHA-512. The following example demonstrates a simple application of SHA-256 to generate a message digest of the string foo:

```
(async function() {
  const textEncoder = new TextEncoder();
  const message = textEncoder.encode('foo');
  const messageDigest = await crypto.subtle.digest('SHA-256', message);

  console.log(new Uint32Array(messageDigest));
})();

// Uint32Array(8) [1806968364, 2412183400, 1011194873, 876687389,
//                 1882014227, 2696905572, 2287897337, 2934400610]
```

Commonly, the message digest binary will be used in a hex string format. Converting an array buffer to this format is accomplished by splitting the buffer up into 8-bit pieces and converting using toString() in base 16:

```
(async function() {
  const textEncoder = new TextEncoder();
  const message = textEncoder.encode('foo');
  const messageDigest = await crypto.subtle.digest('SHA-256', message);

  const hexDigest = Array.from(new Uint8Array(messageDigest))
    .map((x) => x.toString(16).padStart(2, '0'))
    .join('');

  console.log(hexDigest);
})();

// 2c26b46b68ffc68ff99b453c1d30413413422d706483bfa0f98a5e886266e7ae
```

Software companies usually publish a digest of their install binaries so that people who wish to safely install their software can verify that the binary they download is the version that the company actually published (and not one with injected malware). The following example downloads v67.0 of Firefox, hashes it with SHA-512, downloads the SHA-512 binary verification, and checks that the two hex strings match:

```
(async function() {
  const mozillaCdnUrl = '//download-origin.cdn.mozilla.net/pub/firefox/
    releases/67.0/';
  const firefoxBinaryFilename = 'linux-x86_64/en-US/firefox-67.0.tar.bz2';
  const firefoxShaFilename = 'SHA512SUMS';

  console.log('Fetching Firefox binary...');
  const fileArrayBuffer = await (await fetch(mozillaCdnUrl +
    firefoxBinaryFilename))
    .arrayBuffer();

  console.log('Calculating Firefox digest...');
  const firefoxBinaryDigest = await crypto.subtle.digest('SHA-512',
    fileArrayBuffer);

  const firefoxHexDigest = Array.from(new Uint8Array(firefoxBinaryDigest))
    .map((x) => x.toString(16).padStart(2, '0'))
    .join('');

  console.log('Fetching published binary digests...');
  // The SHA file contains digests of every firefox binary in this release,
  // so there is some organization performed.
  const shaPairs = (await (await fetch(mozillaCdnUrl + firefoxShaFilename)).text())
    .split(/\n/).map((x) => x.split(/\s+/));

  let verified = false;

  console.log('Checking calculated digest against published digests...');
```

```
      for (const [sha, filename] of shaPairs) {
        if (filename === firefoxBinaryFilename) {
          if (sha === firefoxHexDigest) {
            verified = true;
            break;
          }
        }
      }

    console.log('Verified:', verified);
  })();

  // Fetching Firefox binary...
  // Calculating Firefox digest...
  // Fetching published binary digests...
  // Checking calculated digest against published digests...
  // Verified: true
```

CryptoKeys and Algorithms

Cryptography would be meaningless without secret keys, and the SubtleCrypto object uses instances of the CryptoKey class to house these secrets. The CryptoKey class supports multiple types of encryption algorithms and allows for control over key extraction and usage.

The CryptoKey class supports the following algorithms, categorized by their parent cryptosystem:

➤ **RSA (Rivest-Shamir-Adleman)**—A public-key cryptosystem in which two large prime numbers are used to derive a pair of public and private keys that can be used to sign/verify or encrypt/decrypt messages. The trapdoor function for RSA is called the *factoring problem*.

➤ **RSASSA-PKCS1-v1_5**—An application of RSA used to sign messages with the private key and allow that signature to be verified with the public key.

> ➤ *SSA* stands for *signature schemes with appendix*, indicating the algorithm supports signature generation and verification operations.

> ➤ *PKCS1* stands for *Public-Key Cryptography Standards #1*, indicating the algorithm exhibits mathematical properties that RSA keys must have.

> ➤ RSASSA-PKCS1-v1_5 is deterministic, meaning the same message and key will produce an identical signature each time it is performed.

➤ **RSA-PSS**—Another application of RSA used to sign and verify messages.

> ➤ *PSS* stands for *probabilistic signature scheme*, indicating that the signature generation incorporates a salt to randomize the signature.

> ➤ Unlike RSASSA-PKCS1-v1_5, the same message and key will produce a different signature each time it is performed.

> ➤ Unlike RSASSA-PKCS1-v1_5, RSA-PSS is provably reducible to the hardness of the RSA factoring problem.

> ➤ In general, although RSASSA-PKCS1-v1_5 is still considered secure, RSA-PSS should be used as a replacement for RSASSA-PKCS1-v1_5.

➤ **RSA-OAEP**—An application of RSA used to encrypt messages with the public key and decrypt them with the private key.

> ➤ *OAEP* stands for *Optimal Asymmetric Encryption Padding*, indicating that the algorithm utilizes a Feistel network to process the unencrypted message prior to encryption.

> ➤ OAEP serves to convert the deterministic RSA encryption scheme to a probabilistic encryption scheme.

➤ **ECC (Elliptic-Curve Cryptography)**—A public-key cryptosystem in which a prime number and an elliptic curve are used to derive a pair of public and private keys that can be used to sign/verify messages. The trapdoor function for ECC is called the *elliptic curve discrete logarithm problem*. ECC is considered to be superior to RSA: although both RSA and ECC are cryptographically strong, ECC keys are shorter than RSA keys and ECC cryptographic operations are faster than RSA operations.

➤ **ECDSA (Elliptic Curve Digital Signature Algorithm)**—An application of ECC used to sign and verify messages. This algorithm is an elliptic curve–flavored variant of the *Digital Signature Algorithm* (DSA).

➤ **ECDH (Elliptic Curve Diffie-Hellman)**—A key-generation and key-agreement application of ECC that allows for two parties to establish a shared secret over a public communication channel. This algorithm is an elliptic curve–flavored variant of the *Diffie-Hellman key exchange* (DH) protocol.

➤ **AES (Advanced Encryption Standard)**—A symmetric-key cryptosystem that encrypts/decrypts data using a block cipher derived from a substitution-permutation network. AES is used in different *modes*, which change the algorithm's characteristics.

➤ **AES-CTR**—The *counter mode* of AES. This mode behaves as a stream cipher by using an incremented counter to generate its keystream. It must also be provided a nonce, which is effectively used as an initialization vector. AES-CTR encryption/decryption is able to be parallelized.

➤ **AES-CBC**—The *cipher block chaining mode* of AES. Before encrypting each block of plain text, it is XORed with the previous block of ciphertext—hence the "chaining" name. An initialization vector is used as the XOR input for the first block.

➤ **AES-GCM**—The *Galois/Counter mode* of AES. This mode uses a counter and initialization vector to generate a value, which is XORed with the plain text of each block. Unlike CBC, the XOR inputs do not have dependencies on the previous block's encryption and therefore the GCM mode can be parallelized. Because of its excellent performance characteristics, AES-GCM enjoys utilization in many networking security protocols.

➤ **AES-KW**—The *key wrapping mode* of AES. This algorithm wraps a secret key into a portable and encrypted format that is safe for transmission on an untrusted channel. Once transmitted, the receiving party can then unwrap the key. Unlike other AES modes, AES-KW does not require an initialization vector.

➤ **HMAC (Hash-Based Message Authentication Code)**—An algorithm that generates *message authentication codes* used to verify that a message arrives unaltered when sent over an untrusted network. Two parties use a hash function and a shared private key to sign and verify messages.

➤ **KDF (Key Derivation Functions)**—Algorithms that can derive one or many keys from a master key using a hash function. KDFs are capable of generating keys of a different length or converting keys to different formats.

➤ **HKDF (HMAC-Based Key Derivation Function)**—A key derivation function designed to be used with a high-entropy input such as an existing key.

➤ **PBKDF2 (Password-Based Key Derivation Function 2)**—A key derivation function designed to be used with a low-entropy input such as a password string.

> **NOTE** *The* CryptoKey *supports a large number of algorithms, but only some algorithms are applicable to some* SubtleCrypto *methods. Refer to the specification for an overview of which algorithms are supported for which methods:* www.w3.org/TR/WebCryptoAPI/#algorithm-overview.

Generating CryptoKeys

Generating a random CryptoKey is accomplished with the SubtleCrypto.generateKey() method, which returns a promise that resolves to one or many CryptoKey instances. This method is passed a params object specifying the target algorithm, a boolean indicating whether or not the key should be extractable from the CryptoKey object, and an array of strings—keyUsages—indicating which SubtleCrypto methods the key can be used with.

Because different cryptosystems require different inputs to generate keys, the params object provides the required inputs for each cryptosystem:

➤ The RSA cryptosystem uses a RsaHashedKeyGenParams object.

➤ The ECC cryptosystem uses an EcKeyGenParams object.

➤ The HMAC cryptosystem uses an HmacKeyGenParams object.

➤ The AES cryptosystem uses an AesKeyGenParams object.

The keyUsages object describes which algorithms the key can be used with. It expects at least one of the following strings:

➤ encrypt

➤ decrypt

➤ sign

➤ verify

➤ deriveKey

➤ deriveBits

➤ wrapKey

➤ unwrapKey

Suppose you want to generate a symmetric key with the following properties:

➤ Supports the AES-CTR algorithm

➤ Key length of 128 bits

➤ Cannot be extracted from the CryptoKey object

➤ Is able to be used with the encrypt() and decrypt() methods

Generating this key can be accomplished in the following fashion:

```
(async function() {
  const params = {
    name: 'AES-CTR',
    length: 128
  };

  const keyUsages = ['encrypt', 'decrypt'];

  const key = await crypto.subtle.generateKey(params, false, keyUsages);

  console.log(key);
  // CryptoKey {type: "secret", extractable: true, algorithm: {...},
  // usages Array(2)}
})();
```

Suppose you want to generate an asymmetric key pair with the following properties:

➤ Supports the ECDSA algorithm

➤ Uses the P-256 elliptic curve

➤ Can be extracted from the CryptoKey object

➤ Is able to be used with the sign() and verify() methods

Generating this key pair can be accomplished in the following fashion:

```
(async function() {
  const params = {
    name: 'ECDSA',
    namedCurve: 'P-256'
  };

  const keyUsages = ['sign', 'verify'];

  const {publicKey, privateKey} = await crypto.subtle.generateKey(params, true,
    keyUsages);

  console.log(publicKey);
```

```
    // CryptoKey {type: "public", extractable: true, algorithm: {...},
    // usages: Array(1)}

    console.log(privateKey);
    // CryptoKey {type: "private", extractable: true, algorithm: {...},
    // usages: Array(1)}
})();
```

Exporting and Importing Keys

If a key is extractable, it is possible to expose the raw key binary from inside the `CryptoKey` object.
The `exportKey()` method allows you to do so while also specifying the target format (`raw`, `pkcs8`,
`spki`, or `jwk`). The method returns a promise that resolves to an `ArrayBuffer` containing the key:

```
(async function() {
  const params = {
    name: 'AES-CTR',
    length: 128
  };
  const keyUsages = ['encrypt', 'decrypt'];

  const key = await crypto.subtle.generateKey(params, true, keyUsages);

  const rawKey = await crypto.subtle.exportKey('raw', key);

  console.log(new Uint8Array(rawKey));
  // Uint8Array[93, 122, 66, 135, 144, 182, 119, 196, 234, 73, 84, 7, 139,
  // 43, 238,    // 110]
})();
```

The inverse operation of `exportKey()` is `importKey()`. This method's signature is essentially a combination of `generateKey()` and `exportKey()`. The following method generates a key, exports it, and
imports it once again:

```
(async function() {
  const params = {
    name: 'AES-CTR',
    length: 128
  };
  const keyUsages = ['encrypt', 'decrypt'];
  const keyFormat = 'raw';
  const isExtractable = true;

  const key = await crypto.subtle.generateKey(params, isExtractable, keyUsages);

  const rawKey = await crypto.subtle.exportKey(keyFormat, key);

  const importedKey = await crypto.subtle.importKey(keyFormat, rawKey, params.name,
      isExtractable, keyUsages);

  console.log(importedKey);
  // CryptoKey {type: "secret", extractable: true, algorithm: {...},
  // usages: Array(2)}
})();
```

Deriving Keys from Master Keys

The `SubtleCrypto` object allows you to derive new keys with configurable properties from an existing secret. It supports a `deriveKey()` method that returns a promise resolving to a `CryptoKey`, and a `deriveBits()` method that returns a promise resolving to an `ArrayBuffer`.

> **NOTE** *The difference between* `deriveKey()` *and* `deriveBits()` *is trivial, as calling* `deriveKey()` *is effectively the same as calling* `deriveBits()` *and passing the result to* `importKey()`.

The `deriveBits()` function accepts an algorithm params object, the master key, and the length in bits of the output. This can be used in situations where two people, each with their own key pairs, wish to obtain a shared secret key. The following example uses the ECDH algorithm to generate reciprocal keys from two keypairs and ensures that they derive the same key bits:

```
(async function() {
  const ellipticCurve = 'P-256';
  const algoIdentifier = 'ECDH';
  const derivedKeySize = 128;

  const params = {
    name: algoIdentifier,
    namedCurve: ellipticCurve
  };

  const keyUsages = ['deriveBits'];

  const keyPairA = await crypto.subtle.generateKey(params, true, keyUsages);
  const keyPairB = await crypto.subtle.generateKey(params, true, keyUsages);

  // Derive key bits from A's public key and B's private key
  const derivedBitsAB = await crypto.subtle.deriveBits(
      Object.assign({ public: keyPairA.publicKey }, params),
      keyPairB.privateKey,
      derivedKeySize);

  // Derive key bits from B's public key and A's private key
  const derivedBitsBA = await crypto.subtle.deriveBits(
      Object.assign({ public: keyPairB.publicKey }, params),
      keyPairA.privateKey,
      derivedKeySize);

  const arrayAB = new Uint32Array(derivedBitsAB);
  const arrayBA = new Uint32Array(derivedBitsBA);

  // Ensure key arrays are identical
  console.log(
      arrayAB.length === arrayBA.length &&
      arrayAB.every((val, i) => val === arrayBA[i]));  // true
})();
```

The deriveKey() method behaves similarly, returning an instance of a CryptoKey instead of an ArrayBuffer. The following example takes a raw string, applies the PBKDF2 algorithm to import it into a raw master key, and derives a new key in AES-GCM format:

```
(async function() {
  const password = 'foobar';
  const salt = crypto.getRandomValues(new Uint8Array(16));
  const algoIdentifier = 'PBKDF2';
  const keyFormat = 'raw';
  const isExtractable = false;

  const params = {
    name: algoIdentifier
  };

  const masterKey = await window.crypto.subtle.importKey(
    keyFormat,
    (new TextEncoder()).encode(password),
    params,
    isExtractable,
    ['deriveKey']
  );

  const deriveParams = {
    name: 'AES-GCM',
    length: 128
  };

  const derivedKey = await window.crypto.subtle.deriveKey(
    Object.assign({salt, iterations: 1E5, hash: 'SHA-256'}, params),
    masterKey,
    deriveParams,
    isExtractable,
    ['encrypt']
  );

  console.log(derivedKey);
  // CryptoKey {type: "secret", extractable: false, algorithm: {...},
  // usages: Array(1)}
})();
```

Signing and Verifying Messages with Asymmetric Keys

The SubtleCrypto object allows you to use public-key algorithms to generate signatures using a private key or to verify signatures using a public key. These are performed using the SubtleCrypto .sign() and SubtleCrypto.verify() methods, respectively.

Signing a message requires a params object to specify the algorithm and any necessary values, the private CryptoKey, and the ArrayBuffer or ArrayBufferView to be signed. The following example generates an elliptic curve key pair and uses the private key to sign a message:

```
(async function() {
  const keyParams = {
```

```
    name: 'ECDSA',
    namedCurve: 'P-256'
  };

  const keyUsages = ['sign', 'verify'];

  const {publicKey, privateKey} = await crypto.subtle.generateKey(keyParams, true,
      keyUsages);

  const message = (new TextEncoder()).encode('I am Satoshi Nakamoto');

  const signParams = {
    name: 'ECDSA',
    hash: 'SHA-256'
  };

  const signature = await crypto.subtle.sign(signParams, privateKey, message);

  console.log(new Uint32Array(signature));
  // Uint32Array(16) [2202267297, 698413658, 1501924384, 691450316, 778757775, ... ]
})();
```

An individual wishing to verify this message against the signature could use the public key and the `SubtleCrypto.verify()` method. This method's signature is nearly identical to `sign()` with the exception that it must be provided the public key as well as the signature. The following example extends the previous example by verifying the generated signature:

```
(async function() {
  const keyParams = {
    name: 'ECDSA',
    namedCurve: 'P-256'
  };

  const keyUsages = ['sign', 'verify'];

  const {publicKey, privateKey} = await crypto.subtle.generateKey(keyParams, true,
      keyUsages);

  const message = (new TextEncoder()).encode('I am Satoshi Nakamoto');

  const signParams = {
    name: 'ECDSA',
    hash: 'SHA-256'
  };

  const signature = await crypto.subtle.sign(signParams, privateKey, message);

  const verified = await crypto.subtle.verify(signParams, publicKey, signature,
      message);

  console.log(verified);  // true
})();
```

Encrypting and Decrypting with Symmetric Keys

The SubtleCrypto object allows you to use both public-key and symmetric algorithms to encrypt and decrypt messages. These are performed using the SubtleCrypto.encrypt() and SubtleCrypto.decrypt() methods, respectively.

Encrypting a message requires a params object to specify the algorithm and any necessary values, the encryption key, and the data to be encrypted. The following example generates a symmetric AES-CBC key, encrypts it, and finally decrypts a message:

```
(async function() {
  const algoIdentifier = 'AES-CBC';

  const keyParams = {
    name: algoIdentifier,
    length: 256
  };

  const keyUsages = ['encrypt', 'decrypt'];

  const key = await crypto.subtle.generateKey(keyParams, true,
      keyUsages);

  const originalPlaintext = (new TextEncoder()).encode('I am Satoshi Nakamoto');

  const encryptDecryptParams = {
    name: algoIdentifier,
    iv: crypto.getRandomValues(new Uint8Array(16))
  };

  const ciphertext = await crypto.subtle.encrypt(encryptDecryptParams, key,
      originalPlaintext);

  console.log(ciphertext);
  // ArrayBuffer(32) {}

  const decryptedPlaintext = await crypto.subtle.decrypt(encryptDecryptParams, key,
      ciphertext);

  console.log((new TextDecoder()).decode(decryptedPlaintext));
  // I am Satoshi Nakamoto
})();
```

Wrapping and Unwrapping a Key

The SubtleCrypto object allows you to wrap and unwrap keys to allow for transmission over an untrusted channel. These are performed using the SubtleCrypto.wrapKey() and SubtleCrypto .unwrapKey() methods, respectively.

Wrapping a key requires a format string, the CryptoKey instance to be wrapped, the CryptoKey to perform the wrapping, and a params object to specify the algorithm and any necessary values.

The following example generates a symmetric AES-GCM key, wraps the key with AES-KW, and finally unwraps the key:

```
(async function() {
  const keyFormat = 'raw';
  const extractable = true;

  const wrappingKeyAlgoIdentifier = 'AES-KW';
  const wrappingKeyUsages = ['wrapKey', 'unwrapKey'];
  const wrappingKeyParams = {
    name: wrappingKeyAlgoIdentifier,
    length: 256
  };

  const keyAlgoIdentifier = 'AES-GCM';
  const keyUsages = ['encrypt'];
  const keyParams = {
    name: keyAlgoIdentifier,
    length: 256
  };

  const wrappingKey = await crypto.subtle.generateKey(wrappingKeyParams,
    extractable,
      wrappingKeyUsages);

  console.log(wrappingKey);
  // CryptoKey {type: "secret", extractable: true, algorithm: {...},
  // usages: Array(2)}

  const key = await crypto.subtle.generateKey(keyParams, extractable, keyUsages);

  console.log(key);
  // CryptoKey {type: "secret", extractable: true, algorithm: {...},
  // usages: Array(1)}

  const wrappedKey = await crypto.subtle.wrapKey(keyFormat, key, wrappingKey,
      wrappingKeyAlgoIdentifier);

  console.log(wrappedKey);
  // ArrayBuffer(40) {}

  const unwrappedKey = await crypto.subtle.unwrapKey(keyFormat, wrappedKey,
      wrappingKey, wrappingKeyParams, keyParams, extractable, keyUsages);

  console.log(unwrappedKey);
  // CryptoKey {type: "secret", extractable: true, algorithm: {...},
  // usages: Array(1)}
})()
```

SUMMARY

HTML5, in addition to defining new markup rules, also defines several JavaScript APIs. These APIs are designed to enable better web interfaces that can rival the capabilities of desktop applications. The APIs covered in this chapter are as follows:

➤ The Atomics API allows you to protect your code from race conditions resulting from multi-threaded memory access patterns.

➤ Clipboard API: provides the ability to programmatically access and manipulate the contents of the clipboard.

➤ Fullscreen API: enables developers to request and exit fullscreen mode for elements on a web page.

➤ Page Visibility API: allows developers to determine the current visibility state of a web page, whether it is visible or hidden to the user.

➤ The URL API: provides a set of methods for parsing, manipulating, and working with URLs in JavaScript.

➤ The Cross-Context messaging API provides the ability to send messages across documents from different origins while keeping the security of the same-origin policy intact.

➤ The Encoding API enables you to seamlessly convert between strings and buffers-an increasingly common pattern.

➤ The File API affords you robust tools for sending, receiving, and reading large binary objects.

➤ The Geolocation API retrieves the geographical location information about a user's device.

➤ The Notifications API gives you a browser-independent way of presenting interactive tiles to the user.

➤ The Streams API affords an entirely new way of incrementally reading, writing, and processing data.

➤ The Timing APIs provide a robust way of measuring latency in and around the browser.

➤ The Web Cryptography API makes cryptographic operations such as random number generation, encrypting, and signing messages first-class citizens.

19

Error Handling and Debugging

WHAT'S IN THIS CHAPTER?

➤ Understanding browser error reporting

➤ Handling errors

➤ Debugging JavaScript code

DOWNLOADS FOR THIS CHAPTER

Please note that all the code examples for this chapter are available as a part of this chapter's code download on the book's website at www.wiley.com/go/ projavascript5e.

JavaScript has traditionally been known as one of the most difficult programming languages to debug because of its dynamic nature and years without proper development tools. Errors typically resulted in confusing browser messages such as "object expected" that provided little or no contextual information. The third edition of ECMAScript aimed to improve this situation, introducing the try-catch and throw statements, along with various error types to help developers deal with errors when they occur. A few years later, JavaScript debuggers and debugging tools began appearing for web browsers. Modern web browsers feature robust suites of JavaScript debugging capabilities.

Armed with the proper language support and development tools, web developers are now empowered to implement proper error-handling processes and figure out the cause of problems.

BROWSER ERROR REPORTING

All modern web browsers have some way to report JavaScript errors to the user. By default, all browsers hide this information, both because it's of little use to anyone but the developer, and because it's the nature of web pages to throw errors during normal operation.

Desktop Consoles

All modern desktop web browsers expose errors through their web console. These errors can be revealed in the developer tools console. In all the previously mentioned browsers, they share a common path to accessing the web console. Perhaps the easiest way to view errors is to right-click on the web page, select *Inspect* or *Inspect Element*, and click the *Console* tab.

To proceed directly to the console, different operating systems and browsers support different key combinations:

BROWSER	WINDOWS/LINUX	MAC
Chrome	Ctrl+Shift+J	Cmd+Opt+J
Firefox	Ctrl+Shift+K	Cmd+Opt+K
Edge	F12, then Ctrl+2	NA
Opera	Ctrl+Shift+I	Cmd+Opt+I
Safari	NA	Cmd+Opt+C

Mobile Consoles

Natively, mobile phones will not offer a console interface directly on the device. However, there are several options for you to use in situations where you would like to inspect errors that are thrown on a mobile device.

Chrome for mobile and Safari on iOS come bundled with utilities that allow you to connect the device to a host operating system running that same browser, and you can then view the errors thrown through the paired desktop browser. This involves physically connecting the device and connecting it to the host system's browser.

ERROR HANDLING

Every major web application needs a good error-handling protocol and most good applications have one, though it is typically on the server side of the application. In fact, great care is usually taken by the server-side team to define an error-logging mechanism that categorizes errors by type, frequency, and any other metric that may be important. The result is the ability to understand how the application is working in the public with a simple database query or report-generating script.

Error handling has slowly been adopted on the browser side of web applications even though it is just as important. An important fact to understand is that most people who use the web are not technically savvy—most don't even fully comprehend what a web browser is, let alone which one they're using. The default browser experience for JavaScript errors is horrible for the end user. In the best case, the user has no idea what happened and will try again; in the worst case, the user gets incredibly annoyed and never comes back. Having a good error-handling strategy keeps your users informed about what is going on without scaring them. To accomplish this, you must understand the various ways that you can trap and deal with JavaScript errors as they occur.

The *try-catch* Statement

The `try-catch` statement is a way to handle exceptions in JavaScript. The basic syntax is as follows, which is the same as the try-catch statement in Java:

```
try {
    // code that may cause an error
} catch (error) {
    // what to do when an error occurs
}
```

Any code that might possibly throw an error should be placed in the `try` portion of the statement, and the code to handle the error is placed in the `catch` portion, as shown in the following example:

```
try {
    window.someNonexistentFunction();
} catch (error){
    console.log("An error happened!");
}
```

If an error occurs at any point in the `try` portion of the statement, code execution immediately skips to the `catch` portion. The `catch` portion of the statement receives the error value.

Most of the time, catch will be handing an error object. The exact information available on this object varies from browser to browser but contains at a minimum:

➤   `message`—A string that contains the error message associated with the error object. It provides a brief description of the error that occurred.

➤   `name` —A string that contains the name of the error. The name property is set to "Error" by default, but it can be overridden to provide more information about the error.

➤   `cause`—The specific original cause of the error. Used when catching and re-throwing an error.

You can display these values as shown in the following example:

```
try {
    window.someNonexistentFunction();
} catch (error){
    console.log(error.message);
}
```

You might encounter situations where the error object is unimportant; only handling the error matters:

```
try {
  throw "foo";
} catch (e) {
  // An error happened, but you don't care about the error object
}
```

ECMAScript allows you to omit the error object assignment and simply ignore the error entirely:

```
try {
  throw "foo";
} catch {
  // An error happened, but you don't care about the error object
}
```

The *finally* Clause

The optional `finally` clause of the `try-catch` statement always runs its code no matter what. If the code in the `try` portion runs completely, the `finally` clause executes; if there is an error and the `catch` portion executes, the `finally` portion still executes. If `finally` is provided, then `catch` becomes optional (only one or the other is required).

There is literally nothing that can be done in the `try` or `catch` portion of the statement to prevent the code in finally from executing, which includes using a `return` statement. Consider the following function:

```
function testFinally(){
  try {
    return 2;
  } catch (error){
    return 1;
  } finally {
    return 0;
  }
}
```

This function simply places a `return` statement in each portion of the `try-catch` statement. It looks like the function should return 2 because that is in the try portion and wouldn't cause an error. However, the presence of the `finally` clause causes that `return` to be ignored; the function returns 0 when called no matter what. If the `finally` clause were removed, the function would return 2.

> **NOTE** *It's very important to understand that any return statements in either the try or the catch portion will be ignored if a finally clause is also included in your code. Be sure to double-check the intended behavior of your code when using finally.*

Throwing Values vs. Error Objects

You can use any value with the `throw` operator, but it is always to your advantage to create a new `Error` object and throw that instead of a value. This will capture the stack trace, which captures valuable information when debugging. This distinction is demonstrated here:

```
function fooError() {
  try {
    throw "foo";
  } catch(e) {
    console.log(e);
  }
}

function barError() {
  try {
    throw new Error("bar");
  } catch(e) {
    console.log(e);
  }
}

fooError();
// foo

barError();
Error: bar
    at barError (?editor_console=true:126:11)
    at ?editor_console=true:133:1
```

Catching and Rethrowing with *error.cause*

Sometimes, you may want to catch an error, handle it in some way, and then rethrow the error so that it can be handled by other parts of your code. When you catch an error using a `catch` block, you can create a new error object and pass a cause property in the `Error` constructor. This allows you to preserve the original error object and its stack trace while providing additional context or information about the error.

```
function rethrow() {
  try {
    throw new Error("foo");
  } catch (e) {
    throw new Error("bar", { cause: e })
  }
}

try {
  rethrow();
} catch (e) {
  console.log(e);
```

```
    // Error: bar
    //    at rethrow (?editor_console=true:120:11)
    //    at ?editor_console=true:125:3
    console.log(e.cause);
    // Error: foo
    //    at rethrow (?editor_console=true:118:11)
    //    at ?editor_console=true:125:3
}
```

Error Types

Several different types of errors can occur during the course of code execution. Each error type has a corresponding object type that is thrown when an error occurs. ECMA-262 defines the following error types:

➤   Error

➤   InternalError

➤   EvalError

➤   RangeError

➤   ReferenceError

➤   SyntaxError

➤   TypeError

➤   URIError

➤   AggregateError

The Error type is the base type from which all other error types inherit. As a result of this, all error types share the same properties (the only methods on error objects are the default object methods). An error of type Error is rarely, if ever, thrown by a browser; it is provided mainly for developers to throw custom errors.

The InternalError type is thrown when the underlying JavaScript engine throws an exception—for example, when a stack overflow occurs from too much recursion. This is not an error type that you would explicitly handle inside your code; if this error is thrown, chances are very good that your code is doing something incorrect or dangerous and should be fixed.

The EvalError type is thrown when an exception occurs while using the eval() function. ECMA-262 states that this error is thrown:

> . . .if value of the eval property is used in any way other than a direct call (that is, other than by the explicit use of its name as an Identifier, which is the MemberExpression in a CallExpression), or if the eval property is assigned to.

This basically means using eval() as anything other than a function call, such as:

```
new eval();  // throws EvalError
eval = foo;  // throws EvalError
```

In practice, browsers don't always throw `EvalError` when they're supposed to. Because of this and the unlikelihood of these patterns being used, it is highly unlikely that you will run into this error type.

A `RangeError` occurs when a number is outside the bounds of its range. For example, this error may occur when an attempt is made to define an array with an unsupported number of items, such as –20 or `Number.MAX_VALUE`, as shown here:

```
let items1 = new Array(-20);            // throws RangeError
let items2 = new Array(Number.MAX_VALUE);  // throws RangeError
```

Range errors occur infrequently in JavaScript.

The `ReferenceError` type is used when an object is expected. (This is literally the cause of the famous "object expected" browser error.) This type of error typically occurs when attempting to access a variable that doesn't exist, as in this example:

```
let obj = x;   // throws ReferenceError when x isn't declared
```

A `SyntaxError` object is thrown most often when there is a syntax error in a JavaScript string that is passed to `eval()`, as in this example:

```
eval("a ++ b");   // throws SyntaxError
```

Outside of using `eval()`, the `SyntaxError` type is rarely used, because syntax errors occurring in JavaScript code stop execution immediately.

The `TypeError` type is the most used in JavaScript and occurs when a variable is of an unexpected type or an attempt is made to access a nonexistent method. This can occur for any number of reasons, most often when a type-specific operation is used with a variable of the wrong type. Here are some examples:

```
let o = new 10;                         // throws TypeError
console.log("name" in true);            // throws TypeError
Function.prototype.toString.call("name"); // throws TypeError
```

Type errors occur most frequently with function arguments that are used without their type being verified first.

A `URIError` occurs only when using the `encodeURI()` or `decodeURI()` with a malformed URI. This error is perhaps the most infrequently observed in JavaScript, because these functions are incredibly robust.

The different error types can be used to provide more information about an exception, allowing appropriate error handling. You can determine the type of error thrown in the catch portion of a try-catch statement by using the `instanceof` operator, as shown here:

```
try {
  someFunction();
} catch (error){
  if (error instanceof TypeError){
    // handle type error
  } else if (error instanceof ReferenceError){
    // handle reference error
  } else {
```

```
      // handle all other error types
    }
  }
```

An `AggregateError` is thrown when multiple errors need to be reported by an operation, such as, for example, by `Promise.any()`. It has an `errors` property that contains an array of all the "wrapped" errors.

```
Promise.any([
  Promise.reject(new Error("foobar")),
]).catch((e) => {
  console.log(e instanceof AggregateError); // true
  console.log(e.errors);                    // [ Error: "foobar" ]
});
```

Checking the error type is the easiest way to determine the appropriate course of action in a cross-browser way because the error message contained in the message property differs from browser to browser.

Throwing Errors

A companion to the `try-catch` statement is the `throw` operator, which can be used to throw custom errors at any point in time. The `throw` operator must be used with a value but places no limitation on the type of value. All of the following lines are legal:

```
throw 12345;
throw "Hello world!";
throw true;
throw { name: "JavaScript" };
```

When the throw operator is used, code execution stops immediately and continues only if a `try-catch` statement catches the value that was thrown.

Browser errors can be more accurately simulated by using one of the built-in error types. Each error type's constructor accepts a single argument, which is the exact error message. Here is an example:

```
throw new Error("Something bad happened.");
```

This code throws a generic error with a custom error message. The error is handled by the browser as if it were generated by the browser itself, meaning that it is reported by the browser in the usual way and your custom error message is displayed. You can achieve the same result using the other error types, as shown in these examples:

```
throw new SyntaxError("I don't like your syntax.");
throw new InternalError("I can't do that, Dave.");
throw new TypeError("What type of variable do you take me for?");
throw new RangeError("Sorry, you just don't have the range.");
throw new EvalError("That doesn't evaluate.");
throw new URIError("Uri, is that you?");
throw new ReferenceError("You didn't cite your references properly.");
```

You can also create custom error types by inheriting from `Error`. You should provide both a `name` property and a `message` property on your error type. Here is an example:

```
class CustomError extends Error {
  constructor(message) {
```

```
      super (message) ;
      this.name = "CustomError";
      this.message = message;
    }
  }

  throw new CustomError ("My message") ;
```

Custom error types that are inherited from `Error` are treated just like any other error by the browser. Creating custom error types is helpful when you will be catching the errors that you throw and need to decipher them from browser-generated errors:

```
class CustomError extends Error {
  ...
}

try {
  throw new CustomError ("My message") ;
} catch (e) {
  if (e instanceof CustomError) {
    // Handle custom error
  } else {
    // Generic error handling
  }
}
```

When to Throw Errors

Throwing custom errors is a great way to provide more information about why a function has failed. Errors should be thrown when a particular known error condition exists that won't allow the function to execute properly. That is, the browser will throw an error while executing this function given a certain condition. For example, the following function will fail if the argument is not an array:

```
function process(values){
  values.sort();

  for (let value of values){
    if (value> 100){
      return value;
    }
  }

  return -1;
}
```

If this function is run with a string as the argument, the call to `sort ()` fails. Each browser gives a different, though somewhat obtuse, error message. None of the error messages are particularly clear as to what happened or how it could be fixed. When dealing with one function, as in the preceding example, debugging is easy enough to handle with these error messages. However, when you're working on a complex web application with thousands of lines of JavaScript code, finding the source of the error becomes much more difficult.

This is where a custom error with appropriate information will significantly contribute to the maintainability of the code. Consider the following example:

```
function process(values){
    if (!(values instanceof Array)){
        throw new Error("process(): Argument must be an array.");
    }

    values.sort();

    for (let value of values){
        if (value> 100){
            return value;
        }
    }

    return -1;
}
```

In this rewritten version of the function, an error is thrown if the values argument isn't an array. The error message provides the name of the function and a clear description as to why the error occurred. If this error occurred in a complex web application, you would have a much clearer idea of where the real problem is.

When you're developing JavaScript code, critically evaluate each function and the circumstances under which it may fail. A good error-handling protocol ensures that the only errors that occur are the ones that you throw.

Throwing Errors versus *try-catch*

A common question that arises is when to throw errors versus when to use try-catch to capture them. Generally speaking, errors are thrown in the low levels of an application architecture, at a level where not much is known about the ongoing process, and so the error can't really be handled. If you are writing a JavaScript library that may be used in a number of different applications, or even a utility function that will be used in a number of different places in a single application, you should strongly consider throwing errors with detailed information. It is then up to the application to catch the errors and handle them appropriately.

The best way to think about the difference between throwing errors and catching errors is this: you should catch errors only if you know exactly what to do next. The purpose of catching an error is to prevent the browser from responding in its default manner; the purpose of throwing an error is to provide information about why an error occurred.

The *error* Event

Any error that is not handled by a try-catch causes the error event to fire on the window object. This event was one of the first supported by web browsers, and its format has remained intact for backwards compatibility in all major browsers. An onerror event handler doesn't create an event object in any browser. Instead, it receives three arguments: the error message, the URL on which the error occurred, and the line number. In most cases, only the error message is relevant because the URL is the same as the location of the document, and the line number could be for inline JavaScript or code in external files. The `onerror` event handler needs to be assigned using the DOM Level 0 technique shown here because it doesn't follow the DOM Level 2 Events standard format:

```
window.onerror = (message, url, line) => {
  console.log(message);
};
```

When any error occurs, whether browser-generated or not, the `error` event fires, and this event handler executes. Then, the default browser behavior takes over, displaying the error message as it would normally. You can prevent the default browser error reporting by returning `false`, as shown here:

```
window.onerror = (message, url, line) => {
  console.log(message);
  return false;
};
```

By returning `false`, this function effectively becomes a `try-catch` statement for the entire document, capturing all unhandled runtime errors. This event handler is the last line of defense against errors being reported by the browser and, ideally, should never have to be used. Proper usage of the `try-catch` statement means that no errors reach the browser level and, therefore, should never fire the error event.

Images also support an `error` event. Any time the URL in an image's `src` attribute doesn't return a recognized image format, the `error` event fires. This event follows the DOM format by returning an `event` object with the image as the target. Here is an example:

```
const image = new Image();

image.addEventListener("load", (event) => {
  console.log("Image loaded!");
});
image.addEventListener("error", (event) => {
  console.log("Image not loaded!");
});

image.src = "doesnotexist.gif";  // does not exist, resoure will fail to load
```

In this example, an alert is displayed when the image fails to load. It's important to understand that once the error event fires, the image download process is already over and will not be resumed.

ERROR HANDLING STRATEGIES

Error-handling strategies have traditionally been confined to the server for web applications. There's often a lot of thought that goes into errors and error handling, including logging and monitoring systems. The point of such tools is to analyze error patterns in the hopes of tracking down the root cause and understanding how many users the error affects.

It is equally important to have an error-handling strategy for the JavaScript layer of a web application. Because any JavaScript error can cause a web page to become unusable, understanding when and why errors occur is vital. Most web-application users are not technical and can easily get confused when something doesn't work as expected. They may reload the page in an attempt to fix the problem, or they may just stop trying. As the developer, you should have a good understanding of when and how the code could fail and have a system to track such issues.

Identifying Where Errors Might Occur

An overwhelming abundance of errors you might encounter can be preemptively handled by using a static code analyzer as part of your application build process. TypeScript is by far the most popular static code analyzer that directly addresses this problem.

Static code analyzers will require you to annotate your JavaScript with types, function signatures, and other directives that describe how the program will run outside of the base executable code. The analyzer will compare your annotations against various parts of your JavaScript codebase that use each other and make you aware of any potential incompatibilities that might manifest inside the actual runtime.

> **NOTE** *As a codebase grows, you will find that static analyzers become increasingly essential—especially as the number of developers working on the same code increases. All major tech companies that maintain extremely large JavaScript codebases use a robust form of static analysis as part of their build processes.*

Common Sources of Error

Since JavaScript is loosely typed and function arguments aren't verified, there are often errors that become apparent only when the code is executed. In general, there are two error categories to watch for:

- ➤ Type coercion errors
- ➤ Data type errors

Type Coercion Errors

Type coercion errors occur as the result of using an operator or other language construct that automatically changes the data type of a value. The two most common type coercion errors occur as a result of using the equal (==) or not equal (!=) operator and using a non-Boolean value in a flow control statement, such as if, for, and while.

The equal and not equal operators, discussed in Chapter 3, "Language Basics," automatically convert values of different types before performing a comparison. Since the same symbols typically perform straight comparisons in nondynamic languages, developers often mistakenly use them in JavaScript in the same way. In most cases, it's best to use the identically equal (===) and not identically equal (!==) operators to avoid type coercion. Here is an example:

```
console.log(5 == "5");    // true
console.log(5 === "5");   // false
console.log(1 == true);   // true
console.log(1 === true);  // false
```

In this code, the number 5 and the string "5" are compared using the equal operator and the identically equal operator. The equal operator first converts the string "5" into the number 5 and then compares it with the other number 5, resulting in `true`. The identically equal operator notes that the two data types are different and simply returns `false`. The same occurs with the values 1 and true: they are considered equal by the equal operator but not equal using the identically equal operator. Using the identically equal and not identically equal operators can prevent type coercion errors that occur during comparisons and are highly recommended over using the equal and not equal operators.

> **NOTE** *Codebase style guides will often assert how === vs. == should be applied. Some style guides subscribe to the notion that if === is always used for comparison, type coercion is a non-issue. Others dictate that an unflinching utilization of === is overkill in all places except for ones in which string/Boolean coercion is possible.*

Type coercion errors also occur in flow control statements. Statements such as if automatically convert any value into a Boolean before determining the next step. The if statement, specifically, is often used in error-prone ways. Consider the following example:

```
function concat(str1, str2, str3) {
    let result = str1 + str2;
    if (str3) {   // avoid!!!
      result += str3;
    }
    return result;
}
```

This function's intended purpose is to concatenate two or three strings and return the result. The third string is an optional argument and so must be checked. Named variables that aren't used are automatically assigned the value of `undefined`. The value undefined converts into the Boolean value `false`, so the intent of the if statement in this function is to concatenate the third argument only if it is provided. The problem is that `undefined` is not the only value that gets converted to `false`, and a string is not the only value that gets converted to `true`. If the third argument is the number 0, for example, the if condition fails, while a value of 1 causes the condition to pass.

Using non-Boolean values as conditions in a flow control statement is a very common cause of errors. To avoid such errors, always make sure that a Boolean value is passed as the condition. This is most often accomplished by doing a comparison of some sort. For example, the previous function can be rewritten as shown here:

```
function concat(str1, str2, str3){
    let result = str1 + str2;
    if (typeof str3 === "string") {   // proper comparison
      result += str3;
    }
    return result;
}
```

In this updated version of the function, the if statement condition returns a Boolean value based on a comparison. This function is much safer and is less affected by incorrect values.

Data Type Errors

Because JavaScript is loosely typed, variables and function arguments aren't compared to ensure that the correct type of data is being used. It is up to you, as the developer, to do an appropriate amount of data type checking to ensure that an error will not occur. Data type errors most often occur as a result of unexpected values being passed into a function.

In the previous example, the data type of the third argument is checked to ensure that it's a string, but the other two arguments aren't checked at all. If the function must return a string, then passing in two numbers and omitting the third argument easily breaks it. A similar situation is present in the following function:

```
// unsafe function, any non-string value causes an error
function getQueryString(url) {
  const pos = url.indexOf("?");
  if (pos> -1){
    return url.substring(pos +1);
  }
  return "";
}
```

The purpose of this function is to return the query string of a given URL. To do so, it first looks for a question mark in the string using indexOf() and, if found, returns everything after the question mark using the substring() method. The two methods used in this example are specific to strings, so any other data type that is passed in will cause an error. The following simple type check makes this function less error prone:

```
function getQueryString(url) {
  if (typeof url === "string") {  // safer with type check
    let pos = url.indexOf("?");
    if (pos> -1) {
      return url.substring(pos +1);
    }
  }
  return "";
}
```

In this rewritten version of the function, the first step is to check that the value passed in is actually a string. This ensures that the function will never cause an error because of a nonstring value.

As discussed in the previous section, using non-Boolean values as conditions for flow control statements is a bad idea because of type coercion. This is also a bad practice that can cause data type errors. Consider the following function:

```
// unsafe function, non-array values cause an error
function reverseSort(values) {
  if (values) {  // avoid!!!
    values.sort();
    values.reverse();
  }
}
```

The `reverseSort()` function sorts an array in reverse order, using both the `sort()` and the `reverse()` methods. Because of the control condition in the `if` statement, any nonarray value that converts to `true` will cause an error. Another common mistake is to compare the argument against `null`, as in this example:

```
// still unsafe, non-array values cause an error
function reverseSort(values) {
  if (values != null) {  // avoid!!!
    values.sort();
    values.reverse();
  }
}
```

Comparing a value against `null` only protects the code from two values: `null` and `undefined` (which are equivalent to using the equal and not equal operators). A `null` comparison doesn't do enough to ensure that the value is appropriate; therefore, this technique should be avoided. It's also recommended that you don't compare a value against `undefined`, for the same reason.

Another poor choice is to use feature detection for only one of the features being used. Here is an example:

```
// still unsafe, non-array values cause an error
function reverseSort(values) {
  if (typeof values.sort === "function") {  // avoid!!!
    values.sort();
    values.reverse();
  }
}
```

In this example, the code checks for the existence of a `sort()` method on the argument. This leaves open the possibility that an object may be passed in with a `sort()` function that is not an array, in which case the call to `reverse()` causes an error. When you know the exact type of object that is expected, it's best to use `instanceof`, as shown in the following example, to determine that the value is of the right type:

```
// safe, non-array values are ignored
function reverseSort(values) {
  if (values instanceof Array) {  // fixed
    values.sort();
    values.reverse();
  }
}
```

This last version of `reverseSort()` is safe—it tests the values argument to see if it's an instance of Array. In this way, the function is assured that any nonarray values are ignored.

Generally speaking, values that should be primitive types should be checked using `typeof`, and values that should be objects should be checked using `instanceof`. Depending on how a function is being used, it may not be necessary to check the data type of every argument, but any public-facing APIs should definitely perform type checking to ensure proper execution.

Distinguishing Between Fatal and Nonfatal Errors

One of the most important parts of any error-handling strategy is to determine whether or not an error is fatal. One or more of the following identifies a nonfatal error:

➤ It won't interfere with the user's main tasks.

➤ It affects only a portion of the page.

➤ Recovery is possible.

➤ Repeating the action may result in success.

In essence, nonfatal errors aren't a cause for concern. For example, Gmail (`https://mail.google.com`) has a feature that allows users to send Hangouts messages from the interface. If, for some reason, Hangouts don't work, it's a nonfatal error because that is not the application's primary function. The primary use case for Gmail is to read and write e-mail messages, and as long as the user can do that, there is no reason to interrupt the user experience. Nonfatal errors don't require you to send an explicit message to the user. You may be able to replace the area of the page that is affected with a message indicating that the functionality isn't available, but it's not necessary to interrupt the user.

Fatal errors, on the other hand, are identified by one or more of the following:

➤ The application absolutely cannot continue.

➤ The error significantly interferes with the user's primary objective.

➤ Other errors will occur as a result.

It's vitally important to understand when a fatal error occurs in JavaScript so appropriate action can be taken. When a fatal error occurs, you should send a message to the users immediately to let them know that they will not be able to continue what they were doing. If the page must be reloaded for the application to work, then you should tell the user this and provide a button that automatically reloads the page.

You must also make sure that your code doesn't dictate what is and is not a fatal error. Nonfatal and fatal errors are primarily indicated by their effect on the user. Good code design means that an error in one part of the application shouldn't unnecessarily affect another part that, in reality, isn't related at all. For example, consider a personalized home page, such as Gmail (`https://mail.google.com`), that has multiple independent modules on the page. If each module has to be initialized using a JavaScript call, you may see code that looks something like this:

```
for (let mod of mods){
    mod.init();   // possible fatal error
}
```

On its surface, this code appears fine: the `init()` method is called on each module. The problem is that an error in any module's `init()` method will cause all modules that come after it in the array to never be initialized. If the error occurs on the first module, then none of the modules on the page will be initialized. Logically, this doesn't make sense because each module is an independent entity that isn't reliant on any other module for its functionality. It's the structure of the code that makes this type of error fatal. Fortunately, the code can be rewritten as follows to make an error in any one module nonfatal:

```
for (let mod of mods){
  try {
    mod.init();
  } catch (ex){
    // handle error here
  }
}
```

By adding a try-catch statement into the for loop, any error when a module initializes will not prevent other modules from initializing. When an error occurs in this code, it can be handled independently and in a way that doesn't interfere with the user experience.

DEBUGGING TECHNIQUES

Before JavaScript debuggers were readily available, developers had to use creative methods to debug their code. This led to the placement of code specifically designed to output debugging information in one or more ways. The most common debugging technique was to insert alerts throughout the code in question, which was both tedious, because it required cleanup after the code was debugged, and annoying if an alert was mistakenly left in code that was used in a production environment. Alerts are no longer recommended for debugging purposes, because several other, more elegant solutions are available.

Logging Messages to a Console

All major browsers have a JavaScript console for debugging, testing, and monitoring JavaScript code. The JavaScript console is accessed via the `console` object.

`console.log()` is used to output messages to the browser's developer console. It can take one or more arguments and outputs them to the console. The messages can be strings, numbers, objects, or any other type of data. `console.log()` is useful for debugging and provides a quick way to check the value of variables or to output messages during the execution of code.

```
console.log("Hello, world!");
// Hello, world!

console.log(`1 + 2 + 3 = ${1+2+3}`);
// 1 + 2 + 3 = 6

console.log("foo", 3, []);
// foo, 3, []
```

Logging messages to the JavaScript console is helpful in debugging code, but all messages should be removed when code goes to production. This can be done automatically, using a code-processing step in deployment, or manually.

> **NOTE** *Logging messages is considered a better debugging method than using alerts, because alerts interrupt program execution, which may affect the result of the code as timing of asynchronous processes are affected. Logging also allows you to print an arbitrary number of arguments and inspect object instances (alerting an object will serialize it to a string before alerting, leading you to all-too-often see* Object[Object] *as the alert message).*

Log Levels

In JavaScript, log levels are used to categorize log messages based on their importance or severity. Different log levels are used to provide a clear distinction between various types of log messages, making it easier to filter and analyze logs. The console object has the following methods for logging:

➤ error(message) —Logs an error message to the console.

➤ warn(message) —Logs a warning message to the console.

➤ log(message) —Logs a general message to the console.

➤ info(message) —Logs an informational message to the console.

➤ debug(message) —Logs a debug message to the console. This message will only appear if enabled in the console.

The message display on the error console differs according to the method that was used to log the message. Error messages contain a red icon, whereas warnings contain a yellow icon. Console messages may be used, as in the following function:

```
function sum(...nums) {
  if (nums.filter(x => typeof x !== "number").length > 0) {
    console.error("Non-number provided to sum(), returning 0");
    return 0;
  }

  if (nums.length === 0) {
    console.warn("No numbers provided");
    return 0;
  }

  console.debug("Before calculation");
  const result = nums.reduce((a, b) => a + b, 0);
  console.debug("After calculation");

  console.info("Exiting sum()");
  return result;
}
```

As the sum() function is called, several messages are output to the JavaScript console to aid in debugging. Browsers allow you to toggle different log levels on or off to filter out noise in the console.

Advanced Console Methods

The `console` object also includes some advanced methods that can make debugging and visualizing data much easier. These methods are *criminally* underutilized by most developers.

`Console.clear()` is used to clear the developer console. It removes all previously logged messages and objects from the console, providing a clean slate for new debugging messages. This can be useful when debugging code, as it allows you to focus on the current debugging messages without being distracted by previous messages. `Console.clear()` can be called at any point during the execution of code, and it does not affect the state of the program in any way.

`Console.assert()` is used to test a condition and output an error message to the console *only* if the condition is `false`. It takes two arguments: a condition to test and an optional message to display if the condition is `false`. If the condition is `true`, `console.assert()` does nothing.

```
Const data = {
  foo: 123
};

console.assert(data.foo, "Object is missing foo property!");
console.assert(data.bar, "Object is missing bar property!");

// Assertion failed: Object is missing bar property
```

`console.group()`, `console.groupEnd()`, and `console.groupCollapsed()` are used to group related console messages together. `console.group()` starts a new group, and `console.groupEnd()` ends the current group, while `console.groupCollapsed()` starts a new group that is initially collapsed. These methods are useful for organizing and structuring console messages, particularly when dealing with complex or lengthy debugging scenarios. The following example shows a sequence of log messages, and Figure 19.1 is a screenshot of what shows up in the browser console:

```
console.log("Ungrouped foo");
console.log("Ungrouped bar");
console.group("My Group");
console.log("Grouped foo");
console.log("Grouped bar");
console.groupEnd();
```

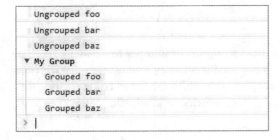

FIGURE 19.1: Grouped console log messages

`console.group()` and `console.groupCollapsed()` can be nested to create hierarchical groups, and `console.groupEnd()` is used to close the current group, effectively behaving as a "group stack."

```
console.group("My Group");           // Start a new group
console.log("Starting loop.");       // Output a message
console.groupCollapsed("Loop");      // Start a new collapsed subgroup
for (let i = 0; i < 5; i++) {
  console.log("Iteration " + i);     // Output a message for each iteration
}
console.groupEnd();                  // End the Loop group
console.log("Loop complete.");       // Output a message
console.groupEnd();                  // End the MyGroup group
```

Figures 19.2 and 19.3 demonstrate the expanded and collapsed subgroup states.

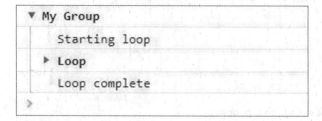

FIGURE 19.2: Nested groups with collapsed subgroup

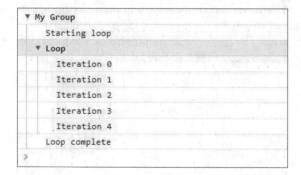

FIGURE 19.3: Nested group with expanded subgroup

`console.count()` and `console.countReset()` are used to count the number of times a particular piece of code is executed. `console.count()` takes an optional label as an argument, and each time it is called with the same label, it increments a counter and outputs the label and counter value to the console. `console.countReset()` resets the counter for a particular label, allowing you to start counting again from one.

```
for (let i = 0; i < 5; i++) {
  console.count("My Loop");
```

```
}

console.countReset("My Loop");
console.count("My Loop");

// My Loop: 1
// My Loop: 2
// My Loop: 3
// My Loop: 4
// My Loop: 5
// My Loop: 1
```

`console.time()`, `console.timeEnd()`, and `console.timeLog()` are used to measure the execution time of code.

`console.time()` starts a timer with a label provided as an argument. When the timer is started, the console records the current time. `console.timeLog()` outputs an intermediate message with the elapsed time since the timer started. `console.timeEnd()` stops the timer with the given label and outputs the elapsed time to the console. The elapsed time is calculated by subtracting the current time from the start time of the timer.

```
console.time("My Timer");
for (let i = 0; i < 1000000; i++) {
  if (i % 100000 === 0) {
    console.timeLog("My Timer", `Finished ${i} items`);
  }
}
console.timeEnd("My Timer");

// My Timer: 0.009033203125 ms Finished 0 items
// My Timer: 1.578125 ms Finished 100000 items
// My Timer: 2.38623046875 ms Finished 200000 items
// My Timer: 3.76513671875 ms Finished 300000 items
// My Timer: 4.132080078125 ms Finished 400000 items
// My Timer: 4.256103515625 ms Finished 500000 items
// My Timer: 4.405029296875 ms Finished 600000 items
// My Timer: 4.574951171875 ms Finished 700000 items
// My Timer: 4.801025390625 ms Finished 800000 items
// My Timer: 5.062255859375 ms Finished 900000 items
// My Timer: 5.320068359375 ms
```

`console.dir()`, `console.dirxml()`, and `console.table()` are used to display objects and arrays in a more readable format. `console.dir()` displays an object in a hierarchical format, allowing you to view its properties and methods. `console.dirxml()` is similar to `console.dir()`, but it is specifically designed for displaying XML and HTML documents in a hierarchical format. These methods are less useful in modern browsers as the modern browser consoles will intelligently display objects and XML when using `console.log()`.

`console.table()` displays an array or object as a table, with each element or property displayed as a row in the table. It can be useful for visualizing data in a more organized and readable format.

```
const myArray = [{
  name: "Alice",
  age: 30
}, {
```

```
      name: "Bob",
      age: 25
    }, {
      name: "Chuck",
      age: 40
    }];
    console.table(myArray);
```

Figure 19.4 demonstrates the tabular formatting printed by `console.table()`

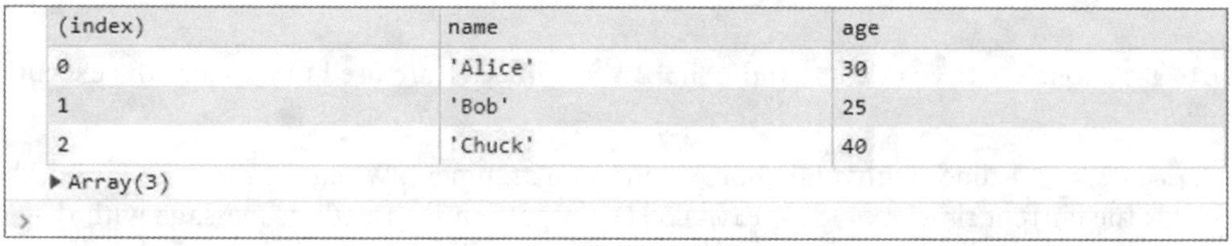

(index)	name	age
0	'Alice'	30
1	'Bob'	25
2	'Chuck'	40
▶ Array(3)		

FIGURE 19.4: Output of `console.table()`

`console.trace()` is used to output a stack trace to the console. A stack trace is a report of the function calls made by a program, along with the line numbers of the calls in the source code. It shows the order in which functions were called as well as how they were nested.

When `console.trace()` is called, it outputs a stack trace to the console, starting with the function that called `console.trace()` and continuing up the call stack. The stack trace includes the names of the functions, along with their file names and line numbers.

```
function foo() {
  console.trace();
}

function bar() {
  foo();
}

bar();
```

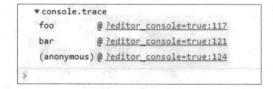

FIGURE 19.5: Output of `console.trace()`

Figure 19.5 demonstrates the stack trace output printed by `console.trace()`

Understanding the Console Runtime

The browser console is a REPL (read-eval-print loop) that is concurrent with the page's JavaScript runtime. It behaves effectively the same way as if the browser were evaluating a newly discovered `<script>` tag inside the DOM. Commands executed from inside the console can access globals and various APIs in the same way that page-level JavaScript can. An arbitrary amount of code can be evaluated from the console; as is the case with any other page-level code it is blocking. Modifications, objects, and callbacks will persist to the DOM and/or runtime.

The JavaScript runtime will restrict what different windows can access, and so in all major browsers you are able to select which window the JavaScript console inputs should execute in. The code you execute does not execute with elevated privilege—it is still subject to cross-origin restrictions and any other controls that are enforced by the browser.

The console runtime also has developer tool integration that offers you some contextual bonus tools to help with debugging that are not available in normal JavaScript. One of the most useful tools is the last-clicked selector, which is available in some form in all major browsers. In the Element tab inside the developer tools, when you click a node in the DOM tree, you gain a reference to the JavaScript instance of that node inside the Console tab by using $0. It behaves as a normal JavaScript instance, so reading properties such as $0.scrollWidth and invoking member methods such as $0.remove() are allowed.

Using the JavaScript Debugger

Also available to you in all major browsers is the JavaScript debugger. As part of the ECMAScript specification, the debugger keyword will attempt to invoke any available debugging functionality. If there is no associated behavior, this statement will be silently skipped as a no-op. The statement can be used as follows:

```
function pauseExecution(){
  console.log("Will print before breakpoint");
  debugger;
  console.log("Will not print until breakpoint continues");
}
```

When the runtime encounters the keyword, in all major browsers it will open the developer tools panel with a breakpoint set at that exact point. You will then be able to use a separate browser console that executes code at the specific lexical scope in which the breakpoint is currently stopped. Additionally, you will be able to perform standard code debugger operations (step into, step over, continue, and so on).

Browsers will also commonly allow you to set breakpoints manually (without using the debugger keyword statement) by inspecting the actual loaded JavaScript code inside the developer tools and selecting the line at which you would like to set the breakpoint. This set breakpoint will behave in the same way, but it will not persist through browser sessions.

Logging Messages to the Page

Another common way to log debugging messages is to specify an area of the page that messages are written to. This may be an element that is included all the time but only used for debugging purposes, or an element that is created only when necessary. For example, the log() function may be changed to the following:

```
function log(message) {
  // Lexical scope of this function will use the following instance
  // instead of window.console
  const console = document.getElementById("debuginfo");
```

```
  if (console === null){
    console = document.createElement("div");
    console.id = "debuginfo";
    console.style.background = "#dedede";
    console.style.border = "1px solid silver";
    console.style.padding = "5px";
    console.style.width = "400px";
    console.style.position = "absolute";
    console.style.right = "0px";
    console.style.top = "0px";
    document.body.appendChild(console);
  }
  console.innerHTML += '<p> ${message}</p>';
}
```

In this new version of log(), the code first checks to see if the debugging element already exists. If not, then a new <div> element is created and assigned stylistic information to separate it from the rest of the page. After that, the message is written into the <div> using innerHTML. The result is a small area that displays log information on the page.

> **NOTE** *As with console logging, page-logging code should be removed before the code is used in a production environment.*

Shimming Console Methods

It is burdensome to a developer to remember to use two different types of log statements—the native console.log(), and a separately defined custom log(). Because console is a global object with writable member methods, it is completely possible to overwrite its member methods with custom behavior and allow log statements sprinkled throughout the codebase to happily log to whatever you have defined.

You can define a shim as follows:

```
// Join all arguments into string and alert the result
console.log = function() {
  // 'arguments' does not have a join method, first convert arguments to array
  const args = Array.prototype.slice.call(arguments);
  console.log(args.join(', '));
}
```

Now, this will be invoked instead of the conventional log behavior. This modification will not persist a page reload, so it is a useful and lightweight strategy for debugging or log interception.

Throwing Errors

As mentioned earlier, throwing errors is an excellent way to debug code. If your error messages are specific enough, just seeing the error as it's reported may be enough to determine the error's source.

The key to good error messages is for them to provide exact details about the cause of the error so that additional debugging is minimal. Consider the following function:

```
function divide(num1, num2) {
  return num1 / num2;
}
```

This simple function divides two numbers but will return NaN if either of the two arguments isn't a number. Simple calculations often cause problems in web applications when they return NaN unexpectedly. In this case, you can check that the type of each argument is a number before attempting the calculation. Consider the following example:

```
function divide(num1, num2) {
  if (typeof num1 != "number" || typeof num2 != "number"){
    throw new Error("divide(): Both arguments must be numbers.");
  }
  return num1 / num2;
}
```

Here, an error is thrown if either of the two arguments isn't a number. The error message provides the name of the function and the exact cause of the error. When the browser reports this error message, it immediately gives you a place to start looking for problems and a basic summary of the issue. This is much easier than dealing with a nonspecific browser error message.

In large applications, custom errors are typically thrown using an assert() function. Such a function takes a condition that should evaluate to true and throws an error if the condition is false. The following is a very basic assert() function:

```
function assert(condition, message) {
  if (!condition) {
    throw new Error(message);
  }
}
```

The assert() function can be used in place of multiple if statements in a function and can be a good location for error logging. This function can be used as follows:

```
function divide(num1, num2) {
  assert(typeof num1 == "number" && typeof num2 == "number",
         "divide(): Both arguments must be numbers.");
  return num1 / num2;
}
```

Using an assert() function reduces the amount of code necessary to throw custom errors and makes the code more readable compared to the previous example.

SUMMARY

Error handling in JavaScript is critical for today's complex web applications. Failing to anticipate where errors might occur and how to recover from them can lead to a poor user experience and possibly frustrated users. Most browsers don't report JavaScript errors to users by default, so you need to enable error reporting when developing and debugging. In production, however, no errors should ever be reported this way.

The following methods can be used to prevent the browser from reacting to a JavaScript error:

➤ The `try-catch` statement can be used where errors may occur, giving you the opportunity to respond to errors in an appropriate way instead of allowing the browser to handle the error.

➤ Another option is to use the `window.onerror` event handler, which receives all errors that are not handled by a `try-catch`.

Each web application should be inspected to determine where errors might occur and how those errors should be dealt with.

➤ A determination as to what constitutes a fatal error or a nonfatal error needs to be made ahead of time.

➤ After that, code can be evaluated to determine where the most likely errors will occur. Errors commonly occur in JavaScript because of type coercion and insufficient data type checking.

Debuggers offer the ability to set breakpoints, control code execution, and inspect the value of variables at runtime.

20

JSON

WHAT'S IN THIS CHAPTER?

➤ Understanding JSON syntax

➤ JSON parsing

➤ JSON serialization

There was a time when XML was the de facto standard for transmitting structured data over the internet. The first iteration of web services was largely XML-based, highlighting its target of server-to-server communication. XML was not, however, without its detractors. Some believed that the language was overly verbose and redundant. Several solutions arose to counter these problems, but the web had already started moving in a new direction.

Douglas Crockford first specified JavaScript Object Notation (JSON) as IETF RFC 4627 in 2006, even though it was in use as early as 2001. JSON is a strict subset of JavaScript, making use of several patterns found in JavaScript to represent structured data. Crockford put forth JSON as a better alternative to XML for accessing structured data in JavaScript because it could be passed directly to eval() and didn't require the creation of a DOM.

The most important thing to understand about JSON is that it is a data format, not a programming language. JSON is not a part of JavaScript even though they share syntax. JSON is also not solely used by JavaScript because it is a data format. There are parsers and serializers available in many programming languages.

SYNTAX

JSON syntax allows the representation of three types of values:

➤ **Simple values**—Strings, numbers, Booleans, and `null` can all be represented in JSON using the same syntax as JavaScript. The special value undefined is not supported.

➤ **Objects**—The first complex data type, objects represent ordered key-value pairs. Each value may be a primitive type or a complex type.

➤ **Arrays**—The second complex data type, arrays represent an ordered list of values that are accessible via a numeric index. The values may be of any type, including simple values, objects, and even other arrays.

There are no variables, functions, or object instances in JSON. JSON is all about representing structured data, and although it shares syntax with JavaScript, it should not be confused with JavaScript paradigms.

Simple Values

In its simplest form, JSON represents a small number of simple values. For example, the following is valid JSON:

```
5
```

This is JSON that represents the number 5. Likewise, the following is also valid JSON representing a string:

```
"Hello world!"
```

The big difference between JavaScript strings and JSON strings is that JSON strings must use double quotes to be valid (single quotes causes a syntax error).

Boolean values and `null` are valid exactly as they are as standalone JSON. In practice, however, JSON is most often used to represent more complex data structures of which simple values represent just part of the overall information.

Objects

Objects are represented using a slight modification of object literal notation. Object literals in Java-Script look like this:

```
let person = {
  name: "Nicholas",
  age: 29
};
```

While this is the standard way that developers create object literals, it's the quoted property format that is used in JSON. The following is exactly the same as the previous example:

```
let object = {
    "name": "Nicholas",
    "age": 29
};
```

The JSON representation of this same object is then:

```
{
    "name": "Nicholas",
    "age": 29
}
```

There are a couple of differences from the JavaScript example. First, there is no variable declaration (variables don't exist in JSON). Second, there is no trailing semicolon (not needed because this isn't a JavaScript statement). Once again, the quotes around the property name are required to be valid JSON. The value can be any simple or complex value, which allows you to embed objects within objects, such as:

```
{
    "name": "Nicholas",
    "age": 29,
    "school": {
        "name": "Merrimack College",
        "location": "North Andover, MA"
    }
}
```

This example embeds school information into the top-level object. Even though there are two properties called "name", they are in two different objects and so are allowed. You do want to avoid having two properties of the same name in the same object.

Unlike JavaScript, object property names in JSON must always be double-quoted. It's a common mistake to hand-code JSON without these double quotes or using single quotes.

Arrays

The second complex type in JSON is the array. Arrays are represented in JSON using array literal notation from JavaScript. For example, this is an array in JavaScript:

```
let values = [25, "hi", true];
```

You can represent this same array in JSON using a similar syntax:

```
[25, "hi", true]
```

Note once again the absence of a variable or a semicolon. Arrays and objects can be used together to represent more complex collections of data, such as:

```
[
    {
        "title": "Professional JavaScript",
        "authors": [
```

```
        "Matt Frisbie"
    ],
    "edition": 5,
    "year": 2023
  },
  {
    "title": "Professional JavaScript",
    "authors": [
        "Matt Frisbie"
    ],
    "edition": 4,
    "year": 2017
  },
  {
    "title": "Professional JavaScript",
    "authors": [
        "Nicholas C. Zakas"
    ],
    "edition": 3,
    "year": 2011
  }
]
```

This array contains a number of objects representing books. Each object has several keys, one of which is `"authors"`, which is another array. Objects and arrays are typically top-level parts of a JSON data structure (even though this is not required) and can be used to create a large number of data structures.

PARSING AND SERIALIZATION

JSON rose to popularity not necessarily because it used familiar syntax. Rather, it became popular because the data could be parsed into a usable object in JavaScript. This stood in stark contrast to XML that was parsed into a DOM document, making extraction of data into a bit of a chore for JavaScript developers. For example, the JSON code in the previous section contains a list of books, and you can easily get the title of the third book via:

```
books[2].title
```

This assumes that the data structure was stored in a variable named books. Compare this to a typical walk through of a DOM structure:

```
doc.getElementsByTagName("book")[2].getAttribute("title");
```

With all of the extra method calls, it's no wonder that JSON became incredibly popular with JavaScript developers. After that, JSON went on to become the de facto serialization standard for web services.

The JSON Object

Early JSON parsers did little more than use JavaScript's eval() function. Because JSON is a subset of JavaScript's syntax, eval() could parse, interpret, and return the data as JavaScript objects and arrays. ECMAScript 5 formalized JSON parsing under a native global called JSON. This object is supported in all major browsers. A shim for older browsers can be found at `https://github.com/douglascrockford/JSON-js`. It's important not to use `eval()` alone for evaluating JSON in older browsers because of the risk of executable code. The JSON shim is the best option for browsers without native JSON parsing.

The JSON object has two methods: `stringify()` and `parse()`. In simple usage, these methods serialize JavaScript objects into a JSON string and parse JSON into a native JavaScript value, respectively. For example:

```
let book = {
  title: "Professional JavaScript",
  authors: [
    "Matt Frisbie"
  ],
  edition: 5,
  year: 2023
};
let jsonText = JSON.stringify(book);
```

This example serializes a JavaScript object into a JSON string using `JSON.stringify()` and stores it in `jsonText`. By default, `JSON.stringify()` outputs a JSON string without any extra white space or indentation, so the value stored in `jsonText` is as follows:

```
{"title":"Professional JavaScript","authors":["Matt Frisbie"],"edition":5,
"year":2023}
```

When serializing a JavaScript object, all functions and prototype members are intentionally omitted from the result. Additionally, any property whose value is undefined is also skipped. You're left with just a representation of the instance properties that are one of the JSON data types.

A JSON string can be passed directly into `JSON.parse()` and it creates an appropriate JavaScript value. For example, you can create an object similar to the book object using this code:

```
let bookCopy = JSON.parse(jsonText);
```

Note that book and `bookCopy` are each separate objects without any relationship to one another even though they do share the same properties.

An error is thrown if the text passed into `JSON.parse()` is not valid JSON.

Serialization Options

The `JSON.stringify()` method accepts two optional arguments in addition to the object to serialize. These arguments allow you to specify alternate ways to serialize a JavaScript object. The first argument is a filter, which can be either an array or a function, and the second argument is an option for indenting the resulting JSON string. When used separately or together, this provides some very useful functionality for controlling JSON serialization.

Filtering Results

If the argument is an array, then `JSON.stringify()` will include only object properties that are listed in the array. Consider the following:

```
let book = {
    title: "Professional JavaScript",
    authors: [
        "Matt Frisbie"
    ],
    edition: 5,
    year: 2023
};
let jsonText = JSON.stringify(book, ["title", "edition"]);
```

The second argument to `JSON.stringify()` is an array with two strings: `"title"` and `"edition"`. These correspond to properties in the object being serialized, so only those properties appear in the resulting JSON string:

```
{"title":"Professional JavaScript","edition":5}
```

When the second argument is a function, the behavior is slightly different. The provided function receives two arguments: the property key name and the property value. You can look at the key to determine what to do with the property. The key is always a string but might be an empty string if a value isn't part of a key-value pair.

In order to change the serialization of the object, return the value that should be included for that key. Keep in mind that returning undefined will result in the property being omitted from the result. Here's an example:

```
let book = {
    title: "Professional JavaScript",
    authors: [
        "Matt Frisbie"
    ],
    edition: 5,
    year: 2023
};
let jsonText = JSON.stringify(book, (key, value) => {
    switch(key) {
        case "authors":
            return value.join(",")
        case "year":
            return 5000;
        case "edition":
            return undefined;
        default:
            return value;
    }
});
```

The function filters based on the key. The "authors" key is translated from an array to a string, the "year" key is set to 5000, and the "edition" key is removed altogether by returning undefined.

It's important to provide a default behavior that returns the passed-in value so that all other values are passed through to the result. The first call to this function actually has key equal to an empty string and the value set to the book object. The resulting JSON string is:

```
{"title":"Professional JavaScript","authors":" Matt Frisbie","year":5000}
```

Keep in mind that filters apply to all objects contained in the object to be serialized, so an array of multiple objects with these properties will result in every object including only the "title" and "edition" properties.

String Indentation

The third argument of JSON.stringify() controls indentation and white space. When this argument is a number, it represents the number of spaces to indent each level. For example, to indent each level by four spaces, use the following:

```
let book = {
    title: "Professional JavaScript",
    authors: [
      "Matt Frisbie"
    ],
    edition: 5,
    year: 2023
};
let jsonText = JSON.stringify(book, null, 4);
```

The following is the string stored in jsonText:

```
{
    "title": "Professional JavaScript",
    "authors": [
        "Matt Frisbie"
    ],
    "edition": 5,
    "year": 2023
}
```

You may have noticed that JSON.stringify() also inserts new lines into the JSON string for easier reading. This happens for all valid indentation argument values. (Indentation without new lines isn't very useful.) The maximum numeric indentation value is 10; passing in a value larger than 10 automatically sets the value to 10.

If the indentation argument is a string instead of a number, then the string is used as the indentation character for the JSON string instead of a space. Using a string, you can set the indentation character to be a tab or something completely arbitrary like two dashes:

```
let jsonText = JSON.stringify(book, null, "--");
```

The jsonText value then becomes:

```
{
--"title": "Professional JavaScript",
--"authors": [
```

```
----"Matt Frisbie"
--],
--"edition": 5,
--"year": 2023
}
```

There is a ten-character limit on the indentation string to use. If a string longer than ten characters is used, then it is truncated to the first ten characters.

The *toJSON()* Method

Sometimes objects need custom JSON serialization above and beyond what JSON.stringify() can do. In those cases, you can add a toJSON() method to the object and have it return the proper JSON representation for itself. In fact, the native Date object has a toJSON() method that automatically converts JavaScript Date objects into an ISO 8601 date string (essentially, the same as calling toISOString() on the Date object).

A toJSON() method can be added to any object, for example:

```
let book = {
  title: "Professional JavaScript",
  authors: [
    "Matt Frisbie"
  ],
  edition: 5,
  year: 2023,
  toJSON: function() {
    return this.title;
  }
};
let jsonText = JSON.stringify(book);
```

This code defines a toJSON() method on the book object that simply returns the title of the book. Similar to the Date object, this object is serialized to a simple string instead of an object. You can return any serialization value from toJSON(), and it will work appropriately. Returning undefined causes the value to become null if the object is embedded in another object or else is just undefined if the object is top-level. Note here that an arrow function is not used for the toJSON() method. This is primarily because the lexical scope of the arrow function will be the global scope, which is unhelpful in this example.

The toJSON() method can be used in addition to the filter function so it's important to understand the order in which the various parts of a serialization process take place. When an object is passed into JSON.stringify(), the following steps are taken:

1. Call the toJSON() method if it's available to retrieve the actual value. Use the default serialization otherwise.

2. If the second argument is provided, apply the filter. The value that is passed into a filter function will be the value returned from Step 1.

3. Each value from Step 2 is serialized appropriately.

4. If the third argument is provided, format appropriately.

It's important to understand this order when deciding whether to create a `toJSON()` method or to use a filter function or to do both.

Parsing Options

The `JSON.parse()` method also accepts an additional argument, which is a function that is called on each key-value pair. The function is called a *reviver* function to distinguish it from the *replacer* (filter) function that `JSON.stringify()` accepts, even though the format is exactly the same: the function receives two arguments, the key and the value, and needs to return a value.

If the reviver function returns undefined, then the key is removed from the result; if it returns any other value, that value is inserted into the result. A very common use of the reviver function is to turn date strings into Date objects. For example:

```
let book = {
  title: "Professional JavaScript",
  authors: [
    "Matt Frisbie"
  ],
  edition: 5,
  year: 2023,
  releaseDate: new Date(2023, 6, 1)
};
let jsonText = JSON.stringify(book);
let bookCopy = JSON.parse(jsonText,
    (key, value) => key == "releaseDate" ? new Date(value) : value);
alert(bookCopy.releaseDate.getFullYear());
```

This code starts with the addition of a `releaseDate` property to the book object, which is a Date. The object is serialized to get a valid JSON string and then parsed back into an object, `bookCopy`. The reviver function looks for the "releaseDate" key and, when found, creates a new Date object based on that string. The resulting `bookCopy.releaseDate` property is then a Date object so the `getFullYear()` method can be called.

SUMMARY

JSON is a lightweight data format designed to easily represent complex data structures. The format uses a subset of JavaScript syntax to represent objects, arrays, strings, numbers, Booleans, and `null`. Even though XML can handle the same job, JSON is less verbose and has better support in Java-Script. What's more, the native JSON object is well supported across all browsers.

ECMAScript defines a native JSON object that is used for serialization of objects into JSON format and for parsing JSON data into JavaScript objects. The `JSON.stringify()` and `JSON.parse()` methods are used for these two operations, respectively. Both methods have a number of options that allow you to change the default behavior to filter or otherwise modify the process.

21

Network Requests and Remote Resources

WHAT'S IN THIS CHAPTER?

➤ Using the Fetch API and Streams API

➤ Cross-domain restrictions

➤ The EventSource API

➤ Web Sockets and beacons

> **DOWNLOADS FOR THIS CHAPTER**
>
> Please note that all the code examples for this chapter are available as a part of this chapter's code download on the book's website at www.wiley.com/go/ projavascript5e.

In 2005, Jesse James Garrett penned an online article titled "Ajax: A New Approach to Web Applications." This article outlined a technique that he referred to as *Ajax,* short for *Asynchronous JavaScript+XML.* The technique consisted of making server requests for additional data without unloading the web page, resulting in a better user experience. Garrett explained how this technique could be used to change the traditional click-and-wait paradigm that the web had been stuck in since its inception.

The key technology pushing Ajax forward was the `XMLHttpRequest` (XHR) object, first invented by Microsoft and then duplicated by other browser vendors. Prior to the introduction of XHR, Ajax-style communication had to be accomplished through a number of hacks, mostly using hidden frames or iframes. XHR introduced a streamlined interface for making server requests and evaluating the responses. This allowed for asynchronous retrieval of additional information from the server, meaning that a user click didn't have to refresh the page to retrieve more data. Instead, an XHR object could be used to retrieve the data and then the data could be inserted into the page using the DOM. And despite the mention of XML in the name, Ajax communication is format-agnostic; the technique is about retrieving data from the server without refreshing a page, not necessarily about XML.

The technique that Garrett referred to as Ajax had, in fact, been around for some time. Typically called *remote scripting* prior to Garrett's article, such browser-server communication has been possible since 1998 using different techniques. Early on, server requests could be made from JavaScript through an intermediary, such as a Java applet or Flash movie. The XHR object brought native browser communication capabilities to developers, reducing the amount of work necessary to achieve the result.

The Fetch API has largely replaced `XMLHttpRequest` (XHR) as the preferred way to make HTTP requests in modern web development. Fetch provides a simpler and more intuitive interface for making network requests, with a more flexible and powerful feature set. In particular, Fetch uses Promises, which provide a simpler and more consistent way to handle asynchronous code compared to the complex and error-prone callbacks used by XHR. Additionally, Fetch supports features such as streaming responses, request cancellation, and automatic request retries, which are not available with XHR. While XHR is still widely used in legacy code, it is recommended to use Fetch in new web applications for its improved functionality and ease of use.

> **NOTE** `XMLHttpRequest`, *though still widely supported, is an artifact of outdated JavaScript specifications and is not covered in this chapter. Its replacement, the Fetch API, is superior is all aspects.*

THE FETCH API

The Fetch API is a WHATWG living standard specification, which can be found at `https://fetch .spec.whatwg.org`. The specification puts it best: "*The Fetch standard defines requests, responses, and the process that binds them: fetching.*"

The Fetch API itself is mostly used for requesting resources and transmitting data in JavaScript, but the API is also relevant in the domain of service workers in that it provides an interface for intercepting, redirecting, and altering requests made via `fetch()`.

Basic API Utilization

The fetch() method is available in any global scope, both in the primary page execution, modules, and inside workers. Invoking it will instruct the browser to send a request to a provided URL.

Dispatching a Request

The fetch() method has only a single required parameter input, which most of the time will be the URL of the resource you wish to fetch. The URL is relative to the page on which the code is called, although an absolute path can be given as well.

This method returns a promise:

```
let r = fetch('/bar');
console.log(r);  // Promise <pending>
```

When the request completes and the resource is available, the promise will resolve into a Response object, which is used as the API wrapper for whatever resource was fetched. This object exposes several properties and methods to inspect the response and convert the payload into a useful form, as shown here:

```
fetch('bar.txt')
  .then((response) => {
    console.log(response);
  });

// Response { type: "basic", url: ... }
```

Reading a Response

The simplest way to read the contents of a response is in the raw text format, which is accessed using the text() method. This method returns a promise that resolves with the full contents of the fetched resource:

```
fetch('bar.txt')
  .then((response) => response.text())
  .then((data) => console.log(data));

// Contents of bar.txt!
```

Handling Status Codes and Request Failures

The Fetch API allows you to inspect the Response object's status code and status text, accessible via the status and statusText properties, respectively. Successfully fetching the resource will typically yield a response code of 200, as shown in this example:

```
fetch('/bar')
  .then((response) => {
    console.log(response.status);      // 200
    console.log(response.statusText);  // OK
  });
```

Requesting a resource that doesn't exist will typically yield a response code of 404:

```
fetch('/does-not-exist')
  .then((response) => {
    console.log(response.status);      // 404
    console.log(response.statusText);  // Not Found
  });
```

Requesting a resource URL that throws a server error will typically yield a response code of 500:

```
fetch('/throw-server-error')
  .then((response) => {
    console.log(response.status);      // 500
    console.log(response.statusText);  // Internal Server Error
  });
```

The behavior of fetch() with respect to redirects can be explicitly set (as detailed later in this chapter), but the default behavior is to follow a redirect and return a response that does not have a response code of 300–399. When a fetch() is followed, the redirected property is set to true on the response object but will still feature a response code of 200:

```
fetch('/permanent-redirect')
  .then((response) => {
    // Default behavior is to follow the redirects until reaching a terminal URL.
    // This example would incur at least two round trip network requests:
    // <origin url>/permanent-redirect -> <redirect url>
    console.log(response.status);      // 200
    console.log(response.statusText);  // OK
    console.log(response.redirected);  // true
  });
```

In all of these examples, notice that the *resolved* handler of the fetch promise is being executed—even when the request could be considered a failure, such as a 500 status. If the server sends a response of any kind, the fetch() promise will resolve. This behavior should make sense: the system-level network protocol has completed a successful round-trip message transmission. What qualifies as a "successful" request should be defined in how that response is handled.

Commonly, a response in the 200s is considered successful, and anything else is considered unsuccessful. To differentiate between these, the Response object's ok property identifies when the response code is between 200–299.

```
fetch('/bar')
  .then((response) => {
    console.log(response.status);  // 200
    console.log(response.ok);      // true
  });
fetch('/does-not-exist')
  .then((response) => {
    console.log(response.status);  // 404
    console.log(response.ok);      // false
  });
```

A true `fetch()` failure—such as a browser timeout where there is no server response—will reject:

```
fetch('/hangs-forever')
  .then((response) => {
    console.log(response);
  }, (err) => {
    console.log(err);
  });

// (after browser timeout duration)
// TypeError: "NetworkError when attempting to fetch resource."
```

The request promise rejects for reasons such as CORS violations, a lack of connection to a network, HTTPS violations, and other browser/network policy violations.

You can inspect the full URL used by `fetch()` when dispatching the request with the `url` property:

```
// Requests made from foo.com/bar/baz
console.log(window.location.href);  // https://foo.com/bar/baz

fetch('qux').then((response) => console.log(response.url));
// https://foo.com/bar/qux

fetch('/qux').then((response) => console.log(response.url));
// https://foo.com/qux

fetch('//qux.com').then((response) => console.log(response.url));
// https://qux.com

fetch('https://qux.com').then((response) => console.log(response.url));
// https://qux.com
```

Custom Fetch Options

When used with only a URL, `fetch()` will dispatch a GET request with a minimal set of request headers. To configure how a request is dispatched, an `init` object can be passed as the optional second argument to `fetch()`. The `init` object should be populated with any number of the keys and corresponding values in the table that follows.

KEY	VALUE
body	Used to specify the body field for requests that make use of a body. Must be any `Blob`, `BufferSource`, `FormData`, `URLSearchParams`, `ReadableStream`, or string instance.

continues

(continued)

KEY	VALUE
cache	Used to control how the browser will interact with the HTTP cache when performing the fetch. For cached redirects to be followed, the request must have `follow` as its redirect value and must also comply with same-origin restrictions.

Must be one of the following string values:

➤ `default`

  ➤ A fresh cache hit is returned from `fetch()`. No request is sent.

  ➤ A stale cache hit will send a conditional request. If the response has changed, the cached value is updated. The cached value is then returned from `fetch()`.

  ➤ A cache miss will send a request and the response is cached. The response is returned from `fetch()`.

➤ `no-store`

  ➤ The browser sends a request without checking the cache.

  ➤ The response is not cached and is returned from `fetch()`.

➤ `reload`

  ➤ The browser sends a request without checking the cache.

  ➤ The response is cached and is returned from `fetch()`.

➤ `no-cache`

  ➤ Both a fresh or stale cache hit will send a conditional request. If the response has changed, the cached value is updated. The cached value is then returned from `fetch()`.

  ➤ A cache miss will send a request and the response is cached. The response is returned from `fetch()`.

➤ `force-cache`

  ➤ Both a fresh or stale cache hit will be returned from `fetch()`. No request is sent.

  ➤ A cache miss will send a request and the response is cached. The response is returned from `fetch()`.

➤ `only-if-cached`

  ➤ Can only be used if the request mode is `same-origin`.

  ➤ Both a fresh or stale cache hit will be returned from `fetch()`. No request is sent.

  ➤ A cache miss will return a response with a status of 504 (Gateway timeout).

Defaults to `default`.

(continued)

KEY	VALUE
credentials	Used to specify if and how cookies should be included with the outgoing request. Must be one of the following string values: ➤ omit—No cookies are sent. ➤ same-origin—Only send cookies when the request URL origin matches the origin of the script executing the fetch. ➤ include—Cookies are included with both same-origin and cross-origin requests. Can also be a FederatedCredential instance or a PasswordCredential instance in browsers that support the Credential Management API. Defaults to same-origin.
headers	Used to specify headers for a request. Must be either a Headers object instance or regular object instance containing header key-value string pairs. Defaults to a Headers object with no key-value pairs. This does not mean the request will be sent with no headers; the browser may still add headers when the request is formally dispatched. This disparity will be invisible to JavaScript but can still be observed in the browser's network inspector.
integrity	Used to enforce subresource integrity. Must be a string containing the subresource integrity identifier. Defaults to an empty string.
keepalive	Used to direct the browser to allow the request to exist beyond the page's lifetime. This is useful for reporting events or analytics metrics to a server when a page unload might occur soon after a fetch is dispatched. Fetch with the keepalive flag can be used as a substitute for navigator.sendBeacon(). Must be a Boolean. Defaults to false.
method	Used to specify the HTTP method of a request. Will almost always be one of the following string values: ➤ GET ➤ POST ➤ PUT ➤ PATCH ➤ DELETE ➤ HEAD ➤ OPTIONS

continues

(continued)

KEY	VALUE
	➤ CONNECT ➤ TRACE Defaults to GET.
mode	Used to specify the mode for the request. The mode determines if a response from a cross-origin request is valid and how much of the response is readable by the client. Requests that violate the specified mode will throw an error. Must be one of the following string values: ➤ cors—Cross-origin requests that comply with the CORS protocol are allowed. The response will be a "CORS-filtered response," meaning the headers accessible in the response are filtered by a browser-enforced whitelist. ➤ no-cors—Cross-origin requests that do not require a preflight request (HEAD, GET, and POST with only CORS-safelisted request headers) are allowed. The response type will be opaque, meaning the content of the response cannot be read. ➤ same-origin—No cross-origin requests of any kind are allowed. ➤ navigate—Intended for supporting HTML navigation, created only when navigating between documents. You will likely never need to use this mode. When a Request instance is manually created via its constructor, defaults to cors. Otherwise, defaults to no-cors.
redirect	Used to specify how redirected responses (defined as a response status code of 301, 302, 303, 307, or 308) should be handled. Must be one of the following string values: ➤ follow—Requests that redirect will be followed and the eventual URL that has a non-redirected response will be returned as the final response. ➤ error—Requests that redirect will throw an error. ➤ manual—Requests that redirect will not follow the redirect and instead return a response with type opaqueredirect while still exposing the intended redirect URL. This allows the redirect to be followed manually. Defaults to follow.

(continued)

KEY	VALUE
`referrer`	Used to specify what should be sent as the HTTP `Referer` header. Must be one of the following string values: ➤ `no-referrer`—Send no-referrer as the HTTP referrer value. ➤ `client/about:client`—Send the current URL or no-referrer (determined by the referrer policy) as the actual HTTP referrer value. ➤ `<URL>`—Spoof the URL sent as the HTTP `Referer`. The origin of the spoofed URL must match the origin of the executing script. Defaults to `client/about:client`.
`referrer-policy`	Used to specify the HTTP `Referer` header. Must be one of the following string values: ➤ `no-referrer` ➤ The `Referer` header is omitted entirely from the request. ➤ `no-referrer-when-downgrade` ➤ For requests sent from a secure HTTPS context to an HTTP URL, the `Referer` header is omitted. ➤ For all other requests, the `Referer` header is set to the full URL. ➤ `origin` ➤ For all requests, the `Referer` header is set to only the origin. ➤ `same-origin` ➤ For cross-origin requests, the `Referer` header is omitted. ➤ For same-origin requests, the `Referer` header is set to the full URL. ➤ `strict-origin` ➤ For requests sent from a secure HTTPS context to an HTTP URL, the `Referer` header is omitted. ➤ For all other requests, the `Referer` header is set to the origin only. ➤ `origin-when-cross-origin` ➤ For cross-origin requests, the `Referer` header is set to the origin only. ➤ For same-origin requests, the `Referer` header is set to the full URL.

continues

(continued)

KEY	VALUE

	➤ `strict-origin-when-cross-origin`
	
	  ➤ For cross-origin requests sent from a secure HTTPS context to an HTTP URL, the `Referer` header is omitted.
	
	  ➤ For all other cross-origin requests, the `Referer` header is set to only the origin.
	
	  ➤ For same-origin requests, the `Referer` header is set to the full URL.
	
	➤ `unsafe-url`
	
	  ➤ For all requests, the `Referer` header is set to the full URL.
	
	Defaults to `no-referrer-when-downgrade`.

`signal`	Used to enable the ability to abort an inflight fetch via an associated `AbortController`. Must be an `AbortSignal` instance. Defaults to an unassociated `AbortSignal` instance.

Common Fetch Patterns

`fetch()` is used both to retrieve data as well as send it. Using the `init` object, `fetch()` can be configured to send an assortment of serializable data types in the request body.

Sending JSON Data

A simple JSON string could be sent to a server as follows:

```
let payload = JSON.stringify({
  foo: 'bar'
});

let jsonHeaders = new Headers({
  'Content-Type': 'application/json'
});

fetch('/send-me-json', {
  method: 'POST',  // Must use an HTTP method which sends a body
  body: payload,
  headers: jsonHeaders
});
```

Sending Parameters in a Request Body

Because the request body supports any string values, it is also easy to send parameters as a serialized body string:

```
let payload = 'foo=bar&baz=qux';
```

```
let paramHeaders = new Headers({
  'Content-Type': 'application/x-www-form-urlencoded; charset=UTF-8'
});

fetch('/send-me-params', {
  method: 'POST',   // Must use an HTTP method which sends a body
  body: payload,
  headers: paramHeaders
});
```

Sending Files

Because the body supports `FormData` instances, a `fetch()` will happily serialize and send a file plucked from a file picker form input:

```
let imageFormData = new FormData();
let imageInput = document.querySelector("input[type='file']");

imageFormData.append('image', imageInput.files[0]);

fetch('/img-upload', {
  method: 'POST',
  body: imageFormData
});
```

Such a `fetch()` implementation can support multiple files as well:

```
let imageFormData = new FormData();
let imageInput = document.querySelector("input[type='file'] [multiple]");

for (let i = 0; i < imageInput.files.length; ++i) {
  imageFormData.append('image', imageInput.files[i]);
}

fetch('/img-upload', {
  method: 'POST',
  body: imageFormData
});
```

Loading Files as Blobs

The Fetch API is able to provide the response as a `Blob`, which in turn is compatible with multiple browser APIs. One common manifestation of this is explicitly loading an image file into memory and attaching it to an HTML image element. To do so, the response object exposes a `blob()` method that returns a promise that resolves to a `Blob` instance. This in turn can be passed to URL `.createObjectUrl()` to generate a valid value for the image element's `src` attribute:

```
const imageElement = document.querySelector('img');

fetch('my-image.png')
  .then((response) => response.blob())
  .then((blob) => {
    imageElement.src = URL.createObjectURL(blob);
  });
```

Sending a Cross-Origin Request

Requesting a resource from a different origin requires the response to have CORS headers for the browser to accept it. Without the headers, the cross-origin request will fail and throw an error.

```
fetch('//cross-origin.com');
// TypeError: Failed to fetch
// No 'Access-Control-Allow-Origin' header is present on the requested resource.
```

If the code does not need access to the response, it is possible to send a no-cors fetch. In this case, the response type property will be opaque, therefore preventing you from inspecting it. This strategy can be useful for sending pings or in cases where the response can be merely cached for later use.

```
fetch('//cross-origin.com', { method: 'no-cors' })
  .then((response) => console.log(response.type));

// opaque
```

Aborting a Request

The Fetch API supports aborting a request via an AbortController/AbortSignal pair. Calling AbortController.abort() terminates all network transmission, so this is especially useful when you wish to halt transferring a large payload. Aborting an inflight fetch() will cause it to reject with an error.

```
let abortController = new AbortController();

fetch('wikipedia.zip', { signal: abortController.signal })
  .catch(() => console.log('aborted!'));

// Abort the fetch after 10ms
setTimeout(() => abortController.abort(), 10);

// aborted!
```

The Headers Object

The Headers object is used as a container for all outgoing requests and incoming response headers. Every outgoing Request instance includes an empty Headers instance accessible via Request .prototype.headers, and every incoming Response instance includes a populated Headers instance accessible via Response.prototype.headers—both of which are mutable properties. You can also create a fresh instance through the constructor via new Headers().

The Headers object has a high degree of overlap with the Map object. This should make sense, as HTTP headers are essentially serialized key-value pairs, and their JavaScript representation is the intermediate interface. The Headers and Map types share a number of instance methods: get(), set(), has(), and delete(). These types can both be initialized with an iterable, and also feature identical keys(), values(), and entries() iterator interfaces.

Unique Features of the Headers Object

The Headers object is not an exact facsimile of a Map. When initializing, a Headers object can be initialized with an object of key-value pairs, whereas a Map cannot:

```
let seed = {foo: 'bar'};

let h = new Headers(seed);
console.log(h.get('foo'));  // bar

let m = new Map(seed);
// TypeError: object is not iterable
```

A single HTTP header may be assigned multiple values, and the Headers object supports this via the append() method. When used with a header that does not yet exist in a Headers instance, append() behaves identically to set(). Subsequent uses will concatenate the header value delimited with a comma:

```
let h = new Headers();

h.append('foo', 'bar');
console.log(h.get('foo'));  // "bar"

h.append('foo', 'baz');
console.log(h.get('foo'));  // "bar, baz"
```

Header Guards

In some cases, not all HTTP headers are mutable by the client, and the Headers object uses guards to enforce this. Different guard settings will change how set(), append(), and delete() behave. Violating the guard restrictions will throw a TypeError.

A Headers instance will behave differently based on its provenance; this behavior is governed by the guard. It is not possible to determine the guard setting of a Headers instance in JavaScript. The table that follows describes the various possible guard settings and the behavioral implications of each.

GUARD	APPLICABLE SCENARIO	RESTRICTIONS
none	Active when a Headers instance is created via its constructor.	None.
request	Active when a Request object is instantiated via its constructor with any mode that is not no-cors.	No modifications are allowed to headers with forbidden header names (https://developer.mozilla.org/en-US/docs/Glossary/Forbidden_header_name).
request-no-cors	Active when a Request object is instantiated via its constructor with a mode of no-cors.	No modifications are allowed to headers that are not simple headers (https://developer.mozilla.org/en-US/docs/Glossary/simple_header).

continues

(continued)

GUARD	APPLICABLE SCENARIO	RESTRICTIONS
response	Active when a `Response` object is instantiated via its constructor.	No modifications are allowed to headers with forbidden response header names (`https://developer.mozilla.org/en-US/docs/Glossary/Forbidden_response_header_name`).
immutable	Active when a `Response` object is instantiated via the `error()` or `redirect()` static methods.	No header modifications are allowed.

The Request Object

As its name indicates, the `Request` object is an interface to the request for a fetched resource. This interface exposes information about the nature of the request as well as different ways of consuming the body of the request.

> **NOTE** *The properties and methods involving the body are covered in the "Requests, Responses, and the Body Mixin" section in this chapter.*

Creating Request Objects

A `Request` object can be instantiated via a constructor. It requires an input argument, which will most commonly be a URL:

```
let r = new Request('https://foo.com');
console.log(r);
// Request {...}
```

The `Request` constructor also accepts a second optional argument, an `init` object. This `init` object is identical to that of `fetch()`, as described earlier in the chapter in the section "Custom Fetch Options." Values not specified inside `init` will be assigned their default values in the `Request` instance:

```
// Creates Request object with all default values:
console.log(new Request(''));

// Request {
//   bodyUsed: false
//   cache: "default"
//   credentials: "same-origin"
//   destination: ""
//   headers: Headers {}
//   integrity: ""
//   keepalive: false
//   method: "GET"
//   mode: "cors"
```

```
//   redirect: "follow"
//   referrer: "about:client"
//   referrerPolicy: ""
//   signal: AbortSignal {aborted: false, onabort: null}
//   url: "<current URL>"
// }

// Creates Request object with specified init values:
console.log(new Request('https://foo.com',
                        { method: 'POST' }));

// Request {
//   bodyUsed: false
//   cache: "default"
//   credentials: "same-origin"
//   destination: ""
//   headers: Headers {}
//   integrity: ""
//   keepalive: false
//   method: "POST"
//   mode: "cors"
//   redirect: "follow"
//   referrer: "about:client"
//   referrerPolicy: ""
//   signal: AbortSignal {aborted: false, onabort: null}
//   url: "https://foo.com/"
// }
```

Cloning Request Objects

The Fetch API offers two slightly different ways of making copies of a Request object: using the Request constructor, and using the clone() method.

Passing a Request instance as the input argument to the Request constructor will make a copy of that request:

```
let r1 = new Request('https://foo.com');
let r2 = new Request(r1);

console.log(r2.url);  // https://foo.com/
```

Values inside the init object will override those of the source object:

```
let r1 = new Request('https://foo.com');
let r2 = new Request(r1, {method: 'POST'});

console.log(r1.method);  // GET
console.log(r2.method);  // POST
```

This copying strategy will not always yield an exact copy. Most notably, it will mark the first request body as used:

```
let r1 = new Request('https://foo.com',
                     { method: 'POST', body: 'foobar' });
let r2 = new Request(r1);

console.log(r1.bodyUsed);  // true
console.log(r2.bodyUsed);  // false
```

If the source object has a different origin than where the new object is created, the referrer property is cleared. Furthermore, if the source object has a mode value of navigate, this will be converted to same-origin.

The second way of cloning a Request object is to use the clone() method, which creates an exact copy with no opportunity to override any values. Unlike the first technique, this will not mark any request body as used:

```
let r1 = new Request('https://foo.com', { method: 'POST', body: 'foobar' });
let r2 = r1.clone();

console.log(r1.url);        // https://foo.com/
console.log(r2.url);        // https://foo.com/

console.log(r1.bodyUsed);   // false
console.log(r2.bodyUsed);   // false
```

Cloning a Request using either technique is not allowed if the bodyUsed request property is false, meaning the body has not yet been read. Once the body is read, attempting to clone will throw a TypeError.

```
let r = new Request('https://foo.com');
r.clone();
new Request(r);
// No error

r.text();  // sets the bodyUsed field to false

r.clone();
// TypeError: Failed to execute 'clone' on 'Request': Request body is already used

new Request(r);
// TypeError: Failed to construct 'Request': Cannot construct a Request with
// a Request object that has already been used.
```

Using Request Objects with *fetch()*

The fact that fetch() and the Request constructor have identical function signatures is no accident. When calling fetch(), you are able to pass an already-created Request instance instead of a URL. As with the Request constructor, values provided in the fetch() init object will override the provided request's values:

```
let r = new Request('https://foo.com');

// send GET request to foo.com
fetch(r);

// send POST request to foo.com
fetch(r, { method: 'POST' });
```

Internally, a fetch is cloning the provided Request object. As with cloning a Request, a fetch cannot be dispatched with a Request that has a used body:

```
let r = new Request('https://foo.com',
                    { method: 'POST', body: 'foobar' });
```

```
r.text();

fetch(r);
// TypeError: Cannot construct a Request with a Request object that has
// already been used.
```

Importantly, using a `Request` in a fetch will also serve to mark the body as used. Therefore, only a single fetch can be performed with a `Request` that has a body. (Requests that do not include a body are not subject to this restriction.) This is demonstrated here:

```
let r = new Request('https://foo.com',
                    { method: 'POST', body: 'foobar' });

fetch(r);

fetch(r);
// TypeError: Cannot construct a Request with a Request object that has
// already been used.
```

In order to invoke `fetch()` multiple times with the same `Request` object that includes a body, `clone()` must be invoked prior to dispatching the first `fetch()`:

```
let r = new Request('https://foo.com',
                    { method: 'POST', body: 'foobar' });

// All 3 succeed
fetch(r.clone());
fetch(r.clone());
fetch(r);
```

The Response Object

As its name indicates, the `Response` object is an interface to the response from a fetched resource. This interface exposes information about the nature of the response as well as different ways of consuming the body of the response.

> **NOTE** *The properties and methods involving the body are covered in the section "Requests, Responses, and the Body Mixin" in this chapter.*

Creating Response Objects

A `Response` object can be instantiated via a constructor. It requires no arguments. Its properties will be populated with default values since this instance does not represent an actual HTTP response:

```
let r = new Response();
console.log(r);
// Response {
//   body: (...)
//   bodyUsed: false
//   headers: Headers {}
//   ok: true
```

```
//    redirected: false
//    status: 200
//    statusText: "OK"
//    type: "default"
//    url: ""
// }
```

The `Response` constructor accepts a first optional argument, a body. This body, which can be `null`, is identical to that of the `init` body, as described earlier in the chapter in the section "Custom Fetch Options." The second optional argument, the `init` object, should be populated with any number of the keys and corresponding values in the table that follows.

KEY	VALUE
headers	Must be either a `Headers` object instance or regular object instance containing header key-value string pairs. Defaults to a `Headers` object with no key-value pairs.
status	The integer indicating the HTTP response status code. Defaults to 200.
statusText	A string describing the HTTP response status. Defaults to an empty string.

The `body` and `init` can be used to build a `Response` as follows:

```
let r = new Response('foobar', {
  status: 418,
  statusText: 'I\'m a teapot'
});
console.log(r);
// Response {
//    body: (...)
//    bodyUsed: false
//    headers: Headers {}
//    ok: false
//    redirected: false
//    status: 418
//    statusText: "I'm a teapot"
//    type: "default"
//    url: ""
// }
```

For most applications, the most common way of producing a `Response` object is by calling `fetch()`; this returns a promise that resolves to a `Response` object that does represent an actual HTTP response. The following code shows an example `Response` object you might expect:

```
fetch('https://foo.com')
  .then((response) => {
    console.log(response);
  });

// Response {
//    body: (...)
//    bodyUsed: false
//    headers: Headers {}
//    ok: true
```

```
//    redirected: false
//    status: 200
//    statusText: "OK"
//    type: "basic"
//    url: "https://foo.com/"
// }
```

The `Response` class also features two static methods for generating `Response` objects, `Response` `.redirect()` and `Response.error()`. `Response.redirect()` accepts a URL and redirect status code (301, 302, 303, 307, or 308) and returns a redirected `Response` object:

```
console.log(Response.redirect('https://foo.com', 301));
// Response {
//    body: (...)
//    bodyUsed: false
//    headers: Headers {}
//    ok: false
//    redirected: false
//    status: 301
//    statusText: ""
//    type: "default"
//    url: ""
// }
```

The provided status code must qualify as a redirect; otherwise an error is thrown:

```
Response.redirect('https://foo.com', 200);
// RangeError: Failed to execute 'redirect' on 'Response': Invalid status code
```

Also available for use is `Response.error()`. This static method produces a response that you would expect from a network error, which would cause a `fetch()` promise to reject.

```
console.log(Response.error());
// Response {
//    body: (...)
//    bodyUsed: false
//    headers: Headers {}
//    ok: false
//    redirected: false
//    status: 0
//    statusText: ""
//    type: "error"
//    url: ""
// }
```

Reading Response Status Information

The `Response` object offers a suite of read-only properties describing how the request completed, as you can see in the table that follows.

PROPERTY	VALUE
`headers`	The `Headers` object associated with the response.
`ok`	A Boolean indicating the nature of the HTTP status code. A status code of 200–299 returns `true`, other status codes return `false`.

continues

(continued)

PROPERTY	VALUE
redirected	A Boolean indicating if the response was subjected to at least one redirect.
status	An integer indicating the HTTP status code of the response.
statusText	A string containing the canonical description associated with the HTTP status code. This value is derived from the optional HTTP Reason-Phrase field, so this field may be an empty string if the server declines to respond with a Reason-Phrase.
type	A string containing the type of response. It will contain one of the following string values: ➤ basic—Indicates a standard same-origin response. ➤ cors—Indicates a standard cross-origin response. ➤ error—Indicates the response object was created via `Response.error()`. ➤ opaque—Indicates a cross-origin response to a `no-cors` fetch. ➤ opaqueredirect—Indicates a response to a request with redirect set to manual.
url	A string containing the URL of the response. For redirected responses, this will be the final URL, which produced a non-redirect response.

The following demonstrates typical response content for URLs that return 200, 302, 404, and 500:

```
fetch('//foo.com').then(console.log);
// Response {
//   body: (...)
//   bodyUsed: false
//   headers: Headers {}
//   ok: true
//   redirected: false
//   status: 200
//   statusText: "OK"
//   type: "basic"
//   url: "https://foo.com/"
// }


fetch('//foo.com/redirect-me').then(console.log);
// Response {
//   body: (...)
//   bodyUsed: false
//   headers: Headers {}
//   ok: true
//   redirected: true
//   status: 200
//   statusText: "OK"
//   type: "basic"
//   url: "https://foo.com/redirected-url/"
```

```
// }

fetch('//foo.com/does-not-exist').then(console.log);
// Response {
//   body: (...)
//   bodyUsed: false
//   headers: Headers {}
//   ok: false
//   redirected: true
//   status: 404
//   statusText: "Not Found"
//   type: "basic"
//   url: "https://foo.com/does-not-exist/"
// }

fetch('//foo.com/throws-error').then(console.log);
// Response {
//   body: (...)
//   bodyUsed: false
//   headers: Headers {}
//   ok: false
//   redirected: true
//   status: 500
//   statusText: "Internal Server Error"
//   type: "basic"
//   url: "https://foo.com/throws-error/"
// }
```

Cloning Response Objects

The primary way of cloning a `Response` object is to use the `clone()` method, which creates an exact copy with no opportunity to override any values. This will not mark any request body as used:

```
let r1 = new Response('foobar');
let r2 = r1.clone();

console.log(r1.bodyUsed);  // false
console.log(r2.bodyUsed);  // false
```

Cloning a `Response` is not allowed if the `bodyUsed` request property is `false`, meaning the body has not yet been read. Once the body is read, attempting to clone will throw a `TypeError`.

```
let r = new Response('foobar');
r.clone();
// No error

r.text();  // sets the bodyUsed field to false

r.clone();
// TypeError: Failed to execute 'clone' on 'Response': Response body
// is already used
```

Only a body read can be performed with a `Response` that has a body. (Responses that do not include a body are not subject to this restriction.) This is demonstrated here:

```
let r = new Response('foobar');

r.text().then(console.log);  // foobar

r.text().then(console.log);
// TypeError: Failed to execute 'text' on 'Response': body stream is locked
```

In order to read the body multiple times with the same `Response` object that includes a body, `clone()` must be invoked prior to performing the first read:

```
let r = new Response('foobar');

r.clone().text().then(console.log);   // foobar
r.clone().text().then(console.log);   // foobar
r.text().then(console.log);           // foobar
```

Alternately, it is also possible to perform a pseudo-clone operation by creating a new `Response` instance with the original body. Importantly, this strategy will not mark the first `Response` as read, but the body is *shared* between the two responses:

```
let r1 = new Response('foobar');
let r2 = new Response(r1.body);

console.log(r1.bodyUsed);    // false
console.log(r2.bodyUsed);    // false

r2.text().then(console.log);  // foobar
r1.text().then(console.log);
// TypeError: Failed to execute 'text' on 'Response': body stream is locked
```

Requests, Responses, and the Body Mixin

Both `Request` and `Response` incorporate the Fetch API's `Body` mixin to accommodate the payload-carrying nature of both types. This mixin confers to each type a read-only body (implemented as a `ReadableStream`), a read-only `bodyUsed` Boolean indicating if the body stream was read, and a handful of methods that read the stream to completion and convert the result into a certain Java-Script object type.

Generally, there are two primary reasons to consume a `Request` or `Response` body as a stream: Either network latency is a factor due to the size of the payload, or the stream API itself is inherently useful for processing the payload. In almost all other cases, the body of a fetched resource will be most useful when consumed all at once.

The `Body` mixin affords you five different methods which flush the `ReadableStream` into a single buffer in memory, cast the buffer into a certain JavaScript object type, and produce it inside a promise. This promise will wait until the body stream reports as finished and the buffer is parsed before resolving. This means you must wait for the fetched resource to be fully loaded on the client before being able to access its contents.

Body.text()

The `Body.text()` method returns a promise that resolves with the flushed buffer decoded as a UTF-8 string. Use of `Body.text()` is shown here with a `Response` object:

```
fetch('https://foo.com')
  .then((response) => response.text())
  .then(console.log);

// <!doctype html><html lang="en">
//   <head>
//    <meta charset="utf-8">
//    ...
```

Use of `Body.text()` is shown here with a `Request` object:

```
let request = new Request('https://foo.com',
                          { method: 'POST', body: 'barbazqux' });

request.text()
  .then(console.log);

// barbazqux
```

Body.json()

The `Body.json()` method returns a promise that resolves with the flushed buffer decoded as JSON. Use of `Body.json()` is shown here with a `Response` object:

```
fetch('https://foo.com/foo.json')
  .then((response) => response.json())
  .then(console.log);

// {"foo": "bar"}
```

Use of `Body.json()` is shown here with a `Request` object:

```
let request = new Request('https://foo.com',
                          { method:'POST', body: JSON.stringify({ bar: 'baz' }) });

request.json()
  .then(console.log);

// {bar: 'baz'}
```

Body.formData()

Browsers are able to serialize/deserialize `FormData` objects as a body. For example, consider the following `FormData` instance:

```
let myFormData = new FormData();
myFormData.append('foo', 'bar');
```

When transmitted via HTTP, a WebKit browser might serialize this as follows:

```
------WebKitFormBoundarydR9Q2kOzE6nbN7eR
Content-Disposition: form-data; name="foo"
```

```
bar
------WebKitFormBoundarydR9Q2kOzE6nbN7eR--
```

The `Body.formData()` method returns a promise that resolves with the flushed buffer decoded as a `FormData` instance. Use of `Body.formData()` is shown here with a `Response` object:

```
fetch('https://foo.com/form-data')
  .then((response) => response.formData())
  .then((formData) => console.log(formData.get('foo')));

// bar
```

Use of `Body.formData()` is shown here with a `Request` object:

```
let myFormData = new FormData();
myFormData.append('foo', 'bar');

let request = new Request('https://foo.com',
                          { method:'POST', body: myFormData });

request.formData()
  .then((formData) => console.log(formData.get('foo')));

// bar
```

Body.arrayBuffer()

You may find the need to inspect and modify the body payload as raw binary. For such a task, the body can be converted to an `ArrayBuffer` instance using `Body.arrayBuffer()`. This method returns a promise that resolves with the flushed buffer exposed as an `ArrayBuffer`. Use of `Body.arrayBuffer()` is shown here with a `Response` object:

```
fetch('https://foo.com')
  .then((response) => response.arrayBuffer())
  .then(console.log);

// ArrayBuffer(...) {}
```

Use of `Body.arrayBuffer()` is shown here with a `Request` object:

```
let request = new Request('https://foo.com',
                          { method:'POST', body: 'abcdefg' });

// Logs the encoded string binary values as integers
request.arrayBuffer()
  .then((buf) => console.log(new Int8Array(buf)));

// Int8Array(7) [97, 98, 99, 100, 101, 102, 103]
```

Body.blob()

You may find the need to use the body payload as raw binary without inspection or modification. For such a task, the body can be used as a `Blob` instance using `Body.blob()`. This method returns a promise that resolves with the flushed buffer exposed as a `Blob`. Use of `Body.blob()` is shown here with a `Response` object:

```
fetch('https://foo.com')
  .then((response) => response.blob())
  .then(console.log);

// Blob(...) {size:..., type: "..."}
```

Use of `Body.blob()` is shown here with a `Request` object:

```
let request = new Request('https://foo.com',
                          { method:'POST', body: 'abcdefg' });

request.blob()
  .then(console.log);

// Blob(7) {size: 7, type: "text/plain;charset=utf-8"}
```

Single-Use Streams

Because the `Body` mixin is built atop a `ReadableStream`, this means that the body stream can only be read a single time. The implication of this is that all of the `Body` mixin methods can only be called a single time; subsequent attempts to invoke a mixin method will throw an error.

```
fetch('https://foo.com')
  .then((response) => response.blob().then(() => response.blob()));

// TypeError: Failed to execute 'blob' on 'Response': body stream is locked
let request = new Request('https://foo.com',
                          { method: 'POST', body: 'foobar' });

request.blob().then(() => request.blob());
// TypeError: Failed to execute 'blob' on 'Request': body stream is locked
```

Even if the stream is merely in the process of being read, all of these methods will place a lock on the `ReadableStream` as soon as they are called and prevent a second reader from accessing the stream:

```
fetch('https://foo.com')
  .then((response) => {
    response.blob();  // First call locks the stream
    response.blob();  // Second call attempts to lock the stream and fails
  });

// TypeError: Failed to execute 'blob' on 'Response': body stream is locked
let request = new Request('https://foo.com',
                          { method: 'POST', body: 'foobar' });

request.blob();  // First call locks the stream
request.blob();  // Second call attempts to lock the stream and fails
// TypeError: Failed to execute 'blob' on 'Request': body stream is locked
```

As part of the `Body` mixin, a `bodyUsed` Boolean property indicates if the `ReadableStream` is *disturbed*, meaning a reader has already placed a lock on the stream. This doesn't necessarily indicate that the stream is fully drained. This property is demonstrated here:

```
let request = new Request('https://foo.com',
                          { method: 'POST', body: 'foobar' });
let response = new Response('foobar');

console.log(request.bodyUsed);     // false
console.log(response.bodyUsed);    // false

request.text().then(console.log);  // foobar
response.text().then(console.log); // foobar

console.log(request.bodyUsed);     // true
console.log(response.bodyUsed);    // true
```

Using a ReadableStream Body

Much of JavaScript programming treats networking as atomic operations; requests are created and sent off all at once, and responses are exposed as a unified data payload that becomes available all at once. This convention hides the underlying messiness, making network-involved code nice to write.

By the very nature of TCP/IP, transmitted data arrives at an endpoint in chunks, and only as fast as the network can deliver those chunks. A receiving endpoint allocates memory and writes what is received over the network as it arrives. The Fetch API allows you to read and manipulate this data as it arrives in real time via a `ReadableStream`.

> **NOTE** *Examples in this section will fetch the HTML of the Fetch specification, found at* `https://fetch.spec.whatwg.org`. *This page has roughly 1MB of markup, which is a large enough payload that the stream examples in this section will arrive in multiple chunks.*

A `ReadableStream`, as defined in the Stream API, exposes a `getReader()` method that produces a `ReadableStreamDefaultReader`, which can be used to asynchronously retrieve chunks of the body as they arrive. Each chunk of the body stream is provided as a `Uint8Array`.

The following snippet invokes `read()` on the reader to log the first available chunk:

```
fetch('https://fetch.spec.whatwg.org/')
  .then((response) => response.body)
  .then((body) => {
    let reader = body.getReader();

    console.log(reader);  // ReadableStreamDefaultReader {}

    reader.read()
      .then(console.log);
  });

// { value: Uint8Array{}, done: false }
```

To retrieve the entire payload as it becomes available, the `read()` method can be called recursively:

```
fetch('https://fetch.spec.whatwg.org/')
  .then((response) => response.body)
  .then((body) => {
    let reader = body.getReader();

    function processNextChunk({value, done}) {
      if (done) {
        return;
      }

      console.log(value);

      return reader.read()
          .then(processNextChunk);
    }

    return reader.read()
        .then(processNextChunk);
  });

// { value: Uint8Array{}, done: false }
// { value: Uint8Array{}, done: false }
// { value: Uint8Array{}, done: false }
// ...
```

Async functions are highly appropriate for use in `fetch()` operations. This recursive implementation can be flattened using `async/await`:

```
fetch('https://fetch.spec.whatwg.org/')
  .then((response) => response.body)
  .then(async function(body) {
    let reader = body.getReader();

    while(true) {
      let { value, done } = await reader.read();

      if (done) {
        break;
      }

      console.log(value);
    }
  });

// { value: Uint8Array{}, done: false }
// { value: Uint8Array{}, done: false }
// { value: Uint8Array{}, done: false }
// ...
```

Alternately, the `read()` method is close enough to the Iterable interface that it is trivial to convert this to use a `for-await-of` loop:

```
fetch('https://fetch.spec.whatwg.org/')
  .then((response) => response.body)
```

```
    .then(async function(body) {
      let reader =  body.getReader();

      let asyncIterable = {
        [Symbol.asyncIterator]() {
          return {
            next() {
              return reader.read();
            }
          };
        }
      };

      for await (chunk of asyncIterable) {
        console.log(chunk);
      }
    });

// { value: Uint8Array{}, done: false }
// { value: Uint8Array{}, done: false }
// { value: Uint8Array{}, done: false }
// ...
```

This can be reduced further into a slightly cleaner generator function. Furthermore, this implementation can be made more robust by allowing for a partial stream read. If the stream terminates either via depletion or throwing an error, the reader should release the lock to allow for a different stream reader to pick up where it left off:

```
async function* streamGenerator(stream) {
  const reader = stream.getReader();

  try {
    while (true) {
      const { value, done } = await reader.read();

      if (done) {
        break;
      }

      yield value;
    }
  } finally {
    reader.releaseLock();
  }
}

fetch('https://fetch.spec.whatwg.org/')
  .then((response) => response.body)
  .then(async function(body) {
    for await (chunk of streamGenerator(body)) {
      console.log(chunk);
    }
  });
```

In these examples, after the current `Uint8Array` chunk goes out of scope, the browser marks it as eligible for garbage collection. This allows for potentially massive memory savings in scenarios where it is suitable to examine a large payload serially and in discrete segments.

The size of the buffer and whether or not the browser waits for it to be filled before pushing it into the stream is subject to the JavaScript runtime's implementation. The browser is sensitive to the fact that it is ideal to wait and fill up an allocated buffer when possible, but at the same time to keep the stream full by sending (sometimes unfilled) buffers as often as possible.

Browsers may vary the size of the chunk's buffer based on factors such as bandwidth or network latency. Furthermore, the browser might decide to send a partially filled buffer to the stream if it decides not to wait for the network. Ultimately, your code should be prepared to handle the following:

➤ `Uint8Array` chunks of variable size

➤ `Uint8Array` chunks being partially filled

➤ Chunks arriving at unpredictable intervals

By default, chunks will arrive in a `Uint8Array` format. Because the termination of a chunk does not respect the encoded content, there may be values such as multi-byte characters split between two separate sequential chunks. There are messy ways to manually account for this, but for many cases there are plug-and-play solutions from the Encoding API.

To convert the `Uint8Array` to readable text, a `TextDecoder` can be passed a buffer and return the converted value. Setting the `stream:true` configuration allows it to keep the previous buffer in memory so that content bridged between the two chunks can be correctly decoded:

```
let decoder = new TextDecoder();

async function* streamGenerator(stream) {
  const reader = stream.getReader();

  try {
    while (true) {
      const { value, done } = await reader.read();

      if (done) {
        break;
      }

      yield value;
    }
  } finally {
    reader.releaseLock();
  }
}

fetch('https://fetch.spec.whatwg.org/')
  .then((response) => response.body)
  .then(async function(body) {
    for await (chunk of streamGenerator(body)) {
```

```
        console.log(decoder.decode(chunk, { stream: true }));
      }
    });

// <!doctype html><html lang="en"> ...
// whether a <a data-link-type="dfn" href="#concept-header" ...
// result to <var>rangeValue</var>. ...
// ...
```

Because a `Response` object can be created using a `ReadableStream`, it is possible to read a stream, pipe it into a newly created secondary stream, and use that secondary stream for `Body` methods such as `text()`. This allows for inspection and manipulation of the stream contents as they become available. This dual-stream technique is shown here:

```
fetch('https://fetch.spec.whatwg.org/')
  .then((response) => response.body)
  .then((body) => {
    const reader = body.getReader();

    // create secondary stream
    return new ReadableStream({
      async start(controller) {
        try {
          while (true) {
            const { value, done } = await reader.read();

            if (done) {
              break;
            }

            // Push the body stream's chunk onto the secondary stream
            controller.enqueue(value);
          }
        } finally {
          controller.close();
          reader.releaseLock();
        }
      }
    })
  })
  .then((secondaryStream) => new Response(secondaryStream))
  .then(response => response.text())
  .then(console.log);

// <!doctype html><html lang="en"><head><meta charset="utf-8"> ...
```

CROSS-ORIGIN RESOURCE SHARING

One of the major limitations of browser networking is the cross-origin security policy. By default, scripts can access resources only on the domain from which the containing web page originates. This security feature prevents some malicious behavior. However, the need for legitimate cross-origin access was great enough for solutions to begin appearing in browsers.

Cross-Origin Resource Sharing (CORS) defines how the browser and server must communicate when accessing sources across origins. The basic idea behind CORS is to use custom HTTP headers to allow both the browser and the server to know enough about each other to determine if the request or response should succeed or fail.

For a simple request, one that uses either GET or POST with no custom headers and whose body is text/plain, the request is sent with an extra header called `Origin`. The `Origin` header contains the origin (protocol, domain name, and port) of the requesting page so that the server can easily determine whether or not it should serve a response. An example `Origin` header might look like this:

```
Origin: https://www.mattfriz.com
```

If the server decides that the request should be allowed, it sends an Access-Control-Allow-Origin header echoing back the same origin that was sent or `"*"` if it's a public resource. For example:

```
Access-Control-Allow-Origin: https://www.mattfriz.com
```

If this header is missing, or the origins don't match, then the browser disallows the request. If all is well, then the browser processes the request. Note that neither the requests nor the responses include cookie information.

Modern browsers support CORS natively. When the browser attempts to open a resource on a different origin, this behavior automatically gets triggered without any extra code. To make a request to a resource on another domain, fetch is used with an absolute URL, such as this:

```
fetch("http://www.somewhere-else.com/page/")
  .then(response => {
    if (response.ok) {
      return response.text();
    } else {
      throw new Error("Request was unsuccessful: " + response.status);
    }
  });
```

Because the same interface is used for both same- and cross-domain requests, it's best to always use a relative URL when accessing a local resource and an absolute URL when accessing a remote resource. This disambiguates the use case and can prevent problems such as limiting access to header and/or cookie information for local resources.

Preflighted Requests

CORS allows the use of custom headers, methods other than GET or POST, and different body content types through a transparent mechanism of server verification called *preflighted requests*. When you try to make a request with one of the advanced options, a "preflight" request is made to the server. This request uses the OPTIONS method and sends the following headers:

➤ `Origin`—Same as in simple requests.

➤ `Access-Control-Request-Method`—The method that the request wants to use.

➤ `Access-Control-Request-Headers`—(Optional) A comma-separated list of the custom headers being used.

Here's an example assuming a POST request with a custom header called FRIZ:

```
Origin: https://www.mattfriz.com
Access-Control-Request-Method: POST
Access-Control-Request-Headers: FRIZ
```

During this request, the server can determine whether or not it will allow requests of this type. The server communicates this to the browser by sending the following headers in the response:

➤   `Access-Control-Allow-Origin`—Same as in simple requests.

➤   `Access-Control-Allow-Methods`—A comma-separated list of allowed methods.

➤   `Access-Control-Allow-Headers`—A comma-separated list of headers that the server will allow.

➤   `Access-Control-Max-Age`—The amount of time in seconds that this preflight request should be cached for.

For example:

```
Access-Control-Allow-Origin: https://www.mattfriz.com
Access-Control-Allow-Methods: POST, GET
Access-Control-Allow-Headers: FRIZ
Access-Control-Max-Age: 1728000
```

Once a preflight request has been made, the result is cached for the period of time specified in the response; you'll only incur the cost of an extra HTTP request the first time a request of this type is made.

Credentialed Requests

By default, cross-origin requests do not provide credentials (cookies, HTTP authentication, and client-side SSL certificates). You can specify that a request should send credentials by setting the `withCredentials` property to `true`. If the server allows credentialed requests, then it responds with the following HTTP header:

```
Access-Control-Allow-Credentials: true
```

If a credentialed request is sent and this header is not sent as part of the response, then the browser doesn't pass the response to JavaScript (`responseText` is an empty string, status is 0, and `onerror()` is invoked). Note that the server can also send this HTTP header as part of the preflight response to indicate that the origin is allowed to send credentialed requests.

THE BEACON API

To maximize the amount of information transmitted about a page, many analytics tools need to send telemetry or analytics data to a server as late in a page's lifecycle as possible. As a result, the optimal pattern is to send a network request on the browser's `unload` event. This event signals that a page departure is occurring and that no more useful information will be generated on that page.

When an `unload` event is fired, analytics tools want to cease collecting information and attempt to ship off what they have to the server. This presents a problem, as the unload event means to the browser that there is little reason to dispatch any pending network requests (since the page is being discarded anyway). For example, any asynchronous requests created in an `unload` handler will be cancelled by the browser. Therefore, a `fetch()` is unsuitable for this task.

To address this issue, a supplemental Beacon API was introduced by the W3C. The API adds a single `sendBeacon()` method to the navigator object. This simple method accepts a URL and a data payload and dispatches a POST request. The optional data payload can be an `ArrayBufferView`, a `Blob`, a `DOMString`, or a `FormData` instance. The method returns `true` if the request was successfully enqueued for eventual transmission, else `false`.

The method can be used as follows:

```
// Sends POST request
// URL: 'https://example.com/analytics-reporting-url'
// Request Payload: '{foo: "bar"}'

navigator.sendBeacon(
  'https://example.com/analytics-reporting-url',
  '{foo: "bar"}'
);
```

This method may seem like mere syntactical sugar for a POST request, but there are several notable features of the method:

➤ `sendBeacon()` is not restricted to the end of a page's lifecycle, it can be used at any time.

➤ Once `sendBeacon()` is called, the browser adds the requests to an internal request queue. The browser will eagerly attempt to send requests in the queue.

➤ The browser guarantees it will attempt to send the request even if the browser has already torn down the original page.

➤ Response codes, timeouts, and any other network failures are totally opaque and cannot be handled programmatically.

➤ The beacon request is sent with all relevant cookies at the time `sendBeacon()` was originally invoked.

WEB SOCKETS

The goal of Web Sockets is to provide full-duplex, bidirectional communication with the server over a single, long-lasting connection. When a Web Socket is created in JavaScript, an HTTP request is sent to the server to initiate a connection. When the server responds, the connection uses the HTTP Upgrade header to switch from HTTP to the Web Socket protocol. This means that Web Sockets cannot be implemented with a standard HTTP server and must use a specialized server supporting the protocol to work properly.

Because Web Sockets use a custom protocol, the URL scheme is slightly different. Instead of using the `http://` or `https://` schemes, there are `ws://` for an unsecured connection and `wss://` for a secured connection. When specifying a Web Socket URL, you must include the scheme since other schemes may be supported in the future.

The advantage of using a custom protocol over HTTP is that very small amounts of data, unencumbered by the byte overhead of HTTP, can be sent between the client and the server. Using smaller data packets makes Web Sockets ideal for mobile applications where bandwidth and latency are a problem. The disadvantage of using a custom protocol is that it has taken longer to define protocol than the JavaScript API.

The API

To create a new Web Socket, instantiate a `WebSocket` object and pass in the URL that will provide the connection:

```
let socket = new WebSocket("ws://www.example.com/server.php");
```

Note that you must pass in an absolute URL to the `WebSocket` constructor. The same-origin policy does not apply to Web Sockets, so you can open a connection to any site. It is completely up to the server whether or not it will communicate with a page from a particular origin. (It can determine from where the request originated using information in the handshake.)

The browser attempts to create the connection as soon as the WebSocket object is instantiated. `WebSocket` has a `readyState` property that indicates the current state. The values are as follows:

➤ `WebSocket.OPENING` `(0)`—The connection is being established.

➤ `WebSocket.OPEN` `(1)`—The connection has been established.

➤ `WebSocket.CLOSING` `(2)`—The connection is beginning to close.

➤ `WebSocket.CLOSE` `(3)`—The connection is closed.

There is no `readystatechange` event for `WebSocket`; however, there are other events that correspond to the various states. The `readyState` always starts at 0.

You can close a Web Socket connection at any time using the `close()` method:

```
socket.close();
```

Upon calling `close()`, the `readyState` immediately changes to 2 (closing) and will transition to 3 when complete.

Sending/Receiving Data

Once a Web Socket is open, you can both send data over and receive data from the connection. To send data to the server, use the `send()` method and pass in a string, `ArrayBuffer`, or `Blob`, as shown here:

```
let socket = new WebSocket("ws://www.example.com/server.php");

let stringData = "Hello world!";
let arrayBufferData = Uint8Array.from(['f', 'o' 'o']);
let blobData = new Blob(['f', 'o' 'o']);
```

```
socket.send(stringData);
socket.send(arrayBufferData.buffer);
socket.send(blobData);
```

When the server sends a message to the client, a message event is fired on the WebSocket object. The message event works similar to other messaging protocols, with the payload available through the event.data property:

```
socket.onmessage = function(event) {
  let data = event.data;
  // do something with data
};
```

Similar to data that is sent to the server via send(), data returned in event.data can be procured as an ArrayBuffer or a Blob. This is governed by the binaryType of the WebSocket object, which can either be "blob" or "arraybuffer".

Other Events

The WebSocket object has three more events that fire during the lifetime of the connection:

➤ open—Fires when the connection has been successfully made.

➤ error—Fires when an error occurs. The connection is unable to persist.

➤ close—Fires when the connection is closed.

The WebSocket object doesn't support DOM Level 2 event listeners, so you need to use DOM Level 0 style event handlers for each:

```
let socket = new WebSocket("ws://www.example.com/server.php");
socket.onopen = function() {
  alert("Connection established.");
};
socket.onerror = function() {
  alert("Connection error.");
};
socket.onclose = function() {
  alert("Connection closed.");
};
```

Of these three events, only the close event has additional information on the event object. There are three additional properties on the event object: wasClean, a Boolean indicating if the connection was closed cleanly; code, a numeric status code sent from the server; and reason, a string containing a message sent from the server. You may want to use this information either to display to the user or to log for analytics:

```
socket.onclose = function(event) {
  console.log(`as clean? ${event.wasClean} Code=${event.code} Reason=${
              event.reason}`);
};
```

THE EVENTSOURCE API

The EventSource API allows the client to receive real-time updates from the server over a single HTTP connection. The EventSource API provides a simple and efficient way to receive real-time updates from the server without the need for a dedicated WebSocket connection. It is supported by most modern web browsers and can be used in combination with SSE to provide real-time updates to web applications.

To use the EventSource API, the server must send events to the client in a specific format called Server-Sent Events (SSE). SSE is a lightweight protocol for sending text-based events from the server to the client over HTTP. Each event consists of a field name and a value, separated by a colon, and multiple events are separated by a double line break. The client can listen for events using an EventSource object, which handles the connection and parsing of the incoming events.

Here's an example of how to use the EventSource API:

```
const eventSource = new EventSource("https://api.example.com/events");
eventSource.onmessage = event => {
  console.log(event.data);
};
eventSource.onerror = error => {
  console.log("Error:", error);
};
```

In this example, an EventSource object is created with the URL "https://api.example.com/events". The onmessage event listener is set to a function that logs the event data to the console. The onerror event listener is set to a function that logs any errors that occur during the connection.

On the server side, the SSE events can be sent using the text/event-stream MIME type and the Cache-Control: no-cache header, which instructs the browser to always request the latest version of the resource.

SUMMARY

The Fetch API is a modern approach for making network requests in JavaScript. It allows you to fetch resources asynchronously from the server, such as JSON data or HTML content, using a simple and concise syntax. The Fetch API returns a Promise that resolves to the response from the server, which can then be parsed or consumed as needed. The Fetch API is considered a preferred approach for making network requests in modern web development due to its ease of use, support for Promises, and ability to handle a wide range of data formats.

Web Sockets are another tool for sending and receiving data between a client and a server. It enables real-time, two-way communication between a client and a server, allowing for push notifications and instant updates. Web Sockets use a persistent connection between the client and server, which allows data to be transmitted in both directions without the need for repeated HTTP requests. Web Sockets are ideal for applications that require real-time updates or streaming data, such as chat applications, multiplayer games, or financial trading platforms.

The EventSource API allows for real-time updates from the server to the client, but while Web Sockets enable two-way communication between the client and server, `EventSource` is primarily used for one-way communication, where the server sends updates to the client in a unidirectional manner. Additionally, `EventSource` uses HTTP as its transport protocol, meaning it works over the same ports and protocols as standard HTTP requests, while Web Sockets use a separate protocol with its own dedicated ports.

22

Client-Side Storage

WHAT'S IN THIS CHAPTER?

➤ Cookies

➤ Browser storage APIs

➤ IndexedDB

DOWNLOADS FOR THIS CHAPTER

Please note that all the code examples for this chapter are available as a part of this chapter's code download on the book's website at www.wiley.com/go/ projavascript5e.

Along with the emergence of web applications came a call for the ability to store user information directly on the client. The idea is logical: information pertaining to a specific user should live on that user's machine. Whether that is login information, preferences, or other data, web application providers found themselves searching for ways to store data on the client. The first solution to this problem came in the form of cookies, a creation of the old Netscape Communications Corporation and described in a specification titled *Persistent Client State: HTTP Cookies* (still available at http://curl.haxx.se/rfc/cookie_spec.html). Today, cookies are just one option available for storing data on the client.

COOKIES

HTTP cookies, commonly just called *cookies*, were originally intended to store session information on the client. The specification called for the server to send a Set-Cookie HTTP header containing session information as part of any response to an HTTP request. For instance, the headers of a server response may look like this:

```
HTTP/1.1 200 OK
Content-type: text/html
Set-Cookie: name=value
Other-header: other-header-value
```

This HTTP response sets a cookie with the name of `"name"` and a value of `"value"`. Both the name and the value are URL-encoded when sent. Browsers store such session information and send it back to the server via the Cookie HTTP header for every request after that point, such as the following:

```
GET /index.jsl HTTP/1.1
Cookie: name=value
Other-header: other-header-value
```

This extra information being sent back to the server can be used to uniquely identify the client from which the request was sent.

Restrictions

Cookies are, by nature, tied to a specific domain. When a cookie is set, it is sent along with requests to the same domain from which it was created. This restriction ensures that information stored in cookies is available only to approved recipients and cannot be accessed by other domains.

Because cookies are stored on the client computer, restrictions have been put in place to ensure that cookies can't be used maliciously and that they won't take up too much disk space.

In general, if you use the following approximate limits, you will run into no problems across all browser traffic:

- ➤ 300 cookies total
- ➤ 4096 bytes per cookie
- ➤ 20 cookies per domain
- ➤ 81920 bytes per domain

The total number of cookies per domain is limited, although it varies from browser to browser. Generally, you should not exceed 60 cookies per domain.

There are also limitations as to the size of cookies in browsers. Most browsers have a byte-count limit of around 4096 bytes, give or take a byte. For best cross-browser compatibility, it's best to keep the total cookie size to 4095 bytes or less. The size limit applies to all cookies for a domain, not per cookie.

If you attempt to create a cookie that exceeds the maximum cookie size, the cookie is silently dropped. Note that one character typically takes one byte, unless you're using multibyte characters— such as some UTF-8 Unicode characters, which can be up to 4 bytes per character.

Cookie Parts

Cookies are made up of the following pieces of information stored by the browser:

➤ **Name**—Unique name to identify the cookie. Cookie names are case-insensitive, so `myCookie` and `MyCookie` are considered to be the same. In practice, however, it's always best to treat the cookie names as case-sensitive because some server software may treat them as such. The cookie name must be URL-encoded.

➤ **Value**—String value stored in the cookie. This value must also be URL-encoded.

➤ **Domain**—Domain for which the cookie is valid. All requests sent from a resource at this domain will include the cookie information. This value can include a subdomain (such as `www.wiley.com`) or exclude it (such as `.wiley.com`, which is valid for all subdomains of `wiley.com`). If not explicitly set, the domain is assumed to be the one from which the cookie was set.

➤ **Path**—Path within the specified domain for which the cookie should be sent to the server. For example, you can specify that the cookie be accessible only from `www.wiley.com/ books` so pages at `www.wiley.com` won't send the cookie information, even though the request comes from the same domain.

➤ **Expiration**—Time stamp indicating when the cookie should be deleted (that is, when it should stop being sent to the server). By default, all cookies are deleted when the browser session ends; however, it is possible to set another time for the deletion. This value is set as a date in GMT format (Wdy, DD-Mon-YYYY HH:MM:SS GMT) and specifies an exact time when the cookie should be deleted. Because of this, a cookie can remain on a user's machine even after the browser is closed. Cookies can be deleted immediately by setting an expiration date that has already occurred.

➤ **Secure flag**—When specified, the cookie information is sent to the server only if an SSL connection is used. For instance, requests to `www.wiley.com` should send cookie information, whereas requests to `www.wiley.com` should not.

Each piece of information is specified as part of the Set-Cookie header using a semicolon-space combination to separate each section, as shown in the following example:

```
HTTP/1.1 200 OK
Content-type: text/html
Set-Cookie: name=value; expires=Mon, 22-Jan-07 07:10:24 GMT; domain=.wiley.com
Other-header: other-header-value
```

This header specifies a cookie called "name" that expires on Monday, January 22, 2007, at 7:10:24 GMT and is valid for `www.wiley.com` and any other subdomains of `wiley.com` such as `p2p.wiley.com`.

The secure flag is the only part of a cookie that is not a name-value pair; the word `"secure"` is simply included. Consider the following example:

```
HTTP/1.1 200 OK
Content-type: text/html
Set-Cookie: name=value; domain=.wiley.com; path=/; secure
Other-header: other-header-value
```

Here, a cookie is created that is valid for all subdomains of `wiley.com` and all pages on that domain (as specified by the path argument). This cookie can be transmitted only over an SSL connection because the secure flag is included.

It's important to note that the domain, path, expiration date, and secure flag are indications to the browser as to when the cookie should be sent with a request. These arguments are not actually sent as part of the cookie information to the server; only the name-value pairs are sent.

Cookies in JavaScript

Dealing with cookies in JavaScript is a little complicated because of a notoriously poor interface, the BOM's `document.cookie` property. This property is unique in that it behaves very differently depending on how it is used. When used to retrieve the property value, `document.cookie` returns a string of all cookies available to the page (based on the domain, path, expiration, and security settings of the cookies) as a series of name-value pairs separated by semicolons, as in the following example:

```
name1=value1;name2=value2;name3=value3
```

All of the names and values are URL-encoded and so must be decoded via `decodeURIComponent()`.

When used to set a value, the `document.cookie` property can be set to a new cookie string. That cookie string is interpreted and added to the existing set of cookies. Setting `document.cookie` does not overwrite any cookies unless the name of the cookie being set is already in use. The format to set a cookie is as follows, and is the same format used by the Set-Cookie header:

```
name=value; expires=expiration_time; path=domain_path; domain=domain_name; secure
```

Of these parameters, only the cookie's `name` and `value` are required. Here's a simple example:

```
document.cookie = "name=Matt";
```

This code creates a session cookie called `"name"` that has a value of `"Matt"`. This cookie will be sent every time the client makes a request to the server; it will be deleted when the browser is closed. Although this will work, as there are no characters that need to be encoded in either the name or the value, it's a best practice to always use `encodeURIComponent()` when setting a cookie, as shown in the following example:

```
document.cookie = encodeURIComponent("name") + "=" +
                  encodeURIComponent("Matt");
```

To specify additional information about the created cookie, just append it to the string in the same format as the `Set-Cookie` header, like this:

```
document.cookie = encodeURIComponent("name") + "=" +
                  encodeURIComponent("Matt") + "; domain=.wiley.com; path=/";
```

To get around the per-domain cookie limit imposed by browsers, some developers use a concept called *subcookies*. Subcookies are smaller pieces of data stored within a single cookie. The idea is to use the cookie's value to store multiple name-value pairs within a single cookie. If you are concerned about reaching the per-domain cookie limit in your work, subcookies are an attractive alternative. You will have to more closely monitor the size of your cookies to stay within the individual cookie size limit.

The most common format for subcookies is as follows:

```
name=name1=value1&name2=value2&name3=value3&name4=value4&name5=value5
```

Subcookies tend to be formatted in query string format. These values can then be stored and accessed using a single cookie rather than using a different cookie for each name-value pair. The result is that more structured data can be stored by a website or web application without reaching the per-domain cookie limit.

> **NOTE** *Because the reading and writing of cookies in JavaScript isn't very straightforward, libraries are often used to simplify cookie functionality. The* `js-cookie` *NPM package is extremely popular for its small size and ease of use.*

Cookie Considerations

There is also a type of cookie called *HTTP-only*. HTTP-only cookies can be set either from the browser or from the server but can be read only from the server because JavaScript cannot get the value of HTTP-only cookies.

Because all cookies are sent as request headers from the browser, storing a large amount of information in cookies can affect the overall performance of browser requests to a particular domain. The larger the cookie information, the longer it will take to complete the request to the server. Even though the browser places size limits on cookies, it's a good idea to store as little information as possible in cookies, to avoid performance implications.

The restrictions on and nature of cookies make them less than ideal for storing large amounts of information, which is why other approaches have emerged.

> **NOTE** *You should avoid storing data such as credit card numbers or personal addresses in cookies; this is not their intended purpose.*

WEB STORAGE

Web Storage was first described in the Web Applications 1.0 specification of the Web Hypertext Application Technical Working Group (WHAT-WG). The initial work from this specification eventually became part of HTML5 before being split into its own specification. Its intent is to overcome some of the limitations imposed by cookies when data is needed strictly on the client side, with no need to continuously send data back to the server.

The most modern edition of the Web Storage specification is its second edition. The two primary goals of the Web Storage specification are:

➤ To provide a way to store session data outside of cookies.

➤ To provide a mechanism for storing large amounts of data that persists across sessions.

The second edition of the Web Storage specification includes definitions for two objects: localStorage, the permanent storage mechanism, and sessionStorage, the session-scoped storage mechanism. Both of these browser storage APIs afford you two different ways of storing data in the browser that can survive a page reload. Both localStorage and sessionStorage are available as global objects.

```
console.log(localStorage);
// Storage {length: 0}

console.log(sessionStorage);
// Storage {length: 0}
```

> **NOTE** globalStorage *was formerly part of the first edition of the Web Storage specification and has since been deprecated.*

The Storage Type

The Storage type is designed to hold name-value pairs up to a maximum size (determined by the browser). An instance of Storage acts like any other object and has the following additional methods:

- ➤ clear()—Removes all values.
- ➤ getItem(name)—Retrieves the value for the given name.
- ➤ key(index)—Retrieves the name of the value in the given numeric position.
- ➤ removeItem(name)—Removes the name-value pair identified by name.
- ➤ setItem(name, value)—Sets the value for the given name.

The getItem(), removeItem(), and setItem() methods can be called directly or indirectly by manipulating the Storage object. Since each item is stored on the object as a property, you can simply read values by accessing the property with dot or bracket notation, set the value by doing the same, or remove it by using the delete operator. Even so, it's generally recommended to use the methods instead of property access to ensure you don't end up overwriting one of the already available object members with a key.

You can determine how many name-value pairs are in a Storage object by using the length property. It's not possible to determine the size of all data in the object.

> **NOTE** *The* Storage *type is capable of storing only strings. Nonstring data is automatically converted into a string before being stored. Keep in mind that this conversion is not undone upon retrieval.*

The *sessionStorage* Object

The `sessionStorage` object stores data only for a session, meaning that the data is stored until the browser is closed. This is the equivalent of a session cookie that disappears when the browser is closed. Data stored on `sessionStorage` persists across page refreshes and may also be available if the browser crashes and is restarted, depending on the browser.

Because the `sessionStorage` object is tied to a server session, it isn't available when a file is run locally. Data stored on `sessionStorage` is accessible only from the page that initially placed the data onto the object, making it of limited use for multipage applications.

Because the `sessionStorage` object is an instance of `Storage`, you can assign data onto it either by using `setItem()` or by assigning a new property directly. Here's an example of each of these methods:

```
// store data using method
sessionStorage.setItem("name", "Matt");

// store data using property
sessionStorage.book = "Professional JavaScript";
```

All modern browsers implement storage writing as a blocking synchronous action, so data added to storage is committed right away. The API implementation might not write the value to disk right away (and prefers to initially use a different physical storage), but this difference is invisible at the JavaScript level, and any writes using some form of Web Storage can immediately be read.

When data exists on `sessionStorage`, it can be retrieved either by using `getItem()` or by accessing the property name directly. Here's an example of each of these methods:

```
// get data using method
let name = sessionStorage.getItem("name");

// get data using property
let book = sessionStorage.book;
```

You can iterate over the values in `sessionStorage` using a combination of the `length` property and `key()` method, as shown here:

```
for (let i = 0, len = sessionStorage.length; i < len; i++){
  let key = sessionStorage.key(i);
  let value = sessionStorage.getItem(key);
  alert(`${key}=`${value}`);
}
```

The name-value pairs in `sessionStorage` can be accessed sequentially by first retrieving the name of the data in the given position via `key()` and then using that name to retrieve the value via `getItem()`.

It's also possible to iterate over the values in `sessionStorage` using a `for-in` loop:

```
for (let key in sessionStorage){
  let value = sessionStorage.getItem(key);
  alert(`${key}=${value}`);
}
```

Each time through the loop, `key` is filled with another name in `sessionStorage`; none of the built-in methods or the `length` property will be returned.

To remove data from `sessionStorage`, you can use either the `delete` operator on the object property or the `removeItem()` method. Here's an example of each of these methods:

```
// use delete to remove a value
delete sessionStorage.name;

// use method to remove a value
sessionStorage.removeItem("book");
```

The `sessionStorage` object should be used primarily for small pieces of data that are valid only for a session. If you need to persist data across sessions, then `localStorage` is more appropriate.

The *localStorage* Object

The `localStorage` object superseded `globalStorage` in the revised HTML5 specification as a way to store persistent client-side data. In order to access the same `localStorage` object, pages must be served from the same domain (subdomains aren't valid), using the same protocol, and on the same port.

Because `localStorage` is an instance of `Storage`, it can be used in exactly the same manner as `sessionStorage`. Here are some examples:

```
// store data using method
localStorage.setItem("name", "Matt");

// store data using property
localStorage.book = "Professional JavaScript";

// get data using method
let name = localStorage.getItem("name");

// get data using property
let book = localStorage.book;
```

The difference between the two storage methods is that data stored in `localStorage` is persisted until it is specifically removed via JavaScript or the user clears the browser's cache. `localStorage` data will remain through page reloads, closing windows and tabs, and restarting the browser.

The *storage* Event

Whenever a change is made to a `Storage` object, the storage event is fired on the document. This occurs for every value set using either properties or `setItem()`, every value removal using either `delete` or `removeItem()`, and every call to `clear()`. The event object has the following four properties:

➤   `domain`—The domain for which the storage changed.

➤   `key`—The key that was set or removed.

➤ `newValue`—The value that the key was set to, or `null` if the key was removed.

➤ `oldValue`—The value prior to the key being changed.

You can listen for the storage event using the following code:

```
window.addEventListener("storage",
    (event) => alert('Storage changed for ${event.domain}'));
```

The `storage` event is fired for all changes to `sessionStorage` and `localStorage` but doesn't distinguish between them.

Limits and Restrictions

As with other client-side data storage solutions, Web Storage also has limitations. These limitations are browser-specific. Generally speaking, the size limit for client-side data is set on a per-origin (protocol, domain, and port) basis, so each origin has a fixed amount of space in which to store its data. Analyzing the origin of the page that is storing the data enforces this restriction.

Storage limits for `localStorage` and `sessionStorage` are inconsistent across browsers, but most will limit the per-origin storage to 5MB. A table containing up-to-date storage limits for each medium can be found at `www.html5rocks.com/en/tutorials/offline/quota-research`.

For more information about Web Storage limits, please see the Web Storage Support Test at `http://dev-test.nemikor.com/web-storage/support-test`.

INDEXEDDB

The Indexed Database API, *IndexedDB* for short, is a structured data store in the browser. IndexedDB came about as an alternative to the now-deprecated Web SQL Database API. The idea behind IndexedDB was to create an API that easily allowed the storing and retrieval of JavaScript objects while still allowing querying and searching.

IndexedDB is designed to be almost completely asynchronous. As a result, most operations are performed as requests that will execute later and produce either a successful result or an error. Nearly every IndexedDB operation requires you to attach `onerror` and `onsuccess` event handlers to determine the outcome.

Databases

IndexedDB is a database similar to databases you've probably used before, such as MySQL or Web SQL Database. The big difference is that IndexedDB uses object stores instead of tables to keep track of data. An IndexedDB database is simply a collection of object stores grouped under a common name—a NoSQL-style implementation.

The first step to using a database is to open it using `indexedDB.open()` and passing in the name of the database to `open()`. If a database with the given name already exists, then a request is made to open it; if the database doesn't exist, then a request is made to create and open it. The call to `indexDB.open()` returns an instance of `IDBRequest` onto which you can attach `onerror` and `onsuccess` event handlers. Here's an example:

```
let db,
    request,
    version = 1;

request = indexedDB.open("admin", version);
request.onerror = (event) =>
  alert(`Failed to open: ${event.target.errorCode}`);
request.onsuccess = (event) => {
  db = event.target.result;
};
```

Formerly, IndexedDB used the `setVersion()` method to specify which version should be accessed. This method is now deprecated; as shown here, the version is now specified when opening the database. The version numbers will be converted to an `unsigned long number`, so do not use decimal points; use whole integers instead.

In both event handlers, `event.target` points to `request`, so these may be used interchangeably. If the `onsuccess` event handler is called, then the database instance object (`IDBDatabase`) is available in `event.target.result` and stored in the database variable. From this point on, all requests to work with the database are made through the database object itself. If an error occurs, an error code stored in `event.target.errorCode` indicates the nature of the problem.

> **NOTE** *Formerly,* `IDBDatabaseException` *was used to indicate the error that IndexedDB experienced. This has been replaced with standard* `DOMExceptions`.

Object Stores

Once you have established a connection to the database, the next step is to interact with object stores. If the database version doesn't match the one you expect then you likely will need to create an object store. Before creating an object store, however, it's important to think about the type of data you want to store.

Suppose that you'd like to store user records containing `username`, `password`, and so on. The object to hold a single record may look like this:

```
let user = {
  username: "007",
  firstName: "James",
  lastName: "Bond",
  password: "foo"
};
```

Looking at this object, you can easily see that an appropriate key for this object store is the `username` property. A username must be globally unique, and it's probably the way you'll be accessing data most of the time. This is important because you must specify a key when creating an object store.

The version of the database determines the database schema, which consists of the object stores in the database and the structures of those object stores. If the database doesn't yet exist, the open() operation creates it; then, an upgradeneeded event is fired. You can set a handler for this event and create the database schema in the handler. If the database exists, but you are specifying an upgraded version number, an upgradeneeded event is fired immediately, allowing you to provide an updated schema in the event handler.

Here's how you would create an object store for these users:

```
request.onupgradeneeded = (event) => {
  const db = event.target.result;

  // Delete the current objectStore if it exists. This is useful for testing,
  // but this will wipe existing data each time this event handler executes.
  if (db.objectStoreNames.contains("users")) {
    db.deleteObjectStore("users");
  }

  db.createObjectStore("users", { keyPath: "username" });
};
```

The keyPath property of the second argument indicates the property name of the stored objects that should be used as a key.

Transactions

Past the creation step of an object store, all further operations are done through *transactions*. A transaction is created using the transaction() method on the database object. Any time you want to read or change data, a transaction is used to group all changes together. In its simplest form, you create a new transaction as follows:

```
let transaction = db.transaction();
```

With no arguments specified, you have read-only access to all object stores in the database. A more targeted strategy is to specify one or more object store names that you want to access:

```
let transaction = db.transaction("users");
```

This ensures that only information about the users object store is loaded and available during the transaction. If you want access to more than one object store, the first argument can also be an array of strings:

```
let transaction = db.transaction(["users", "anotherStore"]);
```

As mentioned previously, each of these transactions accesses data in a read-only manner. To change that, you must pass in a second argument indicating the access mode. This argument should be one of three strings: "readonly", "readwrite", or "versionchange". You can specify the second argument to transaction():

```
let transaction = db.transaction("users", "readwrite");
```

This transaction is capable of both reading and writing into the users object store.

Once you have a reference to the transaction, you can access a particular object store using the `objectStore()` method and passing in the store name you want to work with. You can then use `add()` and `put()` as before, as well as `get()` to retrieve values, `delete()` to remove an object, and `clear()` to remove all objects. Both the `get()` and `delete()` methods accept an object key as their argument, and all five of these methods create a new request object. For example:

```
const transaction = db.transaction("users"),
    store = transaction.objectStore("users"),
    request = store.get("007");
request.onerror = (event) => alert("Did not get the object!");
request.onsuccess = (event) => alert(event.target.result.firstName);
```

Because any number of requests can be completed as part of a single transaction, the transaction object itself also has event handlers: `onerror` and `oncomplete`. These are used to provide transaction-level state information:

```
transaction.onerror = (event) => {
  // entire transaction was cancelled
};
transaction.oncomplete = (event) => {
  // entire transaction completed successfully
};
```

Keep in mind that the event object for `oncomplete` doesn't give you access to any data returned by `get()` requests, so you still need an `onsuccess` event handler for those types of requests.

Insertion

Because you now have a reference to the object store, it's possible to populate the object store with data using either `add()` or `put()`. Both of these methods accept a single argument, the object to store, and save the object into the object store. The difference between these two occurs only when an object with the same key already exists in the object store. In that case, `add()` will cause an error while `put()` will simply overwrite the object. More simply, think of `add()` as being used for inserting new values while `put()` is used for updating values. So to initialize an object store for the first time, you may want to do something like this:

```
// where users is an array of new users
for (let user of users) {
  store.add(user);
}
```

Each call to `add()` or `put()` creates a new update request for the object store. If you want verification that the request completed successfully, you can store the request object in a variable and assign `onerror` and `onsuccess` event handlers:

```
// where users is an array of new users
let request,
    requests = [];
for (let user of users) {
  request = store.add(user);
  request.onerror = () => {
    // handle error
  };
```

```
      request.onsuccess = () => {
        // handle success
      };
      requests.push(request);
    }
```

Once the object store is created and filled with data, it's time to start querying.

Querying with Cursors

Transactions can be used directly to retrieve a single item with a known key. When you want to retrieve multiple items, you need to create a *cursor* within the transaction. A cursor is a pointer into a result set. Unlike traditional database queries, a cursor doesn't gather all of the result set up front. Instead, a cursor points to the first result and doesn't try to find the next until instructed to do so.

Cursors are created using the `openCursor()` method on an object store. As with other operations with IndexedDB, the return value of `openCursor()` is a request, so you must assign `onsuccess` and `onerror` event handlers. For example:

```
const transaction = db.transaction("users"),
    store = transaction.objectStore("users"),
    request = store.openCursor();
request.onsuccess = (event) => {
  // handle success
};
request.onfailure = (event) => {
  // handle failure
};
```

When the `onsuccess` event handler is called, the next item in the object store is accessible via `event.target.result`, which holds an instance of `IDBCursor` when there is a next item or `null` when there are no further items. The `IDBCursor` instance has several properties:

- ➤ `direction`—A numeric value indicating the direction the cursor should travel in and whether or not it should traverse all duplicate values. There are four possible string values: `"next"`, `"nextunique"`, `"prev"`, and `"prevunique"`.

- ➤ `key`—The key for the object.

- ➤ `value`—The actual object.

- ➤ `primaryKey`—The key being used by the cursor. Could be the object key or an index key (discussed later).

You can retrieve information about a single result using the following:

```
request.onsuccess = (event) => {
  const cursor = event.target.result;
  if (cursor) {   // always check
    console.log(`Key: ${cursor.key}, Value: ${JSON.stringify(cursor.value)}`);
  }
};
```

Keep in mind that `cursor.value` in this example is an object, which is why it is JSON encoded before being displayed.

A cursor can be used to update an individual record. The `update()` method updates the current cursor value with the specified object. As with other such operations, the call to `update()` creates a new request so you need to assign `onsuccess` and `onerror` if you want to know the result:

```
request.onsuccess = (event) => {
  const cursor = event.target.result;
  let value,
      updateRequest;
  if (cursor) {  // always check
    if (cursor.key == "foo") {
      value = cursor.value;                     // get current value
      value.password = "magic!";                // update the password
      updateRequest = cursor.update(value);  // request the update be saved
      updateRequest.onsuccess = () => {
        // handle success;
      };
      updateRequest.onfailure = () => {
        // handle failure
      };
    }
  }
};
```

You can also delete the item at that position by calling `delete()`. As with `update()`, this also creates a request:

```
request.onsuccess = (event) => {
  const cursor = event.target.result;
  let value,
      deleteRequest;
  if (cursor) {  // always check
    if (cursor.key == "foo") {
      deleteRequest = cursor.delete();  // request the value be deleted
      deleteRequest.onsuccess = () => {
        // handle success;
      };
      deleteRequest.onfailure = () => {
        // handle failure
      };
    }
  }
};
```

Both `update()` and `delete()` will throw errors if the transaction doesn't have permission to modify the object store.

Each cursor makes only one request by default. To make another request, you must call one of the following methods:

➤ `continue(key)`—Moves to the next item in the result set. The argument `key` is optional. When not specified, the cursor just moves to the next item; when provided, the cursor will move to the specified key.

➤ `advance(count)`—Moves the cursor ahead by `count` number of items.

Each of these methods causes the cursor to reuse the same request so the same `onsuccess` and `onfailure` event handlers are reused until no longer needed. For example, the following iterates over all items in an object store:

```
request.onsuccess = (event) => {
  const cursor = event.target.result;
  if (cursor) {  // always check
    console.log(`Key: ${cursor.key}, Value: ${JSON.stringify(cursor.value)}`);
    cursor.continue();  // go to the next one
  } else {
    console.log("Done!");
  }
};
```

The call to `continue()` triggers another request and `onsuccess` is called again. When there are no more items to iterate over, `onsuccess` is called one last time with `event.target.result` equal to `null`.

Key Ranges

Working with cursors may seem suboptimal given that you're limited in the ways data can be retrieved. *Key ranges* are used to make working with cursors a little more manageable. A key range is represented by an instance of `IDBKeyRange`. There are four different ways to specify key ranges. The first is to use the `only()` method and pass in the key you want to retrieve:

```
const onlyRange  = IDBKeyRange.only("007");
```

This range ensures that only the value with a key of `"007"` will be retrieved. A cursor created using this range is similar to directly accessing an object store and calling `get("007")`.

The second type of range defines a lower bound for the result set. The lower bound indicates the item at which the cursor should start. For example, the following key range ensures the cursor starts at the key `"007"` and continues until the end:

```
// start at item "007", go to the end
const lowerRange  = IDBKeyRange.lowerBound("007");
```

If you want to start at the item immediately following the value at `"007"`, then you can pass in a second argument of `true`:

```
// start at item after "007", go to the end
const lowerRange  = IDBKeyRange.lowerBound("007", true);
```

The third type of range is an upper bound, indicating the key you don't want to go past by using the `upperBound()` method. The following key ensures that the cursor starts at the beginning and stops when it gets to the value with key `"ace"`:

```
// start at beginning, go to "ace"
const upperRange  = IDBKeyRange.upperBound("ace");
```

If you don't want to include the given key, then pass in `true` as the second argument:

```
// start at beginning, go to the item just before "ace"
const upperRange  = IDBKeyRange.upperBound("ace", true);
```

To specify both a lower and an upper bound, use the `bound()` method. This method accepts four arguments, the lower bound key, the upper bound key, an optional Boolean indicating to skip the lower bound, and an optional Boolean indicating to skip the upper bound. Here are some examples:

```
// start at "007", go to "ace"
const boundRange  = IDBKeyRange.bound("007", "ace");
// start at item after "007", go to "ace"
const boundRange  = IDBKeyRange.bound("007", "ace", true);
// start at item after "007", go to item before "ace"
const boundRange  = IDBKeyRange.bound("007", "ace", true, true);
// start at "007", go to item before "ace"
const boundRange  = IDBKeyRange.bound("007", "ace", false, true);
```

Once you have defined a range, pass it into the `openCursor()` method and you'll create a cursor that stays within the constraints:

```
const store = db.transaction("users").objectStore("users"),
    range = IDBKeyRange.bound("007", "ace");
    request = store.openCursor(range);
request.onsuccess = function(event){
  const cursor = event.target.result;
  if (cursor) {  // always check
    console.log(`Key: ${cursor.key}, Value: ${JSON.stringify(cursor.value)}`);
    cursor.continue();  // go to the next one
  } else {
    console.log("Done!");
  }
};
```

This example outputs only the values between keys `"007"` and `"ace"`, which are fewer than the previous section's example.

Setting Cursor Direction

There are actually two arguments to `openCursor()`. The first is an instance of `IDBKeyRange` and the second is a string indicating the direction. Typically, cursors start at the first item in the object store and progress toward the last with each call to `continue()` or `advance()`. These cursors have the default direction value of `"next"`. If there are duplicates in the object store, you may want to have a cursor that skips over the duplicates. You can do so by passing `"nextunique"` into `openCursor()` as the second argument:

```
const transaction = db.transaction("users"),
    store = transaction.objectStore("users"),
    request = store.openCursor(null, "nextunique");
```

Note that the first argument to `openCursor()` is `null`, which indicates that the default key range of all values should be used. This cursor will iterate through the items in the object store starting from the first item and moving toward the last while skipping any duplicates.

You can also create a cursor that moves backward through the object store, starting at the last item and moving toward the first by passing in either `"prev"` or `"prevunique"` (the latter, of course, to avoid duplicates). For example:

```
const transaction = db.transaction("users"),
    store = transaction.objectStore("users"),
    request = store.openCursor(null, "prevunique");
```

When you open a cursor using `"prev"` or `"prevunique"`, each call to `continue()` or `advance()` moves the cursor backward through the object store instead of forward.

Indexes

For some data sets, you may want to specify more than one key for an object store. For example, if you're tracking users by both a user ID and a username, you may want to access records using either piece of data. To do so, you would likely consider the user ID as the primary key and create an index on the username.

To create a new index, first retrieve a reference to the object store and then call `createIndex()`, as in this example:

```
const transaction = db.transaction("users"),
    store = transaction.objectStore("users"),
    index = store.createIndex("username", "username", { unique: true });
```

The first argument to `createIndex()` is the name of the index, the second is the name of the property to index, and third is an `options` object containing the key unique. This option should always be specified so as to indicate whether or not the key is unique across all records. Because `username` may not be duplicated, this index is unique.

The returned value from `createIndex()` is an instance of `IDBIndex`. You can also retrieve the same instance via the `index()` method on an object store. For example, to use an already existing index named `"username"`, the code would be:

```
const transaction = db.transaction("users"),
    store = transaction.objectStore("users"),
    index = store.index("username");
```

An index acts a lot like an object store. You can create a new cursor on the index using the `openCursor()` method, which works exactly the same as `openCursor()` on an object store except that the `result.key` property is filled in with the index key instead of the primary key. Here's an example:

```
const transaction = db.transaction("users"),
    store = transaction.objectStore("users"),
    index = store.index("username"),
    request = index.openCursor();
request.onsuccess = (event) => {
  // handle success
};
```

An index can also create a special cursor that returns just the primary key for each record using the openKeyCursor() method, which accepts the same arguments as openCursor(). The big difference is that event.result.key is the index key and event.result.value is the primary key instead of the entire record.

```
const transaction = db.transaction("users"),
    store = transaction.objectStore("users"),
    index = store.index("username"),
    request = index.openKeyCursor();
request.onsuccess = (event) => {
  // handle success
  // event.result.key is the index key, event.result.value is the primary key
};
```

You can also retrieve a single value from an index by using get() and passing in the index key, which creates a new request:

```
const transaction = db.transaction("users"),
    store = transaction.objectStore("users"),
    index = store.index("username"),
    request = index.get("007");
request.onsuccess = (event) => {
  // handle success
};
request.onfailure = (event) => {
  // handle failure
};
```

To retrieve just the primary key for a given index key, use the getKey() method. This also creates a new request but result.value is equal to the primary key rather than the entire record:

```
const transaction = db.transaction("users"),
    store = transaction.objectStore("users"),
    index = store.index("username"),
    request = index.getKey("007");
request.onsuccess = (event) => {
  // handle success
  // event.result.key is the index key, event.result.value is the primary key
};
```

In the onsuccess event handler in this example, event.result.value would be the user ID.

At any point in time, you can retrieve information about the index by using properties on the IDBIndex object:

➤ name—The name of the index.

➤ keyPath—The property path that was passed into createIndex().

➤ objectStore—The object store that this index works on.

➤ unique—A Boolean indicating if the index key is unique.

The object store itself also tracks the indexes by name in the `indexNames` property. This makes it easy to figure out which indexes already exist on an object using the following code:

```
const transaction = db.transaction("users"),
    store = transaction.objectStore("users"),
    indexNames = store.indexNames
for (let indexName in indexNames) {
    const index = store.index(indexName);
    console.log(`Index name: ${index.name}
                KeyPath: ${index.keyPath}
                Unique: ${index.unique}`);
}
```

This code iterates over each index and outputs its information to the console.

An index can be deleted by calling the `deleteIndex()` method on an object store and passing in the name of the index:

```
const transaction = db.transaction("users"),
    store = transaction.objectStore("users"),
    store.deleteIndex("username");
```

Because deleting an index doesn't touch the data in the object store, the operation happens without any callbacks.

Concurrency Issues

While IndexedDB is an asynchronous API inside of a web page, there are still concurrency issues. If the same web page is open in two different browser tabs at the same time, it's possible that one may attempt to upgrade the database before the other is ready. The problematic operation is in setting the database to a new version, and so version changes can be completed only when there is just one tab in the browser using the database.

When you first open a database, it's important to assign an `onversionchange` event handler. This callback is executed when another tab from the same origin opens the DB to a new version. The best response to this event is to immediately close the database so that the version upgrade can be completed. For example:

```
let request, database;

request = indexedDB.open("admin", 1);
request.onsuccess = (event) => {
  database = event.target.result;
  database.onversionchange = () => database.close();
};
```

You should assign `onversionchange` after every successful opening of a database. Remember, `onversionchange` will have been called in the other tab(s) as well.

By always assigning these event handlers, you will ensure your web application will be able to better handle concurrency issues related to IndexedDB.

Limits and Restrictions

Many of the restrictions on IndexedDB are exactly the same as those for Web Storage. First, IndexedDB databases are tied to the origin (protocol, domain, and port) of the page, so the information cannot be shared across domains. This means there is a completely separate data store for www.foo.com as for cdn.foo.com.

Second, there is a limit to the amount of data that can be stored per origin, but it is significantly larger than Web Storage APIs. Chromium browsers allow up to 80% disk space across all domains and 60% disk space for a single domain. (For example, if you have 10GB, IndexedDB can use up to 8GB of space, and 6GB can be used by a single origin). Firefox allows up to 2GB per origin while Safari allows up to 1GB per origin.

> **NOTE** *Firefox imposes an extra limitation that local files cannot access* IndexedDB *databases at all. Chrome doesn't have this restriction. When running the examples from this chapter locally, be sure to use Chrome.*

Wrapper Libraries

Few developers will need to use the IndexedDB API directly. Wrapper libraries like Dexie.js can simplify the process of using JavaScript storage APIs. These libraries provide a higher-level interface to interact with the storage APIs and abstract away many of the low-level details, making it easier to work with the storage APIs.

The following code borrowed from the Dexie.js documentation demonstrates how easy it is with Dexie.js to initialize and use an IndexedDB database:

```
// Declare DB
const db = new Dexie("MyDatabase");
db.version(1).stores({
    friends: "++id, name, age, *tags",
    gameSessions: "id, score"
});

// Add object
await db.friends.add({name: "Josephine", age: 21});

// Query objects
const someFriends = await db.friends
    .where("age").between(20, 25)
    .offset(150).limit(25)
    .toArray();
```

SUMMARY

Cookies are a simple and widely used mechanism for storing small amounts of data on the client side in web applications using JavaScript. They are small text files that are sent to the browser by a web server and stored on the user's device. Cookies are commonly used to store user preferences, session IDs, and login credentials, among other things. They have a limited storage capacity of around 4KB and can be set to expire after a specific duration or when the user closes their browser. Cookies can be accessed and manipulated using JavaScript, making them a powerful tool for creating more responsive and interactive web applications.

Web Storage defines two objects to save data: `sessionStorage` and `localStorage`. The former is used strictly to save data within a browser session because the data is removed once the browser is closed. The latter is used to persist data across sessions.

IndexedDB is a structured data storage mechanism similar to an SQL database. Instead of storing data in tables, data is stored in object stores. Object stores are created by defining a key and then adding data. Cursors are used to query object stores for particular pieces of data, and indexes may be created for faster lookups on particular properties.

With all of these options available, it's possible to store a significant amount of data on the client machine using JavaScript. You should use care not to store sensitive information because the data cache isn't encrypted.

23

Modules

WHAT'S IN THIS CHAPTER?

➤ Understanding the module pattern

➤ Improvising module systems

➤ Working with pre-ECMAScript module loaders

➤ Working with ECMAScript modules

Writing modern JavaScript essentially guarantees that you will be working with large codebases and using third-party resources. A consequence of these is that you will end up using code broken into different parts and connecting them together in some way.

Prior to the ECMAScript 6 module specification, there was a dire need for module-like behavior even though browsers did not natively support it. ECMAScript did not support modules in any way, so libraries and codebases that wanted to use the module pattern were required to cleverly use JavaScript constructs and lexical features to "fake" module-like behavior.

Because JavaScript is an asynchronously loaded interpreted language, the module implementations that emerged and gained widespread use took on a handful of different forms. These different forms took their shape in order to accomplish different results, but ultimately, they were all implementations of the canonical module pattern.

UNDERSTANDING THE MODULE PATTERN

Splitting code into independent pieces and connecting those pieces together can be robustly implemented with the module pattern. The central ideas for this pattern are simple: break logic into pieces that are totally encapsulated from the rest of the code, allow each piece to explicitly define what parts of itself are exposed to external pieces, and allow each piece to explicitly define what external pieces it needs to execute. There are various implementations and features that complicate these concepts, but these fundamental ideas are the foundation for all module systems in JavaScript.

Module Identifiers

Common to all module systems is the concept of *module identifiers*. Module systems are essentially key-value entities, where each module has an identifier that can be used to reference it. This token will sometimes be a string in cases where the module system is emulated, or it might be an actual path to a module file in cases where the module system is natively implemented.

Some module systems will allow you to explicitly declare the identity of a module, and some module systems will implicitly use the filename as the module identity token. In either case, a well-formed module system will have no module identity collisions, and any module in the system should be able to reference a different module in the system with no ambiguity.

Exactly how a module identifier is resolved to an actual module will be subject to the identifier implementation in any given module system. Native browser module identifiers must provide a path to an actual JavaScript file. In addition to file paths, NodeJS will perform a search for module matches inside the `node_modules` directory, and can also match an identifier to a directory containing `index.js`.

Module Dependencies

The real meat of module systems comes into play when considering how to manage *dependencies*. A module specifying a dependency is entering into a contract with the surrounding environment. The local module declares to the module system a list of external modules—"dependencies"—that it knows exist and are required for the local module to function properly. The module system inspects the dependencies and in turn guarantees that these modules will be loaded and initialized by the time the local module executes.

Each module also is associated with some unique token that can be used to retrieve the module. Frequently, this is a path to the JavaScript file, but in some module systems this can also be a namespace path string declared within the module itself.

Module Loading

The concept of *module loading* is borne out of the requirements of a dependency contract. When an external module is specified as a dependency, the local module expects that when it is executed, the dependencies will be ready and initialized.

In the context of browsers, loading a module has several components. Loading a module involves executing the code inside it, but this cannot begin until all the dependencies are loaded and executed first. A module dependency, if it is code that has not yet been sent to the browser, must be requested and delivered over the network. Once the code payload is received by the browser, the browser must determine if the newly loaded external module has its own dependencies, and it will recursively evaluate those dependencies and load them in turn until all dependent modules are loaded. Only once the entire dependency graph is loaded can the entry module begin to execute.

Entry Points

A network of modules that depend upon each other must specify a single module as the *entry point*, where the path of execution will begin. This should make sense, as the JavaScript execution environment is serially executed and single threaded—so the code must start somewhere. This entry point module will likely have module dependencies, and some of those dependencies will in turn have dependencies. The net effect of this is that all the modules of a modular JavaScript application will form a connected dependency graph starting from a single point.

Dependencies between modules in an application can be represented as a directed graph. Suppose the dependency graph shown in Figure 23.1 represents an imaginary application:

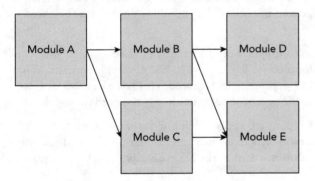

FIGURE 23.1: An example dependency graph

Arrows represent the flow of module dependencies: Module A depends on Module B and Module C, Module B depends on Module D and Module E, and so on. Because a module cannot be loaded until its dependencies are loaded, it follows that Module A, the entry point in this imaginary application, must be executed only after the rest of the application loads.

In JavaScript, the concept of module loading can take a number of different forms. Because modules are implemented as a file containing JavaScript code that will immediately execute, it is possible to request the individual scripts in an order that will satisfy the dependency graph. For the preceding application, the following script order would satisfy the dependency graph:

```
<script src="moduleE.js"></script>
<script src="moduleD.js"></script>
<script src="moduleC.js"></script>
<script src="moduleB.js"></script>
<script src="moduleA.js"></script>
```

Module loading is *blocking*, meaning further execution cannot continue until an operation finishes. Each module progressively loads after its script payload is delivered to the browser, with all its dependencies already loaded and initialized. This strategy has a number of performance and complexity implications; however, loading five JavaScript files sequentially to do the work of one application is not ideal, and managing the correct load order is not an easy task to do by hand.

Asynchronous Dependencies

Because JavaScript is an asynchronous language, it can also be useful to load modules on demand by allowing JavaScript code to instruct the module system to load a new module, and provide the module to a callback once it is ready. At the code level, pseudocode for this might appear as follows:

```
// moduleA definition
load('moduleB').then(function(moduleB) {
  moduleB.doStuff();
});
```

Module A's code is using the `moduleB` token to request that the module system load Module B, and invoke the callback with Module B provided as a parameter. Module B might have already been loaded, or it might have to be freshly requested and initialized, but this code does not care—those responsibilities are delegated to the module loader.

If you were to rework the previous application to use only programmatic module loading, you would only need to use a single `<script>` tag for Module A to load, and Module A would request module files as needed—no generating an ordered list of dependencies required. This has a number of benefits, one of which is performance, as only one file synchronously loading is required on pageload.

It would also be possible to keep these scripts separated, apply a defer or async attribute to the `<script>` tags, and include logic that can discern when an asynchronously script is loaded and initialized. This behavior would emulate what is implemented in the ECMAScript module specification, which is covered later in the chapter.

Programmatic Dependencies

Some module systems will require you to specify all dependencies at the beginning of a module, but some module systems will allow you to dynamically add dependencies inside the program structure. This is distinct from regular dependencies listed at the beginning of a module, all of which are required to load before a module can begin to execute.

The following is an example of programmatic dependency loading.

```
if (loadCondition) {
  require('./moduleA');
}
```

Inside this module, it is determined only at runtime if `moduleA` is loaded. The loading of `moduleA` might be blocking, or it might yield execution and only continue once the module is loaded. Either way, execution inside this module cannot continue until `moduleA` is loaded because the assumption is that `moduleA`'s presence is critical for subsequent module behavior.

Programmatic dependencies allow for more complex dependency utilization, but at a cost—it makes static analysis of a module more difficult.

Static Analysis

The JavaScript that you build into modules and deliver to the browser is often subject to static analysis, where tools will inspect the structure of your code and reason about how it will behave without performing program execution. A module system that is friendly to static analysis will allow module bundling systems to have an easier time when figuring out how to combine your code into fewer files. It will also offer you the ability to perform intelligent autocomplete inside a smart editor.

More complicated module behavior, such as programmatic dependencies, will make static analysis more difficult. Different module systems and module loaders will offer varying levels of complexity. With respect to a module's dependencies, additional complexity will make it more difficult for tooling to predict exactly which dependencies a module will need when it executes.

Circular Dependencies

It is nearly impossible to architect a JavaScript application that is free of dependency cycles, and therefore all module systems including CommonJS, AMD, and ECMAScript—support cyclical dependencies. In an application with dependency cycles, the order in which modules are loaded may not be what you expect. However, if you have properly structured your modules in a way that has no side-effects, the load order should not be a detriment to your overall application.

In the following module (which uses module-agnostic pseudocode), any of the modules could be used as the entry point module even though there are cycles in the dependency graph:

```
require('./moduleD');
require('./moduleB');

console.log('moduleA');
require('./moduleA');
require('./moduleC');

console.log('moduleB');
require('./moduleB');
require('./moduleD');

console.log('moduleC');

require('./moduleA');
require('./moduleC');

console.log('moduleD');
```

Changing the module that is used as the main module will change the dependency load order. If moduleA were to be loaded first, it would print the following, which is indicative of the absolute order of when a module load completes:

```
moduleB
moduleC
moduleD
moduleA
```

The load order can be visualized with the dependency graph in Figure 23.2, where the loader will perform a depth-first load of the dependencies:

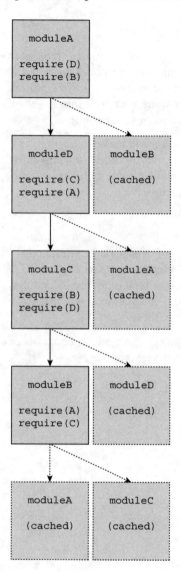

FIGURE 23.2: Depth-first module load with Module A entrypoint

If, instead, moduleC were to be loaded first, it would print the following, which is indicative of the absolute order of module loads:

```
moduleD
moduleA
moduleB
moduleC
```

The load order can be visualized with the dependency graph in Figure 23.3, where the loader will perform a depth-first load of the dependencies:

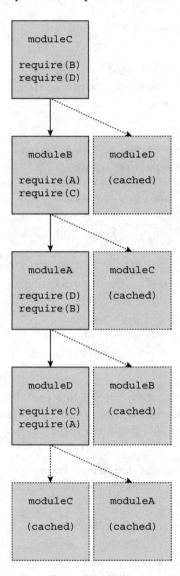

FIGURE 23.3: Depth-first module load with Module C entrypoint

WORKING WITH PRE-ES6 MODULE LOADERS

Prior to the introduction of native ECMAScript module support, JavaScript codebases using modules essentially wanted to use a language feature that was not available by default. Therefore, codebases would be written in a module syntax that conformed to a certain specification, and separate module tooling would serve to bridge the gap between the module syntax and the JavaScript runtime. The module syntax and bridging took a number of different forms, usually either a supplementary library in the browser or preprocessing at build time.

CommonJS

The CommonJS specification outlines a convention for module definition that uses synchronous declarative dependencies. This specification is primarily intended for module organization on the server, but it can also be used to define dependencies for modules that will be used in the browser. CommonJS module syntax will not work natively in the browser.

> **NOTE** *Often, NodeJS and CommonJS will be described as using the same style of module systems, and this is not entirely true. NodeJS uses a slightly modified version of CommonJS, which is appropriate in a server environment because it does not need to deal with the issue of network latency. For consistency, this section will use the NodeJS-flavored module definition syntax.*

A CommonJS module definition will specify its dependencies using `require()`, and it will define its public API using an exports object. A simple module definition might appear as follows:

```
var moduleB = require('./moduleB');

module.exports = {
  stuff: moduleB.doStuff();
};
```

`moduleA` specifies its dependency on `moduleB` by using a relative path to the module definition. What counts as a "module definition," and how a string references that module, is entirely up to the module system's implementation. In NodeJS for example, a module identifier might point to a single file, or it might point to a directory with an `index.js` file inside.

Requiring a module will load it, and assignment of the module to a variable is extremely common, but assignment to a variable is not required. Invoking `require()` means the module will load all the same.

```
console.log('moduleA');
require('./moduleA');  // "moduleA"
```

Modules are always singletons, irrespective of how many times a module is referenced inside `require()`. In the following example, `moduleA` will only ever be printed once because `moduleA` is only ever loaded a single time—even though it is required multiple times.

```
console.log('moduleA');
var a1 = require('./moduleA');
var a2 = require('./moduleA');

console.log(a1 === a2);  // true
```

Modules are cached after the first time they are loaded; subsequent attempts to load a module will retrieve the cached module. Module load order is determined by the dependency graph.

```
console.log('moduleA');
require('./moduleA');
require('./moduleB');  // "moduleA"
require('./moduleA');
```

In CommonJS, module loading is a synchronous operation performed by the module system, so `require()` can be programmatically invoked inline in a module, as well as conditionally.

```
console.log('moduleA');
if (loadCondition) {
   require('./moduleA');
}
```

Here, `moduleA` will load only if `loadCondition` evaluates to `true`. The load is synchronous, so any code that precedes the `if()` block will execute before `moduleA` loads, and any code that follows the `if()` block will execute after `moduleA` loads. All the same load order rules apply, so if `moduleA` had been loaded previously elsewhere in the module graph, this conditional `require()` would only serve to allow you to use the `moduleA` namespace.

In these examples, the module system is implemented inside NodeJS, so `./moduleB` is a relative path to a module target in the same directory as this module. NodeJS will use the module identifier string in the `require()` call to resolve the module reference dependency. NodeJS can use absolute or relative paths to modules, or it can also use module identifiers for dependencies installed in the `node_modules` directory. These details aren't germane to the subject matter of this book, but it's important to know that the module's string reference might be differently implemented inside different CommonJS implementations. However, common to all CommonJS-style implementations is that modules will not specify their identifier; it is derived from their location in the module file hierarchy.

The path to the module definition might reference a directory, or it might be a single JavaScript file—either way, this local module is unconcerned with the module implementation, and Module B is loaded into a local variable. Module A in turn defines its public interface, the `foo` property, on the `module.exports` object.

If another module wanted to use this interface, it could import the module as follows:

```
var moduleA = require('./moduleA');

console.log(moduleA.stuff);
```

Note here that this module does not export anything. Even though it has no public interface, if the module were required in an application, it would still execute the module body on load.

The `exports` object is extremely flexible and can take on multiple forms. If you are looking to export only a single entity, you are able to perform a direct assignment to `module.exports`:

```
module.exports = 'foo';
```

This way, the entire module interface is a string, which can be used as follows:

```
var moduleA = require('./moduleB');

console.log(moduleB);   // 'foo'
```

It is also very common to bundle multiple values into exports, which can either be done with an object literal assignment or a one-off property assignment:

```
// Equivalent:

module.exports = {
  a: 'A',
  b: 'B'
};

module.exports.a = 'A';
module.exports.b = 'B';
```

One of the primary uses of modules is to house class definitions:

```
class A {}

module.exports = A;
var A = require('./moduleA');

var a = new A();
```

It is also possible to assign an instance of a class as the exported value:

```
class A {}

module.exports = new A();
```

Furthermore, CommonJS supports programmatic dependencies:

```
if (condition) {
  var A = require('./moduleA');
}
```

CommonJS relies on several globals such as `require` and `module.exports` to work. For CommonJS modules to be usable in the browser, there needs to be some sort of bridge between its non-native module syntax. There also needs to be some sort of barrier between the module-level code and the browser runtime, as CommonJS code executed without encapsulation will declare global variables in the browser—behavior that is undesirable in the module pattern.

A common solution is to bundle the module files together ahead of time, convert the globals to native JavaScript constructs, encapsulate the module code inside function closures, and serve a single file. Comprehension of the dependency graph is required to bundle the modules in the correct order.

Asynchronous Module Definition

Whereas CommonJS is targeted at a server execution model—where there is no penalty for loading everything into memory at once—the Asynchronous Module Definition (AMD) system of module definition is specifically targeted at a browser execution model, where there *are* penalties from increased network latency. The general strategy of AMD is for modules to declare their dependencies, and the module system running in the browser will fetch the dependencies on demand and execute the module that depends on them once they have all loaded.

The core of the AMD module implementation is a `function` wrapper around the module definition. This prevents the declaration of global variables and allows for the loader library to control when to load the module. The function wrapper also allows for superior portability of module code because all the module code inside the function wrapper uses native JavaScript constructs. This function wrapper is an argument to the define global, which is defined by the AMD loader library implementation.

An AMD module can specify its dependencies with string identifiers, and the AMD loader will call the module factory function once all the dependent modules have loaded. Unlike CommonJS, AMD allows you to optionally specify the string identifier for your module.

```
// Definition for a module with id 'moduleA'. moduleA depends on moduleB,
// which will be loaded asynchronously.
define('moduleA', ['moduleB'], function(moduleB) {
  return {
    stuff: moduleB.doStuff();
  };
});
```

AMD also supports the `require` and `exports` objects, which allow for construction of CommonJS-style modules inside an AMD module factory function. These are required in the same way as modules, but the AMD loader will recognize them as native AMD constructs rather than module definitions:

```
define('moduleA', ['require', 'exports'], function(require, exports) {
  var moduleB = require('moduleB');

  exports.stuff = moduleB.doStuff();
});
```

Programmatic dependencies are supported using this style:

```
define('moduleA', ['require'], function(require) {
  if (condition) {
    var moduleB = require('moduleB');
  }
});
```

Universal Module Definition

In an attempt to unify the CommonJS and AMD ecosystems, the Universal Module Definition (UMD) convention was introduced to create module code that could be used by both systems. Essentially, the pattern defines modules in a way that detects which module system is being used upon startup, configures it as appropriate, and wraps the whole thing in an immediately invoked function expression. It is an imperfect combination, but for the purposes of combining the two ecosystems it is suitable in a surprisingly large number of scenarios.

An example module with a single dependency (based on the UMD repository on GitHub) is as follows:

```
(function (root, factory) {
 if (typeof define === 'function' && define.amd) {
    // AMD. Register as an anonymous module.
    define(['moduleB'], factory);
 } else if (typeof module === 'object' && module.exports) {
    // Node. Does not work with strict CommonJS, but
    // only CommonJS-like environments that support module.exports,
    // like Node.
    module.exports = factory(require(' moduleB '));
 } else {
    // Browser globals (root is window)
    root.returnExports = factory(root. moduleB);
 }
}(this, function (moduleB) {
  //use moduleB in some fashion.

  // Just return a value to define the module export.
  // This example returns an object, but the module
  // can return a function as the exported value.
  return {};
}));
```

There are variations on this pattern that enable support for strict CommonJS and browser globals. You should never be expected to be authoring this exact wrapper by hand—it should be automatically generated by a build tool. Your goal is to be concerned with the content of the modules, not the boilerplate that connects each of them.

Module Loader Deprecation

Ultimately, the patterns shown in this section will become increasingly obsolete as support broadens for the ECMAScript module specification. That being so, it still is quite useful to know what the ECMAScript module specification grew out of in order to learn why design decisions were chosen. The intense conflict between CommonJS and AMD cultivated the ECMAScript module specification that we now enjoy.

WORKING WITH ECMASCRIPT MODULES

One of ECMAScript 6's most significant introductions was a specification for modules. The specification in many ways is simpler than its predecessor module loaders, and native browser support means that loader libraries and other preprocessing is not necessary. In many ways, the ECMAScript module system unifies the best features of AMD and CommonJS into a single specification.

Module Tagging and Definition

ECMAScript modules exist as a monolithic chunk of JavaScript. A script tag with `type="module"` will signal to the browser that the associated code should be executed as a module, as opposed to execution as a traditional script. Modules can be defined inline or in an external file:

```
<script type="module">
  // module code
</script>

<script type="module" src="path/to/myModule.js"></script>
```

Even though they are handled in a different way than a conventionally loaded JavaScript file, JavaScript module files do not have a special content type.

Unlike their traditional script counterparts, all modules will execute in the same order that a `<script defer>` would execute. Downloading a module file begins immediately after the `<script type="module'>` tag is parsed, but execution is delayed until the document is completely parsed. This applies to both inline modules and modules defined in external files. The order in which `<script type="module">` code appears on the page is the order in which it will execute. As is the case with `<script defer>`, changing the location of the module tags—either in <head> or <body>—will only control when the files load, not when the modules are loaded.

The following is the order of execution for an inline module:

```
<!-- Executes 2nd -->
<script type="module"></script>

<!-- Executes 3rd -->
<script type="module"></script>

<!-- Executes 1st -->
<script></script>
```

Alternately, this can be reworked with an external JS module definition:

```
<!-- Executes 2nd -->
<script type="module" src="module.js"></script>

<!-- Executes 3rd -->
<script type="module" src="module.js"></script>

<!-- Executes 1st -->
<script><script>
```

It is also possible to add an `async` attribute to module tags. The effect of this is twofold: the order of module execution no longer is bound to the order of script tags on the page, and the module will not wait for the document to be finished parsing before beginning execution. The entry module must still wait for its dependencies to load.

ECMAScript modules associated with a `<script type="module">` tag are considered to be the entry module for a module graph. There are no restrictions as to how many entry modules there can be on a page, and there is no limit to overlap of modules. No matter how many times a module is loaded in a page, irrespective of how that load occurs, it will only ever load a single time, as demonstrated here:

```
<!-- moduleA will only load a single time on this page -->

<script type="module">
  import './moduleA.js'
<script>
<script type="module">
  import './moduleA.js'
<script>
<script type="module" src="./moduleA.js"></script>
<script type="module" src="./moduleA.js"></script>
```

Modules defined inline cannot be loaded into other modules using import. Only modules loaded from an external file can be loaded using import. Therefore, inline modules are only useful as an entry point module.

Module Loading

ECMAScript modules are unique in their ability to be loaded both natively by the browser as well as in conjunction with third-party loaders and build tools. Some browsers still do not natively support ECMAScript modules, so third-party tooling may be required. In many cases, third-party tooling may, in fact, be more desirable.

A browser that offers full ECMAScript module support will be able to load the entire dependency graph from a top-level module, and it will do so asynchronously. The browser will interpret the entry module, identify its dependencies, and send out requests for its dependent modules. When these files are returned over the network, the browser will parse their contents, identify their dependencies, and send out more requests for those second-order dependencies if they are not already loaded. This recursive asynchronous process will continue until the entire application's dependency graph is resolved. Once the dependencies are resolved, the application can begin to formally load.

This process is very similar to the AMD style of module loading. Module files are loaded on demand, and successive rounds of module file requests are delayed by the network latency of each dependency module file. That is, if entry `moduleA` depends on `moduleB`, and `moduleB` depends on `moduleC`, the browser will not know to send a request for C until the request for B has first completed. This style of loading is efficient and requires no outside tooling, but loading a large application with a deep dependency graph may take too long.

Module Behavior

ECMAScript modules borrow many of the best features from CommonJS and AMD predecessors. To name a few:

➤ Module code is only executed when it is loaded.

➤ A module will only ever be loaded a single time.

➤ Modules are singletons.

➤ Modules can define a public interface with which other modules can observe and interact.

➤ Modules can request that other modules be loaded.

➤ Circular dependencies are supported.

The ECMAScript module system also introduces new behavior:

➤ ECMAScript modules by default execute in strict mode.

➤ ECMAScript modules do not share a global namespace.

➤ The value of `this` at the top-level of a module is `undefined` (as opposed to `window` in the case of normal scripts).

➤ `var` declarations will not be added to the `window` object.

➤ ECMAScript modules are loaded and executed asynchronously.

The behavior described here characterizing an ECMAScript module is conditionally enforced by the browser's runtime when it knows to consider a certain file to be a module. A JavaScript file is designated as a module either when it is associated with a `<script type="module">` or when it is loaded via an import statement.

Module Exports

The public export system for ECMAScript modules is very similar to CommonJS. The `export` keyword is used to control what parts of a module are visible to external modules. There are two types of exports in ECMAScript modules: named exports and default exports. Different types of exports means they are imported differently—this is covered in the following section.

The `export` keyword is used to declare a value as a named export. Exports must occur in the top-level of the module; they cannot be nested inside blocks:

```
// Allowed
export ...

// Disallowed
if (condition) {
  export ...
}
```

Exporting a value has no direct effect on JavaScript execution inside a module, so there is no restriction on the locality of the export statement relative to what is being exported, or what order the export keyword must appear in the module. An export may even precede the declaration of the value it is exporting:

```
// Allowed
const foo = 'foo';
export { foo };

// Allowed
```

```
export const foo = 'foo';

// Allowed, but avoid
export { foo };
const foo = 'foo';
```

A *named export* behaves as if the module is a container for exported values. Inline named exports, as the name suggests, can be performed in the same line as variable declaration. In the following example, a variable declaration is paired with an inline `export`. An external module could `import` this module, and the value `foo` would be available inside it as a property of that module:

```
export const foo = 'foo';
```

Declaration does not need to occur in the same line as the export; you can perform the declaration and export the identifier elsewhere in the module inside an *export clause*:

```
const foo = 'foo';
export { foo };
```

It is also possible to provide an alias when exporting. An alias must occur inside the export clause bracket syntax; therefore, declaring a value, exporting it, and providing an alias cannot all be done in the same line. In the following example, an external module would access this value by importing this module and using the `myFoo` export:

```
const foo = 'foo';
export { foo as myFoo };
```

Because named exports allow you to treat the module as a container, you can declare multiple named exports inside a single module. Values can be declared inside the export statement, or they can be declared prior to specifying it as an export:

```
export const foo = 'foo';
export const bar = 'bar';
export const baz = 'baz';
```

Because exporting multiple values is common behavior, grouping export declarations is supported, as is aliasing some or all of those exports:

```
const foo = 'foo';
const bar = 'bar';
const baz = 'baz';
export { foo, bar as myBar, baz };
```

A *default export* behaves as if the module is the same entity as the exported value. The `default` keyword modifier is used to declare a value as a default export, and there can only ever be a single default export. Attempting to specify duplicate default exports will result in a `SyntaxError`.

In the following example, an external module could import this module, and the module itself would be the value of `foo`:

```
const foo = 'foo';
export default foo;
```

Alternately, the ECMAScript module system will recognize the default keyword when provided as an alias, and will apply the default export to the value even though it uses the named export syntax:

```
const foo = 'foo';

// Behaves identically to "export default foo;"
export { foo as default };
```

Because there are no incompatibilities between named exports and default exports, ECMAScript allows you to use both in the same module:

```
const foo = 'foo';
const bar = 'bar';

export { bar };
export default foo;
```

The two export statements can be combined into the same line:

```
const foo = 'foo';
const bar = 'bar';

export { foo as default, bar };
```

The `export * as <namespace>` syntax allows you to export all the exports from one module as a single namespace object in another module. This can be useful for organizing related exports and making them available through a single, easy-to-use object:

```
// moduleA.js
export const foo = "myFoo";
export const bar = "myBar";
// end moduleA.js



// moduleB.js
export * as myNamespace from './moduleA.js';
// end moduleB.js



import { myNamespace } from './moduleB.js';
console.log(myNamespace.foo);  // myFoo
```

The ECMAScript specification restricts what can and cannot be done inside various forms of an export statement. Some forms allow declaration and assignment, some forms allow only expressions, and some forms only allow simple identifiers. Note that some forms utilize semicolons, and some do not.

```
// Named inline exports
export const baz = 'baz';
export const foo = 'foo', bar = 'bar';
export function foo() {}
export function* foo() {}
```

```
export class Foo {}

// Named clause exports
export { foo };
export { foo, bar };
export { foo as myFoo, bar };

// Default exports
export default 'foo';
export default 123;
export default /[a-z]*/;
export default { foo: 'foo' };
export { foo, bar as default };
export default foo
export default function() {}
export default function foo() {}
export default function*() {}
export default class {}

// Various disallowed forms that will cause errors:

// Variable declarations cannot occur inside inline default exports
export default const foo = 'bar';

// Only identifiers can appear in export clauses
export { 123 as foo }'

// Aliasing only can occur in export clauses
export const foo = 'foo' as myFoo;
```

> **NOTE** *Rules for what can and cannot appear in the same line as the export keyword can be difficult to remember. Generally, it is a good practice to perform declarations and assignments separately, and later on export the identifier. This allows you to easily follow correct export syntax, as well as keep your export statements grouped together.*

Module Imports

Modules can use exports from other modules using the `import` keyword. Like `export`, `import` must appear in the top level of a module:

```
// Allowed
import ...

// Disallowed
if (condition) {
  import ...
}
```

`import` statements are hoisted to the top of the module. Therefore, like the `export` keyword, the order in which import statements appear relative to the use of the imported values is unimportant. It is recommended, however, that imports be kept at the top of the module.

```
// Allowed
import { foo } from './fooModule.js';
console.log(foo);  // 'foo'

// Allowed, but avoid
console.log(foo);  // 'foo'
import { foo } from './fooModule.js';
```

A module identifier can be either the relative path to that module file from the current module or the absolute path to that module file from the base path. It must be a plain string; the identifier cannot be dynamically computed, for example, concatenating strings.

If the modules are being natively loaded in the browser via the path in their module identifier, a .js extension is required for the correct file to be referenced. However, if the ECMAScript modules are being bundled or interpreted by a build tool or third-party module loader, you may not need to include the file extension of the module in its identifier.

```
// Resolves to /components/bar.js
import ... from './bar.js';

// Resolves to /bar.js
import ... from '../bar.js';

// Resolves to /bar.js
import ... from '/bar.js';
```

Modules do not need to be imported via their exported members. If you do not need specific exported bindings from a module, but you still need to load and execute the module for its side effects, you can load it with only its path:

```
import './foo.js';
```

Imports are treated as read-only views to the module, effectively the same as const-declared variables. When performing a bulk import using *, the aliased collection of named exports behaves as if it were treated with `Object.freeze()`. Direct manipulation of exported values is impossible, although modifying properties of an exported object is still possible. Adding or removing exported properties of the exported collection is also disallowed. Mutation of exported values must occur using exported methods that have access to internal variables and properties.

```
import foo, * as Foo './foo.js';

foo = 'foo';         // Error

Foo.foo = 'foo';    // Error

foo.bar = 'bar';    // Allowed
```

The distinction between named exports and default exports is mirrored in the way they are imported. Named exports can be retrieved in bulk without specifying their exact identifier using * and providing an identifier for the collection of exports:

```
const foo = 'foo', bar = 'bar', baz = 'baz';
export { foo, bar, baz }
```

```
import * as Foo from './foo.js';

console.log(Foo.foo);  // foo
console.log(Foo.bar);  // bar
console.log(Foo.baz);  // baz
```

To perform explicit imports, the identifiers can be placed inside an *import clause*. Using an import clause also allows you to specify aliases for the imports:

```
import { foo, bar, baz as myBaz } from './foo.js';

console.log(foo);    // foo
console.log(bar);    // bar
console.log(myBaz);  // baz
```

Default exports behave as if the module target is the exported value. They can be imported using the default keyword and providing an alias; alternately, they can be imported without the use of curly braces, and the identifier you specify is effectively the alias for the default export:

```
// Equivalent
import { default as foo } from './foo.js';
import foo from './foo.js';
```

If a module exports both named exports and default exports, it's possible to retrieve them in the same import statement. This retrieval can be performed by enumerating specific exports, or using *:

```
import foo, { bar, baz } from './foo.js';

import { default as foo, bar, baz } from './foo.js';

import foo, * as Foo from './foo.js';
```

Import Metadata

In JavaScript, the import.meta property provides information about the current module's import metadata. The import.meta object is an immutable object that provides information about the originating URL of the module. Using import.meta outside of a module will throw a SyntaxError. It has one file and one property:

➤ import.meta.url returns the full URL from which the script was obtained.

➤ import.meta.resolve(moduleName) allows a script to access the module specifier resolution algorithm for a module name. The name will be resolved relative to the current module's path. Note that this does not actually perform any module importing.

These properties are demonstrated in the following lines:

```
console.log(import.meta.url)
// https://foo.com/bar.js

const moduleName = "./vendor/baz.js";

console.log(import.meta.resolve(moduleName));
// https://foo.com/vendor/baz.js
```

Dynamic Imports

In addition to static module imports, ECMAScript also supports dynamic module imports via `import(moduleName)`. This is useful in situations where you can defer a module load and programmatically retrieve it based on some observed event or user interaction. The syntax for dynamic module loading is not as flexible as the static `import` keyword, and dynamic imports make analyzing and bundling code via static analysis much harder.

The following is an example of a simple dynamic import:

```
import("./myModule.js").then((myModule) => {
  // myModule is loaded, do stuff with it!
})
```

Calling `import()` returns a promise that will resolve to an object containing all exports from `myModule.js` once the module loads. This object is called a *module namespace object*. The following example demonstrates how a dynamically loaded module can be used:

```
// myModule.js
export const foo = "myFoo";
export const bar = "myBar";
// end myModule.js


import("./myModule.js").then((myModule) => {
  console.log(myModule.foo);   // myFoo
  console.log(myModule.bar);   // myBar
})
```

As you may have realized, this dynamic import resolves to an object that is structured identically, as if you had performed the static import `* as myModule from "./myModule.js"`.

Module Side Effects

Most of the time, you will find modules are the most useful when they are used as bundles of values, methods, and classes. However, since a module is a script that executes upon load, you can structure a module so that the script has valuable *side effects*. For example, suppose you wanted to add some custom properties to the global `window` object.

```
// myModule.js
window.foo = "myFoo";
window.bar = "myBar";
// end myModule.js


import "./myModule.js";

console.log(window.foo);   // myFoo
```

This module is defined without any exports, and is imported purely by module reference. The module loads, applies its side effects, and exits. In many cases, importing this module dynamically might be more useful than statically, as it allows you to control exactly when the side effects are applied.

```
console.log(window.foo);   // undefined
import("./myModule.js");
console.log(window.foo);   // myFoo
```

Module Passthrough Exports

Imported values can be piped directly through to an export. You are also able to convert default to named exports, and vice versa. If you wanted to incorporate all the named exports from one module into another, this can be accomplished with a * export:

```
export * from './foo.js';
```

All named exports in foo.js will be available when importing bar.js. This syntax will ignore the default value of foo.js if it has one. This syntax also requires care around export name collisions. If foo.js exports baz, and bar.js also exports baz, the ultimate export value will be the one specified in bar.js. This "overwrite" will occur silently:

foo.js

```
export const baz = 'origin:foo';
```

bar.js

```
export * from './foo.js';
export const baz = 'origin:bar';
import { baz } from './bar.js';
```

main.js

```
console.log(baz);   // origin:bar
```

It's also possible to enumerate which values from the external module are being passed through to the local exports. This syntax supports aliasing:

```
export { foo, bar as myBar } from './foo.js';
```

Similarly, the default export of an imported module can be reused and exported as the default export of the current module:

```
export { default } from './foo.js';
```

This does not perform any copy of the export; it merely propagates the imported reference to the original module. The defined value of that import still lives in the original module, and the same restrictions involving mutation of imports apply to imports that are re-exported.

When performing a re-export, it is also possible to alter the named/default designation from the imported module. A named import can be specified as the default export as follows:

```
export { foo as default } from './foo.js';
```

Import Maps

Traditionally, the process of resolving module dependencies in JavaScript has been handled by package managers like npm, which uses the `package.json` file to specify dependencies and their versions. With the advent of *import maps*, it's now possible to control module resolution *directly in the browser.*

Specifically, import maps allow you to define a mapping between module specifiers (e.g., the names of modules that your application code imports) and the URLs from which those modules should be loaded. Let's imagine we wish to create an extremely simple script that needs to use Lodash. Begin with the following nonfunctional page:

```html
<html>
  <head>
    <script type="module">
      import _ from 'lodash';

      const numbers = [1, 2, 3, 4, 5];
      const evens = _.filter(numbers, n => n % 2 === 0);

      console.log(evens);
      // [2, 4]
    </script>
  </head>
  <body>
    <div id="root"></div>
  </body>
</html>
```

Of course, this will totally blow up when loaded because the browser has no idea how to resolve the imported module identifier. However, by adding an import map, we can provide a map for the browser to resolve the Lodash identifier:

```html
<html>
  <head>
    <script type="importmap">
      {
        "imports": {
          "lodash": "https://cdn.jsdelivr.net/npm/lodash-es@4.17.21/+esm"
        }
      }
    </script>
    <script type="module">
      import _ from 'lodash';

      const numbers = [1, 2, 3, 4, 5];
      const evens = _.filter(numbers, n => n % 2 === 0);

      console.log(evens);
      // [2, 4]
    </script>
```

```
      </head>
      <body>
        <div id="root"></div>
      </body>
    </html>
```

Now, the browser reads `import _ from "lodash"`, matches `lodash` to the corresponding entry in the import map, and loads that module from the specified CDN. Note that, since this all works using ECMAScript modules, we must import the ESM version of Lodash.

Import maps are generally supported by modern browsers, but you can feature-detect support as follows:

```
if (HTMLScriptElement.supports('importmap')) {
  // Supported!
}
```

Currently there is a limit of one import map per document, though support for multiple maps is on the road map. This limitation can come into play when constructing import maps programmatically.

Worker Modules

ECMAScript modules are fully compatible with `Worker` instances. When instantiating, workers can be passed a path to a module file in the same way you would pass a normal script file. The `Worker` constructor accepts a second argument allowing you to inform it that you are passing a module file. `Worker` instantiation for both types of workers is as follows:

```
// Second argument defaults to { type: 'classic' }
const scriptWorker = new Worker('scriptWorker.js');

const moduleWorker = new Worker('moduleWorker.js', { type: 'module' });
```

In a script worker, modules are imported using the `importScripts()`. In a module worker, modules are imported using the `import` statement.

Backwards Compatibility

Because adoption of ECMAScript module compatibility will be gradual, it is valuable for early module adopters to have the ability to develop for both browsers that support modules and browsers that do not. For users who want to natively use ECMAScript modules in the browser when possible, solutions will involve serving two versions of your code—a module-based version and a script-based version. If this is undesirable to you, utilizing third-party module systems such as SystemJS or transpiling down ECMAScript modules at build time are better options.

The first strategy involves inspecting the browser's user-agent on the server, matching it against a known list of browsers that support modules, and using that to decide which JS files to serve. This method is brittle and complicated, and is not recommended. A better and more elegant solution to this is to make use of the script type attribute and the script `nomodule` attribute.

When a browser does not recognize the `type` attribute value of a `<script>` element, it will decline to execute its contents. For legacy browsers that do not support modules, this means that `<script type="module">` will never execute. Therefore, it is possible to place a fallback `<script>` tag right next to the `<script type="module">` tag:

```
// Legacy browser will not execute this
<script type="module" src="module.js"></script>

// Legacy browser will execute this
<script src="script.js"></script>
```

This, of course, leaves the problem of browsers that *do* support modules. In this case, the preceding code will execute twice—obviously an undesirable outcome. To prevent this, browsers that support ECMAScript modules natively will also recognize the `nomodule` attribute. This attribute informs browsers that support ECMAScript modules to not execute the script. Legacy browsers will not recognize the attribute and ignore it.

Therefore, the following configuration will yield a setup in which both modern and legacy browsers will execute exactly one of these scripts:

```
// Modern browser will execute this
// Legacy browser will not execute this
<script type="module" src="module.js"></script>

// Modern browser will not execute this
// Legacy browser will execute this
<script nomodule src="script.js"></script>
```

SUMMARY

The module pattern remains a timeless tool for managing complexity. It allows developers to create segments of isolated logic, declare dependencies between these segments, and connect them together. What's more, the pattern is one that has proven to scale elegantly to arbitrary complexity and across platforms.

For years, the ecosystem grew around a contentious dichotomy between CommonJS, a module system targeted at server environments, and AMD, a module system targeted at latency-constrained client environments. Both systems enjoyed explosive growth, but the code written for each was in many ways at odds, and often incurred an unholy amount of boilerplate. What's more, neither system was natively implemented by browsers, and in the wake of this incompatibility rose a deluge of tooling that allowed for the module pattern to be used in browsers.

ECMAScript modules take the best of both worlds and combine them into a simpler declarative syntax. Browsers increasingly offer support for native module utilization, but also provide robust tooling to bridge the gap between marginal and full support for ECMAScript modules.

24

Workers

The statement "JavaScript is single-threaded" is practically a mantra for the frontend development community. This assertion, although it makes some simplifying assumptions, effectively describes how the JavaScript environment generally behaves inside a browser. Therefore, it is useful as a pedagogical tool for helping web developers understand JavaScript.

This single-threaded paradigm is inherently restrictive as it prevents programming patterns that are otherwise feasible in languages capable of delegating work to separate threads or processes. JavaScript is bound to this single-threaded paradigm to preserve compatibility with the various browser APIs that it must interact with. Constructs such as the Document Object Model would encounter problems if subjected to concurrent mutations via multiple JavaScript threads. Therefore, traditional concurrency constructs such as POSIX threads or Java's Thread class are non-starters for augmenting JavaScript.

Therein lies the core value proposition of workers: Allow the primary execution thread to delegate work to a separate entity without changing the existing single-threaded model. Although the various worker types covered in this chapter all have different forms and functions, they are all separated from the page's JavaScript environment.

INTRODUCTION TO WORKERS

A single JavaScript environment is essentially a virtualized environment running inside the host operating system. Each open page in a browser is allocated its own environment. This provides each page its own memory, event loop, DOM, and so on. Each page is sandboxed and cannot interfere with other pages. It is trivial for a browser to manage many environments at once—all of which are executing *in parallel*.

Using *workers*, browsers can allocate a second child environment that is totally separated from the original page environment. This child environment is prevented from interacting with single-thread–dependent constructs such as the DOM, but is otherwise free to execute code in parallel with the parent environment.

Comparing Workers and Threads

Introductory resources will commonly draw a comparison between workers and execution threads. In many ways, this is an apt comparison, as workers and threads do indeed share many characteristics:

➤ **Workers are implemented as actual threads.** For example, the Blink browser engine implements workers with a `WorkerThread` that corresponds to an underlying platform thread.

➤ **Workers execute in parallel.** Even though the page and the worker both implement the single-threaded JavaScript environment, instructions in each environment can be executed in parallel.

➤ **Workers can share *some* memory.** Workers can use a `SharedArrayBuffer` to share memory between multiple environments. Whereas threads will use locks to implement concurrency control, JavaScript uses the Atomics interface to implement concurrency control.

Workers and threads have a great deal of overlap, yet there are some important differences between them:

➤ **Workers do not share *all* memory.** In a traditional thread model, multiple threads have the capability to read and write to a shared memory space. With the exception of the `SharedArrayBuffer`, moving data in and out of workers requires it to be copied or transferred.

➤ **Worker threads are not necessarily part of the same process.** Typically, a single process can spawn multiple threads inside of it. Depending on the browser engine's implementation, a worker thread may or may not be part of the same process as the page. For example, Chrome's Blink engine uses a separate process for shared worker and service worker threads.

➤ **Worker threads are more expensive to create.** Worker threads include their own separate event loop, global objects, event handlers, and other features that are part and parcel of a JavaScript environment. The computational expense of creating these should not be overlooked.

In both form and function, workers are not a drop-in replacement for threads. The HTML Web Worker specification says the following:

Workers are relatively heavy-weight, and are not intended to be used in large numbers. For example, it would be inappropriate to launch one worker for each pixel of a four megapixel image. Generally, workers are expected to be long-lived, have a high start-up performance cost, and a high per-instance memory cost.

Types of Workers

There are three primary types of workers defined in the Web Worker specification: the *dedicated web worker*, the *shared web worker*, and the *service worker*. These are all widely available in modern web browsers.

> **NOTE** *The Web Worker specification can be found at* `https://html.spec` `.whatwg.org/multipage/workers.html`.

Dedicated Web Worker

The *dedicated web worker*, also sometimes referred to as a *dedicated worker*, *web worker*, or just *worker*, is the bread-and-butter utility that allows scripts to spawn a separate JavaScript thread and delegate tasks to it. A dedicated worker, as the name suggests, can only be accessed by the page that spawned it.

Shared Web Worker

A shared web worker behaves much like a dedicated worker. The primary difference is that a shared worker can be accessed across multiple contexts, including different pages. Any scripts executing on the same origin as the script that originally spawned the shared worker can send and receive messages to a shared worker.

Service Worker

A service worker is wholly different from that of a dedicated or shared worker. Its primary purpose is to act as a network request arbiter capable of intercepting, redirecting, and modifying requests dispatched by the page.

> **NOTE** *There is a handful of other worker specifications, such as the* `ChromeWorker` *or Web Audio API. These are not widely supported, or they target niche applications and therefore are not included in the book.*

The WorkerGlobalScope

On a web page, the `window` object exposes a broad suite of global variables to scripts running inside it. Inside a worker, the concept of a "window" does not make sense, and therefore its global object is an instance of `WorkerGlobalScope`. Instead of `window`, this global object is accessible via the `self` keyword.

WorkerGlobalScope Properties and Methods

The properties available on self are a strict subset of those available on window. Some properties return a worker-flavored version of the object:

➤ `navigator`—Returns the `WorkerNavigator` associated with this worker.

➤ `self`—Returns the `WorkerGlobalScope` object.

➤ `location`—Returns the `WorkerLocation` associated with this worker.

➤ `performance`—Returns a `Performance` object (with a reduced set of properties and methods).

➤ `console`—Returns the `console` object associated with this worker. No restriction on API.

➤ `caches`—Returns the `CacheStorage` object associated with this worker. No restriction on API.

➤ `indexedDB`—Returns an `IDBFactory` object.

➤ `isSecureContext`—Returns a Boolean indicating if the context of the worker is secure.

➤ `origin`—Returns the origin of the `WorkerGlobalScope` object.

Similarly, methods available on `self` are a subset of those available on `window`. The methods on `self` operate identically to their counterparts on window:

➤ `atob()`

➤ `btoa()`

➤ `clearInterval()`

➤ `clearTimeout()`

➤ `createImageBitmap()`

➤ `fetch()`

➤ `setInterval()`

➤ `setTimeout()`

The `WorkerGlobalScope` also introduces a new global method `importScripts()`, which is only available inside a worker. This method is described later in the chapter.

Subclasses of WorkerGlobalScope

The `WorkerGlobalScope` is not actually implemented anywhere. Each type of worker uses its own flavor of global object, which inherits from `WorkerGlobalScope`.

➤ A dedicated worker uses a `DedicatedWorkerGlobalScope`.

➤ A shared worker uses a `SharedWorkerGlobalScope`.

➤ A service worker uses a `ServiceWorkerGlobalScope`.

The differences between these global objects are discussed in their respective sections in this chapter.

DEDICATED WORKERS

A *dedicated worker* is the simplest type of web worker. Dedicated workers are created by a web page to execute scripts outside the page's thread of execution. These workers are capable of exchanging information with the parent page, sending network requests, performing file I/O, executing intense computation, processing data in bulk, or any other number of computational tasks that are unsuited for the page execution thread (where they would introduce latency issues).

> **NOTE** *When dealing with workers, where a script is executing and where it was loaded from are important concepts. Unless otherwise specified, assume throughout this chapter that* main.js *is a top-level script loaded from and executing on the root path of the* https://example.com *domain.*

Dedicated Worker Basics

Dedicated workers can be aptly described as *background scripts*. The characteristics of a JavaScript worker—including lifecycle management, code path, and input/output—are governed by a singular script provided when the worker is initialized. This script may in turn request additional scripts, but a worker always begins with a single script source.

Creating a Dedicated Worker

The most common way to create a dedicated worker is through a loaded JavaScript file. The file path is provided to the `Worker` constructor, which in turn asynchronously loads the script in the background and instantiates the worker. The constructor requires a path to a file, although that path can take several different forms.

The following simple example creates an empty dedicated worker:

EMPTYWORKER.JS

```
// empty JS worker file
```

> **MAIN.JS**
>
> ```
> console.log(location.href);   // "https://example.com/"
> const worker = new Worker(location.href + 'emptyWorker.js');
> console.log(worker);          // Worker {}
> ```

This demonstration is trivial, but it involves several foundational concepts:

➤ The `emptyWorker.js` file is loaded from an absolute path. Depending on the structure of your application, using an absolute URL will often be redundant.

➤ This file is loaded in the background, and the worker initialization occurs on a thread totally separate from that of `main.js`.

➤ The worker itself exists in a separate JavaScript environment, so the `main.js` must use a `Worker` object as a proxy to communicate with that worker. In the above example, this object is assigned to the `worker` variable.

➤ Although the worker itself may not yet exist, this `Worker` object is available immediately inside the original environment.

The previous example could be altered to use a relative path; however, this requires that `main.js` is loaded from the same directory as `emptyWorker.js`:

```
const worker = new Worker('./emptyWorker.js');
console.log(worker);    // Worker {}
```

Worker Security Restrictions

Worker script files can only be loaded from the same origin as the parent page. Attempts to load a worker script file from a remote origin will throw an error when attempting to construct the worker, as shown here:

```
// Attempt to build worker from script at https://example.com/worker.js
const sameOriginWorker = new Worker('./worker.js');

// Attempt to build worker from script at https://untrusted.com/worker.js
const remoteOriginWorker = new Worker('https://untrusted.com/worker.js');

// Error: Uncaught DOMException: Failed to construct 'Worker':
// Script at https://untrusted.com/main.js cannot be accessed
// from origin https://example.com
```

> **NOTE** *The worker origin restriction does not prevent you from executing code from remote origins. This can be accomplished inside the worker via the use of* `importScripts()`, *which is covered later in the chapter.*

Workers created from a loaded script are not subject to the document's content security policy because workers execute in a separate context from the parent document. However, if the worker is loaded from a script with a globally unique identifier—as is the case when a worker is loaded from a blob—it *will* be subject to the content security policy of the parent document.

> **NOTE** *Creating workers from blobs is covered in the "Creating a Worker from Inline JavaScript" section.*

Using the Worker Object

The `Worker` object is used as the single point of communication with the newly created dedicated worker. It can be used to transmit information between the worker and the parent context, as well as catch events emitted from the dedicated worker.

> **NOTE** *Carefully track references to the* `Worker` *objects associated with each worker you create. Until a worker is terminated, it cannot be garbage collected, and there is no programmatic tool that you can use to regain a reference to an existing worker.*

The `Worker` object supports the following event handler properties:

➤ `onerror`—Can be assigned an event handler that will be called whenever an `ErrorEvent` of type error bubbles from the worker.

   ➤ This event occurs when an error is thrown inside the worker.

   ➤ This event can also be handled using `worker .addEventListener('error', handler)`.

➤ `onmessage`—Can be assigned an event handler that will be called whenever a `MessageEvent` of type message bubbles from the worker.

   ➤ This event occurs when the worker script sends a message event back to the parent context.

   ➤ This event can also be handled using `worker .addEventListener('message', handler)`.

➤ `onmessageerror`—Can be assigned an event handler that will be called whenever a `MessageEvent` of type `messageerror` event bubbles from the worker.

   ➤ This event occurs when a message is received that cannot be deserialized.

   ➤ This event can also be handled using `worker .addEventListener('messageerror', handler)`.

The `Worker` object also supports the following methods:

➤ `postMessage()`—Used to send information to the worker via asynchronous message events.

➤ `terminate()`—Used to immediately terminate the worker. No opportunity for cleanup is afforded to the worker, and the script is abruptly ended.

The DedicatedWorkerGlobalScope

Inside the dedicated worker, the global scope is an instance of `DedicatedWorkerGlobalScope`. This inherits from `WorkerGlobalScope` and therefore includes all its properties and methods. A worker can access this global scope via `self`:

GLOBALSCOPEWORKER.JS

```
console.log('inside worker:', self);
```

MAIN.JS

```
const worker = new Worker('./globalScopeWorker.js');

console.log('created worker:', worker);

// created worker: Worker {}
// inside worker: DedicatedWorkerGlobalScope {}
```

As shown here, the console object in both the top-level script and the worker will write to the browser console, which is useful for debugging. Because the web worker has a non-negligible startup latency, the worker's log message prints after the main thread's log message even though the `Worker` object exists.

> **NOTE** *Using log messages from multiple threads to ascertain order of operation should be done with caution. Note here that two separate JavaScript threads are sending messages to a singular console object, which subsequently serializes the messages and prints them in the browser console. The browser receives messages from two different JavaScript threads and is responsible for interleaving them as it sees fit.*

`DedicatedWorkerGlobalScope` extends the `WorkerGlobalScope` with the following properties and methods:

➤ `name`—An optional string identifier that can be provided to the `Worker` constructor.

➤ `postMessage()`—The counterpart to `worker.postMessage()`. It is used to send messages back out of the worker to the parent context.

➤ `close()`—The counterpart to `worker.terminate()`. It is used to immediately terminate the worker. No opportunity for cleanup is afforded to the worker; the script is abruptly ended.

➤ `importScripts()`—Used to import an arbitrary number of scripts into the worker.

Dedicated Workers and Implicit MessagePorts

You will notice that the dedicated worker object and the `DedicatedWorkerGlobalScope` object share some pieces of interface handlers and methods with `MessagePort`: `onmessage`, `onmessageerror`, `close()`, and `postMessage()`. This is no accident: dedicated workers implicitly use a `MessagePort` to communicate between contexts.

The implementation is such that the object in the parent context and the `DedicatedWorkerGlobalScope` effectively absorb the `MessagePort` and expose its handlers and methods as part of their own interfaces. In other words, you are still sending messages via a `MessagePort`; you just aren't given access to the port itself.

There are some inconsistencies, such as the `start()` and `close()` conventions. Dedicated worker ports will automatically start the sending of queued messages so no `start()` is required. Furthermore, the `close()` method doesn't make sense in the context of a dedicated worker as closing the port would effectively orphan the worker. Therefore, a `close()` called from inside the worker (or `terminate()` from outside) will not just close the port but shut down the worker as well.

Understanding the Dedicated Worker Lifecycle

The `Worker()` constructor is the beginning of life for a dedicated worker. Once called, it initiates a request for the worker script and returns a `Worker` object to the parent context. Although the `Worker` object is immediately available for use in the parent context, the associated worker may not yet have been created due to the worker script's network latency or initialization latency.

Generally speaking, dedicated workers can be informally characterized as existing in one of three states: *initializing*, *active*, and *terminated*. The state of a dedicated worker is opaque to any other contexts. Although a `Worker` object may exist in the parent context, it cannot be ascertained if a dedicated worker is initializing, active, or terminated. In other words, a `Worker` object associated with an active dedicated worker is indistinguishable from a `Worker` object associated with a terminated dedicated worker.

While initializing, although the worker script has yet to begin execution, it is possible to enqueue messages for the worker. These messages will wait for the worker to become active and subsequently be added to its message queue. This behavior is demonstrated here:

INITIALIZINGWORKER.JS

```
self.addEventListener('message', ({data}) => console.log(data));
```

MAIN.JS

```
const worker = new Worker('./initializingWorker.js');

// Worker may still be initializing,
// yet postMessage data is handled correctly.
worker.postMessage('foo');
worker.postMessage('bar');
worker.postMessage('baz');

// foo
// bar
// baz
```

Once created, a dedicated worker will last the lifetime of the page unless explicitly terminated either via self-termination (`self.close()`) or external termination (`worker.terminate()`). Even when the worker script has run to completion, the worker environment will persist. While the worker is still alive, the `Worker` object associated with it will not be garbage collected.

Self-termination and external termination ultimately perform the same worker termination routine. Consider the following example, where a worker self-terminates in between dispatching messages:

CLOSEWORKER.JS

```
self.postMessage('foo');
self.close();
self.postMessage('bar');
setTimeout(() => self.postMessage('baz'), 0);
```

MAIN.JS

```
const worker = new Worker('./worker.js');
worker.onmessage = ({data}) => console.log(data);

// foo
// bar
```

Although `close()` is invoked, clearly execution of the worker is not immediately terminated. `close()` only instructs the worker to discard all tasks in the event loop and prevent further tasks from being added. This is why `"baz"` never prints. It does *not* demand that synchronous execution halt, and therefore `"bar"` is still printed, as it is handled in the parent context's event loop.

Now, consider the following external termination example:

TERMINATEWORKER.JS

```
self.onmessage = ({data}) => console.log(data);
```

```
MAIN.JS
```

```
const worker = new Worker('./worker.js');

// Allow 1000ms for worker to initialize
setTimeout(() => {
  worker.postMessage('foo');
  worker.terminate();
  worker.postMessage('bar');
  setTimeout(() => worker.postMessage('baz'), 0);
}, 1000);

// foo
```

Here, the worker is first sent a `postMessage` with `"foo"`, which it can handle prior to the external termination. Once `terminate()` is invoked, the worker's message queue is drained and locked—this is why only `"foo"` is printed.

> **NOTE** *Both* `close()` *and* `terminate()` *are idempotent operations; they may be called multiple times without harm. These methods merely serve to flag the worker for teardown, so invoking them multiple times will have no ill effects.*

Over its lifecycle, a dedicated worker is associated with exactly one web page (referred to in the Web Worker specification as a *document*). Unless explicitly terminated, a dedicated worker will persist as long as the associated document exists. If the browser leaves the page (perhaps via navigation or closing a tab or window), the browser will flag workers associated with that document for termination, and their execution will immediately halt.

Configuring Worker Options

The `Worker()` constructor allows for an optional configuration object as the second argument. The configuration object supports the following properties:

➤ name—A string identifier that can be read from inside the worker via `self.name`.

➤ type—Specifies how the loaded script should be run, either `"classic"` or `"module"`. `"classic"` executes the script as a normal script; `"module"`, executes the script as a module.

➤ credentials—When type is set to `"module"`, specifies how worker module scripts should be retrieved with respect to transmitting credential data. Can be `omit`, `same-origin`, or `include`. These options operate identically to the `fetch()` credentials option. When `type` is set to `classic`, defaults to `omit`.

Creating a Worker from Inline JavaScript

Workers need to be created from a script file, but this does not mean that the script must be loaded from a remote resource. A dedicated worker can also be created from an inline script via a blob object URL. This allows for faster worker initialization due to the elimination of roundtrip network latency.

The following example creates a worker from an inline script:

```
// Create string of JavaScript code to execute
const workerScript = `
  self.onmessage = ({data}) => console.log(data);
`;

// Generate a blob instance from the script string
const workerScriptBlob = new Blob([workerScript]);

// Create an object URL for the blob instance
const workerScriptBlobUrl = URL.createObjectURL(workerScriptBlob);

// Create a dedicated worker from the blob
const worker = new Worker(workerScriptBlobUrl);

worker.postMessage('blob worker script');
// blob worker script
```

In this example, the script string is passed into a blob instance, which is then assigned an object URL, which in turn is passed to the `Worker()` constructor. The constructor happily creates the dedicated worker as normal.

Condensed, this same example could appear as follows:

```
const worker = new Worker(
 URL.createObjectURL(new Blob([`self.onmessage = ({data}) => console.log(data);`]))
);

worker.postMessage('blob worker script');
// blob worker script
```

Workers can also take advantage of function serialization with inline script initialization. Because a function's `toString()` method returns the actual function code, a function can be defined in a parent context but executed in a child context. Consider the following simple example of this:

```
function fibonacci(n) {
  return n < 1 ? 0
       : n <= 2 ? 1
       : fibonacci(n - 1) + fibonacci(n - 2);
}

const workerScript = `
  self.postMessage(
    (${fibonacci.toString()})(9)
  );
```

```
`;

const worker = new Worker(URL.createObjectURL(new Blob([workerScript])));

worker.onmessage = ({data}) => console.log(data);

// 34
```

Here, this intentionally expensive implementation of a Fibonacci sequence is serialized and passed into a worker. It's invoked as an immediately invoked function expression (IIFE) and passed a parameter, and the result is messaged back up to the main thread. Even though the Fibonacci computation here is quite expensive, all the computation is delegated to the worker and therefore does not harm the performance of the parent context.

> **NOTE** *Importantly, this function serialization method requires that the function passed in does not use any references obtained through a closure, including global variables like* window, *as these will break when executed inside the worker.*

Dynamic Script Execution Inside a Worker

Worker scripts do not need to be monolithic entities. You are able to programmatically load and execute an arbitrary number of scripts with the importScripts() method, which is available on the global worker object. This method will load scripts and *synchronously* execute them in order. Consider the following example, which loads and executes two scripts:

MAIN.JS

```
const worker = new Worker('./worker.js');

// importing scripts
// scriptA executes
// scriptB executes
// scripts imported
```

SCRIPTA.JS

```
console.log('scriptA executes');
```

SCRIPTB.JS

```
console.log('scriptB executes');
```

WORKER.JS

```
console.log('importing scripts');
```

```
importScripts('./scriptA.js');
importScripts('./scriptB.js');

console.log('scripts imported');
```

`importScripts()` accepts an arbitrary number of script arguments. The browser may download them in any order, but the scripts will be strictly executed in parameter order. Therefore, the following worker script would be equivalent:

```
console.log('importing scripts');

importScripts('./scriptA.js', './scriptB.js');

console.log('scripts imported');
```

Script loading is subject to normal CORS restrictions, but otherwise workers are free to request scripts from other origins. This import strategy is analogous to dynamic script loading via `<script>` tag generation. In that spirit, the worker scope is shared with imported scripts.

Delegating Tasks to Subworkers

You may find the need for workers to spawn their own *subworkers*. This can be useful in cases where you have multiple CPU cores at your disposal for parallelization of computation. Electing to use a subworker model should be done only after a careful design consideration: running multiple web workers may incur a considerable computational overhead and should only be done if the gains from parallelization outweigh the costs.

Subworker creation works nearly identically to normal worker creation with the exception of path resolution: a subworker script path will be resolved with respect to its parent worker rather than the main page.

> **NOTE** *Both top-level worker scripts and subworker scripts must be loaded from the same origin as the main page.*

Handling Worker Errors

If an error is thrown inside a worker script, the worker's sandboxing will serve to prevent it from interrupting the parent thread of execution. This is demonstrated here, where an enclosing try/catch block does not catch the thrown error:

MAIN.JS

```
try {
  const worker = new Worker('./worker.js');
  console.log('no error');
} catch(e) {
  console.log('caught error');
}

// no error
```

WORKER.JS

```
throw Error('foo');
```

However, this event will still bubble up to the global worker context and can be accessed by setting an error event listener on the `Worker` object. This is demonstrated here:

MAIN.JS

```
const worker = new Worker('./worker.js');
worker.onerror = console.log;

// ErrorEvent {message: "Uncaught Error: foo"}
```

WORKER.JS

```
throw Error('foo');
```

Communicating with a Dedicated Worker

All communication to and from a worker occurs via asynchronous messages, but these messages can take on a handful of different forms.

Communicating with *postMessage()*

The easiest and most common form of asynchronous worker messaging is accomplished using `postMessage()` to pass serialized messages back and forth. A simple factorial example of this is shown here:

FACTORIALWORKER.JS

```
function factorial(n) {
  let result = 1;
  while(n) { result *= n--; }
  return result;
}

self.onmessage = ({data}) => {
  self.postMessage(`${data}! = ${factorial(data)}`);
};
```

MAIN.JS

```
const factorialWorker = new Worker('./factorialWorker.js');

factorialWorker.onmessage = ({data}) => console.log(data);

factorialWorker.postMessage(5);
```

continues

(continued)

```
factorialWorker.postMessage(7);
factorialWorker.postMessage(10);

// 5! = 120
// 7! = 5040
// 10! = 3628800
```

For simple message passing, using `postMessage()` to communicate between window and worker is extremely similar to message passing between two windows. The primary difference is that there is no concept of a `targetOrigin` restriction, which is present for `Window.prototype.postMessage` but not `WorkerGlobalScope.prototype.postMessage` or `Worker.prototype.postMessage`. The reason for this convention is simple: the worker script origin is restricted to the main page origin so there is no use for a filtering mechanism.

Communicating with MessageChannel

For both the main thread and the worker thread, communication via `postMessage()` involves invoking a method on the global object and defining an ad-hoc transmission protocol therein. This can be replaced by the Channel Messaging API, which allows you to create an explicit communication channel between the two contexts.

A `MessageChannel` instance has two ports representing the two communication endpoints. To enable a parent page and a worker to communicate over a channel, one port can be passed into the worker, as shown here:

WORKER.JS

```
// Store messagePort globally inside listener
let messagePort = null;

function factorial(n) {
  let result = 1;
  while(n) { result *= n--; }
  return result;
}

// Set message handler on global object
self.onmessage = ({ports}) => {
  // Only set the port a single time
  if (!messagePort) {
    // Initial message sends the port,
    // assign to variable and unset listener
    messagePort = ports[0];
    self.onmessage = null;

    // Set message handler on global object
    messagePort.onmessage = ({data}) => {
```

```
      // Subsequent messages send data
      messagePort.postMessage(`${data}! = ${factorial(data)}`);
    };
  }
};
```

MAIN.JS

```
const channel = new MessageChannel();
const factorialWorker = new Worker('./worker.js');

// Send the MessagePort object to the worker.
// Worker is responsible for handling this correctly
factorialWorker.postMessage(null, [channel.port1]);

// Send the actual message on the channel
channel.port2.onmessage = ({data}) => console.log(data);

// Worker will respond on the channel
channel.port2.postMessage(5);

// // 5! = 120
```

In this example, the parent page shares a MessagePort with a worker via postMessage. The array notation is to pass a transferable object between contexts. This concept is covered later in the chapter. The worker maintains a reference to this port and uses it to transmit messages in lieu of transmitting them via the global object. Of course, this format still utilizes a kind of ad-hoc protocol: the worker is written to expect the first message to send the port and subsequent messages to send data.

Using a MessageChannel instance to communicate with the parent page is largely redundant, as the global postMessage affordance is essentially performing the same task as channel .postMessage (not including the additional features of the MessageChannel interface). A MessageChannel truly becomes useful in a situation in which two workers would like to directly communicate with one another. This can be accomplished by passing one port into each worker. Consider the following example where an array is passed into a worker, passed to another worker, and passed back up to the main page:

MAIN.JS

```
const channel = new MessageChannel();
const workerA = new Worker('./worker.js');
const workerB = new Worker('./worker.js');

workerA.postMessage('workerA', [channel.port1]);
workerB.postMessage('workerB', [channel.port2]);

workerA.onmessage = ({data}) => console.log(data);
```

continues

(continued)

```
workerB.onmessage = ({data}) => console.log(data);

workerA.postMessage(['page']);

// ['page', 'workerA', 'workerB']

workerB.postMessage(['page'])

// ['page', 'workerB', 'workerA']
```

WORKER.JS

```
let messagePort = null;
let contextIdentifier = null;

function addContextAndSend(data, destination) {
  // Add identifier to show when it reached this worker
  data.push(contextIdentifier);

  // Send data to next destination
  destination.postMessage(data);
}

self.onmessage = ({data, ports}) => {
  // If ports exist in the message,
  // set up the worker
  if (ports.length) {
    // Record the identifier
    contextIdentifier = data;

    // Capture the MessagePort
    messagePort = ports[0];

    // Add a handler to send the received data
    // back up to the parent
    messagePort.onmessage = ({data}) => {
      addContextAndSend(data, self);
    }
  } else {
    addContextAndSend(data, messagePort);
  }
};
```

In this example, each part of the array's journey will add a string to the array to mark when it arrived. The array is passed from the parent page into a worker, which adds its context identifier. It is then passed from one worker to the other, which adds a second context identifier. It is then passed back up to the main page, where the array is logged. Note in this example how, because the two workers share a common script, this array passing scheme works bidirectionally.

Communicating with BroadcastChannel

Scripts that run on the same origin can send and receive messages on a shared `BroadcastChannel`. This channel type is simpler to set up and doesn't require the messiness of port passing required with `MessageChannel`. This can be accomplished as follows:

MAIN.JS

```
const channel = new BroadcastChannel('worker_channel');
const worker = new Worker('./worker.js');

channel.onmessage = ({data}) => {
  console.log(`heard ${data} on page`);
}

setTimeout(() => channel.postMessage('foo'), 1000);

// heard foo in worker
// heard bar on page
```

WORKER.JS

```
const channel = new BroadcastChannel('worker_channel');

channel.onmessage = ({data}) => {
  console.log(`heard ${data} in worker`);
  channel.postMessage('bar');
}
```

Note here that the page waits 1,000 milliseconds before sending the initial message on the `BroadcastChannel`. Because there is no concept of port ownership with this type of channel, messages broadcasted will not be handled if there is no other entity listening on the channel. In this case, without the `setTimeout`, the latency of the worker initialization is sufficiently long to prevent the worker's message handler from being set before the message is actually sent.

Worker Data Transfer

Workers will often need to be provided with a data payload in some form. Because workers operate in a separate context, there is overhead involved in getting a piece of data from one context to another. In languages that support traditional models of multithreading, you have concepts such as locks, mutexes, and volatile variables at your disposal. In JavaScript, there are three ways of moving information between contexts: the *structured clone algorithm*, *transferable objects*, and *shared array buffers*.

Structured Clone Algorithm

The *structured clone algorithm* can be used to share a piece of data between two separate execution contexts. This algorithm is only implemented by the browser behind the scenes and cannot be invoked explicitly.

When an object is passed to `postMessage()`, the browser traverses the object and makes a copy in the destination context. The following types are fully supported by the structured clone algorithm:

- All primitive types except `Symbol`
- `Boolean` object
- `String` object
- `Date`
- `RegExp`
- `Blob`
- `File`
- `FileList`
- `ArrayBuffer`
- `ArrayBufferView`
- `ImageData`
- `Array`
- `Object`
- `Map`
- `Set`

Some things to note about the behavior of the structured clone algorithm:

- Once copied, mutations to the object in the source context will not be propagated to the destination context object.
- The structured clone algorithm recognizes when an object contains a cycle and will not infinitely traverse the object.
- Attempting to clone an `Error` object, a `Function` object, or a DOM node will throw an error.
- The structured clone algorithm will not always create an exact copy.
- `Object` property descriptors, getters, and setters are not cloned and will revert to defaults where applicable.
- Prototype chains are not cloned.
- The `RegExp.prototype.lastIndex` property is not cloned.

> **NOTE** *The structured clone algorithm can be computationally expensive when the object being copied is large. Avoid large or excessive copying when possible.*

Transferable Objects

It is possible to transfer ownership from one context to another using *transferable objects*. This is especially useful in cases where it is impractical to copy large amounts of data between contexts. Only a handful of types are transferable:

➤ `ArrayBuffer`

➤ `MessagePort`

➤ `ImageBitmap`

➤ `OffscreenCanvas`

The second optional argument to `postMessage()` is an array specifying which objects should be transferred to the destination context. When traversing the message payload object, the browser will check object references against the transfer object array and perform a transfer upon those objects instead of copying them. This means that transferred objects can be sent in a message payload, which itself is copied, such as an object or array.

The following example demonstrates a normal structured clone of an `ArrayBuffer` into a worker. No object transfer occurs in this example:

MAIN.JS

```
const worker = new Worker('./worker.js');

// Create 32 byte buffer
const arrayBuffer = new ArrayBuffer(32);

console.log(`page's buffer size: ${arrayBuffer.byteLength}`);  // 32

worker.postMessage(arrayBuffer);

console.log(`page's buffer size: ${arrayBuffer.byteLength}`);  // 32
```

WORKER.JS

```
self.onmessage = ({data}) => {
  console.log(`worker's buffer size: ${data.byteLength}`);     // 32
};
```

When the `ArrayBuffer` is specified as a transferable object, the reference to the buffer memory is wiped out in the parent context and allocated to the worker context. This is demonstrated here, where the memory allocated inside the `ArrayBuffer` is removed from the parent context:

MAIN.JS

```
const worker = new Worker('./worker.js');

// Create 32 byte buffer
const arrayBuffer = new ArrayBuffer(32);

console.log(`page's buffer size: ${arrayBuffer.byteLength}`);  // 32

worker.postMessage(arrayBuffer, [arrayBuffer]);

console.log(`page's buffer size: ${arrayBuffer.byteLength}`);  // 0
```

WORKER.JS

```
self.onmessage = ({data}) => {
  console.log(`worker's buffer size: ${data.byteLength}`);      // 32
};
```

It is perfectly fine to nest transferable objects inside other object types. The encompassing object will be copied and the nested object will be transferred:

MAIN.JS

```
const worker = new Worker('./worker.js');

// Create 32 byte buffer
const arrayBuffer = new ArrayBuffer(32);

console.log(`page's buffer size: ${arrayBuffer.byteLength}`);  // 32

worker.postMessage({foo: {bar: arrayBuffer}}, [arrayBuffer]);

console.log(`page's buffer size: ${arrayBuffer.byteLength}`);  // 0
```

WORKER.JS

```
self.onmessage = ({data}) => {
  console.log(`worker's buffer size: ${data.foo.bar.byteLength}`);  // 32
};
```

SharedArrayBuffer

> **NOTE** *The* `SharedArrayBuffer` *was disabled across all major browsers in January 2018 due to Spectre* (https://cve.mitre.org/cgi-bin/cvename .cgi?name=CVE-2017-5753) *and Meltdown* (https://cve.mitre.org/ cgi-bin/cvename.cgi?name=CVE-2017-5754) *vulnerabilities. In 2019, some browsers began to gradually re-enable the feature.*

Rather than being cloned or transferred, a `SharedArrayBuffer` is an `ArrayBuffer` that is shared between browser contexts. When passing a `SharedArrayBuffer` inside `postMessage()`, the browser will pass only a reference to the original buffer. As a result, two different JavaScript contexts will each maintain their own reference to the same block of memory. Each context is free to modify the buffer as it would with a normal `ArrayBuffer`. This behavior is demonstrated here:

MAIN.JS

```js
const worker = new Worker('./worker.js');

// Create 1 byte buffer
const sharedArrayBuffer = new SharedArrayBuffer(1);

// Create view onto 1 byte buffer
const view = new Uint8Array(sharedArrayBuffer);

// Parent context assigns value of 1
view[0] = 1;

worker.onmessage = () => {
  console.log(`buffer value after worker modification: ${view[0]}`);
};

// Send reference to sharedArrayBuffer
worker.postMessage(sharedArrayBuffer);


// buffer value before worker modification: 1
// buffer value after worker modification: 2
```

WORKER.JS

```js
self.onmessage = ({data}) => {
  const view = new Uint8Array(data);

  console.log(`buffer value before worker modification: ${view[0]}`);

  // Worker assigns new value to shared buffer
```

continues

(continued)

```
    view[0] += 1;

    // Send back empty postMessage to signal assignment is complete
    self.postMessage(null);
};
```

Of course, sharing the block of memory between two parallel threads introduces a risk of race conditions. In other words, the SharedArrayBuffer instance is effectively being treated as volatile memory. This problem is demonstrated in the following example:

MAIN.JS

```
// Create worker pool of size 4
const workers = [];
for (let i = 0; i < 4; ++i) {
  workers.push(new Worker('./worker.js'));
}

// Log the final value after the last worker completes
let responseCount = 0;
for (const worker of workers) {
  worker.onmessage = () => {
    if (++responseCount == workers.length) {
      console.log(`Final buffer value: ${view[0]}`);
    }
  };
}

// Initialize the SharedArrayBuffer
const sharedArrayBuffer = new SharedArrayBuffer(4);
const view = new Uint32Array(sharedArrayBuffer);
view[0] = 1;

// Send the SharedArrayBuffer to each worker
for (const worker of workers) {
  worker.postMessage(sharedArrayBuffer);
}

// (Expected result is 4000001. Actual output will be something like:)
// Final buffer value: 2145106
```

WORKER.JS

```
self.onmessage = ({data}) => {
  const view = new Uint32Array(data);

  // Perform 1000000 add operations
  for (let i = 0; i < 1E6; ++i) {
```

```
        view[0] += 1;
    }

    self.postMessage(null);
};
```

Here, each worker is executing 1,000,000 sequential operations, which read from the shared array index, perform an add, and write that value back into the array index. A race condition occurs when worker read/write operations are interleaved. For example:

1. Worker A reads a value of 1.

2. Worker B reads a value of 1.

3. Worker A adds 1 and writes 2 back into the array.

4. Worker B, still using the stale array value of 1, writes 2 back into the array.

To address this, the Atomics global object allows for a worker to effectively obtain a lock on the SharedArrayBuffer instance and perform the entire read/add/write sequence before allowing another worker to perform any operations. Incorporating Atomics.add() into this example yields a correct final value:

MAIN.JS

```
// Create worker pool of size 4
const workers = [];
for (let i = 0; i < 4; ++i) {
  workers.push(new Worker('./worker.js'));
}

// Log the final value after the last worker completes
let responseCount = 0;
for (const worker of workers) {
  worker.onmessage = () => {
    if (++responseCount == workers.length) {
      console.log(`Final buffer value: ${view[0]}`);
    }
  };
}

// Initialize the SharedArrayBuffer
const sharedArrayBuffer = new SharedArrayBuffer(4);
const view = new Uint32Array(sharedArrayBuffer);
view[0] = 1;

// Send the SharedArrayBuffer to each worker
for (const worker of workers) {
  worker.postMessage(sharedArrayBuffer);
}

// (Expected result is 4000001)
// Final buffer value: 4000001
```

WORKER.JS

```
self.onmessage = ({data}) => {
  const view = new Uint32Array(data);

  // Perform 1000000 add operations
  for (let i = 0; i < 1E6; ++i) {
    Atomics.add(view, 0, 1);
  }

  self.postMessage(null);
};
```

> **NOTE** *The* `SharedArrayBuffer` *and Atomics API are fully covered in Chapter 18,* *"JavaScript APIs."*

Worker Pools

Because starting a worker is quite expensive, there may be situations where it is more efficient to keep a fixed number of workers alive and dispatch work to them as necessary. When a worker is performing computation, it is marked as busy and will only be ready to take on another task once it notifies the pool that it is available again. This is commonly referred to as a "thread pool" or "worker pool."

Determining the ideal number of workers in a pool is not an exact science, but the `navigator` `.hardwareConcurrency` property will return the number of cores available on the system. Because you will likely not be able to ascertain the multithreading ability of each core, it may be best to treat this number as the upper bound for pool size.

One scenario you may encounter involves a fixed set of workers in a pool all performing the same task that is controlled by a small set of input parameters. By using a task-specific worker pool, you can allocate a fixed number of workers and feed them parameters on demand. The worker will take in these parameters, perform the long-running computation, and return the value to the pool. In turn, the pool will then send the worker additional work to perform. This example will build a relatively simplistic worker pool, but it will cover all the foundational requirements for this concept.

Begin by defining a `TaskWorker`, which extends the `Worker` class. This class has two jobs: keep track of whether or not it is busy performing work, and manage the information and events going in and out of the worker. Furthermore, tasks passed to this worker will be wrapped in a promise and will resolve/reject appropriately. The class can be defined as follows:

```
class TaskWorker extends Worker {
  constructor(notifyAvailable, ...workerArgs) {
    super(...workerArgs);

    // Initialize as unavailable
    this.available = false;
    this.resolve = null;
```

```
      this.reject = null;

      // Worker pool will pass a callback so that the
      // worker can signal it needs another task
      this.notifyAvailable = notifyAvailable;

      // Worker script will send a 'ready' postmessage
      // once fully initialized
      this.onmessage = () => this.setAvailable();
    }

    // Called by the worker pool to begin a new task
    dispatch({ resolve, reject, postMessageArgs }) {
      this.available = false;

      this.onmessage = ({ data }) => {
        resolve(data);
        this.setAvailable();
      };

      this.onerror = (e) => {
        reject(e);
        this.setAvailable();
      };

      this.postMessage(...postMessageArgs);
    }

    setAvailable() {
      this.available = true;
      this.resolve = null;
      this.reject = null;
      this.notifyAvailable();
    }
  }
```

Next, the WorkerPool class definition must make use of this TaskWorker class. It must also maintain a queue of tasks that have yet to be assigned to a worker. Two events can signal that a new task should be dispatched: a new task is added to the queue, or a worker finishes a task and should be sent another. The class can be defined as follows:

```
class WorkerPool {
  constructor(poolSize, ...workerArgs) {
    this.taskQueue = [];
    this.workers = [];

    // Initialize the worker pool
    for (let i = 0; i < poolSize; ++i) {
      this.workers.push(
        new TaskWorker(() => this.dispatchIfAvailable(), ...workerArgs));
    }
  }

  // Pushes a task onto the queue
  enqueue(...postMessageArgs) {
    return new Promise((resolve, reject) => {
```

```
        this.taskQueue.push({ resolve, reject, postMessageArgs });

        this.dispatchIfAvailable();
      });
    }

    // Sends a task to the next available worker if there is one
    dispatchIfAvailable() {
      if (!this.taskQueue.length) {
        return;
      }
      for (const worker of this.workers) {
        if (worker.available) {
          let a = this.taskQueue.shift();
          worker.dispatch(a);
          break;
        }
      }
    }

    // Kills all the workers
    close() {
      for (const worker of this.workers) {
        worker.terminate();
      }
    }
  }
```

With these two classes defined, it is now trivial to dispatch tasks to the worker pool and have them be executed as workers become available. In this example, suppose you wanted to sum 10 million floating point numbers. To save on transfer costs, this will utilize a `SharedArrayBuffer`. The worker definition might appear as follows:

```
self.onmessage = ({data}) => {
  let sum = 0;
  let view = new Float32Array(data.arrayBuffer)

  // Perform sum
  for (let i = data.startIdx; i < data.endIdx; ++i) {
    // No need for Atomics since only performing reads
    sum += view[i];
  }

  // Send the result to the worker
  self.postMessage(sum);
};

// Send messagemessate to TaskWorker to signal worker is
// ready to receive tasks.
self.postMessage('ready');
```

With all this in place, the code that utilizes the worker pools might appear as follows:

```
Class TaskWorker {
  ...
```

```
  ]

  Class WorkerPool {
    ...
  }

  const totalFloats = 1E8;
  const numTasks = 20;
  const floatsPerTask = totalFloats / numTasks;
  const numWorkers = 4;

  // Create pool
  const pool = new WorkerPool(numWorkers, './worker.js');

  // Fill array of floats
  let arrayBuffer = new SharedArrayBuffer(4 * totalFloats);
  let view = new Float32Array(arrayBuffer);
  for (let i = 0; i < totalFloats; ++i) {
    view[i] = Math.random();
  }

  let partialSumPromises = [];
  for (let i = 0; i < totalFloats; i += floatsPerTask) {
    partialSumPromises.push(
      pool.enqueue({
        startIdx: i,
        endIdx: i + floatsPerTask,
        arrayBuffer: arrayBuffer
      })
    );
  }

  // Wait for all promises to complete, then sum
  Promise.all(partialSumPromises)
    .then((partialSums) => partialSums.reduce((x, y) => x + y))
    .then(console.log);

  // (In this example, sum should be roughly 1E8/2)
  // 49997075.47203197
```

> **NOTE** *Blindly introducing parallelization is not a one-size-fits-all upgrade. Performance tuning for worker pools will vary by what the task computation involves and what the system hardware is.*

SHARED WORKERS

A *shared web worker* or *shared worker* behaves like a dedicated worker but is accessible across multiple trusted execution contexts. For example, two different tabs on the same origin will be able to access a single web worker. SharedWorker and Worker feature slightly different messaging interfaces, both externally and internally.

A shared worker is valuable in situations where the developer wishes to reduce computational overhead by allowing multiple execution contexts to share a worker. An example of this could be a single shared worker managing a websocket to send and receive messages for multiple same-origin pages. Shared workers are also useful when same-origin contexts wish to communicate via the shared worker.

Shared Worker Basics

Behaviorally speaking, shared workers can be considered an extension of dedicated workers. Worker creation, worker options, security restrictions, and `importScripts()` all behave in the same way. As is the case with a dedicated worker, the shared worker also runs inside a separate execution context and can only communicate asynchronously with other contexts.

Creating a Shared Worker

As with dedicated workers, the most common way of creating a shared worker is through a loaded JavaScript file. The file path is provided to the `SharedWorker` constructor, which in turn asynchronously loads the script in the background and instantiates the worker.

The following simple example creates an empty shared worker from an absolute path:

EMPTYSHAREDWORKER.JS

```
// empty JS worker file
```

MAIN.JS

```
console.log(location.href);  // "https://example.com/"
const sharedWorker = new SharedWorker(
    location.href + 'emptySharedWorker.js');
console.log(sharedWorker);   // SharedWorker {}
```

The previous example could be altered to use a relative path; however, this requires that main.js is executing on the same path that `emptySharedWorker.js` can be loaded from:

```
const worker = new Worker('./emptyWorker.js');
console.log(worker);   // Worker {}
```

Shared workers can also be created from an inline script, but there is little point in doing so: each blob created from an inline script string is assigned its own unique in-browser URL, and therefore shared workers created from inline scripts will always be unique. The reasons for this are covered in the next section.

SharedWorker Identity and Single Occupancy

An important difference between a shared worker and a dedicated worker is that, whereas the `Worker()` constructor always creates a new worker instance, the `SharedWorker()` constructor will only create a new worker instance if one with the same identity does not yet exist. If a shared worker matching the identity *does* exist, a new connection will be formed with the existing shared worker.

Shared worker identity is derived from the resolved script URL, the worker name, and the document origin. For example, the following script would instantiate a single shared worker and add two subsequent connections:

```
// Instantiates single shared worker
//  - Constructors called all on same origin
//  - All scripts resolve to same URL
//  - All workers have same name
new SharedWorker('./sharedWorker.js');
new SharedWorker('./sharedWorker.js');
new SharedWorker('./sharedWorker.js');
```

Similarly, because all three of the following script strings resolve to the same URL, only a single shared worker is created:

```
// Instantiates single shared worker
//  - Constructors called all on same origin
//  - All scripts resolve to same URL
//  - All workers have same name
new SharedWorker('./sharedWorker.js');
new SharedWorker('sharedWorker.js');
new SharedWorker('https://www.example.com/sharedWorker.js');
```

Because the optional worker name is part of the shared worker identity, using different worker names will coerce the browser to create multiple shared workers—one with name 'foo' and one with name 'bar'—even though they have the same origin and script URL:

```
// Instantiates two shared workers
//  - Constructors called all on same origin
//  - All scripts resolve to same URL
//  - One shared worker has name 'foo', one has name 'bar'
new SharedWorker('./sharedWorker.js', {name: 'foo'});
new SharedWorker('./sharedWorker.js', {name: 'foo'});
new SharedWorker('./sharedWorker.js', {name: 'bar'});
```

As the name implies, shared workers are shared across tabs, windows, iframes, or other workers running on the same origin. Therefore, the following script run on multiple tabs will only create a worker the first time it is executed, and each successive run will connect to that same worker:

```
// Instantiates single shared worker
//  - Constructors called all on same origin
//  - All scripts resolve to same URL
//  - All workers have same name
new SharedWorker('./sharedWorker.js');
```

The script aspect of the shared worker identity is restricted to the URL only, so the following will create two shared workers even though the same script is loaded:

```
// Instantiates two shared workers
//  - Constructors called all on same origin
//  - '?' token differentiates URLs
//  - All workers have same name
new SharedWorker('./sharedWorker.js');
new SharedWorker('./sharedWorker.js?');
```

If this script was run in two different tabs, there would still only be two shared workers created in total. Each constructor would check for a matching shared worker and merely connect to it if it exists.

Using the SharedWorker Object

The `SharedWorker` object returned from the `SharedWorker()` constructor is used as the single point of communication with the newly created dedicated worker. It can be used to transmit information between the worker and the parent context via a `MessagePort`, as well as catch error events emitted from the dedicated worker.

The `SharedWorker` object supports the following properties:

➤ `onerror`—Can be assigned an event handler that will be called whenever an `ErrorEvent` of type `error` bubbles from the worker.

  ➤ This event occurs when an error is thrown inside the worker.

  ➤ This event can also be handled using `sharedWorker .addEventListener('error', handler)`.

➤ `port`—The dedicated `MessagePort` for communication with the shared worker.

The SharedWorkerGlobalScope

Inside the shared worker, the global scope is an instance of `SharedWorkerGlobalScope`. This inherits from `WorkerGlobalScope` and therefore includes all its properties and methods. As with dedicated workers, a shared worker can access this global scope via self.

`SharedWorkerGlobalScope` extends the `WorkerGlobalScope` with the following properties and methods:

➤ `name`—An optional string identifier, which can be provided to the `SharedWorker` constructor.

➤ `importScripts()`—Used to import an arbitrary number of scripts into the worker.

➤ `close()`—The counterpart to `worker.terminate()`. It is used to immediately terminate the worker. No opportunity for cleanup is afforded to the worker; the script is abruptly ended.

➤ `onconnect`—Should be set as the handler for when a new connection is made to the shared worker. `connect` events include a ports array of `MessagePort` instances, which can be used to send messages back up to the parent context.

  ➤ The connect event occurs when a connection is made to the shared worker either via `worker.port.onmessage` or `worker.port.start()`.

  ➤ This event can also be handled using `sharedWorker .addEventListener('connect', handler)`.

> **NOTE** *Depending on the browser implementation, logging to the console inside the* `SharedWorker` *may not print in the default browser console view.*

Understanding the Shared Worker Lifecycle

A shared worker's lifecycle has the same stages and features of a dedicated worker. The difference is that, while a dedicated worker is inextricably bound to a single page, a shared worker will persist as long as at least one context remains connected to it.

Consider the following script, which creates a dedicated worker each time it is executed:

```
new Worker('./worker.js');
```

The following table details what happens when three tabs that spawn workers are opened and closed in sequence.

EVENT	RESULT	TOTAL WORKERS AFTER EVENT
Tab 1 executes `main.js`	Dedicated worker 1 spawned	1
Tab 2 executes `main.js`	Dedicated worker 2 spawned	2
Tab 3 executes `main.js`	Dedicated worker 3 spawned	3
Tab 1 closed	Dedicated worker 1 terminated	2
Tab 2 closed	Dedicated worker 2 terminated	1
Tab 3 closed	Dedicated worker 3 terminated	0

As shown in the table, parity exists between the number of times the script is executed, the number of open tabs, and the number of running workers. Next, consider the following trivial script, which creates or connects to a shared worker each time it is executed:

```
new SharedWorker('./sharedWorker.js');
```

The following table details what happens when three tabs are opened and closed in sequence.

EVENT	RESULT	TOTAL WORKERS AFTER EVENT
Tab 1 executes `main.js`	Shared worker 1 spawned.	1
Tab 2 executes `main.js`	Connects to shared worker 1.	1
Tab 3 executes `main.js`	Connects to shared worker 1.	1
Tab 1 closed	Disconnects from shared worker 1.	1
Tab 2 closed	Disconnects from shared worker 1.	1
Tab 3 closed	Disconnects from shared worker 1. No connections remain, so worker 1 is terminated.	0

As shown in this table, subsequently invoking new `SharedWorker()` in tab 2 and 3 will connect to the existing worker. As connections are added and removed from the worker, the total number of connections is tracked. When the number of connections goes to zero, the worker is terminated.

Importantly, there is no way to programmatically terminate a shared worker. You will notice that the `terminate()` method is absent from the `SharedWorker` object. Furthermore, calling `close()` on a shared worker port (discussed later in the chapter) will not trigger the termination of the worker, even if there is only a single port connected to the worker.

A `SharedWorker` "connection" is uncorrelated with the connected state of an associated `MessagePort` or `MessageChannel`. As soon as a connection to a shared worker is established, the browser is responsible for managing that connection. The established connection will persist for the lifetime of the page, and only when the page is torn down and there are no further connections to a shared worker will the browser elect to terminate the worker.

Connecting to a Shared Worker

A `connect` event is fired inside a shared worker each time the `SharedWorker` constructor is called, whether or not a worker was created. This is demonstrated in the following example, where the constructor is called inside a loop:

SHAREDWORKER.JS

```
let i = 0;
self.onconnect = () => console.log(`connected ${++i} times`);
```

MAIN.JS

```
for (let i = 0; i < 5; ++i) {
  new SharedWorker('./sharedWorker.js');
}

// connected 1 times
// connected 2 times
// connected 3 times
// connected 4 times
// connected 5 times
```

Upon a connect event, the `SharedWorker` constructor implicitly creates a `MessageChannel` and passes ownership of a `MessagePort` unique to that instance of `SharedWorker`. This `MessagePort` is available inside the connect event object as the ports array. Because a connect event will only ever represent a single connection, you can safely assume that the ports array will have a length of exactly 1.

The following demonstrates accessing the event's ports array. Here, a `Set` is used to ensure that only unique object instances are tracked:

SHAREDWORKER.JS

```
const connectedPorts = new Set();

self.onconnect = ({ports}) => {
  connectedPorts.add(ports[0]);

  console.log(`${connectedPorts.size} unique connected ports`);
};
```

MAIN.JS

```
for (let i = 0; i < 5; ++i) {
  new SharedWorker('./sharedWorker.js');
}

// 1 unique connected ports
// 2 unique connected ports
// 3 unique connected ports
// 4 unique connected ports
// 5 unique connected ports
```

Importantly, shared workers behave asymmetrically in terms of setup and teardown. Each new `SharedWorker` connection triggers an event, but there is no corresponding event for when a `SharedWorker` instance disconnects (such as when a page is closed).

In the previous example, as pages connect and disconnect to the same shared worker, the `connectedPorts` collection will become polluted with dead ports with no way to identify them. One solution to this problem is to send an explicit teardown message right as the page is about to be destroyed at the `beforeunload` event, and to allow the shared worker to clean up.

SERVICE WORKERS

A *service worker* is a type of web worker that behaves like a proxy server inside the browser. Service workers allow you to intercept outgoing requests and cache the response. This allows a web page to work without network connectivity, as some or all of the page can potentially be served from the service worker cache. A service worker can also make use of the Notifications API, the Push API, the Background Sync API, and the Channel Messaging API.

Like shared workers, multiple pages on a single domain will all interact with a single service worker instance. However, to enable features such as the Push API, service workers can also survive the associated tab or browser being closed and wait for an incoming push event.

Ultimately, most developers will find that service workers are most useful for two primary tasks: acting as a caching layer for network requests, and enabling push notifications. In this sense, the service worker is a tool designed to enable web pages to behave like native applications.

> **NOTE** *The service worker is an incredibly broad topic that could nearly fill an entire book of its own. To extend your understanding beyond this chapter, consider taking the Udacity course "Offline Web Applications"* (www.udacity.com/course/offline-web-applications--ud899). *Furthermore, Mozilla maintains a service worker cookbook site* (https://serviceworke.rs), *which is an excellent reference for common service worker patterns.*

> **NOTE** *The service worker lifecycle is heavily dependent on the number of open tabs on the same origin (referred to as "clients"), whether the page has undergone a navigation event, and whether the service worker script has changed (among many other factors). Some examples in the "Service Workers" section may not behave as expected if you do not have a good understanding of the service worker lifecycle. The section "Understanding the Service Worker Lifecycle" sheds light on what is happening under the hood.*
>
> *Furthermore, be wary of using the browser's hard refresh feature (Ctrl+Shift+R) when dealing with service workers. A hard refresh will force the browser to ignore all network caches, and a service worker is considered by most major browsers to be a network cache.*

Service Worker Use Cases

One of the most powerful use cases for service workers is their ability to enable offline functionality for web applications. This can greatly improve the user experience by allowing users to continue using the application when they are in areas with poor Internet connectivity or no Internet access at all.

When a user visits an offline-enabled web page, the service worker can check to see if the required resources are available in the cache. If they are, the service worker can serve those resources directly from the cache, without making a network request. If the required resources are not available in the cache, the service worker can display a custom offline page or fallback content.

Service workers are also a key technology that enable the development of *progressive web applications (PWAs)*. PWAs are web applications that are designed to look and feel like native mobile applications. Service workers can be configured to enable home screen installation on desktop and mobile devices, allowing users to add the application to their home screen and launch it like a native application.

In addition to their offline capabilities, service workers also enable push notifications. Service workers run in the background, listen for push notifications, and display them to the user—even when the application is not open.

Service Worker Basics

As a class of web worker, a service worker exhibits many of the same rhythms as a dedicated or shared worker. It exists in a totally separate execution context and can only be interacted with via asynchronous messaging. However, there are a few fundamental differences between service and dedicated/shared.

The ServiceWorkerContainer

Service workers are different from dedicated and shared workers in that they have no global constructor. Instead, a service worker is managed through the `ServiceWorkerContainer`, available via `navigator.serviceWorker`. This object is the top-level interface, which allows you to direct the browser to create, update, destroy, or interact with a service worker.

```
console.log(navigator.serviceWorker);
// ServiceWorkerContainer { ... }
```

Creating a Service Worker

Service workers are similar to shared workers in that a new one will be spawned if it does not yet exist; otherwise a connection is obtained to an existing one. Instead of creation through a global constructor, the `ServiceWorkerContainer` exposes a `register()` method, which is passed a script URL in the same fashion as the `Worker` or `SharedWorker` constructors:

EMPTYSERVICEWORKER.JS

```
// empty service worker script
```

MAIN.JS

```
navigator.serviceWorker.register('./emptyServiceWorker.js');
```

The `register()` method returns a promise, which resolves to a `ServiceWorkerRegistration` object or rejects if registration fails.

EMPTYSERVICEWORKER.JS

```
// empty service worker script
```

MAIN.JS

```
// Successfully registers a service worker, resolves
navigator.serviceWorker.register('./emptyServiceWorker.js')
  .then(console.log, console.error);
```

continues

(continued)

```
// ServiceWorkerRegistration { ... }


// Attempts to register service worker from nonexistent file, rejects
navigator.serviceWorker.register('./doesNotExist.js')
  .then(console.log, console.error);

// TypeError: Failed to register a ServiceWorker:
// A bad HTTP response code (404) was received when fetching the script.
```

The nature of service workers allows you some flexibility with respect to choosing when to begin the registration. Once a service worker is activated after the initial `register()`, subsequent calls to `register()` on the same page and with the same URL are effectively a no-op. Furthermore, even though service workers are not globally supported by browsers, a service worker should be effectively invisible to the page because its proxy-like behavior means actions that would otherwise be handled will merely be dispatched to the network as normal.

Because of the aforementioned properties, an extremely common pattern for service worker registration is to gate it behind feature detection *and* the page's load event. This frequently appears as follows:

```
if ('serviceWorker' in navigator) {
  window.addEventListener('load', () => {
    navigator.serviceWorker.register('./serviceWorker.js');
  });
}
```

Without the load event gating, the service worker's registration will overlap with loading of page resources, which may slow the overall initial page render. Unless the service worker is responsible for managing cache behavior, which *must* occur as early as possible in the page setup process (such as when using `clients.claim()`, discussed later in the chapter), waiting for the load event is usually a sensible choice that still allows the page to enjoy all the benefits of using service workers.

Using the ServiceWorkerContainer Object

The `ServiceWorkerContainer` interface is the top-level wrapper for the browser's service worker ecosystem. It provides facilities for managing service worker state and lifecycle.

The `ServiceWorkerContainer` is always accessible in the client context:

```
console.log(navigator.serviceWorker);

// ServiceWorkerContainer { ... }
```

A `ServiceWorkerContainer` supports the following event handlers:

➤ oncontrollerchange—Can be assigned an event handler that will be called whenever a controllerchange event is emitted from the `ServiceWorkerContainer`.

> ➤ This event occurs when a new activated `ServiceWorkerRegistration` is acquired.

> ➤ This event can also be handled using `navigator.serviceWorker`
   `.addEventListener('controllerchange', handler)`.

➤ onerror—Can be assigned an event handler that will be called whenever an `ErrorEvent` of type `error` bubbles from any associated service worker.

  ➤ This event occurs when an error is thrown inside any associated service worker.

  ➤ This event can also be handled using `navigator.serviceWorker` `.addEventListener('error', handler)`.

➤ onmessage—Can be assigned an event handler that will be called whenever a `MessageEvent` of type `message` is sent from the service worker.

  ➤ This event occurs when the service worker script sends a message event back to the parent context.

  ➤ This event can also be handled using `navigator.serviceWorker` `.addEventListener('message', handler)`.

A `ServiceWorkerContainer` supports the following properties:

➤ ready—Returns a promise, which might resolve with an activated `ServiceWorkerRegistration` object. This promise will never reject.

➤ controller—Returns the activated `ServiceWorker` object associated with the current page, or `null` if there is no active service worker.

A `ServiceWorkerContainer` supports the following methods:

➤ register()—Creates or updates a `ServiceWorkerRegistration` using the provided URL and options object.

➤ getRegistration()—Returns a promise, which will resolve with a `ServiceWorkerRegistration` object that matches the provided scope, or resolve with `undefined` if there is no matching service worker.

➤ getRegistration()—Returns a promise, which will resolve with an array of all `ServiceWorkerRegistration` objects that are associated with the `ServiceWorkerContainer`, or an empty array if there are no associated service workers.

➤ startMessage()—Starts the transmission of message dispatches via `client` `.postMessage()`.

Using the ServiceWorkerRegistration Object

The `ServiceWorkerRegistration` object represents a successful registration of a service worker. The object is available inside the resolved promise handler returned from `register()`. This object allows you to determine the lifecycle status of the associated service worker via several properties.

The registration object is provided inside a promise after `navigator.serviceWorker.register()` is called. Multiple calls on the same page with the same URL will return the same registration object.

```
navigator.serviceWorker.register('./serviceWorker.js')
.then((registrationA) => {
```

```
        console.log(registrationA);

    navigator.serviceWorker.register('./serviceWorker2.js')
      .then((registrationB) => {
        console.log(registrationA === registrationB);
      });
  });
```

A `ServiceWorkerRegistration` supports the following event handler:

➤ `onupdatefound` can be assigned an event handler, which will be called whenever an event of type `updatefound` is fired from the service worker.

> ➤ This event occurs when a new version of this service worker begins installation, signified by `ServiceWorkerRegistration.installing` acquiring a new service worker.

> ➤ This event can also be handled using serv `serviceWorkerRegistration` `.addEventListener('updatefound', handler)`.

A `ServiceWorkerRegistration` supports the following general properties:

➤ `scope`—Returns the full URL path of the service worker's scope. This value is derived from the path from which the service worker's script was retrieved and/or the scope provided inside `register()`.

➤ `navigationPreload`—Returns the `NavigationPreloadManager` instance associated with this registration object.

➤ `pushManager`—Returns the `PushManager` instance associated with this registration object.

A `ServiceWorkerRegistration` also supports the following properties, which can be used to inspect service workers at various stages of their lifecycles:

➤ `installing`—Returns the service worker with a state of `installing` if there is currently one, else `null`.

➤ `waiting`—Returns the service worker with a state of `waiting` if there is currently one, else `null`.

➤ `active`—Returns the service worker with a state of `activating` or `active` if there is currently one, else `null`.

Note that these properties are a one-time snapshot of the state of a service worker. These are suitable for most use cases, as an active service worker will not change state over the lifetime of a page unless coerced to do so with something like `ServiceWorkerGlobalScope.skipWaiting()`.

A `ServiceWorkerRegistration` supports the following methods:

➤ `getNotifications()`—Returns a promise, which resolves with an array of `Notification` objects.

➤ `showNotifications()`—Displays a notification configurable with a title and options arguments.

➤ `update()`—Re-requests the service worker script directly from the server and initiates fresh installation if the new script differs.

➤ `unregister()`—Will attempt to un-register a service worker registration. This allows service worker execution to complete before performing the unregistration.

Using the ServiceWorker Object

The `ServiceWorker` object can be obtained in one of two ways: via the controller property on the `ServiceWorkerController` object, and the active property on the `ServiceWorkerRegistration` object. This object inherits from the `Worker` prototype, and therefore offers all its properties and methods, but notably absent is the `terminate()` method.

A `ServiceWorker` supports the following event handler:

➤ `onstatechange` can be assigned an event handler that will be called whenever a `statechange` event is emitted from the `ServiceWorker`.

    ➤ This event occurs when `ServiceWorker.state` changes.

    ➤ This event can also be handled using `serviceWorker .addEventListener('statechange', handler)`.

A `ServiceWorker` supports the following properties:

➤ `scriptURL`—The resolved URL used to register the service worker. For example, if the service worker was created with the relative path `'./serviceWorker.js'`, then if it were registered on `https://www.example.com` the `scriptURL` property would return `https://www .example.com/serviceWorker.js`.

➤ `state`—Returns a string identifying the state of the service worker. The possible states are `installing`, `installed`, `activating`, `activated`, and `redundant`.

Service Worker Security Restrictions

As a class of web worker, service workers are subject to the normal restrictions with respect to origin matching of the loaded script. (See the section "Worker Security Restrictions" earlier in the chapter for details on this.) Additionally, because service workers are granted nearly unlimited power to modify and redirect network requests and loaded static resources, the service worker API is only available in secure https contexts; in http contexts, `navigator.serviceWorker` will be undefined. To allow for ease of development, browsers make an exemption to the secure context rule for pages loaded locally, either via localhost or 127.0.0.1.

> **NOTE** *A handy tool for assessing if the current context is secure is* `window .isSecureContext`.

The ServiceWorkerGlobalScope

Inside the service worker, the global scope is an instance of `ServiceWorkerGlobalScope`. This inherits from `WorkerGlobalScope` and therefore includes all its properties and methods. A service worker can access this global scope via `self`.

`ServiceWorkerGlobalScope` extends the `WorkerGlobalScope` with the following properties and methods:

> `caches`—Returns the service worker's `CacheStorage` object.

> `clients`—Returns the service worker's `Clients` interface. Used to access underlying `Client` objects.

> `registration`—Returns the service worker's `ServiceWorkerRegistration` object.

> `skipWaiting()`—Forces the service worker into an active state. This is used in conjunction with `clients.claim()`.

> `fetch()`—Performs a normal fetch from inside the service worker. This is used when the service worker determines that an actual outgoing network request should be made (instead of returning a cached value).

Whereas dedicated or shared workers have only a message event as an input, service workers are able to consume a large number of events, which are triggered by actions on the page, notification actions, or push events.

> **NOTE** *Depending on the browser implementation, logging to the console inside the* `SharedWorker` *may not print in the default browser console view.*

A service worker's global scope can listen for the following events, broken down here by category:

Service worker state

> `install` is fired when the service worker enters the `installing` state (visible in the client via `ServiceWorkerRegistration.installing`). You can also set a handler for this event on `self.oninstall`.

>> This is the first event received by a service worker and is fired as soon as worker execution begins.

>> Called only once per service worker.

➤ `activate` is fired when the service worker enters the `activating` or `activated` state (visible in the client via `ServiceWorkerRegistration.active`). You can also set a handler for this event on `self.onactivate`.

  ➤ This event is fired when the service worker is ready to handle functional events and control clients.

  ➤ This event does *not* mean that the service worker is controlling a client, only that it is prepared to do so.

Fetch API

➤ `fetch` is fired when the service worker intercepts a `fetch()` called in the main page. The service worker's fetch event handler has access to the `FetchEvent` and can adjust the outcome as it sees fit. You can also set a handler for this event on `self.onfetch`.

Message API

➤ `message` is fired when the service worker receives data via `postMesssage()`. You can also set a handler for this event on `self.onmessage`.

Notification API

➤ `notificationclick` is fired when the system reports to the browser that a notification spawned by `ServiceWorkerRegistration.showNotification()` was clicked. You can also set a handler for this event on `self.onnotificationclick`.

➤ `notificationclose` is fired when the system reports to the browser that a notification spawned by `ServiceWorkerRegistration.showNotification()` was closed or dismissed. You can also set a handler for this event on `self.onnotificationclose`.

Push API

➤ `push` is fired when the service worker receives a push message. You can also set a handler for this event on `self.onpush`.

➤ `pushsubscriptionchange` is fired when there is a change in push subscription state that occurred outside the control of the application (not explicitly in JavaScript). You can also set a handler for this event on `self.onpushsubscriptionchange`.

> **NOTE** *Some browsers also support a* `sync` *event, which is part of the Background Sync API. This API is not standardized, and therefore it is not included in this book.*

Service Worker Scope Limitations

Service workers will only intercept requests from clients that are inside the service worker's *scope*. The scope is defined relative to the path from which the service worker's script was served. If not specified inside `register()`, the scope becomes the path to the service worker script.

(All the service worker registrations in these examples use absolute URLs for the script to avoid path confusion.) This first example demonstrates a default root scope for a worker script served from the root path:

```
navigator.serviceWorker.register('/serviceWorker.js')
.then((serviceWorkerRegistration) => {
  console.log(serviceWorkerRegistration.scope);
  // https://example.com/
});

// All of the following would be intercepted:
// fetch('/foo.js');
// fetch('/foo/fooScript.js');
// fetch('/baz/bazScript.js');
```

The following example demonstrates a same-directory scope for a worker script served from the root path:

```
navigator.serviceWorker.register('/serviceWorker.js', {scope: './'})
.then((serviceWorkerRegistration) => {
  console.log(serviceWorkerRegistration.scope);
  // https://example.com/
});

// All of the following would be intercepted:
// fetch('/foo.js');
// fetch('/foo/fooScript.js');
// fetch('/baz/bazScript.js');
```

The following example demonstrates a restricted scope for a worker script served from the root path:

```
navigator.serviceWorker.register('/serviceWorker.js', {scope: './foo'})
.then((serviceWorkerRegistration) => {
  console.log(serviceWorkerRegistration.scope);
  // https://example.com/foo/
});

// All of the following would be intercepted:
// fetch('/foo/fooScript.js');

// All of the following would not be intercepted:
// fetch('/foo.js');
// fetch('/baz/bazScript.js');
```

The following example demonstrates a same-directory scope for a worker script served from a nested path:

```
navigator.serviceWorker.register('/foo/serviceWorker.js')
.then((serviceWorkerRegistration) => {
```

```
    console.log(serviceWorkerRegistration.scope);
    // https://example.com/foo/
});

// All of the following would be intercepted:
// fetch('/foo/fooScript.js');

// All of the following would not be intercepted:
// fetch('/foo.js');
// fetch('/baz/bazScript.js');
```

The service worker scope effectively follows a directory permissions model in that it is only possible to reduce the scope of the service worker relative to where the file was served from. Attempting to expand the scope as follows throws an error:

```
navigator.serviceWorker.register('/foo/serviceWorker.js', {scope: '/'});

// Error: The path of the provided scope 'https://example.com/'
// is not under the max scope allowed 'https://example.com/foo/'
```

Typically, service worker scope will be defined as an absolute path with a trailing slash, as follows:

```
navigator.serviceWorker.register('/serviceWorker.js', {scope: '/foo/'})
```

This style of scope path definition accomplishes two tasks: it decouples the relative path of the script file from the relative scope path, and it prevents the path itself from being included in the scope. For example, in the preceding code snippet, it is probably undesirable for the /foo path to be included in the service worker scope; appending a trailing / will explicitly exclude the /foo path. Of course, this requires that the absolute scope path does not expand outside the service worker path.

If you wish to expand the scope of the service worker, there are two primary ways of doing so:

➤   Serve the service worker script from a path that encompasses the desired scope.

➤   Add a Service-Worker-Allowed header to the service worker script response with its value set to the desired scope. This scope value should match the scope value inside register().

The Service Worker Cache

Before service workers, web pages lacked a robust mechanism for caching network requests. Browsers have always made use of an HTTP cache, but this has no programmatic interface available inside JavaScript, and its behavior is governed outside the JavaScript runtime. It was possible to develop an ad-hoc caching mechanism, which cached the response string or blob, but such strategies were messy and inefficient.

JavaScript cache implementations have been tried before. The MDN docs describe it marvelously:

The previous attempt—AppCache—seemed to be a good idea because it allowed you to specify assets to cache easily. However, it made many assumptions about what you were trying to do and then broke horribly when your app didn't follow those assumptions exactly.

One of the major features of service workers is a true network request caching mechanism that can be programmatically managed. Unlike the HTTP cache or a CPU cache, the service worker cache is fairly primitive:

➤ **The service worker cache does not cache any requests automatically.** All cache entries must be explicitly added.

➤ **The service worker cache has no concept of time-based expiration.** A cache entry will remain cached unless explicitly removed.

➤ **Service worker cache entries must be manually updated and deleted.**

➤ **Caches must be manually versioned.** Each time a service worker updates, the new service worker is responsible for providing a fresh cache key to store new cache entries.

➤ **The only browser-enforced eviction policy is based on storage available for the service worker cache to use.** The service worker is responsible for managing the amount of space its cache uses. When the size of the cache exceeds browser limits, the browser will utilize a *least recently used* (LRU) eviction policy to make room for new cache entries.

At its core, the service worker cache mechanism is a two-tier dictionary in which each entry in the top-level dictionary maps to a second nested dictionary. The top-level dictionary is the `CacheStorage` object, which is available on the global scope of a service worker via the `caches` property. Each value in this top-level dictionary is a `Cache` object, which is a dictionary of `Request` objects mapping to `Response` objects.

As with `LocalStorage`, `Cache` objects inside `CacheStorage` persist indefinitely and will survive past the end of a browser session. Furthermore, `Cache` entries are only accessible on a per-origin basis.

> **NOTE** *Although the* `CacheStorage` *and* `Cache` *objects are defined inside the Service Worker specification, they can be used by the main page or other types of web workers.*

The CacheStorage Object

The `CacheStorage` object is a key-value store of string keys mapping to `Cache` objects. The `CacheStorage` object features an API that resembles an asynchronous `Map`. The `CacheStorage` interface is available on the global object via its `caches` property.

```
console.log(caches);  // CacheStorage {}
```

Individual caches inside `CacheStorage` are retrieved by passing their string key to `caches.open()`. Non-string keys are converted to a string. If the cache does not yet exist, it will be created.

The `Cache` object is returned in a promise:

```
caches.open('v1').then(console.log);

// Cache {}
```

Similar to a Map, CacheStorage features has(), delete(), and keys() methods. These methods all behave as promise-based analogues of their Map counterparts:

CACHESTORAGEEXAMPLE01.JS

```
// open a new v1 cache,
// check for the v1 cache,
// check for the nonexistent v2 cache

caches.open('v1')
.then(() => caches.has('v1'))
.then(console.log)    // true
.then(() => caches.has('v2'))
.then(console.log);   // false
```

CACHESTORAGEEXAMPLE02.JS

```
// open a new v1 cache,
// check for the v1 cache,
// delete the v1 cache,
// check again for the deleted v1 cache

caches.open('v1')
.then(() => caches.has('v1'))
.then(console.log)    // true
.then(() => caches.delete('v1'))
.then(() => caches.has('v1'))
.then(console.log);   // false
```

CACHESTORAGEEXAMPLE03.JS

```
// open a v1, v3, and v2 cache
// check keys of current caches
// NOTE: cache keys are printed in creation order

caches.open('v1')
.then(() => caches.open('v3'))
.then(() => caches.open('v2'))
.then(() => caches.keys())
.then(console.log);   // ["v1", "v3", "v2"]
```

The CacheStorage interface also features a match() method that can be used to check a Request object against *all* Cache objects in CacheStorage. The Cache objects are checked in CacheStorage .keys() order, and the first match is the response returned:

CACHESTORAGEEXAMPLE04.JS

```
// Create one request key and two response values
const request = new Request('');
```

continues

(continued)

```
const response1 = new Response('v1');
const response2 = new Response('v2');

// Use same key in both caches. v1 is found first since it has
// caches.keys() order priority
caches.open('v1')
.then((v1cache) => v1cache.put(request, response1))
.then(() => caches.open('v2'))
.then((v2cache) => v2cache.put(request, response2))
.then(() => caches.match(request))
.then((response) => response.text())
.then(console.log);   // v1
```

`CacheStorage.match()` can be configured using an options object. This object is detailed in the next section.

The Cache Object

A `CacheStorage` maps strings to `Cache` objects. `Cache` objects behave similarly to `CacheStorage` in that they, too, resemble an asynchronous `Map`. Cache keys can either be a URL string or a `Request` object; these keys will map to `Response` object values.

The service worker cache is intended to only cache GET http requests. This should make sense: this HTTP method implies that the response will not change over time. On the other hand, request methods such as POST, PUT, and DELETE are, by default, disallowed by the Cache. They imply a dynamic exchange with the server and therefore are unsuitable for caching by the client.

To populate a Cache, you have three methods at your disposal:

➤ `put(request, response)`—Used when you already have both the key (a `Request` object or URL string) and value (Response object) pair and wish to add the cache entry. This method returns a promise, which resolves when the cache entry is successfully added.

➤ `add(request)`—Used when you have only a `Request` object or URL. `add()` will dispatch a `fetch()` to the network and cache the response. This method returns a promise, which resolves when the cache entry is successfully added.

➤ `addAll(requests)`—Used when you wish to perform an all-or-nothing bulk addition to the cache—for example, the initial population of the cache when the service worker initializes. The method accepts an array of URLs or Request objects. `addAll()` performs an `add()` operation for each entry in the requests array. This method returns a promise, which resolves only when every cache entry is successfully added.

Similar to a `Map`, `Cache` features `delete()` and `keys()` methods. These methods all behave as promise-based analogues of their `Map` counterparts:

```
const request1 = new Request('https://www.foo.com');
const response1 = new Response('fooResponse');

caches.open('v1')
.then((cache) => {
  cache.put(request1, response1)
```

```
    .then(() => cache.keys())
    .then(console.log)   // [Request]
    .then(() => cache.delete(request1))
    .then(1) => cache.keys())
    .then(console.log);  // []
});
```

To check a `Cache`, you have two methods at your disposal:

➤ `matchAll(request, options)`—Returns a promise, which resolves to an array of matching cache `Response` objects.

This method is useful in scenarios where you wish to perform a bulk action upon similarly organized cache entries, such as deleting all the cached values inside the /images directory.

The request matching schema can be configured via an options object, described later in this section.

➤ `match(request, options)`—Returns a promise, which resolves to a matching cache `Response` object, or `undefined` if there are no cache hits.

This is essentially equivalent to `matchAll(request, options)[0]`.

The request matching schema can be configured via an options object, described later in this section.

Cache hits are determined by matching URL strings and/or `Request` URLs. URL strings and `Request` objects are interchangeable, as the match is determined by extracting the `Request` object's URL. This interchangeability is demonstrated here:

```
const request1 = 'https://www.foo.com';
const request2 = new Request('https://www.bar.com');

const response1 = new Response('fooResponse');
const response2 = new Response('barResponse');

caches.open('v1').then((cache) => {
  cache.put(request1, response1)
  .then(() => cache.put(request2, response2))
  .then(() => cache.match(new Request('https://www.foo.com')))
  .then((response) => response.text())
  .then(console.log)    // fooResponse
  .then(() => cache.match('https://www.bar.com'))
  .then((response) => response.text())
  .then(console.log);   // barResponse
});
```

The `Cache` object makes use of the `Request` and `Response` objects' `clone()` method to create duplicates and store them as the key-value pair. This is demonstrated here, where the retrieved instances do not match the original key-value pair:

```
const request1 = new Request('https://www.foo.com');
const response1 = new Response('fooResponse');

caches.open('v1')
```

```
  .then((cache) => {
    cache.put(request1, response1)
    .then(() => cache.keys())
    .then((keys) => console.log(keys[0] === request1))          // false
    .then(() => cache.match(request1))
    .then((response) => console.log(response === response1));  // false
  });
```

Cache.match(), Cache.matchAll(), and CacheStorage.matchAll() all support an optional options object, which allows you to configure how the URL matching behaves by setting the following properties:

➤ cacheName—Only supported by CacheStorage.matchAll(). When set to a string, it will only match cache values inside the Cache keyed by the provided string.

➤ ignoreSearch—When set to true, directs the URL matcher to ignore query strings, both in the request query and the cache key. For example, https://example.com?foo=bar and https://example.com would match.

➤ ignoreMethod—When set to true, directs the URL matcher to ignore the http method of the request query. Consider the following example where a POST request can be matched to a GET:

```
const request1 = new Request('https://www.foo.com');
const response1 = new Response('fooResponse');

const postRequest1 = new Request('https://www.foo.com',
                                 { method: 'POST' });

caches.open('v1')
.then((cache) => {
  cache.put(request1, response1)
  .then(() => cache.match(postRequest1))
  .then(console.log)    // undefined
  .then(() => cache.match(postRequest1, { ignoreMethod: true }))
  .then(console.log);   // Response {}
});
```

➤ ignoreVary—The Cache matcher respects the Vary HTTP header, which specifies which request headers may cause the server response to differ. When ignoreVary is set to true, this directs the URL matcher to ignore the Vary header when matching.

```
const request1 = new Request('https://www.foo.com');
const response1 = new Response('fooResponse',
                               { headers: {'Vary': 'Accept' }});

const acceptRequest1 = new Request('https://www.foo.com',
                                   { headers: { 'Accept': 'text/json' } });

caches.open('v1')
.then((cache) => {
  cache.put(request1, response1)
  .then(() => cache.match(acceptRequest1))
  .then(console.log)    // undefined
```

```
    .then(() => cache.match(acceptRequest1, { ignoreVary: true }))
    .then(console.log);  // Response {}
  });
```

Maximum Cache Storage

Browsers need to restrict the amount of storage any given cache is allowed to use; otherwise, unlimited storage would surely be subject to abuse. This storage limit does not follow any formal specification; it is entirely subject to the individual browser vendor's preference.

Using the StorageEstimate API, it is possible to determine approximately how much space is available (in bytes) and how much is currently used. This method is only available in a secure browser context:

```
navigator.storage.estimate()
.then(console.log);

// Your browser's output will differ:
// { quota: 2147483648, usage: 590845 }
```

Per the service worker specification:

> *These are not exact numbers; between compression, deduplication, and obfuscation for security reasons, they will not be precise.*

Service Worker Clients

A service worker tracks an association with a window, worker, or service worker with a `Client` object. Service workers can access these `Client` objects via the `Clients` interface, available on the global object via the `self.clients` property.

A `Client` object features the following properties and methods:

➤ `id`—Returns the universally unique identifier for this client, such as `7e4248ec-b25e-4b33-b15f-4af8bb0a3ac4`. This can be used to retrieve a reference to the client via `Clients.get()`.

➤ `type`—Returns the type of the client as a string. Its value will be one of `window`, `worker`, or `sharedworker`.

➤ `url`—Returns the client's URL.

➤ `postMessage()`—Allows you to send targeted messaging to a single client.

The `Clients` interface allows you to access `Client` objects via `get()` and `matchAll()`, both of which use a promise to return results. `matchAll()` can also be passed an options object that supports the following properties:

➤ `includeUncontrolled`—When set to `true`, returns clients that are not yet controlled by this service worker. Defaults to `false`.

➤ `type`—When set to `window`, `worker`, or `sharedworker`, filters returned clients to only that type. Defaults to `all`, which returns all types of clients.

The `Clients` interface also provides two methods:

➤ `openWindow(url)`—Allows you to open a new window at the specified URL, effectively adding a new `Client` to this service worker. The new `Client` object is returned in a resolved promise. This method is useful when a notification is clicked; the service worker can detect the click event and open a window in response to that click.

➤ `claim()`—Will forcibly set this service worker to control all clients in its scope. This is useful when you do not wish to wait for a page reload for the service worker to begin managing the page.

Service Workers and Consistency

Service workers should be understood through the lens of their overall intended purpose: to enable web pages to emulate native application behavior. Behaving like a native application demands that service workers support *versioning*.

At a high level, service worker versioning ensures that there is *consistency* between how two web pages on the same origin operate at any given time. This consistency guarantee takes two primary forms:

➤ **Code consistency**—Web pages are not created from a single binary like a native application, but instead from many HTML, CSS, JavaScript, image, JSON, and really any type of file assets that a page might load. Web pages will commonly undergo incremental upgrades— versions—to add or modify behavior. If a web page loads 100 files in total, and the assets loaded are a mix of versions 1 and 2, the resulting behavior is completely unpredictable and likely incorrect. Service workers provide an enforcement mechanism to ensure that all concurrently running pages on the same origin are always built from assets from the same version.

➤ **Data consistency**—Web pages are not hermetic applications. They can read and write data on the local device via various browser APIs such as `LocalStorage` or IndexedDB. They can also send and receive data to remote APIs. The format that data is read or written in may change between versions. If one page writes data in a version 1 format, but a second page attempts to read data in a version 2 format, the resulting behavior is completely unpredictable and likely incorrect. The service worker's asset consistency mechanism also ensures that web page I/O behaves identically for all concurrently running pages on the same origin.

To preserve consistency, the service worker lifecycle goes to great lengths to avoid reaching a state that might compromise this consistency. For example:

➤ **Service workers fail early.** When attempting to install a service worker, any unexpected problem will prevent the service worker from being installed. This includes failing to load the service worker script, a syntax or runtime error in the service worker script, failing to load a worker dependency via `importScripts()`, or failing to load even a single cache asset.

➤ **Service workers aggressively update.** When the browser loads the service worker script again (either manually via `register()` or on a page reload), browsers will begin installation of a new service worker version if there is even a single byte of difference between the service worker script *or* any dependencies loaded via `importScripts()`.

➤ **Inactive service workers passively activate.** When `register()` is invoked for the first time on a page, the service worker is installed but will not be activated and begin to control the page until after a navigation event. This should make sense: the current page has presumably already loaded assets, so the service worker should not be activated and begin loading inconsistent assets.

➤ **Active service workers are sticky.** As long as there is at least one client associated with the active service worker, the browser will continue to use it for all pages of that origin. The browser can begin installation of a new service worker instance intended to replace the active one, but the browser will not switch to the new worker until there are 0 clients controlling the active one (or until the service worker is forcibly updated). This service worker eviction strategy prevents two clients from running two different service worker versions at once.

Understanding the Service Worker Lifecycle

The service worker specification defines six discrete states that a service worker might exist in: `parsed`, `installing`, `installed`, `activating`, `activated`, and `redundant`. A full lifecycle for a service worker will always visit these states in this order, although it may not visit every state. A service worker that encounters an error during installation or activation will skip to the `redundant` state.

Each state change will fire a `statechange` event on the `ServiceWorker` object. A handler can be set to listen for this event as follows:

```
navigator.serviceWorker.register('./serviceWorker.js')
.then((registration) => {
  registration.installing.onstatechange = ({ target: { state } }) => {
    console.log('state changed to', state);
  };
});
```

The Parsed State

A call to `navigator.serviceWorker.register()` will initiate the process of creating a service worker instance. The `parsed` state is assigned to that freshly created service worker. This state has no events or `ServiceWorker.state` value associated with it.

> **NOTE** *Although* `parsed` *is a formally defined state in the Service Worker specification,* `ServiceWorker.prototype.state` *will never return parsed. The earliest state that property can return is* `installing`.

The browser fetches the script file and performs some initial tasks to begin the lifecycle:

1. Ensure the service worker script is served on the same domain.

2. Ensure the service worker registration occurs inside a secure context.

3. Ensure the service worker script can be successfully parsed by the browser's JavaScript interpreter without throwing any errors.

4. Capture a snapshot of the service worker script. The next time the browser downloads the service worker script, it will diff it against this snapshot and use that to decide if it should update the service worker or not.

If all these succeed, the promise returned from `register()` will resolve with a `ServiceWorkerRegistration` object, and a newly created service worker instance proceeds to the `installing` state.

The Installing State

The `installing` state is where all service worker "setup" tasks should be performed. This includes work that must occur prior to the service worker controlling the page.

On the client, this phase can be identified by checking to see if the `ServiceWorkerRegistration` `.installing` property is set to a `ServiceWorker` instance:

```
navigator.serviceWorker.register('./serviceWorker.js')
.then((registration) => {
  if (registration.installing) {
    console.log('Service worker is in the installing state');
  }
});
```

The associated `ServiceWorkerRegistration` object will also fire the `updatefound` event any time a service worker reaches this state:

```
navigator.serviceWorker.register('./serviceWorker.js')
.then((registration) => {
  registration.onupdatefound = () => {
    console.log('Service worker is in the installing state');
  };
});
```

In the service worker, this phase can be identified by setting a handler for the install event:

```
self.oninstall = (installEvent) => {
  console.log('Service worker is in the installing state');
};
```

The `installing` state is frequently used to populate the service worker's cache. The service worker can be directed to remain in the `installing` state until a collection of assets is successfully cached. If any of the assets fail to cache, the service worker will fail to install and will be sent to the `redundant` state.

The service worker can be held in the installing state by means of an `ExtendableEvent`. The `InstallEvent` inherits from `ExtendableEvent` and therefore exposes an API, which allows you to delay a state transition until a promise resolves. This is accomplished with the `ExtendableEvent` `.waitUntil()` method. This method expects to be passed a promise that will delay transitioning to the next state until that promise resolves. For example, the following example would delay transition-ing to the installed state by five seconds:

```
self.oninstall = (installEvent) => {
  installEvent.waitUntil(
    new Promise((resolve, reject) => setTimeout(resolve, 5000))
  );
};
```

A more pragmatic use of this method would be to cache a group of assets via Cache.addAll():

```
const CACHE_KEY = 'v1';

self.oninstall = (installEvent) => {
  installEvent.waitUntil(
    caches.open(CACHE_KEY)
    .then((cache) => cache.addAll([
      'foo.js',
      'bar.html',
      'baz.css',
    ]))
  );
};
```

If there is no error thrown or promise rejected, the service worker proceeds to the installed state.

The Installed State

The installed state, also referred to as the waiting state, indicates that the service worker has no additional setup tasks to perform and that it is prepared to assume control of clients once it is allowed to do so. If there is no active service worker, a freshly installed service worker will skip this state and proceed directly to the activating state since there is no reason to wait.

On the client, this phase can be identified by checking to see if the ServiceWorkerRegistration .waiting property is set to a ServiceWorker instance:

```
navigator.serviceWorker.register('./serviceWorker.js')
.then((registration) => {
  if (registration.waiting) {
    console.log('Service worker is in the installing/waiting state');
  }
});
```

If there is already an active service worker, the installed state can be the appropriate time to trigger logic, which will promote this new service worker to the activating state. This might take the form of forcibly promoting this service worker via self.skipWaiting(). It also might take the form of prompting the user to reload the application, thereby allowing the browser to organically promote the service worker.

The Activating State

The activating state indicates that the service worker has been selected by the browser to become the service worker that should control the page. If there is no incumbent active service worker in the browser, this new service worker will automatically reach the `activating` state. If, however, there is an incumbent active service worker, this new replacement service worker can reach the `activating` state in the following ways:

➤ **The number of clients controlled by the incumbent service worker goes to 0.** This often takes the form of all controlled browser tabs being closed. On the next navigation event, the new service worker will reach the `activating` state.

➤ **The `installed` service worker calls** `self.skipWaiting()`. This takes effect immediately and does not need to wait for a navigation event.

While in the `activating` state, no functional events such as `fetch` or `push` are dispatched until the service worker reaches the `activated` state.

On the client, this phase can be partially identified by checking to see if the `ServiceWorkerRegistration.active` property is set to a `ServiceWorker` instance:

```
navigator.serviceWorker.register('./serviceWorker.js')
.then((registration) => {
  if (registration.active) {
    console.log('Service worker is in the activating/activated state');
  }
});
```

Note that the `ServiceWorkerRegistration.active` property indicates that the service worker is in either the `activating` or `activated` state.

In the service worker, this phase can be identified by setting a handler for the `activate` event:

```
self.oninstall = (activateEvent) => {
  console.log('Service worker is in the activating state');
};
```

The `activate` event indicates that it is safe to clean up after the old service worker, and this event is frequently used to purge old cache data and migrate databases. For example, the following example purges all older cache versions:

```
const CACHE_KEY = 'v3';

self.oninstall = (activateEvent) => {
  caches.keys()
  .then((keys) => keys.filter((key) => key != CACHE_KEY))
  .then((oldKeys) => oldKeys.forEach((oldKey) => caches.delete(oldKey));
};
```

An `activate` event also inherits from `ExtendableEvent` and therefore also supports the `waitUntil()` convention for delaying a transition to the `activated` state—or transitioning to the `redundant` state upon a rejected promise.

> **NOTE** *The* `active` *event in a service worker does* not *mean that this service worker is controlling clients.*

The Activated State

The `activated` state indicates that the service worker is in control of one or many clients. In this state, the service worker will capture `fetch()` events inside its scope as well as notification and push events.

On the client, this phase can be partially identified by checking to see if the `ServiceWorkerRegistration.active` property is set to a `ServiceWorker` instance:

```
navigator.serviceWorker.register('./serviceWorker.js')
.then((registration) => {
  if (registration.active) {
    console.log('Service worker is in the activating/activated state');
  }
});
```

Note that the `ServiceWorkerRegistration.active` property indicates that the service worker is in either the `activating` or `activated` state.

A superior indication that a service worker is in the activated state is to check the controller property of the `ServiceWorkerRegistration`. This will return the activated `ServiceWorker` instance, which is controlling the page:

```
navigator.serviceWorker.register('./serviceWorker.js')
.then((registration) => {
  if (registration.controller) {
    console.log('Service worker is in the activated state');
  }
});
```

When a new service worker takes control of a client, the `ServiceWorkerContainer` in that client will fire a `controllerchange` event:

```
navigator.serviceWorker.oncontrollerchange = () => {
  console.log('A new service worker is controlling this client');
};
```

It's also possible to use the `ServiceWorkerContainer.ready` promise to detect an active service worker. This ready promise resolves once the current page has an active worker:

```
navigator.serviceWorker.ready.then(() => {
  console.log('A new service worker is controlling this client');
});
```

The Redundant State

The `redundant` state is the graveyard for service workers. No events will be passed to it, and the browser is free to destroy it and free up its resources.

Updating a Service Worker

Because the concept of versioning is baked into service workers, they are expected to periodically change. Therefore, service workers feature a robust and intricate updating process for safely replacing an outdated active service worker.

This update process begins with an update check, where the browser re-requests the service worker script. A check for an update can be triggered by the following events:

➤   `navigator.serviceWorker.register()` is called with a different URL string than the currently active service worker.

➤   The browser navigates to a page inside the service worker's scope.

➤   A functional event such as `fetch` or `push` occurs *and* an update check has not occurred for at least 24 hours.

The freshly fetched service worker script is diffed against the incumbent service worker's script. If they are not identical, the browser initializes a new service worker with the new script. The updated service worker will proceed through its lifecycle until it reaches the `installed` state. Once it reaches the `installed` state, the updated service worker will wait until the browser decides it can safely obtain control of the page (or until the user forces it to take control of the page).

Importantly, refreshing a page will *not* allow the updated service worker to activate and replace the incumbent service worker. Consider a scenario where there is a single page open with an incumbent service worker controlling it and an updated service worker waiting in the `installed` state. Clients overlap during a page refresh—meaning the new page is loaded before the old page dies—and therefore the incumbent service worker never relinquishes control because it still controls a nonzero number of clients. Because of this, closing all controlled pages is the only way to allow the incumbent service worker to be replaced.

Inversion of Control and Service Worker Persistence

Whereas dedicated and shared workers are designed to be stateful, service workers are designed to be stateless. More specifically, service workers follow the Inversion of Control (IOC) pattern and are built to be event driven.

The primary implication of this is that service workers should have no reliance whatsoever on the global state of the worker. Nearly all code inside the service worker should be defined inside event handlers—the notable exception being global constants such as the service worker version. The number of times a service worker script will execute is wildly variable and highly dependent on browser state, and therefore the service worker script's behavior should be idempotent.

It's important to understand that the lifetime of a service worker is uncorrelated with the lifetime of the clients it is connected to. Most browsers implement service workers as a separate process, and this process is independently managed by the browser. If a browser detects a service worker is idle, it can terminate the worker and restart it again when needed. This means that, while you can rely on a service worker to handle events once activated, you cannot rely on a service worker's persistent global state.

Managing Service Worker File Caching with *updateViaCache*

Normally, all JavaScript assets loaded by the browser are subject to the browser's HTTP cache as defined by their Cache-Control header. Because service worker scripts are not given preferential treatment, the browser will not receive updated service worker script updates until the cached file expires.

To propagate service worker updates as quickly as possible, a common solution is to serve service worker scripts with a `Cache-Control: max-age=0` header. With this, the browser will always fetch the most up-to-date script file.

This instant-expiry solution works well, but solely relying on HTTP headers to dictate service worker behavior means that only the *server* decides how the client should update. To allow the client agency over its updating behavior, the `updateViaCache` property exists to allow for control over how the client should treat service worker scripts. This property can be defined when registering the service worker, and it accepts three string values:

➤ `imports`: the default value. The top-level service worker script file will never be cached, but files imported inside the service worker via `importScripts()` will still be subject to the HTTP cache and `Cache-Control` header.

➤ `all`: No service worker scripts are given special treatment. All files are subject to the HTTP cache and `Cache-Control` header.

➤ `none`: Both the top-level service worker script and files imported inside the service worker via `importScripts()` will never be cached.

The `updateViaCache` property is used as follows:

```
navigator.serviceWorker.register('/serviceWorker.js', {
  updateViaCache: 'none'
});
```

Browsers are still in the process of moving to support this option, so it is strongly recommended that you use both `updateViaCache` and the `Cache-Control` header to dictate caching behavior on the client.

Forced Service Worker Operation

In some cases, it makes sense to coerce a service worker into the activated state as quickly as possible—even at the expense of potential asset versioning conflicts. This commonly takes the form of caching assets at the install event, forcing the service worker to activate, and then forcing the activated service worker to control the associated clients.

A basic version of this might appear as follows:

```
const CACHE_KEY = 'v1';

self.oninstall = (installEvent) => {
  // Populate the cache, then force the service worker
  // into the activated state. This triggers the 'activate' event.
  installEvent.waitUntil(
    caches.open(CACHE_KEY)
    .then((cache) => cache.addAll([
      'foo.css',
      'bar.js',
    ]))
    .then(() => self.skipWaiting())
  );
```

```
  };

  // Force the service worker to take control of the clients. This fires a
  // controllerchange event on each client.
  self.onactivate = (activateEvent) => clients.claim();
```

Browsers will check for a new service worker script on each navigation event, but sometimes this is too infrequent. The ServiceWorkerRegistration object features an update() method that can be used to instruct the browser to re-request the service worker script, compare it to the existing one, and begin installation of an updated service worker if necessary. This might be accomplished as follows:

```
navigator.serviceWorker.register('./serviceWorker.js')
.then((registration) => {
  // Check for an updated version every ~17 minutes
  setInterval(() => registration.update(), 1E6);
});
```

Service Worker Messaging

As with dedicated workers and shared workers, service workers are able to exchange asynchronous messages with clients using postMessage(). One of the simplest ways of accomplishing this is to send a message to the active worker and use the event object to send a reply. Messages sent to the service worker can be handled on the global scope, whereas messages sent back to the client can be handled on the ServiceWorkerContext object:

SERVICEWORKER.JS

```
self.onmessage = ({data, source}) => {
  console.log('service worker heard:', data);

  source.postMessage('bar');
};
```

MAIN.JS

```
navigator.serviceWorker.onmessage = ({data}) => {
  console.log('client heard:', data);
};

navigator.serviceWorker.register('./serviceWorker.js')
.then((registration) => {
  if (registration.active) {
    registration.active.postMessage('foo');
  }
});

// service worker heard: foo
// client heard: bar
```

This can just as easily use the `serviceWorker.controller` property:

SERVICEWORKER.JS

```javascript
self.onmessage = ({data, source}) => {
  console.log('service worker heard:', data);

  source.postMessage('bar');
};
```

MAIN.JS

```javascript
navigator.serviceWorker.onmessage = ({data}) => {
  console.log('client heard:', data);
};

navigator.serviceWorker.register('./serviceWorker.js')
.then(() => {
  if (navigator.serviceWorker.controller) {
    navigator.serviceWorker.controller.postMessage('foo');
  }
});

// service worker heard: foo
// client heard: bar
```

The preceding examples will work every time the page reloads, as the service worker will reply to the new message sent from the client script after each reload. It will also work every time this page is opened in a new tab.

If, instead, the service worker should initiate the message handshake, a reference to the client can be obtained as follows:

SERVICEWORKER.JS

```javascript
self.onmessage = ({data}) => {
  console.log('service worker heard:', data);
};

self.onactivate = () => {
  self.clients.matchAll({includeUncontrolled: true})
  .then((clientMatches) => clientMatches[0].postMessage('foo'));
};
```

MAIN.JS

```
navigator.serviceWorker.onmessage = ({data, source}) => {
  console.log('client heard:', data);

  source.postMessage('bar');
};

navigator.serviceWorker.register('./serviceWorker.js')

// client heard: foo
// service worker heard: bar
```

The preceding example will only work once, as the active event is only fired a single time per service worker.

Because clients and service workers can send messages back and forth, it is also possible to set up a `MessageChannel` or `BroadcastChannel` to exchange messages.

Intercepting a fetch Event

One of the most important features of service workers is their ability to intercept network requests. A network request inside the scope of a service worker will register as a fetch event. This interception ability is not limited to the `fetch()` method; it also can intercept requests for JavaScript, CSS, images, and HTML—including the primary HTML document itself. These requests can come from JavaScript, or they can be requests created by tags such as `<script>`, `<link>`, or `<img>` tags. Intuitively, this should make sense: for a service worker to emulate an offline web app, it must be able to account for all the requested assets needed for the page to function properly.

A `FetchEvent` inherits from `ExtendableEvent`. The valuable method that allows service workers to decide how to handle a fetch event is `event.respondWith()`. This method expects a promise, which should resolve with a `Response` object. Of course, your service worker gets to decide where this `Response` object actually comes from. It could be from the network, from the cache, or created on the fly. The following sections cover a handful of network/cache strategies to employ inside a service worker.

Return from Network

This strategy is a simple passthrough for a fetch event. A good use case for this might be any requests that definitely need to reach the server, such as a POST request. This strategy can be implemented as follows:

```
self.onfetch = (fetchEvent) => {
  fetchEvent.respondWith(fetch(fetchEvent.requeest));
};
```

> **NOTE** *The preceding code is only to demonstrate how to use* event
> .respondWith()*. If* event.respondWith() *isn't called, the browser will send the
> request out to the network.*

Return from Cache

This strategy is a simple cache check. A good use case for this might be any requests that are guaranteed to be in the cache—such as assets cached during the installation phase.

```
self.onfetch = (fetchEvent) => {
  fetchEvent.respondWith(caches.match(fetchEvent.request));
};
```

Return from Network with Cache Fallback

This strategy gives preference to up-to-date responses from the network but will still return values in the cache if they exist. A good use case for this is when your application needs to show the most up-to-date information as often as possible, but would still like to show something if the application is offline.

```
self.onfetch = (fetchEvent) => {
  fetchEvent.respondWith(
    fetch(fetchEvent.request)
    .catch(() => caches.match(fetchEvent.request))
  );
};
```

Return from Cache with Network Fallback

This strategy gives preference to responses it can show more quickly but will still fetch from the network if a value is uncached. This is the superior fetch handling strategy for most progressive web applications.

```
self.onfetch = (fetchEvent) => {
  fetchEvent.respondWith(
    caches.match(fetchEvent.request)
    .then((response) => response || fetch(fetchEvent.request))
  );
};
```

Generic Fallback

Applications need to account for scenarios where both the cache and network fail to produce a resource. Service workers can handle this by caching fallback resources upon install and returning them when both cache and network fail.

```
self.onfetch = (fetchEvent) => {
  fetchEvent.respondWith(
    // Begin with 'Return from cache with network fallback' stragegy
    caches.match(fetchEvent.request)
    .then((response) => response || fetch(fetchEvent.request))
    .catch(() => caches.match('/fallback.html'))
  );
};
```

The catch() clause can be extended to support many different types of fallbacks such as placeholder images, dummy data, and so on.

> **NOTE** *The Google Developers site has a smashing article on network/caching strategies:* https://developers.google.com/web/fundamentals/ instant-and-offline/offline-cookbook.

Push Notifications

For a web application to properly emulate a native application, it must be able to support push notifications. This means that a web page must be able to receive a push event from a server and display a notification on the device—even when the application is not running. With conventional web pages, this, of course is impossible, but the addition of service workers means that this behavior is now supported.

For push notifications to work in a progressive web application, four behavioral aspects must be supported:

➤ The service worker must be able to display notifications.

➤ The service worker must be able to handle interactions with those notifications.

➤ The service worker must be able to subscribe to server-sent push notifications.

➤ The service worker must be able to handle push messages, even when the application is not in the foreground or open.

Displaying Notifications

Service workers have access to the Notification API via their registration object. There is good reason for this: notifications associated with a service worker will also trigger interaction events inside that service worker.

Showing notifications requires explicit permission from the user. Once this is granted, notifications can be shown via `ServiceWorkerRegistration.showNotification()`. This can be accomplished as follows:

```
navigator.serviceWorker.register('./serviceWorker.js')
.then((registration) => {
  Notification.requestPermission()
  .then((status) => {
    if (status === 'granted') {
      registration.showNotification('foo');
    }
  });
});
```

Similarly, a notification can be triggered from inside a service worker using the global registration property:

```
self.onactivate = () => self.registration.showNotification('bar');
```

In these examples, once notification permissions are granted, a foo notification is shown in the browser. This notification will be visually indistinguishable from one generated using `new Notification()`. Furthermore, it doesn't require the service worker to do any work for it to appear. The service worker comes into play when notification events are required.

Handling Notification Events

A notification created via a `ServiceWorkerRegistration` object will send `notificationclick` and `notificationclose` events to the service worker. Suppose the previous example's service worker script was defined as follows:

```
self.onnotificationclick = ({notification}) => {
  console.log('notification click', notification);
};

self.onnotificationclose = ({notification}) => {
  console.log('notification close', notification);
};
```

In this example, both types of interactions with a notification will register inside the service worker. The `notificationevent` exposes a `notification` property, containing the `Notification` object that generated the event. These event handlers can decide what to do after an interaction.

Frequently, clicking a notification means the user wishes to be taken to a specific view. Inside the service worker handler, this can be accomplished via `clients.openWindow()`, shown here:

```
self.onnotificationclick = ({notification}) => {
  clients.openWindow('https://foo.com');
};
```

Subscribing to Push Events

For push messages to be sent to a service worker, the subscription must happen via the service worker's `PushManager`. This will allow the service worker to handle push messages in a push event handler.

The subscription can be done using `ServiceWorkerRegistration.pushManager`, as shown here:

```
navigator.serviceWorker.register('./serviceWorker.js')
.then((registration) => {
  registration.pushManager.subscribe({
    applicationServerKey: key,  // derived from server's public key
    userVisibleOnly: true
  });
});
```

Alternately, the service worker can subscribe itself using the global `registration` property:

```
self.onactivate = () => {
  self.registration.pushManager.subscribe({
    applicationServerKey: key,  // derived from server's public key
    userVisibleOnly: true
  });
};
```

Handling Push Events

Once subscribed, the service worker will receive push events each time the server pushes a message. They can be handled as follows:

```
self.onpush = (pushEvent) => {
  console.log('Service worker was pushed data:', pushEvent.data.text());
};
```

To implement a true push notification, this handler only needs to create a notification via the `registration` object. However, a well-behaved push notification needs to keep the service worker that produced it alive long enough for its interaction event to be handled.

To accomplish this, the push event inherits from `ExtendableEvent`. The promise returned from `showNotification()` can be passed to `waitUntil()`, which will keep the service worker alive until the notification's promise resolves.

A simple push notification implementation might appear as follows:

MAIN.JS

```
navigator.serviceWorker.register('./serviceWorker.js')
.then((registration) => {
  // Request permission to show notifications
  Notification.requestPermission()
  .then((status) => {
    if (status === 'granted') {
      // Only subscribe to push messages if
      // notification permission is granted
      registration.pushManager.subscribe({
        applicationServerKey: key,  // derived from server's public key
        userVisibleOnly: true
      });
    }
  });
});
```

SERVICEWORKER.JS

```
// When a push event is received, display the data as text
// inside a notification.
self.onpush = (pushEvent) => {
  // Keep the service worker alive until notification promise resolves
  pushEvent.waitUntil(
    self.registration.showNotification(pushEvent.data.text())
  );
};

// When a notification is clicked, open relevant application page
self.onnotificationclick = ({notification}) => {
  clients.openWindow('https://example.com/clicked-notification');
};
```

SUMMARY

Workers provide a powerful way to perform complex calculations and data processing without blocking the user interface. The use of workers can significantly improve the user experience, as it allows web applications to remain responsive even when running computationally intensive operations. There are two types of workers: *dedicated workers* and *shared workers*. Dedicated workers are associated with a single web page and can only communicate with the page that created them. Shared workers, on the other hand, can be shared between multiple web pages on the same origin, allowing for more efficient use of system resources and better collaboration between different instances of the same web application.

Service workers are a separate type of worker that are designed to enable advanced web application features such as offline functionality, push notifications, and background syncing. They behave more like a network proxy than a separate browser thread, allowing them to intercept network requests and cache resources. This enables web applications to function even when there is no Internet connection, providing a more consistent and reliable user experience. Service workers can also enable push notifications for progressive web applications, allowing web applications to keep users engaged even when they are not actively using the application.

In addition to their caching and push notification capabilities, service workers can act as a highly customizable network cache. They can cache resources such as HTML, CSS, JavaScript, and images, allowing web applications to load quickly even when there is no network connection. This means that users can continue using the application even when they are offline or have a poor Internet connection, providing a smoother and more reliable user experience.

25

Best Practices

WHAT'S IN THIS CHAPTER?

➤ Writing maintainable code

➤ Ensuring code performance

➤ Deploying code to production

> ### DOWNLOADS FOR THIS CHAPTER
>
> Please note that all the code examples for this chapter are available as a part of this chapter's code download on the book's website at www.wiley.com/go/projavascript5e.

The discipline of web development has grown at an extraordinary rate since 2000. What used to be a virtual Wild West, where just about anything was acceptable, has evolved into a complete discipline with research and established best practices. As simple websites grew into more complex web applications, and web hobbyists became paid professionals, the world of web development was filled with information about the latest techniques and development approaches. JavaScript, in particular, was the beneficiary of a lot of research and conjecture. Best practices for JavaScript fall into several categories and are handled at different points in the development process.

MAINTAINABILITY

In early websites, JavaScript was used primarily for small effects or form validation. Today's web applications are filled with thousands of lines of JavaScript executing all types of complicated processes. This evolution requires that developers take maintainability into account.

As with software engineers in more traditional disciplines, JavaScript developers are hired to create value for their company, and they do that not just by delivering products on time but also by developing intellectual property that continues to add value long after.

Writing maintainable code is important because most developers spend a large amount of their time maintaining other people's code. It's a truly rare occurrence to be able to develop new code from scratch; it's often the case that you must build on work that someone else has done. Making sure that your code is maintainable ensures that other developers can perform their jobs as well as possible.

What Is Maintainable Code?

Maintainable code has several characteristics. In general, code is said to be maintainable when it is all of the following:

➤ **Understandable**—Someone else can pick up the code and figure out its purpose and general approach without a walk-through by the original developer.

➤ **Intuitive**—Things in the code just seem to make sense, no matter how complex the operation.

➤ **Adaptable**—The code is written in such a way that variation in data doesn't require a complete rewrite.

➤ **Extendable**—Care has been given in the code architecture to allow extension of the core functionality in the future.

➤ **Debuggable**—When something goes wrong, the code gives you enough information to identify the issue as directly as possible.

Being able to write maintainable JavaScript code is an important skill for professionals. This is the difference between hobbyists who hack together a site over the weekend and professional developers who really know their craft.

Code Conventions

One of the simplest ways to start writing maintainable code is to come up with code conventions for the JavaScript that you write. Code conventions have been developed for most programming languages, and a quick Internet search is likely to turn up thousands of documents. Professional organizations have long instituted code conventions for developers in an attempt to make code more maintainable for everyone. The best-run open-source projects have strict code convention requirements that allow everyone in the community to easily understand how code is organized.

Code conventions are important for JavaScript because of the language's adaptability. Unlike most object-oriented languages, JavaScript doesn't force developers into defining everything as objects. The language can support any number of programming styles, from traditional object-oriented approaches to declarative approaches to functional approaches. A quick review of several open-source JavaScript libraries can easily yield multiple approaches to creating objects, defining methods, and managing the environment.

The following sections discuss the basics of how to develop code conventions. These topics are important to address, although the way in which they are addressed may differ, depending on your individual needs.

Readability

For code to be maintainable, it must first be readable. Readability has to do with the way the code is formatted as a text file. A large part of readability has to do with the indentation of the code. When everyone is using the same indentation scheme, code across an entire project becomes much easier to read. Indentation is usually done by using a number of spaces instead of by using the tab character, which is typically displayed differently by different text editors. A good general indentation size is four spaces, although you may decide to use less or more.

Another part of readability is comments. In most programming languages, it's an accepted practice to comment each method. Because of JavaScript's ability to create functions at any point in the code, this is often overlooked. Because of this, it is perhaps even more important to document each function in JavaScript. Generally speaking, the places that should be commented in your code are as follows:

➤ **Functions and methods**—Each function or method should include a comment that describes its purpose and possibly the algorithm being used to accomplish the task. It's also important to state assumptions that are being made, what the arguments represent, and whether or not the function returns a value (since this is not discernible from a function definition).

➤ **Large sections of code**—Multiple lines of code that are all used to accomplish a single task should be preceded with a comment describing the task.

➤ **Complex algorithms**—If you're using a unique approach to solve a problem, explain how you are doing it as a comment. This will not only help others who are looking at your code but also help you the next time you look at it.

➤ **Hacks**—Because of browser differences, JavaScript code typically contains some hacks. Don't assume that someone else who is looking at the code will understand the browser issue that such a hack is working around. If you need to do something differently because one of the browsers can't use the normal way, put that in a comment. It reduces the likelihood that someone will come along, see your hack, and "fix" it, inadvertently introducing the bug that you had already worked around.

Indentation and comments create more readable code that is easier to maintain in the future.

Variable and Function Naming

The proper naming of variables and functions in code is vital to making it understandable and maintainable. Because many JavaScript developers began as hobbyists, there's a tendency to use nonsensical names such as `"foo"` and `"bar"` for variables and names such as `"doSomething"` for functions. A professional JavaScript developer must overcome these old habits to create maintainable code. General rules for naming are as follows:

➤ Variable names should be nouns, such as `"car"` or `"person"`.

➤ Function names should begin with a verb, such as `getName()`. Functions that return Boolean values typically begin with is, as in `isEnabled()`.

➤ Use logical names for both variables and functions, without worrying about the length. Length can be mitigated through postprocessing and compression (discussed later in this chapter).

➤ Variables, functions, and methods should begin with a lowercase letter and camelCase, such as getName() and isPerson. Classes like Person and RequestFactory should be capitalized. Constant values should be all uppercase and underscores, such as REQUEST_TIMEOUT.

➤ Be descriptive and sensible with names, but not too verbose. getName() intuitively will return a name value. PersonFactory will be producing some sort of Person object or entity.

➤ It's often helpful to descriptively name a function that has success and failure outcomes. A function that loads and returns user data, or throws an error on network failure, could be named getUserOrError(). A function that searches a list for a user with a certain ID, returns the user on a match, or returns null with no match, could be named findUserOrNull().

It's imperative to avoid useless variable names that don't indicate the type of data they contain. With proper naming, code reads like a narrative of what is happening, making it easier to understand.

Variable Type Transparency

Because variables are loosely typed in JavaScript, it is easy to lose track of the type of data that a variable should contain. Proper naming mitigates this to some point, but it may not be enough in all cases. There are three ways to indicate the data type of a variable.

The first way is through initialization. When a variable is defined, it should be initialized to a value that indicates how it will be used in the future. For example, a variable that will hold a Boolean should be initialized to either true or false, and a variable to hold numbers should be initialized to a number, as in the following example:

```
// variable type indicated by initialization
let found = false;     // Boolean
let count  = -1;       // number
let name = "";         // string
let person = null;     // object
```

Initialization to a particular data type is a good indication of a variable's type. The downside of initialization is that it cannot be used with function arguments in the function declaration.

The second way to indicate a variable's type is to use Hungarian notation. Hungarian notation prepends one or more characters to the beginning of a variable to indicate the data type. This notation is popular among scripted languages and was, for quite some time, the preferred format for JavaScript as well. The most traditional Hungarian notation format for JavaScript prepends a single character for the basic data types: "o" for objects, "s" for strings, "i" for integers, "f" for floats, and "b" for Booleans. Here's an example:

```
// Hungarian notation used to indicate data type
let bFound;     // Boolean
let iCount;     // integer
let sName;      // string
let oPerson;    // object
```

Hungarian notation for JavaScript is advantageous in that it can be used equally well for function arguments. The downside of Hungarian notation is that it makes code somewhat less readable, interrupting the intuitive, sentence-like nature of code that is accomplished without it. For this reason, Hungarian notation has started to fall out of favor among some developers.

The last way to indicate variable type is to use type comments. Type comments are placed right after the variable name but before any initialization. The idea is to place a comment indicating the data type right by the variable, as in this example:

```
// type comments used to indicate type
let found  /*:Boolean*/ = false;
let count  /*:int*/    = 10;
let name   /*:String*/  = "Matt";
let person /*:Object*/  = null;
```

Type comments maintain the overall readability of code while injecting type information at the same time. The downside of type comments is that you cannot comment out large blocks of code using multiline comments because the type comments are also multiline comments that will interfere, as this example demonstrates:

```
// The following won't work correctly
/*
let found  /*:Boolean*/ = false;
let count  /*:int*/    = 10;
let name   /*:String*/  = "Matt";
let person /*:Object*/  = null;
*/
```

Here, the intent was to comment out all of the variables using a multiline comment. The type comments interfere with this because the first instance of /* (second line) is matched with the first instance of */ (third line), which will cause a syntax error. If you want to comment out lines of code using type comments, it's best to use single-line comments on each line (many editors will do this for you).

These are the three most common ways to indicate the data type of variables. Each has advantages and disadvantages for you to evaluate before deciding on one. The important thing is to decide which works best for your project and use it consistently.

> **NOTE** *These strategies are ideal for codebases that only use JavaScript. If using TypeScript is an option, this is a superior choice for typing variables. Read on in the chapter to learn more about TypeScript.*

Loose Coupling

Whenever parts of an application depend too closely on one another, the code becomes too tightly coupled and hard to maintain. The typical problem arises when objects refer directly to one another in such a way that a change to one always requires a change to the other. Tightly coupled software is difficult to maintain and invariably has to be rewritten frequently.

Because of the technologies involved, there are several ways in which web applications can become too tightly coupled. It's important to be aware of this and to try to maintain loosely coupled code whenever possible.

Decouple HTML/JavaScript

One of the most common types of coupling is HTML/JavaScript coupling. On the web, HTML and JavaScript each represent a different layer of the solution: HTML is the data, and JavaScript is the behavior. Because they are intended to interact, there are a number of different ways to tie these two technologies together. Unfortunately, there are some ways that too tightly couple HTML and JavaScript.

JavaScript that appears inline in HTML, either using a `<script>` element with inline code or using HTML attributes to assign event handlers, is too tightly coupled. Consider the following code examples:

```
<!-- tightly coupled HTML/JavaScript using <script> -->
<script>
  document.write("Hello world!");
</script>

<!-- tightly coupled HTML/JavaScript using event handler attribute -->
<input type="button" value="Click Me" onclick="doSomething()"/>
```

Although these are both technically correct, in practice they tightly couple the HTML representing the data with the JavaScript that defines the behavior. Ideally, HTML and JavaScript should be completely separate, with the JavaScript being included via external files and attaching behavior using the DOM.

When HTML and JavaScript are too tightly coupled, interpreting a JavaScript error means first determining whether the error occurred in the HTML portion of the solution or in a JavaScript file. It also introduces new types of errors related to the availability of code. In this example, the button may be clicked before the `doSomething()` function is available, causing a JavaScript error. Maintainability is affected because any change to the button's behavior requires touching both the HTML and the JavaScript, when it should require only the latter.

HTML and JavaScript can also be too tightly coupled when the reverse is true: HTML is contained within JavaScript. This usually occurs when using `innerHTML` to insert a chunk of HTML text into the page, as in this example:

```
// tight coupling of HTML to JavaScript
function insertMessage(msg) {
  let container = document.getElementById("container");
  container.innerHTML = `<div class="msg">
    <p> class="post">${msg}</p>
    <p><em>Latest message above.</em></p>
  </div>`;
}
```

Generally speaking, you should avoid creating large amounts of HTML in JavaScript. This, once again, has to do with keeping the layers separate and being able to easily identify the source of errors. When using this example code, a problem with page layout may be related to dynamically created HTML that is improperly formatted. However, locating the error may be difficult because you would typically first view the source of the page to look for the offending HTML but wouldn't find it there because it's dynamically generated. Changes to the data or layout would also require changes to the JavaScript, which indicates that the two layers are too tightly coupled.

HTML rendering should be kept separate from JavaScript as much as possible. When JavaScript is used to insert data, it should do so without inserting markup whenever possible. Markup can typically be included and hidden when the entire page is rendered such that JavaScript can be used to display the markup later, instead of generating it. Another approach is to make a network request to retrieve additional HTML to be displayed; this approach allows the same rendering layer (PHP, JSP, Ruby, and so on) to output the markup, instead of embedding it in JavaScript.

Decoupling HTML and JavaScript can save time during debugging by making it easier to identify the source of errors, and it also eases maintainability: changes to behavior occur only in JavaScript files, whereas changes to markup occur only in rendering files.

Decouple CSS/JavaScript

Another layer of the web tier is CSS, which is primarily responsible for the display of a page. JavaScript and CSS are closely related: they are both layers on top of HTML and as such are often used together. As with HTML and JavaScript, however, it's possible for CSS and JavaScript to be too tightly coupled. The most common example of tight coupling is using JavaScript to change individual styles, as shown here:

```
// tight coupling of CSS to JavaScript
element.style.color = "red";
element.style.backgroundColor = "blue";
```

Because CSS is responsible for the display of a page, any trouble with the display should be addressable by looking just at CSS files. However, when JavaScript is used to change individual styles, such as color, it adds a second location that must be checked and possibly changed. The result is that JavaScript is somewhat responsible for the display of the page and a tight coupling with CSS. If the styles need to change in the future, both the CSS and the JavaScript files may require changes. This creates a maintenance nightmare for developers. A cleaner separation between the layers is needed.

Modern web applications use JavaScript to change styles frequently, so although it's not possible to completely decouple CSS and JavaScript, the coupling can be made looser. This is done by dynamically changing classes instead of individual styles, as in the following example:

```
// loose coupling of CSS to JavaScript
element.className = "edit";
```

By changing only the CSS class of an element, you allow most of the style information to remain strictly in the CSS. JavaScript can be used to change the class, but it's not directly affecting the style of the element. As long as the correct class is applied, then any display issues can be tracked directly to CSS and not to JavaScript.

Once again, the importance of keeping a good separation of layers is paramount. The only source for display issues should be CSS, and the only source for behavior issues should be JavaScript. Keeping a loose coupling between these layers makes your entire application more maintainable.

Decouple Application Logic/Event Handlers

Every web application is typically filled with lots of event handlers listening for numerous different events. Few of them, however, take care to separate application logic from event handlers. Consider the following example:

```
function handleKeyPress(event) {
  if (event.keyCode == 13) {
    let target = event.target;
    let value = 5 * parseInt(target.value);
    if (value> 10) {
      document.getElementById("error-msg").style.display = "block";
    }
  }
}
```

This event handler contains application logic in addition to handling the event. The problem with this approach is twofold. First, there is no way to cause the application logic to occur other than through the event, which makes it difficult to debug. What if the anticipated result didn't occur? Does that mean that the event handler wasn't called or that the application logic failed? Second, if a subsequent event causes the same application logic to occur, you'll need to duplicate the functionality or else extract it into a separate function. Either way, it requires more changes to be made than are really necessary.

A better approach is to separate the application logic from event handlers, so that each handles just what it's supposed to. An event handler should interrogate the event object for relevant information and then pass that information to some method that handles the application logic. For example, the previous code can be rewritten like this:

```
function validateValue(value) {
  value = 5 * parseInt(value);
  if (value> 10) {
    document.getElementById("error-msg").style.display = "block";
  }
}

function handleKeyPress(event) {
  if (event.keyCode == 13) {
    let target = event.target;
    validateValue(target.value);
  }
}
```

This updated code properly separates the application logic from the event handler. The `handleKeyPress()` function checks to be sure that the Enter key was pressed (`event.keyCode` is 13) and then gets the `target` of the event and passes the `value` property into the `validateValue()` function, which contains the application logic. Note that there is nothing in `validateValue()` that depends on any event handler logic whatsoever; it just receives a value and can do everything else based on that value.

Separating application logic from event handlers has several benefits. First, it allows you to easily change the events that trigger certain processes with a minimal amount of effort. If a mouse click initially caused the processing to occur, but now a key press should do the same, it's quite easy to make that change. Second, you can test code without attaching events, making it easier to create unit tests or to automate application flow.

Here are a few rules to keep in mind for loose coupling of application and business logic:

➤ Don't pass the `event` object into other methods; pass only the data from the `event` object that you need.

➤ Every action that is possible in the application should be possible without executing an event handler.

➤ Event handlers should process the event and then hand off processing to application logic.

Keeping this approach in mind is a huge maintainability win in any code base, opening up numerous possibilities for testing and further development.

Programming Practices

Writing maintainable JavaScript isn't just about how the code is formatted; it's also about what the code does. Web applications created in an enterprise environment are often worked on by numerous people at the same time. The goal in these situations is to ensure that the browser environment in which everyone is working has constant and unchanging rules. To achieve this, developers should adhere to certain programming practices.

Respect Object Ownership

The dynamic nature of JavaScript means that almost anything can be modified at any point in time. It's been said that nothing in JavaScript is sacred, as you're unable to mark something as final or constant. This changed somewhat with ECMAScript 5's introduction of tamper-proof objects, but by default, all objects can be modified. In other languages, objects and classes are immutable when you don't have the actual source code. JavaScript allows you to modify any object at any time, making it possible to override default behaviors in unanticipated ways. Because the language doesn't impose limits, it's important and necessary for developers to do so.

Perhaps the most important programming practice in an enterprise environment is to respect object ownership, which means that you don't modify objects that don't belong to you. Put simply: if you're not responsible for the creation or maintenance of an object, its constructor, or its methods, you shouldn't be making changes to it. More specifically:

➤ Don't add properties to instances or prototypes.

➤ Don't add methods to instances or prototypes.

➤ Don't redefine existing methods.

The problem is that developers assume that the browser environment works in a certain way. Changes to objects that are used by multiple people mean that errors will occur. If someone expects a function called `stopEvent()` to cancel the default behavior for an event, and you change it so it does that and also attaches other event handlers, it is certain that problems will follow. Other developers are assuming that the function just does what it did originally, so their usage will be incorrect and possibly harmful because they don't know the side effects.

These rules apply not only to custom types and objects but also to native types and objects such as Object, String, document, window, and so on. The potential issues here are even more perilous because browser vendors may change these objects in unannounced and unanticipated ways.

An example of this occurred in the popular Prototype JavaScript library, which implemented the `getElementsByClassName()` method on the document object, returning an instance of Array that had also been augmented to include a method called each(). John Resig outlined on his blog the sequence of events that caused the issue. In his post (`http://ejohn.org/blog/` `getelementsbyclassname-pre-prototype-16`), he noted that the problem occurred when browsers began to natively implement `getElementsByClassName()`, which returns not an `Array` but rather a `NodeList` that doesn't have an `each()` method. Developers using the Prototype library had gotten used to writing code such as this:

```
document.getElementsByClassName("selected").each(Element.hide);
```

Although this code worked fine in browsers that didn't implement `getElementsByClassName()` natively, it caused an error in the ones that did, as a result of the return value differences. You cannot anticipate how browser vendors will change native objects in the future, so modifying them in any way can lead to issues down the road when your implementation clashes with theirs.

The best approach, therefore, is to never modify objects you don't own. You own an object only when you created it yourself, such as a custom type or object literal. You don't own `Array`, `document`, and so on, because they were there before your code executed. You can still create new functionality for objects by doing the following:

➤ Create a new object with the functionality you need, and let it interact with the object of interest.

➤ Create a custom type that inherits from the type you want to modify. You can then modify the custom type with the additional functionality.

Many JavaScript libraries now subscribe to this theory of development, allowing them to grow and adapt even as browsers continually change.

Avoid Globals

Closely related to respecting object ownership is avoiding global variables and functions whenever possible. Once again, this has to do with creating a consistent and maintainable environment in which scripts will be executed. At most, a single global variable should be created on which other objects and functions exist. Consider the following:

```
// two globals - AVOID!!!
var name = "Matt";
function sayName() {
  console.log(name);
}
```

This code contains two globals: the variable name and the function sayName(). These can easily be created on an object that contains both, as in this example:

```
// one global - preferred
var MyApplication = {
  name: "Matt",
  sayName: function() {
    console.log(this.name);
  }
};
```

This rewritten version of the code introduces a single global object, MyApplication, onto which both name and sayName() are attached. Doing so clears up a couple of issues that existed in the previous code. First, the variable name overwrites the window.name property, which possibly interferes with other functionality. Second, it helps to clear up confusion over where the functionality lives. Calling MyApplication.sayName() is a logical hint that any issues with the code can be identified by looking at the code in which MyApplication is defined.

An extension of the single global approach is the concept of *namespacing*. Namespacing involves creating an object to hold functionality. The Google Closure library utilizes namespaces to organize its contents. Here are some examples:

➤ goog.string—Methods for manipulating strings.

➤ goog.html.utils—Methods for working with HTML.

➤ goog.i18n—Methods for helping with internationalization (i18n).

The single global object goog serves as a container onto which other objects are defined. Whenever objects are used simply to group together functionality in this manner, they are called *namespaces*. The entire Google Closure library is built on this concept, allowing it to coexist on the same page with any other JavaScript library.

The important part of namespacing is to decide on a global object name that everyone agrees to use and that is unique enough that others aren't likely to use it as well. In most cases, this can be the name of the company for which you're developing the code, such as goog or Wiley. You can then start creating namespaces to group your functionality, as in this example:

```
// create global object
let Wiley = {};

// create namespace for Professional JavaScript
Wiley.ProJS = {};

// attach other objects used in the book
Wiley.ProJS.Chapters = { ... };
Wiley.ProJS.Snippets = { ... };
```

In this example, Wiley is the global on which namespaces are created. If all code for this book is placed under the Wiley.ProJS namespace, it leaves other authors to add their code onto the Wiley object as well. As long as everyone follows this pattern, there's no reason to be worried that someone else will overwrite these values because they will exist on a different namespace.

Although namespacing requires a little more code, it is worth the trade-off for maintainability purposes. Namespacing helps ensure that your code can work on a page with other code in a non-harmful way.

Avoid Null Comparisons

Because JavaScript doesn't do any automatic type checking, it becomes the developer's responsibility. As a result, very little type checking actually gets done in JavaScript code. The most common type check is to see if a value is `null`. Unfortunately, checking a value against `null` is overused and frequently leads to errors due to insufficient type checking. Consider the following:

```
function sortArray(values) {
   if (values != null) {          // AVOID!!
      values.sort(comparator);
   }
}
```

The purpose of this function is to sort an array with a given comparator. The values argument must be an array for the function to execute correctly, but the `if` statement simply checks to see that values isn't `null`. There are several values that can make it past the `if` statement, including any string or any number, which would then cause the function to throw an error.

Realistically, `null` comparisons are rarely good enough to be used. Values should be checked for what they are expected to be, not for what they aren't expected to be. For example, in the previous code, the values argument is expected to be an array, so you should be checking to see if it is an array, rather than checking to see if it's not `null`. The function can be rewritten more appropriately as follows:

```
function sortArray(values) {
   if (values instanceof Array) {  // preferred
      values.sort(comparator);
   }
}
```

This version of the function protects against all invalid values and doesn't need to use `null` at all.

If you see a `null` comparison in code, try replacing it using one of the following techniques:

➤ If the value should be a reference type, use the `instanceof` operator to check its constructor.

➤ If the value should be a primitive type, use the `typeof` operator to check its type.

➤ If you're expecting an object with a specific method name, use the `typeof` operator to ensure that a method with the given name exists on the object.

➤ If you must check for a `null` value, be certain to use the `===` and `!==` strict equivalence operators.

The fewer `null` comparisons in code, the easier it is to determine the purpose of the code and to eliminate unnecessary errors.

Use Constants

The goal of relying on constants is to isolate data from application logic in such a way that it can be changed without risking the introduction of errors. Strings that are displayed in the user interface should always be extracted in such a way as to allow for internationalization. URLs should also be extracted because they have a tendency to change as an application grows. Basically, each of these has a possibility of changing for one reason or another, and a change would mean going into the function and changing code there. Any time you're changing application logic code, you open up the possibility of creating errors. You can insulate application logic from data changes by extracting data into constants that are defined separately.

The key is to separate data from the logic that uses it. The types of values to look for are as follows:

➤ **Repeated values**—Any values that are used in more than one place should be extracted into a constant. This limits the chance of errors when one value is changed but others are not. This includes CSS class names.

➤ **User interface strings**—Any strings that are to be displayed to the user should be extracted for easier internationalization.

➤ **URLs**—Resource locations tend to change frequently in web applications, so having a common place to store all URLs is recommended.

➤ **Any value that may change**—Any time you're using a literal value in code, ask yourself if this value might change in the future. If the answer is yes, then the value should be extracted into a constant.

Using constants is an important technique for enterprise JavaScript development because it makes code more maintainable and keeps it safe from data changes.

Avoid Using *var* Keyword

The `var` keyword can create variables in unexpected places due to JavaScript's function-level scoping rules, leading to bugs and hard-to-read code. In modern JavaScript, there is very rarely a reason to use `var` instead of `const` or `let`. Prefer `let` and `const`, which have block-level scoping.

PERFORMANCE

The amount of JavaScript that developers now write per web page has grown dramatically since the language was first introduced. With that increase came concerns over the runtime execution of JavaScript code. JavaScript was originally an interpreted language, so the speed of execution was significantly slower than it was for compiled languages. Chrome was the first browser to introduce an optimizing engine that compiles JavaScript into native code. Since then, all other major browsers have followed suit and have implemented JavaScript compilation.

Even with the move to compiled JavaScript, it's still possible to write slow code. However, there are some basic patterns that, when followed, ensure the fastest possible execution of code.

Don't Over-Optimize

Modern browsers are already *highly* optimized for JavaScript execution. Their interpreters and compilers are extremely sophisticated and have been designed to handle a wide range of JavaScript code efficiently.

While it's true that optimizing your code can sometimes lead to faster execution times, you will often find that over-optimization can degrade performance. Attempting to outsmart the browser's own optimization mechanisms can often result in unnecessary complexity and slower execution times. Over-optimization can also make your code harder to read and maintain.

Should you find the need to optimize your code, it's essential to test your changes thoroughly to ensure that they *actually* improve performance. Use developer tools like the Chrome DevTools Performance panel to measure the impact of your optimizations on memory, CPU utilization, page load times, and other performance metrics.

Be Scope-Aware

Chapter 4, "Variables, Scope, and Memory," discussed the concept of scopes in JavaScript and how the scope chain works. As the number of scopes in the scope chain increases, so does the amount of time it takes to access variables outside of the current scope. It is always slower to access a global variable than it is to access a local variable, because the scope chain must be traversed. Anything you can do to decrease the amount of time spent traversing the scope chain will increase overall script performance.

Perhaps the most important thing you can do to improve the performance of your scripts is to be wary of global lookups. Global variables and functions are always more expensive to use than local ones because they involve a scope chain lookup. Consider the following function:

```
function updateUI() {
  let imgs = document.getElementsByTagName("img");
  for (let i = 0, len = imgs.length; i < len; i++) {
    imgs[i].title = '${document.title} image ${i}';
  }

  let msg = document.getElementById("msg");
  msg.innerHTML = "Update complete.";
}
```

This function may look perfectly fine, but it has three references to the global `document` object. If there are multiple images on the page, the document reference in the `for` loop could get executed dozens or hundreds of times, each time requiring a scope chain lookup. By creating a local variable that points to the document object, you can increase the performance of this function by limiting the number of global lookups to just one:

```
function updateUI() {
  let doc = document;
  let imgs = doc.getElementsByTagName("img");
  for (let i = 0, len = imgs.length; i < len; i++) {
    imgs[i].title = '${doc.title} image ${i}';
```

```
    }

        let msg = doc.getElementById("msg");
        msg.innerHTML = "Update complete.";
    }
```

Here, the document object is first stored in the local doc variable. The doc variable is then used in place of document throughout the rest of the code. There's only one global lookup in this function, compared to the previous version, ensuring that it will run faster.

A good rule of thumb is to store any global object that is used more than once in a function as a local variable.

Problematic Language Features

Just because JavaScript can do something doesn't mean it's a good idea to do it. There are a handful of language features that should be avoided in almost all situations.

Avoid the *with* Statement

The with statement should be avoided where performance is important. Similar to functions, the with statement creates its own scope and therefore increases the length of the scope chain for code executed within it. Code executed within a with statement is guaranteed to run slower than code executing outside because of the extra steps in the scope chain lookup.

It is rare that the with statement is required because it is mostly used to eliminate extra characters. In most cases, a local variable can be used to accomplish the same thing without introducing a new scope. Here is an example:

```
    function updateBody() {
        with(document.body) {
            console.log(tagName);
            innerHTML = "Hello world!";
        }
    }
```

The with statement in this code enables you to use document.body more easily. The same effect can be achieved by using a local variable, as follows:

```
    function updateBody() {
        let body = document.body;
        console.log(body.tagName);
        body.innerHTML = "Hello world!";
    }
```

Although this code is slightly longer, it reads better than the with statement, ensuring that you know the object to which tagName and innerHTML belong. This code also saves global lookups by storing document.body in a local variable.

Avoid the *delete* Operator

When removing a property from an object, the delete operator can be very slow because it must search the object's prototype chain to find the property. Instead of using delete, consider setting the property to null or undefined to effectively remove it from the object without traversing the prototype chain.

Avoid HTML and JS String Parsing

JavaScript can execute code and generate HTML from strings. Some examples:

```
eval(`alert("foo")`);

new Function(`alert("bar")`)()

setTimeout(`alert("baz")`, 1000);

document.write(`<script>alert("qux")</script>`);
```

Though they may be tempting to use, there is rarely a reason to ever use these features. They are slow and insecure; avoid whenever possible.

Choose the Right Approach

As with other languages, part of the performance equation has to do with the algorithm or approach used to solve the problem. Skilled developers know from experience which approaches are likely to achieve better performance results. Many of the techniques and approaches that are typically used in other programming languages can also be used in JavaScript.

Avoid Unnecessary Property Lookup

In computer science, the complexity of algorithms is represented using O notation. The simplest, and fastest, algorithm is a constant value or $O(1)$. After that, the algorithms just get more complex and take longer to execute. The following table lists the common types of algorithms found in JavaScript.

NOTATION	NAME	DESCRIPTION
$O(1)$	Constant	Amount of time to execute remains constant no matter the number of values. Represents simple values and values stored in variables.
$O(\log n)$	Logarithmic	Amount of time to execute is related to the number of values, but each value need not be retrieved for the algorithm to complete. Example: binary search.
$O(n)$	Linear	Amount of time to execute is directly related to the number of values. Example: iterating over all items in an array.
$O(n^2)$	Quadratic	Amount of time to execute is related to the number of values such that each value must be retrieved at least n times. Example: insertion sort.

Constant values, or $O(1)$, refer to both literals and values that are stored in variables. The notation $O(1)$ indicates that the amount of time necessary to retrieve a constant value remains the same regardless of the number of values. Retrieving a constant value is an extremely efficient process and so it is quite fast. Consider the following:

```
let value = 5;
let sum = 10 + value;
console.log(sum);
```

This code performs four constant value lookups: the number 5, the variable value, the number 10, and the variable sum. The overall complexity of this code is then considered to be O(1).

Accessing array items is also an O(1) operation in JavaScript, performing just as well as a simple variable lookup. So the following code is just as efficient as the previous example:

```
let values = [5, 10];
let sum = values[0] + values[1];
console.log(sum);
```

Using variables and arrays is more efficient than accessing properties on objects, which is an O(n) operation. Every property lookup on an object takes longer than accessing a variable or array, because a search must be done for a property of that name up the prototype chain. Put simply, the more property lookups there are, the slower the execution time. Consider the following:

```
let values = { first: 5, second: 10 };
let sum = values.first + values.second;
console.log(sum);
```

This code uses two property lookups to calculate the value of sum. Doing one or two property lookups may not result in significant performance issues, but doing hundreds or thousands will definitely slow down execution.

Be wary of multiple property lookups to retrieve a single value. For example, consider the following:

```
let query = window.location.href.substring(window.location.href.indexOf("?"));
```

In this code, there are six property lookups: three for `window.location.href.substring()` and three for `window.location.href.indexOf()`. You can easily identify property lookups by counting the number of dots in the code. This code is especially inefficient because the `window.location.href` value is being used twice, so the same lookup is done twice.

Whenever an object property is being used more than once, store it in a local variable. You'll still take the initial O(n) hit to access the value the first time, but every subsequent access will be O(1), which more than makes up for it. For example, the previous code can be rewritten as follows:

```
let url = window.location.href;
let query = url.substring(url.indexOf("?"));
```

This version of the code has only four property lookups, a savings of 33 percent over the original. Making this kind of optimization in a large script is likely to lead to larger gains.

Generally speaking, any time you can decrease the complexity of an algorithm, you should replace as many property lookups as possible by using local variables to store the values. Furthermore, if you have an option to access something as a numeric array position or a named property (such as with `NodeList` objects), use the numeric position.

Optimize Loops

Loops are one of the most common constructs in programming and, as such, are found frequently in JavaScript. Optimizing these loops is an important part of the performance optimization process because they run the same code repeatedly, automatically increasing execution time. There's been a great deal of research done into loop optimization for other languages, and these techniques also apply to JavaScript. The basic optimization steps for a loop are as follows:

1. **Simplify the terminal condition**—Because the terminal condition is evaluated each time through the loop, it should be as fast as possible. This means avoiding property lookups or other O(n) operations.

2. **Simplify the loop body**—The body of the loop is executed the most, so make sure it's as optimized as possible. Make sure there's no intensive computation being performed that could easily be moved to outside the loop.

3. **Use posttest loops**—The most commonly used loops are for and while, both of which are pretest loops. Posttest loops, such as do-while, avoid the initial evaluation of the terminal condition and tend to run faster.

These changes are best illustrated with an example. The following is a basic for loop:

```
for (let i = 0; i < values.length; i++) {
  process(values[i]);
}
```

This code increments the variable i from 0 up to the total number of items in the values array. Assuming that the order in which the values are processed is irrelevant, the loop can be changed to decrement i instead, as follows:

```
for (let i = values.length - 1; i >= 0; i--) {
  process(values[i]);
}
```

Here, the variable i is decremented each time through the loop. In the process, the terminal condition is simplified by removing the O(n) call to values.length and replacing it with the O(1) call of 0. Because the loop body has only a single statement, it can't be optimized further. However, the loop itself can be changed into a posttest loop like this:

```
let i = values.length-1;
if (i > -1) {
  do {
    process(values[i]);
  }while(--i >= 0);
}
```

The primary optimization here is combining the terminal condition and the decrement operator into a single statement. At this point, any further optimization would have to be done to the process() function itself because the loop is fully optimized.

Keep in mind that using a posttest loop works only when you're certain that there will always be at least one value to process. An empty array causes an unnecessary trip through the loop that a pre-test loop would otherwise avoid.

Other Performance Considerations

There are a few other things to consider when evaluating the performance of your script. The following aren't major issues, but they can make a difference when used frequently:

➤ **Native methods are fast**—Whenever possible, use a native method instead of one written in JavaScript. Native methods are written in compiled languages such as C or C++ and thus run much faster than those in JavaScript. The most often forgotten methods in JavaScript are the complex mathematical operations available on the Math object; these methods always run faster than any JavaScript equivalent for calculating sine, cosine, and so on.

➤ `switch` **statements are fast**—If you have a complex series of `if-else` statements, converting it to a single `switch` statement can result in faster code. You can further improve the performance of `switch` statements by organizing the cases in the order of most likely to least likely.

➤ **Bitwise operators are fast**—When performing mathematical operations, bitwise operations are always faster than any Boolean or numeric arithmetic. Selectively replacing arithmetic operations with bitwise operations can greatly improve the performance of complex calculations. Operations such as modulus, logical AND, and logical OR are good candidates to be replaced with bitwise operations.

Minimize Statement Count

The number of statements in JavaScript code affects the speed with which the operations are performed. A single statement can complete multiple operations faster than multiple statements each performing a single operation. The task, then, is to seek out statements that can be combined in order to decrease the execution time of the overall script. To do so, you can look for several patterns.

Multiple Variable Declarations

One area in which developers tend to create too many statements is in the declaration of multiple variables. It's quite common to see code declaring multiple variables using multiple `let` statements, such as the following:

```
// four statements - wasteful
let count = 5;
let color = "blue";
let values = [1,2,3];
let now = new Date();
```

In strongly typed languages, variables of different data types must be declared in separate statements. In JavaScript, however, all variables can be declared using a single `let` statement. The preceding code can be rewritten as follows:

```
// one statement
let count = 5,
    color = "blue",
    values = [1,2,3],
    now = new Date();
```

Here, the variable declarations use a single `let` statement and are separated by commas. This is an optimization that is easy to make in most cases and performs much faster than declaring each variable separately.

Insert Iterative Values

Any time you are using an iterative value (that is, a value that is being incremented or decremented at various locations), combine statements whenever possible. Consider the following code snippet:

```
let name = values[i];
i++;
```

Each of the two preceding statements has a single purpose: the first retrieves a value from values and stores it in name; the second increments the variable `i`. These can be combined into a single statement by inserting the iterative value into the first statement, as shown here:

```
let name = values[i++];
```

This single statement accomplishes the same thing as the previous two statements. Because the increment operator is postfix, the value of `i` isn't incremented until after the rest of the statement executes. Whenever you have a similar situation, try to insert the iterative value into the last statement that uses it.

Use Array and Object Literals

Throughout this book, you've seen two ways of creating arrays and objects: using a constructor or using a literal. Using constructors always leads to more statements than are necessary to insert items or define properties, whereas literals complete all operations in a single statement. Consider the following example:

```
// four statements to create and initialize array - wasteful
let values = new Array();
values[0] = 123;
values[1] = 456;
values[2] = 789;

// four statements to create and initialize object - wasteful
let person = new Object();
person.name = "Matt";
person.age = 29;
person.sayName = function() {
  console.log(this.name);
};
```

In this code, an array and an object are created and initialized. Each requires four statements: one to call the constructor and three to assign data. These can easily be converted to use literals as follows:

```
// one statement to create and initialize array
let values = [123, 456, 789];

// one statement to create and initialize object
let person = {
  name: "Matt",
  age: 29,
```

```
  sayName() {
    console.log(this.name);
  }
};
```

This rewritten code contains only two statements: one to create and initialize the array, and one to create and initialize the object. What previously took eight statements now takes only two, reducing the statement count by 75 percent. The value of these optimizations is even greater in codebases that contain thousands of lines of JavaScript.

Whenever possible, replace your array and object declarations with their literal representation to eliminate unnecessary statements.

> **NOTE** *Reducing statement count in your codebase is a good goal, but not an absolute law. It is possible to condense too much logic into a single statement for it to be easily comprehensible.*

Optimize DOM Interactions

Of all the parts of JavaScript, the DOM is without a doubt the slowest part. DOM manipulations and interactions take a large amount of time because they often require rerendering all or part of the page. Furthermore, seemingly trivial operations can take longer to execute because the DOM manages so much information. Understanding how to optimize interactions with the DOM can greatly increase the speed with which scripts complete.

Minimize Live Updates

Whenever you access part of the DOM that is part of the displayed page, you are performing a *live update*. Live updates are so called because they involve immediate (live) updates of the page's display to the user. Every change, whether it be inserting a single character or removing an entire section, incurs a performance penalty as the browser recalculates thousands of measurements to perform the update. The more live updates you perform, the longer it will take for the code to completely execute. The fewer live updates necessary to complete an operation, the faster the code will be. Consider the following example:

```
let list = document.getElementById("myList"),
  item;

for (let i = 0; i < 10; i++) {
  item = document.createElement("li");
  list.appendChild(item);
  item.appendChild(document.createTextNode('Item ${i}');
}
```

This code adds ten items to a list. For each item that is added, there are two live updates: one to add the `<li>` element and another to add the text node to it. Because ten items are being added, that's a total of twenty live updates to complete this operation.

To fix this performance bottleneck, you need to reduce the number of live updates. There are generally two approaches to this. The first is to remove the list from the page, perform the updates, and then reinsert the list into the same position. This approach is not ideal because it can cause unnecessary flickering as the page updates each time. The second approach is to use a document fragment to build up the DOM structure and then add it to the list element. This approach avoids live updates and page flickering. Consider the following:

```
let list = document.getElementById("myList"),
    fragment = document.createDocumentFragment(),
    item;

for (let i = 0; i < 10; i++) {
  item = document.createElement("li");
  fragment.appendChild(item);
  item.appendChild(document.createTextNode("Item " + i));
}

list.appendChild(fragment);
```

There is only one live update in this example, and it occurs after all items have been created. The document fragment is used as a temporary placeholder for the newly created items. All items are then added to the list, using appendChild(). Remember, when a document fragment is passed in to appendChild(), all of the children of the fragment are appended to the parent, but the fragment itself is never added.

Whenever updates to the DOM are necessary, consider using a document fragment to build up the DOM structure before adding it to the live document.

Use *innerHTML*

There are two ways to create new DOM nodes on the page: using DOM methods such as createElement() and appendChild(), and using innerHTML. For small DOM changes, the two techniques perform roughly the same. For large DOM changes, however, using innerHTML is much faster than creating the same DOM structure using standard DOM methods.

When innerHTML is set to a value, an HTML parser is created behind the scenes, and the DOM structure is created using the native DOM calls rather than JavaScript-based DOM calls. The native methods execute much faster because they are compiled rather than interpreted. The previous example can be rewritten to use innerHTML like this:

```
let list = document.getElementById("myList"),
    html = "";

for (let i = 0; i < 10; i++) {
  html += '<li>Item ${i}</li>';
}

list.innerHTML = html;
```

This code constructs an HTML string and then assigns it to list.innerHTML, which creates the appropriate DOM structure. Although there is always a small performance hit for string concatenation, this technique still performs faster than performing multiple DOM manipulations.

The key to using `innerHTML`, as with other DOM operations, is to minimize the number of times it is called. For instance, the following code uses `innerHTML` too much for this operation:

```
let list = document.getElementById("myList");

for (let i = 0; i < 10; i++) {
  list.innerHTML += '<li>Item ${i}</li>';    // AVOID!!!
}
```

The problem with this code is that `innerHTML` is called each time through the loop, which is incredibly inefficient. A call to `innerHTML` is, in fact, a live update and should be treated as such. It's far faster to build up a string and call `innerHTML` once than it is to call `innerHTML` multiple times.

> **NOTE** `innerHTML` *exposes an enormous XSS attack surface. Any time it is used to interpolate data that you do not explicitly control, an attacker can inject executable code. Use with caution.*

Use Event Delegation

Most web applications make extensive use of event handlers for user interaction. There is a direct relationship between the number of event handlers on a page and the speed with which the page responds to user interaction. To mitigate these penalties, you should use event delegation whenever possible.

Event delegation takes advantage of events that bubble. Any event that bubbles can be handled not just at the event target but also at any of the target's ancestors. Using this knowledge, you can attach event handlers at a high level that are responsible for handling events for multiple targets. Whenever possible, attach an event handler at the document level that can handle events for the entire page.

Beware of HTMLCollections

The pitfalls of `HTMLCollection` objects have been discussed throughout this book because they are a big performance sink for web applications. Keep in mind that any time you access an `HTMLCollection`, whether it be a property or a method, you are performing a query on the document, and that querying is quite expensive. Minimizing the number of times you access an `HTMLCollection` can greatly improve the performance of a script.

Perhaps the most important area in which to optimize `HTMLCollection` access is loops. Moving the `length` calculation into the initialization portion of a `for` loop was discussed previously. Now consider this example:

```
let images = document.getElementsByTagName("img");

for (let i = 0, len = images.length; i < len; i++) {
  // process
}
```

The key here is that the length is stored in the `len` variable instead of constantly accessing the length property of the `HTMLCollection`. When using an `HTMLCollection` in a loop, you should make your next step a retrieval of a reference to the item you'll be using, as shown here, in order to avoid calling the `HTMLCollection` multiple times in the loop body:

```
let images = document.getElementsByTagName("img"),
    image;

for (let i = 0, len=images.length; i < len; i++) {
    image = images[i];
    // process
}
```

This code adds the image variable, which stores the current image. Once this is complete, there should be no further reason to access the images `HTMLCollection` inside the loop.

When writing JavaScript, it's important to realize when `HTMLCollection` objects are being returned so you can minimize accessing them. An `HTMLCollection` object is returned when any of the following occurs:

➤ A call to `getElementsByTagName()` is made.

➤ The `childNodes` property of an element is retrieved.

➤ The `attributes` property of an element is retrieved.

➤ A special collection is accessed, such as `document.forms`, `document.images`, and so forth.

Understanding when you're using `HTMLCollection` objects and making sure you're using them appropriately can greatly speed up code execution.

STRONG TYPING

TypeScript (`www.typescriptlang.org`) was first introduced by Microsoft in October 2012, as an open-source superset of JavaScript. The motivation behind creating TypeScript was to address some of the limitations of JavaScript, specifically around the lack of strong typing. TypeScript adds features such as static type checking, classes, and interface definitions. Developers write their codebases in TypeScript syntax (which browsers cannot natively execute) and then use a TypeScript compiler to convert it into compiled JavaScript.

Of all the JavaScript tooling developed in the past decade, one could make a strong argument that TypeScript is the most powerful and most essential. Open-source projects and company codebases alike have almost universally adopted TypeScript due to its sheer utility. With a strongly typed codebase, a huge swathe of JavaScript development bugs, errors, and headaches is eradicated almost entirely. The modern JavaScript developer has very little excuse to not use TypeScript everywhere: it's easy to set up; all modern JS frameworks offer first-class support for it; and the syntax is simple, intuitive, and highly extensible.

DEPLOYMENT

Perhaps the most important part of any JavaScript solution is the final deployment to the website or web application in production. You've done a lot of work before this point, architecting and optimizing a solution for general consumption. It's time to move out of the development environment and into the web, where real users can interact with it. Before you do so, however, there are a number of issues that need to be addressed.

Build Process

One of the most important things you can do to ready JavaScript code for deployment is to develop some type of build process around it. The typical pattern for developing software is write-compile-test, in that you write the code, compile it, and then run it to ensure that it works. Because JavaScript is not a compiled language, the pattern often becomes write-test, where the code you write is the same code you test in the browser. The problem with this approach is that it's not optimal; the code you write should not be passed, untouched, to the browser, for the following reasons:

> **Intellectual property issues**—If you put the fully commented source code online, it's easier for others to figure out what you're doing, reuse it, and potentially figure out security holes.

> **File size**—You write code in a way that makes it easy to read, which is good for maintainability but bad for performance. The browser doesn't benefit from the extra white space, indentation, or verbose function and variable names.

> **Code organization**—The way you organize code for maintainability isn't necessarily the best way to deliver it to the browser.

For these reasons, it's best to define a build process for your JavaScript files.

File Structure

A build process starts by defining a logical structure for storing your files in source control. It's best to avoid having a single file that contains all of your JavaScript. Instead, follow the pattern that is typically taken in object-oriented languages: separate each object or custom type into its own file. Doing so ensures that each file contains just the minimum amount of code, making it easier to make changes without introducing errors. Additionally, in environments that use concurrent source control systems such as Git, CVS, or Subversion, this reduces the risk of conflicts during merge operations.

Keep in mind that separating your code into multiple files is for maintainability and not for deployment. For deployment, you'll want to combine the source files into one or more rollup files. It's recommended that web applications use the smallest number of JavaScript files possible, because HTTP requests are some of the main performance bottlenecks on the web. Keep in mind that including a JavaScript file via a vanilla <script> tag is a blocking operation that stops all other downloads while the code is downloaded and executed. Therefore, try to logically group JavaScript code into deployment files.

Task Runners

If you're putting together an application that's anything more than a few files, you will likely find yourself reaching for a task runner to automate tasks for you. The task runner can perform jobs such as linting, bundling, transpilation, starting a local server, deployment, or any other scripted program.

Much of the time, jobs that your task runner will perform are available through command-line interfaces, and therefore your task runner will merely be a tool that aids in grouping and ordering complex command line invocations. In this sense, a task runner in many ways is very similar to a `.bashrc` file. In other cases, the tools you wish to use in automated tasks will have designated plugins compatible

If you're using NodeJS and npm to package your JavaScript assets, two popular task runners are Webpack (`https://webpack.js.org`), Grunt (`www.gruntjs.com`) and Gulp (`www.gulpjs.com`). Tools are robust task runners whose jobs and instructions are defined inside configuration files written in plain JavaScript. The benefit of using these task runners is that each enjoys an ecosystem of plugins, which allow the tools to directly interface with npm (`www.npmjs.com`) packages. Details of these plugins can be found in the appendixes.

Tree Shaking

An increasingly common and extremely effective strategy for reducing payload size is tree shaking. As mentioned in Chapter 23, "Modules," using a static module declaration style means that build tools can determine which parts of the codebase depend on other parts. More importantly, tree shaking is also capable of determining which parts of the codebase are not needed at all.

Build tools that implement tree shaking acknowledge that module imports are frequently selective and that entire segments of module files can be ignored in the final bundled file. Suppose this is your example application:

```
import { foo } from './utils.js';

console.log(foo);
export const foo = 'foo';
export const bar = 'bar';   // unused
```

Here, the `bar` export is never used, and static analysis by a build tool can easily determine this is the case. When performing tree shaking, the build tool will completely strip out the bar export from the bundled file. Static analysis also means that the build tool can determine dependencies that are unused and decline to include those as well. By performing tree shaking, the file size savings of the eventual bundle can be enormous.

Tree shaking does not always work. Since it relies on static code analysis, dynamic imports or runtime-generated code will not be eligible for tree shaking. Similarly, if you are using a library or framework that exports everything as a single bundle, it may be difficult or impossible to perform tree shaking on that code.

Module Bundlers

Just because your codebase is written in modules doesn't mean that it should necessarily be served as modules. Often, JavaScript codebases composed of a large collection of modules will be bundled together at build time and served as one or a few different JavaScript files.

The module bundler's job is to identify the landscape of JavaScript dependencies involved in an application, combine them into a monolithic application, make informed decisions about how the modules should be serially organized and concatenated, and generate the output files that will be provided to the browser.

There is an abundance of build tooling that allows you to accomplish such a feat. Webpack and Parcel are just a couple of the many options you have to convert a module-based codebase into a universally compatible page script.

Validation

Even though IDEs that understand and support JavaScript are starting to appear, most developers still check their syntax by running code in a browser. There are a couple of problems with this approach. First, this validation can't be easily automated or ported from system to system. Second, aside from syntax errors, problems are encountered only when code is executed, leaving it possible for errors to occur.

Linters look for syntax errors and common coding errors in JavaScript code. Some of the potential issues they surface are as follows:

➤ Use of `eval()`

➤ Use of undeclared variables

➤ Omission of semicolons

➤ Improper line breaks

➤ Incorrect comma usage

➤ Omission of braces around statements

➤ Omission of break in `switch` cases

➤ Variables being declared twice

➤ Use of `with`

➤ Incorrect use of equals (instead of double- or triple-equals)

➤ Unreachable code

Adding code validation to your development cycle helps to avoid errors down the road. It's recommended that developers add some type of code validation to the build process as a way of identifying potential issues before they become errors.

> **NOTE** *A list of JavaScript linters can be found in Appendix D, "JavaScript Tools."*

Compression

When talking about JavaScript file compression, you're really talking about two things: *code size* and *wire weight*. Code size refers to the number of bytes that need to be parsed by the browser, and wire weight refers to the number of bytes that are actually transmitted from the server to the browser. In the early days of web development, these two numbers were almost always identical because source files were transmitted, unchanged, from server to client. In today's web, however, the two are rarely equal and realistically should never be.

Code Minification

Because JavaScript isn't compiled into byte code and is transmitted as source code, the source code files usually contain additional information and formatting that have no effect on the browser's JavaScript interpreter. A JavaScript minifier will perform transformations on your source code to make the file size as small as possible while retaining identical program flow.

Comments, extra white space, and long variable or function names improve readability for developers but are unnecessary extra bytes when sent to the browser. A minifier can decrease the file size by performing the following duties:

➤ Remove extra white space (including line breaks).

➤ Remove all comments.

➤ Shorten variable names, function names, and other identifiers.

All JavaScript files should be minified with a minification tool before being deployed to a production environment. Adding a step in your build process to compress JavaScript files is an easy way to ensure that this always happens.

> **NOTE** *In the context of web development, the term "minification" is often used interchangeably with "compression." Doing so can be considered a minor faux pas, as the semantics of each have little overlap.*
>
> *Minification is a process where the minified file size is smaller than the original, but the minified file is still syntactically correct code. Generally, minification is only useful for interpreted languages like JavaScript because languages that are formally compiled into a binary will be minified by the compiler as a matter of course.*
>
> *Compression is distinct from minification in that a compressed file is also smaller than the original but is not syntactically correct code. A compressed file must be uncompressed in order to regain the form of readable code. Compression will result in a smaller file size than minification, as compression algorithms do not have to preserve the syntactical structure of the file and therefore can take additional liberties.*

JavaScript Compilation

Similar in spirit to minification, code compilation generally refers to the process of taking source code and converting it into a form that is behaviorally identical but uses fewer bytes of JavaScript. This is distinct from minification in that the post-compilation code structure may be different, but it will still exhibit the same behavior as your original source code. Compilers are able to do this by ingesting the entirety of your JavaScript code and performing robust analysis on program flow.

Compilation might perform some of the following operations:

➤ Remove unused code.

➤ Transform parts of code to use more concise syntax.

➤ Global inlining of function calls, constants, and variables.

JavaScript Transpilation

The code in your project repository will almost never be the exact code that will execute in your browser. The ECMAScript specification is constantly growing, but different browsers will fully implement each of their features at different paces.

Using transpilation will allow you to wield all the newest syntactical specification features without having to worry about backwards browser compatibility. You can transpile your modern code to an older ECMAScript version—typically ES3, ES5, or ES6, depending on your needs—so that your code can work everywhere. Transpilation tools are covered in the appendixes.

> **NOTE** *The terms "transpilation" and "compilation" are often used interchangeably. Compilation is the process of converting source code written in one language into a different language. Transpilation is essentially the same process as compilation, but the end language will have a similar level of abstraction as the original language. Therefore, converting ES6/7/8 code into ES3/5 is technically both compilation and transpilation, although transpilation is a more exact term to describe the process.*

HTTP Compression

Wire weight refers to the actual number of bytes sent from the server to the browser. The number of bytes doesn't necessarily have to be the same as the code size, because of the compression capabilities of both the server and the browser. All major web browsers support client-side decompression of resources that they receive. The server is therefore able to compress JavaScript files using server-dependent capabilities. As part of the server response, a header is included indicating that the file has been compressed using a given format. The browser then looks at the header to determine that the file is compressed, and then decompresses it using the appropriate format. The result is that the amount of bytes transferred over the network is significantly less than the original code size.

For example, using two modules available for the Apache web server (`mod_gzip` and `mod_deflate`) results in savings of around 70 percent of the original file size of JavaScript files. This is largely due to the fact that JavaScript files are plain text and can therefore be compressed very efficiently. Decreasing the wire weight of your files decreases the amount of time it takes to transmit to the browser. Keep in mind that there is a slight trade-off because the server must spend time compressing the files on each request, and the browser must take some time to decompress the files once they arrive. Generally speaking, however, the trade-off is well worth it.

> **NOTE** *Most web servers, both open source and commercial, have some HTTP compression capabilities. Please consult the documentation for your server to determine how to configure compression properly.*

SUMMARY

As JavaScript development has matured, best practices have emerged. What once was considered a hobby is now a legitimate profession and, as such, has experienced the type of research into maintainability, performance, and deployment traditionally done for other programming languages.

Maintainability in JavaScript has to do partially with the following code conventions:

➤ Code conventions from other languages may be used to determine when to comment and how to indent, but JavaScript requires some special conventions to make up for the loosely typed nature of the language.

➤ Because JavaScript must coexist with HTML and CSS, it's also important to let each wholly define its purpose: JavaScript should define behavior, HTML should define content, and CSS should define appearance.

➤ Any mixing of these responsibilities can lead to difficult-to-debug errors and maintenance issues.

As the amount of JavaScript has increased in web applications, performance has become more important. Therefore, you should keep these things in mind:

➤ The amount of time it takes JavaScript to execute directly affects the overall performance of a web page, so its importance cannot be dismissed.

➤ A lot of the performance recommendations for C-based languages also apply to JavaScript relating to loop performance and using `switch` statements instead of `if`.

➤ Another important thing to remember is that DOM interactions are expensive, so you should limit the number of DOM operations.

The last step in the process is deployment. Here are some key points discussed in this chapter:

➤ To aid in deployment, you should set up a build process that combines JavaScript files into a small number of files (ideally just one).

➤ Having a build process also gives you the opportunity to automatically run additional processes and filters on the source code. You can, for example, run a JavaScript verifier to ensure that there are no syntax errors or potential issues with the code.

➤ A compressor can get your files as small as possible before deployment.

➤ Coupling that with HTTP compression ensures that the JavaScript files are as small as possible and will have the least possible impact on overall page performance.

ES.Next

Beginning with ECMAScript 2015 (ES6), the TC-39 committee moved to begin releasing a new ECMA specification each year. Doing so allows them to collect all individual proposals that are at a sufficiently advanced stage and package them as a single bundle. This packaging is of limited importance, however, as browser vendors tend to adopt proposals in a piecemeal fashion. When a proposal has reached stage 4, its behavior will not change, it is likely to be included in the next ECMAScript release, and browsers will begin adopting the proposal's features at their discretion.

This appendix will discuss the handful of late-stage ECMAScript proposals that seem likely to be incorporated into the next formal ECMAScript edition.

> **NOTE** *Because the features described in this chapter are so new, they might have limited browser support. Consult* `https://caniuse.com` *to determine if a browser version supports a certain feature.*

ARRAY FIND FROM LAST METHODS

This proposal adds `.findLast()` and `.findLastIndex()` methods on arrays and typed arrays. These methods are analogous to `.find()` and `.findIndex()`, the only distinction being that they return the last match instead of the first. In other words, `.find()` is equivalent to `.reverse().find()`, but it obviates the need for the intermediate array reversal. This behavior is demonstrated here:

```
const hasFoo = (string) => string.includes("foo");
const strings = ["hello", "foo", "world", "foobar", "baz"];

console.log(strings.find(hasFoo));
// "foo"
console.log(strings.findIndex(hasFoo));
```

```
// 1

console.log(strings.findLast(hasFoo));
// "foobar"
console.log(strings.findLastIndex(hasFoo));
// 3
```

HASHBANG/SHEBANG GRAMMAR

Hashbang, also known as a *shebang*, is a sequence of characters at the beginning of an executable script that defines the interpreter for the program to be run on. Unix-like platforms use it to understand which interpreter to pass the file to for execution. Consider the following example script located at /home/myusername/scripts/myscript.js:

```
#!/usr/bin/env node

console.log("Hello, world!");
```

The program loader is instructed to run the program /usr/bin/env node, passing /home/myusername/scripts/myscript.js as the first argument.

Currently, JavaScript engines do not automatically strip out the hashbang. When the program loader executes a JavaScript program, the host must strip the hashbang to generate a valid source before passing it down to the engine. This proposal moves the stripping out of the hosts and into the engines.

SYMBOLS AS WEAKMAP KEYS

Currently, a WeakMap only allows objects as keys, which can be a limitation for developers who want to use a unique value as a key that can be eventually garbage collected. This proposal suggests extending the WeakMap to allow for a Symbol to be used as a key.

```
const wm = new WeakMap();

const key = Symbol('Key for weak map entry');
const data = {
  // ...
};

myWeakMap.set(key, data);
```

Objects are currently used as WeakMap keys because they share the same identity behavior: the identity of an object can only be verified with access to the original production, and no new object will match a preexisting one in a strict comparison. However, a Symbol is a better fit for certain use cases, and this proposal seeks to enable this feature to enhance the flexibility of the WeakMap.

CHANGE ARRAY BY COPY

This proposal adds .toReversed(), .toSorted(), and .with() methods on arrays and typed arrays and .toSpliced() to only arrays. These methods are analogues of existing array and typed array methods that perform in-place mutation of an array; the new methods *create a shallow copy of the array* and mutate the copied array instead. The distinction is demonstrated here:

```
// This performs an in-place reversal
myArray.reverse();

// This create a copy and reverses the copy
[...myArray].reverse();

// This creates a copy and reverses the copy
myArray.toReversed()
```

➤ `.toReversed()` exhibits the same behavior as `.reverse()`.

➤ `.toSorted(compareFn)` exhibits the same behavior as `.sort()`.

➤ `.toSpliced(start, deleteCount, ...items)` exhibits the same behavior as `.splice()`.

➤ `.with(index, value)` does not have an analogous method. It creates an array copy and replaces the item at `index` with `value`.

These methods are demonstrated here:

```
const myArray = [5,7,3,9,2];

const reversedArray = myArray.toReversed();
console.log(reversedArray);
// [2,9,3,7,5]

const sortedArray = reversedArray.toSorted();
console.log(sortedArray);
// [2,3,5,7,9]

const splicedArray = sortedArray.toSpliced(1,3);
console.log(splicedArray);
// [3,5,7]

const withArray = splicedArray.with(1, 10);
console.log(withArray);
// [3,10,7]

// Unchanged!
console.log(myArray);
// [5,7,3,9,2]
```

B

Strict Mode

ECMAScript 5 was the first to introduce the concept of *strict mode*. Strict mode allows you to opt-in to stricter checking for JavaScript error conditions either globally or locally within a single function. The advantage of strict mode is that you'll be informed of errors earlier, so some of the ECMAScript quirks that cause programming errors will be caught immediately. Strict mode is supported in all major browsers.

OPTING-IN

To opt-in to strict mode, use the strict mode *pragma*, which is simply a string that isn't assigned to any variable:

```
"use strict";
```

Using this syntax, which is valid even in ECMAScript 3, allows seamless fallback for JavaScript engines that don't support strict mode. The engines that support strict mode will enable it, while engines that don't will simply ignore the pragma as an unassigned string literal.

When the pragma is applied globally, outside of a function, strict mode is enabled for the entire script. That means adding the pragma to a single script that is concatenated with other scripts into a single file puts all JavaScript in the file into strict mode.

You can also turn on strict mode within a function only, such as:

```
function doSomething() {
    "use strict";
    // other processing
}
```

If you don't have complete control over all of the scripts on a page, then it's advisable to enable strict mode only within specific functions for which it has been tested.

CLASSES AND MODULES

Classes and modules are two mediums of code containers introduced in ECMAScript 6. There is no concept of an ECMAScript predecessor for either of these, and therefore there is no need to support syntactical compatibility with legacy ECMAScript versions. TC-39 decided that all code defined inside classes and modules by default is in strict mode.

For classes, this includes both class declarations and class expressions; the constructor, instance methods, static methods, getters, and setters are all in strict mode. For modules, all code defined inside them will be in strict mode.

VARIABLES

How and when variables get created is different in strict mode. The first change disallows accidental creation of global variables. In nonstrict mode, the following creates a global variable:

```
// Variable is not declared
// Non-strict mode: creates a global
// Strict mode: Throws a ReferenceError
message = "Hello world!";
```

Even though message isn't preceded by the let keyword and isn't explicitly defined as a property of the global object, it is still automatically created as a global. In strict mode, assigning a value to an undeclared variable throws a ReferenceError when the code is executed.

A related change is the inability to call delete on a variable. Nonstrict mode allows this and may silently fail (returning false). In strict mode, an attempt to delete a variable causes an error:

```
// Deleting a variable
// Non-strict mode: Fails silently
// Strict mode: Throws a ReferenceError
let color = "red";
delete color;
```

Strict mode also imposes restrictions on variable names. Specifically, it disallows variables named implements, interface, let, package, private, protected, public, static, and yield. These are now reserved words that are intended for use in future ECMAScript editions. Any attempt to use these as variable names while in strict mode will result in a SyntaxError.

OBJECTS

In strict mode, object manipulation is more likely to throw errors than in nonstrict mode. Strict mode tends to throw errors in situations where nonstrict mode silently fails, increasing the likelihood of catching an error early on in development.

To begin, there are several cases where attempting to manipulate an object property will throw an error:

➤ Assigning a value to a read-only property throws a `TypeError`.

➤ Using `delete` on a nonconfigurable property throws a `TypeError`.

➤ Attempting to add a property to a nonextensible object throws a `TypeError`.

Another restriction on objects has to do with declaring them via object literals. When using an object literal, property names must be unique. For instance:

```
// Two properties with the same name
// Non-strict mode: No error, second property wins
// Strict mode: Throws a syntax error
let person = {
  name: "Matt",
  name: "Alice"
};
```

The object literal for person has two properties called name in this code. The second property is the one that ends up on person in nonstrict mode. In strict mode, this is a syntax error.

> **NOTE** *The restriction on duplicate property names was removed in ECMAScript 6. Duplicate object literal property keys do not throw an error in strict mode.*

FUNCTIONS

First, strict mode requires that named function arguments be unique. Consider the following:

```
// Duplicate named arguments
// Non-strict mode: No error, only second argument works
// Strict mode: Throws a SyntaxError
function sum (num, num){
  // do something
}
```

In nonstrict mode, this function declaration doesn't throw an error. You'll be able to access the second num argument only by name while the first is accessible only through arguments.

The arguments object also has a slight behavior change in strict mode. In nonstrict mode, changes to a named argument are also reflected in the arguments object, whereas strict mode ensures that each are completely separate. For example:

```
// Change to named argument value
// Non-strict mode: Change is reflected in arguments
// Strict mode: Change is not reflected in arguments
function showValue(value){
```

```
    value = "Foo";
    alert(value);           // "Foo"
    alert(arguments[0]);    // Non-strict mode: "Foo"
                            // Strict mode: "Hi"
}
showValue("Hi");
```

In this code, the function showValue() has a single named argument called value. The function is called with an argument of "Hi", which is assigned to value. Inside the function, value is changed to "Foo". In nonstrict mode, this also changes the value in arguments[0], but in strict mode they are kept separate.

Another change is the elimination of arguments.callee and arguments.caller. In nonstrict mode, these refer to the function itself and the calling function, respectively. In strict mode, attempting to access either property throws a TypeError. For example:

```
// Attempt to access arguments.callee
// Non-strict mode: Works as expected
// Strict mode: Throws a TypeError
function factorial(num){
    if (num <= 1) {
        return 1;
    } else {
        return num * arguments.callee(num-1)
    }
}
let result = factorial(5);
```

Similarly, the caller and arguments properties of a function now throw a TypeError when an attempt is made to read or write them. So in this example, attempts to access factorial.caller and factorial.callee would also throw an error.

Also, as with variables, strict mode imposes restrictions on function names, disallowing functions named implements, interface, let, package, private, protected, public, static, and yield.

The last change to functions is disallowing function declarations unless they are at the top level of a script or function. That means functions declared, for instance, in an if statement are now a syntax error:

```
// Function declaration in an if statement
// Non-strict mode: Function hoisted outside of if statement
// Strict mode: Throws a syntax error
if (true){
    function doSomething(){
        // ...
    }
}
```

This syntax is tolerated on all browsers in nonstrict mode but will now throw a syntax error in strict mode.

Function Parameters

ES6 introduced the rest operator, destructured parameters, and default parameters—a robust collection of new abilities for functions to organize, structure, and define their parameters. A small change introduced in ECMAScript 7 dictates that functions that use any of these advanced parameter features cannot use strict mode inside its function body without throwing an error. Use of global strict mode is still allowed.

```
// ok
function foo(a, b, c) {
  "use strict";
}

// bad
function bar(a, b, c='d') {
  "use strict";
}

// bad
function baz({a, b, c}) {
  "use strict";
}

// bad
function qux(a, b, ...c) {
  "use strict";
}
```

The new features introduced in ES6 expect that the parameters will be parsed in the same mode as the function body. Because the `"use strict"` pragma is encountered inside the function body, the JavaScript parser would need to check for a pragma inside the function body before ingesting the function parameters, introducing a great deal of messiness. Therefore, the ES7 specification introduced this convention in order to allow the parser to definitively know what mode it is operating in before it begins to parse the function.

Using *eval()*

The much-maligned `eval()` function receives an upgrade in strict mode. The biggest change to `eval()` is that it will no longer create variables or functions in the containing context. For example:

```
// eval() used to create a variable
// Non-strict mode: Alert displays 10
// Strict mode: Throws a ReferenceError when alert(x) is called
function doSomething(){
  eval("let x = 10");
  alert(x);
}
```

When run in nonstrict mode, this code creates a local variable x in the function doSomething() and that value is then displayed using alert(). In strict mode, the call to eval() does not create the variable x inside of doSomething() and so the call to alert() throws a ReferenceError because x is undeclared.

Variables and functions can be declared inside of eval(), but they remain inside a special scope that is used while code is being evaluated and then destroyed once completed. So the following code works without any errors:

```
"use strict";
let result = eval("let x = 10, y = 11; x + y");
alert(result);      // 21
```

The variables x and y are declared inside of eval() and are added together before returning their value. The result variable then contains 21, the result of adding x and y, even though x and y no longer exist by the time alert() is called.

eval AND ARGUMENTS

Strict mode now explicitly disallows using eval and arguments as identifiers and manipulating their values. For example:

```
// Redefining eval and arguments as variables
// Non-strict mode: Okay, no error.
// Strict-mode: Throws syntax error
let eval = 10;
let arguments = "Hello world!";
```

In nonstrict mode, you can overwrite eval and assign arguments to a value. In strict mode, this causes a syntax error. You can't use either as an identifier, which means all of the following use cases throw a syntax error:

➤ Declaration using let

➤ Assignment to another value

➤ Attempts to change the contained value, such as using ++

➤ Used as function names

➤ Used as named function arguments

➤ Used as exception name in a try-catch statement

COERCION OF THIS

One of the biggest security issues, and indeed one of the most confusing aspects of JavaScript, is how the value of this is coerced in certain situations. When using the apply() or call() methods of a function, a `null` or `undefined` value is coerced to the global object in nonstrict mode. In strict mode, the `this` value for a function is always used as specified, regardless of the value. For example:

```
// Access a property
// Non-strict mode: Accesses the global property
// Strict mode: Throws an error because this is null
let color = "red";
function displayColor() {
  alert(this.color);
}
displayColor.call(null);
```

This code passes `null` to `displayColor.call()`, which in nonstrict mode means the `this` value of the function is the global object. The result is an alert displaying `"red"`. In strict mode, the `this` value of the function is `null`, so it throws an error when attempting to access a property of a `null` object.

Typically, functions will coerce their `this` value into an object type, a behavior colloquially referred to as "boxing." Primitives will be coerced into their object wrapper equivalents.

```
function foo() {
  console.log(this);
}

foo.call();   // Window {}
foo.call(2);  // Number {2}
```

When executed in strict mode, the `this` value will no longer undergo this boxing:

```
function foo() {
  "use strict";
  console.log(this);
}

foo.call();   // undefined
foo.call(2);  // 2
```

OTHER CHANGES

There are several other changes to strict mode of which you need to be aware. The first is the elimination of the `with` statement. The `with` statement changes how identifiers are resolved and has been removed from strict mode as a simplification. An attempt to use `with` in strict mode results in a syntax error.

```
// Use of the with statement
// Non-strict mode: Allowed
// Strict mode: Throws a syntax error
with(location) {
  alert(href);
}
```

Strict mode also eliminates the *octal literal* from JavaScript. Octal literals begin with a zero and have traditionally been the source of many errors. An octal literal is now considered invalid syntax in strict mode.

```
// Use of octal literal
// Non-strict mode: value is 8.
// Strict mode: throws a syntax error.
let value = 010;
```

ECMAScript 5 changed `parseInt()` for nonstrict mode, where octal literals are now considered decimal literals with a leading zero. For example:

```
// Use of octal literal in parseInt()
// Non-strict mode: value is 8
// Strict mode: value is 10
let value = parseInt("010");
```

JavaScript Libraries and Frameworks

JavaScript *libraries* help to bridge the gap between browser differences and provide easier access to complex browser features. Libraries come in two forms: *general* and *specialty*. General Java-Script libraries provide access to common browser functionality and can be used as the basis for a website or web application. Specialty libraries do only specific things and are intended to be used for only parts of a website or web application. This appendix provides an overview of these libraries and some of their functionality, along with websites that you can use as additional resources.

FRAMEWORKS

The "framework" designation covers a spectrum of different patterns, but in some form they all provide an opinionated organizational structure within which complex applications can take shape. Using a framework allows for applications to maintain consistent code conventions while elegantly scaling in size and complexity. They offer robust mechanisms for common tasks such as component definition and reuse, controlling data flow, routing, and many others.

Increasingly, JavaScript frameworks take the form of a *single page application* (SPA). Single page applications use the HTML5 browser history API to offer an entire application user interface, complete with URL routing, with only a single initial page load. The framework manages the application state as well as all the user interface components during the application's execution. Most popular SPA frameworks have strong developer communities as well as an abundance of third-party extensions.

React

Created by Facebook, the React framework covers the "view" component in the Model-View-Controller model. Its limited purview means it can be used in conjunction with other frameworks or React extensions to attain full MVC coverage. React uses unidirectional data flow, is declarative and component-based, uses a virtual DOM to efficiently rerender the page, and offers a JSX syntax, which allows you to write markup inside JavaScript. Facebook also maintains a complementary framework to React, named "Flux."

License: MIT License

Website: `reactjs.org`

Angular

First released in 2010 by Google, the Angular project is a full-featured web application framework for Model-View-Viewmodel architectures. In 2016, the project forked into two branches: Angular 1.*x*, which is a continuation of the original AngularJS project, and Angular 2, which is a wholly redesigned framework that is built around ES6 constructs and TypeScript. The latest releases of both versions are directive and component-based implementations, and both projects enjoy robust developer communities and third-party add-ons.

License: MIT License

Websites: `angularjs.org` and `angular.io`

Vue

Vue is a full-featured web application framework designed to be less opinionated than frameworks like Angular. Since its release in 2014, its developer community has grown mightily, and many developers reach for Vue because of its ability to offer performance and organizational gains while allowing for less rigorous adhesion to its tenets.

License: MIT License

Website: `vuejs.org`

Alpine.js

Alpine.js is a lightweight JavaScript library that provides an expressive syntax for declaratively adding interactivity to HTML elements without the need for a complex framework. It leverages the power of data binding and event listeners to enable dynamic and responsive user interfaces with minimal code. Alpine.js can be used in combination with other libraries and frameworks, or as a standalone tool, making it a versatile and flexible choice for web developers looking to enhance the functionality and user experience of their applications. With its simple and intuitive syntax, Alpine.js offers a low learning curve and a fast and efficient way to add interactivity to web pages.

License: MIT License

Website: `alpinejs.dev`

Ember

Ember is very similar to Angular in that it is also a Model-View-Viewmodel architecture and uses preferred conventions to fill out a web application. The 2.0 release in 2015 introduced many behavioral characteristics used by the React framework.

> **License:** MIT License
>
> **Website:** emberjs.com

Meteor

Meteor is wholly unlike any other framework in this list because it is an isomorphic JavaScript framework, meaning that client and server share a codebase. It also uses a real-time data updating protocol, which continually pushes fresh data changes from DB to client. Meteor is an extremely opinionated framework; however, the benefit of this is that application features can be developed quickly using its robust out-of-the-box featureset.

> **License:** MIT License
>
> **Website:** meteor.com

Backbone.js

A minimal Model-View-Controller (MVC) open-source library built on top of Underscore.js, *Backbone.js* is optimized for single-page applications, enabling you to easily update parts of the page as application state changes.

> **License:** MIT License
>
> **Website:** backbonejs.org

USEFUL LIBRARIES

JavaScript libraries offer prewritten code to help developers speed up their development process, simplify coding tasks, and enhance the functionality and interactivity of their web applications. From utility libraries like Lodash to data visualization libraries like D3.js, there is a broad and deep collection of libraries to choose from. If you're looking to build something from scratch, chances are there's at least one open-source library that already does it. The following sections cover some actively maintained and popular ones.

jQuery

jQuery is an open-source library that provides a functional programming interface to JavaScript. It is a complete library whose core is built around using CSS selectors to work with DOM elements. Through call chaining, jQuery code looks more like a narrative description of what should happen rather than JavaScript code. This style of code has become popular among designers and prototypers.

> **License:** MIT License or General Public License (GPL)
>
> **Website:** jquery.com

Google Closure Library

The Google Closure Library is an all-purpose JavaScript toolkit, similar in many ways to jQuery. It consists of an extremely broad set of modules covering both low-level operations and high-level components and widgets. The Closure Library is designed so that modules can be included as necessary, and the library is built to work alongside the Google Closure Compiler (covered in Appendix D, "JavaScript Tools").

> **License:** Apache 2.0 License

> **Website:** `developers.google.com/closure/library`

Underscore.js

Underscore.js provides additional functionality for functional programming in JavaScript. The documentation talks about Underscore.js as a complement to jQuery, providing additional low-level functionality for working with objects, arrays, functions, and other JavaScript data types.

> **License:** MIT License

> **Website:** `documentcloud.github.com/underscore`

Lodash

In the same category as Underscore.js, Lodash is also a utility library that provides you with a supplementary JavaScript toolkit. It introduces enhanced methods for native types, such as arrays, objects, functions, and primitives.

> **License:** MIT License

> **Website:** `lodash.com`

D3

Easily the most popular animation library, D3 (for "Data Driven Documents") is the most robust and powerful JavaScript data visualization tool in use today. It has an intensely deep featureset, covering canvas, SVG, CSS, and HTML5 visualizations. The library gives you the capability to control the final rendering with extreme precision.

> **License:** BSD

> **Website:** `www.d3js.org`

three.js

three.js is one of the most popular WebGL libraries available. It offers a lightweight API that allows you to perform complex 3D renderings and animations.

> **License:** MIT License

> **Website:** `threejs.org`

Anime.js

Anime.js is a lightweight JavaScript animation library with a simple yet powerful API. It works with CSS properties, SVG, DOM attributes, and JavaScript objects.

License: MIT License

Website: `animejs.com`

Chart.js

Chart.js provides a set of frequently used chart types, plugins, and customization options. In addition to a reasonable set of built-in chart types, you can use community-maintained chart types. It's also possible to combine several chart types into a mixed chart (essentially blending multiple chart types into one on the same canvas). Chart.js is highly customizable with custom plugins to create annotations, zoom, or drag-and-drop functionalities.

License: MIT License

Website: `chartjs.com`

Leaflet

Leaflet is the leading open-source JavaScript library for mobile-friendly interactive maps. Weighing just about 42 KB of JS, it has all the mapping features most developers ever need. Leaflet is designed with simplicity, performance, and usability in mind. It works efficiently across all major desktop and mobile platforms; can be extended with lots of plugins; and has a beautiful, easy-to-use and well-documented API and simple, readable source code.

License: BSD-2-Clause license

Website: `leafletjs.com`

Axios

Axios is a popular JavaScript library that provides an easy-to-use interface for making HTTP requests from the browser or Node.js. It supports all modern browsers and provides a consistent API that works seamlessly with promises. Axios can handle a wide range of HTTP request and response types, including JSON, XML, and FormData, and supports features such as interceptors, request and response transformations, and automatic handling of response status and headers. Additionally, Axios has built-in support for canceling requests and handling errors, making it a reliable and flexible choice for developers looking to handle HTTP requests in their JavaScript applications.

License: MIT License

Website: `axios-http.com`

Rxjs

RxJS is a popular JavaScript library for reactive programming, which provides an easy-to-use interface for managing asynchronous data streams. It leverages the Observable pattern to represent data streams and provides a range of operators for transforming and combining these streams in powerful ways.

License: Apache 2.0 License

Website: `rxjs.dev`

JavaScript Tools

Writing JavaScript is a lot like writing in any other programming language, with tools designed to make development easier. The number of tools available for JavaScript developers continues to grow, making it much easier to locate problems, optimize, and deploy JavaScript-based solutions. Some of the tools are designed to be used from JavaScript, whereas others can be run outside the browser. This appendix provides an overview of some of these tools, as well as additional resources for more information.

> **NOTE** *You will notice that various tools are included in multiple sections throughout this appendix. Many JavaScript tools available today are meant to be all-in-one project management tools, and thus they relate to multiple domains.*

PACKAGE MANAGERS

JavaScript projects will usually need to leverage third-party libraries and assets to avoid code duplication and speed development. Third-party libraries, referred to as "packages," are hosted on publicly available repositories. Packages can take the form of assets that will be delivered to the browser, JavaScript libraries that will be compiled as part of your project, or even tools for your project development pipeline. These packages are almost always actively developed and undergoing revisions, in addition to having different flavors of releases. JavaScript package managers allow you to manage what packages your projects depend on, how to access and install them, and which versions to install.

Package managers offer a command-line interface for installing or removing project dependencies. The project's configuration will usually be stored in a local project manifest file.

npm

npm, which stands for "Node Package Manager," is the default package manager for the NodeJS runtime. Third-party packages—provided inside the npm registry—can be specified as project dependencies and installed locally via the command line. npm's repository contains both server-side and client-side JavaScript packages.

npm is designed for use on a server, where the size of a dependency graph is less critical. When installing packages, npm uses a nested dependency tree to resolve all project dependencies; each project dependency will install its own version of whatever other packages it depends on. This means that if your project has three package dependencies—A, B, and C—and each of those depends on a different version of package D, npm will install three separate versions of package D, one for each dependency.

> **Website:** www.npmjs.com

Yarn

Developed by Facebook, Yarn is a custom package manager that is, in many ways, a souped-up version of npm. It can access all the same npm packages through the Yarn registry, and it installs them in much the same way as npm. The primary differences between Yarn and npm is that the former offers features that afford you faster installs, package caching, lockfiles, and improved package security features.

> **Website:** yarnpkg.com

Bower

Bower features many of the same rhythms as npm, including package installation and management CLI, but its focus is on managing packages that will be served to a client. One major difference between Bower and npm is that Bower uses a flat dependency structure. This means that project dependencies will share packages they depend on, and the user's job is to resolve these dependencies. For example, if your project has three package dependencies—A, B, and C—and each of those depends on a different version of package D, you will need to find a single version of package D that satisfies the requirements of all these packages because the flat dependency structure dictates that you install a single version of any given package.

> **Website:** bower.io

MODULE LOADERS

Module loaders allow you to request modules from the server on demand as opposed to loading every single JS module or a single bundled JS file all at once. The ECMAScript 6 module specification outlines an eventual target for browsers to natively support dynamic module loading. Module loaders can serve as a sort of polyfill that allows for packages to dynamically load modules from the client.

SystemJS

The SystemJS module loader is geared for either server or client use. It supports all module formats, including AMD, CommonJS, UMD, and ES6. It also supports in-browser transpilation (not recommended for large-scale projects because of performance implications).

> **Website:** `github.com/systemjs`

RequireJS

RequireJS is built atop the AMD module specification and offers exceptional legacy browser support. Although RequireJS is tried and true, the JavaScript community as a whole is largely leaving the AMD module format behind, so beginning a large project with RequireJS is not recommended.

> **Website:** `requirejs.org`

MODULE BUNDLERS

Module bundlers allow you to combine an arbitrary number of modules in various module formats into bundles that can be loaded on the client. The module bundler will keep track of your application's dependency graph and order the modules as necessary. Frequently, the application can be served as a single bundle, but multiple bundle configurations are also possible. Module bundlers also often support bundling raw or compiled CSS assets. Bundles may take the form of a self-executing bundle, or they may remain as concatenated module assets, which will not execute until necessary.

Webpack

Featuring a broad featureset and excellent extensibility, Webpack is overwhelmingly the most popular application bundler in use today. It can bundle different module types, supports a wide array of plugins, and is fully compatible with most templating and transpilation libraries.

> **Website:** `webpack.js.org`

Parcel

Parcel automatically detects dependencies, eliminating the need for complex configuration files. Parcel provides a zero-configuration setup for many common web development workflows, including support for popular frameworks such as React, Vue.js, and Angular. In addition to its powerful bundling capabilities, Parcel also includes features such as hot module replacement, code splitting, and minification.

> **Website:** `parceljs.org`

Rollup

Rollup is similar in many ways to Browserify in its module bundling abilities, but it also introduces tree shaking out-of-the-box. Rollup is able to parse your application's dependency graph and prune off any modules that are not actually used.

> **Website:** `rollupjs.org`

COMPILATION/TRANSPILATION TOOLS AND STATIC TYPE SYSTEMS

Web application code written in the editor is almost never the exact code that will be served to the client. Developers often want to leverage newer ECMAScript specification features that have yet to gain universal browser adoption. Furthermore, developers also often want to augment or enhance their codebase with a static type system or features outside the ECMA specification. There are a range of tools to address different aspects of these needs.

Babel

Babel is one of the most popular tools used for compiling the latest ECMAScript specification features down to a browser-friendly ECMA version. It also features support for React's JSX, accepts a wide range of plugins, and is compatible with all major build tools.

> **Website:** `babeljs.io`

Google Closure Compiler

Google's Closure Compiler is a powerful JavaScript compiler that is capable of varying levels of compilation optimization as well as a robust static type checking system. Type annotations are done in JSDoc-style comments.

> **Website:** `developers.google.com/closure`

TypeScript

Microsoft's TypeScript is a typed superset of JavaScript that introduces robust static type checking and major syntax enhancements. Because it is a strict superset of JavaScript, regular JS programs are valid TypeScript syntax. TypeScript also can use type definition files to specify type information for existing JavaScript libraries.

> **Website:** `typescriptlang.org`

Flow

Facebook's Flow is a simple type annotation system for JavaScript. Its type syntax is very similar to TypeScript, but it does not add additional language features other than type declarations.

> **Website:** `flow.org`

HIGH-PERFORMANCE SCRIPT TOOLS

A common criticism of JavaScript is that it is incredibly slow and inappropriate for computing that requires agility. Whether or not this "slow" designation carries water doesn't change the fact that the language was never built to support nimble computation. To address this, there are a number of projects that attempt to augment code execution paradigms in the browser in order to allow the program to execute at near native speeds and make use of hardware optimizations.

WebAssembly

The WebAssembly project (or *wasm*) is working to implement a language that can run in many locations (portable) and exist as a binary language that can be compiled to from multiple low-level languages such as C++ and Rust. WebAssembly code runs in a totally separate virtual machine from that of JavaScript in a browser, and its ability to interact with various browser APIs is extremely limited. It is possible to interact with JavaScript and the DOM in an indirect and limited fashion, but the bigger goal of WebAssembly is to create an extremely fast language that can run in web browsers (and elsewhere) and offer near-native performance and hardware acceleration. The WebAssembly specification is still being fleshed out and specified, but it is one of the most promising areas in browser technology.

> **Website:** `webassembly.org`

asm.js

asm.js is based around the idea that compiled JavaScript can be run much faster than handwritten JavaScript. asm.js is a subset of JavaScript that low-level language code can be compiled to and executed in a normal browser or Node engine. Modern JavaScript engines infer types at runtime, and asm.js code makes these type inferences (and therefore associated operations) much less computationally expensive by coercing types using lexical hints. It also makes extensive use of TypedArrays, which offer huge performance gains over the traditional associative JS array. asm.js is not as fast as WebAssembly, but it still offers significant performance gains through compilation.

> **Website:** `asmjs.org`

Emscripten and LLVM

While it never executes in the browser, Emscripten is a critical toolkit for compiling low-level code to WebAssembly and asm.js. Emscripten uses the LLVM compiler to compile languages such as C, C++, and Rust into code that can either run directly in the browser (asm.js) or in a virtual machine (WebAssembly).

> **Emscripten Website:** `kripken.github.io/emscripten-site`
>
> **LLVM Website:** `llvm.org`

EDITORS

VIM, Emacs, and their ilk are excellent text editors, but as your build environment and application scale in complexity it becomes increasingly useful for editors to automate common tasks such as autocompletion, file formatting, code linting, and project directory comprehension. A broad range of editors and IDEs that offer these features is available to choose from, both free and paid.

Sublime Text

Sublime Text is a wildly popular closed-source text editor. It can be used for developing in all languages, but it offers an extremely extensive library of plugins maintained by the community. The performance of the editor is among the best in its class.

> **Website:** sublimetext.com
>
> **Price:** Free trial; one-time $80 license

Atom

Github's Atom is an open-source text editor with many of the same features as Sublime Text, including a thriving community and third-party package add-ons. The editor sometimes struggles with performance, but it is continually making strides in this area.

> **Website:** atom.io
>
> **Price:** Free

Brackets

Adobe's Brackets is similar to Atom in that it is open source, but the editor is designed specifically for web developers and offers a number of very impressive and unique features geared toward frontend coding. Accompanying it is a healthy library of plugins.

> **Website:** brackets.io
>
> **Price:** Free

Visual Studio Code

Microsoft's Visual Studio Code is an open-source code editor based on the Electron framework. Similar to other major editors, it is highly extensible via its package library.

> **Website:** code.visualstudio.com
>
> **Price:** Free

WebStorm

JetBrains's WebStorm is an unapologetically high-octane IDE geared to be the ultimate project development toolkit, featuring robust integration with the leading frontend frameworks. It also integrates with most build tools and version control systems.

> **Website:** jetbrains.com/webstorm
>
> **Price:** Free trial; monthly/yearly licensing fees

BUILD TOOLS, AUTOMATION SYSTEMS, AND TASK RUNNERS

The process of transforming a local project directory into an application served in production is usually bundled into a number of tasks. Each of these tasks is often composed of a pipeline of many subtasks—for example, building and deploying an application will involve module bundling, compilation, minification, and pushing static assets, among many other tasks. Running a unit or integration test might involve initialization of test harnesses and spinning up headless browsers. To make management and utilization of these tasks easier, there are a number of tools that allow you to more efficiently compose and organize your application's tasks.

npm

Although not strictly a build tool, npm offers a scripts feature, which many developers have found works nicely as a task runner that works out-of-the-box with no extra frills. Scripts are defined directly inside the NodeJS `package.json`.

> **Website:** `docs.npmjs.com/misc/scripts`

Grunt

Grunt is a NodeJS task runner that uses configuration objects to declaratively define how tasks should execute. It features a healthy community and a large selection of plugins from which to build out your project's tasks.

> **Website:** `gruntjs.com`

Gulp

Similar to Grunt, Gulp is also a NodeJS task runner, which instead uses a Unix-style pipeline approach to task definition, where individual tasks are defined as JavaScript functions. Gulp also features a vibrant community and package library.

> **Website:** `gulpjs.com`

LINTERS AND FORMATTERS

Part of the problem with JavaScript debugging is that there aren't many IDEs that automatically indicate syntax errors as you type. Most developers write some code and then load it into a browser to look for errors. You can significantly reduce the instances of such errors by validating your JavaScript code before deployment. *Linters* check basic syntax and provide warnings about style.

Formatters are tools that implicitly understand the syntactical rules of a language and use a collection of indentation, whitespace, line wrap, and other strategies to give you the capability to automatically neatly organize the content of a file. Formatters will never break or modify the code or semantic meaning of the code, as they are aware of the kinds of modifications that would serve to alter the execution.

ESLint

ESLint is an open-source JavaScript linting utility originally developed by none other than the author of early editions of this very book, Nicholas Zakas. It is designed to be completely "pluggable": it comes out of the box with a commonsense set of default rules, but the rules are totally configurable, and there is a large library of modifiable and toggleable rules that can be used to adjust the linter's behavior.

Website: www.eslint.org

Google Closure Compiler

Built into the Closure Compiler is a linting utility that can be activated using command-line flags. This linter operates on the abstract syntax tree of your code, so it does not perform checks for whitespace, indentation, or other code organization matters that do not affect code execution.

Website: developers.google.com/closure

JSLint

JSLint is a JavaScript validator written by Douglas Crockford. It checks for syntax errors at a core level, going with the lowest common denominator for cross-browser issues. (It follows the strictest rules to ensure your code works everywhere.) You can enable Crockford's warnings about coding style, including code format, use of undeclared global variables, and more. Even though JSLint is written in JavaScript, it can be run on the command line through the Java-based Rhino interpreter, as well as through WScript and other JavaScript interpreters. The website provides custom versions for each command-line interpreter.

Website: www.jslint.com

JSHint

JSHint is a fork of JSLint that provides more customization as to the rules that are applied. Like JSLint, it checks for syntax errors first and then looks for problematic coding patterns. Each JSLint check is also present in JSHint, but developers have better control over which rules to apply. Also similar to JSLint, JSHint can be run on the command line using Rhino.

Website: www.jshint.com

Clang Format

ClangFormat is a set of formatting tools built atop the LibFormat library, based on the Clang project. It uses Clang formatting rules to automatically spatially reorganize your code (without actually changing its semantic structure). It works as a standalone tool that can be used from the command line, but it also features multiple editor integrations.

Website: clang.llvm.org/docs/ClangFormat.html

MINIFIERS

An important part of the JavaScript build process is crunching the output to remove excess characters. Doing so ensures that only the smallest number of bytes are transmitted to the browser for parsing and ultimately speeds up the user experience. There are several such *minifiers* available with varying compression ratios.

Uglify

Uglify, currently in its third release, is a toolkit that allows you to minify, beautify, and compress your JavaScript code. It can be run on the command line, and it offers an extremely wide range of compression options that you can tweak to customize your minification.

> **Website:** github.com/mishoo/UglifyJS2

Google Closure Compiler

Although not strictly a minifier, Closure offers a number of optimization levels that will, as part of their optimization routines, minify your code.

> **Website:** developers.google.com/closure

JSMin

JSMin is a C-based cruncher written by Douglas Crockford that does basic JavaScript compression. It primarily removes white space and comments to ensure that the resulting code can still be executed without issues. JSMin is available as a Windows executable with source code available in C and many other languages.

> **Website:** www.crockford.com/javascript/jsmin.html

UNIT TESTING

Most JavaScript libraries use some form of unit testing on their own code, and some publish the unit-testing framework for others to use. *Test-driven development* (TDD) is a software-development process built around the use of unit testing.

Mocha

One of the most popular unit test frameworks available, Mocha offers excellent configurability and extensibility when developing your unit tests. Tests are quite flexible, and their serial execution means accurate reporting and easier debugging.

> **Website:** mochajs.org

Jest

Jest is designed to be fast and reliable, with features such as parallel test execution and intelligent test watching. Jest provides a range of built-in matchers and assertions, making it easy to write tests that are easy to read and understand. Additionally, it supports mocking and spying on functions and modules, making it easy to isolate and test individual components of a larger application.

> **Website:** jestjs.io

Jasmine

Although it is on the older side of the spectrum of unit test frameworks, Jasmine is still extremely popular. It comes with everything you need out of the box—meaning no external dependencies—and its syntax is simple and easy to read.

> **Website:** `jasmine.github.io`

qUnit

qUnit is the unit-testing framework designed for use with jQuery. Indeed, jQuery itself uses qUnit for all of its testing. Despite this, qUnit has no dependency on jQuery and can be used to test any JavaScript code. qUnit is known for being a very simple unit-testing framework that lets people get up and running easily.

> **Website:** `github.com/jquery/qunit`

JsUnit

The original JavaScript unit-testing library is not tied to any particular JavaScript library. *JsUnit* is a port of the popular JUnit testing framework for Java. Tests are run in the page and may be set up for automatic testing and submission of results to a server. The website contains examples and basic documentation.

> **Website:** `www.jsunit.net`

DOCUMENTATION GENERATORS

Most IDEs include documentation generators for the primary language. Because JavaScript has no official IDE, documentation has traditionally been done by hand or through repurposing documentation generators for other languages. However, there are a number of documentation generators specifically targeted at JavaScript.

ESDoc

ESDoc is capable of generating very advanced documentation pages for your code, including the ability to feature links to source code from the documentation page itself. It also features a library of plugins to extend its features. However, ESDoc requires your codebase to consist exclusively of ES6 modules.

> **Website:** `esdoc.org`

documentation.js

documentation.js processes JSDoc comments inside your code to auto-generate documentation in HTML, Markdown, or JSON. It is compatible with the latest versions of ECMAScript and all major build tools, and also can work with Flow annotations.

> **Website:** `documentation.js.org`

Docco

Per the website, Docco is a "quick and dirty" documentation generator. The motivation behind the tool is that it is a very simple way of generating HTML pages which describe your codebase. Docco is brittle in a few ways, but it offers the fewest barriers to generating documentation from your code.

> **Website:** `ashkenas.com/docco`

JsDoc Toolkit

The *JsDoc Toolkit* was one of the first JavaScript documentation generators. It requires you to enter Javadoc-like comments into the source code, which are then processed and output as HTML files. You can customize the format of the HTML using one of the prebuilt JsDoc templates or you can create your own. The JsDoc Toolkit is available as a Java package.

> **Website:** `github.com/jsdoc3/jsdoc`

INDEX

X

Y